...aland

written and researched by

Laura Harper, Tony Mudd and Paul Whitfield

ROUGH GUIDES

www.roughguides.com

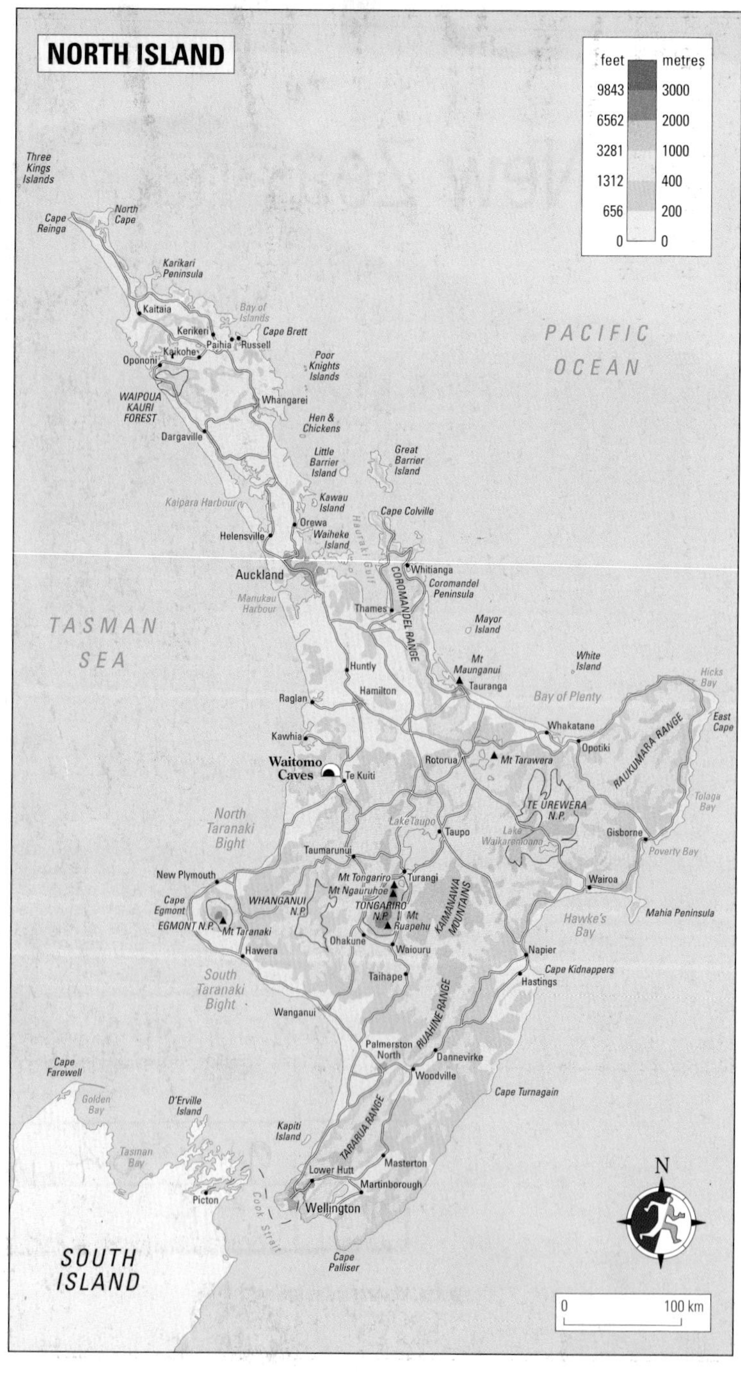
NORTH ISLAND
feet
metres
9843
3000
6562
2000
3281
1000
1312
400
656
200
0
0
Three Kings Islands
Cape Reinga
North Cape
Karikari Peninsula
Kaitaia
Bay of Islands
Kerikeri
Cape Brett
Paihia
Russell
Kaikohe
Opononi
Poor Knights Islands
WAIPOUA KAURI FOREST
Whangarei
Hen & Chickens
Dargaville
Little Barrier Island
Great Barrier Island
Kaipara Harbour
Kawau Island
Cape Colville
Orewa
Hauraki Gulf
Helensville
Waiheke Island
Whitianga
Auckland
COROMANDEL RANGE
Coromandel Peninsula
Manukau Harbour
Thames
PACIFIC OCEAN
TASMAN SEA
Mayor Island
Mt Maunganui
White Island
Huntly
Tauranga
Hicks Bay
Hamilton
Bay of Plenty
Raglan
East Cape
Whakatane
Kawhia
Opotiki
RAUKUMARA RANGE
Rotorua
Mt Tarawera
Waitomo Caves
Te Kuiti
TE UREWERA N.P.
Tolaga Bay
North Taranaki Bight
Lake Taupo
Taupo
Lake Waikaremoana
Gisborne
Poverty Bay
Taumarunui
New Plymouth
Mt Tongariro
Turangi
Mt Ngauruhoe
KAIMANAWA MOUNTAINS
Wairoa
Cape Egmont
WHANGANUI N.P.
TONGARIRO N.P.
Mt Ruapehu
Mahia Peninsula
EGMONT N.P.
Mt Taranaki
Hawke's Bay
Ohakune
Waiouru
Hawera
Napier
Cape Kidnappers
Taihape
Hastings
South Taranaki Bight
RUAHINE RANGE
Wanganui
Palmerston North
Dannevirke
Woodville
Cape Farewell
Cape Turnagain
Golden Bay
D'Erville Island
TARARUA RANGE
Kapiti Island
Tasman Bay
Masterton
Lower Hutt
Martinborough
Picton
Cook Strait
Wellington
N
Cape Palliser
SOUTH ISLAND
0
100 km

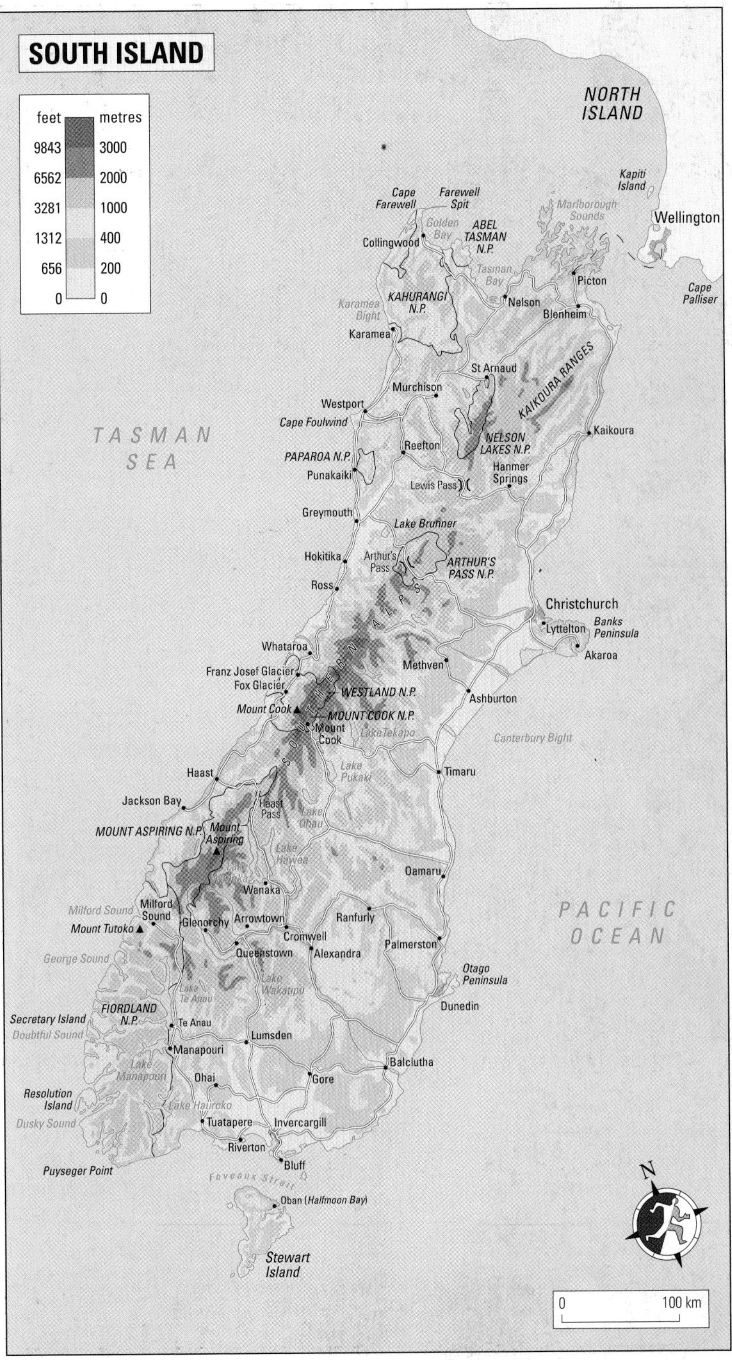
SOUTH ISLAND
feet
metres
9843
3000
6562
2000
3281
1000
1312
400
656
200
0
0
NORTH ISLAND
Kapiti Island
Wellington
Cape Palliser
Cape Farewell
Farewell Spit
Golden Bay
ABEL TASMAN N.P.
Marlborough Sounds
Collingwood
Tasman Bay
Picton
KAHURANGI N.P.
Nelson
Karamea Bight
Blenheim
Karamea
KAIKOURA RANGES
St Arnaud
Murchison
Westport
Cape Foulwind
Kaikoura
TASMAN SEA
NELSON LAKES N.P.
Reefton
PAPAROA N.P.
Punakaiki
Hanmer Springs
Lewis Pass
Greymouth
Lake Brunner
Hokitika
Arthur's Pass
ARTHUR'S PASS N.P.
Ross
SOUTHERN ALPS
Christchurch
Lyttelton
Banks Peninsula
Whataroa
Akaroa
Franz Josef Glacier
Methven
Fox Glacier
WESTLAND N.P.
Mount Cook
Ashburton
MOUNT COOK N.P.
Mount Cook
Lake Tekapo
Canterbury Bight
Haast
Lake Pukaki
Timaru
Jackson Bay
Haast Pass
Lake Ohau
MOUNT ASPIRING N.P.
Mount Aspiring
Lake Hawea
Oamaru
Wanaka
PACIFIC OCEAN
Milford Sound
Milford Sound
Ranfurly
Mount Tutoko
Glenorchy
Arrowtown
Cromwell
Palmerston
Queenstown
Alexandra
George Sound
Lake Wakatipu
Otago Peninsula
Lake Te Anau
FIORDLAND N.P.
Dunedin
Secretary Island
Te Anau
Doubtful Sound
Lumsden
Manapouri
Lake Manapouri
Balclutha
Ohai
Gore
Resolution Island
Lake Hauroko
Dusky Sound
Tuatapere
Invercargill
Riverton
Bluff
Puysegur Point
Foveaux Strait
Oban (Halfmoon Bay)
Stewart Island
N
0
100 km

Introduction to

New Zealand

New Zealand comes with a reputation as a unique land packed with magnificent, raw scenery: craggy coastlines, sweeping beaches, primeval forests, snow-capped alpine mountains, bubbling volcanic pools, fast-flowing rivers and glacier-fed lakes, all beneath a brilliant blue sky. Even Kiwis themselves – named after the endearing, if decidedly odd, flightless bird that has become the national emblem – seem to be filled with astonishment at the stupendous vistas of what they like to think of as "Godzone" (God's own country).

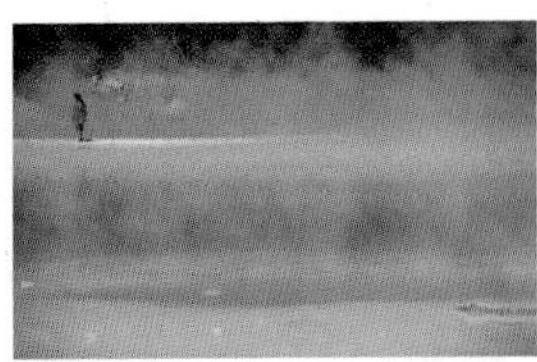

All of this provides a canvas for boundless diversions, from strolls along windswept beaches and multi-day tramps over alpine passes to the adrenalin-charged adventure activities of bungy jumping and whitewater rafting; in fact, some visitors take on New Zealand as a kind of large-scale assault course, aiming to tackle as many adventures as possible in the time available. The one-time albatross of isolation – even Australia is fifteen hundred kilometres away – has become a boon, bolstering New Zealand's clean, **green** image, which is, in truth, more an accident of geography than the result of past government policy.

To a large extent New Zealand lives up to these expectations, and remains unfettered by the crowds you'd find elsewhere. What's more, everything is

Fact file

• Adrift in the south **Pacific Ocean** some 1500km east of Australia, New Zealand is one of the most isolated major land masses and was the last to be peopled, around 1200 years ago.

• At 268,000 square kilometres in **area**, New Zealand is a little larger that the UK and about two-thirds the size of California. With under 4 million **people**, most parts of the country are thinly populated, though Auckland alone has around a million inhabitants.

• Physically, New Zealand is very varied with hairline **fiords** and glacier-weighted **mountains** in the south, rolling green hills fringed with golden **beaches** in the north, and abundant **volcanic** activity producing geysers and natural hot pools.

• For an instinctively conservative nation, New Zealand has often been socially progressive. It was the first country with **votes for women** and workers' **pensions**, and now pursues a **bi-cultural** approach to its race relations.

• New Zealand has almost 40 million **sheep**. That's one for every eleven inhabitants, down from twenty to one in the early 1980s.

• The **economy** has traditionally been agricultural, and dairy products, meat and wool remain central to its continued prosperity, with forestry and fishing also playing a part. There is a growing "knowledge economy" and tourism is a big earner.

• New Zealand's **flora and fauna** developed independently, giving rise to a menagerie of exotica: tall tree ferns, an alpine parrot (kea), a huge ground-dwelling parrot (kakapo), the peculiar kiwi, and many more.

easily accessible, packed into a land area little larger than Britain but with a population of just 3.8 million, over half of it tucked away in the three largest **cities**: Auckland, the capital Wellington, and the South Island's Christchurch. Elsewhere, you can travel miles through steep-hilled farmland and rarely see a soul, and there are even remote spots which, it's reliably contended, no human has ever visited.

Geologically, New Zealand split off from the super-continent of Gondwanaland early, developing a unique **ecosystem** in which birds adapted to fill the role normally held by mammals, many becoming flightless through lack of predators. That all changed around 1200 years ago when the arrival of Polynesian navigators made this the last major land mass to be settled by humans. On sighting the new land from their canoes, Maori named it **Aotearoa** – "the land of the long white cloud" – and proceeded to radically alter the fragile ecosystem, dispatching

forever the giant ostrich-sized moa, which formed a major part of their diet. A delicate ecological balance was achieved before the arrival of Pakeha – white Europeans, predominantly of British origin – who swarmed off their square-rigged ships full of colonial zeal.

The subsequent uneasy coexistence between **Maori** and **European** societies informs both recorded history and the current wrangles over cultural identity, land and resource rights. The British didn't invade as such, and were to some degree reluctant to enter into the 1840 **Treaty of Waitangi**, New Zealand's founding document, which effectively ceded New Zealand to the British Crown while guaranteeing Maori hegemony over their land and traditional gathering and fishing rights. As time wore on and increasing numbers of settlers demanded to buy ever larger parcels of land from Maori, antipathy soon surfaced, eventually escalating to hostility. Once Maori were subdued, a policy of partial integration ensured the rapid dilution of their cultural heritage and all but destroyed **Maoritanga** – the Maori way of doing things. Maori, however, were left well outside the new European order, where difference was perceived as tantamount to a betrayal of the emergent sense of nationhood. Although elements of this still exist and Presbyterian and Anglican values have proved hard to shake off, the Kiwi psyche has become infused with Maori generosity and hospitality, coupled with a colonial mateyness and the unerring belief that whatever happens, "she'll be right". However, an underlying inferiority complex seems to linger: you may well find yourself interrogated as to your opinions of the country almost before you leave the airport. Balancing this out is an extraordinary enthusiasm for **sports** and **culture**, which generate a swelling pride in New Zealanders when they witness plucky Kiwis taking on the world.

Only in the last couple of decades has New Zealand come of age and developed a true national self-confidence, something partly forced on it by Britain severing the colonial apron strings in the early 1970s, and partly by the resurgence of Maori identity. Maori demands have been nurtured by a willingness on the part of most Pakeha to redress the wrongs perpetrated over the last century and a half, as long as it doesn't impinge on their high standard of living or overall feeling of control. More recently, integration has been replaced with a policy of promoting two cultures alongside each other, but with maximum interaction.

The uncertainties of this future are further compounded by extensive recent **immigration**, partly from south Asia but the majority from China and Korea.

Where to go

Tourism is big business in New Zealand but even the key destinations – Queenstown and Rotorua, for example – only seem busy and commercialized in comparison with the low-key Kiwi norm. New Zealand packs a lot into the limited space available and is small enough that you can visit the main sights in a couple of weeks, but for a reasonable look around at a less than frenetic pace, reckon on a month. However long you've got, look at spreading your time between the North and South islands: the diverse attractions of each region are discussed fully in the introduction to each chapter, but here's a quick top-to-toe summary. Obviously, the scenery is the big draw and most people only pop into the big cities on arrival and departure – something easily done with open-jaw air tickets allowing you to fly into Auckland and out of Christchurch.

Certainly none of the cities ranks on an international scale, but in recent years they have taken on more distinct and sophisticated identities. Go-ahead

The Lord of the Rings

Thanks to its part as a backdrop for the majority of the film trilogy, New Zealand has the unusual distinction of possessing, until 2003 at least, a government minister for *Lord of the Rings*, and Wellington's airport even has a sign reading "Welcome to Middle-earth". Chasing down the locations used is a good way of getting to see some of the country's magnificent scenery, and listed below (from north to south) are some that were used, though bear in mind that a good deal of visual enhancement went on in the studio after the shooting.

North Island

Hobbiton was shot near Matamata.

Mount Doom was, in part, Mount Ruapehu.

Trollshaw Forest was the Waitarere Forest.

The hobbits leap aboard the **Bluebury Ferry** at Manukau.

Woodland around Hobbiton is the Otaki Gorge.

Isengard is in part Harcourt Park, near Upper Hutt.

Helm's Deep is Dry Creek Quarry, near Wellington.

Rivendell is, in part, Kaitoke Regional Park.

South Island

Rivendell is, in other parts, Mount Olympus.

Dimrill Dale is Mount Owen.

The Pillars of Argonath were shot in and around Queenstown.

The **Black Riders** chase sequence occurs near Wanaka.

The **Misty Mountains** are the Northwest Lakes.

The **Island of Nen Hithoel** was shot around the Mavora Lakes.

Parts of **Isengard** and **Lothlorien** were filmed in Glenorchy.

Auckland is sprawled around sparkling Waitemata Harbour, an arm of the island-studded Hauraki Gulf. From here, most people head south, missing out on **Northland**, the cradle of both Maori and Pakeha colonization, which comes cloaked in wonderful sub-tropical forest harbouring New Zealand's largest kauri trees. East of Auckland the coast follows the isolated greenery and long, deserted, golden beaches of the **Coromandel Peninsula**, before running down to the **Bay of Plenty** resorts. The lands immediately south are assailed by the ever-present sulphurous whiff of **Rotorua**, with its spurting

The haka

Before every international rugby match, New Zealand's All Blacks put the wind up the opposition by performing an intimidating thigh-slapping, eye-bulging, tongue-poking chant. This is the Te Rauparaha **haka**, just one of many such Maori posture dances, designed to display fitness, agility and ferocity. The Te Rauparaha *haka* was reputedly composed early in the nineteenth century by the warrior Te Rauparaha, who was hiding from his enemies in the *kumara* pit of a friendly chief. Hearing noise above and then being blinded by light, he thought his days were numbered, but as his eyes became accustomed to the light he saw the hairy legs of his host and was so relieved he performed the *haka* on the spot.

Touring teams have performed the *haka* at least since the 1905 All Black tour of Britain, and since the 1987 World Cup for home matches as well. The performance is typically led and spurred on by a player of Maori descent chanting:

Ringa pakia Slap the hands against the thighs
Uma tiraha Puff out the chest
Turi whatia Bend the knees
Hope whai ake Let the hip follow
Waewae takahia kia kino Stamp the feet as hard as you can

After a pause for effect the rest of the team join in with:

Ka Mate! Ka Mate! It is death! It is death!
Ka Ora! Ka Ora! It is life! It is life!
Tenei te ta ngata puhuru huru This is the hairy man
Nana nei i tiki mai Who caused the sun to shine
Whakawhiti te ra Keep abreast!
A upane ka upane! The rank! Hold fast!
A upane kaupane whiti te ra! Into the sun that shines!

geysers and bubbling pools of mud, and the volcanic plateau centred on the trout-filled waters of **Lake Taupo** and three snow-capped volcanoes. Cave fans will want to head west of Taupo to the eerie limestone caverns of **Waitomo**, where you can abseil into, or raft through, the blackness. From Taupo it's just a short hop to the delights of canoeing on the **Whanganui River**, a broad, emerald green waterway banked by virtually impenetrable bush; or if you don't want to get your feet wet, head for the almost perfect cone of **Mount Taranaki**, whose summit is accessible in a day. East of Taupo lie the ranges that form the North Island's backbone, and beyond them the **Hawke's Bay wine country**, centred on the Art Deco city of Napier, and the up-and-coming wine region of Martinborough. Only an hour or so away is the capital, **Wellington**, the most self-contained of New Zealand's cities, with its centre squeezed onto reclaimed harbourside land and the suburbs slung across steep hills overlooking glistening bays. The presence of politicians and bureaucrats gives it a well-scrubbed and urbane sophistication, enlivened by a burgeoning café society and after-dark scene.

The **South Island** kicks off with the world-renowned wineries of **Marlborough** and appealing **Nelson**, a pretty and compact spot surrounded by lovely beaches and within easy reach of the hill country around **Nelson Lakes** and the fabulous sea kayaking of the **Abel Tasman National Park**. From the top of the South Island you've a choice of nipping around behind the 3000-metre summits of the Southern Alps and following the West Coast to the fabulous **glaciers** at Fox and Franz Josef, or sticking to the east, passing the whale-watching territory of **Kaikoura** en route to the South Island's largest centre, straight-laced Christchurch, a city with its roots firmly in the traditions of England. From Christchurch it's possible to head across country to the West Coast via Arthur's Pass on one of the country's most scenic train trips or shoot southwest across the patchwork Canterbury Plains to the foothills of the **Southern Alps** and **Mount Cook** with its distinctive drooping-tent summit.

The flatlands of Canterbury run down, via the grand architecture of **Oamaru**, to the unmistakeably Scottish-influenced city of **Dunedin**, a base for exploring the teeming wildlife of the **Otago Peninsula** with its albatross colony and opportunities for watching penguins. In the middle of the nineteenth century, prospectors arrived here and rushed inland to gold strikes throughout central Otago and around stunningly set **Queenstown**, now a highly commercialized activity centre where bungy jumping, rafting, jet-boating and skiing hold sway. This is also the country's tramping heartland, with the **Routeburn Track** linking Queenstown to the rain-sodden fiords, lakes and mountains of **Fiordland**, and the famous **Milford Track**. The further south you travel, the more you'll feel the bite of the Antarctic winds, which reach their

Bungy jumping

Diving off tall towers with vines tied around the ankles has been a rite of passage for centuries in the South Pacific islands of Vanuatu, but modern **bungy jumping** was actually pioneered in Britain by members of the Oxford University Dangerous Sports Club, who jumped off the Clifton Suspension Bridge near Bristol in 1977, and were promptly arrested. Inspired by this, Kiwi speed skiers A.J. Hackett and Henry Van Asch began pushing the bungy boundaries, culminating in Hackett's jump from the Eiffel Tower in 1987. He too was arrested, but the publicity sparked worldwide interest that continues to draw bungy aspirants to New Zealand's half-dozen supremely scenic bungy operations, an adventure activity boom that shows no sign of slowing up.

Paua

Paua is New Zealand's endemic species of abalone, and is found in shallow waters encrusted in a lime scale. With vigorous polishing this can be removed to reveal a wonderfully iridescent shell, all swirls of silver, blue, green and purple. It was an important resource for early Maori, who fashioned fragments into clasps for capes, used slivers as fishing lures, and inlaid shaped pieces into carvings, especially as the eyes of tiki figures. Its later use in tourist trinkets has also produced some wonderfully kitsch items, but you're more likely to appreciate its use in Maori crafts; perhaps in a catch for a kete (woven basket), incorporated into a brooch, or inlaid into a mirror frame.

peak on New Zealand's third land mass, the tiny and isolated **Stewart Island**, covered mostly by dense coastal rainforest that now forms part of New Zealand's newest national park. Here is your best chance of spotting a kiwi in the wild.

When to go

With over a thousand kilometres of ocean in every direction, it comes as no surprise that New Zealand has a maritime climate: warm through the southern summer months of December to March and never truly cold, even in winter.

Weather patterns are strongly affected by the prevailing westerlies, which suck up moisture from the Tasman Sea and dump it on the western side of both islands. The South Island gets the lion's share, with the West Coast and Fiordland ranking among the world's wettest places. The mountain ranges running the length of both islands cast long rain shadows over the eastern lands, making them considerably drier, though the south is a few degrees cooler than elsewhere, and sub-tropical Auckland and Northland are appreciably more humid. In the North Island, warm, damp summers fade almost imperceptibly into cool, wet winters, but the further south you go the more the year divides into four distinct seasons.

Such regional variation makes it viable to visit at any time of year, provided you pick your destinations. The **summer** months are the most popular and you'll find everything open, though often packed with holidaying Kiwis from Christmas to the end of January. Accommodation at this time is at a premium. In general, you're better off joining the bulk of foreign visitors during the **shoulder seasons** – October to Christmas and February to April – when sights and attractions can be a shade quieter, and rooms easier to come by. **Winter** (June–Sept) is the wettest, coldest and consequently least popular time, though Northland can still be relatively balmy. The switch to prevailing southerly winds tends to bring periods of crisp, dry and cloudless weather to the West Coast and heavy snowfalls to the Southern Alps and Central North Island, allowing New Zealand to offer some of the most varied and least populated (and cheapest) **skiing and snowboarding** anywhere.

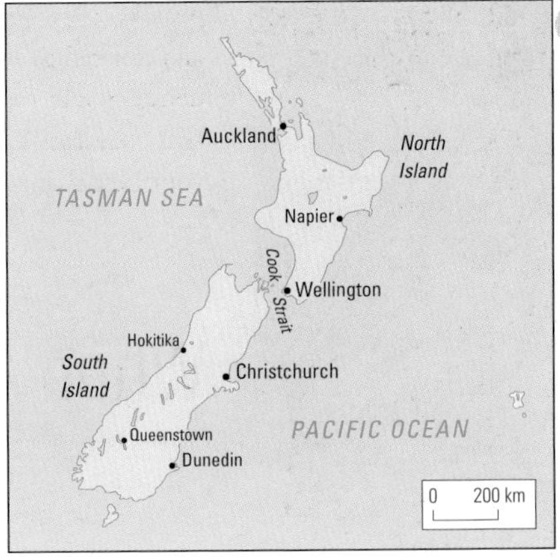

	Jan	Feb	Mar	Apr	May	Jun	Jul	Aug	Sep	Oct	Nov	Dec
Auckland												
av. max. temp. (°C)	23	23	22	19	17	14	13	14	16	17	19	21
av. min. temp. (°C)	16	16	15	13	11	9	8	8	9	11	12	14
av. rainfall (mm)	79	94	81	97	17	137	145	117	102	102	89	79
Napier												
av. max. temp. (°C)	24	23	22	19	17	14	13	14	17	19	21	23
av. min. temp. (°C)	14	14	13	10	8	5	5	6	7	9	11	13
av. rainfall (mm)	74	76	74	76	89	86	102	84	56	56	61	58
Wellington												
av. max. temp. (°C)	21	21	19	17	14	13	12	12	14	16	17	19
av. min. temp. (°C)	13	13	12	11	8	7	6	6	8	9	10	12
av. rainfall (mm)	81	81	81	97	117	117	137	117	97	102	89	89
Christchurch												
av. max. temp. (°C)	21	21	19	17	13	11	10	11	14	17	19	21
av. min. temp. (°C)	12	12	10	7	4	2	2	2	4	7	8	11
av. rainfall (mm)	56	43	48	48	66	66	69	48	46	43	48	56
Hokitika												
av. max. temp. (°C)	19	19	18	16	14	12	12	12	13	15	16	18
av. min. temp. (°C)	12	12	11	8	6	3	3	3	6	8	9	11
av. rainfall (mm)	262	191	239	236	244	231	218	239	226	292	267	262
Queenstown												
av. max. temp. (°C)	21	21	20	7	11	9	9	11	14	18	19	20
av. min. temp. (°C)	10	10	9	7	3	1	0	1	3	5	7	10
av. rainfall (mm)	79	72	74	72	64	58	59	63	66	77	64	62
Dunedin												
av. max. temp. (°C)	19	19	17	15	12	9	9	11	13	15	17	18
av. min. temp. (°C)	10	10	9	7	5	4	3	3	5	6	7	9
av. rainfall (mm)	86	71	76	71	81	81	79	76	69	76	81	89

35 things not to miss

It's not possible to see everything that New Zealand has to offer in one trip – and we don't suggest you try. What follows is a selective taste of the country's highlights: outstanding buildings and natural wonders, adventure activities and exotic wildlife. They're arranged in five colour-coded categories, which you can browse through to find the very best things to see and experience. All highlights have a page reference to take you straight into the guide, where you can find out more.

01 Karori Sanctuary Page **505** • On the edge of Wellington yet seemingly a million miles from anything urban, this beautiful fenced-in nature reserve is concentrating on restocking its 235 hectares with purely native flora and fauna.

02 The Routeburn Track Page **885** • One of the country's finest walks, showcasing forested valleys, rich bird life, thundering waterfalls, river flats, lakes and wonderful mountain scenery.

03 Kiwi spotting Page **782** • Stewart Island's Mason's Bay provides one of the best opportunities to see these rare birds in the wild.

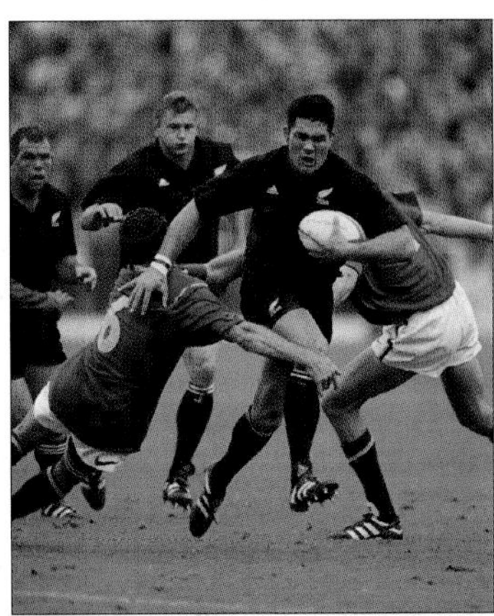

04 Rugby Page **63** • New Zealand's national game; if you get a chance to attend an international match, don't pass it up, not least for a chance to see the All Blacks perform the *haka*.

05 Farewell Spit Page **572** • A stretch of sand reaching out into the sea for 25km that's protected as a nature reserve being home to a whole host of different bird species.

06 Tree ferns Page **992** • New Zealand has a unique flora, its ubiquitous tree ferns sometimes reaching 5m in height and providing shade for more delicate specimens.

07 Wine Page **46** • New Zealand produces some world-beating wines: for wonderful crisp whites, try the wineries around Marlborough; if it's reds you're into, Hawkes Bay can't be bettered.

08 Hot Water Beach Page **401** • Dig yourself a hole in the sand and luxuriate as the underground hot water wells up to mix with the incoming tide.

09 The Catlins Coast Page **757** • The remote, wild Catlins coast is home to rare species of flora and fauna, as well as a petrified forest.

12 Whanganui River Journey Page **265** • This relaxing three-day canoe trip along a historic waterway takes you far away from roads through some of the North Island's loveliest scenery.

10 Surfing at Raglan Page **245** • A left-hand break that's one of the world's longest, coupled with reliable swells, makes Raglan a prime surfing destination.

11 Milford Sound Page **946** • Experience the grandeur and beauty of Fiordland on the area's most accessible fiord, an especially atmospheric place when the mist descends after heavy rainfall.

13 Abel Tasman National Park Page **560** • Kayaking in the waters alongside the Abel Tasman National Park is a great introduction to the area.

14 Ninety Mile Beach Page **215** • This seemingly endless wave-lashed golden strand is a designated highway, plied by tour buses which regularly stop to let passengers boogie board down the steep dunes.

15 Wai-O-Tapu Page **336** • The best of Rotorua's geothermal sites, Wai-O-Tapu offers beautiful, mineral-coloured lakes, plopping mud pools and a geyser that erupts on cue each morning.

16 Kauri Museum Page **229** • The tiny settlement of Matakohe is home to what is one of the country's finest museums, dedicated solely to kauri wood, its extraction, and what you can do with it.

17 Caving and cave rafting Page **254** • Explore Waitomo's labyrinthine netherworld on one of a dozen adventure trips involving super-long abseils and floating underground streams on inner tubes while admiring the glow-worms.

18 **Tongariro National Park** Page **352** • Rafting, kayaking, bramping and slicing – there's an activity to suit most people in this popular area where three great volcanoes dominate the skyline.

19 Penguin watching Page **747** • Penguin Place, on the Otago Peninsula, offers the rare chance to see a penguin nesting area close up thanks to a unique system of hides and tunnels.

20 Moeraki Boulders Page **669** • Don't pass through the area around Oamaru without a visit to the Moeraki Boulders – enormous, perfectly round, naturally formed spheres with a honeycomb centre, just sitting in the surf.

21 Jetboating Page **58** • This countrywide obsession finds its most iconic expression on Shotover River, but there is also good jetboating near Queenstown, in Skippers Canyon, and near Taupo on the Dart River.

22 Bungy jumping Page **58** • New Zealand's trademark adventure sport can be tried at Kawerau Bridge, the original commercial jump site, and some at super-high mega jumps nearby.

23 America's Cup Page **95** • Passions run high in Auckland as the world's most prestigious yachting trophy is contested for on the waters of the Hauraki Gulf.

24 Museum of New Zealand (Te Papa) Page **500** • A celebration of the people, culture and art of New Zealand that's as appealing to kids as it is adults, with an impressive use of state-of-the-art technology.

25 Oparara Basin Page **805** • Stunning karst country, featuring disappearing rivers and dramatic limestone arches.

26 **Dunedin Public Art Gallery** Page **734** • This beautifully designed gallery is one of *the* places to come to for early and contemporary New Zealand art.

27 **Tongariro Crossing** Page **361** • A superb one-day hike through the volcanic badlands of the Tongariro National Park passing the cinder cone of Mount Ngauruhoe, along the shores of turquoise lakes and with long views right across the North Island.

28 White Island Page **426** • Take a boat trip out to New Zealand's most active volcano, and stroll through the sulphurous lunar landscape to peer into the steaming crater.

29 Christchurch Arts Centre Page **616** • Watch the world go by in the grassy quadrangles of the Gothic Revival Arts Centre, then sample ethnic food from around the globe at the weekend arts and crafts market here.

30 Hangi Page **44** • Sample fall-off-the-bone pork and chicken along with sweet potatoes and pumpkin, disinterred after several hours steaming in a Maori earth oven.

31 The glaciers Page **827** • After exploring karst countryside and kayaking along rivers, walking on the Franz Josef or Fox glaciers imparts a real sense of New Zealand's breathtakingly varied scenery.

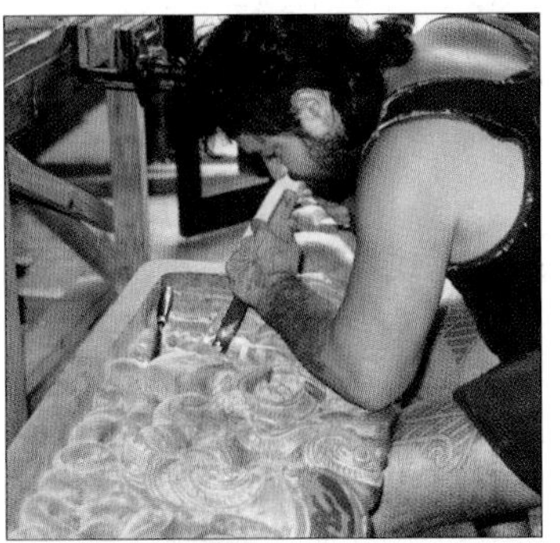

32 Carving Page **818** • Maori motifs are used as the basis for items made from greenstone (jade) and bone, and you can have a go at carving your own in Hokitika.

34 Taieri Gorge Railway Page **740** • Dating back to 1859, the Taieri Gorge Railway penetrates an otherwise inaccessible mountain landscape and provides a dramatic journey at any time of the year.

33 Art Deco Napier Page **460** • The world's finest and most homogeneous collection of small-scale Art Deco architecture owes its genesis to the devastating 1931 earthquake that flattened Napier.

35 Whale watching Page **594** • Whale watching off the Kaikoura Peninsula is justifiably popular, and you don't have to take a boat trip to do it, with plane- and helicopter rides on offer to up the adrenalin ante.

Contents

Using the Rough Guide

We've tried to make this Rough Guide a good read and easy to use. The book is divided into six main sections, and you should be able to find whatever you want in one of them.

Colour section

The front colour section offers a quick tour of New Zealand. The **introduction** aims to give you a feel for the place, with suggestions on where to go. We also tell you what the weather is like and include a basic country fact file. Next, our authors round up their favourite aspects of New Zealand in the **things not to miss** section – whether it's great food, amazing sights or a special hotel. Right after this comes a full **contents** list.

Basics

The Basics section covers all the **pre-departure** nitty-gritty to help you plan your trip. This is where to find out which airlines fly to your destination, what paperwork you'll need, what to do about money and insurance, about internet access, food, security, public transport, car rental – in fact just about every piece of **general practical information** you might need.

Guide

This is the heart of the Rough Guide, divided into user-friendly chapters, each of which covers a specific region. Every chapter starts with a list of **highlights** and an **introduction** that helps you to decide where to go, depending on your time and budget. Likewise, introductions to the various towns and smaller regions within each chapter should help you plan your itinerary. We start most town accounts with information on arrival and accommodation, followed by a tour of the sights, and finally reviews of places to eat and drink, and details of nightlife. Longer accounts also have a directory of practical listings. Each chapter concludes with **public transport** details for that region.

Contexts

Read Contexts to get a deeper understanding of what makes New Zealand tick. We include a brief history, articles about wildlife and the environment, and a detailed further reading section that reviews dozens of **books** relating to the country.

Language

The **language** section gives useful guidance on Maori and Kiwi terms and phrases, and pulls together all the vocabulary you might need on your trip, including a comprehensive menu reader. Here you'll also find a glossary of words and terms peculiar to the country.

Index + small print

Apart from a **full index**, which includes maps as well as places, this section covers publishing information, credits and acknowledgements, and also has our contact details in case you want to send in updates and corrections to the book – or suggestions as to how we might improve it.

Map and chapter list

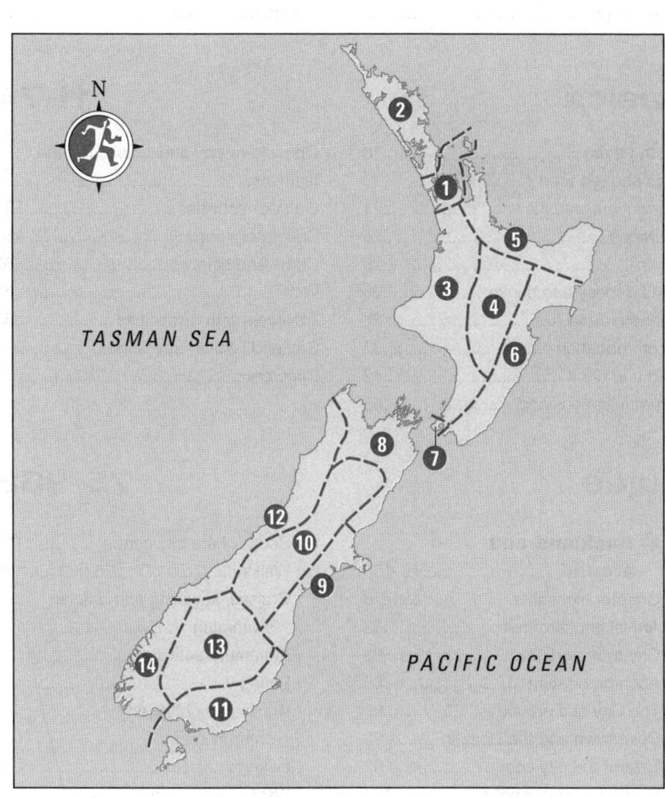

Contents

Colour section i–xxiv

Basics 11–74

Guide 75–962

Contexts 963–1016

Language 1017–1024

Map symbols

maps are listed in the full index using coloured text

- Railway
- State highway
- Road
- Path
- Ferry route
- Waterway
- Chapter division boundary
- Place of interest
- Restaurant
- Hotel
- Campsite
- Hut
- Shelter
- Church (regional maps)
- Castle
- Museum
- Statue
- Public gardens
- Winery
- Swimming pool
- Ski area
- Golf course
- Cave
- Mountains
- Peak
- Viewpoint
- Cliff
- Lighthouse
- Waterfall
- Marshland
- Spring
- Airport
- Parking
- Bus stop
- Toilet
- Hospital
- Tourist office
- Post office
- Telephone
- Internet access
- Fuel station
- Building
- Church
- Cemetery
- Park/National Park
- Beach
- Glacier

Basics

Basics

Getting there

The quickest and easiest way to get to New Zealand is to fly. It is possible to arrive by sea, but unless you own a boat, this means joining a cruise, paying for your passage on a cargo ship or joining a private yacht as crew – all of which are extremely expensive and time consuming.

There are very few charter flights or all-in package deals to New Zealand, so flying there almost always involves **scheduled flights**. Airfares always depend on the **season**, with highest prices being asked during the New Zealand summer (Dec–Feb); fares drop during the shoulder seasons (Sept–Nov & March–May) and you'll get the cheapest prices during the low season (June–Aug). You can often cut costs by going through a **specialist flight agent** – either a consolidator, who buys up blocks of tickets from the airlines and sells them at a discount, or a **discount agent**, who in addition to dealing with discounted flights may also offer student and youth fares and a range of other travel-related services such as insurance, rail passes, car rentals, tours and the like. A further possibility is to see if you can arrange a **courier flight**, although you'll need a flexible schedule, and preferably be travelling alone with very little luggage. In return for shepherding a parcel through customs, you can expect to get a deeply discounted ticket. You'll probably also be restricted in the duration of your stay. See Ⓦwww.aircourier.co.uk for more UK-related information; Ⓦwww.aircourier.org, Ⓦwww.cheaptrips.com, Ⓦwww.courier.org, or Ⓦwww.nowvoyagertravel.com for US details.

If New Zealand is only one stop on a longer journey, you might want to consider buying a **Round-the-World** (**RTW**) ticket. Some travel agents can sell you an "off-the-shelf" RTW ticket that will have you touching down in about half a dozen cities (Auckland is on many itineraries); others will have to assemble one for you, which can be tailored to your needs, though this is liable to be more expensive.

Booking flights online

Many airlines and discount travel websites offer you the opportunity to book your tickets **online**, cutting out the costs of agents and middlemen. Good deals can often be found through discount or auction sites, as well as through the airlines' own websites.

Online booking agents and general travel sites

Ⓦ**www.cheapflights.com** Bookings from the UK and Ireland only. Flight deals, travel agents, plus links to other travel sites.

Ⓦ**www.cheaptickets.com** Discount flight specialists.

Ⓦ**www.etn.nl/discount.htm** A hub of consolidator and discount agent Web links, maintained by the nonprofit European Travel Network.

Ⓦ**www.expedia.com** Discount airfares, all–airline search engine and daily deals.

Ⓦ**www.flyaow.com** Online air travel info and reservations site.

Ⓦ**www.gaytravel.com** Gay online travel agent, concentrating mostly on accommodation.

Ⓦ**www.geocities.com/Thavery2000/** Has an extensive list of airline toll-free numbers and websites.

Ⓦ**www.hotwire.com** Bookings from the US only. Last-minute savings of up to forty percent on regular published fares. Travellers must be at least 18 and there are no refunds, transfers or changes allowed. Log-in required.

Ⓦ**www.lastminute.com** Bookings from the UK only. Offers good last-minute holiday package and flight-only deals.

Ⓦ**www.northsouthtravel.co.uk** Organize low cost fares anywhere in the world.

Ⓦ**www.priceline.com** Name-your-own-price website that has deals at around forty percent off standard fares. You cannot specify flight times (although you do specify dates) and the tickets are non-refundable, non-transferable and non-changeable.

www.skyauction.com Bookings from the US only. Auctions tickets and travel packages using a "second bid" scheme. The best strategy is to bid the maximum you're willing to pay, since if you win you'll pay just enough to beat the runner-up regardless of your maximum bid.

www.smilinjack.com/airlines.htm Lists an up-to-date compilation of airline website addresses.

www.travelocity.com Destination guides, hot web fares and best deals for car hire, accommodation and lodging as well as fares. Provides access to the travel agent system SABRE, the most comprehensive central reservations system in the US.

www.travelshop.com.au Australian website offering discounted flights, packages, insurance, online bookings.

http://travel.yahoo.com Incorporates a lot of Rough Guide material in its coverage of destination countries and cities across the world, with information about places to eat, sleep and etc.

From Britain and Ireland

Over a dozen airlines compete to fly you from Britain to New Zealand for as little as £600, remarkably cheap considering the distances involved but prices depend upon the time of year and rocket at Christmas to around £1500. However, going for the **cheapest flight** typically means sacrificing some comfort, which you may regret, given that your journey will last at least 24 hours, longer if your flight makes more than the obligatory refuelling stop. There are no direct flights to New Zealand from Ireland, and prices are proportionately higher, since the short hop to London (£60–80 return) has to be added on to the fare.

No matter how keen you are to arrive in New Zealand, it makes sense to break the journey, and most **scheduled flights** allow multiple **stopovers** either in North America and the Pacific, or Asia and Australia. The vast majority of direct scheduled flights to New Zealand depart from London's Heathrow, though Garuda Indonesia fly from London Gatwick (1 weekly), and Singapore Airlines use Manchester (around 4 weekly) as well as Heathrow. There are few overseas flights into Wellington or Dunedin, so the only real choice is between the main international airport at Auckland, in the north of the North Island, and the second airport at Christchurch, midway down the South Island. Christchurch receives fewer direct flights, but many scheduled airlines have a code-share shuttle from Auckland at no extra cost. The most desirable option, an open-jaw ticket (flying into one and out of the other), usually costs no more than an ordinary return and means not retracing your steps to get out of the country.

Charter flights to Auckland and Christchurch from London Gatwick with Britannia are currently suspended but may subsequently be reinstated. Contact Austravel (see p.15) for latest details.

The best deals along fixed **Round-The-World** (RTW; usually valid for 12 months) routes include those such as the Aerolineas Argentinas/Thai combo that takes you from London through Buenos Aires, Auckland, Sydney, Perth and Bangkok for £1000–1500, or Alitalia/Air New Zealand's London-based circuit through Bangkok, Singapore, Bali, Auckland, Christchurch, Sydney/Cairns, Los Angeles or New York for £780–950; Trailfinders (see p.16) will usually knock a little off this using a slightly amended route. It is also possible to reduce your flight costs by incorporating an overland section into your round-the-world ticket: common land sectors include Delhi to Kathmandu, Brisbane or Sydney to Cairns, and Buenos Aires to São Paulo. Unusual routes combining the resources of two or more airlines in a RTW ticket are more expensive, but are almost infinitely variable.

If you are planning on doing a lot of travelling within New Zealand, especially between the North and South islands, it may be worth looking into **air passes** offered by Air New Zealand (see "Getting Around", p.29). In addition, if you are combining Australia and New Zealand, there are handy air passes covering internal travel in each country and the joining flight. Air New Zealand do a **G'day Pass** that includes flights to Oz from New Zealand (though not including domestic travel in Oz) based on a zone system. Flying within a single zone is £100, two zones £125 and over a second zone to a third £225. Qantas's **Boomerang Pass** is available to all international travellers (not just Qantas ticket holders), and comprises between two and ten coupons, each valid for a flight within Australasia: a one-zone coupon to fly within New Zealand or short hops in Oz costs around £100, a two-zone trans-Tasman coupon costs £125.

Tourists and those on short-term working visas (see p.66) are generally required by New Zealand immigration to arrive with a ticket out of the country, so one-way tickets are really only viable for Australian and New Zealand residents. If you've purchased a return ticket and find you want to stay longer or head off on a totally different route, it's sometimes possible to cash in the return half of your ticket (though you'll make a loss on the deal) at the same travel agent where you bought it. Alternatively, you could try flogging it on the Internet but don't hold your breath.

Airlines

Aerolineas Argentinas UK ⓣ0845/601 1915, ⓦwww.aerolinas.com.ar. Twice-weekly flights from London Heathrow via Madrid and Buenos Aires to Auckland.
Air New Zealand UK ⓣ020/8741 2299, ⓦwww.airnewzealand.co.nz. Daily to Auckland, via Los Angeles and the popular South Pacific route with a choice of stopovers in Honolulu, Fiji, Western Samoa, the Cook Islands, Tahiti and Tonga. Easy connections to Christchurch.
British Airways UK ⓣ0845/77 333 77, Republic of Ireland ⓣ1800/626 747, ⓦwww.britishairways.com. Daily flights from London Heathrow to Auckland and Christchurch, with stopovers in Australia or America, LA or Brisbane.
Canadian Airlines UK ⓣ0870/5247 226, Republic of Ireland ⓣ01/679 3958, ⓦwww.cdnair.ca. Daily flights from London Heathrow to Auckland via Vancouver and Honolulu.
Cathay Pacific UK ⓣ020/7747 8888, ⓦwww.cathaypacific.com.
Garuda Indonesia UK ⓣ020/7467 8600, ⓦwww.garuda-indonesia.com. London Gatwick to Auckland via Bangkok and Bali.
Japanese Airlines UK ⓣ08457/747 700, ⓦwww.jal.co.jp. Three flights weekly from Heathrow to Auckland, via Tokyo.
Korean Air UK ⓣ0800/0656 2001, Republic of Ireland ⓣ01/799 7990, ⓦwww.koreanair.com. Flights per week vary at different times of the year, running from Heathrow to Auckland and Christchurch via Seoul.
Malaysia Airlines (MAS) UK ⓣ0870/607 9090, Republic of Ireland ⓣ01/676 1561 or 2131, ⓦwww.mas.com.my. Two flights weekly from Heathrow to Auckland via Kuala Lumpur.
Qantas UK ⓣ08457/747 767, ⓦwww.quanta.com.au. Daily scheduled flights from Heathrow to Auckland and Christchurch, via LA, Bangkok, Singapore, Sydney and Melbourne.
Singapore Airlines UK ⓣ0870/608 8886, Republic of Ireland ⓣ01/671 0722, ⓦwww.singaporeair.com. Flights from Heathrow (daily) and Manchester (daily) to Auckland and Christchurch via Singapore, long wait at Singapore on Manchester flights.
Thai Airways International UK ⓣ0870/606 0911, ⓦwww.international-thaiair.co.kr. Four flights weekly from Heathrow to Auckland, via Bangkok and Sydney.
United Airlines UK ⓣ0845/844 4777, ⓦwww.ual.com. Daily flights from Heathrow to Auckland, with various US stopovers, usually LA or Chicago.

Flight and travel agents

Austravel UK ⓣ08701 662 100, ⓦwww.austravel.net. Stopovers in Tokyo, Seoul, Singapore, LA or Fiji; also lays on "Focus Downunder" audio-visual presentations all over the UK to help you plan your trip.
Bridge the World UK ⓣ020/7911 0900, ⓦwww.b-t-w.co.uk. Round-the-world ticket specialist, with good deals aimed at the backpacker market. Agents for Kiwi Experience.
Cresta World Travel, UK ⓣ0870/161 0900, ⓦwww.mytravel.co.uk. Comprehensive range of flights and round-the-world tickets to New Zealand and Australia, with good backpacker deals.
Destination Group UK ⓣ020/7400 7000, ⓦwww.destination-group.co.uk. Good discount fares, especially on Garuda flights; Far East and USA inclusive packages.
Flightbookers UK ⓣ0870/010 7000, ⓦwww.ebookers.com. Low fares on an extensive selection of scheduled flights.
Joe Walsh Tours Dublin ⓣ01/872 2555 or 676 3053, Cork ⓣ021/427 7959, ⓦwww.joewalshtours.ie. General budget fares agent.
Jupiter Travel UK ⓣ020/8296 0309 or 8339 9929. Cheap and reliable agent with multi-stopover and RTW tickets to New Zealand.
London Flight Centre UK ⓣ020/7244 6411, ⓦwww.topdecktravel.co.uk. Long-established agent dealing in discount flights.
North South Travel UK ⓣ & ⓕ01245/608 291, ⓦwww.northsouthtravel.co.uk. Friendly,

competitive travel agency, offering discounted fares worldwide – profits are used to support projects in the developing world, especially the promotion of sustainable tourism.

Quest Worldwide UK ⓣ020/8547 3322, ⓦwww.questtravel.com. Specialists in round-the-world and Australasian discount fares.

STA Travel UK ⓣ08701/600 599, ⓦwww.statravel.co.uk. Worldwide specialists in low-cost flights and tours for students and under-26s, though other customers welcome. Experts on New Zealand travel with branches in major Kiwi cities.

Thomas Cook UK ⓣ08705/666 222, ⓦwww.thomascook.co.uk. Long established one-stop 24-hour travel agency for package holidays or scheduled flights, with bureau de change issuing Thomas Cook travellers' cheques, travel insurance and car rental.

Trailfinders UK ⓣ020/7628 7628, ⓦwww.trailfinders.com, Republic of Ireland ⓣ01/677 7888, ⓦwww.trailfinders.ie. One of the best-informed and most efficient agents for independent travellers; produce a very useful quarterly magazine worth scrutinizing for round-the-world routes.

Travel Bag UK ⓣ0870/900 1350, ⓦwww.travelbag.co.uk. Official Qantas agent. Discount flights to New Zealand, plus tours and adventure trips; agents for Kiwi Experience.

Travel Mood UK ⓣ020/7258 1234. Discount fares and round-the-world tickets; also car rental and bus tours, including Kiwi Experience.

Packages and tours

There are well over a dozen companies offering everything from flexible backpacker-orientated excursions through mainstream bus **tours** to no-expense-spared extravaganzas. If time is limited and you have a fairly clear idea of what it is you want to do, there are good deals going. Even if an all-in package doesn't appeal, there may be some mileage in pre-booking some accommodation, tours or a rental vehicle.

Full "see-it-all" packages can work out to be quite expensive – to say nothing of being rather tame and controlled – but aren't bad value, considering what you'd be spending anyway. Basic bus tours range from 6 days around Northland for about £900 to 17–21 day nationwide tours staying in four-star hotels with all meals, and various cruises and sightseeing included, costing about £3500–4000. A number of companies, most notably Kiwi Experience and Magic Bus, operate flexible bus tours, which you can hop off whenever you like and rejoin a day or two later when the next bus comes through (see "Getting Around", p.31, for details of these).

Pretty much all the major tour operators can also book you onto tramping trips, including some of the guided Great Walks (see p.53); you'll still need to book way in advance, though. Mount Cook organize **skiing** holidays in the South Island, based either at Queenstown for Coronet Peak and The Remarkables or at Methven for Mount Hutt, costing around £400–900 for 6 days, including accommodation, transport from there to the field, ski passes and bus travel from Christchurch. It's also possible – and usually cheaper – to contact ski clubs at the fields direct: check out the contacts at ⓦwww.snow.co.nz.

Australian Pacific Tours UK ⓣ020/8879 7444, ⓦwww.aptouring.co.uk. Massive range of fully inclusive bus tours, a variety of 15-day national tours costing from £2140 with meals, £1795 without.

Contiki ⓣ020/8290 6777, ⓦwww.contiki.com. Bus tours for 18–35s. Itineraries range from 3 days around the Bay of Islands (£105) to a 15-day grand tour (around £600 from Christchurch; £640 from Auckland), with accommodation and most meals included.

Explore Worldwide UK ⓣ01252/760 000, ⓦwww.explore.co.uk. Small-group tours, staying in small hotels and including treks, canoeing and rafting (18 days on South or North islands £2000; 32 days for both £3100).

High Places ⓣ0114/275 7500, ⓦwww.highplaces.co.uk. Trips to NZ specializing in high-country hiking and cycling.

Journeys of Distinction ⓣ01695/578 140. Sedate and exclusive fully escorted tours (27 days £3445; 28 days £3545).

Kuoni Worldwide UK ⓣ01306/741 111, ⓦwww.kuoni.co.uk. A 15- to 17-night bus tour inclusive of flights from Britain and all luxurious accommodation, plus some meals (£2500–2650), as well as more flexible holidays ranging from 3 to 10 days.

Mount Cook Line ⓣ020/8741 5652, ⓕ8741 2125. Major New Zealand holiday and travel company offering tame, planned-itinerary tours as well as flight and bus passes, motorhome rental and ski holidays.

Sunbeam Tours ⓣ01483/454 455. Bus tours,

self-drive car and motorhome holidays, guided Great Walks, semi-independent tours at mid-range prices.

From the US and Canada

Auckland is the only city in New Zealand that has direct, non-stop flights from North America. From there you will find several connections a day to the two other major airports, Wellington and Christchurch. The flying time from Los Angeles to Auckland is approximately 12 hours 45 minutes.

From the US, Air New Zealand, Qantas and United have daily non-stop flights from Los Angeles to Auckland, with connections to Christchurch and Wellington, for a mid-week round-trip Apex fare of $950–1000, rising to about $1600 in peak season. Air New Zealand has special internet fares as low as $810 in low season. It's also possible to fly with Qantas from New York to Sydney and then on to Auckland. Expect to pay an extra $50–100 for weekend travel. Singapore Airlines fly daily from LA to Auckland via Singapore, and 3 days a week to Christchurch, again via Singapore, but their fares are significantly higher, ranging from $1800 to $2100. Don't forget the discount travel companies, which sometimes offer fares for up to $200 less than those quoted above.

Flights from all other US cities are routed via Los Angeles. Air New Zealand and United quote add-on fares of $422–657 (from New York) or $397–632 (from Chicago), but shopping around the discount agents or checking out the newspapers for special offers could save you more than a few bucks.

From Canada, United has daily flights from Vancouver, Toronto and Montreal to Auckland via LA, with Air Canada connections from other Canadian cities. Depending on the season, sample Apex midweek fares are in the following ranges: from Vancouver CAN$1400–2600; from Toronto CAN$1600–3100; from Montreal CAN$1900–3200. Finally, discount travel companies have been known to track down fares from Vancouver for CAN$1004, or from Toronto for CAN$1378.

RTW and Circle-Pacific routes

If New Zealand is only one stop on a longer journey, you might want to consider buying a **Round-the-World** (**RTW**) ticket. A sample itinerary of LA-Tahiti-Cook Islands-Fiji-Auckland-Sydney-Kuala Lumpur-Istanbul-London-LA would cost $2295 (low-season departure). An equally exotic option is a **Circle Pacific** ticket. Air New Zealand offer a ôPacific Escapadeö ticket for $2600, valid for six months, originating from LA and with no limit to stopovers as long as you follow an onward circular route (no backtracking) and do not exceed 20,000 miles. However, a discount agent should be able to put together cheaper itineraries by combining sectors from different airlines, such as LA-Bangkok-Bali-Auckland-LA, starting from $1350.

Airlines in the US and Canada

Air Canada ⓣ1-888/247-2262, ⓦwww.aircanada.ca
Air New Zealand ⓣ1-800/262-1234, in Canada ⓣ1-800/663-5494, ⓦwww.airnz.com
Qantas ⓣ1-800/227-4500, ⓦwww.qantas.com
Singapore Airlines ⓣ1-800/742-3333, ⓦwww.singaporeair.com
United ⓣ1-800/538-2929, ⓦwww.ual.com

Discount flight agents, travel clubs & consolidators

Air Brokers International 150 Post St, Suite 620, San Francisco, CA 94108 ⓣ1-800/883-3273, ⓦwww.airbrokers.com. Consolidator and specialist in RTW and Circle Pacific tickets.
Airtech 588 Broadway, Suite 204, New York, NY 10012 ⓣ1-877/247-8324, ⓦwww.airtech.com. Standby seat broker; also deals in consolidator fares and courier flights.
AirTreks.com 442 Post St, Suite 400, San Francisco, CA 94102 ⓣ1-800/350-0612, ⓦwww.airtreks.com. Round-the-world and Circle Pacific tickets. The website features an interactive database that lets you build your own RTW itinerary.
Council Travel 205 E 42nd St, New York, NY 10017 ⓣ1-800/226-8624, ⓦwww.counciltravel.com. Also has branches in many US cities. Student and budget travel agency.
Skylink 265 Madison Ave, Suite 500, New York,

NY 10016 ⓣ1-800/AIR-ONLY, ⓦwww.skylinkus.com. Also has branches in Chicago, Los Angeles, Miami, Montreal, Ottawa, Toronto, Vancouver and Washington DC. Consolidator.
STA Travel 10 Downing St, New York, NY 10014 ⓣ1-800/777-0112, ⓦwww.sta-travel.com. Also has branches in the Los Angeles, San Francisco and Boston areas. Worldwide discount travel firm; also student IDs, insurance, car rental and travel passes.
Travel CUTS 243 College St, Toronto, ON M5T 1P7 ⓣ1-866/246-9762 & 1-800/667-2887, ⓦwww.travelcuts.com. Other branches all over Canada. Agent specializing in student fares, IDs and other travel services.
Worldtek Travel 111 Water St, New Haven, CT 06511 ⓣ1-800/243-1723, ⓦwww.worldtek.com. Discount travel agency.

Specialist agents and tour operators

Abercrombie and Kent ⓣ1-800/323-7308, ⓦwww.abercrombiekent.com. Upmarket operator with customized tours and set packages. Their 10-day Highlights of New Zealand sightseeing package is priced at $2245 (land costs and internal flights only).
Australian Pacific Tours ⓣ1-800/290-8687, ⓦwww.aptours.com. Various land-only packages from $1430 (8 days) or $3595 (21 days).
Collette Vacations US ⓣ1-800/340-5158, Canada ⓣ1-416/626-1661, ⓦwww.collettevacations.com. Specialists in Australia and New Zealand travel. Their 19-day fully escorted tour of New Zealand's natural areas, including trips to glaciers and rainforests, starts at $1899 (land only).
Contiki Holidays ⓣ1-888/CONTIKI, ⓦwww.contiki.com. Specialists in travel for 18–35s. Their several land packages range from a 3-day Bay of Islands tour ($139) to an 11-day Grand Adventurer ($599).
Elderhostel ⓣ1-877/426-8056, ⓦwww.elderhostel.org. Educational and activity programmes for senior travellers. In addition to joint Australia/New Zealand packages, specialist month-long tours like Land of Geysers and Greenstone ($4445-4810, including return flights).
Inta-Aussie Tours ⓣ1-800/531-9222, ⓦwww.inta-aussie.com. North American agents catering to the cost-conscious, free-wheeling traveller: escorted land tours, such as their Essential New Zealand (10 days; $873-1044), customized packages, transport and accommodation passes and so on.
Inta-G'dAY Tours ⓣ1-888/429-9667, ⓦwww.inta-gday.com. A division of Inta-Aussie that offers customized tours and travel information for gay travellers.
Newmans South Pacific Vacations ⓣ1-888/592-6224, ⓦwww.newmansvacations.com. Specialists in New Zealand vacations, with around 50 different package options in addition to fully independent tours. Their tours include a 12-day guided tour (from $1410, land only) and a 5-day walking tour on the Milford Track (from $781, also land only).
New Zealand Travellers ⓣ1-800/362-2718. Backpacking and day-hiking tours of the South Island from around $2200 (12 days, airfares extra).
Qantas Vacations US ⓣ1-800/641-8772, Canada ⓣ1-800/268-7525, ⓦwww.qantas.com. Highly flexible packages, including fly-drives out of LA. A current special includes two weeks in Australia, New Zealand and Fiji with all accommodations for $1699.
Skylink Women's Travel ⓣ1-800/225 5759. Specialists in tours for lesbian travellers.
Swain Tours ⓣ1-800/22-SWAIN, ⓦwww.swainaustralia.com. South Pacific specialists offering customized individual and group itineraries including walking/trek tours through several national parks for $365–875 (3–5 days, land only).
Sunbeam Tours ⓣ1-800/955-1818, ⓦwww.sunbeamtours.com. Customized tours, along with several set packages. Their 16-day sightseeing tour of the North and South Islands starts at $1799 (land only).
United Vacations ⓣ1-800/917-9246, ⓦwww.unitedvacations-sp.com. Variety of fly-drives, excursions and escorted tours. A 12-day land/air package starts at $2176.

From Australia

Only Qantas and Air New Zealand operate frequent flights between Australia and New Zealand, but competition from the likes of Polynesian Airlines, Aerolinas Argentinas and Thai keeps **prices** reasonable. There's an ever-changing range of special offers, and your best bet is to check the latest with a specialist travel agent (see opposite). All the fares quoted here are for low or shoulder seasons. It's a relatively short hop across the Tasman: flying time from Sydney or Melbourne to Auckland or Christchurch is around three hours.

Qantas and Air New Zealand each have several daily **direct flights** from major cities to Auckland and a smaller number of flights to Wellington and Christchurch. Flights from the eastern states cost around A$700, while flights from Perth start at A$1050; flying to Wellington or Christchurch is likely to cost around the same as a flight to Auckland, and may even be cheaper. Look out for occasional promotional fares (particularly on the companies' websites), which can bring down prices to as low as A$500.

Open-jaw tickets – which let you fly into one city and out of another, making your own way between – can save a lot of backtracking, and add little (if anything) to the total fare. There are also various **air passes** for internal flights available (see "Getting Around", p.29, for details). It may also be worth investigating Air New Zealand's budget wing, **Freedom Air** (Ⓦwww.freedomair.co.nz) who offer considerable savings, but fly infrequently from less popular airports such as Newcastle and Gold Coast as well as Sydney and Brisbane. You can expect a return ticket to Auckland, Hamilton, Palmerston North or Dunedin to cost A$400–500, but there may only be flights two or three days a week.

If you're taking in New Zealand as part of your grand tour, it's worth considering a **Round-The-World** (RTW) ticket also taking in North or South America, Europe and southeast Asia; the scope is enormous and rates start around A$2000.

Cruise ships do pass through the Pacific between November and January, but not on a regular basis; travel agents should be able to advise on which vessels are operating each season.

There's a huge variety of holidays and tours to New Zealand available in Australia. The holiday subsidiaries of airlines such as Air New Zealand and Qantas package short **city-breaks** (flight and accommodation) and **fly-drive** deals for little more than the cost of the regular airfare. In winter, there are accommodation **skiing** packages to New Zealand's skifields; all-inclusive four-day trips to Queenstown start from A$800, rising to A$1000 for a seven-day trip.

Airlines

Aerolineas Argentinas Ⓣ02/9252 5150, Ⓦwww.aerolineas.com.au
Air New Zealand Ⓣ13 2476, Ⓦwww.airnz.co.nz
Freedom Air Ⓣ1800/122 000, Ⓦwww.freedomair.co.nz
Polynesian Airlines Ⓣ300/ 653 737, Ⓦwww.polynesianairlines.co.nz
Qantas Ⓣ13 1313, Ⓦwww.qantas.com.au
Singapore Airlines Ⓣ13 1011, Ⓦwww.singaporeair.com
Thai Airways Ⓣ1300 651 960, Ⓦwwwthaiair.com
United Airlines Ⓣ13 1777, Ⓦwww.unitedairlines.com.au

Travel agents

Anywhere Travel Australia Ⓣ02/9663 0411 & 018/401 014, Ⓔanywhere@ozemail.com.au.
Budget Travel New Zealand Ⓣ09/366 0061 & 0800/808 040, Ⓦwww.budgettravel.co.nz.
Destinations Unlimited New Zealand Ⓣ09/373 4033.
Flight Centres Australia Ⓣ02/9235 3522 or 13 16 00, New Zealand Ⓣ09/358 4310, Ⓦwww.flightcentre.com.au.
Northern Gateway Australia Ⓣ08/8941 1394, Ⓦww.northerngateway.com.au.
STA Travel Australia Ⓣ1300/360 960, Ⓦwww.statravel.com.au, New Zealand Ⓣ0508/782 872, Ⓦwww.statravel.co.nz.
Student Uni Travel Australia Ⓣ02/9232 8444, Ⓔaustralia@backpackers.net.
Thomas Cook Australia Ⓣ 1800/801 002, Ⓦwww.thomascook.com.au, New Zealand Ⓣ09/379 3920, Ⓦwww.thomascook.co.nz.
Trailfinders Australia Ⓣ02/9247 7666.
usit Beyond New Zealand Ⓣ09/379 4224 & 0800/788 336, Ⓦwww.usitbeyond.co.nz.

Packages and tours

Qantas Holidays Ⓣ13 1415, Ⓦwww.qantas.com.au. Week-long South Island ski packages from A$1000.
The Ski & Snowboard Travel Company Ⓣ02/9955 5201, Ⓦwww.skiandsnowboard.com.au. Good deals on custom designed skiing trips to Queenstown, Wanaka and Mount Hutt. Rates vary with dates, standard of accommodation etc.

Sydney International Travel Centre ⓣ02/9299 8000 or 1800/251 911, ⓦwww.sydneytravel.com.au. Excellent resource for flights and car rental.

Value Tours ⓣ1300/ 361 322, ⓦwww.valuetours.com.au. Skiing and snowboarding holidays throughout New Zealand, plus airfares, car and campervan rental and accommodation passes.

Visas and red tape

All visitors to New Zealand need a passport which must be valid for at least three months beyond the time you intend to stay, although if your home country has an embassy or consulate in New Zealand that can renew your passport, you can get away with one month.

On arrival, British citizens are automatically issued with a permit to stay for up to six months, and a three-month permit is granted to citizens of most other European countries, Southeast Asian nations, Japan, the USA and Canada. Australian citizens and permanent residents can stay indefinitely.

Other nationalities need to obtain a Visitor's Visa in advance from a New Zealand embassy, which costs the local equivalent of around NZ$200 and is normally valid for three months. Visas are issued by the New Zealand Immigration Service and in New Zealand (ⓦwww.immigration.govt.nz).

Embassies and consulates abroad

If your country isn't listed here, check at ⓦwww.mft.govt.nz/about/oseas.html.

Australia

High Commission: Commonwealth Avenue, Canberra, ACT 2600 ⓣ02/6270 4211, ⓔnzhccb@austrametro.com.au.
Consulates: Level 14, 1 Alfred St, Circular Quay, Sydney ⓣ02/9247 8567, ⓔnzcgsydney@bigpond.com; 60 Albert Rd, Melbourne ⓣ03/9696 0501; Watkins Place Building, 288 Edward St, Brisbane ⓣ07/3221 9933.

Canada

High Commission: Suite 727, 99 Bank St, Ottawa, Ontario K1P 6G3 ⓣ613/238 5991, ⓔnzhcott @istar.com.
Consulate: Suite 1200, 888 Dunsmuir St, Vancouver, British Columbia, V6C 3K4 ⓣ604/684 7388.

Ireland

New Zealand Consulate General: 37 Leeson Park, Dublin 6 ⓣ01/660 4233, ⓔnzconsul@indigo.ie.

UK

High Commission: The Haymarket, London SW1Y 4TQ ⓣ020/7973 0363.
Consulate: The Ballance House, 118a Lisburn Rd, Glenavy, Co. Antrim ⓣ028/9264 8098.

USA

Embassy: 37 Observatory Circle NW, Washington, DC 20008 ⓣ202/328 4800, ⓦwww.nzemb.org.
Consulates: Suite 1150, 12400 Wilshire Boulevard, Los Angeles ⓣ310/207 1605; Suite 1904, 780 Third Ave, New York 10017 ⓣ212/832 7420.

Customs regulations

In a country all too familiar with the damage that can be caused by the import of non-native plants and animals, New Zealand's Ministry of Agriculture and Fisheries (MAF) takes particular care to minimize the chance of destructive foreign bodies being introduced to the delicate environment of the country. Aircraft cabins are sometimes sprayed with insecticide before passengers are allowed to disembark, to kill off any stowaway insects or micro-organisms; the spray is apparently harmless to humans.

There are certain **prohibited imports**. The following must be declared at customs and will be either treated or confiscated: food, plants or parts of plants (dead or alive), animals (dead or alive), equipment used with animals, camping gear, golf clubs, used bicycles, biological specimens, and footwear (specifically walking boots). If your camping stuff or boots have soil deposits from other countries, they will be cleaned before being returned to you. Although it all seems a bit of a bind, in customs after a long flight, the reasons for these precautions are important and if you flout them you could be liable to fines ($200 on the spot, or higher) or at worse, they won't let you into the country.

The **duty-free allowance** is 200 cigarettes, or 250 grams of tobacco, or 50 cigars; alcohol allowances are a generous 4.5 litres of wine or beer, plus one bottle of not more than 1125ml of spirits. You may also be able to bring in a couple of extra bottles of spirits provided you have not already reached the limit and they do not exceed $50 duty charge.

There are **export restrictions** on wildlife, plantlife, antiquities and works of art. If you're unsure, contact the nearest customs office; there are offices in Auckland, Christchurch, Dunedin, Invercargill, Napier, Nelson, New Plymouth, Tauranga, Mount Maunganui, Timaru, Wellington and Whangarei. A more detailed rundown on these provisions is available on ⓦwww.quarantine.govt.nz.

Information, websites and maps

New Zealand promotes itself heavily and enthusiastically abroad through the New Zealand Tourism Board (see p.22), where enquiries will trigger a deluge of glossy brochures. Much of it comprises inspirational, if rose-tinted, images of the country but is of limited practical use. It is probably more fruitful to spend time surfing their extensive website ⓦwww.purenz.com.

Many of the information centres listed below, as well as some cafés, bars and hostels, keep a supply of **free newspapers** and **magazines** orientated towards backpackers and usually filled with promotional copy, but informative nonetheless. Two of the best are the New Zealand Backpackers News (ⓦwww.backpackernews.co.nz) and TNT (ⓦwww.tntmagazine.com/au).

Visitor centres

Once you arrive you'll soon be weighed down with leaflets advertising just about everything in the country. Every town of any size will have an **official visitor centre**, signified by the green Visitor Information Network (VIN) logo. These are invariably well-stocked, staffed by helpful and knowledgeable personnel and sometimes offer some form of video or slide presentation on the area. Apart from dishing out local maps and leaflets, they offer a **free booking service** for accommodation, trips and activities, and onward travel. In the more popular tourist areas, you'll also come across all manner of places presenting themselves as **independent information centres**, which always follow a hidden agenda, typically promoting a number of allied adventure companies. While these can be useful, it's worth remembering that their advice won't be impartial.

Other useful resources are **Department of Conservation (DOC;** ⓦwww.doc.govt.nz) offices and field centres, usually sited close to wilderness areas and popular tramping tracks, and often serving as the local visitor centre as well. Again these are highly informative and well-geared to trampers' needs, with local weather forecasts, intentions forms and maps. Their website is a motherlode of stuff on the environment and the latest conservation issues plus details on national parks and Great Walks.

Finally, drivers who are already members of motoring associations at home can generally make use of New Zealand's **Automobile Association** (AA; Ⓦwww.nzaa.co.nz), which provides many useful services to drivers (see p.33) and supports a nationwide network of offices (see "Listings" throughout the Guide), stocking excellent maps and providing information on accommodation.

New Zealand tourism board offices

New Zealand PO Box 95, Wellington Ⓣ04/ 917 5400, Ⓕ915 3817.
Australia Level 8, 35 Pitt St, Sydney, NSW 2000 Ⓣ02/9247 5222, Ⓕ9241 1136.
Canada Information line only Ⓣ1-866/639 9325.
United Kingdom New Zealand House, Haymarket, London, SW1Y 4TQ Ⓣ020/7930 1662, Ⓕ7839 8929, premium rated information line Ⓣ09069/101010; also handles enquiries from Ireland.
USA Suite 300, 501 Santa Monica Blvd, Santa Monica, CA 90401 Ⓣ310/395 7480 or 1-800/388 5494, Ⓕ395 5453; Suite 1904, 780 3rd Ave, New York, NY 10017-2024 Ⓣ212/832 8482, Ⓕ832 7602.

Websites

New Zealand has fully embraced the web and throughout the guide we've supplied **websites** for most businesses and any accommodation places which have a web presence. What follows is just a smattering of useful travel planning sites and assorted sites of general Kiwi interest.

Forest and Bird Society Ⓦwww.forest-bird.org.nz Mainstream conservation site with info on biosecurity, at-risk species and a handy bird finding guide.
Kiwi Music Ⓦwww.nzmusic.com Basic portal to websites of most of the more popular and important current Kiwi acts.
Maori Culture Ⓦwww.culture.co.nz Labour-of-love site dedicated to all things Maori with everything from personal profiles and Maori history to an online cookbook.
NZOOM Ⓦwww.nzoom.com TVNZ's "homepage for New Zealanders" with excellent coverage of news, sport entertainment, weather and much more.
NZ Birds Ⓦwww.nzbirds.com Comprehensive site on everything feathery in New Zealand.
NZ Tourism Board Ⓦwww.purenz.com Official site and a good starting point for general travel material.
Search NZ Ⓦwww.searchnz.co.nz Leading NZ-specific search engine.
Stuff Ⓦwww.stuff.co.nz General portal from the parent company of many of New Zealand's leading magazines and newspapers.
The Press Ⓦwww.press.co.nz Excellent site belonging to one of New Zealand's best daily papers: includes the latest news and reviews, plus a good subject search facility.
Women Travel Ⓦwww.womentravel.co.nz Essential information for the woman traveller in New Zealand with links to retreats, women-oriented tour operators and the chance to sign up for their newsletter.

Maps

Specialist outlets (see opposite) should have a reasonable stock of **maps** of New Zealand. The best available is the two-sided 1:1,000,000 edition produced by International Travel Maps (Ⓦwww.itmb.com), with all the important roads, and an attractive and instructive colour scheme giving a good sense of the country's terrain. The 1:2,000,000 maps produced by GeoCentre and Bartholomew come a distant joint second. **Road atlases** are widely available in New Zealand bookshops and service stations; the most detailed are those produced by Kiwi Pathfinder, which indicate numerous points of interest and the type of road surface – though some roads marked as unsealed have since been tar-sealed. The AA (see p.33) provide their members with simple but effective strip maps of major touring routes free of charge.

With a road atlas and our city plans you can't go far wrong on the roads, but more detailed maps may be required for **tramping**. All the major walks are covered by the Trackmap and Parkmap series, complete with photos ($13.50 from DOC offices and bookshops in New Zealand), or go for the larger scale Topo maps ($12.50), which cover the whole country.

Map outlets

Uk and Ireland

Blackwell's Map and Travel Shop 50 Broad St, Oxford OX1 3BQ ⓣ01865/793 550, ⓦhttp://maps.blackwell.co.uk/index.html.
Easons Bookshop 40 O'Connell St, Dublin 1 ⓣ01/873 3811, ⓦwww.eason.ie.
Heffers Map and Travel 20 Trinity St, Cambridge CB2 1TJ ⓣ01223/568 568, ⓦwww.heffers.co.uk.
Hodges Figgis Bookshop 56–58 Dawson St, Dublin 2 ⓣ01/677 4754, ⓦwww.hodgesfiggis.com.
John Smith & Son 100 Cathedral St, Glasgow G4 0RD ⓣ0141/552 3377, ⓦwww.johnsmith.co.uk.
James Thin Booksellers 53–59 South Bridge Edinburgh EH1 1YS ⓣ0131/622 8222, ⓦwww.jthin.co.uk.
The Map Shop 30a Belvoir St, Leicester LE1 6QH ⓣ0116/247 1400, ⓦwww.mapshopleicester.co.uk.
Newcastle Map Centre 55 Grey St, Newcastle upon Tyne, NE1 6EF ⓣ0191/261 5622.
Stanfords 12–14 Long Acre, WC2E 9LP ⓣ020/7836 1321, ⓦwww.stanfords.co.uk, ⓔsales@stanfords.co.uk. Maps available by mail, phone order, or email. Other branches within British Airways offices at 156 Regent St, London W1R 5TA ⓣ020/7434 4744, and 29 Corn St, Bristol BS1 1HT ⓣ0117/929 9966.
The Travel Bookshop 13–15 Blenheim Crescent, W11 2EE ⓣ020/7229 5260, ⓦwww.thetravelbookshop.co.uk.

In Australia and New Zealand

The Map Shop 6–10 Peel St, Adelaide, SA 5000 ⓣ08/8231 2033, ⓦwww.mapshop.net.au.
Specialty Maps 46 Albert St, Auckland 1001 ⓣ09/307 2217, ⓦwww.ubdonline.co.nz/maps.
MapWorld 173 Gloucester St, Christchurch, New Zealand ⓣ0800/627 967 & 03/374 5399, ⓦwww.mapworld.co.nz.
Mapland 372 Little Bourke St, Melbourne, Victoria 3000, ⓣ03/9670 4383, ⓦwww.mapland.com.au.
Perth Map Centre 1/884 Hay St, Perth, WA 6000, ⓣ08/9322 5733, ⓦwww.perthmap.com.au.

In the USA

Adventurous Traveler Bookstore 102 Lake Street, Burlington, VT 05401 ⓣ1-800/282-3963, ⓦwww.adventuroustraveler.com.
Book Passage 51 Tamal Vista Blvd, Corte Madera, CA 94925 ⓣ1-800/999-7909, ⓦwww.bookpassage.com.
Distant Lands 56 S Raymond Ave, Pasadena, CA 91105 ⓣ1-800/310-3220, ⓦwww.distantlands.com.
Elliot Bay Book Company 101 S Main St, Seattle, WA 98104 ⓣ1-800/962-5311, ⓦwww.elliotbaybook.com.
Forsyth Travel Library 226 Westchester Ave, White Plains, NY 10604 ⓣ1-800/367-7984, ⓦwww.forsyth.com.
Globe Corner Bookstore 28 Church St, Cambridge, MA 02138 ⓣ1-800/358-6013, ⓦwww.globercorner.com.
GORP Travel ⓣ1-877/440-4677, ⓦwww.gorp.com/gorp/books/main.htm.
Map Link 30 S La Patera Lane, Unit 5, Santa Barbara, CA 93117 ⓣ805/692-6777, ⓦwww.maplink.com.
Rand McNally ⓣ1-800/333-0136, ⓦwww.randmcnally.com. Around thirty stores across the US; dial ext 2111 or check the website for the nearest location.
The Travel Bug Bookstore 2667 W Broadway, Vancouver V6K 2G2 ⓣ604/737-1122, ⓦwww.swifty.com/tbug.
World of Maps 1235 Wellington St, Ottawa, Ontario K1Y 3A3 ⓣ1-800/214-8524, ⓦwww.worldofmaps.com.

Insurance

New Zealand's Accident Compensation Commission (®www.acc.co.nz) provides limited medical treatment for visitors injured while in New Zealand, but this is no substitute for having comprehensive travel insurance to cover against theft, loss and illness or injury.

Before paying for a new policy, however, it's worth checking whether you are already covered: some all-risks home insurance policies may cover your possessions when overseas, and many private medical schemes include cover when abroad. In Canada, provincial health plans usually provide partial cover for medical mishaps overseas, while holders of official student/teacher/youth cards in Canada and the US are entitled to meagre accident coverage and hospital in-patient benefits. Students will often find that their student health coverage extends during the vacations and for one term beyond the date of last enrolment.

After exhausting the possibilities above, you might want to contact a specialist travel insurance company, or consider the travel insurance deal we offer (see box). A typical travel insurance **policy** usually provides cover for the loss of baggage, tickets and – up to a certain limit – cash or cheques, as well as cancellation or curtailment of your journey. Most of them exclude so-called **dangerous activities** unless an extra premium is paid: in New Zealand this can mean scuba-diving, bungy jumping, whitewater rafting, windsurfing and even tramping under some policies.

Many policies can be chopped and changed to exclude coverage you don't need – for example, sickness and accident benefits can often be excluded or included at will. If you do take medical coverage, ascertain whether benefits will be paid as treatment proceeds or only after return home, and whether there is a 24-hour medical emergency number. When securing **baggage cover**, make sure that the per-article limit – typically under £500 – will cover your most valuable possession. If you need to make a claim, you should keep receipts for medicines and medical treatment, and in the event you have anything stolen, you must obtain an official statement from the police.

Rough Guides travel insurance

Rough Guides offers its own travel insurance, customized for our readers by a leading UK broker and backed by a Lloyds underwriter. It's available for anyone, of any nationality and any age, travelling anywhere in the world.

There are two main Rough Guide insurance plans: **Essential**, for basic, no-frills cover; and **Premier** – with more generous and extensive benefits. Alternatively, you can take out **annual multi-trip insurance**, which covers you for any number of trips throughout the year (with a maximum of 60 days for any one trip). Unlike many policies, the Rough Guides schemes are calculated by the day, so if you're travelling for 27 days rather than a month, that's all you pay for. If you intend to be away for the whole year, the Adventurer policy will cover you for 365 days. Each plan can be supplemented with a "Hazardous Activities Premium" if you plan to indulge in sports considered dangerous, such as skiing, scuba-diving or trekking.

For a policy quote, call the Rough Guide Insurance Line on UK freefone ⓣ0800/015 09 06; US freefone ⓣ1-866/220 5588, or, if you're calling from elsewhere ⓣ+44 1243/621 046. Alternatively, get an **online** quote or buy online at ®www.roughguides.com/insurance.

Health

New Zealand is relatively free of serious health hazards and the most common pitfalls are not taking precautions or simply underestimating the power of nature. No vaccinations are required to enter the country, but you should make sure you have adequate health cover in your travel insurance, especially if you plan to take on the Great Outdoors (see p.56 for advice on tramping health and safety).

New Zealand has a fine health service, despite recent government cuts, and medical services are reasonably cheap by world standards. Although all visitors are covered by the accident compensation scheme, under which you can claim some medical and hospital expenses in the event of an accident, without full accident cover in your travel insurance, you could still face a hefty bill. For more minor ailments, you can visit a **doctor** for a consultation around ($35) and, armed with a prescription, buy any required medication at a reasonable price.

AIDS is as much of an issue in New Zealand as elsewhere but official attitudes are reasonably enlightened, and there are no restrictions on people with HIV or AIDS entering the country. Support organizations include the New Zealand AIDS Foundation, 76 Grafton Rd, Grafton, Auckland (Ⓣ09/303 3124), and the 24-hour HIV/AIDS National Hotline (Ⓣ0800/802 437). For further information you can also contact the New Zealand Aids Foundation on their website Ⓦwww.nzaf.org.nz.

Perhaps the most hazardous element of the whole New Zealand experience is getting there, in the light of a growing realization that long periods of time spent in cramped conditions on aeroplanes can create **deep vein thrombosis** (DVT). All the airlines now have videos telling you to move about, perform stationary callisthenics and drink plenty of water. It also helps to limit the amount of booze you consume and, if you are unsure, contact your GP before travelling to find out if you are predisposed toward this problem and what you can do about it.

The sun

The biggest health problem for visitors to New Zealand is over-exposure to the **sun**, which shines more fiercely here than in the northern hemisphere, its damaging ultra-violet rays reaching a far greater intensity, with a burn time in the spring and summer of as little as ten minutes. You should take extra care, especially at first, to avoid burning. New Zealand has a high rate of **skin cancer**, so it makes sense to slap on maximum-protection sunblock. Remember to re-apply every few hours as well as after swimming, and you should avoid **sunbathing** altogether between 11am and 3pm, when the sun is at its strongest. Keep a check on any moles on your body and if you notice any changes, during or after your trip, see a doctor right away.

Wildlife hazards

Something worth avoiding is **giardia**, a parasite that inhabits rivers and lakes in some national parks. Infection results from drinking contaminated water, with symptoms appearing several weeks later: a bloated stomach, cramps, explosive diarrhoea and wind. The Department of Conservation advises on the likely presence of giardia in national parks around the country. To minimize the risk of infection, purify drinking water by using iodine-based solutions or tablets (regular chlorine-based tablets aren't effective against giardia); by fast-boiling water for at least seven minutes; or by using a giardia-rated filter (obtainable from any outdoors or camping shop).

The relatively rare **amoebic meningitis** is another water-borne hazard, this time contracted from hot thermal pools. The amoeba enters the body via the nose or ears, lodges in the brain, and weeks later causes severe headaches, stiffness of the neck, hypersensitivity to light, and eventually coma. If you experience any of these symptoms, seek medical attention immediately, but to avoid contamination in the first place, simply don't put your head underwater in thermal pools.

Virtually without exception, New Zealand wildlife is harmless. Even **shark** attacks are rare; you are more likely to be carried away by a strong tide than a great white, though it still pays to be sensible and obey any local warnings when swimming.

The country is free of snakes, scorpions and other nasties, and there's only one poisonous creature: the little **katipo spider**. Mercifully rare, this six-millimetre-long critter (the biting female is black with a red patch), is found in coastal areas – except in the far south – and only bites if disturbed. The bite can be fatal, but antivenin is available in most hospitals, is effective up to three days after a bite and no one has died from an encounter with the spider for many years. The West Coast of the South Island in the summer is the worst place for **mosquitoes** and **sandflies**, though they appear to a lesser degree in many other places across the country. They are more irritating than dangerous and a liberal application of repellent keeps most of them at bay, albeit briefly.

Geological hazards

Although common in New Zealand, **earthquakes** are usually minor. If the worst happens, the best advice is to stand in a doorway or crouch under a table. If caught in the open, try to get inside; failing that, keep your distance from trees and rocky outcrops to reduce the chances of being injured by falling branches or debris. New Zealand's **volcanoes** also have a habit of making their presence felt: vulcanologists are often able to predict periods of eruptive activity, and if warnings are issued, get at least as far away as they suggest.

Costs, money and banks

After a few years riding the crest of an economic wave, New Zealand has more recently experienced a downturn in the economy and a resulting dive in the value of the New Zealand dollar. Consequently, most things will seem fairly cheap by European and North American standards. The quality of goods and standards of service you can expect are high and, on balance, the country offers very good value for money, though fluctuating exchange rates introduce some uncertainty.

New Zealanders are a straightforward bunch and the price quoted is what you pay. In almost all cases, the 12.5 percent Goods and Service Tax (GST) is included in the listed price, and no tip is expected.

The **currency** is the Kiwi dollar, or "buck", divided into 100 cents. There are $100, $50, $20, $10 and $5 notes made of a sturdy plastic material, and coins in denominations of $2 and $1, and 50¢, 20¢, 10¢ and 5¢; grocery prices are given to the nearest cent, but the final bill is rounded up or down to the nearest five cents.

Basic costs

With the prevalence of good hostels, single travellers can live almost as cheaply as couples, though you'll pay around thirty percent more if you insist on having a room to yourself. **Accommodation** costs from as little as a couple of dollars for a basic campsite, but a $10-per person pitch or a $15–20 dorm bed in a hostel is more common. Simple double rooms start from as little as $35, though you'll pay $70–90 for a motel unit, $70–120 for homestays and B&Bs, $150–300 for flash international-standard hotels, and anything up to $1000 a person for exclusive retreats. **Food** is good quality and great value; supermarkets are reasonably priced and you can usually find a filling plateful at a pub or café for under $12. A reasonable three-course meal will cost upwards of $35, though you can save on drinks by patronizing **BYO** (Bring Your Own) restaurants, where you can drink wine you've brought with you. Though still quite common in smaller places, these are harder to find in the cities. **Drinking** in pubs and restaurants is substantially more expensive than buying from a bottle shop (liquor store) or from a supermarket.

Given New Zealand's compact size, **transport** costs shouldn't be prohibitive, but if you find yourself moving on every couple of days it can soon add up. Though you are unlikely to return from New Zealand laden with souvenirs, you can completely blow your budget on **adventure trips** – such as a bungy jump (around $130) or tandem parachuting ($170 and up). If you've got the money, by all means spend it; if not, think carefully about how best to get the maximum enjoyment from your visit.

Student **discounts** are few and far between, but you can make substantial savings on accommodation and travel by buying one of the backpacker cards (see p.30 & 31); **kids** and **seniors** enjoy reductions of around fifty percent on most trains, buses and entry to many sights.

Travellers' cheques, credit and debit cards

The safest way to carry your money is still as **travellers' cheques**, which can be exchanged efficiently at banks and bureaux de change all over New Zealand, will be replaced if they are lost or stolen, and usually offer a slightly better exchange rate. Recognized brands – American Express, Thomas Cook, Mastercard and Visa – are accepted in all major currencies and, though travellers' cheques in New Zealand dollars relieve the uncertainty of fluctuating exchange rates, they aren't generally accepted as cash. You usually pay one to two percent commission when you buy travellers' cheques but there is seldom an additional charge when you cash them.

Visitors increasingly rely on **credit cards** – Visa, Mastercard, Bankcard and, to a lesser extent, American Express and Diners Club – which are widely accepted, though some supermarkets and many hostels, campsites and homestays will only accept cash. You'll also find credit cards useful for advance booking of accommodation and trips, and with the appropriate Personal identification Number (PIN) you can obtain **cash advances** through 24-hour ATMs found almost everywhere. You should be aware that such withdrawals may accrue interest immediately or be subject to a two percent premium – check with your bank before you go too wild. Most ATMs also have the facility for international **debit card** transactions using the Plus and Cirrus networks.

Banks and exchange

The best exchange rates are usually from **banks**. ASB, ANZ, BNZ, National Bank and WestpacTrust have branches in towns of any size and are open from Monday to Friday 9.30am to 4.30pm except for public holidays. Outside banking hours, you'll have to rely on **bureaux de change** in the big cities and tourist centres, which are typically open from 8am to 8pm daily. If you get caught short, the larger hotels will often change travellers' cheques at any time, but rates tend to be poor.

Exchange rates tend to be fairly stable in relation to the Australian and US dollars, less so against European currencies. The New Zealand dollar currently trades at NZ$3.1 for £1, NZ$2.1 for US$1 and NZ$1.15 for A$1.

If you are spending some time in New Zealand – say a couple of months or more – you may want to open a **bank account**. The ease of doing so seems to depend largely on the whim of the bank clerk, so shop around: having a New Zealand address you can use for statements helps (though isn't always necessary), and you'll need a couple of pieces of ID.

The big advantage of having an account is that you can get money from branches and ATMs using an **EFTPOS card**, which also enables you to pay for stuff at shops, service stations, restaurants, in fact just about anywhere, by swiping the card and punching in your PIN. Most shops will also give you cash, so you can go for weeks without ever visiting a bank.

Wiring money

The best way to get money sent out is to get in touch with your bank at home and have them **wire money** to the nearest bank. It may take a week but it is relatively cheap – you'll probably pay twice as much to have cash sent through Western Union (Ⓣ0800/270 000; Ⓦwww.westernunion.com) or through the nearest branch of Thomas Cook (Ⓦwww.us.thomascook.com), who offer their own proprietary service and also use the faster Travelers Express MoneyGram (Ⓣ0800/262 263; Ⓦwww.moneygram.com). In all cases, the fees charged are independent of source or destination, and only depend on the amount being transferred: wiring NZ$1000, or equivalent, will cost NZ$70 for example. The funds should be available for collection at the company's local office within minutes of being sent, and by using this service the sender can dispatch cash by phone by using their credit card.

Getting around

New Zealand is a relatively small country and getting around is easy, with some form of transport going to most destinations, though often you may be limited to one or two services per day.

Although it is possible to **fly** to many of the major destinations in New Zealand, there is substantial expense involved. With time to spare you will appreciate the scenery better by travelling at ground level. The **rail** service is very limited and is also quite expensive, while the Interislander **ferries** connecting the North and South islands have hardly any competition but somehow remain quite good value. The cheapest and easiest way to get around is by **bus** or shuttle bus but this is also the most time-consuming mode of travel.

For getting off the beaten track, you'll need a car. **Rental cars** are fine for short periods, but if you are staying in the country for more than a couple of months, it's more economical to **buy** a car. New Zealand is renowned for its green countryside and some travellers prefer to **cycle** their way around.

You'll still need to take to the air or the water (or go tramping) to reach the offshore islands and the remoter parts of the main islands that remain stubbornly impenetrable by road, though as each year passes some areas, such as Fiordland, become progressively easier to access by specialist tour or improved track, road and highway.

Regular long-distance bus, train and plane services are found under "Travel details" at the end of each chapter, with local buses and trains covered in the main text.

Domestic flights

As Air New Zealand have a stranglehold on most **domestic services,** prices remain uniformly high, although there is limited competition from Quantas and Origin Pacific as well as a few tiny schedule and charter operators who tend to concentrate on small areas. Business- and economy-class **fares**, as well as limited-availability advance-purchase ones bookable only in New Zealand, are all on offer; a full-fare economy-class one-way flight from Auckland to Christchurch is currently about $300. There are, however, a number of small companies (most wholly or partly owned by Air New Zealand) flying specific routes that offer good deals from time to time; check the latest with local visitor centres, the airline or your travel agent. Two of the most useful short hops are the very scenic Southern Air flights from Invercargill to Stewart Island around ($120) and the cheap trip over Cook Strait from either the North or South islands for about the same cost as a ferry ticket, but taking only half an hour. Advance-purchase **discounts** (14–21 days for a 30–65 percent on Air New Zealand and Mount Cook flights) must be booked in New Zealand. Standby fares (50 percent off) are available on some Air New Zealand flights to holders of YHA and VIP cards. Over-60s airfares are only available to New Zealand residents.

Air New Zealand **air passes** are good value if you are flying between the major destinations on the main islands but otherwise they don't represent a great saving. The minimum purchase is three coupons ($515) and the maximum is ten (the more you buy up to ten the cheaper each one gets; $1373), each redeemable for one flight. You can get a refund on any leftover coupons so long as you apply before you leave the country.

Domestic flight operators

Adventure Charter ⓣ021/184 1649, ⓦwww.adventurecharter.co.nz.
Air Coromandel ⓣ09/256 7025 or ⓣ09/275 9120, ⓦwww.mountainair.co.nz.
Air New Zealand ⓣ0800/737 000, ⓦwww.airnewzealand.co.nz.
Freedom Air ⓣ0800 600 500, ⓦwww.freedomair.co.nz.
Great Barrier Airlines see Air Coromandel.
Great Barrier Island Express see Air Coromandel.
Mountain Air ⓣ07/892 2812, ⓦwww.mountainair.co.nz.
Mountain Air see Air Coromandel.
Origin Pacific ⓣ0800 302 302, ⓦwww.originpacific.co.nz.
Skylink ⓣ09/275 5885, ⓦwww.skylink.co.nz.
Sounds Air ⓣ03/218 9129, ⓦwww.sirf.to/soundsair.
Stewart Island Flights ⓣ03/218 9129, ⓦwww.stewartislandflights.com.
Tasman Bay Aviation ⓣ03/547 2378, ⓦwww.flytasmanbay.co.nz.

Ferries

The **ferries** you're most likely to use are those plying the Cook Strait between the North and South islands, but there are also ferries to Stewart Island from the South Island and from Auckland to the Hauraki Gulf islands. Information about these short trips is included in our accounts on Invercargill and Auckland.

The **Interislander** fleet (ⓣ0800/802 802, ⓦwww.theinterislander.co.nz) that shuttles between Wellington on the North Island and Picton on the South Island consists of three ferries and the quicker wave-piercing catamaran called the *Lynx*. All the conventional ferries run seven days a week year-round, take around three hours, are very reliable and surprisingly comfortable in most conditions. The *Lynx* is a good deal quicker, takes half the time and, being more modern, is slightly more luxurious. Standard **fares** are around $52, $69 for *Lynx*, one-way, though **reductions** can be had through advance-purchase tickets (on a sliding scale of 15–50 percent discount if booked 7–28 days in advance) on selected sailings, usually early morning or late at night; add $10 each way for a bike, and around $162 for a car. You'll generally get the best deal by booking direct. The *Lynx's* wave-piercing technology makes it an easier ride in lumpy seas and it runs most of the time.

Trains

Tranz Scenic (ⓣ0800/802 802, ⓦwww-tranzscenic.co.nz), the main passenger-carrying service, are in a real mess, and routes and frequencies are disappearing to the point where the government is having to step in to keep some of them running. All that are left are commuter services (good in Wellington; poor in Auckland), passenger trains from Auckland to Wellington, and from Picton to Christchurch, and two of the best rail journeys in the world, the **Tranz Alpine** – a trip to and from Christchurch, through Arthurs Pass, stopping in Greymouth – and the **Taieri Gorge Railway** – from Dunedin to Middlemarch and back. These last two services are scenic trips run almost entirely for the benefit of tourists and are priced accordingly.

Most **carriages** are air-conditioned, with on-board phones and huge picture windows; airline-style meals (including vegetarian options) are served at your seat, and there's also a buffet car. Passengers check in on the platform before boarding (a ticket guarantees a seat) and bags are carried in a luggage van. As a contrast to the trains, **stations** tend to be in a depressingly run-down state.

A standard, non-discounted **fare** from Auckland to Wellington is around $150; Picton to Christchurch will set you back $73. Advance-purchase fares (economy, saver and super saver), offering **discounts** of 25–50 percent, are available in limited numbers; day-excursion fares, also limited in number, are discounted by thirty percent. No Frills tickets, also limited in number, offer significant reductions (around fifty percent) for travelling in older, non-air-conditioned carriages. Discounts of fifteen–thirty percent are available to YHA, BBH and VIP card holders. Over-sixties are entitled to a thirty-percent reduction on all services. Blind and other disabled travellers are entitled to a fifty-percent discount if they present authorization (from the DPA; see p.69).

Tranz Scenic also offers a range of **combined travel passes**; see the box below for more on these.

Public transport buses

Public transport buses and **shuttle buses** (minibuses) will get you to most places. Because of stiff competition, they are the cheapest form of public transport, although note that the big bus operators charge more for South Island journeys than for North due to having more of a monopoly on the transport infrastructure. In general, services are reliable and reasonably comfortable: the larger buses are usually air-conditioned; some have toilets and show feature films and New Zealand promotional material to while away longer journeys.

Standard **fares** from Auckland to Wellington are in the region of $100–110; Christchurch to Queenstown, $140–170; Queenstown to Nelson, $185–210; and Christchurch to Picton, $50–70. Prices often plummet during off-peak periods and a range of discounted fares is available. Advance-purchase fares offer thirty-percent **discounts** for tickets bought five days ahead of travel, and there are a limited number of fifty-percent discounts available on a first-come, first-served basis. YHA, BBH and VIP cardholders get 30 percent **discounts** with InterCity and Newmans.

InterCity (Ⓣ09/913 6100, Ⓦwww.intercitycoach.co.nz) also offer fixed-route **passes** such as the Coromandel Loop Pass (Thames to Coromandel, Whitianga and back; $54); Pacific Coast Traveller (around the east coast to Gisborne and Napier via Rotorua; $209); North Island Value Pass (any route between Auckland and Wellington; $135); and the Forests, islands and geysers (which combines bits of the above for a whole island experience; $341). Prices for their South Island pass options include the West Coast Passport (Nelson to Queenstown; $149); the East Coast Explorer

Combined travel passes

Tranz Scenic's **Best of New Zealand Pass** range (Ⓣ0800/692 378, Ⓦwww.bestpass.co.nz) combines **train, buses,** ferry and **plane travel** on a points system. You buy 600–1000 points, and each journey that you take detracts so many points from your total. Although it involves a lot of pre-planning it is economic, particularly for those with a strict itinerary who book at least a couple of days in advance; 1000 points cost $725 and you'll use up around 115 points for a coach trip to Rotorua from Auckland, or 72 points from Picton to Christchurch. Complicated as it may seem, 600–1000 points would effectively cover all the transport for the length of most holidays, assuming you don't want to stray too far from the beaten track.

Another good travel pass option comes from **New Zealand Travel Pass Ltd** (Ⓦwww.travelpass.co.nz), who offer the option of purchasing 5–22 days of combined travel, with the cost depending upon the various transport modes you choose; five days of coach and ferry travel (the former with either Newmans or Intercity) is $324; with rail options it's $424; add on a short flight and it's $590; while a longer flight increases the price to $757.

(Te Anau to Picton, via Dunedin and Christchurch; $149); and the Milford Bound (Christchurch to Milford, via Mount Cook and Queenstown; $149); a combination of the best bits of the North and South islands is available as a Pathfinder ($408–588).

Newmans (ⓣ09/913 6200, ⓦwww.newmanscoach.co.nz) passes are good value though considerably more restricted in timetable and destination. The deal is for either of the two islands – a look around the major parts of the North or a more limited visit to the South ($99–165). You break your journey where you choose and book buses for the next stage (usually $5 each time you move into a new sector, the country being divided into various sectors for fare purposes).

Note that once you've bought your ticket or pass, you may incur an agent's **reservation fee** of $5 unless you book direct.

Shuttle buses

A host of **shuttle bus** companies fill in the gaps around the country – more on the South Island than the North – linking with the services of the major operators to take you off the beaten track and adding alternative services to the major routes. An ever-growing number of operators also compete with the big companies on the main routes; though generally cheaper, they're not as comfortable over long distances.

Most visitor centres carry **timetables**, so you can compare destinations and fares. **Fares** can be as low as half the price of standard (but not discounted) bus fares, for example Christchurch to Queenstown ($50 plus), Picton to Christchurch ($35 plus), or Queenstown to Dunedin ($35 plus), though these vary with supply and demand.

Backpacker buses

One of the cheapest ways to cover a lot of ground is on a **backpacker bus**, which combines the flexibility of independent travel with the convenience of a tour. You purchase a ticket for a fixed route (valid for up to six months), then either stick with the one bus or stay in some places longer and hop on a later one. The ticket does not cover accommodation, activities (although these are often discounted), side-trips or food.

The best buses and deals are run by **Magic Bus** who work in with the YHA and whose service is pretty comprehensive on both islands, reliable and flexible. Trips are generally less gung-ho than those targeted at the 18–30-something market and target more independently minded travellers (Auckland ⓣ09/358 5600, Wellington ⓣ04/387 2018, Christchurch ⓣ03/377 0951, ⓦwww.magicbus.co.nz) offering well-planned options (2–23 days; $109–985). They also offer a travel pass which includes travel and discounted accommodation but it is only available through travel agents outside New Zealand.

Best known of the backpacker bus operators are **Kiwi Experience** (Auckland ⓣ09/366 1665, Wellington ⓣ04/385 2153, Christchurch ⓣ03/377 0550, ⓔenquiries@kiwiex.co.nz, ⓦwww.kiwiexperience.com), who offer various trips from 1–35 days for $61–1500 that have a reputation for attracting high spirited revellers. However, such is the popularity of these buses that if you decide to break your journey you may have to wait up to a week before being able to continue on another bus, particularly in the summer. That said, YHA, BBH and VIP cardholders get five percent off Kiwi Experience tickets.

Stray (ⓣ07/824 3627, ⓦwww.straytravel.co.nz) are another independent company offering similar tours to Kiwi Experience and Magic, but with smaller groups and a more personal touch.

Specialist tours

Some of the most complete guided **wilderness tours** suitable for anyone who is reasonably fit and wants to see things that few other tourists will are run by New Zealand Nature Safaris, PO Box 93, Lyttelton (ⓣ0800/697 232, ⓕ04/563 7324), on South Island, and Active Earth, PO Box 93, Lyttelton (ⓣ0800/201 040) on North – essentially one company that has split to deal with each island separately. Good-humoured and informative guides take small groups tramping, climbing and wilderness camping in virtually untouched country throughout New Zealand, with almost everything included (around $920 for 10 days), except your own outdoor gear, a daily food and camp-fee kitty (around $18) and any extra adventure activities. More upmarket tours are organized by Kiwi Wildlife Tours (☎09/427 5801, Ⓦwww.kiwi-wildlife.co.nz) who offer three-week-long, small-group specialist birding tours with everything included once you arrive. Prices are around $10,000.

Adventure South (☎03/332 1222, Ⓦwww.advsouth.co.nz) are another small, environmentally conscious company who run guided and self-guided **cycling** and **hiking tours** around the South Island, with accommodation in characterful lodges. They include a two-week "Midlife Adventures" trip designed for "those too young to be called old, and too old to be called young". Trips range from five days ($1365) to twenty days ($6000). Cyclists can also try Pedaltours (☎09/302 0968 & 0800/302 0968, US freephone ☎1-888/222 9187, Ⓦwww.pedaltours.co.nz), who offer guided road and **mountain biking tours** of both islands, from a gentle three-day jaunt around the Marlborough wine country (around $500), to a full nineteen-day Grand Tour of the South Island (around $6000). High-standard accommodation and hearty meals are included, and bikes can be rented from them if needed (around $100 extra a week); there is also often luggage transfer and/or minibus support. Customized tours can be arranged for groups. Cycle Touring Company (☎09/436 0033, Ⓦwww.cycletours.co.nz) also offer tailored tours (self led or guided) of Northland, with several routes of two to twelve days, and the option to have your gear carried for you. Accommodation is in lodges and homestays and prices are around $2000 for a week.

Motorcycle tours can be organized through Adventure New Zealand Motorcycle Tours, 82 Achilles Avenue, Nelson (mobile ☎021/969 071, Ⓦwww.thunderbike.co.nz/anzmtr), who provide boutique, small-group trips around the South Island; itineraries can often be tweaked to suit. Tours are accompanied by a luxury coach, and everything is done to the highest standard. Rates range from $6500 for a standard ten-day trip to $8000 for a fourteen-day deluxe ride. Also providing similar services at the same kind of prices (though starting a little lower at $5970), are New Zealand Motorcycle Rentals/Tours (☎03/337 0663 for Christchurch, ☎09/377 2005 for Auckland, Ⓦwww.nzbike.com). Otherwise try Motorcycling Downunder (☎03/366 0129, Ⓦhttp://1800NZ.com/motorcycles); or Te Waipounamu Motorcycle Tours (☎09/489 9242, Ⓦwww.motorcycle-hire.co.nz).

Women-only tours are run by Wanderwomen, PO Box 68058, Newton, Auckland (☎09/360 7330, Ⓦwww.wanderwomen.co.nz), who provide safe, environmentally aware outdoor activities from a few hours of kayaking or caving ($40–70) to multi-day adventure holidays (roughly $120 a day including accommodation and food) taking in tramping, rock climbing, ice climbing, snorkelling, surfing and other sports. They also do some **family excursions**.

Driving

If your budget will stretch to it, driving is the best way to go, enabling you to get to places beyond the reach of public transport and to set your own timetable, although it's worth being conscious of the damage to the environment cars cause and using more eco-friendly transport wherever possible.

In order to drive in New Zealand you need a valid **licence** from Australia, Britain, Canada, Fiji, Germany, Namibia, The Netherlands, Switzerland or South Africa; citizens of other countries need to obtain an International Driver's Licence before they leave (available from national motoring organizations).

Road rules are similar to those in the UK, Australia and the US, but if you plan to do much driving, you could pick up a copy of *The Road Guide* from AA offices or selected bookshops and newsagents for about $14.95. The one variation peculiar to New Zealand is that you must give way to all traffic crossing or coming from your right; this means that if you are turning left and another car coming from the opposite direction wants to turn right into the same side-road, you must let them go first. Most importantly, drive on the left, and remember that **seat-belts** are compulsory for all occupants. Always park in the same direction as that in which you are travelling; roadside **parking** facing oncoming traffic is illegal.

The **speed limit** for the open road is 100km/hr, reduced to 50km/hr in built-up areas and in limited speed zones (signposted LSZ) when road conditions are deemed unsafe – owing to bad weather, poor visibility, crossing pedestrians, cyclists or excessive traffic. The fine for speeding is currently $120; some drivers warn others of lurking police patrols by flashing their headlights at oncoming cars. **Drink driving** is a major problem in New Zealand: as part of a campaign to cut the death-toll, random breath tests have been introduced, and offenders are dealt with severely.

Unleaded and super unleaded **petrol** and diesel are available in New Zealand. Prices currently hover around 97¢ a litre for unleaded, $1.02 for super unleaded, and 75¢ for diesel, with higher prices in more out-of-the-way places.

If you're driving your own vehicle, check if the **New Zealand Automobile Association** (Ⓦwww.nzaa.co.nz) has reciprocal rights with motoring organizations from your country to see if you qualify for their cover; otherwise, you can join as an overseas visitor. Apart from free 24-hour **emergency breakdown service** (Ⓣ0800/500 222) – excluding vehicles bogged on beaches – membership entitles you to free maps, accommodation guides and legal assistance, discounts on some rental cars and accommodation, plus access to insurance and pre-purchase vehicle inspection services.

Road conditions are generally good: most roads are sealed, although a few have a metalled surface composed of an aggregate of loose chippings. Clearly marked on most maps, these are slower to drive along, are prone to wash-outs and landslides after heavy rain, and demand considerably more care and attention from the driver. Some rental companies prohibit the use of their cars on the worst metalled roads – typically those along Ninety Mile Beach, Skippers Canyon and around the Coromandel Peninsula. Always check conditions locally before setting off on these routes.

Compared with most parts of the world, there are relatively few cars on the roads, but **traffic** can still be a problem around the major cities and on public holidays. Other **hazards** include flocks of sheep and slow, wide farm equipment on country roads, as well as monstrous logging trucks in forested regions, one-lane right-of-way bridges and a paucity of passing lanes.

Vehicle rental

Although you can get good **rental** deals with the major international companies, you'll usually find cheaper rates from local firms if you shop around. Your best bet is to go for mid-range firms rather than those that appear to offer rock-bottom rates; we've listed the more reliable operators throughout the Guide. Vehicle rental is **seasonal**: from December to February prices are at their highest, but for the rest of the year companies will be prepared to make deals, and don't be afraid to haggle.

You need a full, clean **driver's licence** and you must be over 21; drivers under 25 often have to pay more for insurance. For most roads you won't need **4WD** and, since 4WD rental rates are steep (usually $10–20 extra per day), you'll do best to rent for specific areas rather than long term. Daily **car-rental** rates with the major companies are in the region of $80–90 for a small two-door hatchback, or $100 for a medium-sized four-door saloon. With mid-range and smaller companies you can get a car on the road for about $65 a day, although many advertise cheaper rates, then add on extra charges for insurance and mileage. Weekly rates should save you around $5 or $10 per day. One-way rental usually incurs a large drop-off fee, which can be as much as $120–150. However, since most one-way rentals seem to go from north to south, if you're travelling in the opposite direction, you may be able to sweet-talk your way out of drop-off charges. There is often a glut of cars in Queenstown and Christchurch and companies may be glad to get them dropped off in Picton; the same applies in Wellington, if you're heading upcountry to Auckland. Also, by using the cars on the journey you're ensuring that they don't just get returned to their original garage, fouling up the environment for no good reason.

Campervan-rental rates average about $150–180 a day during the high season (Oct–April), dropping to $100–130 the rest of the year. The two most popular rental firms are Maui and Brits, but a few smaller companies offer slightly cheaper rates. Freedom Campervans also have an office in the UK and offer vans for $80–150 a day, depending on season, and Greentours have converted Toyota vans for about $65 a day or $370 a week, year round.

Although no special licence is required to drive a campervan some caution is needed, especially in high winds and when climbing hills and going around tight corners. Bear in mind, too, that you are not allowed to park a campervan in a lay-by overnight – though you're unlikely to be hassled in isolated areas. Finally have some consideration for other road users; in a campervan you are the slowest thing on the road so let people pass wherever possible.

A few things to get straight before signing on the dotted line for any rental:

The **accident cover and bond**. Before giving you a car, rental companies take a credit-card slip or a cash bond from you for anything up to $1000 (usually between $500 and $750). If you have an accident, the bond is used to pay for any damage: in some cases you pay anything up to the value of the bond; in others you pay the entire bond, no matter how slight the damage.

A **Value of Collision Damage Waiver** will cost extra but means that if you have an accident, you won't automatically forfeit your bond.

Check exactly how much **damage** you'll be liable for in the event of an accident. Although some companies only charge a $500 bond, the contract might stipulate that you are in fact liable for the first $1000 worth of damage.

Check the car for any visible **defects**, so you won't end up being charged for someone else's mistakes.

Check whether there are any **restrictions** on driving along certain roads.

If you'll be driving a fair distance, avoid **limited-mileage deals** whereby you pay for each kilometre in excess of a set daily allowance.

Check that **insurance cover** is adequate, bearing in mind any existing travel or vehicle insurance you may have.

Vehicle rental agencies in New Zealand

Adventure Campervans ⓣ0800/844 255, ⓦwww.nzmotorhomes.co.nz
Apex ⓣ0800/93 95 97, ⓦwww.apexrentals.co.nz
Avis ⓣ09/526 2847 & 0800 655 111, ⓦwww.avis.co.nz
Backpackers Campervans ⓣ0800/422 267, ⓦwww.kiwicampa.co.nz
Britz ⓣ0800/831 900, ⓦwww.britz.com
Budget ⓣ0800/652 227 & 09/976 2222, ⓦwww.budget.co.nz
Freedom Campervans Auckland ⓣ09/275 3034, Christchurch ⓣ03/379 3822
Greentours ⓣ0800/399 935
Hertz ⓣ0800/654 321, ⓦwww.hertz.co.nz
Kea Campers ⓣ0800/404 888, ⓦwww.kea.co.nz
Maui Motorhomes ⓣ0800/651080, ⓦwww.maui-rentals.com
National ⓣ0800/800 115 & 03/366 5574, ⓦwww.nationalcar.co.nz
Paradise ⓣ0800/800 987, ⓦwww.paradise.co.nz
Thrifty ⓣ09/309 0111, ⓦwww.thrifty.co.nz

Vehicle rental agencies in Australia

Avis ⓣ13 63 33, ⓦwww.avis.com
Brits: NZ ⓣ1800/331 454
Budget ⓣ1300/362 848, ⓦwww.budget.com
Hertz ⓣ13 30 39, ⓦwww.hertz.com
Maui ⓣ03/8379 8891
Thrifty ⓣ1300/367 227, ⓦwww.thrifty.com.au

Vehicle rental agencies in Ireland

Avis Northern Ireland ⓣ028/9024 0404, Republic of Ireland ⓣ01/605 7500, ⓦwww.avis.co.uk
Budget Northern Ireland ⓣ028/9023 0700, Republic of Ireland ⓣ01/9032 7711, ⓦwww.budgetcarrental.ie or www.budget-ireland.co.uk
Hertz Republic of Ireland ⓣ01/813 3416, ⓦwww.hertz.co.uk

Vehicle rental agencies in North America

Avis US ⓣ1-800/331-1084, Canada ⓣ1-800/272-5871, ⓦwww.avis.com
Budget US ⓣ1-800/527-0700, ⓦwww.budgetrentacar.com
Hertz US ⓣ1-800/654-3001, Canada ⓣ1-800/263-0600, ⓦwww.hertz.com
National ⓣ1-800/227-7368, ⓦwww.nationalcar.com
Thrifty ⓣ1-800/367-2277, ⓦwww.thrifty.com

Vehicle rental agencies In the UK

Avis ⓣ0870/606 0100, ⓦwww.avisworld.com
Brits: NZ ⓣ0990/143 607
Budget ⓣ0800/181 181, ⓦwww.go-budget.co.uk
Freedom Campervans ⓣ0993/823 363
Hertz ⓣ08708/44 88 44, ⓦwww.hertz.co.uk
Maui ⓣ01737/842 735
National ⓣ08705/365 365, ⓦwww.nationalcar.com
Thrifty ⓣ01494/751 600, ⓦwww.thrifty.co.uk

Buying a used car

Buying a used car can be cost-effective if you are staying in the country for more than two months or so. Reselling can recoup enough of the price to make it cheaper than using public transport or renting. The majority of people buy cars in Auckland and then try to sell them in Christchurch, where you'll often have more choice and a better bargaining position.

A **private sale** is a good compromise if you don't know your big end from your steering column. Trawl the local papers or noticeboards at supermarkets and hostels for likely candidates. A decent car bought privately will cost anything from $1500. Auckland, Christchurch and Wellington have plenty of **garages** and **dealerships**; prices begin at around $4500 and some also offer a **buy-back service**, usually paying about fifty percent of the purchase price. If you're confident of your ability to spot a lemon, you can try to pick up a cheap car at an **auction**; they're held weekly in Auckland and Christchurch, and are advertised in the local press. For general **technical pointers**, call the premium-rated AA Techline (Mon–Fri 8.30am–5pm; ⓣ0900/58324 from private lines only; 99¢ per min), who can fill you in on the good and bad points about a range of vehicles.

However you buy, arrange a **vehicle inspection**, either from the AA (contact the local technical centre; numbers listed in AA Services Handbook or call 0800 AACHECK; $90–150) or from Car Inspection Services of Auckland (ⓣ09/309 8084); this will set you back around $80–140, but may give you ammunition to negotiate a price reduction. Finally, before you close a private sale, call Autocheck (ⓣ0800/658 934) **debt check**, which will warn you if there's money owing on a vehicle being sold privately, a debt that a buyer would inherit.

Before they're allowed on the road, all vehicles must have a **Warrant of Fitness** (WOF), which is a test of its mechanical worthiness and safety, just like an MOT in the UK. WOFs are carried out and issued by specified garages and testing stations, and last for six months. Check the expiry date, as the test must have been carried out no more than 28 days before you apply to register the car.

When you buy a car you have to transfer the **vehicle ownership** by filing a form (filled in by buyer and seller) at the post office, but it should already be registered. If it isn't, or in any case when it runs out, you'll have to pay for **registration** (6 months, $110; 12 months, $206). Next you'll need **insurance** (approximately $220 for 6 months) – shop around or use the AA if you're a member. Although it's not compulsory to have insurance in New Zealand, you'll pay through the nose if you risk it and are involved in an accident, whether it's deemed to be your fault or not.

Motorbiking

If you're thinking of **motorbiking**, be prepared for riding on unsealed roads, which can be a far-from-pleasant experience, and be sure you know what you're doing – there's nothing worse than having to push a broken-down bike a few kilometres to the nearest town. Note also that to ride a motorbike your **international licence** must specify motorbikes.

A worthwhile **secondhand bike** will set you back approximately $1200, and the registration procedure is the same as for cars (see above). Motorbikes can be **rented** or bought (outright or on a buy-back basis) from Graham Crosby Motorcycles Ltd, 299 Great North Rd, Grey Lynn, Auckland (ⓣ09/376 2711, ⓕ376 5033), or through the same channels as cars.

Hitching and car shares

Although many travellers enthuse about **hitching** in New Zealand – and it does enjoy a reputation of relative safety – the official advice is don't. Sadly, New Zealand has its share of unpleasant individuals and, with an extensive network of affordable transport and tours at your disposal, there's really little reason to take unnecessary risks. However if you are determined to work those thumbs then try to follow a few **rules**: hitch in pairs (no guarantee of avoiding trouble but safer than going solo); trust your instincts – there will always be another car; ask the driver where they are going, rather than telling them where you're headed; and keep your gear with you so you can make a quick getaway if necessary.

Finding the best hitching spots around the country is generally a matter of common sense, or common knowledge on the travellers' grapevine. Some town and city hostels drop their guests at hitching spots as a matter of course. Pick a spot where you can be clearly seen and drivers can stop safely.

A good compromise is **car share**, where the cost of travel is shared. You can organize this formally through organizations such as Travelpool in Auckland (daily 9am–8pm; ⓣ09/307 0001) and Travelshare in Wellington (daily 8am–9pm; ⓣ04/473 5558), to whom you pay a commission for the introduction service, before signing a contract with the driver to split the cost of the journey; obviously the more of you there are, the cheaper it gets. Casual car shares are also advertised on hostel noticeboards, which saves on commission but demands more trust on both sides.

Cycling

Cycling is an excellent way of appreciating the countryside, especially if you're reasonably fit and keep your time on the main highways to a minimum. Disadvantages are dealing with unsealed roads, which become irksome if you're on them all day and wreak havoc with your tyres (fat tyres limit the damage).

Contrary to what you might think, cycling in New Zealand's mountainous South Island is easier than in the North Island. The South Island's north–south alpine backbone presents virtually the only geographical barrier, while the eastern two-thirds of the island comprise a flat plain. By contrast, in the North Island you can barely go 10km without encountering significant hills – and you have to contend with a great deal more traffic, including overbearing logging trucks. If you do get sick of pedalling, you can always hoick your bike onto a bus, shuttle or train for around $10–15 per trip.

Most people seem to prefer using **mountain bikes** but since the majority of riding is on roads, **touring bikes** are just as good; **helmets** are required by law. If all you want to do is explore locally, some hostels and guesthouses have bikes you can use for a nominal sum, or even for free. **Renting bikes** for more than the odd day can be an expensive option, costing anything from $20–45 a day, depending whether you want a bike with little more than pedals and brakes, a tourer, or a state-of-the-art mountain bike. Specialist cycle shops also do economical monthly rental for around $200 for a touring bike, $350 for a full-suspension superbike.

If you plan on any long-distance cycle-touring, it's generally cheaper to buy, though you have to factor in the cost of transporting the bike by bus or train (see previous page) if you shirk the longer hauls. Hostel noticeboards are the place to look for **second-hand bikes** (between $150 and $300 is a reasonable deal), often accompanied by extras like wet-weather gear, lights, helmet and a pump; some cycle shops will guarantee buy-back at the end of your trip for about fifty percent of the purchase price.

It is possible to bring **your own bike** to New Zealand by plane and if you intend to cycle a lot this is the cheapest option. On most airlines, assuming you prepare and package them appropriately, bikes simply count as a piece of luggage and don't incur any extra cost so long as you don't exceed your baggage limit. It's easy enough to find **spares** in cities and larger country towns but in the more out-of-the-way places you may have to wait some time for spares to be delivered.

Visitors with extensive cycling in mind should get in touch with Adventure Cycles (ⓣ09/309 5566) or Cycle Xpress (ⓣ09/379 0779), both in Auckland. If you're bringing your own bike they'll let you store the bike box you transported your machine in, help you organize an emergency package of spare parts and extra clothing to be forwarded at your request, and give your bike a final once-over before you set off, all for around $30.

Accommodation

Accommodation will make up a fair chunk of your money while in New Zealand, though the expense is ameliorated by excellent standards. Almost every town has a motel or hostel of some description, so finding accommodation is seldom a problem – though it's advisable to book in advance from Christmas through to the end of January when Kiwis take their summer holidays, and a month or two either side when places fill with international visitors.

Kiwis travel widely at home, most choosing to self-cater at the country's huge number of well-equipped motor **camps** (or **holiday parks**, as they now prefer to be known) and **motels**, shunning **hotels**, which cater mainly to package holidaymakers and the business community. An appealing alternative is the range of **guesthouses**, **B&Bs**, **homestays**, **farmstays** and **lodges** which cover the whole spectrum from a room in someone's suburban home to pampered luxury in a country mansion.

In the last fifteen years or so, New Zealand has, together with Australia, pioneered the **backpacker hostel**, a less-regimented alternative to traditional YHAs, which have transformed themselves dramatically to compete. Found all over the country, hostels offer superb value to budget travellers.

Wherever you stay, you can expect unstinting hospitality and a truckload of valuable advice on local activities and onward travel. As far as **facilities** go, there is almost always some form of laundry and low-cost internet access, and tea and coffee are often provided free.

We've included a wide selection of New Zealand's best accommodation throughout the guide, and more detail can be gleaned from specialist accommodation guides.

Accommodation price codes

Accommodation listed in this guide has been categorized into one of nine **price bands**, as set out below. The rates quoted represent the cheapest available double or twin room (single rooms generally cost only ten to twenty percent less) in high season – except for category ❶, which are per-person rates for a dorm bed. Note that fees for tent sites and DOC huts are also per-person, unless otherwise stated. In the lower categories, most rooms will be without private bath, though there may well be a washbasin in the room. From the ❺ band upwards, you'll more than likely have private facilities.

Prices normally include Goods and Services Tax (GST), as do our codes, though some more business-orientated places may give the GST-exclusive price.

❶ under $25 per person	❷ under $50 per room	❸ $50–70
❹ $70–90	❺ $90–120	❻ $120–150
❼ $150–200	❽ $200–250	❾ over $250

Useful accommodation guides and websites

AA Accommodation Guide
Ⓦwww.aaguides.co.nz. Annually published advertising-based guide for the whole country; concentrates on motels and holiday camps but has some coverage of hotels and lodges. Nominally $14 if bought within NZ but available free from most motels.

Charming Bed & Breakfast
Ⓦwww.travelwise.co.nz. Glossy B&B guide ($20) concentrating on mid-range places and with plenty of colour photos.

Friars' Guide
Ⓦwww.friars.co.nz. An advertising-based annual guide with fairly comprehensive coverage of the country's more upscale B&Bs and boutique lodges. Available ($30) from NZ bookshops and vendors listed on their website.

New Zealand Bed & Breakfast Book
Ⓦwww.bnb.co.nz. Annually updated listing of member B&Bs, boutique lodges, homestays and farmstays, covering around 1500 places all over the country. Bear in mind that entries are submitted by the owners, so a little reading between the lines is advisable. Available from many of the places listed on the site, from bookshops and direct from Moonshine Press, PO Box 6843, Wellington (Ⓣ04/385 2615, Ⓔbnb@actrix.gen.nz; $20).

Hotels and motels

In New Zealand, **hotel** is a term frequently used to describe old-style pubs, which were once legally obliged to provide rooms for drinkers to recuperate from their excesses. Many no longer provide accommodation, but some have transformed themselves into backpacker hostels, while others are dedicated to preserving the tradition. At their best, hotels offer comfortable rooms in characterful, historic buildings, though just as often lodgings are rudimentary. Hotel bars are frequently at the centre of smalltown social life and, at weekends in particular, they can be pretty raucous; for the asking price of around $50 a double, you may find a budget room at a hostel a better bet. In the cities and major resorts, you'll also come across hotels in the conventional sense, predominantly business- or tourbus-orientated places with all the usual trappings of international-style establishments. Priced accordingly, they're seldom good value, usually costing $150–300 a room, though at quiet times and weekends there can be substantial discounts; it's always worth asking.

Most Kiwi families on the move prefer the astonishingly well-equipped **motels**, which congregate along the roads running into town, making them more convenient for drivers than for those using trains or buses. They come provided with bed linen, towels, Sky TV, bathroom, a full kitchen and tea and coffee, but are often depressingly functional concrete-block places with little to distinguish one from another. Rooms range from all-in-one **studios** ($70–90 for two), with beds, kettle, toaster and a microwave; through **one-bedroom units** ($80–100 for two), usually with a full and separate kitchen; to two- and three-bedroom **suites**, sleeping six or eight. Suites generally go for the same basic price as a one-bedroom unit, with each additional adult paying $12–18, making them an economical choice for groups travelling together. Anything calling itself a **motor inn** or similar will be quite luxurious, with a bar, restaurant, swimming pool and sauna but no cooking facilities.

Guesthouses, B&Bs and lodges

While families might prefer the freedom and adaptability of a motel, couples are generally better served by a guesthouse, homestay or bed and breakfast (B&B). These terms are used almost interchangeably in New Zealand, though the cheaper places are more likely to call themselves **guesthouses**, offering simple rooms, usually with a bathroom down the hall and a modest continental breakfast included in the price.

A **B&B** may be exactly the same as a guesthouse, but the term also encompasses luxurious colonial homes with well-furnished ensuite rooms and sumptuous home-cooked breakfasts. Those at the top end are now fashioning themselves as **lodges**, **boutique hotels** and "exclusive retreats", where standards of service and comfort are raised to extraordinary levels, with prices to match.

Roughly speaking, **rates** for a double room are around $70–90 at guesthouses, $80–120 at B&Bs, $130–250 at boutique hotels and reach stratospheric levels when it comes to the exclusive retreats, where $800 per person per night is not unheard of, though that includes all meals and drinks. Rates drop in the low season, when these places can often be exceptionally good value. If you're travelling alone and don't fancy hostels, B&Bs can also be a viable alternative, usually charging **lone travellers** 60–80 percent of the double room rate, though some only ask fifty percent.

Homestays and farmstays

Homestays usually offer a guest room or two in an ordinary house where you muck in with the owners and join them for breakfast the following morning. Staying in such places can be an excellent way to meet ordinary New Zealanders; you'll be well looked after, sometimes to the point of being overwhelmed by your hosts' generosity. It is courteous to **call in advance**, and bear in mind you'll usually have to **pay in cash**. Rural versions often operate as **farmstays**, where you're encouraged to stay a couple of nights and are welcome to spend the intervening day trying your hand at farm tasks: rounding up sheep, milking cows, fencing, whatever might need doing. Both homestays and farmstays charge $70–90 for a double room, including breakfast; some cook dinner on request for $15–30 per person, and you may pay a small fee for lunch if you spend the day at the farm.

Hostels, backpackers and YHAs

New Zealand is awash with budget and self-catering places (around four hundred), pretty much interchangeably known as **hostels** or **backpackers** and offering a bed or bunk for around $15–20. As often as not they're in superb locations – bang in the centre of town, beside the beach, close to a skifield or amid magnificent scenery in a national or forest park – and are invariably great places to meet others, hook-up to the travellers' grapevine and pick through the mass of local information, aided by genuinely helpful managers. Many of the best places have been specially built or converted, though some are substantially less appealing, wedged into former hotel rooms above pubs. Wherever you stay, you'll find a fully equipped kitchen, laundry, TV and games room, a travellers' noticeboard, and a stack of tourist information. **Internet access** (typically a coin-op booth) is now pretty standard, though a few rural places foster an away-from-it-all tenor by intentionally eschewing internet access, TV and the like. Often there'll also be a pool, barbecue area, bike and/or canoe rental and information on local work opportunities. For **security**, many of the better places offer cupboards for your gear, though you'll need your own lock. If you **book ahead** – essential in January and February, and preferable in December and March – hostels may even pick you up from the nearest public transport. Almost all hostels in New Zealand are affiliated with local and international organizations that offer **accommodation discounts** to members, along with an array of other travel- and activity-related savings.

Many hostels allow you to pitch a tent in the grounds for $10–12 a person, but generally the most basic and cheapest accommodation is in a 6–12 bunk **dorm** ($15–18), with 3–4 bed rooms (known as **four-shares**) usually priced a dollar or two higher. Most hostels also have **double**, **twin** and **family rooms** ($20–25 per adult), the more expensive ones with ensuite bathrooms. Unless you are planning on using only YHA hostels (where all bedding is provided), you can save money by carrying your own sleeping bag or sleeping sheet.

Around 55 places are classified as **YHA hostels**, which have now abandoned daily chores and arcane opening hours (office hours are still generally limited to 8–11am, 1–3pm & 5–10pm) but maintain a predominance of single-sex dorms. Newer hostels have been purpose-built to reflect the YHA's environmental concerns, promoting recycling and energy conservation; older places are likely to be converted schools or large houses. Hostels are listed in the annual **YHA Hostel Accommodation Guide** and the condensed **Quick Guide** version (both free to all and available from hostels and organization offices). Over half of the places listed are full YHA hostels open only to members: either obtain a **Hostelling International Card** in your own country (see overleaf for contact details), stump up the $30 annual membership or go with the introductory **DownUnder Card** (also valid in Australia) which achieves full membership by allowing you to pay an additional $3 for each of your first ten YHA stays. The rest of the hostels are affiliated **associate hostels**, where no membership card is required, though there is often a discount of a dollar or so for members. At full YHAs all bedding is supplied, whereas associate hostels usually charge a small additional fee if you are not using your own sleeping bag or sheet. You can book ahead either from another hostel or through the YHA National Reservations Centre (see below) using a credit card or bank draft, and through Hostelling International offices in your home country.

YHAs are outnumbered six-to-one by other **backpacker hostels**, where the atmosphere is more variable; some are friendly and relaxed, others are more free-spirited and party-oriented. Most are aligned with the NZ-based **Budget Backpacker Hostels**, and are listed (along with current prices) in the BBH Accommodation guide (or simply "Blue Book") available from hostels and visitor centres. The entries are written by the hostels and don't pretend to be impartial but each hostel is given a percentage rating based on an annual survey of guests, an assessment that is usually a good indicator of quality, though city hostels seldom score as highly as the best rural places. Anyone can stay at BBH hostels, but savings can be made by buying a **BBH Club Card** ($40) which saves the holder $1–4 (although typically $2) on each night's stay in either a bunk or a room. Cards are available from BBH and all participating hostels, and each card doubles as a rechargeable phone card already loaded with $20 worth of calling time.

Around eighty hostels are members of **VIP Backpacker Resorts**, an umbrella organization that offers a dollar off each night's stay to people who buy the annual VIP Discount Card ($30, valid in New Zealand, at 130 hostels in Australia and a few others dotted across Pacific islands). Around twenty others have aligned themselves with **Nomads International**, a smaller but growing organization working on a similar basis who offer the Nomads Adventure Card, a kind of phone card that also offers discounts on hostel accommodation and travel.

Hostel organizations

YHA offices

New Zealand PO Box 436, Christchurch ⓣ03/379 9970, national reservations centre ⓣ03/379 9808, ⓦwww.yha.org.nz or ⓦwww.stayyha.com
Australia ⓣ02/9565 1699, ⓦwww.yha.com.au
Canada ⓣ1-800/663-5777, ⓦwww.hostelingintl.ca
England and Wales ⓣ01727/845047, ⓦwww.yha.org.uk
Ireland ⓣ01/830 4555, ⓦwww.irelandyha.org
Northern Ireland ⓣ028/9031 5435, ⓦwww.hini.org.uk
Scotland ⓣ01786/891 400, ⓦwww.syha.org.uk
USA ⓣ202/783 6161, ⓦwww.hiayh.org

Other backpacker organizations

BBH Club Card ⓦwww.backpack.co.nz
Nomads International ⓣ0800/666 237, ⓦwww.nomads-backpackers.com
VIP Backpacker Resorts ⓣ09/827 6016, ⓦwww.vip.co.nz

For advice on backcountry camping and trampers' huts, see the "Outdoor Activities" section on p.54.

Motorcamps, campsites and cabins

New Zealand has some of the world's best **camping** facilities, so even if you've never been camping before, you may well find yourself using **motor camps** (also known as **holiday parks**), which are geared up for Kiwi families on holiday, with space to pitch tents, hook-ups for campervans and usually a broad range of dorms, cabins and motel units. Elsewhere there is more down-to-earth camping at wonderfully located DOC sites.

Camping is largely a summer activity (Nov–May), especially in the South Island where winters can get very cold. At worst, New Zealand is very wet, windy and plagued by voracious winged **insects**, so the first priority for tent campers is good-quality gear with a fly sheet which will repel the worst that the elements can dish out, and an inner tent with enough bug-proof ventilation for those hot mornings.

Busy times at motor camps fall into line with the school holidays, making Easter and the summer period from Christmas to the end of January the most hectic. Make **reservations** as far in advance as possible at this time and a day or two before you arrive anytime through February and March. DOC sites are not generally bookable, and while this is no problem through most of the year, Christmas can be a mad free-for-all.

Free camping is not strictly legal, though with huge areas of thinly populated land you can probably get away with a dusk-to-dawn stay pretty much anywhere outside the cities. Parking your **campervan** overnight in roadside rest areas is also proscribed, though many do and suffer no adverse consequences. In a few popular areas where this relaxed approach has been abused you'll see abundant "No Camping" signs: respect these, use a little common sense, and you'll have few problems.

Motor camps and cabins

Motor camps are typically located on the outskirts of towns and are invariably well-equipped, with a communal kitchen, TV lounge, games area, laundry, and sometimes a swimming pool; non-residents can often get showers for $2–3. **Campers** usually get the quietest and most sylvan corner of the site and are charged $8–12 per person; we've quoted the per-person tent price throughout the guide. There is often no distinction between tent pitches and **powered sites** set aside for campervans, which are usually charged an extra dollar or so per person for the use of power hook-ups and dump station.

In addition, most sites have some form of on-site accommodation: the basic dorm-style **lodge** ($10–16 per person); **standard cabins** ($30–35 for two, plus $10 for each extra person), often little more than a shed with bunks; larger **kitchen cabins**, previously referred to in the country as tourist cabins ($40–60, plus $12 each extra person) have cooking facilities; and if you step up to **tourist flats** ($45–70 for two, plus $15 each extra person), you also get your own bathroom. The flasher places also have fully self-contained **motel units** ($60–90 for two, plus $15–18 per extra person), usually with a separate bedroom and a TV. Cabins and units generally sleep two to four, but motor-camps generally have at least one place sleeping six or eight. In all but the motel units, **sheets** and **towels** are not generally included, so bring a sleeping bag or be prepared to pay $2–3 a night to rent bed linen. Sometimes pans and plates can be borrowed after handing over a small deposit, though for longer stays it is worth bringing your own.

Campgrounds are independently-run but some have now aligned themselves with nationwide organizations which set minimum standards. Ones to look out for are **Top 10** sites (ⓦwww.topparks.co.nz), which maintain a reliably high standard in return for slightly higher prices than the norm.

DOC campsites

Few motor camps can match the idyllic locations of the two hundred and sixty **campsites** operated by the **Department of Conservation** (DOC) in national parks, reserves, maritime and forest parks, the majority beautifully set by sweeping beaches or deep in the bush. This is back-to-nature camping, low-cost and with simple **facilities**, though sites almost always have running water and toilets of some sort. Listed in DOC's free *Conservation Campsites* leaflet, the sites fall into one of three categories: **informal** (free), often accessible only on foot and with nothing but a water supply; the more common **standard** ($2–6 per person), all with vehicular access and many with barbecues, fireplaces, picnic tables and refuse collection; and rare **serviced** ($6.50–8.50 per person), which are similar in scope to the regular motor camps described above. At any site children aged 5–15 are charged half price, and only the serviced sites can be booked in advance.

Other possibilities for using your tent include pitching in the grounds of many backpackers and along backcountry tramps.

Food and drink

Forget any preconceptions you may have about "slam in the lamb" Kiwi cuisine with a pavlova for dessert, New Zealand's food scene has forged ahead in recent years – both in terms of the quality of the food and the places where it's served.

New Zealand's **gastronomic roots** were nurtured in the British tradition of overcooked meat and two nuked vegetables, an unfortunate heritage that still informs the cooking patterns of older Kiwis and hasn't been completely displaced at some farmstays and guesthouses. Indeed, it is only in the last decade or so that New Zealand's chefs have really woken up to the possibilities presented by a fabulous larder of super-fresh, top-quality ingredients, formulating what might be termed **Modern Kiwi** cuisine. Taking its culinary cues from Californian and contemporary Australian cuisine, it combines traditional elements such as steak, salmon and crayfish with flavours drawn from the **Mediterranean**, **Asia** and the **Pacific Rim**: sun-dried tomatoes, lemongrass, basil, ginger, coconut and many more. Restaurateurs feel duty-bound to fill their menu with as broad a spectrum as possible, lining up seafood linguini, couscous, sushi, Thai venison meatballs and a chicken korma alongside the rack of lamb and gourmet pizza. Sometimes this results in gastronomic overload, but more often the results are sensational.

Meat and fish

New Zealanders have a taste for **meat**. The quality of New Zealand lamb is matched by that of other meats such as beef, chicken and, more recently, farmed venison, which appears on menus as Cervena. Farmed ostrich is also gaining fans for its leanness and superb taste, though the greasy charms of muttonbird remain a mystery to most. A traditional source of sustenance for Maori, each April and May these birds of the shearwater family are still plucked from their burrows on the Titi Islands, off the southwest tip of Stewart Island, and sold through fishmongers in areas with substantial Maori populations.

With the country's long coastline, it's no surprise that **fish** and seafood loom large on the culinary horizon. The white, flaky flesh of the snapper is the most common saltwater fish, though you'll also come across tuna, John Dory, groper (often known by its Maori name of *hapuku*), flounder, blue cod (a speciality from the Chatham Islands), the firm and delicately flavoured *terakihi* and the moist-textured orange roughy. You'll also see a lot of salmon – but not trout, which cannot be bought or sold (an archaic law originally intended to protect sport-fishing when trout were introduced to NZ for the pastime in the nineteenth century), though some hotel restaurants will cook your catch for you. One much-loved delicacy is whitebait, a tiny silvery fish mostly caught on the West Coast and eaten whole in fritters during the August to November season.

Shellfish are a real New Zealand speciality, and the king of them all is the *toheroa*, a type of clam dug from the sands of Ninety Mile Beach on the rare occasions when numbers reach harvestable levels. They are usually made into soups and are sometimes replaced by the inferior and sweeter *tuatua*, also dug from Northland beaches. On menus you're more likely to come across the fabulous Bluff oysters, scallops and sensational green-lipped mussels, which have a flavour and texture that's hard to beat and are grown in the cool clear waters of the Marlborough Sounds, especially around Havelock. Pricey crayfish is also delicious and if you get a chance, try smoked eel and smoked marlin.

Fruit, vegetables and dairy produce

Fruit too is a winner, especially at harvest time when stalls line the roadsides selling apples, pears, citrus and stonefruits for next

Food and drink terms

butternut type of pumpkin
capsicum bell peppers
cervena farmed venison
crayfish a slightly sweeter and pincer-less type of lobster
eggplant aubergine
entree appetizer
feijoa fleshy, tomato-sized fruit with melon-like flesh and a tangy, perfumed flavour
hogget the meat from a year-old sheep. Older and more tasty (though less succulent) than lamb, but not as tough as mutton
hot dog a rather disgusting-looking battered sausage on a stick, dipped in tomato ketchup. What the rest of the world knows as a hot dog is known here as an American hot dog
kiwifruit hairy brown egg-sized fruit with a juicy green centre which swept the world in the 1980s to become the garnish of choice. The New Zealand-grown variety is now marketed as Zespri, and golden-fleshed kiwifruit are now available. Note: they are not called "kiwis".
kumara particularly delicious type of sweet potato and a long-standing Maori staple; often served as kumara chips with sour cream
lamington sponge cake coated in chocolate or pink icing and rolled in desiccated coconut
muttonbird gull-sized sooty shearwater that was a major component of the pre-European Maori diet and is said to taste like oily and slightly fishy mutton – hence the name
paua the muscular foot of the abalone, often minced and served as a fritter
panini near-ubiquitous upmarket toasted sandwich usually with delicious fillings
pavlova sickly meringue confection topped with cream and fruit that's claimed by Kiwis as adamantly as it is by Aussies
pikelets small, thick pancakes served cold with butter and jam or whipped cream
puha type of watercress traditionally gathered by Maori
saveloy particularly revolting but popular kind of sausage served boiled
silverside top-grade corned beef, cured in honey and often served with tangy mustard
swede rutabaga
tamarillo slightly bitter, deep-red fruit, often known as a tree tomato
Vegemite a dark savoury yeast-extract spread that mystifies most people but is much loved by antipodeans, who insist it is far superior to its British equivalent, Marmite

to nothing. Top-quality fruit and dairy products are the starting point for some delicious desserts traditionally variations on the themes of ice cream, cheesecake and pavlova, though now supplemented by rich cakes and modern twists on British-style steamed puddings.

Vegetables are generally fresh and delicious. British favourites – potatoes, carrots, peas, cabbage – along with pumpkin and squash are common in Kiwi homes but on restaurant menus you're far more likely to encounter aubergines (eggplant), capsicums (bell peppers) and tomatoes. Pacific staples to look out for are kumara (sweet potato), which crops up in *hangi* and deep-fried as kumara chips, and the starchy **taro** and sweeter **yam**, both much more rarely seen.

New Zealanders eat a lot of **dairy produce** and all of it is first-rate. Small producers springing up all over the country – but especially around the Kapiti Coast (north of Wellington), Blenheim and Banks Peninsula (east of Christchurch) – are turning out some gorgeous individual cheeses, from the traditional hard cheddar-style to spicy pepper brie. Ice cream of the firm, scooped variety is something of a New Zealand institution, and is available in a vast range of flavours, including intensely fruity ones and the indulgent hokey pokey – vanilla ice cream riddled with chunks of caramel.

Vegetarian food

This abundance of fresh vegetables and superb dairy food means that self-catering **vegetarians** will eat very well, though those who eat in restaurants are less well served. Outside the major centres you'll find few dedicated vegetarian restaurants, and will have to rely on the token meat-free dishes served at most regular restaurants and cafés. Pretty much everywhere you'll be able to get a salad, sandwich, or vegetarian pizza and pasta – but it can get a bit monotonous. **Vegans** can always ask for a simple stir-fry if all else fails. In terms of snacks, you may find yourself developing an unhealthy reliance on nachos (a plateful of tortilla chips with a dollop of refried beans, grilled cheese and a hearty helping of sour cream), and the ubiquitous vegeburger.

If you are taking a rafting expedition or 4WD tour on which food is provided, give them plenty of notice of your dietary needs – otherwise you might be left with bread and salad.

Eating out

The quality of **restaurants** in New Zealand is typically superb, the portions are respectable, and with the current low value of the NZ dollar will seem wonderful value for money – especially at **BYO** establishments, where the cost is eased if you "bring your own" wine, sometimes for a small corkage fee (typically $2–5). In most restaurants you can expect to pay upwards of $15 for a main course, perhaps $35 for three courses without wine. **Service** tends to be unpretentious and helpful without being forced, and there is no expectation of a tip, though a reward for exceptional service is always welcomed.

New Zealand's range of **ethnic restaurants** is meagre by international standards, with only the major influx of east Asian immigrants enlivening the scene and lending a strong Chinese and Japanese flavour to the larger cities, alongside a smattering of Indian and Mexican places. **Maori food** is barely represented in restaurants at all, but you shouldn't miss the opportunity to sample the contents of a *hangi* (see box below), an earth oven producing delectable, fall-off-the-bone meat and delicately steamed vegetables.

Often there is little ground between restaurants and the better **café/bars** that have sprung up all over the land and offer food that's just as good and a few dollars cheaper. Here, dining is less formal and you may well find yourself elbow to elbow with folk only there for the beer or coffee, but dining is very much part of the café/bar scene. Simpler **cafés** may only stretch to breakfasts, panini stuffed with Italian-inspired fill-

The hangi

In New Zealand restaurants you'll find little or no representation of **Maori** or Polynesian cuisines, but you can sample traditional cooking methods at a **hangi** (pronounced nasally as "hungi"), where meat and vegetables are steamed for hours in an earth oven then served to the assembled masses. The ideal way to experience a *hangi* is as a guest at a private gathering of extended families, but most people have to settle for one of the commercial affairs in Rotorua or Christchurch. Though you'll be a paying customer rather than a guest, the *hangi* will be no less authentic.

First the men light a fire and place river stones in the embers. While these are heating, they dig a suitably large pit, place the hot stones in the bottom and cover them with wet sacking. Meanwhile the women prepare lamb, pork, chicken, fish, shellfish and vegetables (particularly kumara), wrapping the morsels in leaves then arranging them in baskets (originally of flax, but now most often of steel mesh). The baskets are lowered into the cooking pit and covered with earth so that the steam and the flavours are sealed in. A couple of hours later, the baskets are disinterred, revealing fabulously tender steam-smoked meat and vegetables with a faintly earth flavour. A suitably reverential silence, broken only by munching and appreciative murmurs, descends.

ings, salads and cakes, but always produce good coffee and keep long hours.

Though common in the more cosmopolitan cities, cafés are less prevalent in the country towns, which are still ruled by traditional **tearooms**, daytime (most close around 5pm), self-service places that are low on atmosphere but high on value. Most are unlicensed, but now come equipped with a coffee machine, though espresso incompetence may mean you're better sticking with the staple of tea, usually accompanied by a packaged sandwich, uninspiring savouries and either Devonshire (cream) Teas or home-style cakes – the carrot cake and ginger crunch are generally good bets. On main tourist routes, long-distance buses usually make their comfort stops at tearooms.

Some of the more civilized bars serve **pub meals**, often the best budget eating around with straightforward plates of steak and chips, lasagne or burritos, all served with salad for around $12. One to look out for here is the nationwide Cobb & Co. chain, formerly used as waystations by stagecoaches and now offering reliable, if uninspired, meals and good breakfasts that will set you up for the whole day.

The country's burgeoning wine industry has spawned a number of **vineyard restaurants**, particularly in the main growing areas of Hawke's Bay and Marlborough. They're almost all geared around shifting their own product but are invariably good places to break your wine tasting. Most have outdoor seating close to or under the vines, and there may well be an area for a post-prandial game of petanque.

Breakfast, snacks and takeaways

New Zealanders generally take a fairly light "continental" **breakfast** of juice, cereals, toast and tea or coffee. Visitors staying at a homestay or B&B may well be offered an additional "cooked breakfast" probably along the lines of the traditional English breakfast of bacon and eggs; if you're staying in motels, hostels or campsites, you'll generally have to fend for yourself. In the bigger towns, you'll often find a **bakery** selling fresh croissants, bagels and focaccia, but increasingly New Zealanders are going out for breakfast or brunch, aided by the proliferation of cafés serving anything from a bowl of fruit and muesli to stupendous platefuls of Eggs Florentine and smoked salmon.

In the cities you'll also come across **food courts**, usually in shopping malls where a central seating area is surrounded by a dozen or so stalls selling bargain plates of all manner of ethnic dishes. Some have outlets for **fast food**, a market dominated by the usual global chains; although undeterred by US fast-food hegemony, traditional **burger bars** continue to serve constructions far removed from the limp franchise offerings: weighty buns with juicy patties, thick ketchup, a stack of lettuce and tomato and that all-important slice of beetroot. **Meat pies** are another stalwart of Kiwi snacking: sold in bakeries and from warming cabinets in pubs everywhere, the traditional steak and mince varieties are now supplemented by bacon and egg, venison, steak and cheese, steak and oyster and many others, though there is seldom a vegetarian version.

Fish and chips (or "greasies") are also rightly popular – the fish is often shark (euphemistically called lemon fish or flake), though tastier species may also be available, and the chips (fries) are invariably thick and crisp. Look out too for paua fritters, a battered slab of minced abalone that's something of an acquired taste.

Self-catering

If you're **self-catering** your best bet for supplies is the local supermarket: the warehouse-style Pak 'n' Save is cheap and found in most large towns and usually stays open until at least 8pm every day. The less common Big Fresh is also good with many products available loose in bins so you can pick as much as you need. Failing that, you'll notice a marked drop in scope and an appreciable hike in prices at the neighbourhood superette – IGA and Four Square are the biggies. Convenient corner shops (or dairies) stock the essentials, but, along with shops at campsites, also tend to have inflated prices, more so if located in isolated areas or anywhere with a captive market. Supermarkets sell **beer** and **wine**, but for anything stronger you'll need to visit a **bottle store**, which may well be attached to the local pub.

Drinking

New Zealand boasts many fine wines and beers, which can be sampled in cafés and restaurants all over the land. But for the lowest prices and a genuine Kiwi atmosphere you can't go past the **pub**, often known as a **hotel** from the days when all drinking establishments were required to have rooms for revellers to sleep off a skinful. The pub is a place where folk stop off on their way home from work, the emphasis being on consumption and back-slapping camaraderie, with ambience and decor taking a back seat. In the cities, where competition from cafés is strong, pubs are sharpening up their act and comfortable, relaxed bars are more common, but in country areas little has changed. Rural pubs can initially be daunting for strangers, but once you get chatting, barriers soon drop. Some pubs are still divided into the **public bar**, a joyless Formica and linoleum place where overalls and work boots are the sartorial order of the day, and the **lounge bar**, where you are expected to dress up and are charged more for the privilege.

There is barely any limitation on the hours you can drink, most bars shutting up around midnight on weeknights if it is quiet, more like 3am at weekends. Until December 1999, arcane Sunday licensing laws forbade the sale of alcohol in shops and pretty much anywhere else unless it was accompanied by a meal. However, on Sundays you can now buy beer as well as wine in supermarkets, and get a drink without eating. The **drinking age** has been lowered to 18 (from 20) and anyone looking under 25 can expect to be asked for identification.

Beer

Beer is drunk everywhere and often in New Zealand. Nearly all beer is produced by two huge conglomerates – New Zealand Breweries and DB – who market countless variations on the lager and Pilsener theme, as well as insipid, deep-brown liquid dispensed from taps and in bottles as "draught" – a distant and altogether feebler relation of British-style bitter. Increasingly, Kiwi beer drinkers are turning to lager, especially their beloved Steinlager, which regularly bags international awards. There really isn't a lot to choose between them except for alcohol content, normally around four percent though five percent is common for premium beers usually described as "export".

To find something truly different, seek out **boutique beers** such as those brewed near Nelson by Mac's. Try their dark and delicious stout-like Black Mac, or wait around for the Oktober Mac, a light and fresh concoction brewed in September and only available until it runs out. Nelson's Pink Elephant brewery also produces a wonderful naturally brewed bitter of the same name which is delicious and packs a punch. Small, regional brewers and in-house micro-breweries are increasingly establishing themselves on the scene – look out for the *Loaded Hog* and *One Red Dog* restaurant/bars. Most bottle shops stock a fair range of foreign brews and the flashier bars are always well stocked with the best of international bottled beers – at a price. On tap, you will only find New Zealand beer, except for the odd ersatz Irish bar pouring Guinness. A good source of information about all things beery in New Zealand is Ⓦwww.brewing.co.nz.

Measures are standard throughout the country: traditionalists buy a one-litre **jug** which is then decanted into the required number of glasses, usually a **seven** (originally seven fluid ounces, or 200ml), a **ten**, or even an elegantly fluted **twelve**. Despite 25 years under the metric system, handled **pints** (roughly half a litre) have now become widespread. Prices vary enormously, but you can expect to pay $4–5 for a pint. It is much cheaper to buy in bulk from a bottle shop where beer is either sold in six-packs or cartons of a dozen ($14–18); serious drinkers go for refillable half-gallon **flagons** (2.25 litres) or their metricated variant, the two-litre **rigger**; these can be bought for around a dollar and filled for $7–9 at taps in bottle shops.

Wines and spirits

Kiwis are justifiably loyal to New Zealand winemakers, who have made great strides in recent years and now produce **wines** that rank alongside some of the best in the world. New Zealand is rapidly encroaching on the Loire's standing as the world benchmark for Sauvignon Blanc, and there is an increasing band of fans for the bold fruitiness of its Chardonnay and the apricot and citrus palate of its Riesling. Certainly wine menus feature few non-Kiwi **whites**, but reds are often of the broad-shouldered Aussie variety. Nevertheless, New Zealand **reds** are rapidly improving and there are some very fine young-drinking varietals using Cabernet Sauvignon, Merlot and, the great red hope, Pinot Noir. A liking for **champagne** no longer implies "champagne tastes" in New Zealand: you can still buy the wildly overpriced French stuff, but good Kiwi Methode Traditionelle (fermented in the bottle in the time-honoured way) starts at around $12 a bottle: Montana's Lindaur Brut is widely available, and justly popular. The latest drinking trend is **dessert wines** (or "stickies") typically made from grapes withered on the vine by the *botrytis* fungus, the so-called "noble rot".

Most bars and licensed restaurants will have a tempting range of wines, many sold by the glass ($4–8, $8 and up for dessert wine), while in shops the racks are groaning with bottles starting from $8 ($12–15 for reasonable quality). Nowadays, the "chateau cardboard" wine bladders are considered passé, so do yourself (and your hosts) a favour and buy a decent bottle if invited to a barbecue or dinner.

If you want to try before you buy, visit a few **wineries**, where you are usually free to sample half a dozen different wines, though there is sometimes a small fee, especially to try the reserve wines. Among the established wine-growing areas, **Henderson** and the **Kumeu Valley**, 15km west of Auckland, is one of the more accessible though its urban nature makes it perhaps the least appealing to tour. On the east coast of the North Island, the area around **Gisborne** is good for a tasting afternoon, but wine connoisseurs are better off in **Hawke's Bay**, where Napier and Hastings are surrounded by almost thirty vineyards open to the public. Further south, **Martinborough** has the most accessible cluster of vineyards, many within walking distance. The colder climate of the South Island effectively limits wine production to the northern part, though there is an increasing number of vineyards in **Central Otago** near Queenstown and Alexandra. The best though are in **Marlborough**, close to Blenheim, which competes with Hawke's Bay for the title of New Zealand's top wine region. A good starting point for information on the Kiwi wine scene is Ⓦwww.nzwine.com.

New Zealand also produces fruit **liqueurs**; some are delicious, though few visitors develop an enduring taste for the sickly sweet kiwifruit or feijoa varieties, which are mostly sold through souvenir shops. International spirits are widely available and their dominance is only challenged by a couple of South Island blended **whiskies**, Wilson's and 45° South.

Soft drinks

New Zealand coolers are stocked with just about every international brand of carbonated soft drink, but one home-grown brand to look out for is L&P – originally **Lemon and Paeroa** after the Hauraki Plains town where it was first made – a genuinely lemon-flavoured pop. **Milkshakes**, **thickshakes** (usually with a dollop of ice cream) and **smoothies** made with blended fruit are popular thirst quenchers, and almost any café worth its salt serves glasses of **spirulina**, a thick, green goo made from powdered seaweed and often mixed with the likes of apple juice and avocado. Advocates claim restorative properties when drunk the morning after a bender.

Tea and coffee

Tea is usually a down-to-earth Indian blend (sometimes jocularly known as "gumboot"), though you may also have a choice of a dozen or so flavoured, scented and herbal varieties. **Coffee** drinking has been elevated to an art form with a specialized terminology: an Italian-style espresso is known as a **short black** (sometimes served with a jug of hot water so you can dilute it to taste); a weaker and larger version is a **long black**, which with the addition of milk becomes a **flat white**; **cappuccinos** come regular or chocolate-laced as a mochaccino; while a milky café **latte** is usually sold in a glass but sometimes in a gargantuan bowl. Better places will serve all these decaffeinated, skinny and even made with soya milk. Flavoured syrups are occasionally available, but are not common, and plunger and drip-style coffee is increasingly rare.

Communications and media

Communications services in New Zealand are generally first-rate, and excellent international networks make it pretty easy to keep in touch. The standard of media coverage sometimes leaves a little to be desired, but for the most part this is a well informed country with relatively sophisticated tastes.

Email

For most people, the easiest way to keep in touch is by **email**, usually using one of the free **web-based email** addresses such as YahooMail or Hotmail – accessible through Ⓦwww.yahoo.com and Ⓦwww.hotmail.com. Once you've set up an account, you can use these sites to pick up and send mail from any internet café, or hotel with internet access.

Almost everywhere you go in New Zealand you'll find someone offering **internet access** and more are springing up all the time. Backpacker hostels almost always have access at reasonable rates, and increasingly motels, hotels and B&Bs will have a computer available. At more expensive places there'll be no charge, and for those carrying a laptop, a **dataport** may also be available. Failing any of these, there are abundant **internet cafés** lining city streets – we've mentioned places in most town accounts, and visitor centres should be able to point you in the right direction. They typically charge $5–8 an hour, and often let you do a free email check on the assumption that you'll stay and reply, for which you'll be charged.

One useful website for details of how to plug your laptop in when abroad, phone country codes around the world, and information about electrical systems in different countries is Ⓦwww.kropla.com.

Mail

Post boxes are white, black and red and found everywhere, usually with some indication of when and how often their contents are collected. Most New Zealand towns used to boast rather grand Victorian or Edwardian **post offices** in or near their centres but these days the majority have been sold off and postal services are now operated from much less picturesque, multi-purpose **post shops** (Mon–Fri 9am–5pm, plus Sat 9am–12.30pm in large towns and cities).

The extremely efficient mail service operates two forms of **domestic delivery**: Standard (40¢, or 80¢ for larger envelopes), delivered to any destination within 2–3 days; and FastPost (80¢, or $1.20 for larger envelopes), delivered in 1 day from cities and 2 from rural areas. **International air mail** takes 3–6 days to reach Australia ($1.50), and 6-12 days to Europe, Asia and the United States ($2), depending on where it's posted; prices are higher for larger envelopes. **Aerogrammes** cost $1.50 to anywhere in the world, as do air-mail **postcards**. Make sure you send your missives by air mail, or the recipients could be in for a long wait. **Stamps** are sold at some newsagents, garages and general stores, as well as at post offices and post shops. For further information, contact NZ Post (Ⓣ0800/736 353; Ⓦwww.nzpost.com). Rival postal services spring up from time to time – note the blue boxes on city streets – but these can generally be ignored.

One post office in each major town operates a **Poste Restante** (or **General Delivery**) service, where you can receive mail; we've listed the major ones in the "Listings" section of each town account, and you can get hold of a list of their addresses from the New Zealand Embassy or Tourism Board in your home country or any Central Post Office in New Zealand. You need a passport or other ID to collect mail, which is returned to the sender after three months – though if you change your plans you can get it redirected (at a charge of $7 within New Zealand, $10–20 internationally) by filling in a form at any post office. Most **hostels** and **hotels** will also keep mail for you, preferably marked with your expected date of arrival. Holders of an American Express card or travellers' cheques can have letters (not packages) sent to **American Express** offices, which will hold them for thirty days; addresses are given in the "Listings" sections throughout the Guide – and you can pick up a booklet of all their locations from any American Express office.

Phones and fax

There are only five **area codes** in New Zealand. The North Island is divided into four area codes, while the South Island makes do with just one; all numbers in the Guide are given with their area code. Even within the same area, you may have to dial the code if you're calling another town some distance away.

On a **private phone**, local calls are either free or cost just 20¢ for as long as you want, and long-distance and international calls cost between a third and a half the daytime rate when dialled outside **peak hours** (Mon–Fri 8am–6pm). Additionally, you can dial ⓣ013 before you make a national call (ⓣ0160 for international) and the operator will call you back when you've finished to tell you the cost; however they will add $2.80 ($5–9 internationally) for the service.

Public telephones generally accept both major credit cards and slot-in phonecards ($5, $10, $20 and $50), which can be bought at post offices, newsagents, dairies, garages, visitor centres and supermarkets. You'll also see phones which accept these cards and coins (10¢, 20¢, 50¢, $1 and $2; no change given); and, rarely, phones which accept only coins. A **local call** on a public payphone costs 50¢ flat rate. Calls outside the local area go up from there, with calls to **mobile phones** (numbers prefixed ⓣ021, ⓣ025 ⓣ027, and ⓣ029) even more expensive. Off-peak calls are half price, though, and any ⓣ0800 and ⓣ0508 numbers are a **free call** nationwide, and require no coins or cards. Calls to **premium-rated** information lines (prefixed ⓣ0900) cannot be made from payphones. Prohibitive **international rates** virtually force you into using an account-based phonecard (see below).

Should you need to send a **fax**, you may well find your hotel, motel, or B&B happy to oblige for a fee of around $5 a page overseas and $1 a page within New Zealand: they'll usually receive for $1 a page. Most post offices offer a fax sending service, charging a basic transaction fee of $2.50 plus a per page fee of $1.50 within New Zealand, $1.60 to Australia, $3 to North America and $4 to Europe and Asia.

Useful phone numbers

National operator ⓣ010 (additional $2.80 for collect or price-required calls)
International operator ⓣ0170 (additional $5–9 for collect or price-required calls)
National directory assistance ⓣ018 (50¢ for up to two numbers)
International directory assistance ⓣ0172 ($1.50 for up to two numbers)
Emergency services Police, ambulance and fire brigade ⓣ111 (no charge)

International dialling codes

To call New Zealand from overseas, dial the **international access code** (ⓣ00 from the UK, ⓣ011 from the USA and Canada, ⓣ0011 from Australia), followed by ⓣ64, the area code minus its initial zero, and then the number.

To dial out of New Zealand, it's ⓣ00, followed by the country code (see below), then the area code (without the initial zero if there is one) and the number. Remember that there'll be a time difference between your country and New Zealand, which can be substantial (check out p.73 to avoid rude awakenings).

Country codes

Remember to dial ⓣ00 first, then:
Australia: 61

Canada: 1
Ireland: 353
UK: 44
USA: 1

Phonecards and calling cards

For **long-distance and international calling** you are best off with pre-paid account-based **phonecards** (denominations from $5 to $50) which can be used on any phone. To make a call you dial the access number, the card number and your password (you choose it when you first use the card) followed by the number you are calling; the cost of the call is then deducted from your account which can be topped up using your credit card. There are numerous such cards around offering highly competitive rates, but be wary of the very cheap ones: they are often internet-based and the voice quality can be poor and delayed. One reliable card is Telecom's Yabba (Ⓣ0800/922 2248, Ⓦwww.yabba.co.nz) which charges 30¢ a minute for calls within NZ, just 25¢ to Australia, Canada, Ireland, the UK and the USA, and 40¢ to South Africa and most of western Europe. Additionally they have a maximum fee for calls up to two hours: $5 nationally, $10 to Australia and $15 to the UK, Ireland, the US and Canada.

There are also **discount phone centres** springing up in major cities and popular tourist destinations, though rates are little better than those offered by the phonecards.

Mobile phones

For sheer convenience you can't do better than a **mobile phone**, and it needn't cost the earth. If you're thinking of bringing your phone from home then you'll find both analogue and digital networks: check with your service to see if your phone needs adapting for use in New Zealand. A simpler approach is to buy a **pre-paid phone** when you get there. There is no account involved, just buy the phone and a pre-paid card which can then be topped up using your credit card. If you are careful and make mostly off-peak calls it can work out to be very good value, though there is usually some clause which requires you to make say $10 of calls per month, which isn't hard to do. Telecom (Ⓦwww.telecom.co.nz) and Vodafone (Ⓦwww.vodafone.co.nz) run the two networks and have outlets in main streets of major towns. They'll both sell you a phone for under $100, and (depending on the special offers at the time) you may even get a pre-paid card thrown in. Shop around for other features like text messaging and voicemail, and if you are planning to spend time in remote areas you might appreciate the wider coverage of Telecom's analogue network.

Opening hours, public holidays and festivals

Opening hours have changed in New Zealand in the last few years, and there's now a marked trend towards Sunday opening in large towns and cities. However, the further out into the wilds you go the more conservative the opening times become, with many small towns being shut up tight from Saturday lunchtime until Monday morning. Holidays result in amiable mayhem, as Kiwis hit the roads en masse.

Opening hours

Banks open Monday to Friday, 9.30am to 4.30pm, with some city branches opening on Saturday mornings (until 12.30pm). **Shops** are usually open Monday to Friday, 9am to 5pm, and until noon on Saturday. The Kiwi tradition of **late-night shopping** until 8 or 9pm on Thursday and Friday nights still hangs on in places, and many tourist-orientated shops open daily until 8pm as a matter of course. In larger towns and cities, many shops stay open on Saturday afternoons and **Sundays**.

An ever-increasing number of **supermarkets** (at least one in or near each major city) now open seven days a week, 24 hours a day and small **"dairies"** (corner shops or convenience stores) also keep long hours and open on Sundays. **Museums** and **sights** usually open around 9am, although small-town museums often open only in the afternoons and/or only on specific days.

Holidays

Christmas falls in the middle of summer in the southern hemisphere, during the school **summer holidays**, which run from mid-December until the end of January. The knock-on effects of this are that there are more people out and about, prices go up, and accommodation and travel can be difficult to book. To help you chart a path through the chaos, visitor centres are open for longer hours, as are some museums and many other tourist attractions. Other **school holidays** last for a week in the middle of April, the second week in July and the first two weeks of October, though these have a less pronounced effect than the main bout of summer madness. **Public holidays** (see below) are big news in New Zealand and it can feel like the entire country has taken to the roads, so it's worth considering staying put rather than trying to travel on these days.

There are a number of **regional festivals** that are usually treated as a showcase for local businesses and artistic talent (see below for some worth looking out for). Cities, towns and villages also take one day a year to celebrate the **anniversary** of the founding of their community. Although this isn't a good time to actually arrive in town, if you're there already you can join in the shenanigans. Festivities usually consist of an agricultural show, horse jumping, sheep shearing, cake baking and best-vegetable contests, plus a novelty event like **gumboot** throwing – all in the salubrious surroundings of the local A&P Showground and accompanied by the acrid smell of fried onions and the excessive consumption of alcohol.

Holidays and festivals

All the festivals listed below are covered in more detail in the relevant section of the Guide.

January

New Year's Day (January 1).

The Gathering rave, Golden Bay (Dec 30–Jan 1).
®www.gathering.co.nz

Whaleboat Racing Regatta, Kawhia (Jan 1).

Public Holiday (Jan 2).

Continues...

Mountain Rock Festival, Manawatu Gorge, between Palmerston North and Napier (second weekend).

Wellington anniversary day (Jan 22).

Wellington Summer Festival (Jan–Feb).

Anniversary day for Auckland, Northland, Waikato, Coromandel, Taupo and the Bay of Plenty, celebrated with a massive regatta on Auckland's Waitemata Harbour (fifth Mon in Jan or first Mon in Feb).

February

Nelson anniversary day (Feb 1).

Taste Nelson food and wine festival (first Sat).

Garden City Festival, Christchurch (Feb 3–14).

Waitangi Day (Feb 6).

Hawke's Bay Harvest food and wine festival (Waitangi holiday weekend).

Marlborough Food and Wine Festival, Blenheim (second weekend).

Art Deco Weekend, Napier (third weekend).

Devonport Food and Wine Festival (third weekend).

International Festival of the Arts, Wellington, in even-numbered years only; roughly coinciding with this, the month-long Wellington Fringe Festival is held every year, and draws acts from all over the world (late Feb to early March).

March

Golden Shears sheep-shearing competition in Masterton (first week). ®www.goldenshears.co.nz.

Wildfoods Festival, Hokitika (second Sat). ®www.hokitika.com/wildfoods

Auckland Round-the-Bays fun run (early March).

New Plymouth Festival of the Arts (Feb–March in odd numbered years).

Ngaruawahia Maori Regatta, near Hamilton (closest Sat to March 17).

Public holiday in Dunedin, Otago and Southland, including Fiordland (third Mon).

Otago and Southland anniversary day (March 23).

Taranaki Anniversary Day (March 31).

April

Arrowtown Autumn Festival (week before Easter).

Good Friday and Easter Sunday (late March to late April).

Waiheke Jazz Festival; Royal New Zealand Easter Show, Auckland; Highland Games, Hastings (Easter week). ®www.waihekejazz.co.nz

ANZAC Day (April 25).

June

Queen's Birthday (first Mon).

July

Auckland International Film Festival (early July).

October

Labour Day (fourth Mon).

Gumboot Day, Taihape (Labour Day).

Public holiday in Hawke's Bay, Gisborne, Marlborough, Nelson (one week after Labour Day).

November

Hawke's Bay and Marlborough anniversary day (Nov 1).

Guy Fawkes' Night fireworks (Nov 5).

Canterbury Show week (second week).

Toast Martinborough food and wine festival (third Sunday). ®www.toastmartinborough.co.nz

December

Westland anniversary day (Dec 1).

Canterbury anniversary day (Dec 16).

Christmas Day (Dec 25).

Boxing Day (Dec 26).

Outdoor activities

Life in New Zealand is very much tied to the Great Outdoors, and no visit to the country would be complete without spending a fair chunk of your time in intimate contact with nature.

Kiwis have long taken it for granted that within a few minutes' drive of their home they can find a deserted beach or piece of "bush" and wander freely through it, an attitude enshrined in the fabulous collection of **national, forest** and **maritime parks**. They are all administered by the **Department of Conservation (DOC**; ⓦwww.doc.govt.nz) which struggles to balance the maintenance of a fragile ecology with the demands of tourism. For the most part it manages remarkably well, providing a superb network of well-signposted paths studded with trampers' huts; operating visitor centres that present highly informative material about the local history, flora and fauna; and publishing excellent leaflets for the major walking tracks.

The lofty peaks of the Southern Alps are perfect for challenging **mountaineering** and great **skiing**, and the lower slopes are ideal for multi-day **tramps** which cross low passes between valleys choked with sub-tropical and temperate rainforests. Along the coasts there are sheltered lagoons and calm harbours for gentle **swimming** and **boating**, but also sweeping strands battered by some top-class **surf**.

Hand in hand with this natural aptitude for outdoor life, the country also promotes itself as the **adventure tourism** capital of the world. All over the country you will find places to go **bungy jumping**, whitewater or cave **rafting, jetboating**, tandem **skydiving, mountain biking**, stunt **flying, scuba diving**, in fact you name it and someone somewhere organizes it. The New Zealand DIY ethic reigns supreme and it sometimes seems as though every Kiwi in possession of a minibus and a mobile phone runs an adventure-tourism business. While thousands of people participate in these activities every day without incident, standards of **instructor training** do vary. It seems to be a point of honour for all male (and they are almost all male) river guides, bungy operators and tandem parachute instructors to play the macho card and put the wind up you as much as possible. Such bravado shouldn't be interpreted as a genuine disregard for safety, but the fact remains that there have been quite a few well-publicized injuries and deaths in recent years – a tragic situation that's finally being addressed by industry-regulated codes of practice and an independent system of accreditation.

Before engaging in any adventure activities, check your insurance cover (see p.24).

Tramping

Tramping, trekking, bushwalking, hiking – call it what you will, it is one of the most compelling reasons to visit New Zealand, and for many the sole objective. Even if the concept sounds appalling, you should try it once; reluctant trampers are frequently bitten by the bug.

Tramps are typically multi-day walks, often taking three to five days and following a well-worn trail through relatively untouched wilderness, more often than not in one of the country's national parks. Along the way you'll be either camping out or staying in idyllically located trampers' huts, and will consequently be lugging a pack over some pretty rugged ground, so a moderate level of **fitness** is required. If this sounds daunting, you can sign up with one of the **guided tramping** companies, which maintain more salubrious huts, provide meals and carry much of your gear, but at a price. Details of these are given throughout the Guide.

The main tramping **season** is in summer, from October to May. Some of the most popular tramps – the Milford, Routeburn and Kepler – are in the cooler southern half of the South Island, where the season is shorter by a few weeks at either end.

The tramps

Rugged terrain and a history of track-bashing by explorers and deer hunters has left New Zealand with a web of tramps following river valleys and linking up over passes, high above the bushline. As far as possible, we've indicated the degree of difficulty of all tramps covered in the Guide, broadly following DOC's classification system: a **path** is level, well-graded and often wheelchair-accessible; **walking tracks** and **tramping tracks** (usually marked with red and white or orange flashes on trees) are respectively more arduous affairs requiring some fitness and proper walking equipment; and a **route** requires considerable tramping experience to cope with an ill-defined trail, frequently above the bushline. DOC's estimated **walking times** can trip you up: along paths likely to be used by families, for example, you can easily find yourself finishing in under half the time specified, but on serious routes aimed at fit trampers you might struggle to keep pace. We've given estimates for moderately fit individuals and, where possible, included the distance and amount of climbing involved to further aid route planning.

Invaluable information on walking directions, details of access, huts and an adequate map are contained in the excellent DOC tramp **leaflets** (usually $1 apiece); as long as you stick to the designated route, there's really no need to fork out for specialized **maps** (see pp.22–23), unless you're keen to identify features along the way. In any case, most trampers' huts have a copy of the local area map pinned to the wall or laminated into the table. In describing tramps we have used "**true directions**" in relation to rivers and streams, whereby the left bank (sometimes referred to as the "true left") is the left-hand side of the river looking downstream.

Eight of New Zealand's finest and most popular tramps (and a river journey) have been classified by DOC as **Great Walks**; all are covered in detail in the text. On the North Island, the gentle **Lake Waikaremoana Circuit** (3–4 days) circumnavigates one of the country's most beautiful lakes; and the **Tongariro Northern Circuit** (3–4 days) takes in the magnificent volcanic and semi-desert scenery of the central part of the island. The popular **Abel Tasman Coastal Track** (2–3 days) skirts the pristine beaches and crystal-clear bays of the northern half of the South Island and avoids the difficult logistics of the **Heaphy Track** (4–5 days), which passes through the Kahurangi National Park, balancing sub-alpine tops and surf-pounded beaches. The tramping heartland is around Queenstown and Fiordland, where there are three magnificent alpine Great Walks: the world-famous **Milford Track** (4 days) passing through stunning glaciated scenery; the equally superb **Routeburn Track** (3 days), which spends much longer above the bushline; and the **Kepler Track** (4 days), intended to take the pressure off the other two, but no less appealing for that. Finally, there's the **Rakiura Track** (3 days) on Stewart Island, conveniently circular and partly along the coast.

Great Walks get the lion's share of DOC track spending, resulting in relatively smooth, broad walkways, with boardwalks over muddy sections and bridges over almost every stream. In short, they represent the slightly sanitized side of New Zealand tramping and are sometimes disparagingly referred to as **hikers' highways**. This is somewhat unfair since, even on the busiest tramps, by judiciously picking your departure time each morning, you can go all day hardly seeing anyone.

Access to tracks is seldom a problem in the most popular tramping regions, though it does require some planning. Most tramps finish some distance from their start, so taking your own vehicle is not much use; besides, cars parked at trailheads are an open invitation to thieves. Great Walks always have transport from the nearest town, but there are often equally stunning and barely used tramps close by which just require a little more patience and tenacity to get to – we've included some of the **best of the rest** in the Guide, all listed under "Tramps" in the index.

Backcountry accommodation: huts and camping

Going bush needn't involve too much discomfort as New Zealand's backcountry is strung with a network of almost nine hundred **trampers' huts**, sited less than a day's walk apart, frequently in beautiful surroundings. They fall into five distinct categories as defined by DOC, which maintains the majority of them, though all are fairly simple, communal affairs.

The simplest huts are the crude **Category 4** (free), mostly used by hunters and rarely encountered on the major tramps. Next up in luxury is **Category 3** ($5 per person per night), basic, weatherproof huts usually equipped with individual bunks or sleeping platforms accommodating a dozen or so, an external long-drop toilet and a water supply. There is seldom any heating and there are no cooking facilities. **Category 2** huts ($10) tend to be larger, sleeping twenty or more in bunks with mattresses; water is piped indoors to a sink – and flush toilets are occasionally encountered. Again, you'll need to bring your own stove and cooking gear, but heating is provided; if the fire is a wood-burning one, you should replace any firewood you use. More sophisticated still are **Category 1** huts, though these are extremely rare as most have been converted to **Great Walk Huts**, found in the most popular walking areas and along the Great Walks. These tend to have separate bunkrooms, gas rings for cooking (but no utensils), gas stoves for heating, a drying room and occasionally solar-powered lighting. Most cost a modest $14 a night, though fees are substantially higher on the Kepler ($20), Milford ($35) and Routeburn ($35) tracks, reflecting the extra costs involved in maintaining these fragile areas. In winter (May–Sept), these huts are often stripped of their heating and cooking facilities and revert to Category 3 status. Children of school age generally pay half the adult fee.

Hut fees are usually paid in advance at the local DOC office, visitor centre or other outlet close to the start of the track. For most tramps you buy a quantity of $5 tickets (valid for 15 months) and give the warden the appropriate number (one for a Category 3 hut, and two for a Category 2 hut; see below for Great Walks huts) or post them in the hut's honesty box. You can sometimes buy tickets direct from wardens, but there is often a 25-percent premium on the price (60 percent on the Milford and Routeburn tracks). If you are planning a lot of tramping outside the Great Walks system, it may be worth buying an **Annual Hut Pass** ($65), which allows you to stay in all Category 2 and 3 huts, but not Great Walk huts except in their downgraded winter format. With the exception of the Milford and Routeburn tracks, having a ticket or an **annual hut pass** doesn't guarantee you a place: bunks are allocated on a **first-come, first-served** basis, so at busy times you may find yourself in an undignified gallop along the trail to stake your claim. Otherwise you'll need to use the Great Walks accommodation booking system. Note that the oversubscribed Milford, Routeburn, Lake Waikaremoana and Abel Tasman tracks require **reservations** as far in advance as possible. The easiest way to do this from overseas is to use a booking agent or book through the relevant DOC office (see Guide accounts of the major tramps), stating where you intend to spend each night. On all other tracks, having a ticket or an annual hut pass doesn't guarantee you a place: bunks are allocated on a first-come, first-served basis, so at busy times you may find yourself in an undignified gallop along the trail to stake your claim.

Camping is allowed on all tracks except the Milford, and generally costs one hut ticket ($5) per night, though there are higher fees for camping on Great Walks: $12 on the Routeburn, $10 on the Lake Waikaremoana and Tongariro Northern circuits, and $6–9 on the others. Rules vary, but in most cases you're required to minimize environmental impact by camping close to the huts, whose facilities you're welcome to use (toilets, water and gas rings where available, but obviously not bunks).

Equipment

Tramping in New Zealand can be a dispiriting experience if you're not equipped for both hot, sunny days and wet, cold and windy weather. The best tramps pass through some of the world's wettest regions, with parts of the Milford Track receiving over six metres of rain a year. **Clothing** wise, it is essential to carry a good waterproof, preferably made from breathable fabric and fitted with a good hood. Keeping your lower half dry is less crucial and most Kiwis tramp in shorts. Early starts often involve wading through long, sodden grass, so a pair of knee-length gaiters can come in handy. Comfortable boots with good ankle support are a must; take suitably broken-in leather boots or lightweight walking boots, and some comfortable footwear for day's end. You'll also need a warm jacket or jumper and a windproof shell, plus a good sleeping bag; even the heated huts are cold at night. All this, along with lighter clothing for sunny days, should be kept inside a robust backpack, preferably lined with a strong waterproof liner such as those sold at DOC offices ($4).

Once on the tramp, you need to be totally self-sufficient. On Great Walks, you need to carry **cooking** gear – a pan or two, a bowl or plate, a mug and cutlery; on other tramps you also need a cooking stove and fuel, both available in New Zealand. **Food** can be your heaviest burden; freeze-dried meals (available from all outdoors shops) are light and reasonably tasty, but they are expensive, and many cost-conscious trampers just carry quantities of pasta or rice, dried soups for sauces, a handful of fresh vegetables, muesli (granola), milk powder, and bread or crackers for lunch. Also consider taking biscuits, trail mix (known in New Zealand as "scroggin"), tea, coffee and powdered fruit drinks (the Raro brand is good), and jam, peanut butter or Vegemite. All huts have a drinkable **water** supply, but DOC advise treating water taken from lakes and rivers to protect yourself from **giardia**; see p.25 for more on this and suitable water-purification methods.

You should also carry basic **medical** supplies: a first aid kit, moleskin to prevent blisters, sunscreen, insect repellent; a **torch** (flashlight) with spare battery and bulb, **candles**, **matches** or a lighter; and a **compass** (though few bother on the better-marked tracks). Don't forget your **camera**, and if you've an interest in New Zealand's flora and fauna you might also want to take relevant guides (see Contexts for some recommendations).

In the most popular tramping areas you can **rent equipment** (stoves, pans, sleeping bags and waterproofs). Most important of all, remember that you'll have to carry all this stuff for hours each day. Hotels and hostels in nearby towns will generally let you leave your surplus gear either free or for a small fee, perhaps $1 a day.

Safety

Most people spend days or weeks tramping in New Zealand with nothing worse than stiff legs and a few irritating sandfly bites, but **safety** is nonetheless a serious issue and every year there are cases of individuals failing to return from tramps. The culprit is usually New Zealand's fickle **weather**. It cannot be stressed too strongly that within an hour (even in high summer) a warm, cloudless day can turn bitterly cold, with high winds driving in thick banks of track-obscuring cloud. Heeding the weather forecast (posted in DOC offices) is some help, but there is no substitute for carrying warm, windproof and waterproof clothing.

Failed **river crossings** are one of the most common causes of tramping fatalities. If you are confronted with something that looks too dangerous to cross, then it is, and you should wait until the level falls (usually as quickly as it rose) or backtrack. If the worst happens and you get swept away while attempting a crossing, don't try to stand up in fast-flowing water; you may trap your leg between rocks and drown. Instead, face downstream on your back and float feet first until you reach a place where swimming to the bank seems feasible.

If you do get lost or injured, your chances of being found are better if you left word of your whereabouts either with a friend or with the nearest DOC office, which stock **intention forms** for you to declare your planned route and estimated finishing time. While on the tramp, fill in the hut logs as you go, so that your movements can be traced, and when you return, don't forget to check in with your contact or with DOC.

Animals are not a problem in the New Zealand bush. Kiwis never tire of reminding you there are no snakes, and there is only one poisonous spider, very rarely encountered. You might stumble upon the odd irate wild pig but the biggest irritants are likely to be **kea**, boisterous green parrots that delight in sliding down hut roofs, pinching anything they can get their beaks into then tearing it apart. If you want to keep your boots, don't leave them outside when kea are around.

Swimming, surfing and windsurfing

Kiwi life is inextricably linked with the beach and from Christmas to the end of March (longer in the warmer northern climes) a weekend isn't complete without a dip or a waterside barbecue – though you should never underestimate the ferocity of the southern **sun** (see p.25 for precautions). Some of the best beaches (often stretching away into the salt-spray) are open to the pounding Tasman surf or Pacific rollers. **Swimming** here can be very hazardous, so only venture into the water at beaches patrolled by **surf lifesaving clubs** and always swim between the flags. For more on the dangers and how best to deal with them, read our box on p.132. Spotter planes patrol the most popular beaches and warn of any **sharks** in the area: if you notice everyone heading for the safety of the beach, get out of the water.

New Zealand's tempestuous coastline offers near-perfect conditions for **surfing** and **windsurfing**. At major beach resorts there is often a kiosk or shop renting out small dinghies, catamarans, canoes and windsurfers; in regions where there is reliably good surf you might also come across boogie boards and surfboards for rent, and seaside hostels often have a couple for guests' use.

Sailing

New Zealand's numerous harbours studded with small islands and ringed with deserted bays make **sailing** one of Kiwis' favourite pursuits. People sail year-round, but the summer months from December to March are busiest. Kids are often introduced to the tiny P-Class dinghies before they're riding bikes, and many grow up to own the yachts which choke the marinas for most of the year. Unless you manage to befriend one of these fortunate folk, you'll probably be limited to commercial yacht **charters** (expensive and usually with a skipper), more reasonably priced and often excellent **day-sailing trips**, or renting a small catamaran for some inshore antics along the bay. Most of what's available is in the northern half of the North Island with Auckland's Hauraki Gulf and the Bay of Islands being the main focal points.

Scuba diving and snorkelling

The waters around New Zealand's coast offer some superb opportunities for **scuba diving** and **snorkelling**. What they lack in tropical warmth and fabulously colourful fish they make up for with the range of diving environments. Pretty much anywhere along the more sheltered eastern side of both islands you'll find somewhere with rewarding snorkelling, but much the best and most accessible spot is the **Goat Island Marine Reserve**, in Northland, where there's a superb range of habitats close to the shore. Northland also has world-class scuba diving at the **Poor Knights Islands Marine Reserve**, reached by boat from Tutukaka; wreck diving on the *Rainbow Warrior*, from Matauri Bay; other good spots lie close to Auckland in the **Hauraki Gulf Maritime Park** and off Great Barrier Island. In the South Island there are the crystal-clear **Pupu Springs**, and fabulous growths of **black and red corals** relatively close to the surface of the southwestern **fiords** near Milford.

For the inexperienced, the easiest way to get a taste of what's under the surface is to take a **resort dive** with an instructor. If you want to dive independently, you need to be PADI qualified, which demands classroom instruction and a series of dives over a minimum period of a week. For more information, pick up the free, comprehensive, bimonthly *Dive New Zealand* brochure from dive shops and the bigger visitor centres, or consult their website at Ⓦwww.dive-newzealand.com.

Rafting

Whitewater rafting is undoubtedly one of the most thrilling of New Zealand's adventure activities, negotiating challenging rapids (see p.59 for details of grading) amid gorgeous scenery. Visitor numbers and weather restrict the main **rafting season** to October to May, and most companies set the **lower age limit** at twelve or thirteen. In general you'll be supplied with a paddle and all the gear you need except for a swimming costume and an old pair of trainers. After safety instruction, you'll be placed in eight-seater rafts along with a guide (usually perched on the back) and directed through narrow, rock-strewn riverbeds, spending an average of a couple of hours on the water, before being ferried back for refreshments.

Thrilling though it undoubtedly is, rafting is also one of the most **dangerous** of the adventure activities, claiming a number of lives in recent years. Operators seem to be cleaning up their act with a self-imposed code of practice, but there are still cowboys out there. It might seem to be stating the obvious, but fatalities happen when people fall out of rafts: heed the guide's instructions about how best to stay on board and how to protect yourself if you do get a dunking.

Both the main islands have a major rafting centre – **Rotorua** on the North Island and **Queenstown** on the South Island – each with an enviable selection of river runs from mildly thrilling to heart-stopping. Less frequented but equally exciting rafting areas include Turangi on the North Island, and central Canterbury and the West Coast in the South Island.

In more remote areas, **helirafting** is common, with rafts and punters airlifted to otherwise inaccessible reaches by helicopter. This can involve a lot of expense and considerable hanging around, so make sure what you are letting yourself in for and be wary of extravagant claims – the water may be no more exciting than more accessible (and cheaper) rivers. That said, if it's a wilderness experience you are after then consider basing yourself in Hokitika, Greymouth or Karamea for the best West Coast rivers.

Rafts are exchanged for inner tubes to undertake **cave tubing**, which involves a generally placid drift through underground waterways, with the emphasis on exploration and viewing glow-worms.

Canoeing and kayaking

New Zealand is a paddler's paradise, and pretty much anywhere with water nearby has somewhere you can rent either **canoes** or **kayaks**. Sometimes this is simply an opportunity to muck around in boats but often there is some kind of instruction or **guided trips** available, with the emphasis being on learning new skills and soaking up the scenery.

Grade II water is pretty much the limit for novices, making the scenic **Whanganui River** a perennial favourite. Despite its riverine nature, the **Whanganui Journey** (3–5 days) operates as a Great Walk and special arrangements apply to access and accommodation; several companies rent out all the necessary gear, often including the DOC hut passes as part of their all-inclusive price. Far shorter trips down similar water are run on the **Matukituki River** near Wanaka and the **Dart River** from Glenorchy.

Casual paddlers are much more likely to find themselves sea kayaking the near-landlocked harbours in Northland or the bays along the Abel Tasman Coastal Path; a perfect way to experience New Zealand's magnificent coastline and to encounter dolphins and seals.

Jetboating

The shallow, braided rivers of the high Canterbury sheep country posed access difficulties for run-owner Bill Hamilton, who got around the problem by inventing the **Hamilton Jetboat** in the early 1960s. His inspired invention could plane in as little as 100mm of water, reach prodigious speeds (up to 80km per hour) and negotiate rapids while maintaining astonishing turn-on-a-sixpence manoeuvrability.

The jetboat carried its first fare-paying passengers on a deep and glassy section of the Shotover River, which is still used by the pioneering Shotover Jet. Over half a dozen companies now run similar deep-water trips around Queenstown, while at nearby Glenorchy there's a wonderful wilderness trip along the shallow and twisting Dart River. Other key sites include the Wilkin River at Makarora and the Waikato River below Taupo's Huka Falls.

Thrills-and-spills **rides** ($65–75) tend to last for around thirty eye-streaming minutes, time enough for as many 360-degree spins as anyone really needs. **Wilderness trips** ($50–100) can last two hours or longer, pacing their antics.

Bungy jumping and bridge swinging

For maximum adrenalin, minimum risk and greatest expense, you can't go past **bungy**

Grading of rivers

Both rivers and rapids are graded according to the six-level **grading system** below, the river grade being dictated by the grade of the most demanding rapid. This lends itself to some creative marketing, and you need to take rafting company promotional material with a pinch of salt – a river hyped as Grade V might be almost entirely Grade III with one Grade V rapid. For maximum thrills and spills, the expression to look out for is "Continuous Grade IV".

I Very easy; a few small waves.

II A flicker of interest with choppier wave patterns. Dunking potential for inexperienced kayakers but no sweat in a raft.

III Bigger but still easily ridden waves make this bouncy and fun. Good proving ground for novice rafters.

IV Huge, less predictable waves churned up by rocks midstream make this excellent fun but dramatically increase the chance of a swim.

V Serious stuff with chaotic standing waves, churning narrow channels and huge holes ready to swallow you up. Best avoided by first-time rafters but thrilling nonetheless.

VI Dicing with death; commercially unraftable and only shot by the most experienced of paddlers.

jumping. Not only is New Zealand the birthplace of commercial bungy jumping, it also has some of the world's finest jump sites – bridges over deep canyons and platforms cantilevered out over rivers. It is a complete head game; there's really nothing to fear but a massive rush of wind that lasts for ten seconds and a huge surge of adrenalin that can linger in the system for days.

The craze was kicked off by Kiwi A.J. Hackett who, after a spectacular and highly-publicized jump from the Eiffel Tower in 1986, set up the first commercial operation just outside Queenstown on the **Kawerau Suspension Bridge** (43m). Its location beside the Queenstown–Cromwell highway, and the chance to be dunked in the river make this the most popular jump site, but there are now several other local sites and a handful of other sites around the country.

Wherever you jump, there'll be a boombox cranking out Limp Bizkit or suchlike while they strap the bungy cord to your legs. You'll be fed the jocular spiel about the bungy breaking (it won't) or not being attached properly (it will be) then you'll be chivvied into producing a cheesy (or wan) grin for a camera or three before shuffling out onto the precipice for the countdown. A swan dive is the traditional first jump, but there is often a substantial discount for second and subsequent jumps on the same day, giving jump veterans the opportunity to try The Elevator (just hopping off the platform, either forwards or backwards) or any number of variations. The pleasure is greatly enhanced by pre-jump banter and post-jump analysis, making the longer trips involving a drive into the site – the Skippers Canyon and Nevis sites in particular – all the more appealing. To show how brave you've been, this will all have been captured on video; there are also souvenir strips of used bungy cord to buy and a T-shirt, sometimes included in the jump package. **Prices** range from $100–160.

There have been a couple of injuries in the past but, on balance, bungy jumping is one of the safest adventure activities. The bungy cords are made from latex rubber (if it's good enough for condoms…) and only used 600 times, a quarter of their expected life. Some folk have been known to notch up over 1500 jumps without adverse effects, though bloodshot eyes aren't uncommon and there have been isolated reports of detached retinas and aggravated back injuries.

A close relative of bungy jumping has hit the scene in recent years, and a couple of places are now offering **bridge swinging**,

Kayak or canoe?

In New Zealand, **canoe** seems to be the generic term for any small craft, whether it be fitted with a closed cockpit – elsewhere known as a kayak – or of the open variety paddled with a single-bladed paddle, sometimes differentiated by the term **Canadian canoe**.

To further confuse matters, some rafting companies run small **inflatable boats** akin to **mini-rafts** and paddled with a double-bladed paddle, which tend to be called **kayaks**.

which involves a gut-wrenching fall and super-fast swing along a gorge while harnessed to a cable.

Canyoning and mountaineering

The easiest way to get your hands on New Zealand rock is to go **canyoning**, which involves following a steep and confined river gorge or streambed down chutes and over waterfalls for a few hours, sliding, jumping and abseiling all the way. This is currently only commercially available in a handful of places, the most accessible being in **Auckland**, **Queenstown**, and **Wanaka**, though there are bound to be more places in the near future.

In the main, New Zealand is better suited to **mountaineering** than rock climbing, though most of what is available is fairly serious stuff, suitable only for well-equipped parties with a good deal of experience. For most people the only way to get above the snow line is to tackle the easy summit of **Mount Ruapehu**, the North Island's highest point, or pay for a guided ascent of one of New Zealand's classic peaks. Prime candidates here are the country's highest mountain, **Mount Cook** (3754m), accessed from the climbers' heartland of Mount Cook Village, and New Zealand's single most beautiful peak, the pyramidal **Mount Aspiring** (3030m), approached from Wanaka. In both areas there is a comprehensive system of climbers' huts used as bases for what are typically twenty-hour attempts on the summit.

Flying, skydiving and paragliding

Almost every town in New Zealand seems to harbour an airstrip or a helipad, and there is inevitably someone happy to get you airborne for half an hour's **flightseeing**. The best of these cross the truly spectacular mountain scenery of the Southern Alps or the ice-sculpted terrain of Fiordland, either from Fox Glacier, Franz Josef Glacier, Mount Cook, Wanaka or Queenstown. Half an hour in a plane will set you back around $100; helicopters cost around fifty percent more and can't cover the same distances but score on manoeuvrability and the chance to land. If money is tight, you could always take a regular flight to somewhere you want to go anyway. First choice here would have to be the journey from either Wanaka or Queenstown to Milford Sound, which overflies some of the very best of Fiordland.

In **tandem skydiving**, a kind of double harness links you to an instructor, who has control of the parachute. After suitable instruction, the plane circles up to around 2500m (or even as high as 4000m) and you leap out together, experiencing around thirty seconds of eerie freefall before the instructor pulls the ripcord. Again the Southern Alps and Fiordland are popular jumping grounds, and Taupo has established itself as a low-cost and reliable venue, charging as little as $190 a shot; elsewhere $200–220 is more common though you may get more personal attention.

A hill, a gentle breeze and substantial tourist presence and you've all the ingredients for **tandem paragliding**, where you and an instructor jointly launch off a hilltop, slung below a manoeuvrable parachute. For perhaps ten minutes of graceful gliding and stomach-churning banked turns, you pay around $150; Queenstown, Wanaka and Nelson are prime spots. You might even come across variations on this theme such as **tandem hang gliding**, **parasailing**, where you are either winched out from the back of a boat then winched back in after a ten minute ride, or a variation on tandem paragliding where you and an instructor are winched way out from the back of a boat then released for a tandem flight back to the beach.

Skiing and snowboarding

New Zealand's **ski season** (roughly June to October or November) starts as snows on northern hemisphere slopes finally melt away. This, combined with the South Island's backbone of 3000-metre peaks and the North Island's equally lofty volcanoes, make New Zealand an increasingly popular international ski destination. Most fields, though, are geared to the domestic downhill market, and the eastern side of the Southern Alps is littered with **club fields** sporting a handful of rope tows, simple lifts and a motley collection of private ski lodges. They're open to all-comers, but some are only accessible by 4WD vehicles, others have a long walk in, and ski schools are almost unheard of. Conversely, lift tickets are only $30–45 a day, queues are short and there's usually a gear-rental shop not too far away. Throughout the country, there are also a dozen exceptions to this norm: **commercial resorts**, with high-speed quad chairs (lift tickets around $55), ski schools, gear rental and groomed wide-open slopes. What you won't find are massive on-site resorts of the scale found in North America and Europe; skiers commute daily to the slopes from nearby après-ski towns. **Gear rental**, either from shops in the nearest town or on the field, ranges from around $30 a day for a full set of decent equipment to around $40–50 for the fancy stuff or for snowboarding tackle.

The best up-to-date source of skiing information is the annual **Ski & Snowboard Guide** published by Brown Bear Publications, PO Box 31207 Ilam, Christchurch (ⓣ03/358 0935, Ⓦwww.brownbear.co.nz). It is freely downloadable from their website, and the printed guide can be picked up from visitor centres and ski area hotels for $2. For each field it gives a detailed rundown of facilities, expected season, lift ticket prices and an indication of suitability for beginners, intermediates and advanced skiers. Heliskiing is also dealt with and there's brief coverage of the main ski towns. Other **websites** for all things skiing in New Zealand are Ⓦwww.snow.co.nz and Ⓦwww.dailyshred.co.nz.

The main **North Island** fields include the country's two largest and most popular destinations, **Turoa** and **Whakapapa**, both on the volcanic Mount Ruapehu, which erupted during the 1995 and 1996 seasons but has remained quiet since. The Southern Alps give the **South Island** a great deal more scope, with the greatest concentration of commercial fields being around Queenstown – **Coronet Peak** and **The Remarkables** – and Wanaka – **Treble Cone**, **Cardrona** and the **Waiorau Nordic Ski Area**, New Zealand's only organized cross-country site. Further north, **Porter Heights** and **Mount Hutt** are within two hours' drive of Christchurch, and the Nelson region is home to New Zealand's newest commercial field, **Mount Lyford**. All these ski areas are covered in the relevant chapters of the Guide.

At weekends and school holidays the tow queues at the major fields can become unfeasibly long, and the ideal solution is **heliskiing**. Guides conversant with the routes and skilled in reading avalanche danger take small parties onto virgin slopes high among the sparkling peaks of the Southern Alps. Provided you are an intermediate skier and are reasonably proficient at skiing powder you should be able to pass the ability questionnaire, but at $650–900 a day it isn't for everyone. If you can't resist, places to consider are the usual suspects of Fox Glacier, Wanaka and Queenstown; in Canterbury, you can ski the wonderful Tasman Glacier from Mount Cook Village or get a taster from the Mount Hutt skifield car park.

Fishing

Kiwis grow up fishing: virtually everyone seems to have fond memories of long days out on a small boat trailing a line for snapper, if only to stock the beachside barbecue. All around the New Zealand coast, but particularly in the north of the North Island, there are low-key canoe, yacht and launch trips on which there is always time for a little **casual fishing**, but you'll also find plenty of trips aimed at more dedicated anglers. Most sea trips aim to land something of modest size with good flavour: snapper, kahawai, moki and flounder being common catches. Bigger boats might hope for hapuku, then there's a step up to the **big-game fishing** boats. From December to May these scout the seas off the northern half of the North Island for marlin, shark and tuna. This is serious business and you're looking at around $200 per person per day to go out on a boat with three others, but on the smaller boats, a day out fishing might cost as little as $60, with all tackle supplied. Regulations and bag limits are covered on the Ministry of Fisheries website Ⓦwww.fish.govt.nz.

Inland, the **rivers** and **lakes** are choked with rainbow and brown trout, quinnat and Atlantic salmon, all introduced for sport at the end of the nineteenth century. Certain areas have gained enviable reputations: the waters of the Lake Taupo catchment are world-renowned for the abundance and fighting quality of the rainbow trout; South Island rivers, particularly around Gore, boast the finest brown trout in the land; and braided gravel-bed rivers draining the eastern slopes of the Southern Alps across the Canterbury Plains bear superb salmon. Archaic laws prohibit the sale of **trout**, so if you want to eat some you've got to go out and catch it.

A national **fishing licence** ($75 for the year from Oct 1 to Sept 30; $30 for 7 days; and $15 for 24 hours) covers all New Zealand's lakes and rivers except for those in the Taupo catchment area, where a local licensing arrangement applies. They're available from sports shops everywhere and directly from Fish and Game NZ (Ⓦwww.fishandgame.org.nz), the government's agency responsible for managing freshwater sportsfish fisheries. The website also lists bag limits and local regulations.

Wherever you fish, the **regulations** are taken very seriously and are rigidly enforced. If you're found with an undersize catch or an over-full bag, heavy fines may be imposed and equipment confiscated. Be sure to find out the local regulations before you set out.

Other fishy **websites** include Ⓦwww.troutnewzealand.com, Ⓦnewzealandfishing.com, and Ⓦwww.fishing.net.nz.

Horse trekking

New Zealand's highly urbanized population leaves a huge amount of countryside available for **horse trekking**, occasionally along beaches, often through patches of native bush and tracts of farmland; there may even be an opportunity to swim the horses. There are schools everywhere and all levels of experience are catered for, but more experienced riders might prefer the greater scope of full-day or even week-long wilderness treks. We've highlighted some of the more noteworthy places and operators throughout the Guide, and there's a smattering of others listed at Ⓦwww.truenz.co.nz/horsetrekking.

Mountain biking

If you prefer a smaller saddle, you'll find a stack of places renting out **mountain bikes**. For a quality machine, you might be paying over $40 a day, but for that you get a bike, a helmet and a headful of advice about local routes. The main trail-biking areas around Rotorua, Queenstown, Mount Cook and Hanmer Springs will often have a couple of companies willing to take you out on **guided rides** (the going rate is about $100 a half-day), usually dropping you at the top of the hill and picking you up at the bottom. For general information about the Kiwi **off-road biking** scene consult Wwww.mountainbike.co.nz.

Mountain bikes aren't allowed off-road in national parks and reserves, and elsewhere you must respect the enjoyment of others by letting walkers know of your presence, avoiding skid damage to tracks and keeping your speed down. For more information, consult the specific biking guides available in New Zealand.

Spectator sports

New Zealanders are an active bunch and most would rather be out fishing or tramping than stuck in some draughty stadium, but following sport remains a national passion. Newspapers and TV news often give it headline prominence and entire radio stations are devoted to sport talkback, often dwelling on Kiwi underdogs overcoming better funded teams from more populous nations.

As elsewhere, most sport now is watched on TV, with all major games televised. Increasingly these are only on subscription channels such as Sky TV, which encourages a devoted following in pubs with large-screen TVs.

Anyone with a keen interest in sport or just a desire to see the less reserved side of the Kiwi character should attend a game. Local papers advertise important games along with ticket booking details. **Bookings** for many of the bigger events can be made through Ticketek (Ⓦwww.ticketek.co.nz), which has a local number in each major centre; look under Ticketek in the white pages. Except for the over-subscribed international matches and season finals you can usually just buy a ticket at the gate.

Rugby

Opponents quake in their boots at the sight of fifteen strapping **All Blacks**, the national **rugby** team, performing their pre-match *haka*, and few spectators remain unmoved. Kiwi hearts swell at the sight, secure in the knowledge that their national team is always amongst the world's best, and anything less than a resounding victory is considered a case for mass mourning and much hand-wringing in the leader columns of the newspapers. Even a narrow win over northern hemisphere sides (until recently the weaker cousins of southern hemisphere rugby) was regarded as a disgrace. This was manifest in 1999 when the All Blacks failed to reach the final of the four-yearly **Rugby World Cup** (after losing to eventual winners France in the semis).

Rugby (or Rugby Union, though it is seldom called this in New Zealand) is played through the winter, the season kicking off with the **Super 12 series** (mid-Feb–May) in which regional southern hemisphere teams (five from NZ, four from Australia and three from South Africa) play each other with the top four teams going on to contest the finals series. In the late 1990s the Auckland-based Blues (Ⓦwww.bluesrugby.co.nz) were dominant but have slipped of late leaving the Christchurch-based Crusaders (Ⓦwww.crusadersrugby.com) and Dunedin's Highlanders (Ⓦhighlanders-rugby.com) to wave the Kiwi flag. The Wellington-based Hurricanes (Ⓦwww.hurricanes.co.nz) and the Waikato Chiefs (Ⓦwww.chiefs.co.nz) have always been also-rans.

Super 12 players make up the All Black team which, through the middle of winter, hosts an international test series or two including the annual **tri-nations series** (mid-July to August) against South Africa and Australia. Games between the All Blacks and Australia also contest the **Bledisloe Cup**.

The international season often runs over into the **National Provincial Championship** (NPC) which is played from the middle of August until the end of October. Each province has a team, the bigger provinces (Auckland, Wellington, Canterbury, Otago and so on) competing in the first division with the minor provinces generally filling up the lower two divisions. Canterbury currently hold the **Ranfurly Shield** (Ⓦwww.ranfurlyshield.com), affectionately known as the "log of wood" (it's a wooden shield). Throughout the season the holders will accept challenges at their home ground, and the winner takes all. Occasionally minor teams will wrest the shield, and in the smaller provinces this is a huge source of pride, subsequent defences prompting a huge swelling of community spirit.

Tickets for Super 12 games cost $25–30, with international games costing a little more and NPC matches considerably less. For more information visit the NZ Rugby Union's official **website** ⓦwww.nzrugby.co.nz, or the more newsy ⓦwww.TheSilverFern.co.nz.

Rugby league (ⓦwww.rugbyleague.co.nz and ⓦwww.nzrl.co.nz) has always been regarded as rugby's poor cousin, though success at international level has raised its profile. Rugby League's World Cup was last held in 2000 with the NZ Kiwis only losing out in the final to their perennial nemesis, Australia. New Zealand's only significant provincial team is the Auckland-based **Warriors** who play in Australia's NRL during the March to early September season. The top eight teams in the league go through to the finals series in September, and though the Warriors haven't done especially well in recent years, they did made it into the final eight in 2001. Home games are usually played at Ericsson Stadium, where you can buy tickets at the gate.

Cricket

Attending a rugby match is something you shouldn't miss, but most visitors spend their time in New Zealand from October to March when the stadiums are turned over to New Zealand's traditional summer sport, **cricket** (ⓦwww.nzcricket.co.nz). The national team – the **Black Caps** – tend to hover around mid-table in international test and one-day rankings but periodic flashes of brilliance – and the odd unexpected victory over Australia – keep fans interested. Unless you are an aficionado, cricket is an arcane game and much of the pleasure of attending a game is sitting in the sun with a beer in your hand soaking up the ambience. This is particularly true of five-day international **test matches** that generally take place at Eden Park in Auckland, the WestpacTrust Stadium and the Basin Reserve in Wellington, Jade Stadium in Christchurch, Carisbrook in Dunedin and a handful of provincial grounds. You can usually just turn up a buy a **ticket** (around $15), though games held around Christmas and New Year fill up fast. The same venues are used for **one day internationals** which are more popular, so it is best to book in advance.

International players are selected from **provincial teams** which contest the league-based championship during the November–March season; Auckland and Wellington are currently the two strongest teams.

Other sports

Other team sports lag far behind rugby and cricket, though women's **netball** (ⓦwww.netballnz.co.nz) has an enthusiastic female following. New Zealand must be one of the few countries to give netball live TV coverage, though usually just for the national team – the Silver Ferns.

Soccer in New Zealand has always been thought of as slightly effete (especially in macho rugby-playing circles) though there are now more youngsters playing soccer than rugby. There was a brief surge of enthusiasm when the national team – the **All Whites** – reached the 1982 World Cup finals in Spain, but with their exit in the first round and subsequent lack of success the fires died out. National pride now rests with the **Football Kingz** (ⓦwww.footballkingz.co.nz), the nation's only representative in the Australian National Soccer League (NSL; ⓦwww.socceraustralia.com.au) and an almost permanent fixture close to the foot of the table. The season runs from October to early April and home games are played (usually on Friday evenings, sometimes Saturday) at Ericsson Stadium in Auckland; **tickets** ($12–20) can be bought at the gate or on the team's website.

Beyond these major team sports there is a reasonable following for women's **softball**, men's and women's **basketball**. In recent years there has been heightened interest in **yachting**: Auckland is a frequent midway point for round-the-world yacht races and in early 2003 is hosting the **America's Cup** (see box, p.94) for the second time.

New Zealand's **Olympic** heritage is patchy with occasional clutches of medals from rowing and yachting and a long pedigree of **middle-distance runners**, particularly in the 1960s with Murray Halberg and Peter Snell, and in the 1970s with John Walker, Dick Quax and Rod Dixon.

Crime and safety

Violent crime was once sufficiently novel in New Zealand that it was reported with front-page relish by the local media. These days it has lost its novelty value, and crime rates approach those in more developed and populated countries. Nonetheless, as long as you use your common sense and don't drop your guard just because you're on holiday, you're unlikely to run into any trouble.

The main source of crime in New Zealand is **car break-ins**, common in cities, in car parks at the beginning of short or long walks, or even just on the roadside while you go to take a picture of a waterfall. **Campervans** are particularly vulnerable, since they contain all your possessions and make obvious and easy pickings. When you leave your vehicle, take your valuables with you, and put packs and bags in the boot or out of sight. If you have a particularly vulnerable vehicle, whether because of age or make, invest in a steering lock or in some way of beefing up the boot lock. When setting out on long walks use a secure car park if possible, where your car will be kept safe for a small sum. There is rarely any stealing in hostels apart from the odd case of mistaken identity when it comes to food in the fridge, although it doesn't do any harm to lock away stuff if you can.

There are a few areas, like K' Road in Auckland, where it is unwise for **lone women** to walk late at night, and obviously the more isolated a spot the less chance of getting help but as long as you are reasonably careful you should be OK. Although this is by no means a rule, another area of difficulty for lone women involves taking up **work** in exchange for board and lodging not arranged through recognized organizations like WWOOF (see overleaf). If you want to taste the country life, stick with the WWOOF booklet when organizing your trip and remember that although it's very good, even so it's not a complete guarantee.

Nude and **topless sunbathing** is not something you will see much in New Zealand except at naturist camps and recognized nudist beaches. New Zealand is by nature a conservative nation and as a matter of consideration to other beach users it's best to seek out one of the numerous secluded, unoccupied coves around the coastline.

Police and the law

The **police** are generally friendly, helpful and, despite a few instances to the contrary, mostly incorrupt. If you do get arrested, you will be allowed one phone call; a solicitor will be appointed if you cannot afford one and you may be able to claim legal aid. It is unlikely that your consulate will take more than a passing interest unless there is something strange or unusual about the case against you.

> **Emergency phone calls**
>
> ☎111 is the free **emergency telephone number** to summon the police, ambulance or fire service.

The laws regarding **alcohol consumption** in public are pretty lenient, and unless you are actively causing trouble, the police will give you a wide berth. The same does not apply to **drink driving** (see p.33), which is taken very seriously. **Marijuana**, less-commonly called "electric *puha*" (taken from the Maori, puha meaning watercress), has a reputation for being very potent and is pretty easily available. It is, however, illegal and although a certain amount of tolerance is sometimes shown towards personal use, the police and courts take a dim view of any tangles with **hard drugs**, handing out long custodial sentences. General folk lore has it that much of the marijuana supply is handled by one of two warring gangs, the Mongrel Mob or Black Power, both identified by gang patches on black leather or denim jackets, tattoos and wrap-around sunglasses, although this is over-simplifying the situation.

Prejudice

Most New Zealanders welcome foreign visitors with open arms and, as a traveller, you're unlikely to experience overt **discrimination** to any great degree. You're unlikely to be refused service because of your race, colour or gender, although on rare occasions (particularly in out-of-the-way rural pubs) you may feel like the cowboy who stops all the music and conversation when he walks through the door, especially if you are a woman.

Despite constant efforts to maintain good relations between **Maori** and Pakeha (white New Zealanders), tensions do exist – inflamed by disproportionately high rates of unemployment and imprisonment among the Maori population. **Asian** immigrants, meanwhile, often bear the brunt of prejudice from both Maori and *pakeha* due to their high profile success in education and business and the perception that they are relative newcomers.

Work

With the current low value of the Kiwi dollar, New Zealand isn't a great place to spend time working. But if you need extra income to fund multiple bungy jumps, skydiving lessons or whatever you can find paid casual work, typically in tourism-linked service industries, or in fruit picking and related orchard work.

If you'd rather not tackle the red tape you can simply reduce your travelling costs without transgressing the terms of your visitor permit by **working for your board**. No money changes hands, but in exchange for four hours work a day, you get free board and lodging.

Working for board and lodging

A popular way of getting around the country cheaply is to **work for your keep**, typically toiling for four hours a day in return for board and lodging. **FHiNZ** (Farm Helpers in New Zealand, 50 Bright St, Eketahuna; ⓣ & ⓕ06/375 8955, ⓦwww.fhinz.co.nz), organize stays on farms, orchards and horticultural holdings for singles, couples and families, and no experience is needed. Over 150 places are listed in their booklet ($25) and accommodation ranges from basic to quite luxurious. An organization run along the same lines is the international **WWOOF** (Willing Workers on Organic Farms, PO Box 1172, Nelson; ⓣ & ⓕ03/544 9890, ⓦwww.wwoof.co.nz), which coordinates some six hundred properties (membership and booklet $30), mostly farms but also orchards, market gardens and self-sufficiency orientated smallholdings, all using organic methods to a greater or lesser degree. They'll expect a stay of at least two nights, though much longer periods are common; armed with the booklet, you then **book direct** (preferably a week or more in advance). Most hosts will work you three to four hours a day and vary the tasks to keep you interested, but there have been occasional reports of taskmasters; make sure you discuss what will be expected of you before you commit yourself. Property managers are vetted but **lone women** may feel happier seeking placements with couples or families.

Visas, permits and red tape

Anyone wanting any other kind of work in New Zealand (except for Australian citizens who are exempt) must first obtain a **Work Visa** (NZ$150 or equivalent), an endorsement in your passport which allows you to enter the country with the intention of working. You must then obtain a **Work Permit** ($90 or equivalent) which actually allows you to work (often with conditions limiting the type of work or even the employer's name). Typically you would apply for both before leaving for New Zealand, but it is possible to arrive on a visitor visa then apply for a Work Permit, though your chances of being granted one are lower and even if granted it will only be for the duration of your original visitor visa. Applications are made through the **New Zealand Immigration Service** (Ⓣ09/914 4100, Ⓦwww.immigration.govt.nz), which has all the details and downloadable forms on its website.

You are only likely to be granted a visa or permit if you have an **offer of employment** for which you are qualified and for which there are no suitable New Zealanders available. With this limitation, some visitors are tempted to **work illegally**, something for which you could be fined or deported. In practice, the authorities sometimes turn a blind eye to infringements especially during the fruit picking season when there isn't enough local labour to fill demand.

The only significant exception to the Work Permit system is the **Working Holiday Scheme** for those aged 18 to 30, which gives you a temporary work permit valid for twelve months. Eight thousand Brits (plus 1000 Irish citizens, 800 Canadians, 500 Dutch and assorted French, Italians, Germans, Japanese, Koreans, Singaporeans and Malaysians) are eligible each year on a first-come-first-served basis starting on July 1; apply as far in advance as you can. You'll need a passport, NZ$90, evidence of a return ticket to New Zealand (or the funds to pay for it), and the equivalent of NZ$4200 (sponsorship from a New Zealand citizen is not accepted in place of this sum).

Anyone working in New Zealand (including, oddly, those working illegally without permits) needs to obtain a **tax number** from your local Inland Revenue office (Ⓦwww.ird.govt.nz), a process that can take from a day to a week. If you don't have a number then you may find your employer has trouble paying you, and that the authorities will be more likely to take an interest in you. The tax department rakes in twenty-four per cent of your earnings and you probably won't be able to reclaim any of this. Many companies will also only pay wages into a **bank account**, so you may need to open one.

Casual work

One of the main sources of casual work is **picking fruit** or related **orchard work** such as packing or pruning and thinning. The main areas to consider are Kerikeri in the Bay of Islands for citrus and kiwifruit, Hastings in Hawke's Bay for apples, pears and peaches, Tauranga and Te Puke for kiwifruit, and Alexandra and Cromwell in Central Otago for stonefruit. Most work is available during the autumn **picking season**, which runs roughly from January to May, but this is also when there are most people looking for work so you can often find something just as easily in the off-season. In popular working areas, some hostels cater to short-term workers and these are usually the best places to find out what's happening.

Picking can be hard and heavy work and **payment** is usually by the quantity gathered, rather than by the hour. When you're starting off, the poor returns can be frustrating but with persistence and application you can soon find yourself pulling in a decent wage. Don't expect to earn a fortune, but in an eight-hour day you should gross $70–100. Rates do vary considerably so it's worth asking around, factoring in any meals and accommodation which are sometimes included. Indoor packing work tends to be paid hourly.

Finding other types of casual work is more ad hoc, with no recognized channels other than newspapers and hostel noticeboards; just keep your ear to the ground, particularly in popular tourist areas – Rotorua, Nelson, Queenstown – where people running **cafés**, **bars** and **hostels** often need extra staff during peak periods. If you have no luck, try your chances in more out-of-the-way locales, where there'll be fewer travellers clamouring for work. Bar and restaurant work usually pays around $9–12 an hour and tips are negligible. Generally you'll need to commit to at least three months. **Ski resorts** occasionally employ people during the June to November season, usually in catering roles. The traditional $9–12 an hour may be supplemented by a lift pass and subsidized food and drink, though finding affordable accommodation can be difficult and may offset a lot of what you gain. Hiring clinics for ski and snowboard instructors are usually held at the beginning of the season at a small cost, though if you are experienced it is better to apply directly to the resort beforehand.

Local hostels and backpackers are always good places to hear about likely work opportunities, and there is a number of handy **resources** and **websites**. Perhaps the best is NZ Job Search, ACB Backpackers, 229 Queen Street, Auckland (Ⓣ09/357 3996, Ⓦwww.nzjobs.go.to), which details the legalities and helps place people in jobs. For fruit picking and the likes it is also worth checking out sites such as: Ⓦwww.seasonalwork.co.nz, Ⓦww.hbgrowers.co.nz; and Ⓦwww.kiwijobs.co.nz.

Volunteering

The Department of Conservation's **Conservation Volunteer Programme** (click "Volunteers" on the Ⓦwww.doc.govt.nz front page) provides an excellent way to spend time out in the New Zealand bush while putting something back into the environment. Often you will get into areas most visitors never see and learn some skills while you're at it. Projects include bat surveys, kiwi monitoring and nest protection, as well as more rugged tasks like track maintenance, tree planting and hut repair – all detailed on the website. You can muck in for just a day or up to a couple of weeks, and sometimes there is a fee (perhaps $50–200) to cover food and transport. Programmes are often booked up well in advance so it pays to send in an application (forms available on the website) before you reach New Zealand.

Travellers with disabilities

New Zealand is disabled-traveller friendly, but that does not mean everything is rosy. Many public buildings, galleries and museums are accessible to disabled travellers, but as a rule restaurants and local public transport make few concessions.

Long-distance transport companies will generally offer disabled travellers help with boarding, but on-board access to toilets and other amenities can be difficult for wheelchair users. All **accommodation** in New Zealand should have at least one room or unit suitable for disabled travellers but the level of facilities and access varies considerably, often depending on the age of the building in question. On the plus side, many **tour operators** are prepared to go to that extra bit of trouble to enable travellers with disabilities to participate in activities.

Planning a trip

There are organized **tours** and **holidays** specifically for people with disabilities – the contacts listed below will be able to put you in touch with any specialists for trips to New Zealand. If you want to be more independent, it's important to become an authority on where you must be self-reliant and where you may expect help, especially regarding transport and accommodation. It is also vital to be honest – with travel agencies, insurance companies and travel companions. Know your limitations and make sure others know them. If you do not use a wheelchair all the time but your walking capabilities are limited, remember that you are likely to need to cover greater distances while travelling (often over rougher terrain and in hotter temperatures) than you are used to. If you use a wheelchair, have it serviced before you go and carry a repair kit.

Read your travel **insurance** small print carefully to make sure that people with a pre-existing medical condition are not excluded. And use your travel agent to make your journey simpler: airline or bus companies can cope better if they are expecting you, with a wheelchair provided at airports and staff primed to help. A **medical certificate** of your fitness to travel, provided by your doctor, is also extremely useful; some airlines or insurance companies may insist on it. Make sure that you have extra supplies of drugs – carried with you if you fly – and a prescription including the generic name in case of emergency. Carry spares of any clothing or equipment that might be hard to find; if there's an association representing people with your disability, contact them early in the planning process. Once you're in New Zealand, several organizations provide information for travellers with disabilities and give practical advice on where to go and how to get there.

Accommodation

The New Zealand Tourism Board's *Where to Stay Guide* provides a few useful pointers on disabled-friendly **accommodation**, with countrywide **listings**, in which disabled facilities are indicated by a wheelchair symbol.

Current New Zealand law stipulates that any newly built hotel, hostel or motel must have at least one room modified for disabled access and use. Many pre-existing accommodation establishments have also converted rooms to meet these requirements, including most YHA hostels, some motels, campsites and larger hotels. Older buildings, homestays and B&Bs are the least likely to lend themselves to such conversions.

Travelling

Few airlines, trains, ferries and buses allow complete independence. Air New Zealand provides a special wheelchair narrow enough to move around in the plane, and the rear toilet cubicles are wider than the others to facilitate access; other **domestic airlines** will provide help, if not always extra facilities. Cook Strait **ferries** have reasonable access for disabled travellers, including physical help while boarding, if needed, and adapted toilets. If given advance warning, trains will provide attendants to get passengers in wheelchairs or sight-impaired travellers on board, but moving around the train in a standard wheelchair is impossible and there are no specially adapted toilets; the problems with **long-distance buses** are much the same.

Some specifically adapted **taxis** (for wheelchairs) are available in the cities, but must be pre-booked; otherwise taxi drivers obligingly deal with wheelchairs by throwing them into the boot and their occupant onto a seat. The **New Zealand Total Mobility Scheme** allows for anyone unable to use public transport to use taxis at a subsidized rate (50 percent); a list of participating areas and companies is available from the Disabled Persons Assembly (see "Useful organizations", below), who will also arrange for the necessary vouchers to be issued. There is also a **parking** concession for people with mobility problems, assuming they bring the relevant medical certificates with them; for more details email Ⓔenabletour@xtra.co.nz. The staff on public buses will endeavour to lend a hand, but buses are difficult to board. Some small minibus conversions are available and shuttle buses will help you board and stow your chair, but it pays to let the operator know beforehand of your particular needs. Enable Tourism (see below) can provide lists of companies with **rental cars** adapted for disabled travellers, while some car rental operators will fit hand controls if they are given advance notice.

Useful organizations

In New Zealand

Disability Information – Project Enable Ⓣ0800/801 981. Information service that can help with advice on travel, accommodation and activities.

Disability Resource Centre PO Box 24-042, Royal Oak, Auckland Ⓣ09/625 8069, Ⓕ624 1633.

Disabled Persons Assembly (DPA) 5th Floor, Central House, 26 Brandon St, Wellington Ⓣ04/472 2626. Worth contacting for local information on access.

Enable Tourism 34 Whittaker Street, Shannon

Ⓣ06/362 7163, Ⓔenabletour@xtra.co.nz. Provides a comprehensive service of contacts and advice.

Galaxy Motors Frank Hall, 274 Great South Road, Takanini, Auckland Ⓣ07/826 4020, Ⓔfhall@xtra.co.nz. Personalized tours with a guide, companion, carer or translator.

New Zealand Disabilities Resource Centre Bennet St, PO Box 4547, Palmerston North Ⓣ06/952 0011 & 0800/171 1981, Ⓦwww.nzdrc.govt.nz; Petone Office, PO Box 38847, Petone, Wellington; Christchurch Office, PO Box 33054, Christchurch. A variety of services including lists of disability friendly accommodation, transport and organizations and contacts with groups who deal with specific types of disability.

Physical Freedom and Manawatu Jet Tours 235 Cambridge Avenue, Ashhurst Ⓣ & Ⓕ06/329 4060, Ⓔmjt@clear.net.nz. Specialize in outdoor pursuits (bungy, whitewater rafting, kayaking, abseiling), have an accessible bus that accommodates five wheel chairs and offer personalized tours.

The Paraplegic and Physically Disabled Association PO Box 610, Hamilton. Provides information (postal enquiries only) on sporting activities across New Zealand.

The Saints Host Service 5 Leaver Terrace, North Beach, Christchurch Ⓣ & Ⓕ03/388 6283. Provides tours and request hosts.

In Australia

ACROD (Australian Council for Rehabilitation of the Disabled) PO Box 60, Curtin ACT 2605 Ⓣ 02/6282 4333; Suite 103, 1st floor, 1–5 Commercial Rd, Kings Grove 2208 Ⓣ02/9554 3666. Provides lists of travel agencies and tour operators for people with disabilities.

In Canada

Jewish Rehabilitation Hospital 205 Place Alton Goldbloom, Chomedy Laval, Quebec H7V 1RT Ⓣ514/688-9550, ext 226. Guidebooks and travel information.

In Ireland

Irish Wheelchair Association Blackheath Drive, Clontarf, Dublin 3 Ⓣ01/833 8241, Ⓔiwa@iol.ie.Provides information for wheelchair travellers intending to go to New Zealand, including travel, accommodation and activities.

In the UK

Access Travel 6 The Hillock, Astley, Lancashire M29 7GW Ⓣ01942/888 844, Ⓦwww.access-travel.co.uk. Tour operator that can arrange flights, transfer and accommodation. They cover NZ and put people in touch with NZ experts.

Holiday Care 2nd floor, Imperial Building, Victoria Rd, Horley, Surrey RH6 7PZ Ⓣ01293/774 535, Minicom Ⓣ01293/776 943, Ⓦwww.holidaycare.org.uk. Provides free list of accessible accommodation in New Zealand.

RADAR (Royal Association for Disability and Rehabilitation) 12 City Forum, 250 City Rd, London EC1V 8AF Ⓣ020/7250 3222, Minicom Ⓣ020/7250 4119, Ⓦwww.radar.org.uk. Produces a holiday guide *Getting There* to long-haul destinations (£5, including p&p) every two years, devoting several pages to New Zealand.

Tripscope Alexandra House, Albany Rd, Brentford, Middlesex TW8 0NE Ⓣ0845/7585 641, Ⓦwww.justmobility.co.uk/tripscope, Ⓔtripscope@cableinet.co.uk. This registered charity provides a national telephone information service offering free advice on UK and international transport for those with a mobility problem.

In the USA

Directions Unlimited 123 Green Lane, Bedford Hills, NY 10507 Ⓣ1-800/533-5343 & 914/241-1700. Tour operator specializing in custom tours for people with disabilities.

Society for the Advancement of Travelers with Handicaps (SATH) 347 5th Ave, New York, NY 10016 Ⓣ212/447-7284, Ⓦwww.sath.org. Non-profit educational organization that has actively represented travelers with disabilities since 1976.

Travel Information Service Ⓣ215/456-9600. Telephone-only information and referral service.

Twin Peaks Press Box 129, Vancouver, WA 98661 Ⓣ360/694-2462 & 1-800/637-2256, Ⓦwww.twinpeak.virtualave.net. Publisher of the *Directory of Travel Agencies for the Disabled* ($19.95), listing more than 370 agencies worldwide; *Travel for the Disabled* ($19.95); the *Directory of Accessible Van Rentals* ($12.95) and *Wheelchair Vagabond* ($19.95), loaded with personal tips.

Wheels Up! Ⓣ1-888/389-4335, Ⓦwww.wheelsup.com. Provides discounted airfare, tour and cruise prices for disabled travelers, also publishes a free monthly newsletter and has a comprehensive website.

Gay and lesbian New Zealand

New Zealand has in recent years become a broadly gay-friendly place, defying the odds in what has always been perceived as a fairly macho country. Certainly there remains an undercurrent of redneck intolerance, particularly in rural areas, but it generally stays well below the surface.

All this has partly come about in response to New Zealand's admirable recent history of resistance to anti-gay bigotry. Homosexuality was decriminalized in 1986 and the **age of consent** was set at sixteen (the same as for heterosexuals). The human rights section of the **legislation** was passed in 1993, with none of the usual exceptions made for the military or the police. This also makes it illegal to discriminate against gays and people with HIV or AIDS, and makes no limitation on people with HIV or AIDS entering the country.

Such is the mainstream acceptance that the New Zealand Symphony Orchestra is quite upfront about one of its most prominent composers, Gareth Farr, doubling as a drag queen – though not mid-concert. This tolerant attitude has conspired to de-ghettoize the gay community; even in **Auckland** and **Wellington**, the only cities with genuinely vibrant gay scenes, there aren't any predominantly gay areas and most venues have a mixed clientele. If things go according to plan, Auckland's gay community will once again be celebrating its existence in 2003 with a two-week celebration of film, theatre, dance and sport that culminates in the **Hero Parade** along Ponsonby Road and an all-night dance party.

Outside the festival season, places slip back into the groove of easy-going **clubbing**. Auckland's scene is generally the largest and most lively, but the intimate nature of Wellington makes it more accessible and welcoming. Christchurch has a small number of predominantly gay venues in the inner city, and Nelson has a moderately active gay community centred on the Spectrum drop-in centre, 42 Franklyn St (Ⓣ03/547 2827). Elsewhere it is hard to find a gay network to plug into; even Queenstown is quiet, though this is beginning to change with a gay information service at Ⓔgay_Queenstown@hotmail.com.

Out in the sticks you'll be relying on the gay press (see below) to make contacts – unless you can time your visit to coincide with the annual **Vinegar Hill Summer Camp**, held just outside the small town of Hunterville, in the middle of the North Island, from Boxing Day to just after New Year. It is a very laid-back affair with perhaps a couple of hundred gay men and women camping out, mixing and partying. There's no charge (except a couple of dollars for camping), no tickets and no hot water, but a large river runs through the grounds and everyone has a great time.

Gay and lesbian contacts

Publications

Express (fortnightly, $2.50; Ⓣ09/361 0190, Ⓦwww.gayexpress.co.nz), sold in almost any decent bookstore, graces the magazine racks of gay-friendly cafés and is often distributed free at gay venues; it is the best source of on-the-ground information and a good way to make contacts. Also keep your eyes skinned for the national bi-monthly **OUT!** ($6, Ⓦwww.outnz.net.nz), and the Wellington-based **Lesbian Quarterly**. The **New Zealand Gay & Lesbian Guide** ($6), which lists a couple of dozen gay accommodation options and a few restaurants, is available through Ron Harris (Ⓣ03/465 1742, Ⓔron.harris@xtra.co.nz).

Travel information and websites

The non-profit **New Zealand Gay and Lesbian Tourism Association**, Private Bag MBE P255, Auckland (Ⓣ09/349 2162 & 0800/123 429, Ⓦwww.nzglta.org.nz) provides travel information aimed at gay, lesbian and bisexual visitors, and vets businesses for standards of service and hospitality. The associated **Gay and Lesbian Visitor**

Information Network (Ⓣ09/374 2162 & 0800/147 465, Ⓦwww.gaynewzealand.com) offers a virtual tour of the country with a gay and lesbian bent visit. Again closely linked, **Gaytravel Net** (Ⓦwww.gaytravel.net.nz) offers a gay online accommodation and travel reservation service. Another useful website is **Ⓦgaynz.net.nz** which gives direct access to all manner of gay, lesbian, bisexual and transgender information including the **New Zealand Pink Pages**, essentially a collection of linked pages including what's on in the gay community and a calendar of events all over the country.

Directory

Airport tax Airport taxes (Auckland $22, Wellington $25, Christchurch $25) are not included in airline ticket prices and must be paid (in NZ dollars; credit cards accepted) by each person aged 12 and over after check-in

Children New Zealand is a child-friendly place: nearly every town of any size has Plunket Rooms, which can be used for changing nappies and sometimes host play groups; family rooms are commonly available in motels, and children are welcomed in most restaurants.

Cigarettes and smoking Smoking is outlawed on most public transport and in many public buildings, and smoking in restaurants is strongly discouraged if not banned. Cigarette advertising has long been outlawed and now sponsorship has gone the same way, with the cigarette-tax-funded Smokefree organization standing in where Rothman's and others have been ousted. Consequently cigarettes are expensive and best bought duty-free on arrival.

Dates New Zealand follows Britain's lead with dates, and 1/4/2004 means April 1 not January 4.

Electricity New Zealand operates a 230/240volt, 50Hz AC power supply, and sockets take a three-prong, flat-pin type of plug. North American appliances require both a transformer and an adaptor, British and Irish equipment needs only an adaptor and Australian appliances need no alteration. Suitable adaptors are widely available in New Zealand and at most international airports.

Emergencies Dial Ⓣ111.

Floors What would be called the first floor in the US is the ground floor in NZ, the one above is

Metric conversion table

	1 centimetre (cm) = 0.394in	1inch (in) = 2.54cm 1 foot (ft) = 30.48cm
1 metre (m) = 100cm 1 kilometre (km) = 1000m	1 metre = 39.37in 1 kilometre = 0.621 miles	1 yard (yd) = 0.91m 1 mile = 1.610km
1 hectare = 10,000 square metres	1 hectare = 2.471 acres	1 acre = 0.4 hectares
	1 litre = 0.22 UK gallons	1 UK gallon (gal) = 4.55 litres
	1 litre = 0.26 US gallons	1 US gallon (gal) = 3.85 litres
1 kilogram (kg) = 1000g	1 gram(g) = 0.035oz 1 kilogram = 2.2lb	1 ounce (oz) = 28.57g 1 pound (lb) = 454g

known as the first, and so on.

Gst A Goods and Services Tax is charged at 12.5 percent on almost all items and services and is included in the price quoted, except for some business hotels where rates will be clearly marked GST-exclusive. GST exemption is available on more expensive items bought at shops bearing the "Duty-Free Shopping" sticker which are to be sent or taken out of the country.

Measurements New Zealand uses the metric system of measurements. Distances are in kilometres, petrol is bought in litres, and food is weighed in kilos (see conversion table on p.72).

Photography Film is widely available, but at a price – and processing is failrly expensive, too. For transparencies, Fujichrome Velvia seems to be particularly good at capturing New Zealand's intense blues and greens and costs around $32 for 36 exposures, plus $20 for processing.

Seasons Don't forget that in the southern hemisphere the seasons are reversed. Summer lasts from November to March, and winter from June to September, with a couple of transitional months that pass for spring and autumn.

Time New Zealand Standard Time (NZST) is 12 hours ahead of Greenwich Mean Time, so at noon in New Zealand, it's midnight in London, 7pm in New York, 4pm in Los Angeles, and 10am in Sydney. From the first Sunday in October to the third Sunday in March, Daylight Saving puts the clocks one hour further forward.

Tipping There is never an expectation of a tip, though reward for exceptional service is always welcomed.

Guide

Guide

1

Auckland and around

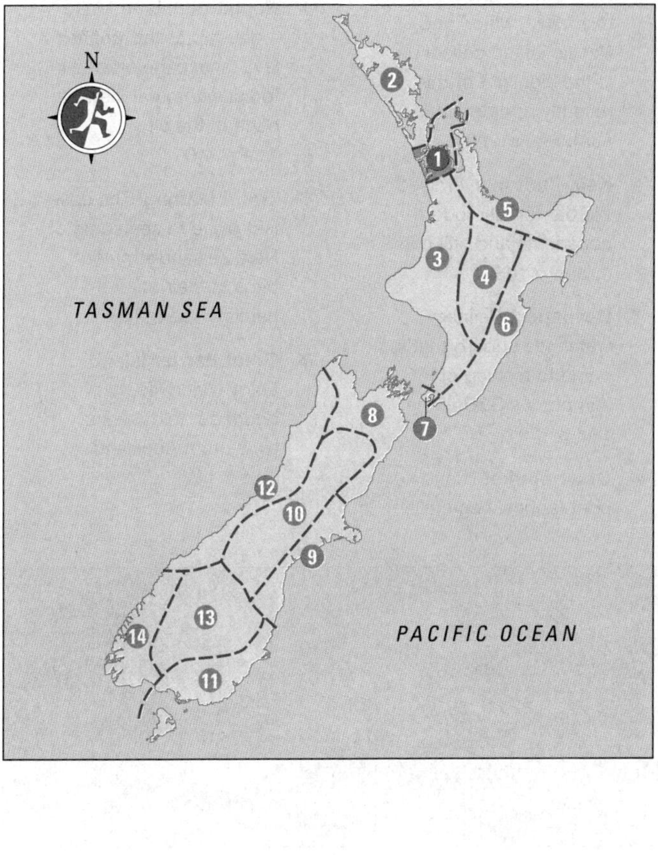
N
TASMAN SEA
PACIFIC OCEAN
1
2
3
4
5
6
7
8
9
10
11
12
13
14

CHAPTER 1

Highlights

* **Karangahape Road** Arguably New Zealand's funkiest street, with designer club-gear, Pacific Island grocers, and some of the city's best ethnic restaurants. See p.99

* **Auckland Museum** An exemplary Maori and Pacific Island collection is the highlight of this recently updated museum. See p.100

* **Kelly Tarlton's** It raised the bar for all modern aquariums and still cuts it. See p.105

* **Devonport** Refined waterside suburb that's home to a swag of sumptuous B&Bs. See p.109

* **Otara Market** Island print fabrics, veg stalls and a lot of life make this New Zealand's finest expression of Polynesian culture. See p.112

* **Ponsonby Road** Auckland's premiere eat street. See p.121

* **Rangitoto Island** Make a day-trip to this gnarled lava landscape draped in forest with great views back to the city. See p.140

* **Tiritiri Matangi** The easiest place to see some of New Zealand's rarest birds in their natural habitat. See p.140

* **Great Barrier Island** Enjoy island life, two hours but thirty years away from Auckland. See p.149

1

Auckland and around

Auckland is New Zealand's largest and most cosmopolitan city and, as the site of the major international airport, is likely to be your introduction to the country. As planes bank high over the island-studded **Hauraki Gulf**, brightly spinnakered yachts tack through the glistening waters towards this "City of Sails". Indeed, Auckland looks its best from the water, the high-rise downtown dwarfed by the Skytower and backed by the low, grassy humps of some of the fifty-odd extinct volcanoes which ring the **Waitemata Harbour**. Beyond the central business district it is a low-slung city, rarely rising above two stories with prim wooden villas, each surrounded by a substantial garden, spreading off into the distance. As a consequence it is one of the least densely populated cities in the world; occupying twice the area of London and yet home to barely a million inhabitants. With its attractive harbour, warm climate and the country's most exciting and vibrant cultural life, Auckland's fans rank it alongside Sydney, though it fails to live up to the claim on most counts. Look beyond the glitzy shopfronts and there's a modest small-town feel and a measured pace, though this can seem frenetic enough in comparison with the rest of the country.

Where Auckland stakes its claim to fame is as the **world's largest Polynesian city**. Almost twenty percent of the city's population declare Maori descent or are the families of migrants who arrived from Tonga, Samoa, the Cook Islands and other South Pacific islands during the 1960s and 1970s. Nevertheless, the Polynesian profile has traditionally been confined to small pockets, notably the nexus of **Karangahape Road** (universally abbreviated to K' Road), and it is only fairly recently, as the second generation reaches maturity, that Polynesia is making its presence felt in mainstream Auckland life, especially in the arts.

Auckland is often regarded very much as a transit place, and many visitors only stay long enough for a quick zip around the smattering of key sights before moving on to far less metropolitan locales. You could be forgiven for doing the same, but don't miss the **Auckland Museum**, with its matchless collection of Maori and Pacific Island carving and artefacts. With more time, dip into the country's strongest collection of New Zealand fine art at the **Auckland Art Gallery**, and delve into the perspex shark tunnels of **Kelly Tarlton's Underwater World**. Auckland is even trying to catch up with the rest of the country by offering a clutch of new adventure activities like the harbour bridge walk and the Sky Jump from the Skytower. Beyond these, the pleasure is in ambling around the fashionable inner-city suburbs of Ponsonby, Parnell and Devonport, and using the city as a base for exploring what's **around Auckland** – the wild and desolate West Coast **surf beaches** less than an hour's drive from downtown, and the **wineries** nearby. Ferries based in the

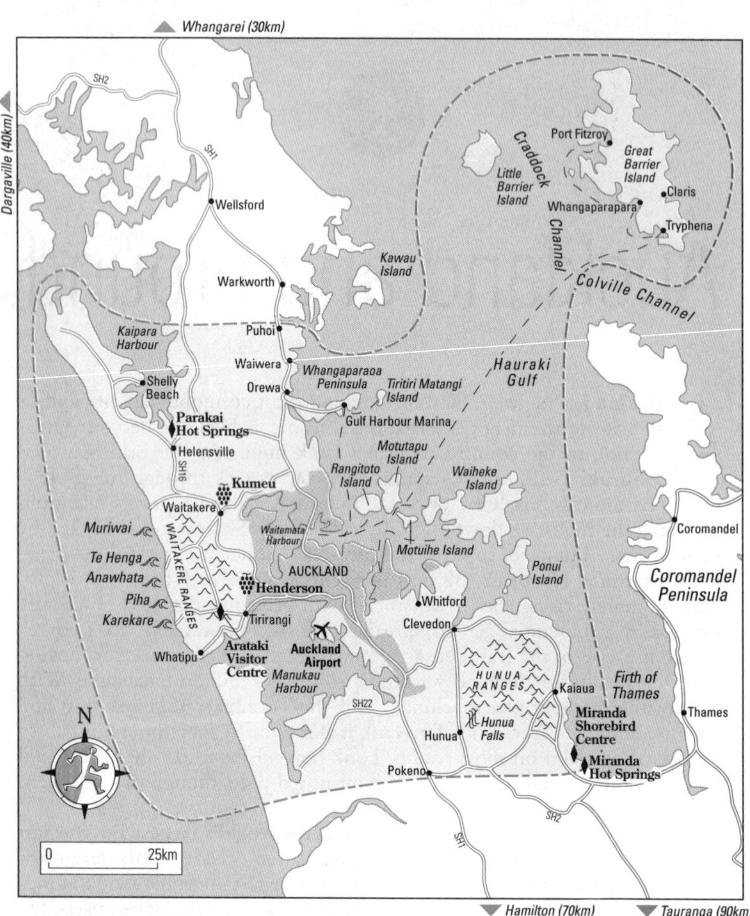

centre of the city open up the **Hauraki Gulf islands**: the botanically and geologically fascinating Rangitoto Island, the sophisticated city retreat of Waiheke Island and the time-warped and isolated Great Barrier Island.

Auckland's **climate** is often described as muggy; it's never scorching hot, and the heat is always tempered by a sea breeze. Winters are generally mild but rainy.

Auckland

AUCKLAND's urban sprawl completely smothers the North Island's wasp waist, a narrow isthmus where the island is all but severed by river estuaries probing inland from the city's two harbours. To the west, the shallow and silted **Manukau Harbour** opens out onto the Tasman Sea at a rare break in the long string of black-sand beaches continually pounded by heavy surf. Maori named the eastern anchorage the **Waitemata Harbour** for its "sparkling waters", which constitute Auckland's deep water port and a focus for the heart of the city. Every summer weekend the harbour and adjoining Hauraki Gulf explode into a riot of brightly-coloured sails.

There could hardly be a more appropriate venue for the **America's Cup**, which was held in the Hauraki Gulf with great fanfare over the summer of 1999–2000 (see box on p.94). Team New Zealand's emphatic victory brings the event back to the Waitemata Harbour over the summer of 2002–2003, and with the infrastructure now firmly in place – there are pavement cafés and trendy restaurants everywhere – Auckland seems set to consolidate its position as New Zealand's most progressive city. Yet despite Auckland's cosmopolitan bustle and harbourside setting, few fall in love with the city on short acquaintance or stick around long enough to scratch below the surface. Those who persist might just find themselves as enthusiastic about the place as Aucklanders.

Some history

The earth's crust between the Waitemata and Manukau harbours is so thin that every few thousand years, magma finds a fissure and bursts onto the surface, producing yet another volcano. The most recent eruption, some six hundred years ago, formed Rangitoto Island, to the horror of some of the region's earliest Maori inhabitants settled on adjacent Motutapu Island. Legend records their ancestors' arrival on the Tamaki Isthmus, the narrowest neck of land between the Waitemata and Manukau harbours. With plentiful catches from two harbours and rich volcanic soils on a wealth of highly defensible volcano-top sites, the land, which they came to know as Tamaki-makau-rau ("the spouse sought by a hundred lovers"), became the prize of numerous battles over the years. By the middle of the eighteenth century it had fallen to **Kiwi Tamaki**, who established a three-thousand-strong *pa* or fortified village on Maungakiekie ("One Tree Hill"), and a satellite *pa* on just about every volcano in the district, but was eventually overwhelmed by rival *hapu* (sub-tribes) from Kaipara Harbour to the north.

With the arrival of musket-trading **Europeans** in the Bay of Islands around the beginning of the nineteenth century, Northland Ngapuhi were able to launch successful raids on the Tamaki Maori which, combined with the predations of smallpox epidemics, left the region almost uninhabited, a significant factor in its choice as the new capital after the signing of the Treaty of Waitangi in 1840. Scottish medic **John Logan Campbell** was one of few European residents when this fertile land, with easy access to major river and sea-borne trading routes, was purchased for £55 and some blankets. The capital was roughly laid out and Campbell took advantage of his early start, wheeling and dealing to achieve control of half the city, eventually becoming mayor and "the father of Auckland". After 1840, immigrants boosted the population to the extent that more land was needed, a demand which partly precipitated the **New Zealand Wars** of the 1860s (see Contexts, p.965).

During the depression that followed, many sought their fortunes in the Otago goldfields and, as the balance of European population shifted south, so did the centre of government. Auckland lost its **capital status** to Wellington in 1865 and the city slumped further, only seeing the glimpse of a recovery when prospectors flooded through on their way to the gold mines around Thames in the late 1860s. Since then Auckland has never looked back, repeatedly ranking as New Zealand's fastest growing city and absorbing waves of migrants, initially from Britain then, in the 1960s and 1970s, from the Polynesian Islands of the South Pacific and, most recently, from Asian countries. Rising with its head high after the depression years of the early 1990s, and a brief slump after the Asian financial melt down, Auckland is confidently leading New Zealand's renaissance as a modern nation, accepted on its own terms.

Arrival and information

As New Zealand's major gateway city, Auckland receives the bulk of **international arrivals**, a few disembarking from stately cruise ships at the dock by the Ferry Building, but the vast majority arriving by air.

Auckland International Airport (Ⓣ09/275 0789) is located 20km south of the city centre in the suburb of Mangere. The international terminal is connected to two domestic terminals – one operated by Air NZ, the other by Qantas – by a shuttle bus (every 20min) but if you've a light load it's only a ten-minute walk. Before leaving the international terminal you can grab a free shower (in most toilets; towels $5), and if you've got a few hours to kill there are even single and double day rooms ($40 for up to 4 hours, $50 for longer) with bed, shower, TV and tea and coffee making facilities. The well-stocked and helpful **visitor centre** (Ⓣ09/275 6467) stays open for all international arrivals and will book you into a city hotel free of charge, or you can make use of the bank of courtesy phones nearby. There's also a branch of the BNZ **bank** which changes money at tolerable rates, and some **duty-free shops**, where inbound passengers can top up their quota.

A **taxi** into the city will set you back around $40, but there are plenty of **minibuses** vying for trade after each arrival, and most offer small discounts to backpackers in possession of a YHA or VIP card. The AirBus (every 20min 6am–10pm; $14 one-way, $22 return) follows a fixed route into the city (roughly 50min). Other buses are more or less door-to-door services and charge around $18 for the first person to any one central destination and $6 for each accompanying person; for Devonport the rates start at around $35. On arrival you just jump into the first one on the rank; for pick up on departure call Super Shuttle (Ⓣ0800/748885 & 09/634 0000). When returning to the airport, ABC Taxis (Ⓣ09/620 3000) do a bargain $25 deal.

InterCity and Newmans operate most of the **long-distance bus services** that use the **Inter City Bus Terminal** under Auckland's Sky City casino complex on Hobson Street. Smaller operators – Northliner, Guthrey's, Go Kiwi and Supa Travel – stop outside the Northliner Travel Centre at 172 Quay Street, opposite the Ferry Building.

Trains pull in ten minutes' walk east of the centre of the city at the station on Beach Road, though by the end of 2003 the station should have moved downtown (see box, below).

Transport changes

After years of prevarication and indecision, Auckland is finally building a **new transport interchange** at the harbour end of Queen Street, and incorporating the old central post office building on QEII Square. Known as **Britomart**, the project is due for completion towards the end of 2003 and will be the new train station and local bus depot. Long distance buses are expected to continue to use their current stops.

Information

Auckland's main **visitor centre**, 287 Queen St (Mon-Fri 9am–5pm, Sat & Sun 9am-6pm; ⓣ09/979 2333, ⓦwww.aucklandnz.com), though often crowded, is fairly efficient at booking and organizing pretty much anything you might want to do in New Zealand. It's often easier to get attention at the second **visitor centre** on the wharf close to the Maritime Museum, Viaduct Harbour (daily 9am-5pm), which shares the same contact details as the former and is equally well stocked with leaflets from around the country.

Both visitor centres, as well as booking agents, hotels and hostels, stock a number of advertisement-heavy **free publications**, the best of which are the annual *Auckland A–Z Visitors Guide* and the bi-monthly *Auckland What's On*. Both have sketch **maps** that are adequate for most purposes, or you could splash out on the spiral-bound *Auckland* KiwiMap ($14).

The compact **Department of Conservation (DOC) office**, in the Ferry Building at 99 Quay St (ⓣ09/379 6476, ⓔaucklandvc@doc.govt.nz; Mon–Fri 10am–5.30pm, Sat 10am–3pm), stocks DOC material and does track bookings for the whole country but specializes in the Auckland and Hauraki Gulf region.

There are also several places specifically geared towards providing **backpacker information**, usually with low-cost internet access, noticeboards for rides, vehicle sales and job opportunities and offering an extensive booking service for onward travel. The larger hostels (especially *Auckland Central Backpackers*) are useful, but the best place to go is the Travellers Contact Point, Dingwall Building, 87–93 Queen St (Mon–Fri 9am–6pm, Sat 10am–2pm; ⓣ09/300 7197, ⓦwww.travellersnz.com), which additionally organizes mobile phones, provides luggage storage (from $10 a week), almost always has people offering drudge work in return for accommodation or somesuch, and offers a worthwhile mail forwarding service. Another good bet is Usit Beyond, 5–7 Victoria St East (ⓣ0508/222572 & 09/300 8266, ⓦwww.usitbeyond.co.nz).

City transport

Auckland's public transport is in a sorry state and periodic moves to improve it are hampered by the city's vast spread and low population density. That said, you'll find you can get to most places **on foot** (notably along the Coast-to-Coast Walkway, see p.93), by local **bus**, or with one of the city tour buses that shuttle between the major sights. Out on the harbour, **ferries** connect the city to the inner suburb of Devonport and numerous islands. **Taxis** are plentiful and can be flagged down, though they seldom cruise the streets and are best contacted by phone (see "Listings", p.129, for numbers). Few visitors will find much use for the Tranz Metro suburban **train** services (call Rideline on ⓣ0800/103080), which start from the station on Beach Road and call at graffiti-covered and inhospitable stations in places that are low on most visitors' must-see lists; the two lines run south through Newmarket and Ellerslie, and west through Henderson then north to Waitakere. **Parking** isn't a major headache, but Auckland **drivers** aren't especially courteous and really you're better off renting a car once you're ready to leave the city. Hilly terrain and motorists' lack of bike-awareness render **cycling** a less than inviting option through city streets, but the situation is redeemed by a few dedicated routes.

Buses

The majority of **local buses** are run by Stagecoach Auckland, who also staff the Rideline **timetable** helpline (ⓣ0800/103080, ⓦwww.rideline.co.nz). The useful *Auckland Busabout Guide* leaflet is available free from visitor centres and newsagents including Victoria Street Lotto & Newsagency, 67 Victoria St (Mon–Fri 7am–6.30pm, Sat 10am–7pm).

The single most useful **route** is the Link (Mon–Thurs 6am–10pm, Fri 6am–11.30pm, Sat & Sun 7am–11pm; $1.20); these flashy white buses ply a continuous loop through the city, Parnell, Newmarket, K' Road and Ponsonby every ten minutes during weekdays and every twenty minutes in the evening and at weekends. Of the remaining services, city-bound buses will be marked "Downtown" if terminating along lower Queen Street, or "Midtown" if ending their run at the corner of Victoria Street and Queen Street.

For buses other than the Link, **fares** are charged according to a zonal system: the inner city, Parnell, Mount Eden and Ponsonby are covered by one zone ($1.20 per journey), from the city to Newmarket is two zones ($2.40), Henderson is five zones ($5), and so on. You can save ten percent by buying a **Ten-trip Ticket** (price determined by the number of zones covered), which is also valid on the trains; for short-stay visitors, a better deal is the one-day **Auckland Pass** ($8 from bus drivers and ferry ticket offices), which gives all-day unlimited travel on the entire bus network (including the Link) and all ferries to the north shore (including Devonport). The same ground is covered with the **three-day Rover** ($18), excellent value if you want to get about a bit.

Tourist buses

To avoid dealing with complex timetables and numerous routes, you'll find it easier to get around the main sights on the hop-on-hop-off **Explorer Bus** (ⓣ0800/439 756, ⓦwww.explorerbus.co.nz; $25 1-day or $40 for a 2-day ticket, pay the driver), which runs every half-hour (May–Sept hourly) between 9am and 4pm, and comes with an en-route commentary. The circuit starts from the Ferry Building on Quay Street and goes along Tamaki Drive to Kelly Tarlton's Underwater World, up to Parnell and the Auckland Museum, and back via Victoria Park Market and Viaduct Harbour. During the summer months (Oct–April) there's a second loop taking in Mount Eden, the Auckland Zoo, MOTAT and the Auckland Art Gallery.

Ferries

The Waitemata Harbour was once a seething mass of ferries bringing commuters in from the suburbs. Services have been rationalized over the years, but the harbour **ferries** remain a fast, pleasurable and scenic way to get around. The main destinations are the Hauraki Gulf islands, but there are also services calling at Devonport, run by Fullers, the principal ferry company (ⓣ09/367 9111, ⓦwww.fullers.co.nz). The **Devonport Ferry** (Mon-Thurs 6.15am-11pm, Fri & Sat 6.30am-1.30am, Sun 7.15am-10pm; every 30min; $8 return, bikes free) is the cheapest of the ferries, takes around fifteen minutes to cross the harbour, and forms part of the Auckland Pass and Rover (see above). There are several other commuter services, the most useful being to Birkenhead, which involves a passage under the harbour bridge.

Driving

With many of the Auckland region's sights conveniently accessible on foot or by public transport, there isn't a huge advantage in having a car while you're in the city, though you'll need one to explore far-flung gems like the Kumeu wineries and the surf beaches of the West Coast. As the main point of entry, Auckland is awash with places to **rent a car** (see "Listings", p.128 for details of outfits in the city); and if you're planning on some serious touring, you may be interested in **buying a car** – see Basics, p.35, for some advice on the pros and cons, as well as the potential pitfalls.

Driving around Auckland isn't especially taxing, though drivers are sometimes aggressive and inconsiderate, and it is worth trying to avoid the rush hours from 7–9am and 4–6.30pm. On first acquaintance, Auckland's urban freeways can be unnerving, with frequent junctions and vehicles overtaking on all sides. Driving is on the left, though if you've just arrived after a long flight, you should consider waiting a day or so before driving at all. Inner-city streets are metered, which means that parking is best done in multi-storey **car parks** which are dotted all over the central city and reasonably well signposted; few are open 24 hours, so check the latest exit time – usually around midnight.

Cycling

Cycling around Auckland's hills can be a tiring and dispiriting exercise. However, a few areas lend themselves to pedal-powered exploration, most notably the harbourside Tamaki Drive east of the city centre, which forms part of a 50km **cycle route** around the city and isthmus – detailed in a free leaflet available from visitor centres. **Rental bikes** cost around $18–25 per day ($80–120 a week), depending on the sophistication of the model; see "Listings", p.127, for details of outlets. In addition, there are several companies that offer monthly rental and **buy-back schemes** for long-stayers (see Basics, pp.36-37).

Accommodation

Auckland has a broader range of accommodation than anywhere else in the country, but that doesn't stop everywhere filling up through December, January and February, when you should definitely **book ahead**. At other times this is less critical, and through the quiet winter months from June to September you'll be spoiled for choice and will find significant discounts on room rates, particularly if you're staying for a few days; it's always worth asking.

Perhaps more than anywhere else in New Zealand, Auckland is a place where you might choose to stay outside the **city centre**. Unless you have a mind to hit the clubs or have arrangements to make in the centre, you may have little cause to spend much time there, and sightseeing can be done just as easily from the **suburbs**. Inner-city suburbs such as **Parnell**, 2km east of the centre; **Ponsonby**, a similar distance west of the centre; **Mount Eden**, 2km south of the central city; and peaceful and salubrious **Devonport**, a short ferry journey across the harbour, all make excellent alternatives. Besides, all four suburbs are well supplied with places to eat and drink, Ponsonby and Parnell's main streets ranking as the city's most vibrant.

The city centre remains the place to find international four- and five-star **hotels**, mostly geared towards business travellers and tour groups; walk-in rates are usually prohibitively high, though there are sometimes tempting weekend deals. Backpacker **hostels** congregate in the inner suburbs, particularly Parnell; **B&Bs** and **guesthouses** are strongest in Devonport and the southern suburbs of Epsom and Remuera; and the widest selection of **motels** is just south of Newmarket in Epsom. Predictably, **campsites** are much further out.

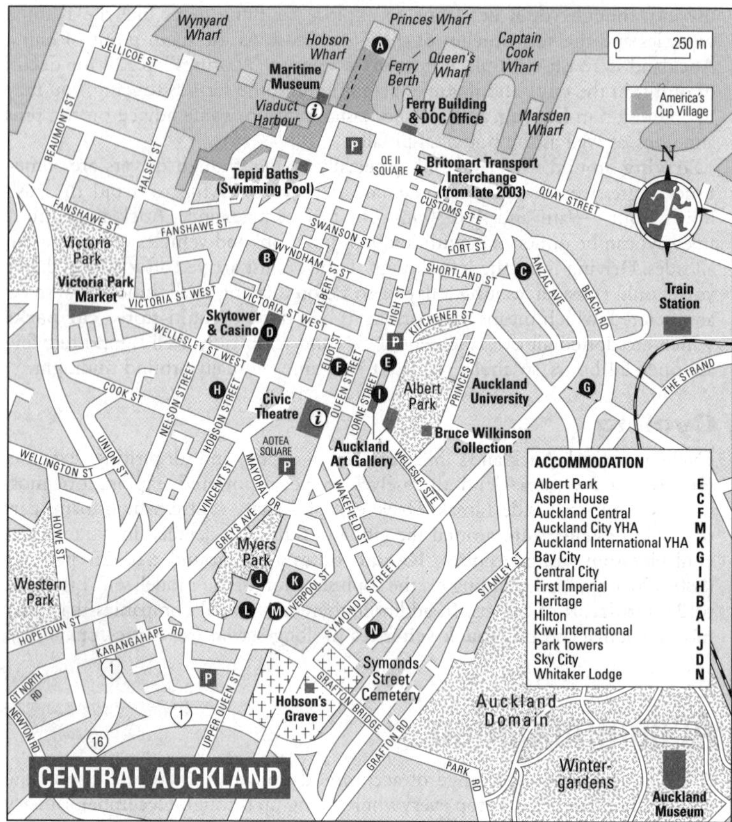

Hotels and motels

As befits New Zealand's largest city, the range of **hotels** and **motels** is second to none. Hotels pepper the city centre and inner suburbs, ranging from places little more salubrious than the hostels up to swanky five-star affairs. High city rents force motels further out and you'll see them just about everywhere, but nowhere more so than the stretch of Great South Road in Epsom, immediately south of the Newmarket shops, where there are at least a dozen places in a kilometre. We've stuck to recommending places that are relatively convenient to the centre and the main sights.

City centre

Aspen House 62 Emily Place ⓣ09/379 6633, ⓦwww.aspenhouse.co.nz, ⓔaspenhouse@xtra.co.nz. Compact hotel right in the heart of the city but surprisingly quiet and with a small garden and deck. Rooms aren't big and don't have private facilities but it's great value and a continental breakfast is included. ④

First Imperial 131–139 Hobson St ⓣ1/800/687968 & 09/357 6770, ⓦwww.firstimperial.co.nz. Spacious, modern and surprisingly quiet business hotel with on-site bar and restaurant and quality rooms, all with private facilities and some with good harbour views. Rooms ❼, apartments ❽

Heritage 35 Hobson St ⓣ09/379 8553 & 0800/368 888, ⓔres.heritageakl@dynasty.co.nz. Top class hotel fashioned from the original Farmers department store – once the city's grandest. Occasional bits of aged planking and wooden supports crop up in public areas, but it has had a major refit to a very high standard and many rooms have views across the harbour or into the glassed-in atrium. There are also tennis courts, a health club, and indoor and outside pools, the latter with views over the city rooftops. ❽–❾

Hilton Princes Wharf, 147 Quay Street, Auckland ⓣ09/978 2000, ⓦwww.hilton.com/hotels/aklhihi. Brand new international class hotel fabulously sited on a wharf jutting into the harbour. Beautifully decorated rooms, all with terrace or balcony, are done in a fairly minimal style and start from around $260 but you'll pay at least $50 more for a good harbour view and fabulous waterside suites are around $1100. ❾

Kiwi International 411 Queen St ⓣ09/379 6487 & 0800/100 411, ⓔkiwihotel@xtra.co.nz. A rather characterless and ageing warren of rooms that compensates with off-street parking and low rates. The standard rooms are fairly comfortable, economy rooms come without a bathroom and there are bunks in dorms, though no self-catering facilities. Dorms ❶, economy rooms ❷, standard rooms ❹

Park Towers 3 Scotia Place ⓣ09/309 2800 & 0800/809 377, ⓔparktowr@ihug.co.nz. One of the best-value hotels in the city with smallish modern rooms, many having expansive views. There's the full range of hotel facilities including bar, brasserie and off-street parking. ❻

Sky City cnr Victoria St & Federal St ⓣ09/363 6000 & 0800/759249, ⓦwww.skycity.co.nz. Part of the casino complex, with all the facilities that entails: rooftop pool, gym, sauna, bars and restaurants. Rooms are standard, international-hotel

Airport accommodation

With a choice of several efficient door-to-door shuttle services into central Auckland there is little reason to stay near the airport except if you arrive at midnight or have a hideously early flight to catch. There is no accommodation actually at the airport site, but a dozen places line Kirkbride Road in Mangere, some 5km away at the end of the approach road and close to many of the car-rental pick-up points. All the places listed below provide their own free shuttle service to the airport (either on a fixed schedule or to order), and have a freephone at the airport: just give them a call and they'll pick you up. Alternatively, a taxi will cost $12–15. There isn't much of interest around the airport hotels, but the better hotels have bars and restaurants, and there are couple of cheap restaurants and takeaways nearby.

Airport Bed & Breakfast 1 Westney Rd at Kirkbride Road ⓣ & ⓕ09/275 0533, ⓔairportbnb@paradise.net.nz. Ten rooms (some en suite) in a converted suburban house well placed for the airport and with a continental breakfast thrown in with the very reasonable price. ❸

Jet Inn 63 Westney Rd ⓣ09/275 4100 & 0800/538 466, ⓔreservations@jetinn.co.nz. New business hotel with all the expected facilities – Sky TV, minibars, lovely outdoor pool – and decor attractively supplemented with traditional arts and crafts from the owners' native South Africa. Rates include a continental breakfast in the hotel restaurant. ❻

Pacific Inn 210 Kirkbride Rd ⓣ09/275 1129 & 0800/504 800, ⓔinfo@pacific-inn.co.nz. Somewhat run-down but reasonably priced hotel with fairly spacious studio rooms, TV and tea- and coffee-making facilities, and a restaurant and bar downstairs. ❹

Skyway Lodge 30 Kirkbride Rd ⓣ09/275 4443, ⓦwww.skywaylodge.co.nz. Several grades of budget accommodation in friendly and relaxed surroundings with a refreshing pool, guests' kitchen and free luggage storage. Accommodation is in 4-bunk dorms, double and twin rooms and self-catering motel units. Dorms ❶, doubles ❷, en-suite doubles & units ❹

style but nicely done, many with good harbour views. Rack rates start high and rise through the stratosphere, but walk-in rates (including breakfast and valet parking) are often lower, especially at weekends and in the winter. Specials ⑧, otherwise ⑨

Whitaker Lodge 21 Whitaker Place ⓣ09/377 3623, ⓦwww.whitakerlodge.co.nz. Auckland's most central motel, tucked down in Grafton Gully and right by the motorway but surprisingly appealing. Choice of smallish rooms without cooking facilities or regular motel units. Rooms ⑤, units ⑥

Parnell

Parnell Inn 320 Parnell Rd ⓣ0800/472763 & 09/358 0642, ⓔparnelin@ihug.co.nz. Compact and simple hotel attached to *The Other Side* café (which does room service) right in the heart of Parnell. Rooms are fairly small, some having cooking facilities, and off-street parking is available. Large rooms with view ⑤, basic rooms ④

Parnell's Village Motor Inn 2 St Stephen's Ave ⓣ09/377 1463, ⓦwww.parnellmotorlodge.co.nz. Well maintained establishment opposite the cathedral with studios and large one- and two-bedroom self-catering units. Studios ⑤, units ⑥

Epsom

Greenpark 66 Great South Rd ⓣ09/520 3038, ⓔgreen.park@xtra.co.nz. Renovated motel with standard and executive suites, all with separate bedrooms and full facilities. ④–⑤

Hansen's 96 Great South Rd ⓣ09/520 2804, ⓕ524 7597. One of the cheapest motels in town with small but perfectly formed self-contained studios and a nice swimming pool. ④

Off Broadway Motel Newmarket 11 Alpers Ave ⓣ0800/427 623 & 09/529 3550, ⓦwww.off-broadway.co.nz. Business-orientated hotel with air-conditioned, soundproofed ensuite rooms. Plump for the much larger suites if your budget allows. Studios ⑤–⑥, suites ⑦.

Siesta 70 Great South Rd ⓣ0800/743 782 & 09/520 2107, ⓔreservations@siestamotel.co.nz. Good modern motel with kitchenless studios and self-catering units. ④–⑤

Tudor Court 108 Great South Rd ⓣ0800/826 878 & 09/523 1069, ⓔstay@tudor.co.nz. Compact motel with small hotel-style rooms and slightly larger ones with kitchenettes. ④

Ponsonby, Herne Bay and Freeman's Bay

Abaco Spa 59 Jervois Rd ⓣ09/376 0119 & 0800/220 066, ⓦwww.abacospamotel.com. Mainstream motel close to Herne Bay and Ponsonby shops and restaurants, with budget kitchenless rooms and larger motel units, some with private spas and distant harbour views. ⑤–⑥

Unicorn 31 Shelley Beach Rd ⓣ0800/864 267 & 09/376 2067, ⓦwww.unicornmotel.co.nz. Top-quality, modern, air-conditioned motel with spacious fully-equipped units; there's a private spa and a pool. ⑥

B&Bs and guesthouses

Auckland's stock of B&Bs and guesthouses is rapidly expanding. New places are continually opening, many pitching for the upper end of the market, with just a few rooms and an almost obsessive attention to the finest detail. Places are scattered widely around the **inner suburbs** on the south side of the harbour, but in recent years the choice in the North Shore suburb of **Devonport** has mushroomed. At last count there were over two dozen high-standard places, not all of them close to the ferry but all willing to pick up and drop off if you arrive that way. Note that airport shuttle buses will drop you in Devonport for only a few dollars more than the central Auckland fare.

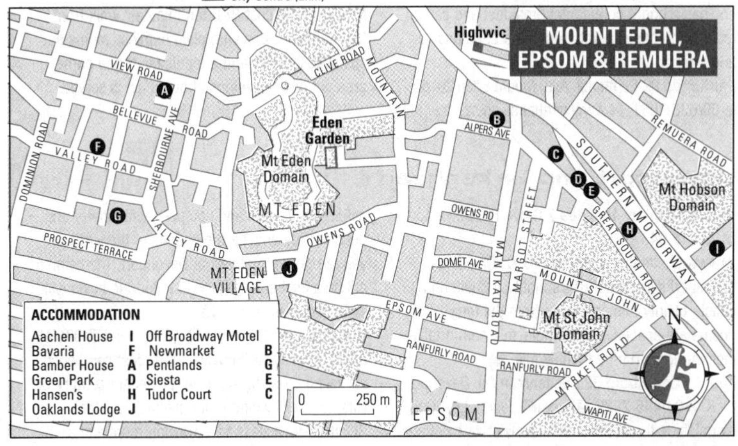

Gay-friendly accommodation

Although Auckland doesn't have any exclusively gay or lesbian hotels, neither does it have a reputation for homophobic proprietors, so you can stay pretty much where you like. There is, however, some gay-friendly accommodation, including the *Brown Kiwi* backpackers, *Aspen House*, a compact **hotel** in the city centre, and several small **guesthouses**: check out *The Great Ponsonby B&B* in Ponsonby, *Herne Bay B&B* in Herne Bay, *St George's Bay Lodge* in Parnell and *Parituhu Beachstay* in Devonport – all reviewed in our main "B&Bs and guesthouses" listings.

Parnell

Birdwood House 41 Birdwood Crescent ⓣ09/306 5900, ⓦwww.birdwood.co.nz. Welcoming B&B in a large 1914 house with Arts and Crafts interiors, well-sited just off Parnell Road and with views of the Domain and museum. Rooms all have their own bathroom, some with tubs, and a gourmet breakfast is served, sometimes out on the deck or in the grounds. ❻

Chalet Chevron 14 Brighton Rd ⓣ09/309 0290, ⓦwww.chaletchevron.co.nz. Comfortable B&B with cheery and colourful en-suite rooms, some with distant sea views, and several well geared for singles. A full breakfast is served and there's free tea and coffee all day. ❺

St Georges Bay Lodge 43 St Georges Bay Rd ⓣ09/303 1050, ⓦwww.stgeorge.co.nz. Gorgeous and welcoming B&B in one of the four original St Georges Bay villas, built in the 1890s and since tastefully and authentically renovated, fitted out in native timbers and hung with New Zealand artworks. Complimentary port and wine, and a full breakfast, are all part of the package. ❼

Mount Eden, Epsom and Remuera

Aachen House 39 Market Rd, Remuera ⓣ09/520 2329 & 0800/222 436, ⓦwww.aachenhouse.co.nz. Elegant boutique B&B in an Edwardian house sumptuously decorated with antiques. Every comfort is catered for: rooms are spacious, beds are huge, bathrooms are beautifully tiled and breakfasts are delicious. ❼–❾

Bavaria 83 Valley Rd, Mount Eden ⓣ09/638 9641, ⓦwww.bavariabandbhotel.co.nz, ⓔbavaria@xtra.co.nz. Eleven-room B&B in a spacious, comfortable villa that boasts a pleasant deck and garden. It's popular with German speakers, has a buffet continental breakfast and can be reached on buses numbered in the 250s and 260s. ❻

Pentlands 22 Pentlands Ave, Mount Eden ⓣ & ⓕ09/638 7031, ⓦwww.pentlands.co.nz. Peaceful, low-cost B&B ten minutes' walk from Mount Eden shops with plain bathless rooms but spacious lounges and a tennis court and barbecue area out back. Continental breakfast is served. ❹

Devonport and Birkenhead

Cheltenham-by-the-Sea 2 Grove Rd, Devonport ⓣ09/445 9437, ⓦwww.cheltenhambythesea.co.nz. One of Devonport's cheapest B&Bs, right by Cheltenham Beach, twenty minutes' walk from the ferry. Rooms are spacious and simple, in a comfortable, modern home run by friendly folk. ❺

The Garden Room 23 Cheltenham Rd, Devonport ⓣ & ⓕ09/445 2472, ⓔb.hall@clear.net.nz. One room inside the house and a lovely private cottage in a leafy garden, all done to a very high standard; sumptuous breakfasts can be served under an arbour or in your room. ❻.

Parituhu Beachstay 3 King Edward Parade, Devonport ⓣ & ⓕ09/445 6559. Excellent budget B&B homestay in the heart of Devonport and overlooking the harbour. There's just the one room, with private bath and access to a secluded garden, and the gay-friendly owners provide a self-service breakfast. ❹

Peace & Plenty Inn 6 Flagstaff Terrace, Devonport ⓣ09/445 2925, ⓦwww.peaceandplenty.co.nz. One of New Zealand's finest B&Bs. Elegantly restored kauri floorboards lead through to a lovely veranda, past exquisite rooms filled with fresh flowers and equipped with sherry and port. Venture outside the bounds of the inn, and you're right in the heart of Devonport. The communal breakfast is a major event, and the hosts will even take you sailing. ❽

Stafford Villa 2 Awanui St, Birkenhead ⓣ09/418 3022, ⓦwww.staffordvilla.co.nz. Just two period furnished en-suite rooms in an elegant century-old villa, with everything to the highest standard. Guests have access to a drawing room and a comfy library (with complimentary port), and are treated to a sumptuous breakfast. It's located on a quiet street in one the North Shore's more venerable waterside suburbs, where there are several good restaurants and the excellent Bridgeway Cinema (see p.127). ❽

Villa Cambria 71 Vauxhall Rd, Devonport ⓣ09/445 7899, ⓦwww.villacambria.co.nz. Beautifully decorated Victorian villa close to Cheltenham beach and fifteen minutes' walk from Devonport with friendly and attentive hosts who provide lovely breakfasts and are relaxed enough to refer to their guests as inn-mates. All rooms en suite with complimentary port. Rooms ❼, large loft room ❽

Ponsonby and Herne Bay

Amitee's on Ponsonby 237 Ponsonby Rd ⓣ & ⓕ09/378 6325, ⓦwww.amiteeson ponsonby.co.nz. Self-styled "urban hotel" right on the Ponsonby strip offering reasonable sized en-suite rooms, all decorated with modern clean lines and interesting artworks, and some with city views. Breakfast is a self-service continental affair. ❻–❼

Freeman's B&B 65 Wellington St, Ponsonby ⓣ09/376 5046, ⓦwww.freemansbandb.co.nz. Good-value B&B well-placed midway between the city and Ponsonby with doubles, spacious self-contained apartments (without breakfast) and a secluded garden. ❺

The Great Ponsonby B&B 30 Ponsonby Terrace, Ponsonby ⓣ09/376 5989, ⓦwww.ponsonbybnb.co.nz. Boutique hotel in a restored 1898 villa three minutes' walk from Ponsonby Road, boldly decorated in ocean tones using native timbers and Pacific artworks and furnishings. All rooms are en suite (some with baths) and come with Sky TV. There are also several self-catering studio units. Everyone has use of the sunny lounge and shaded garden. Rooms ❻

Herne Bay B&B 4 Shelly Beach Rd, Herne Bay ⓣ09/360 0309, ⓦwww.herne-bay.co.nz. Relaxed and very low key, if dowdily decorated, B&B in a large Edwardian house converted to accommodate three classes of room, and with a rooftop turret which is great for watching the sunset. Some rooms share facilities and have access to a small communal kitchen, some have their own kitchen, and the larger ones have a separate living area. Continental breakfast is served. ❹

Hostels

Auckland has stacks of **backpacker hostels**. The scene is highly competitive, and most are very well set up for assisting new arrivals in planning their onward travel, even to the extent of having a fully staffed on-site travel service – sometimes pushing favoured trips and activities, but generally offering fair and impartial advice.

There's a definite trade-off between proximity to the facilities offered by **downtown** hostels, and the relative quiet and comfort of places outside the centre. Those in the centre tend to cram in the beds and, with bars and clubs only a short stagger away, cater to party animals. The emphasis is firmly on having a wild time and the larger places have a reputation for being noisy at night; self-catering facilities seem like an afterthought and serve to encourage guests to eat out. Hostels in the **inner suburbs** – Parnell, Ponsonby and Mount Eden – tend to be less boisterous affairs often in old, converted houses, sometimes with gardens and always with easy parking.

As you'd expect, **prices** are a touch higher than at hostels in the rest of the country, though you can still get dorm bunks around the $18 mark. Small dorms and four-shares hover around $20 and most doubles and twins are $45–50. If you're arriving during the peak summer season, try to book a couple of days in advance to be sure of getting a bed.

City centre

Albert Park 27–31 Victoria St East ⓣ09/309 0336, ⓔbakpak@albertpark.co.nz. Probably the best of the city centre backpackers; small, clean and fairly spacious with some large and several smaller dorms, comfortable doubles, reasonable cooking facilities, bar and pool table. Dorms ❶, rooms ❸

Auckland Central 229 Queen St ⓣ09/358 4877, ⓦwww.acb.co.nz. Long-standing hostel recently relocated to a ten-storey converted office building right in the heart of the city. Despite the inevitable impersonality of housing 600 souls, everything runs smoothly and it seldom feels too crowded. They've thought of everything including a massive internet centre, helpful travel office, large laundry, gear storage and even electronic key access to rooms and public areas. Large mixed dorms sleep up to ten but it is worth the extra $2 to stay in single-sex three- to five-bed dorms supplied with sheets. Twins and doubles come either with or without en-suite bathroom.
Dorms ❶, rooms ❸, en suites ❹

Auckland City YHA cnr City Rd & Liverpool St ⓣ09/309 2802, ⓔyhaauck@yha.org.nz. Large and central YHA with seven floors of mostly twin and double rooms – some with fine city views – plus well-equipped common areas and a large travel centre; even a bistro on site. Single sex dorms ❶, rooms ❷

Auckland International YHA 5 Turner St ⓣ09/302 8200, ⓔyhaakint@yha.org.nz. Just down the hill and even larger than its brother, this purpose-built YHA is thoroughly modern with excellent cooking facilities, spacious rooms, separate TV and smoking lounges, Internet access and a travel centre. Single sex dorms ❶, rooms ❸, en-suite rooms ❹

Bay City 6 Constitution Hill ⓣ09/303 4768, ⓔbed@backpackers.co.nz. The smallest of Auckland's central backpackers fills a couple of houses close to the city and train station and mid-way to Parnell. It's friendly, homely, has a small garden and fairly cramped four- and six-bunk dorms and double rooms. Dorms ❶, rooms ❷

Central City 26 Lorne St ⓣ09/358 5685, ⓦwww.tickit.com/nz/co/ccb/. Large, busy and ever-popular hostel just off Queen Street with a lively atmosphere and stacks of local information plus a travel agency and bar downstairs. Four floors of ten-bunk dorms, four-shares and doubles are well-equipped and fairly spacious. Dorms ❶, rooms ❸

Parnell

City Garden Lodge 25 St Georges Bay Rd ⓣ09/302 0880, ⓕ309 8998. One of the city's finest backpackers in a spacious, well-organized villa surrounded by expansive lawns. For an extra dollar or two, the three- and five-person dorms have beds rather than bunks, and there are some lovely double and twin rooms. Dorms ❶, rooms ❷

International Backpackers 2 Churton St ⓣ & ⓕ09/358 4584, ⓔinternational.bp@xtra.co.nz. Clean, peaceful hostel in a former YHA on a quiet street three minutes from Parnell with parking and a nice fenced garden. Dorms ❶, rooms ❷

Lantana Lodge 60 St Georges Bay Rd ⓣ09/373 4546. Small, spotlessly clean and friendly hostel with reasonable facilities and a homely feel. Dorms ❶, rooms ❷

Mount Eden

Bamber House 22 View Rd ⓣ & ⓕ09/623 4267, ⓦwww.hostelbackpacker.com. Well-run, spacious and very clean hostel with all the facilities you could ask for, lawns right around the house and a great new outdoor pool. The cheapest beds are in a cramped bunkhouse outside, but there are better dorms inside and well-priced doubles. Catch buses #255–258, #265 or #267 from Queen St just up from Victoria St. Dorms ❶, rooms ❷

Oaklands Lodge 5a Oaklands Road ⓣ & ⓕ09/638 6545, ⓦwww.oaklands.co.nz. Former YHA in a big old house right by Mount Eden shops. Beds come in large dorms, four-shares and doubles. Catch buses #274, #275 or #277 from Customs St East, downtown. Dorms ❶, rooms ❷

Ponsonby

Brown Kiwi 7 Prosford St ⓣ09/378 0191, ⓦwww.brownkiwi.co.nz. Lovely little hostel in a restored Victorian villa right in the thick of the Ponsonby café zone but with a peaceful patio and tiny garden at the back. All the usual facilities and a relaxing atmosphere (though it can be a bit noisy at weekends). Daytime parking is poor but it's easily accessible by the Link bus. Dorms ❶, rooms ❷

Ponsonby Backpackers 2 Franklin Rd ⓣ0800/476 676 & 09/360 1311, ⓦwww.ponsonby-backpackers.co.nz. Rambling hostel in a large Victorian house with off-street parking. The rooms are nothing special but prices are low, the place is a good deal more peaceful than the city hostels and you're right by the Ponsonby bars and restaurants. Catch the Link bus from Queen Street. Tents $12, dorms ❶, rooms ❷

Campsites and motor parks

You'd have to travel a long way to find anywhere genuinely attractive to pitch a **tent**, but there are numerous well-equipped motor camps within the city limits which are fine for **campervans** and often have bargain **cabins**. However, without your own vehicle, you'll find yourself spending a lot of time and money on buses, the costs outweighing any saving you may make over staying in town.

Avondale Motor Park 46 Bollard Ave, Avondale ⓣ0800/100 542 & 09/828 7228, ⓦwww.aucklandmotorpark.co.nz. Restful and fairly central site 6km southwest of the city and accessible by buses #210–29 from Victoria St. Camping $10, on-site vans ❷, cabins & flats ❸

North Shore Motels & Top 10 Holiday Park 52 Northcote Rd, Takapuna ⓣ0508/909 090 & 09/418 2578, ⓦwww.nsmotels.co.nz. Well-appointed site on the North Shore, just off the northern motorway, with indoor swimming pool and extensive barbecue areas. Catch Stagecoach buses #921 and #922 from the corner of Victoria and Hobson streets. Camping $30 per site, cabins & motel units ❸–❻

Remuera Motor Lodge and Inner City Camping Ground 16 Minto Rd ⓣ09/524 5126 & 0508/244244, ⓔremlodge@ihug.co.nz. About the most central, convenient and appealing site, 6km east of the city in a quiet, sylvan residential area. There's even a swimming pool. Buses #625, #645 and #655 from Customs St East will get you here.

Camping $13, kitchen cabins & motel units ❹
Takapuna Beach Holiday Park 22 The Promenade, Takapuna ⓣ & ⓕ 09/489 7909, ⓔ takabeach@xtra.co.nz. Beachside caravan park on the North Shore overlooking Rangitoto and within five minutes' walk of the Takapuna shops and restaurants. Stagecoach buses numbered in the 800s from the corner of Victoria and Hobson streets pass nearby. Camping $12, cabins & on-site vans ❷, en-suite cabins ❸, motel units ❺

The City Centre and around

Auckland's city centre clings to the southern shores of the **Waitemata Harbour**, with downbeat **Queen Street**, the main drag, striking south through a business district largely sustained by banks and insurance companies, as the ascendant inner-city suburbs – trendy Ponsonby, affluent Parnell and go-ahead Newmarket – continually erode its mercantile dominance.

Queen Street meets the harbour at the Ferry Building, hub of ferry services to the North Shore, the maritime suburb of **Devonport** and to the islands of the Hauraki Gulf. One of the best ways to begin your exploration of the city is on foot, following the **Coast-to-Coast Walkway** which starts here and winds up through the city past many sights. Skirting **Albert Park**, wedged between the **University** and the **Auckland Art Gallery**, the route then veers towards **The Domain**, an extensive blanket of parkland that represents Auckland's premier green space, laid out around the city's most-visited attraction, the **Auckland Museum**. The Domain divides the city from the inner-eastern suburb of **Parnell**, ecclesiastical heart of the city with the **Cathedral**, one of Auckland's oldest churches and a couple of historical houses, both associated with clergymen. The walkway finishes beside the Manukau Harbour, after climbing to two of Auckland's highest points, **Mount Eden** and its more diverting kin, **One Tree Hill** with its encircling **Cornwall Park**.

To the east of Parnell, the harbourside **Tamaki Drive** runs past **Kelly Tarlton's Underwater World** to the city beaches of Mission Bay and St Heliers. West of the centre, the suburbs spread out beyond the reclaimed basin of Freeman's Bay to Auckland's most concentrated cluster of superb restaurants and cafés along **Ponsonby Road**, and out to Western Springs, home to the **Auckland Zoo** and the transport museum commonly referred to by its abbreviated name, **MOTAT**.

Aucklanders with time on their hands and a penchant for thundering breakers leave the stresses of city behind and head to the surf beaches of the West Coast but there are local spots for a more impulsive dip, particularly compact and often-crowded coves along **Tamaki Drive** and the more expansive strands on the North Shore near **Takapuna**.

Downtown and The Domain

Auckland's central city street names represent a roll call of prime movers in New Zealand's early European history. The city's backbone, Queen Street, along with attendant royal acolytes, Victoria and Albert streets, forms a central grid bedded with thoroughfares commemorating the country's first Governor-General, William Hobson; Willoughby Shortland, New Zealand's first colonial secretary; and William Symonds, who chivvied along isthmus Maori chiefs reluctant to sign the Treaty of Waitangi.

The America's Cup

For a few glorious days in May 1995 **yacht-racing** eclipsed rugby as New Zealand's premier sport as **Peter Blake**, skipper of the *Black Magic* boat, wrested yachting's most valuable prize, the America's Cup, from the Americans (for only the second time in the race's 144-year history). Blake was feted as a national hero and the crew were welcomed down Queen Street with a ticker-tape parade; scenes repeated in March 2000 as New Zealand became the first nation (apart from the United States) to successfully defend the America's Cup, here on the Hauraki Gulf.

The cup was first contested as the **One Hundred Guinea Cup**, with fifteen British boats and one American racing to circumnavigate the Isle of Wight, off the south coast of England, as part of imperial Britain's Great Exhibition in 1851. The schooner *America* romped away with the trophy and the New York Yacht Club held on to it through 23 defences, during which time the race became a battlefield for some of the world's most experienced crews and a proving ground for the latest boat designs, using space-age composite materials.

Finally, in 1983, the Perth Yacht Club's controversial winged-keel **Australia II** showed that the Americans didn't have an inalienable right to the silverware. The America's Cup became something of a holy grail for New Zealanders, and when everything finally came together in 1995, Kiwis went nuts. Peter Blake declared that the red socks he had been wearing were his lucky charm, and the entire nation – Prime Minister Jim Bolger and Governor-General Catherine Tizard included – donned red socks, the proceeds of sales going to fund the *Black Magic* crew, who went on to trounce the Americans five–nil in the final series. Peter Blake subsequently retired from racing to pursue environmental concerns and, sadly, in late 2001, was killed by thieves in the Brazilian Amazon.

The victory in the seas off San Diego earned New Zealand the right to defend the trophy on home turf, in what was to be a five-month jibe-fest through the summer of 1999–2000. A scruffy fishing area known as **Viaduct Harbour** was given a complete makeover with the construction of new yacht berths, several apartment blocks going up, and dozens of flash restaurants opening. It didn't come without controversy and **Maori** groups with claims to the development sites struggled to get some remuneration from the event. For one disgruntled Maori, things came to a head in February 1997 when, driven by frustration, he smashed the cup – then on display in the Royal New Zealand Yacht Squadron's clubhouse – with a sledge hammer.

Nonetheless, by November 1999 half the world's multi-million-dollar superyachts were filling the berths and the frenetic activity around the Viaduct Harbour had become the buzz of the nation. Meanwhile on the waters of the **Hauraki Gulf**, a dozen overseas challengers (five from the United States alone) competed to find who would win the **Louis Vuitton Cup**, and with it the right to challenge the Kiwi defender. The relatively inexperienced (but well-funded) Italian *Prada* team eventually saw off such seasoned competition as Dennis Connor's *Stars and Stripes*. They did it with such grace and style that they gained a place in the hearts of Kiwis, who even hoisted the Italian flag next to the New Zealand ensign on the harbour bridge. There was no love lost at sea, however, and when *Prada* took on the "black boat" of Russell Coutts' Team New Zealand they were trounced 5–0 in the best of nine series.

The Waitemata Harbour will once again host the America's Cup over the summer of 2002–2003 and as the developers and restaurant owners rub their hands in glee, Team New Zealand struggles to rebuild after several of its key personnel succumbed to huge cash offers from rival syndicates. To keep abreast of the lead-up to the America's Cup, surf ⓦwww.americascup.co.nz which relives past triumphs and charts the countdown to the next contest.

The central business district butts up against the **Waitemata Harbour**, formerly divorced from the city by docks, but now reconnected through the development of the **Maritime Museum** and the adjacent waterside rejuvenation of **Viaduct Harbour** and Princes Wharf, essentially flashy restaurants around a marina.

There's little of abiding interest right in the city centre except for the **Auckland Art Gallery**, the country's foremost showcase for fine art. The highbrow theme continues to the east at the excellent **Auckland Museum**, packed with superb Maori and Pacific Island artefacts, which dominates **The Domain**, a vast swathe of trees and lawns sweeping down towards the harbour.

The waterfront

Auckland's waterfront is dominated by the Neoclassical 1912 **Ferry Building**, which is still the hub of the Waitemata Harbour ferry services, though the chaotic bustle of the days before the construction of the harbour bridge is now a distant memory. Nonetheless, there's a constant ebb and flow of commuters and sightseers boarding speedy catamarans to Devonport and Rangitoto, Waiheke and Great Barrier islands.

Since the 1999-2000 America's Cup challenge, the majority of the waterfront activity has shifted a couple of hundred metres west to Viaduct Harbour, where the re-paved wharves are strung with elegant lighting and lined by the endless outdoor seating of the new restaurants. It can seem a little too shiny and pleased with itself, but is fine for a couple of hours strolling past the super-yachts moored alongside, maybe signing up for one of the harbour cruises, and idling away the afternoon over a cappuccino or chardonnay.

The only specific sight is the **National Maritime Museum**, Viaduct Harbour, on the corner of Quay Street and Hobson Street (daily: Nov–Easter 9am–6pm; Easter–Oct 9am–5pm; $12; Ⓦwww.nzmaritime.org), which pays homage to the maritime history of an island nation reliant on the sea for Maori and Pakeha colonization, trade and sport. The short orientational, *Te Waka* video illustrates an imagined Maori migration voyage setting the scene for a display of outrigger and double-hulled canoes from all over the South Pacific. There's a huge variety of designs employed for fishing, lagoon sailing and ocean voyaging – the last represented by the huge 23m-long *Taratai*, which carried New Zealand photographer and writer James Siers and a crew of thirteen over 2400km from Kiribati to Fiji in 1976. Made entirely from traditional materials and propelled by an oceanic lateen sail, its intriguing method of operation is neatly demonstrated on a rig nearby. The creaking and rolling innards of a migrant ship and displays on New Zealand's coastal traders and whalers lead on to a collection of just about every class of yacht, culminating in the devotional exhibits on yacht racing – in particular, comprehensive coverage of the **America's Cup** (see box opposite), its history and detailed scale replicas of key entrants. Other highlights include a very early example of the Hamilton Jetboat, which was designed for shallow, braided Canterbury rivers, and a replica of a classic 1950s holiday *bach* and milk bar, with great archival film footage adding to the nostalgic flavour.

There are interesting guided tours (generally Mon-Fri 11am, Sat 11am or 2pm; free), and the possibility of a one hour **cruise** on the *Ted Ashby* (Tues, Thurs, Sat & Sun noon & 2pm; $15, $19 including museum entry), a 1990s replica of one of the traditional flat-bottomed, ketch-rigged scows that once worked the North Island tidal waterways.

△ A takahe

The city centre

The windswept **Queen Elizabeth II Square**, opposite the Ferry Building, makes an inauspicious and scruffy introduction to the city centre, though things should improve when the Britomart transport interchange (see box, p.82) takes over the Neoclassical 1910 former post office. South, across Customs Street, lies the city's main axis, **Queen Street**, an inelegant canyon lined by shops, banks and offices threaded by arcades – notably Queen's Arcade and The Strand Arcade – running through to the parallel High, Lorne and Elliot streets. The foot of Queen Street once had a three-hundred-metre-long wharf extending out to deep water, but progressive reclamation has shifted the shoreline away from Fort Street (originally Fore Street), which, in keeping with its port-of-call past, is now downtown's red-light district. Jean Batten Place runs south off Fort Street, becoming **High Street**, which is energized by bookshops and trendy clothes shops, and is always the liveliest section of the central city. Most of the action happens around the junction with the former blacksmithing street of **Vulcan Lane**, now equally well-equipped with bars and swanky stores.

The city centre is dominated by the concrete **Skytower**, on the corner of Victoria Street and Federal Street (Sun–Thurs 8.30am–11pm, Fri & Sat 8.30am–midnight; $15, plus $3 for upper viewing deck), built in the mid-1990s as a potent symbol for the city in the run-up to the millennium. At 328m, it is New Zealand's tallest structure (just pipping the Eiffel Tower and Sydney's Centrepoint), and has the obligatory observation decks (192m and 220m) with a café and stupendous views right over the city and Hauraki Gulf. The tower has recently become the focus of a couple of **adventure activities** (see p.113) and you may see SkyJump practitioners hurtling groundwards from the observation area.

The tower sprouts from **Sky City Casino**, a relative newcomer to the city that has managed to carve a niche for itself in a country where temperance is still revered. If you can demonstrate that you're over eighteen and eschew shorts, singlets and thongs (flip-flops), you can get on to a gaming floor awash in deep blue and green decor that's supposed to represent Polynesian demi-god Maui's underwater realm. All the usual distractions intended to separate you from your money are here, along with cafés, bars, a high-roller room and *Alto Casino and Bar* for those who prefer the jacket-and-tie approach. Learner classes are held most mornings.

One of Queen Street's few buildings of any distinction is the Art Nouveau **Civic Theatre**, on the corner of Wellesley Street. The talk of the town when it opened in 1929, the management went as far as to import a small Indian boy from Fiji to complement the ornate Moghul-style decor. After a couple of years of intense renovation it has now reopened in its full splendour complete with a star-strewn artificial sky and an ornate proscenium arch with flanking lions, their eyes blazing red. It's well worth a look, but unless you happen to strike one of the infrequent open days, the only way to get inside is to see a performance (see p.127).

Bang next door, but architecturally miles away, is a chunky post-modern form (previously open as an Imax cinema). Adding little to the block's recent rejuvenation, it flanks **Aotea Square**, which is overlooked on its other sides by the recently refurbished Town Hall and the city's foremost concert hall, the **Aotea Centre**, which opened in a blaze of glory in 1990, with Kiri Te Kanawa honouring a longstanding promise to perform on the inaugural night. On Friday and Saturday, the arts, crafts, vintage clothing, jewellery and Pasifika stalls of the **Aotea Square Markets** bring the square to life.

The Art Gallery and Albert Park

Moving east of Queen Street, Wellesley Street runs up to the **Auckland Art Gallery** (Ⓦwww.akcity.govt.nz/artgallery) which comes in two parts – one predominantly traditional, the other resolutely contemporary – which jointly make up the world's most important collection of Kiwi art. In recognition of this, the fee for any exhibition in the Heritage Gallery that contains mainly New Zealand works is waived on Monday, as is the entry fee to the New Gallery.

The Heritage Gallery

The elaborate mock-French-styled **Heritage Gallery**, on the corner of Wellesley Street and Kitchener Street (daily 10am–5pm; $4, special exhibitions $5–12; free guided tours daily at 2pm; infoline Ⓣ09/379 1349), includes a small but respectable collection of quality works by internationally renowned artists – Brueghel, Corot, Maillol, Liechtenstein – but this is essentially a place to come to appreciate New Zealand art. Works change frequently, but you can expect to find original drawings by the artists on James Cook's expeditions setting the scene for overwrought and often crass oils depicting Maori migrations. These romantic and idealized images of Maori life seen through European eyes frequently show composite scenes that could never have happened, contributing to a mythical view that persisted for decades. Two works show contrasting but equally misleading views: Kennett Watkins' 1912 *The Legend of the Voyage to New Zealand*, with its plump, happy natives on a still lagoon; and Charles Goldie's 1898 *The Arrival of the Maoris in New Zealand*, modelled on Géricault's *Raft of the Medusa* and showing starving, frightened voyagers battling tempestuous seas.

Much of the rest of the early collection is devoted to works by two of the country's most loved artists – both highly respected by Maori as among the few to accurately portray their ancestors. Bohemian immigrant **Gottfried Lindauer** emigrated to New Zealand in 1873 and spent his later years painting lifelike, almost documentary, portraits of *rangatira* (chiefs) and high-born Maori men and women. In the early part of the twentieth century, **Charles F. Goldie** became New Zealand's resident "old master" and earned international recognition for his painterly portraits of elderly Maori subjects regally showing off their traditional tattoos, or *moko*, though they were in fact often painted from photographs (sometimes after the subject's death).

Contemporary landscape painters largely projected their European visions of beauty onto New Zealand landscapes, reducing vibrant visions of shimmering colour into subdued scenes reminiscent of English parkland, drab north European seas and Swiss Alps. It took half a century for more representative images to become the norm – an evolutionary process which continued into the 1960s and 1970s, when many works betray an almost cartoon-like quality, with heavily delineated spaces daubed in shocking colours. Look out for works by **Rita Angus**, renowned for her images of Central Otago in the 1940s, and **Tony Fomison** (1939–90), painter of one of the gallery's most expensive works, *Study of Holbein's "Dead Christ"*. Completed in 1973, it's typical of his later, more obsessive period, combining the artist's passion for art history and his preoccupation with mortality.

The New Gallery and Albert Park

Across the street, the **New Gallery**, on the corner of Wellesley Street and Lorne Street (daily 10am–5pm; $4 for each section), has two light and spacious floors, signalling its more youthful and approachable nature. The exhibitions and site-specific installations by predominantly New Zealand, and particularly Maori, artists vary constantly. One name to look out for is **Colin McCahon**, who died in 1987, but whose fascination with the power and beauty of New Zealand landscape informs so much recent Kiwi art; indeed, there is a whole room set aside for his work. Others, such as **Gordon Walters**, draw their inspiration from Maori iconography, in Walters' case controversially employing vibrant, graphic representations of traditional Maori symbols – spirals, fern-root emblems and stylized human forms (for more on Maori design, see "Maoritanga" in Contexts).

The gallery's works spill outside, with George Rickey's stainless-steel 1984 *Double L Gyratory* and Neil Dawson's monumental semicircular *Throwback* sculpture creeping into **Albert Park**. These formal Victorian-style gardens spread uphill to the university, and are generally thronged with sunbathing students and office workers. Originally the site of a Maori *pa*, the land was successively conscripted into service as Albert Barracks in the 1840s and 1850s, and then as a labyrinthine network of air-raid shelters during World War II, before relaxing into its current incarnation as peaceful parkland. It comes filled with a century's worth of memorials, a floral clock, some beautiful oaks and Morton Bay Fig trees and the 1882 former gatekeeper's cottage containing the **Bruce Wilkinson Collection** (daily 10am–4pm; free), a small display of ornate clocks and figurines amassed by an Auckland businessman and donated to the city.

Karangahape Road

At its southern end, Queen Street climbs to the ridge-top **Karangahape Road**, universally known as K' Road, formerly an uptown residential area for prosperous nineteenth-century merchants, and long associated with Auckland's Polynesian community. For twenty years now, planners have hailed a mainstream shopping renaissance but K' Road remains determinedly niche. Groovy cafés, music shops specializing in vinyl, and clothes shops selling budget designer garb and clubbing gear have gradually gained a foothold, ousting some of the more dowdy shops. Pacific culture remains strong – witness a couple of agents specializing in Pacific Island travel, the Niuean consulate, a Samoan Church and several shops selling island-print fabrics – but increasingly east and south Asians are moving in, adding yet more colour. There are no specific sights, but you can easily pass an afternoon browsing the shops and eating in budget ethnic restaurants.

K' Road is much loved by those who know it and much maligned, even feared, by those who don't – chiefly on account of the notoriety associated with its western end, a two-hundred-metre-long corridor of massage parlours, strip clubs and gay cruising clubs. It is certainly one of the seedier parts of town, but the raunchy places are interspersed with more mainstream nightclubs and there is always a vibrant feel that is seldom intimidating, though the usual precautions should be exercised at night.

Further east, K' Road crosses Symonds Street by the little-known and somewhat neglected **Symonds Street Cemetery**, one of Auckland's earliest burial grounds, with allocations for Jewish, Presbyterian, Wesleyan, Roman Catholic and Anglican faiths – the last two areas largely destroyed by the motorway cut through Grafton Gully in the 1960s. A patch of deciduous woodland shades the grave of New Zealand's first Governor, William Hobson (tucked away on the eastern side of Symonds Street almost under the vast concrete span of Grafton Bridge).

The Domain

Grafton Gully separates the city centre from **The Domain**, a vast swathe of semi-formal gardens draped over the low, irregular profile of an extinct volcano known to Maori as Pukekawa or "hill of bitter memories", a reference to the bloodshed of ancient inter-tribal fighting. In the 1840s, when Auckland was the national capital, Governor Grey set aside the core of The Domain as the city's first park, and it remains the finest, furnished with all the obligatory mid-nineteenth-century accoutrements: a band rotunda, phoenix palms, formal flower beds and spacious lawns. In summer, the scores of rugby pitches metamorphose into cricket ovals and softball diamonds, and every few weeks marquees and stages are erected in the crater's shallow amphitheatre for outdoor musical extravaganzas.

The Domain's volcanic spring was one of Auckland's original water sources. It was used to farm the country's first rainbow trout in 1884, and by the Auckland Acclimatization Society to grow European plants, thereby promoting the rapid Europeanization of the New Zealand countryside. The spirit of this enterprise lingers on in the **Winter Gardens** (Nov–March Mon-Sat 9am-5.30pm, Sun 9am–7.30pm; April–Oct daily 9am–4.30pm; free), a shallow fish-pond in a formal sunken courtyard flanked by two elaborate barrel-roofed glasshouses – one temperate, the other heated to mimic tropical climes – filled with neatly tended botanical specimens. Next door, a former scoria quarry has been transformed into the **Fernz Fernery** (same hours; free), a verdant dell with over a hundred types of fern in dry, intermediate and wet habitats.

Auckland Museum

The highest point on the domain is crowned by the imposing Greco-Roman-style **Auckland Museum** (Te Papa Whakahiku; daily 10am–5pm; $5 donation expected and valid for repeated entry on one day, Ⓦwww.akmuseum.org.nz). Built as a World War I memorial in 1929, the names of World War II battles were duly added to those of earlier bloodbaths around the outer walls. The contents of Auckland's original city museum were moved here and the holdings expanded to form one of the world's finest collections of Maori and Pacific art. After a major revamp in the late 1990s the museum remains traditional in its approach, but now thoroughly contemporary in its execution, with each of the three floors taking on an individual identity – the people (ground), the place (middle), and New Zealand at War (top). Kids are catered for with the **Children's Discovery Centre** on the middle floor and if you're interested in buying Maori crafts while you're in New Zealand, check out the high-quality traditional and contemporary work in the museum **shop**. To round off the experience, head along to the 45-minute **Manaia cultural performance** (11am, noon & 1.30pm; $15) of song and dance, heralded by a conch-blast echoing through the building.

Auckland Museum is on the route of the Coast-to-Coast Walkway and city tour **buses**, and both the Link bus and regular buses #645 and #655 stop on Parnell Road, five minutes' walk away.

Ground Floor

Enter the museum and turn left to reach the **Pacific Lifeways** room, dominated by a simple yet majestic, breadfruit-wood statue from the Caroline Islands depicting **Kave**, Polynesia's malevolent and highest-ranked female deity whose menace is barely hinted at in this serene form. In the main, this room concentrates on the daily life of Pacific peoples, characterized by an elegant vessel for holding kava (a mildly narcotic drink brewed from roots), polished with years of use; stunning tooth and shell necklaces; New Guinean and Solomon Island equipment for preparing betel nuts for chewing; and fine examples of patterned tapa cloth, made from the bark of the mulberry tree. If you're lucky they may even have folk sitting on rush mats and demonstrating the processes involved.

This leads on to **He Taonga Maori**, the extensive Maori collection that's the highlight of the ground floor collection. The transition from purely Polynesian motifs to an identifiably Maori style is exemplified in the **Kaitaia Carving**, a two-and-a-half-metre-wide totara carving thought to have been designed for a ceremonial gateway – guarded by the central goblin-like figure with sweeping arms that stretch out to become lizard forms at their extremities: Polynesian in style but Maori in concept. It was found around 1920 near Kaitaia and is estimated to date from the twelfth or thirteenth century, predating most Maori art so far discovered.

As traditional Maori villages started to disappear towards the end of the nineteenth century, some of the best examples of carved panels, meeting houses and food stores were rescued. Many are currently displayed here, though some of the exhibits are claimed by Maori groups throughout the country and may ultimately be returned to their traditional owners. He Taonga Maori is dominated by **Hotunui**, a large and wonderfully restored carved meeting house (*whare whakairo*), built near Thames in 1878, late enough to have a corrugated iron rather than rush roof, and re-erected here in 1929. Once again the craftsmanship is superb; the house's exterior is all grotesque faces, lolling tongues and glistening paua-shell eyes, while the interior is lined with wonderful geometric *tukutuku* panels. Outside is the intricately carved prow and stern-piece of **Te Toki a Tapiri**, a 25m-long war canoe (*waka taua*), the only surviving specimen from the pre-European era. Designed to seat a hundred warriors, it was hewn from a single totara log near Wairoa in Hawke's Bay in the pre-Colonial era and donated to the museum in 1885. Elsewhere you are bombarded with magnificent work in the shape of storehouses and stand-alone statues, many of them work of the renowned Te Arawa carvers from the Rotorua district. Several were emasculated by prudish Victorians.

Beyond the canoe you're into the main Pacific Island collection, known as **Pacific Masterpieces**, filled with exquisite Polynesian, Melanesian and Micronesian works. Look out for the shell-inlaid ceremonial food bowl from the Solomon Islands; ceremonial clubs; and a wonderfully resonant slit-gong from Vanuatu. The textiles are fabulous too with designs far more varied than you'd expect considering the limited raw materials: the Hawaiian red feather cloak is especially fine.

A couple of smaller but no less interesting galleries are tucked around the back: **Wild Child**, which explores the more entertaining aspects of growing up in the young colony; and **City**, covering how Auckland has grown from a tiny trading post to a million-strong city in the space of two long lifetimes.

Middle Floor

The middle floor of the museum comprises the **natural history galleries**, an unusual combination of modern thematic displays and stuffed birds in cases. It delineates the progress from the "Big Bang" through an exploration of plate tectonics and the break up of Gondwanaland, the geology and seismology of New Zealand and its flora and fauna. Dinosaur skeletons allude to their presence here until 65 million years ago, something scientists had discounted until fairly recently when fossils started turning up. Displays like the three-metre Giant Moa can't be missed, but there's a lot of stuff virtually hidden so be prepared to take your time. Armed with the knowledge of how New Zealand came to be, you proceed to a series of ecosystems such as a reconstruction of a cave in Waitomo complete with stuffed beasts and live animals in tanks and aquariums. Move on to a three-storey-high model of a kauri complete with lighting and sound that compresses a day of birdsong and animal chatter into a few minutes. The live animal theme follows through to the sealife section where you can walk across a tank full of crabs before learning more about how introduced species have affected New Zealand's unique environment.

Top Floor

A multi-levelled approach is used on the top floor in the **Scars on the Heart** exhibition, an emotional exploration of how New Zealanders' involvement in war has helped shape national identity. At any time you are able to divert from the main timeline and explore specific topics in more detail via interactive displays concentrating on personal accounts of the troops' experiences and the responses of those back home. Artefacts aren't completely abandoned, but most of the uniforms, arms and memorabilia are neatly worked into the greater fabric of the exhibition, with the exception of the boldly displayed armoury. You enter through a slightly incongruous mock-up of an 1860s Auckland street that sets the scene for the New Zealand Wars, interpreted from both Maori and *pakeha* perspectives. World War I gets extensive coverage, particularly the Gallipoli campaign in Turkey, when botched leadership led to a massacre of ANZAC – Australian and New Zealand Army Corps – troops in the trenches. Powerful visuals and rousing martial music accompany newsreel footage of the Pacific campaigns of World War II, and finally New Zealand's foray into Vietnam is documented.

East of the city centre

The Auckland Domain separates the city from the fashionable inner suburbs of **Parnell** and **Newmarket**, the former an established, moneyed district of restaurants, boutiques and galleries with a modest line in churches and historical houses, the latter a relative upstart. To the east lies Auckland's prime waterfront, traced by **Tamaki Drive**, a twisting thoroughfare that skirts eight kilometres of some of Auckland's most popular city beaches – **Mission Bay**, Kohimarama and **St Heliers** – and some of the city's most expensive real estate. Throughout the summer it is the favoured hangout of roller-bladers and recreational cyclists, all jockeying for position. **Kelly Tarlton's Underwater World** is the only specific sight, but the harbour views out to Rangitoto and the Hauraki Gulf are excellent both from shore level and from a couple of headland viewpoints. The gentle hills behind are dotted with the secluded mansions of leafy **Remuera**, Auckland's old-money suburb. Further east you're well into the suburban heartland of Panmure, Pakuranga and the former "fencible" settlement of **Howick**.

Parnell

Forty years ago, few would have predicted the transformation of run-down **Parnell**, 2km east of Queen Street, into one of New Zealand's most sought-after addresses with restored kauri villas clamouring around the fashionable shops of the main thoroughfare, Parnell Road.

In fact, the district narrowly escaped the high-rise-concrete fate of many an inner-city suburb in the mid-1960s. Just as the bulldozers were closing in on the quaint but dilapidated shops and houses, eccentric dreamer **Les Harvey**

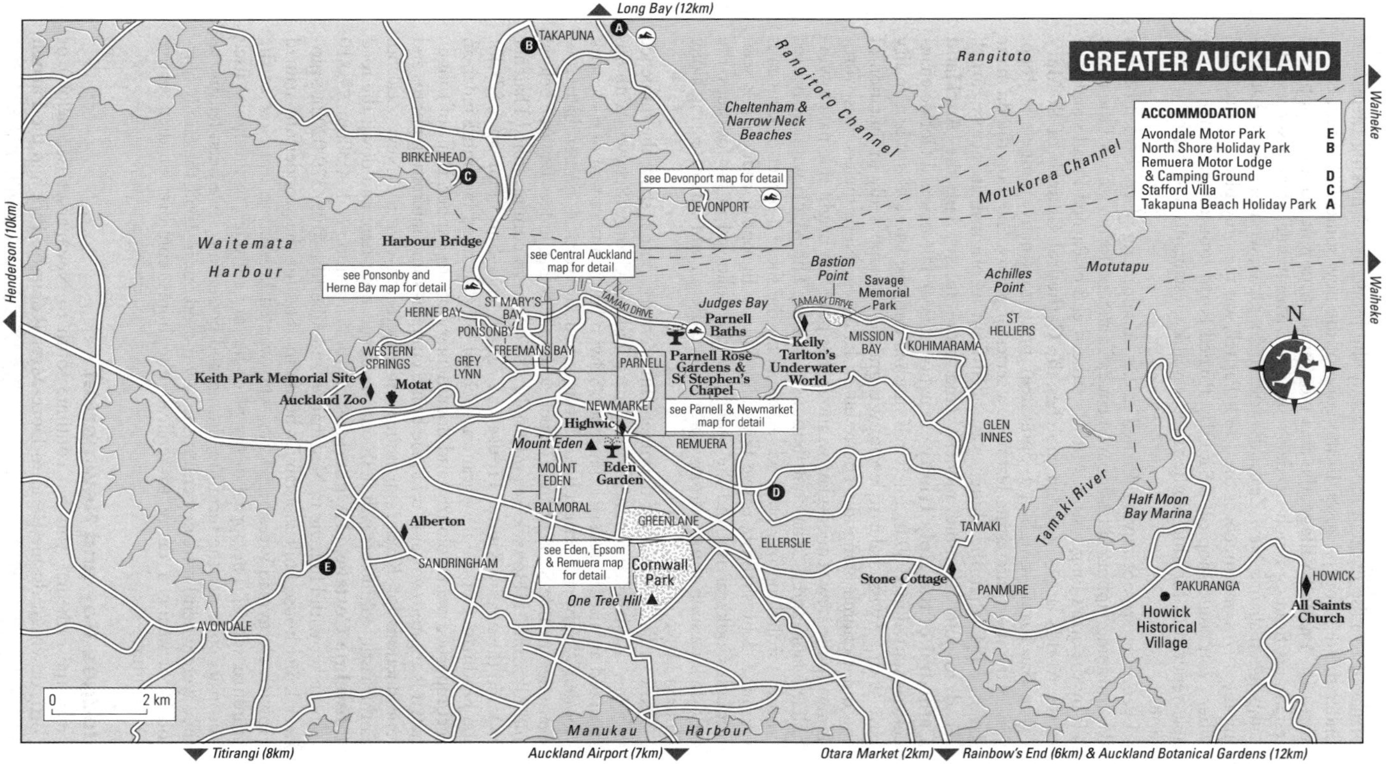

GREATER AUCKLAND

ACCOMMODATION

Avondale Motor Park	E
North Shore Holiday Park	B
Remuera Motor Lodge & Camping Ground	D
Stafford Villa	C
Takapuna Beach Holiday Park	A

Long Bay (12km)
Waiheke
Waiheke
Henderson (10km)
Titirangi (8km)
Auckland Airport (7km)
Otara Market (2km)
Rainbow's End (6km) & Auckland Botanical Gardens (12km)

TAKAPUNA
Rangitoto
Rangitoto Channel
Cheltenham & Narrow Neck Beaches
Motukorea Channel
BIRKENHEAD
see Devonport map for detail
DEVONPORT
Waitemata Harbour
Harbour Bridge
see Central Auckland map for detail
see Ponsonby and Herne Bay map for detail
Bastion Point
Savage Memorial Park
Achilles Point
Motutapu
ST MARY'S BAY
HERNE BAY
PONSONBY
FREEMANS BAY
TAMAKI DRIVE
Judges Bay
Parnell Baths
Kelly Tarlton's Underwater World
MISSION BAY
KOHIMARAMA
ST HELLIERS
WESTERN SPRINGS
GREY LYNN
PARNELL
Parnell Rose Gardens & St Stephen's Chapel
Keith Park Memorial Site
Motat
Auckland Zoo
NEWMARKET
see Parnell & Newmarket map for detail
Highwic
Mount Eden
Eden Garden
REMUERA
GLEN INNES
MOUNT EDEN
BALMORAL
GREENLANE
ELLERSLIE
Tamaki River
Half Moon Bay Marina
Alberton
TAMAKI
SANDRINGHAM
see Eden, Epsom & Remuera map for detail
Cornwall Park
One Tree Hill
Stone Cottage
PANMURE
PAKURANGA
HOWICK
Howick Historical Village
All Saints Church
AVONDALE
Manukau Harbour
0 2 km

managed to raise enough money to buy the properties, whisking them from under the developers' noses. In the guise of the now somewhat dated, ersatz-Victorian **Parnell Village**, the area blossomed, with rent from the shops and restaurants funding much-needed restoration. Meanwhile, Harvey successfully campaigned against New Zealand's strict trading laws, with the result that during the 1970s and much of the 1980s Parnell was the only place in Auckland where you could shop on a Saturday. Parnell Road soon established an enviable reputation for chic clothes shops, swanky restaurants and dealer art galleries.

Even if you're not buying, Parnell makes an appealing place to spend half a day browsing, sipping lattes at pavement cafés and exploring some of the marks left by the area's long history. At the southern end of Parnell Road stands one of the world's largest wooden churches, the **Cathedral Church of St Mary** (Mon–Sat 10am–4pm, Sun 1–5pm; free), built from native timbers in 1886. Inside, the most interesting feature is a series of photos taken on the dramatic day in 1984 when the church was rolled from its original site across Parnell Road to join its more modern (and more messy) kin, the **Auckland Cathedral of the Holy Trinity** (same hours; free). The original Gothic chancel was started in 1959 then left half-finished until the late 1980s, when an airy nave with a Swiss chalet-style roof was grafted on, supposedly in imitation of the older church alongside. The result is shambolic. Nevertheless, it is worth admiring the new stained-glass windows; the bold and bright side panels symbolize Maori and Pakeha contributions to society. The Maori window has sea creatures frolicking in ribbed waves, while on the shore a basket of kumara is surrounded by shellfish, native birds and flowers. European influence is seen through Cook's arrival and the settlement that followed in his footsteps: the city skyline, sunbathing citizens on St Heliers Beach and cars careering along Tamaki Drive.

The Gothic flourishes of the nineteenth-century church show the influence of New Zealand's prominent missionary bishop, George Selwyn. With his favoured architect, Frederick Thatcher, Selwyn left behind a trail of trademark wooden **"Selwyn" churches**, distinguished by vertical timber battens – examples include St Stephen's Chapel, down the hill at Judges Bay (see below) and All Saints' at Howick (see p.106). In 1857, Selwyn commissioned Thatcher to build the nearby **Kinder House**, at 2 Ayr St (Tues–Sun 11am–3pm; $2), for the headmaster of the new grammar school – a post filled by John Kinder, an accomplished watercolourist and documentary photographer. Built of rough-hewn Rangitoto volcanic rock, the house contains some interesting photos and reproductions of Kinder's paintings of nineteenth-century New Zealand. Enthusiastic volunteers will flesh out the details both here and down the road at **Ewelme Cottage**, 14 Ayr St (Fri–Sun 10.30am–noon & 1–4.30pm; $3, $10 joint ticket with Highwic in Newmarket and Alberton; ⓣ09/379 0202), a pioneer kauri house built as a family home in 1864 for the wonderfully named Howick clergyman Vicesimus Lush, who wanted his sons to live close to the grammar school. The appeal of the place lies not so much in the house itself but in its contents: the furniture, fittings and possessions have been left just as they were when Lush's descendants finally moved out in 1968, the family heirlooms betraying a desire to replicate the home comforts of their native Oxfordshire.

Judges Bay and Newmarket

From the cathedral, you can continue south to Newmarket (see below) or north down Gladstone Road to Dove-Myer Robinson Park and the **Parnell**

Rose Gardens (unrestricted entry; free), where five thousand bushes are at their glorious best from October to April. The park sweeps from the rose beds down to **Judges Bay**, named for three officers of the colony's Supreme Court who lived here from 1841, commuting to the courts on Symonds Street by rowboat. Bishop Selwyn used to stay with his friend, the Chief Justice William Martin, and had **St Stephen's Chapel** (usually closed) built nearby on a prominent knoll overlooking the harbour; the waterside Judges Bay Road leads to the open-air saltwater Parnell Baths.

The southern continuation of Parnell Road runs into Broadway, the main drag through newly fashionable **NEWMARKET**, on the eastern flanks of Mount Eden which has several excellent restaurants and numerous motels. Specific sights are few, though you may be tempted by **Lionzone**, 380 Khyber Pass Road (tours daily 9.30am, 12.15pm & 3pm; bookings ⓣ09/358 8366, ⓦwww.lionzone.co.nz; $15), a highly self-promotional introduction to New Zealand's largest brewery involving a historical perspective on beer making, a look at the packing lines and a chance to sample the product. It's better than your average brewery tour, but at almost two hours it's a long-winded way to get a free beer.

If you are staying over this way consider visiting the Gothic timber mansion of **Highwic**, 40 Gillies Ave (Wed–Sun 10.30am–noon & 1–4.30pm; $5, $10 joint ticket with Ewelme Cottage in Parnell and Alberton; ⓣ09/524 5729), built as a "city" property by a wealthy rural auctioneer and landowner in 1862. The estate, complete with its outbuildings and servants' quarters, gives a fair indication of the contrasting lives of the aristocracy and the less fortunate. From here it's a short walk to **Eden Garden**, 24 Omana Ave (daily 9am–4.30pm; $5; ⓦwww.edengarden.co.nz), a verdant enclave created in a former quarry and tended by volunteers. There's year-round interest with a little of everything from watergardens, cacti and proteas to Australasia's largest and most varied collection of camellias, in full bloom from April to October.

Along the Tamaki Drive waterfront

Quay Street runs east from the foot of Queen Street, soon becoming **Tamaki Drive**, which separates Waitemata Harbour from Judges Bay. Crossing the causeway to Okahu Bay brings you to one of the city's foremost attractions, **Kelly Tarlton's Underwater World and Antarctic Encounter**, 23 Tamaki Drive (ⓦwww.kellytarltons.co.nz; daily: Nov–Feb 9am–9pm; March–Oct 9am–6pm; $24).

Underwater World was the brainchild of Kiwi diver, treasure hunter and salvage expert, Kelly Tarlton, who wanted to share the undersea wonders off New Zealand's shores with the non-diving public. Having failed to secure a location in his home town of Paihia in the Bay of Islands, he settled on these huge tanks which, from 1910 until 1961, flushed the city's effluent into Waitemata Harbour on the outgoing tides. Opened in 1985, the aquarium pioneered the walk-through acrylic tunnels (which have since become de rigueur for all self-respecting aquariums), a novelty which lured 100,000 visitors in the seven weeks before Tarlton's untimely death from a heart attack at the age of 47. A moving walkway glides you through two tanks, both sculpted into the gnarled rock walls: the first is dominated by flowing kelp beds, colourful reef fish and twisting eels; the second with graceful rays and smallish sharks, all appearing alarmingly close in the crystal-clear water. You can step off the walkway for closer inspection at any time.

The remaining tanks have since been converted into the **Antarctic Encounter**, a synthesis of Antarctic history and penguin-arium. An earnest video welcome from Sir Edmund Hillary introduces you to an accomplished replica of the prefabricated hut used by Robert Falcon Scott and his team on their ill-starred 1911–12 attempt to be the first to reach the South Pole and plant the British flag there; the original hut still stands at Scott Base, New Zealand's Antarctic foothold. Other Kiwi connections derive from the fact that Scott departed for the ice from Port Chalmers, near Dunedin, after first picking up a pianola donated by the people of Christchurch. Nor is a pianola the only unexpected thing you'll encounter in this capacious shelter. Fittings include a fully-functional laboratory and a printing press – from which the *South Polar Times* rolled every few months throughout the three long years of the expedition. Contemporary footage and tales of their exploits add to the haunting atmosphere. Seamlessly moving from the sublime to the ridiculous, the **Snow Cat** is an inept attempt at a Disney-esque ride made bearable by the close-up views of King and Gentoo penguins shooting through the water and hopping around on fake icebergs. City tour **buses** and Stagecoach buses numbered #74 to 76 all stop outside.

A little further along Tamaki Drive, Hapimana Street leads up onto the grassy range of Bastion Point and the **M. J. Savage Memorial Park**, the nation's austere Art Deco homage to its first Labour prime minister, who ushered in the welfare state in the late 1930s. More recently, **Bastion Point** was the site of a seventeen-month stand-off between police and its traditional owners, the Ngati Whatua, over the subdivision of land for housing. The occupiers were finally removed in May 1977, but the stand helped to galvanize the land-rights movement, and paved the way for a significant change in government attitude. Within a decade, the Waitangi Tribunal recommended that the land be returned, along with a compensatory cash payment.

Bastion Point looks down on **Mission Bay**, the closest of the truly worthwhile city **beaches**, where a grassy waterside reserve is backed by an enticing row of cafés and restaurants. Swimming is best here close to high tide; at other times the water remains shallow a long way out. Similar conditions prevail at the sheltered beaches of **Kohimarama** and **St Heliers Bay**, both a short way further along Tamaki Drive, which finishes on a high note with excellent harbour views from **Achilles Point**.

Panmure and Howick

With your own transport it's easy enough to wind south from St Heliers through the low-rent suburbs of Glen Innes and Tamaki to **Panmure**, one of four **fencible settlements** – Panmure and Howick in the east, Onehunga and Otahuhu in the south – set up around the young capital as a defence against disgruntled Maori and ambitious French. So-called "fencibles" (pensioned British soldiers) were re-enlisted to defend these sites for seven years, in return for free passage and a block of land. Skirmishes were few, and the original shipments of men and their families formed the basis of small towns, all of which were subsequently engulfed by the Auckland conurbation. Panmure has its relocated and restored **Stone Cottage**, at the corner of King's Road and Queen's Road (Fri & Sun 1–3pm; free), but the best place to get a sense of fencible life is at the **Howick Historica Village**, Bells Road, Lloyd Elsmore Park (daily admission 10am–5pm, last admission 4pm; $9; ⓣ09/576 9506, ⓦwww.fencible.org.nz), ten kilometres east of downtown through the numbing suburb of Pakuranga. Over thirty buildings dating from the 1840s and 1870s have been restored and re-sited from the four fencible settlements, and arranged in a believable village setting complete with a pond, a working blacksmith and market gardens. Volunteers role-play the diligently researched lives of real 1850s characters as they amble between the tents and makeshift Maori-style *raupo* huts used on arrival, the officers' cottages, the hostelry, school hall and flower mill.

The colonial village is one kilometre off Pakuranga Road, plied by all Howick & Eastern **buses**, which take about forty minutes to get out here from the Downtown Bus Terminal.

In the last fifteen years, droll Kiwis have dubbed the suburb of **Howick**, a further 5km east, "Chowick" – on account of its popularity with east Asians, who have constructed huge, florid mansions on former farmland to the south of town. For Aucklanders, these have become almost an attraction in their own right, mounting a challenge to Howick's more traditional sight, the distinctive, square-turreted **All Saints' Church**, the country's oldest active "Selwyn" church (see p.104), built in 1847.

West of the city centre

The suburbs of West Auckland developed later than their eastern counterparts, a consequence of their distance from the sea in the days when almost all travel was by ferry. The exceptions were the inner suburbs of Freeman's Bay, **Ponsonby** and Herne Bay, now enjoying renewed desirability for their proximity to the city and an unsurpassed array of the city's best restaurants, cafés and bars. Except for the flagging **Victoria Park Market**, sights are scarce until you get out to **Western Springs**, infant Auckland's major water source. The site of the springs is now part of **MOTAT**, a less than thrilling transport and technology museum, and the small but go-ahead **Auckland Zoo**. To the south stands **Alberton**, once one of the city's grandest residences, but now just a brief distraction before you hit the wineries and West Coast beaches (see "Around Auckland", p.129).

Freeman's Bay, Ponsonby and Herne Bay

Victoria Street climbs the ridge west of Queen Street and descends into **Freeman's Bay**, a flat basin long since reclaimed from the Waitemata Harbour to accommodate early saw-milling operations. The land is now given over to the popular rugby and cricket fields of Victoria Park, all overshadowed by the 38m-high chimney of Auckland's defunct incinerator, occupied since 1984 by **Victoria Park Market** (daily 9am–6pm; Ⓦ www.victoria-park-market.co.nz), a knot of stalls and restaurants. Despite having lost some of its more aspirational patrons to Ponsonby up the road, it's still an interesting enough place to mooch about for reasonably priced clothes and crafts, and a good place to break your walk out to Ponsonby. The **Link bus** passes on its way to Ponsonby, and city tour buses also stop here.

Early in Auckland's European history the areas around **Ponsonby** became fashionable neighbourhoods, only moving downmarket with the arrival of trams at the turn of the century. Inner-city living conditions deteriorated dramatically in the Depression of the 1930s, and the resulting low rents attracted large numbers of Pacific Islanders during the 1950s. Ponsonby took a bohemian turn in the Seventies and before long young professionals were moving in, restoring old houses and spending fistfuls of dollars in the cafés, restaurants and boutiques along Ponsonby Road. The street itself may not be beautiful, but the people sure are: musicians, actors and media folk congregate to lunch, schmooze and be seen in the latest fashionable haunt. There's good reason to brave the poseurs, though, for some of New Zealand's classiest clothes shopping and eating.

Beyond St Mary's Bay and Ponsonby lies **Herne Bay**, which followed its neighbours' economic ebb and flow and now ranks as Auckland's most expensive suburb, the merchants' water-view villas fetching astronomical prices. There's little to see out this way, but you may find yourself staying here or indulging at one of the restaurants and cafés along Jervois Road.

Western Springs: MOTAT and the zoo

In the late nineteenth century the burgeoning city of Auckland, with its meagre supply of unreliable streams, was heavily reliant on the waters of **Western Springs**, 4km west of the city.

The area is now devoted to attractive parkland and two of Auckland's more significant sights. The **Museum of Transport, Technology and Social History** (MOTAT) on Great North Road (daily 10am–5pm; $10; infoline ⓣ09/846 7020) offers a trawl through New Zealand's vehicular and industrial past in a jumble of sheds and halls, but feels half-baked and incomplete – and it's all too obvious that some of the displays haven't been updated in over twenty years. However it might be just the thing if you're newly arrived and have kids to entertain: hidden among the shiny cars and jet-black steam engines are a reconstruction of a Victorian Village, and the Western Springs' pumphouse whose original engine still slowly turns, albeit by electricity rather than steam. The aviation section includes a replica of the home-built plane first flown near Timaru by Richard Pearse.

Admission includes entry to the **Sir Keith Park Memorial Site** (same hours), a kilometre away and linked to the main site by ancient rattling trams (every 10–20min; $2 return). This is one for aeroplane buffs, with a couple of dozen lovingly restored examples slotted into a hangar around the star attractions – one of the few surviving World War II Lancaster bombers, plus a double-decker flying boat, all decked out for dining in a more gracious age, which was used on Air New Zealand's South Pacific "Coral Route" until the mid-1960s.

The tram between the two sites also stops outside the **Auckland Zoo**, Motions Road (daily 9.30am–5.30pm; $13), which has all but overturned the ancient regime of cages, replacing them with naturalistic habitats and captive breeding programmes. The centrepiece is the trailblazing Pridelands development with lions, hippos, rhinos, giraffes, zebras and gazelles all roaming across mock savannah behind enclosing moats. Naturally, New Zealand's wildlife is well represented, with a nocturnal kiwi house, a group of tuatara which form part of conservation work on offshore islands, and a large, walk-through aviary. One of the best displays features the desert-dwelling meerkats: plastic domes placed at ground level enable you to observe their super-cute behaviour at close quarters. Elsewhere, the "rainforest walk" threads its way among artificial islands inhabited by colonies of monkeys, you can walk through the wallaby enclosure unhindered, and the new Sealion and Penguin Shores exhibit brings you face to face with these lovable animals, the former through underwater viewing windows. On overcast days, when the animals tend to be more active, it is particularly good for kids who can also have fun at KidZone, a small farm with keeper talks and animal-feeding sessions held throughout the day.

Western Springs is reached by Stagecoach bus #045 from Custom Street East and is also on city tour **bus** routes.

Alberton

The only other diversion in the western suburbs proper is the imposing mid-Victorian mansion of **Alberton**, 100 Mount Albert Rd (Wed–Sun

10.30am–noon & 1–4.30pm; $5, $10 joint ticket with Highwic in Newmarket and Ewelme Cottage in Parnell), 3km south of the zoo, which began life as a farmstead built in 1863 by Allan Kerr-Taylor. This grand old house achieved its current form – replete with turrets and verandas – through a series of late-nineteenth-century additions befitting the centrepiece for an estate which once stretched over much of western Auckland. The last of Kerr-Taylor's daughters died in 1972 leaving a house little changed in decades: the family furniture and possessions remain surrounded by peeling century-old wallpaper.

The North Shore

Until the 1960s there was very little to the **North Shore**, just a handful of scattered communities linked to each other and the rest of Auckland by a web of ferries crisscrossing the harbour. The completion of the harbour bridge in 1959 provided the catalyst for development. By the early 1970s, the volume of traffic to the booming suburbs log-jammed the bridge – until a Japanese company attached a two-lane extension (affectionately dubbed "the Nippon Clip-ons") to each side. The bridge and its additional lanes can now be seen at close quarters on the Auckland Bridge Climb (see p.114).

The vast urban sprawl marches inexorably towards the Hibiscus Coast (see below), with most interest to be found in the maritime village of **Devonport**, and its quiet adjacent coves of **Cheltenham** and **Narrow Neck**, at the southern end of a long string of calm swimming **beaches** which stretch the length of this coast. Further north, try the more open and busier **Takapuna**, a short stroll from dozens of good cafés and reached by buses #80 and #90, and **Long Bay** (buses #83 & 85), with a grassy reserve and barbecue areas. All to some degree suffer from the Auckland curse of being shallow at low tide but beaches tend to be well attended throughout the summer days. Elsewhere only harbourside **Birkenhead** has a smattering of appeal with its restored cinema and a few places to stay and eat.

Devonport

Devonport is one of Auckland's oldest suburbs, founded in 1840 and still linked to the city by a fifteen-minute ferry journey. The naval station was one of Devonport's earliest tenants, soon followed by wealthy merchants, who built fine kauri villas. Some of these are graced with little turrets ("widows' watches") which served as lookouts where the traders could watch for the arrival of their precious cargoes, and wives could watch hopefully for their returning husbands. Wandering along the peaceful streets and the tree-fringed waterfront past grand houses is the essence of Devonport's appeal, and there's no shortage of tempting bookshops, small galleries, cafés and restaurants along the main street to punctuate your amblings.

On the main street, you can't fail to notice what was once Devonport's post office, now operating as **Jackson's Muzeum** (daily 10am–9pm; $8), bedecked in old New Zealand and British telephone boxes. Longstanding wrangles with the local council over the museum's somewhat unorthodox use of a listed building have seen it closed in recent years but, now open again, it overflows with Bryan Jackson's lifetime collection of collections - a reflection of his philosophy that "more is more". This is an overwhelming hoard of just about everything imaginable: soda siphons, hot-water bottles, gramophones, aquatint postcards, kauri gum, milk bottles and much, much more, ranging from the moderately special to the unbelievably ordinary. Access is through the *Venison Kitchen* restaurant.

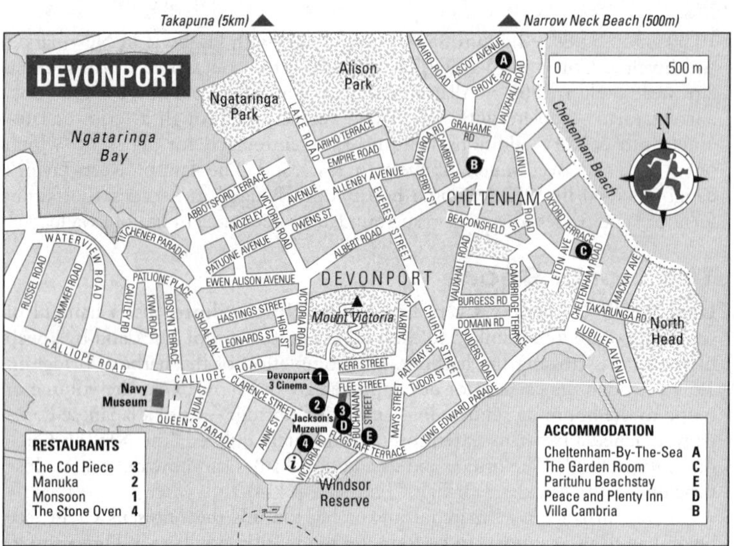

Unless you have a soft spot for lifeless collections of uniforms and guns, you can blithely skip the **Navy Museum**, Spring Street (daily 10am–4.30pm; free), in favour of a stiff walk up one of the two ancient volcanoes that back Devonport. The closest, about fifteen minutes' walk, is **Mount Victoria** (Taka-a-ranga; unrestricted access for pedestrians; closed to vehicles from dusk on Thurs, Fri & Sat), from where you get fabulous city, harbour and gulf views. The hill was once the site of a Maori *pa* and fortified village, and the remains of terraces and kumara pits can still be detected on the northern and eastern slopes. A kilometre east, the grass- and flax-covered volcanic plug of **North Head** (Maungauika; daily 6am–10pm, vehicles 8am–8pm; free) guards the entrance to the inner harbour, a strategic site for Maori before it was co-opted to form part of the young nation's coastal defences. In the wake of the "Russian Scares" of 1884–86, which were precipitated by the opening of the port of Vladivostok, North Head became Fort Cautley, riddled with an extensive system of concrete tunnels linking gun emplacements. Most of the tunnels remain closed to the public, but you are free to poke around some of the peripheral remains and the gulf views are unbeatable.

Devonport is best reached on the **Devonport Ferry** (daily 6am–11pm, every 30min; $7 return, bikes free) which forms part of the Auckland Pass and Auckland Rover (see p.84). There's also a movie and ferry pass ($12) which gets you the ride over from the city and a screening at the Devonport 3 cinema (see p.127) for the same price you'd pay to visit a multiplex. Daytime ferries are met by Fullers' hour-long "Devonport Explorer Tour" (Ⓣ09/367 9111; daily 10am–3pm; $15), but really you're better off calling in to the **visitor centre**, 3 Victoria Rd (daily 9am–5pm; Ⓣ09/446 0677, Ⓔvisitorinfo@nthshore.govt.nz), picking up the free *Old Devonport Walk* leaflet, or a free map, and exploring at your own pace.

If you happen to be here around the middle of February, head for the **Devonport Food and Wine Festival**, where for $15 you can buy the festival glass and spend the day sampling (for a small additional sum) the food and drink on offer from winemakers, market gardeners and restaurateurs.

South of the city centre

The southern tranche of Auckland, arching around the eastern end of Manukau Harbour, is the most neglected by visitors, though the airport at Mangere is where most arrive. In the main there are few unmissable attractions but the city's most lofty volcano, **Mount Eden**, offers superb views, and its near-identical twin, **One Tree Hill**, has some of the best surviving examples of the terracing undertaken by early Maori inhabitants. Further south, Auckland's Polynesian community plies its wares early each Saturday morning at the **Otara Market**.

Mount Eden and One Tree Hill

At 196m, **Mount Eden** (Maungawhau) is Auckland city's highest volcano and is named for George Eden, the first Earl of Auckland. The extensive views from the summit car park, just 2km south of the city, make it extraordinarily popular with tour buses which grind up the steep slope through the day and well into the evening, though you can walk up from Mount Eden Road or take buses #274 or #275 from Custom Street East.

More rewarding, though, is the area around **One Tree Hill** (Maungakiekie; 183m), 5km to the southeast. One of the city's most distinctive landmarks, One Tree Hill is topped by a twenty-metre-tall granite obelisk, and until recently an ageing Monterey pine. For a century, until just before the arrival of Europeans, Maungakiekie ("mountain of the kiekie plant") was one of the largest *pa* sites in the country; an estimated 4000 people were drawn here by the proximity to abundant seafood from both harbours and the rich soils of the volcanic cone, which still bears the scars of extensive earthworks including the remains of dwellings and kumara pits. The site had already been abandoned when it was bought by the Scottish medic and "father of Auckland", Sir John Logan Campbell, who was one of only two European residents when the city was granted capital status in 1840. Through widespread land purchases and the founding of numerous shipping, banking and insurance companies, Campbell prospered, eventually becoming mayor in time for the visit of Britain's Duke and Duchess of Cornwall, in 1901. To commemorate the event, he donated his One Tree Hill estate to the people of New Zealand and named it **Cornwall Park** (daily 7am–dusk; free) in honour of his distinguished guests. The park puts on its best display around Christmas time, when avenues of pohutukawa trees erupt in a riot of red blossom. Campbell is buried at the summit, next to the obelisk, which bears inscriptions in Maori and English lauding Maori–Pakeha friendship. The summit is known in Maori as Te Totara-i-ahua, a reference to the single totara which originally gave One Tree Hill its name. Early settlers cut it down in 1852, and Campbell planted several pines as a windbreak, a single specimen surviving until the millennium. Already ailing from a 1994 chainsaw attack by a Maori activist avenging the loss of the totara, the pine's fate was sealed by a similar attack in 1999. The tree was removed in November 2000 as plans for a replacement totara (or pohutukawa) take shape.

Free leaflets outlining a trail around the archeological and volcanic sites of the hill are available from the **visitor centre** (daily 10am–4pm), which is housed in **Huia Lodge**, originally built on the northern slopes by Campbell as a gatekeeper's house and now containing displays on the park and the man. Immediately opposite is **Acacia Cottage** (dawn–dusk; free), Campbell's original home and the city's oldest building, re-sited from central Auckland in the 1920s. Over the years, it has been heavily restored, but it's worth sticking your head in to see the simple construction and plain furnishings.

Campbell devotees can round off their homage with a visit to the magisterial statue of him in mayoral garb at the northern end of the park by Manukau Road.

Fans of astronomy are better served on the southern side of One Tree Hill at the **Stardome Observatory**, on Manukau Road, where a frequently changing schedule of 45-minute multimedia programmes on the moon and the crystalline stars and distant galaxies of the southern skies is played out on the ceiling of the **planetarium** (Tues–Sat 8pm & 9pm; $10; infoline ⓣ09/625 6945, ⓦwww.stardome.org.nz). Weather and darkness permitting, the shows are followed by thirty minutes or so of telescope viewing; what you see obviously varies, but the moons of Jupiter, binary stars and Saturn's rings are all possibilities.

Most of Cornwall Park is closed after dark but the observatory and the summit are accessible from the southern entrance off Manukau Road, which can be reached on **buses** numbered #302, #305 and #312 from the corner of Queen and Victoria streets.

South Auckland

Head much beyond Cornwall Park and you are venturing into **South Auckland**, the city's poorest sector and the less-then-flatteringly-depicted gangland setting for Lee Tamahori's film *Once were Warriors*. There isn't a great deal to see down here, but neither is it a no-go zone and the **Otara Market** is certainly worth a look. Each Saturday morning, stalls sprawl across the car park of the Otara Town Centre, 18km south of central Auckland. Plausibly billed as the largest Maori and Polynesian market in the world, its authenticity has been somewhat diluted by an influx of market traders flogging cheap clothes and shoddy trinkets. The tat is alleviated by displays of island-style floral print fabrics, reasonably priced Maori carvings and truckloads of cheap fruit and veg, including many varieties peculiar to the islands like taro and yams. Your best bet for a bargain is the food: there are stalls where you can buy home-made cakes and Maori bread, and there's even a van ingeniously kitted out to produce an ersatz *hangi*. The market gets going around 5am and runs through to noon, though by 10am things are winding down, so get there early. Take the Otara exit off the southern motorway or catch buses #487 or #497 for the fifty-minute journey from the corner of Wellesley and Queen streets.

Parents with kids may well want to push on a few kilometres further south to **Rainbow's End**, Great South Road, Manukau City (daily 10am–5pm; adults $35, kids $25; ⓣ09/262 2030 or 24hr infoline ⓣ09/262 2044, ⓦwww.rainbowsend.co.nz), New Zealand's largest theme park, where you get as many goes as you can handle on rides such as the corkscrew roller coaster, log flume, pirate ships, go-karts and flight simulators. Buses numbered #47 come out this way.

If you have your own transport, consider a jaunt to the **Auckland Botanic Gardens**, 102 Hill Road (daily 8am–dusk; free), just by the Manurewa motorway turn-off, 27km south of the city centre. This extensive but relatively young collection of native and exotic plants opened in 1982, but came of age in 1998 when New Zealand's top horticultural show, the **Ellerslie Flower Show** (held annually in mid-Nov), was relocated here. The gardens come complete with interpretative visitor centre (Mon-Fri 9am–4pm, Sat & Sun 10am-4pm), a reference library, a café and a network of walks centred on two ornamental lakes.

Walks, cruises and adventure activities

Few visitors linger long in Auckland, most being content to make travel arrangement then head out to the "real" New Zealand, but if it's activities you're after, Auckland has plenty to offer. The relatively easy Coast to Coast Walkway is supplemented by more ambitious tramps in both the Waitakere (see p.131) and Hunua (see p.138) ranges. There are diverting ways to get out in the harbour, including sailing an America's Cup yacht and swimming with dolphins. And two of Auckland's largest structures provide the framework for the Auckland Bridge Climb and the Skyjump.

In addition, there are sightseeing tours to the city's west coast beaches and gannet colony (see p.134) and **wine tours** to the wineries of Kumeu and Huapai (see p.131).

Walks

The most ambitious walking normally attempted in Auckland is a stroll through The Domain or a more demanding hike up to one of the volcano-top viewpoints. The best of these have been threaded together as the well-marked **Coast to Coast Walkway**, a four-hour, 13-kilometre route straddling the isthmus from the Ferry Building on the Waitemata Harbour to Onehunga on the Manukau Harbour. By devoting a full day to the enterprise you can take in much of the best Auckland has to offer, including excellent harbour views from The Domain and the summits of Mount Eden and One Tree Hill, the Auckland Museum, Albert Park, and numerous sites pivotal to the development of the city. All is revealed in the free "Coast to Coast Walkway" leaflet, which includes an indication of where the walkway intersects with bus routes for walkers who want to tackle shorter sections.

More ambitious hikers can head to Rangitoto Island (see p.140) or out into the hills: west to the Waitakere Ranges (see p.131) or south to the Hunuas (see p.138).

Cruises, kayaking and dolphin swimming

Auckland is so water-focused that it would be a shame not to get out on the harbour at some point; and there is a welter of ways to do just that. The easiest and cheapest way is to hop on one of the **ferries** to Devonport (see p.109), or to one of the outlying islands (see "Islands of the Hauraki Gulf" from p.139), but for prolonged forays, consider one of the many **cruises** available; for a close-up perspective, a **dolphin swimming** or **sea-kayaking** trip offers a more intimate experience.

Cruises and sailing

As well as their ferry services Fullers offer a two-hour **Harbour Cruise** (daily 10.30am & 1.30pm; $30) which tours the inner harbour visiting the America's Cup team bases at Viaduct Harbour and coasting past Devonport and the Harbour Bridge. Similar ground is covered when you crew on *NZL 40* (Ⓣ0800/724569, Ⓦwww.sailnewzealand.co.nz; $75), a **racing yacht** that gives a real sense of power and speed. Built for New Zealand's 1995 America's Cup challenge in San Diego it's now based quayside at the Viaduct Harbour and makes several daily two-hour sailings.

Romantics might prefer a gentler trip **under sail** with Pride of Auckland (Ⓣ09/373 4557, Ⓦwww.prideofauckland.com) who are based at the Maritime

Museum and run a variety of cruises with coffee or a meal served on board: try the 45min basic cruise ($45), the Coffee Cruise (1hr 30min; $55), the Luncheon Cruise (1pm; 1hr 30min; $65) or the Dinner Cruise (7pm; 2hr 30min; $90). All cruises include entry to the Maritime Museum.

On most **summer weekends** you can help sail the *Søren Larsen* (ⓣ0800/707265 & 09/411 8755, ⓦwww.sorenlarsen.co.nz; mid-Nov to mid-Feb Sat 1–4pm, $49, & Sun 10am–3pm, $89 including lunch), a Danish Baltic trader built of oak in 1949 and later fitted with a nineteenth-century sailing rig. This majestic vessel starred in the 1970s TV series *The Onedin Line* and led the First Fleet re-enactment that formed a part of the Australian bicentennial celebrations in 1987. Passengers are free to participate – steering, hauling sheets and climbing the rigging – though maritime instruction tends to be a larger component of the mid-week trips to Hauraki Gulf and Coromandel (2–5 nights; $450–1000).

Dolphin swimming and kayaking

Though few Aucklanders are aware of it, the Hauraki Gulf is excellent territory for spotting marine mammals, best seen on five-hour dolphin and whale watching trips run by **Dolphin Explorer** (ⓣ & ⓕ09/357 6032, ⓦwww.dolphinexplorer.com; $90) from beside the Ferry Building. Educational and entertaining trips head out daily (weather permitting) on a comfortable 20m catamaran, and dolphins are spotted ninety percent of the time (you get a second trip if there is no sighting). Over half the time passengers get to swim with common dolphins, and Bryde's whales are also frequently seen.

Several companies around Auckland will take you **kayaking**. One of the most popular trips is with Fergs Kayaks, 12 Tamaki Drive, Okahu Bay (ⓣ & ⓕ09/529 2230; ⓦwww.fergskayaks.co.nz), kayaking the 7km across to Rangitoto Island (see p.140), watching sundown, hiking to the summit, then paddling back by the light of your torch, and perhaps that of a silvery moon (6–7hr; $60). They also do day-trips to Rangitoto and both day and evening trips 3km to Devonport, with a hike up North Head and a picnic supper (Oct–March daily 5.30pm; 4hr; $60).

If you'd rather go it alone, they offer **kayak rental** in either single sea kayaks ($12/hour, $25 a half-day) or doubles ($25/hour, $50 a half-day).

Adventure activities

Until very recently there were few diverting activities in Auckland, but a glut of recent openings has begun to put Auckland on the adventure map. Opportunities to walk to the top of the Harbour Bridge and jump off the Skytower are supplemented by canyoning trips in the Waitakere Ranges and further afield, and some minor local activities. As well as what's listed below, you could go **roller blading** along the waterfront east of the city where Tamaki Drive provides a smooth path (shared with bikes and pedestrians) and great harbour views; in-line skates can be rented from Fergs Kayaks (see above) for $10–15 per hour or $25–30 for a day.

Harbour Bridge Climb

The most high profile new activity in Auckland is the **Auckland Bridge Climb**, 70 Nelson St (Mon–Fri $125; Sat & Sun $135; ⓣ0800/000 808 & 09/625 0445, ⓦwww.aucklandbridgeclimb.co.nz), which gives you the opportunity to get decked out in natty overalls and sample the excellent city views from the highest point on the city's harbour crossing some 65 metres above the

Waitemata Harbour. The two-and-a-half-hour trip is somewhat misnamed as there is no climbing involved, just strolling along steel walkways under the roadway then emerging onto the upper girders by means of ordinary stairs, all the while clipped by safety harness to a cable which runs the length of the walkway. It is all professionally done with guides relating something of the history of the bridge, along with some of the region's Maori mythology and a good deal of detail on the bridge's fulcrums, pivots and cantilevers.

Bookings are essential and anyone over ten can go. Cameras are not allowed, but there'll be someone on hand to take a snap and sell it to you later. On Saturdays, for an extra $10 you can undertake a **night climb**, starting around 8pm and wearing a head torch.

Skyjump and Vertigo

Auckland's 328-metre Skytower has recently become the venue for two adventure activities, both exploiting its position as New Zealand's tallest building. On the **Skyjump** (Sun–Thurs 10.30am–7pm, Fri & Sat 10.30am–10pm; $195; booking recommended on ⓣ0800/759586) – claimed as the world's highest tower-based jump – you plummet 192m metres to the ground in a kind of arrested freefall with a cable attached to your back. Suitably kitted out in a jumpsuit and full body harness you ascend to the tower's observation area before edging out along a gangplank then flinging yourself off. There's much the same stomach-in-your-mouth feeling as you get bungy jumping, but the cable maintains your descent at around 60km/hr giving you a full 25 second ride until a giant rotating fan brake slows you for a gentle landing. Keep your suit on and you can go again for $75.

If you'd prefer to go up rather than down, consider **Vertigo** (daily 9am–9pm; $95; ⓣ0800/483 784, ⓦwww.4vertigo.com), in which around half a dozen people are led up into the narrow confines of the slender pinnacle which tops the upper observation area. Climbing a vertical internal ladder surrounded by the high-tech cabling that feeds the mast-top broadcast and telecom equipment, you gain a further 50m and top out at the 270-metre level, where an open-air crow's nest gives a stupendous view over the city and Hauraki Gulf.

Book in advance or simply front up at the desk inside the Sky City Casino building, where you'll be kitted out with overalls, body harness, helmet and earpiece then put through a simulator before being given the OK for the climb. Kids can go, provided they pass the simulation, and there are also dawn, sunset and after-dark climbs by arrangement; second-timers get a substantial discount.

Canyoning

About the most fun you can have in a wetsuit around Auckland is to go **canyoning**, a combination of swimming, abseiling, jumping into deep pools and sliding down rock chutes. Two companies operate in the Waitakere Ranges, west of the city, both making pick-ups in Auckland and offering an excellent value day out. Canyonz (ⓣ0800/422 696 & 09/357 0133, ⓦwww.canyonz.co.nz) operates in Blue Canyon with a great variety of activities including an 8m waterfall jump or abseil. The standard full-day trip ($135) can be condensed into a half-day ($105). Awol Adventures (ⓣ09/630 7100, ⓦwww.awoladventures.co.nz) runs similar trip near Piha, with more emphasis on abseils. Join the day trip or go **night canyoning** (both $125), just a head-torch and glowworms for illumination. Both companies' trips often end up with a visit to one of the West Coast surf beaches.

Canyonz also offers Auckland-based day-trips down the magnificent **Sleeping God** canyon near Thames (Oct–May only; $225). In this wonderfully scenic spot you descend 300 metres in a series of twelve drops using slides, and abseils as long as seventy metres (some actually through the waterfall), but also with the opportunity to leap 13m from a rock ledge into a deep pool. It's tough enough to require previous abseiling experience, best done by taking the Blue Canyon/Sleeping God combo ($325) over two days.

Eating

Aucklanders take their eating seriously and there is no shortage of wonderful **restaurants,** with ever more adventurous places opening all the time. They may only be following the trends of London, Australia or California but they're close behind and easily as good. If you're after a more casual eating experience, don't overlook the **pubs** (see "Pubs and bars" listings, starting on p.125), many offering a decent meal for under $15.

For several years, the best areas for grazing have been the inner-city suburbs, chiefly along **Ponsonby Road**, Auckland's culinary crucible; **Parnell Road**, the other main eating street; and **Devonport**, with a more modest but still tempting selection. In the wake of the 2000 America's Cup defence the **city waterfront** has been rejuvenated, with several dozen eating places now ringing the rejuvenated waterside and offering a full range of culinary styles.

Central Auckland and Viaduct Harbour

The centre of Auckland is undoubtedly the best place to grab something quick during the day with dozens of places geared up to cope with the **lunchtime** press of office workers and bank staff. Among the most popular are the **food halls**, seating plazas surrounded by numerous vendors, often tucked away in the basements of the shopping arcades which spur off Queen Street. Downtown's eating scene is spiced up with an increasing number of **Asian restaurants** which cater (sometimes almost exclusively) to the large numbers of recent immigrants who populate the central city apartment blocks. Chinese, Japanese, Korean, Lao, Thai and Indian places are liberally scattered.

The Asian wave continues along **K' Road** which is less influenced by the daytime business crowds; its selection of quirky places can be lively at any hour.

In the evening, parts of the city can feel pretty dead, but if you know where to look – **High Street** and **Lorne Street** are both good hunting grounds – there are plenty of places to eat. Nowhere are the restaurants so densely packed as around the **Viaduct Harbour** area where virtually all the waterside spots are occupied. The restaurants are out to impress just as much as the clientele, though this isn't reflected in the prices which are a dollar or two above the city average.

Food halls

Atrium on Elliot Food Gallery Elliot St. Slightly more salubrious than most of the genre with a wide range of counters – Malay, Thai, burgers, Indian, pizza, kebabs, roasts, Chinese – plus a bakery and decent coffee.

Cuisine Market 106 Customs St West. A kind of food hall crossed with a high-end deli with a few tables to sip coffee while you tuck into delicate savouries and delicious baked goods from the surrounding stalls.

Food Alley 9 Albert St. Spartan two-level food hall with a strong Asian bias exhibited through counters selling Indian, Thai, Korean, Malaysian and Japanese cuisine along with a couple of noodle bars. Open daily until 10pm.

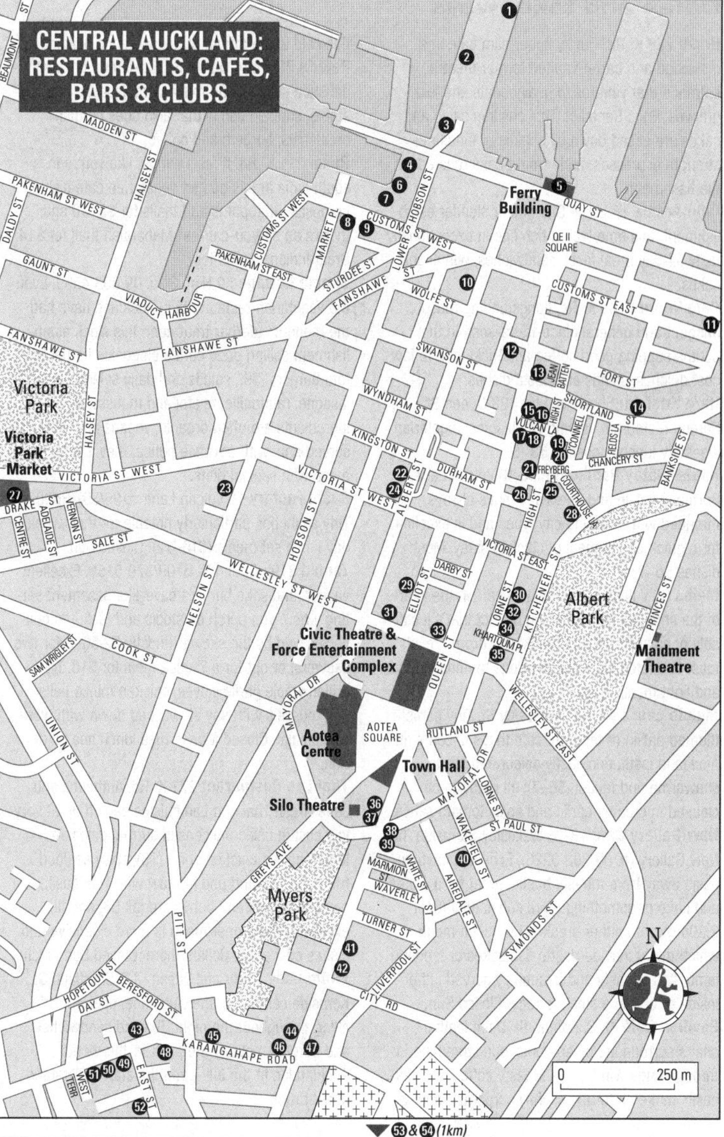

RESTAURANTS, CAFÉS, BARS & CLUBS

Atrium 29
Belgian Beer Café 15
Bellini 1
Brazil 48
Café Aroma 32
Café Verona 46
Caravanserai Tea House 39
Civic Tavern 33
Classic 37
Cuisine Market 8
D72 20
Ding How 22
Dynasty Chinese Restaurant 40
Elbow Room 26
Euro 2
Food Alley 10
Galatos 52
Galbraith's Alehouse 54
Grand Harbour 9
Harbourside Seafood Bar & Grill 5
Hare Krishna: Food for Life 44
Kamo 51
Kermadec 4
Khmer Satay Noodle House 16
Khuja Lounge 47
Kiwi Tavern 11
The Loaded Hog 6
Melba 19
Merchant Mezze Bar 38
Middle East Café 31
Moghul 30
New Gallery Café 35
Otto's 28
Papa Jack's Voodoo Lounge 18
Pavilion Café 14
Peter's Pies 41
Portofino 7
The Power Station 53
Rakino's 21
Rasoi 45
Roots 49
Sake Bar Rikka 27
Shakespeare Tavern 24
Simple Cottage 25
Sri Pinang 50
Sushi Factory 17
Tabac 12
Tanuki 36
Temple 42
Thai Lao Restaurant 43
Tony's 34
Toto' 23
White Lady Diner 13
Wildfire 3

Cafés and takeaways

Brazil 256 K' Rd. Quirky super-slim café in a mosaiced and barrel-vaulted former theatre entrance that vibrates to heavy beats and jazz grooves. Eggs Benedict, Thai chicken salad and cakes are eased down by shakes or industrial-strength espressos made from beans roasted in the basement.

Café Aroma 18 Lorne St. Another slender establishment, this time with a fine line in exceptionally tasty all-day breakfasts, sandwiches, panini and cakes.

Café Verona 169 K' Rd. Longstanding muso hangout and general place-to-be-seen in the booths supping good coffee and tucking in to low-cost quiches, salads and pasta dishes.

Hare Krishna: Food for Life 423 Queen St. Serene restaurant serving wholesome vegetarian weekday lunches costing $3–6.

Khmer Satay Noodle House 10 Vulcan Lane. Burmese eat-in and takeaway that's always thronged with lunching city types and is excellent for a quick cheap meal of chicken satay. Most dishes $5–7.

Melba 33 Vulcan Lane. Reliable café in the heart of the shopping and clubbing district that's justifiably popular for all-day breakfasts (from French toast to sautéd kidneys), delicious muffins, coffee and light meals all day.

Middle East Café 23a Wellesley St. Tiny camel-themed eat-in or take-out café that's become an Auckland institution, justly celebrated for its shawarma and falafel ($6–7), all ready to be cloaked in creamy garlic and spicy tomato sauce.

New Gallery Café 18-26 Wellesley St, inside the New Gallery (ⓣ09/302 0226). Excellent daytime oasis away from the city bustle, great for a coffee and cake or something more substantial (until 2.30pm) from either breakfast or lunch menu which might include risotto fish cakes or tandoori lamb. It 's all tasty and beautifully served either inside or out on a small terrace. Closed Sun.

Pavilion Café 48 Shortland St. Deep leather chairs surrounded by artworks, sun streaming in through huge windows, and tasty coffee and cakes easily make up for the slightly corporate tenor of this café in the atrium of an insurance building.

Peter's Pies 484 Queen St. Eat-in and takeaway pie shop – steak and mushroom, lasagne and vegetable, smoked fish – that also does bargain breakfasts, burgers and coffee.

Rasoi 211 K' Rd. It feels almost like you're in south India in this budget vegetarian café dishing up dosas, uttappams and thalis for $5–10 and there's an all-you-can-eat Maharajah thali for $14. Great Indian sweets too.

Simple Cottage 50 High St ⓣ09/303 4599. Even the vegetarian restaurants in Auckland have had the modern café/bar treatment, this sleek establishment selling good coffee alongside herbal teas, tofu burgers ($9), salads and daily selections of lasagne, ratatouille, falafel and moussaka. Ingredients are often organic, vegans are well served and, with advance notice, they'll cater to those with special diets.

Sushi Factory 15 Vulcan Lane ⓣ09/307 3600. Tiny sushi bar, particularly notable for their weekday lunch set meals ($10–12). Closed Sun.

Tanuki 319b Queen St ⓣ09/379 5151. Excellent yakitori and sake bar in a cave-like basement setting where you perch on stools and tuck into delicacies sold by the skewer (mostly $2.50–3 for two skewers) or opt for a 7-stick meal for $10. Try grilled whole garlic cloves, chicken mince balls and mussels with soy all washed down with wonderful sake. Closed Mon & Tues lunch and all day Sun.

Thai Lao Restaurant 271 K' Rd. Authentic and super fresh Thai and Lao cuisine served up at very low cost in basic unlicensed surroundings. At lunch the red chicken curry ($8), spicy seafood fried rice ($8) and pad krapow with Thai basil, bamboo shoots and baby corn (all $8) are all excellent. The dinner menu is more extensive and dishes cost a few dollars more. Closed Sun lunch.

White Lady Diner cnr Queen St & Shortland St. Kerbside caravan in the club zone, open for refuelling throughout the night. Toasted sandwiches and burgers, notably the pack-in-the-works Aucklander, fit the bill – and the staff understand fluent drunk.

Restaurants

Belgian Beer Café 8 Vulcan Lane. The infatuation with all things Belgian has hit New Zealand and is best manifest in this former pub convincingly converted into a Belgian bar where bargain pots of mussels come dressed with lobster bisque and brandy, mustard and cream, or coconut cream and lemongrass. The expected Hoegaarden, Stella and Leffe are supplemented by bottled fruit beers and a selection of Kiwi wines.

Caravanserai Tea House 430 Queen St. Relaxed Middle Eastern place decked out in Turkish rugs and cushions, some around knee-high tables. The extensive range of mezze, moussaka and kebabs go for around $13, or there are lighter snacks for half that.

D72 Freyberg Place. A Kiwi angle on the traditional American diner with designer plastic chairs outside and booths within where you can tuck into burgers, waffles, Caesar salad, eggs Benedict and much more at slightly inflated prices.

Ding How 2nd floor, 55 Albert St, entrance St Patrick's Square ⓣ09/358 4838. Intimate Cantonese restaurant (reservations advised) with terrific dim sum (11.30am–2.30pm) carried around on trays as the waiters shout out the options; peer under the lids and dive in. There's a full dinner menu too. Licensed and BYO.

Dynasty Chinese Restaurant 57–59 Wakefield St. Large restaurant that's always popular with Auckland's Chinese community especially for Sunday morning yum cha.

Euro Princes Wharf ⓣ09/309 9866. The talk of the town when it opened in time for the America's Cup defence, and still very much the place to be seen, this in no way detracts from the very high quality food and service. Their signature dish of rotisserie chicken on a bed of mashed potato and peanut slaw ($26) is superb, and the appetizers are all pretty fantastic too.

Grand Harbour 18–28 Customs St West ⓣ09/357 6889. More opulent than most of the city's Chinese places, this bustling modern restaurant is always popular for business lunches and serves great yum cha daily.

Harbourside Seafood Bar & Grill 99 Quay St ⓣ09/307 0556. Classy but none-too-formal, award-winning Pacific Rim seafood restaurant upstairs in the Ferry Building. If it's warm, reserve a table on the harbour-view terrace, and feast on beautifully prepared and presented fish and crustaceans. Expect to part with at least $50 for a full meal, plus wine.

Kamo 382 K' Rd ⓣ09/377 2313. Stripped-down rowdy restaurant that is one of the very few serving Pacific-influenced dishes alongside Mediterranean favourites, all at reasonable prices. Try the *ika mata* (literally "fish prepared and eaten"), fresh fish marinated coconut cream and finely diced vegetables.

Kermadec 1st Floor, Viaduct Harbour, cnr Lower Hobson St & Quay St (restaurant ⓣ09/309 0412, brasserie and bars ⓣ09/309 0413). Fashionable and imaginatively decorated seafood emporium, with a large bustling brasserie for classy versions of bistro favourites and the more formal, and expensive, Pacific Room for fine dining.

Merchant Mezze Bar 430 Queen St, cnr Mayoral Drive ⓣ09/307 0349. Buzzing café with a small deck outside and Turkish rugs strewn within. Specializes in dishes from around the Mediterranean, the Middle East and beyond – anything from Spanish tortilla and grilled mushroom on polenta to ceviche and Thai green curry. Soups, salads, mezze ($7–10) and mains ($13–17) are served until 11pm, then drinks and coffee until midnight or later.

Moghul 2 Lorne St ⓣ09/366 0885. Good value Indian curry restaurant that's great at any time but especially notable for $13 lunches comprising five dishes plus rice and naan. Another good bet is the $25 Moghul banquet (minimum two). Licensed and BYO.

Ottos 40 Kitchener St ⓣ09/300 9595. Among the most exalted of Auckland's fine dining restaurants, converted from a former magistrates' court and tastefully decked out in taupe and cream with huge potted palms. You might try a starter of duck confit dressed with coconut and palm sugar and a green paw paw salad, then follow with pan-seared venison, onion ravioli and black fig chutney. Expect $60–80 for three courses, plus drinks.

Portofino Viaduct Harbour ⓣ09/356 7080. The most fashionably sited of a small local chain of Italian places, with seats out by the harbour and in the chic modern interior. The food doesn't quite match the setting and service but is well priced for the location with most dishes served as both appetizer (around $16) and main ($25). Try the calamari Luciana with capers and garlic and the chicken risotto.

Sake Bar Rikka Victoria Park Market ⓣ09/377 8239. Excellent Japanese restaurant: settle down to their formidable platter of tempura, miso, sushi, chicken teriyaki and more for two people (under $40) and every kind of sake known to mankind including chilled versions. Closed Sun.

Sri Pinang 356 K' Rd ⓣ09/358 3886. Simple but ever popular Malaysian restaurant. Start with half a dozen satay chicken skewers ($6) and follow with perhaps sambal okra, beef rendang or clay pot chicken rice (all $11–14) scooped up with excellent roti. BYO only. Closed Mon & Sat lunch, and all day Sun.

ToTo 53 Nelson St ⓣ09/302 2665. One of the city's finest modern Italian restaurants whose airy white, opera-filled room and terrace have become a lunchtime stable for TV execs from across the road. Kick off with exquisite *ripieno* "stuffed breads" ($5) and follow up with roasted scallops with an eggplant puree ($21), lobster and garlic risotto ($30) or a supremely thin *prosciutto e funghi* pizza ($22). Closed Sat & Sun lunch.

Tony's 32 Lorne St ⓣ09/373 2138. Traditional steak restaurant highly regarded for its juicy slabs of prime meat ($25–30), plus cheaper lunches.

Wildfire Princes Wharf ⓣ09/353 7595. Flashy Latin-influenced place with tables by the water or inside where a massive fiery grill flares up from time to time. Gourmet pizzas are overshadowed by the nightly rotisserie specials (quail, duck cervena; $26–28) and the Brazilian *churrascaria*, a vast selection of meats and seafood marinated in herbs and roasted over manuka coals. Served after tapas, the whole shebang costs $40.

Parnell

Parnell's eating places split into two camps; established restaurants with the accent on fine dining, and trendier, cheaper places catering to younger devotees, and backpackers from the nearby hostels.

Antoine's 333 Parnell Rd ⓣ09/307 8756. Enduring restaurant consistently rated among the best in Auckland and much favoured by Parnell and Remuera blue bloods. It's all very professionally, if somewhat conservatively, done, with a "nostalgia" menu full of game, offal and French classics alongside a modern counterpart. Try top-quality lamb and salmon, in mains that start around $40.

Chocolate Café 323 Parnell Rd. Compact chocolate emporium selling handmade choccies and a range of chocolate (and coffee) drinks. Tables inside and out, and it stays open late for that post-dinner dessert.

Iguaçu 269 Parnell Rd ⓣ09/358 4804. Flashy conservatory-style brasserie frequented by a young corporate crowd and wannabes, but worth a look in for a light meal or just a glass of wine. Sunday lunchtime jazz.

Java Room 317 Parnell Rd ⓣ09/366 1606. Intimate restaurant serving loosely Indonesian-influenced dishes but stretching to dim sum, spicy fish cakes, Szechwan prawns and whole snapper in sambal. Licensed and BYO.

The Other Side 320 Parnell Rd. Bright, breezy and reasonably priced café serving good breakfasts and a typical range of Kiwi café food.

Pandoro 427 Parnell Rd. Bakery specializing in Italian-style loaves, stuffed pizza bread – and chocolate brownies.

Portofino 156 Parnell Rd ⓣ09/373 3740. Basic but reliable trattoria without the pretensions of much of this street, but with pasta and pizza favourites all exceptionally well done. Licensed and BYO.

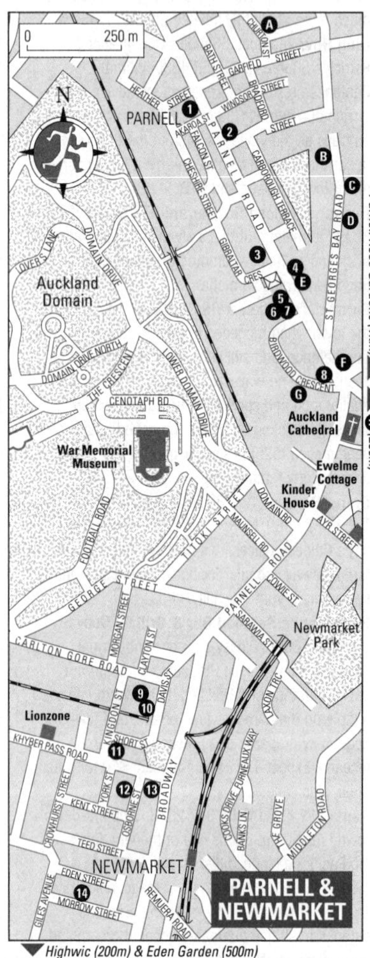

Highwic (200m) & Eden Garden (500m)

ACCOMMODATION	
Birdwood House	G
Chalet Chevron	H
City Garden Lodge	D
International Backpackers	A
Lantana Lodge	B
Parnell Inn	E
Parnell Village	F
St Georges Bay Lodge	C

CAFÉS, RESTAURANTS & BARS	
Antoine's	7
Bodrum	12
Carlton	13
Chocolate Café	6
Cinnamon Twist	11
Iguaçu	3
Java Room	5
Mecca	9
Pandoro	8
Portofino	2
Strawberry Alarm Clock	1
The Other Side	4
Vivo	10
Zarbo	14

Strawberry Alarm Clock 119 Parnell Rd. Low-key café popular perfect for breakfasts, a snack, or just hanging out over good coffee either inside or out in the rear courtyard.

Newmarket

Newmarket is rapidly heading the same way as Parnell, with interesting new places opening up all the time, though unless you are staying nearby it isn't worth making a special effort.

Bodrum 2 Osborne St. Boisterous Turkish restaurant open nightly for feta- and potato-stuffed filo cigars, kebabs in every style imaginable and regional favourites like falafel, moussaka and spanakopita, all at moderate prices. Licensed and BYO.

Cinnamon Twist 4 Kingdon St. Quality French-style bakery producing a delicious range of croissants, brioches, Danishes and a small range of lunchtime savouries. Take out or munch over a coffee or creamy Belgian chocolate drink.

Mecca 61 Davis Crescent. Relaxed café with speedy service dishing up excellent blueberry pancakes with fresh fruit ($11) and a range of fresh and well-presented breakfast and lunch dishes including a Thai chicken curry ($12) and an extensive mezze platter ($9).

Vivo 65 Davis Crescent ☎09/522 0688. Gourmet pizza served in a capacious wood-floored interior or out on the pavement with the denizens of this trendy little street.

Zarbo 24 Morrow St. Auckland's finest deli café with a fabulous range of products from around the world, many of them put to good use in a superb range of breakfast and lunch dishes ($5–15) either ordered from the menu or selected from the counter. Lunch finishes at 3pm but they stay open until five for salads, cakes and coffee.

Tamaki Drive: Okahu Bay and Mission Bay

If you find yourself peckish while visiting Kelly Tarlton's, roller blading along Tamaki Drive or just out for a swim at Mission Bay then head along to one of Mission Bay's cafés; *Hammerheads* is best saved for a more formal lunch or dinner.

Bar Comida 81 Tamaki Drive. Quality version of the typical Kiwi cover-all-the–bases café/restaurant/bar with woodfired gourmet pizza, great coffee and cakes, and a strong line in *pide*, Turkish flatbreads applied to anything from BLT to *lahmejan*, a lamb, parsley and lemon juice combo from Istanbul. Licensed.

Bluefins cnr Tamaki Drive and Atkin Ave ☎09/528 4551. Classy terracotta-tiled seafood restaurant serving delicious seared scallops, tempura dishes and super-fresh daily specials. Mains around $25. Closed Sun & Mon. Licensed.

Hammerheads 19 Tamaki Drive, Okahu Bay, by Kelly Tarlton's ☎09/521 4400. Popular waterfront seafood restaurant that sometimes suffers from slow service. The delectable food is worth the delay, though, and your wait is eased by dynamite cocktails and tremendous views. Licensed.

Ponsonby and Herne Bay

At the cutting edge of Auckland's foodie scene is **Ponsonby Road**, a street where devotion to style is as important as culinary prowess. But don't be intimidated; the food is almost invariably excellent and though prices are generally a notch above those in more downbeat parts of the city, nowhere is prohibitively expensive, and there are several reasonably-priced places hanging in there. Again, popular daytime cafés frequently ease into more rumbustious drinking later on, often until the wee hours.

Atlas Power Café 285 Ponsonby Rd. Small modern café with a strong gay following, pricey but delectable sandwiches and salads for around $14, and their own roast coffee.

Atomic Café 121 Ponsonby Rd. *Atomic*'s own-roast coffee has become a byword for quality espresso all over town and to emphasize the point they've gathered an array of ingenious old coffee makers to grace the walls. Here, at their home base, the muffins reign supreme and macrobiotic and organic food dominates the blackboard. The sandpit in the grapevine-shaded courtyard and fluffies (cappuccino froth adorned with hundreds and thousands) make it a great place for harassed parents. Daytime daily.

Bistro Bambina 268 Ponsonby Rd. Café with a big central table stacked with magazines and newspapers. The food is reliably fresh and tasty from the all-day breakfast – try the ricotta hotcakes with fresh fruit ($11) – through to panini na open Turkish sandwiches. Great coffee too.

Bolliwood 110 Ponsonby Rd ☎09/376 6477. The modern face of Indian restaurants in a vast room with bold colour scheme and a certain theatricality to the proceedings. The menu ranges from dairy-based north Indian dishes to lighter and spicier southern fare such as appam and dosas made from rice flour ground on the premises. Everything is beautifully done, and mains cost around $20.

Café Cézanne 296 Ponsonby Rd. This casual, ramshackle place is a welcome refuge from the glitz of the rest of Ponsonby Road; great for reading the papers over hearty quiches, pizza slices and huge wedges of cake.

Dizengoff 256 Ponsonby Rd ☎09/360 0108. Unlicensed breakfast and lunch café specializing in wonderful bagels, Kosher meals and luscious char-grilled vegetables all at reasonable prices. The mushrooms on toast are particularly creamy.

Food for Life 153 Ponsonby Rd. This breezy café and bar gives the Ponsonby treatment to dishes that are either organic, veggie, sugar-free or non

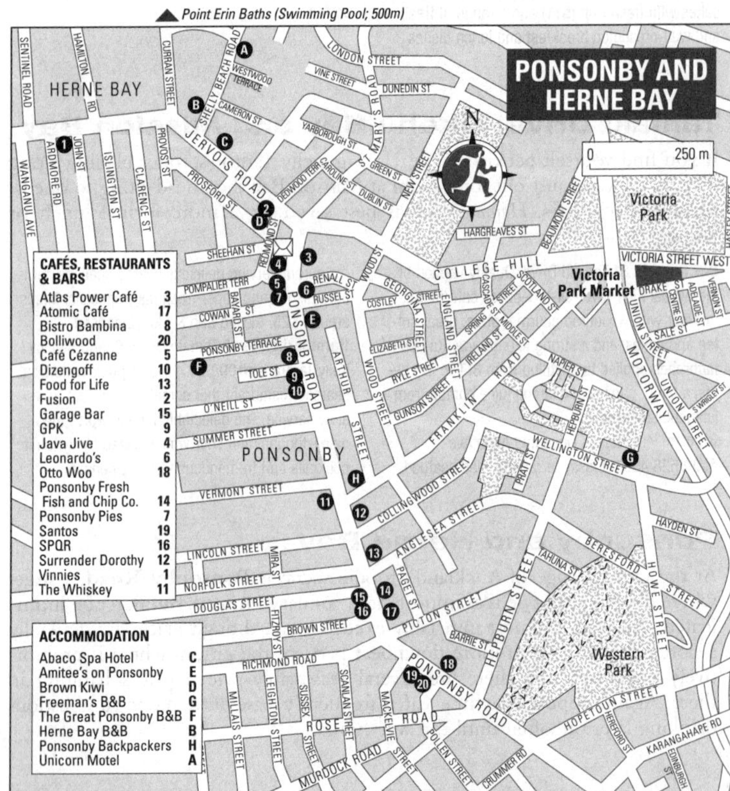

dairy (or all four) offering pies, quiches, roast vegetable dishes, nachos, a range of wholesome cakes and decent coffee.

Fusion 32 Jervois Rd. Enjoyable daytime café that's wonderfully relaxed inside and great out back under the umbrellas. A good range of breakfasts until 12.30pm, plus light lunches, great coffee and flavoursome fruit lassi drinks.

GPK 262 Ponsonby Rd ⓣ09/360 1113. Smart bar and restaurant wood-firing some of the tastiest pizzas in town with avant-garde toppings such as Thai green curry or octopus. They're small, considering the $20 price tag, but well worth it; eat in or take out.

Leonardo's 263 Ponsonby Rd ⓣ09/361 1556. About as authentic an Italian restaurant as you'll find in Auckland. No pizza or risotto but a great antipasto plate ($25 for two), assorted appetizers ($15), pasta and gnocchi dishes (around $20), and segundi piatti ($25–30) such as fish in lemon caper parsley and white wine sauce, all served up with easy charm. Weekend lunches and dinner nightly except Mon.

Otto Woo 47 Ponsonby Rd ⓣ09/360 1989, ⓦwww.ottowoo.com. Excellent unlicensed noodle bar, primarily for take-outs but with a few stools at stark white tables. Choose from freshly prepared chicken bok choy, seafood laksa, satay vegetable noodles and a dozen other dishes (all $9–14) and finish off with some sweet rice balls.

Ponsonby Fresh Fish and Chip Co 127 Ponsonby Rd ⓣ09/378 7885. One of the best basic fish, chips and burger takeaways around, frequently lauded in *Metro* magazine's annual readers' poll and always busy, so call ahead or trot across the road to the SPQR bar and wait. The vegetarian burgers are sensational.

Ponsonby Pies 288 Ponsonby Rd. Basically a takeaway with a few chairs that's great for sumptuous filled focaccia and some of the best pies in the land: apple and pork, silverbeet and cheese, pumpkin and bacon, to name but a few.

Santos 114 Ponsonby Rd. Trendy little spot serving the best cappuccinos on Ponsonby Road and panini to match.

Vinnies 166 Jervois Rd ⓣ09/376 5597. Intimate and expensive restaurant with white linen table cloths that is consistently rated as one of Auckland's finest formal restaurants. Their wood-fired kitchen turns out fine dishes like braised lambs' tongues, perhaps kicked off with snapper ceviche in a raspberry citrus vinaigrette. Expect to pay around $30 for mains.

Devonport

Devonport's range of places to eat is rapidly catching up with Auckland's major foodie hangouts with plenty of worthwhile **lunch stops** and several quality restaurants for **evening dining**.

The following choices are all on the map on p.117.

The Cod Piece 26 Victoria Rd. Sit-in and take-out fish and chip place, cheekily named by the gay owners who earned the wrath of prim Devonport residents for their "more than a mouthful" sign which has since been removed. Gourmet burgers too.

Manuka 49 Victoria Rd. Wood-fired pizza restaurant that's good at any time of the day for light snacks and salads or just for coffee and cake.

Monsoon 71 Victoria Rd ⓣ09/445 4263. There is seldom a bad word said about this excellent value-for-money Thai/Malaysian place with tasty dishes such as fish and Tiger prawns in a red curry sauce for around $18. Evenings only. Licensed and BYO.

The Stone Oven 3 Clarence St. Large, bustling bakery and café with a solid reputation for organic sourdough, black Russian and barley rye breads and cakes and pastries to take away or eat in; also popular for all day breakfasts and light lunches, quiches, pies and panini, accompanied by aromatic coffee.

Drinking, nightlife and entertainment

Auckland has some of New Zealand's best nightlife and, with a million people to entertain, there's always something going on, even if it's just a night down at the local **boozer**. The best way to find out **what's on** is to pick up the *New Zealand Herald*. For gig information, buy the monthly *Real Groove* ($5), available from most record store and magazine shops, pick up the free weekly *Fix* leaflet from the same outlets or surf to the entertainment guide section of the bFM radio station website Ⓦwww.95bfm.co.nz.

New Zealand produces plenty of **bands** and at any time you should be able to find some quality local acts bashing away in a club or dedicated venue; due to New Zealand's remoteness, bands from North America or Europe are less frequent visitors. One of the best ways to see local bands is to attend one of the **free summer concerts** held in Aotea Square, Albert Park and The Domain under the *Free Summer* banner (Ⓣ09/379 2020, Ⓦwww.akcity.govt.nz/freesummer/; mid-Dec to early Feb), mostly on Friday, Saturday and Sunday afternoons.

After a lull of a few years, Auckland's **arts scene** is picking up, and on any night of the week there should be a choice of a couple of plays, comedy and maybe some dance or opera.

Gay and lesbian Auckland

New Zealand has a fairly small but progressive and proactive **gay culture**, and Auckland, the most vibrant of the cities, is at its centre. Until recent times, the annual focus was the Hero Parade and the associated two-week Hero Festival, a smaller and considerably tamer cousin of Sydney's Gay Mardi Gras. Ongoing financial mismanagement and the recent election of the far-from-liberal mayor, John Banks, may scupper plans to revive the festival, though there are hopes for a parade down Ponsonby Road in February 2003.

The best way to find out if the **Hero Parade** is taking place and to generally find out what's happening is to get hold of the fortnightly *Express* magazine ($2.50; Ⓦwww.gayexpress.co.nz), which can be bought from branches of Maggazzino and the Out! bookshop (Ⓣ09/377 7770; 39 Anzac Ave), and is available for browsing in many cafés. It's also worth tuning in to **Round the Bend**, the Sunday evening gay and lesbian interest programme (8–9pm) on 95bFM (Ⓦwww.95bfm.co.nz), preceded by an hour of *The Girls Own Show*. Look out too for **Queer Nation**, sporadically on TV2 late in the evenings.

The gay scene is fairly low-key, gently woven into the café/bar mainstream of Ponsonby, Parnell and Newmarket, with the exception of the western end of K' Road where the strip clubs mingle freely with gay bars and cruise clubs. Among the **cafés** and **bars**, *Atlas Power Café* and *Surrender Dorothy*, both in Ponsonby are good starting points. Along K' Road, *Staircase*, 340 K' Rd (Ⓣ09/374 4278), and the leather-oriented *Urge*, 490 K' Rd, are the places to be. Recently there's been more going on around High Street and the parallel O'Connell Street, specifically at *Wunderbar*, 5 O'Connell St (Ⓣ09/377 9404), *G.A.Y*, 5 High St (Ⓣ09/336 1101) and *Flesh*, 16 O'Connell St, with both lounge and dance club sections.

Useful contacts

Auckland Pride Centre 281 K' Rd; postal address PO Box 5426, Wellesley St Ⓣ09/302 0590, Ⓦwwwpride.org.nz. The best place to tap into the scene, with a drop-in centre (generally Mon–Fri 10am–5pm, Sat 10am–3pm) and a good events noticeboard. Their website has an excellent links section.

Budget Travel 177 Parnell Rd; postal address PO Box 37–259, Parnell Ⓣ09/302 0553, Ⓕ358 1206. This branch of the nationwide chain of travel agencies has a particular interest in helping gay visitors plan their travels

Gay and lesbian helpline Ⓣ09/303 3584; Mon-Fri 10am-10pm, Sat & Sun 5-10pm.

Harvey World Travel 293 Ponsonby Rd Ⓣ376 5011, Ⓦwww.harveyworld.co.nz. Offers a similar service to Budget Travel (see above).

Pubs and bars

In Auckland, as in much of the rest of the country, the distinction between eating and drinking places is frequently blurred, with cafés, restaurants and bars all just points along the same continuum. The factor uniting those listed below is their dedication to **drinking**: some are bars which may serve food but where drinking is the norm; others are old-time hotels in the Kiwi tradition, though even these have been dramatically smartened up and may do a sideline in inexpensive counter meals.

Drinking hours have relaxed markedly over the years to the point where they are almost unlimited and you will find places serving alcohol virtually round the clock. The exceptions are Grey Lynn, which borders Ponsonby, and Mount Eden, which both relinquished their former "dry area" status in recent years but still have few pubs or licensed restaurants.

City centre

Bellini *Hilton Hotel*, Princes Wharf. Polish up your credit cards for this stylish top end cocktail bar with fabulous harbour views from the floor-to-ceiling glass. There's a wonderful range of champagne cocktails ($25), delicious martini variants ($20), a great selection of wines and tasty morsels to keep you going.

Civic Tavern cnr Queen St and Wellesley St. Two-in-one pub that's good for a quick drink before the movies up the road: choose between *Murphy's Irish Bar* downstairs and the *London Bar* upstairs with bistro meals and a hundred brands of bottled beer.

Elbow Room 12 Durham Lane. Fashionable little bar often quiet midweek but with DJs at weekends and no cover.

Kiwi Tavern 3 Britomart Place ⓣ09/307 1717. Top-floor bar with pool tables, and drink discounts that's predictably popular with backpackers for their nightly drink specials, particularly on Tuesdays when there's a "Drink your way around NZ" five-beers-for-$8 deal.

The Loaded Hog Viaduct Harbour. Vast, bustling, glass-walled bar with seating right on the quay, bar food, an impressive range of wines by the glass and four tantalizing micro-brewed beers; beware of the dress standards (no shorts, vests or thongs) enforced in the evenings.

Rakino's 1st floor, 35 High St. Good daytime café with tables shaped like Hauraki Gulf islands (including Rakino Island) which on Thursday, Friday and Saturday evenings transforms into a compact venue serving up anything from live jazz to DJs.

Shakespeare Tavern 61 Albert St. Pub with an in-house micro-brewery producing a thirst-quenching low-alcohol ginger beer and a handful of commendable, stiffer brews – also sold in two-litre bottles to take away.

Tabac 6 Mills Lane. Cosy establishment co-owned by former Crowded House singer/songwriter Neil Finn; good for a drink in the bar or take it through to the sofas of the intimate Velvet Room out back. Closed Sun & Mon.

The suburbs

Carlton cnr Broadway & Khyber Pass Rd, Newmarket. Pub and brasserie offering good-value meals and presenting live music most weekends.

Garage Bar 152 Ponsonby Rd, Ponsonby. Diminutive, smart, barstool-perching place with fine wines by the glass, plenty of top-shelf cocktails and a great window seat. Usually some local DJ on the decks at weekends. Closed Sun.

Galbraith's Alehouse 2 Mount Eden Rd. Former library converted into a microbrew pub with some of New Zealand's finest English-style ales – the warm and flat but wondrously toothsome kind – plus hand-pulled Guinness, Orangeboom, Tuborg, Boddingtons and fifty-odd bottled varieties. Good back-to-basics bar meals include liver and onions and fish and chips along with burgers, curries, hearty soups and desserts, all at very reasonable prices.

SPQR 150 Ponsonby Rd, Ponsonby. Dimly lit and eternally groovy bar with an excellent range of wines (all sold by the glass) and beers, and fine Italian food (especially the pizzas); a good venue for spotting off-duty rock stars and actors.

Surrender Dorothy 175 Ponsonby Rd. An intimate and friendly bar with a strong gay following, that's great for a quiet drink anytime but more lively on Friday and Saturday nights. Closed Sun & Mon.

The Whiskey 210 Ponsonby Rd, Ponsonby. Stylish modern bar with something of the feel of a groovy gentleman's club, all chocolate leather sofas and white brick walls hung with superb photos of Little Richard, the New York Dolls, Jimi Hendrix and more – and they do a particularly fine Manhattan.

Clubs and gigs

Auckland undoubtedly has New Zealand's largest and most exciting club scene and, by sheer weight of population, gets to see more bands than anywhere else; indeed, the bigger international acts often make it no further.

Though the area downtown around the junction of Vulcan Lane and High Street occasionally grasps the **clubbing** torch, the flame currently burns brightest along Karangahape Road, where you can join the nightly flow of bright young things surging between the bars and clubs. Unless someone special is on the decks or a band is playing, few clubs charge more than $5 admission (and many are free), encouraging sporadic and unpredictable exoduses to other venues – just follow the crowds.

Many of the clubs have one area set up as a stage and on any night of the week you might find top Kiwi acts and even overseas **bands** blazing away in the corner; a few pubs may also put on a band from time to time. Bigger acts understandably opt for the larger venues; tickets can be booked through Ticketek (ⓣ09/307 5000).

All venues listed are in the **city centre** unless otherwise specified.

Galatos 17 Galatos St. ⓣ09/303 1928. Lounge bar that's more mellow than most attached to a small venue offering a broad selection of DJ-led dance nights and off-beat live acts. Closed Sun–Tues.

Java Jive 12 Pompallier Terrace, Ponsonby ⓣ09/376 5870. Tiny basement bar with live music from Wednesday to Sunday. Regular acoustic, jazz and blues sessions; call or check local listings magazines for details.

Kings Arms 59 France St, Newton ⓣ09/373 3240. Popular pub and second-string venue hosting local and touring acts who can't quite fill the Power Station.

Khuja Lounge 536 Queen St ⓣ09/377 3711. Currently hot on the weekend circuit this bar/club caters to a slightly-older, more musically inclined crowd, often mixing the styles – khuja means "melting pot" in Arabic. Closed Sun–Tues.

Papa Jack's Voodoo Lounge 9 Vulcan Lane ⓣ09/358 4847. Big bar with a party atmosphere that's heaving at weekends when it stays open to the small hours. Mixed dance and alternative rock DJs occasionally give way to top Kiwi touring bands when there'll be a small cover charge.

The Power Station 33 Mount Eden Rd, Mount Eden ⓣ09/377 7666. Sweaty venue that's usually the most happening place for alternative rock, rap and dance acts.

Roots 322 K' Rd ⓣ09/308 9667. Late-night club that's very much the place to go for DJs spinning reggae, Cuban and African beats.

Temple 486 Queen St ⓣ09/377 4866, ⓦwww.temple.co.nz. Tiny bar that sees emerging and more established Kiwi acoustic and blues acts pretty much every night, and open-mic nights on Monday and Tuesday (usually $3–10 admission). Also pool tables upstairs and pool competition on Wednesday at 8pm.

Classical music, dance, theatre and comedy

Auckland's **theatre** scene is increasingly vibrant; though there is no professional company with a permanent venue, the Auckland Theatre Company (ⓣ09/309 3395, ⓦwww.auckland-theatre.co.nz) is now firmly established at both the Aotea Centre and the Maidment, with occasional performances elsewhere. The Aotea Centre doubles as the major venue for classical music, **opera** and **ballet**, but events are held only sporadically: the New Zealand Symphony Orchestra strikes up every month or so, the Wellington-based New Zealand Ballet calls in during its tours of the provinces from time to time, and the Auckland Opera puts on several shows a year. The **Auckland Philharmonia** (ⓣ0508/266 237, ⓦwww.aucklandphil.co.nz) also put on a number of shows at the Auckland Town Hall and Aotea Centre.

The **comedy** scene is equally lively, with a dedicated venue hosting regular stand-up comedy, while in late April and early May theatres and pubs around town are alive with local stand-up comics and top-flight international acts for the two-week **comedy festival**.

Aotea Centre Aotea Square, Queen St ⓣ09/307 5060. New Zealand's first purpose-built opera house, opened in 1990 and the home stage for New Zealand Symphony Orchestra and the New Zealand Ballet. The Auckland Theatre Company frequently perform in its Herald Theatre.
Civic Theatre cnr Queen St and Wellesley St ⓣ09/307 5058. Wondrously restored theatre (see p.97) worth visiting if there's anything at all on: could be dance, theatre or classic movies.
Classic 321 Queen St ⓣ09/373 4321, ⓦwww.comedy.co.nz. Bar and comedy venue hosting all the best local names and the smaller world-class acts when they're in town. Shows Wed–Sat (and sometimes other nights) but with the best line-ups at weekends when it is $15-20 for the main acts and $8 for the 11pm improv show.
Silo Theatre Lower Grays Ave ⓣ09/366 0339. Small venue specializing in less mainstream plays and events. Success varies, but there's usually something interesting on.
Maidment Theatre cnr Princess St & Alfred St ⓣ09/308 2383. Two university theatres, with mainstream works in the larger venue and more daring stuff in the studio.

Cinema

Suburban multiplexes have virtually killed off smaller cinemas leaving central Auckland with just one twelve-screen monstrosity and one arthouse screen; **repertory** cinemas are more widely scattered, and are listed below. The annual **Auckland International Film Festival**, usually held in early July, presses many of these cinemas into service for arthouse and foreign screenings. **Admission** is around $12, though many cinemas drop their admission to $7 before 6pm on weekdays.

Academy 64 Lorne St ⓣ09/373 2761, ⓦwww.academy-cinema.co.nz. Predominantly arthouse cinema with two screens tucked underneath the main library.
Bridgeway 122 Queen St, Birkenhead ⓣ418 3308. Recently renovated movie theatre on the North Shore that makes cinema-going even more of a pleasure with its intimate feel, good foyer food and coffee, luxurious seating and a wall-to-wall curved screen.
Devonport 3 48 Victoria Rd, Devonport ⓣ09/446 0999. First-run Hollywood movies. Accessible from the city with Fullers' Ferry & Movie Pass for much the same price you'd pay for just the movie on Queen Street.
Lido 427 Manukau Rd, Epsom ⓣ09/630 1500. Grab a beer or wine, sink into super-wide seats, and enjoy mainstream and classic movies with superb digital sound in this renovated suburban cinema.

Listings

Airlines Air New Zealand and Air New Zealand Link ⓣ0800/737 767; Ansett New Zealand ⓣ0800/267 388; British Airways (see Qantas); Canadian ⓣ09/309 0735; Garuda ⓣ09/366 1862; JAL ⓣ09/379 9906; Malaysian ⓣ09/373 2741; Qantas ⓣ09/306 5564; Singapore Airlines ⓣ09/303 2129; Thai ⓣ09/377 3886; United ⓣ09/379 3800.
Automobile Association 99 Albert St ⓣ09/377 4660, ⓦwww.nzaa.co.nz.
Banks and exchange American Express 105 Queen St Mon–Fri 9am–4.30pm, ⓣ379 8286; Interforex 2 Queen St ⓣ09/302 3031 and 99 Quay St ⓣ09/302 3066; Thomas Cook 159 Queen St ⓣ09/379 3924 and 34 Queen St ⓣ09/377 2666; Travelex 32 Queen St ⓣ09/358 9173.
Bike rental Penny Farthing, cnr Khyber Pass Rd & Symonds St (ⓣ09/379 2524, ⓦwww.bikebarn.co.nz) rents entry level mountain bikes for $30 a day; Adventure Cycles, 36 Customs St East (ⓣ09/309 5566, ⓦwww.adventure-auckland.co.nz), has city bikes for $18, mountain bikes

from $25 and offers touring bikes at around $180 a month. Adventure Cycles also offers a service whereby you buy the equipment and they'll buy it back from you at the end of your trip for half the purchase price, a service also offered by Pack & Pedal, 5 Gillies Ave, Newmarket (Ⓣ09/522 2161, Ⓦwww.packnpedal.co.nz).

Bookshops The biggest bookshops are downtown: Borders, at 291 Queen St (Ⓣ09/309 3377), and Whitcoulls, 210 Queen St (Ⓣ09/356 5400). In addition, try the more highbrow Unity Books, 19 High St (Ⓣ09/307 0731); and for a massive selection of secondhand books visit Hard to Find (But Worth The Effort) either at 238 K' Rd (Ⓣ09/303 0555), or over in Devonport at 81a Victoria St (Ⓣ09/446 0300). Out!, 45 Anzac Ave (Ⓣ09/377 7770), is the place for gay-interest books and magazines; and the Women's Bookshop, 105 Ponsonby Rd (Ⓣ09/376 4399), specializes in feminist literature and women's interest books. For maps, make for the Auckland Map Centre, 1a Wyndham St (Ⓣ09/309 7725), or Speciality Maps, 46 Albert St (Ⓣ09/307 2217).

Bus departures InterCity (Ⓣ09/913 6100, Ⓦwww.intercitycoach.co.nz) runs the most comprehensive range of services to many destinations in conjunction with their partner, Newmans (Ⓣ09/913 6200, Ⓦwww.newmanscoach.co.nz). Tickets for InterCity and Newmans can be bought at the office in the Sky City terminal on Hobson St. Guthreys (Ⓣ0800/759 999) runs to Hamilton, Rotorua, Taupo, Waitomo and Tauranga daily and offer very competitive prices.

Buying a car For general advice, consult Basics (see p.35), then peruse the noticeboards in hostels and at the main visitor centre or get along to one of the weekend car fairs, which are typically dominated by private sellers rather than dealers. The major Saturday venue is the Saturday Car Fair, Beach Road, City (Ⓣ09/636 9775; Ⓦwww.saturdaycarfair.co.nz); on Sunday you've a choice of the Auckland Car Fair, Ellerslie Racecourse, Greenlane (Ⓣ09/529 2233, Ⓦwww.carfair.co.nz), and the Manukau Car Fair, Manukau City Shopping Centre (Ⓣ09/358 5000). All take place in the morning from 9am to noon or 1pm (gates usually open around 8am) and are well organized, with qualified folk on hand to check roadworthiness. Alternatively, glance through the page of cars for sale in the weekly *Auto Trader* or *Trade & Exchange* magazines, or pick up Wednesday's or Saturday's *New Zealand Herald* newspaper.

Camping and outdoor equipment Bivouac, 109 Queen St (Ⓣ09/366 1966) and 300 Broadway, Newmarket (Ⓣ09/529 2298), have a good selection of quality gear for sale or rent; Kathmandu, 151 Queen St (Ⓣ09/309 4615), stocks all the major brands; and Canvas City, 171 Hobson St (Ⓣ09/373 5753), have low-cost gear for sale or rent. It's also worth checking the noticeboard in Auckland's main visitor centre and around the hostels for offers of camping and tramping gear for sale.

Car rental The international companies all have depots close to the airport and free shuttle buses to get you to them; smaller companies, frequently offering highly competitive rates in return for older cars and a poorer back-up network, are mostly based in the city or inner suburbs. Call around for the best deals. A2B Rentals Ⓣ09/377 0825 & 0800/616 888, Ⓦwww.a2brentals.co.nz; Apex Ⓣ09/257 0292 & 0800/737 009, Ⓦwww.apexrentals.co.nz; Avis Ⓣ09/379 2650 & 0800/655 111, Ⓦwww.avis.com and airport Ⓣ09/275 7239; Budget Ⓣ09/976 2270 & 0800/283 438, Ⓦwww.budget.co.nz and airport Ⓣ09/256 8447; Hertz Ⓣ09/367 6350 & 0800/654 321, Ⓦwww.hertz.com and airport Ⓣ09/256 8695; National Car Rental Ⓣ09/307 0841 & 0800/800 115 and airport Ⓣ09/275 6573; NZ Rent a Car Ⓣ09/308 9004 & 0800/809 005, Ⓦwww.nzcars.co.nz; Rent-a-Dent Ⓣ09/309 0066 and airport Ⓣ09/275 2044; Thrifty Car Rental Ⓣ09/366 0562 & 0800/737 070, Ⓦwww.thrifty.co.nz and airport Ⓣ09/257 0562.

Consulates Australia Ⓣ09/303 2429; Canada Ⓣ09/309 8516; Netherlands Ⓣ09/379 5399; UK Ⓣ09/303 2973; USA Ⓣ09/303 2724.

Emergencies Police, fire and ambulance, Ⓣ111; Auckland Central police station Ⓣ09/302 6400.

Events Auckland Anniversary Weekend, sailing regatta on the Waitemata Harbour on the last weekend in Jan; Devonport Food and Wine Festival, third weekend in Feb; Pasifika Festival (Ⓦwww.akcity/pasifika), a celebration of Polynesian and Pacific Island culture held at Western Springs Reserve, first or second Saturday in March; Round the Bays Run, when up to 70,000 jog 10km along Tamaki drive, last Sunday in March; Waiheke Jazz Festival, Easter week; Royal New Zealand Easter Show, Easter weekend, family entertainment Kiwi-style with equestrian events, wine tasting and arts and crafts, all held at the showgrounds along Greenlane; International Comedy Festival, late April and early May; Auckland International Film Festival, early July.

Internet access and discount phone centres There are places all over the central city mostly charging $3–7 an hour: try Cyber Max, behind the Queen St visitor centre; the 24hr *Cyber Gates*, 409

Queen St; the 24hr Hot Shotz, 13 Customs St East; or Cyber City, 29 Victoria St, next to *Albert Park Backpackers*.

Laundry Clean Green Laundromat, 18 Fort St ⓣ09/358 4370; Mon–Sat 9am–8pm.

Left luggage Lockers at the Sky City Bus Terminal, Hobson St, and many hostels also have long-term storage for one-time guests at minimal or no charge.

Library Auckland Public Library, 44–46 Lorne St ⓣ09/377 0209; Mon–Fri 9.30am–8pm, Sat 10am–4pm, Sun noon–4pm.

Medical treatment Auckland Hospital, Park Rd, Grafton ⓣ09/379 7440; Travelcare, 5th Floor, 87 Queen St ⓣ09/373 4621, offers diving medicals, physiotherapy, X-rays and dental treatment. Registered medical practitioners are listed separately at the beginning of the *White Pages* phone directory.

Newspapers and magazines Auckland's morning paper is the anodyne *New Zealand Herald* (ⓦwww.nzherald.co.nz), the closest New Zealand gets to a national daily. The best selection of international newspapers – mostly from Australia, UK and the US – is at Borders, 291 Queen St. This is also your best bet for specialist magazines, which are also sold at branches of Magazzino (123 Ponsonby Rd, Ponsonby; and 3 Mortimer Passage, Newmarket). These shops also sell *Metro*, Auckland's city monthly which, if nothing else, offers an insight into the aspirations of upwardly mobile Aucklanders.

Pharmacy The most convenient late-opening pharmacy is the Auckland City Urgent Pharmacy, 60 Broadway, Newmarket (Mon–Fri 6am–1am, Sat & Sun 9am–1am); emergency departments of hospitals (see "Medical treatment" above) have 24hr pharmacies.

Post office Auckland's main post office is just off Queen St in the Bledisloe Building, 24 Wellesley St (Mon–Fri 8.30am–5pm), and has poste restante facilities.

Swimming Central pools include the indoor Edwardian-style Tepid Baths, 102 Customs St West (ⓣ09/379 4745), the open-air saltwater Parnell Baths, Judges Bay Rd (ⓣ09/373 3561), and the heated outdoor Point Erin Baths, cnr Shelley Beach Rd & Sarsfield St, Herne Bay (ⓣ09/376 6863). Otherwise, simply head for one of the beaches (see "The North Shore", p.109).

Taxis Alert ⓣ09/309 2000; Co-op ⓣ09/300 3000; Corporate ⓣ09/631 1111.

Travel agencies Budget Travel, 33 Lorne St (ⓣ09/366 4645 & 0800/808 040), and STA Travel, 10 High St (ⓣ09/309 0458), are good for internal and international travel, or visit one of the specialist backpacker places (see p.91).

Women's centres Auckland Women's Centre, 4 Warnock St, Grey Lynn (Mon–Fri 9am–4pm; ⓣ09/376 3227, ⓦwww.womenz.org.nz), offers counselling, health advice, massage and a library.

Around Auckland

For many, the best Auckland has to offer lies in the immediate vicinity, with its verdant hills, magnificent beaches and appealing seaside communities. Few would argue that the **Waitakere Ranges**, to the **west** of the city, rank among New Zealand's most spectacular landscapes, but their proximity makes them a viable break from the urban bustle. The hills also serve to deflect the prevailing westerly winds, providing shelter for the **vineyards** of the Henderson Valley and Kumeu, home base for many of the country's top winemakers, most of which offer tastings.

Spectacular expanses of sand which can't be beaten for long moody strolls are found pretty much the full length of New Zealand's western seaboard, but it is only at Auckland's **West Coast beaches** that you will find surf-lifesaving patrols in reassuring numbers. Heading **north**, Auckland infringes on southern Northland, making the **Hibiscus Coast** a virtual suburb, enormously popular with day-trippers and holiday-home owners. South of Auckland, the **Hunua Ranges** offer a few modest walks and again provide a windbreak, this time for the **Seabird Coast**, where low shingle banks and extensive mudflats form an excellent breeding ground for dozens of migratory species.

Moving on from Auckland

Moving on from Auckland is a straightforward business, with frequent **buses** following the main routes north and south to most major destinations, and **trains** (Tranz Scenic ⓣ0800/802 802, ⓦwww.tranzscenic.co.nz) leaving daily for Hamilton, Palmerston North and Wellington. If you are **driving**, you have a couple of alternatives if you're heading north. You can take SH1 directly over the harbour bridge and make for Orewa, or go west around the head of the Waitemata Harbour past the wineries, West Coast Beaches and Waitakere Ranges to meet up with SH1 at Wellsford. **Cyclists** must use the Devonport Ferry rather than the harbour bridge if heading directly north but will do well to take the western route, possibly riding a suburban train to Waitakere (bikes carried free outside peak hours). Southbound cyclists are better off following the Seabird Coast, avoiding the Southern Motorway, the main route south out of the city for motorists.

The network of **ferries** and **flights** linking the islands in the Hauraki Gulf presents more interesting ways to get out of the city. By linking them together you can visit a few islands and continue on to Whitianga on the Coromandel Peninsula or Whangarei without returning to Auckland. The most useful combination is to take a ferry to Great Barrier Island (see p.149) and catch a flight from there, possibly adding Waiheke Island to your itinerary; contact Fullers (ⓣ09/367 9111) and Great Barrier Airlines (ⓣ09/256 6500 & 0800/900 600) for schedules and fares. Finally, if you're on your way out of New Zealand, remember to keep $22 aside for your **airport tax**, as this is payable on site, rather than being included in the price of your ticket.

West of Auckland

Auckland's suburban sprawl peters out some 20km west of the centre among the enveloping folds of the **Waitakere Ranges**. Despite being the most accessible expanse of greenery for almost a million people, the hills remain largely unspoiled, with plenty of trails through native bush. On a hot summer day, thousands head up and over the hills to one of half a dozen thundering **surf beaches**, all largely undeveloped but for a few holiday homes (known to most Kiwis as *baches*) and the odd shop. The soils around the eastern fringes of the Waitakeres nurture long established **vineyards**, mainly clustered in the Henderson Valley but also stretching north to Kumeu, just short of the Kaipara Harbour town of **Helensville** and the **hot pools** at Parakai.

You'll need your own transport to do justice to the beaches and most of the ranges, unless you join one of the West Coast **tours**: Bush & Beach (ⓣ09/575 1458, ⓦwww.bushandbeach.co.nz) runs a half-day trip out west ($65) and a more satisfying full-day tour ($99) which takes in the Muriwai gannets; and GeoTours (ⓣ09/525 3991, ⓦwww.geotours.co.nz) do a Gannets & Volcanics of the West trip (half-day; $69) concentrating on landforms. You can also see something of the area on canyoning trips (see p.115) from Auckland.

As far as public transport goes, the Tranz Metro **trains** make it as far as Henderson and Waitakere – a boon for cyclists keen to get out of the city quickly – and Richies **buses** #054, #055, #064 & #066 run through Henderson to Kumeu.

The Henderson and Kumeu wineries

Much of New Zealand's enviable reputation as a producer of quality wine is the result of vintages emanating from West Auckland, the historical home of the country's viticulture. The bigger enterprises now grow most of their grapes in Marlborough, Gisborne and Hawke's Bay, but much of the production process is still centred 20km west of central Auckland around the suburban Henderson Valley, or 15km further north around the contiguous and equally characterless villages of **Kumeu** and **Huapai**.

As early as 1819 the Reverend Samuel Marsden planted grapes, ostensibly to produce sacramental wine, in Kerikeri in the Bay of Islands, but commercial winemaking didn't really get under way until Dalmatians turned their hand to growing grapes after the kauri gum they came to dig ceased to be profitable (see box on p.225 for the finer points of gum digging). Many of today's thriving businesses owe their existence to these immigrant families, a legacy evident in winery names such as Babich, Delegat, Nobilo and Selak. Today, the region is producing some quality wines and winning prestigious awards, usually with the key varietals of Cabernet Sauvignon, Merlot, Pinot Noir and Chardonnay. More than anywhere else in the country, this is where you can taste wines produced throughout New Zealand in one day.

The free *Winemakers of Auckland* leaflet available from Auckland visitor centres details the **wineries** which can be visited; most offer tastings. Give Henderson a miss and head out to the rural and broadly more appealing Kumeu where half a dozen places do tastings, notably Coopers Creek, SH16, Huapai (Ⓣ09/412 8560, Ⓦwww.cooperscreek.co.nz; Mon–Fri 9.30am–5.30pm, Sat 10.30am–5.30pm), Kumeu River, SH16 Kumeu (Ⓣ09/412 8415, Ⓦwww.kumeuriver.co.nz; Mon–Fri 9am–5.30pm, Sat 11am–5.30pm), Nobilo, Station Road, Huapai (Ⓣ09/412 9148, Ⓦwww.nobilo.co.nz; Mon–Fri 9am–5pm, Sat 10am–5pm, Sun 11am–4pm), and Matua Valley, Waimauku Valley Road, Waimauku (Ⓣ09/411 8301, Ⓦwww.matua.co.nz; Mon–Fri 9am–5pm, Sat 10am–5pm, Sun 11am–4.30pm). At the last, reserve a table to eat at the wonderful, if pricey, *Hunting Lodge* **restaurant** (Ⓣ09/411 8259; lunch Fri–Sun; dinner Thurs–Sun; $25–30 for main dishes), which is beautifully set beside the vines. For more modest eating, visit *Carriages*, SH15 in Huapai, where excellent café-style food is served on a large deck or inside a couple of old railway carriages.

If you plan to do some serious tasting, designate a non-drinking driver or leave the car behind and join one of the West Coast tours (see opposite) which visit wineries as part of wider explorations. Better still, spend the day with Fine Wine Tours (Ⓣ & Ⓕ09/849 4519, Ⓦwww.insidertouring.co.nz), which offers a selection of specialist small-group wine tours around west Auckland, some also visiting gannet colony. Their half-day tour ($95) visits three or four wineries, and allows time for a relaxed lunch, and there are full day tours ($115–130) which might include extra wineries and extensive gourmandising.

The Waitakere Ranges and the West Coast beaches

Auckland's western limit is defined by the bush-clad **Waitakere Ranges**, which rise up to five hundred metres. At less than an hour's drive from the city, the hills are a perennially popular weekend destination for Aucklanders intent on a picnic and a bit of a stroll. The western slopes roll down to the wild, black-sand **West Coast beaches**. Pounded by heavy surf and punctuated by precipitous headlands, these tempestuous shores are a perfect counterpoint to the calm, gently shelving beaches of the Hauraki Gulf.

The Kawarau a Maki people knew the region as Te Wao Nui a Tiriwa or "the Great Forest of Tiriwa", aptly describing the kauri groves that swathed the hills

Always swim between the flags

The New Zealand coast is frequently pounded by ferocious surf and even strong swimmers can find themselves in difficulty in what may seem relatively benign conditions. Most **drownings** happen when people swim outside areas patrolled by volunteer lifeguards. Every day throughout the peak holiday weeks (Christmas–Jan), and at weekends through the rest of the summer (Nov–Easter), the most popular surf beaches are monitored daily from around 10am to 5pm. Lifeguards stake out a section of beach between two red and yellow flags and continually monitor that area: always swim between the flags.

Before entering the water, watch other swimmers to see if they are being dragged along the beach by a strong along-shore **current** or **rip**. Often the rip will turn out to sea at some point leaving a "river" of disturbed but relatively calm water through the pattern of curling breakers. On entering the water, feel the strength of the waves and current before committing yourself too deeply, then keep glancing back to where you left your towel to judge your drift along the shore. Look out too for **sand bars**, a common feature of surf beaches at certain tides: wading out to sea, you may well be neck deep, then suddenly be only up to your knees. The corollary is that moments after being comfortably within your depth you'll be floundering around in a **hole**, reaching for the bottom. Note that **boogie boards**, while providing flotation, can make you vulnerable to rips, and riders should always wear fins (flippers).

If you do find yourself in **trouble**, try not to panic, raise one hand in the air and yell to attract the attention of other swimmers and surf rescue folk. Most of all, don't struggle against the current; either swim across the rip or let it drag you out. Around 100–200 metres offshore the current will often subside and you can swim away from the rip and bodysurf the breakers back to shore. If you have to be rescued (or are just feeling generous), a large donation is in order. Surf lifeguards are dedicated volunteers, always strapped for cash and in need of new rescue equipment.

before the arrival of Europeans. By the turn of the century, diggers had pretty much cleaned out the kauri gum, but logging continued until the 1940s, by which time the land was economically spent. The Auckland Regional Council bought the land, built reservoirs and designated a vast tract as the Centennial Memorial Park, with two hundred kilometres of walking tracks leading to fine vistas and some of the numerous waterfalls which cascade off the escarpment.

The easiest access to the majority of the walks and beaches is the **Waitakere Scenic Drive** (Route 24), which winds through the ranges from the dormitory suburb of **Titirangi**, in the foothills, to the informative **Arataki visitor centre** (Sept–May daily 9am–5pm, June–Aug Mon–Fri 10am–4pm Sat & Sun 9am–5pm). From here, walkways forge into the second-growth forest, where panels identify a multitude of species, all readily visible from a series of nature trails (20min–1hr) which loop around the centre, the longest visiting one of the few mature kauri stands to survive the loggers' onslaught. One recently felled kauri has been transformed by Kawarau a Maki carvers into a striking *pou*, or guardian post, the largest of several fine carvings around the centre. Arataki is also the place to pick up **camping** permits (call the Parksline in advance on ⓣ09/303 1530) for the twelve backpacker sites ($4 per person) scattered through the ranges and located on the *Waitakere Ranges Recreation and Track Guide* map ($8, available from the visitor centre).

Beyond the visitor centre, the scenic drive swings north along the range, passing side roads to the **beaches**, noted for their foot-scorching, golden-black sands and demanding swimming conditions. Before entering the water, study the box (above), and heed all warning signs.

No **buses** run out this way, but Piha Surf Shuttle (Ⓣ025/227 4000; $20 each way) picks up in Auckland around 8am and leaves Piha for the city at 4pm; otherwise you're on your own.

Whatipu

Whatipu is the southernmost of the West Coast surf beaches, 45km from central Auckland and located by the sand-bar entrance to Manukau Harbour, the watery grave of many a ship. The wharf at Whatipu was briefly the terminus of the precarious coastal **Parahara Railway**, which hauled kauri from the mill at Karekare across the beach and headlands during the 1870s. The tracks were continually pounded by surf, but a second tramway from Piha covered the same treacherous expanse in the early twentieth century. Scant remains are visible, including an old tunnel which proved too tight a squeeze for a large steam engine whose boiler still litters the shore.

Over the last few decades, the sea has receded more than half a kilometre leaving a very broad beach backed by wetlands colonized by cabbage trees, tall *toe toe* grasses and waterfowl. It's a great place to explore, particularly along the base of the cliffs to the north where, in 30min, you can walk to the **Ballroom Cave**, fitted with a sprung dancefloor in the 1920s that apparently still survives, buried by five metres of sand that has drifted into the cave in the intervening years.

The only sign of civilization here now is *Whatipu Lodge* (Ⓣ09/811 8860, Ⓔwhatipulodge@xtra.co.nz; tent sites $12 per site, in this case it is better just to say tent sites because there are no powered sites, rooms ❸). Occupying a 120-year-old former mill manager's house, the lodge only has electricity when the generator is fired up each evening, but has extensive communal cooking facilities, hot showers, a tennis court, a cosy library and a full-size billiard table.

Karekare, Piha and Te Henga

You can walk 5km north along the beach from Whatipu to **KAREKARE**, otherwise reached by a 17km road from Arataki visitor centre. Perhaps the most intimate and immediately appealing of the West Coast settlements, Karekare has regenerating manuka, pohutukawa and cabbage trees running down to a deep, smooth beach hemmed in by high promontories and only a smattering of houses more or less successfully integrated into the bush. In one hectic year, this dramatic spot was jolted out of its relative obscurity, providing the setting for beach scenes in Jane Campion's 1993 film *The Piano* and, at much the same time, the inspiration for Crowded House's *Together Alone* album. Spikes that once secured the Parahara railway tracks to the wave-cut platform around the headland to the south can still be seen from the **Gap Gallery Track** (15min each way), which winds around Korekau Point to the seemingly endless beach beyond – but beware, the track is submerged at high tide. The Karekare Surf Club patrols a safe swimming area on summer weekends, or there is the pool below **Karekare Falls**, a five-minute walk on a track just inland from the road. Despite the presence of the fine colonial Winchelsea House, which took guests for its first fifty years, there is nowhere to stay and no facilities at Karekare.

For decades **PIHA**, 20km west of the visitor centre at Arataki and 40km west of central Auckland, has been an icon for Aucklanders. It is the quintessential West Coast beach with its string of low-key weekend cottages and crashing surf that lures day-tripping families as well as a youthful partying set whose New Year's Eve antics hastened in a dusk-till-dawn alcohol ban on holiday weekends. Piha feels on the brink of change; in the last few years some of the quaint old-time *baches* have been displaced by condo-style developments, and gentrification seems inevitable.

For the time being, though, a 3km-long sweep of gold and black sand is hemmed in by bush-clad hills and split by Piha's defining feature, the 101m **Lion Rock**. This former *pa* site, with some imagination, resembles a seated lion staring out to sea; the energetic climb to a shoulder two-thirds of the way up (20–30min return) is best done as the day cools and the sun casts a gentler light. The **Tasman Lookout Track** (30–40min return) leaves the south end of the beach, climbing up to a lookout over the tiny cove of The Gap where a spectacular blowhole performs in heavy surf.

Most **swimmers** flock to South Piha, the quarter of the beach south of Lion Rock where the more prestigious of the two surf-lifesaving clubs hogs the best **surf**. North Piha Road follows the beach north of Lion Rock for 2km to the second surf club. If battling raging surf isn't your thing, head for the cool **pool** below Kitekite Falls, a three-stage plunge reached on a loop track (1hr 30min) that starts 1km up Glen Esk Road, which runs inland opposite Piha's central Domain.

Most of Piha's visitors are day-trippers so facilities are limited to a general store, a fine traditional burger bar at South Piha, and a surf shop, Piha Surf (ⓣ09/812 8723, ⓦwww.surf.co.nz/piha/), a couple of kilometres before the beach on the road in. There are a few **places to stay** including self-contained caravans at the Surf Shop (❶), and the poorly shaded, year-round *Piha Domain Motor Camp* (ⓣ09/812 8815; tent sites $10; on-site vans ❷), which is slightly set back from the beach and best booked in advance. For something a little more upmarket try *Piha Lodge*, 117 Piha Rd, 3km before you reach the beach (ⓣ 09/812 8595, ⓦwww.pihalodge.co.nz; ❻), which has comfortable rooms and an outdoor pool.

The smaller and much less popular **TE HENGA** (also known as Bethell's Beach) lies at the end of a long road from Waitakere 8km north along the coast. Less dramatic than Karekare, Piha or Muriwai, Te Henga is correspondingly less visited, making it good for escaping the crowds at the height of summer. There are no shops, but there is a surf club and **accommodation** – at either the elegant pohutukawa-shaded *Te Koinga Cottage*, which can house up to seven but comfortably sleeps two couples, or *Turehu Cottage*, a smaller studio sleeping two; both have kitchen facilities (ⓣ09/810 9581, ⓦwww.bethellsbeach.com; ❼–❽).

Muriwai

MURIWAI, the most populous of the West Coast beach settlements, lies 15km north of Piha, and 10km coastwards from Huapai. Again, there's wonderful surf and a long beach stretching 45km north to the heads of Kaipara Harbour. The main attraction here, though, is at the southern end of the beach where a **gannet colony** occupies Motutara Island and Otakamiro Point, the headland between the main beach and the surfers' cove of Maori Bay. The gannets breed here between September and March before migrating to sunnier Australian climes, a few staying behind with the fur seals which inhabit the rocks below. Gannets normally prefer the protection of islands and this is one of the few places where they nest on the mainland, in this case right below some excellent viewing platforms from where you can observe them gracefully wheeling on the up-draughts. Short paths lead up here from near the surf club and off the road to Maori Bay. The beach, dunes and exotic, planted forests to the north are best explored on **horse treks** run by the Muriwai Riding Centre, 290 Oaia Rd (ⓣ09/411 8480; 2hr; $45).

The Waterfront **general store** serves coffee and light meals, and you can **stay** at either the *Muriwai Beach Motel*, 280 Motutara Rd (Ⓣ09/411 8780, Ⓕ411 9202; ❹), half a kilometre back from the beach, or the shaded *Muriwai Beach Motor Camp*, (Ⓣ09/411 9262; tent sites $10). For those without transport, Bush & Beach Ltd (see p.130) run half-day and full day-trips out here.

The southern Kaipara: Helensville and Parakai

Venture beyond the vineyards of Kumeu and you'll soon find yourself in uninspiring **HELENSVILLE**, 45km from Auckland but more closely associated with Kaipara Harbour (see p.135). Like many Kaipara towns, Helensville was founded on timber which, following the completion of the rail link to Auckland in 1881, was floated here in huge rafts then loaded onto wagons. Dairying has replaced the kauri trade and, though the spread of the Auckland conurbation is threatening, Helensville just potters along. Photos of busier days are displayed at the **Helensville Pioneer Museum**, on Commercial Street (daily 1–3.30pm; $3 suggested donation) but you'll get a better idea of what the kauri logging days were like with Kaipara Tours (Ⓣ09/420 8466; Dec to mid-March, according to demand but mostly weekends), which ply the waters of Kaipara Harbour, visiting kauri mills and bush camps. The three-hour Historical and Nature Cruise costs a bargain $15, while the full-day "Go North" Bus 'n' Boat Adventure ($50) links up with a 4WD sand bus to take you into Dargaville (see p.227) along Ripiro Beach. Depending on the tide, boats leave either from the wharf at Springs Road in Parakai, just north of the Aquatic Park (see below), or from Shelly Beach wharf, 20km north of Helensville.

To get to either wharf, you have to drive through **PARAKAI**, 3km north of Helensville and chiefly noted for its Aquatic Park (Ⓣ09/420 8998; daily 10am–10pm; $10, private spa $5 extra per hour), where a series of enclosed and open pools are filled by natural hot springs; entry includes free use of a couple of buffeting water chutes.

Practicalities

Richies **buses** #066, #067 & #069 (Ⓣ0800/103080; Mon–Sat only) operate from the corner of Customs and Lower Albert streets in central Auckland to Parakai and Helensville, with one evening service continuing on to Orewa (see below). There's a **visitor centre**, 27 Commercial Rd (daily 9am–6pm; Ⓣ09/420 7468, Ⓦwww.helensville.co.nz), right in the heart of town.

The best **place to stay** is the central *Malolo House*, 110 Commercial Rd (Ⓣ0800/286 060, Ⓣ & Ⓕ09/420 7262, Ⓔmalolo@xtra.co.nz), which operates as a high-standard backpackers with four-shares (❶) and doubles (❷) and a beautifully decorated B&B with ensuite rooms (❺), lavish breakfasts and an outdoor hot tub. If this doesn't suit, try the *Mineral Park Motel*, 3 Parakai Ave (Ⓣ & Ⓕ09/420 8856; ❹), where each room has its own outdoor mineral pool, or the **campsite** adjacent to Parakai's Aquatic Park (Ⓣ09/420 8998; tent sites $15 including pool entry).

Helensville is basically **takeaway** land, with the notable exception of *Café Regent* (Ⓣ09/420 9148; licensed and BYO), at 14 Garfield Road, the northern continuation of Commercial Road. Here, the foyer of an Art Deco cinema has been decorated with old movie posters and offers good snacks and coffee as well as an imaginative range of full meals at very reasonable prices.

North of Auckland

The straggling suburbs of north Auckland virtually merge into **The Hibiscus Coast**, which starts 40km north of the city and is increasingly favoured by retirees and long-distance commuters. The region centres on the suburban Whangaparaoa Peninsula, the launching point for trips to Tiritiri Matangi Island (see p.140), and the pleasant beachside community of **Orewa**, now mostly bypassed and somewhat quietened by an extension of the northern motorway. Immediately to the north, the hot springs at **Waiwera** herald the beach-and-barbecue scene of **Wenderholm** and the wonderful **Puhoi** pub. Travelling north, the account continues on p.165 with Warkworth.

Orewa

The most striking of the Hibiscus Coast beaches is the three-kilometre strand backed by **OREWA**, the region's main town, which garners just about all the accommodation and restaurants. Swimming aside, there isn't a great deal to do here, though the visitor centre can point you towards pleasant bushwalks and minor diversions such as the town's stern-looking statue of Edmund Hillary.

South of Orewa, the **Whangaparaoa Peninsula** juts out 12km into the Hauraki Gulf, its central ridge traced by Whangaparaoa Road, which passes the small-time, narrow-gauge **Whangaparaoa Railway**, 400 Whangaparaoa Rd (Sat & Sun 10am–5pm, plus school holidays Mon–Fri 10am–4pm; $5) on the way to **Shakespear Regional Park** (8am–dusk; free), a pleasant enough place to swim and wander through regenerating bush spotting pukeko, red-crowned parakeets and tui. The peninsula's most enticing diversion, though, is a trip to the bird sanctuary of Tiritiri Matangi (see p.140), with boats leaving from the vast Gulf Harbour Marina just before Shakespear Park.

Practicalities

Auckland's Stagecoach **buses** (call Rideline ⓣ0800/103080) run a complex timetable from downtown Auckland to the Hibiscus Coast, often requiring a transfer at Silverdale, just south of Orewa. These, and Northland-bound InterCity and Northliner buses, stop in central Orewa after passing the well-stocked **visitor centre**, 214a Hibiscus Coast Highway (Mon–Fri 9am–5pm, Sat & Sun 10am–4pm; ⓣ09/426 0076, ⓦwww.orewa-beach.co.nz). Bus routes #898 and #899 run along Whangaparaoa Road to Shakespear Park several times a day, passing within 2km of the Tiritiri Matangi wharf.

The most convenient budget **accommodation** is *Pillows Travellers Lodge*, 412 Hibiscus Coast Hwy (ⓣ09/426 6338, ⓔpillows.lodge@xtra.co.nz), which has modern dorms and four-shares (❶) and rooms, some en suite (❷–❸); while the very relaxing *Marco Polo Backpackers*, 2d Hammond Ave, 2km north at Hatfields Beach (ⓣ09/426 8455, ⓦwww.marcopolo.co.nz), has some very nice dorms (❶) and rooms (❷) set around a lush garden. **Motels** that line Orewa's main drag, the Hibiscus Coast Highway, tend to be quite expensive during the summer months but try: the beachfront *Edgewater Motel*, at #387 (ⓣ09/426 5260, ⓕ426 3378; ❹); and the budget *Hibiscus Palms*, at #416 (ⓣ & ⓕ09/426 4904, ⓔhibiscuspalms@xtra.co.nz; ❸). Though it isn't beside the beach, the best **campground** is the peaceful *Puriri Park Holiday Complex*, Puriri Ave (ⓣ0508/478 747 & 09/426 4648, ⓕ426 2680; tent sites $10, cabins ❷, tourist flats ❸). If you fancy pampering yourself and don't mind staying out of town, try *The Ridge*, Greenhollows Road (ⓣ0508/843 743, ⓦwww.theridge.co.nz; ❽), about 10km north of Orewa, though accessed via Puhoi (see p.137; call for directions). A luxurious eco-friendly lodge with panoramic views of the sea, farmland and bush, everything here is beautifully presented, with bush walks fanning out from the house and three-course dinners available ($45).

For straightforward **eating** try *Creole Bar & Brasserie*, 310 Hibiscus Coast Hwy, which does decent Mexican, Thai and burgers at modest cost, and stays open late at weekends when there is usually some live entertainment. For something more fancy, visit *Il Veneziano*, Red Beach Shopping Centre, Red Beach Road, 2km south of Orewa (ⓣ09/426 5444; closed Mon), where the menu justifiably effuses over the modern Italian dishes, priced around the $23 mark.

Waiwera and Wenderholm

The main highway north of Orewa (and bus #895) runs through the cluster of holiday and retirement homes that make up Hatfields Beach to **WAIWERA**, 6km north of Orewa, where Maori once dug holes in the sands to take advantage of the naturally hot springs. Bathing is now formalized in the **Waiwera Thermal Resort**, Waiwera Road (ⓦwww.waiwera.co.nz; daily 9am–10pm; $17), a vast complex of suicidal water slides and over twenty indoor and outdoor pools naturally heated to between 28 and 43°C. Private pools can be rented at $25 each per hour.

Occupying a high headland between the estuaries of the Puhoi and Waiwera rivers, **Wenderholm Regional Park** was the first of Auckland's regional parks and is still one of the most celebrated. Its sweeping golden beach is backed by pohutukawa-shaded swathes of grass and is often packed with barbecuing families on summer weekends. Walking tracks ranging from twenty minutes to two hours wind up to a lovely headland viewpoint through nikau palm groves which have been turned into a "mainland island". By trapping and poisoning, the headland is kept free of introduced predators, allowing native birds to return, some reintroduced from Tiritiri Matangi (see p.140). You can also take a peek at **Coudrey House** (Jan daily 1–4pm, Feb–Dec Sat & Sun 1–4pm; $2), an 1860s colonial homestead.

The #895 bus terminates here on summer Sundays, and if you need to stay there's a nicely sited water-and-toilets **campground** ($5) with grassy plots and a barbecue beside the mangroves.

Puhoi

The village of **PUHOI**, 6km north of Waiwera, is now attracting attention from Auckland lifestylers, but for the moment remains a bucolic place which was settled by staunchly Catholic Bohemian migrants who arrived here in 1863 from Egerland, in what was then the Austro-Hungarian Empire. Their descendants still form a small proportion of Puhoi's tiny population. As the land was found to be poor, the settlers were forced to eke out a living by cutting the bush for timber, and the horns of some of the more famed bullock teams are still ranged around the walls of the historic **Puhoi Tavern**, a single-roomed bar festooned with all manner of pioneering paraphernalia and photos of harder times. Buy a beer, charm the bartender and you may be invited to see the side room hung with what is claimed to be New Zealand's largest collection of paintings of Maori chiefs and princesses. Come on the second or last Friday of each month to see ageing members of a local Bohemian band playing their accordions and supping jugs of beer.

Few visitors get much further than the pub, but there is an interesting **Puhoi Historical Society Museum** (Christmas–Easter daily 1–4pm; Easter–

Christmas Sat, Sun & school holidays 1–4pm; $1 donation requested) in the former Convent School, with a model of the village as it once was and a phalanx of volunteers brimming with tales of the old days.

For some gentle activity, you can **kayak** or paddle an open canoe along a tidal section of the river (kayak $15 per hour; canoe $25) or continue downstream to Wenderholm (2hr; kayak $30, canoe $60, including pick-up at the far end) with Puhoi River Canoe Hire (☎09/422 0891). For refreshments, drive 3km north to *The Art of Cheese* café with lawns running down to a small stream and a reasonable selection of snacks and light meals, several including some of the cheeses made on site.

Details on points north of here can be found in the Northland chapter, starting on p.162.

Southeast of Auckland

Most southbound travellers hurry along Auckland's southern motorway to Hamilton or turn off to Thames at Pokeno – either way missing out on the (admittedly modest) attractions of the **Hunua Ranges** and **The Seabird Coast** on its eastern shore. For **cyclists** in particular the coast road is an excellent way into and out of Auckland, avoiding the worst of the city's traffic, following Tamaki Drive from the city centre then winding through Panmure, Howick and Whitford to Clevedon and the coast.

Even for Auckland day-trippers the older and more rounded Hunuas definitely play second fiddle to the more ecologically rich Waitakeres, but there are a few decent walks – notably those around the **Hunua Falls**. There are greater rewards further south with excellent seabird viewing and hot pools at **Miranda**.

The Hunua Ranges

A considerable amount of rain is dumped on the 700m-high **Hunua Ranges**, 50km southeast of Auckland, and flows down into a series of four dams which jointly supply sixty percent of the city's water. The bush surrounding the reservoirs was once logged for kauri but has largely regenerated, providing a habitat for birds; bellbirds, long since extinct in the city, can sometimes be heard here.

Access to the region is easiest through the village of **CLEVEDON**, home to Auckland's polo club (games Dec–April; ☎09/292 8556), and with a couple of restaurants and a smattering of craft shops. Pressing on south to Hunua, you'll come across the **Hunua Ranges Park visitor centre** (daily 8am–4.30pm), which sells the *Hunua Recreation & Track Guide* ($8) – invaluable for extended walks in the ranges. The best of the walks are around the thirty-metre Hunua Falls, around 5km east, where the Wairoa River carves its way through the crater of an ancient volcano. A good half-day hike, passing some lovely swimming holes, crosses the Wairoa River at the falls and follows Massey Track to Cossey's Dam and back down the Cossey Creek Track to the falls.

The Seabird Coast and Miranda

The Hunua Ranges are bounded to the east by the Firth of Thames, a sheltered arm of the Hauraki Gulf which separates South Auckland from the Coromandel Peninsula. Its frequently windswept western littoral has become known as **the Seabird Coast**, in recognition of its international importance for migrating shorebirds; almost a quarter of all known species visit the region. During winter, the vast inter-tidal flats support huge 30,000-strong flocks of birds, with over fifty percent of the entire world population of the wrybill plover over-wintering here. During the southern summer (Sept–March), the arctic migrants are more significant – notably bar-tailed godwits and lesser knots, as well as turnstones, curlews, sandpipers and red-necked stints – who fly 15,000 kilometres from Alaska, Siberia and Mongolia.

The tidal flats butt up against the geologically significant "chenier plain" around Miranda, where the land has been built up from successive depositions of shell banks; much has been converted to farmland but newer shell banks in the making can be seen along the coast.

From Clevedon the coast road winds 35km past the small beach settlements of Kawakawa Bay and Orere Point, and the **Tapapakanga Regional Park** (primitive camping $5) to **KAIAUA**. Here you'll find the *Kaiaua Motor Camp* (Ⓣ09/232 2712; tent sites $9, cabins ❷) and a couple of places to eat in the form of the *Bay View Hotel*, which does a good grilled snapper, and the adjacent *Kaiaua Fisheries*, which has twice been voted the best **fish and chip** shop in the land (though not recently) and now operates a licensed seafood restaurant in the evening.

The coast's birdlife is thoroughly interpreted at the **Miranda Shorebird Centre**, 7km south of Kaiaua (daily 9am–5pm, and often later; Ⓦwww.miranda-shorebird.org.nz); they'll fill you in on the current hot sightings and point you in the direction of the best viewing spots. With a sunny veranda for viewing, the centre also has good self-catering accommodation (Ⓣ09/232 2781 or see the warden in the cottage next door; dorms ❶, flat ❸). A further 7km south are the slightly alkaline **Miranda Hot Springs** (Mon–Thurs 8am–9pm, Fri–Sun 8am–10.30pm; $8, private spa $4 extra per half hour), with a large warm, open pool surrounded by grassy lawns and barbecue areas with private kauri spa tubs. Guests at the adjacent and upmarket *Miranda Holiday Park* (Ⓣ0800/833144, Ⓣ & Ⓕ07/867 3205, Ⓦmirandaholidaypark.virtualave.net/; tent sites $14, dorms ❶, cabins ❺) have access to their own new and nicely landscape mineral pool as well as a tennis court.

From here it's a twenty-minute drive to Thames (see p.385).

Islands of the Hauraki Gulf

One of Auckland's greatest assets is the island-studded **Hauraki Gulf**, a seventy-kilometre-square patch of ocean to the northeast of the city, host in 2003 to New Zealand's second defence of the America's Cup. In Maori, Hauraki means "wind from the north" – though the gulf is somewhat sheltered from the prevailing winds and ocean swells by the islands of Great Barrier and Little Barrier, creating benign conditions for Auckland's legions of yachties. Most are content just to sail but those who wish to strike land can choose from some of the 47 islands, administered by the Department of Conservation, and designated either for recreational use, with full access, or as sanctuaries for endangered wildlife, requiring permits.

Auckland's nearest island neighbour is uninhabited **Rangitoto**, a flat cone of gnarled and twisted lava which dominates the harbourscape. The most populous of the gulf islands is **Waiheke**, increasingly a commuter suburb of Auckland – but one with sandy beaches and a delightfully slow pace, enlivened by some quality wineries and an improving range of restaurants. Such sophistication is a far cry from the largest island hereabouts, **Great Barrier**, which until recently seemed trapped in a thirty-year time warp. However, the advent of fast ferries has put its sandy surf beaches, hilly tramping tracks and exceptional fishing within easy reach of holidaying Aucklanders and international visitors, many of whom continue on to the Coromandel (see p.383). DOC's happy compromise of allowing access to wildlife sanctuaries is wonderfully demonstrated at **Tiritiri Matangi**, where a day-trip gives visitors an unsurpassed opportunity to see some of the world's rarest bird species. **Little Barrier Island** resists any such interference, and is pretty much off-limits except to researchers.

Frequent **ferries** run to the more popular islands from the wharves around Auckland's Ferry Building, at the foot of Queen Street; there's a DOC **information** centre conveniently located in the same complex. Around the corner is the Fullers Cruise Centre (Mon–Fri 7.30am–5.30pm, Sat & Sun 8am–5pm; bookings and enquiries ⓣ09/367 9111, timetable information ⓣ09/367 9102, ⓦwww.fullers.co.nz,), which sells tickets for most island-bound boats. For more on cruising and kayaking the gulf, see "Adventure activities" starting on p.114.

Rangitoto and Motutapu islands

The distinctive, low, conical shape of **Rangitoto**, 10km northeast of the city centre, is a familiar sight to every Aucklander – yet few Aucklanders have actually set foot on the island. They miss out on a freakish land of fractured black lava, with the world's largest pohutukawa forest clinging precariously to the

Rangitoto summit walk

The best way to appreciate Rangitoto Island is on foot; but bear in mind that, though not especially steep, the terrain is rough and it can get very hot out there on the black lava. Consequently the best walks are those that follow shady paths to the summit rather than the more open roads. A favourite is the clockwise **Summit/Coastal Path loop** (12km; 5–6hr; 260m ascent) around the southeast of the island. Turn left just past the toilets at Rangitoto Wharf and follow signs for the **Kowhai Grove**, a typical Rangitoto bush area with an abundance of the yellow-flowering kowhai that blossoms in September. Turn right onto the coastal road from Rangitoto Wharf then left into **Kidney Fern Grove**, which is packed with unusual miniature ferns that unfurl after rain. The well-worn **Summit Track** winds through patches of pohutukawa forest. Around three-quarters of the way to the summit, a side track leads to the **lava caves** (20min return), which probe deep into the side of the volcano. Further along the main track a former military observation post on the **summit** provides views down into the bush-shrouded sixty-metre-deep crater and out across Auckland city and the Hauraki Gulf.

Continue northwards to the east–west road across the island and follow it towards Islington Bay; from there, pick up the **coastal track** south, initially following the bay then cutting inland through some little-frequented forests back to Rangitoto Wharf.

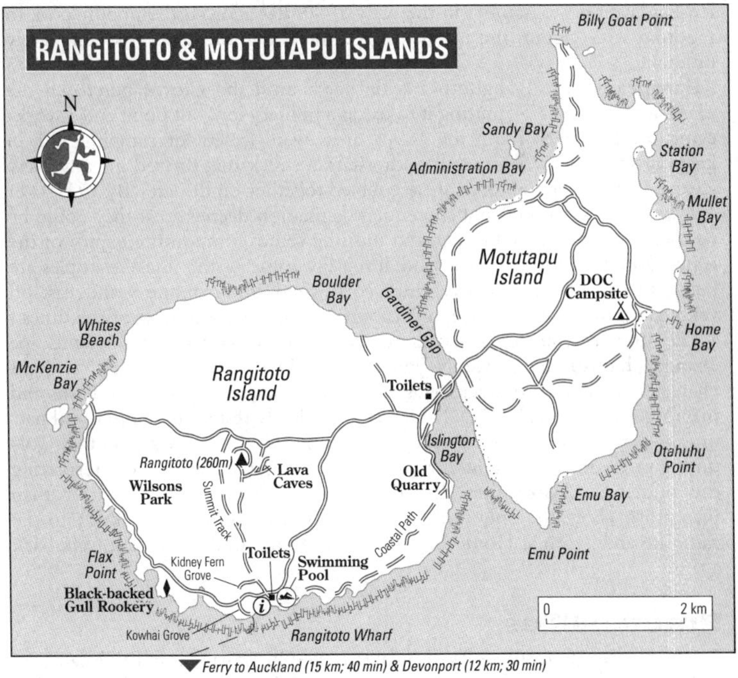

RANGITOTO & MOTUTAPU ISLANDS

Ferry to Auckland (15 km; 40 min) & Devonport (12 km; 30 min)

crevices. Alongside lies the much older and geologically quite distinct island of **Motutapu** or "sacred island", linked to Rangitoto by a narrow causeway.

A **day-trip** is enough to get a feel for Rangitoto, make the obligatory hike to the summit and tackle a few other trails, but **longer stays** are possible if you're prepared to pitch your tent at the primitive campsite at Home Bay on Motutapu.

Rangitoto is Auckland's youngest and largest **volcano**. Molten magma probably pushed its way through the bed of the Hauraki Gulf around six hundred years ago – watched by Motutapu Maori, who apparently called the island "blood red sky" after the awesome spectacle that accompanied its creation. Others attribute the name to a contraction of Te Rangi i totongia a Tamatekapua ("the day the blood of Tamatekapua was shed"), recalling an incident when chiefs of the Arawa and Tainui clashed at Islington Bay.

Rangitoto's youth, lack of soil and the porous nature of the rock have created unusual conditions for **plant life**, though the meagre supply of insects attracts few birds, making things eerily quiet. Pohutukawa trees seeded first, given a head start by their roots, which are able to tap underground reservoirs of fresh water up to 20 metres below the surface, then smaller and fleshier plants established themselves under the protective canopy. Harsh conditions have led to some strange botanical anomalies: both epiphytes and mud-loving mangroves are found growing directly on the lava, an alpine moss is found at sea level, and the pohutukawa has hybridized with its close relative, the northern rata, to produce a spectrum of blossoms ranging from pink to crimson. Sadly, the succulent pohutukawa leaves were a big hit with **possums** and wallabies which were introduced in the 1880s and proceeded to ravage the forests.

An eradication programme in the early 1990s has allowed the pohutukawa to rebound with vigour, and in fifty years' time Rangitoto will look completely different.

Europeans gave Rangitoto a wide berth until the Crown purchased the island for £15 in 1854, putting it to use as a military lookout point and a work-camp for prisoners. From the 1890s, areas were leased for camping and, in keeping with the defiantly anti-authoritarian streak that thrived in early New Zealand, unauthorized *baches* were cobbled together on the sites. By 1937, over 120 *baches* had sprouted, but subsequent legislation decreed that they could be neither sold nor handed down, and must be removed upon the expiry of the lease. Only thirty-four remain and, ironically, some of the finest examples are being preserved for posterity, their corrugated iron chimneys and cast-off veranda railings used as fenceposts capturing the make-do spirit of the times.

The moment you step across the **causeway** onto **Motutapu**, the landscape changes dramatically; suddenly, you are back in rural New Zealand with its characteristic grassy paddocks, ridge-top fencelines, corrugated iron barns and macrocarpa windbreaks. DOC's plan is to gradually restore its cultural and natural landscape, replanting the valleys with native trees – you can join their volunteer programme (see p.68 for details) – restoring wetlands and interpreting the numerous Maori sites. Currently though Motutapu is drearier than Rangitoto: about the only thing to do is walk the Motutapu Walkway to the campsite and beach at Home Bay (6km; 1hr 30min one-way), then walk back again.

Practicalities

Fullers **ferries** (Christmas–April 3 daily; May–Christmas Mon–Fri 2 daily, Sat & Sun 3 daily; time of last returning ferry varies throughout the year; $20 return) take forty minutes to reach Rangitoto Wharf, where there is an **information kiosk**, which opens to coincide with summer ferry arrivals; here you'll find a few bags of potato chips, a toilet block, the island's only **drinking water**, and a sun-warmed saltwater swimming pool (filled naturally by the high tide) that's great for kids. Apart from more toilet facilities at Islington Bay there's nothing else on the island, so bring everything you need – including strong shoes to protect you from the sharp rocks, sun hat, raincoat and, if you're planning a walk, carry plenty of water. Boats are met by the only transport on the island, a kind of tractor-drawn buggy which operates the two-hour **Volcanic Explorer Tour** ($49 including cost of ferry), a dusty summit trip with a full and informative commentary; the final 900m is on foot along a boardwalk.

The DOC has intentionally done all they can to ensure that the twin islands are the preserve of day-trippers. As a concession to the hardy and determined, there is a primitive but pleasant beachside DOC **campsite** ($6), with toilets and water, at Home Bay on the eastern side of Motutapu, over an hour's walk from Islington Bay and almost three hours' walk from Rangitoto Wharf.

Waiheke Island

Pastoral **WAIHEKE**, 20km east of Auckland, is the second-largest of the gulf islands and easily the most populous, particularly on summer weekends when Auckland day-trippers and weekenders quadruple the island's 8000 resident population. The traffic isn't all one-way, though, and a fast and frequent ferry service makes it feasible for a tenth of the islanders to leave every day for work in the city – a trend that threatens to turn Waiheke into just another suburb. For the moment, with its chain of sandy beaches along the north coast and a climate that's slightly warmer and a lot less humid than Auckland, Waiheke retains its sybaritic character – and is increasingly being discovered by international visitors in search of a peaceful spot to recover from jet lag or to idle away their last few days before flying out.

The **earliest settlers** on Waiheke trace their lineage back to the crew of the Tainui canoe which landed at Onetangi and gave the island its first name of Te Motu-arai-Roa, "the long sheltering island". Waiheke, or "cascading waters", originally referred to a particular creek but was assumed by European settlers to refer to the whole island. Among the first **Europeans** to set foot on Waiheke was Samuel Marsden, who preached here in 1818 and established a mission near Matiatia. The island went through the familiar cycle of kauri logging, gum digging and clearance for farming. Gradually, the island's magnificent coastal scenery gained popularity as a setting for grand picnics, and hamper-encumbered Victorians, surreally attired in formal dress, arrived in boatloads.

Development was initially sluggish, but the availability of cheap land amid dramatic landscapes drew painters and **craftspeople** to the island's shores; others followed as access from Auckland became easier and faster. Since the mid-1980s, the city has been less than forty minutes away, and Waiheke has become increasingly **sophisticated**: dilapidated shacks have been replaced by swanky condos, cafés and restaurants are a match for many in Auckland and boutique **wineries** produce some of the finest Cabernet Sauvignon blends in the country.

Arrival, information and getting around

Fullers operate fast **ferries** (Ⓣ09/367 9111; 40min; $24 return, bikes free) from the Ferry Building in Auckland to the Matiatia Wharf at the western end of Waiheke, just over a kilometre from the main settlement of Oneroa, every hour or two. If you're staying for a couple of days or longer, you may find it cost-effective to bring your vehicle over using the daily **car ferry**, a flat-deck barge run by Subritzky Line (Ⓣ0800/478 274 & 09/534 5663, Ⓦwww.subritzky.co.nz; $106 return for a car only, plus $24 per passenger) from Half Moon Bay near Pakuranga in Auckland's eastern suburbs to Kennedy Point. With frequent fast ferries there is little advantage in **flying** here, though if you are planning to visit Great Barrier Island and don't need to return to Auckland you can fly there with Waiheke Air Services (Ⓣ09/372 5000; 2 daily; $70). The **airport** is 3km east of Ostend and is reached by taxi (see "Listings", p.149) for around $10 from Oneroa.

Information

Waiheke's main source of information is the efficient **visitor centre**, 2 Korora Rd, Oneroa (Mon–Sat 9am–5pm, Sun 9am–4pm; Ⓣ09/372 1234, Ⓦwww.gotowaiheke.com/vin.html), which can organize most things on the island, and stores bags for $2 apiece. **Shops**, a couple of **banks** and a post office are also clustered in Oneroa. The weekly *Gulf News* ($1.50) comes out on Thursday afternoons and has details of **what's on**, as well as a rundown of arts and crafts outlets. The island goes mad at Easter for the four days of the **Waiheke Island Jazz Festival**, which is held at venues and cafés all over the island.

Getting around

Ferry arrivals and departures connect with Stagecoach buses (ⓣ366 6400) which operate along four **bus routes**, #1 to Onetangi via Oneroa, Surfdale and Ostend, and #2 to Rocky Bay via Oneroa, Little Oneroa and Palm Beach being the most useful. Tickets and a $5 day pass (which becomes worthwhile for return trips between Oneroa and Onetangi) are available on the bus. For more flexibility, rent a vehicle from Waiheke Rental Cars (ⓣ09/372 8635), at Matiatia Wharf and beside the tourist office, who **rent cars** ($50 a day plus 50¢/km) 4x4s ($65 plus 50¢/km) and scooters ($45). **Bikes** cost around $25 per day, from Wharf Rats Trading Co (ⓣ09/372 7937) at the Matiatia wharf, and Blue Bikes, cnr Oceanview Rd and Korora Rd, Oneroa (ⓣ09/372 3143); bear in mind that Waiheke is very undulating and you'll need to be pretty fit.

Day-trippers are well catered for by a number of **island tours**. Among those departing from Auckland, and including the return ferry trip, are Fullers Island Explorer (daily year-round departing Auckland 10am; $45.60), which includes an hour-and-a-half island tour, plus an all-day bus pass so you can explore further on your own, and their half-day Vineyard Explorer Tour (Dec–Feb daily, March–Nov Sat & Sun departing Auckland noon; $65.60) which spends three hours sightseeing and visiting the Mudbrick, Peninsula and Stonyridge vineyards: both tours allow a return to Auckland at a later date. On balance, this is the best way to tour the wineries, some of which are otherwise only open by appointment.

Island-based operators include Ananda Tours (ⓣ09/372 7530, ⓦwww.waiheke.co.nz/anandatours.htm) who run personalised wine, eco, art and scenic tours around the island costing around $55 per person. For basic transport contact Waiheke Island Shuttles (ⓣ09/372 7756) or the taxi companies (see "Listings", p.149), which all run tours and **drop-offs** at accommodation around the island, with prices depending on numbers and destination.

Accommodation

If your visit coincides with the Jazz Festival, the peak Christmas and January season, or any weekend, be sure to **reserve** a room as far **in advance** as you can, though this tends to be less critical at the backpacker hostels dotted along the north coast beaches. At other times, accommodation is fairly plentiful, especially if you follow Aucklanders' lead and go for **B&Bs**; most are registered with the visitor centre and with the Fullers Cruise Centre at the Ferry Building in Auckland.

Camping is restricted to the grounds of the various hostels and a simple but attractive site at *Whakanewha Regional Park* ($5, reservations through the Parksline ⓣ09/303 1530) on the tidal Rocky Bay, with safe swimming, composting toilets, drinking water, cold showers and pleasant walks through the park. It is a couple of kilometres' walk from the nearest bus stop, though there are rumours of extending the bus route to the campsite.

Though there's a lot to be said for basing yourself at one of the quieter and more relaxing **beaches** like Palm Beach and Onetangi, many people prefer to stay close to Oneroa, for the convenience of being near the buses, restaurants, shops and other facilities.

Hotels, motels and B&Bs

Island View 9 Hauraki Rd, Palm Beach ⓣ09/372 9000, ⓔwaiheke@ihug.co.nz. A friendly, modern B&B with good sea views, but a fifteen-minute trek to the beach. ❺

Jungle's Edge 5a Crescent Rd West, Palm Beach ⓣ & ⓕ09/372 2283, ⓦhomepages.win.co.nz/windsors. Gay-run and gay-orientated B&B in a big modern home with a large secluded deck in the bush, ten minutes'

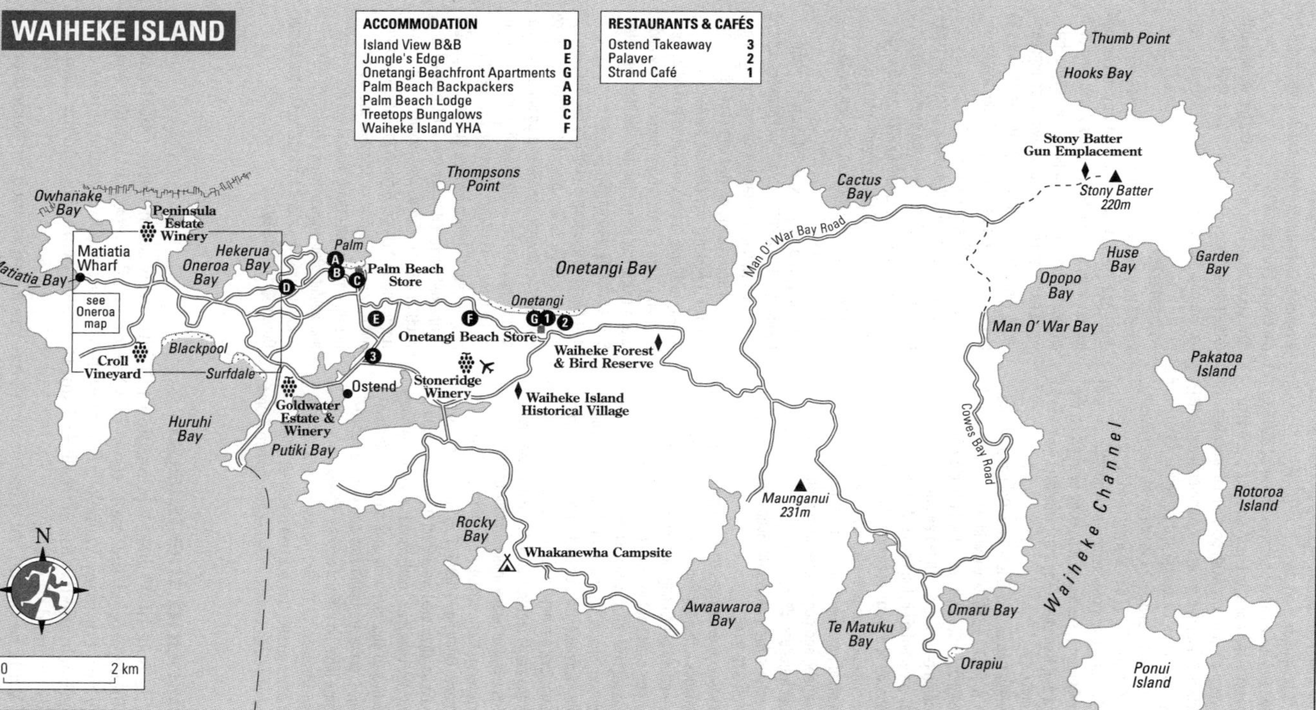
WAIHEKE ISLAND
ACCOMMODATION
Island View B&B D
Jungle's Edge E
Onetangi Beachfront Apartments G
Palm Beach Backpackers A
Palm Beach Lodge B
Treetops Bungalows C
Waiheke Island YHA F
RESTAURANTS & CAFÉS
Ostend Takeaway 3
Palaver 2
Strand Café 1
Auckland (20 km; 40 min)
Half Moon Bay (15 km; 1 hr 20 min)
Thumb Point
Hooks Bay
Stony Batter Gun Emplacement
Stony Batter 220m
Cactus Bay
Man O' War Bay Road
Garden Bay
Huse Bay
Opopo Bay
Man O' War Bay
Pakatoa Island
Cowes Bay Road
Waiheke Channel
Rotoroa Island
Ponui Island
Omaru Bay
Orapiu
Te Matuku Bay
Maunganui 231m
Awaawaroa Bay
Whakanewha Campsite
Rocky Bay
Thompsons Point
Onetangi Bay
Onetangi
Onetangi Beach Store
Waiheke Forest & Bird Reserve
Waiheke Island Historical Village
Stoneridge Winery
Palm
Palm Beach Store
Ostend
Goldwater Estate & Winery
Putiki Bay
Huruhi Bay
Surfdale
Blackpool
Croll Vineyard
see Oneroa map
Matiatia Wharf
Matiatia Bay
Owhanake Bay
Peninsula Estate Winery
Hekerua Bay
Oneroa Bay
N
0 2 km

stroll from Palm Beach. Includes cooked breakfast, pick up and drop off. ❻

Kiwi House 23 Kiwi St, Oneroa ⓣ09/372 9123, ⓔkiwihouse@clear.net.nz. A sociable place with several good rooms (with continental breakfast included); all have access to communal self-catering facilities, a TV lounge and barbecue. ❹

Palm Beach Lodge 23 Tiri View Rd, Palm Beach ⓣ & ⓕ09/372 7763, ⓦwww.ki-wi.co.nz/palmlodge.htm. Luxurious salmon-pink guesthouse with lovely rooms, each with a balcony overlooking the sea and free use of kayaks, mountain bikes and a dinghy. ❽

Punga Lodge 223 Ocean View Rd, Little Oneroa ⓣ & ⓕ372 6675, ⓦwww.ki-wi.co.nz/punga.htm. Delightful B&B, well set in the bush close to Oneroa beach, and with tea and muffins on tap all day provided by helpful hosts. Accommodation consists of a range of comfortable and spacious en-suite doubles with verandas, and four self-catering apartments of different sizes. There's a spa pool, and good-value off-season deals. Free boat transfers. ❺–❻

Treetops Bungalows Hill Road, Palm Beach ⓣ09/372 5146, ⓦwww.gotowaiheke.co.nz/tree.html. Two gorgeous cottages (often booked well ahead at weekends) beautifully set among verdant gardens. For character you can't beat the Treetops bungalow, an ancient bush cabin which sleeps three, has a full kitchen, phone, TV, stereo and laundry and comes with a continental breakfast; or go for the Luxury bungalow, a romantic self-contained hideaway with all the same features done to a higher standard plus a hydrotherapy mineral water bath. ❺–❼

Onetangi Beachfront Apartments 27 The Strand, Onetangi ⓣ09/372 7051, ⓦwww.onetangi.co.nz. Upgraded waterfront motel units with kayaks, volleyball court, sauna and two spa pools all free to guests. Some units are quite old fashioned, some are brand new and well-equipped, some have beachfront access. ❺–❼

Twin Gables 17 Tiri Rd, Oneroa ⓣ09/372 9877. Another goodie, this bed and breakfast offers excellent sea views from attractive modern rooms with shared facilities. ❺

Women's Guesthouse Hekerua Bay; call for directions ⓣ09/372 9284, ⓔw.guesthouse@clear.net.nz. Budget women-only retreat near a secluded bay with bush walks nearby. Evening meals available. ❸

Hostels

Fossil Bay Lodge 58 Korora Rd, Oneroa ⓣ09/372 7569. A haphazard and very relaxed collection of huts, small dorms and self-catering units all located five minutes' walk from an all-but private beach, a kilometre from town on an organic farm. Tent sites $10, dorms ❶, rooms ❷, units ❸

Hekerua Lodge 11 Hekerua Rd, Little Oneroa ⓣ & ⓕ09/372 8990, ⓦwww.ki-wi.co.nz/hekerua.htm. Peaceful and friendly, pool-equipped backpackers set in the bush ten minutes' walk from Little Oneroa Beach and Oneroa shops, and with additional private rooms and a self-contained unit. Tent sites $15, dorms ❶, rooms ❸, unit ❹

Palm Beach Backpackers 54 Palm Rd, Palm Beach ⓣ09/372 8662. Lively backpackers right by the beach with nice verandas, grassy lawns for camping and chalets divided into small dorms and doubles. Breakfast and evening barbecues are usually available, there are kayaks and bikes for rent, and there's a full programme of winery and island tours, kayaking trips and the like. Tent sites $12, dorms ❶, rooms ❷

Red Earth Homestay 6 Kennedy Rd, Surfdale ⓣ09/372 9975. A very peaceful and relaxed place that falls somewhere between a backpackers and a homestay with space for just five people (a twin and a three-bed dorm). There's a nice deck and easy access to beach and the Surfdale shops. ❶

Waiheke Island YHA Seaview Rd, Onetangi ⓣ & ⓕ09/372 8971, ⓔrobb.meg@bigfoot.com. A well-run associate YHA set high on the hill overlooking the beach, with a host of activities available to guests – mountain-biking, kayaking and snorkelling. Call Jaguar Tours (ⓣ09/372 7312) before leaving Auckland for transport to the hostel. Dorms ❶, rooms ❷

Around the island

The bulk of Waiheke's population inhabits the western quarter of the island, chiefly around the main town of **Oneroa**, a kilometre east of the Matiatia Wharf. For many, Waiheke's finest beaches lie east of Oneroa: the almost circular Enclosure Bay for snorkelling, Palm Beach for swimming, and the more surfie-oriented Onetangi.

Waiheke has no shortage of diversions once you've tired of baking on the beaches and cooling off in the surf. The lovely bays and headlands lend themselves to some short but often steep **walks** detailed in the free *Waiheke Island Walkways* leaflet, available from the visitor centre in Oneroa. One of the best and most accessible coastal tracks leads from Oneroa past Little Oneroa around to Enclosure Bay, while inland there's a shady stroll through the regenerating bush of the **Waiheke Forest and Bird Reserve**, up behind Onetangi. If you're still restless, take your pick from horse riding, kayaking, sailing and so on (see "Listings" on p.149).

Oneroa and around

The settlement of **ONEROA** is draped across a narrow isthmus between the sandy sweep of Oneroa Bay – one of the best and most accessible beaches on the island – and the shallow and silty Blackpool Beach. The ridge-top main street runs up to the island's visitor centre (see p.143), where you can pick up the free *Waiheke Winegrowers' Map* and a free leaflet about the *Arts & Crafts Trail* around the scattered **studios** of Waiheke's numerous artists and craftspeople; studio opening times tend to be erratic, so call ahead if you're set on visiting particular workshops (phone numbers are in the leaflet). Local artists' work is also displayed in the adjoining Artworks gallery (daily 10am–4pm; free). In the same building is the slightly eccentric **Whittaker's Musical Experience** (daily except Tues 10am–4pm; $3; ⓦwww.musical-museum.org), a room full of flageolets, piano accordions, player pianos, xylophones and more, some dating back two hundred years and all ably demonstrated during the "musical experience" performance (at 1pm; 1hr 30min; $10). Two of Waiheke's **vineyards** are easily accessible from Oneroa: the Peninsula Estate, 52a Korora Rd, 1km northwest of town (ⓣ09/372 7866; sales daily 1–4pm in summer; free tours and tastings by appointment only); and the more casual Mudbrick, 2km west on Church Bay Road (ⓣ09/372 9050, ⓦwww.mudbrick.co.nz; tasting daily in summer), where you should also investigate the attached *Mudbrick Vineyard Restaurant* (see "Eating and entertainment" on p.148).

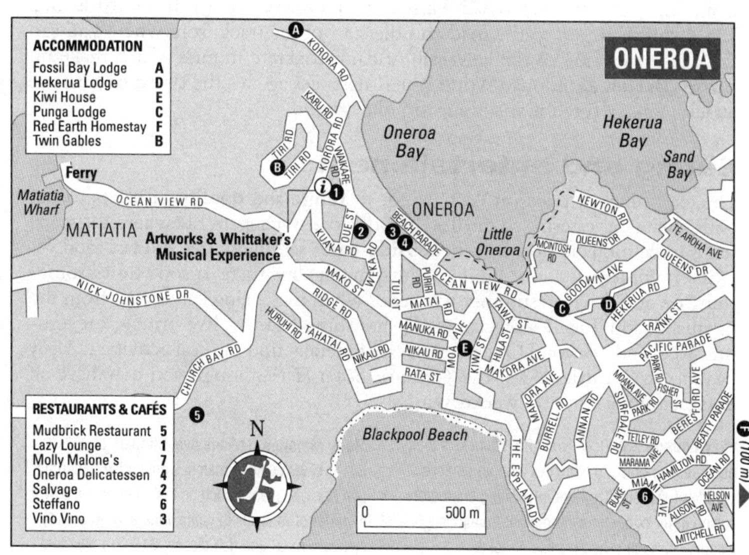

The rest of the island

What passes for a main road on Waiheke winds east from Oneroa through the contiguous settlements of Little Oneroa, Blackpool and Surfdale, and across the lagoon at Putaki Bay to **Ostend**. The island's light-industrial heart, far from any appealing beaches, Ostend is best ignored except on Saturday mornings (8am–1pm) when the Ostend Hall, corner of Ostend Rd and Belgium St, is given over to the **Ostend Market**, a very Waiheke affair with organic produce, arts and crafts, food stalls, massage, iridology readings and local entertainers.

A couple of Waiheke's most reputable **wineries** lie between here and Onetangi. At Goldwater Estate, 18 Causeway Rd (Ⓣ09/372 7493, Ⓦwww.goldwaterwine.com; sales and tastings daily 11am–4pm in summer), you can picnic in style, accompanied by one of their fine wines; you'll need to bring your own provisions, but there's no charge for glasses if you buy wine (typically $15 plus a bottle). The organic, hand-tended vineyards of Stonyridge, 80 Onetangi Rd (Ⓣ09/372 8822, Ⓦwww.stonyridge.co.nz), produce the world-class Larose, one of New Zealand's top Bordeaux-style reds. Each vintage is sold out before it's even bottled so there are often no cellar-door sales, but the **tour and tasting** (Sat & Sun 11.30am; $10) is entertaining and you can stick around for an excellent, al fresco meal in view of the vines, olive trees and cork oaks.

Six kilometres east of Oneroa, **Palm Beach** takes a neat bite out of the north coast, with houses tumbling down to a small sandy beach separated by a handful of rocks from the nude bathing zone at the western end. The Palm Beach Store rents boogie boards at $10 per day. Waiheke's longest and most exposed beach is **ONETANGI**, popular in summer with surfers, board riders and swimmers, and an occasional venue for beach horse races, usually Waitangi weekend at the beginning of February. The beachside Onetangi Beach Store rents waveskis ($10 an hour) and boogie boards ($5 an hour).

There are no shops or restaurants east of Onetangi, just tracts of open farm land riddled with fledgling vineyards and bordered by fine swimming beaches. One of the best of these is **Cactus Bay**, which is accessible down a short track from Man O' War Bay Road, 6km east of Oneroa. Jaguar Tours (Ⓣ09/372 7312) runs trips out to the road end the start of the track from where you can walk just over 1km to the labyrinth of dank concrete tunnels which make up **Stony Batter**, abandoned World War II defences against the threat of Japanese attack – take a torch if you want to poke around.

Eating and entertainment

Oneroa is unchallenged on Waiheke for its **range** and **quality** of places to eat, with restaurants catering to the demands of city day-trippers. Elsewhere, the scene tends to be more ad hoc, with **beachside cafés** serving snacks and fast food.

Entertainment is more limited and sporadic, but there is sometimes something on at *Salvage* on summer weekends when they bring bands over from the mainland, and *Vino Vino* occasionally has some form of **live music** on summer weekends. Beyond Oneroa, you can generally find musical activity at *Molly Malones* in Surfdale and at the *Onetangi Beach Hotel*, though you may have an enforced quiet time on weekday nights.

Lazy Lounge 139 Oceanview Rd. Waiheke's loosest café. The place to hang out with an endless parade of the island's more interesting characters calling in for coffee, mushroom and pumpkin lasagne, pizza or a hearty slice of cake.

Molly Malones 6 Miami Ave, Surfdale Ⓣ09/372 8011, Ⓦwww.molly-malones.com. Irish restaurant and bar with dishes such as Irish beef stew ($14), a starter of mussels in white wine and garlic ($8), standard meat and fish dishes ($18–25) plus that all important Guinness and Kilkenny. Live music at weekends and garden seating.

Mudbrick Vineyard Restaurant Church Bay Road, 2km west of Oneroa ☎09/372 9050. Expensive but highly regarded restaurant serving delicious Mediterranean-inspired meals, often with a lot of game on the menu. Lunch & dinner daily in summer with mains approaching $30.

Oneroa Delicatessen 153 Ocean View Rd, Oneroa. The best, though somewhat pricey, place in town for wholesome quiches, panini, sumptuous cakes and a range of breakfast and lunch dishes served with good coffee.

Ostend Takeaways 30 Belgium St, Ostend ☎09/372 8463. The island's best chippy and burger bar, and they deliver.

Palaver The Strand, Onetangi ☎09/372 8028. Lounge bar in the *Onetangi Beach Hotel* also serving fairly standard bar food at modest prices.

Pizzeria and caffe da Stefano Miami Ave, Surfdale ☎09/372 5309. Coffee, panini and good pizza restaurant that will deliver for larger orders. BYO only. Closed Mon.

Salvage Pendragon Mall, Oneroa ☎09/372 2273. Opposite *Vino Vino*, and in a similar vein – but with higher prices, grander aspirations and variable results.

Strand Café At the beach store, The Strand, Onetangi. Casual place, serving breakfasts, light meals and takeaways.

Vino Vino 153 Ocean View Rd, Oneroa ☎09/372 9888. Hard to beat for light meals, extending to bruschetta, warm salads and daily blackboard specials. Eat inside, or out on the deck with fabulous views across to the Coromandel.

Listings

Horse riding Shepherd's Point Riding Centre, 91 Ostend Rd, Ostend (☎09/372 8104) has a two-hour beach ride ($60), or a full-day bush-and-beach session ($100, including lunch).

Internet access There's a cybercafé at the *Lazy Lounge* (see p.148) and internet access at Rafael's Gallery, in the ArtWorks complex beside the visitor centre.

Kayaking Ross Adventures (☎09/372 5550, Ⓦwww.kayakwaiheke.co.nz) runs from Matiatia and offers four-hour paddles ($60), moonlit evening trips (3hr; $60), full-day trips including a shuttle back to your starting point ($110) and round-the-island camping trips (2–4 days; $110 per day). They also rent sea kayaks from $30 a half-day. The Kayak Company (☎09/372 2112, Ⓦwww.thekayakcompany.co.nz) offers an almost identical range of tours at similar prices.

Medical emergencies Waiheke Island Community Health Services, 5 Belgium St, Ostend (☎09/372 5005).

Sailing Matangi Sailing Adventures (☎09/372 3377, Ⓔwaihekebooking@actrix.co.nz) runs half-day, full-day and overnight sailing trips, providing fishing lines and the chance to barbecue your catch, for roughly $80 a day with a two-person minimum.

Taxis Dial-a-Cab ☎09/372 3000; Waiheke Taxi ☎09/372 8038; Waiheke Tuk Tuk ☎09/372 6127.

Great Barrier Island (Aotea)

Rugged and sparsely populated **Great Barrier Island** (Aotea) lies 90km northeast of Auckland on the outer fringes of the Hauraki Gulf and, though only 30km long and 15km wide, packs in a mountainous heart which drops away to deep indented harbours in the west and eases gently to golden surf beaches in the east. It's only a two-hour ferry or half-hour plane ride from the big city but seems a world apart, almost anachronistic in its lack of mains electricity or a reticulated water supply. There are no towns to speak of, no industry and no regular public transport, lending Great Barrier that sense of peace and detachment unique to island life, enhanced by **beaches**, **hot springs** and **tightly packed mountains** clad in bush and spared the ravages of deer and possums.

Ferries arrive in **Tryphena**, the southern harbour and major settlement, some continuing up the west coast to the minuscule hamlets of **Whangaparapara** and **Port Fitzroy**, both ideal jumping-off points for tramps in the Great Barrier Forest. **Claris**, in the east, is the site of the main airport and is convenient for the best beaches at **Medlands** and **Awana Bay**.

Some history

Great Barrier is formed from the same line of extinct **volcanoes** as the Coromandel Peninsula, and shares a common geological and human past. Aotea was one of the places first populated by **Maori**, and the Ngatiwai and Ngatimaru people were occupying numerous *pa* sites when Cook sailed by in 1769; recognizing the calming influence of Aotea and neighbouring Hauturu on the waters of the Hauraki Gulf, Cook renamed them Great Barrier Island and Little Barrier Island. The vast stands of kauri all over the island were soon seized upon for ships' timbers, the first load being taken in 1791. Kauri **logging** didn't really get under way until the late nineteenth century but continued until 1942, outliving some early copper mining at Miners Head and sporadic attempts to extract gold and silver from a large quartz intrusion in the centre of the island. Kauri logging and gum digging were replaced by a short-lived whale-oil extraction industry at Whangaparapara in the 1950s, but the Barrier soon fell back on tilling the poor clay soils and its peak population of over 5000 dropped back to little more than 1000.

The space and tranquillity of the island appealed to budding alternative lifestylers, many of whom trickled across from the mainland in the 1960s and 1970s. Much of the Seventies idealism has been supplanted by a more modern pragmatism, but **self-sufficiency** remains. Now more of a necessity in the face of isolation than a lifestyle choice, many people grow their own vegetables; everyone has their own water supply and the load on diesel generators is eased by wind-driven turbines and solar panels. However, **agriculture** is beginning to take a back seat to **tourism** and second-home-owners – a trend resisted to some degree by islanders, who fear that the Barrier will become just another commuter suburb for Auckland. Despite the island's inclusion within the domain of Auckland City Council in 1993, at present this seems unlikely, especially since the fast ferry service introduced in 1992 recently cut back services to just a couple of months over the summer. Still, a new entrepreneurial spirit has resulted in dilapidated lodges being bought by ambitious owners keen to make the Barrier a real destination.

Arrival, information and getting around

Points of entry are the **airport** at Claris on the east coast, the grass airstrip at Okiwi in the north, and the three main **harbours** of Port Fitzroy, Whangaparapara and Tryphena Harbour. Around the first two ports there's little more than a couple of lodges and a shop, leaving the bulk of the activity to the four main bays of Tryphena Harbour. Ferries arrive at Shoal Bay, from where shuttle buses run to Mulberry Grove, where there's a motel, or on to Stonewall Village, where there are several places to stay and eat, and a shop. Puriri Bay is a short walk along the coast from Stonewall Village. **Bad weather** occasionally causes ferries to be cancelled, but you can pre-empt the inconvenience this may cause by buying a boat/fly deal ($125), flying back or out and taking the ferry the other way.

The vast majority of visitors arrive from Auckland over the summer months aboard Fullers **ferries** (ⓣ09/367 9111; Christmas to early Jan daily, Labour weekend (at the end of October), plus early Dec–Christmas & early Jan–Feb 3–4 weekly; 2hr), which runs to Tryphena for $99 ($89 if booked 3 days in advance; bikes free). Shuttle buses meet the ferry, charging around $5–10 to Stonewall Village, $10–15 to Medlands: ask around when you arrive.

With less urgency (or a desire to bring a car), travel with Sealink (ⓣ09/373 4036 & 0800/732 546, ⓦwww.subritzky.co.nz), which runs two comfortable barges carrying passengers, cars and just about all the island's freight, leaving Wynyard Wharf in Auckland (Christmas–Jan daily, Feb–Christmas 5 weekly; 4hr) for Tryphena, with one service a week (Tues) continuing to Port Fitzroy. Fares are $75 return for foot passengers and $250 return for a car ($440 in Dec & Jan).

To slot into the island pace as soon as you leave Auckland, travel from Marsden Wharf, close to Auckland's Ferry Building, with Great Barrier Shipping Co. (in Auckland ⓣ09/307 1405, on the island ⓣ09/429 0431, ⓕ307 0475; $50 return) which uses a former lighthouse service ship for its twice weekly six-hour service. The Tuesday service calls at Whangaparapara, Tryphena and then back to Auckland; the Thursday run goes to Tryphena, Whangaparapara and Port Fitzroy where it stays overnight, returning to Auckland the next day.

Some visitors prefer the reliability of daily **flights**. The two main players are Great Barrier Airlines (ⓣ09/275 9120 & 0800/900 600, ⓔgba@gbair.co.nz; $189) and Great Barrier Xpress (ⓣ0800/222 123 & 09/256 7025, ⓦwww.mountainair.co.nz; $174 return), both of which operate at least three scheduled flights a day from Auckland International Airport to Claris; services are met by shuttle buses which drop off in Medlands ($10 each way) and Tryphena ($12 each way). GBA also flies from the Barrier to Whangarei, Whitianga and Tauranga around three times a week.

Information

The island's **visitor centre** (daily 9am–4pm; ⓣ & ⓕ09/429 0033, ⓦwww.greatbarrier.co.nz) is opposite Claris airfield. The main **DOC office** is the well-stocked and informative Port Fitzroy Field Base (Mon–Fri 8am–4.30pm; ⓣ09/429 0044, ⓕ429 0071), ten minutes' walk west of the Port Fitzroy wharf. Note that there are **no banks** or ATMs on the island but several places have EFTPOS facilities.

Getting around

Great Barrier has no scheduled public transport in the usual sense, though there is a **bus service** run by Aotea Bus (Nov–March daily, April–Oct Mon–Fri only; ⓣ0800/426 832 & 09/429 0055) which travels from Tryphena to Port Fitzroy and back once a day; their Super Travel Pass ($40 for seven days unlimited travel) may be useful. They also run a shuttle service which meets planes and ferries, as do *Stray Possum Lodge* (see p.154). Prices depend on numbers but expect from $10 from Tryphena to Medlands and $15 to continue on to the hot springs. Safari Tours & Travel (ⓣ09/429 0448) do a good all-day island **tour** ($45) in direct competition with Bob's Island Tours (ⓣ09/420 0988; $45), which venture off the beaten track a little more. Both these companies also operate as the island's **taxi** services.

Many people **rent a car** for at least part of their stay, but rates are high, at around $85 for one day, dropping to $60 a day for longer rentals; note that all roads are gravel except for the run from Tryphena to Claris. **Mountain bikes** can be rented for around $25 a day, though the hills are steep and the roads dusty and hot in summer. See "Listings", p.157, for details of car- and bike-rental outfits.

Accommodation

Accommodation on Great Barrier is broad ranging. Walkers and campers are well catered for with some pleasant but basic campsites, a trampers' **hut** and a

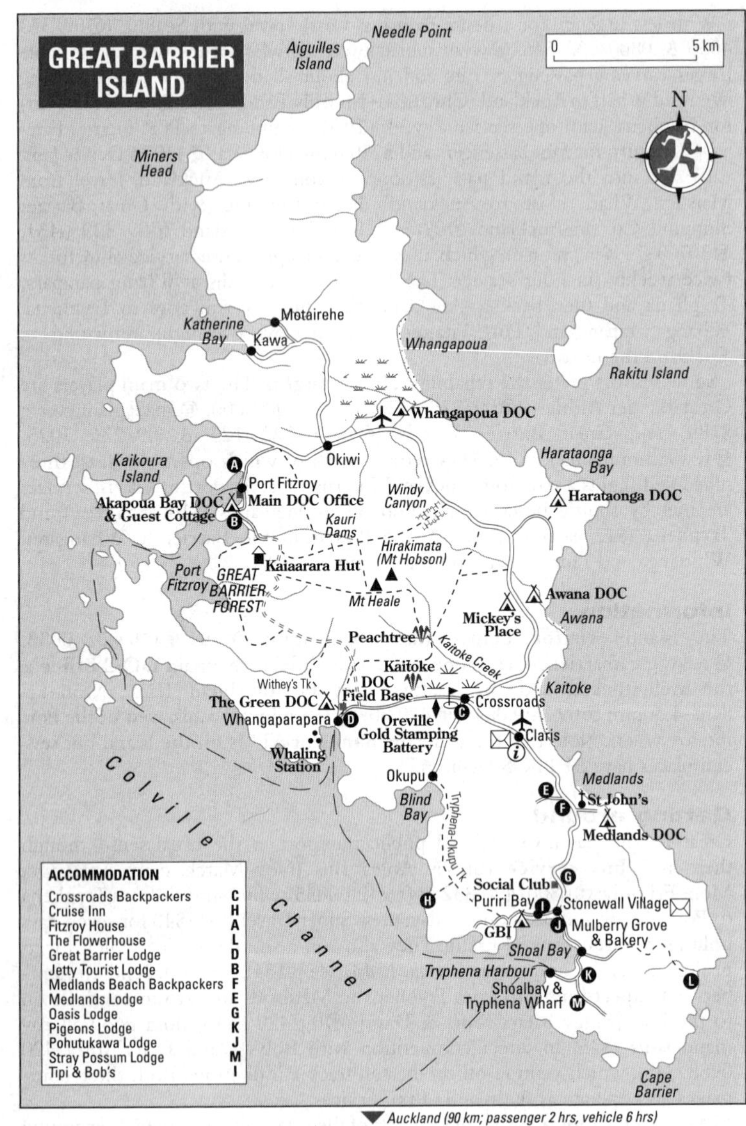

cabin, which is well set up for groups. Most of these are towards the north of the island, close to the Great Barrier Forest: all six **DOC campsites** are marked on the map above, and tend to be empty most of the year except for Christmas to the end of January when you should definitely book in advance (☎09/429 0044); note that camping is not permitted outside designated campsites. There are several backpacker **hostels** scattered across the island, but most of the rest of the accommodation is concentrated around Tryphena Harbour and ranges from comfortable guesthouses to high-class **lodges**. Some of the best of the island's **self-catering cottages** are given below, but there are many more on lists held by the visitor centre; the owners often live close by and can arrange breakfast and sometimes dinner. In fact, given the dearth of places to eat, many lodges and **guesthouses** also have self-catering units.

Some places **pick up** from the harbours and airport, though those in Tryphena and Medlands will expect you to catch the transport which meets each boat or plane. The island's remoteness means that accommodation is generally more **expensive** than the mainland, particularly through the summer; some places further boost their rates from Christmas to the end of January when visitor numbers are at their peak – and you'll need to **book well ahead** to stand any chance of finding a place to stay. The price codes we've given below are based on standard summer prices.

Lodges, guesthouses and cottages

DOC Guest Cottage Port Fitzroy ⓣ09/429 0044. Fully-equipped cottage sleeping up to ten, with gas cooking and wood supplied for barbecues. It is beautifully sited at Port Fitzroy adjacent to the DOC office and campsite and ten minutes' walk from the wharf. ❸

The Flowerhouse Rosalie Bay ⓣ09/429 0464, ⓔflower@greatbarrier.co.nz. One beautiful guest room in a retreat tucked away in a remote valley, where the emphasis is on peace and healthy living. The room is let on a full-board basis, with meals made from home-grown organic produce. Free pick-up from Tryphena. ❼

Fitzroy House Glenfern Rd, Port Fitzroy ⓣ09/429 0091, ⓦwww.fitzroyhouse.co.nz. One very comfortable self-contained cottage sleeping six, with views over the northern shore of the inner harbour. The emphasis here is on nature tourism with free use of canoes and a dinghy (sea kayaks are extra), a lovely walkway with a bridge to the top of a kauri, and combination walks where you get dropped off by Unimog (a kind of 4WD German military truck), do a hike, then get picked up by yacht. Bring your own food. ❻

Great Barrier Lodge Whangaparapara Harbour ⓣ09/429 0488, ⓦwww.greatbarrierlodge.com. This is pretty much all there is at Whangaparapara, and the comfortable harbourside lodge also serves as the local shop. Accommodation is in cottages and studio units, and the main building houses a bar and restaurant serving home-style meals. Mountain bikes and kayaks are free for guests and there are rental cars from $95. Bunkroom $30pp, rooms & studios ❻

Jetty Tourist Lodge Kaiaarara Bay, Port Fitzroy ⓣ09/429 0050, ⓕ429 0908. Superbly sited place with bar and restaurant overlooking Kaiaarara Bay, around 2km from Port Fitzroy Wharf. B&B accommodation is in nicely decorated, self-contained chalets. ❻

Medlands Lodge Masons Rd ⓣ09/429 0352, ⓕ429 0993. Two self-contained units in a rural setting 2km from the beach with an on-site restaurant. ❻

Oasis Lodge Stonewall, Tryphena ⓣ09/429 0021, ⓦwww.barrieroasis.co.nz. One of the finest places on the island, with lovely en-suite rooms and great valley views and a couple of separate self-contained units. Rooms are let on a B&B basis, though you are encouraged to go full-board with delicious Asian-influenced meals included. Unit ❼, rooms ❽

Pigeons Lodge Shoal Bay Rd, Tryphena ⓣ09/429 0437, ⓦwww.pigeonslodge.co.nz. Small, comfortable and classy B&B nestled in the bush near the sea, with en-suite accommodation, a self-catering chalet and a good licensed restaurant. ❺

Pohutukawa Lodge Stonewall, Tryphena ⓣ09/429 0211, ⓔplodge@xtra.co.nz. The pick of the places around Tryphena, homely, small and welcoming, with a great pub and restaurant spilling out onto the veranda and peaceful garden, all conveniently close to the shop; there are international newspapers on hand, and aromatherapy massage is available. Attractive rooms are let on a B&B basis, and there are compact three-bed backpacker dorms. Dorms ❶, B&B ❺

Tipi & Bob's Waterfront Lodge Puriri Bay Rd, Tryphena ⓣ & ⓕ09/429 0550, ⓦwww.waterfrontlodge.co.nz. Good but pricey motel rooms, some with fine sea views, plus a self-contained cottage. ❺–❻

Hostels

Cruise Inn Schooner Bay Rd ⓣ025/534 134. Beautifully sited but simple backpacker dorm accommodation that takes a bit of effort to reach but is well worth it for the isolation and the alternative lifestyle it espouses. It's about three hours' walk through bushland from Stonewall or about an hour's paddle by kayak (see "Listings" on p.157). Phone for directions, and remember to bring all the food you'll need unless you arrange full board (from $45 per person). ❶

Crossroads Backpackers Lodge 1 Blind Bay Rd, Crossroads ⓣ09/429 0889, ⓦwww.scwl.demon.co.uk/crossroads/. Newish hostel with cabins let by the person, and double rooms, well sited in the middle of the island, close to the airport and facilities in Claris and within walking distance of the hot springs and island tramps. Beds ❶, rooms ❸

Medlands Beach Backpackers 9 Mason Rd ⓣ09/429 0320, ⓦwww.medlandsbeach.com. Basic and low-key backpackers with two- and four-bed dorms, doubles and a secluded chalet on a small farm ten minutes' walk from Medlands Beach – making this place popular with surfers. There are boogie boards, mountain bikes and snorkelling gear for guests' use, but there are no meals and no shops nearby, so bring all your food with you. ❶–❸

Stray Possum Lodge Shoal Bay ⓣ0800/767 786 & ⓣ & ⓕ09/429 0109; ⓦwww.straypossum.com. Very much part of the backpacker circuit, this activity-orientated hostel has a bar and on-site licensed pizza restaurant (which also serves breakfast) set in a spacious clearing in attractive bush. Beds are in four- to six-bed dorms or in well-appointed self-contained chalets ideal for groups of up to six. Daily trips visit the hot springs or drop-off for walks and horse rides, and there are mountain bikes, kayaks, snorkelling gear and surfboards for rent (see also "Tours" in Listings on p.157 for details of package deals from Auckland). Tent sites $12, dorms ❶, made-up rooms ❸, chalets ❻

Campsites

Akapoua DOC Campsite Orama. Harbour-edge site right by the DOC office and an easy walk to the harbour and shop at Port Fitzroy. It comes equipped with coin-operated barbecues, cold showers and toilets. Tent sites $7.

Awana DOC Campsite Awana. Exposed site with separate tent and vehicle sites, all 400m from a good surf beach. Cold showers and toilets. Tent sites $7.

GBI Campground Puriri Bay, Tryphena ⓣ09/429 0184. A quiet sheltered campground nestled in bush by a fresh water stream near a safe swimming beach, 20min walk to shops. $8.50 per person.

The Green DOC Campsite Whangaparapara. Basic campsite with barbecues, water and toilets but without vehicular access. No showers but it's close to the sea and there's a stream to wash in. Tent sites $7.

Harataonga DOC Campsite Harataonga. Shady site 300m back from the beach, equipped with toilets and cold showers. Tent sites $7.

Medlands DOC Campsite Medlands Beach. Attractive beach-back site that gets very crowded in the peak season. Cold showers, stream water and toilets. Tent sites $7.

Mickey's Place Awana ⓣ09/429 0170. Hospitable commercial campsite 25km north of Tryphena that's less well-sited than the nearby DOC site but features hot showers, toilets and a cookhouse, all for $5.

Around the island

Places which would be regarded as sights in the usual sense are thin on the ground on Great Barrier, and most of those that do exist require some perseverance to get to. Much of the pleasure here is in lazing on the beaches and striking out on foot into the **Great Barrier Forest**, a rugged chunk of bush and kauri-logging relics that takes up about a third of the island between Port Fitzroy and Whangaparapara. If you're looking for more structure to your day, there are a few small-time operators keen to keep you entertained by means of various activities and tours (see "Listings", p.157, for details). Tryphena has a particular dearth of things to do, though there is the appealing **Tryphena to Okupu Walking Track** (4hr) from Puriri Bay around coastal headlands to Okupu on Blind Bay.

Most people head straight for **Medlands Beach**, a long sweep of golden sands broken by a sheltering island and often endowed with some of the Barrier's best surf – though, be warned, there is no patrolled area. The pretty blue and white **St John's Church** looks somewhat out of place – and it is, having only been moved here in 1986, making the journey from the mainland by barge before being dragged over the dunes.

North of Medlands, the road leaves the coast for the airport at **Claris**, where the post office runs the gimmicky **Great Barrier Pigeon-Gram Service** (summer only; $20 to send a pigeon-gram letter) in imitation of the original pigeon-mail service – said to be the world's first airmail service – set up in 1898 after it took a sobering three days to notify Auckland that the SS *Wairarapa* had been wrecked on the northwest coast. Birds took under two hours to cover the same distance, and were used until 1908 when a telephone was finally established. One or two letters are now attached to birds which fly to Auckland, where the letters are forwarded anywhere in the world.

Crossroads, 2km north of Claris, is just that – the junction of roads to Okupu, Port Fitzroy and the north of the island, and Whangaparapara. The Whangaparapara road runs past the scant roadside remains of the **Oreville gold stamping battery** (unrestricted entry) and the start of a path to **Kaitoke Hot Springs** (4km; 1hr 20min return; also on the Great Barrier Forest Tramp – see box on p.156–7), sulphurous dammed pools that aren't especially pretty but are perfect for an hour's wallowing. At Whangaparapara itself, a short stroll around the bay brings you to the foundations of a whaling station built here in the 1950s.

North from Crossroads, the Port Fitzroy road passes two excellent camping spots by the surf beach at Awana Bay, then the start of a short track to **Windy Canyon** (1km; 20–30min return), a narrow defile that gets its name from the eerie sounds produced by certain wind conditions. A narrow path winds through nikau palms and tree ferns to a viewpoint that gives a sense of the island's interior, as well as fabulous coastal views.

The island's highest point, Hirakimata, can be reached in three hours from here or a similar time from **PORT FITZROY**, whose harbour remains remarkably calm under most wind conditions, a property not lost on the dozens of yachties who flock here in summer. Apart from the shop and a few places to stay there's not a lot here, but Port Fitzroy makes the best base for **tramping** or shorter day-walks to some fine **kauri dams** (see box overleaf for details of long and short routes). For three years from 1926, the Kauri Timber Company hacked trees out of the relatively inaccessible Kaiaarara Valley, shunning the tramways and trestle bridges employed in more manageable terrain in favour of six kauri dams – wooden structures up to twenty metres high and spanning the valley floor. Logs were cut and rolled into the reservoirs as the stream built up the water level behind the dams. The upper dams were then tripped, followed seconds later by the lower dams; the combined releases sent a torrent of water and logs sluicing down to Kaiaarara Bay, where they were lashed together in rafts and floated to Auckland.

Eating and drinking

The absence of stand-alone **restaurants** forces pretty much everywhere that provides a bed for the night to offer meals and drinks for both guests and non-residents; always book in advance. There's also a couple of shops where you can get snacks when you're on the move and pick up picnic provisions. **Drinking** tends to happen in bars attached to accommodation establishments or in the social clubs at Tryphena and Claris.

Barrier Oasis Lodge Stonewall, Tryphena ⓣ09/429 0021, ⓦwww.barrieroasis.co.nz. Delicious meals using local and home-grown produce (including their own Cabernet Sauvignon and olive oil), frequently with Thai, Indian or seafood themes. The luncheon platter costs around $20,

The Great Barrier forest tramp

The only decent walking map is the 1:50,000 Great Barrier Island Holidaymaker *($15); DOC also print a* Track Information *leaflet ($2 from DOC offices) which will just about do for most purposes.*

The **Great Barrier Forest**, New Zealand's largest stand of possum-free bush, offers a **unique** tramping **environment**. Because the area is so compact, in no time at all you can find yourself climbing in and out of little subtropical gullies luxuriant with nikau palms, tree ferns, regenerating rimu and kauri, up onto scrubby manuka ridges with stunning coastal and mountain views. Many of the tracks follow the routes of mining tramways past old kauri dams.

Access and huts

The tramp can be done equally well from Port Fitzroy or Whangaparapara, both having a reasonably well-stocked shop, a campsite and other accommodation. Port Fitzroy also has a 24-bunk **hut** nearby (Category 2; $10), with the advantage of the main DOC office (☎09/429 0044; Mon–Fri 8am–4.30pm), which sells hut **tickets** and **maps**; the Whangaparapara DOC residence has leaflets available in the porch. In addition, Port Fitzroy's beautifully sited *Akapoua Bay* **campsite** ($7) is superior to Whangaparapara's simple site, *The Green* ($7).

If you have come specifically to tramp it is best to catch a ferry direct to Port Fitzroy, or call one of the shuttle operators in advance to organize transport from the airport or Tryhphena.

The tramp

From the wharf at **Port Fitzroy**, follow the coast road fifteen minutes south to the DOC office. From there the road climbs for half an hour over a headland with views over Kaiaarara and Rarohara bays, to a gate. The Kaiaarara Hut is roughly fifteen minutes on, along a 4WD track and across a couple of river fords. From **Kaiaarara Hut to Whangaparapara** (13km; 7–9hr; 800m ascent), the track soon leaves the 4WD track and crosses the Kaiaarara Stream several times as it climbs steeply to the first and most impressive **kauri dam** (see p.155), reached in under an hour. The well-defined path continues for another fifty minutes to one of the upper dams then

while evening meals are table d'hôte and will set you back $40.

Claris Texas Café Claris ☎09/429 0811. Easily the best café on the island with a sunny deck and a grassy patch for the kids. It's open 8am–5pm daily for light meals, panini, great desserts and excellent coffee; then for a la carte evening meals (summer nightly, winter Thurs–Sat) which might include chargrilled calamari or pan-fried sole with ginger and chive hollandaise.

Currach Irish Pub Stonewall, Tryphena. An Irish Pub that's about as traditional as you can get on a South Pacific island – a lot of the paraphernalia came from the owner's grandmother's pub, in County Kerry, which closed in 1950. What's more they have Murphy's and Kilkenny on tap, and there's often live acoustic music, especially on Thursday when anyone is welcome to jam. Full breakfasts are served until 9.30am, and in the evening you might expect seafood chowder ($7.50), sirloin steak "pohutukawa" ($18.50), fish 'n' chips ($11), or one of the chef's daily specials.

The Flowerhouse Rosalie Bay ☎09/429 0464. Lunches made from home-grown organic produce, including olives, their own fresh pasta and delicious cheese, for around $23. Reservations are essential and they'll pick you up from Tryphena.

Great Barrier Island Sports & Social Club Whangaparapara Road, at the foot of the road to Medlands Beach ☎09/429 0260. Cavernous public bar with pool tables and bar meals (Wed, Fri & Sat).

Great Barrier Lodge Whangaparapara Harbour. Bar and restaurant serving home-style meals indoors or on the spacious deck with harbour views.

Jetty Tourist Lodge Kaiaarara Bay, Port Fitzroy ☎09/429 0050. Spacious restaurant with a large deck and a bar overlooking the bay. Hearty Kiwi meat and seafood dishes go for around $20, and

begins a long and arduous series of boardwalks and wooden steps designed to keep trampers on the path and prevent the disturbance of nesting black petrels. It'll take a good thirty to forty minutes to reach the summit of the 621-metre **Hirakimata** (Mount Hobson), where you'll be amply rewarded by panoramic views.

Less extensive boardwalks extend south around the dramatic spire of Mount Heale towards the junction of **two paths**. To the right a path follows the south branch of the Kaiaarara Stream **back to the Kaiaarara Hut** in around an hour and a half, making a four-to-five-hour circuit from the hut. The leftmost path follows an undulating but gradually descending route into Kaitoke Creek No.1 eventually reaching the edge of Kaitoke Swamp right by the hard-to-locate **Peach Tree Hot Spring**. Originally dug by kauri loggers, the pools here are hotter than the more widely used **Kaitoke Hot Springs** – the latter reached along a ten-minute track which spurs off south twenty minutes ahead; the more attractive hollows are to be found upstream. Back on the main track, you soon reach the 4WD forest road: follow it south for a hundred metres or so, then join the signposted track to the former site of Whangaparapara Hut, fifteen minutes on. From here it's ten minutes' walk to the DOC residence and half an hour to the Whangaparapara Wharf.

There are two main routes from **Whangaparapara to Kaiaarara Hut**, the direct and dull route following the Pack Track due north of the former site of Whangaparapara Hut and the 4WD forest road (11km; 5hr; 200m ascent), and the more appealing semi-coastal Kiwiriki Track (12km; 6hr; 300m ascent) which branches off the 4WD forest road just north of its junction with the Pack Track. The track cuts west from the forest road by the rocky knob of Maungapiko, leading to the picnic area at Kiwiriki Bay then climbing steeply over a ridge to Coffins Creek before a relatively gentle walk to a second picnic area at **Kaiaarara Bay.** From here it is half an hour to Kaiaarara Hut and another hour or so to the Port Fitzroy Wharf.

An alternative start to either route eschews the Pack Track and follows the far more interesting **Withey's Track**, which starts between the Whangaparapara DOC field base and the former hut site; it takes half an hour longer, but goes through some lovely bush with delightful streamside nikau groves.

breakfasts, lunches and Devonshire teas are also served.

Pigeons Lodge Shoal Bay Rd, Tryphena ⓣ09/429 0437. Guests and visitors alike can avail themselves of this guesthouse's charming licensed restaurant and eat out on the deck (mains around $20).

Tipi & Bob's Waterfront Lodge Puriri Bay, Tryphena ⓣ09/429 0550. The rather soulless public bar and leafy garden bar are always popular spots, as is the spartan seafood restaurant serving $20–25 mains and cheaper takeaways.

Listings

Bike rental *Stray Possum Lodge* and *Great Barrier Lodge* both rent bikes to guests, or try Great Barrier Hire Centre in Claris (ⓣ09/429 0417), which rents machines to all comers.

Car rental On the southern half of the island, try Tryphena's Better Bargain Rental (ⓣ09/429 0092), and in the north call Aotea Rentals (ⓣ & ⓕ09/429 0055).

Fishing To test Great Barrier's enviable reputation, head out for a day's fishing in the Colville Channel aboard any of the Tryphena-based boats who charge $400–500 a day for four people: try the *Vitamin C* (ⓣ09/429 0949) or the *Mokum* (ⓣ09/429 0485).

Golf Pioneer Park, Whangaparapara Rd, Claris (ⓣ09/429 0420; green fee $10, club rental $5), is a nine-hole par-three course surrounded by bush and with pukeko strutting across the fairways; every Thursday and Sunday the lively bar serves cheap drinks and decent meals.

Horse riding Great Barrier Island Adventure Horse Treks (ⓣ09/429 0274) will take you out onto the

beach and hinterland for $30 per hour.
Internet *Crossroads Backpackers Lodge* (see p.154) has internet facilities open to all.
Kayaking Tryphena-based Great Barrier Island Kayak Hire (ⓣ 09/429 0520, ⓔ bruce@islands.co.nz) rents double and single kayaks at $10/hr or $40 a day; and *Great Barrier Lodge* and *Fitzroy House* both rent kayaks. Aotea Kayak (ⓣ 09/429 0664) operates all year and run short paddling trips ($30), and joint 4–5hr kayak and snorkelling trips ($55).
Scuba diving Tryphena-based Destination Aotea (ⓣ 09/429 0449) runs dives with all equipment included ($130) exploring some of New Zealand's best locations, with wrecks, varied undersea terrain and stacks of marine life to explore, all in conditions of good visibility (especially in autumn).
Tours *Stray Possum* (ⓣ 0800/767 786) offers the "Possum Pursuit Pass" ($45), which includes mountain biking, kayaking, trips and activities for as long as you stay at the lodge; package deals include the pass plus ferry transport to and from Auckland ($120), a loop from Auckland to the Barrier by ferry, a flight on to Whitianga with Coromandel Air then bus back to Auckland, or vice versa ($155), and a weekend package ($155) including return ferry trip from Auckland, island transport, a Saturday night barbecue and two nights accommodation.

Tiritiri Matangi

No one with even the vaguest interest in New Zealand's wonderful birdlife should pass up the opportunity to visit **Tiritiri Matangi**, a low island 4km off the tip of the Whangaparaoa Peninsula and 30km north of Auckland. Tiritiri Matangi is run as an "open sanctuary", and visitors are free to roam through the predator-free bush where, within a couple of hours, it's quite possible to see takahe, saddlebacks, whiteheads, North Island robins, kokako, parakeets and brown teals. To stand a chance of seeing the little-spotted kiwi, you'll have to be here at night.

Judging by evidence from *pa* sites on the island, Tiritiri Matangi was first populated by the Kawerau **Maori** and later by the Ngati Paoa, both of whom are now recognized as the land's traditional owners. They partly **cleared the island** of bush, a process continued by Europeans who arrived in the mid-nineteenth century to graze sheep and cattle. Fortunately, **predators** such as possums, stoats, weasels, deer, cats, wallabies and the like failed to get a foothold on Tiritiri, so after farming became uneconomic in the early 1970s it was singled out as a prime site for helping to restore barely viable bird populations. The cacophony of birdsong in the Tiritiri bush is stark evidence of just how catastrophic the impact of these predators has been elsewhere.

When grazing stopped, a **reforestation** programme was implemented: a quarter of a million saplings raised from seeds found on the island have been planted out to form rapidly regenerating bush, though it is still far from mature. The **birds** seem to like it, however, and are mostly thriving – with nesting boxes standing in for decaying trees, and feeding stations equipped with video cameras and pressure-sensitive perches that weigh birds each time they alight.

Three of the species released here are among the rarest in the world, with total populations of around a couple of hundred. The most visible are the flightless **takahe**, lumbering blue-green turkey-sized birds long thought to be extinct (see p.932 for more on these ungainly critters); birds moved here from Fiordland have bred well and are easily spotted as they seem unafraid of humans and are very inquisitive. **Saddlebacks** and **stitchbirds** (of which only seventy survive anywhere) both stick to the bush, but often reveal themselves if you sit quietly for a few moments on some of the bush boardwalks. **Northern blue penguins** also frequent Tiritiri, and can be seen all year round – but are more in evidence in March, when they come ashore to moult, and from September to December, when they nest in specially constructed viewing boxes located along the seashore path just west of the main wharf.

Practicalities

Tiritiri Matangi is typically visited as a **day-trip**, giving almost five hours on the island; you'll need to take your own **lunch**, as there is no food available. The most reliable way to get here is with Fullers (☎09/367 9111), who depart from the Auckland Ferry Building (Oct–April Thurs–Sun 9am, May–Sept not Friday; $45 return) for the forty-minute run up to Gulf Harbour Marina on the Whangaparoa Peninsula, 30km north of Auckland (see p.136), from where it makes the twenty-minute crossing ($25 return) to Tiritiri. On other weekdays (particularly Wednesday), the ferry is often chartered for school trips and you are usually welcome to tag along. Boats depart the island for Gulf Harbour and Auckland at 3.30pm.

Visitors arriving on scheduled ferries can join extremely worthwhile **guided walks** (1hr; $5), which leave from the wharf and are led by volunteers and DOC rangers steeped in bird-lore. Otherwise, you're free to wander the island at will or indulge in a little **swimming** from Hobbs Beach, a ten-minute walk west of the wharf (turn left as you step ashore), and the only sandy strand on Tiritiri.

It's also possible to **stay overnight** in a self-contained bunkhouse – bring a sleeping bag and food – near the lighthouse (call the rangers on ☎09/476 0010; ❶), but weekends are booked months ahead and even for week nights you'll need to book at least two weeks in advance; you can also get **general information** on this phone number.

Other gulf islands

There are dozens of other islands scattered around the Hauraki Gulf, several of them privately owned but more forming part of the Hauraki Gulf Maritime Park. The most easily accessible is the DOC-managed recreation reserve of **Motuihe Island**, just 3km south of Motutapu Island, a popular day-trip destination for Aucklanders keen to laze on the sheltered sandy beaches of the northwestern peninsula and spend three or four hours exploring the easy walking trails. The majority of the island is farmland, with small patches of bush around its fringes. The northwestern end of the island, where the boats dock, has had something of a chequered history. It was used as a smallpox and influenza quarantine station from 1873 until after World War I, doubling up as prisoner-of-war camp; during World War II, the same buildings served as a naval base associated with gun emplacements built in the northern tip of the island. Motuihe is most easily visited on Fullers Island Hopper service (early Nov–Feb 4 daily; $20 return) giving up to six hours on the island and allowing you to combine your visit with a trip to Rangitoto. If you want **to stay** longer there are boats on Friday evening allowing you to stop over in a well-supplied farmhouse sleeping up to twelve ($12 per person, $60 minimum nightly charge), a bunkhouse (❶) and a campsite ($5). All are booked through the **kiosk** (☎09/534 8095), which is open daily in summer for groceries and takeaways.

Very few visitors make it out to **Little Barrier Island** (Hauturu), 80km north of Auckland, a nature reserve barred to those without the necessary DOC permit (contact the Warkworth DOC office ☎09/425 7812). Although around a third of its trees were felled for timber before the government acquired the island and set it aside as a wildlife sanctuary in 1884, mountainous Little Barrier remains largely unspoiled, its vast forests unaffected by introduced pests. The island is home to fascinating creatures – including giant earthworms up to a metre long, the prehistoric tuatara and a mouse-sized version of the grasshopper-like weta – and once cats were eradicated in 1975 Little Barrier also became a refuge for birds under threat on the mainland, such as the kakapo, kaka, stitchbird and the kokako.

Travel details

Trains

From Auckland to: Hamilton (2 daily; 2hr); National Park (2 daily; 5hr 30min); Ohakune (2 daily; 6hr); Otorohanga (2 daily; 3hr); Palmerston North (2 daily; 8–9hr); Wellington (2 daily; 11hr).

Buses

From Auckland to: Cambridge (4 daily; 3hr); Dargaville (2–3 daily; 3hr 15min); Gisborne (1 daily; 9hr); Hamilton (14–16 daily; 2hr); Hastings (3 daily; 7hr 30min); Helensville (Mon–Fri 8 daily; 1hr 10min); Kaitaia (1 daily; 7hr); Kerikeri (2 daily; 5hr); Kumeu (4–6 daily; 35min); Mangonui (1 daily; 6hr 30min); National Park (1 daily; 5hr 30min); Napier (3 daily; 7hr); New Plymouth (3 daily; 6–7hr); Ohakune (1 daily; 6hr); Opononi (3 weekly; 5hr 40min); Orewa (hourly; 45–60min); Paihia via Whangarei (3–6 daily; 4hr 20min); Paihia via Opononi (3 weekly; 8hr 30min); Palmerston North (4 daily; 9hr); Rotorua (8 daily; 4hr); Taupo (4 daily; 4–5hr); Taihape (3 daily; 6hr 30min); Tauranga (4–6 daily; 3hr 40min); Thames (5 daily; 2hr); Warkworth (8 daily; 1hr); Waipu (4–6 daily; 2hr 20min); Waitomo (3 daily; 3hr 15min); Whangarei (4–6 daily; 3hr); Wellington (4 daily; 11hr).
From Helensville to: Orewa (1 Mon–Fri; 40min).
From Orewa to: Auckland (hourly; 45–60min); Helensville (1 Mon–Fri; 40min); Waiwera (hourly; 15min); Wenderholm (summer Sundays 4 daily; 15min).

Ferries

From Auckland to: Devonport (every 30min; 10min); Great Barrier (2–5 weekly; 2–6hr); Motuihe (2–3 weekly; 50min); Rangitoto (2–4 daily; 40min); Tiritiri Matangi (4 weekly; 1hr 30min); Waiheke (7–10 daily; 40min).
From Gulf Harbour Marina to: Tiritiri Matangi Island (4 weekly; 20min).
From Half Moon Bay to: Waiheke (6–9 daily; 1hr).

Flights

From Auckland to: Bay of Islands (3–4 daily; 50min); Blenheim (2–3 daily; 1hr 20min); Christchurch (13 daily; 1hr 20min); Dunedin (3 daily; 2hr 30min); Gisborne (3–5 daily; 1hr); Great Barrier Island (5–10 daily; 30min), Hamilton (1–2 daily; 35min); Kaitaia (1 daily; 1hr), Napier (7–10 daily; 1hr); Nelson (2 daily; 1hr 30min); New Plymouth (5–8 daily; 50min); Palmerston North (5–8 daily; 1hr 10min); Queenstown (4 daily; 1hr 40min); Rotorua (4–5 daily; 45min); Taupo (2 daily; 50min); Tauranga (5–7 daily; 40min); Wanganui (2–3 daily; 1hr); Wellington (20–25 daily; 1hr); Whakatane (3–5 daily; 50min); Whangarei (5–7 daily; 40min).
From Great Barrier Island: to Whangarei (2 weekly; 30min); Whitianga (3 weekly; 20min).
From Waiheke Island to: Great Barrier Island (2 daily; 30min).

2

Northland

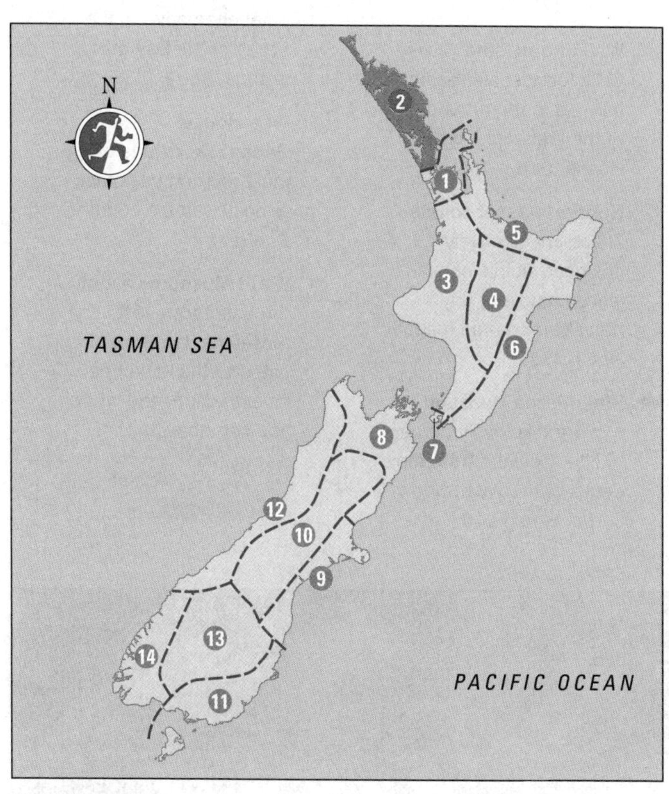

CHAPTER 2 Highlights

* **Poor Knights Islands** One of the world's ten best dive spots with caves, rock arches, abundant fish, and even a couple of wrecks. See p.179
* **Waikokopu Café** Classy yet informal café, beautifully set in the grounds of the Waitangi Treaty House. See p.192
* **Hundertwasser toilets** These imaginatively-designed public conveniences have put tiny Kawakawa on the map. See p.193
* **Whangaroa Harbour** Explore this lovely corner of New Zealand from the decks of the yacht *Snow Cloud*. See p.206
* **Swamp Palace** Oddball rural cinema specialising in cult movies as well as the latest releases. See p.208
* **Hokianga Harbour** The quiet alternative to the frenzy of the Bay of Islands. See p.219
* **Tree House Backpackers** One of the most relaxing backpacker hostels in the country. See p.221
* **Kauri Museum** One of the country's finest museums, totally dedicated to the kauri tree, its extraction, and what you can do with it. See p.229

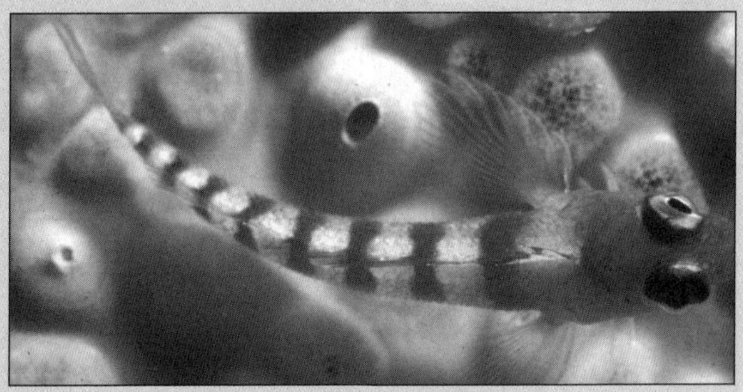

2

Northland

The narrow and staunchly Maori province of **Northland** (Taitokerau; Ⓦwww.northland.org.nz) thrusts 350km out from Auckland into the subtropical north, separating the Pacific Ocean from the Tasman Sea – two oceans which meet in the maelstrom off Cape Reinga, New Zealand's most northerly accessible road. The province is often described as the "Winterless North", and though the name only really holds true in the topmost part of the region, it rightly suggests that palms, citrus fruit and even bananas thrive here, that frosts are rare, and that the waters off its many gorgeous beaches stay warmer than elsewhere.

Scenically, Northland splits down the middle. The **east coast** comprises a labyrinth of straggling peninsulas, with hidden coves set between plunging headlands. The beaches tend to be calm and safe, their waters becoming choppy only during occasional Pacific storms, whose force is broken by clusters of protective barrier islands. There could hardly be a greater contrast than that with the **west coast**, one enormous dune-backed beach pounded by powerful Tasman breakers and broken by occasional harbours. Tidal rips and holes make swimming dangerous here, and there are no lifeguard patrols. Some beaches are even designated as roads, but are full of hazards for the unwary – and rental cars aren't insured for beach driving. Exploration of the undulating **interior** is both hampered and enlivened by the roads: the major routes are inland and often well away from the unspoiled and deserted beaches that are the main event in these parts, leading to long forays down twisting side roads.

North of Auckland's urban sprawl, the short **Kowhai Coast** begins to feel more genuinely rural and is popular with yachties sailing around Kawau Island, and snorkellers exploring the underwater world of the **Goat Island Marine Reserve**. The broad sweep of **Bream Bay** runs from the Scottish settlement of Waipu up to the dramatic crags of Whangarei Heads at the entrance to Northland's major port and the associated town of **Whangarei**. Off the coast here lie the **Poor Knights Islands**, New Zealand's premier dive spot. Tourists in a hurry tend to make straight for the **Bay of Islands**, a jagged bite out of the coastline dotted with islands perfect for cruising, diving and swimming with dolphins, and steeped in early New Zealand history. Everything north of here is loosely referred to as **The Far North**, a region characterized by the quiet remoteness of the **Whangaroa Harbour**, the popular resorts of **Doubtless Bay**, and the **Aupori Peninsula**, which backs **Ninety Mile Beach** all the way up to **Cape Reinga**.

The west coast feels very different from the east, marked by economic neglect over the last fifty years as kauri logging ended and dairying never successfully replaced it. First stop is the fragmented **Hokianga Harbour**, one of New

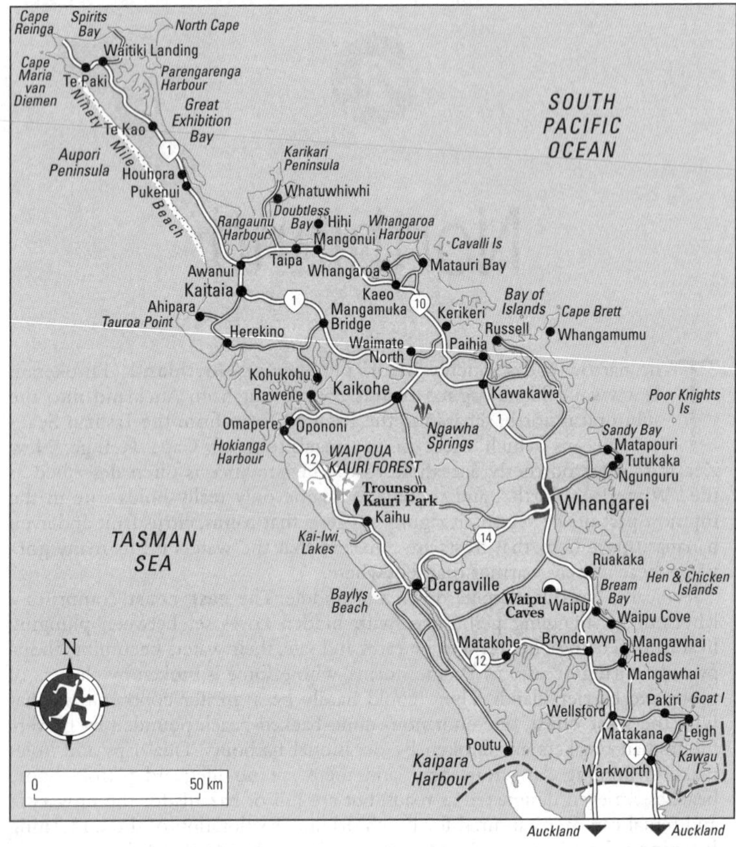

Zealand's largest, with some fine sand dunes gracing the north head. South of here you're into the **Waipoua Forest**, all that remains after the depredations of the loggers, a story best told at the excellent **Matakohe Kauri Museum** on the shores of the Kaipara Harbour.

Northland has no passenger train services so **getting around** by public transport means travelling by **bus**. Kaitaia and the Bay of Islands airports have direct **flights** to Auckland and each other, Whangarei has flights to Auckland and Great Barrier Island, and Kerikeri has flights to Auckland and Kaitaia, but distances are relatively short and high prices act as a deterrent. Details of frequencies and journey times are given in "Travel details" at the end of the chapter (see p.230). If you're **driving** the choices are limited to a major road up each side of the peninsula. This forms a logical loop which has recently been formalized as the **Twin Coast Discovery route** (Ⓦwww.twincoast.co.nz): there's no need to follow it slavishly, but the small brown signs emblazoned with a curling wave form a good starting framework.

Some history

Northland was the site of most of the early contact between **Maori** and **European settlers**, and the birthplace of New Zealand's most important document, the **Treaty of Waitangi**. Maori legend tells of the great Polynesian explorer Kupe discovering the Hokianga Harbour and, finding the climate and abundance of food to his liking, encouraging his people to return and settle there. It was their descendants in the Bay of Islands who had the dubious honour of making the first contact with Europeans, as whalers plundered the seas and missionaries sought converts. Maori society was ill-prepared for this onslaught, and their leaders petitioned Britain to step in. Without fully appreciating the implications or understanding the duplicity of the Pakeha, the northern chiefs signed away their **sovereignty** in return for assurances on land and traditional rights, which were seldom respected. There is still a perception among Maori in the rest of the country that the five northern *iwi* gave Aotearoa away to the Pakeha, and resentment lingers.

As more fertile farmlands were found in newly settled regions further south, Northland fell into decline and the pattern became one of exploitation rather than development. Rapacious **kauri loggers** and **gum diggers** cleared the bush and, as extractive industries died away, pioneers moved in, turning much of the land to **dairy country**. Local dairy factories closed as larger semi-industrial complexes centralized processing, leaving small towns all but destitute, though the planting of fast-growing exotic trees and sporadic pockets of horticulture keep local economies ticking over, aided by the cultivation of marijuana, a major cash crop in these parts.

The Kowhai Coast to Bream Bay

Auckland's influence begins to wane by the time you reach the **Kowhai Coast** around 50km north of central Auckland, a thirty-kilometre stretch of shallow harbours, beach-strung peninsulas and small islands. Freed from the shackles of the city, a more individual character becomes apparent, particularly once you pass sleepy **Warkworth** and head out either to **Kawau Island**, one-time home of Governor General George Grey, or up the coast to Leigh and the snorkelling and diving nirvana of **Goat Island Marine Reserve**.

There's little to detain you on SH1 between Warkworth and Waipu as it passes through dull Wellsford and the road junction and bus interchange at **Brynderwyn**, where SH12 loops off to Dargaville, the Waipoua Kauri Forest and the Hokianga Harbour. If you're heading north and want a scenic route, it's better to stay on the coast and follow **Bream Bay**, named by Cook when he visited in 1770 and his crew hauled in tarakihi, which they mistook for bream. The bay curves gently for 20km from the modest, rocky headland of Bream Tail in the south, past the entrance to Whangarei Harbour to the dramatic and craggy Bream Head. There are no sizeable towns here, only the small beach communities of **Mangawhai Heads** and **Waipu Cove**, looking out to the **Hen and Chicken Islands**, refuges for rare birds like the handsome wattled saddleback.

Warkworth and around

The economic focus of the Kowhai Coast is the easy-going small town of **WARKWORTH**, at the head of Mahurangi Harbour, and sheltered from the sea by its eponymous peninsula. For much of the year Warkworth is a peaceful and slow-paced rural town, only coming to life at the peak of the summer season, when thousands of yachties descend, mooring their boats in the numerous estuaries and coves nearby. For a century onwards from the late 1820s, the languid stretch of river that flows behind the town seethed with boats shipping out kauri, initially as spars for the Royal Navy and later on as sawn planks. A high-grade limestone deposit was subsequently discovered here in 1865, and cement production became important for a while.

To learn more about the town's past, head 3km south to the **Warkworth and Districts Museum**, on Tudor Collins Drive, signposted off the main road (daily: Nov–Easter 9am–4pm; Easter–Oct 9am–3.30pm; $5), which offers a fairly dull exploration of the region's history through re-created rooms, examples of kauri gum and a five-metre-long, 130-link chain carved from a single piece of kauri. The two ancient kauri outside mark the start of two well-presented twenty-minute boardwalk nature trails through the **Parri Kauri Park** (9am–dusk; donation), an appealing stand of bush that was preserved as a public amenity at the end of the nineteenth century. A couple of kilometres further south along SH1, the **Honey Centre** on Perry Road (daily 9am–5pm) is the place to buy some honey or see bees building their own honeycombs.

Following SH1 north, it's 5km to the entertaining **Sheep World** (daily 9am–5pm; $10), where you can see lambs being bottle-fed or try your hand at a little shearing. The complex also contains a campground and a backpackers (see below), plus the **Matakana Co-op Market** (daily 10am–4pm), a quality craft, plants and produce co-op that's worth a quick peek. The **Dome Forest Walkway** begins 2km further north on SH1, leading up through native forest to a lookout point (40min return), before climbing steeply to the summit (1hr 30min return) for superb views and continuing gently down to the twenty magnificent trees of the Waiwhiu Kauri Grove (3hr return).

Practicalities

Warkworth's **visitor centre**, 1 Baxter St (Christmas–Feb Mon–Fri 8.30am–6pm, Sat & Sun 9am–4.30pm; March–Christmas Mon–Fri 9am–5pm, Sat & Sun 9am–3pm; ⓣ09/425 9081, ⓦwww.warkworth-information.co.nz), is right in the centre of town at the junction of Queen Street and Neville Street, where InterCity buses stop. Northliner buses pull up on SH1 near the ambulance station.

Central **accommodation** includes *The Warkworth Inn Backpackers*, 9 Queen Street (ⓣ09/425 8569, ⓔwwinn@maxnet.co.nz; dorms ❶, rooms ❸), Warkworth's original 1860 hotel, with pleasant rooms and dorms; campervans can park outside and use the facilities for $20. The *Central Motel* on Neville Street (ⓣ & ⓕ09/425 8645, ⓔcentralmotel@xtra.co.nz; ❹) has twelve units, plus a spa and swimming pool. North of town, *Sheep World Caravan Park and Camping Ground* (ⓣ & ⓕ09/425 9962, ⓦwww.sheepworldcaravanpark.co.nz; tent and van sites $13, dorms ❶, vans and cabins ❷, chalets ❹) has on-site vans and a range of cabins, and also operates as a VIP backpackers). The best of several good **B&Bs** and **homestays** is *Saltings Guest House*, 1210 Sandspit Rd (ⓣ09/425 9670, ⓦwww.saltings.co.nz; ❻), a standard 1970s Kiwi home tastefully restyled along Mediterranean lines; fine breakfasts are served. It overlooks Sandspit, 7km from Warkworth, within walking distance of the Kawau ferry wharf and the adjacent *Sandspit Motor Camp*, 1334 Sandspit Rd (ⓣ & ⓕ09/425 8610; tent sites $10, cabins ❷).

Daytime **eating** is best done at *Ducks Crossing Café*, which serves good quiche, salads, cakes and coffee in the River View Plaza down by the river; at the *Queen Street Corner Café*, on the corner of Queen Street and Neville Street; or at the restaurant out at Heron's Flight (see p.168). In the evening, make for the *Pizza Co.*, 18 Neville St (BYO & licensed), which serves fine traditional pizza, superb vegetable soup and a spicy peperoni Garibaldi stew, or drive 8km out to Snell's Beach, where *Pizza Construction* (book in advance on ⓣ09/425 5555) has garnered quite a reputation for its delicious pizzas and high-quality fish dishes, especially the spicy scallops and prawns.

Kawau Island

KAWAU ISLAND holds a special place in the hearts of the Hauraki Gulf yachting fraternity, as much for the safety of its straggling harbours as for the sandy coves wedged between modest cliffs. With a meagre resident population of around a hundred, the island is chiefly given over to holiday homes – including some multimillion-dollar affairs with helipads – whose bristling jetties choke the shoreline. As a casual visitor, you can't do much without your own boat except visit the Mansion House on the unimaginatively named Mansion House Bay, and the sumptuous exotic grounds thereabouts.

Once farmed, the island is slowly reverting to kanuka scrub and isn't an especially appealing place to walk around, while access is difficult to all but the DOC-managed southwestern tenth of the island. This area is where one of New Zealand's first export industries sprang up around a briefly profitable **copper trade** in the 1840s and 1850s. Mines in Dispute Cove yielded copper ore, which was processed at Smeltinghouse Bay on Bon Accord Harbour, the inlet that nearly cuts the island in two. The industry was defunct by 1862, when George Grey, then doing his second stint as New Zealand's governor, was looking for a private home and bought the mine manager's house and adjacent assay office, linking the two with his own larger-roomed extension to form the **Mansion House** (daily 10am–3.30pm; $4). Grey was an austere man and there's little flamboyance in the construction, the rooms being simply decorated using kauri and totara panels and – the sole nod to his position – some kauri pillars which were sent to England for turning. Grey sold up in 1888, after which the house became a hotel, sprouting ugly extensions which had to be stripped away during restoration. Apart from a collection of silverware, there's little in the house that belonged to Grey himself, though most of the furniture is contemporary with his tenure.

Grey's pursuit of the Victorian fashion for all things exotic resulted in grounds stocked with flora and fauna imported from all over the world. Though much of it was ill-tended after his departure, the dell running back from the house is still a gracious place. Chilean wine palms, coral trees, Moreton Bay figs and a smattering of native species stud the formal lawns, where peacocks – one completely white – strut by, weka scurry around and rosellas screech overhead. Grey also brought in four species of **wallaby** – most easily seen in a large compound in the dell – which have overtaken the island to the extent that they are now regularly culled, and residents construct impenetrable fences to protect their gardens. There is even talk of complete eradication.

A path runs through the gardens to the tiny beach at **Lady's Bay** and on to a network of short tracks that drop down to the coves on Bon Accord Harbour and the ruins of the old copper mine, a walk of about forty minutes each way.

Practicalities

Boats to Kawau Island leave from **Sandspit** (all-day parking $5), a small road-end community on the Matakana Estuary, 8km east of Warkworth. Throughout the year, Kawau Kat Cruises (ⓣ0800/888 006) operate the **Royal Mail Run** (daily 10.30am; 4hr; $39; $49 with barbecue lunch), delivering mail, papers and groceries to all the wharves on the island and giving you about two hours ashore at Mansion House Bay; their direct service (2pm, plus extra services Christmas–Easter; $24) gives you more time at the bay. For a cheaper and more leisurely option, try the **Coffee Cruise** on the MV *Matata* (Ⓣ025/960910; Christmas–Easter daily 10am & 2pm; Easter–Christmas Mon & Wed–Sat 10am, Thurs 7.15am, 10am & 2.30pm, Fri 10am, 3pm & 7pm, Sun 10am & 3pm; $25), which follows a similar itinerary to the Royal Mail Run – though you'll need to go out on the early boat and come back on the later one (return boats are at 1pm & 4pm) if you want to linger on the island. Both companies run a range of other cruises in summer. Bring whatever you need to Kawau as there are no stores or cafés.

There are several **places to stay** on Kawau, including *Pah Farm*, Moores Bay (Ⓣ09/422 8765, Ⓔpah.farm@ihug.co.nz; tent sites $10, four-shares ❶, rooms ❷), and a simple, self-contained two-bedroom DOC house, *Sunny Bay Cottage* (Ⓣ09/422 8882; ❸), fifteen minutes' walk from Mansion House – it's let for a minimum of two nights. There's also *The Beachhouse*, Vivian Bay (Ⓣ09/422 8850, Ⓔbeachhouse@paradise.net.nz; ❾), geared more towards romantic weekends away and charging from $300 with all meals included.

Anyone keen to put in a week's **voluntary work** can stay free in a DOC bunkhouse at Mansion House Bay; consult the website (Ⓦwww.doc.govt/volunteers) for details.

Matakana

MATAKANA, 8km northeast of Warkworth, is little more than a road junction at the heart of a fledgling wine-making region, though the surrounding area is now dotted with the workshops of craftspeople who have set up shop far enough from Auckland to discourage the weekend masses but close enough to lure interested buyers. The catalyst for the region's development was the **Morris & James Pottery & Tileworks**, Tongue Farm Road (Mon–Fri 8.30am–4.30pm, Sat & Sun 10am–5pm; free), which in the late 1970s exploited New Zealand's fortress economy by producing otherwise unobtainable handmade terracotta tiles and large garden pots made from local clay. Since then, its distinctive designs, executed in lustrous, multi-layered salt glaze, have been sold into ceramics shops throughout the country. You can watch wall tiles being hand decorated in the workshop, then catch a free tour of the pottery (daily 11.30am) before a visit to the café.

Despite received wisdom about high humidity and proximity to the sea being bad for viticulture, half the valley seems to have been planted with **vineyards** during the last ten years. The free and widely available *Matakana Wine Trail* leaflet currently details half a dozen wineries offering tastings, whilst two of the most interesting have restaurants attached. First stop should be *Heron's Flight*, 49 Sharp's Rd (Ⓣ09/422 7915, Ⓦwww.heronsflight.co.nz), which has styled itself along Tuscan lines, planting Sangiovese vines with considerable success. Mulberries, figs and olives are also grown on site and sold in the deli, as well as being used in dishes served up in the lovely **restaurant**, which overlooks the vines. You can taste four wines (including the pricey Sangiovese) for $6. Another good bet is *Ascension Vineyard & Café* (Ⓣ09/422 9601, Ⓔascension@xtra.co.nz), prominently situated on Matakana Rd, which also has a very respectable café-restaurant and offers a tasting of their complement of wines for $8. If you just fancy a little **free tasting**, try Matakana's original winery, *Hyperion Wines* (Ⓣ09/422 9375, Ⓦwww.hyperion-wines.co.nz), on Tongue Farm Road near Morris & James.

Leigh and Goat Island

East of Matakana, the road runs 13km to the clifftop village of **LEIGH**, which boasts a picturesque harbour bobbing with wooden fishing boats, as well as the fine sandy bay of **Mathesons Beach**, 1km to the west. The presence of so many boats attests to the abundance of fish here where ocean currents meet the waters of the Hauraki Gulf. Overfishing has taken its toll, however, something which underlines the importance of the **Goat Island Marine Reserve** (officially **Cape Rodney–Okakari Marine Reserve**, but usually known as Goat Island), located around some 4km northeast of Leigh. Established in 1975, this was New Zealand's first marine reserve, stretching 5km along the shoreline and 800m off the coast – it's named for its most prominent feature, a small, bush-clad island 300m offshore. Two angling- and shellfishing-free decades later the undersea life is thriving, with large rock lobster and huge snapper. Feeding is discouraged but commonly practised – blue maomaos in particular seem to have developed a taste for frozen peas, and frequently mob swimmers and divers.

Easy beach access, wonderfully clear water, rock pools on wave-cut platforms, a variety of undersea terrains and relatively benign currents combine to make this an enormously popular year-round **diving** spot, as well as a favourite summer destination for sun-seeking families. **Snorkellers** get a lush world of kelp forest with numerous multi-coloured fish; those who venture deeper will find more exposed seascapes with an abundance of sponges. Snorkelling and diving gear (from $13 for mask, snorkel and fins to $75 for complete diving gear) can be rented from **Seafriends** (Ⓣ09/422 6212, Ⓦwww.seafriends.org.nz), just over a kilometre up the Goat Island access road. Non-divers wanting a taste of what's down there can visit a series of **aquariums** at Seafriends that re-create different Goat Island ecosystems and, in fine weather, join 45-minute tours around the island with Glass Bottomed Boat Habitat Explorer on the beach at the marine reserve (call in advance to check times and weather conditions on Ⓣ09/422 6334; $18).

Practicalities

There's no public transport to Leigh or Goat Island, and the facilities are limited once you get here. You can **stay** at the welcoming if slightly shabby *Goat Island Backpackers* (Ⓣ09/422 6185, camping $10, dorms ❶, cabins and on-site vans ❷, self-contained unit ❹), about 1km back from the reserve on the way to Goat Island (about 1km before you get there), where there are grassy sites with great bay views and a selection of simple but appealing accommodation options. In Leigh, the *Leigh Sawmill Café*, 142 Pakiri Road (Ⓣ09/422 6019, Ⓦwww.sawmillcafe.co.nz), has five appealing en-suite doubles (❺) and two bunkrooms (❶); while the *Leigh Motel*, 15 Hill St (Ⓣ & Ⓕ09/422 6179, Ⓔliegh.motel@xtra.co.nz; ❹), has good two-night deals outside of January.

Eating is a big surprise. The slick *Leigh Sawmill Café* (see above), a vast sawmill sensitively converted into a smart café/bar, serves fine gourmet pizza and a range of well-presented dishes, often supplemented by daily specials based around an Indian, Thai or Japanese theme; weekends typically draw touring bands. Good alternatives include Leigh's fish-and-chip takeaway, and the BYO and licensed restaurant at Seafriends (see above; daily: Oct–Apr 9am–8pm; May–Sept 10am–4pm), both serving excellent seafood, even if coming at it from very different angles.

Pakiri

Heading north up the coast, it's possible to reach Mangawhai Heads (see below) from Leigh via a string of dirt roads through steep green hills over boggy farmland and scrubby bush. It's not an especially striking journey, though, and you'll do as well to return to SH1 in Warkworth unless you want to visit the long, dune-backed white strand of **Pakiri**, with its few houses scattered about, 10km north of Leigh. It's a gorgeous long beach with good surf, but the main attraction here is **horse-riding** with the highly professional Pakiri Beach Horse Riding, Rahuikiri Road (ⓣ09/422 6275, ⓦwww.horseride-nz.co.nz). Rides range from a brief jaunt along the beach and through a *pohutukawa* glade to full-blown safaris through stands of native bush and along the tops of seacliffs. Outings leave daily at 10am & 2pm, and there are many more departures in the peak summer season ($35 for an hour, $55 for two hours, $75 for half a day). They also arrange sunset rides in summer, as well as moonlight rides and overnight trips year-round. If you'd like to stay over they have some attractive **accommodation** in backpacker dorms (❶), self-contained beachside and riverside cabins (❺), farmstay (❺, including dinner and breakfast), and a luxurious beach house ($300) sleeping three couples. **Campers** can stay nearby at the *Pakiri Beach Motor Camp*, Pakiri Beach Road (ⓣ09/422 6199; tent sites $11, cabins ❶, motel units ❹).

Mangawhai Heads and around

Back on SH1 and heading north, your next chance to turn off towards the coast is at the small roadside settlement of **KAIWAKA**, from where a winding country road runs 13km inland to tiny **MANGAWHAI**, little more than a crossroads until the recent arrival of the *Smashed Pipi*, 40 Moir St (ⓣ09/431 4847; closed evenings Sun–Tues), an upscale gallery with attached café and bar that draws the Auckland and Whangarei weekend set. If this doesn't appeal, try the lovingly produced pasta and pizza dishes across the road at *Quatro Café* (ⓣ09/431 5226).

The road continues 3km north to meet the coast at **MANGAWHAI HEADS** at the mouth of the Mangawhai Harbour, now marked by an expanding cluster of holiday homes straggling over the hillsides behind a fine surf beach. Long a Kiwi summer holiday favourite, Mangawhai Heads tends to be bypassed by outsiders due its lack of specific attractions, but that's part of the charm, and a day or two here lazing on the beach and body surfing can be wonderfully relaxing. If you're feeling more energetic, there's also the scenic **Mangawhai Cliffs Walkway** (2–3hr). Walk north along the beach for fifteen minutes then follow the orange markers up through bush-backed farmland along the top of the sea cliffs until the path winds back down to the beach. Provided the tide is below half, you can then return along the beach through a small rock arch and past numerous rock pools.

Practicalities

The *Mangawhai Heads Motor Camp*, Mangawhai Heads Road (ⓣ & ⓕ09/431 4675, ⓔcampnewing@xtra.co.nz; tents $8, powered sites $10, cabins and units ❹), is a perfectly good place to stay, right by the calm waters of Mangawhai Harbour, but Mangawhai Heads excels in more luxurious **accommodation**. Reserve as far in advance as you can to stay at *Milestone Cottages by the Sea*, 27 Moir Point Rd (ⓣ & ⓕ09/431 4018, ⓦwww.friars.co.nz/hosts/milestones.html; studio ❺, cottages ❻), a cluster of beautifully turned-out cottages set amid sumptuous gardens within sight of the sea. They're all self-catering and equipped with everything you might need, including a barbecue deck, TV and VCR, and guests have free use of a lap pool and kayaks. If it's tremendous sea views and a more personal touch you want, then opt for *Mangawhai Lodge*, 4 Heather St (ⓣ09/431 5311, ⓦwww.seaviewlodge.co.nz; ❻), set high on the hill with tastefully furnished rooms and a wraparound veranda that surveys the whole town, its beaches and out to the Hen and Chicken Islands.

Good **eating** abounds. In Mangawhai Heads, the licensed *Naja Garden Café*, 5 Molesworth Drive (ⓣ09/431 4111), makes a fine stop for a coffee among the plants of the associated garden centre and also serves great breakfasts, gourmet sandwiches and panini ($6). It's also open for dinner (summer nightly, winter Thurs–Sat) serving the likes of warm Greek salad with lamb ($15), tomato and field mushroom risotto ($20) or scallop and dory potato lasagne ($20). If that doesn't suit, retreat to either of the two restaurants listed in Mangawhai (see above).

Lang's Beach and Waipu Cove

You know you're getting close to the Scottish enclave of Waipu when you reach the delightful **Lang's Beach**, 12km north of Mangawhai Heads, with its tree-backed strand and the *Lochalsh B&B* (ⓣ & ⓕ09/432 0053, ⓔlangs@xtra.co.nz; ❹), overlooking the beach from its perch above the main road, and offering two double rooms. From here it's a further 4km to the top surf beach of **WAIPU COVE**, a cluster of houses by a sweeping stretch of Bream Bay. Again, accommodation is limited. There's camping at the *Waipu Cove Reserve Camp*, 897 Cove Rd (ⓣ09/432 0410; tent and powered sites mid-Dec to mid-Feb $12.50, rest of the year $8), and rooms at the *Cove Beach Motel*, 891 Cove Rd (ⓣ09/432 0348, ⓔann@covebeach.co.nz; ❹, 2-bedroom units ❻), both right by the beach.

Waipu and around

Driving through it, you wouldn't pick nondescript **WAIPU** as being different from any other small Kiwi town but for an Aberdeen granite monument surmounted by a Scottish lion rampant in the middle of the main street. Erected in 1914 to commemorate the sixtieth anniversary of the town's founding, the monument recalls the Scottish home of the settlers who arrived here by way of Nova Scotia, following the charismatic preacher, the Reverend Norman McLeod. Like numerous other crofters dispossessed by the Highland clearances and enticed by stories of the New World, McLeod left Scotland in 1817 with as many as he could persuade to follow him and set down roots in St Ann's, Nova Scotia, where they stayed until famine and a series of harsh winters in the late 1850s drove them out. Some went to Australia, but most decamped to Waipu, forming a self-contained and deathly strict Calvinist community that eked a living from farming and forestry. The town is proud of its heritage, and every year someone is sponsored to study pipes, drum or Scottish country dancing at the Gaelic College of Arts and Crafts in Nova Scotia. The biggest event of the year is Waipu's annual New Year's Day **Highland Games** (ⓦwww.highlandgames.co.nz), in which competitors heft large stones, and toss cabers and sheaves in the Caledonian Park. The Scottish history and genealogy of the settlers is recounted in the **Waipu House of Memories** on the main street (daily 9.30am–4pm; $4), which is jammed full of photos of anxious first-boat arrivees and their personal effects.

Unless you happen to coincide with the Highland Games, there's nothing much to do in Waipu, though there's a popular excursion to the **Waipu Caves** (unrestricted entry), a 200-metre glow-worm-filled passage forming part of an extensive underground system in the limestone country 16km to the west. Obtain a map from the visitor centre in Waipu (see below), take a couple of good torches – it's pitch-black and very disorientating inside the caves – and explore: there are no guides, so use your judgement as to how far to go in. The cave is signposted from Waipu Caves Road and is impenetrable when wet; you'll get muddy even in dry weather.

North from Waipu, the road runs parallel to Bream Bay, though occasional turnings give access to the long white **beach** that lies to the east. The best place to head down to the sands is at **Uretiti**, 6km north of Waipu, where there's a primitive DOC camping area ($6), with water and cold showers and an adjacent nudist beach. Four kilometres north, Ruakaka marks a turn-off for the **Marsden Point Oil Refinery** (daily 10am–5pm; free), 10km to the north, where a couple of continuously running videos offer heavy-handed self-promotion as you stroll around a vast scale model of New Zealand's only oil refinery.

Practicalities

InterCity and Northliner **buses** drop off and pick up on request outside Bargain Buys, on the main street, which also acts as a ticket agent (Ⓣ09/432 0046). Nearby, the Waipu House of Memories (see above) contains the town's **visitor centre** (daily 9.30am–4pm; Ⓣ & Ⓕ09/432 0746, Ⓦwww.waipu.co.nz). Waipu has no banks or ATMs, but you can change travellers' cheques (Mon, Wed & Fri 10am–2pm only) at the Waipu Cyber Centre, opposite the visitor centre, which also has **internet access**.

The best budget **accommodation** is at the very welcoming and super-relaxed *Ebb & Flow Backpackers*, 3km southeast of Waipu (Ⓣ09/432 1288, Ⓦwww.ebbandflow.co.nz; tents $13, dorms ❶, rooms ❷; no credit cards). Perched on the edge of the Waipu Estuary wildlife reserve, it enjoys lovely sea views out to the Hen and Chicken Islands and lures backpackers for an extra day or two with free bikes and kayaks, pick-up from Waipu and an impressive collection of old vinyl. You can save a dollar or so by staying in Waipu at the *Waipu Wanderers*, 25 St Mary's Rd (Ⓣ09/432 0532, Ⓔskyla@ihug.co.nz; dorms ❶, rooms ❷), which has just eight ready-made beds in a separate house with its own kitchen and bathroom.

For tasty **meals**, *The Pizza Barn 'n' Bar*, 2 Cove Rd (Ⓣ09/432 0737), serves a range of well-priced lunches and dinners, including pizzas, in Waipu's former post office, either in the cosy log-cabin dining room or out in the garden. For basic Kiwi fare, head to *Granz Café*, opposite the visitor centre, which dishes up all-day breakfasts, lunch and afternoon tea.

Whangarei and around

On initial acquaintance, **WHANGAREI** is a bit of a disappointment. If you've come from the south, Bream Bay's sweeping coastline and the attractive Whangarei Harbour seem to promise more than Northland's provincial capital is able to deliver. But Whangarei does have redeeming features, not least the riverside **Town Basin**, where sleek yachts are moored outside a renovated settler-style shopping and restaurant complex. Elsewhere there's a smattering of

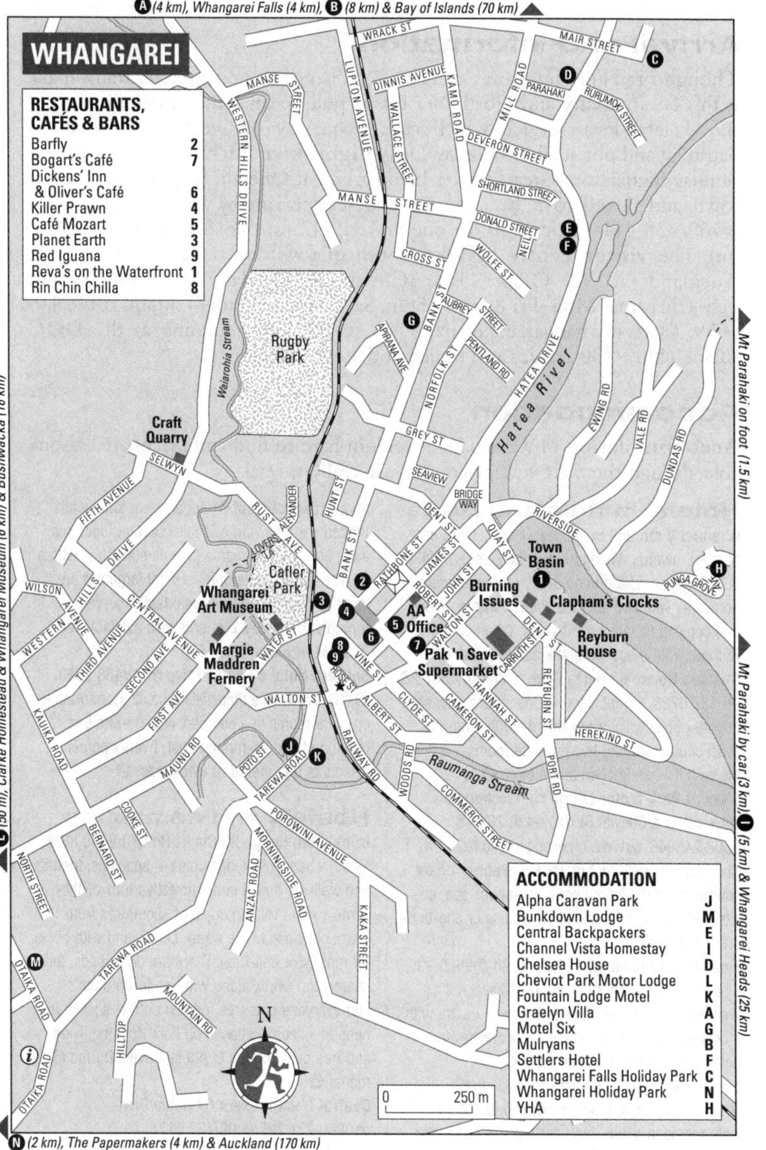

modest museums and sights and a few pleasant walks, but Whangarei is perhaps best used as a base either for a swimming and walking day-trip out to Whangarei Heads, or for diving and snorkelling around the **Poor Knights Islands**.

Arrival and information

Though a rail line runs from Auckland to Whangarei, no passenger trains make it this far. InterCity and Northliner **buses** pull up on Rose Street, the hub of the skeletal local service which runs frequently on weekdays, less so on Saturday, and not at all on Sunday. Daily **flights** from Auckland and Friday and Sunday flights from Great Barrier Island arrive at Onerahi Airport, 5km east of town and linked to it by a shuttle taxi service run by Kiwi Carlton Cabs (ⓣ09/438 4444; around $8 for one person, $12 for two, $16 for three and so on). The **visitor centre** lies 2km south of town on the main route from Auckland at 92 Otaika Rd (Christmas–Jan daily 8.30am–6.30pm; Feb–Christmas Mon–Fri 8.30am–5pm, Sat & Sun 9.30am–4.30pm; ⓣ09/438 1079, ⓦwww.whangareinz.co.nz) – it's in the same building as the **DOC office** (ⓣ09/430 2007; same hours) and a decent café.

Accommodation

Accommodation in Whangarei is seldom hard to find and prices are reasonable, though there are few places that are really special.

Hotels, motels and B&Bs

Channel Vista 254 Beach Rd, Onerahi, 5km east of town towards Whangarei Heads ⓣ & ⓕ09/436 5529, ⓔtancred@igrin.co.nz. Luxurious modern homestay with two luxurious suites with en-suite and cooking facilities overlooking Whangarei Harbour, with a cooked breakfast included. ❺

Chelsea House 83 Hatea Drive ⓣ0508/243573 & 09/437 0728, ⓔmel.clarke@clear.net.nz. Pleasant double-gabled villa, a ten-minute walk from the town centre, offering two en-suite rooms – a double with its own kitchen and a twin. ❹

Cheviot Park Motor Lodge cnr Western Hills Drive (SH1) & Cheviot St ⓣ09/438 2341 & 0508/243846, ⓦwww.cheviot-park.co.nz. Cheerful and well-kept motor lodge about 1.5km southwest of the town centre, with pool, spa, on-site restaurant and a choice of studios or one-bedroom suites. ❹

Fountain Lodge Motel 17 Tarewa Rd ⓣ0800/999 944, ⓣ & ⓕ09/438 3532, ⓔghen@clear.net.nz. Well-appointed motel close to the town centre with a couple of kitchenless studio units and several units with bathroom and kitchen. ❹

Graelyn Villa 166 Kiripaka Rd, Tikipunga ⓣ09/437 7532, ⓔgraelyn@xtra.co.nz. Three en-suite rooms in a hundred-year-old suburban villa surrounded by lush gardens in a tranquil setting close to Whangarei Falls. In summer, the tasty full breakfast is served on the terrace. ❹

Motel Six 153 Bank St ⓣ09/438 9219,ⓔmotel6@xtra.co.nz. Standard, decent motel ten minutes' walk from the centre with spa pool and in-house video. Studios ❸, units ❹

Mulryans Crane Rd ⓣ09/435 0945, ⓦwww.mulryans.co.nz. Elegant and welcoming country B&B about 10km north of Whangarei, set amid well-tended gardens with a tennis court, outdoor spa and pool. The two rooms (one en suite, one with a private but separate bath) are not large but are tastefully appointed and breakfast is served throughout the day. Dinner is also available for $45–55, including wine. ❻

Settlers Hotel 63 Hatea Drive ⓣ09/438 2699, ⓕ438 0794, ⓔsettlers@ihug.co.nz. Comfortable en-suite rooms in a complex with on-site bar, restaurant and swimming pool. Twenty percent discounts are offered at weekends. ❺

Hostels and campsites

Bunkdown Lodge 23 Otaika Rd ⓣ09/438 8886, ⓦwww.bunkdownlodge.co.nz. A spacious, friendly and well-run hostel in an attractive turn-of-the-century kauri villa a couple of kilometres from town, but close to the visitor centre and with bikes for rent ($5 a half-day). There are dorm beds, four-shares and twins, along with made-up doubles, and everyone gets free tea and coffee, access to a heap of videos, guidance on Poor Knights diving and free guided tours of Abbey Caves. Dorms ❶, rooms ❷

Central Backpackers 67 Hatea Drive ⓣ0800/227 222 or 09/437 6174, ⓔcentralback@xtra.co.nz. Slightly cramped but clean hostel in a converted suburban house with dorms, doubles and a couple of compact units with fridge and stove. Guests can rent kayaks at bargain prices and join coastal kayak trips ($35). Dorms ❶, rooms and units ❷

Whangarei Falls Holiday Park Ngunguru Rd, 6km from town near Whangarei Falls ⓣ & ⓕ09/437 0609, ⓦwww.whangareifalls.co.nz. Less convenient than the other campsites, but the setting – on the edge of the countryside, and with a pool and spa – compensates. Tent sites $10, dorms ❶, cabins ❷

Whangarei Holiday Park 24 Mair St ☎09/437 6856, ⓔwhangareiholiday@actric.co.nz. Small, tranquil and well-maintained site 2km from town with a range of accommodation from tents and powered sites to en-suite cabins. Tents $10, dorms ❶, on-site vans and cabins ❷

Whangarei Manaki Tanga YHA 52 Punga Grove Ave ☎09/438 8954, ⓔyhawhang@yha.org.nz. Intimate hilltop hostel a steep fifteen-minute walk up from the centre of Whangarei, with good views over the town and glow-worms a ten-minute walk away into the bush. Accommodation is in twins, doubles and four- and six-bed dorms, and there are Friday-night barbecues in summer, plus free bikes. Dorms ❶, rooms ❷

The Town

The working port that originally brought Whangarei its prosperity is a few kilometres out of town, leaving the renovated **Town Basin** to restaurants and a smattering of tourist sights. Nearby, ranks of car sales-yards and print shops press in on the central grid of streets where the museum, fernery and craft quarry can occupy half a day. There's more interest just out of town at the cluster of museums around the **Clarke Homestead**, at Whangarei Falls, and in the smattering of local **walks**.

Central Whangarei

Whangarei's greatest concentration of sights is around the **Town Basin**, a prettified zone of upmarket galleries, shops and restaurants based around an 1880s villa. Amble around, calling in at the kauri and fudge shops and perhaps wrestling with the pieces on the giant chess board outside the **Burning Issues Gallery** (daily 10am–5pm; free), a glass and ceramics studio where you can watch glass-blowing most days. The only essential sight is **Clapham's Clocks** (daily 9am–5pm; $5), right by New Zealand's largest sundial, and packed with 1500 clocks, ranging from mechanisms taken out of church towers to cuckoo clocks, by way of work-time recorders, domestic timepieces and all manner of ornamental clocks. Nearby, Whangarei's oldest kauri villa, **Reyburn House** (Tues–Fri 10am–4pm, Sat & Sun 1–4pm; free), hosts the Northland Society of Arts' exhibition gallery, usually containing a few quality pieces.

On the western side of the town centre, the small but well-kept **Cafler Park** makes a pleasant place for a stroll – head for the Rose Gardens and the adjacent **Whangarei Art Museum** (Tues–Fri 10am–4pm, Sat & Sun noon–4pm; donation), which has a small permanent collection of New Zealand art and frequently changing exhibitions that showcase Kiwi artists. A footbridge crosses the stream running through Cafler Park to the restful and cool **Margie Maddren Fernery**, First Avenue (daily 10am–4pm; free), a compact collection of native ferns packed into half a dozen specially built compounds. These are flanked by two glasshouses: the **Filmy Fern House** provides a damp, draught-free environment for New Zealand's more delicate fern species, while the **Snow Conservatory** contains a steamy tropical hothouse and a desert room packed with cacti. From here, it's ten minutes' walk to the **Craft Quarry** artists' co-operative, Selwyn Avenue (daily 10am–4pm; free), something of a focus for the vibrant crafts community in this part of Northland. You're free to wander among anarchic shacks built from adobe, timber and corrugated iron, watch the artisans at work (though few are on hand at weekends) and, of course, to buy their handiwork.

Suitably inspired, you may fancy having a go at making your own paper and cards at **The Papermakers**, 4km south on SH1 at Otaika (book ahead on ☎09/438 2652; daily $4, or $6 to make paper), where an interesting range of handcrafted paper is produced from recycled materials in an eighteenth-century cottage – don't let the period costumes put you off.

The Clarke Homestead and Whangarei Museum

There's another collection of museums ($3 each, or $7 combined ticket) 6km southwest of Whangarei on SH14 in Maunu, in the grounds of the **Clarke Homestead** (daily 10am–4pm), a rare example of an unrestored original homestead. Built in 1886 for a Scottish doctor, Alexander Clarke, the house was at its most vibrant in the 1930s, when Alexander's son James hosted high-society parties here, and much of what you see dates from that era. Among the accumulated possessions of the three generations, the highlight is the unkempt, boys-own bedroom of Alexander's grandson, Basil, complete with hunting gear, drum kit and an impressive shelf of medicines.

The **Whangarei Museum** (same hours; $3), housed in a modern building in the homestead grounds, has an intriguing selection of objects relating to local history, flora and fauna, plus a small but good Maori collection. Among the clubs, fishing lures and agricultural implements is a lovely feather cloak, but the prize exhibit is the *waka tupapuka*, a unique sixteenth-century wooden funerary chest decorated with bird-form carvings, as opposed to the more common human forms. The museum's **Kiwi House** (same hours; $3) is one of the best of its ilk, nicely laid out and with good visibility. On several Sundays through the summer the complex holds themed "live days", when $5 gets you the run of the place along with, say, vintage transport buffs or log-skidding experts.

Eating, drinking and entertainment

When it comes to **eating**, Whangarei has more choice than anywhere between Auckland and the Bay of Islands. A selection of popular **fast-food** franchises line Bank Street, while more imaginative **restaurants** cluster around the Town Basin and along Cameron Street. For **groceries**, Pak 'n' Save, on the corner of Robert Street and Carruth Street, has the best prices. Look out too for draft microbrews produced by the local Northland Breweries, available at several locations around town.

For details of **live music** gigs, check "The Leader" pullout from Tuesday's *Northern Advocate* newspaper.

Barfly 13 Rathbone St. Friendly all-day café/bar known locally for its excellent coffee, wood-fired pizzas, vegetarian dishes and lavish desserts.

Bogart's 84 Cameron St. Easy-going licensed restaurant that's always lively at weekends, serving crispy gourmet pizzas and a range of appealing mains for under $20; also opens during the day for coffee and snacks.

Café Mozart 60 Cameron St ☎09/438 1116. Swiss-run café and licensed restaurant in a former pharmacy which still retains much of its original woodwork and many of its glass cases. An eclectic menu – steaks, curries, kebabs and salads – also includes a nod in the direction of the owner's heritage, with Swiss sausage soup and a Zurich-style chicken breast, plus some delicious fruit tarts, all at modest prices. Mozart plays on the stereo. Closed Sun.

Killer Prawn 28 Bank St. Conservatory-style café, bar and restaurant that's the place to be seen in Whangarei, with a multitude of dishes ranging from sashimi to steaks, plus many offerings featuring prawns. Light snacks start at around $5; enormous mains at around $25.

Parua Bay Tavern Parua Bay Rd ☎09/436 5856. Waterside pub 20km out of town on the road to Whangarei Heads which frequently hosts live bands; listen to local radio for details or check "The Leader".

Planet Earth Bank St, near cnr Vine St. A big, colourful and kicking bar where live bands play from time to time as the mood takes them. There's standard bar food – burgers, pizzas and nachos – too. Closed Sun.

Hikes and activities around Whangarei

Perhaps Whangarei's most appealing feature is the number of small parks and easy **walks** within a few minutes of the town, the best of which are outlined in the *Whangarei Walks* leaflet, available free from the visitor centre. Views over the harbour and town are the reward for making it up to the ugly sheet-metal war memorial atop the 240m **Mount Parahaki**, which can be approached by car along Memorial Drive (off Riverside Drive; 3km) or on foot along the steep Ross Track (40min ascent) from the end of Dundas Road.

Most visitors, however, prefer the twenty-minute stroll around the broad curtain of the **Whangarei Falls**, where the Hatea River cascades over a 26-metre basalt ridge into a popular swimming hole. The falls are 5km northeast of the town centre; Kamo-bound buses pass close by. The road out to the falls passes Whareora Road, which runs 1.5km to the **A. H. Reed Memorial Kauri Park**, where shady paths through native bush pass several mature kauri – look out especially for the ten-minute Alexander Walk, which follows a sinuous boardwalk high across a creek, looking down on palms and ferns before reaching some fine kauri.

Three kilometres further along the same road, the fluted and weather-worn limestone formations of **Abbey Caves** (unrestricted access) invite comparison with Henry Moore sculptures. Though the caves are open to anyone, you really need some caving experience to enter them; the best bet is to enrol on a one-hour-plus **guided tour** from Whangarei (☎09/437 6174; $15).

Some 18km southwest of town on SH14, the **Bushwacka Experience** (reserve in advance on ☎09/434 7839) offers fun packages of outdoor adventures amid interesting geology and thick bush hidden away on a dairy farm. You can tailor your visit from a range of activities including 4WD safaris, exploring the "Squeeze" or one of the other deep volcanic rock crevices, abseiling into the "Black Hole", hiking to some giant kauri or just relaxing over a barbecue. The cost is $55 for two hours, $85 for half a day, including pick up from Whangarei.

Red Iguana In the *Grand Hotel*, cnr Bank St & Rose St. Nicely modernized version of a traditional Kiwi bar, mainly devoted to bar-propping, boozing and sports-watching, but also serving $8 lunches and hosting live bands at weekends.
Reva's On The Waterfront Town Basin ☎09/438 8969. A Whangarei institution, with breezy quayside seating and a broad range of daily specials (around $25) from char-grilled peppers and Bream Bay seafood to gourmet pizzas.
Rin Chin Chilla 6 Vine St ☎09/438 5882. Small and cheery coffee and snack bar with a small but well formed appealing range of kebabs, felafel, tortilla wraps and nachos (mostly $6–9), plus good coffee and shakes, to eat in or out. Closed Mon.

Around Whangarei

The best reason to spend some time in Whangarei is to explore the surrounding area, particularly the areas east and north of the town where the craggy, weathered remains of ancient volcanoes abut the sea. Southeast of the town **Whangarei Heads** is the district's volcanic heartland, where dramatic walks follow the coast to calm harbour beaches and windswept coastal strands. To the northeast, **Tutukaka** acts as the base for dive trips to the undersea wonderland around the **Poor Knights Islands**. Heading north from Whangarei or Tutukaka to the Bay of Islands, don't miss the **Hundertwasser toilets** in Kawakawa (see p.193).

There's no useful **public transport** to any of these places, and the rugged terrain can make cycling a challenge, but dive-trip operators run trips out from Whangarei.

△ Hundertwasser toilets

Whangarei Heads

The winding road around the northern side of Whangarei Harbour runs 35km southeast to **Whangarei Heads**, a catch-all name for a series of small beach communities scattered around jagged volcanic outcrops that terminate at Bream Head, the northern limit of Bream Bay. Numerous attractive bays provide safe swimming – **McLeod Bay** in particular – but there's really no special reason to stop until the road leaves the harbour and climbs to a saddle at the start of an excellent, signposted **walk** (3km return; 2hr–2hr 30min; 200m ascent) up the 430m **Mount Manaia**, the heads' most distinctive summit, crowned with five deeply eroded pinnacles, whose unusual shape is shrouded in legend. One tells of a jealous dispute between two chiefs, Manaia, whose *pa* (fortified village) stood atop Mount Manaia, and the lesser chief, Hautatu, from across the water at Marsden Point, who was married to the beautiful Pito. Hautatu was sent away on a raid, leaving the coast clear for Manaia to steal Pito. Hautatu returned and was chasing Manaia, his two children and Pito across the hilltop when all five were struck by lightning, leaving the figures petrified on the summit. These pinnacles remain *tapu*, but you can climb to their base through native bush, passing fine viewpoints.

Beyond Mount Manaia, the road runs for 5km to **Urquharts Bay**, where a short walk (20min each way) leads to the white-sand **Smugglers Cove**. A longer trail (3hr return) continues to **Peach Cove**, and very keen walkers could press on to **Ocean Beach** (5hr one way), a wild surf beach that's also accessible by road.

Tutukaka and the Poor Knights

The Tutukaka coast means one of two things to New Zealanders: big-game fishing or scuba diving – both based in tiny **TUTUKAKA**, set on a beautiful, deeply incised harbour 30km northeast of Whangarei. Boats leave from here for one of the world's premier dive locations, the **Poor Knights Islands Marine Reserve**, 25km offshore. Here the warm East Auckland current swirling around Cape Reinga and the lack of run-off from the land combine to create wonderfully clear water – visibility approaches 30m most of the year, though in spring (roughly Oct–Dec) a profusion of plankton can reduce it to 15–20m. These waters are home to New Zealand's most diverse range of sea life, including some subtropical species found nowhere else around its shores, as well as a striking underwater landscape of near-vertical **rock faces** which drop down almost 100m through a labyrinth of caves, fissures and rock arches teeming with rainbow-coloured fish, crabs, soft corals, kelp forests and shellfish. The Poor Knights also lie along the migratory routes of a number of **whale** species, so blue, humpback, sei and minke whales, as well as dolphins, are not uncommon. As if that weren't enough, the waters north and south of the reserve are home to two navy **wrecks**, both deliberately scuttled. The survey ship HMNZS *Tui* was sunk in 1999 to form an artificial reef, and such was its popularity with both divers and marine life that the obsolete frigate *Waikato* followed two years later.

Everything is protected within the Poor Knights reserve, but free-ranging species such as marlin, shark and tuna which stray outside the reserve are picked off by **big-game anglers** during the December to May season. Anglers wanting to rent a quarter-share of a charter game-fishing boat for the day should expect to pay $200 or more: contact the Whangarei Deep Sea Anglers Club (☎09/434 3818).

The reserve also contains myriad **islands**, though you're not actually allowed to land on any of them. Many of these were cultivated by Maori until a nineteenth-century massacre, after which they became *tapu* – they're now a safe haven for geckos, skinks and thousands of tuatara, the sole survivors of a branch of prehistoric lizards the rest of which became extinct sixty million years back.

Practicalities

About the only amenities you'll find around the harbour at Tutukaka are **restaurants**, most notably the *Schnappa Rock Café*, Marina Road (ⓣ09/434 3774), a stylish and casual bar-restaurant in modern Kiwi mode with seating inside and out, and a tempting range of dishes including pasta and succulent burgers ($12–15), plus evening mains (around $25). The *Blue Marlin Restaurant*, upstairs at the Whangarei Deep Sea Anglers Club beside the Tutukaka harbour, offers a range of dishes for around $20 – pasta, cajun chicken and, not surprisingly, seafood – as well as a cheaper bistro menu.

Local **accommodation** is mostly on the headland just south of Tutukaka or 5km back towards Whangarei in **NGUNGURU**, which is strung along an attractive, sandy estuary that's fine for swimming if you dodge the jet-skis. Here you'll find camping and cabins at the waterside *Ngunguru Motor Camp*, Papaka Road (ⓣ & ⓕ09/434 3851; tent sites $25 for two, cabins ❷–❸). For something a bit smarter, and pleasantly located right beside the sands of Whangamumu Bay, on the headland south of Tutukaka, make for *Sands Motel* (ⓣ09/434 3747, ⓕ434 3192; ❹), 4km off the highway along Tutukaka Block Road, with self-contained two-bedroom units each with TV, plus access to a smokehouse for your day's catch. Nearby, try the tranquil, self-contained suites at *Pacific Rendezvous*, 73 Motel Rd, off the Tutukaka Block Road (ⓣ0800/999 800 & 09/434 3847, ⓦwww.oceanresort.co.nz; ❻), fabulously sited on the peninsula that forms the southern arm of Tutukaka's harbour. In the same general area, diving groups are welcome at the two spacious and fully self-contained units (one sleeping 4, the other 8) set in a secluded subtropical garden at *Malibu Mals*, Tutukaka Block Road, Kowharewa Bay (ⓣ09/434 3450 ⓔmalibumal@xtra.co.nz; ❹).

Beaches north of Tutukaka

Settlements get smaller north of Tutukaka, with most comprising nothing more than a few holiday homes ranged behind the beach. Day-trippers flock from Whangarei for safe swimming in gorgeous bays tucked between headlands and dotted with numerous islets. Favourites include the village of **MATAPOURI**, 6km from Tutukaka, which backs a curving white-sand bay bounded by bushy headlands, and the pristine **Whale Bay**, 1km further north and reached by a twenty-minute bush walk. The only facilities along this stretch are *Dreamstay* (ⓣ09/434 3059, ⓔdreamstay@able.net.nz; ❺), a stunningly located B&B set high above Sandy Bay, just north of Whale Bay, and a shop and takeaway at Matapouri.

Heading inland from here the road is sealed all the way to **Hikurangi**, where it joins SH1. The coastal section between here and the Bay of Islands is most easily reached from Russell (see p.193).

The Bay of Islands

THE BAY OF ISLANDS, 240km north of Auckland, is one of the brightest stars in New Zealand's tourism firmament, luring thousands to its beautiful coastal scenery, scattered islands and clear blue waters. It's an undoubtedly

Diving and snorkelling around the Poor Knights

You'll need some prior diving experience to sample the best the **Poor Knights** have to offer, but there's plenty for novices and even snorkellers. Both Tutukaka and Whangarei can be used as **diving** bases, though **boats** all leave from Tutukaka. These offer broadly the same deal, with a full day out (8.30am–4pm), two dives and all the equipment you need costing $160–180, including transport from Whangarei. This comes down to $100–140 if you can provide some or all of your own gear, and a day's **snorkelling** starts at $90. First-time divers can try a **resort dive** ($210) with full gear and one-to-one instruction; a PADI open-water dive qualification will cost about $550 and take four or five days, two of them out at the Poor Knights.

Half a dozen companies run daily trips in the main season (Nov–April), and usually at least one of them goes out most days throughout the rest of the year. The visitor centre in Whangarei (see p.174) has a full list of current **operators**, but the most prominent and one of the most professional in Tutukaka is Dive Tutukaka, Marina Rd, Tutukaka (Ⓣ0800/288 882 & 09/434 3867, Ⓦwww.diving.co.nz), who offer wreck dives and trips to the Poor Knights, ensuring that you're on a boat with similarly skilled divers, and even catering to non-divers with kayaking and snorkelling. In Whangarei, good deals are available at The Dive Connection, 140 Lower Cameron St (Ⓣ09/430 0818) and Dive HQ, 41 Clyde St (Ⓣ09/438 1075).

Non-divers can appreciate these waters from the safety of a **cruise** on the *Wairangi* (Ⓣ09/434 3350, Ⓔritchie@ihug.co.nz; $60) – an ex-pilot boat skippered by a knowledgeable marine biologist. Day-trips leave from Tutukaka marina, stopping for snorkelling en route, and dolphin sightings are common. The *Wairangi* also operates overnight charters, comfortably accommodating twelve people (prices vary and are negotiable).

appealing place, but for scenery alone it is really no more stunning than several other spots along the Northland coast, such as Whangaroa and Hokianga harbours. What sets it apart is the ease with which you can get out among the islands, and also the bay's rich history – this was the cradle of European settlement in New Zealand, a fact abundantly testified to by the bay's churches, mission stations and orchards. It's also a focal point for Maori on account of the **Treaty of Waitangi** (see box on p.191) – still, despite its limitations, New Zealand's most important legal document.

Perhaps surprisingly, much of your time in the Bay of Islands will be spent on the mainland. There are no settlements on the islands, and there's only one on which you are allowed to stay overnight. The vast majority of visitors base themselves in beachside **Paihia**, which is well set up to deal with the hordes who come here eager to launch themselves on the various cruises and other excursions, as well as being the closest town to the Treaty House at **Waitangi**. The compact town of **Russell**, a couple of kilometres across the bay by passenger ferry, is prettier and more restrained, though almost equally convenient for cruises. To the northwest, away from the bay itself, **Kerikeri** is intimately entwined with the area's early missionary history, while **Waimate North**, inland to the west, was another important mission site and still has its Mission House, though the regional focus has now moved further south to **Kaikohe**.

As the main tourist centre in Northland, the Bay of Islands acts as a staging post for forays further north, in particular for day-long **bus tours** to Cape Reinga and Ninety Mile Beach – arduous affairs lasting eleven hours, most of them spent stuck inside the vehicle. You're better off making your way up to Mangonui or Kaitaia and taking a trip from there, though if time is short you

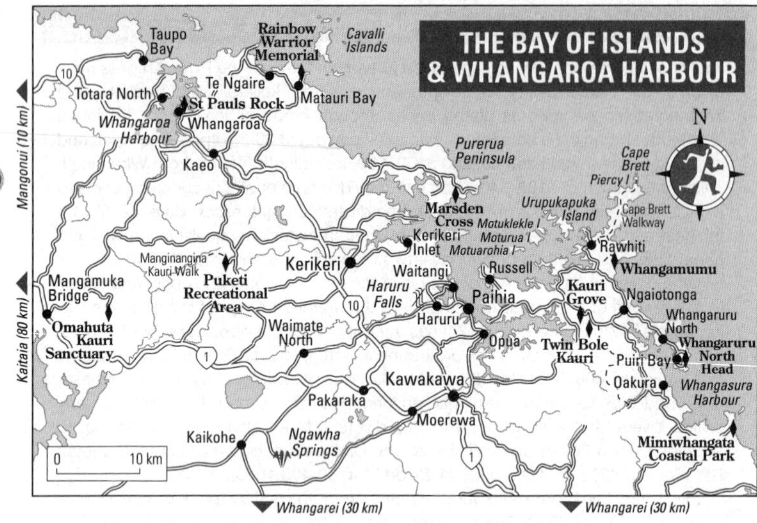

can take your pick from a wide range of Paihia-based excursions, including scenic flights over Northland.

Some history

A warm climate, abundant seafood and deep, sheltered harbours all contributed to dense pre-European **Maori settlement** in the Bay of Islands, with every headland seeming to support a *pa*. The sheltered bay also appealed to **Captain Cook**, who anchored here in 1769 and prosaically noted in his journal, "I have named it the Bay of Islands on account of the great number which line its shores, and these help to form several safe and commodious harbours". Cook landed on Motuarohia Island at what became known as Cook's Cove, where he forged generally good relations with the inhabitants. Three years later the French sailor **Marion du Fresne**, en route from Mauritius to Tahiti, became the first European to have sustained contact with Maori, though he ultimately fared less well. He stayed three months while his crew recovered their health and the ship was refitted, but a misunderstanding, probably over *tapu*, soured their initial accord and du Fresne and 26 of his crew were killed. The French retaliated, destroying a *pa* and killing hundreds of Maori.

Despite amicable relations between the local Ngapuhi Maori and Pakeha whalers in the early years of the nineteenth century, the situation gradually deteriorated to the point where historian Robert Hughes described the mid-nineteenth-century Bay of Islands as "a veritable rookery of absconders ... littered with grim little communities and patriarchal clans of convicts". With increased contact, firearms, grog and Old World diseases spread and the fabric of Maori life began to break down, a process accelerated by the arrival in 1814 of Samuel Marsden, the first of many **missionaries** intent on turning Maori into God-fearing Christians. In 1833, James Busby was sent as the "British resident" to secure British interests and prevent the brutal treatment meted out to the Maori by whaling captains, though lacking armed back-up or judicial authority, he had little effect. The signing of the **Treaty of Waitangi** in 1840 brought effective policing, but heralded a decline in the importance of the Bay of Islands, as the capital moved from its original site of Kororareka (now Russell), first to Auckland and later to Wellington.

The Bay of Islands regained some degree of world recognition in 1927, when American writer **Zane Grey** came here to fish for striped and black marlin, making the area famous with his book *The Angler's El Dorado*. Every summer since, the bay has seen game-fishing tournaments and glistening catches strung up on the jetties.

The islands

The only island which accommodates overnight guests is **Urupukapuka Island**, where Zane Grey, author of best-selling westerns and avid hooker of marlin, set up a fishing resort at Otehei Bay. The resort largely burned down in 1973, but you can still stay in the accommodation units, which now operate as the *Zane Grey Lodge* (Ⓣ09/403 7009, Ⓔreservations@zanegrey.co.nz; $20 per person), with spartan, private rooms, full kitchen and optional linen rental ($5). The adjacent *Zane Grey* restaurant is a frequent stopping point for Fullers cruises, which provide regular access to the island; lodge guests pay the concessionary $35 return fare. There are also basic DOC **campsites** ($6) in all except the western bays of the island and there's a range of Maori *pa* and terrace sites, which can be explored in a few hours by following signs on the island and the free *Urupukapuka Island Archeological Walk* leaflet.

Of the bay's other six large islands, by far the most popular is **Motuarohia**, more commonly known as **Roberton Island** after John Roberton, who moved here in 1839. The Department of Conservation manages the most dramatic central section, an isthmus almost severed by a pair of perfectly circular blue lagoons. Understandably, it's immensely popular with both private boaties and commercial cruises, and DOC have even gone to the trouble of installing an undersea nature trail for snorkellers, waymarked by inscribed stainless-steel plaques. The wildlife sanctuary of **Moturua** lies adjacent, offering a network of walks through bush alive with spotted kiwi, saddlebacks and North Island robins.

Other sights which often feature on cruise itineraries include **the Black Rocks**, bare islets formed from columnar jointed basalt – these rise only 10m out of the water but plummet a sheer 30m beneath, allowing boats to inspect them at close quarters. At the outer limit of the bay is the craggy peninsula of **Cape Brett**, named by Cook in 1769 after the then Lord of the Admiralty, Lord Piercy Brett. Cruises also regularly pass through the **Hole in The Rock**, a natural tunnel through Piercy Island, an activity made more exciting when there's a swell running.

Exploring the bay

Wherever you turn in the Bay of Islands you'll find people keen to take you yachting, scuba-diving, dolphin-watching, kayaking or fishing. The vast majority of trips start in Paihia, but all the major **cruises** and bay **excursions** also pick up from Russell wharf around fifteen minutes later. Occasionally there are no pick-ups available, but the **ferry** between Paihia and Russell only costs $5 each way. The Bay of Islands is popular and prices can be quite high, especially during the summer months when demand outstrips supply and everything should be booked at least a couple of days in advance. Most hotels and motels will book these trips for you and hostels can usually arrange some sort of "backpacker" discount of around ten percent, though better deals can sometimes be obtained by booking direct. Almost all bookings can be made in or around the Maritime Building on Marsden Road either with the main **tour operators**: King's (Ⓣ0800/222 979 & 09/402 8288, Ⓦwww.dolphincruises.co.nz); Fullers (Ⓣ0800/653 339 & 09/402 7421, Ⓦwww.fullers-bay-of-islands.co.nz); or their adventure-oriented offshoot Awesome Adventures (Ⓣ09/402 6985, Ⓦwww.awesomeadventures.co.nz). All are open until around 6pm in winter, 9pm in summer.

In addition to the water-based activities covered below you can see the bay in style on **flights** offered by Paihia-based Salt Air (Ⓣ0800/472 582 & 09/402 8338, Ⓦwww.saltair.co.nz), who charge $95 for thirty minutes, $145 for an hour, and also offer island stopovers.

Cruises

Unless you get out onto the water you're missing the essence of the Bay of Islands. There are three cruise companies vying for business, all based in or around the Maritime Building, by the wharf: the longstanding Fullers operates large and stable craft, while the family-run King's and relative newcomers Dolphin Discoveries run similar trips in smaller boats. Expect the boats to be full during peak season, and book in good time.

For 35 years from 1919, **Fullers** boats collected cream from dairy farms around the perimeter of the bay, but as the infrastructure improved, the cream took to the roads and the boats began to take passengers. By the 1950s, the cream trade had died and the boat trip had been transformed into the leisurely Cream Trip that now forms part of the Supercruise (Sept–May daily; June–Aug Mon, Wed, Thurs & Sat; 6–7hr; $85), which still delivers groceries and mail to wharves all around the bay and includes a cream tea, for old time's sake. This cruise also visits the Hole in the Rock and spends ninety minutes at Otehei Bay. If that's too much boating for one day, try the Hole in the Rock Cruise (1–2 daily; 4hr; $60), which speeds out through the islands to Cape Brett and, when conditions permit, edges through the hole itself – by splitting your journey between the two daily summer trips, you can spend a few hours on Urupukapuka. Those wanting to maximize their time on Urupukapuka might prefer Island Time (Dec–Feb daily; $35). This gives you up to seven hours ashore, during which you could take a trip on Nautilus ($12), a kind of deep-hulled boat with undersea viewing windows which putters out into the bay for twenty minutes to a spot where fish are fed.

King's, meanwhile, offer a Hole in the Rock Scenic Cruise (1–2 daily; 3hr; $58), which makes no island stops but includes a *powhiri* (welcome) and onboard Maori legend commentary, and the Day in the Bay trip (Oct–May daily; 6hr; $83), taking in the Hole in the Rock, an approximation of the Cream Trip and an island stop of the captain's choice.

Dolphin Discoveries ($60) run a three- to four-hour fast cat around the bay with no fixed schedule or pre-set island stops, giving added flexibility.

Fast boats

The two main cruise companies each work in conjunction with **fast-boat operators**. King's led the field by introducing *Mack Attack* (mid-Dec to May; 5 daily; 1hr 30min; $60; Ⓔkingsnz@voyager.co.nz), an adrenalin-pumping blast out to the Hole in the Rock and back in an open catamaran driven by 1200hp engines. Even on fine days you're kitted out in windproof and waterproof gear, protective glasses and life jacket, but despite the unpleasantness of having rain driven into your face at sixty kilometres-plus an hour, they still go in all but the worst weather. *The Excitor* (6 daily in summer, 2 daily in winter; 1hr 30min; $60; Ⓣ09/402 7020, Ⓦwwwexcitor.co.nz) is basically the same thing.

Sailing

For **day-trips**, Fullers' *R. Tucker Thompson,* a Northland-built schooner in the "tall ship" tradition, sails out into the islands and anchors for a swim and barbecue lunch (late Oct–April daily; 7hr; $89). Smaller yachts usually take less than a dozen passengers: competition is tight and the standards high, with all having snorkelling and fishing gear on board and typically going out for six hours and including lunch. Pick of the bunch are *Carino* ($60, plus $5 for BBQ lunch; Ⓣ09/402 8040, Ⓔcarinonz@voyager.co.nz), a large red catamaran based in Paihia skippered by a woman who also offers swimming with dolphins; the nine-metre catamaran, *Straycat* ($72; Ⓣ09/402 6130); and the twenty-metre yacht *Gungha* ($75; Ⓣ0800/478 900, Ⓦwww.bayofislandssailing.co.nz).

If you fancy more than a day-trip, you should seriously consider a **three-day sail** on the twenty-two-metre twin-masted *Manawanui* with Ecocruz ($350; Ⓣ0800/432 627, Ⓦwww.bigblueandgreen.co.nz), which takes up to twelve people out around the Bay with the emphasis on exploration and appreciation of the natural environment. Excellent meals are all included along with on-board dorm-style accommodation, use of kayaks, snorkel gear, fishing tackle and a good deal of local knowledge and enthusiasm.

Kayaking

Lack of previous experience is no impediment to going kayaking in and around Paihia, with plenty of operators offering **guided trips**. Coastal Kayakers, based by the Waitangi Bridge (Ⓣ09/402 8105, Ⓕ403 8550), operate year-round and run half-day trips upstream to Haruru Falls ($43) and full-day trips ($65), which also includes paddling around Motumaire Island; longer excursions operate from November to June and cost around $110 a day. Island Kayaks, based at Pipi Patch Lodge, 18 Kings Rd (Ⓣ09/402 7111, Ⓔisland-kayaks@acb.co.nz), also operate all year, offering half-day and twilight trips exploring the inner islands and bays ($49).

If you want to go it alone, there are also various **rental outfits** to choose from. Bay Beach Hire, at the south end of Paihia Beach (Ⓣ09/402 7905) rents double and single open kayaks ($10 per hour, $40 a day), windsurfers ($25 per hour) and catamarans ($25 per hour); Coastal Kayakers (see above) also rent out kayaks for two or more people at a time, for safety's sake ($12 per hour, $30 per half-day, $45 a day), and catamarans (Dec–March; $20–30 an hour).

Dolphin watching and swimming

Relatively warm water all year round and an abundance of marine mammals make the Bay of Islands one of the best places to go **dolphin watching**. You're likely to see bottlenose and common dolphins in pretty much any season, orca from May to August and Minke and Bryde's **whales** from August to January. If you don't see anything, most companies will take you out for a second chance, though lack of a swim doesn't usually earn a repeat cruise.

Though cruise boats and yachts will detour for a positive cetacean sighting, the best way to see dolphins and whales is on a cruise with one of the four companies licensed to actively search for and swim with dolphins. There's no swimming when dolphins are feeding or if they have juveniles with them, and only a dozen people are allowed in the water at a time. Since most trips carry around 35 people in the peak season, you can expect to be in the water about a third of the time that the dolphins are about. The pioneers, **Dolphin Discoveries**, Marsden Road, opposite the visitor centre (Ⓣ09/402 8234, Ⓔdolphin@igrin.co.nz; $95), are sensitive to the needs of the dolphins and claim a ninety-five percent success rate, while Fullers' **Dolphin Adventures** ($95) include the option of a stopover on Urupukapuka for a few hours if you take the early boat. King's swim with dolphins as part of their Day in the Bay cruise (see above), and finally, *Carino* (see p.185) takes you on a day-trip around the islands, with a chance to swim with the dolphins if you come across them in the right conditions.

Diving and fishing

The main people running **scuba-diving** trips are Paihia Dive (Ⓣ09/402 7551, Ⓕ402 7110, Ⓔdivepaihia@xtra.co.nz), who will take you **snorkelling** ($75) and diving in the Bay of Islands (from $90 with no gear supplied; from $150 with all gear) or on the wreck of the *Rainbow Warrior* (see p.205; $160). The smaller Dive North (Ⓣ09/402 7345, Ⓔdivenorth@xtra.co.nz) charge similar prices for comparable trips.

There is a wider range and greater choice of **fishing trips** than any other activity: everything from a little line fishing for snapper to big game boats in search of marlin, shark, tuna and kingfish. The best method is to ask around and speak to the skippers to make sure you get a trip that suits; daily charter rates range around $60 to $500 for the big game boats.

Parasailing, horse riding and zorbing

For a serene scenic view over the bay combined with the fun of **parasailing** you can spend time airborne with Flying Kiwi Parasail (Ⓣ09/402 6078), who'll winch you off the back of a speedboat up to around 200m ($60) or 300m ($70), either solo for ten minutes or tandem for twenty minutes, then winch you back in again – all without getting your feet wet.

Should you wish to stay on dry land there are a couple of activities to keep you entertained, not least **horse riding** with Big Rock Springs Trail Rides (Ⓣ09/405 9999) who charge $70 for a full day out with four to five hours riding around the hills near Waimate, swimming the horses in the river and viewing glow-worm caves. If you're searching for something a little odd-ball try **Zorb** ($40; Ⓣ025/208 1319), which takes place 5km west of Haruru Falls on Puketona Rd.

Paihia and Waitangi

PAIHIA is where it all happens. In its own way, it is just as historically important as Russell, Waitangi and Kerikeri, but this two-kilometre-long string of waterside motels, restaurants and holiday homes has been completely overrun by the demands of tourism. Its location on three flat bays looking out towards Russell and the Bay of Islands is pleasing enough and the encircling forested hills make an attractive backdrop, but the town itself could hardly be called pretty. Nevertheless, abundant well-priced accommodation, several good restaurants, a couple of boisterous bars and endless possibilities to get out on the water make this the goal of the vast majority of visitors to the Bay of Islands.

Legend has it that the town was named in 1823 by the less than accomplished Maori scholar, the Reverend Henry Williams, when he was looking for a site to establish the Church Missionary Society's third mission. He apparently exclaimed, "*pai* [good] here!" – unlikely, but it makes a nice story. At the time, Maori were overwhelmed by the influx of Europeans and looked to the missionaries to intercede on their behalf. A plaque outside the current St Paul's Anglican Church on Marsden Road marks the spot where, in 1831, the north-

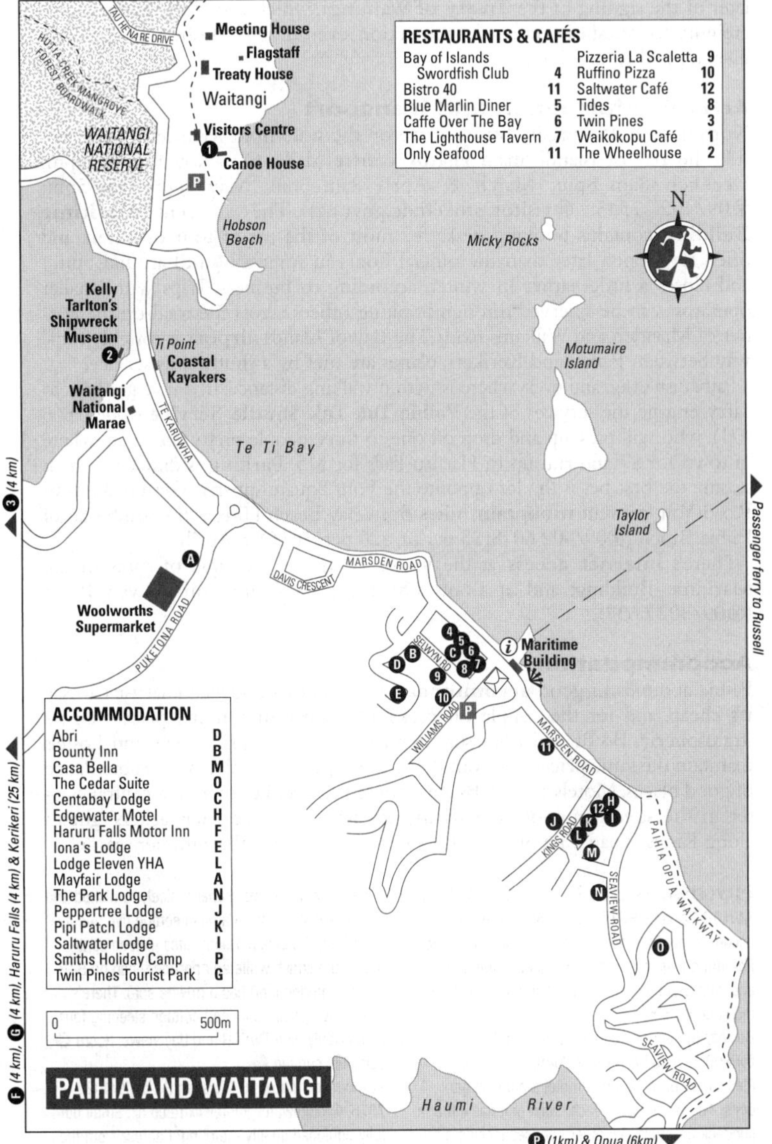

ern chiefs petitioned the British Crown for a representative to establish law and order. In 1833 King William IV belatedly addressed their concerns by sending the first British resident, James Busby. He built a house on a promontory 2km north across the Waitangi River in **WAITANGI** – the scene some seven years later of the signing of the **Treaty of Waitangi**, which ceded the nation's sovereignty to Britain in return for protection, even though Busby was singularly ill-equipped to provide it.

Arrival, information and transport

Northliner and InterCity **buses** arrive on the waterfront Marsden Road outside the Bay of Islands' main **visitor centre** (daily: Oct–Nov 8am–6.30pm; Dec–Feb 8am–8pm; March & April 8am–6pm; May–Sept 8am–5pm; ⓣ09/402 7345, ⓔvisitorinfo@fndc.govt.nz). The adjacent **Maritime Building** contains booking desks for most of the major tour operators and often stays open later than the official hours in summer (until around 9pm), and closes a little earlier in winter, according to business. Trips with smaller operators can be reserved through booking offices across the road on the corner of Marsden and Williams roads. The Bay of Islands **airport** is roughly midway between Paihia and Kerikeri; planes are met by a shuttle bus service.

Paihia isn't big, and everywhere is within walking distance. If you've got bags to carry, engage the services of the **Paihia Tuk Tuk Shuttle Service** (ⓣ025/866 071), who will pick up and drop off one to three people pretty much anywhere in town for $7 and run up to Haruru Falls for $15. **Parking** is difficult in high season; the best bet is the lot opposite the Four Square supermarket on Williams Road. You can rent **mountain bikes** from Bay Beach Hire, at the south end of Paihia Beach (ⓣ09/402 6078; $5 per hr, $20 per day; Oct–April).

There's **internet access** at the visitor centre; at a couple of spots in the Maritime Building; and at Boots Off Travellers Centre on Selwyn Road (ⓣ09/402 6632).

Accommodation

Paihia abounds in good **accommodation** to suit all budgets. That isn't to say it's cheap, and for the couple of weeks after Christmas, motel prices can be stratospheric. B&Bs and homestays tend to vary their prices less, and hostels maintain the same prices year round, and are kept competitive by the abundance of good places. Motels and B&Bs are scattered all over but there is a central cluster in the streets opposite the wharf, and it's a veritable backpackers' ghetto along Kings Road. The price codes given below are for the summer season.

Hotels, motels and B&Bs

Abri 10 Bayview Rd ⓣ09/402 8003, ⓦwww.abri-accom.co.nz. Two modern and very private studio apartments appointed to the highest standards and with great views over the town and bay from the sundecks. ❽

Bounty Inn cnr Bayview Rd & Selwyn Rd ⓣ0800/117 897 & 09/402 7088, ⓕ402 7081. Pleasant central yet quiet motel amid lush gardens, 100m from the beach. Each unit has either a sundeck or a balcony; other bonuses include a private spa, on-site restaurant and ample off-street parking. ❺

Casa Bella 3 MacMurray Rd ⓣ09/402 7387,ⓔcasa.bel@xtra.co.nz. Simple, recently renovated rooms around a quiet stuccoed courtyard with a heated pool and spa. ❺

The Cedar Suite 5 Sullivan's Rd ⓣ09/402 8516, ⓔcdr.swt@xtra.co.nz. Superb, nicely furnished and very hospitable B&B in a bush setting five minutes' walk from the beach. Room rates include continental breakfast, while an apartment can be B&B or self-catering (and has a private spa). There's also a lovely self-contained cottage sleeping four comfortably with TV/VCR and bay views. Room ❺, suite ❻, cottage ❻

Edgewater Motel 10 Marsden Rd ⓣ09/402 7875, ⓔedgewater_motel@xtra.co.nz. Small but fully equipped quality motel right across from the beach with video, a spa pool, and a fenced playground for kids. ❺

Iona's Lodge 29 Bayview Rd ⓣ & ⓕ09/402 8072, ⓦwww.ionaslodge.com. Central, self-contained units with a wonderful panoramic view of the bay, and very reasonable rates which include a breakfast tray. ❹

Hostels

Centabay Lodge 27 Selwyn Rd Ⓣ09/402 7466, Ⓕ402 8145, Ⓔcentabay@xtra.co.nz. Central hostel near the beach and shops, with decent three- to five-bunk dorms, twins and doubles (with and without private bath) and motel-style self-catering studios. Guests get free use of kayaks. Dorms ❶, rooms ❷, ensuite rooms ❸, studios ❹

Lodge Eleven YHA cnr Kings Rd & MacMurray Rd Ⓣ09/402 7487, Ⓔlodgeeleven@hotmail.com. Good-value central hostel with eight-bunk and four-share dorms, plus rooms that are en suite, as well as airy motel-style doubles and twins, all serviced daily. There's also bike rental, a barbecue area and tennis courts next door. Dorms ❶, rooms ❷

Mayfair Lodge 7 Puketona Rd Ⓣ & Ⓕ09/402 7471, Ⓔmayfair.lodge@xtra.co.nz. Paihia's smallest hostel, at the Waitangi end of town, with a friendly atmosphere and some of the cheapest dorm beds around in spacious six-bunk dorms, as well as unmade twins and made-up doubles. Other facilities include a spa pool and a games room, free kayaks and bike rental. Tents $12, dorms ❶, rooms ❷

Peppertree Lodge 15 Kings Rd Ⓣ & Ⓕ09/402 6122, Ⓔpeppertree.lodge@xtra.co.nz. Deluxe, quiet and central hostel with spacious eight-bunk dorms, four-bunk dorms with bathroom, and particularly nice en-suite doubles. The games room, TV room, quiet lounge and fully equipped kitchen are all in tip-top condition without seeming sterile. Be sure to book ahead from October to May. Dorms ❶, rooms ❸, self-contained flat ❹

Pipi Patch Lodge 18 Kings Rd Ⓣ09/402 7111, Ⓔpipipatch@acb.co.nz. Central converted motel now operating as a VIP hostel that's popular with Kiwi Experience, making it a party place. Accommodation is in dorms (sleeping up to eight) and fully self-contained twins or doubles. There's also a communal kitchen, spa, plunge pool and bar. Dorms ❶, rooms ❸

Saltwater Lodge 14 Kings Rd Ⓣ0800/002 266 & 09/402 7075, Ⓦwww.saltwater.co.nz. Very new, clean and efficiently laid out hostel, if lacking in character, with six- and four-share dorms, each with its own bathroom and a locker for each guest (bring a lock), and attractive motel-style rooms on the upper floor with great sea views. Facilities include a large lounge with video library, a barbecue area, small gym and free bikes, tennis and kayaks. Dorms ❶, rooms ❺

Campsites

Haruru Falls Motor Inn and Camping Ground Puketona Rd Ⓣ09/402 7816, Ⓔbookings@falls.co.nz. Tent sites down by the river facing Haruru Falls, 4km north of Paihia, and motel units around a nice pool with commanding views of the falls. Tents $12, motel units ❸

The Park Lodge cnr Seaview Rd & MacMurray Rd Ⓣ09/402 7826, Ⓔparklodge@xtra.co.nz. Average hotel backed by Paihia's most central campsite, now equipped with new kitchen facilities. Tents $12.

Smith's Holiday Camp Opua Rd, 3km south of Paihia Ⓣ09/402 7678, Ⓔsmithshc@xtra.co.nz. Small and peaceful waterside site with a range of cabins and units, as well as dinghies for rent. Tent sites $12.50, cabins and units ❷–❺

Twin Pines Tourist Park Puketona Road Ⓣ & Ⓕ09/402 7322, Ⓔenquiries@twinpines.co.nz. Attractive, well laid out and recently upgraded site by Haruru Falls, 4km north of Paihia. Tents $12, cabins ❸, motel units ❹

The Town

Paihia is primarily a base for exploring the bay, and there are really no sights in town itself. Around a kilometre north, the Waitangi River separates Paihia from Waitangi and provides a mooring for the *Tui*, a three-masted barque, built as a sugar lighter in 1917, which now accommodates **Kelly Tarlton's Shipwreck Museum** (daily 10am–6pm; $7.50). Kelly Tarlton was New Zealand's foremost wreck diver and this museum demonstrates the scale of his pioneering excavations. A salty soundtrack accompanies you through the bowels of the ship, where the expected bounty of nails, pottery and tankards is spiced up with a bottle of 1903 whisky, found by laboratory testing to be almost identical to the day it was bottled, and a collection of strangely dated-looking sunglasses and calculators from the *Mikhail Lermontov*, a Soviet cruise ship that went down in the Marlborough Sounds in 1986. Somewhat more venerable hauls include a rudder gudgeon from Cook's *Endeavour*, assorted domestic articles from the *Boyd*, and a mouth organ and salt and pepper shakers from the *Wahine*, which foundered in Cook Strait in 1968.

Waitangi National Reserve

Crossing the bridge over the Waitangi River from the shipwreck museum you enter the **Waitangi National Reserve** (unrestricted access), the single most symbolic place in New Zealand for Maori and Pakeha alike, and a focal point for the modern nation's struggle for identity. It was here in 1840 that Queen Victoria's representative William Hobson and nearly fifty Maori chiefs signed the Treaty of Waitangi (see box opposite), ceding Aotearoa's sovereignty to Britain, whilst ostensibly affording the Maori protection and guaranteeing them rights over land and resources. When the area was gifted to the people of New Zealand in 1932 by Governor-General Lord Bledisloe, the Treaty House was being used as a sheep shelter and the grounds were neglected, but a sudden desire to commemorate the 1940 centennial of the signing in fitting fashion provoked a flurry of restoration. The house is now the centrepiece of the **Waitangi Visitor Centre and Treaty House** (daily: Dec–Feb 9am–6pm; March–Nov 9am–5pm; $9), where a twenty-minute audio-visual presentation sets the historical framework, bolstered by a small exhibition of Maori artefacts, including a musket owned by Hone Heke, the first Maori chief to sign the Treaty of Waitangi, and a portrait of him blithely entitled *Johny Heke*.

The **Treaty House** itself was built in Georgian colonial style in 1833–34. Once described as "only a couple of rooms separated by a lobby", it's a thoroughly unprepossessing structure, largely because James Busby's superiors in Sydney failed to supply the requisite materials. The original part of the house is furnished as it would have been in Busby's time, while the wings added in the 1880s contain displays on Busby, Waitangi life and the treaty itself. The front windows look towards Russell over sweeping lawns, where marquees were erected on three significant occasions: in 1834, when Maori chiefs chose the Confederation of Tribes flag, which now flies on one yard arm of the central flagpole; the meeting a year later at which northern Maori leaders signed the Declaration of Independence of New Zealand; and, in 1840, the signing of the Treaty of Waitangi itself.

The northern side of the lawn is flanked by the *whare runanga*, or **Maori meeting house**, built between 1934 and 1940. Though proposed by Bledisloe and northern Maori chiefs, the construction of the house was a co-operative effort between all Maori and is unique in that it is pan-tribal. A short audio-visual presentation highlights and explains key elements on the richly carved panels, introducing the major themes and legends depicted. Housed in a specially built shelter in the Treaty House grounds is another centennial project, the world's largest **war canoe** (*waka*), the Nga Toki Awhaorua, named after the vessel navigated by Kupe when he discovered Aotearoa. It's an undoubtedly impressive boat, built over two years from two huge kauri by members of the five northern tribes and measuring over 35m in length. It has traditionally been launched each year on Waitangi Day, propelled by eighty warriors, though the future of the launching, along with the Waitangi Day commemoration ceremony, is uncertain (see box opposite).

Westwards, the Waitangi National Reserve extends beyond the Waitangi Golf Course to the scenic viewpoint atop **Mount Bledisloe**, 3km away. Two kilometres beyond are the **Haruru Falls**, formed where the Waitangi River drops over a basalt lava flow – though not that impressive by New Zealand standards, there's good swimming at their base. Haruru Falls are also accessible from the Treaty House grounds via the very gentle **Hutia Creek Mangrove Forest Boardwalk** (2hr return).

The Treaty of Waitangi

The Treaty of Waitangi is the **founding document** of modern New Zealand, a touchstone for both Pakeha and Maori, and its implications permeate New Zealand society. Signed in 1840 between what were ostensibly two sovereign states – the United Kingdom and the United Tribes of New Zealand, plus other Maori leaders – the treaty remains central to New Zealand's **race relations**. The Maori rights guaranteed by it have seldom been upheld, however, and the constant struggle for recognition continues.

The treaty at Waitangi

Motivated by a desire to staunch French expansion in the Pacific, and a moral obligation on the Crown to protect Maori from rapacious land-grabbing by settlers, the British instructed naval captain William Hobson to negotiate the transfer of sovereignty with "the free and intelligent consent of the natives", and to deal fairly with the Maori. Within a few days of his arrival, Hobson, with the help of James Busby and others, drew up both the English Treaty and a Maori "translation". On the face of it, the treaty is a straightforward document, but the complications of having two versions (see Contexts, p.969) and the implications of striking a deal between two peoples with widely differing views on land and resource ownership and usage have reverberated down the years.

The treaty was unveiled in grand style on February 5, 1840, to a gathering of some 400 representatives of the five northern tribes in front of Busby's residence in Waitangi. Presented as a contract between the chiefs and Queen Victoria – someone whose role was comprehensible in chiefly terms – the benefits were amplified and the costs downplayed. As most chiefs didn't understand English, they signed the Maori version of the treaty, which still has *mana* (prestige) among Maori today.

The treaty after Waitangi

The pattern set at Waitangi was repeated up and down the country, as seven copies of the treaty were dispatched to garner signatures and extend Crown authority over parts of the North Island that had not yet been covered, and the South Island. On May 21, before signed treaty copies had been returned, Hobson claimed New Zealand for Britain: the North Island on the grounds of cession by Maori, and the South Island by right of Cook's "discovery", as it was considered to be *in terrorium nullis* ("without owners"), despite a significant Maori population.

Maori fears were alerted from the start, and as the settler population grew and demand for land increased, successive governments passed laws that gradually stripped Maori of control over their affairs – actions which led to the New Zealand Wars of the 1860s (see Contexts, p.970). Over the decades, small concessions were made, but nothing significant changed until 1973, when **Waitangi Day** (February 6) became an official national holiday. From 1971, Maori groups, supported by a small but articulate band of Pakeha, began a campaign of direct action, increasingly disrupting commemorations, thereby alienating many Pakeha and splitting Maori allegiances between angry young urban Maori and the *kaumatua* (elders), who saw the actions as disrespectful to the ancestors and an affront to tradition. Many strands of Maori society were unified by the *hikoi* (march) to Waitangi to protest against the celebrations in 1985, a watershed year in which Paul Reeves was appointed New Zealand's first Maori Governor General and the **Waitangi Tribunal** (see Contexts, p.981) was given some teeth.

Protests have continued in the years since – including several infamous flag-trampling, egg-pelting and spitting incidents – as successive governments have vacillated over maintaining the commemorations at Waitangi or trying to defuse the situation by promoting a parallel event at the Governor General's residence in Wellington.

Eating, drinking and entertainment

Paihia's range of **places to eat** is unmatched anywhere in the Bay of Islands and competition keeps prices tolerable. Though nowhere is actually on the waterfront, many establishments have sea views and salty menus by way of compensation. The restaurants are also good places to stick around for post-prandial drinking, though there are a couple of more raucous **bars** in town and a popular **live music** and comedy venue out of town.

If you fancy eating on the water, **Bay of Islands Mini Cruises** ($45; ⓣ09/402 7848) putter about the Waitangi Estuary below Haruru Falls for a couple of hours while you tuck into pan-fried fish, T-bone steak or a veggie dish. They depart from the Old Wharf at Haruru Falls – you'll need to bring your own drinks. For something more cultural, Kawa Performing Arts offer a **hangi** ($50; reserve on ⓣ09/402 5570) in conjunction with a roster of traditional Maori poi dances and action songs. A more contemporary approach to presenting Maori culture (but without the hangi) is used at **The Story of the Treaty of Waitangi** (Oct–April nightly; $45; ⓣ09/402 5990, ⓦwww.culturenorth.co.nz), which combines dancing with local history, related by an elder – it's held either in the meeting house at Waitangi or outside in front of the treaty house. There's also a seasonal diversion in the form of Paihia's **jazz festival**, usually held during the second weekend in August (a $30 pass admits you to any of the venues in town).

Bay of Islands Swordfish Club Marsden Rd. Private club, overlooking the bay, which welcomes visitors outside the peak summer season for some of the cheapest drinks in town. Temporary membership (available at any time of year) costs $2.50. Simple but good-value food is served from 6pm.

Bistro 40 40 Marsden Rd ⓣ09/402 7444. Sister restaurant to *Only Seafood* (see below), located in the same big atmospheric villa and open nightly for dinner. White tablecloths and polished glassware set the tone for sumptuous meals from an eclectic menu that's strong on high-quality beef and lamb dishes (around $25), as well as seafood dishes.

Blue Marlin Diner Marsden Rd. Cheap and cheerful licensed café and takeaway, serving breakfast from $7 and, later in the day, steaks and seafood platters for $16.

Caffé Over the Bay Paihia Mall, Marsden Rd. A good place for a daytime coffee on the veranda but also worth a visit for good salmon-bagel breakfasts and reasonably priced lunches and dinners with an international slant. Dinners in summer only. Licensed.

The Lighthouse Tavern Upstairs in the Paihia Mall. A lively drinking spot and traditional Kiwi bar that later turns into Paihia's only nightclub, though it's more small-town than you might expect for such a touristy place. Open until 2.30am at weekends.

Only Seafood 40 Marsden Rd. As the name implies, it's seafood only at what is one of Paihia's finest restaurants, with mains ($20–26) such as a raw-fish salad of lemon-marinated hapuka and coconut cream, or the day's gamefish served with roasted cashews and bamboo shoots.

Pizzeria La Scaletta Selwyn Rd ⓣ09/402 7039. Gourmet pizza bar with beer on tap and outside dining. Takeaway also available.

Saltwater Backpacker Café & Bar 14 Kings Rd. Boisterous restaurant and bar catering mainly (though not exclusively) to backpackers, with decent beer on tap, a selection of shooters (the alcoholic variety), good and moderately priced gourmet pizza, one of the country's very few shuffleboard tables, and nightly giveaways of fast-boat cruises, dolphin trips and the like.

Tides Williams Rd ⓣ09/402 7557. Highly regarded, innovative and well-priced breakfasts, lunches and dinners, with the emphasis on fresh seafood and top-quality lamb, though the portions can be rather small. Closed Tues in winter.

Twin Pines Puketona Rd, Haruru Falls ⓣ09/402 7195. Fine old villa shipped from Auckland in 1980 and refitted as a restaurant and bar that often puts on live bands and occasionally comedy. A courtesy bus runs from Paihia during the peak summer season. Closed Mon & Tues in winter.

Waikokopu Café Treaty House Grounds, Waitangi ⓣ09/402 6275. Outstanding licensed café surrounded by lawns and a fish pond. The relaxed indoor and outdoor seating areas are perfect for tucking into unusual and beautifully prepared breakfasts and lunches ($12–15) such as smoked mushroom, roast pumpkin and feta salad, plus an excellent range of cakes and great coffee. They're also open for dinner in summer (Nov–Dec Sat only, Jan nightly; mains $20–25).

Around Paihia: Opua and Kawakawa

Drivers travelling between Paihia and Russell will need to cross the narrow Veronica Channel at **OPUA**, 6km south of Paihia, where the small vehicle **ferry** leaves every ten to twenty minutes (daily 7am–10pm; every 10min until 5.30pm, every 20min thereafter; car & driver $8 each way, pedestrians $1). Fans of mangroves and estuarine scenery can tackle the gentle **Paihia–Opua Coastal Walkway** (6km; 90min–2hr one-way) to get here.

As the Bay of Islands' only deepwater port, Opua was once an important freight entrepot, with rail connections south to Whangarei and beyond. The track now only extends 13km south to **KAWAKAWA**, a bog-standard Kiwi small town principally distinguished by having train tracks running down the middle of its only significant street. Regular passenger services last rumbled through town in the 1960s, and the Opua–Kawakawa route carried its final freight in 1986, but the line is still maintained by the non-profit **Bay of Islands Vintage Railway** (ⓣ09/404 0684). Services are currently suspended but should restart late in 2002. A steam locomotive and restored 1930s rolling stock can still be seen at the station at the end of the main street.

A potentially more pressing reason to stop is to visit Kawakawa's celebrated **toilets**, created in 1997 by the reclusive Austrian émigré **Friedrich Hundertwasser**, a painter, architect, ecologist and philosopher who made Kawakawa his home from 1975 until his death early in 2000, aged 71. The ceramic columns supporting the entrance are fashioned from old bits of terracotta, glazed plant pots and brick, and hint at the complex use of broken tiles and found objects within. In the Gents, a mosaic fish is sculpted onto one wall, while next door in the Ladies, Maori fern imagery is used to good effect. Light is shed through wall panels made of bottles, and the roof sports a flourishing garden. Most visitors take a peek at both sides after suitable warning. The style of the columns found on the loo is echoed by more columns in same style across the road outside. The Grass Hut, 35–37 Giles St, is a gift shop selling Hundertwasser prints, cards and bookmarks.

Russell

New Zealand's most historic village, the small hillside settlement of **RUSSELL** is for much of the year a sleepy place favoured by city escapees, its isolation on a narrow peninsula with poor road but good sea access giving it an island ambience. During the summer, by contrast, it's swamped with day-trippers piling off the passenger ferries from Paihia, a couple of kilometres across the water, who come to explore the village's historic buildings and stroll along its appealing Pohutukawa-lined waterfronts.

Evenings are more peaceful – the major exception being **New Year's Eve**, when half the nation's youth seem to descend and the all-night revelry harks back to the 1830s when **Kororareka**, as Russell was then known, was a swashbuckling town full of whalers and sealers with a reputation as the "Hell Hole of the Pacific". As one observer noted in 1836, it was "notorious at present for containing, I should think, a greater number of rogues than any other spot of equal size in the universe", while a missionary found it "a dreadful place – the very seat of Satan". Savage and drunken behaviour served as an open invitation to **missionaries**, who gradually won over a sizeable congregation and left behind Russell's two oldest buildings, the church and a printing works which was used for producing religious tracts. By 1840, Kororareka was the largest settlement in the country, but after the

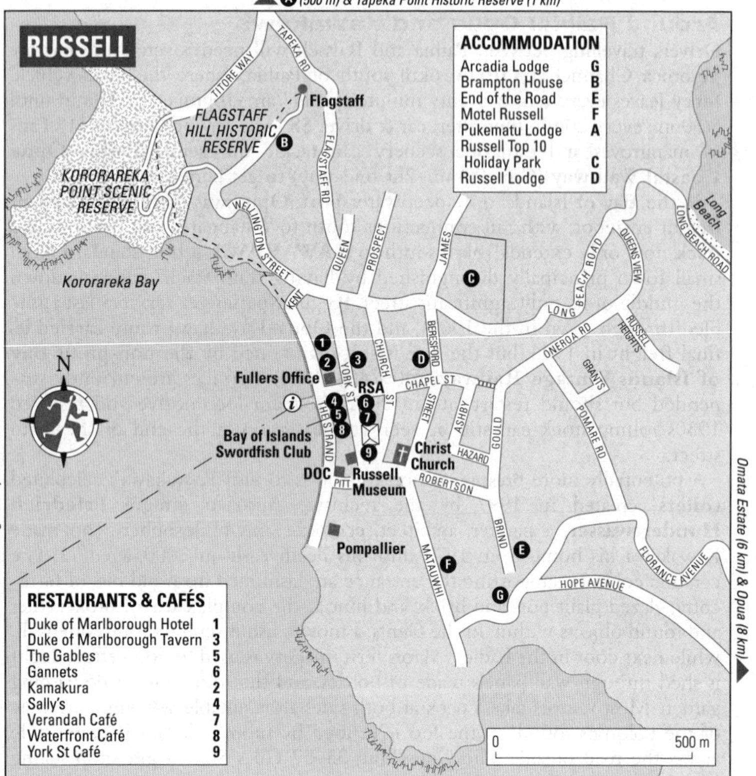

signing of the Treaty of Waitangi, Governor William Hobson fell out with both Maori and local settlers and moved his capital progressively further south.

Meanwhile, initial Maori enthusiasm for the Treaty of Waitangi had faded: financial benefits had failed to materialize and the Confederation of Tribes flag that flew from Flagstaff Hill between 1834 and 1840 had been replaced by the Union Jack. This came to be seen as a symbol of British betrayal, and as resentment crystallized it found a leader in **Hone Heke Pokai**, Ngapuhi chief and son-in-law of Kerikeri's Hongi Hika. Between July 1844 and March 1845, Hongi and his followers cut down the flagstaff no less than four times, the last occasion sparking the first **New Zealand War**, which raged for nearly a year, during which Kororareka was sacked and all but destroyed.

The settlement rose from the ashes under a new name, Russell, and though it never really flourished, it grew slowly around its beachfront into the delightful and peaceful village which attracts so many visitors today. Though far fewer people stay here than in Paihia on account of the limited range of budget **accommodation**, Russell makes a perfectly good base for exploring the rest of the bay. The main **cruises** (see p.184) all call here some fifteen minutes after leaving Paihia, though it's important to reserve in advance so that they know to pick you up. If you're only passing through, everything can be seen comfortably in a day.

Arrival and information

Most visitors arrive in Russell by way of **ferries**. Pedestrians and cyclists can get directly from Paihia to Russell by passenger ferry (Oct–May 7am–10.30pm; June–Sept 7.30am–7pm; $5 each way), which runs every twenty to thirty minutes (about a 15min journey); buy your ticket on the boat. If you're **driving** from Paihia and SH1 you'll typically cross the narrow strait 9km south of Russell at Opua (see p.193) by vehicle ferry.

Information is available from **Russell Information**, at the end of the wharf (daily 8am–5pm, Christmas–Jan until 7pm; ⓣ & ⓕ09/403 8020), and, to a lesser degree, from the Fullers office, Cass Street (7.30am–5pm, until 6–7pm in high season; ⓣ & ⓕ09/403 7866). For specific walking and environmental information make for DOC's **Bay of Islands Maritime & Historic Park Visitor Centre**, The Strand (daily: Nov–April 9am–5pm; May–Oct 9am–4.30pm; ⓣ09/403 9003, ⓕ403 9009), which is full of interesting displays and sells the useful *Russell Heritage Trails* leaflet ($1.20). Few places are more than half a kilometre away from the wharf, though if time is limited you may fancy the **Russell Mini Tour** (5–6 daily; 1hr; $16), which leaves from outside the Fullers office and visits the major sights. There's **internet access** at Enterprise Russell on York St (ⓣ09/403 8843).

Accommodation

Accommodation in Russell is much more limited than across the water in Paihia and tends to be more upmarket, in keeping with Russell's quieter and more refined image. Apart from a handful of motels, hotels and backpacker lodges, most accommodation is in B&Bs and homestays; as well as those listed below, Russell Information or the visitor centre in Paihia can help you pick one out. Don't expect to find many vacancies in the three weeks after Christmas, when you'll have to book well ahead and pay inflated rates, which continue to the end of February.

Arcadia Lodge, Florance Ave ⓣ09/403 7756, ⓦwww.bay-of-islands.co.nz/accomm/arcadia.html. One of Russell's gems: a historic, rambling wooden house encircled by decks overlooking luxuriant English cottage gardens and the bay. It's a five-minute stroll from the village and some of the half-dozen characterful, wood-floored rooms and suites enjoy sea views, while most have en-suite bathrooms. Full breakfast is included, along with free use of bikes. Rooms ❻, suites ❼

Brampton House 79 Wellington St ⓣ & ⓕ09/403 7521, ⓔbrampton@xtra.co.nz. Two spotless and well-appointed suites (with separate entrances and terraces) in the highest house in Russell, surrounded by bush and commanding fabulous views all around. Deft touches such as complimentary wine and sumptuous breakfasts make this a treat. ❻

End of the Road Backpackers Brind Rd ⓣ09/403 7632. Small home-style hostel with just six beds in the main house and an additional twin and a double in a self-contained house with a sunny veranda across the road. Dorm ❶, rooms ❷

Motel Russell Matauwhi Bay Rd ⓣ09/403 7854 & 0800/240 011, ⓔmotelrussell@xtra.co.nz. Despite the lack of sea views, this is the pick of Russell's motels, with pleasant self-contained units and hotel-style rooms, plus an attractive pool and spa. Studios ❹, one-bedroom units ❺

Pukematu Lodg Flagstaff Hill ⓣ09/403 8500, ⓦwww.pukematu.co.nz. Beautifully sited boutique lodge with great views and two spacious suites furnished in recycled rimu(a type of wood). A delicious breakfast is included, plus muffins and tea on arrival. ❽

Russell Lodge cnr Chapel St & Beresford St ⓣ09/403 7640 & 0800/478 773, ⓔrussell_lodge@hotmail.com. Combined backpackers and motel in a garden setting right in the heart of Russell. There's a range of accommodation, including four-bunk cabins (each with its own bathroom), studio, family units and a communal kitchen, as well as a pool, barbecue area and kids' playground. Dorms ❶, budget rooms ❸, studios ❹, units ❺

Russell Top 10 Holiday Park Longbeach Rd

☎09/403 7826, ©russell.top10@xtra.co.nz. Central, well-ordered and spotless campsite with tent and sites with power hook-up for campervans, backpacker bunks (except in peak season) and an extensive range of high-standard cabins and motel units. Tent sites $11–13, dorms ❶, cabins ❷, kitchen cabins ❸, units ❺–❻

The Town

Several historic buildings and Flagstaff Hill constitute the main sights in Russell, supplemented by a few diverting craft shops. Arriving on the passenger ferry, the single most striking building at the southern end of town is **Pompallier** (daily: Dec–April open access 10am–5pm; May–Nov fifty-minute guided tours only at 10.15am, 11.15am, 1.15pm, 2.15pm & 3.15pm; $5), the last surviving building of Russell's Catholic mission, which was once the headquarters of Catholicism in the western Pacific. New Zealand's oldest industrial building, Pompallier was built in 1842 as a printing works for the French Roman Catholic bishop Jean Baptiste François Pompallier, who had arrived three years earlier and found the Catholic word of God under siege from Anglican and Wesleyan tracts, translated into Maori. Lacking money to import all the timber needed to erect a conventional building, the missionaries instead built an elegant rammed-earth structure in a style typical of Pompallier's native Lyon. The hipped roof was flared out to protect the earth walls, and thought was also given to security, since the printing press's lead type could be melted down for shot, and the paper used for making cartridges. The press and paper were imported, and a tannery installed to make leather book-bindings, after which the bishop set about printing over a dozen titles during the next eight years, comprising a total of more than thirty thousand volumes. These were some of the first books printed in Maori, *Ako Marama* being typical, with its pastoral letter, prayers, hymns, psalms and burial service.

The printing operation only lasted until 1850 and the property subsequently became a private house, though restoration work has now largely restored it to its 1842 state, with austere wooden floors and lime-washed walls. Displays chart the changes the house has undergone over the years, while artisans are now once again producing handmade books – the production processes are explained in each room, and you can even get your hands dirty having a go in what is New Zealand's only surviving colonial tannery. Outside, the grounds have been restored to their late nineteenth-century grandeur, and make a perfect place for a picnic or a game of croquet.

The only other building surviving from the same era is the prim, white, weatherboard **Christ Church**, Robertson Road, built in 1836 and now New Zealand's oldest surviving church – earlier examples at Kerikeri and Paihia having been lost. Unlike most churches of similar vintage, it was not a mission church but was built by local settlers: an appeal for public donations loosened the purse strings of Charles Darwin, who passed through the Bay of Islands at the time, long before he fell out with the church over his theory of evolution. In the mid-nineteenth century the church was besieged during skirmishes between Hone Heke's warriors and the British, leaving several still-visible bullet holes; the neat graveyard contains some of the oldest European graves in the country and numerous headstones inscribed in Maori.

The small **Russell Museum** (Te Whare Taonga o Kororareka), close by on York Street (daily: late Dec to early Feb 10am–5pm; mid-Feb to mid-Dec 10am–4pm; $3), contains ageing exhibits on Russell's whaling days, a few Maori pieces, fishing tackle, binoculars and clothing once used by American writer Zane Grey, and an impressive one-fifth scale model of Cook's *Endeavour*, which called in here in 1769. From the museum, a stroll along The Strand passes the rooms of the prestigious Bay of Islands Swordfish Club, which was founded in 1924, and the *Duke of Marlborough Hotel* – the original building on this site held New Zealand's first liquor licence.

At the end of The Strand, a short track (30–40min return) climbs steeply to **Flagstaff Hill** (*Maiki*). The current flagpole was erected in 1857, some twelve years after the destruction of the fourth flagpole by Hone Heke (see Contexts, p.971), as a conciliatory gesture by a son of one of the chiefs who had ordered the original felling. The Confederation of Tribes flag, abandoned after the signing of the Treaty of Waitangi, is now flown on twelve significant days of the year, such as the anniversary of Hone Heke's death and the final day of the first New Zealand War. From Flagstaff Hill it's a further kilometre to the **Tapeka Point Historic Reserve**, a former *pa* site on a headland at the end of the peninsula – a wonderfully defensible position with great views and abundant evidence of terracing.

Another worthwhile stroll is to **Oneroa Bay** (Long Beach), 1km east of Russell on the far side of the peninsula, where you'll find a gently shelving beach sheltered from the prevailing wind and safe for swimming.

Eating and drinking

The range of **restaurants** in Russell is not especially varied, and prices are relatively high. **Drinking** options are no better, though there are a number of cheap private clubs – the RSA on Cass Street and the Bay of Islands Swordfish Club on The Strand, for example – which often welcome visitors, though officially you should be with a member.

The Duke of Marlborough Hotel The Strand ☎09/403 7829. Well-prepared traditional food is served in New Zealand's oldest licensed establishment, now a pricey hotel. The verandahed bar is a good place to idle over a daytime coffee.

The Duke of Marlborough Tavern York St. Unreconstructed Kiwi pub with a lively atmosphere and mainstream bar meals (from around $14) in the *Bounty Bistro*, plus occasional bands at weekends.

The Gables The Strand ☎09/403 7618. Formal waterfront dining in a lovely wood-panelled candlelit restaurant (originally built in 1847) serving superb and varied dishes from a crispy Thai salad appetizer ($16) to chicken livers in brandy ($29) and ostrich steaks ($32).

Gannets cnr Chapel St & York St ☎09/403 7990. The decor may be uninspired, but the eclectic selection of food is always tasty and many of the dishes can be had as either a starter ($10–15) or main ($20–25).

Kamakura The Strand ☎09/403 7771. Modern, licensed waterfront restaurant with an understated Japanese ambience and a varied menu of pricey but tasty and beautifully presented dishes (around $25), such as pumpkin gnocchi, crayfish bisque or sashimi.

Omata Estate Aucks Rd, Opua, 6km from Russell ☎09/403-8007, www.omata.co.nz. Delightful café, restaurant and bar overlooking young vineyards with the inner bay as a backdrop. In summer you'll need to reserve a table, Dishes include starters such as bocconcini and grilled pepper tart ($16) or mezze ($37), and mains including grilled Cervena (venison), and confit of duck leg with honey-roasted yams for around $30. Alternatively, just drop in for a coffee or a sundowner on the patio. The adjacent tasting room offers samples of six wines ($5) – the grapes for the chardonnay and syrah are grown on site.

Sally's 25 The Strand ☎09/403 7652. Relaxed and convivial restaurant, strong on modestly priced seafood and open for lunch and dinner, though it's worth booking ahead in peak season. Licensed & BYO.

Verandah Cafe York St ☎09/403 7167. Licensed daytime café with plenty of garden seating, a selection of homebaked goodies and good espresso, plus various breakfasts and lunches.

Waterfront Café The Strand. Simple café with the best coffee in town, as well as snacks, all-day breakfasts and an ice-cream parlour in summer.

York Street Café Traders Mall, York St. Relaxing and unpretentious café popular with locals for reliable fare ranging from full breakfasts ($11) to dinner dishes of Thai prawns ($25), fish of the day ($22) or pizza ($14).

Around Russell: Whangaruru Harbour

To the south and east of Russell lies the mixed kauri forest of the **Ngaiotonga Scenic Reserve** and some wonderful coastline around the **Whangaruru Harbour**. The sealed Russell coast road twists through the region, closely tracing the shore from Orongo Bay, just south of Russell. Just beyond the Waikare Road turn-off for Kawakawa and Paihia, a signposted side road leads to some fine stands of kauri which can be visited on the **Ngaiotonga Kauri Grove Walk** (1km; 20min), the **Twin Bole Kauri Walk** (around 200m; 5min), and the **Ngaiotonga–Russell Forest Walkway** (21km; 9hr); the last is best tackled over two days with a tent (more information is available from DOC in Russell).

Continuing along the Russell coast road, you'll reach the turn-off to the scattered and predominantly Maori village of **Rawhiti**, the start of the challenging but rewarding **Cape Brett Tramping Track** (20km; 8hr each way; $8 track fee, payable in advance; hut bookings essential at the DOC Bay of Islands Visitor Centre in Russell). The walk follows the hilly ridge along the centre of the peninsula with sea occasionally visible on both sides, and terminates at the end of the peninsula, where you turn around and come back along the same route. A former lighthouse keeper's house at the cape has been turned into a trampers' hut (21 beds, $8; annual hut pass not valid) with gas cooking stove and fuel, but no cooking utensils. The track crosses private land and you should check with DOC in Russell for the latest news about access to sections of the peninsula, where possum control is periodically undertaken. The base of the Cape Brett peninsula is crossed by the **Whangamumu Walking Track** (4km; 1hr), which starts close to the Rawhiti Road junction, and runs through forest to a beach where the remains of a 1920s whaling operation can be seen.

At **Ngaiotonga**, 20km south of Rawhiti, a dirt road runs 8km through hilly farmland to the broad sweep of **Bland Bay**, with great beaches on both sides of the isthmus. You can camp at the simple *Bland Beach Motor Camp* (Ⓣ09/433 6759; tent sites $9) or press on a further 2km to **Whangaruru North Head Scenic Reserve**, with yet more lovely beaches, fine walks around the end of the peninsula and a DOC campsite ($6; closed Easter–Nov) with water and toilets.

The main settlement on the mainland side of the Whangaruru Harbour is **OAKURA**, 12km south of Ngaiotonga along Russell Road. Not a great deal happens here, but that is exactly its appeal, and there's no shortage of places to swim and walk, as well as impressive sea and island views. There are a few **places to stay**, including the *Whangaruru Harbour Motor Camp*, Ohawiri Road (Ⓣ09/433 6806; tent sites $9, cabins ❷, motel units ❹), and the *Oakura Bay B&B*, 24 Rapata Rd (Ⓣ & Ⓕ09/433 6066; ❶–❷), which has a self contained one-bedroom flat for $20 per person, plus evening meals ($20) and kayak rental ($5 per hour).

Kerikeri

KERIKERI, 25km northwest of Paihia, is both central to the history of and yet geographically removed from the Bay of Islands. On initial acquaintance it's an ordinary-looking service town, strung out along the main road and surrounded by the orchards that form Kerikeri's economic mainstay and offer abundant opportunities for casual work. Two kilometres to the east of town, the thin ribbon of the Kerikeri Inlet forces its way from the sea to its tidal limit at **Kerikeri Basin**, the site chosen by Samuel Marsden for the Church Missionary Society's second mission in New Zealand. John Butler, the first Anglican missionary, arrived here in 1819 but struggled to win the trust and assistance of the Ngapuhi, since he was unable to sell them the muskets they so wanted. As missions opened in the new settlements that sprang up after 1840, Kerikeri's importance waned.

In the 1920s the area was planted with the subtropical crops which continue to thrive here – mainly citrus fruit, along with tamarillos, feijoas, melons, courgettes, peppers and kiwi fruit. For most of the year it's possible to get **seasonal work** in the orchards, either weeding, thinning or picking. Work is most abundant from January through to July, but this is also when competition for jobs is greatest, and you may find that your chances are just as good any month except August and perhaps September. The best contacts are the managers of the hostels and campgrounds (see especially *Aranga* and *Hideaway*), many of which also offer good weekly rates. In recent years Kerikeri has earned itself a reputation for its **craft shops**, scattered among the orchards and frequently featuring on tour-bus itineraries.

Arrival, information and accommodation

Air New Zealand **flights** from Auckland land 5km out of town towards Paihia at Bay of Islands Airport, from where Paihia Taxis operate an airport shuttle ($10 per person to Kerikeri, $15 to Paihia). Northliner and InterCity **buses** stop on Cobham Road, with several services to Paihia but just one bus heading north to Kaitaia daily: book through the Kerikeri Travel Shop on Fairway Drive (ⓣ09/407 8013). There's no official visitor centre, but the the leaflets in the unmanned foyer at the library on Cobham Road (Mon–Fri 10am–5pm, Sat 10am–noon; ⓣ09/407 9297) supply local **information**, and there's a **DOC office** at 34 Landing Rd (ⓣ09/407 8474), which can advise on local walks and more ambitious treks into the Puketi and Omahuta forests (see p.203). For **internet access** try Scottronic Technologies Ltd, a computer store in Hub Mall on Kerikeri Road (ⓣ09/407 8932).

Kerikeri is fairly well endowed with **accommodation** in all categories, but is particularly strong in budget places – a consequence of the area's popularity with long-stay casual workers. Seasonal price fluctuations are nowhere near as marked as in Paihia, though it's still difficult to find a place in January, when places are correspondingly expensive; prices quoted here are outside this post-Christmas period.

Motels and B&Bs

Abilene Motel 136 Kerikeri Rd ⓣ09/407 9203, ⓔabilene@kerikeri-nz.co.nz. Standard, centrally located motel in a garden setting with pool, spa and Sky TV. ❹

Central Motel 58 Kerikeri Rd ⓣ0800/867 667 & 09/407 8921, ⓔewrigley@voyager.co.nz. Aptly named motel, and about the cheapest in town, with some newish and some older rooms, all with full kitchens, set around a pleasant pool and spa. ❹

Kemp Lodge 134 Kerikeri Rd ⓣ & ⓕ09/407 8295. Three pleasant and modern self-contained cottages close to town, complete with TV and video, solar-heated pool and spa. ❹

Kerikeri Village Inn 165 Kerikeri Rd ⓣ09/407 4666, ⓦwww.kerikerivillageinn.co.nz. Attractive modern home, with long views over rolling country and comfy en-suite rooms brightened with fresh flowers. Complimentary port, chocolates and a tasty breakfast included. ❻

The Summer House Kerikeri Road ⓣ09/407 4294, ⓦwww.thesummerhouse.co.nz. Classy ecologically-conscious boutique inn done out in French provincial style with just three rooms, all with en-suite bathrooms (one also has self-catering facilities). Sumptuous breakfasts are served, and dinner ($45) is available by arrangement. ❼

Hostels and campsites

Aranga Holiday Park Kerikeri Rd ⓣ0800/272 642 or 09/407 9326, ⓦwww.aranga.co.nz. Large stream-side site on the edge of town with a spacious camping area, well-equipped standard cabins, comfortable kitchen cabins and single rooms for long-stayers at a bargain $90 a week. There's a big barbecue on Friday nights. Tents $9, ❶, cabins ❷, flats ❸

Gibby's Place Kerikeri Rd ⓣ09/407 9024, ⓔgibbysplace@xtra.co.nz. Cosy, quiet campsite in a big tree-filled garden with a small pool. Tent and powered sites $18, cabins ❷, en-suite doubles ❸, en-suite family room ❹

Hideaway Lodge Wiroa Rd, 4km west of Kerikeri ⓣ0800/562 746 & 09/407 9773, ⓕ407 9793. Large well-appointed hostel, some way out of town and catering almost exclusively to seasonal workers, who appreciate the reduced weekly rates and the large pool and games room after a hard day in the orchards. Free trips into town, and free shonky bikes for guests' use. Tent sites $9, dorms ❶, rooms ❷

Hone Heke Lodge 65 Hone Heke Rd ⓣ & ⓕ09/407 8170, ⓔhoneheke@xtra.co.nz. Pleasant hostel with six-bed dorms, each with a fridge and cooking gear, and doubles and twins, some en suite. There's also a games room and barbecue area. Tent sites $10, dorms ❶, rooms ❷

Kerikeri Farm Hostel SH10, 5km west of Kerikeri ⓣ09/407 6989, ⓔkkfarmhostel@xtra.co.nz. Top-class hostel on an organic citrus orchard, with comfortable dorms and rooms in a lovely wooden house. Rates are a dollar or so higher than in other Kerikeri hostels, but it's well worth it. Dinner ($10–15) and breakfast are also available. Dorms ❶, rooms ❷

Kerikeri YHA 114 Kerikeri Rd ⓣ09/407 9391, ⓔyhakeri@yha.org.nz. Well-placed hostel close to the centre but showing its age. Dorms ❶, rooms ❷

The Town

The only way to get a sense of Kerikeri's past importance is to make straight for **Kerikeri Basin**, nearly 2km northeast of the current town. It was here, in 1821, that mission carpenters started work on what is now New Zealand's oldest European-style building, **Kemp House** (daily: Nov–April 10am–5pm; May–Oct 10am–4pm; $5, combined entry with Old Stone Store $6), a restrained, two-storey Georgian colonial affair which has miraculously survived fire and periodic flooding. The first occupants, missionary John Butler and family, soon moved on, and by 1832 the house was in the hands of lay missionary and blacksmith James Kemp, who extended the three-up, three-down design. Since the last of the Kemps moved out in the early 1970s it has been restored and furnished in mid-eighteenth century style.

Next door is the only other extant building from the mission station and the country's oldest stone building, the **Old Stone Store** (same times as Kemp House; $2.50), constructed mostly of local stone, with keystones and quoins of Sydney sandstone. Completed in 1835 as a central provision store for the Church Missionary Society, it successively served as a munitions store for troops garrisoned here to fight Hone Heke, then a kauri trading store and a shop, before being opened to the public in 1975. The ground-floor **store** sells goods almost identical to those on offer almost 170 years ago, including the once-prized Hudson Bay trading blankets, copper and cast-iron pots, jute sacks, Jew's harps, gunpowder tea, old-fashioned sweets, and preserves made from fruit grown in the mission garden next door. The two **upper floors** house a museum stocked with old implements including a hand-operated flour mill from around 1820, thought to be the oldest piece of machinery in the country, and a box of flintlock muskets. There's also a library used by Bishop Selwyn which is now full of photocopied documents, among them Kemp's diaries and the store's day book.

Opposite the Old Stone Store, a path along the river leads to the site of local chief Hongi Hika's **Kororipo Pa**, passing the place where, in the 1820s, he had a European-style house built. The *pa* commands a hill on a prominent bend in the river, a relatively secure base from which attacks were launched on other tribes using newly acquired firearms. Signs help interpret the dips and humps in the ground, but you'll get a better appreciation of pre-European Maori life from **Rewa's Village**, 1 Landing Rd (daily 9.30am–4.30pm or later; $2.50), a

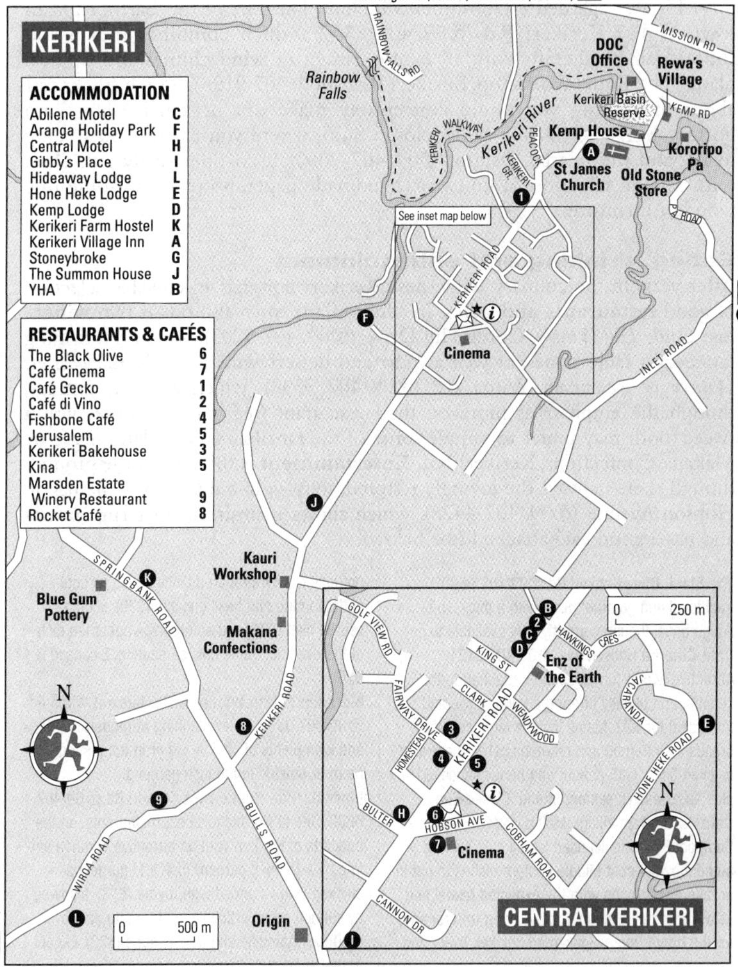

1969 reconstruction of a fishing village across the river from the *pa* site. It comes complete with *marae*, weapons and *kumara* stores, as well as an authentic *hangi* site with an adjacent shell midden; the entrance kiosk screens a short video on the history of the area. Opposite is the **Kerikeri Basin Reserve** and the start of a track past the site of Kerikeri's first hydroelectric station (15min each way) and the swimming holes at Fairy Pools (35min each way) to the impressively undercut **Rainbow Falls** (1hr each way). The latter are also accessible off Waipapa Road, 3km north of the Basin.

Elsewhere, Kerikeri is dominated by orchards and the roads running between them (especially SH10 and Kerikeri Road), which are studded with **craft outlets**. The free and widely available *Kerikeri Art & Craft Trail* leaflet advertises the major ones; they're mostly open daily from 10am to 5pm, and you could easily spend a day trawling round them all. A few of the most highly regarded establishments include The Enz of the Earth, right in town at 127 Kerikeri Rd (☎09/407 8367), which combines Indian and Indonesian handicrafts with an exotic garden of wind chimes and tropical plants; The Kauri Workshop, Kerikeri Rd (☎09/407 9196), which stocks just about everything you could conceivably make out of kauri; Blue Gum Pottery, SH10 (☎09/407 9008; closed Sun), where you can see pots being made; and the nearby Origin (☎09/407 9065), a co-operatively run place with a wide selection of knitwear, handmade paper, pottery and some fine wooden furniture.

Eating, drinking and entertainment

After years in the culinary wilderness, Kerikeri now has an enviable selection of good **restaurants and cafés**. In addition, the town also boasts two **wineries**: *Cottle Hill Winery*, Cottle Hill Drive (☎09/407 5203), which offers a big range of a table wines, as well as port and dessert wines; and *Marsden Estate Winery & Restaurant*, Wiroa Rd (☎09/407 9398), which also has tastings, though the emphasis is more on their restaurant (see below). Those with a sweet tooth may prefer to sample some of the tantalizing chocolates made by Makana Confections, Kerikeri Rd. **Entertainment** is thinner on the ground, though there's always the lovingly restored, sixty-year-old Cathay Cinema, on Hobson Avenue (☎09/407 4428), which shows mainstream first-run movies and has a good café attached (see below).

The Black Olive Kerikeri Rd ☎09/407 9693. Good traditional and gourmet pizza with a thick, soft-dough base, though currently only available to go.

Café Cinema Hobson Ave ☎09/407 9121. Attractive, wood-furnished café attached to the cinema, and usually offering a good movie and meal deal for $22. Mains include lamb sweetbreads with Pernod and croutons ($19), marinated chicken fillets with peanut and honey sauce ($18), plus an extensive seafood menu. Closed Sun.

Café Jerusalem Village Mall ☎09/407 1001. Compact BYO and licensed Israeli café serving authentic, low-cost Middle Eastern dishes to eat in or take away. Along with the expected falafel and schwarma they also offer *levivot* (veg fritters) and, for the brave, *morav* (pan-fried chicken livers and hearts). Closed Sun.

Fishbone Café 88 Kerikeri Rd ☎09/407 6065. Very good licensed café in the modern Kiwi mould, perennially popular for its high-quality fusion food. It's open all day in summer, when there's outdoor seating, and for more limited hours in winter. Thurs–Sat only; booking essential for dinner.

Kerikeri Bakehouse Fairway Drive. The best baked goods in town: sandwiches, pastries, superlative vegetarian pies and good coffee.

Kina Village Mall, 132 Kerikeri Rd ☎09/407 7669. Convivial and bustling restaurant serving hearty portions of well-prepared dishes such as courgette, tomato and basil gnocchi ($20), scotch-seared fillet ($23) and an organic vegetarian dish of the evening. Some outside seating. Licensed & BYO.

Marsden Estate Winery & Restaurant Wiroa Rd ☎09/407 9398. Relaxed dining at moderate prices and with plenty of choice, either in the tasting room or outside in the lush gardens.

Marx Garden Restaurant Kerikeri Rd ☎09/407 6606. One of Northland's best restaurants, on the outskirts of Kerikeri with an attractive veranda setting by a tranquil garden. Tuck into gorgeous chicken livers sautéed with thyme ($13), followed by salmon on an artichoke and tomato risotto ($30) or ratatouille and feta lasagne ($23). Expect to pay at least $50 for three courses, excluding wine. Closed Sun. Licensed.

Rocket Café Kerikeri Rd, 3km west of town ☎09/407 3100. Excellent modern café on the site of Robbs Fruit Winery, an orchard specializing in feijoa, kiwi fruit and boysenberry wines and preserves. Dishes include a fine range of quiches, pizzas and filo rolls stuffed with imaginative fillings, plus larger meals such as pork vindaloo ($17) and lamb and apricot tajine ($16). Great coffee too, served outside or in the airy interior. Open for breakfast and lunch. Licensed.

Around Kerikeri

Some 15km southwest from Kerikeri is **WAIMATE NORTH** and the colonial Regency-style **Te Waimate Mission House**, set in lush gardens (Nov–April Mon–Wed, Sat & Sun 10am–5pm; May–Oct Sat & Sun 10am–5pm, or by appointment on ⓣ09/405 9734; $5), New Zealand's second-oldest European building. Now pretty much in the middle of nowhere, in the 1830s this was the centre of a vigorous **Anglican mission**, the first to be established on an inland site, chosen for its fertile soils and large Maori population. At the time, missionaries were keen to add European agricultural techniques to the literacy and religion they were teaching the Maori, and they made use of the grounds already cultivated by the missionaries' friend and Ngapuhi chief, Hongi Hika. By 1834 locally grown wheat was being milled at the river, orchards were flourishing and crops were sprouting – all duly impressing Charles Darwin, who visited the following year. For two years from 1842 this was the home of Bishop Selwyn and headquarters of the Anglican church in New Zealand, but ultimately shifting trade patterns made this first European-style farm uneconomic, and the mission declined. The house itself was built by converts in 1831–32 and fashioned almost entirely of local kauri. Though slightly modified over the years, it has now been restored as accurately as possible to its original design and the rooms stocked with period furniture and personal effects, giving some insight into the early missionary lifestyle. Guided tours highlight prize possessions including a pre-1840 wheelwright's lathe, some furniture which the first missionaries brought with them in 1814, and one of the earliest pieces of New Zealand-made furniture, a fairly rudimentary chaise longue whose scrolled back was intended to lend it a touch of Regency elegance. The modest mission **Church of St John the Baptist** nearby is also open daily during daylight hours (free).

Ngapha Springs and the Puketi Forest

The nearest substantial town to Waimate North is **KAIKOHE**, almost equidistant from both coasts. There's little reason to stop, though you might like to soak your bones at **Ngawha Springs** (daily 7am–9.45pm; $4), 3km south of SH1 just east of Kaikohe, where naturally heated waters fill the Waiariki Pools, a series of eight tanks surrounded by wooden boardwalks but otherwise untouched by tourist trappings.

The stands of the **Puketi and Omahuta native forests**, 20km north of Kaikohe, jointly comprise one of the largest continuous tracts of kauri forest in the north. The easiest and most rewarding access is to the east of the forest: head north off SH1 at Okaihau, or west off SH10 just north of Kerikeri along Pungaere Road. Both routes bring you to the **Puketi Recreation Area**, where there's a basic $6 campsite and a trampers' hut (see the Kerikeri DOC for keys) at the start of the twenty-kilometre **Waipapa River Track** – best done in one short (5hr) and one long (8hr) day, camping midway. This and several other worthwhile tracks are detailed in DOC's *Puketi and Omahuta Forests* leaflet ($1) which, along with camping and hut details, can be obtained from the DOC office in Kerikeri.

For a short visit, a better destination is the **Manginangina Kauri Walk**, 2km further north, where a ten-minute wheelchair-accessible boardwalk curves elegantly through the forest past numerous medium-sized kauri.

North to Doubtless Bay

North of the Bay of Islands everything gets a lot quieter. There are few towns of any consequence along the coast and it is the peace and slow pace that attract visitors to an array of glorious beaches and the lovely Whangaroa Harbour. The first stop north of Kerikeri is tiny **Matauri Bay**, where a hilltop memorial commemorates the Greenpeace flagship, *Rainbow Warrior*, which was sunk in Auckland Harbour in 1985. The wreck now lies off the coast of Motutapere Island, a site which can be dived from here. A mostly unsealed backroad continues north, offering fabulous sea views and passing gorgeous headlands and beaches including **Te Ngaire**, **Wainui Bay**, **Mahinepua Bay** and **Tauranga Bay**, before delivering you to **Whangaroa Harbour**, one of the most beautiful in Northland, and an excellent place to go sailing or kayaking.

Further north is the huge bite out of the coast called **Doubtless Bay**, which had two celebrated discoverers: Kupe, said to have first set foot on Aotearoa in Taipa; and Cook, who sailed past in 1769 and pronounced it "doubtless, a bay". The French explorer Jean François Marie de Surville was also close by and, a week later, became the first European to enter the bay, though he departed in an undignified hurry after a dispute with local Maori over a missing dinghy – and it was Cook's moniker that stuck. Bounded on the west and north by the sheltering **Karikari Peninsula**, the bay offers safe boating and is popular with Kiwi vacationers. In January you can barely move up here and you'll struggle to find accommodation, but the shoulder seasons can be surprisingly quiet, and outside December, January and February room prices drop to more affordable levels. Most of the bay's facilities cluster along the southern shore of the peninsula in a string of beachside settlements – **Coopers Beach**, **Cable Bay** and **Taipa Bay** – running west from picturesque Mangonui.

Matauri Bay

Some 20km north of Kerikeri, a high inland ridge provides a dramatic first glimpse of the long and sandy **MATAURI BAY** as it stretches north to a stand of Norfolk pines and the offshore **Cavalli Islands**. The northern limit of the main bay is defined by Matauri Bay Hill, topped by a distinctive stone and steel memorial to the *Rainbow Warrior* (see box on p.205), now scuttled off Motutapere Island, one of the Cavalli Islands.

Missionary Samuel Marsden first set foot in Aotearoa in 1814 at Matauri Bay, where he mediated between the Ngati Kura people – who still own the bay – and some Bay of Islands Maori, a process commemorated by the quaint wooden **Samuel Marsden Memorial Church** on the road in, and a small memorial behind the beach. The strength of Maori culture in the bay is evident from the finely carved *Mataatua II waka* further north along the beach: constructed in the early 1990s, its name echoes the Ngati Kura's ancestral *waka*, which lies in waters nearby. The resonance of this legendary canoe partly led the Ngati Kura to offer a final resting place to the wreck of the *Rainbow Warrior*.

Sculptor Chris Booth's **Rainbow Warrior Memorial** comprises a stone arch (symbolizing a rainbow) and the vessel's salvaged bronze propeller. It's reached by a well-worn path from near the holiday park at the foot of the hill. Two-tank **dive trips** out to the wreck, ten minutes by boat, can be organized through Matauri Kat Charters (☎09/405 0525), at the holiday park, who charge $95 for one dive, $145 for two – there are substantial discounts if you've got your own gear. The best visibility is typically in April; from September to November plankton sometimes obscure the view.

French nuclear testing in the Pacific

The French government has always claimed that nuclear testing is completely safe, and for decades has persisted in conducting tests on the tiny Pacific atolls of **Mururoa** and **Fangataufa**, a comfortable 15,000km from Paris, but only 4000km northeast of New Zealand.

In 1966 France turned its back on the 1963 Partial Test Ban Treaty, which outlawed atmospheric testing, and relocated Pacific islanders away from their ancestral villages to make way for a barrage of tests over the next eight years. The French authorities claimed that "Not a single particle of radioactive fallout will ever reach an inhabited island" – and yet radiation was routinely detected as far away as Samoa, Fiji and even New Zealand. Increasingly antagonistic public opinion forced the French to conduct their tests underground in deep shafts, where another 200 detonations took place, threatening the geological stability of these fragile coral atolls. Surveys with very limited access to the test sites have since revealed severe fissuring; there is also evidence of radioactive isotopes in the Mururoa lagoon, as well as submarine slides and subsidence.

In 1985, Greenpeace co-ordinated a New Zealand-based protest flotilla, headed by its flagship, the **Rainbow Warrior**, but before the fleet could set sail from Auckland, the French secret service sabotaged the *Rainbow Warrior*, detonating two bombs below the waterline. As rescuers recovered the body of Greenpeace photographer Fernando Pereira, two French secret service agents posing as tourists were arrested. Flatly denying all knowledge at first, the French government was finally forced to admit to what David Lange (then Prime Minister of New Zealand) described as "a sordid act of international state-backed terrorism". The two captured agents were sentenced to ten years in jail, but France used all its international muscle to have them serve their sentences on a French Pacific island; they both served less than two years before being honoured and returning to France.

In 1995, to worldwide opprobrium, France announced a further series of tests. Greenpeace duly dispatched *Rainbow Warrior II*, which was impounded by the French navy on the tenth anniversary of the sinking of the original *Rainbow Warrior*. In early 1996 the French finally agreed to stop nuclear testing in the Pacific, paving the way for improved diplomatic relations between the French and New Zealand, and the following year the two foreign ministers met for the first time since the bombing of the *Rainbow Warrior*.

Accommodation in the bay is limited to the family-oriented *Matauri Bay Holiday Park* (Ⓣ & Ⓕ09/405 0525, Ⓦwww.matauribay.co.nz/camp.html; tent sites $10, powered sites $3 extra; on-site vans ❷) and, around the corner, *Ocean's Holiday Village* (Ⓣ & Ⓕ09/405 0417, Ⓦwww.matauribay.co.nz/oceans; lodges & units ❻), a self-contained family and fishing resort with spacious units, houses (containing up to four bedrooms), a licensed **restaurant** (open daily in summer, weekends only in winter) and dinghies and kayaks for rent.

Whangaroa Harbour

Inland from Matauri Bay on SH10 the small town of **KAEO** heralds the virtually landlocked and sheltered **Whangaroa Harbour**. Time spent around here is the perfect antidote to Bay of Islands commercialism. The scenery, albeit on a smaller scale, is easily a match for its southern cousin and, despite the limited facilities, you can still get out onto the water for a cruise or to join the big-game fishers. Narrow inlets forge between cliffs and steep hills, most notably the two bald volcanic plugs, **St Paul and St Peter**, which rise up behind the harbour's two settlements, **WHANGAROA** and **TOTARA NORTH**.

The harbour wasn't always so quiet though, being among the first areas in New Zealand to be visited by European pioneers, most famously those aboard the *Boyd*, which called here in 1809 to load kauri spars for shipping to Britain. A couple of days after its arrival, all 66 crew were killed and the ship burned by local Maori in retribution for the crew's mistreatment of Tara, a high-born Maori sailor who had apparently transgressed the ship's rules. A British whaler avenged the incident by burning the entire Maori village, thereby sparking off a series of skirmishes that spread over the north for five years, substantially reducing European enthusiasm for the harbour. Nonetheless, the vast stands of kauri were soon being hacked away and the harbour was said by contemporary observers to be choked with logs; some were rafted to Auckland, while others were milled at Totara North, which claims the oldest mill in the country still operating (though only just).

The single best thing to do around Whangaroa is to spend a day on the eleven-metre *Snow Cloud* **yacht** (ⓣ09/405 0523, ⓦwww.kerikeri.net/snowcloud; 10–11hr; $65, including meals) – trips typically involve sailing out to the Cavalli Islands, stopping to let passengers snorkel, sunbathe and walk. Alternatively, **kayak** trips can be arranged with the knowledgeable Northland Sea Kayaking, on the northeastern flank of the harbour (ⓣ09/405 0381, ⓔnorthlandseakayaking@xtra.co.nz); half- day-trips start at $50, a full day costs $70, overnight camping trips are available, and there's even self-catering accommodation (❶) at the kayaking base. Two-tank **dive trips** to the *Rainbow Warrior* run from the Whangaroa Harbour Motor Camp (see below) and cost $75 plus gear hire ($65). Land-based activities primarily mean **walks**, two of the most rewarding being the short hike up St Paul from the top of Old Hospital Road in Whangaroa and DOC's Lane Cove Walk (1hr 30min–2hr each way) from Totara North, past freshwater pools, mangroves and viewpoints to the Lane Cove Cottage (❶) on the Pekapeka Bay, which sleeps sixteen people, but only opens for a minimum of four. It has a solar-heated shower, water, toilets and plenty of sandflies, but you'll need your own cooking gear. Book well in advance in summer.

Even if you're just passing through, it's worth driving the 4km along the northern shore of the harbour to Totara North, passing a boatyard or two and a sawmill, the last commercial remnants of this historic community. You'll also pass *The Gumstore* (see below) and, at the end of the road, reach *The Store*, which is great for a coffee or an ice cream on the sunny deck overhanging the water.

Practicalities

Though a combined InterCity and Northliner **bus** plies SH10 at the head of the harbour, public transport reaches neither the small community of Whangaroa, 6km off SH10 on the southern side of the harbour, nor tiny Totara North, 4km off the highway on the northern side.

Most of the harbour's limited **accommodation** clusters along the road to Whangaroa, first up being the tree-shaded *Whangaroa Harbour Motor Camp* (ⓣ & ⓕ09/405 0306, ⓔdyleewhangaroa@xtra.co.nz; tent sites $11, dorms ❶, cabins ❸), 3km south of the centre and with its own small grocery and shop selling takeaway food. The *Sunseeker Lodge*, Old Hospital Road (ⓣ & ⓕ09/405 0496, ⓦwww.sunseeker.co.nz; camping $12, dorms ❶, rooms ❷, motel units ❹), perched on the hill overlooking the harbour, benefits from a personable host and a relaxed atmosphere, plus great sea views from the new spa, a kids' play area, and cheap sea kayak and fishing gear rental. The extremely welcoming *Kahoe Farms Hostel* (ⓣ09/405 1804, ⓔkahoefarms@xtra.co.nz; tents $10, dorms ❶, rooms ❷), on SH10 1.5km north of the Totara North turn-off, is a beautifully restored homestead tucked into a corner of a working cattle farm, where people come to kickback for days, fuelled by fine pizza, bread and espresso. The attractive accommodation is in a six-bed dorm and three private rooms, and there are also free bikes, kayak rental ($30 per day) and hiking trails to some superb swimming holes.

As for **eating**, there's decent seafood at the *Whangaroa Gamefish Club*, while Totara North's *Gumstore Bar and Grill*, 2km off SH1 (℡09/405 1703), serves reasonable bar-style meals ($15–20) and takeaways, and is festooned with the owner's collections of ships, tableware, lifebelts and golliwogs. Around 10km south near Kaeo there's a little touch of America at *Janit's Texas Diner* (Jan & Feb daily; Nov, Dec & March–May Wed–Sun; ℡09/405 0569), which has its own Wild West minigolf course. Small **shops** in Whangaroa and Totara North provide for self-caterers.

Mangonui and around

There's an undeniably antiquated air to the village of **MANGONUI**, attractively strung out along a sheltered half-kilometre of harbour off Doubtless Bay. A handful of two-storey buildings with wooden verandas have been preserved and a couple of craft shops nestle between a clutch of cafés, but this is still very much a working village, with a lively fishing wharf and a traditional grocery perched on stilts over the water. It makes the most obvious stopping point on the way north, with excellent beaches nearby and a waterfront where you can successfully catch your supper over an afternoon beer and have it cooked up at any of the local restaurants.

Mangonui means "big shark", a name recalling an incident when the legendary chief Moehuri's *waka* was led into the harbour by such a fish. But it was whales and the business of provisioning **whaling** ships that made the town: one apocryphal story tells of a harbour so packed with ships that folk could leap between the boats to cross from the Mangonui side over to the diminutive settlement of Hihi. As whaling diminished, the kauri trade took its place, chiefly around Mill Bay, the cove five minutes' walk to the west of Mangonui.

While ships were being repaired and restocked at Mangonui, barrels were being fixed a couple of kilometres west beside a stream crossing the strand that became known as **COOPERS BEACH**. This glorious and well-shaded sweep of sand is now backed by a string of motels and blighted by a rash of construction sites for big new homes. The beach is popular in January and at weekends, but at other times you might still find you have it pretty much to yourself.

Another couple of kilometres west, the smaller settlement of **CABLE BAY** owes its existence to its short-lived role as the terminus of the 1902 trans-Pacific cable; in 1912, the telegraph station was moved to Auckland. Again, the water is the focus of the modern community, with the excellent swimming beach and good surf. The Taipa River separates Cable Bay from the beachside village of **TAIPA**, now the haunt of sunbathers and swimmers, but historically significant as the spot where Kupe, the discoverer of Aotearoa in Maori legend, first set foot on the land.

To get a feel for the layout of the bay and a sense of how attractively sheltered it must have seemed to early whalers, wander up to the views at **Rangikapiti Pa Historic Reserve**, off Rangikapiti Rd (unrestricted entry), between Mangonui and Coopers Beach. For a deeper understanding though you'll need to drive 15km around the head of the harbour to Hihi and the waterside **Butler House and Whaling Museum** (open by appointment only on ℡09/406 0006; $7.50, grounds only $5). Butler House was originally built in 1847 by whaler, ship owner and local MP William Butler (and incorporates

The Swamp Palace

If you are staying anywhere around Doubtless Bay and have your own transport, don't pass up an evening at **The Swamp Palace** (Ⓣ09/408 7040 for screening info; $8, backpackers $6; closed Nov & Dec), a quirky cinema in the Oruru Community Hall, seven kilometres south of Taipa in the middle of nowhere. It caters to an eclectic mix of tastes – cult and classic movies, as well as the very latest releases – each introduced with an informed talk by the proprietor.

a still earlier house of 1843, which was floated across the bay from Mangonui), and is now filled with early colonial and Victorian furniture. The adjacent whaling museum has a well restored whaling boat complete with replica try-works (where blubber was boiled down), assorted harpoons and blubber spades. Scrimshaw, in the form of carving and images etched into whalebone, along with knot boards, hint at the boredom of ship life, though when it turned brutal the whalers had to rely on the shipboard doctor with his fearsome-looking instruments and medicine chest. All this is set in the lovely grounds of **Butler Point**, which occupies a former *pa* site studded with mature trees, including a magnificent magnolia planted by Butler and several enormous pohutukawas – one seven-hundred-year-old specimen has a trunk almost eleven metres in diameter, the fattest in the country.

In Mangonui, don't miss the reasonably priced selection of handmade **woven flax items**, shells and other locally made crafts at Flax Bush, The Waterfront (daily 10am–5pm): the deals on woven baskets (*kete*) are some of the best you'll find. Art of a different kind is to be found along the Waterfront in the old courthouse at **Exhibit A** (Ⓣ09/406 0455; 9am–5pm most days), where Annie Tothill makes and sells vibrant wall-hangings, throws and clothes from natural fabrics, and exhibits work from a roster of Far North artists.

For something more active, **dolphin watching and swimming** can be arranged with Doubtless Bay Adventures (book through the visitor centre at Mangonui; $80), while Seabed Safaris (Ⓣ09/408 5885) offer **diving** off the Karikari Peninsula and elsewhere: resort dives from the shore go for $145 (second dive $100), boat dives start at $95, and for $135 you can dive the *Rainbow Warrior* wreck – there are big discounts if you have your own gear. Mangonui also makes a good base for organized trips to **Cape Reinga and Ninety Mile Beach** (see box on p.214).

Practicalities

SH10 bypasses the Mangonui waterfront, which is reached on a two-kilometre loop road plied by the joint Northliner and InterCity **bus** service, which runs once a day in each direction between Paihia and Kaitaia. Buses stop outside the BP station (Ⓣ09/406 0024) which sells tickets, as does the adjacent Mangonui Stationery (Ⓣ09/406 0024). The **visitor centre** next door (daily 9am–4pm; Ⓣ & Ⓕ09/406 2046, Ⓦwww.doubtlessbay.co.nz) has **internet access** and can point you to accommodation, both here and along the coast.

Accommodation

Backpackers Beach Resort 4 Taipa Point Rd, Taipa Ⓣ09/406 0789, Ⓔtaipabeach@hotmail.com. A row of self-catering motel units let either as made-up doubles or by the bed – very comfortable and spacious, if lacking in atmosphere. Tents $10, beds ❶, rooms ❷

Beach Lodge SH10, Coopers Beach Ⓣ & Ⓕ09/406 0068, Ⓔbeachlodge@paradise.net.nz. Luxurious self-catering one-bedroom apartments sleeping four, with waterfront balconies, full kitchen, satellite TV and VCR, free boogie boards and kayaks, and a small gym. ❼

Heath's B&B Homestay Hihi Rd, Hihi, 12km from Mangonui ⓣ & ⓕ09/406 0088. Pleasant homestay in a modern home with distant views across the water to Mangonui. En-suite rooms come with continental breakfast and freshly baked bread, and dinners are available on request. ④

Mac 'n' Mo's, SH10, Coopers Beach ⓣ & ⓕ09/406 0538, ⓔmacnmo@xtra.co.nz. Welcoming homestay with good views and en-suite rooms. ④

Macrocarpa Cottage 2 Bush Point Rd, Taipa ⓣ09/406 1245, ⓦwww.doubtlessbay.co.nz/macrocarpa/macrocarpa.htm. An open-plan, self-catering cottage at the water's edge with one double, and two single beds on a mezzanine, full kitchen and cable TV, plus fabulous views across the Taipa Estuary. Great for couples. ⑥

Mangonui Hotel Waterfront Rd, Mangonui ⓣ09/406 0003, ⓕ406 0015. Turn-of-the-century hotel, opposite the harbour and with an excellent upstairs veranda for whiling the day away. Rooms are fairly plain and the best ones with harbour views go quickly, so book ahead or arrive early. ④

Old Oak Inn Waterfront Rd, Mangonui ⓣ & ⓕ09/406 0665. Ancient hotel with a few small but characterful rooms upstairs, let either by the bed or by the room. Beds ①, rooms ③

San Marino San Marino Drive, off Kupe Road, Coopers Beach ⓣ09/406 0345, ⓕ406 0202. Standard motel units, each with a small deck, and all wonderfully sited with direct access to the beach. ④

Time Out 6 Heretaunga Crescent, Cable Bay ⓣ09/406 0101, ⓦwww.taketimeout.co.nz. Just one idyllic studio unit with full self-catering facilities, stylish decor and direct beach access through subtropical vegetation. ⑥

Eating and drinking

Doubtless Bay has the best range of **places to eat** north of Kerikeri, though admittedly it doesn't have much competition. Committed **drinking** mostly happens at the *Mangonui Hotel*, which often has bands at weekends.

Fresh & Tasty Waterfront Road, Manganui. Rival chippy to its more famous neighbour, the *Manganui Fish Shop*, and much frequented by locals happy to trade location for lower prices and equally good tucker.

Mangonui Fish Shop Waterfront Road, Mangonui. A better-than-average fish-and-chip restaurant, hyped as being "world famous", that is descended upon each evening by several of the Cape Reinga tour buses. Guaranteed fresh, you can select your fillet from the catch of the day, watch while it's weighed, priced and deep fried in front of you, then retire to the great licensed deck perched out over the water.

Mangonui Hotel Waterfront Rd, Mangonui. Moderately priced bistro meals inside or out at the *Clansman*, and more formal dining in the *Donnybrook Restaurant*, where half a dozen oysters ($10) might be followed by a scotch fillet ($20) or the daily pasta dish ($15).

Pamir Restaurant SH12, Coopers Beach ⓣ09/406 0860. Imaginative and well-executed meals, featuring steaks, vegetarian dishes and plenty of seafood, with Thai mussels or scallop mornay setting you up for salmon fillet on basil mash ($25) or the fabulous "Kai Moana" seafood platter ($33) with lobster, prawns, oysters and a seafood chowder. Closed Mon & Tues.

Waterfront Café Waterfront Road, Mangonui ⓣ09/406 0850. Reliable café and bar opening out to pavement seating just over the street from the harbour. Stop by for the best coffee in the district, light lunches or mains such as lemon chicken with tzatziki and Greek salad ($22), or one of their fine pizzas.

The Karikari Peninsula

Doubtless Bay to the east and Rangaunu Harbour to the west are both bounded by the crooked arm of the **Karikari Peninsula** as it strikes north, swathed in unspoiled golden- and white-sand beaches which, at least outside the peak Christmas to mid-February season, have barely a soul on them. There's no public transport, facilities are limited and, without diving or fishing gear, you'll have to resign yourself to lazing on the beaches and swimming from them – and there can be few better places to do just that.

The initial approach across a low and scrubby isthmus is less than inspiring, though it's worth stopping briefly at **Lake Ohia**, 1km off SH10, which has gradually drained to reveal the stumps of a 40,000-year-old kauri forest thought to have been destroyed by some prehistoric cataclysm. A kilometre on, the **Gum Hole Reserve** has a short trail past holes left by kauri gum diggers (see box on p.225 for more on their exploits). Eight kilometres later, a side road leads to the peninsula's west coast and the **Puheke Scenic Reserve**, a gorgeous, dune-backed beach that's usually deserted. There's another fine strand nearby at the beachside hamlet of **RANGIPUTA**, with the *White Sands Motor Lodge* (Ⓣ09/408 7080, Ⓕ408 7580; ❹) and, 1km back down the road, the attractive, spa-equipped *Reef Lodge*, Rangiputa Road (Ⓣ09/408 7100, Ⓔreeflodge@clear.net.nz; ❺), set among lawns and backed by a golden beach.

The peninsula's main road continues past the Rangiputa junction to the community of **TOKERAU BEACH**, a cluster of houses and a couple of shops at the northern end of the grand sweep of Doubtless Bay. The only accommodation here is the well-run *Whatuwhiwhi Holiday Park*, Whatuwhiwhi Rd (Ⓣ09/408 7202, Ⓔwhatuwhiwhi@xtra.co.nz; tents $12, cabins ❷, units ❸, self-catering cabins ❹), set back from a gorgeous beach. One kilometre north of Tokerau Beach at the Carrington Club golf course, the *Fairway Café* (Fri & Sat 11am–9pm, Sun 11am–3pm, longer in summer; Ⓣ09/408 7208) is, takeaways apart, the only place **to eat** on the peninsula.

The Karikari Peninsula saves its best until last: **Maitai Bay**, 20km north of SH10, is a matchless double arc of golden sand split by a rocky knoll, all encompassed by the *Maitai Bay Campground* ($6 per adult), the largest DOC campsite in Northland. Much of the site is *tapu* to local Maori, and you are encouraged to respect the sacred areas.

Kaitaia

KAITAIA, 40km west of Mangonui, is the Far North's largest commercial centre, but suffers from one of the highest unemployment rates in the country and is a place of little charm or excitement. With your own transport you might want to whizz round the sights, refuel and push on, but it does make a convenient base for some of the best bus trips to Cape Reinga and Ninety Mile Beach (see p.215), although you might prefer to base yourself at the beach in Ahipara (see p.213).

A Maori village already flourished here when the first missionary, Joseph Matthews, came looking for a mission site in 1832. The protection of the mission encouraged other European pastoralists to establish themselves here, but by the 1880s they found themselves swamped by the gum diggers who had come to plunder the underground deposits around Lake Ohia (see p.209) and Ahipara (see p.213). Many early arrivals were young Dalmatians (mostly Croats) fleeing tough conditions in what was then part of the Austro-Hungarian Empire, though the only evidence of this today is a telephone directory full of Croat names, a Serbo-Croat welcome sign at the entrance to town, and a cultural society that holds a traditional dance each year.

The Town

The best place to gain a sense of the area is the surprisingly good **Far North Regional Museum**, 6 South Rd (Mon–Fri 10am–5pm; $3.50), with arresting displays on pretty much every aspect of local life and history. The room of Ngati Kahu pieces is particularly striking; you enter under one of three copies

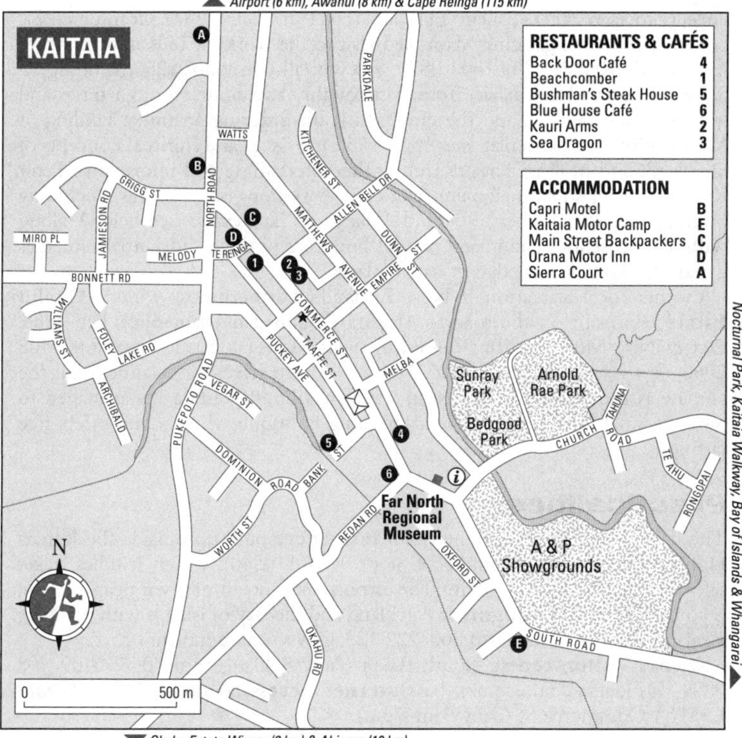

of the twelfth- or thirteenth-century **Kaitaia Carving**, found around 1920 on the outskirts of Kaitaia, an example of the transitional period during which Polynesian art began to take on Maori elements; the original is held in the Auckland Museum (see p.100). Another rare find is the series of boards from **palisades** which once surrounded *pa* sites: these were mostly burned or rotted away, but several surviving examples are on display here. Elsewhere in the room, beautifully woven and decorative flax-and-kiwi-feather cloaks contrast with utilitarian items – a carved canoe bailer, collections of clubs, spears and oratory staffs – and a complete skeleton of a juvenile kuri, the Polynesian dog brought to New Zealand by early Maori settlers, which died out around a century ago. Pride of place in the main room goes to the earliest European artefact to be left in New Zealand: a huge one-and-a-half-tonne **anchor**, one of three abandoned by de Surville when he departed in haste in 1769 (see p.204). The maritime theme continues through a collection of ships in glass cases, including a fine whaler made of matchsticks, and sundry bits and pieces from the *Rainbow Warrior*. Photographs of early gum-digging operations are supported by examples of the diggers' tools and polished pieces of prize gum in shades from pale amber to deep treacle.

As elsewhere throughout the north, Maori people make up a large proportion of the population and influence the local culture strongly, though on a short visit this may not be particularly evident. One way to explore this influence is to join the excellent Tall Tale Travel 'n' Tours, 237a Commerce St, behind *KFC*, on a genuine Maori-led visit to the working Te Rarawa **marae**, just outside Kaitaia (Ⓣ09/408 0870, Ⓦwww.tall-tale.co.nz; $25, including $5 donation to the local *marae*). Tours last roughly two hours, though times and itineraries are flexible, and the emphasis is on fostering an understanding of Maori culture, in particular *marae* protocol, land issues and spiritual concepts of life, death and healing. They're run by the entertaining and informative Peter Kitchen, who also runs all manner of craft workshops (same details), including bone carving ($50). They're behind *Main Street Backpackers* (see below), along with a shop selling handmade natural bodycare potions and herbal remedies based on Maori knowledge of native plants.

Another local attraction is New Zealand's northernmost winery, **Okahu Estate**, 3km out on the road to Ahipara (Dec & Jan 10am–6pm; Feb–June, Oct & Nov Mon–Sat 10m–6pm; July–Sept Mon–Fri 10am–6pm; Ⓣ09/408 2066, Ⓦwww.okahuestate.co.nz). Though experts have long claimed that the climate is too moist for successful wine making, the estate has managed to produce small quantities of award-winning boutique wines – and offers free tastings.

Practicalities

The daily InterCity–Northliner joint **bus** service pulls up outside the Kaitaia Holiday Shoppe, 170 Commerce St (Ⓣ09/408 0540), which handles ticket sales (as does the visitor centre). The airport, 6km north of town near Awanui, is connected by direct **flights** to Auckland and the Bay of Islands with Air New Zealand and Air Kaitaia (Ⓣ0800/222 123, Ⓦwww.mountainair.co.nz).

Kaitaia's **visitor centre**, South Road (daily 8.30am–5pm; Ⓣ & Ⓕ09/408 0879, Ⓔfndckta@xtra.co.nz), has **internet access**, as does *Hackers Internet Café*, 84 Commerce St (daily 9am–7pm).

Accommodation

Accommodation can be tight in peak season, but prices are generally lower than at the coastal resorts to the east.

Capri Motel 5 North Rd Ⓣ0800/422 774 & 09/408 0224, Ⓔcaprimotel@xtra.co.nz. Basic but perfectly adequate motel with some recently refurbished units. ❸

Kaitaia Motor Camp 69 South Rd Ⓣ09/408 1212. Small and fairly ordinary campsite with tent sites ($8), powered sites ($10), communal kitchen, games room and barbecue area.

Main Street Backpackers, 235 Commerce St Ⓣ09/408 1275, Ⓦwww.tall-tale.co.nz/mainstreet. Welcoming YHA-associate hostel which actively promotes itself as New Zealand's first Maori backpackers and offers the opportunity to hand-carve bone pendants ($20) and join the activities at the carving workshop next door (see above). They also rent out bikes ($10 a day), provide free sand-toboggans and rent camping gear for use at Cape Reinga. Tent sites $10, dorms ❶, rooms ❷

Sierra Court 65 North Road Ⓣ0800/666 022 & 09/408 1461, Ⓔsierracourt.Kaitaia@xtra.co.nz. Attractive motor lodge with swimming and spa pools along with a selection of studios and larger units. ❹

Eating and drinking

Back Door Café 51 Commerce St, behind Aqua Pulse. Kaitaia's best espresso is served in what amounts to little more than a wide passage beside the Aqua Pulse shop with a few tables outside – they also dish up muffins, sandwiches, nachos and the like.

Beachcomber Restaurant 222 Commerce St Ⓣ09/408 2010. Slightly formal licensed restaurant, predictably strong on seafood – scallops, squid, rock oysters – but also with steaks ($23), salmon and ostrich. The lunch menu also offers lighter fare such as omelettes, burgers and pasta dishes for around $12. Closed Sat lunch and all day Sun.

Blue House Café 14 Commerce St. Probably the pick of Kaitaia's cafés, open from breakfast until late and serving up large portions of hearty Kiwi food at modest prices, and with a lively bar at one end.

Bushman's Steak House 7 Bank St ⓣ09/408 4320. Licensed restaurant decorated in rustic style with corrugated iron and rough-hewn timber, serving a wide range of burgers, curries, chicken dishes, fish and steaks at decent prices.

Kauri Arms Commerce St. Possibly the most popular of Kaitaia's workaday pubs, drumming up custom with local bands at weekends.

Sea Dragon 185 Commerce St. Reasonably priced BYO Chinese restaurant and takeaway.

Ahipara and the gumfields

Bus tours along Ninety Mile Beach turn off long before its final southern curl around to **AHIPARA**, a scattered village 15km west of Kaitaia that grew up around the Ahipara gumfields. A hundred kilometres of sand recede into sea spray to the north, while to the south the high flatlands of the Ahipara Plateau tumble to the sea in a cascade of golden dunes. Beach and plateau meet at **Shipwreck Bay**, a surf and rough swimming beach named for the paddle-shaft of the *Favourite*, wrecked in 1870, which still sticks out of the waves. At low tide you can pick mussels off the rocks as you follow the wave-cut platform some 5km around to some big sand dunes; great for sand boarding if you drag one along.

At their peak in the early twentieth century, the **gumfields,** on a sandy dune plateau to the south of town, supported three hotels and two thousand people. Unlike most fields, where experimental probing and digging was the norm, here the soil was methodically excavated, washed and sieved to extract the valuable kauri gum (see box on p.225). None of the machinery or dwellings remain on the plateau, but gum can still be found – particularly in the stream that washes down into Shipwreck Bay.

The best way to explore the dunes and gumfields is on four-wheel motorbikes with Tua Tua Tours (ⓣ & ⓕ09/409 4875, ⓦwww.ahipara.co.nz/tuatuatours; call them and they'll pick you up) whose excursions include the ninety-minute coastal Reef Rider ($80) to the excellent three-hour Gumfields Safari ($145), which includes some sand boarding. Two can share a bike for $10–20 more. If you can manage without the local knowledge and riding instruction, head out on your own with quad bikes from the Ahipara Adventure Centre, Takahe St (ⓣ09/409 2055, ⓦwww.Ahipara.co.nz/adventure; $50 for 1hr, $110 for 3hr). They also rent out sand toboggans, fishing gear and blokarts (a kind of mini sand yacht; $25 for 30min), and run gentle horse-riding trips ($25 for first hour, $20 per hour thereafter).

Keen hikers might prefer to tackle the same area on the tide-dependent **Gumfields Walk** (29.5km; 12hr round trip; free maps from *Main Street Backpackers* in Kaitaia), which takes you into an eerie and desolate landscape of wind-sculpted dunes and an ancient kauri forest uncovered by the sand, and back around the coast. Let someone know where you're going, and keep your eyes peeled for dull lumps of kauri gum which can be polished up later. Finally, **scenic flights** over Shipwreck Bay and the gumfields from Kaitaia Airport are organized by Blue Sky Scenics (ⓣ09/406 7320; $55).

Practicalities

Basing yourself in Ahipara is a broadly more appealing proposition than **staying** in Kaitaia, viable, though when it comes to **eating** there's just a couple of takeaways and one restaurant, the *Bayview Restaurant*, at 22 Reef View Rd (ⓣ09/409 4888), which has acceptable if uninspired licensed dining with good sea views.

Beach Abode 11 Korora St ⓣ & ⓕ09/409 4070, ⓦwww.beachabode.co.nz. Two well appointed and tastefully decorated beachfront units (one studio, the other with additional bedroom) each with a full kitchen, barbecue, deck and great views over low dunes to the sea. Meals are available on request (breakfast $9; three-course dinner $35). ❺

Foreshore Lodge 269 Foreshore Rd ⓣ & ⓕ09/409 4860, ⓦwww.ahipara.co.nz/foreshore. Two en-suite self-contained units each with a small terrace and sea views. ❹

Pine Tree Lodge Motor Camp ⓣ09/409 4864, ⓔpinetree@xtra.co.nz. Basic campsite away from the sea with tent sites ($8) and basic cabins (❷).

Shipwreck Lodge 70 Foreshore Rd ⓣ09/409 4929, ⓦwww.shipwrecklodge.co.nz. Luxurious B&B right on the beachfront with sparsely but stylishly furnished en-suite rooms, each opening out onto a small private balcony with great sea views; there's also a guest lounge with satellite TV and stereo. Full breakfast is included, and dinner ($50) is available on request. ❼–❽

Getting to the Cape

The best way to experience the phenomenal length and wild beauty of Ninety Mile Beach is to take one of the **bus tours** based in Kaitaia, Mangonui and Paihia in the Bay of Islands. Those from Paihia are the most numerous but are also the longest (11hr); tours starting further north mean you spend less time in the bus and have more time to explore. Paihia-based buses will often pick up along the way. Their content varies but in essence they do the same trip, a loop up the Aupori Peninsula and back, travelling SH1 in one direction and Ninety Mile Beach in the other, the order being dictated by the tide. Highlights include boogie boarding or tobogganing down the sand dunes that flank Te Paki Stream, and the rambling collection of the Wagener Museum.

From Kaitaia there are currently two bus companies which run virtually identical trips to the cape: Harrison's Cape Runner, 123 North Rd (ⓣ09/408 1033 & 0800/227 373, ⓦwww.ahipara.co.nz/caperunner; $40), or Sand Safaris, 221 Commerce St (ⓣ09/408 1778 & 0800/869 090, ⓦwww.sandsafaris.co.nz), who charge around $5 more. Both collect you up from your accommodation around 9am and return around 5pm – they'll also drop you off and pick you up later if you want to do the three-day walk at Cape Reinga. Alternatively, it's worth trying to get a group together (minimum 6) for the small-group trips run by Tall Tale Travel 'n' Tours, 237a Commerce St (ⓣ09/408 0870, ⓦwww.tall-tale.co.nz; $95), which emphasize the spiritual significance of the area for Maori through traditional stories, and usually includes shellfish gathering and a barbecue. **From Mangonui**, Paradise Connexion Tours (ⓣ0800/494 392, ⓣ & ⓕ09/406 0460, ⓔconnexion@xtra.co.nz) charge $55 for a bus tour including pick-up from your accommodation, and also have 4WDs for customized tours for up to four people ($450 day).

From Paihia, the two big cruise companies, King's and Fullers, dominate the Cape Reinga tour market. Most trips run daily, leaving at around 7.30am, returning about eleven hours later, and going via Kerikeri, Mangonui and Awanui in one direction and passing Kaitaia and the kauri trees of the Puketi Forest in the other. King's (ⓣ09/402 8288) run the all-in Cape Reinga Scenic ($85, plus $10 for picnic lunch). Fullers (ⓣ09/402 7421) operate swanky, custom-designed buses on the Cape Reinga Heritage tour ($110, including barbecue lunch), which includes a *marae* visit, and the more sightseeing-oriented Cape Reinga Wanderer (Oct–May only; $89, $99 including box lunch), with sand tobogganing, swimming and shellfish digging. Both companies offer ten percent discounts if you sign up for both a cruise and a cape trip. Those with a more adventurous spirit generally go with either Awesome Adventures

Ninety Mile Beach and Cape Reinga

Northland's final gesture is the **Aupori Peninsula**, a narrow, 100km-long finger of consolidated and grassed-over dunes ending in a lumpy knot of 60-million-year-old marine volcanoes. To Maori it's known as *Te Hika o te Ika* ("The tail of the fish"), recalling the legend of Maui hauling up the North Island ("the fish") from the sea while in his canoe (the South Island).

The most northerly accessible point on the peninsula is **Cape Reinga**, believed by Maori to be the "place of leaping", where the spirits of the dead depart. Beginning their journey by sliding down the roots of an 800-year-old pohutukawa into the ocean, they climb out again on Ohaua, the highest of the

(☎09/402 6985; $79) or one of the smaller operators, who use more modest vehicles and take a less rigid approach, letting the group fine-tune the itinerary and not fussing overly if things run past the scheduled return time: Northern Exposure Tours (☎09/402 8644 & 0800/573 875; $70) use a minibus and include a beachside picnic lunch; they also pick up from **Kerikeri**; 4x4 Dune-Rider (☎ & ℗09/402 8681, ⓦwww.dunerider.co.nz; $77) make the cape trip in a 4WD, so you can get right off the beaten track; they also pick up in **Kaeo**, **Mangonui**, **Taipa** and **Awanui**, and will drop you off and pick you up another day at no extra cost.

If you're intent on seeing Cape Reinga and not bothered about driving along Ninety Mile Beach, you can **drive to the Cape** via the main road and avoid the beach altogether. Alternatively you can **fly** there from Paihia with Salt Air Paihia (☎0800/475 582 & 09/402 8338; $285), who land at Te Paki station and cover the last section by road and 4WD; or with Kaitaia-based Blue Sky Scenics (☎09/406 7320; $145).

Going it alone on Ninety Mile Beach

Rental cars and private vehicles are not insured to drive on Ninety Mile Beach – and for good reason. Vehicles frequently get bogged in the sand and abandoned by their occupants, who return home with salutary photos of the roof sticking out of the surf. If you get stuck there are no rescue facilities near enough to get you out before the tide comes in, and mobile phone coverage is almost nil: you could end up with a long walk.

If you are determined to take your own vehicle for a spin on the beach, seek local advice and prepare your long-suffering car by spraying some form of water repellent on the ignition system – CRC is a common brand. Schedule your trip to coincide with a receding tide, starting two hours after high water and preferably going in the same direction as the bus traffic that day; drive close to the water's edge, avoiding any soft sand, and slow down to cross streams running over the beach – they often have deceptively steep banks. If you do get stuck in soft sand, lowering the tyre pressure will improve traction. There are several access points along the beach, but the only ones realistically available to ordinary vehicles are the two used by the tour buses: the southern access point at **Waipapakauri Ramp**, 6km north of Awanui, and the more dangerous northern one along **Te Paki Stream**, which involves negotiating 3km of quicksand – start in low gear and don't stop, no matter how tempting the dunes look.

Three Kings Islands, to bid a final farewell before returning to their ancestors in Hawaiiki. The spirits reach Cape Reinga along **Ninety Mile Beach** (which is actually around 64 miles long), a wide band of sand running straight along the western side of the peninsula. Most visitors follow the spirits, though they do so in modern buses specifically designed for belting along the hard-packed sand at the edge of the surf – officially part of the state highway system – then negotiating the quicksands of Te Paki Stream to return to the road. The main road runs more-or-less down the centre of the peninsula, while the western ocean is kept tantalizingly out of sight by the thin pine ribbon of the **Aupori Forest**. The forests, and the cattle farms that cover most of the rest of the peninsula, were previously the preserve of gum diggers, who worked the area intensively early this century.

If you've made it this far north, you'll already be familiar with the paucity of facilities in rural Northland, so the Aupori Peninsula doesn't come as much of a surprise. There's sporadic **accommodation** along the way, ranging from some beautifully sited DOC campsites to motels, lodges and hostels. Most are reasonably priced, reflecting the fact that many visitors pass through without stopping; however, all are very busy immediately after Christmas. There are a few **places to eat**, though nothing stays open after around 8pm. Pukenui and Waitiki both have a shop and expensive **petrol**.

Awanui

AWANUI, 8km north of Kaitaia on SH1, is a dilapidated rural backwater notable chiefly for being the meeting point of the eastern and western roads north. The name is Maori for "Big River", though all you'll find is an attractive bend in a narrow tidal creek that makes a great setting for the *Big River Café*, which has some of the best eating hereabouts, including panini, wraps, burgers (including ostrich) and full meals from breakfast until around 9pm. Across the road, Te Whenua, offers locally made Maori arts.

Almost all buses to Cape Reinga stop 1km north at the **Ancient Kauri**

The legend of To Houtaewa and the marathon

Each year competitors from around the world take part in a series of running and walking events on Ninety Mile Beach in mid-March, originally inspired by the tale of a great Maori athlete.

According to legend, **Te Houtaewa**, the fastest runner of his day, enjoyed playing pranks on the enemies of his people. One day his mother asked him to collect some *kumara* from the gardens at Te Kao towards the northern end of the beach, but instead Te Houtaewa ran off south over the hard sands to annoy the **Te Rarawa** people living in Ahipara. Soon after, Te Houtaewa was spotted filling two large *kete* (baskets) from the Te Rarawa storehouse, and a line of people gathered to block his way back to the beach. Sprinting up a hill, Te Houtaewa drew his enemies in pursuit. After waiting for the Te Rarawa to draw close, Te Houtaewa (still clasping the baskets) ran back onto the beach, sending his pursuers sprawling. The Te Rarawa dispatched their best athletes in response, but despite his heavy load Te Houtaewa outran and outwitted them, arriving home to find the *hangi* hot, in readiness for his stolen *kumara*.

Today events range from the mammoth **Te Houtaewa Challenge**, a sixty-kilometre open marathon run by international competitors, to a six-kilometre **Walk for Life**. Call Tall Tale Promotion (☎09/408 0870) for entry forms; fees are $50–70, depending on the event.

Kingdom (daily 9am–5pm; free), a defunct dairy factory now operating as a sawmill, cutting and shaping huge peat-preserved kauri logs hauled out of swamps where they have lain for between 30,000 and 50,000 years. You can wander around parts of the factory and watch slabs of wood being fashioned into all manner of things. Predictably, the emphasis is on the shop, where along with assorted wooden trinkets there are some expensive dining suites, coffee tables and bowls, and some admittedly impressive but astonishingly ugly sofas with polished roots and branches forming arms and legs. Be sure to climb up to the mezzanine on the spiral staircase hewn out of the centre of the largest piece of swamp kauri trunk ever unearthed, a monster three and a half metres in diameter.

Some 12km to the north of the Kauri Kingdom, 3km off SH1, the **Gumdiggers Park** (Tues–Sun 9am–5pm; donation requested) features an easy twenty-minute trail through manuka forest, leading past holes in the ground excavated by diggers early last century and revealing massive kauri roots and small piece of kauri gum uncovered when the site was tidied up for display. Everything is well explained, and there's even a primitive replica diggers' camp.

The main southern entrance to Ninety Mile Beach, the **Waipapakauri Ramp**, is just south of the Gumdiggers Park turn-off.

Houhora and Pukenui

Around 30km north of Awanui are the Aupori Peninsula's two largest settlements: scattered **HOUHORA**, and the working fishing village of **PUKENUI**, 2km to the north, where good catches are to be had off the wharf. At Houhora, a three-kilometre side road turns east to **Houhora Heads** and the **Wagener Museum Complex** (daily 9am–4.30pm or later; $6), a golf course, campsite, licensed café with great harbour views and twin museums that are on the itinerary of several cape-bound tour buses. It was here in 1860 that Polish pioneers used locally hewn timbers and mortar made from powdered seashells to build the **Subritzky Homestead** (open morning or afternoon depending on the tour-bus schedules, or by arrangement on ⓣ09/409 8850; $3). Although now largely restored to its original state, some rooms still reflect the style of later inhabitants, particularly the last resident, Uncle Fred, who lived here until 1960 in a simple room with a bed made of gum sacks. When descendants of the Subritzkys decided to restore the homestead in the late 1960s, they could only obtain the original furniture as part of a large purchase that included the makings of the ever-expanding **Wagener Museum** (daily: Christmas–Jan 7am–7pm; Feb–Christmas 8am–6pm; $6). This somewhat random, something-for-everyone assemblage includes one of the world's largest collection of seashells, along with a similarly superlative array of nearly 500 chamber pots, musical instruments, Victorian arcade games, guns, polished kauri gum, ancient washing machines and Maori artefacts.

Practicalities

The area around Houhora and Pukenui has the greatest concentration of **places to stay** on the Aupori Peninsula. There are two options close to the Wagener Museum: the spacious A-frame chalets of the *Houhora Chalets Motor Lodge*, cnr SH1 & Houhora Heads Rd (ⓣ409 8860, ⓔchalets@xtra.co.nz; ❸); and the beautifully sited but kitchen-less *Houhora Heads Motor Camp*, Houhora Heads Road (ⓣ09/409 8564, ⓕ409 8880; sites $7–9, on-site vans ❷). **In Pukenui**, *Pukenui Lodge,* cnr SH1 & Wharf Rd (ⓣ09/409 8837, ⓔpukenui@igrin.co.nz; dorms ❶, rooms ❷, units ❹), offers plain, self-catering motel units, as well as doubles and dorms in a separate house, all occupying a lush, landscaped site on a small rise with harbour views, a nice pool and spa (for guests staying in units only), barbecue area and bikes for rent. Some 6km north, a side road winds 6km east to the excellent YHA-associate *North Wind Lodge Backpackers*, Otaipango Road, Henderson Bay (Ⓣ & Ⓕ09/409 8515, Ⓔnorthwindldge@xtra.co.nz; dorms ❶, rooms ❷; no credit cards), a modern house not far from a fine beach with very welcoming hosts, good facilities (including a small shop) and pick-ups from Pukenui.

The only **places to eat** are the café at the Wagener Museum and the *Harbour View* restaurant and takeaway at Pukenui (Tues–Sun 11.30am–9pm; Ⓣ09/409 8816), but you can always seek refuge at the waterside *Houhora Tavern*, 2km north of Pukenui, which is often claimed as New Zealand's northernmost pub.

The Parengarenga Harbour, Te Kao and Waitiki Landing

Beyond Houhora the road runs out of sight of the sea, though side roads give opportunities to reach the east coast, particularly at **Rarawa**, 10km north of Pukenui, where the fine sandy beach is as white as you'll find anywhere, and comes backed by a shady streamside DOC **campsite** ($6), 4km off SH1.

The white sands stretch over thirty kilometres north of Rarawa to the straggling **Parengarenga Harbour**, a place largely forgotten by most New Zealanders until 1985, when it was identified as the drop-off point for the limpet mines (delivered by yacht from New Caledonia) that were used to sabotage the *Rainbow Warrior.* Bends in the road occasionally reveal glimpses of the silica sands of the harbour's southern headland, which are pure white except in late February and early March, when hundreds of thousands of bar-tailed godwits turn the vista black as they gather for their 12,000km journey to Siberia.

This whole area is intensely Maori. The Ngati Kuri people own much of the land and comprise the bulk of the population, particularly in the settlement of **TE KAO**, just south of the harbour on SH1. The only reason to stop here, however, is for the twin-towered Ratana Temple, one of the few remaining houses of the Ratana religion, which combines Christian teachings with elements of Maori culture and spiritual belief.

The last place of any consequence before the land sinks into the ocean is **WAITIKI LANDING**, the end of the tarmacked road 21km from Cape Reinga and home to a petrol station, shop and the *Waitiki Landing Complex* (Ⓣ & Ⓕ09/409 7508, Ⓔwaitiki.landing@xtra.co.nz; tent sites $7, powered sites $9, cabins ❸), with its campsite, kitchen cabins, and restaurant serving steak, chicken and fish dinners (around $17) and takeaways. The complex also rents boards for riding the dunes ($8 for 4hr) and can arrange transport for trampers wanting to be dropped off or picked up at the start or end of a walk. Alternatively you could join one of the guided **hikes or kayak trips** run by Pack or Paddle Fishing Adventures (Ⓣ09/409 8445), based 2km south of Waitiki Landing beside SH1. Trips can be designed to suit, but expect to pay $125 a day, including backpacker-style accommodation.

From Waitiki Landing, a dirt road twists 15km to the gorgeous and usually deserted seven-kilometre sweep of **Spirits Bay** (Kapowairau), where you'll find a DOC **campsite** ($5) with pitches in manuka woods and cold showers. The main road continues towards Cape Reinga, passing a turn-off after 6km to the **Te Paki Stream entrance** to Ninety Mile Beach, where there's a small picnic area and parking, plus a twenty-minute hike to some huge sand dunes.

Cape Reinga

The last leg to **Cape Reinga** runs high through the hills before revealing the Tasman Sea and the huge dunes that foreshadow it. Magnificent seascapes unfold until you are deposited at the scruffy Cape Reinga car park, where you'll find toilets but little else. A well-trodden ten-minute path heads from here to the Cape Reinga **lighthouse**, dramatically perched on a headland 165m above Colombia Bank, where the waves of the Tasman Sea meet the swirling currents of the Pacific Ocean in a boiling cauldron of surf. On clear days the view from here is stunning: east to the Surville Cliffs of North Cape, west to Cape Maria van Diemen, and north to the rocky **Three Kings Islands**, 57km offshore, which were named by Abel Tasman, who first came upon them on the eve of Epiphany 1643.

Several dramatic **walks** radiate from the car park. Only avid beach nuts should attempt the long and sandy trudge along the **Cape Reinga Walkway** (134km), which runs the length of Ninety Mile Beach. It can be walked in either direction and will take at least three days, though with no facilities, limited fresh water and a cavalcade of buses passing each day – to say nothing of the sandflies, which are massive up here, especially in summer – you're unlikely to get much pleasure from it. The walk does, however, provide a starting point for shorter strolls: west to **Te Werahi Beach** (30min one way), and steeply east to **Sandy Bay** (30min one way) and the lovely Tapotupotu Bay (2hr one way) – the latter can also be reached by road and is a popular lunchtime picnic stop for tour buses.

The only place to stay hereabouts is the beautifully located DOC **campsite** at Tapotupotu Bay ($6), which comes with toilets and cold showers.

Hokianga Harbour

South of Kaitaia, the narrow, mangrove-flanked fissures of **Hokianga Harbour** snake deep inland past tiny and almost moribund communities. For a few days' relaxation, the tranquillity and easy pace of this rural backwater are hard to beat. You are likely to spend most of your time on the southern shores, from where the harbour's striking, deep-blue waters beautifully set off the mountainous sand dunes of North Head. The dunes are best seen from the rocky promontory of South Head, high above the treacherous Hokianga Bar, or reached by boat for a little sand tobogganing. The high forest ranges immediately to the south make excellent hiking and horse-trekking territory, and the giant kauri of the Waipoua Forest are within easy striking distance, but the focus is definitely the harbour.

It was from here that the great Polynesian explorer **Kupe** left Aoteaora to go back to his homeland in Hawaiiki during the tenth century, and the harbour thus became known as Hokianganui-a-Kupe, "the place of Kupe's great return". Cook saw the Hokianga Heads in 1770 but didn't realize what lay beyond, and it wasn't until a missionary crossed the hill from the Bay of Islands in 1819 that Europeans became aware of the harbour's existence. Catholics, Anglicans and Wesleyans soon followed, converting the local Ngapuhi, gaining their trust, intermarrying with them and establishing the well-integrated Maori and European communities that exist today. The Hokianga area soon rivalled the Bay of Islands in importance and notched up several firsts: European boat building was begun here in 1826; the first signal station opened two years later; and the first Catholic Mass was celebrated in the same year.

With the demise of kauri felling and milling (for more on which, see p.225), Hokianga became an economic backwater, with little industry, high unemployment and limited facilities. Over the last couple of decades, however, city dwellers, artists and craftspeople have snapped up bargain properties and moved up here in a small and fairly inconspicuous way, settling in **Kohukohu** on the north shore, **Rawene**, a short ferry ride away to the south, and the two larger but still small-time resorts of **Opononi** and **Omapere**, opposite the dunes near the harbour entrance.

On a practical note, you'll need to stock up with cash before exploring the harbour and kauri forests: there are **no banks** between Kaitaia and Dargaville, 170km away to the south, though all towns have EFTPOS facilities and the *Omapere Tourist Hotel and Motel* in the centre of Omapere will often change travellers' cheques, but at poor rates. The Hokianga region is served by a **visitor centre** in Omapere on SH12 (see p.223).

Kohukohu and the northern Hokianga

Heading south from Kaitaia, the hilly SH1 twists its way through the forested Mangamuka Ranges for 40km to reach **Mangamuka Bridge**, the western entrance to the Omahuta Forest (see p.203), from where a narrower and equally tortuous road heads towards the north shore of the Hokianga Harbour. An alternative route from Kaitaia winds 23km south from the Ahipara road to tiny **HEREKINO**, just a pub, a few houses and the *Tui Inn*, Puhata Road (☎09/409 3883; beds $12), a fairly primitive backpackers with bargain tent sites, where the main lure is the rural Kiwi tenor fostered by the owner, who offers superb horse trekking for around $45 for the day, fishing trips and maybe even some pig-hunting – an entertaining if somewhat brutal business.

Both routes converge on **KOHUKOHU**, a blink-and-you-miss-it waterside village on the northernmost arm of Hokianga Harbour. Kohukohu was once the hub of Hokianga's kauri industry, but the subsequent years of decline have only partly been arrested by the recent influx of rat-race refugees, resulting in today's low-key settlement, which is almost entirely made up of attractive, century-old wooden houses. Four kilometres further east at Narrows Landing is the northern terminus of the **Rawene Vehicle Ferry** (☎09/405 2602; daily 7.45am–8pm; car and driver $14 one way, $19 return, pedestrians $2 each way), which runs across the harbour to Rawene, on the hour southbound and half-hour northbound.

The beauty of staying on the north side of the harbour is that there's almost nothing to do. You could try some **bone carving** at Kohukohu Carving Studio, 2km up Rakautapu Road ($40 per person; ☎09/405 5802), or spend a few hours **kayaking** around the mangroves and harbour with Misty Waters Kayaks (☎09/405 5806), who do tours from a one-hour paddle through the mangroves ($15) to half-day trips to the sand dunes ($35); they also rent out kayaks for $25 per half day. Those in search of real tranquillity might fancy the forty-kilometre drive northwest (half of it on gravel) to the coastal hamlet of **Mitimiti**, little more than a few houses, a *marae*, and the *Manaia Hostel*, West Coast Road (☎09/405 5855, Ⓔmitimiti@xtra.co.nz; ❶ & ❷) where $20 gets you a bed in a double or twin room.

Practicalities

The Kohukohu area makes a delightful place for a brief sojourn on account of its excellent **places to stay**. Foremost among them is the TV-free *Tree House* (ⓣ09/405 5855, ⓦwww.treehouse.co.nz; tent sites $11–12, dorms ❶, cabins ❷), at Motukaraka, 2km west of the ferry, where people often stay a lot longer than they planned, lulled into submission by the ultra-relaxing surroundings. There are never more than about twenty guests scattered among the spacious four-bunk dorms and double cabins which are scattered around the grounds, but you'll need to bring food and expect to cook. For harbour views from a sunny deck, make for the relaxed *Bag End Adobe Lodge*, Yarborough St, Kohukohu (ⓣ09/405 5806; dorms ❶, rooms ❷), a very small backpackers with doubles, twins and four-shares. The tasteful and aptly named *Harbour Views Guesthouse*, Rakautapu Road, Kohukohu (ⓣ & ⓕ09/405 5815; ❹), also makes a lovely spot for a peaceful night or two, with shady verandas, nicely decorated rooms and dinner for $20.

The Kohukohu scene, such as it is, has recently seen a resurgence, with the old pub and grocery store now supplemented by quality burgers (mushroom, lentil, chicken satay and so on), smoothies and espresso available from *The Palace Flophouse and Grill*, cnr Beach Rd (April–Nov closed Mon; ⓣ09/405 5858), and the prospect of more cafés on the way.

Rawene

The Rawene Vehicle Ferry shuttles from Narrows Landing across to appealing **RAWENE**, a slightly livelier village than Kohukohu which occupies the tip of Herd's Point, a peninsula roughly halfway up the harbour. Though almost isolated by the mud flats at low tide, Rawene's strategic position made it an obvious choice for the location of a timber mill, which contributed material for the town's attractive wooden buildings, some perched on stilts out over the water.

On a sunny day it's a pleasant place to saunter around, perhaps strolling along Clendon Esplanade to reach the **Mangrove Walkway**, a pleasant boardwalk through the coastal shallows. Along the way you pass the town's only significant distraction, **Clendon House** (Nov–April Sat, Sun & Mon 10am–4pm; $3), on a hillside overlooking the harbour. This was the last residence of James Clendon, a pivotal figure in the early life of the colony, who served as US honorary consul, justice of the peace and member of the First Legislative Council before taking up a position as resident magistrate of the Hokianga district in 1861. The house wasn't finished until 1868 and Clendon only lived in it for the four years prior to his death, leaving his part-Maori second wife, Jane, and eight kids. The colonial-era contents of the two-storey house owe more to Jane than to James, but nonetheless reflect the family's relative wealth, with much of the stuffy furniture emanating from Britain. The upper floor has been restored as a child's playroom and schoolroom, and one room beside the veranda has been retained as the post office it once was.

Practicalities

Rawene's proximity to the Rawene Vehicular Ferry makes it an ideal base for exploring both sides of the harbour. The main thoroughfare, Parnell Street, passes the most convenient **accommodation**, the *Masonic Hotel* (ⓣ09/405 7822, ⓔmasonic@igrin.co.nz; ❸), with small but decent traditional hotel rooms. The hilltop *Rawene Motor Camp*, Marmon Street, 1.5km from the ferry landing (ⓣ & ⓕ09/405 7720; tent sites $8, on-site vans and cabins ❷), has tent sites and self-catering cabins tucked away in bush enclaves, and a pool.

For such a small place you can **eat** well. First stop should be the relaxed, *Boatshed Café* (breakfast and lunch only), on Clendon Esplanade, which is built out over the water and offers a stack of magazines to read on the sunny deck as you tuck into snacks such as filo parcels or pizza slices, cakes and the best espresso for miles around. Next door, *Hokianga Wholefoods* stocks wholesome groceries and sells great shakes; while the *Masonic Hotel* (see above) does good bar meals and reasonably priced à la carte dinners, has a peaceful veranda to sup away the afternoon and hosts bands most summer weekends.

Opononi and Omapere

The two small-time resorts of **OPONONI** and **OMAPERE**, some 20km west of Rawene, run seamlessly for 4km along the southern shore of the Hokianga Harbour, with great views across to the massive sand dunes on the north side. Kiwis of a certain age will be able to tell you all about Opononi and the eventful summer of 1955–56 when a wild bottlenose dolphin, dubbed "Opo", took a shine to the local populace and started playing with the kids in the shallows and performing tricks with beach balls. At the time, New Zealand still had whaling factories on its shores, dolphin-watching trips were decades away and signs had to be erected discouraging people from shooting the precocious dolphin. And yet Opo's antics captivated the nation: Christmas holidaymakers jammed the narrow dirt roads; film crews were dispatched; protective laws were drafted; and bandwagon-jumping Auckland musicians Pat McMinn, Bill Langford and The Crombie Murdoch Trio cobbled together the novelty song, "Opo The Crazy Dolphin". Written and recorded in a day, the tape arrived at the radio station for its first airing just as news of Opo's untimely death broke – the song was a hit nonetheless.

Opononi has dined out on its fifteen minutes of fame ever since, though the only concrete reminders are a statue of Opo outside the *Opononi Resort Hotel* and her grave next door outside the War Memorial Hall. To get a better sense of the frenzied enthusiasm for Opo, head to Omapere – just a roadside string of clapboard houses and a few places to stay and eat – where the local museum inside the visitor centre (see below) shows a short video in classic corny-yet-charming 1950s documentary style.

The only other attraction is **Labyrinth Woodworks**, Waiotemarama Gorge Road, 8km southeast of Opononi (☎09/405 4581), one of the region's better craft shops, whose wares include carved kauri pieces and excellent woodblock prints by noted local craftsman Allan Gale. There are also all manner of puzzles to play with and, from mid-December to April, a maize maze, the pathways cut through the cornfield.

Activities and walks

Opononi and Omapere make good bases for exploring the surrounding area. The biggest of all the kauri trees, **Tane Mahuta**, is only 22km south of Omapere, and boats ply across the harbour to the sand dunes – though the vistas from the south side are so striking that it's enough just to visit the viewpoints. The most notable of these are immediately west of Omapere: **Arai te Uru Reserve**, along Signal Station Road, and the magical **Pakia Hill**, on SH12.

The **dunes** are most easily visited by boat from the Opononi wharf: Hokianga Express water taxi (☎09/405 8872) will drop you off and pick you up a couple of hours later for around $18, and also supply sand toboggans; Muddy Mullet Kayak Tours (☎025/791181) run a number of guided kayak trips around the harbour, including a half-day jaunt ($35) across to the dunes, with some sand boarding. There are also **harbour cruises** (Nov–April; $20) on the *Alma*, a century-old kauri scow which works pretty much on demand provided they get the numbers – January and February are your best bets unless you have a group (around a dozen). On land, Okopako Horse Trekking, at *Okopako Lodge* (see below), will take you riding ($20 per hour) into the bush and the hills, with views over the entire Hokianga Harbour.

The best and most popular of the short walks in the district is the **Waiotemarama Walk**, a two-kilometre loop through a lovely bush-clad valley full of ferns, nikau palms and kauri. From Labyrinth Woodworks, a ten-minute walk gets you to an attractive waterfall with a small swimming hole, and after another ten minutes you reach the first kauri. Another popular outing is the **Hokianga Track** (8km; 3–4hr), which heads from Hokianga South Head along Kaikai Beach and up the Waimamaku River back to SH12. More ambitious walkers could set two or three days aside for the **Waipoua Coast Walkway**, a fifty-kilometre coastal trek that continues south from the Hokianga Track to Maunganui Bluff and on to Kai Iwi Lakes (see p.227). Details are available in DOC's *Waipoua & Trounson Kauri Forests* leaflet ($1) and from visitor centres, though there are few facilities along the track.

Practicalities

Westcoaster run a limited **bus service** through the Hokianga on behalf of InterCity and Northliner (whose passes you can use on them), with a southbound service on Monday, Wednesday and Friday and northbound runs on Tuesday, Thursday and Saturday. They stop by the wharf in Opononi and on the main road in Omapere, outside the Hokianga **visitor centre** (daily 8.30am–5pm; ⓣ09/405 8869, ⓦwww.hokianga.co.nz), where you can book and buy bus tickets, and get information on the Waipoua Kauri Forest (see p.226), as well as on the more immediate area.

Top-end accommodation is hard to find around the Hokianga, but the twin towns are well served with **hostels**, the pick being the small and cosy *House of Harmony*, SH12, Opononi (ⓣ & ⓕ09/405 8778, ⓦwww.geocities.com/harmonybak; tent sites $10, dorms ❶, rooms ❷). The combined B&B and YHA-associated *Okopako Lodge: The Wilderness Farm*, Mountain Road (ⓣ & ⓕ09/405 8815; tent sites $9, dorms ❶, rooms ❷), is good and welcoming, and has panoramic views from its hilltop position 5km east of Opononi and 1.5km up a twisting unsealed road. Mostly organic farmhouse dinners are available for under $20. In Omapere, there's accommodation at *Globe Trekkers*, SH12 (ⓣ & ⓕ09/405 8183, ⓦglobetrekkerslodge@hotmail.com; tent sites $8, dorms ❶, rooms ❷).

The best of the **hotels** is the *Omapere Tourist Hotel & Motel*, SH12 (ⓣ09/405 8737, ⓔicesam@ihug.co.nz; sites $9, rooms ❺, beachfront rooms ❻), which is beautifully set opposite the dunes and has a heated pool, bar and restaurant. For **B&B**, try *Harbourside B&B*, SH12 at the western end of Omapere (ⓣ09/405 8246; ❹), which has en-suite rooms and harbour views; or *Solitaire Historic Homestay*, SH12, 10km south (ⓣ & ⓕ09/405 4891, ⓔlesjenread@xtra.co.nz; ❺), located 10km south of Omapere towards the kauri forests and offering comfortable rooms (some en suite), set in attractive gardens. **Campers** are best served at the hostels or the spacious, harbourside *Opononi Holiday Park*, SH12, Opononi (ⓣ & ⓕ09/405 8791, ⓔharrybarlow@xtra.co.nz; sites $10, cabins ❷, self-catering cabins ❸).

Eating possibilities are severely limited. In Opononi there's just *Opo Takeaways* and the *Opononi Resort Hotel*, which offers the district's best eating, both bar food and à la carte. In Omapere the *Omapere Tearooms* dish up light meals in plastic surroundings, while the *Omapere Tourist Hotel* serves pretty reasonable meals in its *Harbourmaster's Restaurant*, but the bar is pleasanter, with great views over the lawns and harbour to the sand dunes. *Calypso's* café, on SH12, 2km to the west, is better known for its view than its middle-of-the-road food.

The Kauri Forests and the northern Kaipara Harbour

Northland, Auckland and the Coromandel Peninsula were once covered in mixed forest dominated by the mighty kauri (see box opposite), the world's second largest tree after the Californian sequoias. By the early years of the twentieth century, rapacious Europeans had felled nearly the lot, the only extensive pockets remaining in the **Waipoua and Trounson kauri forests** south of the Hokianga Harbour. Though small stands of kauri can be found all over Northland, three-quarters of all the surviving mature trees grow in these two small forests, which between them cover barely 100 square kilometres. Walks provide access to the more celebrated examples, which dwarf the surrounding tataire, kohekohe and towai trees.

This area is home to the Te Roroa people who, like their kin in the north, traditionally used the kauri sparingly. Simple tools made felling and working these huge trees a difficult task, and one reserved for major projects such as large war canoes. Once the Europeans arrived with metal tools, bullock trains, wheels and winches, clear felling became more manageable, and most of the trees had gone by the end of the nineteenth century. The efforts of several campaigning organizations eventually bore fruit in 1952, when much of the remaining forest was designated the Waipoua Sanctuary. It's now illegal to fell a kauri except in specified circumstances, such as culling a diseased or dying tree, or when constructing a new ceremonial canoe.

Driving through miles of farmland it's often hard to imagine the same landscape covered in dense forest. This is certainly true of the lands to the south around the muddy shores of **Kaipara Harbour**, a labyrinth of mangrove-choked inlets, drowned valleys and small beaches which constitutes New Zealand's largest harbour. The harbour once unified this quarter of Northland, with sailboats plying its waters and linking the dairy farming and logging towns on its shores. Kauri was shipped out from the largest northern town, **Dargaville**, though the fragile boats all too often foundered on the unpredictable Kaipara Bar and were eventually washed up on **Ripiro Beach**, a fabulous salty strand which just pips Ninety Mile Beach to the title of New Zealand's longest, running for 108km. Since the decline of harbour traffic, modern Dargaville itself survives on horticulture and a constant stream of tourists, bound for the kauri forests, who pause to explore the beach and the windswept Kaipara Heads. If you're pushed for time, skip the town in favour of a couple of hours at the **Matakohe Kauri Museum**, 45km south, which gives the best sense of what the kauri meant to the Northland economy and their spiritual significance for Maori.

Very infrequent **buses** run through the kauri forests from Omapere to Dargaville (northbound on Tues, Thurs & Sat; southbound on Mon, Wed &

Fri), making a brief stop to glimpse the biggest tree; in addition, two or three buses a day run south from Dargaville, so judicious timing should enable you to see the Kauri Museum and get back again.

The kauri and its uses

The **kauri** (*agathis australis*) isn't the tallest species of tree, nor does it boast the greatest girth, but as its gargantuan trunk barely tapers from roots to crown it ranks alongside the sequoias, or redwoods, of California as one of the largest trees in existence. Unlike the redwoods, which are useless as building timber, kauris produce beautiful wood, a fact which hastened their demise and spawned the industries that dominated New Zealand's economy in the latter half of the nineteenth century.

The kauri is a type of pine which now grows only in New Zealand, though it once also grew in Australia and southeast Asia, where it still has close relations. Identifiable remains of kauri forests are found all over New Zealand, but by the time humans arrived on the scene its range had contracted to Northland, Auckland, the Coromandel Peninsula and northern Waikato. Individual trees can live up to 2000 years, reaching 50m in height and 20m in girth, finally toppling over as the rotting core becomes too weak to support its immense weight.

Kauri loggers

Maori have long used mature kauri for dugout canoes, but it was the young "rickers" (young trees) that first drew the attention of **European loggers** since they formed perfect spars for sailing ships. The bigger trees didn't escape attention for long, soon earning an unmatched reputation for their durable, easy-to-work and blemish-free wood, with its straight, fine grain. Loggers' ingenuity was taxed to the limit by the difficulty of getting such huge logs out of the bush. On easier terrain, bullock wagons with up to twelve teams were lashed together to haul the logs on primitive roads or tramways, horse-turned winches were used on steeper ground and, where water could be deployed to transport the timber, dams were constructed from hewn logs. In narrow valleys and gullies all over Northland and the Coromandel, loggers constructed kauri dams up to 20m high and 60m across, with trap doors at the base. Trees along the sides of the valley were felled while the dam was filling, then the dam was opened to flush the floating trunks down the valley to inlets where the logs were rafted up and towed to the mills.

Gum diggers

Once an area had been logged, the **gum diggers** typically moved in. Like most pines, kauri exudes a thick resin to cover any scars inflicted on it, and huge accretions form on the sides of trunks and in globules around the base, further hardening off in time. In pre-European times, Maori chewed the gum, made torches from it to attract fish at night and burned the powdered resin to form a pigment used for *moko* (traditional tattoos). Once Pakeha got in on the act, it was exported as a raw material for furniture varnishes, linoleum, denture moulds and the "gilt" edging on books. When it could no longer be found on the ground, diggers – mostly Dalmatian, but also Maori, Chinese and Malaysian – thrust long poles into the earth and hooked out pieces with bent rods; elsewhere, the ground was dug up and sluiced to recover the gum. Almost all New Zealand gum was exported, but by the early twentieth century synthetic resins had captured the gum market. Kauri gum is still considered one of the finest varnishes for musical instruments, though prices don't justify collecting it; occasional accidental finds supply such specialist needs.

Waipoua and Trounson kauri forests

South of the Hokianga Harbour, SH12 twists and turns through nearly 20km of mature kauri in the **Waipoua Kauri Forest**, following the contours of the hills and skirting around the base of the big trees so as to cause minimal damage to their fragile and shallow root system. Just after you enter the forest you reach a small car park (there's often an enterprising attendant who charges $2 to look after your vehicle), from where's it's a three-minute walk to New Zealand's mightiest tree, the 1200-year-old **Tane Mahuta**, "Lord of the Forest". A vast wall of bark six metres wide rises up nearly 18m to the lowest branches, where it seems that half the forest's epiphytes have lodged. A kilometre or so further south on SH12, another car park marks the beginning of a ten-minute track to a clearing where three paths lead off to notable trees. The shortest (5min return) runs to the **Four Sisters**, relatively slender kauri all growing close together on the same mound of shed bark. A second path (30min return) twists among numerous big trees to the Big Daddy of them all, **Te Matua Ngahere**, the "Father of the Forest", ranked as the second largest tree in New Zealand on account of its shorter stature than Tane Mahuta but, if anything, more richly festooned in epiphytes than its brothers. The third, the **Yakas Track** (6km; 3hr), leads to the Waipoua Forest visitor centre (see below); even if you don't fancy the full track, walk the first thirty minutes to Cathedral Grove, a dense conglomeration of trees, the largest being the **Yakas Kauri**, named after veteran bushman Nicholas Yakas.

In the heart of the Waipoua forest, a side road leads 1km to the **Waipoua Forest visitor centre** (Oct–April Mon–Fri 8.30am–6pm, Sat & Sun 9am–6pm; May–Sept Mon–Fri 8.30am–4.30pm, Sat & Sun 9am–4.30pm; ⓣ09/439 3011, ⓔdanderson@doc.govt.nz). The grounds contain **Maxwell Cottage** (daylight hours; free), a woodcutter's cottage from 1900 built with vertical kauri paling, and a DOC **campsite** (book through the visitor centre; tent sites $7, 2-bed cabins $14 per person, 4-bed cabins $10 per person) with hot showers and a kitchen but no utensils. South of here the highway runs through farmland 6km to the nearest formal **accommodation**, *Waipoua Lodge*, SH12 (ⓣ & ⓕ09/439 0422, ⓦwww.waipoualodge.co.nz; ❺–❻), with attractively self-contained doubles in a converted woolshed, stables and calf pen – they're much more luxurious than they sound, and are set amid landscaped gardens and bush; there's also an on-site restaurant, which serves fine evening meals ($25) incorporating produce from the lodge's organic vegetable garden.

Immediately south of Waipoua Lodge, a side road leads to another small but superb stand of kauri, the **Trounson Kauri Park**, which since 1997 has been subject to intensive trapping and poisoning of native-bird predators – possums, stoats, weasels, feral cats, dogs and hedgehogs – to create a "mainland island" where North island brown kiwi can thrive. Numbers are up significantly, and you can join two-hour long guided night-time walks ($15) to see kiwi, weta, glow-worms and more from *Kauri Coast Holiday Park*, Trounson Park Road (ⓣ0800/807 200, ⓣ & ⓕ09/439 0621, ⓔkauricoast.top10@xtra.co.nz; tent sites $10, dorms ❶, standard and self-catering cabins ❷, motel units ❹). The forest can also be seen from a short track from the car park or from the simple but popular DOC campsite ($7).

A further 9km south of the Trounson turn-off, Aranga Coast Road branches west to the 460m **Maunganui Bluff**, the northern limit of Ripiro Beach (see p.228). Budget accommodation is available at the appealingly rural *Kaihu Farm Hostel*, on SH12 some 4km south of Aranga Coast Road (ⓣ09/439 4004; dorms ❶, rooms ❷), from where it's an easy walk to the Trounson kauris.

Kai Iwi Lakes

The **Kai Iwi Lakes**, 11km west of SH12 and 20km south of Trounson, are a real change, with pine woods running down to fresh, crystal-blue waters fringed by silica-white sand. All three are dune lakes – relatively common along Northland's western seaboard – fed by rainwater and with no visible outlet. Though the largest, **Taharoa**, is less than a kilometre across, and **Waikere** and **Kai Iwi** are barely a hundred metres long, they constitute the deepest and some of the largest dune lakes in the country. Families flock here in the summer to swim, fish and waterski, but outside the first weeks in January you can usually find a quiet spot. There's no public transport to the lakes, but once here you'll find **accommodation** at the large and well-equipped *Kai Iwi Lakes Campground* (Ⓣ09/439 8360; tent sites $8), which comprises the Pine Beach site on the gently shelving shores of Taharoa Lake, with water, toilets and cold showers; and the more intimate Promenade Point site with just pit toilets. The more substantial motel-style *Waterlea*, neighbouring Lake Taharoa (Ⓣ09/439 0727, Ⓔkaiiwilakes@xtra.co.nz; ❹), serves meals, rents mountain bikes and kayaks, and organizes trout-fishing trips ($65 an hour).

Walkers can follow the beach north from here to Maunganui Bluff (2hr one way) and either walk back, follow Aranga Coast Road inland to pick up a bus on SH12, or continue north along the Waipoua Coast Walkway to the Hokianga Harbour.

Dargaville and around

Sleepy **DARGAVILLE**, 30km south of Kai Iwi Lakes, is trying to shake off its cow-town image by pitching itself as the capital of the so-called Kauri Coast, an amorphous region encompassing everywhere south from the Hokianga down and around the Kaipara. In reality, it's more a service town for the region's farming community, traditionally dairy-based but more recently burgeoning into the country's top kumara-growing district. The town was founded as a port in 1872, 64km up the strongly tidal but navigable Northern Wairoa River, by an Australian, Joseph McMullen Dargaville. Ships came to load kauri logs and transport gum (see box on p.225) extracted by Dalmatian settlers who, by the early part of the twentieth century, formed a sizeable portion of the community. A building on Normanby Street still proclaims itself the Yugoslav Social Hall, and a statue on Hokianga Road of a jolly little gum digger commemorates their presence.

The town

The only specific sight is the **Dargaville Museum** (daily 9am–4pm; $3), in the hilltop Harding Park, 2km west of town and marked by two masts rescued from the *Rainbow Warrior* (see box on p.186) and containing extensive displays of artefacts recovered from the shifting dunes, which occasionally reveal old shipwrecks. An uncovered piece of sixteenth-century Spanish helmet has led local experts to contend that the Spaniard Juan Fernandez was the first European to visit New Zealand in 1576, a full 66 years before Abel Tasman's more widely recognized "discovery". Naturally, this is highly controversial, and most of the evidence is circumstantial, though Ross Wiseman makes a strong case for Fernandez in his book *The Spanish Discovery of New Zealand in 1576* (see p.965). Remains from later wrecks are on show along with photos of their excavation, the only pre-European artefact being the Ngati Whatua *waka* which lay buried under the sands of the North Head of the Kaipara Harbour from 1809 until 1972, and is a rare example of a canoe hewn entirely with stone tools. A recent addition proudly displays the museum's fine collection of kauri gum, pride of place going to an 84kg piece, reputed to be the largest ever found.

Back in town at the **Woodturners Kauri Gallery & Working Studio**, 4 Murdoch St (Ⓣ09/439 4975, Ⓔkauri4u@hotmail.com), leading woodturner Rick Taylor demonstrates what can be done with the extraordinarily varied grains and colours of kauri, and runs courses for those prepared to dedicate a week or more. There's a more industrial approach at **Zizania**, 101 River Rd, a working paper mill which puts the Manchurian wild rice grasses that grow hereabouts to good use in all manner of paper products. Tours ($3; Ⓣ09/439 0217) take place when numbers warrant, but you can always visit the shop (Mon–Fri 9am–5pm).

Baylys Beach and Ripiro Beach

West of Dargaville a minor road runs 14km to **Baylys Beach**, a conglomeration of mostly holiday homes on a central section of **Ripiro Beach**. The sands of Ripiro Beach are renowned for their mobility, with several metres of beach often being shifted by a single tide, and huge areas being reclaimed over the centuries; the anchors or prows of long-lost wrecks periodically reappear through the sand. As elsewhere on the West Coast, tidal rips and holes make swimming dangerous and there are no beach patrols. Beach driving is no less fraught with danger and shouldn't be undertaken without prior local consultation; vehicles frequently get stranded. Nevertheless, it's a fine place for long moody walks, digging up tua tua, the locally renowned shellfish (you find them with your feet by doing a sort of twist), and spotting seals and penguins in winter. When easterlies are blowing the coastline is adorned with kites, flown out from the shore and drawing fishing lines for anything up to a kilometre. They're left for twenty minutes or so then kite and line are hauled in, hopefully heavy with fish.

Several local operators run trips on Ripiro Beach and around the northern Kaipara Harbour, sometimes linking together to offer interesting combinations. Call in advance, though, as minimum numbers apply, and outside the peak summer season you may find little happening. If you fancy riding along the sands, try the excellent three-hour horse-riding trips run by Baylys Beach Horse Treks (Ⓣ09/439 6342; $33). Taylor Made Tours (Ⓣ09/439 1576) run a specially designed 4WD truck along a wild and exposed section of Ripiro Beach to the disused Kaipara lighthouse of 1884 (2hr; $45); 4x4 Sandcruiser Tours (Ⓣ09/439 8360) offer a shorter tour but combine it with a short harbour cruise on the *Kewpie To*. Both hook up with Pouto 4x4 Quad Tours (Ⓣ09/439 8360; $45 per hour), who organize quad-biking over the sand and dunes. To get to the quad bikes you can either go along the beach, or go across water in a jetboat (Ⓣ & Ⓕ09/431 7493, Ⓔjetboat@kauricoast.co.nz). The jetboat company also do parasailing, for $55 (tandem $65). Finally, Kaipara Kat (Ⓣ09/439/1401), run trips in a powerful catamaran from Dargaville to Pouto Point ($85 return).

Practicalities

Two **bus** services stop on Kapia Street in Dargaville: InterCity (operated by Westcoast) runs between Paihia and Brynderwyn, where it connects with services to Auckland; and Mainline (Ⓣ09/278 8070) run direct from Dargaville to Auckland. Tickets for both are available from the **visitor centre**, 65 Normanby St (Nov–March Mon–Fri 8.30am–5.30pm, Sat & Sun

9am–4.30pm; April–Oct Mon–Fri 8.30am–5pm, Sat & Sun 10am–4.30pm; ⓣ0800/528 744 & 09/439 8360, ⓔinfo@kauricoast.co.nz), which also has comprehensive accommodation listings for the region.

The best budget **place to stay** is the *Greenhouse Hostel*, 13 Portland St (ⓣ09/439 6342, ⓕ439 6327; tent sites $10, dorms ❶, rooms ❷), a former 1920s schoolhouse. Traditional pub beds are available at the *Northern Wairoa Hotel*, on the corner of Victoria Street and Hokianga Road (ⓣ09/439 8923; ❸), and there are several reasonable motels such as the *Dargaville Motel*, 217 Victoria St (ⓣ & ⓕ09/439 7734; ❹). Dargaville's grandest rooms are at the engagingly low-key *Kauri House Lodge*, Bowen Street (ⓣ & ⓕ09/439 8082, ⓔkaurihouse@infomace.co.nz; ❼), which has comfortable en-suite rooms set in a vast kauri house complete with billiard room, library and swimming pool. Campers can choose between *Dargaville Holiday Park*, 10 Onslow St, Dargaville (ⓣ0800/114 441, ⓣ & ⓕ09/439 8296; tent sites $10, dorms ❶, cabins ❷–❹), which operates as a VIP hostel, and the *Baylys Beach Motor Camp*, 22 Seaview Rd (ⓣ & ⓕ09/439 6349; tent sites $9, cabins ❷–❸). For a little isolation, drive an hour south to Pouto Point and *Lighthouse Lodge* (ⓣ0800/439 515 & 09/439 5150, ⓦwww.lighthouse-lodge.co.nz; ❻), which has fantastic harbour and sea views, comfortable en-suite rooms and three-course dinners for $25.

Eating in Dargaville is nothing special, though the *New Asian Restaurant*, 114 Victoria St (BYO & licensed), dishes up tolerable Chinese meals, while the *Northern Wairoa Hotel* is locally renowned for its bargain pub meals and juicy Sunday roasts served in an unusually elegant restaurant. You'll do better driving out to Baylys Beach to the *Funky Fish*, 34 Seaview Rd (reserve in advance on ⓣ09/439 8883), a casual modern café and bar with great fish and chips – beer-battered dory with chargrilled lemon and salad – a range of burgers, stuffed baguettes and a varied evening menu.

Matakohe and the Kauri museum

South of Dargaville, SH12 runs 45km south to Matakohe, passing through countryside that is mostly flat except for the knobby **Tokatoka Peak**, 17km south of Dargaville. There are wonderfully panoramic views from the 180-metre summit of this extinct volcanic plug, reached in ten breathless minutes from a trailhead 1km off SH12 near the *Tokatoka* pub.

If there's one museum you must see in the north it's the **Kauri Museum**, Church Road (daily: Nov–April 8.30am–5.30pm; April–Oct daily 9am–5pm; $9; ⓦwww.kauri-museum.com), on the outskirts of the village of **MATAKOHE**, 45km south of Dargaville. One of the best in the country, and deserving at least a couple of hours, the museum focuses on the way the kauri shaped the lives of pioneers in Northland, focusing on the makeshift settlements around logging camps, the gumfields, and the lives of merchants who were among the few who could afford to buy the fine kauri furniture or beautifully carved kauri gum. A 22-metre-long vertical slice of cut kauri makes an impressive start, providing a canvas for a photographic essay of its felling in 1994 after it was struck by lightning. Mock-ups of the various ways in which the huge logs are transported – kauri dams, wooden sleds, bullock trains and winches – lead on to a pit-saw operation and a steam-driven breaking-down mill where planks were shaped. Fine examples of cut boards surround the wall, some exhibiting the dark staining of swamp kauri where water in the peat bogs has penetrated the grain, others showing blemishes where gum climbers punctured the bark, a process which eventually killed many trees. Matakohe has the most extensive display of kauri gum anywhere, with glass cases stuffed full of everything from vast lumps of the raw material to finely worked pieces in every imaginable form down to strands braided into a plait. The rather lifeless tableaux of wealthy Victorian families at play in kauri-panelled rooms are perhaps the only weakness among rooms groaning with magnificently detailed furniture and fascinating photos.

Three mildly diverting **wooden buildings** (open during museum hours) have been moved into the museum grounds from the surrounding area: a one-room schoolhouse, used for nearly a century until 1972, a 1909 post office and a diminutive pioneer church dating back to 1867. By the latter is the 1950 Coates Memorial Church, built in honour of locally raised Joseph Gordon Coates, who in 1925 became the country's first New Zealand-born prime minister.

Practicalities

By using two different **bus services**, it's possible to travel along SH12 with a stop of two to three hours at the museum. Alternatively, you can stay the night nearby, though none of the options are outstanding. Possibilities in Matakohe include *Matakohe House* (ⓣ09/431 7091, ⓔmathouse@xtra.co.nz; ❺), a new B&B right next to the museum with simply furnished en-suite rooms opening out onto a deck; and the nearby *Matakohe Holiday Park*, Church Road (ⓣ0800/431 643, ⓣ & ⓕ09/431 6431; sites $10; vans and cabins ❷; units ❸). Slightly further afield, there's a warren of rooms at the *Old Post Office Guest House*, SH12, 7km east in Paparoa (ⓣ & ⓕ09/431 6444; dorms ❶, B&B rooms ❹); and backpacker accommodation at the *Travellers Lodge*, on SH16 in Ruawai, 15km west of Matakohe (ⓣ09/439 2283; tent sites $10, dorms ❶, rooms ❷). There are a couple of decent **cafés** right by the Kauri Museum.

Travel details

Buses

Two major bus companies serve Northland. The most comprehensive operation is InterCity, who in combination with West Coaster (ⓣ09/913 6100) run two routes, one up the eastern side from Auckland's Sky City depot through Warkworth, Brynderwyn, Whangarei, Paihia, Kerikeri and Mangonui to Kaitaia, the other spurring off at Brynderwyn and covering Dargaville, the Waipoua Forest, Omapere, Opononi and Kaikohe on the way to Paihia. Their Twin Coast Kauri Discovery pass ($99) is valid for three months and covers a loop from Auckland to Paihia and back through Opononi, the Waipoua Forest and Dargaville, or vice versa. Northliner Express (ⓣ09/307 5873 in Auckland, ⓣ09/438 3206 in Whangarei; ⓦwww.nzinfo.com/northliner) run almost identical services with a similar frequency from 172 Quay St, opposite Auckland's ferry building. North of Paihia InterCity and Northliner run a joint service. Northliner sell three useful passes, all valid for a month and all requiring some form of backpacker or student ID: the Bay of Islands Pass ($53) covers Auckland to Kerikeri via Paihia, the Loop Pass ($83) is identical to InterCity's Twin Coast Kauri Discovery, and the Northland Freedom Pass ($115), adds the leg up to Kaitaia. There is also one short-range operator: Mainline Coaches (ⓣ09/278 8070), who also serve Warkworth and continue on to Dargaville.

From Dargaville to: Auckland (2–3 daily; 3hr 15min); Opononi (3 weekly Tues, Thurs & Sat; 2hr 20min).

From Kaitaia to: Auckland (1 daily; 7hr).

From Kerikeri to: Auckland (2 daily; 5hr); Paihia (2 daily; 25min).

From Mangonui to: Auckland (1 daily; 6hr 30min).

From Opononi/Omapere to: Auckland (3 weekly Mon, Wed & Fri; 5hr 40min); Paihia (3 weekly Tues, Thurs & Sat ; 2hr), Dargaville (3 weekly Mon, Wed & Fri; 2hr 30min).

From Paihia to: Auckland via Whangarei (4–6 daily; 4hr 20min); Auckland via Opononi and Dargaville (3 weekly Mon, Wed & Fri; 8hr 30min);

Kaitaia (2 daily; 2hr); Kerikeri (1 daily; 20min); Mangonui (1 daily; 1hr 20min).
From Waipu to: Auckland (4–6 daily; 2hr 20min); Whangarei (3–4 daily; 30min).
From Warkworth to: Auckland (7–8 daily; 1hr 15min).
From Whangarei to: Auckland (4–6 daily; 3hr); Paihia (4–6 daily; 1hr 15min); Warkworth (4–6 daily; 1hr 45min).

Ferries

From Kohukohu to: Rawene (hourly; 20min).
From Opua to: Okiato (every 10–20min; 15min).
From Paihia to: Russell by passenger ferry (every 20min; 20min).
From Rawene to: Kohukohu (hourly; 20min).

Flights

From Bay of Islands (Paihia/Kerikeri) to: Auckland (3–4 daily; 50min).
From Kaitaia to: Auckland (1 daily; 1hr).
From Whangarei to: Auckland (5–7 daily; 40min); Great Barrier Island (2 weekly; 30min).

3

Western North Island

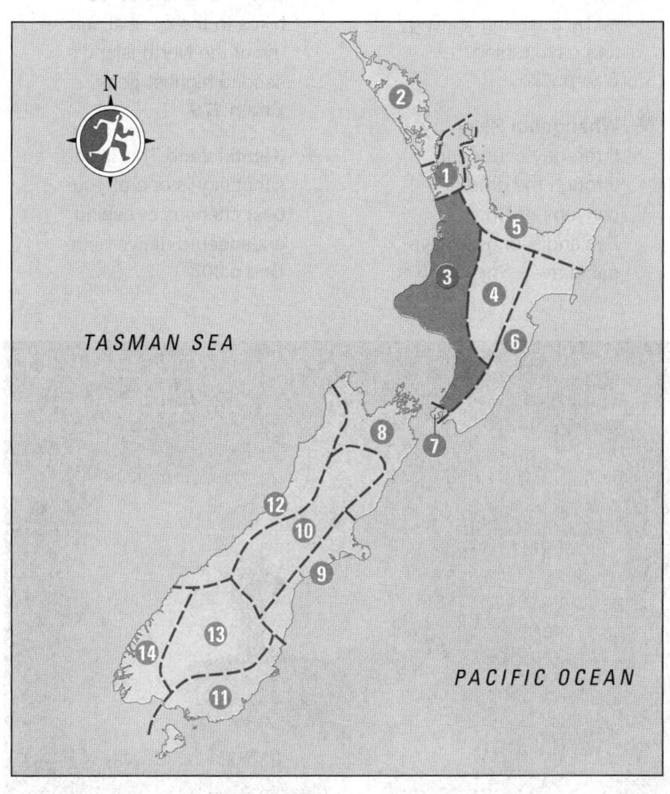

CHAPTER 3

Highlights

* **Raglan** Pretty and sociable harbourside town within easy reach of some of New Zealand's finest surf. See p.245

* **Waitomo** A labyrinthine underworld illuminated by glow-worms, all visited by abseiling, caving and cave tubing. See p.252

* **Whanganui River** Try a three-day canoe trip through the green canyons of New Zealand's longest navigable river. See p.265

* **Wind Wand** This iconic 45-metre carbon fibre sculpture swaying in the breeze was designed by Kiwi artist Len Lye. See p.274

* **Egmont National Park** Easy walks and steep hikes to the conical summit of the North Island's second highest peak. See p.279

* **Kapiti Island** This island sanctuary is one of your best chances of seeing endangered native birds. See p.303

3

Western North Island

Much of the **Western North Island** is ignored by visitors, who make a beeline for the netherworld wonders of Waitomo and perhaps pay a visit to New Plymouth and the graceful Mount Taranaki then continue on to somewhere else. In fact, there's much more to the area and perhaps more than anywhere it is a place to absorb slowly, spending an afternoon in some timewarped fishing community or driving slowly along almost forgotten highways sampling their small time charms and meeting the locals.

Much of the appeal is tied to its extraordinary **history** of pre-European settlement and post-European conflict. This region is deeply rooted in **Maori** legend and history, for it was on the west coast at **Kawhia** that the Tainui people first landed in New Zealand. Kawhia was also the birthplace of **Te Rauparaha**, the great Maori chief who led his people from Kawhia to escape the better-armed tribes of the Waikato down the west coast to Kapiti Island and on to the South Island, pursuing his individual road to justice, fame and glory.

Approaching the region from the north you're into **the Waikato**, important farming country but with little of interest to the visitor. Much the same can be said of its provincial capital **Hamilton**, the fourth largest city in the land but only worth half a day of your time. It is far better to head to the west coast and **Raglan**, a wonderfully relaxed town with a laid-back surf culture and a great selection of places to stay and eat. The surf itself is world class.

Backroads lead you south to harbourside **Kawhia**, a historic spot but a place you'll have to make your own entertainment, perhaps soak in hot springs at the edge of the surf. Inland, this rich dairying and agricultural region benefits from the fecund soil scattered by long-extinct volcanoes. Prim **Cambridge** exploits the rich grass by breeding thoroughbreds, while **Te Awamutu** is renowned for breeding roses, and producing two of New Zealand's most celebrated musicians, the brothers Finn.

South of the Waikato is the **King Country**, which took its name from the King Movement (see box on p.251) and was the last significant area in New Zealand to succumb to the onrush of European colonization. At one time a densely forested and inhospitable hinterland, a number of stalwart communities coexist with some extraordinary natural features – most famously the **Waitomo Caves**, where unusual rock formations surmount a netherworld of glow-worm-filled caverns. The farming towns of **Te Kuiti** and **Taumarunui** aren't much in themselves, but the former provides access to the tall-canopied **Pureora Forest Park**, while the latter is one of the main jumping-off points for wonderful canoe trips along the **Whanganui River** thorough the heart of the **Whanganui National Park** to the Bridge to Nowhere.

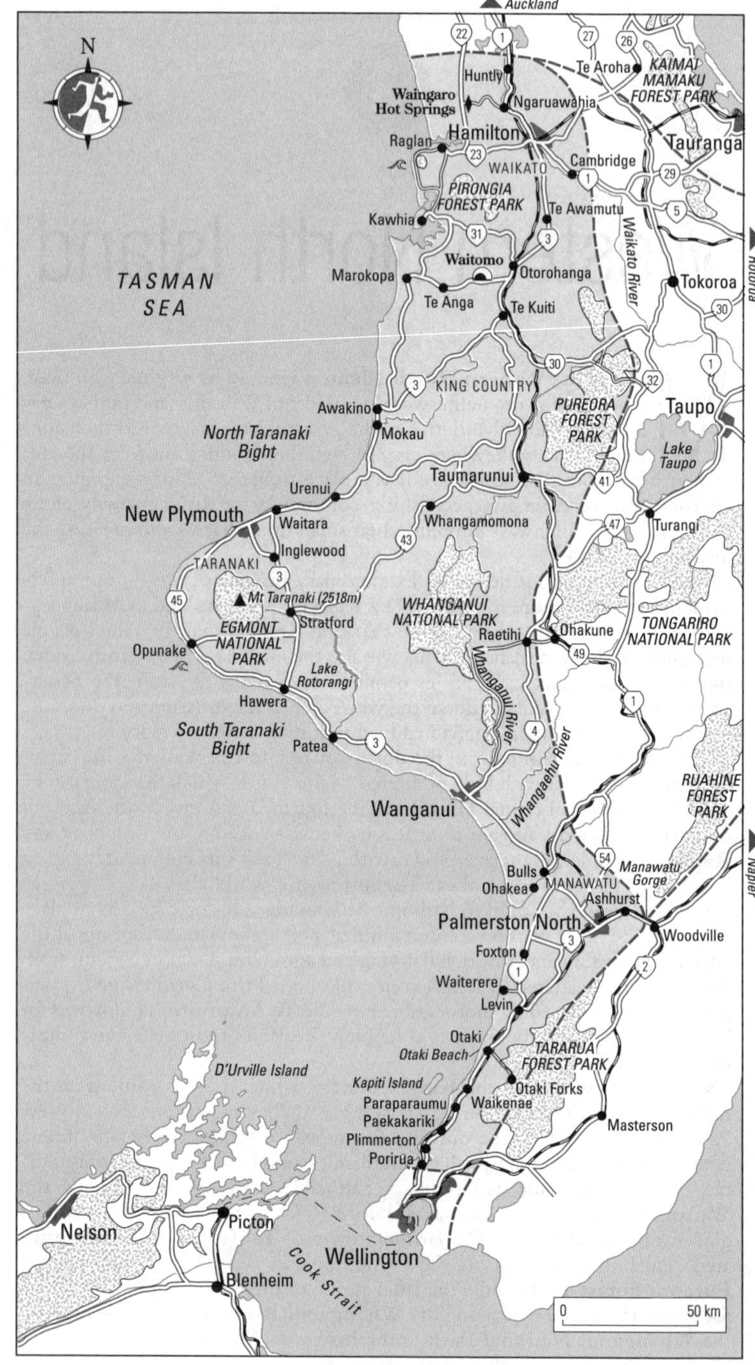
Auckland
N
Huntly
Waingaro Hot Springs
Ngaruawahia
Te Aroha
KAIMAI MAMAKU FOREST PARK
Tauranga
Hamilton
Raglan
Cambridge
WAIKATO
PIRONGIA FOREST PARK
Kawhia
Te Awamutu
Waikato River
Rotorua
Waitomo
Otorohanga
Marokopa
Tokoroa
TASMAN SEA
Te Anga
Te Kuiti
KING COUNTRY
Awakino
PUREORA FOREST PARK
Taupo
Mokau
North Taranaki Bight
Lake Taupo
Taumarunui
Urenui
New Plymouth
Waitara
Whangamomona
Turangi
Inglewood
TARANAKI
Mt Taranaki (2518m)
WHANGANUI NATIONAL PARK
Stratford
TONGARIRO NATIONAL PARK
EGMONT NATIONAL PARK
Raetihi
Ohakune
Opunake
Lake Rotorangi
Whanganui River
Hawera
South Taranaki Bight
Patea
Whangaehu River
RUAHINE FOREST PARK
Wanganui
Napier
Bulls
Manawatu Gorge
Ohakea
MANAWATU
Ashhurst
Palmerston North
Woodville
Foxton
Waiterere
Levin
Otaki
Otaki Beach
TARARUA FOREST PARK
D'Urville Island
Kapiti Island
Otaki Forks
Paraparaumu
Waikenae
Paekakariki
Masterson
Plimmerton
Porirua
Picton
Nelson
Wellington
Cook Strait
Blenheim
0
50 km

To the west, the giant thumb-print peninsula of **Taranaki** is dominated by the symmetrical cone of the 2500-metre **Mount Taranaki** (2518m), the location of some superb hiking in the **Egmont National Park**. At its feet, the **New Plymouth** warrants time spent at its excellent contemporary art gallery.

A multitude of surf beaches line the Taranaki coast, becoming wilder as they head south towards **Wanganui**, a small, ordered city where you can relive its river port past on an elderly paddle steamer. The university city of **Palmerston North** is at the centre of the rich farming region of **Manawatu** and has some interesting architecture and a museum to show for its importance and prosperity. A cluster of small communities line the highway to the south, the former flax-weaving town of **Foxton** providing the most interest until you reach the **Kapiti Coast**. Here, **Paraparaumu** is the launch point for boat trips out to the wonderful bird sanctuary on **Kapiti Island**.

Paraparumu is less than an hour from Wellington and now you're firmly into commuter territory with only a couple of small towns warranting a brief stop, though **Waikanae**, **Plimmerton** and **Porirua** can all be decent bases from which to visit the capital.

South from Auckland

Heading south from Auckland into the northern Waikato there's little reason to delay your progress into Hamilton. At **Huntly**, 95km south of Auckland along SH1, it is enough to gaze across the Waikato River at the twin 150m-high chimneys of New Zealand's largest power station, and perhaps pay a brief visit to the **Waikato Coalfields Museum**, 26 Harlock Place (Mon–Fri 10am–3pm, Sat 1–3pm; $3), with its reconstructed mine tunnel, miner's cottage and displays on early life in the Waikato coalfield which provides fuel for the power station.

The most interesting and culturally significant spot in these parts is **NGARUAWAHIA**, 14km further south on SH1, a farming centre at the junction of the Waikato and Waipa rivers. Both rivers were important Maori canoe routes, and the area has long held great significance for Maori: it is here that the **King Movement** (see box on p.251) has its roots, and the town is home to the current monarch, Te Arikinui Dame Te Atairangikaahu. It was also the scene of the signing of the Raupatu Land Settlement, whereby the New Zealand government agreed to compensate the Tainui for land confiscated in the 1860s.

The Maori heritage is most evident on **Regatta Day** (the closest Sat to March 17) when the waters of the two rivers host a parade of great war canoes before the Maori queen, and hurdle races and the like take place at the **Turangawaewae Marae** (generally closed except on Regatta Day; enquiries ⓣ07/824 5189) on River Road, off SH1 just north of the river bridge. For the rest of the year you'll have to content yourself with a view of the perimeter fence, made of the dead trunks of tree ferns interspersed with robustly sculpted red posts and a couple of fine carved entranceways. Through these you can glimpse the main features: the strikingly carved and decorated **Mahinarangi House**, which houses the Maori throne; **Turongo House**, the official residence of the present queen; and the Kimi-ora Cultural Complex, with its spectacular mural and a conspicuous octagonal roof.

On the opposite side of the river and road is **Turangawaewae House**, on

Eyre Street, built in 1920 as the intended home of the Maori parliament. It isn't open to the public and is really just an ordinary Edwardian-style stucco building, except for the red-, black- and white-painted doors, carved barge boards and *pou* (guardian post).

Twenty-three kilometres west of Ngaruawahia, at the junction with SH22, are the popular though slightly run-down **Waingaro Hot Springs**, Waingaro Road (daily 9am–10pm; $6), a large pool complex based around a series of natural springs, which tends to get busy on summer weekends. Nearby *Worsp's Farm* (Ⓣ07/825 4515, Ⓔsrworsp@xtra.co.nz; ❸), north of the springs via Matira Road, offers **accommodation** and is the base for the **Hole Adventure**, an enjoyable four-hour caving, riding the flying fox (zip wire) and abseiling trip with a "Jurassic stroll" through prehistoric caves and ancient bushland ($95, min 4 people). Also offered is a ninety-minute caving stroll ($25, no min number of people).

Hamilton

Most visitors only pass through **HAMILTON**, 136km south of Auckland. Certainly there are few genuinely compelling reasons to come here, but it is a pretty enough place, well sited on the banks of the languid green Waikato River and surrounded by parks. If you're using public transport you'll probably pass through at some point, and it is worth devoting a few hours to visit the excellent **Museum of Art and History** and the tranquil **Hamilton Gardens**. And as befits New Zealand's fourth-largest city, there's a decent-sized student population, and a lively term-time nightlife.

Archeological evidence indicates that the **Tainui** settlement of **Kirikirioa** had existed on the current site of Hamilton for at least two hundred years before the **Europeans** arrived in the 1830s. The newcomers named their riverside settlement after **John Fane Charles Hamilton**, an officer of the Royal Navy who had died, either bravely or foolishly (depending whose interpretation you believe), at the battle of Gate Pa, near Tauranga, a few months earlier; a fictionalized account of the events leading up to his death appears in Maurice Shadbolt's excellent novel *The House of Strife*. The river remained the only supply route for the city until the railway came in 1878, effectively opening up the country to more European immigration, farming and commercial expansion.

Arrival, information and city transport

Hamilton **airport**, 12km south, is connected to the city by the door-to-door Super Shuttle (Ⓣ07/843 7778 & 0800/748 885; $10), which meets all arrivals. The **train** station is on Fraser Street (Ⓣ07/846 8353) in the suburb of Frankton, a twenty-minute walk west of the city centre, or catch the #8 bus straight to the modern **Transport Centre**, right in the centre of town at the corner of Anglesey and Bryce streets, which is the hub for local and long-distance **buses**. Tickets are for sale inside at the **visitor centre** (Mon–Fri 9am–5pm, Sat & Sun 10am–4pm; Ⓣ07/839 3580, Ⓦwww.hamiltoninfo.co.nz), where there is also **internet access** and some **left luggage** lockers. The **DOC office** is five minutes' walk north at Level 4, 18 London St (Mon–Fri 8.30am–4.30pm; Ⓣ07/838 3363, Ⓕ839 0794).

Most of Hamilton's attractions are within walking distance of the centre; for

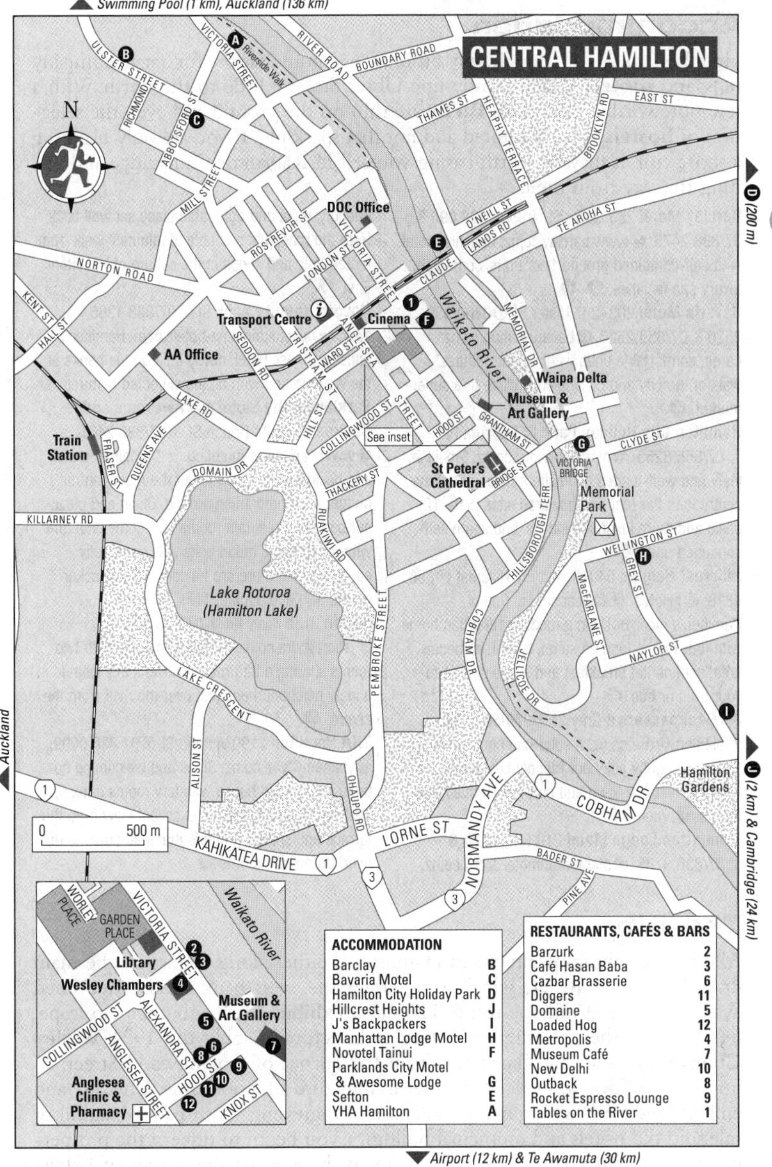

those further afield pick up the BusIt timetable ($1) or call the information line on ⓣ0800/428 754; fares are $1.80 a ride. Local **bus** companies also run scheduled services to the neighbouring communities of Paeroa, Raglan, Thames and Te Awamutu; Roadcat Transport (ⓣ07/823 2559) runs to and from Auckland as does Guthreys (ⓣ0800/759 999).

Accommodation

Hamilton excels in downtown business accommodation for farm company reps, and **motels** which mostly line Ulster Street a little to the north. With a few noteworthy exceptions **B&Bs** are thin on the ground and even the selection of **hostels** is fairly limited and not that sparkling. If you are only planning a short visit, it may be worth basing yourself in Raglan or Cambridge and visiting the city from there.

Barclay Motel 280 Ulster St ⓣ0800/808 090 & 07/838 2475, ⓦwww.barclay.co.nz. Upscale motel with self-contained ground-floor units, some with luxury spa facilities. ❺–❻

Bavaria Motel 203–207 Ulster St ⓣ0800/839 2520 & 07/839 2520, ⓔbavaria@ihug.co.nz. Large, comfortable units within eight minutes' walk of the city and conveniently close to a supermarket. ❹

Hamilton City Holiday Park 14 Ruakura Rd ⓣ07/855 8255, ⓔm.walsh@xtra.co.nz. Smallish, leafy and well-tended campsite a mile east of the centre with flat tent and powered sites ($10–12), basic and more luxurious cabins, and some self-contained units. ❷

Hillcrest Heights 54 Hillcrest Rd, Hillcrest ⓣ856 4818, ⓔhillcrest.bb@clear.net.nz. One of Hamilton's nicer B&Bs in a modern suburban home with four rooms (one en suite), a pool, barbecue area, continental breakfast and a free shuttle to your train or bus. ❹

J's Backpackers 8 Grey St ⓣ07/856 8934, ⓔbiddlem@xtra.co.nz. A suburban house converted into a slightly poky but friendly hostel, around 2km southeast of town and on the #10 bus route. Dorms ❶, rooms ❷

Manhattan Lodge Motel 218 Grey St ⓣ & ⓕ07/856 3785, ⓔmanhattanmotel@xtra.co.nz. Friendly, quiet and agreeable place set well back from the road, just a couple of minutes' walk from restaurants and shops in the suburb of Hamilton East. ❹

Novotel Tainui 7 Alma St ⓣ07/838 1366, ⓦwww.novoteltainui.nz-hotels.com. Hamilton's finest business hotel, newly built on the banks of the Waikato and with all the expected features. ❽

Parklands City Motel and **Awesome Lodge Backpackers** 24 Bridge St ⓣ07/838 2461, ⓦwww.parklands-motel.co.nz. Combined motel and backpackers that's about the most central budget accommodation around. Clean and pleasant bed and breakfast rooms (❹) come with and without en suite, motel units (❺) come fully equipped, and there are functional backpacker dorms (❶) and doubles (❷). ❶–❺.

Sefton 213b River Rd ⓣ07/855 9046, ⓔjshort@xtra.co.nz. Simple homestay with two rooms sharing a bathroom, conveniently located in a leafy neighbourhood just over the river from the centre. ❺

YHA Hamilton 1190 Victoria St ⓣ07/838 0009, ⓔyhaham@yha.co.nz. Small and welcoming hostel in a large, old house with airy rooms (max 5), well-equipped kitchen, an excellent view from the terrace and superb grounds that lead down to the river. Dorms ❶, rooms ❷

The City

Almost everything of interest in Hamilton is either along or just off the main drag, **Victoria Street**, which runs along the west bank of the tree-lined Waikato River. While the rest of Hamilton exhibits a low, suburban cityscape, here at least there's some interesting architecture, notably the 1924 **Wesley Chambers** (now the *Grand Hotel*) on the corner of Collingwood Street, an imposing edifice influenced by the architecture of boomtime Chicago and embellished with wrought-iron balconies. Progressing south past a handful of splendid old hotels and municipal buildings, you begin to discern the prosperity that farming and trade have brought to the area. At the corner of Bridge Street, the rough-cast concrete **St Peter's Cathedral** was built in 1915 but was modelled on a fifteenth-century Norfolk church.

Waikato Museum of Art and History

The single significant sight in central Hamilton is the **Waikato Museum of Art and History**, 1 Grantham St (daily 10am–4.30pm; ⓦwww.waikaotmuseum.org.nz; donation), which occupies a challenging modern construction full of airy spaces stepping down on five levels to the river, which can be viewed through the large windows. The content of most of the exhibition spaces is rotated regularly, but one enduring feature is a section devoted to **Tainui culture**, with some superb examples of domestic items, woven flax, tools, ritual artefacts and fine examples of wood and stone carving. Pride of place goes to the magnificent *Te Winika* war canoe, surrounded by contemporary Tainui carvings plus worked elements from the entry to a meeting house, and *tukutuku* panels made from flax, leather and wood. Also worth checking out is *Tainui, Ngati Koroki* the detailed wood-carved model of a *waka* by Fred Graham.

You may also see something from the museum's huge collection of Australasian paintings and photographs, and a good deal on European settlement and development, including the *Bullock Webster Diary*, which contains amusing cartoons of long-dead settlers and accounts of their dealings with the author/artist, a local diarist.

The building is also home to **Exscite** ($5), a hands-on series of science displays intended for children and school groups; the **Film Archive** which is usually showing something interesting along the lines of local documentaries and historical footage; and a quality **café** (see "Eating and drinking", below.

Parks and gardens

From the museum, the pretty **Riverside Walk** runs along the left bank. It's a pleasant place for a stroll, but there's more interest across the river in **Memorial Park**, where the pitiful remains of the *Rangiriri*, an 1864 sternwheel steamer, gaze longingly at the river. In a much healthier state the old paddle steamer *Waipa Delta* (Thurs–Sun only; ⓣ0800/472 335, ⓦwww.waipadelta.co.nz) still **cruises** sedately along the Waikato River leaving the Memorial Park jetty at 12.30pm ($35, including lunch); 3pm ($20, including afternoon tea); and 7pm ($45, including smorgasbord).

From Memorial Park, another riverside path heads 2km south to the youthful but ever improving **Hamilton Gardens**, Cobham Road (always open; free; ⓦwww.hamiltongardens.co.nz), with extensive massed displays of roses, tropical plants, chrysanthemums, rhododendrons and cacti. Pick up the free *Layout and Attractions* brochure from the gardens' visitor centre (daily 9am–4pm), then duck next door to the inner sanctum of the **Paradise Gardens Collection** (daily 7.30am–dusk; free), six small enclosures each planted in a different style. Sit and enjoy the contemplative raked-stone Zen stillness of the Japanese Garden, stop and smell the flowers in the English Garden, visit the idealized world of the Chinese Scholar's Garden, and catch a view of the Waikato from the terrace in the Italian Renaissance Garden. A surprise highlight is the American Modernist Garden, with aloe and grass mass plantings around a shallow pool ringed with bright yellow loungers and a huge Marilyn Monroe.The final plot will be the Indian Char Bagh Garden.

Back by the Hamilton Gardens visitor centre, the artificial Turtle Lake manages to look natural and is well worth strolling round, or at least observing from the *Garden Terrace* café, a nice enough place for a coffee.

Eating, drinking and nightlife

The nucleus of Hamilton nightlife lies on Hood Street and around the corner, along the southern end ofVictoria Street, where several places start as daytime **cafés** and progressively transform themselves into **restaurants** and then **bars** as the day wears on. Only Alma Street, further north along Victoria Street, has anything like a similar concentration. The standard is generally high and the prices moderate with a few pricey exceptions.

Many of the places more oriented towards drinking branch out into live **music** and dancing on Friday and Saturday nights, while theatres often act as concert venues for touring bands and classical music. The Village 7 multiplex **cinema**, in the Centreplace Mall on Ward Street, shows the usual mainstream releases. Check the daily *Waikato Times* for details of these and other happenings; comprehensive events and entertainment **listings** are in the Friday and Saturday editions.

The Bank Bar and Brasserie cnr Hood St & Victoria St. A former bank that has been transformed into a cleanly decorated restaurant with lots of wood, loud music and the feel of a big-city bistro. There's always a crowd for the substantial snacks and $20 mains, or just for a drink, and at weekends DJ-instigated dancing kicks in from 10pm.

Barzurk Gourmet Pizza Bar 250 Victoria St. Excellent pizzas with a variety of toppings ($16–20). Lunch Wed–Sun, dinner daily.

Café Hasan Baba 228 Victoria St. A cheap and cheerful café serving authentic Turkish, Greek and Middle Eastern dishes. BYO & licensed.

Cazbar Brasserie The Marketplace, off Hood St. Stylish, dinner/night spot with more champagne chic than its neighbours. Snacks are served all day, and globally inspired dinner mains go for under $20. Live music Tues–Sat until 3am.

Diggers 17 Hood St. A real drinkers' den, with a long kauri bar that's open till midnight and provides welcome respite from the trendy city bars. It's also the liveliest place on a Sunday night, with regular live gigs and a great atmosphere.

Domaine 575 Victoria St ⓣ07/839 2100. Vibrant modern restaurant with streetside seating and booths in the back, both good for cafe dining throughout the day and a more formal evening approach with perhaps wild mushroom ravioli ($13) followed by venison steak ($22).

Loaded Hog 27 Hood St. One of the most attractive bars in the city, this large double-gabled building is dotted with rural New Zealand memorabilia and has tables on the street out front. The usual array of excellent home-brewed ales is supplemented by a broad selection from around the country and full menu. DJ-cranked dancing on Fri & Sat night.

Metropolis 211 Victoria St. A hip all-day café that serves an eclectic range of tasty food for lunch and dinner, including a broad range of veggie and vegan options and some good coffee and liqueurs. Closed Mon.

Museum Café 1 Grantham St ⓣ07/839 7209. Relaxed and stylish restaurant justly popular with Hamilton's dining cognoscenti for its considered menu of beautifully prepared Modern Kiwi meals. There are superb beef and lamb dishes, but concoctions might also include spinach and roast garlic gnocchi or twice-baked duck with mash and sweet soy jus. Lunch dishes are around $15, dinner mains $20–25, and there's live jazz on Thursday evenings. Dinner reservations only.

New Delhi 15 Hood St ⓣ07/838 1053). Quality curry joint in a relaxed setting, with all the north Indian and tandoori favourites plus daily $8 lunch specials and $10 dine-in offers on Monday and Tuesday night. Licensed & BYO.

Outback Inn The Marketplace, off Hood St. Big, loud and boisterous bare-boards drinking hole that's always popular with students downing a good selection of beers and some alcohol-absorbing snacks. The place exists symbiotically with the *Cue Bar* pool hall next door.

Rocket Espresso Lounge 181 Victoria St. The attached coffee-roasting operation ensures quality java at this relaxed and intimate café, where alfresco blue chairs are the place to tuck into a limited range of tasty breakfast dishes, cakes and muffins.

Tables on the River 12 Alma St ⓣ07/839 6555. Sophisticated semi-formal riverside dining with an accent on fusion cuisine offering dishes like snap-seared scallops ($19) and rack of lamb with a pistachio crust ($28).

Listings

Automobile Association 295 Barton St ⓣ07/839 1397.

American Express Calder and Lawson Travel Ltd, 455 Grey St ⓣ07/856 9009.

Bike rental R&R Sport, 943 Victoria St ⓣ07/839 3755 & 0800/777 767. About $25 a day for a mountain bike.

Bookshops Dimensions Women's Bookshop, 266

Victoria St; Browsers, 221 Victoria St; Crows Nest Books, Arcadia Building, Worley Place; and Nonesuch, 192 Victoria St. The last two both buy and sell secondhand books.
Car rental Budget ⓣ07/838 3585; Cambridge Car Rentals ⓣ07/823 0990; Hertz ⓣ07/839 4824; Rent-a-Dent ⓣ07/839 1049; Waikato Car Rentals ⓣ07/855 0094.
Library Central Hamilton library, Garden Place, off Victoria St (Mon–Fri 9am–8.30pm, Sat 9am–4pm, Sun noon–3.30pm), has internet access.
Medical treatment Anglesea Clinic and Pharmacy, cnr Anglesea St & Thackeray St (daily 7.30am–11pm; ⓣ07/858 0775) offers consultations and fills prescriptions.
Post offices The main post office is in Bryce St near Victoria St.
Taxis Dial a Cab ⓣ07/847 5050 & 0800/342 522. The principal taxi rank is outside the Transport Centre.
Thomas Cook Garden Place ⓣ07/838 0149.
Travel agents Air New Zealand Travel Centre, 25 Ward St ⓣ07/839 9835; and STA, 42 Ward St ⓣ07/839 1833.

Around Hamilton and the coast

Hamilton may not detain you for long, but there's plenty to soak up a couple of days' exploration in the immediate vicinity. South of the city, the genteel English charms of **Cambridge** contrast with the turbulent history of the former garrison township of **Te Awamutu**, but the region's real draws lie further west. Foremost among them is the sand-swathed coast principally the surfie Mecca of **Raglan**, which has a curiously enduring appeal. South of Raglan the surf-lashed coast borders the **Pirongia Forest Park**, a great spot for walks leading to the summit of wind-buffeted hills where you can appreciate the grisly, rough-hewn coastline to the south. It extends to **Kawhia**, a moribund little community on the site of the Tainui people's first landfall in Aotearoa – and still their spiritual home. The beaches south of Kawhia are typically black sand, steeped in isolation and lashed by wind and sea, though a little comfort can be taken in the thermal pools that bubble up at the shoreline close to Kawhia.

Cambridge

There's a peaceful understated air to the small town of **CAMBRIDGE**, 24km southeast of Hamilton. Founded as a militia settlement at the navigable limit of the Waikato River in 1864, Cambridge is now marooned in a broad agricultural belt renowned for stud farms. Attractive in a bucolic sort of a way, it has a spacious village green, tree-lined avenues and the elegant white weatherboard **St Andrew's Anglican Church**, at the corner of Victoria Street and SH1, with its tall steeple, fine dark-wood interior and original stained-glass. Opposite the church lies the semi-formal **Te Koutu Park**, ranged around a picturesque sunken lake and threaded by tracks through stands of tall chestnut and oak trees; pick up the free *Cambridge Town of Trees* brochure from the visitor centre (see below) to get the best from your amblings.

Cambridge has long been associated with breeding and training thoroughbred racehorses, a business celebrated at **New Zealand Horse Magic**, 6km southeast of the town on SH1 (ⓣ07/827 8118, ⓦwww.cambridgethoroughbredlodge.co.nz), where their hour-long show (Tues–Sun 10.30am; $12) puts a number of breeds through their paces and includes show jumping, a dressage demonstration and a short stint in the saddle; call for reservations.

Practicalities

InterCity and Newmans **buses** between Hamilton and Taupo stop at the Cambridge Travel Centre, Alpha Street, while Cambridge Travel Lines

(Ⓣ07/827 7363) run a local service from Hamilton which stops right by St Andrew's church. Both stops are two minutes' walk from the **visitor centre** at the corner of Queen Street and Victoria Street (Mon–Fri 9am–5pm, Sat & Sun 10am–4pm; Ⓣ07/823 3456, Ⓕ823 3457).

Just steps from the visitor centre overlooking the leafy Victoria Square, *Park House*, 70 Queen St (Ⓣ07/827 6368, Ⓦwww.parkhouse.co.nz; ❻), provides a good reason to **stay**, in an elegantly furnished 1920s house where service is handled with an easy grace. For something cheaper, try *Colonial Court Motel*, 37 Vogel St, off SH1 (Ⓣ0800/525 352; Ⓦwww.nzmotels.co.nz/colonial.cambridge; ❹), or *Cambridge Motor Camp*, 32 Scott St (Ⓣ07/827 5649; camping $10, cabins ❷, kitchen cabins ❸) ten minutes' walk west of town over the river.

Daytime **eating** is best done either at *Fran's Café*, 62 Victoria St, where you can grab simple **snacks** and light meals for under $10, while enjoying local art displayed on the walls. In the evening try the upscale *Oasis*, 35 Duke St, or the more value-for-money oriented English pub-style *Prince Albert*, Victoria Plaza, off Victoria Street.

Te Awamutu and around

The birthplace of fraternal Kiwi pop music icons Tim and Neil Finn, **TE AWAMUTU**, 30km south of Hamilton, is a placid place, surrounded by rolling hills, hedgerowed dairy pasture and overlooked by prominent Mount Pirongia.

Local Maori trace their descent to the Tainui Canoe (see p.249), and by the nineteenth century there was a heavy Maori presence on the land, as evidenced by the many *pa* sites in the loops of rivers and on steep hill tops – the earthwork foundations of which are still visible today. During the 1863 **New Zealand Wars**, Te Awamutu was a garrison for government forces, and one of the most famous battles of the conflict was fought at the hastily constructed Orakau *pa*, where 2000 soldiers were held at bay for three days by just 300 Maori, an incident touchingly remembered in the local church.

The Town

Te Awamutu is locally renowned for its extensive **rose gardens**, at the corner of Gorst and Arawata streets, at their best between November and May. Immediately across the road is the visitor centre (see p.245), where fans of **Split Enz** and **Crowded House** won't be able to resist picking up the leaflet (50 cents) for the self-guided tour around frankly dull places of significance in the Finn brothers' formative years. The visitor centre also holds the key to **St John's Church**, just across Arawata Street, the very existence of which is a poignant reminder of the New Zealand Wars. Built as a garrison church in 1854, it was spared as other European buildings burned around it, because the Maori chieftain, Te Paea Potatau, had placed her *mana* upon it. Inside the church, a tribute from a British regiment, written in Maori, honours their Maori enemies, many of whom crawled, under fire, onto the battlefield to give water to their wounded British foes. The church also contains one of the oldest figurative, painted stained-glass windows in New Zealand.

Te Awamutu Museum, on Roche Street, about ten minutes' walk west of the visitor centre (Ⓦwww.tamuseum.org.nz; Mon–Fri 10am–4pm, Sat & Sun 10am–1pm; free), contains an excellent collection of early Maori artefacts (tools, clothes, carving and household relics). The museum's pride and joy is *Uenuku*, a striking darkwood carving representing a traditional god as a rainbow. This sacred relic of the Tainui people is thought to have been carved around 1400AD. Along with displays about the European settlers and the New Zealand Wars there's the True Colours exhibit, a corner devoted to the Finn brothers, but concentrating on the life and times of Split Enz.

Te Awamutu practicalities

Trains on the main Auckland–Wellington line stop on Station Road, about 2km west of the visitor centre – a short walk, or call any of the cabs advertising at the station. All the **bus** companies drop off at Stuart Law's Garage, 90 Mahoe St, which also acts as a ticket office. The **visitor centre** is at corner of Gorst Avenue and Arawata Street (Mon–Fri 9am–4.30pm, Sat & Sun 9.30am–3pm; ⓣ07/871 3259, ⓦwww.teawamutu.co.nz), and just about everything in town is a short walk away. Te Awamutu's **accommodation** and eating options are very limited. A safe bet, just a few minutes' walk from the visitor centre, are the clean, comfortable serviced units at the *Road Runner Motel*, 141 Bond St (ⓣ07/871 7420), which has a campsite ($10), cabins (❷) and units (❹). The **eating** situation is a little better with *Robert Harris*, 39 Arawata Street, being good for breakfast and coffee, and the *Rose and Thorn*, 32 Arawata St, the best bet for inexpensive and generous **dinners**. The French *pâtissier* at Salvador's, 50 Alexandra St, produces indifferent savouries but tasty pastries.

Yarndley's Bush and Pirongia

There is little to stop for along the straight highway north of town, except the atmospheric **Yarndley's Bush** (dawn–dusk; free), one of the largest remaining stands of the towering kahikatea on the North Island. To reach the bush reserve, turn off SH3 4km north of Te Awamutu, on to Ngaroto Road, and continue for 1500m to the signposted entrance. A **loop walk** (20min) winds through the reserve, past huge root buttresses, and midway along, a raised platform gives you a bird's eye view of the constantly moving canopy. The drainage of marshland for farming and the use of odourless kahikatea wood to make boxes to transport butter overseas have hastened the demise of these magnificent native trees.

Dominating the landscape to the west of Te Awamutu is **Mount Pirongia**, scarred by redoubt trenches from the New Zealand Wars. The peak lies within the **Pirongia Forest Park**, an area traversed by a series of interesting nature **walks** described in the DOC *Pirongia Forest Park* leaflet ($1, from Te Awamutu visitor centre). Five **tramping routes** converge on the 959-metre summit, the most rewarding and one of the easiest being the Mahaukura Track (4–6km each way; 4hr up), from the education centre at the end of Grey Road, 16km west of Te Awamutu. The more direct (and steeper) Wharauroa Route (5km; 3.5hr), begins at O' Shea Road, 3km west of the township of Pirongia. The summit ridge even has DOC's **Pahautea Hut** (8 bunks; $5), which allows you to split your exploration over two days.

Raglan and around

Visitors often stay far longer than they intended at the small town of **RAGLAN** which hugs the south side of the large and picturesque Raglan Harbour some 48km west of Hamilton. Long a popular holiday and weekend destination from the provincial capital, it is now seeing something of a renaissance, gaining permanent residents drawn by the town's bohemian arts-and-crafts tenor and the laid-back spirit engendered by the surf community. In fact, Raglan has an international reputation among **surfers** for having the best left-handed break in the world, the lines of perfect breakers appearing like blue corduroy at Manu Bay and Whale Bay, both around 8km south of town.

Almost everything of note lines **Bow Street**, its central row of Phoenix palms shading banks, several good restaurants and a selection of shops selling sculpture, pottery and antique clothing. At the street's western end it butts up against the sparkling harbour, where a slender footbridge over one arm provides access to the main campsite and a safe swimming **beach**.

To the south the horizon is dominated by **Mount Karioi** (site of an excellent hike; see p.249), which, according to Maori legend, was the goal of the great migratory canoe *Tainui*. They travelled towards it for a very long time, but when they reached the mouth of the harbour a bar blocked their way, so they named the harbour Whaingaroa ("long pursuit") and paddled south where they could finally land. The shortened epithet, Whangaroa, was the name used for the harbour until 1855, when it was renamed Raglan after the officer who led the Charge of the Light Brigade.

Arrival, information and accommodation

Pavlovich Coachlines run **buses** from Hamilton (Mon–Fri 3-4 daily; ⓣ07/856 4579), stopping outside the library on Bow Street, just across from the **visitor centre**, 4 Wallis St (Nov–May Mon–Fri 10am–5pm, Sat & Sun 10am–4pm; April–Oct daily 10am–4pm; ⓣ07/825 0556, ⓦwww.raglan.net.nz). Raglan Harbour Cruises run a **water taxi** service (ⓣ07/825 0300) to various points around the bay. For explorations further afield contact Raglan Taxi (ⓣ07/825 0506). Raglan Video, 9 Bow St, has **internet** access.

One of the reasons you may overdo your expected stay here is the abundance of excellent **accommodation** at all levels, some of the best located out by Whale Bay.

Accommodation

Belindsay's 28 Wallis St ⓣ & ⓕ07/825 6592. Central accommodation in the style of an upmarket backpackers, set in a lovely 1930s house with polished wood floors, stained glass and a deep bath. There are three-bed shares and doubles, all with bedding and towels supplied, sunny lounge and kitchen, and surprisingly low prices. Dorms ❶, rooms ❷

11 Earles Place 11 Earles Place, Whale Bay, 6km south of Raglan ⓣ07/825 6519. Lovely self-contained one-bedroom holiday home with private entrance, TV, stereo, stupendous surf views and breakfast available on request. ❺

Harbour View Hotel ⓣ07/825 8010, ⓕ825 8107. Pleasant rooms in the town's archetypal, two-storey hotel, some of them with a veranda overlooking the main street. ❹

Raglan Backpackers & Waterfront Lodge 6 Nero St ⓣ07/825 0515. One of the finest backpackers around these parts – small but clean, comfortable and exceptional friendly, and beautifully laid out around a courtyard that backs onto the estuary. It is also very centrally located and has free kayaks ($5 for 2hr for non-guests), rental surfboards ($10 per session) and surf lessons ($15 per hr including gear). Dorms ❶, rooms ❷

Raglan Kopua Holiday Park Marine Parade ⓣ07/825 8283, ⓕ825 8284. Central campsite that's 1km by road from town, but is quickly accessible by footbridge, and is well-sited next to Te Kopua, the harbour's safest swimming beach. Tents $8, dorms $❶, cabins ❷, kitchen cabins ❸

Raglan Wagon Cabins Wainui Road, about 2km south of Raglan ⓣ07/825 8268. Idiosyncratic accommodation in the form of brightly painted, sometimes grubby, converted train carriages set on top of a windswept hill with panoramic views. Camping $9, dorms ❶, cottages ❹

Whale Bay Villas 14 Calverts Rd, Whale Bay ⓣ07/825 6831, ⓦwww.whalebayvillas.co.nz. Sumptuously furnished, very tasteful and fully-self-contained villas all with gorgeous views, and with the option of having someone come in to prepare a meal for you ($55). Very indulgent. ❽

The Town

It's easy to pass a couple of hours just wandering along the foreshore, but there is little specific to see in town. The two-storey *Harbour View Hotel* looks suitably impressive overlooking the junction of Bow Street and Wainui Road, and there are plenty of shops selling alternative art, tat and jewellery, the most worthwhile of which is Show Off, 2 Bow St, a harbour of handmade danglies, rings and bracelets.

Housed in an old police station, the **Raglan Museum**, Wainui Street (Sat & Sun 1–3.30pm; donation), has a modest local history collection. For a more colourful version of local lore, you'd do better to hop aboard a **Raglan Harbour Cruise** (90min; $15; book ahead Dec–March on ⓣ07/825 0300), which leaves from the jetty at the bottom of Bow Street at times dependent on the tides. The skipper keeps passengers amused with a seemingly endless string of amusing facts and fictions woven around the historic sites the boat passes. The trip also takes in the so-called pancake rocks, sedimentary limestone formations which appear to be made of a pliable dough. The same stuff can be seen a lot quicker (though with a good deal more noise) with Jet Safari Tours (ⓣ07/825 0556) who run **jetboat** trips around the harbour ($35 for 30min; $50 for 1hr) from the campsite over the footbridge.

Raglan has long been known as a prime **surfing** destination but is now making more of this asset; the local high school even has a surf academy. Most of the action happens 8km south of town around **Manu Bay** and **Whale Bay**, but the town still exudes a surf spirit, with board-topped old Holdens and Falcons parked outside the surf shop and a lot of baggy pants in the cafés. There are opportunities for novices to try their hand; guests at *Raglan Backpackers* (see above) can get low-cost lessons from the manager, but otherwise contact the Raglan Surfing School (ⓣ07/825 7873, ⓦwww.raglansurfingschool.co.nz) who charge $70 for a two-hour lesson including all gear and transport. They also operate a shack at **Ngarunui** (aka **Ocean Beach**), 3km west of Raglan off Wainui Road, where you can rent boards ($10/hr), boogie boards ($5/hr) and wetsuits ($5/hr).

You can **rent surf gear** in town from Gag Raglan, 9a Bow St (ⓣ07/825 8702, ⓦwww.gagraglan.com), in the centre of town, open roughly 9am to 5pm, with boards ($25-35 a day) and kayaks ($35/day) for rent.

Eating and drinking

The explosion of surfers and travellers has spawned a minor **eating** revolution in Raglan with almost everywhere of note congregating around the intersection of Bow and Wainui streets.

Molasses 17 Bow St. A bright comfortable bar/café offering excellent coffee, muffins, fry-ups and internet access, plus frequent live music at weekends.

Raglan Club 22 Bow St. The atmosphere's nothing to shout about but there's good basic fare such as fish and chips and chicken salad around the $10 mark.

Tongue and Groove 19 Bow Street. Another lively place with a great range of imaginative café fare and great coffee. Licensed & BYO.

Vinnie's World of Eats 7 Wainui Road ⓣ07/825 7273. The place that trailblazed the café scene hereabouts over a decade ago and remains excellent whether for weekend breakfast or lunch and dinner throughout the week. There's everything from kumara chips with honey garlic sauce and crab wontons to New Orleans seafood gumbo ($25), and gourmet pizza (from $10) plus a great smoothies bar. BYO.

△ Egmont National Park

Around Raglan

With a little time to spare it is well worth exploring the area south of Raglan around the **Karioi Range**, where the **Te Toto Gorge** track (8km return; 5-6hr) climbs steeply up to the 755-metre summit of **Mount Karioi**. Starting 12km south of Raglan along Whaanga Road, the track heads up a gorge and, after a strenuous and difficult climb within a cliff-lined cut to a lookout, reaches an easier final section to the summit and excellent views of the mouth of Raglan Harbour and up and down the storm-battered coast.

Inland, a much easier walk (10min each way) leads to the **Bridal Veil Falls** hidden in dense native bush 23km southeast of Raglan. Water plummets 55m down a sheer rock face into a green pool; some droplets evaporate before they hit the bottom, creating a shimmering veil, adorned with ethereal rainbows in sunny weather. From the Kawhia Road, a signpost indicates the track to the falls, which is about a ten-minute stroll beside a small stream.

These can be combined on a winding gravel-road loop around the Karioi Range, which might also include **horse riding** with Magic Mountain Horse Treks, 334 Houchen Rd (Ⓣ07/825 6892, Ⓦwww.magicmountain.co.nz), who charge $30 for an hour, $50 for two hours and $60 for a trek to Bridalveil Falls. To get here, head 8km east of Raglan on SH23, then 6km up Te Mata Road, and 3km up Houchen Road; pick-ups can be arranged from the Bridal Veil Falls. They also have accommodation (❻).

Kawhia

Sleepy **KAWHIA**, 55km south of Raglan, perches prettily on the northern side of the large Kawhia Harbour. The town itself is little more than the harbourside Jervois Street, lined by a couple of petrol stations, a handful of combined shops and cafés, and the quaint little **Kawhia Museum** (Nov–March Wed–Sun 10am–4pm and by appointment; free; Ⓣ07/871 0161), which reveals much about Maori culture (see p.982) and early European settlers, and includes an original kauri whaleboat built in the 1880s. In summer the resident population of 450 swells to 4000 when holidaying Kiwi families flock to the Ocean Beach and the **Te Puia Hot Springs**, which bubble up from beneath the black sand between two hours either side of low tide (check times at the museum or in any of the local stores). Drive 4km along the unsealed Taunui/Kawhia Forest Road then hike over the dunes and branch slightly right to find the spot, or hope there are others to show you and share the hole they've dug: be warned that the black sand can scorch bare feet. The climb over the sand dunes is rewarding in its own right, revealing views of Mount Karioi to the north and Albatross Point to the south. Four-wheel-drive Sand Rover Trips ($8) run here from the Kawhia Camping Ground.

Kawhia is the spiritual home of the **Tainui** people, whose legends tell of their 1350 arrival from the homelands of Hawaiki in the ancestral *waka* (canoe), or the **Tainui Canoe**. Kawhia Harbour was so bountiful that the Tainui lived on its shores for some three hundred years, until tribal battles over the rich fishing grounds forced them inland. In 1821, after constant attacks by the better-armed Waikato Maori, the great Tainui chief Te Rauparaha led his people to the relative safety of Kapiti Island. On arrival, the *waka* was tied to a pohutukawa tree, Tangi te Korowhiti, which still grows in the grounds of the **Maketu Marae**, 800m west of the museum and reached along a waterside footpath; enquire at the museum in advance about gaining access as there is no one willing to show you around. The Tainui Canoe itself is buried on a grassy knoll above the beautifully carved and painted **meeting house** with Hani and Puna stones marking its stern and prow.

With the arrival of **European** settlers and missionaries in the 1830s, Kawhia became a highly prosperous port, providing a gateway to the fertile King Country, although its fortunes declined in the early years of the twentieth century, owing to its unsuitability for deep-draught ships. These days the settlement is known throughout New Zealand for annual **whale-boat races** (Jan 1), when eleven-metre, five-crew whaling boats are rowed across the bay. To sample something of this maritime spirit, join a **cruise** around the harbour with Kawhia Harbour Cruises (Ⓣ07/871 0149; about $15), or Dove Charters (Ⓣ07/870 3493; $55 a day).

Practicalities

Kawhia Bus and Freight **bus** service from Te Awamutu (Mon–Sat; Ⓣ07/871 0701) drops off in the centre close to the museum (see above) which acts as an unofficial **visitor centre**, dispensing free maps and details of local attractions.

Campers should stay at *Kawhia Camping Ground*, 73 Moke St (Ⓣ07/871 0863; tents $7, powered sites $9, cabins ❷), or the waterfront *Kawhia Beachside S–cape*, 225 Pouewe St (Ⓣ07/871 0727, Ⓕ871 0217; tent sites $9, dorms ❶, cabins ❷), which rents kayaks cheaply. For a basic, spacious holiday flat/backpackers try *Wee Knot Inn*, Jervois Street (Ⓣ & Ⓕ07/871 0778; dorm ❶, room ❷); and there's **B&B** at *Rosamond House*, Rosamond Terrace (Ⓣ & Ⓕ07/871 0681; ❹) with swimming pool, mountain bikes and kayaks for guests' use.

The best place to get a **drink** is the *Wee Knot Inn*, a locals' haunt with a variety of beers, snacks, coffee – and usually a story or some advice. Also on Jervois Street, the Beachside Store serves burgers, fish and chips, and a variety of other **snacks** during the day; and when you fancy something a bit more substantial in a nice setting visit *Annie's Café* (Ⓣ07/871 0198), adjacent to *Wee Knot Inn* – if you arrive after 6.30pm just give her a ring and she'll come and cook for you. Last but not least are the excellent **fish and chips** at *Kawhia Seafoods*, on the quay opposite the museum (Wed–Sun, closes 6.30pm).

The King Country

The rural landscape inland from Kawhia and south of Hamilton is known as the **King Country**, an area that derive its name from more uncertain times when it became the refuge of **King Tawhiao** and members of the **King Movement** (see box opposite), as they were driven south in defeat during the New Zealand Wars. The area soon gained a reputation as an inhospitable Maori stronghold, renowned for difficult terrain and the type of welcome that meant few, if any, Europeans had the nerve to enter. However, the forest's respite was short-lived: when peace was declared in 1881, eager loggers descended in droves.

These days the most famous place in the King Country is **Waitomo**, a tiny village that sits at the heart of a unique and dramatic landscape, honeycombed by limestone caves eerily illuminated by millions of glow-worms, and overlaid by a geological wonderland of karst features. North of Waitomo is the small dairying town of **Otorohanga**, with the unexpected pleasure of a kiwi house and large aviary.

Workaday **Te Kuiti** remains devoted to sheep farming and bills itself as the shearing capital of the world. In the 1860s, the town provided sanctuary for

Maori rebel Te Kooti, who reciprocated with a beautifully carved meeting house. Further south is the **Pureora Forest Park**, an enclave of rich lowland podocarp forest that was the site of a conservation battle in the late 1970s, and now provides access to some excellent walks and a home for the rare **kokako** bird, which seems to prefer an ungainly walk to flight. The last community in the King Country, the rather jaded town of **Taumarunui** provides access to the Whanganui River, a historic drive to Stratford and the spectacular coastal road via **Mokau**, a tiny and intriguing coastal settlement, before heading through the Taranaki coastal plains to New Plymouth.

Otorohanga

Surrounded by sheep and cattle country some 30km south of Te Awamutu, **OTOROHANGA** (meaning "food for a journey") is primarily of interest as a base for Waitomo (see p.252) and for the unusually visible birds at the **Kiwi House Native Bird Park**, Alex Telfer Drive, off Kakamutu Road (daily: Sept–May 9.30am–5pm; June–Aug 9am–4.30pm; $9; Ⓦwww.kiwihouse.org.nz), five minutes' walk from the town centre. The lifestyle of the kiwi is amply explained by attendants in the well laid out nocturnal house, which

The King Movement

Before Europeans arrived on the scene, Maori loyalty was solely to their immediate family and tribe, but wrangles with acquisitive European settlers led many tribes to discard age-old feuds in favour of a common crusade against the Pakeha. Initially a response to poor communication and administration, **Maori nationalism** hardened in the face of blatantly unjust decisions and increasing pressure to "sell" their ancestral lands.

In 1856, the influential Otaki Maori sought a chief who might unite the disparate tribes against the Europeans, and in 1858 the Waikato, Taupo and some other tribes (largely originating from the Tainui Canoe; see p.249) chose **Te Wherowhero** as their leader. Taking the title of **Potatau I**, the newly elected king established himself at Ngaruawahia – to this day the heartland of the **King Movement**. The principal tenet of the movement was to resist the appropriation of Maori land and to provide a basis for a degree of self-government. Whether out of a genuine misunderstanding of these aims or for reasons of pure economic expediency, the settlers interpreted the formation of the movement as an act of rebellion – despite the fact that Queen Victoria was included in its prayers – and tension heightened. The situation escalated into armed conflict later in 1858 when the Waitara Block near New Plymouth was confiscated from its Maori owners. The fighting spread throughout the central North Island: the King Movement won a notable victory at Gate Pa, in the Bay of Plenty, but were eventually overwhelmed at Te Ranga. Seeing the wars as an opportunity to settle old scores, some Maori tribes sided with the British and, in a series of battles along the Waikato, forced the kingites further and further south, until a crushing blow was struck at Orakau in 1864. The king and his followers fled south of the Puniu River into an area that, by virtue of their presence, became known as the **King Country**.

They remained there, almost devoid of all European contact, until 1881, when **King Tawhiao**, who had succeeded to the throne in 1860, made peace. Gradually the followers of the King Movement drifted back to Ngaruawahia. Although by no means supported by all Maori, the loose coalition of the contemporary King Movement plays an important role in the current reassessment of Maori–Pakeha relations, and the reigning Maori queen, **Te Arikinui Dame Te Atairangikaahu**, has been the recipient of many state and royal visits.

leads on to a section devoted to native lizards, geckos and the prehistoric lizard-like tuatara. Outdoor enclosures are given over to just about every species of New Zealand native bird, many in extensive walk-through aviaries: the kea and it's cousin the kaka are always entertaining but there are also parakeets, tui, morepork, and myriad less sexy species.

Nearby on Kakamutu Road, the small **Otorohanga Museum** (Sun 2–4pm; other times by arrangement, ⓣ07/873 8849; donation) presents Maori flax weavings, dog-hair cloaks, and a splendid portrait of Wahanui Huatare, a one-time local elder, in traditional costume. A separate room houses the 110-year-old wheelbarrow used in the inaugural ceremony for the railway, which finally opened up the King Country to Pakeha settlement.

In recent times, Otorohanga has taken it upon itself to celebrate all things archetypally Kiwi through a series of light-hearted shop-window Kiwiana displays along the main **Maniopoto Street**. Take a few minutes to glance in Giltrap Gifts at #58 for the pavlova, Otorohanga Sheepskins at #52 for Marmite, and the kiwi bird itself at the visitor centre. Following a similar theme, check out the Karam and John Haddad Menswear Store, 65–71 Maniapoto St, a stockist of Swandri bushwear and Kiwi Stockman waxed coats, plus bucket loads of other great stuff, for men and women – vital accessories if you want to be taken seriously in rural New Zealand and considerably cheaper than elsewhere.

Practicalities

Auckland to Wellington **trains** pull in just off the main street 50 metres from the **visitor centre**, 57 Maniapoto St (Mon–Fri 9am–5pm, Sat & Sun 10am–3pm; ⓣ07/873 8951, ⓔoto-kiwi@xtra.co.nz), which is where InterCity and Newmans **buses** stop. Bill Miller, the doyen of Otorohanga Taxis (ⓣ07/873 8279 & 0800/808 279, ⓕ873 8214), runs **guided trips** as well as a **taxi** service; there's not much about Otorohanga that Bill doesn't know, and his enthusiasm is infectious.

If you want to **stay**, try the *Oto-Kiwi Backpackers*, 1 Sangro Crescent (ⓣ07/873 6022, ⓔoto-kiwi@xtra.co.nz; dorms ❶, rooms ❷), a small, comfortable hostel with friendly owners, or the *Otorohanga Kiwi Town Holiday Park*, Domain Road (ⓣ07/873 8214; tent sites $7, powered $8), a well-kept, sheltered campsite where you can hear the call of the kiwis at night. Moving upscale there's the *Palm Court Motel*, cnr Clarke & Maniopoto streets (ⓣ0800/686764 & 07/873 7122, ⓔpalmcourt@xtra.co.nz; ❹), and luxurious farmstay at *Kamahi Cottages* (ⓣ & ⓕ 07/873 0849, ⓦwww.kamahi.co.nz; ❽), around 15km southeast of Otorohanga.

Eating in Otorohanga mostly revolves around the tearooms and takeaways along Maniapoto Street. *Toni's Café*, at #13, is good for coffee, snacks and lunches, while the *Otorohanga Club*, at #107, serves up hearty evening meals and sells cheap booze: you're supposed to be a member, but visitors are always welcomed; just sign yourself in at the door.

Waitomo

WAITOMO, 8km west of SH3 some 16km south of Otorohanga, is a diminutive village with an outsize reputation for its wonderful **cave trips** and magnificent **karst limestone features** all around – dry valleys, streams that disappear down funnel-shaped sinkholes, craggy limestone outcrops, fluted rocks, and potholes and natural bridges caused by cave ceiling collapses. Below ground, seeping water has sculpted the rock into eerie and extraordinarily beautiful shapes visited on a number of tours from a gentle underground float through grottoes illuminated by **glow-worms**, to full-on wetsuit-clad adventure caving trips involving hundred-metre abseils (rappels) into the void and tight squeezes

Appropriately enough, Waitomo means "water entering shaft" and, for over a hundred years, visitors have flocked here to explore the surrounding caves. Passages were first discovered in 1887 by Maori chief **Tane Tinorau** and English surveyor **Fred Mace**, who built a raft of flax stems and drifted along an underground stream, with candles as their only source of light. So impressed were they that further explorations ensued, and within a year the enterprising Tane was guiding tourists to see the spectacle. In a patronising move typical of the era, the government took over the operation in 1906 and it was not until 1989 that the caves were returned to their traditional Maori owners who now receive a percentage of all the revenue generated and participate in the site's management. Only a fraction of the forty-five kilometres of cave passages under Waitomo can be visited on **guided tours**, and the only caves you can safely explore **independently** are the Piripiri Caves west of the village (see p.258).

The ongoing process of **cave creation** involves the interaction of rainwater and carbon dioxide from the air which together form a weak acid that flows down cracks in the rock; as more carbon dioxide is absorbed from the soil the acid grows stronger, dissolving the limestone and enlarging the cracks and joints and eventually forming the varied caves you see today. Each year a further seventy cubic metres of limestone (about the size of a double-decker bus) is dissolved; at the present rate, the caves will be entirely eroded in less than two million years.

Arrival, information and accommodation

Trains and InterCity **buses** stop in Otorohanga, from where Waitomo Shuttle (Ⓣ0800/808 279; $7 each way) ferry people to Waitomo, with Otorohanga departures at 9am, 11.15am and 3.30pm. Newmans buses run daily to Waitomo on their Hamilton–Rotorua run, and there is also the Waitomo Wanderer (Ⓣ07/873 7559) which runs here daily from Rotorua. Buses stop in the centre of the village opposite the **visitor centre** (daily: Jan & Feb 8am–8pm; Oct–Dec & March 8am–5.30pm, April–Sept 8.30am–5pm; Ⓣ07/878 7640, Ⓔwaitomomuseum@xtra.co.nz), which takes cave trip bookings.

Although backpackers are well provided for in Waitomo, other **accommodation** options are fairly limited. To make sure you get what you want, **book in advance**, particularly during December and January.

Accommodation

Abseil Inn 709 Waitomo Caves Rd, 300m east of the museum Ⓣ07/878 7815, Ⓔabseilinn@xtra.co.nz. Stylish B&B on the top of a hill with great views over the local countryside. Rooms (some en suite) are all done with bare boards, bold colours and no frills, a style continued in the TV-equipped guest lounge where great breakfasts are served. ❺

Dalziels B&B Waitomo Caves Rd Ⓣ07/878 7641, Ⓕ878 7466. Comfortable, clean, spacious rooms and a friendly welcome. ❹

Glow Worm Motel cnr SH3 & Waitomo Caves Road, 8km east Ⓣ07/873 8882, Ⓕ873 8856. Straightforward motel with nine comfortable, self-contained units, and swimming and spa pools. ❹

Hamilton Tomo Group Lodge 1.7km west of Waitomo Ⓣ07/878 7442. Caving-club lodge that welcomes visitors and plies them with local knowledge. Large and clean, if simple, dorms are very cheap and have access to kitchen facilities and a wide sunny deck. ❶

Juno Hall Waitomo Caves Rd, 1km east of Waitomo Ⓣ07/878 7649. Comfy hostel in a modern all-wood building nicely set on a low hill with a lovely saltwater pool, barbecue on the deck and free transfers to and from the centre of Waitomo. Camping $10, dorms ❶, rooms ❷, en suites ❸

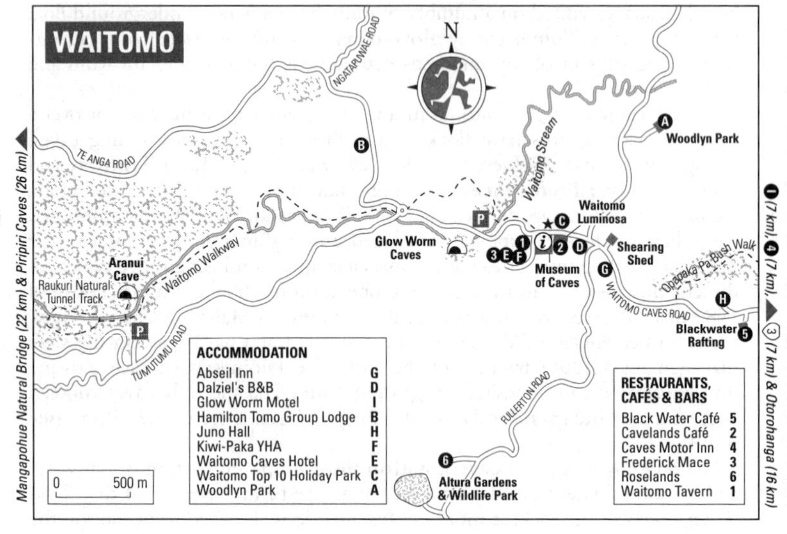

Kiwi-Paka YHA Waitomo Hotel Road ⓣ07/878 3395, ⓦwww.kiwipaka-yha.co.nz. Brand new, purpose–built hostel right in the heart of Waitomo with beds in four-share dorms, and twins and doubles. There's a café, travel-booking desk, and some chalets with private bathrooms are planned for 2003. ❶–❸

Waitomo Caves Hotel and Hostel, up the steep hill beside the Museum of Caves ⓣ07/878 8204, ⓦwww.waitomocaveshotel.co.nz). Sadly, this once grand 1908 hotel should now be considered a last resort when everywhere else is full. Economy rooms are pretty good value but the premium rooms are overpriced and the backpacker sections are dispiritingly soulless. ❶–❻

Waitomo Top 10 Holiday Park, Waitomo Caves Rd ⓣ0508/498666 & 07/878 7639, ⓔstay@waitomopark.co.nz. Spacious campsite conveniently sited in the heart of town. Camping $10, cabins ❷, self-catering units ❹

Woodlyn Park, 700m up Waitomo Valley Rd, off Waitomo Caves Rd ⓣ07/878 6666, ⓕ878 8866. A 1950s railway carriage converted into a three-room motel unit located on the site of the Heritage Show (see opposite). ❹

The Village

Above ground there's not much to **Waitomo Village** apart from the *Waitomo Caves Hotel*, which sits atop its hill, brooding like an ancient castle over all it surveys. At its feet lie a campsite, a few places to stay, the general store and pub and some offices for booking cave trips.

To enhance your cave experience, first stop should be a visit to the **Museum of Caves**, beside the visitor centre (daily 8.30am–5pm; $5; ⓦwww.waitomomuseum.co.nz), which has entertaining and informative displays on the geology and history of the caves and both their exploration and exploitation. With hands-on and interactive exhibits it's a great place for kids, who will appreciate the displays on life cycle of glow-worms and that of cave wetas, an otherworldy insect that looks like a large spikey grasshopper: apparently its appearance influenced the modelmakers working on the *Aliens* films. To test your aptitude for claustrophobic underground spaces before signing up for an adventure trip, try to wriggle through some of the tight crawl holes provided throughout the museum.

Waitomo's original cave experience is **Waitomo Glow Worm Caves**, 500m west of the centre (daily 9am–5pm; $24), now very much geared to tour bus passengers who are herded through on forty-minute tours which begin every half hour. Paved walkways, and lighting that picks out the best of the stalactites and stalagmites, makes for a gentle cave experience, nicely finished off with a boat ride through the cave grotto, where glow-worms shed pinpricks of ghostly pale-green light resembling constellations in the night sky of another planet. The best **tours** are the first and last of the day, when there are fewer tourists.

The office here also sells tickets for the forty-five minute tours around the **Aranui Cave**, 3.5km east of the visitor centre (daily 10am, 11am, 1pm, 2pm & 3pm; $24), which is only 250m long, but is geologically more spectacular, with high-ceilinged chambers and magnificent stalactites and stalagmites. A two-cave combo costs $40, and a museum-and-cave special is $25.

If you want a more gentle cave experience, no getting wet and almost an hour underground, consider **Black Water "Dry"** (3hr; $35), run by Black Water Rafting (see p.256), which involves a four-wheel-drive trip across a farm, followed by an underground hike through tunnels and caves, then twenty minutes or so floating in a raft with a galaxy of glow-worms just above your head. If serious cave trips are your thing, then see p.256.

Other attractions include **Woodlyn Park**, 700m up Waitomo Valley Road from the village (Ⓣ07/878 6666, Ⓦwww.woodlynpark.co.nz), where a rustic barn hosts the endearing hour-long **Pioneer Heritage** show (daily 1.30pm, $13) which presents the history of logging and farming in an off-beat way, with loads of audience participation. Outside, you can pilot powerful single-seater jetboats around an exceedingly tight course ($42 for 8 laps). You can also tackle the rugged karst countryside around Waitomo on 4WD **quad bikes** with Waitomo Big Red (book through the visitor centre; $65), and there's more sedate activity **horse riding** with Waitomo Caves Horse Treks (Ⓣ07/878 5065; 1hr $40; 2hr $50; 4hr $90).

Only incorrigible lovers of extreme fluffiness will enjoy the **Shearing Shed**, Waitomo Caves Road (daily 9.30am–4.30pm, shearing 1pm; free), where Angora bunnies get shorn and their fur gets made into heart-stoppingly expensive goods. In the same cutesy vein, **Altura Gardens and Wildlife Park**, 4km south on Fullerton Road (daily 10am–4pm; $7), presents seventy varieties of birds and animals in picturesque grounds and the chance of a free pony ride.

Glow-worms

Glow-worms are found all over New Zealand, mostly in caves but also on overhanging banks in the bush where in dark and damp conditions you'll often see the tell-tale bluey-green glow. A glow-worm isn't a worm at all, but the matchstick-sized larval stage of the fungus gnat (a relative of the mosquito), which attaches itself to the cave roof and produces around twenty or thirty mucus-and-silk threads or "fishing lines", which hang down a few centimetres. Drawn by the highly efficient chemical light, midges and flying insects get ensnared in the threads and the glow worm draws in the line and eats the insect.

The six- to nine-month larval stage is the only time in the glow-worm **lifecycle** that it can eat so it needs to store energy for the two-week pupal stage when it transforms into the adult gnat, which has no mouthparts. It only lives a couple of days, during which time the female has to frantically find a mate in the dark caves (the glow is a big help here) and lay her batch of hundred-odd eggs. After a two- to three-week incubation, these hatch into glow-worms and the process begins anew.

Adventure caving

While the gentle cave trips (see p.255) are a good way to see glow-worms and cave features, Waitomo really excels in **adventure caving trips**, which should be **booked in advance**, especially in December and January. The adrenalin factor varies considerably and the trick is in picking a trip that is exciting enough but won't scare you witless – most trips are not really recommended for borderline claustrophobics. Operators are pretty adept at matching patrons with the appropriate trip, most of which involve getting kitted out in your own swimwear plus wetsuit, caver's helmet with lamp and rubber boots, and combine two or more adventure elements as outlined below.

Cave tubing generally involves a gentle float through a pitch-black section of cave with your bum wedged into a truck's inner tube as you gaze at the glow-worms overhead, unsure whether the cave roof is one or one hundred metres above your head. Access into some caves is by **abseiling** (rappelling) down a long rope, always with some safety system. Once underground you may do some genuine **caving**, working your way along passages, through fairly tight squeezes, clambering over rocks and perhaps jumping into deep pools. In all cases, **heavy rain** can lead to cancellation, so it pays to have a day or two to spare. **Kids** under twelve are not usually allowed on adventure trips, and the wilder trips are for those fifteen and over.

Serious cavers with experience should contact the **Waitomo Cave Club** (through the *Hamilton Tomo Group Lodge*, see "Accommodation", p.253), who can usually arrange contacts or a trip.

Adventure caving operators

The Waitomo Luminosa office in the centre of town is the base for **Waitomo Adventures** (ⓣ07/878 7788 & 0800/924866, ⓦwww.waitomo.co.nz), a highly professional operation who offer a number of trips: Tumu Tumu Toobing (4hr; $70), a combination of walking, tubing and swimming through a particularly spectacular cave; Haggas Honking Holes (4hr; $135), a madcap series of abseils, climbs and crawl-throughs; and Lost World Abseil (4hr; $195), a wetsuit-free "dry" trip involving a 100-metre rappel into the gaping fern-draped mouth of a spectacular pothole, followed by a short cave walk before climbing out on a seemingly endless ladder – the first trip of the day is best. Cave junkies should go for the Lost World Epic (7hr; $300), with the abseil followed by several hours working your way through squeezes, behind a small waterfall and into a glittering glow worm-grotto.

Roughly 1km east, Waitomo's original cave-tubing company, **Black Water Rafting** (ⓣ07/878 6219 & 0800/228464, ⓦwww.blackwaterrafting.co.nz), run two wetsuit-clad trips: Black Water I (3hr, 1hr underground; $69) involves a short jump from an underground waterfall and an idyllic float through a glow-worm cave; and the more adventurous Black Water II (5hr, 2–3hr underground; $140) which adds abseiling and an eerie flying fox ride into the darkness. Museum of Caves entry is included in Black Water Rafting trips, and they also run the Black Water "Dry" trip (see above).

Rap, Raft & Rock (ⓣ0800/228 372, ⓦwww.caveraft.com), a small company that offers a four-hour trip ($75), give maximum value for money with small-group trips that start with a 27-metre abseil into a glow-worm-filled cave, where you explore partly on foot and partly floating on a tube, then finish up with a rock-climb out to your starting point. Entry to the Museum of Caves (see p.254) is included. There's also a high ropes course ($50 per half-day) set among plantation pines close to the cave entrance, with all manner of confidence-testing escapades – trapeze, wobbly bridges, jumps and a big swing

– plus some limestone bluffs for rock climbing. A one-day cave and ropes combo costs $110.

Walks in and around Waitomo

Waitomo Village and the Aranui Cave are linked by the **Waitomo Walkway** (10km; 3hr return), which starts opposite the museum, passes through the car park for the Waitomo Glow Worm Caves, then largely follows the Waitomo Stream to the Aranui Cave. The trail saves the best until last in the form of the **Raukuri Natural Tunnel** track (2km return; 30min), surely one of the most impressive short walks in the country. It starts from the car park for the Aranui Cave on Tumutumu Road, and follows the Waitomo Stream on boardwalks and mostly level walkways past cave entrances you could carefully explore. Ducking and weaving through short tunnel sections, you eventually reach a huge cave where the stream temporarily threads underground. Do the walk at night and the light from the banks of glow-worms almost obviates the need for a torch.

Lastly, at the eastern end of the village, the **Opapaka Pa Bush Walk** (2km return; 45min) climbs past plants and trees traditionally used in Maori medicine to an original *pa* site, which is thought to have been established in the 1700s.

Eating and drinking

Despite its position as one of New Zealand's tourist hot spots, Waitomo has a fairly limited range of **eating** options, particularly in winter, when opening times become severely restricted. Still, there are several daytime **cafés**, a good **espresso cart** beside the museum most days, and a **pub** with reliable low-cost meals.

Black Water Café 1km east of the museum. Cooked breakfasts ($7), Waitomo's best coffee, simple snacks and light meals are served from early morning to around 4pm in this spacious room always alive with people setting off on caving trips, playing pool, or hanging out on the sunny deck.

Cavelands Café just east of the museum. Decent if uninspired soups, pizza, burgers, fish and salads, cakes and coffee at low prices.

Caves Motor Inn cnr SH3 & Waitomo Caves Road ☎07/873 8109. Some of the best and most reliable meals in these parts are served upstairs at this out-of-town motel. The decor could hardly be less inviting, but stick around for large portions of king prawns ($15), or their excellent chowder ($8) followed by beautifully tender steak ($20–25).

Frederick Mace Restaurant *Waitomo Caves Hotel*, see p.254. Fine dining in a grand room with linen tablecloths and polished glassware, where you might expect seafood chowder ($10) or Thai fish cakes ($14) followed by Cajun pork sirloin ($25) or chicken fettuccini ($19). There are great desserts, a kids' menu and an adjacent bar for an aperitif or digestif.

Roselands Restaurant 4km south along Fullerton Rd. Splendid buffet lunches (11am–2pm) of char-grilled meat and fish with salad, fruit, tea and coffee ($22), served in a beautiful bush setting. Licensed.

Waitomo Tavern immediately west of the museum. Almost everyone eventually turns up at this unreconstructed Kiwi pub either for convivial boozing or large and good-value meals in the steak, pasta and burger tradition. There is occasional live music.

Around Waitomo: towards the coast

If you can't get enough of limestone scenery, or would prefer a less commercialised experience, drive Te Anga Road for three free sights which kick off with the **Mangapohue Natural Bridge**, 24km west of Waitomo. An easy fifteen-minute loop trail winds through forest to a riverside boardwalk into a delightful, narrow limestone gorge topped by a remarkable natural double bridge formed by the remains of a collapsed cave roof. Dramatic at any time, it is especially picturesque at night when the underside of the bridges glimmer with myriad glow-worms. In daylight don't miss the rest of the walk which loops through farmland past fossilised examples of 35 million year old giant oysters.

Four kilometres further west, the **Piripiri Caves** are reached by a short path (5min each way) through a forested landscape full of weathered limestone outcrops. Inside the cavern you'll need a decent torch (and an emergency spare) to explore the Oyster Room which contains more giant fossil oysters. A kilometre or so on, a track (5min each way) accesses the dramatic **Marokopa Falls** through a forest of tawa, pukatea and kohekohe trees. The sense of anticipation is heightened by the sound of falling water, which grows gradually louder as you approach the broad, multi-tiered cascade.

The road continues west past tiny **TE ANGA**, with an archetypal country pub, the *Te Anga Tavern*, and on towards the wind-lashed communities and long black-sand beaches of the coast. At **MAROKOPA**, stop at the Albatross Anchor, at the end of the road overlooking the beach, saved from the ship of the same name which foundered crossing the harbour bar, and take in the spot where the river meets the roaring white-capped waves – but be careful, the sea is dangerous and sometimes even fishermen get dragged in. **Kiritehere Beach**, about 3km south of Marokopa, has a variety of unusual rock formations and a number of ancient fossils scattered among the sands.

Te Kuiti and around

The hills narrow around the plain town of **TE KUITI**, 19km south of Waitomo, a regional farming centre that isn't much in itself but makes reasonable base for Waitomo. On the main north–south rail line it sits near the junction of three routes: SH3, heading southwest to the coast and Taranaki; SH4, running south towards Taumarunui and the Tongariro National Park; and SH30, weaving south then east into the Pureora Forest Park.

Te Kuiti hosts the annual **New Zealand Shearing and Wool Handling Championships**, which are held in late March or early April, and the town's primacy in the competitive world of shearing is reinforced by the seven-metre-high statue of a man shearing a sheep at the southern end of Rora Street. More intriguingly, Te Kuiti also has a proud Maori history, for it was here that King Tawhiao and his followers fled after the battle of Rangiriri in 1864. Eight years later, Maori rebel Te Kooti (see box on p.456) also sought refuge here and lived under the Maori King's protection until he was pardoned. In return for sanctuary, Te Kooti left a magnificently carved **meeting house**, Te Tokanganui-a-noho, opposite the south end of Rora Street, on Awakino Road; ask at the visitor centre and they'll secure you permission to look around.

Practicalities

The **train station** is on Rora Street, just a few steps from *Tiffany's Restaurant*, on the corner of Rora and Lawrence streets, where InterCity and Newmans **buses** stop. Smaller services such as Perry's Bus (which runs a regular **shuttle** to Waitomo and across to the coast) pick up at the **visitor centre** (Oct–April Mon–Sun 9am–5pm, May–Sept Mon–Fri 9am–5pm, Sat & Sun 10am–4pm; Ⓣ07/878 8077, Ⓔthcomf@mtxlink.co.nz), next to the train station. The **DOC office**, 78 Taupiri St (Mon–Fri 8am–4.30pm), has details of the Pureora Forest Park (see below).

Accommodation is available at the rural *Casara Mesa Backpackers*, Mangarino Rd (Ⓣ07/878 6697, Ⓔcasara@xtra.co.nz; dorms ❶, rooms ❷),

3km to the south but with free pick-up from the visitor centre. Bedding is supplied either in the house or in en-suite cabins outside. There are also rooms at the *Panorama Motor Inn,* 59 Awakino St (ⓣ07/878 8051; ❹), and the attached restaurant serves wholesome country food, or settle for the *Te Kuiti Camping Ground,* 1 Hinerangi St (ⓣ07/878 8966; tent sites $7, on-site vans & cabins ❷), along the bank of the Mangaokewa River.

The most lively place to **eat and drink** is *Tiffany's Restaurant,* at the corner of Rora and Lawrence streets, which has reasonable snacks and meals at low prices. There is better food a couple of kilometres north at the daytime-only *Bosco,* 57 Te Kumi Rd (ⓣ07/878 3633), a promotional effort for New Zealand's plantation forest industry using renewable softwoods and glass in a modern structure to give a light and airy effect. Political implications aside, it is a great place for wraps, inventive sandwiches, mains such as chicken satay and lasagne, as well as desserts like sweet polenta and plum cake, and good coffee. Back in town, *Riverside Lodge,* beside the river off King Street (ⓣ07/878 8027), runs a café/bar that does good pizza.

Pureora Forest Park

Straddling the Hauhungaroa Range some 50km southeast of Te Kuiti, the **Pureora Forest Park** only narrowly escaped clear-felling in 1978, when it became the site of a successful tree-top protest. Along with Little Barrier Island (see p.159) and a few pockets around Rotorua, this broad-leaf forest environment is now one of the few remaining habitats of the rare North Island **kokako**, a bluish-grey bird distinguished by the bright blue patches on either cheek. Poor fliers, they prefer to hop among the braches and nest close to the ground, making them vulnerable to introduced predators. On-going trapping and poisoning programmes attempt to redress the balance and give the kokako a fighting chance.

There is no public transport to the park, but SH30 provides access from the west, running 46km from Te Kuiti to the **DOC Pureora Field Centre** (Mon–Fri 7.30am–4pm; ⓣ07/878 1080), at the entrance to the forest. Here you can pick up leaflets describing various walks in the park ($1), and get details of the simple *Ngaherenga* DOC **campsite** ($7), 1km to the north. Half a kilometre north of the field centre, you can follow the wheelchair-accessible **Totara Walk** (800m loop; 15–30min), which winds through giant podocarps, past matai, rimu, tawa, kahikatea, ferns, vines and perching plants, with a screeching accompaniment from kaka high up in the leafy canopy. Immediately south of the campsite, a signposted road runs 3km to the **Forest Tower**, which gives a twelve-metre-high protestor's-eye view of the surrounding area, close to the site of the landmark anti-logging protest. It's a fifteen-minute drive north of the field centre to reach the **Pouakani Tree**, the largest totara ever recorded.

Link Road (also called Kakaho Road) runs east through the Pureora Forest to SH32, which provides access to the forest from the area around Lake Taupo. Along Link Road, coming from the field centre, there's challenging hiking and excellent views from the **Mount Pureora Summit Track** (4km return; 2–3hr; 300m ascent), which starts 10km east of the field centre; and the relatively easy but rewarding **Rimu Walk** (1.5km loop, 30min–1hr; 100m ascent), which goes through some lovely podocarp forest – predominantly rimu – and, after five minutes, past a nice but cool swimming hole. The walk begins a further 16km east beside DOC's *Kakaho* **campground** ($7). From here it is 6km to SH32 which runs along the western side of Lake Taupo (see p.340).

The coast road to Taranaki

Heading southwest from Te Kuiti, **SH3** makes a beeline for the Tasman Sea, and the small but appealing coastal town of **Mokau**, then twists its way through tiny communities, sandwiched between the spectacular black beaches and steep inland ranges. Opportunities for exploration focus on walks near the **Tongaporutu** rivermouth, and there's refreshment a little further on at an excellent microbrewery. Eventually the scenery opens out onto the **Taranaki Plains** just north of New Plymouth; our coverage of New Plymouth and Taranaki starts on p.270.

Mokau

The first significant place to stop is the tiny community of **MOKAU**, 73km southwest of Te Kuiti, perched on a rise above the **Mokau Estuary** where the 85-year-old historic creamboat, MV *Cygnet* (☎06/752 9775; daily 11am & summer weekends 3pm; $30), runs **cruises** up river past a number of points of historic interest, old coal workings and abandoned farms. The river is noted for its run of whitebait, and in season (Aug 15–Nov 30) you'll find this fishy delicacy available in Mokau; look for signs. The estuary also has good swimming though the two local black-sand surf **beaches** – Mokau and Rapanui – are dangerous and best left to surfers and those after the region's abundant **shellfish**. The wild scenery hereabouts provided the backdrop for several scenes from Jane Campion's 1993 film *The Piano*, particularly in the bush scenes and the fence line, seen in silhouette, along which the daughter dances.

In town, the local **Tainui Museum** (daily 10am–4pm; donation $1), charts the history of the small Maori settlements on either side of the Mokau rivermouth and of the 1840 European settlement beside the coal-rich river. Just over 2km north along SH3 the **Maniaroa Marae** and *pa* is the resting place of the Tainui Canoe's anchor stone from the alleged Great Migration, a historic *waka* and some excellent wood carvings; on entering the *marae* driveway, keep left to reach the cemetery where you must observe the anchor stone form outside the cemetery gates.

Buses between Auckland and New Plymouth stop outside the *Whitebait Inn* (☎06/752 9713; tent sites $6, cabins ❷), where you can get **accommodation** and simple meals. From there it is 100m north to the cosy and well-kept *Palm House Backpackers* (☎06/752 9081; dorms ❶, room ❷), and a similar distance to the museum, which acts as an unofficial **visitor centre**, and the *Mokau Roadhouse*, which has a limited supply of groceries, sells takeaways and serves basic bistro-style **meals**.

Tongaporutu and White Cliffs Brewery

Continuing south down the coast, after 18km you come to a fascinating **sea cave** just south of the **Tongaporutu rivermouth**. Conveniently signalled by two rock stacks on the beach opposite the entrance, the cave bears ancient footprints on its upper walls, about four metres up from the floor. For many years this coastal, tide-dependent route was the only access for Maori travelling between the Waikato and Taranaki districts, and this cave provided shelter. Local lore has it that the infamous chief Te Rauparaha, along with his most trusted female companion, rested in a sea cave to recover from a debilitating attack of boils. When the boils were lanced, the chief braced himself against the cave wall and, due to the combination of the sudden pain and his great strength, left impressions of his hands and feet in the rock. The chief was reputed to have six toes – as do eight of the foot imprints in the cave.

Just over 30km on keep your eyes skinned for a final worthwhile stop at **White Cliffs Brewery** (daily 10am–6pm, ⓣ06/752 3676, ⓦwwwbrewing.co.nz/mikes.htm; free), a tiny organic microbrewery of international standing which produces just one super brew. The delicious Mike's Mild Ale will make you well disposed towards the entire region even if it's raining, and Mike may well be available for a quick tour of the facilities before selling you a few bottles.

Taumarunui and around

With its declining population and dwindling industries, five-thousand-strong **TAUMARUNUI**, 82km south of Te Kuiti, feels rather run-down. For most travellers the only reason to stop is to use the town as a base for canoe or jetboat forays into the Whanganui National Park (see p.262) or to follow the **Taumarunui–Stratford Heritage Trail** towards Taranaki.

Surrounded by national parks and forests at the confluence of the Ongarua and Whanganui rivers, Taumarunui was one of the last places to be settled by Europeans, who didn't arrive in large numbers until 1908, when the railway came to town. Finding a suitable route for the track on its steep descent towards Taumarunui from the area around the Tongariro National Park proved problematic, but surveyor R.W. Holmes proposed the what's now known as the **Raurimu Spiral**, a remarkable feat of engineering combining bridges and tunnels to loop the track over itself. The spiral can be seen from a signposted viewpoint 37km south of Taumarunui on SH4 (and actually closer to National Park; see p.363), and is still part of the Auckland–Wellington train line. Rail fans will want to view the model of the spiral in the Taumarunui visitor centre and make the two-hour **train trip** ($28, departs daily 1pm; book at the visitor centre) to National Park and back, which negotiates the spiral in both directions.

Practicalities

Buses stop on Hakiaha Street (SH4) outside the **train station**, which contains the **visitor centre** (Mon–Fri 9am–4.30pm, Sat & Sun 10am–4pm; ⓔtaumarunui.vic@xtra.co.nz). Staff here sell Whanganui National Park passes and hut tickets and offer general information, but for specific enquiries visit the **DOC office** (nominally Mon–Fri 8am–noon & 1–4.30pm, but often closed) in Cherry Grove, off Taumarunui Street, about fifteen minutes' walk to the south. The library, opposite the ANZ Bank on Hakiaha Street (Mon noon–5pm, Tues–Fri 10am–5pm, Sat 9am–noon), has **internet access**.

Motel **accommodation** is available at *Calverts Spa Motel*, 6 Marae Street (ⓣ07/895 8501, ⓔcalvertsmotel@xtra.co.nz; ❹), which has quiet, comfortable motel rooms with continental breakfast included; or there's camping and decent cabins at *Taumarunui Holiday Park*, 4km south on SH4 (ⓣ07/895 9345, ⓔtaumarunui-holiday-park@xtra.co.nz; camping $8, cabins ❷), wedged between a patch of native bush and the Whanganui River. If you don't mind being a little out of town, try *Orangi Farmstay*, Orangi Rd, 10km east (ⓣ & ⓕ07/896 6035; ❹).

Hakiaha Street has several **eating** places, though none are particularly special. The 24-hour *Main Trunk Café*, a converted railway carriage at the east end of town, serves filling burgers, steaks, fish, good toasted sandwiches and full cooked breakfasts from 10am to 10pm; or the *Rivers II Café*, 43 Hakiaha St, Taumarunui's version of a modern Kiwi café with decent coffee, calzone, pies, steaks and various veggie options.

The Taumarunui–Stratford Heritage Trail

For a taste of genuinely rural New Zealand it is hard to beat the Taumarunui–Stratford Heritage Trail (SH43), a rugged but mostly sealed 155-kilometre road that twists through the hills west of Taumarunui and is described in the *Taranaki & SH43 Heritage Trail* leaflet (free from visitor centres). Recently re-branded the "Forgotten World Highway", it skirts the northern reaches of the Whanganui National Park and is bordered by farmland, scenic reserves and about thirty points of historic and geographical interest. Some are very minor but others are worth a brief stop: we've outlined the best, and you should allow a minimum of three hours to travel the route, considerably longer if you want to spend time at any of the diversions along the way.

The first notable stop is **Maraekowhai Reserve**, signposted 18km down an unsealed road. A track from the road end follows a creek to a lookout over the **Ohura Falls** (10min). Just before the falls, another track branches off to the left over a small plank bridge, climbing to a former stronghold of the Hau Hau (see p.429) and site of some **nui poles**, which is also accessible from the Whanganui River (see p.268). Here in 1862 the Hau Hau erected a war pole, **Rongo-nui**, with four arms indicating the cardinal points of the compass, intended to call warriors to their cause from all over the country. At the end of hostilities, a peace pole, **Rerekore**, was erected close by.

Back on SH43, the road snakes through the sedimentary limestone of the Tangarakau Gorge, where a small sign directs you along a short trail to the picturesque site of **Joshua Morgan's grave**, the final resting place of an early surveyor. At the crest of a ridge you pass through the dark **Moki Tunnel** then descend to join a little used rail line which runs parallel to the road as far as the village of **WHANGAMOMONA**, around 90km from Taumarunui. It only has around seventy residents, but on October 28, 1989, it declared itself a republic after the government altered the provincial boundaries, taking it out of Taranaki. The declaration is celebrated every second year – the next on January 18, 2003 – with the swearing in of the president, whip-cracking, gum-boot-throwing competitions, and a good deal of drinking and eating, all shared by hordes who come to witness and partake; special trains even run from Hamilton and Auckland.

Celebrations revolve around the only significant business, the 1911 *Whangamomona Hotel*, Ohura Road (ⓣ06/762 5823), where you can get your passport stamped or buy a Whangamomonian version ($2), while wetting your whistle. The **hotel** offers dinner, bed and breakfast for $45 a head, and serves **meals** and is open daily from 11am till the barman goes to bed. A kilometre down the road, the simple *Whangamomona Domain Camping Ground* (ⓣ06/762 5595) has **tent** sites and space in cabins for $5 per person.

Climbing beside steep bluffs, SH43 passes a couple of saddles with views down the valley and across the **Taranaki Plains** before descending to flat dairy pasture, eventually rolling into **Stratford** (see p.284) as the permanently snow-capped Mount Taranaki looms into view.

Whanganui National Park

A vast swathe of barely inhabited and virtually trackless bush country immediately southeast of Taumarunui is taken up by the **Whanganui National Park**. Through it run the emerald-green waters of the Whanganui River, which tumble 329km from the northern slopes of Mount Tongariro to the Tasman

Sea at Wanganui. The park itself sits on a bed of soft sandstone and mudstone (*papa*) that has been eroded to form deep gorges, sharp ridges, sheer cliffs and waterfalls. On this grows one of the largest remaining tracts of lowland forest in the North Island. Beneath the canopy of broad-leaved podocarps and mountain beech, an understorey of tree ferns and clinging plants extends down to the riverbanks, while abundant and vociferous **birdlife** includes the kereru (native pigeon), fantail, tui, robin, grey warbler, tomtit and brown kiwi.

Visiting the park is most commonly done on wonderful multi-day canoe trips and on jetboat rides, which penetrate the interior and usually take in a visit to the intriguing Bridge to Nowhere. You can also hike through it, but this is tough country and most who aren't taking a river trip are content to drive the roads that nibble at the fringes. SH43 provides limited access to the north-west, but only the slow and winding **Whanganui River Road** stays near the river for any length of time. This runs off SH4 near Ohakune, an easy 70km drive south of Taumarunui.

Information on the national park and the river is most readily available from DOC offices and visitor centres in Taumarunui and Wanganui, and directly from the widely available *In and Around the Whanganui National Park* booklet ($2.50).

Some history

This is New Zealand's longest navigable river, and one much respected by **Maori**, who hold that each bend of the river had a *kaitiaki* (guardian), who controlled the *mauri* (life force). The *mana* of each settlement depended upon the way in which the food supplies and living areas were maintained: sheltered terraces on the riverbanks were cultivated and elaborate weirs were constructed to trap eels and lamprey. **European** missionaries started arriving in the 1840s, after which traders began to exploit this relatively easy route into the interior of the North Island, and from 1891 a regular boat service carried passengers and cargo to the settlers establishing towns at Pipiriki and higher up at Taumarunui. For the first two decades of the twentieth century, **tourists** came too, making the Whanganui New Zealand's equivalent of the Rhine with paddle steamers plying the waters to reach the occasional elegant hotel en route to Mount Ruapehu and central North Island.

European attempts to stamp their mark on this wild landscape have often been ill-fated. In 1917 the **Maungpurua Valley**, in the middle of the park, was opened up for settlement by servicemen returning from WWI, who little realized they were trading one battlefield for another. Plagued by economic hardship, remoteness and difficulty of access, many had abandoned their farms by the 1920s. A bridge over the Maungpurua Valley was subsequently opened in 1936, but after a major flood in 1942 the government declined to make any further funds available for road maintenance, and the bridge was cut off, the three remaining families ordered out, and the valley officially closed.

With the coming of the railway and better roads, the riverboat tourist-trade dwindled then ceased in the 1920s. Farms along the Whanganui continued to support a cargo and passenger service until the 1950s, but with the final loss of river traffic the region's isolation returned. This attracted recluses and visionaries fleeing the excesses of the civilized world, the most celebrated being poet **James K. Baxter** who set up a commune in the 1970s and was held in great affection by local Maori. Today, the only signs that the valley was ever inhabited are the disappearing road, old fence lines, stands of exotic trees planted by the farmers, occasional brick chimneys and the poignant **Bridge to Nowhere**, which can be reached from the river or on the three-day Mangapurua Track.

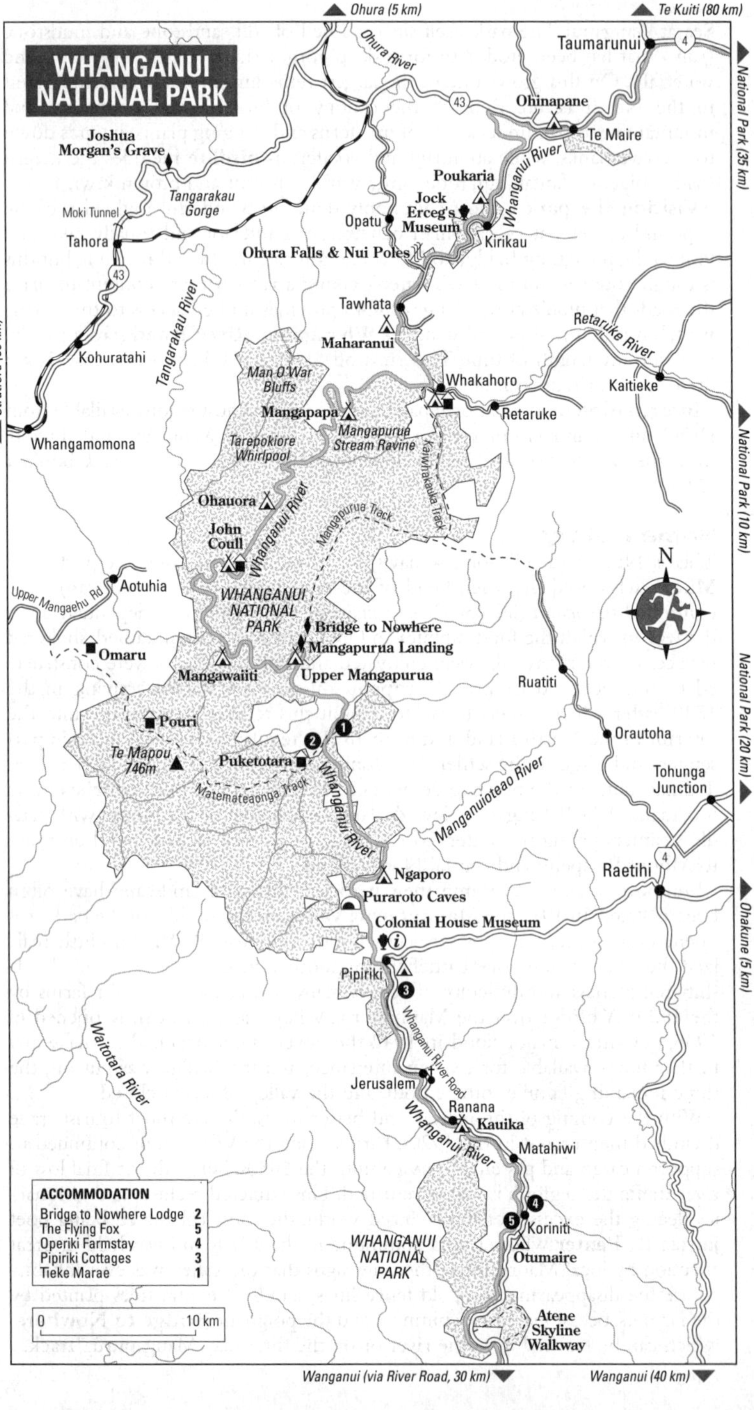

WHANGANUI NATIONAL PARK

Ohura (5 km)
Te Kuiti (80 km)
National Park (35 km)
National Park (10 km)
National Park (20 km)
Ohakune (5 km)
Stratford (50 km)
Wanganui (via River Road, 30 km)
Wanganui (40 km)

Taumarunui
Ohinapane
Te Maire
Ohura River
Joshua Morgan's Grave
Tangarakau Gorge
Moki Tunnel
Tahora
Poukaria
Jock Erceg's Museum
Opatu
Kirikau
Ohura Falls & Nui Poles
Tawhata
Maharanui
Tangarakau River
Kohuratahi
Retaruke River
Man O'War Bluffs
Whakahoro
Kaitieke
Retaruke
Mangapapa
Mangapurua Stream Ravine
Whangamomona
Tarepokiore Whirlpool
Kaiwhakauka Track
Ohauora
Mangapurua Track
John Coull
Whanganui River
Aotuhia
Upper Mangaehu Rd
WHANGANUI NATIONAL PARK
Bridge to Nowhere
Mangapurua Landing
Omaru
Mangawaiiti
Upper Mangapurua
Ruatiti
Pouri
Orautoha
Te Mapou 746m
Puketotara
Matemateaonga Track
Manganuioteao River
Tohunga Junction
Raetihi
Ngaporo
Puraroto Caves
Colonial House Museum
Pipiriki
Waitotara River
Whanganui River Road
Jerusalem
Ranana
Kauika
Matahiwi
Koriniti
Otumaire
WHANGANUI NATIONAL PARK
Atene Skyline Walkway

ACCOMMODATION	
Bridge to Nowhere Lodge	2
The Flying Fox	5
Operiki Farmstay	4
Pipiriki Cottages	3
Tieke Marae	1

0 10 km

Whanganui River trips

The best way to explore the Whanganui National Park is on a trip down the **Whanganui River**, which provides a safe and reliable route to the wilderness and is well furnished with riverside campsites as well as *marae* and farmstay accommodation. Canoes, kayaks and jetboats all work the river, allowing you to tailor trips to your needs; see below for a list of operators. When steamboats regularly plied these waters, captains concerned about navigation with paddle steamers noted 239 rapids on their charts, but many of these were, in reality, just shallows, and the flow is rarely violent – mostly Grade I with the occasional Grade II rapid. This makes it an excellent canoeing river for those with little or no experience.

The navigable section of river starts at Cherry Grove in Taumarunui (see p.261) where there is a DOC office. From here it is about two days' paddle to **Whakahoro**, essentially just a DOC hut and a boat ramp at the end of a 45km mostly-gravel road running west from SH4. Between these two points the river runs partly through farmland with roads nearby, and throws up a few rapids appreciably larger than those downstream (but still only Grade II). The journey also takes you past several spectacular water cascades and the niu poles (see p.262), and **Jock Erceg's Museum** (open sporadically; free) with its collection of river memorabilia.

Downstream from Whakahoro you'll see the Mangapapa Stream Ravine, the **Man-o-war Bluff** (named for its supposed resemblance to an old iron-clad battleship) and the **Tarepokiore Whirlpool**, which once completely spun a river steamer. At Mangapurua Landing everyone stops for the forty-minute walk through the bush to the **Bridge to Nowhere**, a trail that becomes the Mangapurua Track to Whakahoro. Further downstream you come to **Tieke Marae**, a former DOC hut built on the site of an ancient *pa* that has been re-occupied by local Maori; it's possible to stay here, and across the river at *Bridge to Nowhere Lodge*. The last stretch runs past the **Puraroto Caves** and into Pipiriki.

River practicalities

The best source of practical **information** for river trips is the *Whanganui Journey* leaflet ($1) available from visitor centres and DOC offices in the region. It explains how all overnight river users must buy a **DOC Facility User Pass** ($25 in advance, $35 from rangers in the park), which covers the cost of staying up to six nights in DOC campsites and huts: these are scattered along the river and are marked on our map. All river users can buy passes from DOC offices and the Taumarunui visitor centre; those going on organized canoe trips will generally find that the pass is not included, but operators can often arrange one for you.

There are no shops along the river, so you need to take all your **supplies** with you – and don't drink the river water unless you have boiled it first.

Apart from the huts and campsites, you can find **accommodation** at the *Bridge to Nowhere Lodge* (Ⓣ025/480 308, Ⓦwww.wanganui.com/ramanui), which is only accessible from the river but manages a licensed **restaurant** and bar, and offers rooms in the lodge (❸), a cabin (❶) and camping ($5). A full dinner, bed and breakfast package with jetboat transfer from Pipiriki costs $175. Across the river is the Tieke *marae*, where you can stay in the hut for a small donation, and if any of the residents are about you'll be treated to an informal cultural experience. Booze is not allowed here.

The quickest way to get about on the river is on **jetboat trips** (see below for operators and details): Whanganui River Jet run from Whakahoro; and Bridge to Nowhere Jet Boat Tours and River Sprint Jet operate from Pipiriki. They'll run you to the end of tramping tracks, drop you off for a few days' fishing and take you pretty much anywhere else you fancy going, but the main destination is the Bridge to Nowhere, which is appreciably closer to Pipiriki.

The real beauty, tranquillity and remoteness of the river is best appreciated on **canoe** and **kayak trips**. These range from one to six days, with most companies offering both **guided trips** and canoe or kayak **rentals** for independent paddlers. Companies supply pretty much everything you'll need (except possibly sleeping bags and tents for longer trips) and generally include transport to and from the river. Taumarunui, National Park and Ohakune are the most common bases.

Two-day canoe and kayak trips are normally on the upper section from Taumarunui to Whakahoro, but most people prefer the more scenic three- to four-day run between Whakahoro and Pipiriki. Five- and six-day marathons cover the whole stretch from Taumarunui to Pipiriki; few continue downstream from there. The river is accessible all year, but the paddling **season** is generally from November to April.

Tour and rental operators

Bridge to Nowhere Jet Boat Tours ⓣ06/385 4128, Ⓔbookings@bridgetonowhere.co.nz. Popular and regular jetboat tours upstream from Pipiriki including: Bridge to Nowhere, which builds in a walk up to the bridge itself ($75); an afternoon tour with *powhiri* at the Tieke *marae* ($85; 4–5hr; min 4 people); and an evening barbecue tour ($105). They also work in with Hiruharama-based Wairua Hikoi Tours.

Blazing Paddles 1033 SH4, Taumarunui ⓣ07/895 5261 & 0800/252 946, Ⓦwww.blazing-paddles.co.nz. Gear rental with prices including drop-off, pick-up and looking after your vehicle (1 day for $50 per person, 2 days for $75, 3 days for $110, 4 days for $115 & 5 days for $125); they can also organize guides.

Canoe Safaris, 5 Miro St, Ohakune ⓣ06/385 9237 & 0800/272 335, Ⓦwww.canoesafaris.co.nz. Professional outfit offering all-inclusive guided canoe trips from $290 for two days up to $755 for five days. They also do canoe and kayak rentals for self guided trips charging $115 per person for a 3-day trip, $130 for four and $145 for five; rental prices include transport to and from the river from Ohakune.

Plateau Outdoor Adventure Guides Uwha Road, Raurimu ⓣ07/892 2740, Ⓦwww.kiwiadv.co.nz/volcanic/plateauguides.htm. Fully inclusive guided canoe and kayak trips (2 days $260, 3 days $390, 4 days $520, 5 days $650). Self-guided trips involve renting a canoe ($40 a day) or kayak ($35 day) and paying $50 each for transport to and from the river.

River Spirit Jetboat Tours ⓣ06/342 1748, Ⓦwww.riverspirit.co.nz. Jetboat day-trips from Wanganui to the *Flying Fox* ($100) and from Pipiriki to the Bridge to Nowhere ($80), as well as a package including the Bridge to Nowhere and an overnight stay and dinner at the *Bridge to Nowhere Lodge* ($170).

Wades Landing Outdoors /Whanganui River Jet ⓣ07/895 5995, Ⓦwww.kiwiadv.co.nz/volcanic/wadenav.htm. Whakahoro-based operator running jetboat trips (Whakahoro to the Bridge to Nowhere for $95) and self-guided canoe and kayak trips (2 days for $70 per person, 3 days for $115, and five days for $130). You can also kayak during the day downstream and catch a jetboat back ($75).

Wairua Hikoi Tours Hiruharama, contact through Bridge to Nowhere Jet Boat Tours above. Gentle canoeing trips on the lower reaches of the river ($75 guided; $45 self-guided) incorporating a visit to the *Flying Fox* (see p.269), and a commentary focusing on Maori folklore, stories and insights into the use of herbal medicines.

Whanganui National Park Rural Mail Tour ⓣ06/344 2554 & 0800/377 311, Ⓦwww.rivercitytours.co.nz. This is a genuine mail delivery service which doubles as a Whanganui-based full-day tour (take a packed lunch) calling at sites of interest along the Whanganui River Road and offering the opportunity to spread your trip over several days taking jetboat rides into the heart of the park and canoeing back down. Trips depart Mon–Fri at 7.30am ($30).

Yeti Tours ⓣ06/385 8197 & 0800/322 388, ⓦwww.canoe.co.nz. Ohakune-based guided paddling trips including gear, food and transport. Prices range from $295 for two-days to $875 for six, and there's canoe and kayak rental ($125 per person for 3 days, $165 for 5).

Whanganui Park hikes

With the undoubted lure of canoe trips down the Whanganui River few people bother to tackle serious **hikes** in the area. In fact the country is so rugged that few tracks trace the deep valleys and bush-clad slopes, and those that do spend much of their time in the forest with only occasional lookouts revealing distant views. The prime hiking **season** is October to April, when track conditions are at their best, but track maintenance has been sporadic in the past and it always pays to check current conditions at DOC offices. **Huts** along the way are managed by DOC and you'll need to buy hut tickets or an annual hut pass before setting out. Unless you fancy doing the walks in both directions, you'll also want to arrange for a **jetboat pick-up** either with Wades Landing Outdoors or Bridge to Nowhere (see opposite).

For general **advice** on tramping, see Basics, p.53; the best **map** is the 1:80,000 Whanganui National Park Parkmap ($13.50).

The Kaiwhakauka / Mangapurua Track

The park's most manageable and appealing multi-day tramp follows the **Kaiwhakauka and Mangapurua Track** (40km one way; 3 days; 660m ascent) from Whakahoro south past the **Bridge to Nowhere** to Mangapurua Landing where you can be picked up by jetboat. There is a **hut** near the start of the track at Whakahoro, but otherwise you stay overnight in clearly marked **camping** areas, with side streams providing water. Day one (8hr) follows old road routes and consists of easy riverside walking up the Kaiwhakauka Valley before dropping into the Mangapurua Valley, where you pitch camp. Day two (6hr) heads through bush and along sections hewn from sheer papa bluffs, but day three (6hr) is the highlight, taking in the atmospheric Bridge to Nowhere and beyond to the Mangapurua Landing, where signs mark the **pick-up point** and another **camping** spot.

The Matemateaonga Track

The isolated **Matemateaonga Track** (42km one way; 4 days; 732m ascent), starts on the western side of the park just off the Upper Mangaehu Road at a turning off SH43, 48km from Stratford. Using old Maori trails, you are able to push deep into the dense forest before emerging at the river for a pre-arranged pick-up.

Day one (1hr 30min) heads up the Kohi Saddle overlooking the Matemateaonga Range and along to the **Omaru Hut** (12 bunks; $10). On day two (5hr), the track continues along the range through dense bush with occasional small clearings; after about three hours, you can take the side-track to Mount Humphries (90min return), for spectacular views across the park to mounts Taranaki and Tongariro, before continuing along the main track to the **Pouri Hut** (12 bunks; $10). Day three (7hr) is an easy gradient along a well-defined track, mostly along a ridge crest, before ascending to a clearing where the **Ngapurua Shelter** provides an ideal spot for lunch, before the final descent to the **Puketotara Hut** (12 bunks; $10). The last day (1hr) comprises a steep descent from the hut to the river, where a large sign marks the **pick-up point**.

The Whanganui River Road

Canoe and jetboat trips navigate the main body of the Whanganui National Park, but there are outlying sections to the south which can be accessed along the **Whanganui River Road**. Accessed either from Raetihi, a small town near Ohakune, or Wanganui, the River Road hugs the river's left bank from the riverside hamlet of **Pipiriki** 78km downstream to Upokongaro, just outside **Wanganui**. It is a rough, twisting and only partially sealed road which is prone to floods and land slips, and even in the best conditions will take you a minimum of two hours.

Opened in 1934, the road is wedged between river, farmland and heavily forested outlying patches of the Whanganui National Park, and forms the supply route for the four hundred people or so who live along it. **Facilities** along the way are almost non-existent with no shops, pubs or petrol stations and only one café and a handful of places to stay.

If you don't fancy the drive, consider joining the **Whanganui National Park Rural Mail Tour** (see p.266), which leaves Wanganui each weekday for the four hour run along the River Road up to Pipiriki, then back on the same day.

Pipiriki and around

The southern reaches of the Whanganui National Park are accessed from Raetihi along the winding 27km Pipiriki–Raetihi Road which meets the river at **Pipiriki**. While this is the most important community on the river road, and a major gateway and exit for the park, with most operators finishing canoe trips here, and a couple of jetboat companies running trips upstream, it comprises little more than a few houses. There's also a free **campsite** with toilets and water, and a **DOC office** (Oct–April daily 10am–4pm) inside the **Colonial House Museum** (same hours; $1), which is full of pictures, articles and information about the river. The other point of historical interest in the village is the 1904 **MV Ongarue**, the longest-serving riverboat on the middle reaches of the river, though these days the vessel sits high and dry on the riverbank and is in a sorry state. The signposted **Pukehinau Walk** (1km return; 30min) climbs above the settlement to the hilltop site of a former Hauhau stronghold.

Two kilometres south along the Whanganui River Road, the *Shining Cuckoo Garden Café* serves light **meals** and refreshments, acts as the contact point for Bridge to Nowhere jetboat trips (see p.266) and is also the site of *Pipiriki Cottages* (Ⓣ06/385 4128; s/c ❷, B&B ❸) with secluded **cottages** let on a self-catering or bed-and-breakfast basis, with dinner an option.

The road south passes the **Omorehu Waterfall Lookout**, overlooking one of many impressive waterfalls that cascade into the Whanganui River, and the highest point on the river road, marked by a picnic site, with excellent views of the national park.

Hiruharama

HIRUHARAMA (Maori for Jerusalem), 10km south of Pipiriki, was originally a Maori village and Catholic mission but is now best known as the site of the **James K. Baxter commune**, which briefly flourished here in the early 1970s. Baxter, one of New Zealand's most (in)famous poets, attracted upwards of two hundred of his followers to the area. A devout Roman Catholic convert, but also firm believer in free love in his search for a "New Jerusalem", he became father to a flock of his own, the *nga moki* (fatherless ones), who soon dispersed after his death in 1972. The main commune house is situated high on a hill to the right of the road, and Baxter is buried just below the house. To pay homage at his grave, ask for directions from the three remaining Sisters of Compassion, who still live beside the 1892 **church**, which features a Maori-designed and carved altar; also in the church is a photo of Mother Mary Joseph Aubert (1835–1926), who established the first community of sisters in 1892, and a portrait of Baxter, looking suitably messianic. The original convent now offers basic self-catering **accommodation** ($10) in dorms with beds separated by curtains.

From Moutoa Island to Koriniti

A couple of kilometres to the south lies **Moutoa Island**, scene of a famous and vicious battle in 1864 when the lower-river Maori defeated the rebellious Hauhau warriors, both protecting the *mana* of the river and saving the lives of European settlers downstream at Wanganui. A cluster of houses 1km on marks **RANANA** (London) where there's a Roman Catholic mission church that's still in use today, and the *Kauika* **campsite** (Ⓣ06/342 8061; tent sites $6), adjacent to the river, with toilets, showers, fresh water and a kitchen.

A further 4km downstream a hundred-metre track leads down to the two-storey 1854 **Kawana Flour Mill**. One of a number of water-powered flour mills that once operated along the river road, it's the only one that's been restored to its original condition (though it's not operational), along with the adjacent miller's cottage.

The only real settlement of note in these parts is **KORINITI** (Corinth), roughly half-way along the river road and home to a lovely small church and a trio of traditional Maori buildings, the best being a 1920s **meeting house**. It is a fairly private community and you'll have to content yourself with driving down a side road off the highway and enjoying the view from the road.

The immediate environs of Koriniti offer a couple of **accommodation** options, not least the welcoming *Operiki Farmstay*, 1km north of Koriniti (Ⓣ06/342 8159; ④), surrounded by lush gardens, offering dinner for $20 and accepting campervans for $15 a head. There's also the wonderful *Flying Fox*, immediately south of Koriniti (Ⓣ & Ⓕ06/342 8160, Ⓦwww.theflyingfox.co.nz), an ecologically conscious lodge which can only be accessed from the river or by the eponymous aerial cableway. Once there you can camp ($10) or stay in one of the comfortable cottages (self-catering, ④; dinner, bed and breakfast basis, $80–85 per person) making use of the solar showers, wood-fired bath and dine on mostly organic produce largely grown on site. They even have home-brew beer.

Around 2km south of Koriniti is the simple Otumaire **campsite** ($8).

From Atene to SH4

Almost 10km south of Koriniti, a few occupied houses mark what's left of **ATENE** and the start of the **Atene Skyline Track** (18km loop; 6–8hr), which makes a wide loop, finishing with a two-kilometre walk along the road back to your vehicle. From the upriver trailhead the track climbs up to an old road that follows a gently ascending ridge line to a clearing, where there's the hike's only potable water supply, toilets and space for **camping**. Shortly after this you reach the highest point, before skirting some impressive sandstone bluffs and descending steeply back to the river road. A shorter **nature trail** (20min) shares the same starting point, taking you past examples of the flora and fauna of the region.

A few kilometres further on, you will pass **Oyster Shell Bluffs**, small road-side overhangs with oyster-shell deposits embedded in them, and **Hipango**

Park, a scenic reserve on the riverbank that's only accessible from the river.

Finally, just 3km from the point where the Whanganui River Road meets SH4, the road winds up to the summit lookout of **Aramoana**, the starting point of the **Aramoana Walkway** (closed Sept–Oct for lambing), which heads inland for about 40min – you can only go up one side and back the same way. It's an easy enough amble, heading through farmland, a plantation of pine, banks and cuttings. On a clear day, there are views of the northeast horizon dominated by Mount Ruapehu, and the northwest horizon dominated by Mount Taranaki.

Taranaki

The province of **Taranaki** juts out west from the rest of the North Island forming a blunt peninsula centred on **Maunga Taranaki** (aka **Mount Egmont**), an elegant conical volcano rising 2500m from the subtropical coast to its icy summit. Taranaki means "peak clear of vegetation", an appropriate enough description of the upper half of "the mountain" (as locals know it), but a name also adopted by one of the local Maori *iwi*, and the colonists when the province was formed.

As you tour the region the mountain remains a constant presence, though much of the time it is likely to be obscured by cloud. Local wags are likely to trot out the old chestnut that if you can see the mountain, it's going to rain, and if you can't, it's raining already. The fact is you'll often see the summit in the early morning and just before sunset, though cloud frequently forms through the middle of the day – the bane of summit aspirants who put in all the hard work for no view.

Much of your time in Taranaki is likely to be spent in **New Plymouth**, the vibrant provincial capital with its collection of worthwhile sights and a decent selection of places to stay and eat. It makes a good base for a couple of days, perhaps for day trips into the **Egmont National Park** that surrounds the mountain or for short forays out to the surfing and windsurfing hotspot of **Oakura** or historic **Waitara**.

While New Plymouth and Egmont National Park are the undoubted highlights of the province, rural Taranaki has its share of minor attractions best sampled on a one- or two-day loop around the mountain – and everywhere you go, provided the weather plays ball, you'll have fabulous views of Mount Taranaki. On the coastal SH45 **Surf Highway** west around the mountain, these are supplemented by ocean views from the multitude of surf beaches, and there's a hub of interest at **Hawera**, where there are a couple of entertaining museums and the opportunity to go **dam dropping**. The swift, virtually uninterrupted progress of the inland SH3 from New Plymouth to Hawera is dull by comparison to the Surf Highway, but compensates with good mountain access and also ends up at Hawera.

Some history

According to Maori, the mountain-demigod Taranaki fled here from the company of the other mountains in the central North Island. He was certainly firmly in place when spotted by the first European in the area, **Cook**, who named it Egmont after the first Lord of the Admiralty. In the early nineteenth century few **Maori** were living in the area as annual raids by northern tribes had forced many to migrate with Te Rauparaha to Kapiti

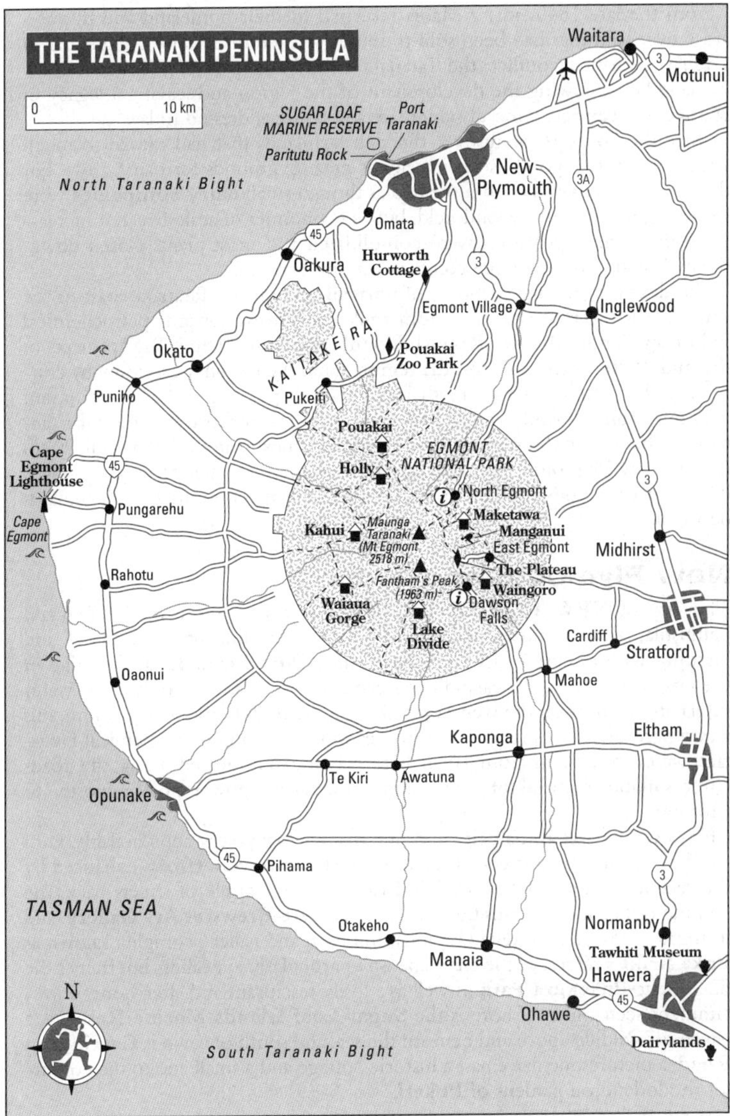

Island. This played into the hands of John Lowe and Richard Barrett who in 1828 established a trading and whaling station on the Ngamotu Beach on the northern shores of the peninsula.

In 1841, the **Plymouth Company** dispatched six ships of English colonists to New Zealand settling at Lowe and Barrett's outpost. Mostly from the West Country, the new settlers named their community **New Plymouth**, which has grown into the region's largest city.

From the late 1840s many Maori returned to their homeland and disputes arose over land that had been sold to settlers, which from 1860 culminated in a ten-year armed conflict, the Taranaki Land Wars, part of the wider New Zealand Wars, slowing the development of the region and leaving a legacy of **Maori grievances**, some of which are still being addressed today.

Once the hostilities were over, the rich farmlands that had caused so much strife were put to good use, primarily as grazing grounds for dairy cattle. For the next seventy years or so it seemed as though small **dairy companies** were springing up in every second field, but as economies of scale became increasingly important operations were consolidated and most plants closed down, finally leaving just one huge complex outside Hawera.

The discovery of large deposits of **natural gas** off the Taranaki coast in the early 1970s diverted attention from milk and cheese towards petrochemical industries. Prime Minister Rob Muldoon's grandiose "Think Big" projects of the mid-1980s sought to boost the region's (and the nation's) economy by converting the natural gas into methanol and even petroleum. The government paid huge sums to American and Japanese firms for prefabricated modular factories, which were shipped over and assembled, mostly around Motonui, 20km east of New Plymouth, yet although they continue to operate, as gas supplies decline over the next decade or so their long-term economic benefit remains debatable.

New Plymouth and around

The city of **NEW PLYMOUTH**, on the northern shore of the Taranaki peninsula, is the commercial heart of Taranaki, bustling with prosperity and bristling with a sense of its own importance. **Port Taranaki**, at the edge of the city, serves as New Zealand's western gateway and is the only deep-water international port on the west coast. During the mid-1980s energy boom, this was where the huge prefabricated pieces of the region's petrochemical factories were brought in from Japan before being transported along the roads (after suitable removal of cables and bridges and power poles), mostly to Motonui.

However, it's still a small city and one that's actually very approachable, with a tight grid of central streets flanked by an attractive **waterfront** enhanced by the recent addition of Len Lye's **Wind Wand**. A couple of streets back, the commercial centre contains the admirable **Govett-Brewster Art Gallery**, and from mid-2003, a brand new regional museum and gallery complex known as **Puke Ariki**. The rest of the cityscape isn't particularly appealing, but there's the fine public **Pukekura Park** as well as a lively restaurant and after-hours entertainment scene. Just offshore is the **Sugar Loaf Islands Marine Reserve**, a haven for wildlife above and beneath the sea, and south of town is **Carrington Road**, a picturesque drive past a historic cottage and a small zoo to the colourful rhododendron gardens of **Puketi**.

Arrival, information and transport

From the **airport**, 12km northeast of town, Withers Coachlines shuttle into the city on request (ⓣ06/751 1777; $12). Long-distance **buses** drop off at the Travel Centre, 32 Queen St, in the centre. The **visitor centre** (Mon–Fri 8.30am–5pm, Sat & Sun 9am–5pm; ⓣ06/759 6080, ⓦwww.newplymouthnz.com) is at the corner of Leach Street and Liardet Street, but is scheduled to move into the new museum complex near the waterfront around June

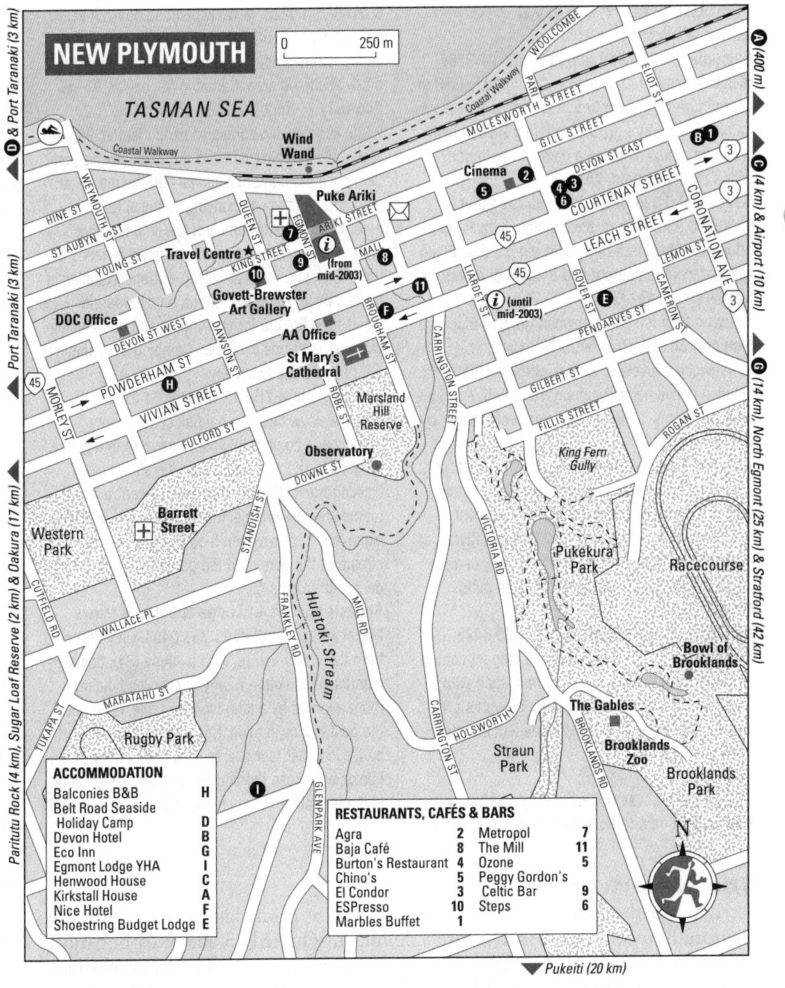

2003. For specific information on Egmont National Park (see p.279), visit the **DOC office**, 220 Devon St West (Mon–Fri 8.30am–4.30pm), which sells hut tickets.

Local bus services are run by Okato Bus Lines (☎07/758 2799) but there are few useful routes and services are infrequent; the mountain can be reached with Mountain Shuttle (see p.279).

Accommodation

New Plymouth has a reasonable range of **accommodation** with modest prices, but you might like to consider staying outside of town, either at Oakura, or up on the flanks of the mountain.

Hotels, farmstays and B&Bs

Balconies 161 Powderham St ⓣ06/757 8866, ⓔbalconies@paradise.net.nz. Comfortable B&B in a large turn-of-the-century manor-style house surrounded by mature grounds offering B&B in high-ceilinged rooms all using a common bathroom with a claw-foot bath. ❹

Devon Hotel 390 Devon St ⓣ06/759 9099 & 0800/800 930, ⓦwww.devonhotel.co.nz. A smart, refurbished business hotel with a heated pool and spa, a decent restaurant and a range of rooms, as well as suites. ❹–❼

Henwood House 314 Henwood Rd, Bell Block, 5km east off SH3 ⓣ & ⓕ06/755 1212, ⓔhenwood.house@xtra.co.nz. Grand 1890s wooden house nestled among trees, with spacious en-suite rooms, a lounge and sun deck. Dinner by arrangement ($35). ❻

Kirkstall House 8 Baring Terrace ⓣ06/758 3222, ⓔkirkstall@xtra.co.nz. An intimate and friendly B&B in a 1920s house with lovely views over a garden that slopes down to the Te Henui River, about fifteen minutes' walk from the city centre. Characterful rooms, one of which is en suite. ❹–❺

Nice Hotel 71 Brougham St ⓣ06/758 6423, ⓦwww.nicehotel.co.nz. Small and elegant central city hotel with just six stylish rooms, each with a designer bathroom, contemporary artworks and luxurious fittings. There's also a decent on-site restaurant. ❽

Hostels and campsites

Belt Road Seaside Holiday Camp 2 Belt Rd ⓣ & ⓕ06/758 0228, ⓦwww.beltroad.co.nz. A scenic cliff-top site, twenty minutes' walk from the city centre, with camping and cabins (some en suite) in a tidy sheltered area. Camping $9, cabins ❷–❸

Eco Inn 671 Kent Rd, 15km south ⓣ06/752 2765, ⓦwww.myaddress.co.nz/tourism/ecoinn. A real (if distant) alternative to the town hostels just 3km from the Egmont National Park boundary, an eco farm (with accompanying animals) fully embracing the self-sufficient low-impact ethos. Wind, water and solar energy supply the needs of the hostel, and there are sleep-out opportunities in a tree house, along with an organic garden, a wood-fired hot tub for relaxing in, and good hiking close by. Pick-ups available. Camping $10, singles ❶, doubles and twins ❷

Egmont Lodge YHA 12 Clawton St ⓣ06/753 5720, ⓦwww.taranaki-bakpak.co.nz. A very friendly and comfortable associate YHA in a peaceful garden, reached along a gentle streamside walking track (15min) from the city centre. The rooms are comfortable, the facilities well kept and clean, and you can even feed the eels in the stream at the bottom of the garden. Camping $10, dorms ❶, rooms ❷

Shoestring Budget Lodge & Cottage Mews Motel 48 Lemon St ⓣ06/758 0404. Only 350m from the visitor centre, with a sauna ($4), this self-catering joint, with a roomy kitchen and dining room adorned by a long wooden table, is one of the best places in town. Stay in the charming old house in either four shares with beds rather than bunks, or choose the doubles and twins next door in the bargain motel units. ❶–❹

The waterfront

Arriving in the centre of New Plymouth you're immediately drawn towards the foreshore and the **Wind Wand**, a slender, bright-red 45-metre carbon-fibre tube topped with a light globe that glows red in the dark and sways mesmerizingly in the wind. Designed by Len Lye (see box opposite) in 1962, it wasn't erected until 2000, since when it has fast established itself as a regional icon, appearing on postcards and shop signs. Though a smaller version was constructed in Greenwich Village in 1962, and another slightly larger one at the Toronto International Sculpture Symposium in 1966, due to the constraints of contemporary technology his true vision couldn't be brought to life. However, more recent advances in polymer engineering allowed his successors to gradually scale up to the current full-size model. That said, Lye's vision was greater still, but it seems unlikely that his forest of 125 such wind wands all swaying in the breeze together will be built in the near future.

Landscaping and pathways stretch a couple of hundred metres either side of the Wand making up a waterfront park that's pleasant for an evening stroll. More ambitious walkers can follow the **Coastal Walkway** which stretches some 3km in each direction.

Len Lye

All of a sudden it hit me – if there was such a thing as composing music, there could be such a thing as composing motion. After all, there are melodic figures, why can't there be figures of motion?

Len Lye

Until recently, New Zealand-born sculptor, film-maker and conceptual artist **Len Lye** (1901–1980) was little known outside the art world, but his work is now beginning to get some well-deserved recognition. An Australasian tour in 2001 and 2002 prompted a profile on Lye in *Newsweek*, and MTV in Europe has occasionally run his amazingly modern-looking animated films (see below) as channel branding, and now there's New Plymouth's *Wind Wand* (see opposite).

Born in Christchurch, Lye developed a fascination with movement, which in his late teens expressed itself in early experiments in kinetic sculpture. His interest in Maori art encouraged him to travel more widely studying both Australian Aboriginal and Samoan dance. Adapting indigenous art to the precepts of the Futurist and Surrealist movements coming out of Europe, he experimented with sculpture, batik, painting, photography and animated "cameraless" films (he painstakingly stencilled, scratched and drew on the actual film). He spent time working on his films in London, but towards the end of World War II he joined the European artistic exodus and ended up in New York where he returned to sculpture, finding that he could exploit the flexibility of stainless-steel rods, loops and strips to create abstract "tangible motion sculptures" designed to "make movement real". These motor-driven sculptures are erratic in their movement, lending them an air of anarchy that induces a certain primal fear, and nowhere is this more evident than in what is probably his best-known work, 1977's *Trilogy* – more commonly referred to as *Flip and Two Twisters* – three motorized metal sheets that shake and contort madly until winding down before a final convulsion.

Lye envisaged his works as being monumental and set outdoors, but was always cognizant of the technical limitations of his era and considered his projects to be works of the twenty-first century. Just before his death in New York in 1980, friend, patron and New Plymouth resident, John Matthews, helped set up the Len Lye Foundation, which brought most of Lye's scattered work to New Plymouth's Govett-Brewster Art Gallery – the most forward-thinking gallery at the time. The foundation has been instrumental in furthering Lye's work and the *Wind Wand* is the most visible largest yet.

If you're inspired and have a spare $50, get hold of Roger Horrocks' biography *Len Lye*, available in the gallery book shop.

Downtown New Plymouth

The commercial heart of New Plymouth lies barely 200m back from the waterfront, with shops and cafés lining Devon Street. At its junction with Queen Street lies the **Govett-Brewster Art Gallery**, 42 Queen Street (daily 10.30am–5pm; free; Ⓦ www.govettbrewster.org.nz), which is home to the **Len Lye Foundation**, the driving force behind the construction of the *Wind Wand*. The gallery has a huge permanent collection of Lye's work, and although only a small amount is likely to be on show at any one time you can still watch some of Len Lye's films and a documentary on his life and work; if none are showing, just ask.

The gallery has no permanent exhibits, but puts on a changing roster of summer and winter exhibits, usually challenging and always full of interest. The focus is contemporary and the collection is especially strong from 1970 onwards often with a Pacific Rim bias, but there are also travelling national and international exhibitions, and a good shop selling a wide range of material including the gallery's own publications. The on-site café (see p.278) is excellent.

New Plymouth's major new building project is **Puke Ariki**, Ariki St (Ⓦwww.pukeariki.com), two minutes' walk east of the Govett-Brewster. This is due to open in the middle of 2003 and will contain the visitor centre, town library and a vastly updated and expanded version of the former Taranaki provincial museum. This will include a large and permanent collection of local and national New Zealand paintings, ranging from 1834 pen-and-ink sketches through to contemporary works, such as those of John Bevan Ford (see p.296), and an extensive Maori section. Highlights include the anchor from the Tokomaru Canoe, which brought Taranaki Maori to New Zealand; the Tokomaru *waka*; an intricate *tauihu* (canoe prow), thought to be one of a number carved for Te Rauparaha in the 1830s; volcanic rock carvings and wood carvings of a style unique to Taranaki with three-dimensional figures, unlike many Maori carvings which are reliefs on a flat background. The museum site also encompasses the period-furnished **Richmond Historic Cottage**, a stone cottage built in 1854 for local MP Christopher William Richmond, and moved to its current site in 1962.

Following Brougham Street south from Puke Ariki you reach Vivian Street and the Frederick Thatcher-designed **St Mary's Cathedral**, the oldest stone church in New Zealand. It was built in 1845 along austere lines that are now marred by a modern annexe, though it is worth visiting for its imposing gabled dark-wood interior and atmospheric graveyard dotted with ancient knotted trees and gravestone testaments to disease and war. Also inside the cathedral is a striking Maori memorial with carvings by John Bevan Ford and tukutuku panels by Min Crawford; unveiled in 1972, the memorial invites forgiveness for past injustices by telling the story of Raumahora and Takarangi whose love for each other united two warring *iwi*.

Immediately behind the cathedral, Marsland Hill Reserve contains **The Observatory**, Robe St (Tues: summer 8–10pm, winter 7.30–9.30pm; $2), where you are guided around the **night sky** using their telescope.

Pukekura Park

Downtown New Plymouth is backed by the broad, hilly swathe of **Pukekura Park and Brooklands** (daily dawn–dusk; free), a tranquil oasis that constitutes one of New Zealand's finest city parks. The Pukekura section is mostly semi-formal with ornamental fountains, a bandstand, lawns, glasshouses, lily ponds and a boating lake, but there are also paths threading through the fern-clad tunnels of **King Fern Gully**. The more free-range Brooklands section occupies the grounds of a long-gone homestead and includes the **Bowl of Brooklands** outdoor amphitheatre, and numerous mature native and exotic trees including a 2000-year-old Puriri and a lovely large Ginkgo. Nearby a former colonial hospital from 1847 is now **The Gables** (Jan daily 1–4pm; Feb–Dec Sat & Sun 1–4pm; free), containing an art gallery and a small and mildly diverting medical museum. Here too is the **Brooklands Zoo** (daily 8.30am–5pm; free), that's firmly oriented towards children, with an animal petting section, plenty of entertaining Capuchin monkeys and playful otters, all very tastefully presented. The whole area is a great place to wander at any time, but is better still on summer evenings when the Pukekura section is given over to the **festival of lights** (Christmas to early Feb nightly dusk–10.30pm; free) when families and courting couples promenade along gorgeously lit pathways between illuminated trees, and take out rowboats festooned with lights.

Paritutu Rock and the Sugar Loaf Marine Reserve

New Plymouth's port and a rather ugly power station lie 4km west of the town centre at the foot of the 200-metre-high **Paritutu Rock**, a feature of great cultural significance to Maori and a near-perfect natural fortress that still marks the boundary between Taranaki and Te Atiawa territories. Despite its importance you are free to climb it from a car park on Centennial Drive, signposted off Vivian Street. It's a steep scramble (20–40min return) with a steel rope providing guidance and support, but the reward is a great view of the coast and out to sea, where a cluster of steep-sided rocky islands comprise the DOC-administered **Sugar Loaf Marine Reserve**. These eroded remnants of ancient volcanoes were long occupied by Maori, but were given their current name by Captain Cook in 1770, who was struck by Moteroa Island's similarity to the conical sugar loaves produced in Britain at the time. These days the islands provide a sanctuary for rare plants, little blue penguins, petrels and sooty shearwaters, while the surrounding waters harbour abundant marine life, including 67 species of fish and a wealth of multicoloured anemones, sponges and seaweeds in the undersea canyons. Humpback whales (Aug–Sept) and dolphins (Oct–Dec) migrate past the islands, and New Zealand's northernmost breeding colony of fur seals populate tidal rocks.

The islands themselves are off-limits, but Happy Chaddy's Charters (daily at 11.30am, 1.30pm & 3pm; $20; ⓣ06/758 9133) run excellent if slightly eccentric hour-long **trips** around the islands in an old lifeboat launched from its shed at Ocean View Parade marina about 3km west of downtown.

Carrington Road

With your own wheels it makes a pleasant outing to follow Carrington Road south of the city towards the Taranaki foothills. First stop, 8km south, is the historic **Hurworth Cottage**, 906 Carrington Rd (open by appointment on ⓣ06/753 3593; $3.50). Built in 1856,and restored to its original appearance and furnished accordingly, it is the only survivor of a settlement called Hurworth, which was abandoned during the New Zealand Wars. The original occupier went by the name of Harry Atkinson, a young lawyer, who became New Zealand's Prime Minister four times – though two of these terms were only a year and one was just six days – and was one of the first politicians to advocate women's suffrage and welfare benefits.

Some 5km further south, the **Pouakai Zoo Park**, 1296 Carrington Rd (Tues–Sun 10am–4.30pm; $5), has an interesting walk-through bird enclosure, but the rest of the areas are pretty lacklustre. Around 20km from New Plymouth lies **Pukeiti**, 2290 Carrington Rd (daily: Oct–March 9am–5pm April-Sept 10am–3pm; $8; ⓦwww.pukeiti.org.nz), a gorgeous rainforest garden spread of 360 hectares with New Zealand's largest collection of rhododendrons and azaleas. There's always something in bloom – though it is perhaps best in October and November when a **rhododendron festival** is held – and there's a café in the gardens serving light lunches, morning and afternoon teas.

Eating, drinking and entertainment

The majority of the cafés, **restaurants** and clubs are on what is known as the **Devon Mile**, on Devon Street between Dawson and Eliot streets. You'll seldom need to stay far from here for **drinking** either, though some exploration may be needed to track down the excellent Mike's Mild Ale (see p.261). The Top Town Cinema 5, 119–125 Devon St (ⓣ06/759 9077), shows mainstream **movies**.

For those of a more cultural persuasion, the biennial **Festival of the Arts** takes place at venues all over town during March every odd-numbered year, and showcases classical concerts, pop concerts, performance artists, comedy, parades and a searchlight tattoo.

Agra 151 Devon St ⓣ06/758 0030. Reasonably authentic curry restaurant with the usual north Indian favourites, and free delivery in New Plymouth. Licensed & BYO.

Baja Café Bar 17–19 Devon St West. Popular and fairly groovy restaurant serving an excellent selection of international cuisine, including Mexican and Thai for under $22. The dance club out the back goes off Thurs–Sat nights and settles into a sports bar/pool hall for the rest of the week.

Burton's Restaurant *State Hotel*, cnr Gover St & Devon St. Moderately priced breakfasts, lunches, snacks and dinners, all in fearsome portions, plus drinks served in a bar bedecked with rural memorabilia.

El Condor 170 Devon St East ⓣ06/757 5436. Small and very simple Argentine-run place with value-for-money pasta and gourmet pizza along with the likes of Cajun blackened fish, sautéed chicken livers and oven-baked beef fillet, mostly for under $20. They do takeaway orders too. Licensed and BYO; closed Mon.

ESPresso Govett-Brewster Gallery, cnr Queen St & King St. One of the most stylish and imaginative daytime cafés in town for carnivores and vegetarians, with great variety (all meals under $15), a deli counter, good wine, luscious cakes and excellent coffee.

Marbles Buffet *Devon Hotel*, 390 Devon St East ⓣ06/759 9099. Worth a visit for its excellent evening $30 smorgasbord with cabaret-like entertainment at the weekends, when it gets crowded.

Metropol 32a Egmont St ⓣ06/758 9788. A relaxed and airy restaurant with an imaginative menu exhibiting a broad palette of European influences in dishes around the $20 mark. They're well presented, tasty and accompanied by a select range of wines (many by the glass).

The Mill 2 Courtenay St. A massive converted flour mill with many bars for the late-night crowd, a wide range of beers and snacks, and live bands (or more likely a DJ playing Top 40 hits) at weekends.

Ozone 117 Devon St East. Specialist coffee roaster and groovy daytime café, with a small but well made selection of panini, bagels, wraps and great coffee. Closed Sun.

Peggy Gordon's Celtic Bar cnr Egmont St & Devon St. With pictures of Irish and Scottish folk heroes on the walls, an extensive range of single malt whiskies, twelve beers on tap, and live Irish music on Fri & Sat, it's no surprise that this is a popular haunt of both locals and travellers. The basement *Cotton Club* carries on after hours (Thurs–Sat).

Steps 37 Gover St ⓣ06/758 3393. Widely and rightly regarded as New Plymouth's top restaurant, *Steps* is housed in a renovated villa with a nice brick courtyard. Smart but unfussy service ensures that dishes from the Mediterranean-inspired menu arrive promptly, and there's a short but well-chosen wine list. Licensed & BYO; closed Sun & Mon.

Listings

Automobile Association 49–55 Powderham St ⓣ06/757 5646.

Banks and exchange All the major banks have branches along Devon St or within one block of the city centre, and there's also Thomas Cook, 55–57 Devon St ⓣ06/757 5459.

Bike rental Raceway Cycles, 207 Coronation Ave ⓣ06/757 9260; $20 a day.

Camping and outdoor equipment Kiwi Outdoors, 18 Ariki St, rent and sell outdoor gear and camping equipment. They also have kayaks from $45 a day.

Car rental Avis ⓣ06/757 5736; Hertz ⓣ06/758 8189; Thrifty ⓣ06/757 4500.

Internet access At the public library (see below) and at *Flicks Café*, 125 Devon St.

Library The public library is temporarily located at the corner of Devon and Brougham streets (Mon, Wed & Fri 10am–8.30pm, Tues & Thurs 10am–5.30pm, Sat 10am–4pm, Sun 1–5pm), and has internet access. From mid-2003 the library will be in the new museum complex.

Medical treatment There's medical and dental care and a 24hr pharmacy at Medicross, Richmond Centre, Egmont St ⓣ06/759 8915.

Post office The main post office, with a poste restante service, is at 21 Currie St (Mon–Fri 7.30am–5.30pm, Sat 9am–1pm).

Swimming The Fletcher Challenge Aquatic Centre, Buckley Terrace, Kawaroa Park (ⓣ06/758 6496), is a massive complex with indoor and outdoor pools, wave machine, gym and fitness suite.

Egmont National Park

The province of Taranaki, and pretty much the whole western third of the North Island, is dominated by **Taranaki** (or Mount Egmont) a dormant strato-volcano that last erupted in 1755. From most angles its profile is an unblemished cone rising to a 2518-metre summit, a purity of form favourably compared to Japan's Mount Fuji. In winter, snow blankets almost the entire mountain, but as summer progresses this melts leaving only the crater filled with snow. The mountain is the focal point for **Egmont National Park**, the boundary of which forms a ten-kilometre-radius arc around the mountain interrupted only on its north side where it encompasses the **Kaitake Range**, an older and more weathered cousin of Taranaki created by the same volcanic hotspot.

Farmland lies all about, but within the national park the mountain's lower slopes come cloaked in native bush, which gradually changes to stunted flag-form trees, lopsidedly shaped by the constant buffeting of the wind higher up. Higher still vegetation gives way to loose scoria slopes, hard work for those hiking to the summit.

Three sealed roads climb up the sides of the mountain, all on the eastern side and all ending a little under half way up at car parks from where the park's 140km of walking tracks spread out in all directions. **North Egmont** is the most easily accessible from New Plymouth, but you can get higher up the mountain on the road through **East Egmont** to The Plateau, and there's particularly good walking (and the best alpine accommodation) around **Dawson Falls**.

Both the DOC office and visitor centre in New Plymouth also have **information** on the park, and anyone interested in relatively easy hikes should obtain DOC's *Short Walks in Egmont National Park* brochure ($2.50). The main **visitor centre** is in North Egmont (see below).

With **accommodation** high on the mountain slopes close to all three major trailheads, it makes sense for avid hikers to base themselves inside the park. Day visitors can easily visit from New Plymouth, Stratford or Hawera, with all trailheads accessible in less than an hour by **car**. If you're relying on **buses**, your best bet is Mountain Shuttle (Ⓣ06/758 3222, Ⓔkirkstall @xtra.co.nz; $35 return) which departs New Plymouth daily at 7.30 for North Egmont. It leaves for the return journey at 4.15pm giving just enough time for a summit attempt. Competitive alternatives include Withers Coachlines (Ⓣ06/751 1777) and Seaspray Tours (Ⓣ06/758 9676).

If you'd rather go on **guided walks**, call either MacAlpine Guides (Ⓣ025/417 042, after hours 06/751 3542), Top Guides (Ⓣ0800/448 433, Ⓦwww.topguides.co.nz) or Mountain Guides (Ⓣ06/758 8261, Ⓦwww .mountainguides.co.nz). All offer bush walking, guided summit treks and a range of more technical stuff. Guides will normally take up to four or five clients for summer hiking and summit attempts, but perhaps only two clients for winter expeditions, rock climbing or instruction. Guiding rates are around $250–300 for two or three people, and you can add $60 each per day if you need instruction.

Finally, if you're here in February, you can join one of the local **alpine clubs**' inexpensive day trips to the summit; book through the North Egmont visitor centre.

Egmont Village and North Egmont

The easiest access point to the park, and the closest to New Plymouth, is tiny **Egmont Village**, 13km southeast of New Plymouth on SH3. From here, the

16km sealed Egmont Road runs up the mountain to **North Egmont** (960m) by far the most popular base for summit ascents. Before heading up (or on any of the numerous easier tracks) be sure to call at the park's main information source, the **North Egmont visitor centre** (daily 8am–4.30pm; Ⓣ06/756 0990, Ⓔnevc@doc.govt.nz), which has interesting displays about the mountain, maps of all the tracks, good viewing windows, weather updates and a decent café.

Short walks around North Egmont include the unusual and atmospheric **Ngatoro Loop Track** (1km loop; 45min–1hr; 100m ascent), which winds through the hidden valley of the Goblin Forest, with its kaikawaka trees, alpine plants and gnarled trunks hung with ferns and cushioning mosses. There's also the **Veronica Loop Track** (2.5km loop; 2hr; 200m ascent) which climbs up to a ridge through mountain forest and scrub with fine views of the ancient lava flows known as Humphries Castle, and beyond to New Plymouth and the coast. Note that **water supplies** at North Egmont are limited and you should bring some with you.

With the embarrassment of good hiking, you may want a **place to stay** around these parts, something easily found at *The Camphouse* (book through the visitor centre; ❶), a large corrugated-iron hut built in 1891 and now renovated for trampers, with four bunkrooms (each sleeping 8; bring a sleeping bag), a communal lounge with electric heating, full kitchen and hot showers. Alternatively, stay at the foot of the mountain in Egmont Village at *The Missing Leg*, SH3 (Ⓣ06/752 2570, Ⓔjo.thompson@xtra.co.nz; camping $8, dorms ❶, rooms ❷), a fairly basic but hospitable and low-cost backpackers 300m south of the Egmont Road/SH3 junction, which has functional bikes for rent.

East Egmont

The highest road on the mountain goes through **East Egmont**, simply a parking area and the site of the *Mountain House* (see below). From here, the **Curtis Falls Track** (3.5km return; 2–3hr; 120m ascent) traces the Te Popo Stream, via steps and ladders, to the Manganui River Gorge, then follows the riverbed past two waterfalls, and the **Enchanted Track** (3km one-way; 3hr; 300m ascent) heads through dense vegetation before climbing up to The Plateau (see below).

East Egmont is reached from Stratford (see p.284), from where Pembroke Road runs 14km west to East Egmont then a further 3.5km to **The Plateau**, a rugged and windswept spot 1172m up on Taranaki's flanks, which is on the upper route of the Around the Mountain Circuit (see box on p.283) and acts as the wintertime parking area for the **Manganui Skifield** (see box on p.281).

Accommodation is at the *Mountain House* (Ⓣ & Ⓕ06/765 6100, Ⓦwww.mountainhouse.co.nz; e–f), a beautifully sited but flagging **hotel**, 846m above sea level with en-suite rooms (❺), some with spa-bath (❻), and self-contained chalets (❺) each with two rooms. They have a **restaurant** with a slight bias towards game and quality Swiss dishes (mains $20–25), and also manage *Anderson's Alpine Lodge* (same contact details; ❻), a lovely, modern chalet-style building offering B&B located 5km downhill right on the edge of the national park.

Dawson Falls

The most southerly access up Taranaki follows Manaia Road to **Dawson Falls**, roughly 23km west of Stratford and 900m above sea level. Here you'll find the **Dawson Falls visitor centre** (daily 8am–4.30pm; Ⓣ025/430 248), with a few displays including a mock-up of Syme Hut, a mountaineers' hut actually located high up on the mountain. Several tracks branch off from the

Manganui Skifield

Committed skiers who fancy sampling a simple club field can hike thirty minutes from The Plateau at the top of Pembroke Road to **Manganui Skifield** (late June to mid-Oct daily 9am–4pm; ⓣ06/765 7669, ⓦwww.snow.co.nz/manganui), with its 420-metre vertical drop served by three rope tows and a T-bar ($30 per day). The slopes are rarely crowded and the skiing and snowboarding is most suited to intermediate and advanced skiers. Ski and snowboard **rental** is available at the *Mountain House Motor Lodge*, Pembroke Rd (ⓣ06/765 6100), and Stratford Taxis (ⓣ06/765 5651) will run you up to the top of the road for around $30.

visitor centre, most notably to the seventeen-metre-high **Dawson Falls** (400m return; 20min; 30m ascent), which plummet over an ancient lava flow. This hike can be extended along the **Kapuni Walk** (1km; 1hr; 50m ascent). Another good walk leads to **Wilkies Pool** (1km loop; 1hr; 100m ascent), where the waters of the Kapuni Gorge rush through a staircase of rock pools, and there's a tougher hike to **Hasties Hill** (2km loop; 1hr 30min–2hr; 100m ascent) involving a passage across the flank of the mountain to a lookout and returning via **Kaupokponui Falls**. Experienced hikers can also tackle the summit from here (see p.279).

At Dawson Falls there's budget **accommodation** at *Konini Lodge* (reserve through the visitor centre; ❶), a kind of oversized hikers' hut with separate bunk rooms mostly sleeping eight (bring a sleeping bag), a communal lounge, hot showers and a kitchen equipped with stoves and fridges. You can also go more upmarket at the nearby *Dawson Falls Mountain Lodge* (ⓣ0800/695 634 & 06/765 5457, ⓦwww.dawson-falls.co.nz), a lovely lodge where you keep out the mountain chill around the fire or in the sauna. There are pleasant enough studios (❺) and appreciably nicer suites (❻) plus a **restaurant** (breakfast from $14, 4-course table d'hôte dinner $43), **bar** and daytime **café**.

Along SH45: the Surf Highway

Despite its name, the **Surf Highway** (or SH45), running from New Plymouth to **Hawera**, mostly runs around 3km inland with myriad roads running down to tiny uninhabited bays. It's only just over a hundred kilometres in length, but with its beachy charms it can easily consume half a day, longer if you've a mind to sample the surf for which the coast is becoming increasingly known. Even among surfers it is still something of a backwater, but few who've sampled its glassy, even breaks doubt that this coast offers New Zealand's most consistent surfing. **Windsurfing** is good too, with near constant onshore winds that buffet the coastal trees.

Surf beaches are everywhere, but the only surf-oriented communities are **Oakura**, which is becoming increasing populated by New Plymouth commuters, and **Opunake**, which retains its beach resort feel. Between lies Cape Egmont with its picturesque **lighthouse**.

Oakura

Heading west through New Plymouth's suburbs you're briefly into the fields before arriving at **OAKURA**, 17km west of town. Rapidly becoming a dormitory community, it still retains a counter-culture tenor thanks to the boardriders here to surf the local breaks and experience the best windsurfing beach in Taranaki.

Taranaki summit hikes and the Around the Mountain Circuit

The majestic conical shape rising direct from the surrounding sea makes Taranaki an obvious target for summit aspirants. Although it is an exhausting hike, it is quite possible in a day for anyone reasonably fit, but don't underestimate the mountain. Essentially the upper mountain is off limits to ordinary hikers in winter, but even during the summer **hiking season** (Jan to mid-April) bad weather, including occasional snow, sweeps in frighteningly quickly, and hikers starting off on a clear fine morning frequently find themselves groping through low cloud before the day is through. Deaths occur far too often: be sure to consult our **hiking advice** in Basics (see p.56); get further advice and an up-to-date **weather forecast** from one of the visitor centres; and leave a **record of your intentions** before you set out.

There are two main **summit routes**, both requiring a full day, so you'll need to set off early, say around 7.30am. If you want to spend longer than a day on the mountain and are happy to forgo the goal-driven dash to the summit, the spectacular and testing **Around the Mountain Circuit** might fit the bill.

Summit routes

The **Northern Route** (10km return; 6–8hr; 1560m ascent) is by far the most popular summit route from North Egmont – there's good bus access from New Plymouth, handy accommodation at the trailhead, and the path is reasonably well defined. It begins at the top car park at North Egmont and initially follows the gravel Translator Road and then a wooden stairway to *Tahurangi Lodge*, a private hut run by the New Zealand Alpine Club. After negotiating the North Ridge you're onto loose slopes of scoria (a kind of jagged volcanic gravel) up the Lizard Ridge which leads to the crater. After crossing the crater ice and a short scoria slope, you reach the summit rocks. After (hopefully) taking in views that stretch over half the North Island, return by the same route.

The longer and poorly marked **Southern Route** to the summit (11km return; 8–10hr; 1620m ascent) is a more exacting proposition best left to those with mountain experience. The route starts at the Dawson Falls car park and climbs through bush before making a rapid ascent up a staircase to the Lake Dive Track. From there on it is a steep and exhausting series of zig-zags up scoria slopes.

For **surfboard rental**, go to Vertigo, 605 Main St (Ⓣ06/752 7363, Ⓔvertigosurf@xtra.co.nz), who have learner, slalom and wave boards, and also run a **surf school** (Ⓣ06/752 8283; $60 for a 2hr lesson for 2 people). Standing up is virtually guaranteed with Tandem Surfing (Ⓣ06/752 7734, Ⓔgregpage@cookietime.co.nz), where for $75 an hour you get to ride two-up on a specially elongated board.

While in Oakura, a visit to the **Koru pa** is well worth a brief detour: turn towards Mount Taranaki on the Wairau Road and left into Surrey Road, from which an easy walk (15min) brings you to the stronghold of the Nga Mahanga, its stone-faced ramparts now mostly strangled by native vegetation.

If you want a **place to stay**, try the beachside *Oakura Beach Camp*, 2 Jans Terrace (Ⓣ06/752 7861, Ⓔoakurabeachcamp@internet.co.nz; camping $8, cabins ❷), or head 4km southwest along SH45 to *The Wavehaven*, 1518 South Rd (Ⓣ & Ⓕ06/752 7800, Ⓔwave.haven@clear.net.nz; dorm ❶, rooms ❷), a backpackers frequented by avid surfers. It's opposite Ahu Ahu Road, which runs for 3km down to the coast and to *Ahu Ahu Beach Villas*, 321 Ahu Ahu Rd (Ⓣ06/752 7370, Ⓦwww.ahu.co.nz; ❻), some gorgeous self-contained villas sleeping four, built on a rise overlooking the ocean from an intriguing blend of salvaged materials and luxurious modern fittings.

The Around the Mountain Circuit

The well-marked **low-level Around the Mountain circuit** 44km; 3–5 days) makes an irregular loop around Taranaki varying in altitude from 500m to 1500m. During the middle of summer (generally Dec–Feb) the snow melts enough for hikers to tackle the more strenuous **high-level route**, which is essentially the same but makes a few shortcuts by heading higher up the slopes. In this way you can shave a day or so off the lower circuit. Both routes, and their practical details, are all fully explained in DOC's *Around the Mountain Circuit* **leaflet** ($1). There are six well-spaced **huts** along the way, all costing $10 except for the tiny *Kahui Hut* ($5); use your DOC annual hut passes or buy hut tickets from one of the DOC visitor centres. **Camping** is allowed anywhere on the circuit (free), but it's best to camp beside the huts so you can use their facilities (except the bunks) and pay half the hut fee.

Since the circuit passes through or close to North Egmont, The Plateau and Dawson Falls, you can start anywhere and go in either direction; here we've described it clockwise, starting from North Egmont. Heading from there to **Maketawa Hut** (2.7 km; 1–2hr), you initially loop downhill, then uphill, to join the Maketawa Track to the hut. From *Maketawa Hut* to **Waingongoro Hut** (6.5km; 4–5hr), the low-level track heads across the mountain to the *Mountain House*, diving down into gullies then climbing out all the way to the *House*. It is then another couple of hours to the *Waingongoro Hut*. Leaving there for **Lake Dive Hut** (8km; 4–5hr), there's an initial steep climb before you drop down to Dawson Falls then traverse around the mountain to the waterside hut. The hike from *Lake Dive Hut* to **Waiaua Hut** (11km; 6–7hr) provides the toughest day of all, involving a long descent down to 550m, then a gradual ascent along the Taungatara Track to the hut, the last section involving negotiating a ladder out of a gorge. The longest day is from *Waiaua Hut* to **Holly Hut** (12km; 5–7hr), along the way passing *Kahui Hut* where you can break your journey. The last day takes you from *Holly Hut* to **North Egmont** (6km; 3–4hr), though frustratingly the track meets the road 2km downhill from the visitor centre and you'll have to hike up for your hard-earned refreshments.

Cape Egmont and Opunake

At Pungarehu, about 25km further on, Cape Road cuts 5km west to the white-painted cast-iron tower of **Cape Egmont Lighthouse**, moved here in 1877 from Mana island north of Wellington. Now automated, it perches on a rise on the westernmost point of the cape and overlooking Taranaki's windswept coast; a great spot around sunset with the mountain glowing behind. As the wind and tidal conditions alter, surfers range along this coast but the real surfing hub in these parts is 20km on at **OPUNAKE**, a large village that hopes to put itself on the map by installing an artificial reef just offshore that should almost guarantee great year-round waves. Reef or no reef, there's still a great golden beach and a relaxed atmosphere engendered by there being little to do but swim, surf and cast a line.

If you fancy **staying**, try the *Opunake Beach Camp*, Beach Rd (Ⓣ & Ⓕ06/761 755; camping $9, on-site vans ❷), or *Opunake Motel and Backpackers*, 36 Heaphy Rd (Ⓣ06/761 8330, Ⓔopunakemotel@xtra.co.nz), which has a four-bunk room (❶), doubles (❷), cottages (❸) and one bedroom motel units (❹). You can eat well at *Volcanic Café & Surf Shop* at 55 Tasman St.

Along SH3 and SH3A: between New Plymouth and Wanganui

The quickest way to the upper slopes of the mountain, and the fastest road south to Wanganui, is **SH3** which runs 74km to Hawera where it meets the coastal SH45 Surf Highway. Along the way it passes through minuscule **Egmont Village** where a good road accesses the mountainside trailhead at North Egmont (see p.279). At **Inglewood** SH3 is joined by **SH3A** from **Waitara**, a small coastal settlement worth a brief exploration. **Stratford** is the starting point for two more roads that head up walking trails in Egmont National Park. Stratford itself shouldn't detain you long from pressing on to **Hawera**, the most substantial and interesting town in rural Taranaki, or tiny **Patea** on the coast road to Wanganui.

Waitara and around

Leaving New Plymouth on the inland route south it's only a short detour to the small coastal settlement of **WAITARA**, 15km to the northeast. Once an important port, it is now quiet but marks the beginning of the **Waitara Campaign Trail**, a nineteen-kilometre drive marked by boards and plaques which traces the culture clash that sparked the first Taranaki Land War. For more details call at the Waitara **visitor centre**, 39 Queen St (Mon–Fri 9am–4pm; ⓣ06/754 4405, ⓔwaitarapr@xtra.co.nz).

Should you fancy sampling or buying fruit wines – particularly kiwifruit and boysenberry – along with killer golden scrumpy and some hair-raising gin, visit the **Sentry Hill Winery**, 152 Cross Rd (Dec & Jan daily 10am–5pm; Feb–May & Sept–Nov Wed–Sun same hours; June–Aug Sat & Sun same hours), signposted 4km off the SH3a some 8km south of Waitara.

Inglewood and Stratford

SH3 and SH3a meet at diminutive **INGLEWOOD**, a nondescript farming service town worth a brief stop to sample the excellent *MacFarlane's Café*, at the corner of Kelly and Matai streets.

Just over halfway between New Plymouth and Hawera and 23km south of Inglewood is the small town of **STRATFORD**, which provides direct access to the slopes of Mount Taranaki, particularly East Egmont and the Manganui Skifield (see box on p.281). Stratford isn't an especially attractive place, made less so by the presence of a truly grotesque mock-Elizabethan **clock tower** (built in 1996 to hide the 1920s version), from which lifesize figurines of Romeo and Juliet emerge to mark the hour at 10am, 1pm and 3pm. Milking the town's nominal association with the Bard's birthplace, several streets have Shakespearean names, but that's about it. If you're bound for the centre of the North Island, Stratford marks the start of the **Taumarunui–Stratford Heritage Trail**, covered from p.261.

Intercity and Newmans **buses**, as well as locally based Dalroy Express (ⓣ0508/465 622), stop outside the **visitor centre** on Broadway close to the clock tower (Mon–Fri 8.30am–5pm & Sat 10am–3pm; ⓣ & ⓕ06/765 6708, ⓔstratford@info.stratford.govt.nz).

There are a couple of **places to stay**, mostly patronized by the ski crowd: the well-cared-for *Stratford Top 10 Holiday Park*, 10 Page St (ⓣ & ⓕ06/765 6440, ⓔstratfordholpark@hotmail.com; camping $9, dorms ❶, cabins ❷, cabins ❸), is central and has bike rental for $25 a day; and *Taranaki Accommodation Lodge*, 7 Romeo St (ⓣ & ⓕ06/765 5444, ⓔmttaranakilodge@hotmail.com; dorms ❶, rooms ❷) occupies a former nurses' home, with mostly twin rooms.

For something a little good deal more rural, visit *Sarsen House Country Retreat*, 636 Stanley Rd (Ⓣ & Ⓕ06/762 8775, Ⓦwww.tepopo.co.nz; ❻), 15km north-east of Stratford but worth the journey for relaxed accommodation set amid lovingly tended gardens. Rooms are en suite and well appointed with fires for winter and balconies for summer. You can self-cater or join the congenial hosts for dinner ($30).

Stratford's **eating** scene is limited, but you won't go far wrong at the *Backstage Café*, 234 Broadway (licensed & BYO; closed Mon), which serves good coffee, big snacks and some thoughtful and tasty main courses for under $20.

Hawera

The eastern and western routes around Taranaki meet at **HAWERA**, a tidy and well presented town of eight thousand surrounded by gently undulating dairy country. Primarily a service and administration centre for the district's farmers, its survival is largely dependent on the fortunes of Kiwi Co-op Dairies, the world's largest **dairy factory** complex just south of town. Through the peak of the milk production season around the end of October the plant processes thirteen million litres a day, equivalent to a tanker every two-and-a-half minutes around the clock. Year-round it handles twenty percent of the country's milk production, mostly gathered from the rich volcanic soils of Taranaki but also brought by rail from other parts of the North Island.

You can't visit the complex, but should call in at the **Dairylands** visitor centre, see how a former dairy factory has been transformed into the **Tawhiti Museum**, arrange to visit a fabulous **Elvis collection** and consider **dam dropping**.

The town and around

Hawera was the birthplace and home of one of New Zealand's most celebrated authors, **Ronald Hugh Morrieson** (see Contexts, p.1004) who loved jazz, wrote well-observed and amusing novels about small-town life and liked a drink or two. Appropriately, the only memorial to his existence here is *Morrieson's Café and Bar* on Victoria Street, which contains a few of his books, his old staircase, and tabletops made from timbers salvaged when his house was demolished to make way for KFC.

The only other sight in Hawera is the irresistible **Elvis Presley Memorial Record Room**, 51 Argyle St (visits by appointment, Ⓣ06/278 7624, Ⓦwww.digitalus.co.nz/elvis; donation), a garage shrine to the King where the owner often dresses the part. It is about ten minutes' walk from the visitor centre, and contains thousands of rare recordings, photographs and memorabilia.

Elements of kitsch also poke through at **Dairyland**, SH3, 3km south of town (Mon & Tues 9am–5pm, Wed–Sun 9am–8.30pm; $3), the public face of the local dairy industry. It is a kind of museum to all things lactic, where you're greeted by a couple of fibreglass cows, then treated to an insightful series of displays to a constant soundtrack of lowing. Some of the content is fairly technical, and a good deal more is blatant industry promotion, but there are highlights including a couple of "moovies" and an engaging day-in-the-life-of-a-delivery-truck video, complete with road vibration. Afterwards, retire to the café (known as *The Grasserie*) which is designed with a revolving floor meant to replicate a rotary milking shed. Here you can tuck into excellent café fare and gaze out at Mount Taranaki until the cows come home.

Economy of scale has put paid to many of the dozens of small dairy factories that once dotted the surroundings. Many of the buildings survive in other guises, about the most interesting being the **Tawhiti Museum and Bush Railway**, 401 Ohangai Road (10am–4pm: Christmas–Jan daily; Sept–Christmas & Feb–May Fri–Mon; June–Aug Sun; $6.50), just off Tawhiti Road, 4km east of Hawera. The unique exhibits really bring the past to life, using sixty-odd lifesize figurines modelled on local people by owner, creator and visionary, Nigel Ogle. The social and technological heritage of both Maori and Pakeha is explored through the extensive use of photographs, models and dioramas, some of the most impressive being representations of *pa* sites. Note the model of the virtually impregnable Turuturumokai *pa*, and the changes to fortifications demanded by the advent of musket warfare. Other highlights include a record of the life of Chew Chong, a widely respected Chinese migrant who initiated the export of local fungi to China, a working pottery and the small-scale **bush railway** (first Sun in the month, every Sun during school holidays & every public hol; $3) that trundles 1km through displays recounting the logging history of Taranaki.

For something more active, try **dam dropping**, a variation on whitewater sledging conducted by Kaitiaki Adventures (ⓣ06/278 4452; ⓦwww.kaitiaki.co.nz). As long as you can swim, you'll be equipped with a wetsuit, helmet and buoyant plastic sledge, and will then be ready to slide between six and nine metres down the face of a dam. This is more fun (and less scary) than it sounds, and you can do it as many times as you care to before the gentle scenic float down the docile Wainongoro river with the guide, who imparts local Maori history and folklore. You can choose to go dam dropping only ($40; 1hr), or take the full three-hour trip downstream ($80).

Practicalities

Long-distance **buses** travelling between New Plymouth and Wanganui stop at the **visitor centre**, 55 High St (Mon–Fri 8.30am–5pm, plus Nov–March Sat & Sun 10am–3pm; ⓣ06/278 8599, ⓔvisitorinfo@stdc.govt.nz), easily found at the base of the now-redundant water tower that dominates the townscape. There's no local transport, but Hawera Taxis (ⓣ06/278 7171) will run you out to the Tawhiti Museum and other local sights.

Hawera has a reasonable range of **accommodation**, most cheaply at either the *King Edward Park Motorcamp*, 70 Waihi Rd (ⓣ & ⓕ06/278 8544; camping $8, cabins ❷), right in town, or *Wheatley Downs*, 46 Ararata St, 4km past the Tawhiti Museum (ⓣ06/278 6523, ⓦwww.taranaki-bakpak.co.nz; dorms ❶, rooms ❷, self-catering unit ❸), a friendly farmstay and backpackers with views of Mount Taranaki.

Back in town, there are comfortable units at the *Furlong Motor Inn*, 256 Waihi Rd (ⓣ06/278 5136, ⓕ278-5134; ❹), and delightful **B&B** in a grand 1875 *kauri* mansion called *Tairoa Lodge*, at the corner of Puawai Street and SH3 (ⓣ & ⓕ06/278 8603, ⓦwww.tairoa-lodge.co.nz; ❺), with a pool, mature grounds, comfy en-suite rooms and dinners on request (from $30).

When it comes to daytime eating, head for *The Caff*, 79 High St (closed Sun), purveyor of coffee, tea, toast, bacon and eggs from early morning to late afternoon, *Morrieson's* for bar meals, or time your explorations to dine at the cafés at Dairylands or the Tawhiti Museum. In the evening make straight for the *White Elephant Restaurant and Lounge Bar*, 47 High St (ⓣ06/278 7424), a relaxed bar with an à la carte restaurant where you might expect pumpkin and thyme risotto with truffle oil ($21), or roasted pork loin ($24), followed by chocolate-and-banana steamed pudding with crème anglaise ($9).

Patea and around

Cutting through heavily cultivated farmland, SH3 splits **PATEA**, the only major community between Hawera and Wanganui. The township has a large model of the Aotea Canoe in the main street, commemorating the settlement of the area by Turi and his *hapu*, a good surfing beach at the mouth of the Patea River and a safe freshwater swimming hole, overlooked by the Manawapou Redoubt and *pa* site.

Some 47km south of Patea is the turn-off for **Bushy Park Historic Homestead and Scenic Reserve**, 796 Rangitautau East Road (daily 10am–5pm; $3), well signposted 8km off SH3. The park contains a large stand of native bush thick with vines, creepers and supplejack, the largest rata tree in New Zealand (3.5m in diameter and 43m tall) and a 1906 homestead. Notable features in the house include a striking stained-glass window, a carved overmantel and fireplace and a huge five-metre Chesterfield in the entrance hall; you can even soak up the gracious surroundings while **staying** (Ⓣ06/342 9879, Ⓦwww.bushypark-homestead.co.nz), either on a B&B basis in the homestead (❺), self catering in the chalet (❶) or at one of the motorhome sites ($25 per site).

Wanganui and around

There's something of an archaic feel to **WANGANUI**, with its slow pace and its obvious sense of civic pride evident in its museums and well-tended streetscape. Founded on the banks of the **Wanganui River** – the longest navigable watercourse in New Zealand – Whanganui is one of New Zealand's oldest cities and was the hub of early European commerce by virtue of its access to the interior and coastal links with the ports of Wellington and New Plymouth. The river traffic has long gone and the port is a shadow of what it was, but the city has given itself a facelift in recent years with an eye to the settlement's colonial past: the late Victorian and early Edwardian facades have been refurbished, mock gaslamps have been installed along re-cobbled streets, and there seem to be flowers everywhere. With its riverbank charm, it is a pleasant little place to spend a day or two, perhaps taking a ride on a restored **river steamer**, visiting the excellent museum, and idling an hour away in the nationally renowned **art gallery**. Perhaps best of all you can join a **rural mail delivery** as it visits the tiny settlements alongside the Whanganui River (see p.266).

By the time **Europeans** arrived in the 1830s, the Maori population was well-established, and land rights quickly became a bone of contention. Transactions Maori perceived as a ritual exchange of gifts, the New Zealand Company took as a successful negotiation for the purchase of Wanganui and a large amount of surrounding land. Settlement went ahead regardless of the misunderstanding, and it was not until the **Gilfillan Massacre** of 1847 that trouble erupted again. When a Maori was accidentally injured, his tribesmen took *utu* (retribution), massacring four members of the Gilfillan family. Further violent incidents culminated in a full-scale but inconclusive **battle** at St John's Hill. The next year the problems were apparently resolved by a payment of £1000 to the Maori; local tribes took no action during the wars in Taranaki, even helping European settlers by defeating Hauhau warriors at Moutoa Island in 1864. More recently, tensions came to a head in town at **Moutoa Gardens** (see p.289), though this is once again a peaceful patch of urban greenery.

Whanganui versus Wanganui

Visitors are often confused by the variant spellings of **Whanganui** (the original Maori), which is retained for the river and the national park, and **Wanganui** (the Anglicized version), which has been adopted by the city. Explanations of the discrepancy cite the silent "H" in spoken Maori being omitted when the name was written down, or the H being dropped over time as a result of common early English usage. A debate has been raging in the council chambers for some time about whether to restore the original Maori name to the city, but don't hold your breath.

Arrival, information and city transport

The **airport** is 5km southwest of the city centre and is linked by Ash Mayor Transport shuttles (ⓣ06/347 7444). **Buses** drop off at various places around town: InterCity and Newmans stop at 156 Ridgway St (ⓣ06/345 4433), and White Star at 161 Ingestre St (ⓣ06/347 6677).

The **visitor centre**, 101 Guyton St (Mon–Fri 8.30am–5pm, Sat & Sun 10am–3pm; March–Oct closes 2pm Sat & Sun; ⓣ06/349 0508, ⓦwww.destinationwanganui.com), has **internet** access, and provides useful **maps** and leaflets, including timetables for Wanganui Buses (ⓣ06/345 5566), who run a limited Monday to Saturday **bus service** round the city and to the beaches at the rivermouth. If the buses don't suit then either walk (the city centre is easily manageable on foot) or try River City Cabs (ⓣ06/345 3333). The **DOC office**, 74 Ingestre St (Mon–Fri 8am–4.30pm), sells leaflets on the Whanganui National Park, plus hut and camping tickets.

Banks are all on Victoria Ave or within one block of it, the **post office** is at 60 Ridgway St, and the **AA office** can be found at 78 Victoria Ave (ⓣ06/348 9160).

Accommodation

With a reasonable range of accommodation that seldom seems to be completely booked you should have little trouble finding somewhere suitable to stay in Wanganui, and rates are modest.

Hotels, motels and B&Bs

Acacia Park Motel 140 Anzac Parade ⓣ06/343 9093 & 0800/800 225, ⓔacacia.park.motel@xtra.co.nz. Simple, clean rooms set in extensive grounds overlooking the river. ❹

Arlesford House 202 SH3, 7km north of Wanganui ⓣ06/347 7751, ⓦwww.arlesford-house.co.nz. Situated in six acres of well-tended garden, this friendly spot offers respite from the city. It's also a fine example of a 1930s house, with rimu floors and spacious rooms boasting pastoral views. ❻

Avenue Hotel 379 Victoria Ave ⓣ06/345 0907, ⓦwww.theavenuewanganui.com. A range of rooms, from clean and budget ones to plush spacious suites. On-site restaurant and swimming pool. ❹–❻

Bradgate 7 Somme Parade ⓣ & ⓕ06/345 3634. An agreeable spot with comfortable, high-ceilinged rooms in a house overlooking the river, an easy walk from the city centre. ❹

Crellow House 274 Taupo Quay ⓣ06/345 0740. Bargain B&B in small riverview home done in Victorian Gothic style. Rooms are comfortable and the welcome warm. ❸

Rutland Arms Inn cnr Victoria Ave & Ridgeway St ⓣ06/347 7677, ⓦwww.rutland-arms.co.nz. Luxurious central accommodation in an historic building, the top end of all the town's accommodation. ❻

Hostels and campsites

Aramoho Top 10 Holiday Park 460 Somme Parade, 6km north ⓣ06/343 8402 & 0800/272 664, ⓔaramoho.holidaypark@xtra.co.nz. Well-tended site 6km from the city centre, by the river in the shade of giant trees. Camping $10, cabins

❷–❸, motel units ❹.

Castlecliff Holiday Park 1a Rangiora St, Castlecliff, 9km west of town ⓣ06/344 2227, ⓔtokiwipark@xtra.co.nz. Close by the beach, bus stop and general store, this site offers camping and a range of on-site accommodation. Camping $9, cabins ❷, kitchen cabins ❸

Riverside Inn 2 Plymouth St ⓣ & ⓕ06/347 2529. Combined guesthouse and associate YHA in a large 1895 homestead surrounded by lawns with a thoroughly equipped kitchen and cosy lounge. There are airy and quiet B&B rooms with a bathroom down the hall plus backpacker doubles and dorms bunks. ❶–❹

Tamara Lodge 24 Somme Parade ⓣ06/347 6300, ⓦwww.tamaralodge.com. A large historic building with plenty of space, pretty gardens and a friendly atmosphere, just three minutes' walk from the city centre. Offers free bike usage and lots of neat, comfortable dorms and doubles and a balcony with a river view. Dorms ❶, rooms ❷

The City

The cultural heart of Wanganui beats around Pukenamu, a grassy hill that marks the site of Wanganui's last tribal war in 1832. Now known as **Queens Park**, it contains a trio of the city's most significant buildings. Architecturally, the most impressive is the gleaming white hilltop **Sarjeant Gallery** (Mon–Fri 10.30am–4.30pm & Sat–Sun 1–4.30pm; free), an engaging 1917 building of Oamaru stone with a magnificent dome that filters natural light to illuminate the exhibits. The highly regarded permanent collection concentrates on contemporary New Zealand art and photography and is augmented by various touring exhibitions. Immediately north of the gallery sits one of Wanganui's oldest buildings, the white, weatherboarded **Tylee Cottage**, at the corner of Cameron and Bell streets, which was built in 1853 and now provides accommodation for the artists in residence at the Sarjeant Gallery.

Southwest of the gallery, the Veteran Steps lead towards the centre of the city past the **Whanganui Regional Museum** (Mon–Sat 10am–4.30pm, Sun 1–4.30pm; $2), which was founded in 1892. It contains an outstanding collection of Maori artefacts, tools, weapons, *tukutuku*, garments, ornaments, musical instruments and three impressive canoes, all displayed in Te Ati Haunui-a-Paparangi, the central court that is shaped like a traditional meeting house. Hung around the collection and in smaller galleries off the main area are portraits of Maori in full ceremonial dress and *moko* (traditional tattoos) by Gottfried Lindauer. Though these portraits are sometimes criticized for the sitters' passivity, if you look at them long enough the strongest impression is of great *mana* (dignity and pride). Other exhibits include a reconstruction of an early street in the Pakeha settlement, photographs and displays on New Zealand geology and natural history, including a large number of moa skeletons.

Towards the river, on Somme Parade, lie the historic **Moutoa Gardens**, just a small peaceful patch of grass, but a historic one. Traditionally Maori had lived at Moutoa during the fishing season until it was co-opted by Pakeha settlers, who renamed the area Market Square. It was here that Maori signed the document agreeing to the "sale" of Wanganui, an issue revisited on Waitangi Day 1995 when simmering old grievances and one or two more recent ones reached boiling point. Maori occupied Moutoa Gardens, claiming it as Maori land, and began an 83-day occupation. This ended peacefully in the High Court, but created much bitterness on both sides, neither of which particularly distinguished themselves during the occupation. By 2001 a more creative atmosphere prevailed, and the government, city council and local *iwi* agreed to share management of the Gardens.

Following Ridgeway Street until it meets the main Victoria Avenue you reach the pretty **Watt Fountain**, which is surrounded by a number of ornate classi-

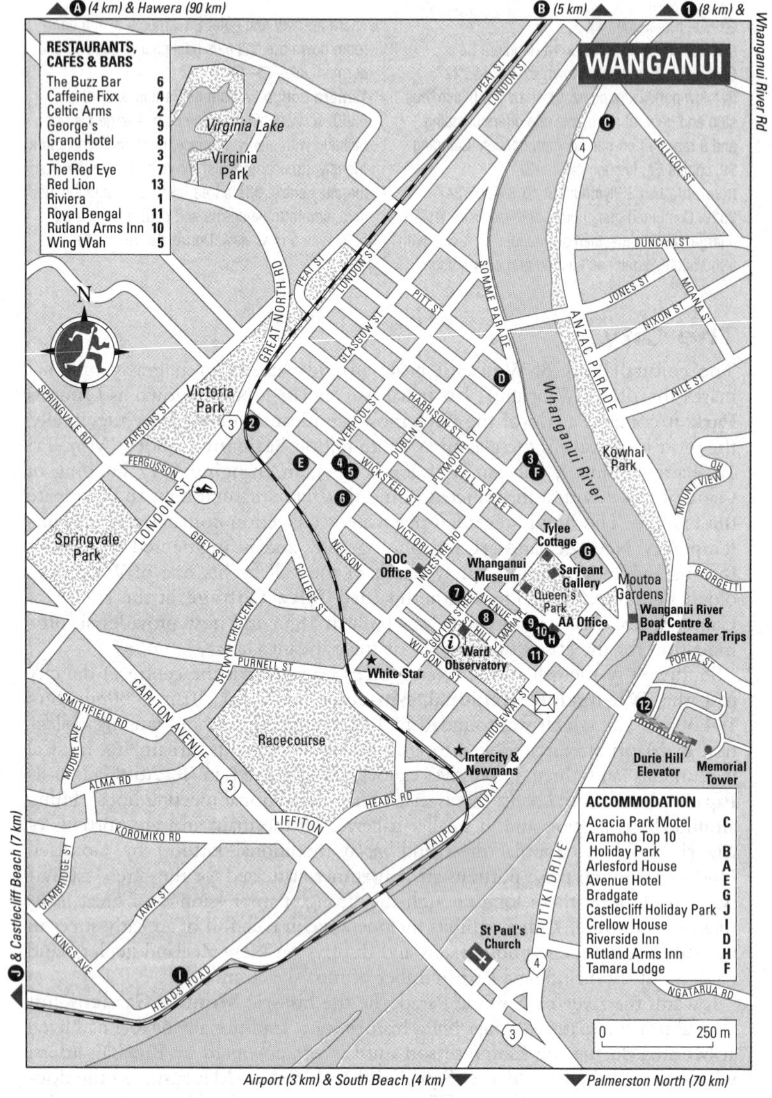

cal buildings, including the old Post Office and the striking Rutland Building. The Cinema 3 Complex provides a welcome counterpoint in the form of a stylish Art Deco (although actually built in the early 1950s) exterior, foyer and mezzanine lounge, not to mention luxurious ladies' powder rooms.

Continuing west you come to **Cook's Gardens**, known in New Zealand as the place where in 1962 local hero **Peter Snell** set a new world mile record of 3min 54.4sec, on grass. There's still a running track here along with a velodrome and the 1903 **Ward Observatory**, where you can look through the

24-centimetre refractor, the largest still in use in New Zealand (Friday 9.30pm in summer, otherwise by arrangement on ⓣ06/345 6954; $2).

The evening is also the best time to take a stroll around **Virginia Park**, almost 3km north on SH3, where there's a colourful ornamental fountain in Virginia Lake, trees are illuminated alongside paths and there's even an imitation glow-worm bank.

The river

Wanganui's history is inextricably tied with the Whanganui River, and though commercial river traffic has virtually stopped you can still ride the *Waimarie* **paddle steamer**, Taupo Quay (daily 2pm; $25; ⓣ06/347 1863, ⓦwww.riverboat.co.nz; bookings advisable), New Zealand's last surviving paddlesteamer, which makes a two-hour run up a tidal stretch of the river. It is a relaxing trip with the huffing of the coal-fired steam engine and the slosh of the paddles a soothing background to an afternoon sunning yourself on deck or retiring to the wood-panelled saloon for cakes and tea, the water boiled by heat from the engines.

The *Waimarie* was built by Yarrow and Company of London, in 1899, to a shallow-draught design with a tough hull making it suitable for river work. It was transported to New Zealand in kit form, then put to work on the Whanganui River, where it saw service during the pre-Great War boom in tourism in the region. when thousands of people from all over the world came to travel up the Whanganui River and stay at the hotel at Pipiriki. In 1949 the *Waimarie* made her last voyage and three years later sank at her moorings. It wasn't until 1993 that the boat was salvaged and, after 67,000 hours spent using skills passed on from half a century ago, the ship finally returned to the river in 1999.

The restoration took place at the admirable **Whanganui River Boat Centre** (Mon–Fri 9am–4pm, Sat & Sun 10am–4pm; donation), which sits flanked by old warehouses and stores at Taupo Quay. Housed in an 1881 two-storey timber-framed building, the centre's museum concentrates on the river and its history in relation to the town.

The left bank

Crossing City Bridge to the east bank of the river you're walking straight towards the **Durie Hill Elevator** (Mon–Fri 7.30am–6pm, Sat 9am–5pm, Sun 11am–5pm; $1 each way), where a Maori carved gateway marks the entrance to a 213-metre tunnel at the end of which a historic 1919 elevator carries passengers 66m up through the hill to the summit. Once at the top of the hill there are two excellent vantage points, both granting extensive views of the city, beaches and inland. The viewpoint atop the elevator's machinery room is the easy option, but the best views are 176 steps up at the top of the 34-metre **Memorial Tower** (daily 8am–dusk; free). Once you've seen enough back to town using the 191 steps to the river – it only takes about ten minutes, and provides some satisfying views of the surrounding area.

It is about 2km south along Putiki Drive to **St Paul's Memorial Church**, Anaua Street (donation requested), which looks like any other small whitewashed weatherboard church but contains magnificent Maori carvings adorned with *paua*, a painted rib ceiling (as in Maori meeting houses), beautiful etched-glass windows and *tukutuku* panels. The church is sometimes locked, but you can get a key from the house on the corner or a small wooden box near the church entrance.

The beaches

Wanganui isn't noted for its great swimming beaches, but the strands either side of the mouth of the Wanganui River are great places for moody walks. Around 5km southwest of town, **South Beach** is a vast desolate tract of sand accessible from the old airport road, while north of the mouth **Castlecliff Beach** offers a broad sweep of black iron-sand and the usual motley collection of driftwood: it is around 8km west of town along Heads Road. For swimming head 20km north along SH3 for **Mowhanau Beach**, a spectacular beach surrounded by papa cliffs (sandstone and mudstone) and renowned for good windsurfing.

Eating, drinking and entertainment

There are few culinary stars in Wanganui's firmament, but if you've just emerged after days in the Whanganui National Park the range of dining and drinking options is a welcome sight. Either way, there's enough choice to keep you sated for the night or two you'll be here.

For entertainment there's the Embassy 3 **cinema**, 34 Victoria Avenue (☎06/345 7958). If you happen to be here in late February and early March look out for the two-week **Wanganui Arts Festival** which has events all over town. For **listings** of any gigs or events check out the Friday edition of the *Wanganui Chronicle*.

Cafés and restaurants

Caffeine Fixx 71 Liverpool St. Great little café with bright blue outdoor seating, as well as sofas in which to relax over panini, salads and aromatic coffee. Also has internet access.

George's 40 Victoria Ave. Old-fashioned fish-and-chip shop also selling good-value fresh fish.

Grand Hotel 99 Guyton St. Cobb and Co franchise, dishing up simple food in large portions.

Legends' 25 Somme Parade ☎06/348 7450. Self-styled café, restaurant and cigar house with a sunny deck and river views that are always popular. Drop in for a coffee or something from the modern menu, which might extend to Thai fishcakes with manuka honey and wasabi mayo ($9) and Hokkien noodles with shiitake mushrooms ($20).

The Red Eye 96 Guyten St ☎06/345 5646. The hippest café in town, with eye-brightening coffee, an alternative art-student atmosphere and tasty, mostly organic food for lunch or dinner, including Tandoori chicken, Indonesian stir fry pizza slices and traditional New Zealand favourites. They occasionally have acoustic live music at weekends. Licensed and BYO.

Riviera Upokongaro, 11km north on SH4 ☎06/345 6459. The best and most authentic Italian restaurant in the area – fresh pasta, great coffee, home-made ice cream – and nothing on the menu costs more than $22. Lunch Thurs–Sun, dinner Wed–Sun; licensed; book Fri & Sat dinner.

Royal Bengal 7 Victoria Ave ☎06/348 7041. Respectable no-nonsense curry restaurant and takeaway serving tasty samosa ($3) and dishes such as chicken dupiaza, prawn madras and chicken tikka masala for around $13. Licensed & BYO.

Wing Wah 330 Victoria St. Good-quality Chinese restaurant and take away offering reasonable prices, with generous banquet meals for two or more.

Bars

Buzz Bar 321 Victoria Ave. Popular neon-, mirror- and chrome-decorated sports bar with big-screen TV, all-day bar snacks, Friday happy hours (3.30–7.30pm) and an upstairs nightclub called Metro, with a DJ and dance music from Thurs to Sat night.

Celtic Arms 437 Victoria Ave. Bargain pub food, including fry-up breakfasts, fish'n'chips, pan-fried snapper or steak, plus live folk, jazz or rock on Fri.

Red Lion 45 Anzac Parade. An atmospheric pub with a wide selection of beers and bar meals, just about the best place to see live music at weekends. Daily 11am–3am.

Rutland Arms Inn 48–52 Ridgway St. A pseudo old-style pub, with 14 beers on tap and a full range of mainstream meals served up in a sunny courtyard.

South to Palmerston North

Southbound traffic along both SH1 and SH3 meets at **BULLS**, 44km north of Palmerston North, worth a brief pause to marvel at how the locals have let their sense of humour get the better of them with their signage. The police station comes billed as Const-a-Bull, the medical centre as Medic-a-Bull, the town hall as Soci-a-Bull, and even the litter bins get hopefully labelled Respons-i-Bull.

At **OHAKEA**, 7km south, anyone with an aeronautical bent should stop off at the **Airforce Museum**, SH3 (daily 9.30am–4.30pm; $8), where you can browse through the remnants of old planes, make pretend on flight simulators, pick up some history or just gaze from the café window at the RNZAF base next door.

Palmerston North and around

PALMERSTON NORTH is the thriving capital of the province of Manawatu, and with around 75,000 people it's one of New Zealand's largest landlocked cities. The term-time presence of students from **Massey University** makes the city a lively place with plenty of action around the restaurants and bars, but during the day there's no single must-see attraction, and the place tends to get ignored by most tourists.

After the arrival of the rail line in 1886, Palmerston North grew from little more than a crossroads to a city with its roots in commercial supply, something maintained by its pivotal position at the junction of road and rail routes. Today its identity is reflected in some fine civic buildings, notably an excellent **museum** and **gallery** and a stunning **library**.

Arrival, information and accommodation

Frequent Air New Zealand flights from Auckland, Wellington and Christchurch land at Palmerston North's **airport**, 3km northeast of the city, from where **taxis** run into town: try Palmerston North Taxis (ⓣ06/355 5333 & 0800/355 5333). The **train station** is on Matthews Avenue, about 1.5km northwest of the city centre, and **long-distance buses** stop at the Palmerston North Travel Centre, at the corner of Pitt and Main streets, which is the focal point for all **local bus** services. These run in a series of loops from the terminal to various parts of the city ($1.50) with reduced services outside of term time. Timetables can be obtained from the helpful **visitor centre**, 52 The Square (Mon–Fri 9am–5pm, Sat & Sun 10am–3pm; ⓣ06/354 6593, ⓦwww.manawatunz.co.nz), which is packed to the gills with information on the area, including an excellent weekly events sheet.

There's a perfectly decent range of **accommodation**, though the paucity of tourists means most places are geared towards university business and visiting parents.

Acacia Court Motel 374 Tremaine Ave ⓣ06/358 3471, ⓕ37 5871. A friendly welcome and clean, fully self-contained, ground-floor units. ④

Birch Trees Lodge 97 Tremaine Ave ⓣ06/356 1455, ⓕ356 1458. Six self-contained modern units and four well-kept studios, all spacious and comfortable. ④

Contact House 186 Fitzherbert House ⓣ06/355 3653, ⓔcontact.house@clear.net.nz. The pick of the bunch in terms of value for money, with modern colourful rooms only five minutes' walk from the square. Breakfast is simple but it's so hospitable here that you'll feel spoiled. ❸

The Gables 179 Fitzherbert Ave ⓣ06/358 3209, ⓔthegables.pn.nz@xtra.co.nz. Attractive and very welcoming B&B in a 1930s house set in mature grounds, with comfortable rooms that share a bathroom, and a separate self-contained cottage. ❹–❺

King Street Backpackers 95 King St ⓣ06/358 9595, ⓔparadise@bopis.co.nz. Clean and spacious hostel close to the centre with all the expected facilities. Dorms ❶, rooms ❷

Palmerston North Holiday Park 133 Dittmer Drive ⓣ06/358 0349. Spacious campsite close to the Manawatu River with a wide range of accommodation and excellent facilities. Camping $9, cabins ❷, self-catering units ❸

The Palm & Oaks 183 Grey St ⓣ06/359 0755, ⓦwww.thepalm-oaks.co.nz. Supremely luxurious and private self-contained accommodation (with breakfast provided) in a modern Italian Deco-style villa with four double rooms. There are top-quality fittings everywhere, an outdoor hot tub, and everything has been thought of right down to floor tiles that are heated or cooled on demand. ❾

Pepper Tree YHA 121 Grey St ⓣ06/355 4054, ⓔpeppertreehostel@clear.net.nz. A comfortable associate YHA hostel within easy walking distance of the central square. Run by friendly and helpful folk, this is a small place, so phone ahead. Dorms ❶, rooms ❷

Quality Hotel 110 Fitzherbert Ave ⓣ06/356 8059 & 0800/808 228, ⓦwww.qualitypalmerston.co.nz. A modern comfortable hotel only five minutes' walk from the square, offering a variety of accommodation largely for corporate custom. Prices drop from May–Sept and there is a lively bar often frequented by students and a reasonably priced carvery restaurant, popular with families, attached to the hotel. ❺

The City

Palmerston North centres on **The Square**, a simple grassy expanse marred by car parking in the middle and the ugly intrusion of the Civic Centre, which occupies part of the western side. The Square is improved by **Te Marae o Hine**, or the Courtyard of the Daughter of Peace, an open area largely populated by skateboarders but with a couple of five-metre-high Maori figures carved by John Bevan Ford (see p.296). The Maori name for the area is the one suggested for the settlement's central square by the chief of the Ngati Raukawa in 1878, in the hope that love and peace would become enduring features in the relationship between the Manawatu Maori and incoming Pakeha.

Around The Square, the mish-mash of architectural styles – classical Victorian and Edwardian, Art Deco and so on – serves to enhance the impact of seeing the **City Library** (Mon–Fri 10am–6pm, Sat 10am–4pm & Sun 1–4pm), a post-modern conversion sensitively poking its nose from behind the classical facade of the 1927 C.M. Ross building on the southeast side. Designed by Ian Athfield (see box on p.497) and opened in May 1995, the exterior hides a challenging environment full of colour and contrast, light and texture in which all the reading materials are arranged according to "subject living rooms" furnished with armchairs and sofas.

Immediately west of the square lies **Te Manawa** (daily 10am–5pm) the city's main cultural focus. It is divided into three parts centred on the **Life Galleries** (free), a museum devoted to the history and culture of the Manawatu region. Much of the space is given over to high-standard touring exhibitions, but one room is devoted to a large Maori exhibit where carvings, weapons, tools, baskets and figureheads are mounted in a specially designed environment that recreates the ambience of bush, trees and meeting houses. In the same building, **Mind Galleries** ($6) offers top quality hands-on science displays and experiments predominantly aimed at children and changing every couple of months. Adjacent stands the **Art Gallery** (free), which displays Pakeha and Maori art from its permanent collection alongside touring exhibitions.

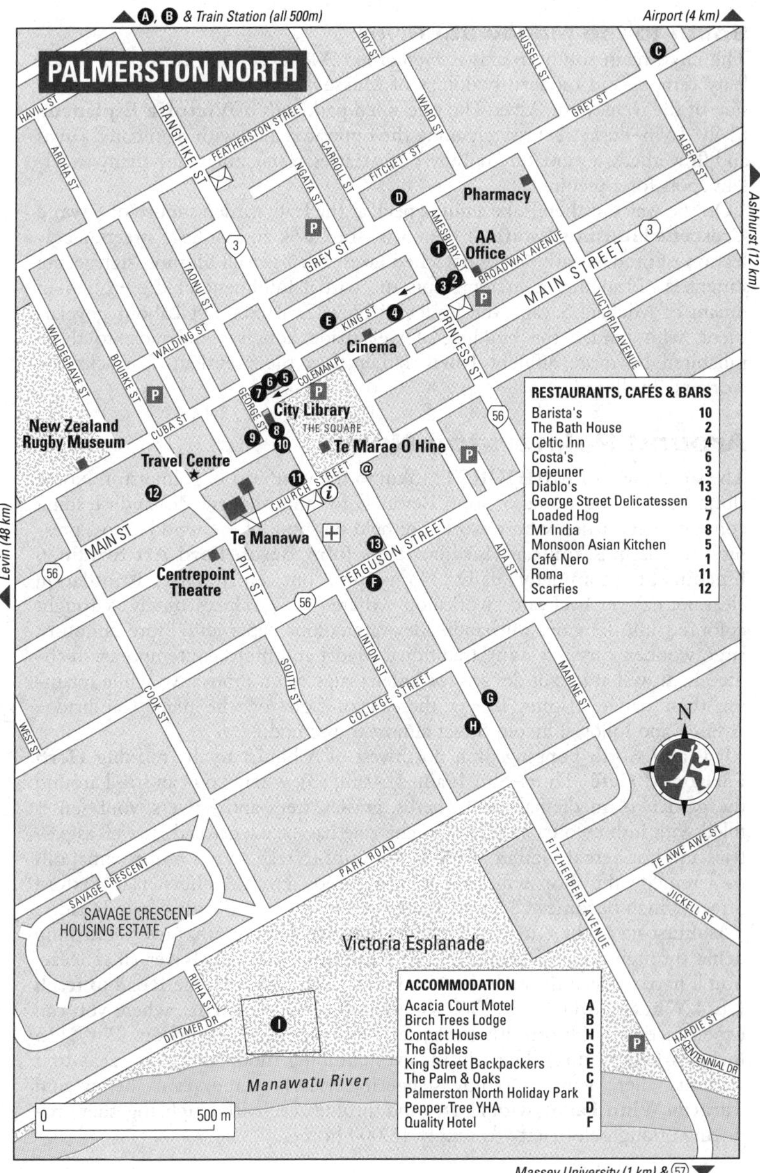

A short stroll northwest of the square, the **New Zealand Rugby Museum**, 87 Cuba St (Mon–Sat 10am–noon & 1.30–4pm, Sun 1.30–4pm; $4), is chiefly for die-hard rugger fans who can marvel at caps, ties, blazers, jerseys, balls, cups, cartoons, photographs, a reference library of games on video and the bronzed boots of famous players.

South to the Manawatu River

The city's main southern axis is Fitzherbert Avenue, which runs 3km to the leafy campus and modern buildings of **Massey University**, on the southern side of the Manawatu River. The tree-filled parklands of **Victoria Esplanade** (daily dawn–dusk; free) stretch along the opposite bank, with manicured lawns and flowerbeds, a miniature railway, bird aviaries, rose gardens and many excellent spots for a picnic.

On the way out there, take a quick peek at the leafy garden suburb of **Savage Crescent Housing Estate**, at the corner of Cook and College streets, a collection of modest early 1940s detached houses that is well off most sightseeing itineraries. Nonetheless, it represents the partial fulfilment of the egalitarian dream of Michael Savage, the leader of New Zealand's first Labour government, who funded the building of well-made houses comparable to those inhabited by more affluent Kiwis, rather than the prevalent "barracks-like workers' dwellings".

Around Palmerston North

The small town of **ASHHURST**, 13km to the northeast of Palmerston North along SH3, is the home of John Bevan Ford, one of New Zealand's leading contemporary artists whose works are held by some of the world's most prestigious museums. You can visit him at the **John Bevan Ford Art Studio**, 6 Lincoln St (nominally daily 11am–4pm, but email first; Ⓔfordart@clear.net.nz), a backyard workshop where he produces finely wrought coloured-ink drawings on handmade watercolour paper and, more famously, large wooden carvings using traditional Maori and more contemporary techniques, as well as bright designs for Dilena rugs, again innovative while retaining their native origins. To get there, turn right off the main Cambridge Avenue and follow Lincoln Street almost to the end.

It is also worth popping 3km northwest of Ashhurst to the relaxing **Herb Farm and Café** (Thurs–Sun 10am–4.30am; $3), where you can stroll around the garden of medicinal plants, herbs, grasses, trees and flowers, your senses filled with lush colours and aromas. The café has excellent salads as well as pastries and hot herbal toddies, while if you want to take away some essential oils or a remedy, the shop will cater to your needs. From Ashhurst take Oxford Street, which becomes Cloyton Road, then turn down North Grove Road.

Ashhurst sits at the entrance to the **Manawatu Gorge**, a narrow 10km-long defile through which a train line, SH3 and the Manawatu River all squeeze. You'll have to head through there and travel 3km down Gorge Road to reach **Go 4 Wheels** (Ⓣ06/376 7136, Ⓔgo4wheels@amcom.co.nz), where you can experience one of North Island's better 4WD motorbike excursions (2hr; $115 includes bike tuition). The trip involves climbing modified cattle tracks to a summit where you can enjoy staggering views of the plains below and **Tararua Wind Farm**, with its 48 wind turbines, each 40m high, together producing enough electricity to supply 15,000 homes.

Eating, drinking and entertainment

With its prosperous business community and large student population, Palmerston North supports a lively **restaurant** scene that ranges from straightforward cafés serving reliable filling fare to fancy restaurants. Many places morph into vibrant **bars**, some of the best lining **George Street**, home of Palmerston North's café society.

For entertainment, there's the **Centrepoint Theatre**, cnr Church and Pitt streets (☎06/354 5740, Ⓦwww.centrepoint.co.nz), an intimate purpose-built performance space, with a pleasant pre-show and interval bar; and **movies** at the Downtown Cinema 8, on Broadway Avenue between Princess Street and The Square (☎06/355 5655). "The Pulse" pull-out section of Saturday's *Evening Standard* has entertainment **listings**.

Barista's Espresso Bar George St. Modern minimalist café, with a corrugated-iron counter bar where they grind their own coffee and serve amazing cakes, snacky meals ($6–18), mains around the $20 mark and bagels for breakfast.

The Bath House 161 Broadway Ave. A restaurant and lounge bar in a bathhouse wittily decorated in "fall of the Roman Empire" bacchanalia, plus courtyard dining. Food is suitably decadent – French- and Italian-influenced meals, finger food, and brunches.

Café Nero 36 Amesbury St ☎6/354 0312. Congenial café, restaurant and bar in a large gabled house with sofas for relaxing over a coffee or glass of wine, and tables (inside and out) for dishes such as smoked-beef salad ($15), gourmet pizza ($17) and larger mains around $24.

Costa's 282 Cuba St; book Fri & Sat ☎06/356 6383. Evening restaurant with arched windows looking down on the street. The food is inexpensive (mains under $20) and includes nachos, beef satay, pasta, Tex-Mex, Chinese and Thai. Licensed & BYO.

Dejeuner 159 Broadway Ave ☎06/356 1449, Ⓦwww.dejeuner.co.nz. The finest restaurant hereabouts and longstanding city, favourite offering French/Asian fusion cuisine such as fresh tiger prawns ($19) followed by venison on roasted pumpkin ($30). Licensed & BYO; closed Sun.

Diablo's 96 Fitzherbert Ave. Popular bar that's worth visiting late in the week when the party is DJ piloted and always lively, and there's outdoor seating where you can cool off after dancing up a sweat..

George Street Delicatessen 82 George St. The best espresso daytime bar/deli in the city, with sandwiches, quiches, bagels, bargain breakfasts, and mixed platters for two, spring salad, hash browns full of pumpkin and kumera, all for under $20. You can also buy cheeses, other deli goods and wonderful breads at the counter. Licensed & BYO.

Loaded Hog cnr George St & Coleman Mall. A well-managed incarnation of this Kiwi chain with rural Kiwiana on the walls and a range of home-brewed natural ales and good food. Always busy at weekends.

Monsoon Asian Kitchen 200 The Square. Value-for-money Chinese, Malaysian and Singaporean cuisine serving the likes of hot and sour soup ($6) and Indonesian fried chicken ($17). It isn't licensed but they will order drinks for you from the bar across the street.

Mr India 79e George St ☎06/345 5075. Superb, authentic and charismatic restaurant where you always get too much to eat without destroying your bank account. Licensed & BYO.

Roma 51 The Square ☎06/952 5579. Authentic Italian restaurant with a cosy atmosphere, easy-going service and many dishes available as a starter or a main. Dishes include an antipasto plate ($10), ham, pea and mushroom risotto ($9–16) and panfried veal ($26) as well as thin-crust pizza.

Scarfies cnr David St & Main St. A three bar extravaganza, at least one of which has live entertainment Wed–Sat.

Listings

AA (Automobile Association) office 185 Broadway Ave ☎06/357 7039.

Banks and exchange Most banks are within a couple of blocks of The Square; there's also *Thomas Cook*, cnr Broadway Ave & Princes St ☎06/356 4800.

Bookshop Best in the region is Bruce McKenzie Booksellers, 51 George St ☎06/356 9922.

Internet access There are fast machines, good prices and long hours at *i Café*, cnr The Square & Fitzherbert Ave ☎06/353 7899.

Medical treatment Accident and Family Medical Clinic, 27 Linton St ☎06/354 7737 (daily 8am–9pm). Full facilities and a pharmacy on-site.

Post office The main post office is at 338 Church St, right by the visitor centre.

South to the Kapiti Coast

To the south of Palmerston North and the Manawatu, the peaks of the rugged and inhospitable **Tararua Mountains** corral the **Horowhenua** region into a strip along the coast. Renowned for its gentle landscape, lakes, walkways, fruit and vegetable growing, rivers and beaches, the area has a few mildly diverting settlements, but lacks any substantial attractions. The northern towns are popular with retirees, but as you head south you're firmly into the commuter belt, just an hour or so from Wellington. This is the **Kapiti Coast** – named for the island 5km offshore – a narrow coastal plain between the mountains and sweeping beaches that comes peppered by dormitory suburbs and golf courses.

Transport-wise, the coastal towns are served by the main north–south rail link between Auckland and Wellington and the main bus companies, but once you get off your options are limited: it is a region best explored by car.

If you choose to stop, then the best bet is tourist-orientated **Foxton**, with its plethora of museums and an extraordinary long flat beach facing its seaside offshoot of **Foxton Beach**. Workaday **Levin** only really warrants a stop if you're intent on exploring the **Tararua Forest Park** to the east, though this rugged bush country is more easily accessible from **Otaki Forks**, accessible from the small town of **Otaki**.

For waterfowl and a kiwi house visit the Nga Manu Sanctuary at **Waikanae**, but otherwise press on to burgeoning **Paraparaumu**, home to the comestible pleasures of the Lindale Farm Complex, a launching point for trips to the wonderful bush-covered bird sanctuary and marine reserve of **Kapiti Island**, 5km offshore.

Further south, **Paekakariki** offers the adrenalin rush of Fly by Wire, in marked contrast with the more relaxed charms of **Plimmerton** on the shores of Porirua Harbour. **Porirua** itself only warrants a brief stop if you're into the history of law enforcement, then it is just 20km into Wellington.

Foxton

The most interesting little town around these parts is **FOXTON**, 38km southwest of Palmerston North, a place where you step back in time: the town has old-style shop facades, cobblestoned paving and several **museums**, along with some heritage attractions and decorative murals painted on prominent buildings.

Archeological evidence suggests that there was a semi-nomadic **moa-hunter** culture in this area between 1400 and 1650 AD, pre-dating larger tribal settlements. **Europeans** came to the area in the early 1800s and settled at the mouth of the Manawatu River, but struck problems with land purchases and soon retreated to found Foxton. It soon became the **flax-milling** capital of New Zealand, adopting and adapting the techniques perfected by local Maori who had long relied on handmade flax items for their everyday needs. Flax was exported from the small river port for use in woolpacks, binder twine, fibrous plaster lashings, upholsterers' tow and carpet. In an effort to streamline the stripping and weaving processes, mills were constructed alongside swamps and on riverbanks in Manawatu and Horowhenua in the 1880s, and the history of this industry is recounted in the pick of the town's museums, the **Flax Stripper Museum**, Main St (daily 1–3pm; $3). Just behind the museum, a hundred-metre-long strip of riverbanks has been given over to the flaxwalk, a display of sixty-five types of flax, all growing in an unkempt manner. There are no signs to tell you what's what, so you'll need the free explanatory leaflet available from the visitor centre or the museum.

At the north end of Main Street, in Coronation Hall, the **Museum of Audio Visual Arts and Sciences**, Avenue Rd (Tues–Fri 1–3pm Sat & Sun 2–4pm; $4), offers an insight into early broadcasting and home entertainment through its collection of over 14,000 records going back to the early 1890s, assorted gramophones, cameras, projectors, restored Pianola rolls, and vintage radios and televisions. Only museum addicts will want to go for a hat-trick by visiting the **Trolley Bus Museum and Doll Gallery**, 55 Main St (Tues–Sun 11am–4.30pm; $2), with its surreal juxtaposition of a 1953 London Bus and an assortment of ancient and modern dolls, some looking remarkably sinister. Time is better spent cruising on the **MV Corsair** (ⓣ06/363 8897, ⓔrivercruises@e3.net.nz; $10 for 35min), an old boat whose skipper will fill you in on the Maori and European history of the river and the town.

Foxton Beach is 5km away on the coast, where there's a long sandy beach with good surfing, safe swimming areas and abundant birdlife around the Manawatu River estuary. The small community by the beach is full of *baches* for vacationing New Zealanders. The beach stretches 20km north of here making it a perfect spot for sand-yachting, a sport mostly conducted at the settlement of **Himatangi Beach**, 10km north.

Practicalities

Long-distance **buses** stop outside the **visitor centre**, 80–88 Main St (daily 8.30am–5pm; ⓣ06/363 8940), which is located in the old rail and tram station, now also housing a good daytime **café**, and a horse-drawn tram that is hauled out every summer for tourist rides around town (15min; $2). When **food** cravings hit, make for the *Laughing Fox*, easily spotted on SH1 by its odd-looking turret, offering filling snacks, quiches, satay, salads, curries and pastries and lavish cakes.

Levin and around

The main southbound road routes converge 19km south of Foxton at **LEVIN**, the principal community in the Horowhenua region. The town makes a living from clothes manufacturing and horticulture – witness the abundance of **factory shops** flogging discount clothing – and the orchards where **fruit-picking** work can often be had (Nov–May). If neither of these grab you, just take a quick spin around the nearby coast and mountains.

Drivers on SH1 need only take a two-kilometre detour to reach the **Papaitonga Scenic Reserve**, 4km south of Levin, for a gentle boardwalk stroll to the Papaitonga Lookout (20min return) and great **views** of Lake Papaitonga and the surrounding wetlands, which provide a refuge for many **rare birds**, including the spotless crake, Australasian bittern, and New Zealand dabchick. It's a further ten-minute walk to the Otomuiri Lookout, though the views are no better.

It takes considerably more commitment to tackle the near impenetrable barrier of the Tararua Range immediately east of Levin, specifically the hikes within the rugged **Tararua Forest Park**. The tracks are narrow, poorly marked and subject to fog, high winds and snow funnelled from the Cook Strait, and the huts are basic, but if you're still keen, consider one of the shorter walks such as the **Mount Thompson Track** (2–4hr). This ascends one of the smaller peaks in the range, but nonetheless offers good views of the coast and Kapiti Island. The walk begins around 100m past the Panatewaewae car park on North Manakau Road, a side road off SH1 some 10km south of Levin.

Alternatively, engage the services of Back to Basics Guided Walks (ⓣ06/368 6306), who offer guided **tailored hikes** ($50–95 a day), also passing on esoteric bush skills – the subtle art of navigation without benefit of a map or compass.

Practicalities

Auckland–Wellington **trains** stop on SH1 in the centre of town, and **buses** pull into the Levin Mall car park. The **visitor centre**, 93 Oxford St (Mon–Fri 9am–5.30pm, Sat & Sun 10am–3pm), is five minutes' walk from both the station and the bus stop.

Fantails B&B, 40 MacArthur St (ⓣ06/368 9011, ⓦwww.fantails.co.nz; ❺), provide excellent, well-appointed **rooms** in a verdant setting, or for something cheaper try *Mountain View Motel*, The Avenue (ⓣ06/368 5214, ⓕ368 4091; ❹), where most units have cooking facilities.

The best **place to eat** in Levin is *Italian Flame*, 104 Oxford St (closed Sun; licensed), where you can enjoy a relaxed, authentic and very filling Italian dinner without breaking the bank. The café attached to *Fantails* (see above) is also good set in pretty tree-filled gardens and has a variety of snacks, light meals and excellent ice cream, and you can grab a reasonable coffee at *The Café Club*, 7 Bath St.

Otaki and around

OTAKI, 20km south of Levin, marks the northern gateway to the Kapiti Coast, and sits beside a broad, braided section of the Otaki River, in a rich fruit-growing area. For most of the year, this is a quiet place with a strong Maori heritage but, like other towns along this coast, it changes beyond recognition during the high-summer months of December to March, when its population of 4500 swells by a further 2000 or so mainly Kiwi tourists – and that increase mostly in just the Christmas to January period.

The smattering of services along the highway is only the outskirts of Otaki proper, which is 2km towards the sea along Mill Road. Here, Te Rauparaha Street leads for 200m to the barren plot of land which, until a devastating fire in 1995, was the site of the 1849 **Rangiatea Church**, the finest Maori church in New Zealand. All that's left is the graveyard, and across the street, a monument to the Maori chief Te Rauparaha who is though to be buried on Kapiti Island.

A further 2.5km along Mill Road brings you to the long gently curving, dune-backed **Otaki Beach**, which is rendered safe for swimming in summer by the presence of a surf patrol.

Otaki Gorge and Otaki Forks

A kilometre south of the town, the scenic and partly unsealed **Otaki Gorge Road** branches off SH1 and threads 19km into the hills along the picturesque gorge of the Otaki River to **Otaki Forks**, the main western entrance to the **Tararua Forest Park**.

Most of the forest park is accessible only to serious trampers, though there are a few shorter and less intimidating **walks** from a series of three parking areas, all close to each other at the end of Otaki Gorge Road. First up is the **Boielle Flat** picnic area, immediately followed by **Gibbons Flat**, where a resident ranger provides assistance and information, and keeps an intentions book. Nearby, crossing a swing bridge over the river and walking 200m brings you to Parawai Lodge, a **trampers' hut** where those with a sleeping bag and cooking equipment can stay ($5). Half a kilometre up the road from Gibbons Flat there's a basic **campsite** ($5), and there's another 1.5km further on at the road end.

Armed with the free *Otaki Forks* leaflet (available from area visitor centres) you can explore the region and its remains of old boilers, stone walls, and remnants of abandoned logging and farming endeavours that are gradually being engulfed by regenerating bush. One good bet is the **Fenceline Walk** (3km; 2hr), which offers excellent views of the river flowing down the valley to the coast.

Otaki practicalities

There's a **train station** in the centre of town, two minutes' walk away from the **visitor centre**, at the corner of SH1 and Mill Rd (Mon–Fri 8.30am–5pm, Sat & Sun 9am–4pm, with extended hours in summer; ⓣ06/364 7620, ⓔkapiti.info@clear.net.nz), where **buses** stop. The visitor centre has free town maps and sells **hut passes** for tracks in the Tararua Forest.

It is just five minutes' walk across the rail tracks to pleasant backpacker **accommodation** at *Otaki Oasis*, 33 Rahui St (ⓣ06/364 6860, ⓔoobackpackers@xtra.co.nz; dorms ❶, rooms ❷) set on an orchard with free range eggs and animals to feed. Out at Otaki Beach try the simple but well kept *Otaki Beach Motor Camp*, 40 Moana St (ⓣ06/364 7107, ⓕ364 8123; camping $9, cabins & on-site vans ❷), just one block back from the beach, or *Byron's Resort*, 20 Tasman Rd (ⓣ06/364 8121 & 0800/800 122, ⓦwww.byronsresort.co.nz; camping $11, tourist flats ❸, motel units ❹, beachside cottage ❺), a multi-faceted complex with a restaurant, bar, spa and swimming pool

Eating in Otaki is best done at *Brown Sugar*, on SH1 at the southern outskirts of town, just over the Otaki River bridge (daily 9am–5pm). Probably the best little **café** on the Kapiti Coast, it serves the likes of veg somosa or feta, sun-dried tomato and olive salad on focaccia, along with delicious cakes and great coffee, either inside or in a leafy garden. Otherwise try the **restaurant** at *Byron's Resort* (see above), which offers good-quality dinners at moderate prices, plus daytime snacks and light meals.

Waikanae

WAIKANAE, 10km south of Otaki, is divided between the highwayside settlement and a beach community, 4km away along Te Moana Road where the broad, dune-backed **beach** has safe swimming.

The only reason to stop is the **Nga Manu Nature Reserve**, a large man-made bird sanctuary (daily 10am–5pm; $7.50), with easy walking tracks and some picnic spots. A circular track (1.5km) cuts through a variety of habitats, from ponds and scrubland to swamp and coastal forest, which attract all manner of birds. There is also a nocturnal house containing kiwi, morepork and tuatara, plus eels which are fed at 2pm daily. To get here, follow Te Moana Road off SH1 for just over a kilometre and turn right at Ngarara Road; the sanctuary is a further 3km.

About 3km south of Waikanae, the **Southward Car Museum**, Otaihanga Road (daily 9am–4.30pm; $5), presents a stunningly comprehensive collection of veteran and vintage cars, kept in mint condition and displayed in rotation in a specially built showroom, each accompanied by a detailed history. Gems include Marlene Dietrich's Rolls-Royce, a 1915 Stutz Racer, a gull-winged Mercedes Benz and a Chicago gangster's armour-plated Cadillac.

The library in Mahara Place shopping centre contains the **visitor centre**

(Mon–Fri 9.30am–3pm, Sat 9am–noon; ⓣ04/293 3278). The Kapiti Coast's main **DOC office** is also here, at 10 Parata St, one street west of the main highway (ⓣ04/296 1112, ⓕ296 1115; Mon–Fri 8am–12.30pm & 1–4.30pm), and can advise on Kapiti Island permits but does not sell them.

Paraparaumu and around

PARAPARAUMU, 7km south of Waikanae, is the Kapiti Coast's largest settlement and the only jumping-off point to Kapiti Island (see overleaf). Though 45km short of Wellington it is a burgeoning dormitory community, with commuters lured here by the proximity of the long and sandy **Paraparaumu Beach**, 3km to the west along Kapiti Road, which is safe for swimming and looks directly out onto Kapiti Island.

There's precious little land-based interest in town, though tour buses all flock to the touristy **Lindale Farm Complex**, 2km north on SH1 (daily 9am-5pm; free), where you can sample the excellent cheese and ice-cream at **Kapiti Cheeses**, both among New Zealand's finest, which are made in the complex and sold in a small shop. Its success has attracted a number of other shops - wood-turning, honey, olive products and so on - and there is now a kind of petting zoo (farm walk $5) and an excellent well-priced **café**, *The Farm Kitchen*, (daily 7am–5pm), offering hearty snacks, light lunches and great cakes and coffee.

Those with a sweet tooth might prefer the **Nyco Chocolate Factory**, at the corner of SH1 and Raumati Rd, 1km south of Paraparaumu (daily 9am–5pm), which produces 90,000 chocolates daily and sells them through a shop stuffed with goodies. A short guided tour (by appointment on ⓣ04/299 8098; $1) lets you see work in action.

Practicalities

The **visitor centre**, SH1 by the Coastlands shopping centre (Mon–Sat 9am-4pm, Sun 10am-3pm; ⓣ & ⓕ04/298 8195, ⓔkapiti.info@clear.net.nz), has local and DOC information. InterCity and Newmans' **buses** drop off at the **train station** opposite, as do local services from Wellington. There are few genuinely tempting **places to stay**, though *Barnacles Seaside Inn*, 3 Marine Parade, Paraparaumu Beach (ⓣ04/902 5856, ⓔlin&lois@xtra.co.nz; singles ❶, doubles ❷), is a comfortable enough place, with backpacker accommodation in twin rooms. There's more luxury at the beachside motel *Wrights by the Sea*, 387 Kapiti Rd (ⓣ04/902 7600, ⓔwrights@paradise.net.nz; ❹), while one of the newer of the motels in the main town is *Lindale Lodge*, on SH1, 2km north of Coastlands (ⓣ04/298 7933, ⓔlindale_lodge@xtra.co.nz; ❺). Just north of town, off SH1, is the *Lindale Motor Park* (ⓣ & ⓕ04/298 8046; camping $9, cabins ❷, kitchen cabins ❸).

Apart from *The Farm Kitchen* at Kapiti Cheeses (see above), **eating** is best done at Paraparaumu Beach where the intimate *Brier Patch*, 9 Maclean St (ⓣ04/902 5586; book ahead Thurs–Sat evenings; BYO & licensed), specializes in superb, moderately priced Creole and Cajun food for lunch (Wed–Fri), dinner (daily from 6pm) and weekend brunch (10am–3pm); there's a separate bar for casual drinking, coffee and desserts. Otherwise settle for the cheap and cheerful *Fagins Eatery*, in the *Copperfield Motel* complex, 7–13 Seaview Rd, a cosy BYO restaurant that dishes up traditional roast beef and Yorkshire pudding. They also do an all-day breakfast for $10, and snacks along the lines of savoury pancakes with brie, avocado and bacon.

Kapiti Island

One of the few easily accessible island **nature reserves** in New Zealand, the 10km-long by 2km-wide **Kapiti Island** is a magical spot, its bush, once cleared for farmland, now home to birdlife that has become rare or extinct on the mainland. In 1822, infamous Maori chief **Te Rauparaha** captured the island from its first known Maori inhabitants and, with his people the Ngati Toa, used it as a base until his death in 1849: it's thought that he may be buried somewhere on the island, but the site of his grave is unknown. For this, and other reasons, the island is considered extremely spiritual to Maori, and was designated a reserve in 1897.

Late January and February are the best months to visit, when the **birdlife** is at its most active, but at any time of the year you're likely to see kaka (bush parrots that may alight on your head or shoulder), weka, kakariki (parakeets), whiteheads (bush canaries), tui, bellbirds, fantails, wood pigeons, robins and a handful of the 200 takahe that exist in the world. The island can be explored on three **walking tracks**, two of them linking up to lead to the island's highest point (521m), which gives spectacular views, though the best variety of birdlife is found along the lower parts of the tracks - take your time, keep quiet and stop frequently (allow about 3hr for the round-trip). Most visitors only have time to go to the top and back, most easily achieved by ascending **Trig Track** and returning along the steeper, and sometimes slippery, **Wilkinson Track**. The third option (2–3hr), **North Track**, follows the coast to the island's northern end, climbing quite steeply in places to about fifty metres above sea level and leading to a lagoon thronged with waterfowl such as royal spoonbills.

The exceptionally clear waters of the marine reserve make for great **snorkelling** around the rocks close to the shore and **scuba diving** (see below for dive operators), particularly to the west and north of the island, where there are some interesting formations such as a rock archway known as the Hole-in-the-Wall. Three types of habitat – a boulder bottom, sheltered reef and sand bottom – are home to a rich variety of marine life, including orange and yellow sponges (some very rare), and luxuriant seaweed beds feeding kina and paua. Visiting ocean fish like moki and kingfish are common, and occasionally you'll see rare and subtropical fish.

Practicalities

DOC manage the island but allow limited numbers of visitors on **day-trips** (daily except Christmas Day & New Year's Day). Obligatory **landing permits** ($9 per person, valid for 6 months in case weather prevents a crossing) limit visitation to fifty a day: **book** a few days in advance but note that weekends from December to March are filled three months ahead. This can be done either through DOC in Wellington (see p.494), the Paraparaumu visitor centre or directly with the two **launch operators**: Kapiti Marine Charter (Ⓣ04/297 2585 & 0800/433779), or Kapiti Tours (Ⓣ0800/527484, Ⓦwww.kapititours.co.nz); both trips depart from Paraparaumu Beach at 9am and return around 3.30pm, charging $30 return per person for the ten- to fifteen-minute trip. DOC are so sensitive about the reintroduction of pests that they insist your bags are checked before leaving for the island. On arrival, you are greeted by the ranger, who will explain what there is to do and see on the island; a copy of the informative DOC booklet, *Kapiti Island Nature Reserve* (usually $2), is included in the price of the landing permit. There will also be someone leading a **guided walk** (1hr; $10), which focuses on cultural and history.

PADI-qualified **divers** can arrange a full-day trip with New Zealand Sea

Adventures, 65 Omapere St, Wellington (Ⓣ04/236 8787; full day $80), who can supply gear and transport. The island has a single toilet at the landing point, and if you take a picnic lunch be sure to bring back all the rubbish.

Paekakariki

There'd be no reason to stop in **Paekakariki**, 10km south of Paraparaumu, were it not for a good backpacker hostel and the **Fly by Wire**, SH1 (Ⓣ0800/359299, Ⓕ03/442 2116, Ⓦwww.flybywire.co.nz), hidden away in a narrow valley just five minutes' walk off the main road. Here, wires strung across this grassy bowl create an anchor point from which a one-person, propeller-driven plane is suspended. Part with $99 and you'll be strapped in and hoisted up ready for a six-minute blast, swooping round on the end of the 55-metre cable with you (hopefully) in control as you alternate between weightlessness at the top of an arc to a maximum of 3G in descent.

If you want to **stay** here, visit *Paekakariki Backpackers*, 11 Wellington Rd (Ⓣ04/902 5967, Ⓔpaekakbackpack@paradise.net.nz; tents $10, dorms ❶, rooms ❷), a lovely, peaceful spot with ocean views but close to the train station for trips into Wellington. Wood floors and tasteful decor set the tone in the share-rooms and in the two en-suite rooms in the house as well as the separate cabin located beside the new barbecue area.

Plimmerton and Porirua

South of Paekakariki the highway cuts inland for a few kilometres and rejoins the sea at **PLIMMERTON**, which hugs the shores at the mouth of the double-armed Porirua Harbour. Beautifully set and with a peaceful character it may lure you into just resting up a while, though with a good train service and even late-night buses at weekends it makes a decent base for the capital. There's more bustle 7km south at the rapidly growing settlement of **PORIRUA,** booming on account of its proximity to Wellington just over the hills to the southeast. For the passing visitor there are few reasons to stop, though **Titahi Bay**, 4km off SH1 along Titahi Bay Road, is a great little surfing beach.

In central Porirua the **Pataka Porirua Museum of Arts and Cultures** (Mon–Sat 10am–5pm, Sun 11am–4.30pm; free), at the corner of Norrie and Parumoana streets, shows local works, plus exhibitions by leading contemporary New Zealand artists, and hosts regular Maori and Pacific Island dance performances. You can watch them practise in the dance rehearsal rooms if you ask first.

More of a curiosity, the **New Zealand Police Museum** (Wed–Sun 10am–4pm; Ⓣ04/238 3141, Ⓔmuseum@police.govt.nz; $5), signposted from the Papakowhai exit off SH1, 1km north of Porirua, details New Zealand police history, with particular emphasis on the sinking of the *Rainbow Warrior* (see box on p.965) and the 1981 Springbok Tour (see p.965). See the *Rainbow Warrior*'s engine-room clock, stopped at the moment the blast ripped through the hull, and a mounted Springbok head given by the rugby team to the New Zealand Police to thank them for their efforts in policing the tour. Bus #30 leaves Porirua station on the half hour for the museum or walk it in half an hour.

For a change of pace, tackle the moderately hard **Colonial Knob Walkway** (7.5km loop; 3–4hr), a track across forested hills to the west of Porirua reaching the 468-metre Colonial Knob, the highest point within the Wellington urban area, from where there are amazing **views** of Mana and Kapiti islands, Mount Taranaki to the north, and south as far as the Kaikoura Ranges. This and many other local walks are detailed in the free *Walking Tracks in Porirua* leaflet.

Practicalities

TranzMetro trains and local buses between Wellington and the Kapiti Coast stop at the combined bus and train station, a few minutes walk from Porirua's **visitor centre**, 8 Cobham Court (Mon–Sat 9am–5pm, Sun 11–3pm; ⓣ04/237 8088, ⓔporiruainfo@visitorshop.co.nz), which acts as an agent for buses, trains and ferries, and can help you find somewhere to stay that's near the capital but out of the hubbub.

For the budget-conscious, the best **accommodation** bet is the wonderful *Moana Lodge*, 49 Moana Rd, Plimmerton (ⓣ04/233 2010, ⓔmoanalodge@clear.net.nz; dorms ❶, rooms ❷), nicely located on the shoreline with some rooms offering views out to Mana Island. Clean, immaculately kept and with all bedding and towels supplied, it is a cut above most, and offers free kayak and mountain-bike usage, as well as stacks of local advice from the enthusiastic hosts. They're happy to put you in touch with local operators offering windsurfing, rock climbing, diving, visits to the local *marae*, and even out to the offshore bird sanctuary of Mana Island.

For something more upmarket, try the relaxing *Braebyre B&B*, Flightys Road, Pauatahanui, north of Porirua (ⓣ0800/369311 & 04/235 9311, ⓔbraebyre@paradise.net.nz; ❺–❻), a rural homestay in a big modern house set amid rolling hills and with a small mohair-goat farm in the grounds. A private guest wing has five mostly en-suite rooms along with a log fire and indoor spa, and great dinners on request ($40).

Travel Details

Trains

A single train line (with one daytime and one overnight service) runs south from Auckland to Wellington through Hamilton, Te Awamutu, Otorohanga, Te Kuiti, Taumarunui, National Park, Ohakune, Palmerston North, Levin and Paraparaumu. Frequent commuter services run from Wellington as far as Paraparaumu.

From Hamilton to: Auckland (2 daily; 2hr); Ohakune (2 daily; 3hr 40min); Otorohanga (2 daily; 40min); Palmerston North (2 daily; 6hr 40min); Te Awamutu (1 daily; 20min); Wellington (2 daily; 8hr 40min).

From Levin to: Paraparaumu (2 daily; 40min); Wellington (2 daily; 1hr 30min).

From Otorohanga to: National Park (2 daily; 1hr 40min); Palmerston North (2 daily 6hr).

From Palmerston North to: Auckland (2 daily; 8–9hr); Hamilton (2 daily; 6hr 40min); Wellington (2 daily; 2hr).

From Paraparaumu to: Paekakariki (half-hourly or more; 8min); Plimmerton (half-hourly or more; 25min); Porirua (half-hourly or more; 35min); Wellington (half-hourly or more; 50min–1hr).

From Taumarunui to: Hamilton (2 daily; 2hr 20min); Palmerston North (2 daily; 4hr 20min); Wellington (2 daily; 6hr 15min).

Buses

From Cambridge to: Auckland (4 daily; 3hr); Hamilton (7 daily; 20min).

From Hamilton to: Auckland (14–16 daily; 2hr); Cambridge (7 daily; 20min); Ngaruawahia (11 daily; 15min); New Plymouth (3 daily; 4hr 20min); Otorohanga (4 daily; 45min); Paeroa (1 daily; 1hr 30min); Raglan (4 daily; 45min); Te Aroha (1 daily; 1hr 10min); Te Awamutu (5 daily; 30min); Te Kuiti (5 daily; 1hr 20min); Rotorua (8 daily; 1hr 45min); Taupo (3 daily; 2hr 30min); Tauranga (1–2 daily; 2hr); Thames (3 daily; 1hr 50min); Wanganui (2 daily; 6–8hr), Wellington (4 daily; 9hr).

From Otorohanga to: Hamilton (4 daily; 45min); Te Kuiti (4 daily; 25min); Waitomo (6 daily; 30min).

From New Plymouth to: Auckland (3 daily; 6–7hr); Hamilton (3 daily 4hr 20min); Te Kuiti (3 daily; 2hr 40min); Wanganui (1 daily; 3hr); Wellington (3 daily; 6hr 45min).

From Palmerston North to: Auckland (4 daily; 9hr); Hastings (4 daily; 3hr); Levin (6 daily; 45min); Masterton (4 daily; 1hr 35min); Paraparaumu (6 daily; 1hr 15min); Rotorua (2 daily; 5hr 30min); Taupo (3 daily 3hr 30min); Wanganui (3 daily; 1hr 5min); Wellington (6 daily; 2hr).

From Taumarunui to: Te Kuiti (1 daily; 1hr);

Wanganui (1 daily; 3hr).
From Te Awamutu to: Hamilton (5 daily; 30min); Kawhia (Mon–Sat 1; 1hr 30min); Otorohanga (5 daily; 25min).
From Te Kuiti to: New Plymouth (3 daily; 2hr 40min); Taumarunui (1 daily; 1hr).
From Wanganui to: Hamilton (2 daily; 6–8hr); New Plymouth (1 daily; 3hr); Palmerston North (3 daily; 1hr 5min); Taumarunui (1 daily; 3hr).
From Waitomo to: Auckland (3 daily; 3hr 15min); Rotorua (2 daily; 2hr–2hr 30min).

Flights

From Hamilton to: Auckland (3 daily; 30min); Nelson (1 daily; 1hr 15min); Palmerston North (1–2 daily; 1hr); Wellington (8 daily; 50min).
From New Plymouth to: Auckland (5–7 daily; 50min); Nelson (1 daily; 1hr); Wellington (5 daily; 55min).
From Palmerston North to: Auckland (5–8 daily; 1hr 10min); Christchurch (4–6 daily; 1hr 25min); Hamilton (1–2 daily; 1hr); Nelson (1 daily; 50min); Wellington (6 daily; 35min).
From Wanganui to: Auckland (2–3 daily; 1hr).

4

Central North Island

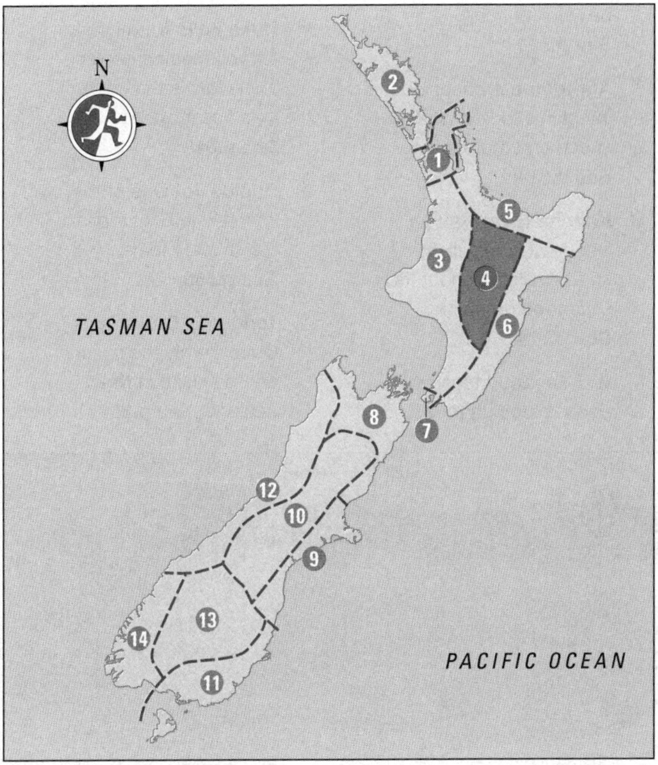
N
TASMAN SEA
PACIFIC OCEAN
1
2
3
4
5
6
7
8
9
10
11
12
13
14

CHAPTER 4

Highlights

* **Polynesian Spa** Bathe in outdoor mineral pools or opt for the landscaped luxury of the massage and spa section. See p.319

* **Maori cultural performance** Chants, dance, songs, humour and a belly full of *hangi*. See p.321

* **Agrodome** A cheesy but infectious look at sheep, sheep and more sheep. See p.324

* **Kaituna River** Raft (or sledge) this excellent short river and shoot its seven-metre fall. See p.324

* **Wai-O-Tapu** Iridescent pools, glooping mud and a performing geyser make this the best of Rotorua's thermal areas. See p.336

* **Lake Taupo** Cruise it, haul trout out of it, or approach while high speed skydiving. See p.340

* **Huka Falls** Not high, but for volume and power alone this is the country's finest waterfall. See p.348

* **Rapids Jet** One of the very few jetboat trips to tackle real rapids. See p.350

* **Tongariro Crossing** Quite simply the finest one-day hike in New Zealand. See p.361

4

Central North Island

The landlocked **Central North Island** contains more than its fair share of New Zealand's star attractions. The area is delineated by three defining geological features: Lake Taupo, the country's largest; Tongariro National Park, with its trio of active volcanoes; and the volcanic field that feeds colourful and fiercely active thermal areas, principally around the Arawa heartland of **Rotorua**. If you are ticking off Kiwi icons, then time is well spent around Rotorua, where boiling mud pools plop next to spouting geysers fuelled by superheated water, which is drawn off to fill the hot pools found all over town. To complete this quintessential New Zealand experience, here you'll also find the most accessible expression of Maori culture, with highly regarded Arawa carvings and any number of groups ready to perform traditional dances and *haka*, and feed you with fall-off-the-bone meat cooked in a *hangi* steam oven.

The dramatic volcanic scenery is all the more striking for its contrast with the encroaching pines of the **Kaingaroa Forest**, one of the world's largest plantation forests, with serried ranks of fast-growing conifers marching to the horizon. When the country was being carved up for farming, the central North Island was all but abandoned as cattle grazed here soon contracted "bush sickness" and died. In the 1930s, scientists discovered that the disease was caused by an easily rectified deficiency of the mineral cobalt, but by this stage the free-draining pumice soils had already been planted with millions of radiata (Monterrey) pine seedlings by gangs of convicts and Great Depression relief workers. Since then, sylviculture has continued to consolidate its position as the region's chief earner through pulp and paper mills at Kinleith, near Tokoroa, and Kawerau.

The rest of the region is loosely referred to as the **Volcanic Plateau**, a sometimes-bleak high country that is overlaid with a layer of rock and ash expelled two thousand years back when a huge volcano blew itself apart, the resultant crater being filled by **Lake Taupo**. This serene lake, and the streams and rivers feeding it, have since become a fishing mecca for anglers keen to snag brown and rainbow trout, but the area is no less appealing for the lure of its watersports and the thundering rapids of the Waikato River, which drains the lake. South of Lake Taupo rise the three majestic volcanoes of **Tongariro National Park**, created in 1887, since when it has become a winter playground for North Island skiers and a summer destination for trampers intent on bagging a couple of magical walks.

If you're hot-footing it to this region from Auckland, you've got a choice of **routes**: the direct SH1 through Hamilton; or the faster, less congested and broadly more appealing journey along SH2, which branches east at Pokeno,

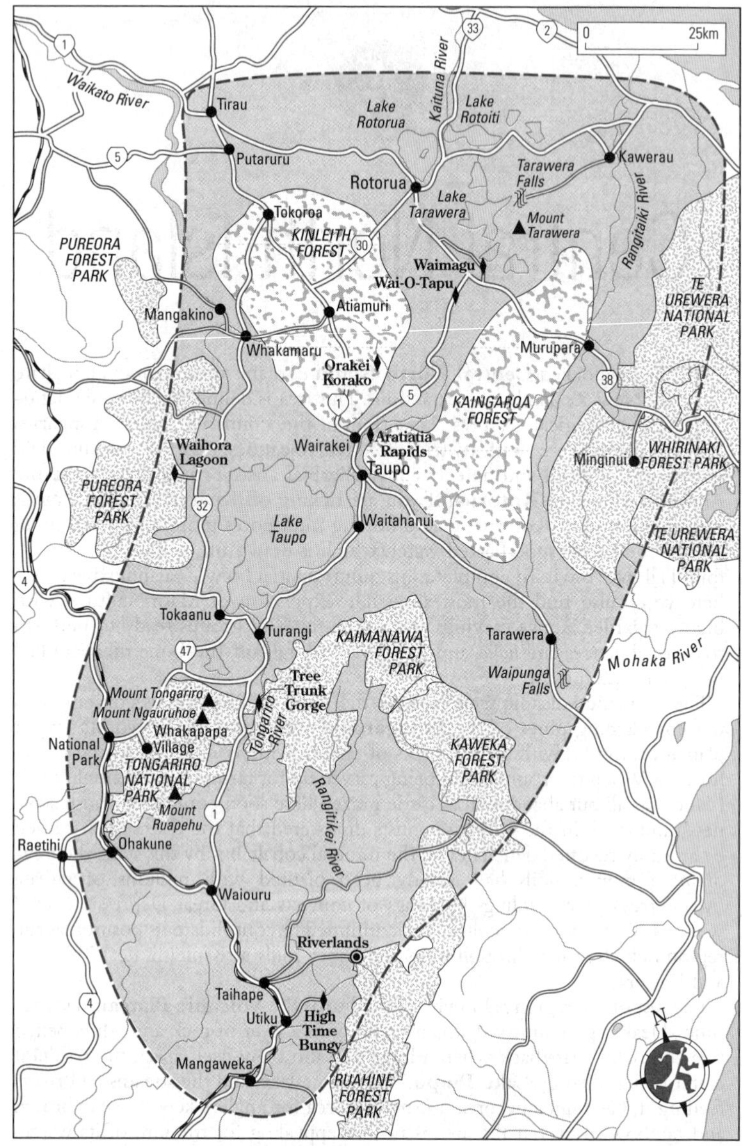

50km south of Auckland, then along SH27 as it cuts south across the fringes of the Hauraki Plains. The two routes converge on the small town of Tirau, where SH1 heads almost 100km south to Taupo and SH5 crosses the Mamaku Plateau to Rotorua, 52km away to the east.

Climate wise, the altitude of the Volcanic Plateau lends Taupo, the Tongariro National Park and environs a refreshing crispness even in high summer, when it is a welcome retreat from the stickiness of Auckland and the north. Spring and autumn are tolerably warm and have the added advantage of freedom from the summer hordes, though the often freezing winter months from May to October are best left to winter-sports enthusiasts. The Rotorua area is more balmy on the whole, but can still be cool in winter, making the thermal areas steamier and the hot baths all the more appealing.

Rotorua and around

There is little doubt that the "Sulphur City" of **Rotorua** is New Zealand's tourist destination par excellence. For this is one of the world's most concentrated and accessible geothermal areas, where twenty-metre geysers spout among kaleidoscopic mineral pools, steam wafts over cauldrons of boiling mud and terraces of encrusted silicates drip like stalactites. Everywhere you look there's evidence of vulcanism: birds on the lakeshore are relieved of the chore of nest-sitting by the warmth of the ground; graves in Ohinemutu and Whakarewarewa churchyards have to be built topside, as digging the ground is likely to unearth a hot spring; and hotels are equipped with geothermally-fed hot tubs, perfect for easing your bones after a hard day's sightseeing. Throughout the region, sulphur and heat combine to form barren landscapes where only the hardiest of plants brave the trickling hot streams, sputtering vents and seething fumaroles. Plant life may be absent, but there is no shortage of colour from iridescent mineral deposits lining the pools: bright oranges juxtaposed with emerald greens and rust reds. The underworld looms large in Rotorua's lexicon: there is no end of "The Devil's" this and "Hell's" that, a state of affairs that prompted George Bernard Shaw to ruminate on his colourful past while visiting the Hell's Gate thermal area and famously quip, "It reminds me too vividly of the fate theologians have promised me".

But hydrothermal activity is only part of Rotorua's appeal. The naturally hot water lured **Maori** to settle around Lake Rotorua and Lake Tarawera, using the hottest pools for cooking, bathing in cooler ones and building their *whare* (houses) on the hot ground to drive away the winter chill. Here they managed to hang on to their traditions and tribal integrity more than almost anywhere else in the country, forging a strong and vibrant culture that is part of the daily life of a third of the region's people. Despite the inevitably diluting effects of tourism, there is no better place to get an introduction to Maori values and traditions, dance and song than at one of the concert and *hangi* evenings held all over Rotorua and on nearby *marae*.

Maori-owned and operated tour companies often make the most educational, not to say entertaining, ways of exploring Rotorua's surrounding area. To the south and east, the forests are punctuated by two dozen **lakes** tucked into bush-girt hollows and overlooked by the mountainous products of ancient volcanic activity and its more recent manifestation, the shattered five-kilometre-long chasm of **Mount Tarawera**. During one cataclysmic night of eruptions in 1886 this chain of volcanoes split in two, destroying the region's first tourist attraction, the Pink and White Terraces, entombing the nearest settlement, the so-called **Buried Village**, and creating the **Waimangu Thermal Valley**. Waimangu is just one of four magnificent thermal areas open to the public; the Pohutu Geyser at **Whakarewarewa**, on the outskirts of Rotorua, and the Lady Knox Geyser at **Wai-O-Tapu**, to the south of Waimangu, also demand particular attention.

Some history

The Rotorua region is home to the Arawa people, who trace their ancestry back to the **Arawa canoe** which struck land at Maketu, at the mouth of the Kaituna River on the Bay of Plenty, after its long journey from the Polynesian homelands of Hawaiki sometime in the fourteenth century. The leader of one of the first parties to explore the interior was the *tohunga* (priest), **Ngatoroirangi**, who made it as far as the freezing summit of Mount Tongariro, where he feared he might die from cold. His prayers to the gods of Hawaiki were answered with fire, which journeyed underground, first surfacing at the volcanic White Island in the Bay of Plenty, then at several more points in a line between there and the three central North Island volcanoes. Ngatoroirangi was saved, and he and his followers established themselves around Lake Rotorua, where they lived contentedly until another Arawa sailor, the wily **Ihenga**, duped Ngatoroirangi out of his title to the land. The victor named the lakes as he reached them along the Kaituna River: Lake Rotoiti ("small lake") and Lake Rotorua ("second lake").

In revenge for an earlier raid on an island in nearby Green Lake, the Northland Ngapuhi chief, **Hongi Hika**, led a war party here in 1823. The Arawa got wind of the attack and retreated to the sanctuary of Mokoia Island, in the middle of Lake Rotorua; undaunted, Hongi Hika and his warriors carried their canoes overland between lakes (the track between Lake Rotoiti and Lake Rotoehu still bears the name Hongi's Track). The Ngapuhi, equipped with muskets traded with Europeans in the Bay of Islands, defeated the traditionally armed Arawa then withdrew, leaving the Arawa to regroup in time for the New Zealand Wars of the 1860s, in which the Arawa supported the government. This worked in their favour when, in 1870, **Te Kooti** (see box on p.456) attacked from the east coast, and the colonial troops helped turn them back.

By this time a few **Europeans** – notably a Danish trader Philip Hans Tapsell and the missionary Thomas Chapman – had already lived for some years in the Maori villages of Ohinemutu and Whakarewarewa, but it wasn't until Te Kooti had been dispatched that Rotorua came into existence. **Tourists** began to arrive in the district to view the **Pink and White Terraces** using Ohinemutu, Whakarewarewa and Te Wairoa as staging posts. The Arawa, who up to this point had been relatively isolated from European influence, were quick to grasp the possibilities of tourism and helped turn Rotorua into what it is today.

Rotorua

You smell **Rotorua** long before you see it. Hydrogen sulphide drifting up from natural vents in the region's thin crust means that the whiff of rotten eggs lingers in the air, but after a few hours you barely notice the smell. No amount of bad odour, however, will keep visitors away from this small, ordered place clinging to the southern shores of the near-circular **Lake Rotorua**. Rotorua's northern and southern limits are defined by the two ancient villages of the

Arawa sub-tribe, Ngati Whakaue. The lakeshore **Ohinemutu** and the inland **Whakarewarewa** were the only settlements before the 1880s, when Rotorua became New Zealand's only city with its origins firmly rooted in tourism. Specifically, Rotorua was set up as a **spa town** on land leased from the Ngati Whakaue, under the auspices of the 1881 Thermal Springs Districts Act. By 1885, the fledgling Rotorua boasted the Government Sanatorium Complex, a spa designed to administer the rigorous treatments deemed beneficial to the "invalids" who came to take the waters. The original **Bath House** and recreational **Blue Baths**, both set amid the oh-so-English **Government Gardens**, are now part of the **Rotorua Museum** which successfully puts these early enterprises into context.

Arrival and information

InterCity and Newmans **buses** pull up outside Tourism Rotorua (see below), as do Guthreys (ⓣ0800/759 999), who run here from Auckland via Hamilton. Air New Zealand **flights** from Auckland, Wellington and Christchurch land 8km northeast of town at the lakeside airport (ⓣ07/345 6175). The door-to-door Super Shuttle (ⓣ07/349 3444) charges $10 for the first passenger and $2 for each extra to the same place, and **taxis** (see Listings, p.329) run into town for around $15.

For **information**, Tourism Rotorua, at 1167 Fenton St, contains a foreign exchange counter and an efficient but often busy visitor centre (daily: Nov–Easter 8am–6pm, Easter–Oct 8.30am–5.30pm; ⓣ07/348 5179, ⓦwww.rotoruanz.co.nz) that has two sections: one dealing with local tourism, the other with New Zealand-wide travel and ticketing. For DOC bookings, track hut tickets, countrywide maps and lots of local outdoorsy information visit The Map Shop & Track, 1225 Fenton St (daily 9am–6pm; ⓣ &ⓕ07/349 1845, ⓦwww.maptracknz.com).

For a general round up of what's happening around town, pick up the free weekly *Thermal Air Visitor's Guide*, and if there are two of you spending a few days sightseeing around Rotorua, you can make good savings by buying the **Rotorua Good Time Card** ($25), which gives two-for-the-price-of-one deals on many of the sights and activities around town, plus discounts on movie tickets and even meals.

Note that Central Rotorua **addresses** are subject to a block-based numbering system that increases south and west from the corner of Whakaue and Hinemaru streets near the lake, starting with the 1000 block. Confusingly, outlying areas haven't been numbered in the same way, so some streets – such as Fenton Street – increase from 1000 to around 1600 then start again at about 200.

City transport

Richies Coachlines (ⓣ07/345 5694) provide the most basic level of urban **bus** transport, centred on Pukuatua Street between Tutanekai and Fenton streets. Buses leave daily for Ngongotaha, passing Rainbow Springs and Whakarewarewa (roughly every 90min), and costing $2.20 each way or $7 for an all-day pass.

The "Magic of the Maori" **sightseeing shuttle** (ⓣ0800/021 987, ⓦwww.maorimagic.com; daily 9am–5pm) is generally more convenient, completing a circuit of Whakarewarewa, the Polynesian Spa, Rainbow Springs, Skyline Skyrides, the Agrodome and the visitor centre every hour and a half or so. Day passes ($12) are available, as well as section fares ($4 to Whakarewarewa, $5 to the Agrodome). There are also any number of **tours**, most geared towards the more distant sights (see "Around Rotorua", p.329).

The points visited by the sightseeing shuttle are mostly within 7km of central Rotorua and there are no substantial hills, so **cycling** is a viable way to go; **car-rental** rates are also fairly competitive here (see "Listings", p.329, for details of bike- and car-rental outlets).

Accommodation

Rotorua's accommodation has one big advantage: no matter how low your budget, you can stay somewhere with a **hot pool**, and for a little more you might even get a private tub in your room. In fact there is barely a place in town without a hot pool – the best of them directly fed with mineral water, but most are now artificially heated.

The range is wide, including a clutch of quality **hostels**, all close to the city centre, all eager to advise on local activities and many offering small discounts on trips and tours. There must be more **motels** in Rotorua than just about anywhere else in the country, most of them lining Fenton Street, which runs south towards Whakarewarewa. Competition is fierce and at off-peak times you may well get rock bottom prices, but it is a busy road and you might find it quieter in motels tucked away down side roads. **B&Bs** and **guesthouses** come liberally scattered around Rotorua and maintain a typically high standard, while **hotels** mostly cater to bus-tour groups and charge prohibitive prices if you just walk in off the street; though again, surprisingly good deals can be struck in the off season. We've mainly recommended **campsites** right in town, but there are dozens of others scattered around the region; most are listed with the visitor centre, who can advise on availability.

Between Christmas and March you would do well to make **reservations** a few days in advance.

Hotels and motels

Amber Pacifica Lodge 1296 Hinemaru St ⓣ0800/426 237 & 07/348 0595, ⓕ348 0795. Middle-of-the-road motel with only average rooms but well situated close to the town centre. ❹

Gibson Court Motel 10 Gibson St ⓣ07/346 2822, ⓕ348 9481. Small motel in a quiet location, simply decorated but with nice private mineral pools. ❹

Havana Motor Lodge 1078 Whakaue St ⓣ07/348 8134 & 0800/333 799, ⓕ348 8132. Quiet, well-sited motel close to the lakefront with spacious grounds, a heated pool and two small mineral pools. Decent units are gradually being renovated. ❹

The Princes Gate 1057 Arawa St ⓣ07/348 1179 & 0800/696 963, ⓦwww.scenic-circle.co.nz. The sole survivor from the days when all of Hinemaru Street was lined with hotels catering to the ailing, who took the waters at the bathhouse across the road. This lovely old wooden hotel is now restored with en-suite rooms fronting onto lovely wide verandas, a tennis court and in-house video. Off-peak B&B specials are sometimes available. ❼

Regal Geyserland Hotel 424 Fenton St ⓣ07/348 2039 & 0800/881 882, ⓔgeyserland@silveroaks.co.nz. Book early to get a third- or fourth-floor room with unsurpassed views over the Whakarewarewa thermal area; watch the mud volcanoes plopping below your balcony while you wait for Pohutu to perform. The rooms and public areas have seen better days, but are quite adequate and there's an outdoor pool, small gym and restaurant/bar. Some viewless rooms are ❺, but that rather defeats the object of staying here. ❻

Royal Lakeside Novotel Lake end Tutanekai St ⓣ07/346 3888 & 0800/444 422, ⓦwww.novotel.co.nz. Swankiest of the big hotels, with elegant modern rooms, some with lake views, and all the usual facilities, plus thermal pool and massage facilities. The rack-rate comes out at ❾,though for most of the year there are specials at ❼–❽

Silver Fern Motor Inn 326 Fenton St ⓣ07/346 3849 & 0800/118 808, ⓦwww.silverfernmotorinn.co.nz. Modern top-of-the-line motel with studios and one-bedroom units, all with spa baths, Sky TV, sunny balconies and oodles of space. ❻–❼

B&Bs and guesthouses

Ariki Lodge 2 Manuariki Ave, Ngongotaha ⓣ07/357 5532, ⓦwww.arikilodge.co.nz, ⓔrgforgie@xtra.co.nz. Excellent, welcoming B&B perched right beside the lake, the views of which are framed by Phoenix palms and extensive lawns. The rooms, one with excellent lake views, are both en suite, and there's an enormous suite with spa bath and a separate sitting area. Sumptuous breakfasts are served. Ariki Lodge is located around 8km northwest of Rotorua and is reached from central Ngongotaha along Taui St. ❺–❼

Best Inn Rotorua 1068 Whakaue St ⓣ & ⓕ07/347 9769. Pristine, modern B&B right in the centre with attractively simple, clean rooms and Japanese-style Onsen mineral baths. ❺

Eaton Hall with ensuites as well as rooms with shared facilities, right in the heart of town. Friendly and well-priced, with a full cooked-breakfast served. ❷–❺

Jack & Di's 21 Lake Rd ⓣ07/346 8482, ⓕ346 8486. Welcoming and attractively decorated B&B right by Ohinemutu with good lake views and three en-suite rooms. Continental breakfast is served and there's free tea, coffee, biscuits and fresh fruit all day. ❹

Lake House 6 Cooper Ave ⓣ07/345 3313 & 0800/002 863, ⓦbabs.co.nz/lakehouse. Spacious B&B in a 1930s house beautifully sited right on the lakeshore with views across lawns to Mokoia Island from both rooms and from the veranda. As well as a comfortable lounge, guests have free use of kayaks, catamaran and windsurfers and can swim safely from the beach. Breakfast is substantial and there's a four-course dinner on request ($35). Located just off Robinson Ave, itself off SH30 7km north of Rotorua. ❺–❻

Lynmore Hilton Rd ⓣ345 6303, ⓔkibble@xtra.co.nz. Comfortable B&B in the suburb of Lynmore, just off the Tarawera Rd 4km from central Rotorua, with very welcoming well-travelled hosts, nicely appointed rooms, lush gardens, a separate guest lounge, and tasty breakfasts. ❺

Namaste Point 187 Te Akau Rd, Lake Rotoiti ⓣ07/362 4804, ⓦmysite.xtra.co.nz/~namastepoint. A kind of homestay/apartment beautifully sited beside Lake Rotoiti some 20km north of Rotorua near Okere Falls. Perfect as a rural retreat, you get a beautifully decorated self-contained suite with, TV, stereo, fresh flowers and gourmet breakfast supplied. Guests have free use of the spa pool, canoe, dinghy and a jetty for swimming or fishing. ❼

Peacehaven, 10 Peace St ⓣ & ⓕ07/348 3759, ⓔpeacehaven@clear.net.nz. Suburban homestay close to Whakarewarewa with friendly hosts, comfortable rooms, a large thermally heated pool in the back yard and a lovely little mineral pool. ❹

Sandi's B&B, 103 Fairy Springs Rd ⓣ07/347 0034, ⓔsandi.mark@xtra.co.nz. Just one good-value, comfortable and nicely decorated en-suite room close to Rainbow Springs, with continental breakfast. ❹

Hostels

Cactus Jack Downtown Backpackers 1210 Haupapa St ⓣ0800/122 228, ⓔcactusjackbp@xtra.co.nz. A snazzy paint job and enthusiastic staff add character to this ageing warren of rooms and cabins with reasonably spacious dorms, twins and doubles, and bike rental for $20 a day. A large spa pool and pool table ensure it is always pretty lively. ❶–❷

Central Backpackers 10 Pukuatua St ⓣ & ⓕ07/349 3285, ⓔrotorua.central.bp@clear.net.nz. Small but spacious, homely and easygoing hostel in an immaculately kept, large house, with beds rather than bunks in the four- and six-bed dorm rooms. There's low-cost bike rental and a spa pool too. ❶–❷

Crash Palace 1271 Hinemaru St ⓣ07/348 8842, ⓦwww.crashpalace.co.nz. Revamped former YHA with spacious and airy public areas, a spa pool and rooms, four-shares and doubles all made up with sheets. ❶–❸

Funky Green Voyager 4 Union St ⓣ07/346 1754, ⓕ350 1100. Very relaxed hostel in a suburban house, ten minutes' walk from downtown with an easy-going communal atmosphere fostered by the idiosyncratic owner. Cooking facilities in particular are excellent and there's a hot tub and a cosy, TV-less lounge. Dorms, doubles and ensuites ❶–❷

Hot Rock 1286 Arawa St ⓣ07/347 9469, ⓦwww.acb.co.nz/hotrock. Large, lively and, at weekends, noisy hostel, a perennial favourite with patrons of the backpacker tour buses, kept entertained in the two mineral pools, a heated outdoor swimming pool and the *Lava Bar* next door. Accommodation is in four-shares or larger dorms, each with private bathroom, and there are backpacker doubles, and nicer ensuites with kitchens as well. ❶–❸

KiwiPaka YHA 60 Tarewa Rd ⓣ07/347 0931, ⓦwww.kiwipaka-yha.co.nz. Huge and well-organized modern complex on the far side of Kuirau Park, with camping space and a series of accommodation blocks ranged around a pool and a low-cost café and bar. Six- and four-bunk dorms are good value, and the doubles and modern chalets are a bargain too. Tent $9, vans $10.50. ❶–❸

The Wall 1140 Hinemoa St ⓣ0800/843 392 & 07/350 2040, ⓦwww.thewall.co.nz. Brand new, central and well-appointed backpackers with separate music, TV and games rooms, a lively bar on site and a 20m indoor climbing-wall. Standards are high, so prices are a dollar or two more expensive than some other hostels, but drink and climbing-wall discounts redress the balance. City bikes rented for $25 a day. Dorms, four-shares, singles doubles and ensuites ❶–❸

Campsites and motor parks

Blue Lake Top 10 Holiday Park Tarawera Road, Blue Lake ⓣ0800/808 292 & 07/362 8120, ⓦwww.topparks.co.nz. Large and well-organized site 9km from Rotorua on the way to the Buried Village and just across the road from Blue Lake. Extensive facilities include games room, spa pool, and aquatic paraphernalia for rent. Tents $10, powered sites $11, cabins & kitchen cabins ❷, s/c unit ❸, motels ❹

Cosy Cottage Holiday Park 67 Whittaker Rd ⓣ07/348 3793, ⓔcosycottage@xtra.co.nz. Excellent holiday park a couple of kilometres from town with an extensive range of comfortable cabins and tourist flats, powered and tent sites, some of which are on geothermally-heated ground – great in winter but less appealing in summer. Along with all the usual facilities, there's a swimming pool, a couple of pleasant mineral pools, naturally fed steam-boxes for *hangi*-style cooking, and bikes for rent ($16 a day). Tents $11, powered sites $12, cabins ❷, flats ❸

Lakeside Thermal Holiday Park, 54 Whittaker Rd ⓣ & ⓕ07/348 1693, ⓔrelax@lakesidethermal.co.nz. Small and compact lakefront motor camp 2km from the city, with kayaks for guests' use, a barbecue overlooking the lake, a genuine mineral-water pool and mineral water baths where you can adjust the temperature to suit. Tent and van sites $10, cabins ❷, kitchen cabins ❸

Rotorua Top 10 Holiday Park, 137 Pukuatua St ⓣ07/348 1886, ⓦwww.rotoruatop10.co.nz). Very well-appointed holiday park that's the closest to the city centre, with an outdoor pool and spa. A spacious camping area has tent and powered sites, basic but serviceable cabins, and more luxurious self-catering tourist flats as well as motel units. Tents $10, vans $11, cabins ❷, flats ❸, units ❹

The Town, Lake Rotorua and Whakarewarewa

Rotorua's sights are scattered: even those around the centre of town require some form of transport, though half a day can be spent on foot visiting the fine collection of Maori artefacts and bath-house relics in the **Rotorua Museum**, located in the former bathhouse in the formal **Government Gardens**, then strolling around the shores of **Lake Rotorua** to Ohinemutu, the city's original Maori village with its neatly carved church. For a soak in a hot pool in the slightly surreal setting of a native bird sanctuary, catch a boat out to **Mokoia Island**, the romantic setting for the tale of two lovers, Hinemoa and Tutanekai.

The majority of sights require a little more effort, though a shuttle bus (see p.313) does the rounds. Top of most sightseeing lists is **Whakarewarewa**, a large thermal reserve now divided into two sections: the **Thermal Village**, where folk still go about their daily lives amid the steam and boiling pools; and the **Maori Arts and Crafts Institute**, with its two large geysers and a fascinating carving and weaving school. Where Rotorua's northwestern suburbs peter out, Mount Ngongotaha rises up, providing the necessary slope for a number of gravity-driven activities at the **Skyline Skyrides**. In its shadow, **Rainbow Springs** provides a window into the life cycle of trout, with some fine specimens swimming in pools richly draped in ferns, while Rainbow Farm offers a slightly different twist on the sort of sheep-centred farmshow pioneered by the **Agrodome**, nearby.

Government Gardens and around

In the early years of the twentieth century, Rotorua was already New Zealand's premier tourist town, a fact it celebrated in confident civic style by laying out the **Government Gardens** east of the town centre. With their juxtaposition of the staid and the exotic the gardens are like some bizarre vision of an antipodean little England. White-suited bowls players mill around sulphurous steaming vents, palm trees loom over rose gardens, and, commanding the centre, there's the neo-Tudor **bathhouse**, built in 1908 in a style commensurate with the expectations of patrons familiar with European spas. Heralded as the greatest spa in the South Seas, "antagonistic" waters were supplied from the nearby Rachel and Priest springs to 84 baths, all fitted with the latest balneological equipment. But this was no pleasure palace, more a state-of-the-art non-residential hospital where patients suffering from just about any disorder – arthritis, alcoholism, nervousness – underwent ghoulish treatments involving electrical currents and colonic irrigation as well as the more traditional pampering. However, the bathhouse opened as the era of the grand spas was coming to a close; it limped along until 1963, when a combination of low patronage and maintenance costs hiked up by corrosive hydrogen sulphide in the waters hastened its demise.

Other than the attractions within the gardens themselves, on their southwestern edge you'll find the **Tamaki Trading Post**, a meeting point on the corner of Hinemaru St and Pukuatua St for Tamaki Tours (see p.328) and the site of the poor but improving **Orchid Gardens** (daily 8am–7pm; $10), a hothouse full of orchids, plus a second hothouse gradually being replanted in native species, especially those with medicinal or spiritual significance for Maori.

The Rotorua Museum and the Blue Baths

The building now houses the **Rotorua Museum of Art and History** (daily: Nov to mid-March 9.30am–6pm, mid-March to Oct 9.30am–5pm; $9), where one of the principal attractions is the old baths themselves, complete with gloomy green and white tiling and exposed pipes. Several rooms have been preserved in a state of arrested decay and filled with photos of the glory days. The rest of the building is devoted to three main exhibitions. The small but exquisite and internationally significant **Te Arawa** display showcases the long-respected talents of Arawa carvers who made this area a bastion of pre-European carving traditions. Many pieces have been returned from European collections, and the magnificent carved figures, dog-skin cloaks, *pounamu* (greenstone) weapons and intricate barge-boards are all powerfully presented. Prized pieces include the flute played by the legendary lover Tutanekai (see below), an unusually fine pumice goddess, and rare eighteenth-century carvings executed with stone tools. The photos around the walls depict faces tattooed with detailed *moko* (traditional tattoos), and a portrait of the Tarawera guide standing outside the Whakarewarewa meeting house. Much of the remainder of the museum covers the dramatic events surrounding the **Tarawera eruption**. The extensive displays include an informative relief map of the region, eye-witness accounts and reminiscences, and photos of the ash-covered Temperance Hotel at Te Wairoa and of the similarly smothered Rotomahana Hotel, both now demolished. The small section on the exploits of the **Maori battalion** during WWII is mainly for war buffs, but the half-hour video is very moving and well worth a look.

The main bathhouse promoted health: when the adjacent **Blue Baths** (daily 9.30am–5pm; included with Rotorua Museum entry) opened in 1933, it promised only pleasure. Designed in the Californian Spanish Mission style so popular at the time, this was one of the first public swimming pools in the world to allow mixed bathing. Like its neighbour, the Blue Baths hit hard times and closed in 1982, not reopening until 1999. You can still swim in an ancillary outdoor pool ($7), though the bulk of the building is now a museum charting its decades at the centre of Rotorua's social whirl. People's recollections are posted on panels amid the old changing cubicles, and serve to reinforce the sense of loss you get strolling around the main pool, now filled in and grassed over.

The Polynesian Spa

Immediately to the south lies the **Polynesian Spa**, Hinemoa Street (daily 6.30am–11pm; Polynesian Pools $10, Lake Spa $25; ⓣ07/348 1328, ⓦwww.polynesianspa.co.nz), a mostly open-air complex landscaped for lake views and comprising three separate areas. The main Polynesian Pools section comprises thirty-odd hot mineral pools claimed to treat all manner of ailments, principally arthritis and rheumatism. The vast majority of visitors bathe in either the slightly alkaline main pool or the small and turbid Radium and Priest pools, where the acidic waters bubbling up through the bottom of the tub vary from 33°C to 43°C. Private pools (an additional $10 per person for 30min), where you can adjust the temperature yourself, are ranged around the Radium and Priest pools, but for real exclusivity, opt for the adjacent **Lake Spa** section, with four attractively landscaped shallow rock pools of differing temperatures along with private relaxation lounge and bar. Reserve in advance for the hedonistic pleasures of the enormous range of massages, body scrubs, mud wraps and general pampering, from thirty minutes ($60, includes Lake Spa entry) to varying full-day detox programmes ($500–620). Families are catered for in the new **Family Spa** ($24 for up to two adults and four kids), with one chlorinated 33°C pool, a couple of small mineral pools and a water slide.

Lake Rotorua

From the Government Gardens it is a short walk along the waterfront to the Lakefront Jetty, the starting point for trips onto **Lake Rotorua** and out to **Mokoia Island**, 7km to the north of the jetty. New Zealand's only inland, predator-free bird sanctuary, Mokoia is the scene of a successful and long-standing breeding programme for saddlebacks and North Island robins – often spotted at the feeder stations – and a fledgling one for the little spotted kiwi. The island is better known, however, for the story of **Hinemoa and Tutanekai**, the greatest of all Maori love stories and widely considered to be more truth than legend. It tells of two lovers, the young chief Tutanekai of Mokoia Island, and his high-born paramour, Hinemoa, whose people lived along the western shores of the lake. Hinemoa's family forbade her from marrying the illegitimate Tutanekai and prevented her from meeting him by beaching their heavy *waka* (canoe), but the strains of Tutanekai's lamenting flute still wafted across the lake nightly and the smitten Hinemoa resolved to swim to him. One night, buoyed by gourds, she set off towards Mokoia, but by the time she got there Tutanekai had returned to his *whare* (house) to sleep. Hinemoa arrived at the island but, without clothes, was unable to enter the village, so she immersed herself in a hot pool. Presently Tutanekai's slave came by to collect water, and Hinemoa lured him over, smashed his gourd and sent him back to his master. An enraged Tutanekai came to investigate, only to fall into Hinemoa's embrace. The site of Tutanekai's *whare* and **Hinemoa's Pool** can still be seen, along with the grave of the first Pakeha born in the Rotorua district._

There are a couple of ways to get out on the lake and to Mokoia Island. The unfortunately named Scatcat tour (ⓣ07/347 9852; 4 daily; $25) takes a speedy **catamaran** around the island on their hour-long trip, and if you catch one of the early boats you can be put ashore on Mokoia Island ($20 additional landing fee) and picked up by a later boat, leaving time for an extended soak or to wander the trails with an eagle eye out for native birdlife. Clearwater Charters (ⓣ07/348 4186) offer comfortable self-piloted **pontoon boats** carrying up to eight (1hr $75, 3hr or more $55 an hour), which can be taken to Mokoia Island or used for lake fishing; and rent an assortment of kayaks and peddle boats.

If it is just a cruise you are after, consider the leisurely *Lakeland Queen* (ⓣ0800/862 784, ⓦwwww.lakelandqueen.co.nz), a replica **paddle steamer** that runs a series of hour-long trips named after the meal provided on board – the Morning Tea Cruise (10am; $20); Lunch Cruise (12.30pm; $30); and Afternoon Tea Cruise (2.30pm; $20). They also do occasional dinner cruises ($50).

Ohinemutu

Before the town of Rotorua grew up around its government buildings, the principal settlement in the area was at **Ohinemutu**, 500m north of the centre, on the lakeshore. It occupies a site chosen for its proximity to fishing and transport on the lake, and to hot springs along its shore perfect for washing and cooking. Ohinemutu remains an overwhelmingly Maori village centred on the springs and the small wooden **St Faith's Anglican Church**, built in 1914 to replace its 1885 predecessor. The church's simple half-timbered neo-Tudor exterior gives no hint of the gloriously rich interior where there is barely a patch of wall that hasn't been carved or covered with *tukutuku* (ornamental latticework) panels. Everything has been intricately worked, from pew ends and support beams to the entrance to the chancel, which has been made to look like the barge-boards (*maihi*) of a meeting house. Even the pulpit has been inlaid with geometrically patterned cloth. Wonderful though all this is, it is treated as a sideshow to the main attraction, a window with the figure of Christ, swathed in a Maori cloak and feathers, etched into it and positioned so that he appears to be walking on the lake. Outside is the grave of Gilbert Mair, a captain in the colonial army who twice saved Ohinemutu from attacks by rival Maori and became the only Pakeha to earn full Arawa chieftainship.

At the opposite end of the small square in front of the church stands the **Tamatekapua Meeting House**, again beautifully carved, though the best and most ancient of the work, some dating back almost two hundred years, is inside, which, unfortunately, is currently inaccessible. Between the two buildings, a signed passage leads down to Ohinemutu Maori Handicrafts, Mataiamutu St (ⓣ07/350 3378), a small gallery where Tony Kapua, a locally renowned carver, turns out fine Maori pieces.

Immediately south of Ohinemutu, on Ranolf Street, lies **Kuirau Park**, its northern end pockmarked by fairly modest steaming hot pools, while the southern end has some minor thrills for kids: crazy-golf, a miniature railway, play areas and the like.

Whakarewarewa thermal reserve and forest park

To New Zealanders, mention of Rotorua immediately conjures up images of the **Whakarewarewa Thermal Reserve** – or Whaka, as it is more commonly known – the closest thermal area to the city. Until 1998 this was a single entity, but local in-fighting over ownership of the rights to the thermal area has now thrown up a barrier through the middle leaving two entirely separate complexes. Around two-thirds of the active thermal zone and the lion's share of the infrastructure have been inherited by the **NZ Maori Arts & Crafts Institute**, Hemo Road, 3km south of central Rotorua (daily: Nov–March 8am–6pm, April–Oct 8am–5pm; $18; ⓦwww.nzmaori.co.nz), which is the start of a series of walkways past glooping pools of boiling mud, sulphurous springs and agglomerations of silica stalactites. The main attractions are New Zealand's most spectacular geysers, the ten-metre **Prince of Wales' Feathers** and the granddaddy of them all, the twenty-metre **Pohutu** ("big splash"), which once performed several times a day until 2000, when it surprised everyone by spouting continuously for an unprecedented 329 days. It has since settled back to jetting water into the air for around eighty percent of the time.

Ambling around is undoubtedly more appealing when the weather is good, but don't be too dismayed if the weather is poor: low barometric pressures often bring out the best in the geysers, while cool winter conditions condense the steam into thick clouds, making the place even more ethereal. Free hour-long guided tours leave on the hour.

The area would be worth visiting if that was all there was, but it also contains a **nocturnal house** with kiwi, a replica of a traditional Maori **village**, its entrance marked by a carving of lovers Tutanekai and Hinemoa embracing, and the **Arts and Crafts Institute** itself (same hours; included with entry). The institute serves both to teach young Maori the traditional carving and weaving techniques and to demonstrate those same skills to visitors. Half an hour spent here can be wonderfully inspirational and informative, as skilled artisans produce flax skirts and carvings, which can be bought in the classy but expensive shop. The institute also hosts **Mia Ora** (6.15pm; $65; ⓣ0800/494 252) comprising a Maori welcome, concert and steam-cooked feast.

The remainder of the Whakarewarewa thermal area falls under the auspices of the **Maori Village of Whakarewarewa**, Tryon St, 3km south of central Rotorua (daily 8.30am–5pm; $18), which, unlike the other thermal areas, is a living village founded in pre-European times and enlarged by an influx of displaced people in the aftermath of the Tarawera eruption. With the division of the thermal area, you can't get really close to the geysers and the more dramatic geothermal manifestations from here, but there is considerable compensation in being able to wander around the houses, many of them fairly new constructions as the hydrogen sulphide issuing from the ground tends to rot concrete. You might even see people using steam boxes for cooking, though the most common experience of geothermally cooked food is the sweetcorn stand near the entrance. You can wander at leisure past assorted souvenir shops demonstrating carving and weaving skills, attend a free **cultural performance** (11.15am & 2pm), and partake in a **hangi** (served at 12.30; $22).

The western fringe of the Whakarewarewa thermal area borders the **Whakarewarewa Forest**, experimentally planted a century back to see which exotic species would grow well under New Zealand conditions. Redwoods were found to grow three times faster than in their native California, creating the impressive **Redwood Grove**, which is threaded by a number of short paths. The **Fletcher Challenge Forests' Visitor Centre**, Long Mile Road (Oct–March Mon–Fri 8.30am–6pm, Sat & Sun 10am–4pm; April-Sept Mon–Fri 8.30am–5pm, Sat & Sun 10am–4pm; ⓣ07/346 2082), has details of these on its free *The Redwoods* recreation guide, and information on the excellent **mountain-biking trails**. The Forest is also the venue for **horse rides** with the Maori-run Peka Horse Trekking (ⓣ07/346 1755), who offer one-hour ($25), two-hour ($40) and longer treks at competitive prices.

West of the Lake: Around Ngongotaha

Aside from visits to the thermal areas, much of Rotorua's daytime activity takes place between five and ten kilometres northwest of central Rotorua around the flanks of **Mount Ngongotaha**, which is increasingly being surrounded by the city's suburbs. Closest to downtown, there's all manner of gravity-driven activities at the **Skyline Skyrides** site, and gentler pursuits at either **Rainbow Springs** or around the mountain at **Paradise Valley Springs**. Sheep take centre stage (literally) a little further out at the **Agrodome**, centrepiece of an adventure park that is trying to wrestle the adrenaline torch from the Skyline Skyrides.

Skyline Skyrides, Rainbow Springs and Paradise Valley Springs

First stop, around 4km from town, is the **Skyline Skyrides**, an aerial gondola (daily 9am–6pm or later; $13.50) that whisks you 200m up to the station part way up the mountain for superb views across the lake and town, scenic but uninspired dining in the restaurant (which stays open until 10–11pm; the gondola runs return trips until then) and café, and a bevy of adventure activities. Among these, most fun is to be had on the **luge** ($5 per ride; gondola plus 5 rides $28), a kind of plastic tray on wheels on which you hurtle down 5km of banked concrete tracks on three courses, achieving speeds of up to 60km per hour on the steepest sections – a kind of concrete, less severe toboggan run. A chair lift carries you back up to the top for subsequent runs. The adjacent **Skyswing** ($30) involves you and up to two others being strapped firmly into a seat that's attached to a forty-metre-long cable then winched up and released – just like a huge playground swing, with enough freefall to leave your stomach far behind. Air guns, a flight simulator and helicopter flights complete the summit set-up.

At the foot of the hill lies **Rainbow Springs** (daily 8am–5pm; $20), an all-too-neat series of trout pools linked by nature trails which, along with the adjacent and now integrated Fairy Springs, has been admitting visitors since 1898, when a *tapu* (taboo) on the springs was lifted. Fresh water flows through the crystal-clear pools, some with glass sides for superb viewing of some of the largest rainbow, brown and North American brook trout you will ever see. Adult fish all have free access to the lake, but know when they're on to a good thing and return for the near-constant supply of food tossed in by visitors, something that may well help account for their size. Other marginal attractions include animal pens, an aviary, a freshwater aquarium, a kiwi house and an extensive collection of ferns, but it all feels far too regimented and unless you're here early in the day it can be very crowded. You can usually escape the crush at the quieter Fairy Springs section, which has more of the same stuff. Across the road is the **Rainbow Farm** section (included in ticket price; shows at 10.30am, 11.45am, 1pm, 2.30pm & 4pm), with a huge fluffy shop and a covered area from where you can watch sheepdogs rounding up a flock, followed by a fake auction and a display of shearing prowess.

For even more trout, but in the company of lions rather than sheep, eschew Rainbow Springs in favour of **Paradise Valley Springs**, 13km west of Rotorua on Paradise Valley Road (daily 8am–5pm; $15; Ⓦ www.paradisev@xtra.co.nz). It's an altogether more peaceful setting, with boardwalks guiding you past pools of trout, native birds and an attractive wetland area. The biggest draw is the breeding pride of lions, who are fed at 2.30pm; if you catch it lucky there may be lion cubs on hand, which can be petted (under guidance) until they are six months old.

Trout superfans should continue along Paradise Valley Road to reach the **Ngongotaha Hatchery** (daily 9am-4pm; free) where a small hatchery and a succession of rearing ponds gives an insight into the activities of government-run Fish & Game New Zealand, the outfit that stocks most of the lakes around these parts. Paradise Valley Road continues to the Agrodome.

△ Maori cultural performance

The Agrodome and Agrodome Adventure Park

Just about every bus touring the North Island stops 10km north of Rotorua at the **Agrodome**, Western Road, Ngongotaha (☎07/357 1050; shows at 9.30am, 11am & 2.30pm; show $15, farm tour $18, combined price $27), where the star attraction is a slick 45-minute **sheep show**, a legacy of the 1970 Osaka World's Fair. Though undoubtedly corny, the popular spectacle is engaging and always entertaining: rams representing the nineteen major breeds farmed in New Zealand are enticed onto the podium; a sheep is shorn; lambs are bottle-fed; and there's an impressive sheepdog display. Afterwards, the dogs are put through their paces outside – rounding up sheep into pens and so on – and you can watch a 1906 industrial carding machine turn fleece into useable wool, and there's a 45-minute farm tour complete with honey tasting, deer viewing and, between April and June, kiwifruit picking.

A totally different market is catered for at the adjacent **Agrodome Adventure Park** (daily 9am–5pm or later), where they've gone all out to lure adrenaline junkies. Rotorua now has a **bungy jump** ($80) from a huge metal arm which is hoisted into the air to create a platform for a 43m plummet. The same arm, along with a couple of stayed towers, creates **Swoop** ($45 for one, $40 each for two, $35 each for three), in which up to three of you are lashed into a hang-gliding harness, winched up to 40m and released for a giant swing at speeds of up to 130km per hour: a larger number produces greater momentum and higher speeds. All this overlooks the **Agrojet** ($35) where tiny racing jetboats, de-tuned but still pumping out 450 horsepower, hurtle around a short artificial course. You get less than five minutes, but are left breathless.

Nearby at the **Zorb** (one go $40, two goes $60) you can dive into the centre of a three-metre diameter clear plastic ball and roll down a two-hundred-metre hill. You can either do it "dry" ($40), harnessed in for a head-over-heels roll; or "wet" ($40 for one person, $30 each for two, $25 each for three), with no harness but a couple of buckets of water, so you slosh around inside madly. It is a fair bit of cash for a small thrill, but it's quite a laugh all the same, and even kids can have a go in a smaller, more sedate version. There are discounts for second runs, and combo packages with the Swoop, bungy and Agrojet which will suit just about anyone's desires.

A **free shuttle bus** runs out to the Agrodome and Adventure Park (4 daily) from the visitor centre and some of the backpackers.

Activities

As you might expect in a place which attracts visitors in such numbers, numerous companies have sprung up in Rotorua to offer all manner of adventure activities – rafting, kayaking, mountain biking or even fishing. The **adventure tourism** scene hasn't quite snowballed to the degree it has in Queenstown, but there is still loads to keep you occupied. In addition to the activities detailed below, brochures everywhere advertise water-skiing on Blue Lake, horse riding, quad biking, hot-air ballooning plus particularly scenic **skydiving** with Tandem Skydiving Rotorua (☎07/345 7520; around $180).

Rafting

Rotorua has developed a considerable reputation for its rafting trips; in fact, there's a better range of trips available here than anywhere else in New Zealand. Much of the hype (which includes inflating the river grading) is reserved for the Grade IV **Kaituna River**, or at least the two-kilometre section of it after it leaves Lake Rotoiti 20km north of Rotorua and enters a narrow, verdant gorge. As the river twists around rocky bluffs, it periodically plummets over vertical drops, including the spectacular seven-metre **Tutea's Falls**, which operators use to justify their claims of offering Grade V rafting. The trip is a short one, only spending around forty minutes on the water, and everyone comes out wanting more. In the summer, the half-dozen or so companies operating out of Rotorua take several trips a day, charging around $65–75, and even in the depths of winter someone's bound to be running the river.

While the Kaituna is a great trip, the river to go for, if you can get the timing right, is the Grade IV-plus **Wairoa River**, 80km by road from Rotorua, on the outskirts of Tauranga, which relies on dam-releases for raftable quantities of white water (Dec–March every Sun; Sept–Nov & April–May every second Sun). This is on-the-edge rafting and one of the finest short trips in the world, negotiating a dangerous and immensely satisfying stretch of water, and shooting rapids such as Mother's Nightmare, Devil's Hole and the Toaster, which has a nasty habit of tipping rafts over immediately above the toughest rapid on the river, the Roller Coaster. They accept all comers, but this is essentially a trip for those with some rafting experience and a good appreciation of the hazards of white water; several companies do the run, charging around $70-85 for the six-hour trip from Rotorua (90min actually on the water), often including a post-deluge barbecue. Some companies offer a double run for around $150.

If your tastes lean more towards appreciation of the natural surroundings with a bit of a bumpy ride thrown in, opt for the Grade III **Rangitaiki River**, which also shoots Jeff's Joy, a Grade IV drop that's the highlight of the trip. Trips from Rotorua cost $85–90. With more time, and money on your hands, it is well worth considering a **multi-day wilderness rafting trip** on Eastland's **Motu River** (see box, p.430).

Currently over half a dozen **operators** run trips from Rotorua, all rafting the same stretches of water at pretty much the same prices, though it pays to ask around for special offers and backpacker discounts. There's little to choose between them, but Kaitiaki Adventures (Ⓣ0800/338 736, Ⓦwww.raft-it.com) run a particularly tight ship and add a cultural dimension, explaining the significance of the river to Maori. Other contenders include Kaituna Cascades (Ⓣ0800/524 886, Ⓔkaituna.cascades@clear.net.nz), and River Rats (Ⓣ0800/333 900, Ⓦwww.riverrats.co.nz).

Whitewater sledging and kayaking

To up the ante a few notches, consider **whitewater sledging** with Kaitiaki Adventures ($110), who equip you with a wetsuit, full-face helmet, fins and a buoyant plastic sledge before guiding you down the Kaituna (or when unsuitable, the Rangitaiki). Extra vulnerability, eye-level intimacy with the water and the trepidation induced by a seven-metre waterfall up ahead makes this a good deal more exciting and potentially more risky than rafting, but thorough training, committed guides and the odd prayer to the river before the biggest drops allay the fears of most.

Excitement and risk come together in similar proportions with **tandem kayaking**, undertaken by Kaituna Kayaks (Ⓣ0800/465 292, Ⓦwww.kaitunakayaks.com) on the Kaituna River and including the 7m Tutea's Falls. If you are physically fit and have a spare $95 you'll be stuck in the front of a double kayak, given basic instruction then steered down the river by an experienced paddler in the driving seat behind you.

If any of this inspires you to **rent kayaks** or undertake **kayaking courses**, get in touch with the Sun Spots Kayak Shop, SH33, Okawa Bay (Ⓣ07/362

4222, ⓦwww.sunspots.co.nz), 14km north of Rotorua. They rent recreational kayaks ($20 per half-day), sea kayaks ($30 per day), and full whitewater set-ups ($30 per day) and run all manner of courses including the half-day introduction to kayaking ($90). Kaituna Kayaks also run half-day kayak lessons ($120 for one, $70 each for two to four), and offer a two hour lesson plus their tandem trip down the Kaituna for $180. For a more leisurely approach, contact Adventure Kayaking (ⓣ07/348 9451, ⓦwww.adventurekayaking.co.nz) who rent sea kayaks ($35 a day) and undertake **guided kayaking trips** on several of the larger lakes in the region with the emphasis on scenic appreciation, soaking in hot pools and maybe a little fishing. Try the Twilight Paddle ($60) on Lake Rotoiti, the Lake Tarawera Full Day Tour ($75), or the Kayak Camp Out ($120) with a hot swim, barbecue dinner and cooked breakfast.

Mountain biking

Some of the country's finest and most accessible **mountain biking** lies just fifteen minutes' ride from central Rotorua, with large areas of the Whakarewarewa Forest's redwoods, firs and pines threaded by single-track trails especially constructed with banked turns and jumps under a sub-canopy of tree ferns. Altogether there's over 40km of track, divided into a dozen circuits in five grades of difficulty and all explained and colourfully illustrated on the waterproof **trail map** ($2.50) available in town from the Map and Track Shop (see p.313), or out at the forest from the Fletcher Challenge Forests' Visitor Centre.

There is **no charge** to enter the forest or use the trails, which are most easily accessed from the obvious car park on Waipa Mill Road, 5km south of town off SH38. On summer weekends Planet Bike (ⓣ07/348 9971, ⓦwww.planetbike.co.nz) **rent bikes** here, or sturdy front- and full-suspension machines are available from one of the bike rental places in town (see p.329); most models available at hostels aren't up to the task. If you prefer **guided mountain biking**, Planet Bike run trips through the forest at all experience levels ($49–59 for 2hr) as well as night rides ($69), half-day scenic rides ($79); they even offer "women guides for women's rides".

Fishing

The Rotorua Lakes District has a reputation for trout fishing only matched in the North Island by the rivers and streams flowing into Lake Taupo. With two dozen gorgeous lakes, the angling could hardly be more scenic and almost all the lakes are stocked with strong-fighting rainbow trout; a typical summer catch is around 1.5kg, though in winter this can creep up towards 3kg. The proximity of **Lake Rotorua** makes it a perennial favourite, reached by charter boats from the Lakefront Jetty (2hr minimum; $80–90 an hour, including tackle but not licences – see below).

If you are going it alone, obtain up-to-date information on lake and river conditions from either the Map and Track Shop (see "Arrival and information", p.313) or sports shops such as O'Keefe's, 1113 Eruera St (ⓣ07/346 0178, ⓔcotter@thenet.net.nz). Both also stock the free *Lake Rotorua & Tributaries* leaflet published by Fish & Game NZ that explains the rules of the fishery (which in broad terms is open year round), and will provide contacts for fly-fishing guides which will generally set you back around $500 a day. **Licences** (24hr, $15; 7 days, $30; year, $75), which are valid for the whole country except for the Taupo fishery region, can be bought with a credit card from the free licence helpline (ⓣ0800/542 362).

Eating, drinking and entertainment

In recent years Rotorua has made great culinary strides and there are now quite a few quality **restaurants**, most congregated along a short strip at the lake end of Tutanekai Street – known as "The Streat". Nowhere is outrageously expensive, but the assiduously budget-conscious will fare better at less flashy places further from the main drag. Unlike the shops, which close up for much of the weekend, the restaurants and bars are generally open all week, most staying open as long as custom demands; unless you're part of a large group, there's little need to reserve a table.

Despite its exalted status as New Zealand's tourist mecca, Rotorua remains a small city and the nightlife is correspondingly limited. There are a few lively **bars** to keep you entertained, but almost everyone spends one evening of their stay attending one of the **hangi** and **Maori concerts** in one of the tourist hotels or, preferably, at one of the outlying *marae*.

Restaurants and cafés

Bath House Café Blue Baths (see p.318). Gracious tea rooms re-created in the renovated Blue Baths complex complete with potted palms, linen napkins, cakes off an Art Deco trolley and a couple of huge portraits of the Queen and Duke of Edinburgh. Pick a window seat and watch the bowls outside in Government Gardens while you indulge in tiffin ($16.50), Devonshire tea ($11.50), or lunches such as shepherds pie or calzone.

Bistro 1284 1284 Eruera St ⓣ07/346 1284. White linen tablecloths belie the relatively relaxed atmosphere in what is one of Rotorua's better restaurants, though it is only a couple of dollars pricier than many inferior places downtown. Try the artichoke risotto with grilled mushrooms and caper sauce ($23) or lamb shanks with rosemary jus on kumara ($25), but leave space for the lemon and passionfruit brûlée. Dinner only; closed Sun & Mon.

Café DNA 1151 Arawa St. One of the best places in town to relax over a coffee and a magazine, especially if you can land the sofas in the window. They also do a wide range of light meals throughout the day, serve dinner in the evening (mains $20), and stay open until the small hours when it becomes more like a convivial bar.

Fat Dog 1161 Arawa St. Always lively café and bar, with a relaxed atmosphere engendered by mismatched furniture, eclectic wall hangings and music. Drop in for coffee and cake or a plate of wedges, or go for the wide-ranging selection of hearty mains ($12-20) which come in large helpings.

Freos 1103 Tutanekai St. Quality modern Kiwi café dining at reasonable prices both inside and out. Good for burgers, focaccia sandwiches, pasta dishes and chargrilled meats. Licensed & BYO.

Landing Café Tarawera Rd, 18km southeast of Rotorua ⓣ07/362 8595. Quality food at moderate prices make this waterside café, restaurant and bar – with great views across to Lake Tarawera towards Mount Tarawera – an essential stop if you're out this way, and even justify a trip from town. During the day it is informal with brunch and lunch dishes mostly at $10–15, but from 6pm (generally Wed–Sat) à la carte dining offers the likes of gravalax and marinated vegetables with wasabi mayonnaise ($15) followed by pork loin with roasted parsnips ($25) then lime and passionfruit mascapone tart ($10). Evening reservations required.

Mitas 1114 Tutanekai St ⓣ07/349 6482, ⓦwww.mitas.co.nz. Beautifully prepared and presented southeast Asian fusion cuisine, and although they do serve an excellent rijstaffel banquet ($39 per person), don't expect plates of Indonesian staples; instead try the duck in Balinese orange sauce served with Asian mixed mushrooms ($29) or the delicious Chicken Borobudur ($26). Original desserts can be washed down with java roasted on the premises. Dinner only; closed Mon.

Swiss Cake and Confectionery Shop 1230 Tutanekai St. Excellent pastries and handmade chocolates to take away.

Tastebuds Mexican Cantina 1213 Fenton St. Ever-popular Mexican eat-in and takeaway, serving hefty helpings of Tex-Mex staples at low prices.

Tutanekai Espresso 1226 Tutanekai St. Daytime café with a good line in panini, crepes and BLTs, plus good coffee. Closed Sun.

La Vega 1158 Whakaue St. Bustling restaurant and bar concentrating on gourmet pizzas cooked in a wood-fired oven, pasta and steaks.

Zippy Central 1153 Pukuatua St. Rotorua's grooviest restaurant, with haphazard retro 1950s and 1960s pop decor. Purple and green walls and

Formica tables only temporarily distract you from the great coffee and small selection of imaginative and well-prepared food, from bagels and smoothies to marinated lamb and tabouleh salad or pumpkin gnocchi ($12–15). Licensed and BYO.

Bars and clubs

Barbarella 1263 Pukuatua St ⓦwww.barbarella.co.nz. Rotorua's coolest club, dark and definitely the place to be seen, chiefly for underground dance nights, visiting DJs and occasional bands. Usually Wed–Sat 10pm–3am.

Fuze 1122 Tutanekai St ⓣ07/349 6306. Upscale downtown bar with comfortable seating and DJs or live music most nights. Closed Mon.

Lava Bar 1286 Arawa St. A house converted into a bar that's found favour with backpackers, rafting guides and local youth. Basic meals are available and there's an early-evening happy hour, pinball machines and a pool table – if you can get to them.

O'Malley's 1287 Eruera St. Ersatz Irish bar with a strong line in draught Irish beers and bargain meals. Live entertainment every Fri with happy hour.

Outlaws, 1140 Hinemoa St. Saloon-style bar in the same building as *The Wall* backpackers, with big windows overlooking the climbing wall. Good for a few beers and some pool anytime, and several nights a week they lure in the adrenalin freaks with competitions for free adventure trips.

Pig & Whistle, cnr Haupapa St & Tutanekai St. Lively bar in a former police station with good locally brewed beers on tap, a garden bar, and rock and pop covers bands at weekends, when tidy dress is required and a small cover charge applies. There are also large and reasonably priced bar meals, the burgers and sandwiches served with pigtail fries.

Hangi and Maori concerts

Rotorua is far and away the best place to sample food steamed to perfection in the Maori earth oven or **hangi** and watch a **Maori concert**, typically an hour-long performance of traditional dance, song and chants. Although not entirely satisfactory introductions to Maori culture, these are at least accessible and good value. Almost a dozen groups vie for your custom, with offerings that fall into two distinct camps: extravaganzas laid on at the major hotels (typically $45–50); and packages operated and organized by Maori groups ($63–70). All trips run for three or four hours, most starting around 6 or 7pm, with buses picking up and dropping off at hotels and hostels around town; some of the hotels offer *hangi*-only or concert-only deals for about half the cost.

The two groups running **out-of-town packages** are distinctly different, though they follow largely the same format, giving instruction on *marae* customs and protocol (see "Maoritanga" in Contexts, p.982) as you are driven out to a Maori village, followed by a formal welcome. By far the most popular is Tamaki Tours (ⓣ07/346 2823, ⓔtamaki@wave.co.nz; $70), where you, and several more busloads, are driven out to a specially built "Maori village" south of town for a spine-chilling welcome. Everything is so professionally done that it is hard to quibble, though parts can feel a little voyeuristic. Its popularity has become its biggest downfall and sightlines can be restricted at the busier times of year. In contrast, Rotoiti Tours (ⓣ0800/476 864 & 07/348 8969, ⓔrotoititours@xtra2.co.nz; $63) lack some of the panache, but offer a much more engaging (and in some ways more authentic) affair, with almost the whole *whanau* (extended family group) contributing to the proceedings, which take place in the beautifully decorated meeting house on the Rakeiao Marae at Tapuaekura Bay on the shores of Lake Rotoiti some 20km north of Rotorua.

The big **hotels** take a more cabaret approach to the whole affair, usually eating first and relegating the concert to a form of after-dinner entertainment. The food is four-star-hotel standard, though in a misguided desire to present imaginative salads and precisely carved slices of meat they veer away from the more robust *hangi* style, usually resorting to steam boxes rather than traditional earth ovens. The content of the concert is almost identical to the *marae*-based shows but the tone is less intimate and more consciously choreographed, with sophisticated lighting and a disembodied voice commentating. There's little to choose between the hotels though the *Grand Tiara*, Fenton Street, near Whakarewarewa (☎07/348 7139; $49), and the Novotel's *Matariki* show, Tutanekai Street (☎07/346 3888; *rotorua@novotel.co.nz*; $55), both have good reputations.

If none of these suit, the Ohinemutu Cultural Group conduct Rotorua's original **concert-only** Magic of the Maori (☎07/349 3949 & 0508/300 333, Ⓦwww.magicmaori.com; 8pm; $19), and there are concerts held at Whakarewarewa (see p.316) at both the NZ Maori Arts & Crafts Institute and The Thermal Village.

Listings

Airlines Air New Zealand Travelcentre, 1103 Hinemoa St: domestic ☎07/348 7159; international ☎07/347 9564; arrival and departure info ☎07/345 6299.
American Express Galaxy United Travel, 1315 Tutanekai St ☎07/347 9444.
Automobile Association 1191 Amohau St ☎07/348 3069.
Banks and exchange ANZ, cnr Hinemoa St & Amohia St ☎07/348 2169; BNZ, cnr Haupapa St & Tutanekai St ☎07/348 1099; National, cnr Fenton St & Hinemoa St ☎07/349 5300; Westpac, cnr Hinemoa St & Tutanekai St. See also American Express and Thomas Cook.
Bike rental Planet Bike (☎07/348 9971, Ⓦwww.planetbike.co.nz) offer city bikes ($15 half day, $25 full day), mountain bikes suitable for Whakarewarewa Forest trails ($30 for 2hr and $5 per hr thereafter), and a range of guided bike tours; call them and they'll deliver a machine to you. Rotorua Cycle Centre, 1120 Hinemoa St (☎07/348 6588), have similar rental deals and Edzone Bike (☎07/346 1717) offer rentals and a deal where you use the gondola to whisk you to the top of the track.
Bookshops Idle Hour Book Inn, 1186 Eruera St for secondhand books; Whitcoulls, 1238 Tutanekai St for new.
Car rental Link, 1222 Fenton St (☎07/349 1629 & 0800/652 565, Ⓦwww.autohire.co.nz), offers a fully insured unlimited mileage runabout for $59 a day (3-day minimum). Budget, 1230 Fenton St (☎07/348 8127, Ⓦwww.budget.co.nz), matches these rates most of the time, and U-Drive (☎0800/837 483) usually undercuts them both with four-day deals from $40 a day.
Cinema Hoyts Movieland 5, 1263 Eruera St.
Internet access Numerous places around town, especially along Fenton St, where there's fast access at the Map & Track Shop, #1225, and a larger number of machines at Contact Cyber Café, #1217, and Nomads Cyber Café, #1195.
Left luggage At Tourism Rotorua ($2 for 3hr, $4 per day).
Library The public library is on Haupapa St (☎07/348 4177).
Medical treatment For emergencies and urgent healthcare go to Lakes Primecare, cnr Arawa St & Tutanekai St ☎07/348 1000. Daily 8am–11pm.
Pharmacy Lakes Care Pharmacy, cnr Arawa St & Tutanekai St ☎07/48 4385. Daily 9am–9.30pm.
Police 64–98 Fenton St ☎07/348 0099.
Post office The main post office, with poste restante facilities, is at 79–85 Hinemoa St ☎07/349 2397.
Taxis Fast Taxis ☎07/348 2444; and Rotorua Taxis ☎07/348 1111.
Thomas Cook/Travelex, Air New Zealand Travelcentre, 1103 Hinemoa St ☎07/343 1103, Ⓕ343 1101.
Travel agents Budget Travel, cnr Fenton St & Eruera St ☎07/348 4152; Flight Centre, 1228 Tutanekai St (☎07/346 3145); Galaxy United Travel, 1315 Tutanekai St ☎07/347 9444.

Around Rotorua

Much of the best Rotorua has to offer lies outside the city among the lakes to the north and east and around the most dramatic of the volcanic zones half an hour's drive south towards Taupo. Shuttles and tours run by numerous companies (see the box on p.331) mean that just about any combination of sights can be packed into a full day-trip, while if travelling independently, minor sights along the eastern shore of Lake Rotorua can be quickly dispatched, leaving time for the seldom-crowded **Hell's Gate** thermal area and the opportunity to watch terrified rafters plunging over **Tutea's Falls**. Hiring a boat opens up the best of lakes Rotoiti, Rotoehu and Rotama, though they're pleasing enough just to drive past on the way to Whakatane and the East Cape. Rewards are more plentiful to the east and south especially around Mount Tarawera which, in 1886, showered tonnes of ash on the **Buried Village**, where partly-interred Maori dwellings graphically illustrate the volcano's immense power. As the village and the Pink and White Terraces were being destroyed, the

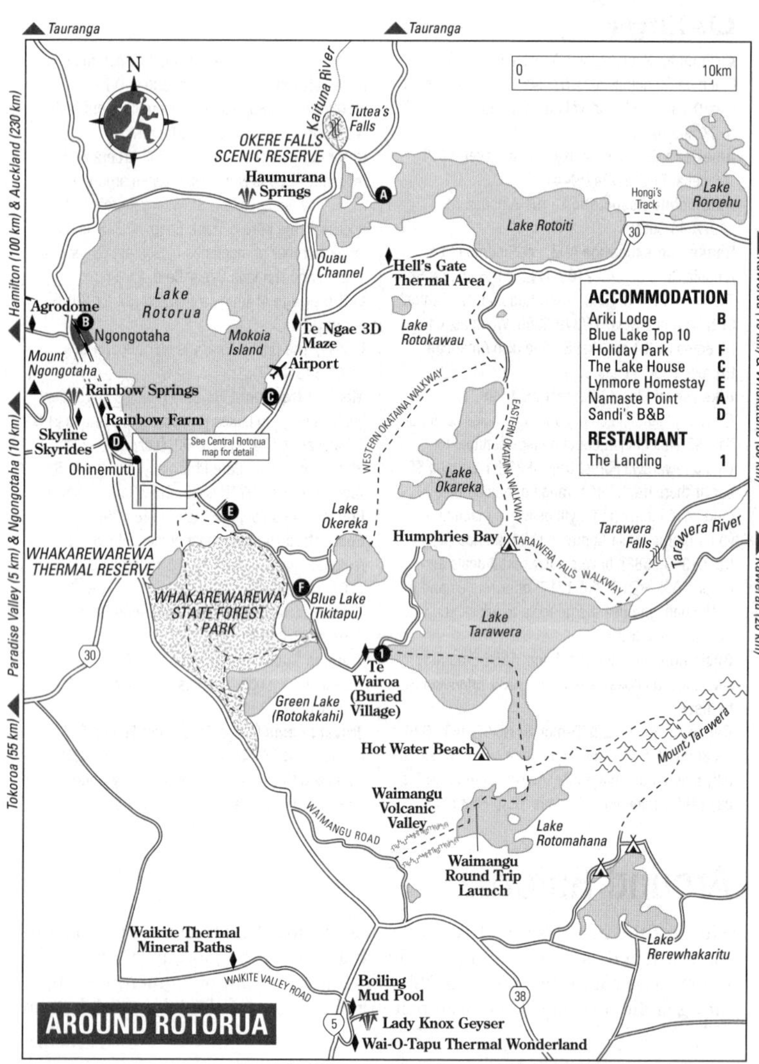

Tours and flights around Rotorua

To get out to the sights around Rotorua without your own transport, you've got a choice of shuttles, which just do the running around, and a bewildering array of minibus tours, ranging from a couple of hours to a full day. The latter all include admission to sights, have a commentary of some description and the itineraries can be quite flexible, particularly when numbers are small.

Most comprehensive of the **shuttle** operators is Cultural Thermal Shuttle (ⓣ0800/287 296) who make four daily circuits of Wai-O-Tapu, Waimangu, Tamaki Maori Village and the Waikite hot pools, picking up at hostels around Rotorua. A $20 all-day pass lets you get on and off as you please and includes an afternoon run out to the Buried Village. Santa Fe Shuttle (ⓣ07/345 7997) will run you out to Wai-O-Tapu ($10 return), throw in Waimangu ($45 return), or just run you to Hell's Gate ($15 return); and Dave's Shuttle (ⓣ0800/328 329) do a couple of runs out to Wai–O-Tapu and Waimangu for $24, including entrance to the former.

Of the **minibus tours**, Carey's Tours, 1108 Haupapa St (ⓣ07/347 1197) run a vast array of trips, including the Geothermal Wonderland (4hr; $70) out to Wai-O-Tapu and Waimangu; and the scenic Waimangu Round Trip (9hr; $145) which visits the Waimangu Thermal Valley, cruising across Lake Rotomahana, then bushwalking to a second cruise on Lake Tarawera, ambling around the Buried Village and finishing with a soak in the Polynesian Spa. Their backpacker-oriented trips – known as Carey's Capers – include lunch and a dip in natural hot pools in the bush but are otherwise almost identical. For a more personalized experience, join one of two entertaining and informative Maori-run tours giving a native perspective on the local sights: Sonny's World (ⓣ07/349 0290, ⓦwww.sonnysworld.co.nz), offer a half-day tour ($55) including a *marae* visit; TeKiri Trek (ⓣ07/345 5016, ⓔtekiri@ihug.co.nz), carry a maximum of five for a full day ($120) taking in Wai-O-Tapu and Waimangu, a 4WD safari through native forest, a big meal in the bush and a little hot-pool bathing. One destination that isn't accessible with your own vehicle is the shattered line of craters atop **Mount Tarawera**, which can be reached on foot (see box on p.332) and on tours with Mt Tarawera NZ (ⓣ07/349 3714, ⓦwww.mt-tarawera.co.nz) who have sole rights to the mountain. Either join their shuttle (3hr; $80) from near the base of the mountain, or take their Rotorua-based half-day tour ($110). However, the majesty of Mount Tarawera is best appreciated from the air; **plane flights** start from as little as $50 for a quick spin over the lake, $165 for Tarawera flights and something closer to $300 for an overflight of White Island out in the Bay of Plenty; Volcanic Wunderflites (ⓣ0800/777 359, ⓔwunderflites@xtra.co.nz), Volcanic Air Safaris (ⓣ0800/800 848, ⓦwww.volcanicair.co.nz) and Lakeside Aviation (ⓣ0800/535 363) all run competitive trips. For something a little different, consider biplane flights with either Red Cat (ⓣ0800/733 228, ⓦwww.redcat.co.nz) or Adventure Aviation (ⓣ07/345 6780) who both do scenic flights (15–20min for $120–140) and offer acrobatics for just a little more.

Helicopter flights will set you back a little more, with a short flight to Mount Tarawera and fifteen minutes on the ground going for $270 with Mt Tarawera NZ. Agrodome-based HeliPro (ⓣ07/357 2512, ⓦwww.helicopteradventures.com) and Wai-O-Tapu-based Heli-Kiwi (ⓣ07/366 6611, ⓦwww.helikiwi.co.nz) both offer a range of flights, some overflying Mount Tarawera and combining with jet boat trips and the like.

Waimangu Thermal Valley was created and now ranks as one of the finest collections of geothermal features in the region alongside kaleidoscopic **Wai-O-Tapu**, with its daily-triggered **Lady Knox Geyser** and multicoloured pools.

Walks in the Rotorua area

Although Rotorua isn't especially well endowed with serious tramps, it does work well as a staging post for forays into the Whirinaki Forest (see p.337) and further afield to Waikaremoana (see p.337). If you're keen to stretch your legs around these parts, you are best off with there-and-back day-walks. Trying to link up multi-day hikes is all but impossible without a compliant driver to pick you up at the other end. The best **map** is the 1:60,000 Holidaymaker *Rotorua Lakes* map ($14).

Blue Lake (Tikitapu; 5.5km loop; 2hr; 500m ascent). A pleasant and none-too-arduous loop around the Blue Lake through regenerating bush then Douglas firs and past some sandy beaches perfect for a dip. The single major climb takes you away from the lake to a viewpoint over the Blue and Green lakes. Starts at the eastern end of the beach opposite the Blue Lake Holiday Park, 9km southeast of Rotorua.

Mount Tarawera (14km return; 4–5hr; 400m ascent). If you've got a car and don't want to pay for a 4WD ascent of Mount Tarawera, the alternative is to drive as far as you can then get out and walk; though it will cost you $23 per person to cross Ngati Rangitihi land. The reward is a fifteen-kilometre-long gash of craters that can be explored for as long as you wish, always keeping an eye out for cloud which can quickly disorientate in this trackless domain. The hike starts on Bob Annett Road, off SH38 around 35km by road southeast of Rotorua. If road conditions are good and you have reasonable clearance on your rig, you should make it to the car park where you pay the fee, then continue on foot with 4WD vehicles and mountain bikes periodically clattering by.

Okere Falls Scenic Reserve (2.5km return; 40min–1hr). An easy stroll with river views and spectacular angles on rafters shooting Tutea's Falls (see opposite). Starts 18km north of Rotorua.

Tarawera Falls Walk (1–8km return; 30min–4hr; 100m ascent). Gorgeous bush walk to a great view of Tarawera Falls (see opposite), and on past swimming holes to the outlet of Lake Tarawera. Starts 80km by road from Rotorua, 24km south of Kawerau, and you can walk as far as you fancy before returning.

Northeast of Lake Rotorua: Hell's Gate and the northern lakes

SH30 hugs the eastern shores of Lake Rotorua, bound for Whakatane and passing through the region's greatest concentration of lakes and plenty of twisting hill country. Scenery aside, there isn't a great deal to stop for along the way apart from the **Fairbank Maze**, opposite the airport, 7km northeast of Rotorua (daily 10am-5pm; $5), which ranks as the largest hedge maze in the country, and **Te Ngae 3D Maze**, 3km further on (daily 9am–5pm; $5), a wooden affair with bridges linking separate sections and complicating things immeasurably.

Immediately north, SH30 veers off right to Whakatane while SH33 continues north to Te Puke and Tauranga. A couple of kilometres along the latter and you'll cross the riverine Ohau Channel, which links lakes Rotorua and Rotoiti. Haumurana Road then spurs left around the shores of Lake Rotorua passing **Haumurana Gardens**, 773 Haumurana Rd (daily 9am–5pm; $5), which boast the largest natural spring in the North Island – though in a land where crystal clear waters are commonplace it seems strange to pay to see a spring.

Sticking with SH33, you soon come upon signs to the **Okere Falls Scenic Reserve**, which surrounds the rafting mecca of the Kaituna River - follow signs up Trout Pool Road, 4km north of the Haumurana Road junction. From the first car park, 400m along Trout Pool Road, a broad track follows the river to a second car park (2.5km return; 40min–1hr) passing glimpses of the churning river below, and a viewing platform that's perfect for observing rafters plummet over the seven-metre **Tutea's Falls**. From here, steps descend through short tunnels in the steep rock walls beside the waterfall to **Tutea's Caves**, thought to have been used as a safe haven by Maori women and children during attacks by rival groups.

Most of the traffic out this way sticks to SH30, the route to **Hell's Gate** (Tikitere; daily 9am–5pm, and often later; $12; Ⓦwww.hellsgaterotorua.co.nz), 14km northeast of Rotorua. The least-visited and smallest of the major thermal areas, this is also one of the fiercest and most active, with an abundance of bubbling mud and seething gunmetal-grey waters. Its fury camouflages a lack of notable features, however, and the only real highlights are the bubbling mud of the Devil's Cauldron and the hot **Kakahi Falls**, whose soothing 38°C waters once made this a popular bathing spot (though now off-limits to bathers). By way of compensation you can bath in the hot waters ($10) and even take a mud bath ($25, including hot swim).

Beyond Hell's Gate lies **Lake Rotoiti**, which translates as "little lake", though it is in fact the second-largest in the region and is linked to Lake Rotorua by the narrow Ohau Channel. This passage, along with the neighbouring **Lake Rotoehu** and **Lake Rotama**, traditionally formed a part of the canoe route from the coast. A section of this route, apparently used on a raid by the Ngapuhi warrior chief Hongi Hika, is traced by **Hongi's Track** (3km; 1hr return; negligible ascent), a beautiful bushwalk which runs through to Lake Rotoehu passing the Wishing Tree, which is often surrounded by plant offerings.

Kawerau and Tarawera Falls

Around 6km beyond Lake Rotama, a good sideroad leads to the planned timber-mill town of **Kawerau**, which sits on a flood plain of the Tarawera River at the foot of the distinctive hump of Mount Edgecumbe (Putauaki). You are unlikely to want to stay longer than it takes to visit the **visitor centre**, Plunket St (Mon–Fri 8.30am–4.30pm, Sat & Sun 10am–3pm; Ⓣ07/323 7550), for the compulsory **permit** ($2 here, or free from the Fletcher Challenge Forests' Visitor Centre in Rotorua) and directions to the region's main attraction, **Tarawera Falls**, 24km to the south. It is at its most impressive when the underground Tarawera River appears to burst in a solid stream out of the cliff face. It is less impressive after a dry spell, but still worth the fifteen-minute walk (mostly flat) along the Tarawera Falls/Tarawera Outlet walkway to the falls viewpoint. You can see where the Tarawera River dives underground a further 10–20min walk upstream (and uphill), and by pressing on a further 5min you come across a wonderful safe swimming hole with natural diving spots and a rope swing. The track continues a further hour to DOC's popular lakeside Tarawera Outlet **campsite** ($5; toilets and water only), also accessible by forest road. Note that **driving can be hazardous** on metalled forest roads – keep your headlights on at all times and steer well clear of the billowing clouds of dust thrown up by huge logging trucks.

Southeast of Rotorua

Volcanic activity again provides the main theme for attractions southeast of Rotorua, most having some association with **Lake Tarawera** and the jagged line of volcanic peaks and craters along the southeastern shore, collectively known as **Mount Tarawera**, which erupted in 1886.

Before this, Tarawera was New Zealand's premier tourist destination, with thousands of visitors every year crossing lakes Tarawera and Rotomahana in whale boats and *waka*, frequently guided by the renowned Maori guide Sophia, to the **Pink and White Terraces**, two separate fans of silica that cascaded down the hillside to the edge of Lake Rotomahana. Boiling cauldrons bubbled away at the top of each formation, spilling mineral-rich water down the hillside where, over several centuries, it formed a series of staggered cup-shaped pools, the outflow of one filling the one below. The White Terraces (Te Tarata or "Tattooed Rock") were the larger, but most visitors favoured the Pink Terraces (Otukapuarangi or "Cloudy Atmosphere"), which were prettier and better suited to sitting and soaking. The chemical reaction that gave them the pink tint was explained in the 1980s, since when there has been much idle talk of trying to re-create the terraces.

All this steamy bliss came to an abrupt end on the night of June 10, 1886, when the long-dormant Mount Tarawera ripped itself asunder, creating 22 craters along a 17km rift, and covering over 15,000 square kilometres in mud and scoria. The Pink and White Terraces were shattered by the buckling of the earth, covered by ash and lava, then submerged deep under the waters of Lake Rotomahana which, dammed by earth upheavals, grew to twenty times its previous size.

The cataclysm had been foreshadowed eleven days earlier, when two separate canoe loads of Pakeha tourists and their Maori guides saw an ancient *waka* glide silently out of the mist, with a dozen warriors paddling furiously, then vanish just as suddenly; this was interpreted by the ancient *tohunga* (priest) Tuhoto Ariki as a sign of imminent disaster. The fallout from the eruption buried five villages, including the staging post for the Pink and White Terrace trips, **Te Wairoa**, where the *tohunga* lived. In a classic case of blaming the messenger, the inhabitants refused to rescue the *tohunga* and it wasn't until four days later that they allowed a group of Pakeha to dig him out. Miraculously, he was still alive, though he died a week later.

The chain of eruptions that racked the fault line during that fateful night in 1886 created an entirely new thermal valley, **Waimangu**, running southwest from the shores of the newly enlarged Lake Rotomahana. Still geothermally active, Waimangu struggles to outdo the supremely colourful thermal area of **Wai-O-Tapu**, a few kilometres further south.

Beyond the volcanic zone, the Kaingaroa Forest stretches away east to the little-visited tramping territory of the **Whirinaki Forest Park**, and the Kinleith Forest straggles west to **Tirau**, **Putaruru** and **Tokoroa**, minor way-stations on the route from Auckland to Taupo and the Tongariro National Park.

The Blue and Green lakes, the Buried Village and Lake Tarawera

To nineteenth-century tourists Rotorua was merely a staging post before they continued their journey to the shores of **Lake Tarawera**, 15km southeast, where canoes would take them across to view the Pink and White Terraces. Latter-day sightseers still follow the same route, passing a ridge-top viewpoint that overlooks the iridescent waters of **Blue Lake** (Tikitapu) and **Green Lake** (Rotokakahi), which get their hues from subterranean mineral activity.

The road reaches the shores of Lake Tarawera just past the Te Wairoa **Buried Village** (daily: Nov–April 8.30am–5.30pm; May–Oct 9am–4.30pm; $14.50; ⓣ07/362 8287, ⓦwww.buriedvillage.co.nz), the partly excavated and heavily reconstructed remains of a pre-European settlement that, at the time of the Tarawera eruption, was larger than contemporary Rotorua. Numerous houses collapsed under the weight of the two or three metres of ash that settled on Te Wairoa on June 10, 1886; others were saved by virtue of their inhabitants hefting ash off the roof to lighten the load. Much of the village was excavated in the 1930s and 1940s, though work continues slowly today. Free **guided tours** take place on the hour (11am–3pm), or you can make your own way through the grounds where there is less of a sense of an archeological dig than of a manicured orchard: half-buried *whare* and the foundations for the Rotomahana Hotel sit primly on mown lawns among European fruit trees gone to seed, marauding hawthorn and a perfect row of full-grown poplars fostered by a line of fenceposts. Many of the *whare* contain small collections of implements and ash-encrusted household goods, contrasting with the stark simplicity of other dwellings such as **Tohunga's Whare**, where the ill-fated priest lay buried alive for four days before being released from his ashen tomb. Look out too for the extremely rare, carved-stone *pataka* (storehouse), and the bow section of a *waka* once used to ferry tourists on the lake and allegedly brought to the district by Hongi Hika when he invaded in 1823.

Beyond the formal grounds, a sequence of steep steps and slippery boardwalks dives down the hill alongside **Te Wairoa Falls**, then climbs up through dripping, fern-draped bush on the far side. By the entrance to the Buried Village complex is a new **museum** which does a great job of capturing the spirit of the village in its heyday and the aftermath of its destruction, through numerous photos, some fine aquatints of the Pink and White Terraces and more ash-encrusted knick-knacks.

Two boats run **cruises** on Lake Tarawera. From Tarawera Landing, 2km east of the Buried Village, Lake Tarawera Launch Services (Ⓣ07/362 8595) operate the *Reremoana* on a 45-minute scenic cruise on the lake (summer 1.30pm, 2.30pm & 3.30pm, winter 1.30pm; $17.50), and the Eruption Trail Cruise (11am; 2hr 30min; $27) which takes you to the approximate site of the Pink and White Terraces and includes a short bush walk. Boatshed Bat, 1km east of Tarawera Landing, is the base for summer-only cruises aboard the restored, coal-burning *SS James Torrey* (bookings recommended Ⓣ07/362 8698, Ⓦwww.steamboat.co.nz; $36) to Hot Water Beach where you can spend an hour soaking. Both companies will also do drop-offs for campers wanting to stay at any of the three DOC campsites around the lake.

Tamaki Maori Village

Heading south from Rotorua, bound for Waimangu and Wai-O-Tapu, you'll pass the palisades and red-painted warrior statues of **Tamaki Maori Village**, a modern creation built as a base for the Tamaki Tours concert and *hangi* (see p.328). It is an attractive site, nestled beside a patch of native bush, with *whare* (houses) ranged around the central **Tribal Market** (daily 9am–4pm; $15), which is little more than a few shops selling quality Maori crafts and clothing in the *whare*, and is pretty lacklustre during the day.

Waimangu

At the southern limit of the volcanic rift blown out by Mount Tarawera lies **Waimangu Volcanic Valley** (daily 8.30am–5pm; $18; Ⓦwww.waimangu.co.nz), 19km south of Rotorua on Waimangu Road, via SH5, and 5km off the highway. Among the world's youngest thermal areas, this is also New Zealand's largest and most lushly vegetated.

A visitor centre by the entrance hints at the sights lining the streamside path, which cuts through a valley choked with scrub and native bush that has re-established itself since 1886. The regeneration process is periodically interrupted by smaller eruptions, including one in 1917 which created the 100m-diameter **Frying Pan Lake**, the world's largest hot spring. Impressive quantities of hot water welling up from the depths is the attraction of the **Inferno Crater**, an inverted cone where mesmerizing steam patterns partly obscure the powder-blue water. The water level rises and falls according to a rigid 38-day cycle – filling to the rim for 21 days, overflowing for 2 days then gradually falling to 8m below the rim over the next 15 days. More run-of-the-mill steaming pools and hissing vents line the stream, which also passes the muddy depression where, from 1900 to 1904, the **Waimangu Geyser** regularly spouted water to an astonishing height of 400m, carting rocks and black mud with it.

The path through the valley ends at the wharf on the shores of Lake Rotomahana, where the rust-red sides of Mount Tarawera dominate the far horizon. From here, frequent free shuttle buses run back up the road to the visitor centre and gentle, commentated, 45-minute **cruises** (6 daily; $22) chug around the lake past steaming cliffs, fumaroles and over the site of the Pink and White Terraces.

Wai-O-Tapu

The tussle for Rotorua's geothermal crown is principally fought between Waimangu and the **Wai-O-Tapu Thermal Wonderland** (daily 8.30am–5pm; $15), 10km south of Waimangu (and 30km from Rotorua), just off SH5. This combines a vast expanse of multi-hued rocks and pools, New Zealand's largest and most impressive lake of boiling mud and the **Lady Knox Geyser**, which is ignominiously induced to perform on schedule, at 10.15am daily. Buy your entrance ticket at the main entrance then double back 1km along the road to the geyser where, as the crowds fill the serried ranks of benches, a staff member pours a packet of soap flakes into the vent. Within a few minutes, the soap reduces the water's surface tension, and superheated steam and water are released in a jet which plays initially to around 10m and continues at half that height for anything up to an hour. Everyone then bundles into their vehicles and drives back to the main site for the crawl around the hour-long walking loop track as it wends its way through a series of small lakes which have taken on the tints of the minerals dissolved in them – yellow from sulphur, purple from manganese, green from arsenic and so on. The gurgling and growling black mud of the **Devil's Ink-Pots** and a series of hissing and rumbling craters pale beside the ever-changing rainbow colours of the **Artist's Palette** pools and the gorgeous, effervescent **Champagne Pool**, a circular bottle-green cauldron wreathed in swirling steam and fringed by a burnt-orange shelf. The waters of the Champagne Pool froth over **The Terraces**, a rippled accretion of lime silicate that glistens in the sunlight.

As you drive back to the main road, follow a short detour to a huge and active **boiling mud pool** which plops away merrily, forming lovely concentric patterns. On the opposite side of SH5, Waikite Valley Road runs 6km to **Waikite Valley Thermal Pools** (daily 10am–10pm; $5), a naturally fed geothermal pool that's a good deal more low-key than the pools in Rotorua, but hardly justifies a special journey; guests at the adjacent motor camp (tent sites $10) get in free.

Whirinaki Forest Park and the road to Lake Waikaremoana

Midway between Waimangu and Wai-O-Tapu, some 25km south of Rotorua, SH38 spurs southeast, running arrow-straight through the regimented pines of the Kaingaroa Forest towards the jagged peaks of Te Urewera National Park, a vast tract of untouched wilderness which separates the Rotorua lakes from Poverty Bay and the East Cape. The Kaingaroa Forest finally relents 40km on, as the road crosses the Rangitaiki River by the predominantly Maori timber town of **MURUPARA**. Apart from a couple of shops and takeaways, the only reason to pull over is DOC's **Rangitaiki Area Visitor Centre**, 1km south-east of town on SH38 (Dec–March daily 8am–5pm; April–Nov Mon–Fri 8am–5pm; ⓣ07/366 1080, ⓕ366 1082), with diverting displays and a stack of information on Te Urewera National Park and the Lake Waikaremoana region.

Particular emphasis is given to the easily accessible **Whirinaki Forest Park**, a wild and wonderful slice of country that harbours some of the densest and most impressive stands of bush on the North Island: podocarps on the river flats, and native beech on the steep volcanic uplands between them, support a wonderfully rich birdlife with tui, bellbirds, parakeets and even the rare brownish-red kaka. The forest is now protected from the loggers' chainsaw, after a close shave in the late 1970s and early 1980s, when it saw one of the country's fiercest and most celebrated **environmental battles**. In early 1978, protesters had succeeded in preventing logging by occupying trees in the Pureora State Forest to the west of Lake Taupo. Anticipating similar action at Whirinaki and fearing for their livelihood, the local Ngati Whare people blockaded the road into the forest; conflict was only avoided through intense negotiation. By 1987 logging of all native timber had ceased (except for totara cut for ceremonial-carving purposes), the mill had closed and the entire logging village of **MINGINUI**, 25km south of Murupara, was unemployed. Today, this moribund village ticks by on a trickle of tourism: even the sole community shop is only open sporadically.

River Road runs 8km south from Minginui to the Whirinaki car park, from where, in four hours or so, you can sample some of the best of the Whirinaki Forest Park – the Whirinaki Falls, where the Whirinaki River cascades over an old lava flow, and the churning Te Whaiti-nui-a-tio Canyon – on the first stretch of the **Whirinaki Track** (27km; 2 days). To penetrate deeper into the forest, you can follow the rest of this gentle track, though you'll need to carry your own cooking stove, food and sleeping bag. By linking several tracks and staying in some of the nine Category 3 **huts** ($5) that pepper the park, more robust walkers can tramp for four or five days. DOC's *Whirinaki Forest Park* leaflet ($1) covers the main routes, with expanded coverage on their *Whirinaki Short Walks and Tracks* leaflet ($1.50) and on the NZMS 260 series V18 *Whirinaki* map. It is also possible to explore the area with Rotorua-based Whirinaki Trax (ⓣ07/366 4756; 1 day; $70), which offers a pick and drop-off service for the Whirinaki Track ($60), and uses Maori guides for its one-day **guided treks** that also visit a local vineyard.

Practicalities

For details of **transport** out this way contact the Rangitaiki Area Visitor Centre (see above) for advice, as it can be difficult to get to Whirinaki or through to Lake Waikaremoana without your own wheels. Even a car can be a liability as vehicles left at the Whirinaki car park aren't safe, so the best bet is to enlist the assistance of *Whirinaki Forest Holidays*, on Minginui Road, 1km south of its junction with SH38 (ⓣ & ⓕ07/366 3235). As well as running a pick-up service from Rotorua or Taupo ($25 each way), and a trampers' shuttle service for the Whirinaki Track (price dependent on numbers), the lodge also offers **accommodation** in comfortable dorms, cottages and motel units, or in the lodge with all meals included (dorms ❶, cottages ❷, units 3, lodge ❺), and organizes horse treks ($15 per hour). *Jail House*, 2km south along Minginui Road (Ⓣ07/366 3234; ❹), also operates track transport from their self-contained jail-turned-chalet, which sleeps up to seven. Minginui itself has the informal riverside *Mangamate Waterfall campsite* ($6 per tent).

West of Rotorua: Tirau, Putaruru and Tokoroa

Fifty-odd kilometres northwest of Rotorua, SH5 and SH1 meet at the small farming settlement of **TIRAU**, a highwayside strip adorned with a wonderfully kitsch corrugated-iron sheep housing a wool shop. It has become something of a town icon and has spawned a sheet-metal biblical shepherd in the grounds of the church next door, and a similarly constructed sheepdog containing the **visitor centre** (Ⓣ & Ⓕ07/883 1202, Ⓔthedogtirau@xtra.co.nz; daily 9am–5pm). Here you can obtain the free *Tirau Visitors' Guide*, which highlights the town's recent reinvention of itself as something of an antique and crafts centre – several such shops now line SH1 and Hillcrest Street at the eastern end of town, some of which are quite interesting.

There is a handful of **places to eat** along SH1, notably the *Alley Cats Espresso Café*, opposite the dog, which serves good quiches, pizza slices and cakes, and the *Loose Goose* (closed Tues) further east on SH1, which serves more substantial meals. If you need to break your journey, **stay** at the well-priced *OK Tirau Motor Inn*, SH1 (Ⓣ07/883 1111, Ⓕ883 1999; rooms ❹, units ❺), which has modern rooms and large self-contained units.

Okoroire Street, beside the sheep, runs 8km to the lovely **Okoroire Hot Springs**, a couple of private, concrete pools located (one open-air with a sandy bottom) in a glade by a cascading stream, each accommodating a dozen or more sybaritic souls. The pools cost $10 an hour, and can be booked at the adjacent *Okoroire Hot Springs Hotel* (Ⓣ & Ⓕ07/883 4876, Ⓦwww.okohotel.co.nz), which has backpacker rooms for $25 per person, recently renovated en-suite rooms (❹) and some chalets (also ❹) and allows camping ($10 per tent) among the mature poplars and conifers; the hotel also has a bar, serves meals, and lets you onto their nine-hole golf course for $10 a day.

East of Tirau the roads split again, with SH5 forging on to Rotorua, while SH1 turns southeast towards Taupo, passing through **PUTARURU**, 8km further on, and the **Putaruru Timber Museum** (Ⓣ07/883 7621; daily 9am–4pm; $5), a further 2km south, where the region's timber-milling heritage is pulled together in a well-laid-out collection of minor historic buildings relocated from around the district. If you do nothing else, climb the totara-built 1930s fire lookout to get an inkling of just how extensive the Kaingaroa Forest really is.

SH1 continues through rolling farmland to pungent **TOKOROA**, 25km southeast, a modern place downwind of the nearby Kinleith pulp mill, the principal reason for the town's existence. There's little to stop for, but it is almost 70km to Taupo, the next place of any consequence, so those needing a **place to stay** might choose to overnight at the barely acceptable *Tokoroa Motorcamp*, 22 Sloss Rd (Ⓣ & Ⓕ07/886 6642; tent & power sites $9, cabins & flats ❷–❸), at the northern entrance to town, or at the quiet and clean *Mayfair*

Court Motel, 3 Logan St (ⓣ & ⓕ07/886 7399; ❹). Newmans and InterCity **buses** stop outside the visitor centre, on SH1 (Nov–March Mon–Fri 8.30am–5.30pm, Sat & Sun 9am–3pm; shorter weekend hours in winter; ⓣ07/886 8872, ⓔtokoroa.info@xtra.co.nz). If the fast-food joints beside the highway aren't to your taste, try *Scoffers Café* on Rosebery Street, which runs parallel to the main highway.

The Western Bays Highway

Most likely you'll want to stick on SH1 to Taupo, but if the Tongariro National Park beckons, follow SH32 30km south from Tokoroa to Whakamaru and turn left (south) for the **Western Bays Highway** (still SH32) direct to Turangi. The road flanks the eastern side of the Pureora Forest, mostly accessed along Kakaho Road, 19km south of Whakamaru, but with additional interest 10km further south where a short side road leads to the **Waihora Lagoon Walk** (500m return; 15min), which ends at a gorgeous lake surrounded by rimu and kahikatea.

There are very few facilities down this way, but one lovely place to break your journey is *South Claragh*, 12km south of Whakamaru (ⓣ07/372 8848, ⓔlhill@reap.co.nz; room ❺, self-catering cottage ❹), situated on a small working livestock farm where you are encouraged to join the family for an excellent three-course dinner with wine ($40). Either stay in the house on a B&B basis or in the cottage in the grounds with no meals provided.

Taupo and around

Taupo, 80km south of Rotorua and slap in the centre of the North Island, is very much a Kiwi holiday resort slung around the northern shores of New Zealand's largest lake, Lake Taupo. Views stretch 30km southwest towards the three snow-capped volcanoes of the Tongariro National Park, the reflected light from the lake's glassy surface combining with the 360m altitude to create an almost alpine radiance. Here, the impossibly deep-blue waters of the Waikato River ("flowing water" in Maori) begin their long journey to the Tasman Sea, and both lake and river frontages are lined with parks, lending Taupo a slow pace and an undeniably appealing tenor.

For decades, Kiwi families have been descending en masse for a couple of weeks' holiday, bathing in the crisp cool waters of the lake, fishing its depths and lounging around their holiday homes that fringe the lakeshore. Although you could easily follow their lead and spend a relaxing few days here, there is no shortage of stuff to see and do, most notably around the spectacular rapids and geothermal badlands of **Wairakei Park**, immediately north of town. Thousands more come specifically for the **fishing**: the Taupo area is perhaps the most fecund trout fishery in the world, extending south to Turangi and along the Tongariro River and with an enviable reputation for the quality and fighting-spirit of its fish. Year-round, you'll see boats drifting across the lake with lines trailing and, particularly in the evenings, rivermouths choked with fly casters in chest-high waders.

Lake Taupo itself is a geological infant, born just two thousand years ago when a massive volcano erupted, spewing out 24 cubic kilometres of rock, debris and ash – ten times more than was produced by the eruptions of Krakatoa and Mount St Helens combined – and covering much of the North Island in a thick layer of pumice. Ash was ejected so high into the atmosphere that it was carried around the world, enabling historians to pinpoint the date of the **eruption** as 186 AD – when the Chinese noted a blackening of the sky and Romans recorded that the heavens turned blood-red. As the underground magma chamber emptied, the roof slumped, leaving a huge steep-sided **crater**, since filled by Lake Taupo. It is hard to reconcile this placid and beautiful lake with such colossal violence, though the evidence is all around: entire beaches are composed of feather-light pumice which, when caught by the wind, floats off across the lake. **Geologists** continue to study the causes and effects of the eruption and treat the lake as a kind of giant spirit-level, in which any tilting could indicate a build-up of magma below the surface that might trigger an eruption.

The local Tuwharetoa people ascribe the lake's formation to their ancestor, **Ngatoroirangi**, who cast a tree from the summit of Mount Tauhara, on the edge of Taupo, and where it struck the ground water welled up and formed the lake.

Taupo

Nowhere in **TAUPO**'s compact low-rise core is more than five minutes' walk from the waters of the Waikato River or Lake Taupo, which jointly hem in three sides. The fourth side rises up through the gentle slopes of Taupo's suburbs. Most of the commercial activity happens on, or just off, SH1, which passes through the middle of town as the main Tongariro Street and the aptly named Lake Terrace. Room for expansion is limited to the southeastern quarter, where ever more motels and timeshares are springing up along the lakeshore.

Although Taupo bears little trace of the vigorous Tuwharetoa settlement that existed into the middle of the nineteenth century, there was scant European interest in the area until the New Zealand Wars of the 1860s, when the Armed Constabulary were trying to track down **Te Kooti** (see box on p.456). They set up camp one night in June 1869 at Opepe, 17km southeast of Taupo (beside what is now SH5), and were ambushed by Te Kooti's men, who killed nine soldiers. Garrisons were subsequently established at Opepe and Taupo, but it was Taupo that flourished, enjoying a more strategic situation and being blessed with hot springs for washing and bathing. By 1877, Te Kooti had been contained, but the Armed Constabulary wasn't finally disbanded until 1886, after which several soldiers and their families stayed on, forming the nexus of European settlement.

Taupo didn't really flourish as a resort until the prosperous 1950s, when the North Island's roads had improved to the point where Kiwi families – equipped with caravans, boats and all manner of playthings – could easily drive here from Auckland, Wellington or Hawke's Bay. For the most part, the town just languishes by the lake, with what diversions there are limited to tacky tourist fodder, but Taupo makes a great base for exploring the natural wonders of the surrounding area.

Arrival, information and transport

InterCity and Newmans **buses** (with direct connections from Rotorua, Tauranga, Hamilton, Auckland, Napier, Palmerston North and Wellington) stop at the Taupo Travel Centre bus station, 16 Gascoigne St (Ⓣ07/378 9032), around two hundred metres from Taupo's **visitor centre**, Tongariro Street (daily 8.30am–5pm; Ⓣ07/376 0027, Ⓦwww.laketauponz.com), right in the heart of town. Taupo's **airport**, 10km south of the centre, is served by Air New Zealand flights; Airporter Shuttle (Ⓣ07/378 5713) meets all planes for costs $12 for the first person, then less for others to the same destination, this cost depending on numbers.

As for **getting around**, almost everything you'll want to visit in the centre can be reached either on foot or with Top Cabs (Ⓣ07/378 9250) and Taupo Taxis (Ⓣ07/378 5100). To visit the surrounding sights without your own vehicle, use the Hot Bus (daily 10am–6pm), which makes an hour-long circuit of all the main sights (except Aratiatia Rapids) plus a few hostels, Taupo Hot Springs and the visitor center. You pay $2 each time you hop on, and the sixth ride is free. Alternatively join a **guided tour** with Paradise Tours (Ⓣ07/378 9955; 2hr 30min; $25) who visit most of the same places, including the Aratiatia Rapids.

Renting a bike gives greater freedom: the most sophisticated machines will set you back roughly $25 a half-day and $35 a day (see p.347 for rental outlets). For **car-rental**, try the Rental Car Centre, 7 Nukuhau St (Ⓣ06/378 2740), which undercuts the big guys.

Accommodation

Taupo manages to maintain a very high standard of accommodation for all budgets. Finding somewhere to stay is unlikely to be a problem except when the crush is on (Christmas to end-Feb), when you should **book** several days in advance, especially at weekends. As befits a Kiwi holiday resort, there is no end of places catering to families, with much of the lakefront taken up by **motels**, and grassy spots on the fringes of town given over to **campsites**. **Hostels** are abundant too and uniformly good, though differing in style.

Hotels and motels

Baycrest Lodge 79 Mere Rd Ⓣ07/378 3838 & 0800/229 273, Ⓦwww.gisnz.com/baycrest. Luxuriously appointed top-of-the-range motel with spacious multi-room units, a heated pool, poolside bar and Sky TV. ❼

Cascades SH1, Two Mile Bay Ⓣ07//378 3774 & 0800/996 997, Ⓦwww.cascades.co.nz. Classy motel with units either on the waterfront or with access to an attractive pool. Studio and family units are all spacious with deluxe fittings, a full kitchen, mezzanine sleeping area, a patio and a spa bath. ❻

Clearwater Motor Lodge 229 Lake Terrace Ⓣ07/377 2071 & 0800/639 639. Beautiful lakeside accommodation with great views, in-room spas and some rooms with small balconies. ❻

Continental Motel 9 Scannell St Ⓣ & Ⓕ07/378 5836. Comfortable, low-cost, central motel with small, well-maintained units. ❹

Dunrovin Motel 140 Heu Heu St Ⓣ & Ⓕ07/378 7384 & Ⓣ0800/386 768, Ⓔinfo@dunrovintaupo.co.nz. Older, budget units that are well-kept and characterful, being built of wood rather than the ubiquitous concrete blocks. ❹

Huka Lodge Huka Falls Rd, 4km north of Taupo Ⓣ07/378 5791, Ⓦwww.hukalodge.com. One of the first and still the best-known of New Zealand's exclusive lodges, located just upstream from Huka Falls. It costs a cool $900 a night for a double, including cocktails, five-course dinner and breakfast. ❾

Mountain View Motel 12 Fletcher St Ⓣ07/378 9366 & 0800/146 683, Ⓔmt-view-motel@xtra.co.nz. Budget, central motel with spa pool, Sky TV, games room and kids' play area. The family units are huge, and the studios are at the bottom end of this price code. Studios ❹, family units ❺

B&Bs and guesthouses

Bickers Homestay 190 Spa Rd ⓣ07/377 0665, ⓔorbiii@reap.org.nz. Plain, simple and friendly non-smoking homestay made special by its sunny garden, on the cliffs high above the Waikato River and the views of Cherry Island and the Taupo Bungy. ❹

Beside the Lake 8 Chad St, 5km south of Taupo ⓣ & ⓕ07/378 5847, ⓔfoote.tpo@xtra.co.nz. Two modern, tasteful and well-appointed luxury rooms (one with private bath, one en suite) beside a small park which fronts the lake. Rooms have lake views, a/c, and a terrace that catches the afternoon sun. A full breakfast is served. ❻

Bradshaw's 130 Heu Heu St ⓣ07/378 8288, ⓕ378 8282. Good-value guesthouse with pleasant floral decorated rooms with showers, let at very reasonable rates, with breakfast an optional extra. There are also new and good three-bedroom units that can be good value for groups. ❸

Bramham Lodge 7 Waipahihi Ave ⓣ07/378 0064, ⓦwww.bramham-bed-and-breakfast.com. Spacious homestay with expansive lake and mountain views, a couple of comfortable rooms with private facilities, and delicious breakfasts. ❺

Paeroa Lakeside Homestay 21 Te Kopua St, Acacia Bay ⓣ07/378 8449, ⓦwww.taupohomestay.com. Luxurious homestay in a lush garden setting with great lake views five minutes' drive southwest of Taupo, with en-suite double all with balconies. ❼

Hostels

Action Downunder 56 Kaimanawa St ⓣ07/378 3311, ⓕ378 9612. Modern associate YHA hostel close to town and with good lake and mountain views from the kitchen and barbecue balcony, and a spa pool. Dorms sleep three–five, there are doubles and twins, and bikes can be rented for $20 a day. Dorms ❶, rooms ❷

Berkenhoff Lodge 75 Scannell St ⓣ & ⓕ07/378 4909, ⓔbhoff@reap.org.nz. Bustling and slightly cramped hostel fifteen minutes' walk from the centre. The games room and on-site bar are perennially popular and they run a barbecue every evening by the pool and spa. Each dorm has a bathroom, and doubles and twins come with linen. Dorms ❶, rooms ❷

Go Global Central Backpackers, cnr Tongariro St & Tuwharetoa St ⓣ0800/464 562 & 07/377 0044, ⓦwww.go-global.co.nz. Large, central hostel above a bar and popular with the backpacker buses. The dorms and a multitude of rooms are all clean and comfortable and there's bike rental for $28 per day, as well as Internet access, though self-catering facilities are a bit cramped. Dorms ❶, rooms ❷

Rainbow Lodge 99 Titiraupenga St ⓣ07/378 5754, ⓔrainbowlodge@clear.net.nz. Spacious, relaxed and spotless purpose-built backpackers with a comfortable lounge, coin-op sauna, bike rental at $15 a day and fishing gear for $11 a day, a stack of local information and little touches that create a homely atmosphere. Dorms have six–nine beds and there are spacious triples and doubles, many of them en suite. Dorms ❶, rooms ❷

Sunset Lodge 5 Tremaine Ave ⓣ07/378 5962, ⓔsunset@reap.org.nz. Small, low-key and friendly hostel at Two Mile Bay some 3km from town but with courtesy pick-ups, low-cost bike rental and daily drop-offs at the Craters of the Moon. The more spacious three-bed rooms are worth the extra dollar over the larger dorms. Dorms ❶, rooms ❷

Campsites and motor parks

All Seasons Holiday Park 16 Rangatira St ⓣ07/378 4272 & 0800/777 272, ⓦwww.destinations-nz.com/allseasons. Compact site just over 1km from town, with tent sites scattered among nice new cabins and a range of good tourist flats. Tent sites $11, cabins ❷, flats ❸

Lake Taupo Top 10 Holiday Park 28 Centennial Drive ⓣ & ⓕ07/378 6860, ⓦwww.taupotop10.co.nz. Wonderfully spacious site 2km from town with good communal facilities and excellent range of clean and new tourist cabins, tourist flats and fully self-contained cottages, and easy access to the A.C. Baths. Tent sites $12, cabins, flats & cottages ❸–❹

Reids Farm 3km north of Taupo on Huka Falls Rd. Spacious free campsite right by the Waikato River just upstream of Huka Lodge. The makeshift slalom course makes it a popular spot with kayakers.

Taupo Motor Camp 15 Redoubt Rd ⓣ & ⓕ07/377 3080, ⓦwww.taupomotorcamp.co.nz. Very handy site on the banks of the Waikato River right in town. Tent sites $11, cabins ❷, on-site vans ❸

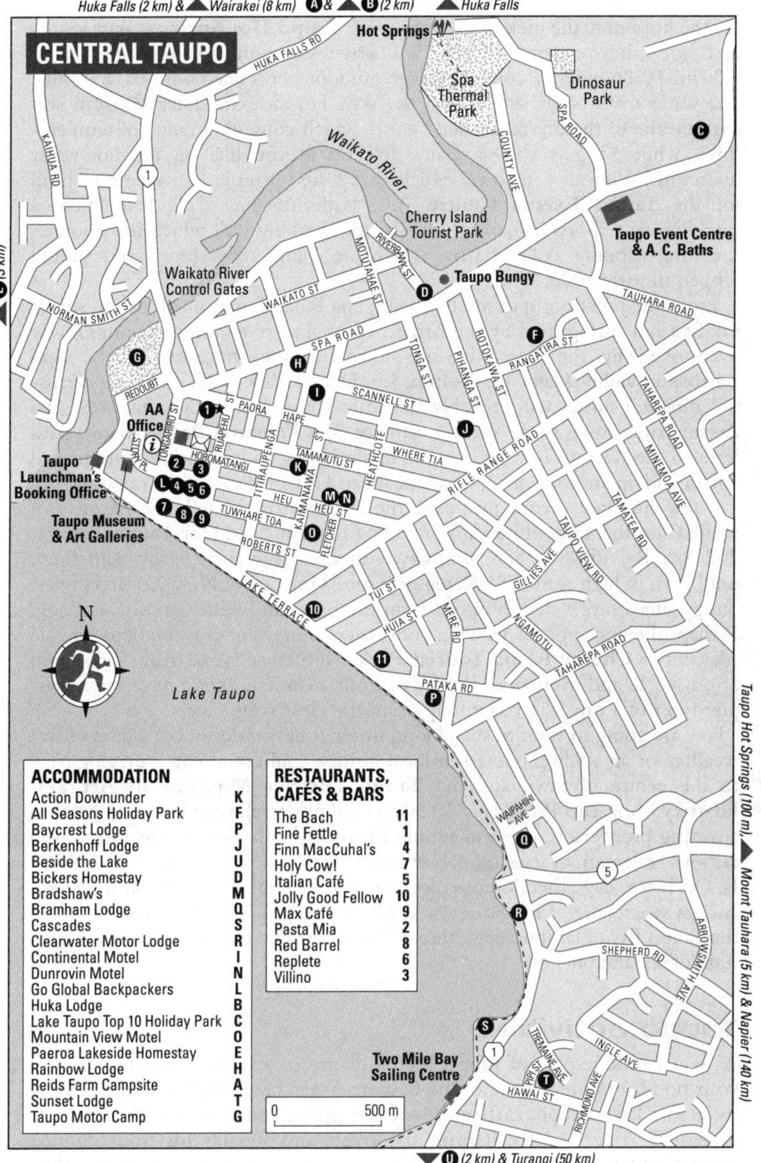

The Town

True to its family-resort status, Taupo specializes in entertainment for the kids and adventure activities for adults. Perhaps the best all-round crowd-pleasers are the hot pools; the pick of the two being **Taupo Hot Springs**, 3km southeast of the centre on SH5 (Ⓦwww.taupohotsprings.com, daily 7.30am–9.30pm; $8), a couple of large outdoor pools filled with natural mineral water that's oddly slippery on the skin. For an extra dollar you can also soak in one of the private mineral pools, which come in a range of temperatures, while $5 gets you as many descents as you like on the hot-water hydroslide. Without your own vehicle, you'll find it more convenient to head for the **Taupo Events Centre**, A.C. Baths Avenue (daily 8am–9pm), a sparkling new sports hall and twelve-metre climbing wall which incorporates the long-standing **A.C. Baths**, which are being redeveloped and should reopen in early 2003.

From the junction opposite the baths, Spa Road forges north to the site of the first hot spring used by the Armed Constabulary and now ignominiously overlooked by the thirty life-size ferro-concrete dinosaurs of the **Spa Dinosaur Valley** (daily 10am–4pm; $5). Jurassic Park it ain't, but the "realistic" dinosaur noises will probably still scare young kids witless. Just west, Spa Avenue runs down to the green swathe of **Spa Thermal Park**, where a path leads to the Waikato River past some naturally hot bathing pools (unrestricted entry) and, in an hour or so, downstream to Huka Falls (see box opposite).

A few hundred metres upstream, the river swirls through the narrows of Hell's Gate, the 45m white cliffs providing the launch pad for **Taupo Bungy**, 202 Spa Rd (Ⓣ0800/888 408, Ⓦwww.taupobungy.co.nz; daily 9am–5pm, until 7pm in high season; $100, repeat jumps $45), one of New Zealand's finest bungy sites cantilevered 20m out from the bank, and with optional dunking. Perhaps the best spot for viewing your mates' bungy antics is the outdoor café adjacent to **Cherry Island Tourist Park**, Motutahae Road (daily 9am–5pm; $8), a feeble and overpriced display of trout, deer and exotic birds that occupies most of a tiny islet beautifully set in the clear river waters.

Few are going to want to spend long summer days indoors, but a dose of wet weather, or an abiding interest in local history, could send you scurrying back to the centre of town and the **Taupo District Museum of Art and History**, Tongariro Park (daily 10.30am–4.30pm; free), with its varied exhibits covering pioneering days and fishing in some depth, before moving on to a curious collection of scale models of every plane which took part in World War II. On better days, there's more pleasure in lolling about outside on the pleasant grassy expanse of Tongariro Park, which sweeps down to the lakeshore and the Taupo Boat Harbour, departure-point for cruises, fishing trips and a multitude of aquatic pursuits.

Taupo activities

As you would expect of Taupo, there's plenty of activities to relieve you of your holiday money. Some of the best are water-based, either **cruising** gently across Lake Taupo, **rafting** down the raging waters of the Tongariro or Rangitaiki rivers or **fly-fishing** the rivers and streams for trout. Taupo's magnificent scenery has also given it something of a name for tandem **skydiving**.

Cruises, boat trips and watersports

One of the most satisfying ways to relax in Taupo is to take one of the **lake cruises**, run from the Taupo Boat Harbour and setting course for some striking modern Maori rock carvings, which can only be seen from the water at Mine Bay, 8km southwest of town. The carvings, dating from the late 1970s,

Walks around Taupo

There are a few relatively easy **walks** near town. By far the most popular is the **Great Lake Walk**, which is more modest than it sounds: just follow the lakeshore east from town, covering as much of its 7km as you like, passing hot springs right at the water's edge.

On the northern edge of town, County Avenue leads to the **Spa Thermal Park**, where there's a pleasant thirty-minute bushwalk, which can be combined with a riverbank walk to **Huka Falls** (4km; 1hr one-way), and further extended to the Aratiatia Rapids (8km; 2hr one-way), though you've then got to get back – if you set off early, you could conceivably walk back via the Wairakei visitor centre and the Craters of the Moon (12km; 3hr).

Finally, if you have your own transport and a taste for magnificent lake and town views, try the track to the summit of **Mount Tauhara** (6km; 2–3hr return), the hill behind Taupo, which is approached on Mountain Road, which turns off SH5 to Napier after 6km.

depict a stylized image of a man's face heavy with *moko*, together with tuatara (lizard-like reptiles) and female forms draped over nearby rocks. The most characterful of the trips – as much for the sea-dog skipper as the boat – is aboard *The Barbary* (☎07/378 3444; 10am & 2pm; 2hr 30min; $25), a 1926 ketch once owned by Eroll Flynn (who, it is colourfully claimed, won it in a card game) and subsequently co-opted into the 1973 Greenpeace anti-nuclear-testing flotilla that sailed to Mururoa Atoll. If you're not too bothered about seeing the carvings, take the summer-time-only sunset trip which is a little shorter and only costs $20.

For a touch of gin-palace style, opt for the *Cruise Cat* (☎07/378 0623 & 0800/252 628; 11.30am; 1hr 30min; $26), which motors past the carvings. Different atmospherics are offered by the *Ernest Kemp* (☎07/378 3444; daily: Dec–Feb 10am, 2pm & 4.15pm; Oct–Nov & March–April 10am & 2pm; May–Sept 2pm; $22), a replica 1920s steamboat that chugs to the carvings and back in a couple of hours. Finally, you can compress the carvings trip into one eye-streaming hour ($29) on the *Superjet* (☎0800/278 737, Ⓦwww.superjet.co.nz), a powerful catamaran that also does a two-hour circuit around most of the lake for $59.

To experience the lake at a more sedate pace, join Eco-Explorer (☎0800/529 255, Ⓦwww.kayakingkiwi.com) for **kayak tours**, which use a launch to get you to interesting sections of coastline and act as a base while you paddle around. Three- to four-hour trips (Nov–April 8am, 1pm & 6.30pm; May–Oct 10am; $75) require no prior experience and take an educational, eco-sensitive approach.

There are no whitewater rivers right on Taupo's doorstep, but the town makes a viable base for **rafting**. The main rivers run from Taupo are the Tongariro (covered under Turangi – see p.354), the Rangitaiki and the Wairoa, and a two-day trip on the relatively gentle upper section of the Mohaka, camping on the riverbank overnight. Rapid Sensations (☎07/378 7902 & 0800/227 238, Ⓦwww.rapids.co.nz) run the Tongariro for $85, and Kiwi River Safaris (07/377 6597 & 0800/723 857, Ⓦwww.krs.co.nz) organize trips to the Wairoa ($85), the Rangitaiki ($85) and the overnight Mohaka trip ($275, including meals). Closer to town, Kayak New Zealand (☎0800/529 256) offer guided **kayaking** trips on the Waikato (2hr, $40), with a welcome emphasis on scenic appreciation.

Bookings can be made either direct with operators, through the visitor centre or with the Taupo Launchmen's Booking Office, Redoubt Street (Ⓣ07/378 3444; 8am–5pm). The latter can point you in the direction of other lake-based watersports, such as **parasailing** (150m ascent for $59, 300m ascent for $85), **waterskiing** ($70 per half-hour for up to four skiers), and **jetbiking** ($80 per hour).

If you'd rather be self propelled, head around the lake to Two Mile Bay, where U-Sail-It Sailing Centre (Ⓣ025/967 350; daily 9am–6pm in summer, otherwise sporadically) rents rowboats ($20 per hr), self-drive boats for four ($40–60 per hour), kayaks and canoes ($20 per hr), **windsurfers** ($25) and **catamarans** ($40).

Fishing

New Zealand's arcane fishing rules dictate that trout can't be sold, so if you've got a taste for their succulent flesh you'll have to catch it yourself. No one is going to guarantee you'll land a fighting rainbow or brown but the chances are better here than most places. If dinner is more of an incentive than sport, then your best approach is to fish the lake on a boat chartered through the visitor centre or directly from the Taupo Launchmen's Booking Office. Smaller **boats** go out for a minimum of two hours, but more usually three or four, and cost $70 an hour, taking up to four people. **Book in advance** from mid-December to February – and at any other time of year if you want the booking offices to help reduce your costs by matching you up with other interested parties. Boat operators have all the tackle you need and will organize a Taupo District Fishing Licence ($12.50 per day, $27 per week, $37 per month and $58 for the full July-to-June year) for you.

The rivers flowing into Lake Taupo are the preserve of **fly-fishers**, particularly from March to September when mature rainbow trout enter the mouths of the streams and rivers and make their way upstream to shallow gravel hollows where they spawn. Brown trout are also in these waters, but they tend to be more wily. You can **rent tackle** from Taupo Rod & Tackle, 34 Tongariro St (Ⓣ07/378 5337), and the Fly & Gun Shop, Heu Heu Street (Ⓣ07/378 4449), and pick your own spot, but average catches are much larger if you engage the services of a **fishing guide**, which will set you back close to $250 for half a day with gear and licence: the tourist office has a list of guides.

Skydiving and scenic flights

Taupo has rapidly gained a reputation as one of the cheapest places to go tandem **skydiving** – and one of the best, with magnificent scenery all around, if you dare to look. At times it can feel like a production line, with two very professional companies putting through dozens of customers a day, and each offering an array of videos, photos and T-shirts, some included in the quoted prices. Great Lake Skydive (Ⓣ0800/373 335 & 07/378 4662, Ⓦwww.freefly.co.nz) and Taupo Tandem Skydiving (Ⓣ0800/275 934 & 07/377 0428, Ⓦwww.tts.net.nz) currently vie for your business, both offering jumps from 9000ft ($190–195) which give around 30 seconds freefall, the popular 12,000-foot jump ($200–215) with 45 seconds freefall, and the whopping one minute freefall from 15,000 feet ($300–345), a height which occasionally warrants a few breaths of supplemental oxygen before you exit.

If you'd prefer to stay in the plane, there are fixed-wing **scenic flights** over Wairakei Thermal Area and the Huka Falls on a float plane from the Taupo Boat Harbour with ARK Aviation (Ⓣ07/378 7500; 10min; $60). An extensive range of longer flights down to the volcanoes are operated by Skytrek Aviation (☎07/378 0172; 15min–2hr; $50–300). Helistar Helicopters (☎0800/435 478, Ⓦwww.helistar.co.nz) offer **helicopter** flights over the Huka Falls and Craters of the Moon (10min; $80), along with a bunch of longer flights.

Eating, drinking and nightlife

Taupo's culinary stock has risen in recent years with new places opening all the time, many making use of settings with great views across the lake. A sprinkling of modern cafés supplement more traditional tearooms, and the better lakefront motor lodges all have pricey **restaurants**, some of them very good. For a small provincial town, there's a reasonable nightlife, with holidaymakers converging on several **pubs** and **clubs**.

Restaurants and cafés

The Bach 2 Pataka Rd ☎07/378 7856. Modern dining in an easy-going atmosphere. Choose from wood-fired crispy pizza, a select range of $30 mains such as seared venison tenderloin with roast garlic potatoes, and an extensive selection of cellared New Zealand wines by the bottle and glass. Closed lunchtime Mon–Fri in low season.

Fine Fettle 39 Paora Hape St. Daytime organic wholefood (but not entirely vegetarian) café that's good for breakfasts, including buckwheat pancakes ($8.50) and eggs Benedict ($14.50). Lunches include hearty soups ($8), panini and salads, many served with organic bread, which is also available by the loaf.

Italian Café 28 Tuwharetoa St. Reliable Italian trattoria of the gingham-tablecloth-and-Chianti-bottle ilk, with a range of traditional pizza and pasta ($17) and meat and fish dishes (around $20). Takeaways also available. Licensed & BYO.

Jolly Good Fellow 76–80 Lake Terrace. The nearest Taupo gets to an English pub, nothing like one in style but with over a dozen English and Irish beers on tap, most of which seem to have travelled well. There are also pub meals in the English tradition with fish and chips ($17), toad-in-the-hole ($15) and breakfast served all day.

Max Café 38 Roberts St. Taupo's fast-food mainstay, serving a good standard of burgers, toasties and steak 'n' chips meals 24hr a day, and with lake views to boot.

Pasta Mia 7 Horomatangi St. Relaxed daytime café with a small but immaculate line in simple pasta dishes ($10–18) and the best coffee in town.

Replete 45 Heu Heu St. Despite inconsistent service, this remains Taupo's finest deli and daytime café, run by a former chef from the esteemed *Huka Lodge* and serving excellent quiches, pizza slices, cakes and coffee until 5pm Mon–Fri, 3pm Sat & Sun.

Villino 45 Horomatangi St ☎07/377 4478. Classy downtown restaurant and café open daily for lunch and dinner and serving a typically eclectic range of dishes which lean towards German and Italian, though they also do wonderful Pacific oysters for under $20. Mains ($26–28) might include prime rib with truffled mash or crispy duck confit.

Bars and clubs

Finn MacCuhal's cnr Tongariro St & Tuwharetoa St. Ersatz Irish bar very popular with the locals as well as the backpackers staying upstairs at *Go Global*. You come here for the Guinness, but they also do good-value steaks, pasta dishes and salads.

Holy Cow! 11 Tongariro St. The liveliest late-night bar in town, spinning an eclectic selection of rock and dance tunes and turning clubby late on. Very popular with backpackers who can soak up their excesses with burgers, toasties and the like.

Jolly Good Fellow (see above). An excellent range of hand-pulled ales and much more.

Red Barrel, 4 Roberts St. Traditional beer-and-pool pub with decent bar meals and seats outside with lake views.

Listings

Automobile Association 93 Tongariro St ☎07/378 6000.

Bike rental Most of the hostels have basic bikes for guests' use: *Rainbow Lodge* and *Go Global* backpackers also rent to non-guests.

Horse riding Taupo Horse Treks, Karapiti Rd (☎07/378 0356), do one-hour ($30) and two-hour ($50) treks through the pine forests around the Craters of the Moon (see p.350), and will do courtesy pick-up for booked two-hour jaunts.

Internet access Cheapest rates are at *Central Plateau Reap*, cnr Heu Heu St & Kaimanawa St (☎07/378 8109) though there are longer opening hours at *Contact Cyber Café*, 10 Roberts St (☎07/378 3697) where you can do your laundry while you surf.
Left-luggage Lockers are available at the Superloo, Tongariro St. Daily: Dec–Jan 7.30am–9pm; Feb–Nov 7.30am–5.30pm. $1 a day.
Medical treatment Taupo Health Centre, 115 Heu Heu St ☎07/378 7060.
Pharmacy Main Street Pharmacy, cnr Heu Heu St & Tongariro St, is open daily until 8.30pm ☎07/378 2636.
Police Story Place b ☎07/378 6060.
Post office cnr Horomatangi St & Ruapehu St, with poste restante facilities ☎07/378 9090.
Travel Agents Budget Travel, 37 Horomatangi St ☎07/378 9799; United Travel, Taupo Travel Centre, 40 Heu Heu St ☎07/378 9709; James Travel Holiday Shoppe, 28 Horomatangi St ☎07/378 7065.

Around Taupo

Taupo's town attractions are in many ways upstaged by those immediately to the **north**, a fabulously concentrated collection of natural wonders. Within a few minutes of each other you can find boiling mud, hissing steam harnessed by the Wairakei power station and the clear, blue Waikato River, which cuts a deep and swirling course northwards, occasionally turning wild as it squeezes through some of the country's most powerful rapids. The highlights – **Huka Falls**, **Aratiatia Rapids** and the **Craters of the Moon** geothermal area – are all within 10km of Taupo, but you'll have to venture further to reach a second thermal park, **Orakei Korako**, 40km north. To get out this way, you'll need your own vehicle, or the services of one of Taupo's tour companies (see "Listings" above).

Moving **south** from Taupo, SH1 follows the lakeshore to Turangi, while heading east along SH5 towards Napier, there are a couple of things to detain you along the way.

Along Huka Falls Road

The bulk of the sights and activities around Taupo flank the Waikato River as it wends its way north, and are lumped together under the collective title of **Wairakei Park**. The park is reached via Huka Falls Road, which loops off SH1 a couple of kilometres north of Taupo and passes the Reids Farm free campsite and the exclusive *Huka Lodge* (see p.341) en route to the first point-of-call, the impressive and justly popular **Huka Falls** (*hukanui*, or "great body of spray"). Here the full flow of the Waikato River, one of New Zealand's most voluminous rivers, funnels into a narrow chasm then plunges over a ten-metre shelf into a seething maelstrom of eddies and whirlpools; the sheer power of some four hundred tonnes of water per second make it a far more awesome sight than its relatively short drop would suggest. A footbridge spans the channel, providing a perfect vantage point for watching the occasional mad kayaker making the descent, usually on weekend evenings. The parking lot, toilets and snack stand are only open until around 6pm but you can park outside and walk in at any time.

A large Russian helicopter marks the launch pad for Helistar flights en route to the cutaway hives and educational video at the **Honey Hive** (☎07/374 8553; daily 9am–5pm; free), 1km further north along Huka Falls, which shouldn't divert you long, though they do have an excellent range of honey varieties, including the wonderful *manuka*. Press on to the **Volcanic Activity Centre** (Mon–Fri 9am–5pm & Sat–Sun 10am–4pm; $5), a highly

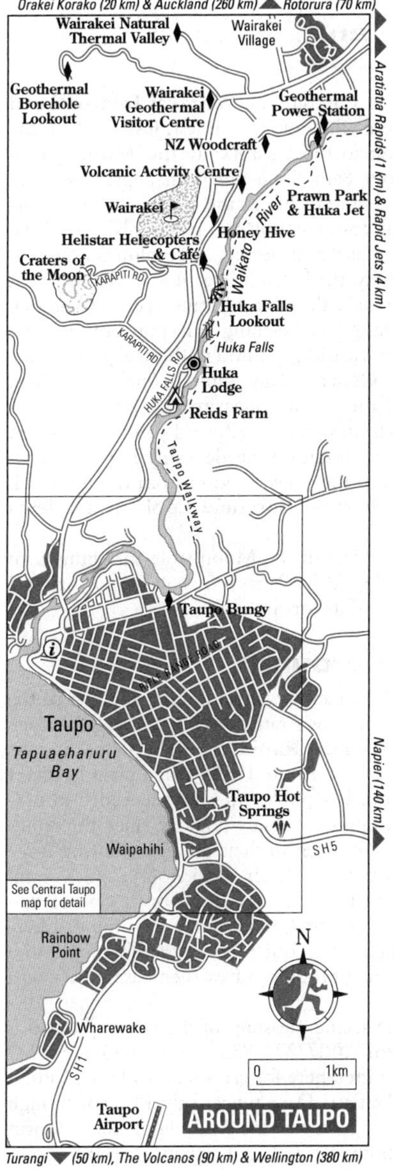

instructional museum where the dense text is alleviated by striking photos and interactive computer displays on all things tectonic. Watch one of several films run continuously then check out the seismograph linked to sensors on Mount Ruapehu, an earthquake simulator and a large relief map of Taupo Volcanic Zone, which extends from Mount Ruapehu to White Island.

Moving swiftly past **NZ Woodcraft** (Ⓣ07/374 8555), essentially a shop selling turned native woods, you'll come to the Wairakei geothermal power station. Most of the excess heat generated by the station is discharged into the river, though a portion is channelled into large open ponds, where tropical Malaysian prawns are raised in an enterprise known as the **Prawn Park** (daily: Jan 10am–4pm, Feb–Dec 11am–4pm, tours hourly; $6). Even if the "Day in the life of a Prawn" tour of the complex doesn't stir your imagination, you can at least indulge in the scrumptious platters dished up by the *Prawn River Restaurant* while seated by the deep-blue water of the Waikato.

The peace is periodically shattered by the **Huka Jet** (Ⓣ07/374 8572 & 0800/485 2538, Ⓦwww.hukajet.co.nz; 30min; $59) as it roars along the river between Huka Falls and the Aratiatia Dam. The boats leave from a jetty by the Prawn Park (courtesy bus from Taupo), and play all the usual tricks – close encounters with rock faces and 360-degree spins – but if you are looking for thrill opt for Rapids Jet (see below) or save your money for the jetboating heartland around Queenstown.

Craters of the Moon and the Wairakei Valley

The Huka Falls loop road rejoins SH1 opposite the **Wairakei International Golf Course** (☎07/374 8152), one of the country's finest. Just south of the intersection, Karapiti Road runs west to the **Craters of the Moon** (unrestricted entry but custodian on duty 8am–6pm; donation appreciated), an other-worldly geothermal area that sprang to life in the 1950s, after the construction of the Wairakei geothermal power station had drastically altered the underground hydrodynamics. What it lacks in geysers and colourful lakes, it more than makes up for in hyperactivity: the belching steam is so vigorous that you should wear closed footwear to walk the 2km of trails that wind among roaring fumaroles and huge rumbling pits belching out pungent bad-egg smells. The culprit can only be visited vicariously through the self-promotional **Wairakei Geothermal Visitor Centre** (daily 9am–4.30pm; free), 3km north on SH1, with its relief map of the whole Tongariro and Waikato power schemes, an explanatory video shown on demand ($2), and plenty of stuff on the intricacies of harnessing the earth's bounty. Outside, shiny high-pressure-steam pipes twist and bend the 2km to the power station from the borefield, which can be viewed from the **Geothermal Borefield Lookout** just down the road.

The same forces that created the Craters of the Moon stole the thunder of the **Wairakei Natural Thermal Valley** (daily 9am–5pm; $6), Taupo's original thermal area but now a mere shadow of its former self.

Aratiatia Rapids and around

Around 2km downstream from the Wairakei power station lies the first of the Waikato River's eight hydroelectric dams, the Aratiatia Dam, which holds back the Waikato immediately above the **Aratiatia Rapids**, a long series of cataracts that were one of Taupo's earliest attractions. In the 1950s, when plans to divert the waters around the rapids were revealed, public pressure succeeded in preserving the rapids; though it's something of a hollow victory, since the rapids are left empty most of the time and only seen in their full glory during three or four thirty-minute periods each day (Oct–March 10am, noon, 2pm & 4pm; April–Sept 10am, noon & 2pm). Stand on the dam itself or at one of two downstream viewpoints reached by an easy trail, and wait for the siren that heralds the bizarre spectacle of a parched watercourse being transformed into a foaming torrent of waterfalls and surging pressure waves, then easing back to a tame trickle.

An amiable way of appreciating the scenic pleasures of the river upstream is to board the paddle-wheeler **Otunui** (☎07/374 8338; 90min; $30), a 1907 Whanganui riverboat that has been shifted here for cruises up to Huka Falls. It leaves a small landing right by the Aratiatia Dam twice daily. Pleasant though these daytime cruises are, the one to go for is the Moonlight Glow Worm Cruise, which drifts along while spotlights pick out aquatic life and glow-worms illuminate the gorge walls.

Small discounts are available if you book the Otunui and a trip with the top-value **Rapids Jet** (☎07/378 5828 & 0800/727437; $65), located on Rapids Road 3km beyond the Aratiatia Dam. This is no slick bus-them-in operation, but New Zealand's only true commercial whitewater jetboating run, taking you down and up Fuljames rapid and throwing in a good deal of local lore and entertaining patter to boot. The entire boat gets airborne and the company makes no secret of having sunk three boats on the rapid, but no one has been injured: just listen closely to the safety spiel, hang on and prepare to get very wet.

If this is your kind of thing, you might also want to trip along to **Rock 'n' Ropes**, a maze of high ropes and wires on SH5 16km north of Taupo (Ⓣ07/374 8111 & 0800/244 508, Ⓦwww.rocknropes.co.nz; daily 8.30am–4.30pm or later), where you can ride the Giant Swing ($15), a fifteen-metre swoop that's as heart-stopping as many a bungy and a whole lot cheaper. The swing is included in the Adrenaline Combo ($35), where you are attached to a climbing harness for a nerve-wracking walk along a horizontal pole suspended 15m above the ground, then goaded into leaping off the top of a pole and grabbing a trapeze. Those with nerves of steel might prefer the Half Day ($59), which includes all of the above plus the opportunity to learn how to belay then work in pairs around the rest of the ropes course. For the Half Day there's free courtesy transport from Taupo.

The site is also home to the **Crazy Catz Adventure Park** (Ⓦwww.crazycatz.co.nz; same hours) where the farm tour, mini golf and maze are no match for riding go-carts around a dirt track ($15 for 8min), or trying to steer around a track in a VW Beetle with its steering mechanism reversed ($10) – when you turn left, the car turns right. There's also the Gravatac ($20), where up to four are strapped into seats then raised up a tower and released for a forty-metre freefall before being gently lowered to the ground.

Orakei Korako

There's yet more geothermal activity 40km north of Taupo at **The Hidden Valley of Orakei Korako** (daily: 8am–4.30pm in summer, 4pm in winter; $19; Ⓣ07/378 3131), which is reached by travelling 14km east off SH1 or 23km west off SH5. The site's main distinguishing feature is its means of access, via a short shuttle-boat journey across a dammed section of the Waikato River, which drops you at the foot of a large silica terrace tinged orange, pink and green by heat-loving algae. From here, an hour-long self-guided walking trail loops past bubbling mud pools, through an active geyser field, and down into the mouth of Ruatapu Cave, a sacred site once used by Maori women to prepare themselves for ceremonies – hence *Orakei Korako*, "a place of adorning".

You can **stay** on the opposite side of the river at *Orakei Korako Lodge* (Ⓣ07/378 3131, Ⓦwww.orakeikorako.co.nz; dorms ❶, units ❹) in self-catering bunk-style budget accommodation and new motel units, with a big lounge, a pool table, hot tubs, and canoes for rent at $8 an hour.

The Napier–Taupo Road

Travelling beyond the immediate vicinity of Taupo, SH1 hugs the lake as it heads southwest to Turangi (see p.354), while SH5 veers southeast along the **Taupo–Napier Road**, a twisting but increasingly speedy ninety-minute run through some of the North Island's remotest country. Much of the early part of the journey crosses the Kaingaroa Plains, impoverished land cloaked in pumice and ash from the 186 AD Taupo volcanic eruption and of little use save for the pine plantations which stretch 100km north. The history of this route to Napier is traced by the **Taupo–NapierHeritage Trail**; pick up a free booklet from Taupo or Napier visitor centres. Many of the 35 stops are of limited interest, but be sure to call in at **Opepe Historic Reserve**, 17km from Taupo, where, on the north side of the road, a cemetery contains white wooden slabs marking the graves of nine soldiers of the Bay of Plenty cavalry, killed by followers of maverick Maori leader Te Kooti in 1869. A half-hour bush walk winds through a fine stand of totara, rimu and kahikatea alive with birdsong. Across the road, a couple of trails lead to a well, water trough and a sawpit used by the Armed Constabulary during the construction of the Taupo–Napier telegraph line.

After another 11km, Clements Mill Road leads 30km south into the northern reaches of the **Kaimanawa Forest Park**, a remote rugged mountain wilderness, almost untouched, and little-visited by recreational trampers, but a perennial favourite with deer hunters and anglers. There is no public transport out this way and tracks are not well marked, but if you are experienced and determined, get hold of the detailed *Guide to Kaimanawa State Forest Park* map and set off on the remote **Te Iringa–Oamaru Circuit** (60km; 4–5 days), staying in a series of Category 3 huts ($5 per night). Some 25km southeast of the Clements Mill Road turn-off, the Waipunga River, a tributary of the Mohaka, plummets 30m over the **Waipunga Falls**, and continues beside SH5 through the lovely Waipunga Gorge, packed with tall native trees and dotted with picnic sites which double as overnight "freedom" **campsites** with no facilities but river water. Soon, the highway descends to the Mohaka River and the appealing riverside accommodation at the *Riverlands Outback Adventures*, 5km south of SH5 (Ⓣ06/834 9756, Ⓔriverlnds@xtra.co.nz; camping $8, dorms ❶, rooms ❷, self-contained units ❸), a residential multi-activity centre where the prime attractions are **horse trekking** (2hr, $30; 4hr, $45) along farm trails and down to the river; and **whitewater rafting** on Grade I–II stretches of the Mohaka (2hr, $60), or the more exciting and wonderfully scenic Grade III section (full day; $80), which runs through a narrow gorge that's just great for jumping off the cliffs either side. Beyond the Mohaka River, the highway climbs the Titiokura Saddle before the final descent through the grape country of the **Esk Valley** into Napier (see p.460).

Tongariro National Park and around

New Zealand's highly developed network of national parks owes much to Te Heu Heu Tukino IV, the Tuwharetoa chief who, in the Pakeha land-grabbing climate of the late nineteenth century, recognized that the only chance his people had of keeping their sacred lands intact was to donate them to the nation – on condition that they could not be settled nor spoiled (see the box on p.355 for more on this). His 1887 gift formed the core of the country's first major public reserve, **Tongariro National Park**. In the north a small, outlying section of the park centres on **Mount Pihanga** and the tiny **Lake Rotopounamu,** but most visitors head straight for the main body of the park, dominated by three great volcanoes, which rise starkly from the desolate plateau to pierce the hard blue sky: the broad-shouldered ski mountain,

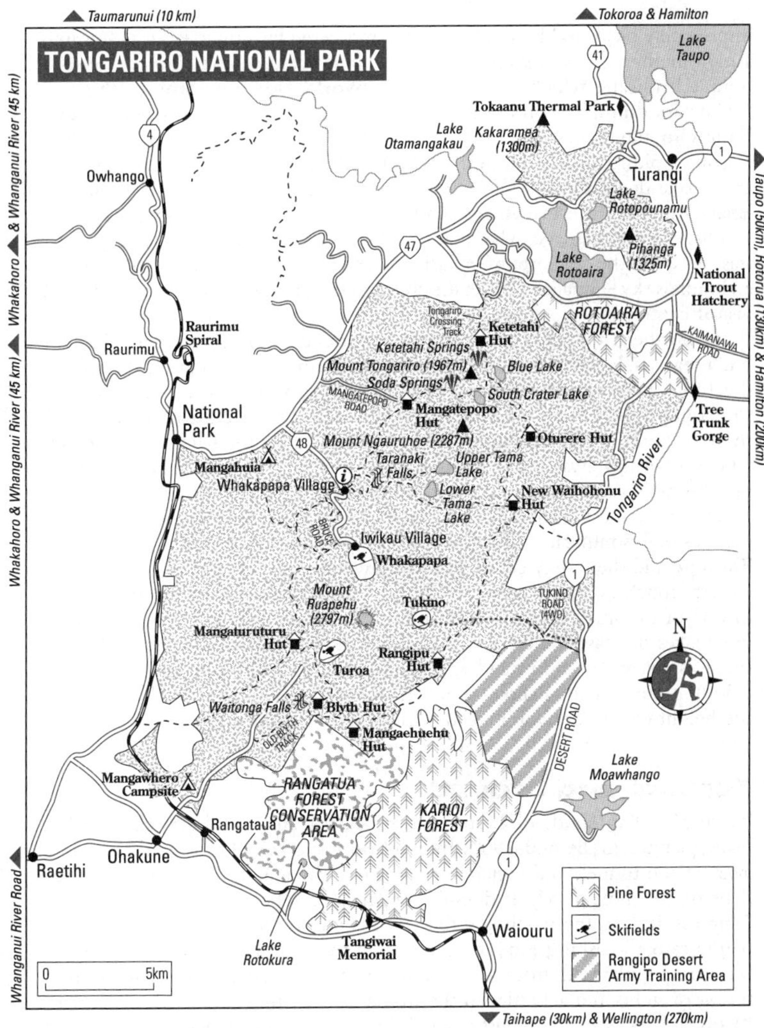

Ruapehu (2797m), its squatter sibling, **Tongariro** (1968m), and, wedged between them, the conical **Ngauruhoe** (2287m).

Within the boundaries of the park is some of the North Island's most striking scenery – semi-arid plains, crystal-clear lakes and streams, steaming fumaroles, virgin rainforest, an abundance of ice and snow – and two supremely rewarding tramps, the one-day **Tongariro Crossing** and the three-to-four-day **Tongariro Northern Circuit**, one of New Zealand's Great Walks. The undulating plateau to the west of the volcanoes is vegetated by bushland and golden tussock, while on the eastern side the rain shadow of the mountains produces the **Rangipo Desert**. Although this is not a true desert, it is still an impressively bleak and barren landscape, smothered by a thick layer of volcanic ash from the 186 AD Taupo eruption. These features combine to create a unique landscape, which was designated a **World Heritage Site** in 1991.

The park captured world headlines in 1995 and again in 1996 when **Mount Ruapehu**, the highest and most massive of the three volcanoes, burst into life, blasting a plume of ash and dust 12km into the atmosphere and emptying the crater lake down the side of the mountain in great muddy deluges known as lahars. Although the **eruptions** drastically curtailed the ski season, they have had little lasting damage; what made them newsworthy was the dramatic contrast between the black spume of ash and the pristine snowy peak, all offset by a cloudless sky – images now endlessly recycled on the walls of local cafés and visitor centres.

The northern approach to the region is through **Turangi**, not much in itself but a reasonable base both for the Tongariro tramps and for rafting and fishing the Tongariro River. What it lacks is a sense of proximity to the mountains – something much more tangible in the service town of **National Park**, and more so again in **Whakapapa Village**, 1200m up on the flanks of Ruapehu. The southern gateway is **Ohakune**, a more appealing place than National Park but distinctly dead outside the ski season. Heading south, the Army Museum at Waiouru marks the southern limit of the Volcanic Plateau, which tails off into the pastoral southern half of the island around the agricultural town of **Taihape** and the bungy centre at **Mangaweka**.

Pretty much everyone comes to the park either to **ski** or to **tramp**, staying in one of the small towns dotted around the base of the mountains. While a **car** makes life easier, there is a reasonable network of **minibuses** plying the more useful routes and providing trailhead transport for trampers (see box on p.360). Note that this whole region is over 600m above sea level, so even in the height of summer you'll need some **warm clothing**.

Turangi and around

Turangi, 50km south of Taupo, is a small, flat and seemingly characterless place, planned in the mid-1960s and built almost overnight for workers toiling away at the tunnels and concrete channels of the ambitious Tongariro Power Scheme (see box, p.357). It doesn't even make the best of its location – Lake Taupo is 4km to the north and the town centre is separated by SH1 from its trump card, the fishing and rafting waters of the Tongariro River. Nonetheless, it is very popular with trout fishers, and works well enough as a base for a smattering of sights and activities in the immediate vicinity and for the Tongariro National Park (see p.360), just beyond the steep volcanic range to the south. It has also become a major jumping-off point for the Tongariro Crossing (see p.361) with a selection of hostels offering transport to and from the trailheads.

European settlement began early this century soon after trout were released into the Taupo fishery, but although the collection of fishing lodges warranted a shop and post office, no town existed until 1964 when well-paid work on the power scheme lured workers to the area, notably Italian tunnellers, many of whom subsequently settled here.

Arrival, information and accommodation

Alpine Scenic Tours and Tongariro Expeditions (see box on p.360) both run low cost daily **bus** services from Taupo dropping off pretty much where you want. InterCity and Newmans both pull in at the Turangi Bus & Travel Centre, Ohunga Road (Mon–Fri 9am–5pm; ⓣ07/386 8918, ⓕ386 8397), which sells

The Maori mountain legends

According to Maori, there used to be a lot more mountains in the Tongariro area, dominated by the chiefly **Ruapehu**, **Tongariro**, **Ngauruhoe** and **Taranaki**. Around them clustered smaller mountains including the beautiful **Pihanga** in the northern section of the park, whose favours were widely sought. Pihanga loved only Tongariro, the victor of numerous battles with her other suitors, including one that had brought him to his knees, striking off the top of his head, giving him him his present shape. Taranaki, meantime, defeated Ngauruhoe, but when he came to face Ruapehu, he was exhausted and badly wounded. He fled, carving out the Whanganui River as he made for the west coast of the North Island. Meanwhile the smaller **Putauaki** got as far north as Kawerau; but **Tauhara** was reluctant to leave and continually glanced back, so that by dawn, when the mountains could no longer move, he had only reached the northern shores of Lake Taupo, where he remains to this day, "the lonely mountain".

To the local Tuwharetoa people these mountains were so sacred that they averted their eyes while passing and wouldn't eat or build fires in the vicinity. The *tapu* stretches back to legendary times when their ancestor **Ngatoroirangi** came to claim the centre of the island. After declaring Tongariro *tapu* he set off up the mountain, but his followers broke their vow to fast while he was away and the angry gods sent a snow storm in which Ngatoroirangi almost perished before more benevolent gods in Hawaiki saved him by sending fire to revive his frozen limbs.

tickets when open. Otherwise buy them from the visitor centre, Ngawaka Place (daily 8.30am–5pm; ⓣ07/386 8999 & 0800/288 726, ⓦwww.laketauponz.com, ⓔturangivc@laketauponz.com), which is packed with local **information**, including informative panels on trout fishing and a relief model of the Tongariro Power Scheme. They also sell Taupo fishing licences, topo maps, DOC tramping brochures and hut tickets, though if you have detailed tramping enquiries you can trot down the street to the small **DOC office**, Turanga Place (Mon–Fri 8.30am–5pm; ⓣ07/386 8607, ⓕ386 7086).

Turangi's need to cater to anglers, skiers and trampers bound for the Tongariro National Park has left it with a decent range of **accommodation**; the budget places congregate in the town centre, while the plusher lodges and B&Bs line the Tongariro River to the east, though nowhere backs right onto the river.

Bellbird Lodge cnr Tautahanga Road and Rangipoia Place ⓣ07/386 8281, ⓔbookings@bellbird.co.nz. A popular and homely backpackers occupying several suburban houses, with home-made cakes each evening. Dorms ❶, rooms ❷

Club Habitat 25 Ohuanga Road ⓣ07/386 7492, ⓔhabitat@voyager.co.nz. An activity-oriented associate YHA that comes with a spacious games bar and dining complex, a spa and sauna, and is a favourite with the backpacker tour buses. Tent sites $8, dorms ❶, cabins ❸, self-contained units ❹

Creel Lodge 183 Taupahi Rd ⓣ & ⓕ07/386 8081. A simple, low-cost, fishing-oriented motel comprising a cluster of self-contained one- and two-bedroom units in grounds running down to the river edge with communal fish smoker and barbecue. ❹

Extreme Backpackers 26 Ngawaka Place ⓣ07/386 8949, ⓔebpcltd@xtra.co.nz. Worth paying the extra dollar or so over the other hostels for superior, simply decorated rooms in this purpose-built backpackers set around a central courtyard, with spacious common areas and amenable hosts who sometimes run guests to the Tokaanu hot pools in the evening. Tents $10, dorms ❶, rooms ❷, ensuites ❸

Ika Lodge 155 Taupahi Rd ⓣ & ⓕ07/386 5538, ⓦwww.ika.co.nz. This superior homestay-cum-fishing lodge by the Tongariro River has three en-suite rooms and succulent game and fish dinners for $40. ❻

Parklands cnr SH1 & Arahori Street ⓣ0800/456 284 & 07/386 7515, ⓔinfo@prklands.co.nz. An extensive motor lodge with an outdoor pool, private hot tubs, games room and a small restaurant serving home-style dinners. Tents and vans $10, studios ❹, units ❺

River Birches 21a Koura St ⓣ & ⓕ07/386 5348, ⓔgillo@voyager.co.nz. A lovely two-bedroom self-contained house in the woods a stone's throw from the river and right by the start of the Tongariro River Walk. Everything is laid on with full cooking facilities, a range of teas and coffees, extensive library, complimentary pre-dinner drinks in the main house and breakfast included. ❻

Around Turangi

The massive amount of trout fishing in this area makes it essential that rivers are continually restocked with fingerlings raised at fish-breeding facilities such as the **Tongariro National Trout Hatchery**, on SH1, 5km south of Turangi (daily 10am–3pm; free), set among native bush between the Tongariro River and one of its tributaries, the Waihukahuka Stream. Ever since its inception in 1927 the centre has used wild rainbow trout collected from the stream – as opposed to the more common practice of using hatchery-raised fish – and stripped them of their eggs and milt to produce fry that are genetically more varied and disease-resistant. The fish are then left to grow for around a year until they reach 150mm before being released into streams all over the country. There isn't a lot to see, but you are free to wander through buildings where tanks hold the tiniest fish, among the rearing ponds outside and into an underground viewing chamber where you can view wild trout in the Waihukahuka Stream.

Fauna in its natural state is best seen on the educational two-hour-plus **Tongariro River Delta Wetland Tour** run by Tongariro River Rafting (see "Activities" below; around dawn & dusk; $40). Aboard a specially designed shallow-draught boat, you putter around the fringes of the lake while guides well-versed in local ecosystems explain the dynamics of one of the country's largest delta wetlands, which is home to black swans, dabchicks, four species of cormorant, white-faced heron and Canada geese.

Heading away from the delta region, the **Tongariro River Loop Track** (4km; 1hr) is a pleasant trail that starts from the Major Jones footbridge at the end of Koura Street on the edge of town and follows the right bank of the river north past a couple of viewpoints and over a bluff then crosses the river and returns along the opposite side. Ten kilometres south of Turangi, off SH47, the **Lake Rotopounamu Circuit** (5km; 90min) encircles a pristine lake surrounded by bush alive with native birds.

Activities

Four companies offer rafting year round on the lower reaches of the Tongariro River, which runs through one of the most scenic and accessible river gorges in the country. The river's natural flow patterns have been modulated by the Tongariro Power Scheme, limiting the possibilities of a really wild time on the Grade II and Grade III rapids, but what sets the Tongariro apart is the range of trips you can do on one piece of water – some involving a two-hour run in traditional river rafts, some employing sit-on kayaks and some combining fishing with the rafting.

All **operators** charge $85: handiest are Tokaanu-based Rock 'n' River Rafting (ⓣ07/386 0352, ⓦwww.laketaupo.co.nz/rafting) and Turangi-based Tongariro River Rafting, Atirau Road (ⓣ07/386 6409 & 0800/101024, ⓔrafting@xtra.co.nz). Taupo's Rapid Sensations (ⓣ0800/227238 & 07/378 7902, ⓦwww.rapids.co.nz, ⓔinfo@rapids.co.nz) and Kiwi River Safaris (ⓣ07/377 6597, ⓦwww.krs.co.nz) are also very competitive. All offer straightforward whitewater-rafting trips, though Tongariro River Rafting also allow you to paddle yourselves with a guide in hailing distance, and offer the Tongariro Duo

The Tongariro Power Scheme

The **Tongariro Power Scheme** provides an object lesson in harnessing the power of water with minimal impact on the environment. Its two powerhouses produce around seven percent of the country's electricity, while the outflows that feed into Lake Taupo add flexibility to the much older chain of eight hydroelectric dams along the Waikato River. While some argue it is unacceptable to tamper with such a fine piece of wilderness, and while it has caused fluctuations in the levels of nutrients in the Tongariro River and erosion along some of the service tracks, the scheme has many admirers.

In fact, if it weren't for the scale models in visitor centres and the ugly bulk of the Tokaanu power station, only astute observers would be aware of the complex system of tunnels, aqueducts, canals and weirs unobtrusively going about their business of diverting the waters of the Tongariro River and myriad streams running off the mountain slopes, back and forth around the perimeter of the national park, using modified natural lakes for storage. Mount Ruapehu poses its own unique problems: the threat of **lahars** is ever-present and, after the 1995 eruption, **tephra** (a highly abrasive volcanic ash) found its way into the turbines of the Rangipo underground powerhouse, causing an unscheduled seven-month shutdown.

($120), which spends the best part of a day careering along mountain-biking trails and then rafting the river.

Big rafts make the modest scale of the lower Tongariro seem a little tame, and more fun can be had on Tongariro River Rafting's **sit-on kayak** trips ($65 for 2hr) on a lower stretch of Grade II whitewater.

If you're keen to try hauling a trout from Lake Taupo or one of the local rivers, the visitor centre will help pair you with a **fishing** guide to match your experience and aspirations; expect to pay around $100 for a couple of hours with gear and guiding. You can rent a boat and tackle at moderate prices from the Motuoapa Marina (☎07/386 7000, $30 per hr), 8km north of Turangi on SH1. River fishing takes place pretty much year-round, but the the spawning season is from April to October.

To combine the last two activities, Tongariro River Rafting will take you for a full day **raft fishing** (Dec–May only) which involves rafting the Grade III section of the Tongariro, stopping off at otherwise inaccessible pools along the way to cast a fly. Rates are $500 a day for two people – roughly the same as you'd pay for a fishing guide alone.

If you'd prefer to just take off on a **mountain bike**, call Tongariro River Rafting who rent bikes at $20 for two hours ($40 per day) and can provide transport and guides for the 42 Traverse, an exhausting full-day trek along forest roads – a group of three or four will bring prices down to manageable levels.

Eating and drinking

Eating in Turangi is more limited than the range of accommodation would indicate, but you can eat tolerably well for a couple of nights with many of the best places attached to lodges.

Brew Haus Bar & Restaurant at *Club Habitat* on Ohuanga Rd ☎07/386 7492. Simple restaurant serving moderately priced hearty meals at breakfast (7–9.30am) and dinner (6–9pm), with a range of beers brewed on site.

Grand Central Fry cnr Ohuanga Rd & Ngawaka Place ☎07/386 3344. Easily the best of the town's several takeaways.

Kaimanawa Bistro 258 Taupahi Rd ☎07/386 8709. Dinner-only restaurant outside the town centre towards the Tongariro River where you might expect beef satay on jasmine rice ($10) followed by mustard glazed rack of lamb or salmon steak ($25). Closed Sun & Mon.

Mustard Seed Café 91 Ohuanga Rd. Casual modern café with the usual range of breakfasts, panini, salads and cakes, plus decent espresso and internet access.

Valentino's, Ohuanga Road ⓣ07/386 8812. Mainstream and modestly priced restaurant serving reasonable Italian and Kiwi mains ($18–22) in drab surroundings. Closed Tues.

Tokaanu

Turangi's smaller neighbour, **Tokaanu**, 5km west, was the main settlement in the area in pre-European times. Maori were drawn by the geothermal benefits of what is now the **Tokaanu Thermal Park** (unrestricted entry; free), a compact patch of low scrub, beautifully clear hot pools and plopping mud threaded by a fifteen-minute trail. The adjacent **Tokaanu Thermal Pools**, Mangaroa Road (daily 10am–10pm; $4), are great for soaking your bones after a day's tramping in the national park, with an open-air public pool and hotter, partly enclosed and chlorine-free private pools ($6 per hour, close at 9.30pm). Nearby you can spend a very pleasurable hour or two gently paddling along a narrow, lush, bush-fringed channel, past the hot tubs and back gardens of the locals in **boats** rented from Tokaanu Kayaks (ⓣ07/386 7558, ⓔkayaks@reap.org.nz; daily 10am–5pm). They charge $25 for an hour, $45 for two and will even provide transport if you don't fancy paddling back upstream. Take the Tokaanu road out of Turangi and look for the sign on the left, just over the bridge.

To **stay** in Tokaanu, try the *Oasis Motel and Tourist Park*, SH41 (ⓣ07/386 8569, ⓕ386 0694; tents $9, cabins ❷, studios & units ❸), an extensive campsite with mineral hot pools, spa pools and simple but well priced on-site accommodation.

Whakapapa and around

Tiny **Whakapapa**, the only settlement set firmly within the boundaries of the Tongariro National Park, hugs the lower slopes of Mount Ruapehu some 45km south of Turangi on SH48, which spurs off SH47. Approaching from the north, an open expanse of tussock gives distant views of the imposing form of the *Grand Chateau* hotel, framed by the snowy slopes of the volcano behind and overlooked by the arterial network of tows of the Whakapapa skifield.

From Whakapapa, SH48 continues as Bruce Road 6km to **Iwikau Village** (known locally as the "Top o' the Bruce"), an ugly jumble of ski-club chalets which, from late June through to mid-November, and in exceptional circumstances as late as Christmas, becomes a seething mass of wrap-around shades and baggy snowboarders' pants. Outside the ski season, the village dies, leaving only a couple of chair lifts (mid-Dec to mid-April; $15 return) to trundle up to the *Knoll Ridge Café*, New Zealand's highest at 2020m above sea level.

Arrival and information

The only **bus services** to Whakapapa are the once-daily shuttle buses from Turangi and National Park (see box on p.360), which drop off close to DOC's helpful **visitor centre** (daily: Dec–March 8am–6pm, April–Nov 8am–5pm; ⓣ07/892 3729, ⓔ*whakapapavc@doc.govt.nz*). The centre is stocked with all the maps and leaflets you could need and is equipped with extensive displays on the park, including the tiny Ski History museum and a couple of videos that are shown on demand – *Volcanoes of the South Wind* (15min) is a fairly simplistic discussion of vulcanism in general and its manifestations here, including the

'95 and '96 eruptions, while *The Sacred Gift of Tongariro* (25min) combines Maori legends surrounding Tongariro with impressive footage of the landscape through the seasons and the activities that take place in it. Each costs $3, or you can see both for $5.

Accommodation

There's not much to Whakapapa beside a café and three **places to stay**, all within a couple of minutes' walk of each other and all often booked up in advance. You'll do well to reserve as far ahead as possible through the ski season and over the Christmas and January school holidays. The most prominent is the *Grand Chateau* (ⓣ07/892 3809 & 0800/242832, ⓦwww.chateau.co.nz; ❻), a vast brick edifice built in 1929 with gracious public areas including a huge lounge with full-size snooker table and great mountain views. Guests have use of the highest nine-hole golf course in New Zealand, tennis courts, gym and a small indoor pool, and stay in rooms modernized to international hotel standard; you'll need a premium room (❼) to get plenty of space and good views, and can save money in spring and autumn when there are often discounts of around thirty percent. The *Chateau* also has self-contained chalets (❼), some sleeping up to six; and organizes the Tongariro trek (see p.362). The only other hotel is *Skotel* (ⓣ07/892 3719 & 0800/756 835, ⓦwww.skotel.co.nz; backpacker beds ❶, standard rooms ❺, chalets ❻), a rambling place with a sauna and a range of rooms from self-catering hostel-style affairs (with very limited kitchen facilities) to relatively luxurious rooms, some with views of Ngauruhoe and Tongariro. Note that rates are hiked up considerably in the ski season (cheapest room ❹). The best budget option is the *Whakapapa Holiday Park* (ⓣ07/892 3897, ⓔwhakapapaholpark@xtra.co.nz; camping $8, dorms ❶, cabins ❷, flat ❸), nicely set in a patch of bushland with spacious tent and powered sites, simple cabins that are let as backpacker dorms in summer, and a more luxurious en-suite tourist flat. There is also DOC's toilets-and-water self-registration *Mangahuia campsite* ($4), on SH47 close to the foot of the Whakapapa access road.

Iwikau Village has no public accommodation, only ski-club lodges and a daytime café that's open throughout the year.

Around Whakapapa

Outside the skiing season (see box on p.364), Whakapapa is a lot less frenetic but is still alive with trampers, since it makes a fine base for both short walks and long tramps. The Tongariro Northern Circuit and the Round the Mountain track (see p.362) can both be tackled from here, but there are also easier strolls covered by DOC's *Whakapapa Walks* leaflet ($1). Three of the best of these are the **Whakapapa Nature Walk** (1km; 20–30min), highlighting the unique flora of the park; the **Taranaki Falls Walk** (6km; 2hr return), which heads through open tussock and bushland to where the Wairere Stream plunges 20m over the end of an old lava flow; and the **Silica Rapids Walk** (7km; 2hr 30min return), which follows a stream through beech forests to some creamy-coloured geothermal terraces.

Eating and drinking

You can eat **lunches** and **snacks** cheaply at *Fergussons Café*, opposite the visitor centre, though you might prefer the better quality across the road at the Chateau's *Pihanga Café*, which serves the region's best coffee and the likes of Cajun beef on jambalaya rice ($14) and seafood pasta ($10) from 11am to 11pm. Alternatives are *Skotel*, which serves breakfast (continental $13, cooked

$19) and good-value bistro meals, or pizza at *Trails Bar*, which also boasts the cheapest **drinks** in the village. If you want to reward yourself for the successful completion of a major tramp, the place to do it is the Chateau's *Ruapehu Room*, with very good à la carte meals that might include dill- and vodka-cured salmon on green salad ($13) followed by roasted venison on kumara rosti ($30).

Tramping in Tongariro National Park

Tongariro National Park contains some of the North Island's finest walks. The **Tongariro Crossing** alone is rated as the best one-day tramp in the country, but there are many longer possibilities, notably the three- to four-day **Tongariro Northern Circuit**, which rates as one of the New Zealand Great Walks; both pass through spectacular and varied volcanic terrain. Mount Ruapehu has the arduous but rewarding **Crater Rim Walk** and a circuit, the **Round the Mountain Track**, which offers a narrower variety of terrain and sights than the Tongariro tramps, but is consequently less used.

Practicalities

The 1:80,000 *Tongariro Park* **map** ($15) is ideal for these tramps, but **DOC leaflets** ($1 each) covering the tramps separately are informative and perfectly

Getting to and around Tongariro National Park

The major bus companies don't run through the Tongariro National Park, leaving several smaller companies, many associated with backpacker hostels, to fill the void. Several of those servicing the Tongariro Crossing offer an Early Bird service getting you to the trailhead before the masses, though some only run at peak times.

From Taupo, Alpine Scenic Tours (☎07/378 7412, Ⓦwww.alpinescenictours.co.nz) pick up and drop off Tongariro Crossing-bound trampers ($25 return), will provide wet weather gear and walking poles, and since it is a scheduled service, will even go when the weather is poor. Tongariro Expeditions (☎0800/828763 & 07/377 0435, Ⓦwww.tongariroexpeditions.com; $25 return) compete directly, but only go when the crossing is viable.

From Turangi, Alpine Scenic Tours (☎07/386 8918, Ⓔalpine.scenic@xtra.co.nz) do a particularly useful run three times a day, calling at Whakapapa and the start and end of the Tongariro Crossing including one run (11am from Turangi) going right through to National Park. Bellbird Connection, based at the *Bellbird Lodge* (☎07/386 8281), *Club Habitat* (☎07/386 7492), and *Extreme Backpackers* (☎07/386 8949) run a similar service open to everyone, with most offering an early bus giving you a head start on the pack. Fares are very competitive – each charges $20 for the Tongariro Crossing drop-off and pick-up and $15–20 one-way to either Whakapapa or National Park. Alpine becomes a skifield shuttle in winter.

From Whakapapa, Tongariro Track Transport (☎07/892 3716) runs a daily shuttle leaving the visitor centre at 8am for the start of the Tongariro Crossing ($15 return), and meeting you at Ketetahi at either 4.30pm or 6pm.

From National Park, shuttle buses serve the trailheads in summer and skifields in winter. All the hostels will arrange transport, but the biggest operator is *Howard's Lodge* (☎07/892 2827) which runs its own all-comer buses, charging $16 for drop-off and pick-up at either end of the Tongariro Crossing. Tongariro Track Transport (see above) picks up in National Park at 7.45am then continues to Whakapapa and Mangatepopo.

From Ohakune, Tongariro National Park Shuttle Transport (☎0800/825 825) do door-to-door Tongariro Crossing shuttles ($25 return) and include a free DOC brochure. They're also helpful for linking Ohakune with National Park and Whakapapa.

adequate. The main **points of access** to the walks are Mangatepopo Road and Ketetahi Road for the Tongariro Crossing and Tongariro Northern Circuit; and Whakapapa for the Tongariro Northern Circuit, the Ruapehu Crater Rim and the Round the Mountain Track. Shuttle **buses** serve the trailheads from Turangi, National Park and Whakapapa, with the exception of the unmarked Crater Rim walk, the tracks are all well maintained and sporadically signposted, so you can judge your progress if you've a bus to catch.

Other than accommodation in Whakapapa Village, the only places to stay are the **trampers huts**, all of which have adjacent **campsites**. In summer (roughly late Oct–May), huts on the Tongariro Northern Circuit – Mangatepopo, Ketetahi, Waihohonu and Oturere – are classed as Great Walk huts ($14); in winter they lose their cooking facilities and revert to Category 2 ($10, camping $5). Hut tickets do not guarantee a bunk, so at busy times you could still find yourself on the floor. Campers (summer $10, winter $5) stay close to the huts and use the same facilities. Huts on the Round the Mountain Track – Whakapapaiti, Mangaturuturu, Blyth, Mangaehuehu and Rangipo – are Category 2 huts all year ($10, camping $5). Hut tickets can be bought in advance from DOC in Whakapapa and Ohakune, or DOC and the visitor centre in Turangi; if bought from a hut warden you pay an extra $4.

There are several **organized treks**, too: the *Grand Chateau* hotel in Whakapapa Village runs the Tongariro Trek (mid-Dec to mid-April; $1215; ⓣ07/892 3809 & 0800/242 832, ⓦwww.trek.co.nz), which combines the Ruapehu Crater Rim walk, the Tongariro Crossing and four nights to recover from it all at the Chateau. The Whakapapa Skifield Guided Walk (ⓣ07/892 3738; mid-Dec to mid-April daily 9.30am; $55, including chair-lift ride) ascends to the Ruapehu Crater Rim, providing interesting commentary on the geology and flora en route.

The **weather** in the mountains is extremely changeable, and the usual provisos apply. Even on apparently scorching summer days, the increased altitude and exposed windy ridges produce a wind-chill factor to be reckoned with, and storms roll in with frightening rapidity. Any time from the end of March through to late November there can be snow on the tracks, so if you are planning a tramp during this period, enquire locally about current conditions. Always take warm **clothing** and rain gear – and if you plan to scramble up and down the volcanic cone of Mount Ngauruhoe, take gloves and long trousers for protection from the sharp scoria rock.

Tongariro Crossing

The **Tongariro Crossing** (16km; 6–8hr; 750m ascent) is by far the most popular of the major tramps in the region and for good reason. Within a few hours you climb over lava flows, cross a crater floor, skirt active geothermal areas, pass beautiful and serene emerald and blue lakes and have the opportunity to ascend the cinder cone of Mount Ngauruhoe. Even without this wealth of highlights it would still be a fine tramp, traversing a mountain massif through scrub and tussock, before descending into virgin bush for the final half-hour. It can be a long day out if you're not particularly fit, but it's not excessively arduous. Note too that this isn't a wilderness experience – on weekends and through the height of summer well over a thousand people complete the Crossing, so it pays to aim for spring or autumn, or stick to weekdays.

Car parks at both ends of the track have a reputation for break-ins and it is a good idea to leave your vehicle in Turangi, National Park or Whakapapa and make use instead of the many shuttle buses (see box opposite). The track can be walked in either direction but by going from west to east you save 400m of ascent: all shuttle buses are conveniently scheduled around a west to east traverse, usually depositing their charges at Mangatepopo Road End, six gravel kilometres east of SH47, at about 8.30am and picking up at Ketetahi Road around 4.30pm. Some shuttle operators do a 6pm pick-up allowing you to tack on an ascent of Ngauruhoe; ask when you book. To avoid the worst of the crush, steal a march on the others by choosing a shuttle operator prepared to drop-off at Mangatepopo Road a little earlier; or dawdle behind the mob and plan to stay the night at Mangatepopo Hut; or get dropped off at Ketetahi Road late in the day and sleep at Ketetahi Hut ready for a crack-of-dawn start next day.

From Mangatepopo Road End the first hour is fairly gentle, following the Mangatepopo Stream through a barren landscape and passing the Mangatepopo Hut. The track gradually steepens as you scale the fractured black lava flows towards the **Mangatepopo Saddle**, passing a short side-track to the **Soda Springs**, a small wildflower oasis in this blasted landscape. The Saddle marks the start of the high ground between the bulky and ancient Mount Tongariro and its youthful acolyte, **Mount Ngauruhoe**, which fit walkers can climb (2km return; 2hr return; 600m ascent) from here and still make the shuttle bus at the end of the day. The two-steps-forward-one-step-back ascent of this thirty-five-degree cone of red and black scoria must be one of the most exhausting and dispiriting walks in the country, but it is always popular – both for the superb views from the toothy crater rim and for the thrilling headlong descent among a cascade of tumbling rocks and volcanic dust.

From the Mangatepopo Saddle, the main track crosses the flat pan of the South Crater and climbs to the rim of **Red Crater**, with fumaroles belching out steam, which obscures the banded crimson and black of the crater walls. Colours get more vibrant still as you begin the descent to the Emerald Lakes, opaque pools shading from jade to palest duck-egg, and beyond to the crystal-clear Blue Lake. Sidling around Tongariro's **North Crater**, you begin to descend steeply on golden tussock slopes to **Ketetahi Hut**, a major rest stop with views of Lake Rotoaira and Lake Taupo. From here you pass close to the steaming Ketetahi Springs, then begin the final descent through cool stream-side bush to the car park on Ketetahi road.

Tongariro Northern Circuit – and the Round the Mountain track

If the Tongariro Crossing appeals, but you are looking for something a little more challenging, the answer is the **Tongariro Northern Circuit** (49km; 3–4 days), one of New Zealand's Great Walks. The section from **Whakapapa to Mangatepopo Hut** (9km; 2–3hr; 50m ascent) is boggy after heavy rain but usually passable, though you could always get a shuttle to Mangatepopo. If you decide to walk you'll find the track undulating through tussock and crossing numerous streams before meeting the Tongariro Crossing track close to Mangatepopo Hut. From **Mangatepopo Hut to Emerald Lakes** (6km; 3–4hr; 660m ascent), you follow the Tongariro Crossing (described above), then have the choice of continuing on the Crossing **to Ketetahi Hut** (4km; 2–3hr; 400m descent) and returning to this point the next day, or branching right **to Outere Hut** (5km; 1–2hr; 500m descent), descending steeply through fabulously contorted lava formations towards the Rangipo Desert. The initial section from **Outere Hut to Waihohonu Hut** (8km; 2–3hr; 250m descent) crosses open, undulating country, then descends into the beech forests before a final climb over a ridge brings you to the hut, where you can drop your pack and press on for twenty minutes to the cool and clear Ohinepango Springs. The final day's walk, from **Waihohonu Hut to Whakapapa** (14km; 5–6hr; 200m ascent), cuts between Ngauruhoe and Ruapehu, passing the Old Waihohonu Hut (no accommodation) that was built for stage coaches on the old road in 1901. The path then continues alongside Waihohonu Stream to the exposed **Tama Saddle** and, just over a kilometre beyond, a junction where side tracks lead to Lower Tama Lake (20min return) and Upper Tama Lake (1hr return), both in-filled explosion craters. It is only around two hours' walk from the saddle back to Whakapapa, so you should have time to explore the **Taranaki Falls** before ambling back through tussock to the village.

If you'd prefer to steer clear of the popular Northern Circuit but still circle around a mountain, try the **Round the Mountain Track** (71km; 4–5 days) which loops around Mount Ruapehu, most easily tackled from Whakapapa. This track can also be combined with the Northern Circuit to make a mighty five- or six-day **circumnavigation** of all three mountains. For these two you need backcountry hut tickets or an annual hut pass. Huts are Cat 2 ($10) and camping is $5. A Great Walks pass is necessary for Waihohonu hut which is also part of the Northern Circuit Great Walk.

Ruapehu Crater Rim

The ascent to the **Ruapehu Crater Rim** takes around eight hours return from the Top o' the Bruce (15km), and a much more appealing five hours from the top of the **Waterfall Express chair lift** (9km), avoiding a long slog through a barren, rocky landscape. Even from the top of the chair lift, this is one of New Zealand's more gruelling short hikes, but the destination makes it all worthwhile. Volcanic instability makes it dangerous to go beyond the **Dome Shelter** (no accommodation), at 2672m the highest structure in the country and typically surrounded in snow. It perches on the rim of the crater, with great views across the upper reaches of a small glacier to the dramatic silhouettes of Cathedral Rocks, west to Mount Taranaki and down into the crater lake, currently in the process of refilling after thousands of tonnes of water were ejected during the 1995 and 1996 eruptions. The route is not waymarked, but from Christmas until the first snows arrive, the ascent can usually be made in ordinary walking boots without crampons or an ice axe. If you are in any doubt or would appreciate some commentary, join an organized trek (see p.364).

National Park

The evocative moniker attached to **National Park**, 15km west of Whakapapa Village, belies the overwhelming drabness of this tiny settlement – a dispiriting collection of A-frame chalets sprouting from a scrubby plain of pines, eucalyptuses and flax, with only the superb views of Ruapehu and Ngauruhoe to lend it any grace.

Arrival and information

National Park comprises a grid of half a dozen streets wedged between SH4 and the parallel rail line. **Trains** stop at the deserted platform on Station Road, while InterCity **buses** pull up outside what used to be the National Park Store, now just a telephone box 100m north on Carroll Street. Bus tickets can be bought a further 100m up the road at *Howard's Lodge* (see below). There are no banks or cash machines in National Park so unless you have an EFTPOS card, bring plenty of cash.

Mount Ruapehu skifields

When the snows come, around two-thirds of New Zealand's skiers generally turn their attention to Mount Ruapehu, home to the North Island's only substantial **skifields.** Every weekend from around **late June to early November**, cars pile out of Auckland and Wellington (and pretty much everywhere in between) for the four-hour drive to either Whakapapa, the more extensive skifield on the northwestern slopes of Mount Ruapehu, or Turoa, easily beaten into second place on the south side. Both fields have excellent reputations for pretty much all levels of skier and the orientation of volcanic ridges lends itself to an abundance of dreamy, natural half-pipes for snowboarding. Only members of the Tukino Ski Club are allowed onto the tiny Tukino field on the eastern flank of the mountain, which they battle their way to in 4WDs.

With over thirty groomed runs, a dozen major chair lifts and T-bars and the dedicated learners' area of Happy Valley, **Whakapapa** is New Zealand's largest and busiest ski area. It offers the longest North Island season (usually late June to early Nov and sometimes through to Christmas), 675 vertical metres of snow, plus snow-making equipment, ski schools, a huge gear-rental operation, crèche and a couple of cafés. **Access** is along the toll-free, sealed Bruce Road. Chains are sometimes required, in which case a fitting service miraculously appears at a parking area beside the road. Car parking is free and there is a free courtesy bus from the lower car parks. Shuttle buses run from Whakapapa Village, National Park, Turangi and Taupo.

Turoa (typically mid- to late June through to late October) has developed in a much more controlled fashion than Whakapapa, and offers the country's greatest vertical drop – 720m – a skiable area almost as extensive as Whakapapa's with wide groomed trails particularly aimed at intermediate skiers and, at Ohakune, the region's best après ski. It is usually possible to drive straight up the sealed, toll-free, 17km **access** road from Ohakune without chains, and park for nothing. Again, the skifield operators will fit chains ($20) when needed, or you can rent from shops in Ohakune for a little less and fit them yourself. Several shuttle buses run up from Ohakune, charging around $15 return.

Practicalities

After recent rationalization brought on by short seasons, the two fields have now amalgamated under one company (ⓣ07/892 3738, ⓦwww.mtruapehu.com). **Lift passes** at either fields cost $54 a day, $216 for five days, and there is both a Discover Ski pack ($55) and a Discover Snowboard pack ($70) that includes gear rental, an hour-and-a-half lesson and a learners' area lift pass. On-site **ski rental** for one day costs $29–45, $40 for snowboard and boots, and there are discounts for rentals of five or more days. Several places in National Park and Ohakune also offer competitive rates and a wide selection of equipment.

Neither field has public **accommodation** on site. Ski clubs maintain dozens of chalets at the foot of the main tows in Whakapapa's Iwikau Village, but casual visitors (unless they can get invited to a lodge as a guest) have to stay 6km downhill at Whakapapa Village or 22km away at National Park (see opposite). Almost everyone skiing Turoa stays in Ohakune (see opposite).

Accommodation

Accommodation is in great demand during the **ski season** – when prices will be at least one price code higher than those given here – and can fill up from Christmas to the end of January, but otherwise it's plentiful. *Pukenui Lodge*, SH4 (ⓣ0800/785 368, ⓦwww.tongariro.cc; tents $8, dorms ❶, rooms ❸, en suites ❸, units ❺), offers a spacious lounge with great mountain views, a spa pool, plenty of assistance arranging activities, and a range of accommodation from plain and comfortable dorms and doubles, some en suite, to self-contained motel units. Similar standards are maintained at *Howard's Lodge*, 9 Carroll Street (Ⓣ & Ⓕ07/892 2827, Ⓦwww.howardslodge.co.nz; dorms ❶, rooms ❷, deluxe rooms ❸), which has its own track transport, a spa pool, and two accommodation sections – one catering to backpackers and the other offering plusher kitchen and lounge for the better-heeled guests. Rooms range from basic dorms (separate for men and women) and doubles to appreciably more modern and comfortable en-suite rooms; mountain bikes are available to rent ($20 for 2hr), as is tramping and climbing gear. Alternatives include the *Plateau Lodge*, Carroll Street (Ⓣ07/892 2993 & 0800/861 861, Ⓔplateaulodge@xtra.co.nz; dorms ❶, units ❷), offering marginally the cheapest dorms and some ageing but perfectly functional motel units; and National Park Backpackers, Finlay Street (Ⓣ & Ⓕ07/892 2870, Ⓔnat.park.backpackers@xtra.co.nz; tents $10, dorms ❶, rooms ❷, made-up doubles ❸), with and outdoor hot tub and generally good facilities, but chiefly notable for being built around an indoor climbing wall ($8, plus $2 for boots and harness). Guests only pay once for climbing during their visit.

The Town

Though initially founded as a way station on the main Auckland–Wellington train line, National Park owes its continued existence to skiers and trampers bound for the adjacent Tongariro National Park, and paddlers heading for **Whanganui River trips** (see p.265). With the limited accommodation at Whakapapa Village, visitors to Tongariro, Ngauruhoe and the northern side of Ruapehu are all but forced to stay in National Park, using shuttle buses (see box on p.360) to get to Whakapapa and the Tongariro tramps.

In National Park itself, there is precious little to do except for a couple of adventure activities. To go **mountain biking**, sign up with Pete Outdoors (Ⓣ07/892 2773), who rent bikes for $30 a half day and offer guides for $25 an hour; or Go For It Tours, based beside the train station (Ⓣ07/892 2705), who operate guided trips through rivers and along muddy tracks on motorbikes or two-rider **quad bikes** (1hr 30min; $80).

Eating and drinking

All lodges serve breakfast for guests, but for main **meals** you're limited to steaks and bar-style meals at the typically rowdy *Schnapps Bar*, on SH4, next to Pukenui Lodge, or you can get fish 'n' chips and a jug of **beer** at the *National Park Hotel* on Carroll Street. National Park's best restaurant burnt down late in 2001 but the owner vows to return; look out for the new *Eivins* at the corner of Carroll Street and SH4.

Ohakune and around

Ohakune, 35km south of National Park, welcomes you with a huge carrot, celebrating its position at the heart of one of the nation's prime market-gardening regions. This is easily forgotten once you are in town among the chalet-style lodges and ski-rental shops geared to cope with the massive influx of winter-sports enthusiasts who descend from mid-June to early November for the **skiing** at Turoa (see box opposite), 20km north up Ohakune Mountain Road.

Arrival and information

Ohakune is strung between two centres. The Auckland–Wellington rail line passes through **Ohakune Junction** where there's the **train station** and a cluster of hotels and restaurants mostly serving the skiing fraternity. **Central Ohakune**, the commercial heart of the town, lies 2km to the southwest, where InterCity **buses** on the Hamilton–Taumarunui–Wanganui run (daily except Sat) stop close to the **visitor centre**, 54 Clyde St (Mon–Fri 9am–5pm, Sat & Sun 9am–3.30pm; ⓣ06/385 8427, ⓔruapehu.vic@xtra.co.nz), which has all the general information you'll need and sells both bus and train tickets. For more specific tramping information, the mountain weather forecast and a detailed low-down on local flora and fauna, make for the DOC **field centre** at the foot of Ohakune Mountain Road (school and public holidays daily 9am–4pm; all other times Mon–Fri 9am–3pm; ⓣ06/385 0010, ⓔohakunevc@doc.govt.nz); weather and tramping information is available in the foyer which stays open 24hr. **Internet access** is available at The Video Shop, 53 Clyde St.

There are no regular buses around Ohakune, so you might want to rent a **mountain bike** from either the Powderhorn Chateau, 194 Mangawhero Terrace ($25 per half-day, $35 full-day), or from Turoa Sports Ski Shed, 71 Clyde St (ⓣ06/385 8887) where the machines range in quality and start from $15 for 2hr (tandems $25).

Accommodation

Ohakune has stacks of **places to stay**, though several of them close outside the ski season and are packed once the snows arrive – when prices get hiked up by around thirty percent more than those quoted here. Enough places are open in summer to satisfy almost all budgets, the most comprehensive and appealing being *Rimu Park Lodge*, 27 Rimu St, Ohakune Junction (ⓣ06/385 9023, ⓦhomepages.ihug.co.nz/~rimulodg; dorms ❶, rooms and cabins ❷, units and carriages ❹, chalets ❹–❺), a 1914 villa containing spacious six-bunk dorms and comfortable doubles. The grounds are dotted with simple cabins, en-suite units with TV and fridge but no kitchen, fully self-contained chalets sleeping between four and ten, and several railway carriages fitted out as self-contained units with separate lounge and sleeping quarters. Also in Ohakune Junction you'll find the top-of-the-range *Powderhorn Chateau*, 194 Mangawhero Terrace, at the base of Ohakune Mountain Road (ⓣ06/385 8888, ⓦwww.powderhorn.co.nz; ❻), an immense log-cabin style edifice with a lovely indoor swimming pool ($6 for nonguests), sun beds, and en-suite rooms, the best with balconies and forest views.

Folk arriving by bus will find it more convenient to stay in the main town, where there's budget accommodation at the clean and spartan *Matai Lodge*, 17 Clyde St (ⓣ06/385 9169, ⓔmatai.lodge@xtra.co.nz; dorms ❶, rooms ❷); and next door at the small and old but well maintained *YHA*, 15 Clyde St (ⓣ & ⓕ06/385 8724, ⓔyhaohak@yha.org.nz; dorms ❶, rooms ❷), which only operates during the ski season (June–Oct). Good budget beds can also be found at the *Alpine Motel Lodge*, 7 Miro St (ⓣ & ⓕ06/385 8758, ⓦwww.alpinemotel.co.nz; dorms ❶, rooms ❷, units & chalets ❹), with basic four-share dorms and rooms, and some nicer studio units and fully self-contained chalets, all with access to Sky TV, a spa and drying room. For B&B try the cosy, welcoming and very reasonable *Penguins*, 56 Goldfield St (ⓣ & ⓕ06/385 9411, ⓔdouglas.richard@xtra.co.nz; ❹), which has a shared bathroom and separate guest lounge; or the very tasteful and amiable *Whare Ora*, 14 Kaha St (ⓣ & ⓕ06/385 9385, ⓔwhareora@xtra.co.nz; ❼), 6km east in the village of Rangataua, with two rooms (one with spa bath and both with diverting modern art works), a lounge with unsurpassed mountain views, and delicious dinners available on request ($45 per person with wine).

Campers have a choice of the *Ohakune Top 10 Holiday Park*, 5 Moore St (Ⓣ & Ⓕ06/385 8561, Ⓔohakune_holiday_park@xtra.co.nz; tents $10, cabins & kitchen cabins ❷, motel units ❸–❹), right on the edge of the bush but still central, and DOC's toilets-and-water *Mangawhero Campsite* ($4), 1.5km up Ohakune Mountain Road from the field centre.

The Town and around

For four short months Ohakune comes alive, bars and restaurants swing into action, everyone makes their money for the year and then shuts up until next season. Consequently it is pretty quiet in summer, but once the snows have melted, the trails are open for tramping, mountain biking and horse trekking.

Unlike at Whakapapa, the Turoa chairlifts rarely run outside the ski season, but the 17km Ohakune Mountain Road makes an impressive drive through stands of ancient rimu and provides access to a number of fine **walks**, including the Round the Mountain track (see p.362). The pick of the shorter trails are: the **Mangawhero Forest Walk** (3km return; 1hr), a short and well-marked loop track from opposite the DOC field centre; the **Waitonga Falls Walk** (4km return; 1hr 10min) to a spectacular waterfall, starting 11km up the Mountain Road; and the hike to **Lake Surprise** (12km return; 5hr), an undulating route along the Round the Mountain track to a shallow lake which starts from the 15km mark on Ohakune Mountain Road and passes evidence of volcanic debris which swept down the mountain during the 1975 and 1995 eruptions.

Most of the walking tracks, and any inside the bounds of the national park, are off-limits for **mountain biking**, but you can coast 17km down Ohakune Mountain Road on The Ohakune Mountain Ride, 16 Miro St (Ⓣ06/385 8257; Nov–June; $30), or rent a bike (see above) and head 12km east to the forest roads around Rangataua; consult DOC or the visitor centre for more details.

A less arduous approach is to let **horses** take the strain at *Ruapehu Homestead*, 4km east on SH49 (Ⓣ06/385 8799), which runs back-country trail rides through bush and rivers (2hr; $38), as well as easier trips for the less experienced.

Eating, drinking and nightlife

During the ski season, Ohakune Junction is very much the happening place to spend your evenings. In summer though, when hardly any of the half-dozen restaurants, bars and clubs bother to open, you're better off in **central Ohakune**, where the tastiest meals are served at the daytime *Utopia*, 47 Clyde St (closed Sunday in summer), an ideal spot for idling away an hour or two over great coffee and sumptuous all-day brunches; you might even catch them open in the evening, but don't bank on it. Other good bets are succulent gourmet kebabs from *Mountain Kebabs*, 29 Clyde St (generally winter only), where chicken, lamb, seafood and vegetarian fillings are doused with a stack of tasty sauces; and *O Bar and Restaurant*, 72 Clyde St, inside the Ohakune Country Hotel, a kind of upscale bar with pool table, roaring fire in winter and an extensive range of $15–20 dishes including pizza, steaks and Thai curry.

At the **Ohakune Junction**, the *Powderhorn Chateau* harbours two restaurants: the excellent fine-dining *Matterhorn* (Ⓣ06/385 8888), serving the likes of venison medallions on ratatouille, and rack of lamb on a carrot and parsnip mash ($25–30); and the more modest *Powderkeg* brasserie/bar, which serves full bar meals in winter, when you'll need to fight for a prized place on the balcony (they don't take bookings). Next door, the *Fat Pigeon Garden Café*, Mangawhero Terrace, serves excellent café-style meals and coffee, but in summer is often only open weekends. In winter, *Margarita's*, 5 Rimu St, do warming and tasty enchiladas, tostadas and other faux-Mexican favourites, and *Lido*, 30 Thames St, kicks up a storm until the early hours.

Dine early, and you'll have time to catch Kiwi Encounters (☎06/385 9505), who take highly informative three-hour kiwi-spotting trips into the Waimarino Forest ($35; minimum two people) leaving around 7.45pm, and with a fair chance of an encounter.

The Desert Road and Waiouru

South of Turangi, and past the trout hatchery, SH1 sticks to the east of the Tongariro National Park running roughly parallel to the Tongariro River. This is the **Desert Road** (SH1), which climbs up over an exposed and barren plateau. This isn't a true desert (the rainfall is too high), but it's about as near as you'll get anywhere in New Zealand. Road cuttings reveal the cause as they slice through several metres of volcanic ash - a timeline of past eruptions - that's so free-draining that any vegetation struggles to take hold.

Initially you're deep in pine forest with side roads periodically ducking off to the east and the assortment of hydro-electric tunnels, intakes and tailraces of the Tongariro River. Some 9km south of Turangi, Kaimanawa Road runs 2km down to the river and beyond to a good free camping area by a stream (best found in daylight). After crossing the river, keep left on a tarmac road following signs to Waihaha Valley. The site is 500m back from the substation at the end of the road, and a narrow track through the bush leads to some toilets. A further 5km south along SH1, Tree Trunk Gorge Road leads again to the Tongariro River at a spot where it squeezes through a narrow fissure known as **Tree Trunk Gorge** - one for river devotees mainly.

Back on the highway you soon climb out of the forest for great views of the three volcanoes off to the west and the blasted territory ahead. It is a dramatic scene, somehow made even more elemental by the three lines of electricity pylons striding off across the bleak tussock towards Waiouru.

Waiouru and the Army Museum

The Desert Road and the roads flanking the western side of Ruapehu, Ngauruhoe and Tongariro meet at **WAIOURU**, an uninspiring row of service stations and tearooms perched 800m above sea level on the bleak tussock plain beside New Zealand's major **army base**. The serene view of the mountains from here can be fabulous but the peace is often disturbed by troop movements and even target practice.

The place to take cover is in the three concrete bunkers of the **QEII Army Memorial Museum** (daily 9am–4.30pm; $8), a showcase of national military heritage from the New Zealand Wars through the Anglo-Boer and two World Wars to New Zealand's involvement in Vietnam. Mannequins in regimental regalia set in lifeless dioramas do little to prepare you for the impact of the *Roimata Pounamu* ("Tears on Greenstone") **wall of remembrance**, where a veil of tears symbolizes mourning and cleansing as it streams down a curving bank of heavily veined greenstone tiles while the name, rank and place of death of each of the 33,000 New Zealanders who have died in the various wars is recited. A twenty-minute audio-visual presentation sets the scene for the rest of the chronologically arranged exhibits, which are brought to life by oral histories, including some heart-rending ones that recount the bungled Gallipoli campaign of World War I. The emphasis is small-scale and personal: one particularly affecting case contains artefacts made by soldiers in the trenches – cribbage boards, chess sets and a cigarette holder that completely encased the cigarette so it could be smoked at night without risk of the enemy seeing the telltale glow.

The *Rations* **café**, inside the Army Museum, is as good as any hereabouts. Should you need to **stay**, try the budget *Oasis Hotel and Motel*, SH1 (Ⓣ & Ⓕ06/387 6779; ❸), with mostly twin rooms and some motel units.

Northern Rangitikei: Taihape and Mangaweka

Continuing south along SH1, you descend from the volcanic plateau into the **Rangitikei District**, with the Rangitikei River never far away, though seldom seen as its waters have carved down through some of the youngest and softest rock in New Zealand to leave off-white cliffs as the only evidence of the river's course. This is prime farming country, pretty much the Kiwi archetype of sheep farms stretching to the horizon over angular green hills characterized by "terracettes" – a kind of corrugated effect caused by minor slumping on land too steep to support grass. The pastoral nature of the region is reflected in the character of the region's largest town, **Taihape**, an agricultural service centre of only passing interest, though it works well enough as a base for some superb whitewater rafting, a bungy jump and some fine gardens.

Taihape

For want of any more interesting features, the small town of **TAIHAPE**, 30km south of Waiouru, pronounces itself "New Zealand's one and only Gumboot City", something it showcases each year on Labour Day in late October with **Gumboot Day**, a tongue-in-cheek celebration of this archetypal Kiwi footwear that culminates in a gumboot-throwing competition. Said boots are increasingly hard to find in the hardware stores and farm-supply shops that line the main street, though gumboot-shaped postcards and souvenirs seem all the rage. The horticultural theme continues in several showpiece **gardens** all listed and pinpointed in the *Garden Guide of The Rangitikei* leaflet available free from the Taihape visitor centre, in the Town Hall, Hautapu Street (daily: Nov-March 9am–5.30pm, April-Oct 9am-5pm; Ⓣ06/388 0350, Ⓦwww.rangitikei.com). The best of the gardens are around twenty minutes' drive northwest of Taihape. They're unexpectedly sited amid farmland and relish the cool inland high-country climate. Outside the peak summer season it pays to call before heading out to either the hillside **Rongoiti** (Ⓣ06/388 7866; Oct-April daily 10am-5pm; $5), noted for its giant Himalayan lilies and woodland setting, or the hilltop **Waitoka** (Oct–May daily 10am–5pm; $7), a more formal affair with broad lawns, formal vegetable garden and mature exotic trees.

For most it is enough to stop for a bite to eat, and Taihape has the best **eating** on SH1 between Taupo and Wellington. The main contenders here are: *The Venison Kitchen*, 65b Hautapu St, which claims to be the only farmed venison café in the country, and serves it in burgers, souvlaki and pies for under $10; the cottagey *Brown Sugar Café*, Huia Street (Ⓣ06/388 1880), which serves excellent light meals, cakes and coffee during the day, as well as dinner on Friday and Saturday evenings (booking advisable); and the more modern *Café Exchange,* Huia St (Ⓣ06/388 0599), which has a good deli selection, breakfast and snacks throughout the day and a few more substantial dishes in the evening. *Brown Sugar* and *Exchange* both have garden seating.

Places to stay include the rock-bottom rooms at the *Gretna Hotel*, corner of SH1 and Hautapu Street (ⓣ06/388 0638; dorms ❶, rooms ❷); units at the *Safari Motel*, SH1, 1km north (ⓣ0800/200 046, ⓕ06/388 1116; ❹); and hilltop homestay at *Korirata*, 25 Pukeko St (ⓣ & ⓕ06/388 0315, ⓔkorirata@xtra.co.nz; ❹), which has great views over Taihape and Mount Ruapehu. There's **camping** at the *Abba Motor Camp* (ⓣ06/388 0718, abbamotorcamp@xtra.co.nz; tents $20 per site, cabins ❷, tourist flat and motel ❸), 3km north of town on the Old Abattoir Road.

Around Taihape

Driving through Taihape, there is little to suggest that the hilly country to the east hides one of New Zealand's most thrilling whitewater-rafting trips and the North Island's highest bungy jump.

The Grade V gorge section of the **Rangitikei River** is one of the toughest regularly used sections of **whitewater-rafting** river in the country. Ten major rapids are packed into the 2-3hr run. Operators will take first-timers, but newbies can make it safer for everyone if they choose to raft elsewhere first. Trips on the Rangitikei are run from Mangaweka (see below), or more directly from *River Valley*, Pukoekahu (ⓣ06/388 1444, ⓦwww.rivervalley.co.nz; ❶–❸), a mostly backpacker-oriented complex well-sited right by the Rangitikei at the pull-out point for the rafting trips some 30km east of Taihape. Morning, and occasionally afternoon, trips ($95) are run throughout the year, though when water levels are low, rafts are replaced by paddle-yourself one-person inflatable kayaks (also $95) launched in convoy with guides helping out the more tentative paddlers. *River Valley* also offer scenic rafting ($95; 5hr) down the quieter Grade II section immediately downstream of the lodge, **kayaking** ($40 per half day), **horse trekking** ($45 for 2hr), **mountain biking** ($35 per day), **abseiling** down a 40m cliff ($25) and 9-hole **pitch-and-putt** ($10). There's even a tempting $229 combo with a raft trip, a night at the lodge, a bungy and a Jet Sprint ride (see both below).

Customers, many of them from the Kiwi Experience buses which call nightly, typically stay in sixteen-bunk or slightly pricier six-berth dorms (❶), pleasant double or twin rooms (❸), tents ($10), or ten-minutes up the road in shearers' quarters nicely converted into a self-contained house (❶). Straightforward low-cost meals are served and there's a bar on site.

With a detailed map you can follow the backroads from *River Valley* to the eighty-metre HighTime **bungy** (ⓣ0800/802864, ⓦwww.hightimebungy.co.nz; $99), though it is simpler to turn off SH1 at Uhutu, 7km south of Taihape, and follow the signs 15km east. You jump from a bridge over Rangitikei River far below, get lowered onto a raft, then get spirited back to the bridge on a water-balanced chair lift, a ride available separately for non-jumpers ($25 for two people).

Mangaweka

The brightly-painted form of a DC3 airplane beside SH1, 24km south of Taihape, is about the only indication that there might be a reason to stop in the dilapidated hamlet of **MANGAWEKA**, scattered across a plain high above the Rangitikei River. The *DC3 Café* is cheap, basic and an obvious lure, but there is more of interest at the adjacent service station, from where Rangitikei River Adventures (ⓣ & ⓕ06/382 5747, ⓦwww.rra.co.nz) operate **whitewater rafting** on the Grade V Rangitikei Gorge (see above; $119 including transport to the river), along with more family-oriented fun rafting down a gentle stretch of the river (1hr $30, half-day $55).

Unless you are planning to stay – and good reasons to do that are listed opposite - continue 6km south to *Flat Hills Park*, a café complex that's a popular refreshment stop for InterCity and tourist buses. A better reason to pause is **Flat Hills Jet Sprint** (daily 8.30am-5pm; $25), a short, sharp burst of adrenaline delivered by having 450 horses right behind your head as you hurtle around an artificial course in a de-tuned three-seater racing jetboat. It might not be scenic and you only get five minutes, but you'll remember the G-forces and the engine heat on the back of your neck.

From here it is 60km to Bulls, with little to see in between. You may, however, want to stay, either at the bargain *Mangaweka Motor Camp*, Ruahine Road, by the river 1.5km north of town (ⓣ07/382 5730; $8 per tent, $10 per van); or 11km further along Ruahine Road at the excellent *Mairenui Rural Retreat*, (ⓣ06/382 5564, ⓦwww.mairenui.co.nz; villa ❸, retreat ❺, homestead ❻), on a working farm in typical Rangitikei sheep country. Here you have a choice of simple rooms with self-catering facilities in a colonial villa ($30 a head), self-contained accommodation in a modernist secluded retreat, or lovely en-suite B&B rooms in the homestead. Tasty evening meals start at $30 (including a pre-dinner drink), and self-catering guests can get breakfast from $10.

Travel details

Trains

From National Park to: Auckland (2 daily; 5hr 30min); Ohakune (2 daily; 30min); Palmerston North (2 daily; 3hr 30min); Waiouru (2 daily; 1hr); Wellington (2 daily; 5hr 30min).
From Ohakune to: Auckland (2 daily; 6hr); Wellington (2 daily; 5hr).

Buses

From Kawerau to: Rotorua (2 daily; 45min); Whakatane (2 daily; 45 min).
From National Park to: Auckland (1 daily; 5hr 30min); Ohakune (1 daily; 30min); Wellington (1 daily; 5hr 40min).
From Ohakune to: Auckland (1 daily; 6hr); Wellington (1 daily; 5hr 15min).
From Rotorua to: Auckland (8 daily; 4hr); Gisborne (1 daily; 4hr 30min); Hamilton (8 daily; 1hr 45min); Kawerau (2 daily; 45min); Opotiki (1 daily; 2hr 10min); Palmerston North (2 daily; 5hr 30min); Taupo (4 daily; 1hr); Tauranga (4 daily; 1hr 30min); Waitomo (2 daily; 2hr–2hr 30min); Whakatane (2 daily; 1hr 30min).
From Taihape to: Auckland (3 daily; 6hr 30min); Taupo (3 daily; 2hr); Turangi (3 daily; 1hr 10min); Wellington (3 daily; 4hr).
From Taupo to: Auckland (4 daily; 4–5hr); Hamilton (3 daily; 2hr 30min); Hastings (3 daily; 2hr 30min); Napier (3 daily; 2hr); Palmerston North (3 daily; 3hr 30min); Rotorua (4 daily; 1hr); Taihape (3 daily; 2hr); Tauranga (4 daily; 2hr 30min); Turangi (3 daily; 45min); Wellington (3 daily; 6hr).
From Tokoroa to: Hamilton (2 daily; 1hr 45min); Taupo (2 daily; 45min).
From Turangi to: The Chateau (4 daily; 1hr).

Flights

From Rotorua to: Auckland (4–5 daily; 45min); Christchurch (2 daily; 1hr 15min); Wellington (4–5 daily; 1hr 10min).
From Taupo to: Auckland (2 daily; 50min); Wellington (3 daily; 1hr).

Travel details

5

The Coromandel, Bay of Plenty and Eastland

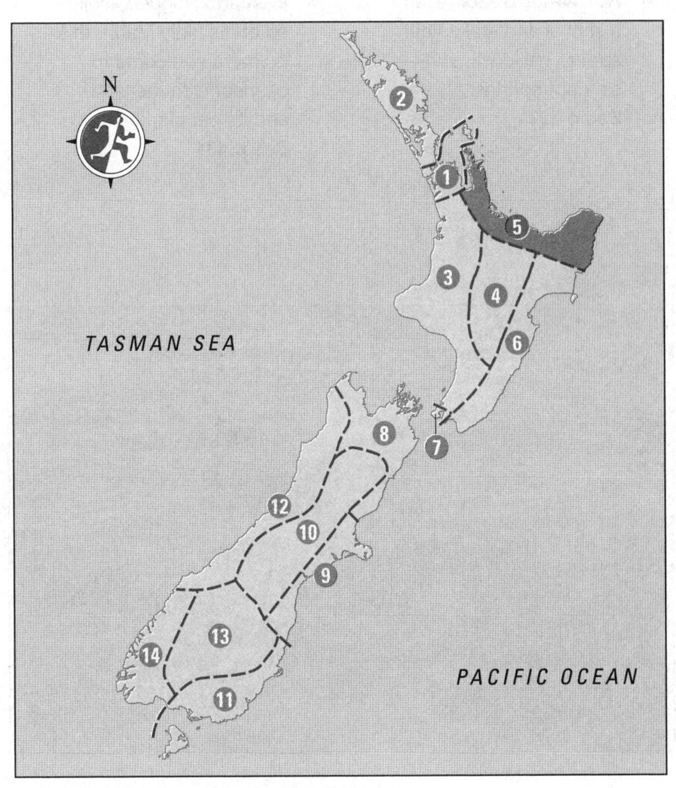

CHAPTER 5

Highlights

* **Coromandel Peninsula** Untouched beaches, rich bush and a slow pace lull you into Peninsula time. See p.383
* **Driving Creek Railway** This modern narrow-gauge line climbs high through the bush for long coastal views. See p.383
* **Hot Water Beach** Grab a shovel and stake your spot to wallow in surf-side hot springs. See p.397
* **White Island** Visit the otherworldly moonscape and sulphur deposits of New Zealand's most active volcano. See p.426
* **Dolphin Swimming** There's always a high success rate in the waters off Whakatane. See p.427
* **Eastland** Rugged, isolated and solidly Maori, this is where you come to connect with the land and its people. See p.431

5

The Coromandel, Bay of Plenty and Eastland

The long coastal sweep to the east of Auckland is split into three distinct areas, among them two of the most popular summer-holiday destinations on the North Island; the other is one of the least-visited parts of the country, whatever the time of year. Heading east from Auckland by road you'll first cut across at least a portion of the **Hauraki Plains**, a wedge of dairy country at the foot of the Coromandel Peninsula with a few pleasant surprises for anyone willing to dawdle for a day or so. In the spa town of **Te Aroha** you can languish in a private soda bath, while at nearby **Paeroa** there are pleasant walks in the lush **Karangahake Gorge**, once the scene of intensive gold mining.

Directly across the Hauraki Gulf from Auckland, the long and jagged **Coromandel Peninsula** is blessed with some of the country's best sandy beaches and a gorgeous climate. But if this conjures up images of overcrowding and overdevelopment, then think again. This is a place of great coastal scenery, solitude, walks to pristine beaches, and tramps in luxuriant mountainous rainforest. Its two coasts are markedly different, the east supplying the softer, more idyllic tourist beaches and short coastal walks, while the west has a far more rugged and atmospheric coastline, plus easier access to the volcanic hills and ancient kauri trees of the **Coromandel Forest Park**. All this countryside is best explored from bases such as **Thames**, a small town rich in gold-mining history, or tiny **Coromandel**, set in rolling hills beside an attractive harbour. The principal towns in the east are **Whangamata** and **Whitianga**, both blessed with long, luxurious, sandy beaches. The latter is also handy for **Hot Water Beach**, where natural thermal springs bubble up through the sand lapped by the Pacific Ocean, and **Cathedral Cove Marine Reserve**, ideal for dolphin spotting and snorkelling.

From the open-cast gold-mining town of **Waihi** at the base of the Coromandel Peninsula, the **Bay of Plenty** sweeps down and east to Opotiki, punctuated by an outstanding sequence of golden beaches and great surf, and

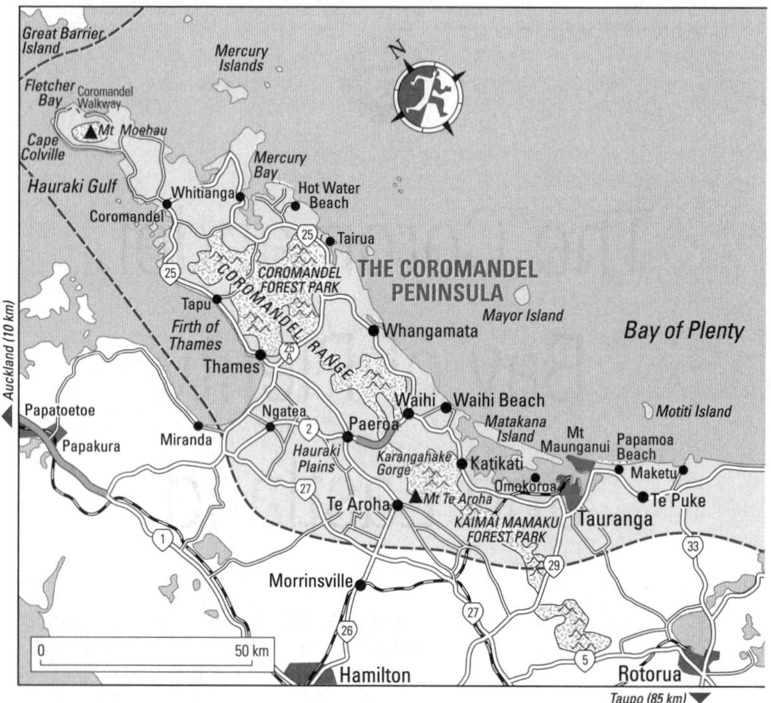

traced along its length by the Pacific Coast Highway (SH2), which links Auckland with Gisborne. The bay earned its name from **Captain Cook**, who sailed in on the *Endeavour* in 1769 and was struck by the number of thriving Maori settlements living off the abundant resources, as well as by the generous supplies they gave him. This era of peace and plenty was shattered by the **New Zealand Wars** of the 1860s, as fierce fighting led to the establishment of garrisons at both Tauranga and Whakatane, and the easternmost town of Opotiki gained notoriety as the scene of the death of a European missionary – allegedly murdered by a Maori prophet.

This area has the best climate on the North Island, making it a fertile fruit-growing region – particularly citrus and kiwifruit – and another much-visited resort area. The coast, though popular with Kiwi holidaymakers, has remained relatively unspoiled, offering great surf beaches, a good variety of offshore activities and walks in the forest-clad hills of the inland **Kaimai-Mamaku Forest Park**. On top of that, the region is home to one of the country's fastest-growing urban areas, centred on modern, vigorous **Tauranga** and the contiguous beach town of **Mount Maunganui**.

The eastern Bay of Plenty revolves around sunny **Whakatane**, primarily of interest for boat excursions to the fuming, volcanic **White Island**, opportunities to swim with dolphins, and as a base for wilderness rafting on the remote Motu River.

Contrasting with these two regions is the splendid, rugged and isolated **Eastland**, once a wealthy part of New Zealand but today run-down and

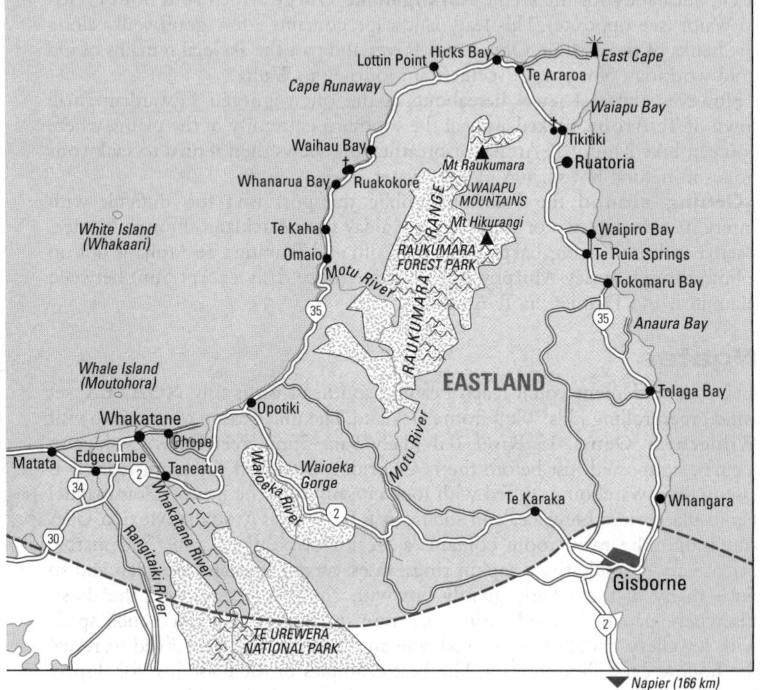

sparsely populated. With a dramatic coastline, and a rich and varied Maori history, this region provides a taste of a secluded way of life long gone in the rest of the country. At its easternmost point – the **East Cape** – is a lighthouse that overlooks East Island, the first place in the country to see the sunrise. All of the region's small communities, each with its own distinctive personality, are dotted along the coastline, against the dramatic backdrop of the **Waiapu Mountains**.

The Hauraki Plains

Approach the Coromandel Peninsula from the west and you can't help but pass through at least a part of the fertile **Hauraki Plains**, a wedge of former swamp at the peninsula's southern end. It's bordered to the north by the Firth of Thames, final destination for a number of meandering rivers which drain this sweep of rich pastoral farmland. Attractions are admittedly limited, and most people rush through on their way to the scenic splendour to the north and further east, missing out on at least a couple of sights worth a minor detour.

Journeying southeast from Auckland on SH2 you'll first strike the tiny settlement of **Ngatea**, worth a fleeting visit for the curiosity value of a warehouse crammed with rock crystals. The hub of the plains is **Paeroa**, not much in itself, but handy for the scenic **Karangahake Gorge** which runs from Paeroa to Waihi (see opposite). This leafy landscape contains a few good walks along the banks of the rushing Ohinemuri River and past the skeletal remains of old gold workings, plus a short scenic train journey to Waihi.

However, the real jewel hereabouts is the often-ignored Edwardian small town of **Te Aroha**, tucked away at the southern extremity of the plains, where you can hike Mount Te Aroha for breathtaking views then return to soak your bones in natural hot springs of soda water.

Getting around the Plains by public transport isn't too difficult with InterCity running two or three services a day from Auckland through Ngatea, Paeroa and the Karangahake Gorge to Waihi and Tauranga. Te Aroha is out on a limb though Turley-Murphy run a service (once daily except Sun) between Hamilton and Thames via Te Aroha.

Ngatea

The first settlement you'll reach heading southeast on is tiny **NGATEA**, set amid green rolling hills 70km from Auckland. The only reason to stop is to visit **Wilderness Gems**, 13 River Rd (daily 9am–5pm; free; Ⓦwww.wildgems.co.nz), signposted just before the river bridge, 200m off the main road. It is essentially a warehouse stuffed with rock crystals from the nearby Coromandel Peninsula, around New Zealand and from as far away as Australia, Mexico, USA and India. The main room contains a wealth of polished stone and marble ornaments – candlesticks, napkin rings, vases, carved animals, chess sets and so on – many of them fairly ghastly but with choice pieces among the dross. Elsewhere petrified wood, agates and rose quartz compete for bench space with jewellery crafted from carved jade and bone, and geodes sliced to reveal the hollow crystalline interior. The best examples of these are just for display but some pretty snazzy specimens are available for as little as $3 – and as much as $3000. You can catch a glimpse of the cutting and polishing operation through a window, or press on to the dark and pokey Fluorescent Room, where a five-minute programme illustrates how a range of minerals react to UV light, vibrantly glowing bright yellow, green, purple and red.

From here the highway continues to Paeroa, where you can branch off on SH26 northwards to the Coromandel Peninsula or southwards to Te Aroha.

Paeroa

Continuing 25km southeast from Ngatea on SH2 you reach the small and rather dreary **PAEROA**, which briefly became a significant port during the early gold-mining days when boats from Auckland could go no further up the Ohinemuri River. This facet of the town's past is poorly illustrated at the well-publicized **Maritime Museum** (Mon–Fri 10am–4pm; $4), which includes a desultory collection near the site of the original jetty and the rotting remains of an old paddle steamer, inexplicably marooned on a riverbank within the grounds.

To Kiwis, Paeroa is simply the birthplace of **Lemon and Paeroa** (L & P), a homegrown soft-drink which still holds its own against international competition, despite substituting the original natural mineral water, discovered here in the nineteenth century, with water from an Auckland bottling plant. Undaunted by this harsh reality, a giant brown L & P bottle stands at the junction of SH2 and SH26, greeting those entering town from the south, and Paeroa gets as much mileage as it can from the drink's promotional catchphrase "World Famous in New Zealand".

On Paeroa's main thoroughfare, Belmont Road, the pleasant but limited **Paeroa Museum**, at no. 37 (Mon–Fri 10.30am–3pm; $2), avoids the usual mind-boggling clutter, and has neatly displayed exhibits covering the town's history, early shipping and gold mining in the Karangahake Gorge. Of particular interest is a huge collection of Royal Albert bone china, while among the few Maori artefacts is a stack of collection drawers containing tools and ornaments: stone adzes, cutting tools, bone fish-hooks and carved *tiki* (pendants).

Practicalities

Paeroa's **main street** is Belmont Road (SH2), which runs south through town before becoming Normanby Road; the town centre is concentrated into a small area wedged between the Domain and the junction with SH26. InterCity, Guthreys and Turley-Murphy **buses** stop outside the **visitor centre**, 1 Belmont Rd (Oct–April Mon–Fri 9am–5pm, Sat & Sun 10am–3pm; May–Sept Mon–Fri 9am–5pm; ⓣ & ⓕ07/862 8636), which is well stocked with bumph on the Coromandel Peninsula and makes a point of selling cans of L & P.

There are a couple of reasonable **places to stay**, including the wooden, nineteenth-century *Criterion Hotel*, 147 Normanby Rd (ⓣ & ⓕ07/862 7983; ❶–❸), with recently refurbished rooms and prices as low as $20 per person. There's little to choose between the motels, but try the comfortable units at the pleasant *Racecourse Motel*, 68 Thames Rd (ⓣ07/862 7145, ⓕ862 7131; ❸), 1km north of town along SH26. An appealing rural alternative lies 8km east in the Karangahake Gorge (see below).

Café culture has come to Paeroa in the form of the *Lazy Fish*, 56 Belmont St (licensed & BYO), so you can **eat** well on Mediterranean-inspired mains, or just grab a coffee and muffin. Otherwise, you're limited to fairly standard, inexpensive cafés such as the licensed *Tui Coffee Lounge*, 18 Belmont Rd, and the more modern *World Famous in New Zealand* café and bar, almost opposite the visitor centre.

The Karangahake Gorge

Paeroa visitors bound for the Coromandel Peninsula (see p.383) should still take time to explore the leafy tranquillity of the magnificent **Karangahake Gorge** immediately east of Paeroa. This was the scene of the Coromandel's first gold rush, in 1875, where independent miners, armed only with picks and sluice pans, were quickly superseded by large companies that could afford the powerful equipment needed to extract the metal. Today it's hard to envisage such frenetic activity in this scenic spot. The steep-sided gorge begins 8km east of Paeroa along the narrow, snaking continuation of SH2 as it traces the Ohinemuri River to Waihi. The **Karangahake Gorge Historic Walkway** (fully described in a $1 leaflet available from the Paeroa visitor centre) covers 7km of a former rail line and is accessed from several points along the gorge, the best being the **Karangahake Reserve**, at the start of the gorge. Here a new pedestrian suspension bridge crosses the river to join the **loop walk** (3km; 1hr) which heads upstream alongside the Ohinemuri River past remnants of the gold workings and into the Karangahake Gorge hugging the cliffs and winding through regenerating native bush. The loop is completed by crossing the river and walking right through a 1km-long tunnel (usually lit). This walk encircles the site of the Karangahake township, now reduced to the reliable *Talisman Café*, and the *Ohinemuri Estate Winery and Café*, Moresby St (ⓣ07/862 8874, ⓔohinemuri-wines@paradise.net.nz; ❺), which has a delightful courtyard where you can sample the wines and tuck into well-prepared examples of the usual Kiwi café fare (daily in summer; Fri–Sun in winter). On summer Sunday afternoons there's a classical guitarist on duty, and you can even **stay** in a smart, self-contained apartment built into the hay loft.

At the eastern end of the gorge, the tiny village of **WAIKINO** comprises little more than a train station which acts as the western terminus for the Goldfields Railway. Inside there are displays on local history and walks in the area, while out on the platform is a café that has outside seating whenever the weather dictates.

Heading south from here, Waitawheta Camp Road runs for 8km along the rugged **Waitawheta Valley** to a trailhead for hikes into the scenic **Kaimai-Mamaku Forest Park**. Tracks follow old logging routes and rivers through a diverse mix of regenerating bush and podocarp forest, all described in DOC's *Kaimai-Mamaku Forest Park Day Walks* leaflet ($1).

Te Aroha

On the fringes of the Hauraki Plain, 21km south of Paeroa on SH26, the dairy-farming settlement town of **TE AROHA** is not really on the way to anywhere; something of an outlier despite its status as New Zealand's only intact **Edwardian spa**. It benefits from relative obscurity, and those prepared to make the journey are rewarded with a neat little town hunkered below the imposing bush-clad slopes of the **Kaimai-Mamaku Forest Park**. The 954-metre **Mount Te Aroha** rears up immediately behind the town centre providing a reasonably challenging goal for determined hikers, while gentler pleasures are pursued in hot **soda baths**.

The town itself was founded in 1880 at the furthest navigable extent of the Waihou River and the following year rich deposits of gold were found on Mount Te Aroha, sparking a full-scale **gold rush**, with the reefs of gold-bearing quartz producing handsome yields until 1921. Within a few months of settlement, the new townsfolk set out the attractive hilly Hot Springs Domain around a cluster of soda springs which, by the 1890s, was New Zealand's most popular mineral spa complex, frequently compared with those of Vichy or Baden. People flocked to enjoy the therapeutic benefits of its waters – the hottest soda springs in the country at 38–41°C – and enclosures were erected for privacy, most rebuilt in grand style during the Edwardian years early in the twentieth century. Spas went out of favour in the 1950s, but today the fine suite of original buildings has been beautifully restored and integrated with more modern pools fed by the hot soda springs. Perhaps the only drawback to a peaceful half-day spent here are the strong and biting winds that assault the town from time to time.

The Town

Te Aroha's centrepiece is the **Hot Springs Domain**, a 44-acre **thermal reserve** of formal gardens, rose beds and a bandstand only brought into the modern age by the skate park adjacent to the croquet lawns. To find the baths, just follow your nose; a slightly smoky yet not unpleasant smell emanates from the modern **Spa Baths** complex (daily 10am–10pm; $7–8 Mon–Fri, $10 Sat & Sun), which comprises five private, enclosed pools each with hydro-therapeutic water jets. Choose a stainless steel one if you fancy adding aromatherapy oils (not supplied); otherwise the wooden tubs are more comfy and spacious. A ten-minute soak followed by a prolonged spa bath is said to extract polluting heavy metals from your system – shower first to open up your pores

Walks in and around Te Aroha

The most rewarding of Te Aroha's **walks** is undoubtedly the ascent of **Mount Te Aroha**, which tops out on the crest of the Kaimai Range from where there are sweeping views down to the Bay of Plenty and, on exceptionally clear days, across to mounts Ruapehu and Taranaki. The **Te Aroha Mountain Track** (8km return; 3hr 30min; 950m ascent), starts from just behind the Mokena Geyser in the Domain and climbs steeply through native bush, zigzagging up a well-defined path to a viewing platform at **Whakapipi** (or Bald Spur), before dipping to a small saddle. From here, the final climb (which can be muddy and slippery after rain) becomes increasingly arduous, and you'll need to use your hands to pull yourself up in places, but the stunning views make it all worthwhile. To return, follow the **Tui Mine Track**, which drops through a stark, heavily mined landscape to link with the Tui Road back to town in one direction, and with the **Tui–Domain Track** in the other, a pleasant bush-walk past a waterfall back to the Domain. If the thought of an uphill slog right to the top is too much, the **sector** as far as the **Whakapipi Lookout** (2km; 50min) gives good views over the town and its surroundings.

Other walks of varied grades and duration lie south of Te Aroha in the **Waiorongomai Valley**, part of the **Kaimai-Mamaku Forest Park**. Formerly the scene of intense mining activity, several tracks following historic miners' trails are described in the leaflet *Guide to the Waiorongomai Valley* ($2.50), available from Te Aroha visitor centre (see p.382). Access is from a car park on the Waiorongomai Loop Road, which is signposted 4km south of town off the Shaftesbury Road – but note that this is an extremely rugged area punctuated by old mines and shafts that are dangerous to enter. **Overnight hikes** should only be attempted by experienced, fit and well equipped trampers; hut tickets can be bought from the visitor centre in Te Aroha.

and be sure to drink plenty of water afterwards to help counteract the dehydrating effects of the mineral-rich water. You could also visit the nearby Te Aroha Domain Therapy Clinic (ⓣ07/884 8717) and indulge in Swedish massage, aromatherapy, acupressure and all manner of holistic jiggery pokery ($20 for 30min).

Nearby, a brand-new outdoor **Wyborn Leisure Pool** complex ($4) contains one of the original communal bath houses, the 1878 **No. 2 Bathhouse** (daily: Nov–March 11am–9pm, April-Oct 11am–7pm; $7 per person per half-hour), best suited to larger groups of up to fifteen, with one large pool which, at 32°C, is slightly cooler than the Spa Baths.

Just uphill from the baths is the erratic **Mokena Geyser**, which spurts to impressive heights on good days, going off roughly every half-hour. From here, a **trail** (see box, above) leads to the top of **Mount Te Aroha** which, legend has it, was named by a young Arawa chief, Kahumatamomoe, who climbed it after losing his way in the region's vast swamp while on his way home to Maketu in the Bay of Plenty. Delighted to see the familiar shoreline of his homeland, he called the mountain *Te Aroha*, meaning "love", in honour of his father and kinsmen.

An old sanatorium, just below the spa baths and in front of the croquet lawn, houses the town **museum** (Dec–March Sat & Sun 11am–4pm; April–Nov Sat & Sun 1–4pm; donation). There are three exhibit-packed rooms and two finely decorated Royal Doulton Victorian lavatories. A large part of one room is given over to a selection of wind-up gramophones, another to a collection of black-and-white photos of the town and its people, plus a chemical analysis of the local soda water. There are also memorabilia of an old silent movie called *Tilly of Te Aroha*, made when the film industry was in its infancy, and a racy picture for its time.

By the Boundary Street exit from the Domain you'll find the 1926 **St Mark's Anglican Church**, on the corner of Church Street and Kenrick Street, insignificant but for the incongruously sited 1712 organ, said to be the oldest in the southern hemisphere. Built in England by Renatus Harris, it is the sole survivor of ten built after Queen Anne petitioned Parliament to raise taxes so that the finest pipe organs of the day could be put into ten London churches. Brought to New Zealand in 1926, this particular organ was restored in 1985 by an Auckland firm who found that part of the finely carved English heart oak casework predates the organ and probably came from the famed Grinling Gibbons's workshop. If you can get a group together and are prepared to make a small donation, an organ recital can be arranged through the visitor centre.

Practicalities

The town's main street is Whitaker Street and everything of interest – banks, post office, library with internet access – is along it or close by: the **visitor centre** (Sept–April Mon–Fri 9am–5pm, Sat & Sun 10am–3pm; May–Aug Mon–Fri 9.30am–4.30pm, Sat & Sun 10am–3pm; ⓣ07/884 8052, ⓦwww.tearoha-info.co.nz) is at 102 Whitaker St by the entrance to the Domain, and has DOC information for the local area.

For a small place, Te Aroha has a reasonable choice of **accommodation**. The *YHA* on Miro Street, off Burgess Street (ⓣ07/884 8739, ⓔtearoha.yha@xtra.co.nz; office open 5–8.30pm; dorms ❶, room ❷), is one of the simplest in New Zealand, about ten minutes' walk from the visitor centre in an attractive cottage on the lower slopes of Mount Te Aroha, with great views and a pretty garden. The hostel has just two bunkrooms and one twin room, and a charming kitchen stocked with plenty of basic cooking ingredients. Beside the Domain is the *Te Aroha Motel*, at 108 Whitaker St (ⓣ07/884 9417; ❹), with functional, well-kept units. Campers should head 4km out on the road to Hamilton (SH26) to the delightful *Te Aroha Holiday Park*, 217 Stanley Rd (ⓣ07/884 9567, ⓕ889 7910; tent sites $9, on-site vans ❷, cabins & flats ❸), set among well-established oak trees with a few free-range chickens strutting around and free use of bikes.

Two cosmopolitan **cafés** vie for your business: *Café Banco*, 174 Whitaker St (no credit cards), occupies a former bank and dishes up daytime meals mainly based on Italian flatbreads along with evening meals ($20–25) such as Cajun chicken with roasted vegetables and salad; *Ironique*, 159 Whitaker St, does good coffee, nachos, panini and salads in a place where almost everything – the wine racks, door handles, even washbasins – is made of black iron.

If you'd rather dine within the sylvan confines of the Domain, try the *Domain House Restaurant*, where lunch and dinner is served in a lovely 1906 colonial building with broad verandas; dishes such as chicken breast filled with camembert on fettuccine and pork fillets on wild rice with prune and red wine sauce go for $20–25. The low-key *Mokena Restaurant*, in a rambling old wooden hotel at 6 Church St (ⓣ07/884 8038; licensed), is a big hit with locals, offering evening **smorgasbords** (Fri–Sun from 6pm; $26; book ahead) of fresh, home-cooked fare.

The Coromandel Peninsula

Auckland's Hauraki Gulf is separated from the Pacific Ocean by the long, broad thumb of the **Coromandel Peninsula**, a mountainous and bush-cloaked interior fringed with beautiful surf and swimming beaches, all basking in a balmy climate. This happy combination of natural features is an understandable lure, and it seems that almost every visitor has the Coromandel Peninsula on their itinerary even if they're not quite sure why. Certainly the genuine sights are few, but there's no denying the allure of a relaxing few days spent exploring or just lazing on a beach.

The peninsula's two coasts are starkly different. In the **west**, cliffs and steep hills drop sharply to the sea leaving only a narrow coastal strip shaded by **pohutukawa** trees which erupt in a blaze of rich red from mid-November to December. The beaches are sheltered, safe and ripe for exploration, but most are only good for **swimming** when high tide obscures the mud flats. Except for the attraction of a couple of interesting small west coast towns, most people prefer the **east coast**, a land of sweeping white-sand beaches pounded by impressive but often perilous **surf**. This is where Kiwis flock for long weekends and summer holidays, and the more fashionable beaches are lined with the holiday homes of Aucklanders and rich Waikato farmers. Increasingly people are finding ways to live here permanently, and one-time *baches* are being replaced by million-dollar beachfront properties.

Elsewhere on the peninsula, low property prices in declining former gold towns, combined with the wonderful juxtaposition of bush, hills and beaches, have exerted a powerful effect on hippies, **artists** and New Agers. Keep your eyes peeled and you'll spot folk eking out a living from the land, running holistic healing centres and holding quasi-religious retreats. Less vigilance is required to find painters, potters and **craftspeople**, many of them very good, often hawking the fruit of their labours from their homes and studios. The free and widely available *Coromandel Craft Trail* leaflet details thirty-odd mostly rural craft outlets all over the peninsula, selling items ranging from silk flowers to bronze and concrete sculpture. Unsurprisingly, the evil weed is also prevalent, and (if you hang out in the right places) it won't be long before you'll meet someone passing around a joint. This all adds up to large-scale support of the Green Party, and sure enough, at the end of 1999, the Coromandel's Jeanette Fitzsimmons became New Zealand's first elected **Green MP**.

Maori spirituality is also important in the peninsula. The **Coromandel Range** which runs through the interior – sculpted millions of years ago by volcanic activity into a jagged and contorted skyline, since clothed in dense rainforest – is interpreted as a canoe, with **Mount Moehau**, at the peninsula's northern tip, as its prow, and Mount Te Aroha in the south, bordering the Hauraki Plains, as its sternpost. The **summit** area of Mount Moehau is sacred Maori-owned land, the legendary burial place of Tama Te Kapua, the commander of one of the Great Migration canoes, *Te Arawa*.

Notwithstanding the bohemian flavour and scenic splendour, there's not much to do here, though a few towns warrant attention. At the base of the peninsula, the former gold town of **Thames** exhibits its heritage and makes a good base for exploring the forested **Kauaeranga Valley** with its walking tracks into the steep hills. Further north the lovely little town of **Coromandel** offers the opportunity to ride the narrow-gauge **Driving Creek Railway** and is close to the trans-peninsula **309 Road** where the **Waiau Waterworks** and an impressive stand of **kauri** are the main attractions. For really remote country

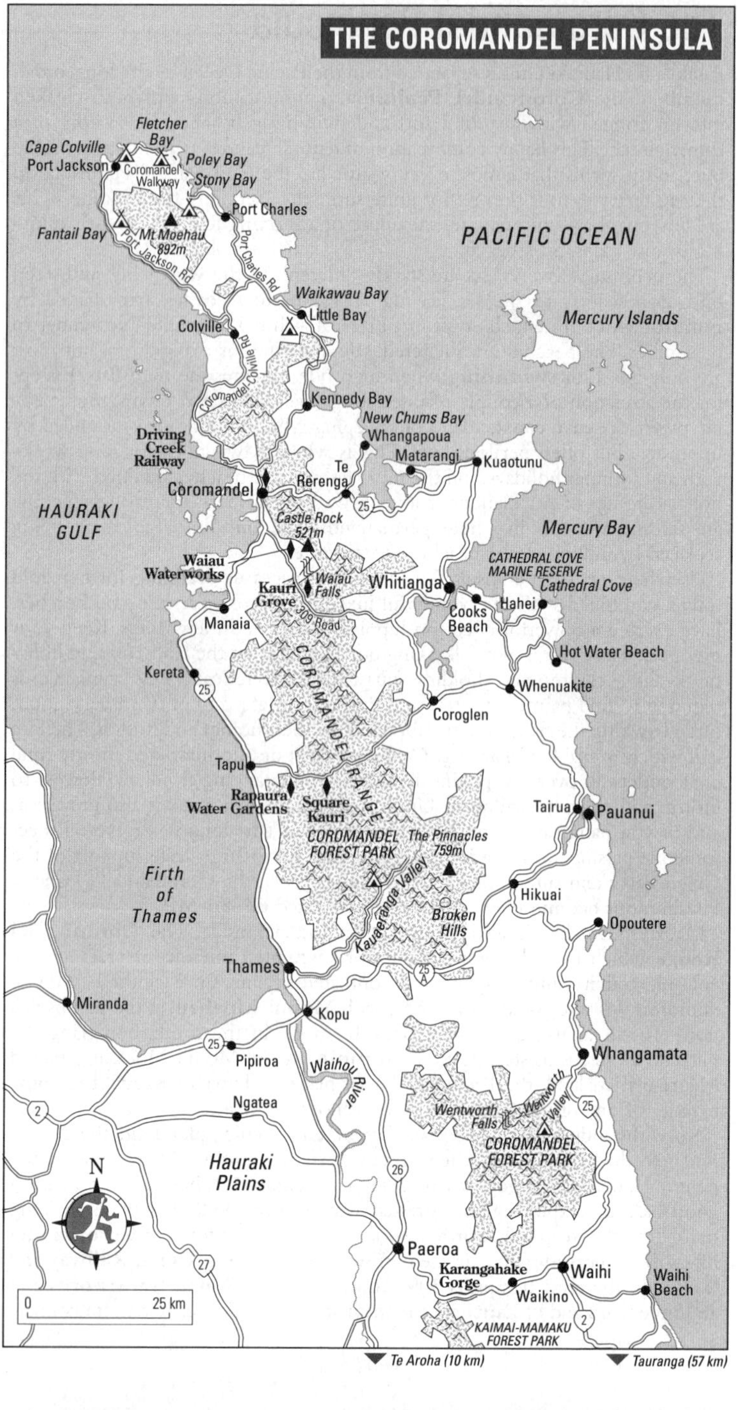

THE COROMANDEL PENINSULA

PACIFIC OCEAN
Cape Colville
Fletcher Bay
Port Jackson
Coromandel Walkway
Poley Bay
Stony Bay
Port Charles
Fantail Bay
Mt Moehau 892m
Port Jackson Rd
Port Charles Rd
Waikawau Bay
Little Bay
Colville
Coromandel-Colville Rd
Mercury Islands
Kennedy Bay
New Chums Bay
Whangapoua
Driving Creek Railway
Matarangi
Kuaotunu
Te Rerenga
Coromandel
HAURAKI GULF
Castle Rock 521m
Mercury Bay
Waiau Waterworks
CATHEDRAL COVE MARINE RESERVE
Cathedral Cove
Kauri Grove
Waiau Falls
Whitianga
Hahei
Cooks Beach
Manaia
309 Road
Hot Water Beach
COROMANDEL RANGE
Kereta
Whenuakite
Coroglen
Tapu
Rapaura Water Gardens
Square Kauri
Tairua
Pauanui
COROMANDEL FOREST PARK
The Pinnacles 759m
Firth of Thames
Kauaeranga Valley
Hikuai
Broken Hills
Opoutere
Thames
Miranda
Kopu
Whangamata
Pipiroa
Waihou River
Ngatea
Wentworth Valley
Wentworth Falls
COROMANDEL FOREST PARK
Hauraki Plains
N
Paeroa
Karangahake Gorge
Waihi
Waikino
Waihi Beach
0 25 km
KAIMAI-MAMAKU FOREST PARK
Te Aroha (10 km)
Tauranga (57 km)

head up to tiny **Colville** and the peninsula's northern tip, but the paved highway continues east to **Mercury Bay**, centred on the appealing town of **Whitianga**. Nearby, digging a hole to wallow in surf-side hot springs lures hundreds to **Hot Water Beach**, while brilliant snorkelling and gorgeous bays draw others to the **Cathedral Cove Marine Reserve**. Yet more beaches string the coast further south, some of the best (and most populated) around **Whangamata** and at **Waihi Beach**, the coastal acolyte of **Waihi**, the peninsula's southernmost town, which still produces gold from its open-cast mine.

Peninsula practicalities

As one of the North Island's principal holiday spots, the Coromandel Peninsula becomes the scene of frenetic activity from **Christmas** until the end of January, when finding accommodation can become near impossible – book well ahead. Numbers are more manageable for the rest of the summer, and in **winter** much of the peninsula is deserted, even though the **climate** remains mild for most of the year.

It's easiest to negotiate the Peninsula by **car**. The main roads are mostly sealed, and though many to the more out-of-the-way stretches are gravel, very few pose any real danger if you take it steadily – even the infamous roads beyond Colville to the northern tip are a lot better than they once were. **Bus** travel is a little more problematic and limiting, but still pretty good. Timetables all but dictate that you cover the peninsula in a clockwise direction, with InterCity providing a regular loop service from Thames, north to Coromandel, across to Whitianga and back down and across to Thames: the **Coromandel Trail** ticket costs $101 and incorporates the fare from Auckland to Rotorua. Go Kiwi (Ⓣ0800/446 549) offers a very competitive door-to-door service between Whitianga, Tairua, Thames and Auckland, running to Auckland in the morning and back in the afternoon.

Flying to the peninsula is only really feasible if you have a Stray Possum **travel pass** (Ⓣ0800/767 786), which allows you to make a cost-effective loop from Auckland to the Coromandel by bus, a flight from Whitianga to Great Barrier Island, another on to either Auckland ($165) or Whangarei in Northland ($235), an option which includes a bus ride up to the Bay of Islands then back to Auckland ($235).

Thames and around

The small and rather dull former gold town of **THAMES** is home to just seven thousand, packed into a coastal strip between the Firth of Thames and the Coromandel Range. It is the peninsula's main service town with a variety of accommodation, a few reasonable places to eat and transport connections for both the immediate surroundings and the rest of the peninsula.

The first big discovery of gold-bearing quartz was made in a Thames creek bed in 1867, but mining activity tailed off during the 1880s, and little remained after 1913. Nonetheless, the legacy of the **mining** heyday forms the basis of the town's attractions, and you can easily spend half a day visiting them and wandering backstreets liberally dotted with the erstwhile owners' grand homes. Also within easy reach is the **Kauaeranga Valley**, a popular centre for hikers visiting the Coromandel Forest Park that's often busy at weekends.

Arrival, information and transport

InterCity, Guthreys and Go Kiwi **buses** drop off all over town, including outside the **visitor centre**, 206 Pollen St (Mon–Fri 8.30am–5pm, Sat & Sun

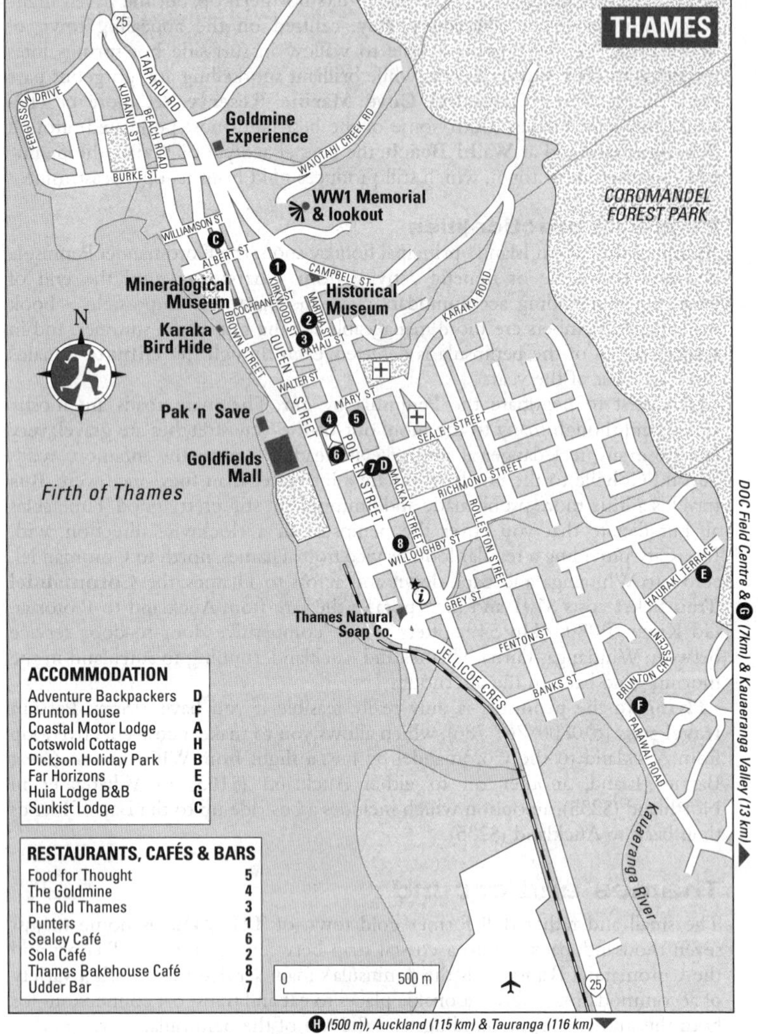

9am–4pm; ☎07/868 7284, ⓔthames@ihug.co.nz), which has stacks of literature on the town and the Coromandel Peninsula (including Hot Water Beach tide times), and acts as the local AA office. Pollen Street, the main shopping thoroughfare, is home to what is left of Thames' traditional gold-era hotels, and has a number of **banks**, and the **post office**. Nowhere is far from here, but you can get around with **taxis** from Thames Gold Cabs (☎07/868 6037), or **rental bikes** from Paki Paki Bike Shop, in the Goldfields Mall (☎07/868 8311). There's also **car rental** from The Rental Car Centre, 733 Pollen St (☎07/868 8556, ⓔthames@therentalcarcentre.co.nz), which allows its budget cars onto the peninsula's roughest roads.

Accommodation

Accommodation in Thames is rather scattered, most of it lying outside the town centre, though it's generally of a good standard and there's plenty of choice.

Adventure Backpackers Coromandel (ABC) 476 Pollen St ⓣ & ⓕ07/868 6200. Good clean low-cost hostel above the *Udder Bar* and *Krazy Cow* nightclub in the centre of town, with 4- to 8-bed dorms and ensuite doubles with TV. Dorms ❶, rooms ❷

Brunton House 210 Parawai Rd ⓣ & ⓕ07/868 5160, ⓔbruntonhouse@xtra.co.nz. A fine, large Victorian villa within easy walking distance of the centre. Three rooms share one guest bathroom and there's a swimming pool and tennis court. Dinner ($25) is also available by arrangement; room rates are at the lower end of this price code. ❺

Coastal Motor Lodge 608 Tararu Rd, SH25, 2.5km north of town ⓣ07/868 6843, ⓦwww.nzmotels.co.nz/coastal. A complex of pleasant "cottage" units and modern A-frame chalets (all self-contained), overlooking the Firth. Predictably, the best views are from the pricier chalets. ❺–❻

Cotswold Cottage 46 Maramarahi Rd, 3km south of town ⓣ & ⓕ07/868 6306. Grand old villa set in mature grounds on the outskirts of Thames, with canoes for exploring the adjacent river. En-suite rooms are richly furnished and delicious breakfasts are included in the price. ❻

Dickson Holiday Park Victoria St ⓣ07/868 7308, ⓔyha@dicksonpark.co.nz. Large, well-run campsite and associate YHA in a pretty valley 3.5km north of the centre. Excellent facilities include a pool and bus pick-up from Thames. Tent sites $10, backpacker cabins ❶, cabins ❷, flats ❸, units ❹

Far Horizons 204 Hauraki Terrace ⓣ07/868 9711, ⓔt1p1@xtra.co.nz. Budget B&B in a single studio unit with good views and continental breakfast. Transport by arrangement, but it is only a 15-min walk from the visitor centre. ❸

Huia Lodge B&B 589 Kauaeranga Valley Rd ⓣ & ⓕ07/868 6557. A wonderfully peaceful setting right in the valley, amid bush and pasture, 8km from town. Two modern and comfortable en-suite units, dinner available for $20. Free transport from Thames. ❹

Sunkist Lodge, 506 Brown St ⓣ07/868 8808 & 0800/767 786, ⓔsunkist@xtra.co.nz. An atmospheric backpacker hostel in a historic building; dorms hold 4–10 bunks, and there are also a few double rooms. Facilities include a well-equipped kitchen, sun deck and garden, and baggage storage; and the InterCity bus stops outside. Dorms ❶, rooms ❷

The Town

The best introduction to the town's gold-mining past is at the **Goldmine Experience**, Tararu Road (Dec–April daily 10am–4pm; May–Nov by reservation; $10; ⓣ & ⓕ07/868 8514, ⓦwww.goldmine-experience.co.nz), where you join an informative tour through the old battery: machines are fired up for a couple of minutes, which is ample considering the racket as quartz gets crushed then transferred to the shaking table, where the minerals are separated according to their weight, gold being the heaviest. The tour continues underground along a narrow horizontal shaft originally cut by hand and just high enough to clear a miner's head. Life down the mine is convincingly portrayed through sound effects, realistic-looking mannequins, anecdotes from guides all related to the original Cornish miners, and an extensive historical photo museum.

The **Mineralogical Museum**, on the corner of Brown and Cochrane streets (daily: Nov–April 11am–4pm, May–Oct 11am–3pm; $3.50), continues the mining theme with a vast collection of quartz, crystals, rocks and fossils displayed in cases – one for geology freaks only. Neither is the Victoriana-stuffed **Historical Museum**, on the corner of Pollen Street and Cochrane Street (daily 1–4pm; $2.50), anything to write home about.

Fans of natural lotions and potions should pay a visit to the EcoPeople store, on the corner of Pollen and Grey streets, where you can nip out the back to take a one-hour tour of the **Thames Natural Soap Co** factory (Mon–Fri

11am, 1pm & 3pm; $10), complete with 150 essential oils to sniff and a complimentary bar of soap.

At the junction of Brown Street and Cochrane Street, a boardwalk across the mangroves leads to the **Karaka Bird Hide**: a couple of hours either side of high tide is the optimum time to spot migratory birds such as knots, godwits, shags and terns, especially between October and February. An information board details the species which frequent the mangroves. Flying creatures can also be seen at the family-oriented **Butterfly and Orchid Garden** some 3km north, at the *Dickinson Holiday Park* on SH25 (daily: Nov–March 10am–4pm, April–Oct 11am–3pm; $8), where you can wander around a hothouse hoping a butterfly will land on your shoulder.

You can get a good view over the town and the Firth of Thames from the **lookout** at the war memorial; walk or drive up Waiotahi Road and Monument Road to a car park just below the monument, then follow a short flight of stone steps leading up to the viewpoint.

Kauaeranga Valley

The steep-sided **Kauaeranga Valley**, to the east of town, stretches towards the spine of the Coromandel Peninsula, a jagged landscape of bluffs and gorges topped by **The Pinnacles** (759m), with stupendous views to both coasts across native forest studded with original giants such as rata, rimu and the occasional kauri. All this is reached along a scenic and mostly-sealed road snaking beside the river, providing access to some of the finest walks in the Coromandel Range, and the only backcountry DOC hut on the entire peninsula. *Sunkist Lodge* (see p.387) runs a shuttle bus along the road on request (roughly $35 return); or you can **drive** by heading out of the southern end of Thames, along Parawai Road, which becomes Kauaeranga Road. Thirteen kilometres along you reach the **DOC office** (daily 8am–4pm; ⓣ07/867 9080, ⓕ867 9095), where you can stock up on maps, buy hut tickets and examine displays on early kauri logging in the valley. From here a loop track (500m; 10min) leads to a scale model of a kauri driving dam, the type once used extensively in this forest. Along the eight unsealed kilometres beyond the DOC office to the road-end, an assortment of tracks (see box opposite) lead off into the bush that's full of "pole stands" of young kauri that have grown since the area was logged a century back: only a handful in each stand will reach maturity. Most of the hikes head into the bush near one of the half-dozen simple roadside **campsites** ($7; toilets and water) dotted the length of the stretch.

To really get off the beaten track consider **canyoning** down the Sleeping God canyon with Canyonz (see p.115), whose trips begin in Auckland but will pick up in Thames.

Eating and entertainment

Thames' staple of old-style tearooms and traditional bars is now being supplemented by a couple of more modern places, though evening entertainment still revolves mostly around the pub.

Food for Thought 574 Pollen St. This small, central café specializes in pastries, lasagne, cakes and *pastizzi* (Lebanese pies), much of it vegetarian; and does good coffee too.

The Goldmine cnr of Pollen & Mary streets. Excellent-value restaurant serving mainstream meals in gargantuan portions. Try the T-bone and chips ($14) or the beer-battered fish and chips ($18).

The Old Thames cnr of Pollen & Pahau streets. Evening restaurant popular among families for its broad range of moderately priced seafood, steaks,

Kauaeranga walks

The Kauaeranga Valley is blessed with a wonderful range of easily accessible tramps ranging from a twenty-minute stroll to a satisfying two-day circuit with a night spent at the large and relatively plush **Pinnacles Hut** (80 bunks; $15; advance booking essential ☎07/867 9080). There are also a couple of remote and very basic DOC **campsites**: one near the Pinnacles Hut and another at Billygoat Basin (both $7.50). The *Kauaeranga Kauri Trail* DOC leaflet ($1) covers the basics, though you might prefer the detail provided by the 1:50,000 Thames topo map ($12): both are available from DOC office and the Thames visitor centre.

Billygoat Landing (1.5km return; 20–30min). The shortest walk in the valley, giving excellent views of the 180-metre Billygoat Falls.

Edwards Lookout (1km loop; 40min–1hr). A fine viewpoint over manuka-towai forest from a rocky saddle reached by a track starting 5km beyond the DOC office.

Pinnacles Circuit (14km loop; 2 days). This is the way to really get to grips with the region, following the **Kauaeranga Kauri Trail** and overnighting in the *Pinnacles Hut* (see above) about a third of the way along. It is really just a day and a half, starting at the road end and spending the first 2–3hr following Webb Creek up to *Pinnacles Hut* and the well-restored Dancing Camp kauri dam. From the hut there is a steep 50min climb to The Pinnacles themselves. The second day is longer (7–8hr) and passes the sad remnants of a couple of kauri dams, an old logging camp and some more fine viewpoints. A there-and-back trip to the Pinnacles can be done in 6–7hr.

Short Trestles Walk (5km return; 2hr). The most satisfying walk if you've only got a couple of hours, climbing up above the Atuatumoe (Billygoat) Stream to the Short Trestles, one of the last remnants of an old logging tramway. Return the same way, and see if you can find a path down to the stream and a good swimming hole a couple of hundred metres down from the lowermost trestle.

Wainora Track (6km return; 2–3hr). Moderate, well formed track to a couple of large kauri – pretty much the only ones left standing hereabouts – that starts from the Wainora campsite, 6km beyond the DOC office.

pizzas and generous desserts. Licensed.

Punters 719 Pollen St ☎07/868 9178. Popular, friendly and airy, with eclectic food and a garden bar. The menu ranges from light snacks to reasonably priced dinners. Lunch & dinner daily; book ahead for Sun brunch; DJ or live music Fri & Sat nights.

Sealey Café 109 Sealey St. Laid-back place in an attractive, high-ceilinged house with a pleasant courtyard. Light lunches of burgers and big sandwiches go for around $10, while dinner mains ($20–25) might include rack of organic lamb or pork fillet with juniper berries. Daily from 11am; licensed & BYO.

Sola Café 720b Pollen St. Modern vegetarian café and restaurant where you might drop in for excellent coffee and cake or stay for panini, pizza slices or frittata. Open evenings (Thurs–Sun) for excellent-value mains such as pumpkin and rosemary risotto. BYO.

Thames Bakehouse Café 326 Pollen St. Very traditional daytime tearooms serving pies, toasted sandwiches, burgers and cakes at low prices.

Udder Bar 476 Pollen St. Sparsely furnished bar with a value-for-money line in bar meals and a lively clientele who dutifully spill into the Krazy Cow nightclub (in the same building) on Fri & Sat nights.

North to Coromandel

From Thames, SH25 snakes 58km north to Coromandel (the town after which the peninsula is named), tracing the grey rocky shoreline of the "**Pohutukawa Coast**" past a series of tiny, sandy bays, most with little more than a few houses and maybe a campsite. Hills and sand-coloured cliffs rise dramatically from the roadside for the first 19km to **Tapu**, where the **Tapu–Coroglen Road** peels off to the Coromandel's east coast. It is a wonderfully scenic 28km run of narrow, unsealed but manageable driving, leaving behind the marginal farmland on the coast and climbing over the peninsula's mountainous spine. Even if you aren't tackling the traverse, it is worth making a detour 6.5km along the road (and just beyond the end of the asphalt), to **Rapaura Water Gardens** (mid-Sept to May daily 10am–5pm; $8), a cleverly landscaped "wilderness" of bush and blooms, punctuated by lily ponds and a trickling stream. Hidden away against a backdrop of bush and threaded by numerous paths, the gardens fully tap into the Coromandel ethos by posting philosophical messages urging you to stop and think awhile, and it's easy enough to spend half a day doing just that – though you could get around most of the gardens in an hour. One of the highlights is a lovely three-tiered Rapaura Falls, reached by a well-kept track from the car park at the entrance (15min). There are verdant and shady picnic areas, and they serve excellent cream teas.

The road continues for 3km on to the (easily missed) "square kauri" signpost near the road's summit, opposite a rough lay-by and just before a small bridge. Steep steps through bush (175m; 10min) lead to this giant of a tree (1200 years old, just over 41m high and 9m wide), whose unusual, angular shape saved it from loggers. From here it's another rough and windy 19km across the peninsula to Coroglen, linking with the main road between Whitianga and Whangamata, or 9.5km back to Tapu and the continuation of SH25 north.

Back on **SH25** the road lurches inland soon after Kereta (about 12km north of Tapu), snaking over hills to the roadside **Manaia-Kereta Lookout** (206m), which has great views of the northern peninsula, the majestic Moehau Range and Coromandel Harbour. Beyond, Great Barrier Island may be visible on a clear day – a giant block of rock with vertical cliffs rising from the sea. Ducking and diving in and out from the rocky shoreline and the blue-green vistas of the Firth of Thames, SH25 continues for 20km to the turn-off to 309 Road, 3km south of Coromandel, which cuts across to Whitianga by way of a few roadside attractions, all within 8km of Coromandel (see "East to Whitianga", p.395).

Coromandel

The northernmost town of any substance is the pretty, spruce little **COROMANDEL**, 58km north of Thames, huddling beneath high, craggy hills at the head of Coromandel Harbour. It is known to many simply as the jumping-off point for the **Coromandel Walkway** (see box on p.395), 57km away amid the jagged landscape of the northern peninsula, but it's worth taking time to soak up the atmosphere of this old gold town and ride its **scenic railway** into the local hills.

The town and peninsula took their name from the geographically dissimilar Coromandel Coast, south of Madras in India; an anomaly which stems from the visit here of the British Admiralty supply ship *Coromandel* which called into the harbour in 1820 to obtain kauri spars and masts and to extend Captain Cook's brief survey of the Hauraki Gulf.

A more mercenary European invasion was precipitated by the 1852 discovery of **gold**, near Driving Creek, in the northern part of town. The subsequent boom left its mark with a string of fine wooden buildings along the main street, though these days the town just ticks by as a local service centre and minor tourist hub. There are a couple of supermarkets and petrol stations, a BNZ bank, a cluster of cafés and a broad range of accommodation.

Moving on you've a choice of striking **east to Whitianga**, via the continuation of SH25 (see p.396) past the deserted beaches of Whangapoua and Kuaotunu, or taking the more rugged 309 Road (see p.395).

Arrival, information and transport

The combined **visitor centre** and **DOC office**, 355 Kapanga Rd (Nov–Easter daily 9am–5pm, Easter–Oct Mon–Fri 9am–5pm, Sat & Sun 11am–3pm; ⓣ07/866 8598, ⓦwww.coromandeltown.co.nz), is at the northern end of town, just over the bridge. Daily InterCity and Turley Murphy **buses** pull into the car park opposite. The only **car rental** firm in town is Rent-a-Dent, 226 Wharf Rd (ⓣ07/866 8736), which also allows its cars onto the unsealed roads north of Colville. There's **mountain bike rental** from Expedition, 5 Kapanga Rd (ⓣ07/866 8189), for around $30 a day.

Accommodation

For a small place, Coromandel offers a good range of **places to stay**, from a campsite in the town centre through to a luxurious lodge in an idyllic setting a few kilometres north. Most are within easy walking distance of the town centre.

Buffalo Lodge 860 Buffalo Rd, signposted north of town past the Gold Stamper Battery ⓣ & ⓕ07/866 8960, ⓦwww.buffalolodge.co.nz. Luxurious, award-winning accommodation in an architect-designed house set high up in the bush, with superb views across the Hauraki Gulf. Run by two Swiss artists, the three en-suite double rooms are modern and elegant; two of them have private decks. Superb dinners are offered to guests for $85 a head. Reserve well in advance; closed May–Sept. ❽.

Celadon Lodge Motel & B&B Alfred St, about 1km north of town ⓣ & ⓕ07/866 8058, ⓦwilsonmc@wave.co.nz. This charming self-contained A-frame on a bush-clad hillside, with town and harbour views, operates as a motel. There are two double rooms and a couple of two-bed bunkrooms plus a separate B&B section that has two en-suite rooms with sun decks. ❹.

Coromandel Colonial Cottages 1737 Rings Rd, 1.5km north of town ⓣ0508/222 688 & 07/866 8857, ⓦwww.corocottagesmotel.co.nz. Tranquil, luxury cottages sleeping two to six people. Excellent facilities include a swimming pool and BBQ area. Good value for money. ❹

Coromandel Town Backpackers 732 Rings Rd ⓣ & ⓕ07/866 8327. Modern, spick-and-span hostel close to the centre of town with budget bunks and some clean and attractive rooms. Dorms ❶, rooms ❷

Jacaranda Lodge 3km south on SH25 ⓣ07/866 8002, ⓔlightning.prohosting.com/~bowler. A modern house in farmland offering B&B in extremely comfortable and spacious rooms. Breakfasts are made from organic ingredients, dinner is available on request ($30–40), and the single room rate makes it good value for lone travellers. ❺

Lion's Den 126 Te Tiki Rd ⓣ & ⓕ07/866 8157. Very appealing, communally inclined hostel that's a great place to relax for a couple of days, perhaps lying in the hammock over the stream feeding the eels. Stay in the villa or out in a former house truck. Camping $12, four-shares ❶, house truck ❷

Long Bay Motor Camp 3200 Long Bay Rd, 3km west of town ⓣ07/866 8720, ⓔlbmccoromandel@paradise.net.nz. Attractive beachfront campsite with safe swimming and good facilities including kayak, dinghy and fishing tackle rental plus some basic new units, and some fridge- and microwave-equipped cabins which sleep up to six. Additional tent sites ($8) are located at the secluded Tucks Bay, a 1.5km drive through the bush or a five-minute walk around the headland. Tent sites $9, units ❷, cabins ❸

Tidewater Tourist Park 270 Tiki Rd ⓣ07/866 8888, ⓦwww.tidewater.co.nz. Combined motel and associate YHA set in large, leafy grounds right in town and by the harbour, with barbecue area, sauna and low-cost bike rental. Dorms ❶, flats ❸, units ❹

Tui Lodge 600 Whangapoua Rd, just off SH25 ⓣ07/866 8237. Good-value backpacker ten minutes' walk south of town (and right on the InterCity bus route), set in a relaxed, rambling house by an orchard. Perks include free linen, laundry, tea and coffee, fruit (in season) and use of bikes. Tent sites $10, dorms ❶, chalet & rooms ❷

△ Driving Creek Railway

The Town and around

The town centre, such as it is, spreads along the main road, with a few old buildings left from gold-mining days. From the south, SH25 becomes Tiki Road and then splits into two: to the left is Wharf Road, which skirts the harbour; to the right you immediately enter the heart of the town, on Kapanga Road, lined with shops and cafés. A couple of blocks further on, it becomes Rings Road, before heading northwards out of town as Colville Road.

About 300m north of the visitor centre is the small **Coromandel Historical Museum**, at 841 Rings Rd (Oct–March daily 10am–4pm; April–Sept Sat & Sun only 1–4pm; $2). Based in the old School of Mines (1898), this is a mishmash of domestic items and mining memorabilia, including a number of evocative black-and-white photographs from early mining days. The original jailhouse is around the back.

The main attraction in the immediate vicinity is **Driving Creek Railway and Potteries**, Driving Creek Road, 3.5km north of town (daily 10am–5pm; ⓣ07/866 8703, ⓦwww.drivingcreekrailway.co.nz). Built mostly by hand over twenty years, this is the country's only narrow-gauge hill railway, the brainchild of Barry Brickell, an eccentric local potter and rail enthusiast who wanted access into the clay-bearing hills. Wood is still brought down to fire the kilns, though the railway, which runs through bush where 13,000 native saplings have been planted over the last 25 years, is now mainly used to carry visitors on a delightfully shambolic hour-long **train trip** (daily 10.15am & 2pm, extra trains at 9am, 12.45pm & 4.30pm during holidays; $15) for which bookings are advised. The track is only 381mm wide and carries specially designed, articulated diesel trains, which climb 120m over a distance of about 3km. The rewards of this leisurely, commentated trip are spectacular views and extraordinary feats of engineering, including a series of viaducts, spirals and tunnels, a zigzag section, and a unique steel "double-decker" viaduct straddling a deep ravine, as well as increasingly elaborate embankments and cuttings, initially built of wine and beer bottles and later lined with inventive murals. At the end of the line is a lookout point with panoramic views of Coromandel town, over the Hauraki Gulf and Waiheke Island, and across the Firth of Thames to the Hunua Ranges. The journey starts and ends at the **workshops**, kilns and sheds, where you can see various types of **pottery**: stoneware and earthenware items for the home and garden, and sculptures made from terracotta that has been wood-fired to produce a variety of subtle colours.

Around 1.5km north is the turn-off to the **Gold Stamper Battery**, another 300m or so along Buffalo Road (daily: Oct–Dec 10am–4pm, Jan–March 10am–5pm; guided tour $6), where the 100-year-old machinery is operated briefly to demonstrate the processing of gold. Outside is a pleasant garden scattered with old bits of machinery and picnic tables by a stream where, for an extra $5, you can try your hand at gold panning.

Eating and entertainment

For a small town, Coromandel is surprisingly well endowed with decent places to eat, with several good **cafés** touting for your business and a couple of fancier restaurants. Evening **entertainment** is restricted to live bands (summer weekends only) at the *Pepper Tree* bar and the pub.

Assay House Café 2 Kapanga Rd. Cheerfully painted, bare-boards café usually hung with local artworks and serving great coffee, loose-leaf tea and cakes as well as more substantial dishes like empanadas, ostrich burgers and a great eggs Benedict. There's courtyard seating too.

Coromandel Café 36 Kapanga Rd. Middle-of-the-road snacky place that's a good deal cheaper than most of the places on the main street. BYO.

Peppertree 31 Kapanga Rd. A very popular bar

and restaurant, with main courses for $20–25 and an all-day snack menu ($10 or less); eat indoors or on the veranda. Open daily; live bands on weekend nights in summer.

The Success Café & Restaurant 102 Kapanga Rd ⓣ07/866 7100. An intimate place with smart white tablecloths and covered outdoor dining at the back. Plenty of seafood and steak, and superb garlic mussels, mostly around the $22 mark. Licensed & BYO.

Top Pub *Coromandel Hotel*, 611 Kapanga Rd. An evening bistro, good for its seafood, but also serving steaks and other meat dishes as a set three-course meal for under $20. Closed Sun May–Sept.

North to Fletcher Bay and Port Charles

The landscape **north of Coromandel** is even more rugged than the rest of the peninsula, its green hills dropping down to seemingly endless beaches, clean blue sea and white surf. The tourist authorities have dubbed the area the **Pohutukawa Cape**, and indeed the dirt roads are lined with ancient pohutukawa trees, blazing red from early November until just after Christmas. With its erstwhile dairy farms long deserted it is a virtually uninhabited land and there are **few facilities**: one café and a couple of places to stay pretty much wraps it up – so replenish your supplies in Coromandel town. As elsewhere on the peninsula, signs have sprung up to deter freelance **camping** outside the few commercial sites between Coromandel and Colville. The Department of Conservation has responded by opening five waterside campsites around the northern peninsula. For the two weeks after Christmas the campsites will be full, but for most of the rest of the year you'll have this unspoilt area to yourself.

From Coromandel, the road snakes for some 20km along the coast, then cuts inland to the tiny settlement of **COLVILLE**, little more than a post office, a petrol pump and the Colville General Store, set in a quiet green valley that greatly appealed to counter-culture aspirants in the 1970s. The spirit of those times lives on in the distinctly bohemian BYO *Colville Caff*, that's great for breakfast, lunch or just to stock up on food – especially pastries – for the Coromandel Walkway (see box below) and to check on the state of the road north of Port Jackson. If you fancy **staying** up this way, you can't go far wrong with *Colville Farm*, Main Road, 1.5km south of Colville (ⓣ & ⓕ07/866 6820; camping $5–9, dorms ❶, rooms ❷, bush lodge ❸, house ❹), a very relaxing spot on a sheep and cattle farm with the opportunity to go hiking, horse trekking or hand-milk a cow. Accommodation ranges from bush and pasture campsites, to backpacker dorms in a piano-equipped cottage, a couple of bush lodges, and two self-contained houses with TV and fabulous views. To be closer to the beach, try *Colville Bay Lodge Motel*, Wharf Road (ⓣ & ⓕ07/866 6814; camping $8, units ❹), the Coromandel peninsula's northernmost motel with units and campsites all overlooking Colville Bay.

Beyond Colville the road is unsealed, and becomes narrower, rougher and dustier the further north you go, though there's really nothing difficult about driving up here. Most of all, it is best taken at a steady pace, all the better to fully appreciate the tiny bays flanked by shelves of volcanic grey rock. Three kilometres north of Colville the road splits, with the right fork heading east over the hills to Stony Bay and the southern end of the Coromandel Walkway (see box opposite). The left fork runs 35km north to Port Jackson and Fletcher Bay at the very tip of the peninsula, following the coast all the way. Halfway along, an abandoned **granite wharf** marks the spot where a small harbour was once fashioned for loading rock from a nearby quarry. A couple of kilometres beyond, you'll find the diminutive and lovely *Fantail Bay Recreation Reserve* ($7), the first of the DOC **campsites**, which come equipped with toilets and a water supply. The road then cuts briefly inland, over hills rising straight from the shore, to reach **PORT JACKSON**, just two houses and a one-kilometre sandy crescent of beach. It's safe for swimming and backed by a grassy DOC reserve, where you can **camp** ($7) with views across to Great Barrier and Little Barrier islands. From here the road deteriorates further for the final 7km to **FLETCHER BAY**, probably the best beach of all, its eastern end marking the start of the **Coromandel Walkway** (see box below). The beach is backed by yet another DOC **campsite** ($7), with flush toilets and cold showers; and there's also accommodation at the small and comfortable *Fletcher Bay Backpackers* (Ⓣ & Ⓕ07/866 6712, Ⓔjs.lourie@xtra.co.nz; ❶) set 400m back from the beach up on a hill overlooking the bay.

Stony Bay, at the southern end of the Coromandel Walkway, is reached by two perilously twisty gravel roads – one across the Coromandel Range from Coromandel, the other traversing the Moehau Range from just beyond Colville. The latter runs 14km from Colville to the small holiday settlement of **Port Charles**, and a further 6km to Stony Bay, where there's another DOC campsite ($7), also with flush toilets and cold showers.

East to Whitianga

The drive east from Coromandel to Whitianga can be done in under an hour, but you could easily spend much of a day on either of two highly **scenic roads** which cross the mountains: the more direct, snaking, gravel **309 Road** (33km; no public transport) spends much of its time in the bush, while the main (and mostly sealed) **SH25** climbs through forested hills before switch-backing down to the coast, 46km away.

Coromandel to Whitianga: the 309 Road

From the junction with SH25, 4km south of Coromandel, the 309 Road twists 5km east to **Waiau Waterworks** (daily 9am–5pm; $8; Ⓦwww.waiauwater-works.co.nz), a garden carved from the bush and liberally dotted with whimsical water-powered contraptions and contrivances. It is the product of twelve years' work (so far) by one Chris Ogilvie, who is realizing his lifelong passion to do "fun stuff with water". And it is a great success; quirky at every turn yet

The Coromandel Walkway and cycle route

Other than a bit of swimming, fishing or lolling around on the beaches, the only activity in the far north of the peninsula is to hike from Fletcher Bay to Stony Bay along the **Coromandel Walkway** (7km; 3hr one way), a gentle and clearly route-marked path with lovely sea views. The walk starts at the far end of the beach in Fletcher Bay and heads off into a no-man's-land, first following gentle coastal hills that alternate between pasture and bush, then giving way to wilder terrain as you head further south past a series of tiny bays. Several hilltop **vantage points** punctuate the walk, yielding spectacular vistas of the coast and Pacific Ocean beyond, before the track dips once more into pockets of dense bush. From the pretty, rocky inlet of **Poley Bay** a steep, short climb out cuts through regenerating bush to **Stony Bay**, a sweep of pebbles with a bridge across an estuary and safe swimming.

Mountain bikers can make a complete circuit of the northern peninsula by going off-road from Fletcher Bay to Stony Bay using a longer route further inland which starts and finishes at the same points as the walkway.

The only bus company serving both ends of the track recently went out of business, but ask in Coromandel to see if anyone has filled the gap.

explained in enough detail to satisfy the more engineering minded. You are greeted with a waterwheel built from construction helmets, teapots and gumboots and continue through the gardens, occasionally coming across a static bicycle shooting a jet of water when you peddle or a raised waterway where you can play an elaborate form of pooh sticks. Perhaps the highlight is a huge clock powered by jets playing against a row of empty pop bottles arranged on a pendulum: apparently it keeps remarkably good time unless the wind blows the pendulum off kilter. Allow a couple of hours and bring a picnic, especially if you've got kids who'll appreciate the swimming hole and flying fox.

One hundred metres past the waterworks, an access road on the left climbs steeply for 3km to the trailhead for the track to **Castle Rock** (2km return; 40min–1hr 30min), the most easily accessible peak on the Coromandel Peninsula. It is a climb that gets progressively steeper towards the final tree-root claw onto the 521-metre summit of this old volcanic core, but your efforts are well rewarded by fantastic views to both coasts: the Whangapoua peninsula and the Mercury Islands on the east coast, and Coromandel and the Firth of Thames to the west.

A further 2.5km along the 309 Road, the **Waiau Falls** crash over a rockface into a pool below. They're not that impressive, but they are right next to the road and offer a gorgeous spot to cool off on a hot day. Half a kilometre further on, a car park heralds the easy bush track to the magnificent **Kauri Grove** (1km return; 30min). Fortuitous gaps in the bush make this one of the best places in the country to really get a sense of the size of the kauri, and appreciate just how they stand head and shoulders above the rest of the forest trees: a boardwalk allows you to get face-to-bark with these delicate-rooted giants.

The road then tops out at the 306m saddle and descends towards Whitianga, passing a couple of relaxing riverside **accommodation** options which we've covered under our Whitianga account (see opposite).

Coromandel to Whitianga: SH25

From Coromandel, **SH25** follows an attractive route through lush native forest passing a couple of isolated but pretty beachside settlements with campsites. About 14km from Coromandel is the five-kilometre turn-off to the secluded village and beach of **WHANGAPOUA**, whose long stretch of white sand is lined by *baches* and a single general store/petrol station. At the end of the road is a pleasant walk to the idyllic sandy beach of **New Chums Bay** (4km return; 1hr): from the beach, cross the estuary and follow the bushline around the headland to a saddle; on the other side is New Chums Bay (accessible at low tide only). A basic but scenic **campsite**, *Whangapoua Beach Camping Ground* (tent sites $9), lies 300m along the left fork as you enter town. Continuing along SH25, about 34km from Coromandel, you drop down to diminutive **KUAOTUNU**, beside a lovely beach. There's a range of especially good **accommodation** here: the shady and well-equipped *Kuaotunu Motor Camp*, Bluff Road (Ⓣ07/866 5628, Ⓕ866 4061; tent sites $10); the relaxed, well-maintained *Black Jack Backpackers*, SH25 (Ⓣ07/866 2988, Ⓦwww.blackjack.co.nz; camping $12, dorms beds ❶, doubles and en-suite doubles ❸), where you can rent mountain bikes and kayaks at reasonable rates; the highly recommended *Drift In B&B*, 16 Grays Ave (Ⓣ07/866 4321, Ⓦwww.bnb.co.nz/hosts /driftinbb.html; ❹); and *Kuaotunu Bay Lodge*, SH25 (Ⓣ07/866 4396, Ⓦwww.kuaotunubay.co.nz; ❻), set on a rise with excellent sea views, with one self-contained unit, B&B doubles and dinner ($45) by arrangement.

About 4km past Kuaotunu, on SH25, is Twin Oaks Riding Ranch, the base for extremely scenic two-hour **horse treks** (book ahead on Ⓣ07/866 5388;

daily 10am & 2pm, plus twilight trek at 6pm Nov–March; $30), offering breathtaking views of Mercury Bay and the northern Coromandel; transport from Whitianga can also be arranged. From here, SH25 continues through farmland to Whitianga and the stunning expanse of Mercury Bay.

Whitianga and around

The attractive town of **WHITIANGA** clusters where the estuarine Whitianga Harbour meets the broad sweep of **Mercury Bay**. This huge bite out of the Coromandel Peninsula coastline was named by Captain Cook who stopped here in 1769 so that his party of scientists could observe Mercury pass across the face of the sun: the ostensible justification for his South Pacific peregrinations. Now a popular Kiwi summer-holiday destination, the population of about 4000 swells dramatically during January as vacationers flock to the town's **Buffalo Beach**, a long sweep of surf-pounded white sand.

Whitianga makes a good base from which to make a series of half-day and **day-trips** to some wonderfully secluded spots, so allow a couple of days here. Just across the narrow harbour mouth and strung along Mercury Bay's eastern shore are several unusual beaches, reached by passenger ferry to **Ferry Landing**, from where you can catch a **bus** or strike out along scenic coastal tracks. The area is also served by roads branching off the southbound SH25, which loops around the deeply indented harbour. Two gems here are **Cathedral Cove**, a stunning geological formation, and **Hot Water Beach**, renowned for its natural hot-water springs bubbling beneath the sand. Bordering part of the eastern shore is **Cathedral Cove Marine Reserve**, whose protected waters are a great spot for snorkelling and scuba diving. In addition, **boat trips** to the outer reaches of Mercury Bay and the volcanically formed **Mercury Islands**, 25km offshore, explore pristine waters and shoreline – and search for bottlenose **dolphins** and **whales**. Whitianga is also one of the best places in New Zealand to try your hand at **bone carving**, creating your very own *tiki* in as little as half a day, while 10km north of town you can enjoy astounding views of the whole region on a **scenic horse trek** (see above).

Arrival, information and transport

SH25 runs right through town becoming Albert Street along the main shopping thoroughfare, then Buffalo Beach Road along the shore. Pretty much everything happens on these two streets or The Esplanade which branches off and leads to the wharf and ferry.

InterCity and Go Kiwi **buses** drop off at accommodation around town and outside the **visitor centre** at the corner of Albert Street and Blacksmith Lane (daily 9am–5pm; ⓣ07/866 5555, ⓔwhitvin@ihug.co.nz), which has **internet access**, and **bike rental** for $25 a day. Air Coromandel (ⓣ0800/900 600) flights from Auckland (2 daily) and Great Barrier Island (3 weekly) land at the **airport,** 3km south of the town centre and reached by a $5 ride with Mercury Bay **Taxis** (ⓣ07/866 5643).

The surrounding **beaches** are served by ferry and buses. The **passenger ferry** to Ferry Landing (daily 7.30am–6.30pm, until midnight in summer; $1 each way) takes three minutes and leaves from The Esplanade. Hot Water Beach Connection (ⓣ07/866 2478) runs hop-on, hop-off **excursion buses** from Ferry Landing to Cooks Beach, the Purangi Winery, Hahei and Hot Water Beach (3–5 daily; $20 all-day pass), with some services continuing to Whenuakite on SH25 for connection with buses to Auckland and Whitianga;

it costs $10 from Ferry Landing to Hot Water Beach, while a $35 pass allows you to explore the region for three days.

Accommodation

As one of the Coromandel's main tourist centres, Whitianga itself has plenty of **accommodation** to suit all tastes. Further out, beside the secluded **beaches** of Mercury Bay, is a small selection of perfect places to unwind, mostly at Hot Water Beach and Hahei; and it is worth considering a couple of places along the 309 Road, around 12km southwest of town (listed below), and some more around 12km north at Kuaotunu. Throughout summer you'll need to **book ahead**, and during the peak month of January places get booked up about two months beforehand. Also, be prepared for **higher prices** than on the rest of the peninsula, especially at any place with a sea view, and particularly from Christmas to January when motels and campsites hike their prices.

Central Whitianga

Buffalo Beach Resort Eyre St ⓣ07/866 5854, ⓔbuffalo@xtra.co.nz. Extremely well-equipped campsite adjacent to the beach, in shaded parkland a 3-min walk from the town centre. Fishing tackle, kayak and bike rental available. Camping $10, chalets & units ❸–❺

Cat's Pyjamas Backpackers 4 Monk St ⓣ07/866 4663 & 0800 666 237, ⓔcatspyjamas@xtra.co.nz. Small, friendly, clean place with two dorms and two doubles, a couple of minutes' walk from the wharf. Perks include free linen, tea and coffee, and occasional fresh fruit and seafood. Dorms ❶, rooms ❷

Cottage by the Sea 11 The Esplanade ⓣ07/866 0605, ⓦwww.acottagebythesea.com. Very central B&B decorated with heavy wooden furniture and offering accommodation that's with both en-suite and shared facilities. ❺

Mana-Nui Motor Lodge 20 Albert St ⓣ07/866 5599, ⓔmananui@xtra.co.nz. Centrally located, comfortable and well-kept motel with seven fully self-contained units. ❺

Mercury Bay Beachfront Resort 111–113 Buffalo Beach Rd ⓣ07/866 5637, ⓦwww.beachfrontresort.co.nz. Luxurious motel right on the beach with eight excellent spacious units, half with great sea views and half having direct access to a garden with spa pool and barbecue area. There are kayaks, a dinghy, fishing rods, boogie boards and bikes for guests' use, and courtesy transport from the airport and bus depot avoids the 25-min walk from the centre. ❼

Mercury Bay Motor Camp 121 Albert St ⓣ & ⓕ07/866 5579. Large, sheltered and well-equipped site about 400m from the town centre with bargain kayak and bike rental, a pool and spa. Camping $10, cabins & apartments ❷–❺

On the Beach Backpackers 46 Buffalo Beach Rd ⓣ07/866 5380, ⓔcorobkpk@wave.co.nz. Ten minutes' walk from town, overlooking the bay, this is a particularly welcoming and well-equipped associate YHA hostel, with bikes for rent, and free use of kayaks, fishing lines, spades for Hot Water Beach and courtesy transport. Dorms ❶, rooms ❷

Whitehouse B&B 129 Albert St ⓣ07/866 5116, ⓔwhitehousebb@paradise.net.nz. Pleasant B&B with views over the estuary, a lot of white decor and hearty breakfasts. Shared bath ❺, en suite ❻

Hotel Whitianga The Esplanade ⓣ & ⓕ07/866 5818. Pleasant, old-fashioned harbourside hotel with nine well-tended rooms, most of them en suite and all with TV and washbasin. Can get noisy on Fri and Sat nights, with live music in the bar. Shared bath ❸, en suite ❹

Around Whitianga

309 River Lodge 309 Rd ⓣ07/866 51511, ⓦwww.bushcreek.co.nz. Backpacker-style place on a smallholding (with animals) run along sustainable organic principles and located 12km southwest of Whitianga. There's dormitory accommodation and doubles in a kauri cottage complete with communal kitchen and eating area and great sunny veranda overlooking the river and swimming hole. Bring a sleeping bag and food. Camping $10, dorms ❶, doubles ❷

Auntie Dawn's Place Radar Rd, Hot Water Beach ⓣ07/866 3707, ⓔauntiedawn@wave.co.nz. Tranquil modern hillside house overlooking the beach with simple but comfortable self-contained apartments, plus backpacker beds. ❶–❹

Hahei Holiday Resort Harsant Ave, Hahei ⓣ & ⓕ07/866 3889, ⓔinfo@haheiholidays.co.nz. Located on half a kilometre of beachfront and within an easy walk of Cathedral Cove, this enormous site is close to a shop and restaurants and has accommodation ranging from dorms to luxurious self-contained villas right on the beachfront.

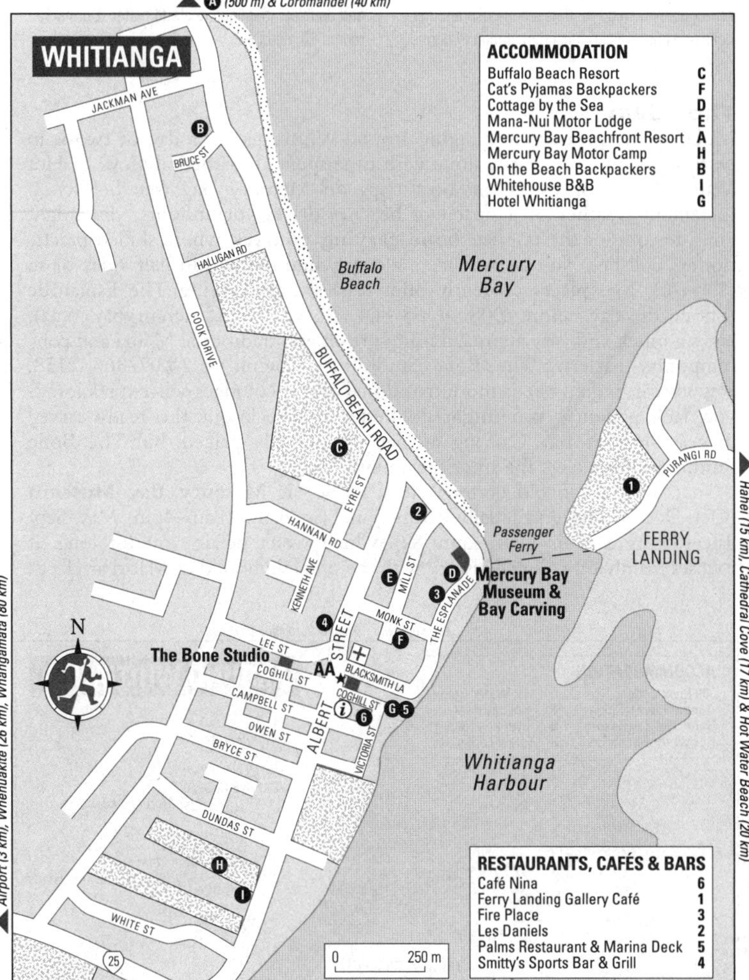

Tent sites $10, dorms ❶, cabins & on-site vans ❷, kitchen cabins ❹, units ❺, villas ❻, seaview villas ❼

Hot Water Beach B&B 48 Pye Place ⓣ07/866 3991 & 0800/146 889, ⓦwww.hotwaterbedand-breakfast.co.nz. Comfortable and very welcoming B&B perfectly sited close to the beach and with great sea views. En-suite rooms have access to sunny decks and spa pool and there's even a full-sized snooker table. ❼

Hot Water Beach Holiday Park adjacent to the general store, Hot Water Beach ⓣ07/866 3735. Well-kept site right by the beach. Tent sites $12, plus $1 for a power hook-up.

Riverside Retreat 309 Rd ⓣ & ⓕ07/866 5155, ⓦwww.riversideretreat.co.nz. A single, self-contained wooden cottage ten minutes' drive south-west of Whitianga, where the sound of a burbling stream wafts in through the window. Continental breakfast is provided. ❻

Tatahi Lodge Grange Rd, Hahei ⓣ07/866 3992, ⓔtatahi_lodge@xtra.co.nz. Several comfortable self-contained wooden units set in bush and gardens, plus backpacker accommodation in dorms and doubles; free linen, tea and coffee. Dorms ❶, rooms ❷, units ❺

The Town

Much of the pleasure in hanging around Whitianga for a day or two is in getting out of town, easily done with time spent at Cathedral Cove or Hot Water Beach, or by taking boat trips on Mercury Bay (see below). If inclement weather or a surfeit of beaches drives you indoors, you might consider one of the popular **bone-carving courses**, where skilled practitioners will help you to produce a glossy, white *tiki* within half a day or so ($30–40). Two places currently offer classes: Bay Carving, The Esplanade (phone the day before ⓣ0800/158 864, ⓔbaycarving@mercurybay.co.nz), takes a quick and easy approach using pre-drawn traditional Maori and contemporary patterns; The Bone Studio, 16 Coghill St (ⓣ07/866 2158, ⓦwww.carving.co.nz), is more traditional and encourages self-expression. If you lack patience, you might do better to check out the ready-carved pieces: those at Bay Carving are very reasonably priced, but The Bone Studio tends to have the finer specimens.

Next door, in an old butter factory, is the big **Mercury Bay Museum** (Oct–Dec & Feb–April daily 10am–3pm, Jan daily 10am–4pm, May–Sept Tues–Thurs & Sun 11am–2pm; $2), which won't detain you for long. It focuses mainly on colonial history with the usual slight nod to Maori artefacts.

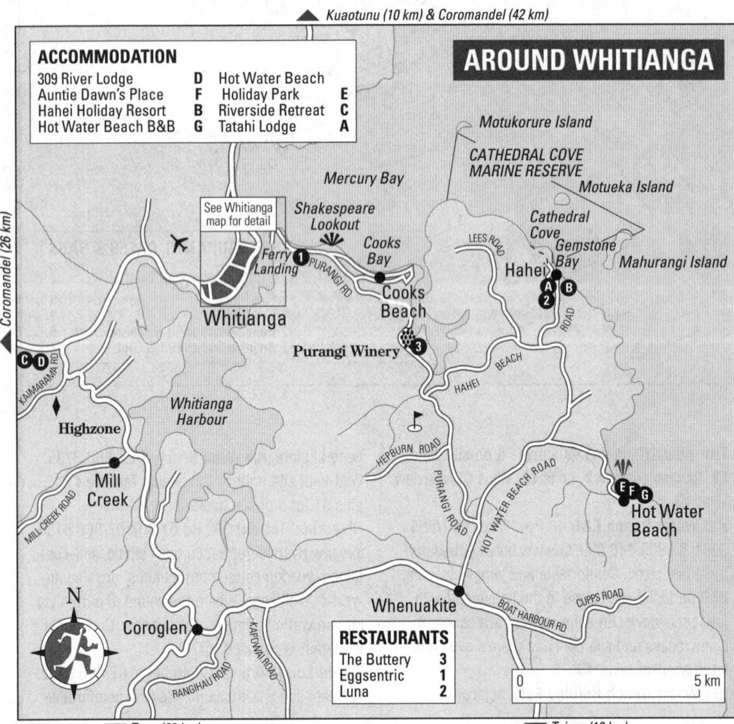

Points of interest are an extensive exhibition on Captain Cook and his discovery of the peninsula, and informative displays on kauri-gum digging (including carved blackjack gum), minerals and local shipwrecks.

Ferry Landing and the beaches

The beaches across the estuary are accessible by passenger ferry to **Ferry Landing**, where buses continue on to the beaches; by boat (see "Exploring Mercury Bay", below); or by car from Whitianga. The longer **road route** travels south along SH25, skirting the harbour and cutting inland through hill country to a signposted turn-off at Whenuakite, 26km from Whitianga, which strikes north towards Mercury Bay.

From Ferry Landing the first point of interest is **Shakespeare Lookout**, atop a cliff which, when viewed from the sea, is said to resemble the Bard's profile. From the lookout – signposted 1.5km along the road, and reached after another kilometre uphill to a car park – panoramic views stretch east to Cooks Beach and across Mercury Bay, west to Buffalo Beach, and north towards Mount Maungatawhiri. A memorial plaque commemorates James Cook's anchorage in Mercury Bay in 1769. Signposted tracks lead from the car park to the secluded Lonely Bay and on to the popular family holiday spot of **Cooks Beach** (2km one way; 20min), which is also accessible from the main road 2km further east.

About 3km southeast of Cooks Beach on the main road is **Purangi Winery and Brasserie** (daily 9am–5.30pm, often later in summer; ⓦwww.purangi.co.nz), which offers free tastings of their fruit wines and liqueurs made from kiwifruit, plums, apples and just about anything they can lay their hands on. The results are variable to say the least, but it is worth hanging around to soak up the rustic atmosphere, perhaps having lunch at *The Buttery* (see p.403) and checking out progress on the fledgling Eco Village, a self-sufficient rural refuge for writers, artists and gardeners.

A few hundred metres south, Hahei Beach Road runs 6km to the tiny beachside community of **HAHEI**, a viable alternative place to stay if you don't fancy the bustle of Whitianga. The main attraction here is **Cathedral Cove**, reached along a hilly **coastal track** which starts at Hahei Beach (1hr 20min to Cathedral Cove), though you can join it at a car park at the western end of the village (30–40min to Cathedral Cove). The walk is steep in places, with patches of pine-dominated bush, and affords great views out to sea. Five minutes' walk from the car park, a track leads down to the rocky **Gemstone Bay**, where DOC has set up a snorkelling course around three buoys to show off the undersea wonders of the **Cathedral Cove Marine Reserve**. Most visitors continue to Cathedral Cove itself; striking white cliffs hugging a long, sheltered, sandy beach and bisected by an impressive rock arch which vaults out over the beach like the nave of some great cathedral. A walk through the arch reveals another delightful beach on the other side, while offshore the remains of several arches are stranded at sea. Bring a towel and a picnic, sink into the sand and relax to the deceptively gentle sound of the waves.

If there is one place hereabouts that trumps Cathedral Cove, it is **Hot Water Beach**, 5km along Hot Water Beach Road, the last place you'll come to from Ferry Landing and the first you'll reach arriving by road from Whitianga via SH25. The beach itself is split in two by a rocky outcrop which creates dangerous tidal rips (read our surf warning, see box p.132), but also provides the setting for the hot springs which give the beach its name. Be sure to visit an hour and a half either side of **low tide** (check tide times at the visitor centre or in the local paper), then dig a hole and you can sit in the hot water while being refreshed by waves of incoming sea water. In summer, the springs area will be pockmarked by other visitors' diggings, but if no one has been here before you, you'll need to **rent a spade** from the **general store** (daily 9am–5pm; $4 for 2hr, plus $20 deposit); the store also sells burgers, toasted sandwiches, hot dogs, tea and coffee, ice cream and milk shakes. There's almost nothing else at Hot Water Beach save for a few houses, some of which offer accommodation.

Exploring Mercury Bay

The waters around Whitianga have developed something of a reputation for opportunities to **swim with dolphins**; no one is currently offering such adventures, but **dolphin sightings** are always possible on rigid-hull-inflatable trips run by Cave Cruzer Adventures (Ⓣ07/866 2275, Ⓦwww.cavecruzer.co.nz). The most popular of its excursions is the two-hour Scenic & Sounds ($60) trip, which visits Cathedral Cove, the nearby marine reserve, blowholes, a waterfall, and sea caves where guides put on a wonderfully resonant performance with didgeridoo, African drums and Maori instruments.

Riverboat Cruises (Ⓣ867 1055, Ⓔriverboatcruises@xtra.co.nz) operates more leisurely cruises on the Whitianga Estuary complete with a barbecue and full bar service: choose from the lunch cruise (12.30pm; 2.5hr; $35), the dinner cruise (6pm; 2.5hr; $35) or the extended run upstream to Coroglen (tide dependent; 3.5hr; $45).

Great boat trips are also run **from Hahei**, where Hahei Explorer (book previous evening or before 9am on the day on Ⓣ07/866 3910) specializes in hour-long cave trips, visiting a blowhole between Cathedral Cove and Hot Water Beach with an entertaining commentary (year-round; $40), and guided snorkelling trips (gear rental $30 a day). If you'd rather propel yourself, join one of the excellent **guided sea kayak tours** run from Hahei by Cathedral Cove Sea Kayaking (Ⓣ07/866 3877): its half-day trip ($55) visits Cathedral Cove, its full-day outing ($95) calls at Hot Water Beach, and there are lovely sunset trips ($50).

Scuba diving in Cathedral Cove Marine Reserve can be arranged through Hahei-based Cathedral Cove Dive (Ⓣ07/866 3955): a one-dive trip costs $80, two-dives $150, less if you have your own gear. **Non-divers** can learn basic scuba skills ($110), and it also runs other PADI courses, from beginners to advanced.

Land-based activities

If the water's not for you, there's considerable pleasure to be had **horse riding** either 8km north of Whitianga at Twin Oaks Riding Ranch (see p.396), or 8km south at Ace Hi Ranch (Ⓣ07/866 4897, Ⓦwww.pubcrawlnz.com), which offers two-hour trekking trips ($30) and half-day river rides ($70), and a "Pub Crawl on Horseback" ($200) – a day-long ride to the Coroglen pub for dinner, much beer and backpacker-style accommodation, with a day-long return the next day.

For a bit more adrenaline, sign up for the jumps, swings and balance exercises at the High Zone **ropes course**, 49 Kaimanama Rd, 8km south off SH25 (Ⓣ07/866 2113, Ⓦwww.highzone.co.nz; $15–60).

Eating and entertainment

Whitianga and its environs are well supplied with places to **eat**, many of the better places clustered along The Esplanade close to the marina, just as they should be. Entertainment options are more limited though live **bands** occasionally play the *Hotel Whitianga* (see p.398) in summer.

Whitianga

Café Nina 20 Victoria St. Excellent bare-boards café with seating inside and out. Tasty food, all carefully made to order, with vegetarian and vegan options. Try the signature seafood chowder ($7), the chicken and mushroom pie or the delicious peach upside-down cake.

Les Daniels 21 The Esplanade ☎07/866 5209. Fairly upmarket à la carte dining from a pleasant first-floor vantage point overlooking the beach. Seafood is the speciality, with the oysters ($11 per half -dozen) and market-priced crayfish particularly recommended.

The Fire Place 9 The Esplanade. Smart but casual restaurant that brings big-city style to Whitianga with a lovely deck overlooking the water. Wonderful gourmet pizzas ($18) are helped down with the likes of haloumi, asparagus and prosciutto salad ($10) and followed by desserts such as white chocolate steamed pudding ($10).

Palms Restaurant & Marina Deck in the *Hotel Whitianga*, The Esplanade. An airy, comfortable restaurant overlooking the marina that's especially good for à la carte mains ($18–25) but also specializes in Thai dishes mostly around the $15 mark.

Smitty's Sports Bar & Grill 37 Albert St. Popular sports bar with big-screen TVs and a lively atmosphere. Great for a few beers but also serving well-priced grilled meats and excellent burgers, though they make a few concessions to vegetarians. Dine in the barn-like interior, or out on the deck.

Around Whitianga

The Buttery Purangi Winery, 450 Purangi Rd, near Hahei ☎07/866 3724. Rustic, secluded brasserie in a picturesque setting serving high-quality snacks, barbecued steak, seafood and yummy sausages, all for $20 and under, supplemented by the winery's own produce.

Eggsentric 1047 Purangi Rd, Ferry Landing ☎ 07/866 0307. A relaxing place for a daytime meal or coffee but best in the evening when there's almost always live music (or poetry, or theme evening) to accompany the broad range of moderately priced dinners. Closed Mon & Aug; licensed & BYO.

Ferry Landing Gallery Cafe 1134 Purangi Rd, Ferry Landing. About 100m up the hill from the wharf, this attractive garden café is perfect for light meals, coffee, and a rest among flowers and greenery or watching resident potters at work. Closed Tues in winter.

Luna Beach Rd, Hahei. Airy daytime café with good coffee and cakes, and mains such as beef lasagne and zucchini bake. Licensed & BYO.

South to Whangamata

The run along SH25 from Whitianga **south to Whangamata** is a pleasant enough journey, though you seldom get a good eyeful of coastal scenery, and when you do it has often been spoiled by over-development. To some degree this is true of **Tairua**, the midway point, and especially so of its neighbour across the harbour, the luxury retirement and holiday resort of **Pauanui**; reminiscent of the worst excesses of Florida, and best avoided altogether. All is not lost though; there is great bush country just inland, with the **Broken Hills** area particularly rich in gold-mining relics. Unspoilt beaches can also be found, particularly the delightful **Opoutere**, a tiny harbourside retreat at the foot of a mountain, with a wild sweep of beach and a beautifully situated hostel. From there, you're best off making a beeline for Whangamata.

Tairua

The small but overdeveloped beachside town of **TAIRUA** lies on SH25, 16km south of the turn-off to Hot Water Beach and 42km from Whitianga. It huddles between pine-forested hills and the calm estuary of the Tairua River, separated from the crashing Pacific breakers by two opposing and almost touching peninsulas. One is crowned by the imposing volcanic Mount Paku and the other is entirely covered by the suburban sprawl of exclusive **Pauanui**, accessible by a five-minute passenger ferry ride from Tairua (roughly hourly; $4 return), or a 25km drive. The combination of surf and sheltered waters makes Tairua popular in summer with holidaying Kiwis, who also find it a good base for Hot Water Beach, more easily reached by car from here than from Whitianga.

With time on your hands, you could stop briefly for a dip, or to climb **Mount Paku** (15min up) for spectacular views over the town, its estuary and beaches; the track starts at the end of Paku Drive, reached by following the estuary around to the north. You could also contact Tairua Dive & Fish Inn (ⓣ & ⓕ07/864 8054) which deals with just about anything to do with the sea hereabouts, or hook up with Kiwi Dundee Adventures (see p.406), for one of its extremely informative and light-hearted **eco-tours**, or try your hand at windsurfing (see p.407).

InterCity **buses** from Whitianga and Thames drop off a couple of times a day at Tairua post office, a few steps from the **tourist office**, Main Road (Mon–Sat 9am–4pm; ⓣ07/864 7575, ⓔtairua.info@xtra.co.nz). Go Kiwi buses pass through once a day in each direction dropping off at the numerous motels and at *Tairua Backpackers*, 200 Main Rd (ⓣ07/864 8345, ⓔtairuabackpackers@xtra.co.nz; dorms ❶, rooms ❷), the best hostel in town. South of the centre across the river bridge, it is set among trees near the water's edge, with free use of canoes, shonky bikes (better models are $15 a day), windsurfers (tuition available at $10 a session), and you can help yourself to the garden's fruit, vegetables and eggs when available. There's even a free car to Hot Water Beach. Also recommended is the pleasant *Annju'bro Cottage*, Main Road, 1.3km south (ⓣ07/864 8840; ❺), with just one twin chalet and a lovely garden.

For **eating**, head to the base of Mount Paku and *The Upper Deck*, 1 Main Rd (ⓣ07/864 7499), located on the upper deck of the *SS Ngoiro*, a restored former ferry which once plied Auckland's Waitemata Harbour.

Broken Hills

Upstream from Tairua, the Tairua River emerges from the peninsula's mountainous spine at **Broken Hills**, an unsung but attractive swathe of bush reached along a 7km spur off SH25 17km south of Tairua, immediately opposite the road to Pauanui. Several tracks (listed in DOC's *Broken Hills* leaflet; $1) disappear into the bush, mostly in pursuit of relics from the early years of the twentieth century when the small town of Puketui (now gone) was the focus of fevered gold mining and kauri logging. Most are short, and you can knock off a few in a day, or base yourself at DOC's *Broken Hills Campground* ($7; toilets and water) for more extensive explorations. The easiest trail is the **Gem of the Boom Creek Walk** (500m loop, 15min) which visits the site of the former town jail, essentially an abandoned mining tunnel. For something more strenuous, try the **Golden Hills Mine Track** (7km loop; 3hr) which climbs steeply before plunging into a 500m-long tunnel, emerging near the remains of a stamper battery and finishing through mature podocarp forest.

Opoutere

Around ten kilometres south of the Broken Hills junction is a 5km side road to **Opoutere**, barely a settlement at all, but a gorgeous and usually deserted 4km-long surf beach backed by pines, and behind them a campsite, YHA and a few houses. The pohutukawa-fringed road hugs the shores of the Wharekawa Harbour where wetlands make good bird-watching spots, mudflats yield shellfish and the relatively calm waters are good for canoeing.

From a signposted parking area a small bridge leads to two paths, both leading to the beach in ten minutes or so: the **left-hand fork** runs straight through the forest to the beach; the **right-hand track** follows the estuary to the edge of a protected sandspit where endangered New Zealand dotterels breed from November to March. The white-sand Opoutere Beach can have a strong undertow and there are no lifeguards, so swim with caution.

For a wider view over the estuary and the coastline out towards the Mayor and Aldermen islands, tackle the track up **Mount Maungaruawahine** (2km return; 40–50min) which climbs through gnarled pohutukawa and other native trees to the summit.

The summit track begins by the gate to the relaxed and old-fashioned **YHA** (Ⓣ07/865 9072, Ⓔyhaopout@yha.org.nz; tent sites $12, dorms ❶, rooms ❷), set in an old schoolhouse and associated buildings in mature grounds with estuary views. There are also free canoes and the chance for some nocturnal glow-worm spotting. The small **campsite**, *Opoutere Park Beach Resort* (Ⓣ & Ⓕ07/865 9152; tent sites $10, flats & chalet ❷–❹), is about 700m up the road towards the beach.

There's no regular **bus** service, but drop-offs can be arranged – call the YHA or campsite in advance – and remember to bring all your food as both places have only basic **provisions** for sale.

Whangamata and the Wentworth Valley

The long, straggling resort of **WHANGAMATA**, on SH25 towards the southern end of the Coromandel Peninsula, is bounded on three sides by estuaries and the ocean, and on the fourth by bush-clad hills: nowhere else on the Coromandel do bush and beach sit so closely together. This single-storey town of 4500 grows tenfold in January, when holiday-makers flock to its four-kilometre **Ocean Beach**, a crescent of white sand that curves from the harbour entrance to the mouth of the **Otahu River**. The bar at the harbour end has an excellent break making this one of New Zealand's true **surfie** meccas.

Arrival, information and accommodation

Whangamata's layout is initially confusing, but the **main street**, Port Road, runs straight through the small town centre, linking it with the highway. **Buses** drop off outside the centrally located **visitor centre**, 616 Port Rd (Mon–Sat 9am–5pm, Sun 10am–4pm; Ⓣ07/865 8340, Ⓔinfo-whangamata@xtra.co.nz), and most places are within easy walking distance of here.

Kiwis flock to this small town from Christmas until the middle of January when **accommodation** is very scarce and already high prices are jacked up by as much as fifty percent. For the rest of the year it's pretty quiet.

Brenton Lodge 1 Brenton Place Ⓣ & Ⓕ07/865 8400, Ⓦwww.brentonlodge.co.nz. Very attractive retreat right on the edge of Whangamata with sea views from the two cottages and one suite. Lovely understated decor, fresh flowers and delicious breakfasts, all for $250. ❾

Bushland Park Lodge 7km southwest of town in the Wentworth Valley Ⓣ07/865 7468, Ⓦwww.wellness.co.nz. A very appealing hideaway and classy restaurant (see "Eating and drinking", p.406) in private grounds close to the start of the track to Wentworth Falls. Four immaculate and cheerfully decorated en-suite doubles, with on-site therapies – sauna, hydrotherapeutic spa, yoga, t'ai chi and massage – to help you completely unwind (at extra cost). Rooms ❼, suites ❽

Garden Tourist Lodge cnr Port Rd & Mayfair Ave Ⓣ07/865 9580, Ⓔgardenlodge@xtra.co.nz. An immaculate motel and backpackers. The well-equipped hostel section has four-shares, double rooms, free use of surfboards and transport to walks. The motel has well-appointed, smart and spacious motel units, some with full kitchen. Four-shares ❶, rooms ❷, units ❹

Palm Pacific Resort 413 Port Rd Ⓣ07/865 9211, Ⓦwww.palmpacificresort.co.nz. The biggest motel in town, offering fairly modern, spacious units sleeping up to eight. Facilities include a barbecue, several bars, a bistro, tennis courts, large pool, spas and sauna. ❺

Pinefield Top 10 Holiday Park 207 Port Rd ⓣ07/865 8791, ⓔpinefield@xtra.co.nz. An excellent, shady site that gets very busy over summer weekends. On-site accommodation comes well-equipped; there's a barbecue and a large swimming pool. Camping $11; cabins, flats & units ❷–❺

Wentworth Valley Campground, end of Wentworth Valley Rd. Lovely DOC campsite with streamside pitches, barbecues and cold showers right by the start of the track to Wentworth Falls, 7km southwest of Whangamata. $7.

The Town and around

Surfies should make straight for the well-stocked Whangamata Surf Shop, 634 Port Rd (daily 9am–5pm), owned by surfing legend Bob Davie and heaped with designer gear to keep the coolest of customers happy. It is the only place in town where you can **rent a surfboard** ($10 per hr, $18 half-day, $25 full-day) or a **boogie board** ($5 per hr, $12 half-day, $16 full-day); wetsuits and fins are available for $5 per day. The Windsurfing School, up the harbour past the boat ramp (ⓣ07/865 8186), operates daily during summer holidays for up to three hours either side of high tide (and throughout the year on bookings); **sailboard** rental costs $20 per hour, a group lesson $25, and a private lesson $30.

Aside from enjoying the surf, there are only a couple of other diversions in the foothills of the Coromandel Range, right on the edge of town. One is a pleasant **walk to Wentworth Falls** (10km return; 2hr) in the nearby Wentworth Valley. Take SH25 south for 2km to the signposted turn-off to Wentworth Valley Road; at its end (4km) is a campsite (see above) and the start of the track through regenerating bush past numerous small swimming holes ideal for wallowing away a couple of hours in the heat of the day. The track continues into the heart of the mountains, but most turn around at the two-leap Wentworth Falls, best viewed from a small deck from where it is possible to scramble steeply down to the pool at the bottom of the falls. The other reason to come here is to join one of the extremely popular **eco-tours** run by Kiwi Dundee Adventures (ⓣ07/865 8809, ⓦwww.kiwidundee.co.nz; book as far ahead as possible). For over twenty years, the passionate conservationist Doug Johansen (popularly known as "Kiwi Dundee") has been getting his message across in his own distinctive way, generally accompanied by a good deal of showmanship. Operating year-round, the company offers a variety of tours including the full-day "Nature Experience, Gold Mines & Coastal" trip ($150), taking small groups off the beaten track for a day or more to explain history, geology, Maori medicines and natural history, with departures from Tairua, Pauanui and Whangamata.

Eating and drinking

Port Road is lined with **tearooms**, takeaways and **restaurants**, but few stand out, so you might want to venture further afield for more inspiring fare.

Caffe Rossini 646 Port Rd. Modern café serving the town's best range of panini, cakes, good coffee and pizzas, either inside or on tables on the street.

Nero's Port Rd. The best pizzas in town (around $17), mostly gourmet style with combinations like salmon and shrimp, chicken and mango and plain vegetarian ($16). They also do mains such as Moroccan chicken ($22).

Nickel Strausse 7km southwest of town on the Wentworth Valley Rd ⓣ07/865 7468. Excellent and good-value dining in an intimate restaurant set in rural surroundings. A charming German couple serve typical Black Forest lunches ($15–25) and three-course dinners (around $60), including exquisite Black Forest gateau made fresh daily. Booking required for dinner.

Whangamata Ocean Sports Club harbour end of Port Rd. Private club and home of the Whangamata Boat & Gamefishing Club that's open to non-members when they're not busy; ask at the bar. It is worth the effort for great harbour and sea views, cheap drink and hearty fare such as chicken chimichangas ($13), sirloin steak ($20) and fish and chips ($18).

Waihi and Waihi Beach

SH25 continues 30km south from Whangamata to the town of **WAIHI**, where it meets SH2 at the entrance to the Karangahake Gorge (see p.379). Gold was first discovered at Waihi in a reef of quartz in 1878, but it was not until 1894 that a boom began with the first successful trials in extracting gold using cyanide solution at Karangahake. By 1908 Waihi was the fastest-growing town in the Auckland Province, and today it remains a mining district some five thousand strong. Although underground mining came to a halt in 1952, extraction was cranked up again in 1987 when the focus of activity moved to the opencast but well hidden Martha Mine. You can visit the mine, learn about its past in a good **museum**, or hop on a steam train for a scenic ride into the nearby **Karangahake Gorge**.

And, if you're in need of some light relief, the popular surf beach of **WAIHI BEACH** lies 12km east of town, off SH2: its long, thin strip of golden sand stretches for 8km and is one of the safest ocean beaches in the country.

The Town

At the eastern end of town, **Martha Mine** still produces gold (and silver) to the value of about one million dollars a week, and is one of the few working mines in New Zealand that you can visit. **Guided tours** (book a couple of days ahead, ⓣ07/863 9880; Mon–Fri, according to demand; 75–90min; $2) take visitors around the opencast gold mine and processing areas, providing background history and details of the environmental work the company is supposedly doing. The company's operations recently came into question when several houses sank into a hole which suddenly appeared, apparently because of the collapse of old underground mine workings. Even if you decide against the gold-mine tour, it's worth heading a couple of hundred metres up Moresby Avenue from the main street to the mine **viewing platform**, from where you can peer down into the vast red-earth pit where the laden trucks are dwarfed by the sheer scale of the earthworks, and the noise of the mechanical diggers labouring at the bottom are strangely muffled by the distance. Meanwhile, out of sight, a two-kilometre-long conveyor belt transports about 30,000 tonnes of ore a day through a tunnel to the treatment plant just outside town.

There are explanatory signs at the platform, but for more background visit the **Gold-mining Museum & Art Gallery**, 54 Kenny St (Mon–Fri 10am–4pm, Sun 1.30–4pm; $3). More than anything else, this is a showcase for the fine and intricately detailed models on mining themes that were made between 1976 and 1986 by ship's engineer, Tom Morgan, in his spare time. You can't help but admire the effort that went into the working model of a miniature stamper battery, which makes almost as much racket as the original, or the delightful working model of Waihi's pump house. There are also some evocative dioramas depicting miners at work, interesting ephemera about their lives, and historical accounts of the violent Waihi Strike of 1912 which helped galvanize the labour movement and eventually led to the creation of the Labour Party. The small art gallery in the same building exhibits the work of local and invited artists.

At the western end of town, the ramshackle wooden station at the end of Wrigley Street is home to the **Goldfields Railway**, which operates scenic 6km rail trips in summer to Waikino in the Karangahake Gorge (daily 11am, 12.30pm & 2pm, with extra services on Sun, returning from Waikino 45min later; 20min each way; $7 one way, $10 return; ⓣ07/863 8251). An old steam engine pulls 1930s carriages over a stretch of track built between 1900 and 1905 by gold-mining companies; travelling alongside SH2, you get spectacular views of the Ohinemuri River.

Practicalities

Both InterCity **buses** and Whangamata Buses (ⓣ07/865 7088) pull up at Rosemont Road Service Station, just a hundred metres from the **visitor centre** (daily: Oct–April 9am–5pm, May–Sept 9am–4.30pm; ⓣ07/863 6715), currently in a temporary location on Seddon Street in the centre of town.

There are several **places to stay** in Waihi itself and a few others at the beach (see below). A ten-minute walk from town, the *Waihi Motor Camp*, 6 Waitete Rd, off Seddon Rd (ⓣ07/863 7654; camping $8.50, dorm bunks ❶, cabins & flats ❷–❸), enjoys a quiet creekside setting, while the *Waihi Motel*, on Tauranga Road/SH2 (ⓣ07/863 8095, ⓕ863 8094; ❹), two minutes' walk south of the centre, has good-sized units and a spa pool; and the central *Chez Nous B&B*, 41 Seddon Ave (ⓣ07/863 7538; ❹), offers quiet rooms in a pleasant modern house, and dinner by arrangement.

At the western end of town, on Waitete Road, the pleasant daytime *Waitete Orchard* **winery** and **café** serves great-value, freshly cooked snacks, light meals, fresh fruit juices and naturally brewed beer; they use organic produce wherever possible and sell organic fruit and vegetables, too. Favourites are their authentic samosas ($8) and the delicious fruit ice cream. Just up the road is an excellent licensed and BYO **restaurant**, *Grandpa Thorn's*, 4 Waitete Rd (ⓣ07/863 8708; Tues–Sun evenings only; book ahead); diners travel from as far afield as Tauranga and Hamilton to eat high-quality country-style Kiwi cuisine ($20–25 a main course), such as rack of lamb with leek and mint compôte, in this log-cabin setting.

At **Waihi Beach** a few **accommodation** places are strung along the waterfront Seaforth Road. Try the small *Shalmar Motel*, 40 Seaforth Rd (ⓣ & ⓕ07/863 5439; ❺), near the shops, or the secluded *Bowentown Beach Holiday Park* (ⓣ & ⓕ07/863 5381; camping $11, cabins & flats ❷–❹), which sits right at the southern end of the beach. Good beachside fodder can be found at *Cactus Jack's*, 31 Wilson Rd, a BYO sit-in and takeout burger bar perfect for a chilli burger and shake.

Katikati and around

Waihi and the Karangahake Gorge mark the southern limit of the Coromandel Peninsula. From here on the coast begins to curl eastwards into the Bay of Plenty leaving behind the bush-clad mountains and taking on a gentler, more open aspect of rolling hills carved up by tall evergreen shelter belts which provide protection for valuable hectares of kiwifruit vines. In summer, numerous roadside stalls spring up selling ripe fruit straight from the orchards, often at knockdown prices. It takes less then an hour to drive from Waihi to Tauranga, but you may be induced to pause a while over the **murals** of Katikati or press on to the swimming beach at Omokoroa and the hot pools at Plummers Point.

Although, strictly speaking, **Rotorua** lies in the Bay of Plenty, it is covered along with the rest of the volcanic plateau region in Chapter Four, starting on p.307.

Katikati

Some twenty kilometres south of Waihi you arrive in **KATIKATI**, an ordinary little town which was dealt a devastating economic blow when the price of kiwifruit collapsed in the late 1980s. The town reacted by fashioning itself as "Mural Town", a fairly desperate but reasonably successful attempt to catch passing tourist traffic. Colourful and well-painted murals have since sprung up on buildings all over town, many reflecting the heritage of the original settlers from Ulster and the growth of the town: a couple of the best are "Waitekohe No. 3", on a block wall on the right as you enter the main street from the north, and the photo-realist "Central Motors", a little further along on the left. More information on the town and its murals is available in the volunteer-staffed **visitor centre**, 36 Main Rd/SH2, in the library building (daily 10am–4pm; Ⓣ07/549 1658).

For something to **eat** try *The Landing*, a café/bar on Main Road that does a good beef salad ($15), lamb shanks and mash ($16) and wood-fired pizzas. If you fancy **staying overnight** in these parts, head 6km south and turn up Thompson's Track to *Jacaranda Cottage*, 2.3km along at #230 (Ⓣ & Ⓕ07/549 0616, Ⓔjacaranda.cottage@clear.net.nz; backpacker beds ❶, cottage & B&B ❹), a homestay with individual beds let to backpackers (bring a sleeping bag), and a self-catering cottage with extensive Kaimai Range views. The genial host also takes folk horse riding in the woods nearby for a modest fee.

Around 8km south of Katikati on SH2 the South African **Cape Dutch-style** architecture of the *Morton Estate* winery (sales and tastings daily 10.30am–5pm) hoves into view. It is a charming place ringed by mountains and standing at the foot of a sloping vineyard with roses planted at the end of each row, in classic French tradition. Much of the grape juice is tankered here from their more extensive plantings in Hawke's Bay but it is here they produce an extensive range of quality wines, and offer **tastings**, free except for a few of their finer drops which cost $2 a sample, refunded if you make a purchase. You can also **eat** at *The Vineyard* (reservations advised Ⓣ07/552 0620; closed Sun evening & Mon), where the likes of chicken and pear salad and garlic rack of lamb are served in an airy conservatory or outside by the vines.

Omokoroa Beach

A further 19km on, and still 17km short of Tauranga, a dead-end road spurs 5km to pretty **OMOKOROA BEACH** (no bus service), a safe swimming beach backed by a grassy reserve. From the point you can gaze across to Matakana Island, accessible from here by ferry (3 daily; foot passengers $2 return, cars $45 return), though since you can't access the island's beaches there's little point making the journey.

You can **stay** at the quiet beachside *Omokoroa Tourist Park*, 165 Beach Rd (Ⓣ & Ⓕ07/548 0857; tent sites $10, cabins & chalets ❷–❸, motel units ❹), but it is more enjoyable to stay a few kilometres away at the *Plummers Point Caravan Park* (Ⓣ & Ⓕ07/548 0669; tent sites $11, on-site vans and tourist cabins ❷), where there are well-tended **hot mineral pools** (free to guests, otherwise $2.50). They're 3km along Plummers Point Road, which runs off SH2 2km south of the Omokoroa turn-off. From here it is a fifteen-minute drive into Tauranga, reached through Te Puna (home of the Paparoa Marae; see p.419), and the satellite community of **Bethlehem** (see p.420).

The western Bay of Plenty: Tauranga and Mount Maunganui

The western end of the **BAY OF PLENTY** centres on the prosperous port city of **TAURANGA** ("safe anchorage"), and its beachside acolyte, **Mount Maunganui**, effectively a suburb of Tauranga. This amorphous settlement, sprawled around the numerous glittering tentacles of Tauranga Harbour, is currently one of the **fastest-growing cities** in the land and will soon overtake Dunedin as New Zealand's fifth-largest urban area. A combination of warm dry summers and mild winters initially attracted retirees, followed in recent years by telecommuters and folk who have worked out how to run their profitable small businesses from home. The result is a wealthy community that has fuelled increasing expansion – driving into the area you see new, often spacious, housing developments everywhere – and helped create a vibrant café society.

Once through the protecting ring of suburbs, it's apparent that rampant development hasn't spoilt central Tauranga, which occupies a narrow peninsula with several city parks and gardens backing a lively waterfront area. Progress has been less kind to the over-commercialized beach resort of **Mount Maunganui**, which huddles under the extinct volcanic cone of the same name – a landmark visible throughout the whole western Bay of Plenty. "The Mount", as hill and town are often known, was once an island but is now connected to the mainland by a narrow neck of dune sand (a tombolo) covered with apartment blocks, shops, restaurants and houses. The Mount's saving grace is a 20km-long golden strand of Ocean Beach that's wonderful for swimming and surfing. No surprise, then, that the area's a big draw for Kiwi **holidaymakers** throughout January and on summer weekends, when Tauranga and Mount Maunganui can be rather overwhelming and accommodation hard to come by.

Visit outside the three peak weeks of summer madness and the region's charms quickly become apparent – though you'll do best if you have access to the surrounding area. Beyond the beach and a couple of walks around the volcano, Mount Maunganui's appeal runs only to a flourishing **restaurant** and **bar scene**. This it shares with Tauranga, which is best used to get out on the water: trips primarily head to **Matakana Island**, which acts as a barrier to Tauranga Harbour, and **Mayor Island**, a bush-clad retreat out in the Bay of Plenty. Boats also take clients out to **swim with dolphins**, cruise the harbour, or on excellent full-day **sailing trips**.

Beyond the city limits, there are opportunities to go **kayaking**, scale an outdoor climbing wall, ride horses, and wrangle quad bikes at a couple of adventure parks, or engage in more peaceful pursuits like **wine tasting** or picnicking beside some delightful swimming holes at **McLaren Falls**.

Finally, Tauranga is in a major **kiwifruit picking region**, but be warned, it's tough and prickly work and you must commit yourself to a minimum of three weeks (if this doesn't put you off, check out "Listings" on p.420).

Arrival, information and transport

The **airport** receives daily Air New Zealand flights from Auckland and Wellington, and lies midway between Tauranga and Mount Maunganui, roughly 3km from each: a taxi (see "Listings", p.420) to either costs about $8. Tauranga no longer has a train service, but InterCity and Newmans **buses** generally stop at the visitor centres in both towns. The Tauranga **visitor centre**, 95 Willow St (Mon–Fri 7am–5.30pm, Sat & Sun 8am–4pm; ⓣ07/578 8103, ⓔinfo@nztauranga.com), handles transport and accommodation bookings, as well as selling town plans (50¢) and more substantial maps ($3.75). There is a **DOC office**, 253 Chadwick Rd, Greerton (Mon–Fri 8am–4.40pm; ⓣ07/578 7677), inconveniently sited some 6km south of central Tauranga. For topographic **maps** try Absolute Adventure, 94 Willow St, by the visitor centre. The Mount Maunganui **visitor centre** is on Salisbury Avenue (Mon–Fri 9am–5pm, Sat & Sun 9am–4pm; ⓣ07/575 5099).

Visitor centres stock timetables for the local **Hopper Bus** (ⓣ0800/422 928, ⓦwww.baylinebus.co.nz), which runs Monday to Saturday services that cover most places in the immediate vicinity, including an hourly Tauranga–Mount Maunganui run ($5 all-day ticket from driver). These dry up around 5pm; after that you'll have to shell out for a taxi ($15–20), either from the **taxi** stand in The Strand in Tauranga or by calling one of the radio-cab companies (see "Listings", p.420). During summer, there's also a daytime **ferry** (Christmas–Easter; $6 each way) to Salisbury Wharf in Mount Maunganui from Coronation Wharf on The Strand in Tauranga. For **bike and car rental** see "Listings" on pp.419–20.

Accommodation

On arrival, your first move is to decide which side of the water you want to stay. If you've got a car you might prefer to stop in **Tauranga**, where the choice is wider and prices tend to be a little lower, though you're further from the beach. Without your own transport, you'll have to balance the advantages of proximity to the surf in **Mount Maunganui** against the wider range of restaurants, nightlife and access to offshore islands that Tauranga offers.

Alternatively, you might like to stay further afield at the **beachside campsites** out of town and commute in as necessary. Likely candidates are Omokoroa and Plummers Point to the west (see p.409) or Papamoa Beach to the east (see p.421).

Tauranga

Tauranga has many **hostels**, **motels** and **B&Bs** all within walking distance of the centre, and plenty more in the suburbs and out into the hinterland. A plethora of motels line Fifteenth Avenue, some offering good deals at slack times of year.

Hotels and motels

Ambassador Motor Inn 9 Fifteenth Ave ⓣ07/578 5665 & 0800/735 294, ⓦwww.ambassador-motorinn.co.nz. Well-appointed motel with a heated pool a short drive from the city centre and near the harbour. Popular, well-equipped budget units and more luxurious ones, each with a spa and some with water views. Studios ❹, with spa bath ❺

Harbour City Motor Inn 50 Wharf St ⓣ07/571 1435, ⓔtaurangaharbourcity@xtra.co.nz. Centrally located upmarket motel with tasteful designer decor, spa baths throughout, a/c, dataports, spectacularly comfy beds and a full kitchen equipped with real coffee. There's a complimentary drink on arrival and you can have breakfast (not included) delivered to your room. Studio ❺, one-bedroom ❻

Harbour View Motel, 7 Fifth Ave East ⓣ07/578 8621, ⓔharbview@wave.co.nz. Small, quiet and fairly simple place a stone's throw from the bay. ❹

Strand Motel 27 The Strand ⓣ & ⓕ07/578 5807. Budget, central and near the waterfront, but on a noisy corner. Sea views from the decks of most of the fully equipped units. ❹

B&Bs and guesthouses

The Palms 241 Beach Rd, Matua ⓣ07/576 7687, ⓔdonbrebs@xtra.co.nz. Well-sited B&B away from

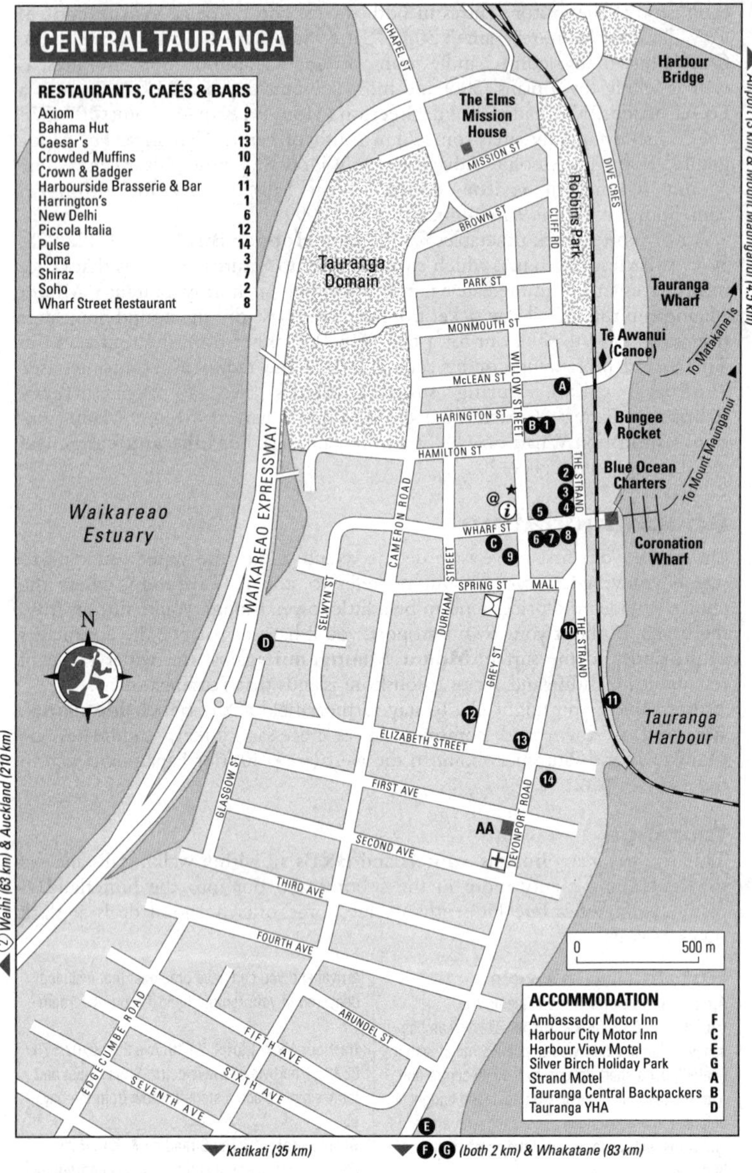

the city centre but with great harbour views from all rooms. 5

Tauranga Bed & Breakfast 4 Ninth Ave ⓣ07/577 0927, ⓕ577 0954. Pleasant and fairly central homestay with en-suite facilities and full breakfast. 4

Hostels and campsites

Apple Tree Cottage 47 Maxwell Rd ⓣ07/576 7404. A suburban house 1.5km from the centre of Tauranga with a limited supply of doubles and dorm beds around a garden equipped with plunge pool, barbecue and a covered cooking area. Relaxed and friendly. Dorms ❶, rooms ❷

Bell Lodge 39 Bell St, off Waihi Rd ⓣ07/578 6344, ⓦwww.bell-lodge.co.nz. A clean, modern and comfortable backpackers 3km from the centre with spacious dorms, comfortable en-suite rooms and some brand-new motel units. Excellent facilities including barbecue and free daily pick-ups and transport to Mount Maunganui. Tent sites $10, dorms ❶, rooms ❷, units ❸

Just the Ducks Nuts 6 Vale St ⓣ07/576 1366. A small backpackers just over 2km from the centre, with great views of the harbour and the Mount, and budget bikes for rent. Camping $10, dorms ❶, rooms ❷

Silver Birch Holiday Park 101 Turret Rd ⓣ07/578 4603, ⓔsilverbirch@xtra.co.nz. Fairly central campsite right on the harbour's edge with a family atmosphere and thermal pools. Tent sites $10, cabins ❷–❸

Tauranga Central Backpackers 64 Willow St ⓣ571 6222, ⓔcentralbackpack@xtra.co.nz. Comfortable hostel that primarily benefits from its location right in the heart of Tauranga. Dorms ❶, rooms ❷

Tauranga YHA 171 Elizabeth St ⓣ07/578 5064, ⓔyhataur@yha.org.nz. Recently refurbished, well equipped and very hospitable, this hostel lies in secluded grounds a 5min walk from the centre. Barbecue, volleyball, minigolf; bikes and body-boards for rent. Tent sites $10, dorms ❶, rooms ❷

Mount Maunganui

Mount Maunganui is close to the surf and though much of the accommodation is geared towards **long-staying** Kiwi holidaymakers you'll also find several motels and a couple of hostels.

Belle Mer 57 Marine Parade ⓣ07/575 0011 & 0800/100 235, ⓦwww.bellemer.co.nz. Plush apartments with modern decor, just across the road from the beach. All have sea views, luxurious kitchens, stereo and access to a heated lap pool. ❼

Classic Accommodation 16b Ulster St ⓣ07/574 1776, ⓔinfo@mctours.co.nz. Great value B&B in a stylish modern home close to the beach. One en-suite room and a self-contained unit, and breakfast is $10 extra. ❹

Links Motel 209 Valley Rd ⓣ07/575 5774, ⓕ575 6495. Good clean low-cost motel close to the beach, with Sky TV spa pool, free newspaper and breakfast served in your room if required. ❹

Mount Backpackers 87 Maunganui Rd ⓣ07/575 0860, ⓔmountinternet@xtra.co.nz. Small and somewhat cramped hostel right in the thick of things – close to restaurants, bars and the beach. Low-cost bike and boogie board rental. Dorms ❶, rooms ❷

Mount Maunganui Domain Motor Camp 1 Adams Ave ⓣ07/575 4471, ⓔmtdomain@xtra.co.nz. A sizeable, terraced campsite very close to the beach in a pleasant spot beside the hot saltwater pools and right at the foot of the Mount. Camping $22 per site.

Ocean Waves Motel 74 Marine Parade ⓣ07/575 4594, ⓔoceanwaves@xtra.co.nz. Nicely located motel as close as you'll get to the popular end of the beach with ocean views from many units. ❺

Pacific Coast Backpackers 432 Maunganui Rd ⓣ07/574 9601 & 0800/666 237, ⓦwww.pacific-coastlodge.co.nz. Vast, rambling hostel with good facilities (spacious dorms, comfy rooms with sheets, large kitchen, games room, barbecue area) and a strong eco/recycling ethic, but a little soulless and well away from the restaurants and the fashionable end of the beach. Dorms ❶, rooms ❷

The city of Tauranga

Tauranga's flat **city centre** is concentrated between Tauranga Harbour and Waikareao Estuary. It's a dense kernel of shops, restaurants and bars where you'll find just about everything you need, but little of abiding interest other than boat trips out onto the bay and its islands (see p.417). Downtown Tauranga is a pleasant spot though, and you can easily spend half a day strolling along the waterfront or mooching around the couple of minor sights.

First stop should be the ornately carved traditional **war canoe** – *Te Awanui*

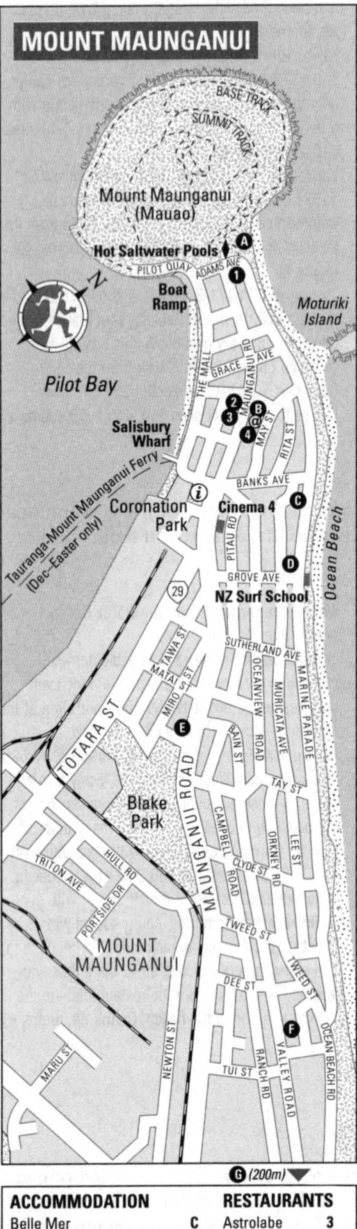

ACCOMMODATION		RESTAURANTS	
Belle Mer	C	Astrolabe	3
Classic Accommodation	F	Hasan Baba	2
Links Motel	G	Sidetrack Café Pacifica	1
Mount Backpackers	B	Volantis	4
Mount Maunganui Domain Motor Camp	A		
Ocean Waves Motel	D		
Pacific Coast Backpackers	E		

stands proudly in a shelter on the corner of Dive Crescent and McLean Street, and is used on ceremonial occasions on the harbour. About one block up and entered from Cliff Street is **Robbins Park** (dawn–dusk; free), an attractive swathe of green equipped with a rose garden and begonia house, and boasting fine views across to Mount Maunganui. At the northern end of The Strand, Mission Street is home to **The Elms Mission House** (Sun 2–4pm, and by appointment on ☎07/577 9772; $5). One of the country's oldest homes, it was built between 1835 and 1847 by an early missionary, Archdeacon A.N. Brown, who tended the wounded of both sides during the **Battle of Gate Pa** (see box, p.416). The house has been restored to its original form complete with Brown's thousand-volume library. However, unless you strike it lucky and catch it when it is open, you'll only get to see the pretty **garden** (dawn–dusk; free), including an English oak planted by Brown in 1838 and a reconstruction of the original chapel. Inside is a dining table at which Brown entertained several British officers on the eve of the Battle of Gate Pa, little suspecting that over the next few days he would bury most of them.

Back on the waterfront, you might want to experience the 5g acceleration meted out by the **Bungee Rocket** (daily 10am–5pm, and later in summer; $35), a kind of cross between a fairground ride and a reverse bungy jump in which two people sit strapped into a tubular metal cocoon attached by two bungy cords to 30m

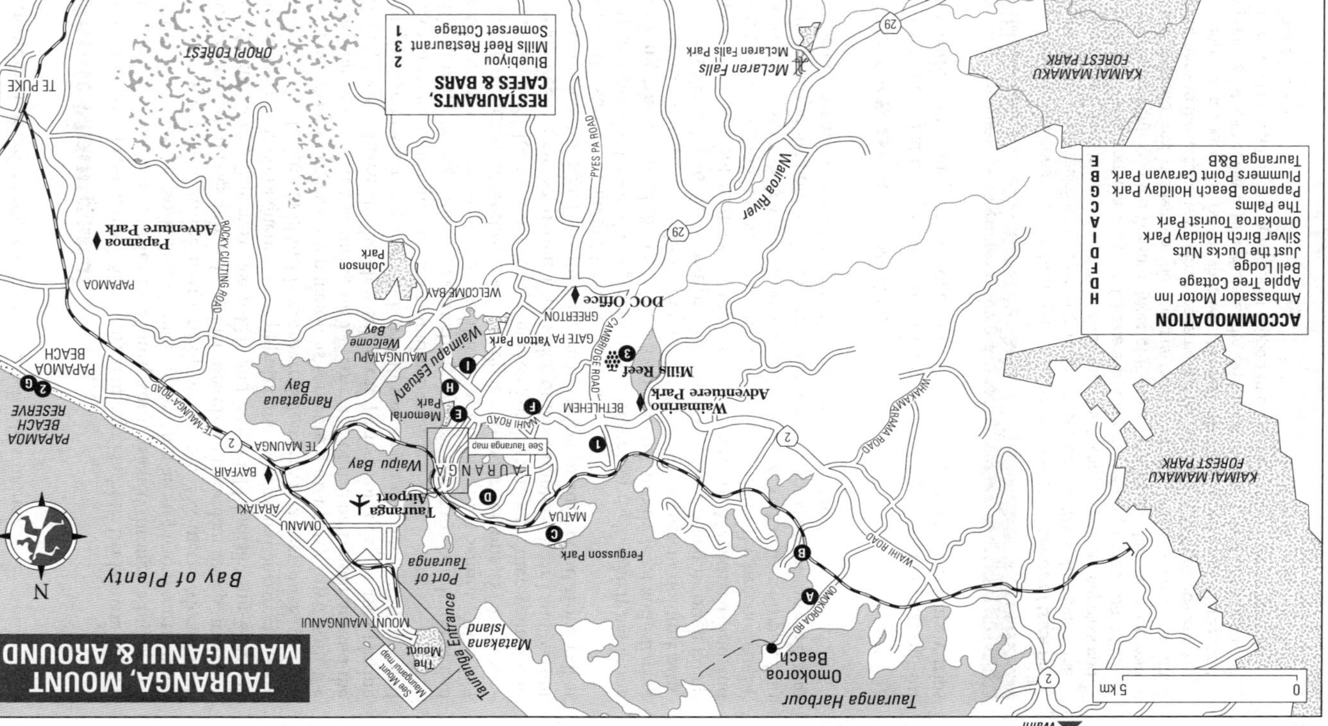
TAURANGA, MOUNT MAUNGANUI & AROUND
Bay of Plenty
N
Whakatane (55 km)
Waihi
0
5 km
ACCOMMODATION
Ambassador Motor Inn H
Apple Tree Cottage D
Bell Lodge F
Just the Ducks Nuts D
Silver Birch Holiday Park I
Omokaroa Tourist Park A
The Palms C
Papamoa Beach Holiday Park G
Plummers Point Caravan Park B
Tauranga B&B E
RESTAURANTS, CAFÉS & BARS
Bluebiyou 2
Mills Reef Restaurant 3
Somerset Cottage 1
TE PUKE
OROPI FOREST
PAPAMOA BEACH RESERVE
PAPAMOA BEACH
PAPAMOA
Papamoa Adventure Park
ROCKY CUTTING ROAD
TE MAUNGA ROAD
Johnson Park
WELCOME BAY
Welcome Bay
MAUNGATAPU
Rangataua Bay
Waimapu Estuary
Memorial Park
TE MAUNGA
BAYFAIR
ARATAKI
OMANU
MOUNT MAUNGANUI
The Mount
See Mount Maunganui map
Tauranga Airport
Waipu Bay
TAURANGA
See Tauranga map
Port of Tauranga
Tauranga Entrance
Matakana Island
MATUA
Fergusson Park
WAIHI ROAD
GATE PA
Yatton Park
GREERTON
DOC Office
CAMBRIDGE ROAD
PYES PA ROAD
BETHLEHEM
Mills Reef
Waimarino Adventure Park
Wairoa River
McLaren Falls
McLaren Falls Park
KAIMAI MAMAKU FOREST PARK
WHAKAMARAMA ROAD
OMOKOROA RD
Omokoroa Beach
Tauranga Harbour
2
29

towers. When the catch is released you rocket skywards: less intimidating than a traditional bungy jump, but as much fun for less money.

Mount Maunganui

From the eastern end of the 3.5km-long Tauranga Harbour Bridge, you are still 3km short of the heart of **Mount Maunganui**, reached through a big industrial estate of cement works and a bitumen plant: not an auspicious start. Things improve as you head to the northern tip where the 232-metre Mount itself (*Mauao* in Maori) rises above the golden **beach**, an unbroken sweep stretching over 20km east to Papamoa (see p.421) and beyond. Habitually sun-kissed in the summer, it is consequently very popular, and condos and apartments have colonized the beach's fashionable northern kilometre in a very un-Kiwi fashion. The Mount also has a reputation as something of a party town with the New Year revelry often featuring on TV coverage of bad behaviour around the country. Nevertheless the beach is still great, perfect for a day or two playing volleyball and swimming while still within easy reach of good restaurants and bars where everyone gravitates for sundowners.

If you fancy trying your hand at **surfing**, wander along the beach to the end of Grove Avenue, where teachers at the New Zealand Surf School (ⓣ07/574 1666, ⓔnzsurfschool@yahoo.com) conduct two-hour **lessons** ($70) on specially designed longboards; they guarantee you'll stand up. After your lesson you are free to practise as long as you like; others can rent a board and wetsuit for two hours for $20. For other gear and advice on **surf conditions** call at any of the surf shops along Maunganui Road.

Apart from the beach, the big draw is the mountain itself, which has a fine **walking track** around the base (3km loop; 45min), mostly level and offering a great sea and harbour outlook from under the shade of ancient pohutukawas. You can also **hike to the summit** (2km one way; 1hr), which is tough going towards the top but well worth the effort for views of Matakana Island and along the coast. Both tracks start from the northern end of the beach, right by the outdoor **Hot Saltwater Pools**, Adams Way (Mon–Sat 6am–10pm, Sun 8am–10pm; public pool $2.50, private $3.50 per half hour; use of towel $2, togs $2), which form Mount Maunganui's other main attraction.

Cruises and day-trips

It would be a shame to come to the western Bay of Plenty and not get out **on the water**, something easily done from the Tauranga Wharf, with many trips

The Battle of Gate Pa

In 1864 the tiny community of Tauranga became the scene of the **Battle of Gate Pa**, one of the most decisive engagements of the **New Zealand Wars**. In January the government sent troops here to build two redoubts, hoping to prevent supplies and reinforcements from reaching the followers of the Maori King (see box on p.250), who were fighting in the Waikato. Most of the local Ngaiterangi hurried back from the Waikato and challenged the soldiers from a *pa* they quickly built near an entrance to the mission land, which became known as Gate Pa. In April, government troops surrounded the *pa* in what was New Zealand's only naval blockade, and pounded it with artillery. Nonetheless, the British lost about a third of their assault force and at nightfall the Ngaiterangi slipped through the British lines to fight again in the Waikato.

also picking up at Salisbury Wharf in Mount Maunganui. A full range of boats is ready to take you cruising, fishing, sailing, parasailing and **swimming with dolphins**.

The island retreats of Matakana and Mayor are both prime Bay of Plenty boat-trip destinations. Strictly speaking the former is, in fact, two islands: the tiny **Rangiwea** and the long sheltering sweep of **Matakana**, nestled close to Tauranga Harbour and used primarily for farming and forestry. **Mayor Island** is the cone-shaped dormant volcano, protruding from the Bay of Plenty 40km off the coast of Tauranga and increasingly geared towards eco-tourism.

Boat trips on the bay

About the cheapest way to get on the water is on a six-hour **harbour cruise** aboard the 1938 line-fishing boat *Ratahi* (Ⓣ07/578 9685; $25) as it chugs across the bay to Omokoroa and back; there's afternoon tea on the way.

An equally leisurely day out at sea, but with the option of **swimming with dolphins**, is run by The Tauranga Dolphin Company on its yacht *Gemini Galaxsea* (book a day ahead Ⓣ07/578 3197 & 0800/836 574; $90, take your own lunch). The skipper, Graham Butler, is a good-natured sea dog and militant greenie who has a high success rate of finding dolphins. His secret is to allow plenty of time, so don't be surprised if you're out well into the evening; if there's time you also get to snorkel around a reef. Trips run most of the year, but only in good weather conditions. If you are on a tight schedule and still want to swim with dolphins, try the Mount Maunganui-based Dolphin Seafaris, 90 Maunganui Rd (Ⓣ07/575 4620 & 0800/326 874; $100), which runs half-day trips in the morning and afternoon in its launch.

Scores of boats are available for **fishing charters**, many through Blue Ocean Charters, Tauranga Wharf (Ⓣ07/578 9685, Ⓦwww.blueoceancharters.co.nz): game fishing for marlin tuna and kingfish (Dec–April) is likely to cost about $250 a day per person, but if you go out for the bottom fish (snapper and tarakihi) it's cheaper at around $50 per half day.

Matakana Island

MATAKANA ISLAND has 24km of beach and great surfing on its eastern side, not to mention a general store and pub for more mundane requirements. However, much of the island is Maori land with limited access, so even if you take your own wheels on the ferry from Omokoroa, you will be fairly restricted. The best way to experience the island is to join the tribal owners on Matakana Island Tours' day-long trip (book through Blue Ocean Charters, see above; Nov–March; $75) from Tauranga by boat to Matakana and then in a restored 1914 covered wagon hauled by Clydesdale horses to a barbecue in the shade of walnut trees.

Mayor Island (Tuhua)

Dormant volcano, **MAYOR ISLAND**, has a crater now virtually overgrown and a third of its coast designated a **marine reserve** in readiness for low-key eco-tourism. There are some great **walking tracks** around the island's base and through its centre, and boats coming out here will rent snorkelling gear ($10 per day) so you can explore the aquatic world. The area, however, is particularly well endowed with **wasps** and anyone allergic to stings should pack medication or just not risk it.

As the island is privately owned by the Tuhua Trust Board, all visitors are charged a **landing fee** which is included in commercial boat fares. Blue Ocean Charters (see above) organizes **boats** to the island leaving Tauranga for Mount Maunganui then on to the island's only landing site, Opo Bay, at the south end – though sailings are often cancelled in rough weather. Regular services operate in summer (Nov to mid-April), but the rest of the year you may need to charter a boat; contact Tauranga visitor centre for details and the going rates. The **crossing** usually takes two to three hours depending on boat and conditions, and will cost you $60, though there are sometimes trips including lunch and off-shore fishing for $75.

Your only **accommodation** option on the island is the *Tuhua Campsite* at Opo Bay (☎07/577 0531; tent sites $10, bunks ❶, cabins ❷) which sits beneath tall pohutukawa trees behind an idyllic bay. It has showers and toilets, but you'll need to bring a cooking stove, all utensils and food.

Eating

Tauranga and Mount Maunganui have both fully embraced modern café/bar culture, Tauranga in particular rating as something of a regional culinary hotspot. As elsewhere, distinctions between eating and drinking places are becoming ever more blurred and you may well find yourself enjoying a drink at one of the places listed below.

In **Tauranga**, most of the cafés and restaurants are right in the centre – a slew of them strung along Devonport Road with a bunch more lining The Strand and the streets running back from it. **Mount Maunganui** doesn't have Tauranga's selection, but you'd have to be finicky not to be able to find something appealing on the half-dozen blocks of Maunganui Road that make up the centre.

Tauranga and Bethlehem

Axiom 131 Willow St. Smart, modern café that's almost too cool for its own good, but serves excellent coffee and delightful little savouries and cakes.

Caesar's cnr Devonport Rd & Elizabeth St. Basic buffet restaurant noted for its bargain all-you-can-eat buffets; lunch (Mon–Fri $16, Sat & Sun $18), dinner (Mon–Thurs $20, Fri–Sun $27).

Crowded Muffins 22 Devonport Rd. Daytime joint with great, cheap muffins to enjoy over a coffee or take away.

Harbourside Brasserie & Bar under the railway bridge at the southern end of The Strand. A big, airy building right on the harbour, with great views and a sizeable deck built over the water where you can feed the fish below; in summer, boats moor alongside. Lively cosmopolitan ambience and food, with mains for $20–25 and cheaper light meals.

Mills Reef Restaurant 143 Moffat Rd, Bethlehem ☎07576 8800. Highly regarded winery restaurant that's Tauranga's favourite lunch spot in an elevated position overlooking the vines. Great gourmet pizzas and an à la carte menu that might include whole baby pumpkin stuffed with mushrooms, feta and coriander ($19) and pork vindaloo with okra, lime and mustard seed pickle ($18). Afterwards, you can enjoy a post-prandial game of petanque in the grounds. Lunch daily and dinner most evenings.

New Delhi 20 Wharf St ☎07/578 5533. Recently opened and unpretentious Indian restaurant with a good range of north Indian mains including vegetarian dishes. The chicken tikka masala ($13) goes nicely with a mint paratha. Delivery available. Licensed & BYO.

Piccola Italia 107 Grey St ☎07/578 8363. Admirable northern Italian café and restaurant with wonderfully prepared authentic dishes served with aplomb. Highlights include pork ravioli ($16), perfect gnocchi ($16), and baked fish with lemon, pine nuts and olive oil ($24). Open for lunch Thurs & Fri, and dinner Mon–Sat.

Pulse 130 Devonport Rd. Laid-back, groovy little café ideal for reading the paper over a coffee and a muffin. BYO.

Shiraz 12 Wharf St ☎07/577 0059. Tasty Middle Eastern and Mediterranean food, excellent service and reasonable prices for lunch (under $15) and dinner (under $20) make this a popular and often packed place; reservations recommended. Leisurely eating in a small café and covered courtyard. Closed Sun.

Soho 59 The Strand ☎07/577 0577. Relaxed and

welcoming restaurant that has brought French provincial (and assorted European) dining to the Tauranga waterfront. Dishes include herb-crusted lambs' brains ($14), leek, thyme and mushroom risotto ($21) and lime and passionfruit soufflé ($10), all served with Gallic panache. Closed Sun.
Somerset Cottage 30 Bethlehem Rd, Bethlehem ⓣ07/576 6889. An extremely popular and traditional restaurant that oozes charm and serves excellent value mains (around $25).
Wharf Street Restaurant, cnr Wharf St & The Strand ⓣ07/578 8322. Upper-floor brasserie and bar with great views over the harbour and a seafood-dominated menu – crab and sweetcorn fritters ($15), salmon fillet on parsley mash ($24), and a sumptuous seafood platter for two ($110). Closed Sun.

Mount Maunganui

Astrolabe 82 Maunganui Rd. A large and popular diner-cum-drinking hole, with a beachy and slightly upmarket tenor and some late-night dancing. Open for lunch and dinner, with salads and pasta, char-grilled steak and fish, and a large range of beers.
Hasan Baba 16 Pacific Ave. Well-prepared Middle Eastern dishes, delicately flavoured and served in relaxed surroundings at moderate prices.
Sidetrack Café Pasifica Marine Parade. A great place to go for breakfast or morning coffee, when you can gaze across the beach to the ocean in the warming early sun.
Volantis105 Maunganui Rd. One of the best spots on the strip for a casual coffee, or snacks along the lines of Thai chicken soup ($9) and gourmet burgers, with several vegetarian options. Dinner mains ($20) might be lamb curry or fish and cashew filo parcel. Licensed & BYO.

Drinking, nightlife and entertainment

In both Tauranga and Maunganui the restaurants double as **bars**: neither town is especially jumping in the off season, but come summer the evenings hot up, with Mount Maunganui earning a reputation for boisterous behaviour. Of the two only Tauranga boasts a couple of dedicated watering holes and a **nightclub** or two, all in the same downtown area. **Films** are shown at Cinema 6 on Elizabeth Street in Tauranga (infoline ⓣ07/577 0800) and at Cinema 4 on Maunganui Road in The Mount (infoline ⓣ07/577 0900). Screening times are listed in Friday's *Bay of Plenty Times*, which is the best general source of entertainment **listings**.

For something completely different, consider a visit to **Paparoa Marae**, Paparoa Road, 15km west of Tauranga (ⓣ & ⓕ07/552 5796), which puts on professional but low-key cultural performances complete with traditional *wero* (challenge), a visit to the simple meeting-house, where the carvings are explained, and a display of Maori crafts. Performances are only put on for groups (or when there's a cruise ship in town), but you may be able to tag along (around $40), and evening events may also include a *hangi*.

Tauranga clubs and bars

Bahama Hut 19 Wharf St. Popular surf bar with a big central brazier, pool tables and surfboards everywhere.
Crown & Badger cnr The Strand & Wharf St. Lively (sometimes frenetic) Irish-cum-English pub with a good range of beers from both nations and pub-style meals mostly for under $10.
Harington's 10 Harington St. A bar-cum-nightclub, usually packed by midnight and open until 5am. Mostly dance music. During the summer holidays they often hold theme evenings and beach parties. Oct–April nightly; May–Sept Thurs–Sat.
Roma 65 The Strand. One of the more upmarket bars, open from 4pm, serving gourmet pizzas until 2am or so, and often with live jazz, plus dancing on Fri & Sat nights. Closed Mon.

Listings

Automobile Association cnr First Ave & Devonport Rd, Tauranga ⓣ07/578 2222.
Bike rental Around $20 a day from Bike and Pack Warehouse, 1 Dee St, Mount Maunganui (ⓣ07/575 2189), and several of the hostels have cheaper machines – some available to non-guests.

Buses InterCity and Newmans (both ⓣ07/578 2825) run several daily services to Mount Maunganui, Auckland, Hamilton, Rotorua, and Thames (via Katikati, Waihi and Paeroa).
Car rental Budget deals from Johnny's Rentals, at the airport (ⓣ07/575 9204) as well as international companies in Tauranga, notably Budget (ⓣ07/578 5156).
Internet access Tauranga Library, in the Civic Shopping Centre behind the visitor centre, has internet access at reasonable rates.
Kiwifruit picking The best time for picking is late April to mid-June, but pruning is also necessary from mid-June to early Sept and again from end-Oct to Jan. For picking, you're paid by the bin, so speed is of the essence; an average rate is $70 a day, but quick workers can earn $100. The best sources of up-to-date information are the backpacker hostels which will often help you to find work.
Medical treatment After-hours medical care and an emergency pharmacy is available at the Baycare Medical Service Centre, cnr Edgecumbe Rd & Tenth Ave ⓣ07/578 8111; Mon–Fri 5pm–8am, Sat & Sun 24hr.
Post office The post office, 17 Grey St, Tauranga (Mon–Fri 9am–5pm, Sat 9am–12.30pm) has poste restante facilities.
Taxis Citicabs ⓣ07/577 0999; Coast Line ⓣ07/571 8333; Tauranga Taxis ⓣ07/578 6086.
Thomas Cook 63 Devonport Rd ⓣ07/578 3119.

Around Tauranga and Mount Maunganui

Unless you are happy spending days on the beach, or are keen to explore the Bay of Plenty and its islands, you'll soon exhaust the temptations of Tauranga and Mount Maunganui. Help is at hand in the hinterland, where **Mills Reef winery** drapes across fertile countryside backed by the angular peaks of the Kaimai-Mamaku Forest Park. Rivers cascading down the slopes and across the coastal plain supply water for assorted activities at **Waimarino Adventure Park**, and periodically fire up **McLaren Falls**, where shallow rock pools make great swimming holes. At the coast, the great sweep of Mount Maunganui's Ocean Beach extends to **Papamoa Beach**, great for surfing and swimming away from the glitz of the mount.

Bethlehem: Mills Reef winery and Waimarino Adventure Park

The suburb of **Bethlehem** justifies a little of your time, particularly if you fancy a visit to the Art Deco-style **tasting rooms** at *Mills Reef*, 143 Moffat Rd (daily 10am–5pm; ⓦwww.millsreef.co.nz), where you can sample, and of course buy, bottles: the Reserve Chardonnay and Elspeth Chardonnay are usually very good, and they also produce Rieslings, Sauvignons, some sparkling wines and Cabernet Sauvignons. There's also a classy on-site restaurant and another, *Somerset Cottage*, just a couple of kilometres back towards Bethlehem (for both, see "Eating" on pp.418-9).

All this eating and wine tasting could work as a perfect finale to a half a day spent at the riverside **Waimarino Adventure Park**, 34 Taniwha Place (daily 10am–6pm; ⓣ07/576 4233, ⓦwww.waimarino.com), which conducts a huge range of mainly water-based courses and activities. The most accessible are the **activity sessions** around the centre ($12–25 per person depending on what you opt for) which all include rope swings, a hydro-slide, spa pool, ropes course and trampolines ($12 per person) and can include water-bikes and kayaks ($20) and the climbing wall ($25). **Kayaking** trips start with the Wairoa River Trip (3hr; $25), a tide assisted and unguided flatwater paddle down a lower stretch of the Wairoa River to the adventure park; a moonlit version costs $35 and booking is essential. If whitewater rafting isn't thrilling enough for you, try the Extreme Boating (3hr; $140–150), where you are stuck at the sharp end of a double kayak and guided down either the Wairoa (certain Sundays only; Grade IV+) or the Kaituna (Grade III–IV).

McLaren Falls

Most summer Sundays, **McLaren Falls**, signposted 11km south of Tauranga off SH29, becomes the scene of frenetic activity as hundreds of rafters and kayakers congregate to run the Grade IV+ rapids of the Wairoa River. The ten-metre cataract itself is only worth viewing on the Sundays when the upstream dam releases its charge (Dec–March every Sun; Sept–Nov & April–May every second Sun) but pretty much every day of the summer locals flock here to wallow in a lovely series of shallow pools hewn out of the bedrock. It can get crowded, but a few minutes rock-hopping should secure you a pool to yourselves: bring a picnic and some sunscreen.

The dam that holds back the Wairoa River forms Lake McLaren, centrepiece for **McLaren Falls Park**, 1km upstream from McLaren Falls (daily: Nov–March 8am–7.30pm, April–Oct 8am–5.30pm; free), a large area of parkland, native bush and exotic trees, with barbecue areas and the freedom to **camp** anywhere ($7). To use the shower and cooking facilities, campers will need to make arrangements with the two basic on-site **hostels** (Ⓣ07/577 7000; ❶), which are open to backpackers.

Kaimai-Mamaku Forest Park

Tauranga and Mount Maunganui have a deserved reputation for balmy weather, a result of the rain shadow cast by the broad, forested spine of the **Kaimai Range** which rises up south of the Karangahake Gorge and extends 70km south. This rugged landscape was created about five million years ago when vast quantities of lava, scoria and ash were spewed across the region, forming a chain of large **volcanic cones**. The entire range falls within the **Kaimai-Mamaku Forest Park**, not the most hospitable nor accessible of the tramping regions, though it contains some **tracks** worthy of exploration, scenic lookouts and a network of back-country **huts**, which can be reached either from Te Aroha in the west (see p.380), the Karangahake Gorge in the north (see p.379) and from Tauranga. The northern sector of the park is an extension of the Coromandel Range and has been intensively mined for gold and logged for its kauri, while the southern sector is largely plateau country, much of it dissected by deep streams. DOC produce a useful leaflet on the area ($1), as well as several booklets detailing walks in the park.

Papamoa Beach

Mount Maunganui's stunning Ocean Beach stretches 20km east to **Papamoa Beach**, a burgeoning community accessed off SH2. Backed by the dramatic Papamoa Hills, it makes a pleasant spot for a beach break away from the city, facilitated by the extensive *Papamoa Beach Top 10 Holiday Park*, 535 Papamoa Beach Rd (Ⓣ07/572 0816, Ⓦwww.papamoabeach.co.nz; camping $12, cabins ❷–❸, units ❹–❺, villas ❻), with a broad selection of accommodation including beachfront campsites and some gorgeous villas with wonderful sea views. The licensed, nautically themed *Bluebiyou* café/restaurant next door has a covered deck that leads right on to sand and surf, and a kitchen that serves light meals all day, lunch, dinner and Sunday brunch.

In the hills a couple of kilometres back from the beach, there's fun to be had at **Papamoa Adventure Park**, 1162 Welcome Bay Rd (Ⓣ07/542 0972, Ⓔpapamoa.adventure.park@xtra.co.nz), where they'll take you **horse trekking** ($30 per hour) over open hill country and through forest tracks. For something more energetic you can career down a steep dirt track at frighteningly high speed in a wheeled buggy known as the **luge** (1 ride $15, 2 for $25), join a forty-minute **quad bike** tour ($20), or head into the forest for a **paint-**

ball game (from $25). It is a great spot to spend a few hours, and there's farm animal feeding to entertain young children.

The eastern Bay of Plenty

Moving away from Tauranga toward the **eastern Bay of Plenty**, along what's been dubbed the Pacific Coast Highway, the urban influence wanes noticeably; the pace slows and everything seems that much more rural, with orchards and kiwifruit vines gradually giving way to sheep country. You'll also find a gradual change in the racial mix, for the Eastern Bay of Plenty is increasingly Maori country; appropriate since some of the first **Maori** to reach New Zealand arrived here in their great *waka* (war canoes). In fact Whakatane is sometimes known as the birthplace of Aotearoa, for it was here that the Polynesian navigator **Toi te Huatahi** first landed.

The westernmost town, **Te Puke**, is very much New Zealand's kiwifruit capital, and is well inland, but the sea is still the focus of the region. The heyday of its port has long passed, but **Whakatane** remains the largest town, prettily set between cliffs and a river estuary, and currently improving its image with new street paving and feature lighting on the town waterfall. It makes a great base for forays out to volcanic **White Island**, or the bird reserve of **Whale Island**. Further east, **Opotiki** is the gateway to Eastland in one direction and to Gisborne in the other, as well as providing access to some interesting walks in the hills to the south and to trips on the remote and scenic **Motu River**.

Te Puke

Te Puke, 31km southeast of Tauranga on SH2, comes justifiably billed as the "kiwifruit capital of the world", a claim driven home at **Kiwifruit Country**, 6km east of Te Puke (daily 9am–5pm; 30–40min guided tours $10), a massive orchard and processing plant that also operates as a horticultural theme park, with a surreal, giant slice of kiwifruit standing close by its gateway. The complex is as tacky and commercialized as you would expect, but it's the only place to be if you're curious about how these little green, furry fruits grow and are harvested. The "Kiwi Kart" guided tours tell you everything you ever wanted to know about them (and much more besides), and there's an overpriced souvenir stall and café.

Next door to Kiwifruit Country is the **Vintage Auto Barn** (daily 9am–5pm; $7), literally a big barn of some ninety-odd vintage and classic cars from 1906 to 1970, all kept in exceptional condition. One of the more touching exhibits is The Beast, a racing car hand-built in the late 1950s by a young man dying of cancer. For his "final fling" he sped around the streets of Pirionga (near Te Awamutu) in this jalopy. Among the older models is a 1912 Model C Renault in pristine condition, complete with wooden-spoked wheels, and assorted models up for sale at prices that are astonishingly low given the amount of work that's gone into them. Car fanatics might easily lose a few hours in the extensive motoring library.

From Te Puke it's 66km along SH2 to Whakatane, the road hugging the coast for much of the way, but with little worth breaking your journey for. The one possible exception is **Longridge Park**, SH33, 3km south of its junction with SH2 (daily 9am–5pm; ⓣ07/533 1515), where kids can feed farm animals and see captive eels ($1.50), and adults can take a highly scenic **jetboat** ride up the Kaituna River ($59), spend 45 minutes driving an **off-road 4WD** through all manner of devious mud traps and bogs ($60), or take a more sedate tour of the kiwifruit vines and working farm ($12).

Whakatane and around

The main settlement of the Eastern Bay of Plenty is **WHAKATANE**, a 17,000-strong town sprawled across flat farmland around the last convulsions of the Whakatane River, before it spills into the sea. The dull suburbs surround a genuinely attractive centre wedged between the river and bush-clad hills which rise steeply from the town. Here, the **Pohaturoa** rock outcrop provides a focal point, and the **museum** and **gallery** provides wet-day distraction. Whakatane's real appeal lies off the coast, either swimming with **dolphins**, or on trips to the bird sanctuary of **Whale Island**, and to the active, volcanic **White Island**, billowing white plumes of smoke into the sky. Back on land, there are walks along the spine of hills above the town out to the viewpoint at **Kohi Point**, and body surfing and sunbathing to be done at the broad expanse of **Ohope Beach**.

The Whakatane area seems to have had more than its fair share of dramatic events. The **Maori** word Whakatane means "to act as a man" and comes from a legendary incident when the women of the *Mataatua* canoe were left aboard while the men went ashore; the canoe began to drift out to sea, but touching the paddles was *tapu* for women. Undeterred, the high-spirited Wairaka took matters into her own hands and paddled back to the safety of the shore, shouting *Ka Whakatane Au i Ah au* ("I will act as a man"), and a statue at Whakatane Heads commemorates her heroic act. The first **Europeans** to set foot in the area, apart from a brief sortie by Cook, were flax traders in the early 1800s and a trader called Philip Tapsell, who established a store in 1830. The next turning point in Whakatane's history came when, in March 1865, missionary **Carl Volkner** was killed at Opotiki, and a government agent, **James Falloon**, arrived to investigate. At this unwelcome intrusion, supporters of a fanatical Maori sect, the Hau Hau, attacked Falloon's vessel, killing him and his crew. In response, the government declared **martial law**, and by the end of the year a large part of the Bay of Plenty had been confiscated and Whakatane was being peopled by military settlers. The memory of this led **Te Kooti** (see box on p.456) to choose Whakatane as his target for a full-scale attack by his Maori force in 1869, burning and looting buildings before being driven back into the hills of Urewera. In more **recent times**, Whakatane has led a relatively quiet life as a trading area and service town for the surrounding regions, and as a tourist attraction with access to many areas of natural beauty.

Arrival, information and accommodation

Long-distance **buses** running between Rotorua and Gisborne (along SH2) stop once a day in each direction outside the brand-new **visitor centre**, corner of Quay Street and Kakahoroa Drive (Christmas–Feb Mon–Fri 8.30am–5.30pm, Sat & Sun 9am–4pm, March–Christmas Mon–Fri 9am–5pm Sat & Sun 10am–3.30pm; ⓣ07/308 6058, ⓦwww.whakatane.com), which is well-stocked with DOC leaflets for the local area. **Internet access** is pricey in Whakatane, but cheapest at *Friends*, a café at 122 The Strand. The **post office**, corner of Commerce Street and The Strand (ⓣ07/307 1155), has poste restante facilities.

There's a reasonable selection of **accommodation** in Whakatane, much of it firmly mid-range with a preference for motels and campsites. Luxurious places are fairly thin on the ground and there is only one hostel.

Alton Lodge Motel 76 Domain Rd ⓣ07/307 1003 or 0800/500 468, ⓔaltonlodge@wave.co.nz. Comfortable modern motel with eleven luxury units with full kitchens and an indoor pool; good value. ❺

Briar Rose 54 Waiewe St ⓣ 07/308 0314, ⓔbriarrosewhk@hotmail.com. Very welcoming homestay B&B 1.5km uphill from the centre of Whakatane and surrounded by bird-filled bush. There's one room in the house and one self-contained cottage but you are encouraged to socialize in the house, and even stay for dinner ($25 by arrangement) which may well be wild pork or venison. ❹

Clifton Manor 5 Clifton Rd ⓣ & ⓕ07/307 2145, ⓣ0800/307 214, ⓔcliftonmanor@xtra.co.nz. Lovely, friendly old home with a large swimming pool, three well-kept guest rooms (some with private bath) let on a B&B basis, and two self-contained motel units. ❹

Karibu Backpackers 13 Landing Rd ⓣ & ⓕ07/307 8276. A suburban house converted into a well-maintained and welcoming hostel a short walk from town, with free bikes and free pick-up from the bus stop. Tent sites $10, dorm and four-share rooms ❶, made-up doubles ❷

Motuhora 2 Motohura Rise ⓣ07/307 0224, ⓔjtspell@xtra.co.nz. Attractive top-end B&B high above the town, with just two tastefully decorated, well-appointed rooms sharing access to an outdoor spa pool. ❼

Ohope Beach Top 10 Holiday Park Harbour Rd, 10km east of Whakatane ⓣ & ⓕ07/312 4460, ⓔohopebeach@xtra.co.nz. Upscale holiday park right behind at Ohope Beach with a pool complex, camping ($11) and a range of cabins, kitchen cabins, self-contained units and motel units. ❷–❹

Tourist Court Motel 50 Landing Rd ⓣ07/308

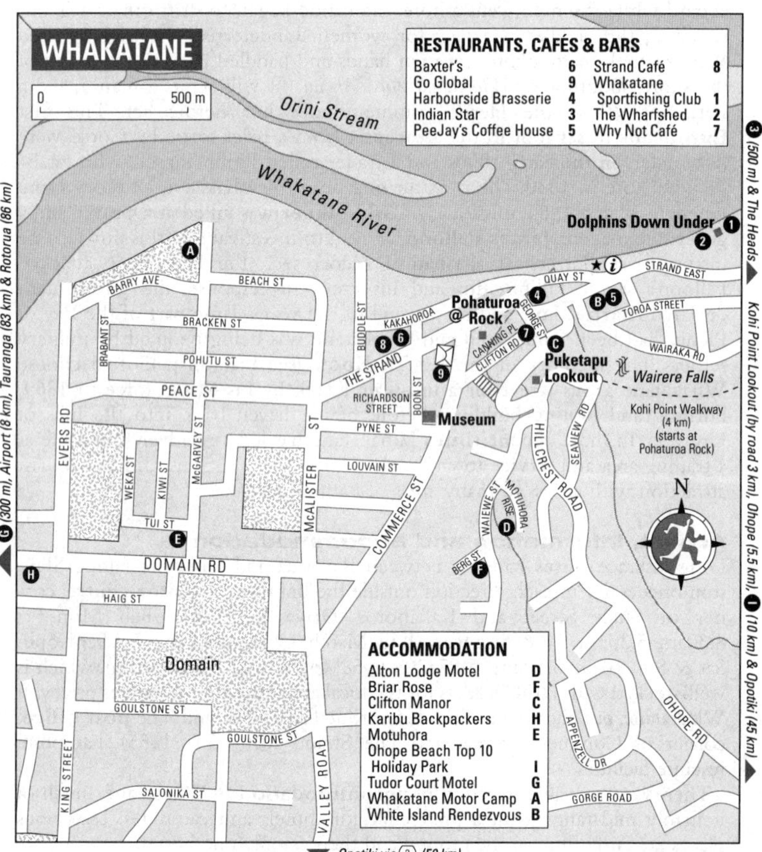

7099, Ⓕ307 0821. A very friendly establishment with eight fully self-contained, clean and comfortable units and a retro 1970s feel. ❸

Whakatane Motor Camp McGarvey Rd Ⓣ07/308 8694, Ⓕ308 2070. A reasonable, sheltered campsite ten minutes' walk from The Strand. Tent sites $10, cabins ❷

White Island Rendezvous 15 The Strand Ⓣ07/308 9500 & 0800/242 299, Ⓦwww.whiteisland.co.nz. Smart, modern motel with clean rooms (some with spa) attractively decorated in blues and greens, and equipped with Sky TV and microwave. Downstairs units have polished wooden floors, upstairs units have sea views. ❺

The Town

Driving into Whakatane, Commerce Street hugs cliffs which were once lapped by the sea. The junction with The Strand is effectively the town centre, marked by Whakatane's defining feature, a large rock outcrop called **Pohaturoa** ("long rock"). The place is sacred to Maori and the small park surrounding the rock contains a canoe, carved benches and a black marble monument to Te Hurinui Apanui, a great chief who propounded the virtues of peace and is mourned by Pakeha and Maori alike. This site was once a shrine where rites were performed by Maori priests, and the seed that grew into the karaka trees at its base are said to have arrived on the *Mataatua* canoe. From here, it is a short walk along Canning Street to the base of **Wairere Falls** (see box below) from where you can rejoin The Strand and stroll a kilometre along the river to the heads, a lovely late afternoon walk rewarded by the sight of the bronze statue of Wairaka on top of the rock, often behatted by local wags after a good night out.

Back in town, the **Whakatane & Districts Museum and Gallery** (Mon–Fri 10am–4.30pm, Sat 11am–1.30pm, Sun 2–4pm; $2 donation; Ⓦwww.whakatanemuseum.co.nz) lies on Boon Street with a steam engine from Tunnicliffe's Sawmill outside. Travelling exhibitions occupy the small gallery section, adjacent to which is the main museum, just one room packed with well-conceived displays on geological, Maori and European history – particularly as they relate to the Eastern Bay of Plenty. The collection is rich and varied with over 25,000 photographs and an important collection of Maori

Kohi Point Lookout walk

There are several interesting **walks** in the area, all detailed in the *Walks Around Whakatane* booklet available free from the visitor centre. Easily the best is to **Kohi Point Lookout** (8km loop; 3hr 30min), combining part of the Whakatane Town Centre Walk with the Nga Tapuwae o Toi ("Sacred Footsteps of Toi") Walkway, which traverses the domain of the great chieftain Toi, and ends at Kohi Point with panoramic views of Whakatane, Whale and White islands and Te Urewera National Park.

The walk starts in Commerce Street, from where you turn right between the escarpment and Pohaturoa, climb the steps to Hillcrest Road, then cross over to Seaview Road, where you will find the track leading to **Ka-pu-Terangi**, which passes the head of the **Wairere Falls**, a cool and peaceful spot. From here you walk through regenerating bush to the **Toi pa**, reputedly the oldest in New Zealand. The track continues along the cliff top past a number of other *pa* sites and food pits through more bushland, including honeysuckle and pohutukawa, before emerging onto flax and scrub towards the Kohi Point. If you wish, you can continue from here along the headlands to **Otarawairere Bay**, an excellent swimming and picnic spot; the steep walk down to the bay is quite beautiful, as is the bay itself. From here you can press **on to Ohope**, but the scenery doesn't get any better and the return journey makes for a long and tiring day.

taonga (treasures) from the local *iwi*, tracing their descent from the *Mataatua* canoe.

As regards activities in and around town, you can get out on the local **Rangitaiki River** with Kiwi Jetboat Tours (Ⓣ & Ⓕ07/307 0663 or Ⓣ0800/800 538, Ⓔkiwijet@xtra.co.nz; 1hr 15min; $60), run by an ex-world champion jetboat racer who will take you from the Matahina Dam, 25km south of Whakatane, to the beautiful Aniwhenua Falls over a number of modest whitewater sections. There are also innumerable **fishing** guides, mostly working on a charter basis from the local marina; check at the visitor centre for the best deals.

Ohope

Seven kilometres east of Whakatane, the tiny settlement of **OHOPE** extends along the beach in a thin ribbon to the entrance of **Ohiwa Harbour**. Ohiwa ("a place of watchfulness") is the site of a natural shellfishery for pipi and cockles, and a place of numerous *pa* sites, signifying the importance of a convenient and renewable food source to the Maori way of life. Its fecund waters can be explored on two-hour **eco-tours** with Ohiwa Harbour Tours (Ⓣ07/308 7837;

Whale Island and White Island

Whale Island (Motohora), 10km offshore from Whakatane, is a DOC-controlled haven where, in the 1980s, considerable efforts were made to eradicate goats and rats. Native bush is now rapidly returning and the island has become a bird reserve and safe environment for saddlebacks, grey-faced petrels, sooty shearwaters, little blue penguins, dotterels, oystercatchers, as well as three species of lizard – geckos and speckled and copper skinks – and the reptilian tuatara; there are also occasional visits made by the North Island kaka and falcon, as well as fur seals.

Once the site of a **pa**, the island's inhabitants sent out several canoes when Cook was tacking near its coastline and some **trading** took place. The history of the island is quiet from then until 1829, when a trading schooner, *Haweis*, was attacked by the Nga Tiwawa chief, who wanted to get hold of the muskets aboard the ship to defend himself against neighbouring *iwi*. The attack took place while some members of the crew were ashore on the island, salting pork. Noticing something was amiss, they rowed for their lives to Tauranga, where they met the schooner *New Zealander*, which duly sailed back and regained control of the *Haweis*.

Access to the island is on one of only half a dozen full-day **guided tours** a year (between Dec and mid-Feb), which depart from Whakatane and can be arranged through the visitor centre for around $50 per person. If you can face a 7am start, you're likely to be rewarded by calm seas and light winds on a **dolphin swimming** tour (3–4hr; $100) with Dolphins Down Under, 2 The Strand (Ⓣ07/308 4636 & 0800/354 773, Ⓦwww.dolphinswim.co.nz), who also do excellent **snorkelling trips** around Whale Island (Christmas to mid-Jan; 6pm; $35). All gear is supplied and you should book a couple of days in advance between December and February.

White Island

Many people ignore Whale Island in favour of the more obvious and spectacular attractions of **White Island** (Whaakari), so named by Cook for its permanent shroud of mist and steam. Over twice the size of Whale Island, White Island lies a sometimes-rough 50km offshore. Neither this nor its seething vulcanism deters visitors, who flock to appreciate its desolate, other worldly landscape, with its billowing towers of gas, steam and ash, spewing from a crater lake sixty metres

$55), with a very knowledgeable guide imparting much of the area's history and giving a insight into the birdlife and estuarine ecology. Trips depart from the wharf at the eastern end of Ohope, generally around high tide, and pickups can be arranged. Otherwise, this is very much a beach resort, and when you've had enough of the surf and sand you'll want to press on, though Ohope makes a pleasant enough base from which to explore Whakatane and its surroundings. Ohope's **accommodation** is crammed to bursting between December and the end of January – when you'll be lucky to find anything and will probably have to retreat to Whakatane – but is quiet the rest of the year (see p.423–425 for listings). If you're just after supplies of fresh seafood, stop off at the *Ohiwa Oyster Farm* (daily 10am–7pm), a shack beside Ohiwa Harbour, 1km south of the beach and the road to Opotiki.

Eating, drinking and entertainment

Whakatane isn't quite up to speed with café culture, but it is getting there with decent espressos available and a couple of appealing waterside **restaurants** doubling as good spots for an evening tipple. There's virtually no entertainment, except for the **Cinema 5** multiplex, 99 The Strand (☎07/308 7623).

below sea level, and to marvel at the smaller fumaroles surrounded by garish yellow and white crystal deposits that re-form in new and bizarre shapes each day.

Whaakari is a living embodiment of the ongoing clash between the Indo-Australian Plate and the Pacific Plate which has been driven beneath it for the last two million years. This resulted in the upwards thrust of super-heated rock through the ocean floor creating a massive **volcanic** structure. **Sulphur**, for use in fertilizer manufacture, was sporadically mined on the island from the 1880s, but all enterprises were plagued by catastrophic eruptions, landslides and economic misfortune. The island was abandoned in 1934, and these days is home only to 60,000 grey-faced **petrels** and 10,000 **gannets**.

An excellent **guided boat trip** to White Island is run from Whakatane by PeeJay Charters (☎07/308 9588 & 0800/733529, ⓦwww.whiteisland.co.nz; daily 8.30am; 5hr; $110, including lunch); book at least a couple of days in advance. After a fairly precarious transfer to the shallow-water jetty, the two-hour tour of the island begins at the site of a 1924 sulphur processing factory, which is gradually being eaten away by the high sulphur content of the atmosphere, and progresses to the open-sided crater. Here, amid pools of bubbling mud and skyscraper pillars of smoke and steam, you get the chance to stand in the wind-driven clouds (with a gas mask on) and experience a spooky and disorienting white-out.

With plenty of cash and clement weather, you can also visit White Island by **helicopter** with Vulcan Helicopters (☎07/308 4188 & 0800/804 354, ⓦwww.vulcanheli.co.nz; 3hr; $375, including a walking tour of the island). East Bay Flight Centre (☎07/308 8446 & 0800/550 880, ⓦwww.ebfc.co.nz) operates a number of **scenic flights** over White Island (45min; $170; min 2 passengers).

An often-spotted resident pod of common dolphins, clear water and stacks of fish make White Island a great place to go **swimming with dolphins**. Dolphins Down Under (see above) runs trips out to the island (5–6hr; $135) departing at 11am, with good views into the crater as an added bonus. For more committed undersea explorers, Dive White Island, 186 The Strand (☎0800/348 394, ⓦwww.divewhite.co.nz) offers **dive trips** (usually with 2 dives) out to the waters off White Island where visibility is commonly around 20m. Costs range from $125 with your own gear, to $189 for full rental and $250 for a beginner's dive with an instructor.

Baxter's 208–210 The Strand. A simple but good-value daytime establishment with a traditional tea-room atmosphere. Closed Sun.

Go Global cnr The Strand & Commercial St. A pleasant first-floor bistro-style place with balcony views. The menu plunders the world with the likes of Thai seafood hotpot, Madras curry, kangaroo loin fillet and vegetarian enchilada, plus a good range of fresh seafood, all around $20. Closed Sun; licensed & BYO.

Harbourside Brasserie 62 The Strand ⓣ07/308 6721, reservations recommended. A light and airy, popular family restaurant, serving the biggest and meanest steaks in town at reasonable prices. Also a selection of lamb and poultry dishes of equally large proportions.

Indian Star The Heads, Muriwai Drive. Decent curry restaurant with all the usual favourites, well sited overlooking Whakatane Harbour entrance.

PeeJay's Coffee House 15 The Strand. The best espressos in town help wash down mostly vegetarian quiches, salads, muffins and cakes. Located in the *Rendezvous Motel* building.

Pohutukawa Café 19 Pohutukawa Ave, Ohope. A stylish café and bar out at Whakatane's best beach, serving coffees and an eclectic range of dishes from $10–25.

Strand Café 214 The Strand. The best place to eat in town at any time of the day. A relaxed café with simple, colourful decor and reasonable prices. A variety of excellent breakfasts, snacks and main courses such as lamb kebabs, seafood and steaks, and some mouth-watering desserts.

Whakatane Sportfishing Club The Strand. Spacious public bar with huge windows overlooking the boats and river, great for cheap drinks, good-value bar meals at lunch and dinner, and a Friday and Saturday evening smorgasbord ($17). It is a private club, but visitors can just stroll up to the bar and ask to be signed in.

The Wharfshed The Strand ⓣ07/308 5698. Smart, modern café that's great for watching the sun set over the river while tucking into the like of sautéed scallops on oven-roasted tomatoes ($14) and beer-battered tarakihi with fries and tomato mayo ($22).

Why Not Café in the *Whakatane Hotel*, cnr The Strand & George St. A friendly and welcoming little eatery and bar, serving lunches and dinners ($17–23), including steaks and delicious seafood fettuccine. Daily 11am–midnight.

Opotiki

The small settlement of **OPOTIKI**, 60km east of Whakatane, is the easternmost town in the Bay of Plenty and makes a useful stopping-off point for exploring its beautiful surroundings. Though it doesn't amount to much in itself, it does act as an effective gateway to Eastland and is your last place to stock up on supplies and petrol before heading on.

From Opotiki, **SH2** strikes inland **to Gisborne**, while **SH35** meanders along the more circumspect roads around the perimeter of **Eastland**, never straying far from its rugged and windswept coastline.

Arrival, information and accommodation

InterCity **buses** from Whakatane and Gisborne drop off on Bridge Street near its junction with Opotiki's main drag, Church Street. From here it is five blocks to the combined **visitor centre** and **DOC office**, on the corner of St John and Elliott streets (Mon–Fri 8am–5pm, plus mid-Dec to Jan Sat & Sun 10am–3pm; ⓣ07/315 8484, ⓦwww.eastlandnz.com), a good place to pick up information and advice for Opotiki and the whole of the Eastland region.

For **accommodation** Opotiki has a couple of very good **hostels**: the cosy and friendly *Central Oasis Backpackers*, 30 King St (ⓣ07/315 5165, ⓔcentraloasis@hotmail.com; camping $8, dorms ❶, rooms ❷), in a hundred-year-old renovated kauri villa right in town and with free bikes; and the laid-back *Opotiki Backpackers Beach House*, 7 Appleton Rd, 5km west of Opotiki on SH2 (ⓣ07/315 5117; tents $10, dorms ❶, room ❷), right by the beach and with free use of kayaks, body boards, fishing rods and so forth. *Eastland Pacific Motor Lodge*, 44 St Johns St (ⓣ07/315 5524 & 0800/103 003, ⓦwww.eastlandpacific.co.nz), is probably the best of the **motels**, with comfortable modern

The Hau Hau

Missionaries encouraged many Maori to abandon their belief structure in favour of a zealous **Christianity**, but as land disputes with settlers escalated the Maori increasingly perceived the missionaries as agents for land-hungry Europeans.

When **war** broke out and the recently converted Maori suffered defeats, they felt betrayed not only by the Crown but also by their newly acquired god, and some formed the revivalist **Hau Hau** movement, based on the Old Testament. Dedicated to routing the interlopers, disciples danced around **nui poles**, chanting for the *Pakeha* to leave the country. The name is derived from the **battle cry** of the warriors, who flung themselves at their enemies with their right arms raised to protect them from bullets, believing that true faith prevented them from being shot. The movement began in 1862 and by 1865, having capitalized on widespread Maori unrest at the land situation, there was a *nui* pole in most villages of any size from Wellington to the Waikato. The Hau Hau were some of the most feared **warriors** and involved in the bloodiest and bitterest battles, but the movement began to fade after their **leader** and founder, Te Ua Haumene, was captured in 1866. Some of the sect's ideas were **revitalized** when the infamous rebel **Te Kooti** (see box on p.456) based parts of his **Ringatu** movement on Hau Hau doctrine.

units (❹–❺), some with spa baths; but *Fantail Cottage* **B&B**, 318 Ohiwa Harbour Rd, 9km west of Opotiki (Ⓣ07/315 4981; ❹, dinner by arrangement $25), is a more peaceful and intimate place to stay, in a house with panoramic harbour views and an outdoor spa. Heading 15km south on SH2, you'll find *Riverview Cottage* (Ⓣ & Ⓕ07/315 5553, Ⓔriverview.cottage@xtra.co.nz; ❻), a modern and spacious two-bedroom cottage on a property that runs down to the Waioeka River where the hosts run kayak trips (see p.430).

Campers wanting to stay centrally should try the sheltered and well-kept *Opotiki Holiday Park* (Ⓣ & Ⓕ07/315 6050; camping $9, on-site vans & cabins ❷–❹), on the corner of Potts Avenue and Grey Street: follow Elliot Street west to the war memorial then 100m right along Potts Avenue. For a more rural setting, head 6km east along SH35 to *Tirohanga Beach Holiday Park* (Ⓣ & Ⓕ07/315 7942; camping $9, bunks ❶, cabins ❷), right by the beach.

The Town and around

Opotiki has few sights of interest to delay your departure for the wilds of Eastland or the bright lights of Gisborne, but it does have some lush countryside and beaches around it. All the significant historic buildings cluster around the junction of Church and Elliot streets, including the **Opotiki Museum**, 123 Church St (Mon–Sat 10am–3.30pm, Sun 1.30–4pm; $2), which occupies the site of the livery stables once used by the overland stagecoach to Whakatane. Its collection is garnered from the local area, resulting in the usual ill-assorted domestic, farming and military bric-a-brac, here ameliorated by an extensive range of black and white photographs. Opposite, the innocent-looking white clapboard **St Stephen's Church**, set among trees and chirruping birds, was once the scene of a notorious murder, for it was here, in March 1865, that local missionary **Carl Völkner** was allegedly killed by a prophet, Kereopa Te Rau, from the militant Hau Hau sect (see box above). The case is far from clear-cut, however: at the time, many Maori believed that missionaries doubled as spies, duly reporting their findings to the settlers and military, and it appears that Völkner had indeed written many letters to Governor Grey espousing settlers' land-grabbing ambitions. Local Maori claim Völkner was justly executed after being confronted with the evidence and denounced as a traitor. Whatever the truth, the settlers used the story as propaganda, fuelling intermittent skirmishes over the next three years. The museum will usually let you have a key so that you can nip in and see the gorgeous *tukutuku* panels around the altar and Völkner's grave beside it.

The small and unspoiled **Opotiki (Hukutaia) Domain** (dawn–dusk; free) is full of native palms, lianas and trees, including a two-century-old puriri tree once used as a burial tree by local Maori. There is also a good lookout over the Waioeka Valley and a series of short but interesting rainforest tracks. To get to the domain, head south from the centre of town on Church Street as far as the Waioweka River Bridge, cross it and then bear left along Woodlands Road for 7km.

Getting a little more active, there are water-based activities either on the **Waioeka River** south of town, or on the **Motu River** which surges through the hills to the east of Opotiki and meets the sea 45km to the northeast. On the former, Waioeka River Kayak Trips (ⓣ & ⓕ07/315 5553, ⓔriverview.cottage@xtra.co.nz) runs gentle three-hour paddles down a beautiful stretch of river for $39($49 with barbecue lunch). There are superb backcountry **rafting trips** (see box, below) on the Motu River, and scenic flat-water **jetboating** with either Motu River Jet Boat Tours (ⓣ07/315 8107) or Motu AAA (ⓣ025/686 6489); both offer comparable trips (booking essential) from $30 for half an hour to around $80 for the full two and half hours on the lower 50km.

Eating

There are a number of small daytime **cafés** in town, the best being the *Flying Pig*, right in town at 97 Church St, and the *Hot Bread Shop Café*, on the corner of Bridge and St John streets, which does the town's best coffee. Once these close, things get pretty sketchy with only a handful of burger bars, some doing sit-in steak and egg dinners until around 7.30pm. Decent, traditional **meals** are served at the *Masonic Hotel*, a large colonial-style building on Church Street, but in fine weather you could do a lot worse than a newspaper full of **fish and chips** from the *Ocean Seafoods Fish and Chips* at 88 Church St.

Wilderness rafting on the Motu River

Some of the best **wilderness rafting** trips in New Zealand are on the Grade III–IV **Motu River**, which is hidden deep in the mountain terrain of the remote Raukumara Ranges, with long stretches of white water plunging through gorges and valleys to the Bay of Plenty coast. In 1981, after a protracted campaign against hydro dam builders, the Motu became New Zealand's first designated "wild and scenic" river. Access by 4WD, helicopter and jetboat makes one- and two-day trips possible, but to capture the essence of this remote region you should consider one of the longer trips when you'll see no sign of civilization for three days – a magical and eerie experience.

Rotorua-based Wet 'n' Wild Rafting (ⓣ07/348 3191 & 0800/462 723, ⓦwww.wetnwildrafting.co.nz) starts trips from Opotiki, generally using 4WD vehicles to get you in there. On all but the dedicated wilderness trips, the final flat drift to the coast is skipped in favour of a jetboat ride. Trips range from a two-day trip ($535; with helicopter access $690), to the full four-day adventure ($635) from the headwaters to the sea. In all cases transport, camping equipment and food are provided, though you may need to supply your own sleeping bag.

The Inland Route to Gisborne

From Opotiki, **SH2** strikes out south to **Gisborne** (137km away), dotted with tiny settlements as it twists its way through the scenic and bush-clad **Waioeka Gorge**. Following the river for 30km, the route becomes increasingly narrow and steep before emerging onto rolling pastureland on the Gisborne side and dropping to plains. From there it runs straight as an arrow through orchards, vineyards and sheep farms to Gisborne (covered in Chapter Six; see p.442). The only part of the route worth breaking your journey for, or exploring from Opotiki, is the first 72-kilometre stretch to Matawai, along which a number of interesting **walks** branch off either side of the road. Ten scenic tracks through forest, ranging from fifteen minutes to ten hours one way, are described in the DOC leaflet *Walks in Waioeka and Urutawa* ($1), available at Opotiki visitor centre. This is also where you'll find *Riverview Cottage* and Waioeka River Kayak Trips (see both above).

Eastland

Eastland, the nub of land jutting northeast of Opotiki and Gisborne out into the South Pacific, is one of the most sparsely populated areas in New Zealand, rarely visited and something of a backwater lost in time. Between Opotiki and Gisborne, the Pacific Coast Highway (SH35) runs 330 scenic kilometres around the peninsula hugging the rugged coastline much of the way and providing spectacular views out to sea on a fine day.

As soon as you enter the region you'll notice a change of pace, epitomized from time to time by the sight of a lone horseback rider clopping along the road. This is one of the most unspoiled parts of the North Island, steeped in **Maori** history (see box overleaf) and not to be rushed. Contemporary Maori, who make up a significant percentage of Eastland's population, draw on their strong culture to cope with the hardships of this untamed landscape and uncertain economic prospects. Over eighty percent of land tenure here is in Maori hands, something which sits well with the people: most feel in greater control of their destiny than Maori do elsewhere.

Eastland is a reminder of how New Zealand once was, and the response to strangers splits into two camps: generally people are warm, friendly and uncommonly welcoming, though sometimes there's a slightly intimidating standoffishness, which usually evaporates with a little openness and acceptance on your part. As for the **climate**, it tends towards extremes – hot in summer, wet in winter, and extremely changeable at any time of year.

The **coast** is very much the focus here, and whatever time isn't spent gazing out of the car or bus window is likely to be consumed on the beach or in the water. That said, there are limited hiking opportunities, and just about everywhere you go there will be someone happy to take you **horse trekking**, either along the beach or into the bush. In general, the **towns**, such as they are, don't have much to recommend them and you're better off planning to stay between towns, though at weekends you might like to find a pub if you fancy a country music jukebox singalong.

Inland, a central core of mountains runs through Eastland: the inhospitable **Waiapu Mountains**, encompassing the northeastern Raukumara Range and the typical native flora of the Raukumara Forest Park. The isolated and rugged peaks of Hikurangi, Whanokao, Aroangi, Wharekia and Tatai provide a spectacular backdrop to the coastal scenery, but are only accessible through **Maori**

land and **permission** must be sought (further information is available at the DOC offices in Gisborne and Opotiki).

Eastland practicalities

The road is completely sealed all the way round the coast, but twists in and out of small bays so much that driving right around takes a full six hours, though three or four days is better. The further around you go, the fewer the **services**, including food stores and petrol pumps.

Public transport in Eastland is limited; a few **shuttle bus** services do exist but timetables change frequently and you'll need to call to check. Currently there is no service doing the whole Opotiki–Gisborne run in one day so you'll need to break your journey in Hicks Bay or Te Araroa. For more information contact the Gisborne or Opotiki visitor centres, or call Polly's Couriers (☎06/864 4728), Cook's Couriers (☎06/ 864 4711) or Matakaoa Coastline (☎0800/628 252). Note that Saturday service is very limited and there are no buses on Sunday, but with detailed planning you could manage half a dozen stops in three or four days.

Campsites are the staple accommodation along much of the route, though free beachside camping (once the norm) is now outlawed just about everywhere. **Hostels** are fairly liberally scattered along the route along with the odd motel and B&B, but upscale accommodation is almost non-existent.

Legends of the Eastland Maori

According to legend, a great *ariki* (leader) from Eastland was drowned by rival tribesmen and his youngest daughter swore vengeance: when she gave birth to a son called **Tuwhakairiora**, she hoped he would make good her promise. As a young man, Tuwhakairiora travelled and encountered a young woman named **Ruataupare**; she took him to her father, who happened to be the local chief. A thunderstorm broke, signalling to the people that they had an important visitor among them, and Tuwhakairiora was allowed to marry Ruataupare and live in Te Araroa. When he called upon all the *hapu* of the area to gather and avenge the death of his grandfather, many warriors travelled to Whareponga and sacked the *pa* there. Tuwhakairiora became renowned as a famous warrior, dominating the area from **Tolaga Bay** to Cape Runaway, and all Maori families in the region today trace their descent from him.

Ruataupare, meanwhile, grew jealous of her husband's influence. While their children were growing up, she constantly heard them referred to as the offspring of the great Tuwhakairiora, yet her name was barely mentioned. She returned to her own *iwi* in **Tokomaru Bay**, where she summoned all the warriors together and started a war against rival *iwi*; victorious, Ruataupare became chieftainess of Tokomaru Bay.

The other legend that has shaped this wild land is one of rivalry between two students – **Paoa**, who excelled at navigation, and **Rongokaka**, who was renowned for travelling at great speed by means of giant strides. At the time, a beautiful maiden, Muriwhenua, lived in Hauraki and many set off to claim her for their bride. Paoa set off early but his rival took only one step and was ahead of him; this continued up the coast, with Rongokaka leaving huge footprints as he went – his imprint in the rock at Matakaoa Point, at the northern end of Hicks Bay, is the most clearly distinguishable. En route, they created the **Waiapu Mountains**: Paoa, flummoxed by Rongokaka's pace, set a snare for his rival at Tokomaru Bay, lashing the crown of a giant totara tree to a hill; recognizing the trap, Rongokaka cut it loose. The force with which the tree sprang upright caused such vibration that Mount Hikurangi partly disintegrated, forming the other mountain peaks. Finally, Rongokaka stepped across the Bay of Plenty and up to Hauraki, where he claimed his maiden.

Notwithstanding a couple of steak-and-chips places attached to pubs and motels, there isn't anywhere in Eastland that you'd describe as a real **restaurant**. Unless you've arranged to stay in B&Bs which serve meals you really need to be prepared for self-catering, or accept a diet of toasted sandwiches and fish and chips.

Opotiki to Waihau Bay

The road from Opotiki to **Waihau Bay** covers 103km, generally sticking close to the sea, but frequently twisting up over steep bluffs only to drop back down to desolate beaches heavy with driftwood logs. These have been washed down from the Raukumara Range by the numerous rivers which reach the sea here, typically forming delightful fresh-water swimming holes. This is probably the section of East Cape where you'll want to spend most of your time. You'll find family campsites every few kilometres, none of them far from the beach but never right beside it either. Nonetheless, most make the best of their proximity to the sea with a wealth of aquatic activities offered to guests – from boogie boards and canoes to half-day fishing and dive trips – along with horse riding and bikes to search out your own secluded cove.

Omaio and Te Kaha

Leaving Opotiki you soon hit a section of the coast which sets the scene for the next couple of hours of driving. Swimming beaches are scarce initially and, once past Tirohanga, the only place you are likely to want to stop is *Oariki Farm House*, almost 40km east of Opotiki (Ⓣ & Ⓕ07/325 2578, Ⓔoariki@clear.net.nz; ❺), a gorgeous B&B and separate self-catering cottage completely surrounded by gardens and native bush and overlooking the sea. Call for directions, and either cook your own meals or eat three-course dinners ($30) made largely from organically grown produce. Some rooms have a balcony with views of White Island, and there are opportunities to go fishing and diving.

Continuing, you soon cross the Motu River and after 11km reach **Omaio** where there is a store with a petrol pump, and one of the very few places in these parts that you can **camp** free: turn sharp left onto Omaio Marae Road by the store. A further 13km on, the *Te Kaha Hotel* (Ⓣ & Ⓕ07/325 2830; ❹) marks the beginning of **Te Kaha**, a region which spreads 7km along the highway in a beautiful crescent shape, with spectacular headlands and a deserted beach strewn with driftwood. You can swim safely here and, 2km past the hotel, there's the *Te Kaha Holiday Park & Motels* (Ⓣ & Ⓕ07/325 2894; tent sites $9, dorms ❶, cabins ❸, motels ❹), a **campsite** with a store, post office and takeaway food as well as access to the shoreline.

Whanarua Bay

Te Kaha is about the closest land to White Island, 50km offshore, which remains in view as you continue 6km to the hospitable *Waikawa B&B* (Ⓣ & Ⓕ07/325 2070, Ⓔwaikawa.bnb@xtra.co.nz; ❹), a nice little spot above a rocky cove with a couple of en-suite **rooms** and cooked breakfast. The adjacent communities of **Whanarua Bay** and **Maraehako Bay**, 10km further on, make another ideal opportunity to stop and enjoy the beaches and rugged countryside. What's more there's abundant **budget accommodation**. At Whanarua Bay you can stay comfortably at *Robyn's Place* (Ⓣ07/325 2904; bunks ❶, room ❷), a small hostel with a personal touch and sea views from the veranda; or next door at the family-oriented *Rendezvous on the*

Coast Holiday Park (ⓣ & ⓕ07/325 2899, ⓔrotchp@clear.net.nz; tents $8, dorms ❶, cabins & flats ❷–❸), a large **campsite** with its own takeaway van, mountain bikes and kayaks. Continue half a kilometre and down a narrow drive to reach *Maraehako Bay Retreat* (ⓣ07/325 2648, ⓔthumbloon@paradise.net.nz; dorms ❶, rooms ❷), a small and intimate backpackers wonderfully located less than 10m from the water and with abundant opportunities to go kayaking, swimming and fishing, or out checking the crayfish pots with Pihi, the owner. If you're looking for something more basic, go no further than the beachside *Maraehako Camping Ground* (ⓣ07/325 2942; tents and campers $7), 400m along SH35 at the far end of Maraehako Bay, which has toilets and solar-heated showers.

Waihau Bay

Still hugging the coast, SH35 winds 13km to **Ruakokore**, where a picture perfect, white clapboard Anglican church stands on a promontory framed by the blue ocean. From here it is five minutes' drive to **Waihau Bay**, another sweeping crescent of sand and grass that's ideal for swimming, surfing and kayaking. The abundance of shellfish and flat fish here might encourage you to sling a line for a tasty supper from the wharf beside the *Waihau Bay Lodge*, which serves meals to unsuccessful fishers. There's also a store and post office, and 3km further on, the *Waihau Bay Holiday Park* (ⓣ07/325 3844, ⓕ325 3980; tents $9, dorm & on-site vans ❶, cabins ❷, motels ❹), which caters to campers with another store and the closest thing to a modern café – there's an espresso machine – between Opotiki and Gisborne. The best place to **stay** is the hospitable and friendly *Waihau Bay Homestay* (ⓣ07/325 3674, ⓔn.topia@clear.net.nz; ❹–❺), 1km on at the far end of the bay, with self-contained accommodation and an en-suite room (in a house overlooking the beach); book in advance for a superb $25 seafood dinner.

Lottin Point to Te Puia Springs

Beyond Waihau Bay the highway continues close to the water for a few more kilometres before veering inland at Cape Runaway, Eastland's northernmost point. For the next 125km you hardly see the coast again, with the significant exception of the area around Hicks Bay, Te Araroa and East Cape, the only real points of interest along this stretch. Further on, the church at Tikitiki, the East Cape's largest community at Ruatoria and the hot springs at Te Puia will only briefly distract you.

Keen anglers might want to make a 4km detour from the small community of Potaka, 25km east of Waihau Bay, north to **Lottin Point**, said to offer the best angling for **king fish** in New Zealand. **Accommodation** needs are catered for at the *Lottin Point Motel* (ⓣ & ⓕ06/864 4455; ❹) which has simple rooms, a restaurant, gear rental and bait.

Hicks Bay

The small coastal township of **HICKS BAY** (*Wharekahika*), 44km from Waihau Bay, shelters between headlands and rock bluffs about halfway along SH35. It was named after Lieutenant Zachariah Hicks of Cook's *Endeavour* expedition, who was the first to sight its black volcanic beach and popular sandy beach. Take time to explore the Hicks Bay region if you're interested in the numerous *pa* sites in varying states of repair, some of which were modified for musket fighting during the 1860 Hau Hau uprising.

Entering Hicks Bay on SH35 there's upmarket **accommodation** at *Te Puna*

Frontier (Ⓣ & Ⓕ06/864 4862, Ⓔtepuna@paradise.net.nz; ❻), a very attractive **B&B** with en-suite cottages each set in their own little garden, and a three-course dinner for $35. The owners also do a range of guided **horse treks** – from twilight rides to Tahuroa Plateau overlooking the bay, followed by mugs of manuka tea (2hr; $35), to all-day rides along the Wharekahia River with a campfire lunch ($70). Beachside accommodation in the area is provided by *Hicks Bay Backpackers Lodge*, Onepoto Beach Road (dorms ❶, rooms ❷), a pleasant, comfortable little **hostel** with a variety of canoes, bikes, fishing lines and wave skis to keep you amused.

Alternatively continue 2km east of Hicks Bay along SH35 to *Hicks Bay Motel Lodge* (Ⓣ06/864 4880 & 0800/200 077, Ⓕ864 4708; ❹–❺, where around a third of the units have cooking facilities; the motel also has a licensed **restaurant**, a **bar** and access to a glow-worm grotto for evening entertainment.

Te Araroa

From Hicks Bay SH35 climbs over a hill and drops back to the coast, 6km on, at the well-run *Te Araroa Holiday Park* (Ⓣ06/864 4873, Ⓕ864 4473; tent sites $8.50, dorms ❶, cabins ❷–❸), which has a handy shop, a takeaway van, and a small indoor **cinema** (the most easterly in the land) that screens recent releases during the summer and Easter school holidays; ask at the shop for programme details and tickets.

From here it is 4km to **East Cape Manuka Oil** on SH35 (Ⓦwww.manuka-products.com), a small producer of essential oils extracted from the genetically distinct manuka trees grown on the East Cape. A shop selling medicinal manuka oil products is soon to be supplemented by a café.

A further 2km on, the broad surf-washed shore of Kawakawa Bay is graced by the drab village of **TE ARAROA** ("long pathway") which marks the midway point between Opotiki and Gisborne. Te Araroa was once the domain of the famous Maori warrior Tuwhakairiora and of the legendary figure of Paikea, who is said to have arrived here on the back of a whale. Ironically, the first Europeans in the area occupied a **whaling station** not far from the present township. These days the settlement contains little more than a pub, petrol station, store and a takeaway selling spanking fresh **fish and chips**. In the grounds of the local school stands a giant pohutukawa tree, reputedly the largest in New Zealand.

East Cape Lighthouse

The New Zealand mainland's easternmost point is marked by the **East Cape Lighthouse**, reached by a good, partly sealed 21km road from Te Araroa: follow the sign east along the foreshore. It is a dramatic coastal run which ends in a car park from where you clamber up seven-hundred-odd steps to the lighthouse perched atop a 140m hill – an atmospheric spot with views inland to Raukumara Range, and seaward towards East Island, just offshore.

If you're relying on public transport along SH35, you can still get to East Cape on 4WD sunrise **trips** (Ⓣ06/864 4775; $25), which pick up at accommodation in the area before dawn in order to see the sunrise from the lighthouse.

Tikitiki, Ruatoria and Te Puia Springs

From Te Araroa SH35 cuts inland through 24km of sheep-farming country, before reaching **TIKITIKI**, a village which will only delay you long enough to peek inside the modest and recently restored Anglican **church**, on a rise as you enter the town. The plain wooden exterior hides a treasure trove of elaborate and fine Maori design, *tukutuku* and carving; unusually, the stained glass is also in Maori designs, and the rafters come painted in the colours of a Maori meeting-house.

Inland **RUATORIA**, 19km south of Tikitiki, is the largest town since Opotiki some two hundred kilometres back, though that's not saying much. The main highway skirts the town and only counts a petrol station, a pub, a couple of grocery shops and the *Kai Kart* takeaway (all on the main street) as temptation to visit. Alternatively, stay on SH35 for the *Mountain View* café and *Blue Boar* tavern, two kilometres south of town where you can tuck into chicken, fish and steak dinners for under $15, then lose to the locals at pool.

The hill country to the west of Ruatoria comes under the jurisdiction of the Raukumara Conservation Area, which includes the upper catchments of several rivers that drain into the Bay of Plenty. The desolate terrain and limited access discourage most visitors from exploring the park, but it is possible to tackle the tough, full-day trek up the 1754m **Mount Hikurangi** (the highest peak in the range), offering the early riser the opportunity of being among the first in New Zealand to see the sunrise. The local Ngati Porou control the land and you should consult local visitor centres for the latest access details.

At Kopuaroa, around 15km south of Ruatoria, a rough and unsealed loop road heads 6km to **Waipiro Bay**, a busy port in its heyday, but now a beautiful and secluded inlet. Phone ahead for instruction if you want to **stay** at the welcoming *Waikawa Lodge Backpackers* (Ⓣ06/864 6719; ❸), which has just two double rooms with stupendous views in a unique bush setting where you can muck in, or cater for yourself.

The loop road to Waipiro Bay rejoins SH35 at the small settlement of **TE PUIA SPRINGS**, where a small lake picturesquely surrounded by deciduous trees comes as something of a surprise after miles of green paddocks and cabbage trees. The eponymous sulphur-rich **hot springs** (roughly daily 6am–midnight; private pools $2 per person for 30min) gained popularity during the early 1900s as a way of easing aching bones, but have declined to comprise just one ivy-hung tank accommodating around six people. They sit behind the *Te Puia Hot Springs Hotel* (Ⓣ06/864 6755; ❸), which has a bar serving pub meals, simple rooms, and a basic campsite ($5).

Tokomaru Bay to Gisborne

At **Tokomaru Bay** the road emerges from the inland bush and pastoral country to reveal the North Island's east coast in all its glory. For the remaining 80km to **Gisborne** you stay mostly inland but catch frequent glimpses of yawning bays and crashing surf, accessed either on SH35 itself, or by taking short side roads to little-visited coves. In the days before a decent road was put in, this was a thriving area with coastal traders calling to drop off supplies and pick up sheep (or their dressed carcasses). The subsequent decline is most evident at Tokomaru Bay, though things pick up progressively as you approach Gisborne.

Tokomaru Bay

TOKOMARU BAY (or just "Toko"), 11km south of Te Puia Springs, makes a pretty decent place to idle away a couple of relaxed days exploring the steep green hills, rocky headlands and the broad expanse of **beach**, dotted with driftwood and pounded by surf. The Maori who settled here trace their descent to

Toi te Huatahi, the great navigator and the first to arrive from the ancestral home of Hawaiki. In 1865 the Mawhai Pa was the scene of several attacks by a party of Hau Hau, but they were repulsed by a small garrison of old men and women.

At the northern end of town, a long wooden wharf and ruined buildings of a freezing works (abattoir) testify to the former prosperity of this once-busy port, which thrived until improved road transport forced the factory's closure in 1953. The town now gets by on the merest hint of a craft industry; call at the irregularly open **craft shop** on Waitangi Street to see locals making flax goods, possum-fur hats, pottery and more.

There isn't a great deal to do here except take long walks on the beach or the short **waterfall walk** (3.5km; 45min) through regenerating bush – take the road along the beach towards the wharf, cross the concrete bridge and go through the gate on the other side, then follow the river round to the start of the track. If you tire of surfing and swimming, you can **explore on horseback** with a series of bush and beach treks (from $35 for 2hr) available at *Brian's Place* (see below), where the owner knows the country like the back of his hand.

Budget **accommodation** starts with the *Mayfair Camping Ground*, Waitangi Street (ⓣ & ⓕ06/864 5843; tent sites $8.50, cabins ❷), conveniently located beside the general store and petrol station. **Backpackers** should head to either the *House of the Rising Sun* on Potae Street (ⓣ06/864 5858, ⓔrising.sun.back.packers@xtra.co.nz; tents $10, dorms ❶, rooms ❷), which has good facilities and a great sunny veranda with sea views, or up the hill to *Brian's Place*, also on Potae Street (ⓣ06/864 5870; tents $10, dorms ❶, rooms ❷), a very small and welcoming place on the hill with two doubles (one with sunny balcony) and a loft dorm: horse riding and hunting trips optional.

Te Puka Tavern on Beach Road serves inexpensive pub **meals** in hefty portions but, as elsewhere in Eastland, self-catering is the way to go, and Toko even has a small supermarket, open daily on Waitangi Street. The pub is the only place in town for a drink and can be quite boisterous at the weekend.

Anaura Bay

Some 22km south from Tokomaru, a 6km-long sealed side road runs to rugged **ANAURA BAY**, a prized surf spot with a broad sweep of sand and jagged headlands. At the north end of the bay the **Anaura Scenic Reserve** harbours a large area of mixed broadleaf bush noted for its large puriri trees and abundance of native birds. Starting near the end of the road, and signposted to the west by the reserve, is the **Anaura Bay Walkway** (3.5km loop; 2hr), which follows the course of the Waipare Stream into thick green bush, up a gently climbing valley and then out into scrubland before turning back towards the bay and a lookout point with magnificent views.

Beside the beach immediately beyond the start of this walk there's a very basic DOC **campsite** (free), and at the opposite end of the bay, superbly sited just back from the beach, the simple *Anaura Bay Motorcamp* (ⓣ06/862 6380; camping $9), which always has a relaxed feel. Facilities are in the former schoolhouse and there's a store selling essentials: if they're not too busy the owners might arrange a visit to the local *marae*.

Tolaga Bay to Gisborne

TOLAGA BAY (*Uawa*), 36km from Tokomaru, is the first place since Opotiki with the tenor of a thriving, viable town; six hundred strong and one of the better-serviced communities in Eastland. Once again, rugged headlands enclose the bay which was the scene of a 1769 visit by Captain Cook and his crew. They are commemorated in the town's street names: Banks, Solander, Forester and, of course, Cook.

Cook, anchoring to replenish his stocks of food and water, named the bay "Tolaga", owing to a misinterpretation of the Maori name for the prevailing wind (correctly called *teraki*). One character who stayed a little longer – and may well have provided the historical basis for the character played by Harvey Keitel in the film *The Piano* – was an early flax trader called Barnet Burns. He wore full *moko*, and stayed in the bay for three years, marrying a Maori woman and fathering three sons, before decamping; his wife, Amotawa, went on to marry the great Maori chief Te Kani-a-Takirau.

Just over 1km south of town, Wharf Road cuts seaward past the start of **Cooks Cove Walkway** (2.6km; 45min), which involves a steep and often muddy climb through bush and birdlife, rewarding the effort with good views across the bay. Another 300m along Wharf Road you'll find the 660m-long concrete **wharf** itself, the longest concrete jetty in the southern hemisphere, jutting out past steep sandstone cliffs. Built in the late 1920s to service coastal shipping, it soon became redundant and is now in a near-ruinous state, and with no safety rails. It hasn't been used commercially since 1963, and is no longer strong enough for vehicles, though you can wander to the end which makes a picturesque spot for a picnic. A determined bunch of local residents are now trying to raise $3 million to preserve the structure and a collection vault is located by the entrance to the wharf.

Having seen the sights there's little reason to linger, but there is **accommodation** at the incongruous mock-Tudor *Tolaga Bay Inn*, on the corner of Solander and Cook streets (Ⓣ06/862 6856; ❹), with bright and cheerful rooms, meals served to guests, and a bar which occasionally sees live bands at weekends. There's also self-contained **homestay** at *Papatahi*, SH35, 3km north (Ⓣ & Ⓕ06/862 6623; ❹), and beachfront accommodation at *Tolaga Bay Motor Camp*, Wharf Road (Ⓣ & Ⓕ06/862 6716; tent sites $9, cabins & cottages ❷), which has a store and great views.

The 47-kilometre stretch from Tolaga Bay to Gisborne, via the small settlement of **Whangara**, becomes both tamer and bleaker the further south you travel, the land despoiled by clearance for farming. The road climbs in and out of more small bays, occasionally providing panoramic vistas of sea and close-ups of the slate-grey rock shelves that characterize this coast. Eventually, the comparatively enormous town of Gisborne (see p.444) looms into view.

Travel details

Buses

From Coromandel to: Thames (2–3 daily; 1hr 15min); Whitianga (1 daily; 1hr)
From Opotiki to: Gisborne, via SH2 (1 daily; 2hr); Hicks Bay via SH35 (2 daily; 3hr); Rotorua (1 daily 2hr 10min); Whakatane (1 daily; 40min).
From Paeroa to: Auckland (3 daily; 2hr 30min); Hamilton (1 daily; 1hr 30min).
From Tauranga to: Auckland (4–6 daily; 3hr 40min); Hamilton (1–2 daily; 2hr); Rotorua (4 daily; 1hr 30min); Taupo (4 daily; 2hr 30min).
From Te Aroha to: Hamilton (1 daily; 1hr 10min).
From Thames to: Auckland (5 daily; 2hr); Coromandel (2–3 daily; 1hr 15min); Hamilton (2 daily; 1hr 30min); Mount Maunganui (3 daily, 2hr);

Tauranga (3 daily; 1hr 45min); Whitianga (3 daily; 1hr 40min).
From Whakatane to: Gisborne (1 daily; 3hr); Kawerau (2 daily; 45min); Opotiki (1 daily; 40min); Rotorua (2 daily; 1hr 30min).
From Whitianga to: Coromandel (1 daily; 1hr); Thames (3 daily; 1hr 30min).

Flights

From Tauranga to: Auckland (5–7 daily; 40min); Wellington (2–3 daily; 1hr 20min).
From Whakatane to: Auckland (3–5 daily; 45min).
From Whitianga to: Auckland (2 daily; 30min), Great Barrier Island (3 weekly; 30min).

6

Poverty Bay, Hawke's Bay and the Wairarapa

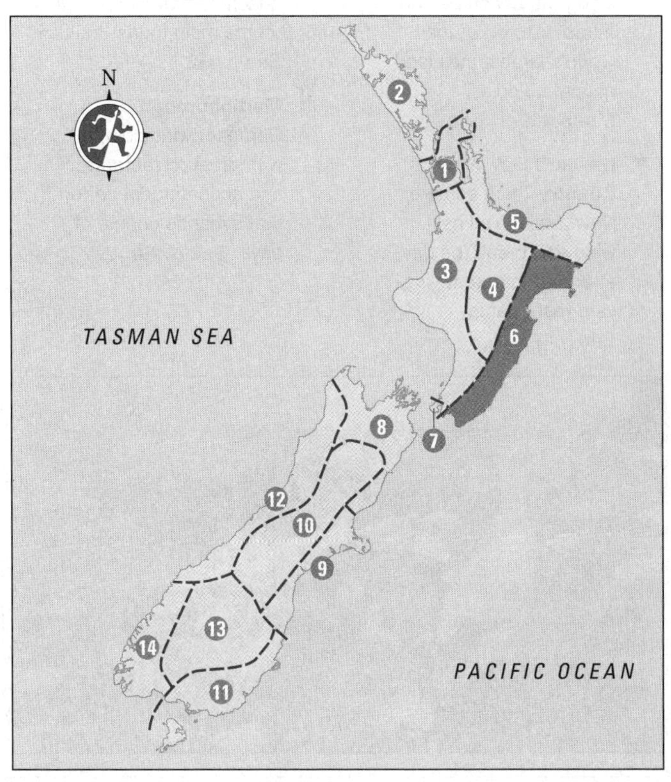

CHAPTER 6 Highlights

* **Lake Waikaremoana** Great bush scenery and a superb round-the-lake tramp. See p.455

* **Art Deco Napier** The world's finest collection of small scale Art Deco architecture is to be found in this pleasant town. See p.464

* **Cape Kidnappers** Ride along the beach behind a tractor to on of the world's largest mainland gannet colonies. See p.469

* **Hawke's Bay Wine Country** Taste some of New Zealand's finest wine and break the day at one of the great vineyard restaurants. See p.471

* **Rush Munroe's** Long-standing purveyor of rich and supremely fruity ice cream. See p.477

* **Golden Shears** Be in Masterton in early March for this Olympiad of sheep shearing. See p.481

* **Castlepoint** Wild and appealing, this isolated beach community is well off the main tourist trail. See p.482

* **Martinborough** Compact wine country with great restaurants and accommodation for that sybaritic couple of days. See p.484

6

Poverty Bay, Hawke's Bay and the Wairarapa

From the tip of Eastland, the North Island's mountainous backbone runs 650km southwest to the outskirts of Wellington, defining and isolating the **East Coast**. A region comprising the characteristically dry and sunny provinces of Poverty Bay, Hawke's Bay and the Wairarapa, this is sheep country. Large stations command the rich pastures of the expansive Heretaunga Plains around central Hawke's Bay and the sharp-ridged hill country to the north, the land frequently contoured into small terraces that are hallmarks of a young land eroded by overgrazing. But the region isn't all pastoral: the contiguous Raukumara, Kaweka, Ruahine, Tararua and Rimutaka mountain ranges protect much of the coast from the prevailing westerlies and cast a long rain shadow, the bane of farmers who watched their land become parched dirt, the grass leached to a dusty brown. Increasingly, these rain-shadow pastures are being given over to viticulture, and all three provinces are now noted **wine** regions. Any tour of the wineries would have to take in **Poverty Bay**, a major grape-growing region, where the main centre of **Gisborne** is both the first city in the world to see the light of the new day and was the first part of New Zealand sighted by Cook's expedition in 1769. Finding little but apparently hostile natives, he named it Poverty Bay and sailed off south across Hawke's Bay – named after Admiral Sir Edward Hawke, a boyhood hero of Cook's – to a second disastrous encounter with Maori at **Cape Kidnappers**, now the location of an impressive gannet colony.

The surrounding region of **Hawke's Bay** has long been dubbed "the fruit bowl of New Zealand", famed for orchard boughs sagging under the weight of prime apples, pears and peaches. In recent years the torch has passed to grapes, which have been producing the sort of fine vintages that enhance the Hawke's Bay wine country's reputation as one of the foremost in the country. The district is best visited from **Napier**, the single most appealing city on the East Coast, as much for its seafront location and range of minor attractions as for the wealth of Art Deco buildings constructed after the city was flattened

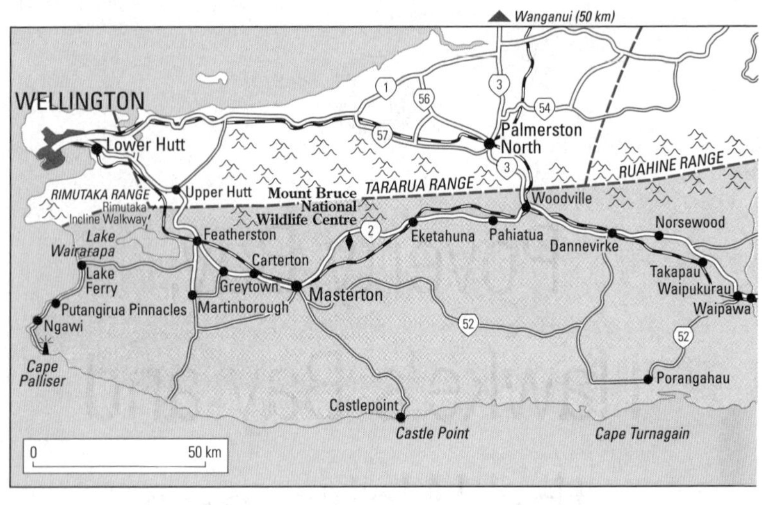

by a massive earthquake in 1931. Nearby **Hastings** suffered much the same fate and wove Spanish Mission-style buildings into the Art Deco fabric, though this won't delay you long from pressing on south through the uninspiring "Scandinavian" towns of southern Hawke's Bay. These run almost seamlessly into the similarly lacklustre settlements in the sheep lands of the **Wairarapa**, which takes its name from Lake Wairarapa ("glistening waters"), the eye in the fish that is the North Island, according to Maori legend. Unless you've a taste for the competitive sheepmanship of the Golden Shears competition in **Masterton**, the main goal in this region is **Martinborough**, surrounded by another collection of fine vineyards, most of which can be visited on foot.

Access to the mountainous **interior** of this region is limited, with only six roads winding over or cutting through the full length of the ranges. The most tortuous and one of the most scenic of these is SH38, which forges northwest from the small town of **Wairoa**, midway between Gisborne and Napier, to Rotorua. En route it wends its way through the remote wooded mountains of **Te Urewera National Park**, past beautiful Lake Waikaremoana, which is encircled by the four-day **Lake Waikaremoana Circuit** tramping route, as well as many appealing shorter lakeside strolls.

The East Coast is privileged to have the North Island's most appealing summertime **climate**: the grape-ripening heatwaves come with just enough sea breeze to make vigorous activity tolerable. The slight chill of spring and autumn mornings has its advocates, but winter can be cold and damp. As elsewhere, the **Christmas and January** madness packs out the motor camps and motels, but even Napier, the most visited destination, is manageable at this time.

Gisborne and around

The small city of **GISBORNE**, is New Zealand's easternmost city – and the first in the world to see the light of the new day. It is also one of New

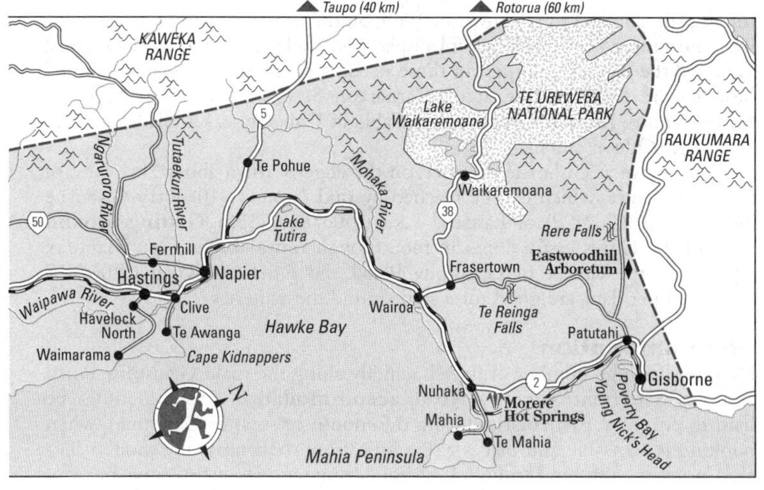

Zealand's more relaxing and gently appealing places, not overly endowed with brash entertainments, but easy-going enough for a peaceful day or so and with the chance to try surfing or view sharks in their natural habitat. Broad streets come lined with squat weatherboard houses, which are warmed by long hours of sunshine, and are interspersed with parkland hugging the flanks of the Pacific, the harbour and three rivers – the Taruheru, Turanganui and Waimata.

Gisborne holds a special place in the European history of New Zealand, for it was here in October 1769 that **James Cook** first set foot on the soil of *Aotearoa* – and immediately ran into conflict with local Maori, killing several before sailing away empty-handed. He named the landing site **Poverty Bay**, since "it did not afford a single item we wanted, except a little firewood". The fertility of the surrounding lands belies the appellation, but the name stuck and looks set to prevail, despite the wishes of some **Maori** who would rename it Turanganui a Kiwa – in honour of a Polynesian navigator, rather than continually harking back to that unfortunate first Maori–Pakeha encounter. Early nineteenth-century Poverty Bay remained staunchly Maori and few Pakeha moved here, discouraged by both the Hau Hau rebellion and Te Kooti's uprising (see box on p.456). It wasn't until the 1870s, when these had been contained, that **Europeans** felt safe enough to flock here in numbers to farm the rich alluvial river flats. A decent port wasn't constructed until the 1920s, after which sheep farming and market gardening really took off, activities only recently challenged by the ascendant grape harvest and the rise of plantation forestry.

Arrival, information and accommodation

Gisborne sits near the junction of the region's two main highways, SH35, which skirts the rugged coast of Eastland, and the inland SH2, which straddles the Raukumara Range and continues south to Napier. **Buses** along these route all converge on the **visitor centre**, 209 Grey St (daily 8.30am–5.30pm; ⓣ06/868 6139, ⓦwww.gisbornenz.com), which is heralded by a Canadian totem pole donated to the town in 1969, on the bicentennial of Cook's landing. The visitor centre has helpful displays on walks in Te Urewera National Park and the Waioeka Gorge, but those needing specialist outdoor info should head to the **DOC office** at 63 Carnarvon St (☎06/867 8531; Mon–Fri 8am–4.30pm). **Internet access** is available at Cyberzone, 83 Gladstone Rd, beside the Odeon cinema.

Flights arrive at Gisborne **airport**, on the edge of town about 2km west of the town centre, which can be reached by **taxi** (around $10) – try Gisborne Taxis (☎06/867 2222) or Eastland Taxis (☎06/868 1133). **Getting around** most of the city is easily done on foot, though **rental bikes** from Maintrax Cycles, on the corner of Gladstone Road and Roebuck Road (☎06/867 4571; $15 per day), are good for a spin around the wineries.

Accommodation

Despite the huge number of motels, chiefly along the main Gladstone Road and the waterfront Salisbury Road, **accommodation** can sometimes be hard to come by, particularly during the month or so after Christmas, when booking is advisable and prices rise a little from their normally modest levels. Campsites also tend to be full of holidaying families at this time, but you should be able to get into one of the Gisborne's clutch of mostly below-par hostels. B&Bs are relatively rare, but there are a few good places around the city.

Motels, B&Bs and homestays

Blue Pacific Beachfront 90 Salisbury Rd ☎06/868 6099, ⓦwww.seafront.co.nz. Presentable beachfront motel with fully-equipped units, a sauna and spa pool. ❺

Cedar House 4 Clifford St ☎06/868 1902, ⓦwww.cedarhouse.co.nz. Very appealing boutique B&B in a large Edwardian house with spacious, well appointed and tastefully decorated rooms. Breakfasts are great, and last all day. Rooms ❻, ensuites ❽

Endeavour Lodge Motel 525 Gladstone Rd ☎06/868 6075, ⓔendeavourlodge@telstra.co.nz. One of Gisborne's cheapest motels, but maintained to a high standard and equipped with an attractive pool. ❹

Sea View 68 Salisbury Rd ☎06/867 3879 & 0800/268 068, ⓔraewyn@regaleggs.co.nz). Attractive, modern beachfront B&B, a 10min walk into town. Both double rooms have their own bathrooms. ❺

Thomson Homestay 16 Rawiri St ☎ & ⓕ06/868 9675. Modest homestay with pleasant rooms, all sharing bathrooms; substantial breakfasts feature home-preserved fruit. Canoe available for guests' use. ❹

Whispering Sands 22 Salisbury Rd ☎06/867 1319 & 0800/405 030, ⓔwhisperingsandsmotel@xtra.co.nz. Luxurious beachfront motel with large modern units, all with great sea views. ❻

Hostels and campsites

Flying Nun 147 Roebuck Rd ☎06/868 0461, ⓔyager@xtra.co.nz. Reasonable hostel a 15min walk from town in a former convent, with a pool table in the chapel, where sofas take the place of the altar and the confessionals have become phone booths. Some of the spacious dorms front onto verandas, and singles cost little more than dorm beds; doubles tend to be a bit cramped. Campsites are available in the extensive grounds and there's Sky TV. Tent sites $10, dorms ❶, rooms ❷

Gisborne Backpackers/Sycamore Park 690 Gladstone Rd ☎06/868 1000, ⓔgisbornebp@xtra.co.nz. Somewhat sterile former orphanage but with good, clean facilities and a 15min walk from the centre. Doubles are especially spacious, dorms less so, and there's plenty of camping space in the grounds. Camping $10, dorms ❶, rooms ❷

Gisborne YHA 32 Harris St ☎06/868 3269, ⓔyha.gisborne@clear.net.nz. Well-run associate hostel in a large house with big grounds, conveniently close to town. Camping $10, dorms ❶, twins and doubles ❷

Showgrounds Park Motor Camp 20 Main Rd ☎06/867 5299, ⓦwww.gisborneshow.co.nz. The more distant of the two campsites, but with perfectly reasonable facilities and rock-bottom prices. Camping $12 per site, cabins ❷

Waikanae Beach Holiday Park Grey St

☎06/867 5634, ©motorcamp@gdc.govt.nz. Wonderfully sited motor park right by Gisborne's main beach and five minutes' walk from town, with tennis courts and comfortable cabins and flats. Camping $10, cabins ❷, kitchen cabins ❸

The Town

Perhaps more than any other East Coast town, Gisborne makes the best of its location, with almost everywhere in this compact city an easy stroll from the excellent and popular swimming and sunbathing strand of **Midway Beach**. Elsewhere, pleasant parks and green spaces run along the three rivers which converge at the largely disused harbour, below the steep hummock of Kaiti Hill.

Most of Gisborne's sights are connected in some way to the historical accident of Cook's landing and the dynamic between Maori and Pakeha cultures it engendered. The first of James Cook's crew to spy the mountains of *Aotearoa*, a couple of days before the first landing, was the twelve-year-old surgeon's boy **Nick Young**, who thereby claimed the gallon of rum Cook had offered as a reward. Honouring a second pledge, Cook recorded this white-cliffed promontory, 10km south of Gisborne across Poverty Bay, on his chart as Young Nick's Head. Young's keen eyes are commemorated with a pained-looking statue on the western side of the rivermouth in Gisborne, next to a modern millennial **statue of Cook** looking commanding in a tricorn hat atop a stone hemisphere.

Three long blocks to the northeast in Heipipi Park, early Maori explorers are commemorated with **Te Tauihu Turanga Whakamana** – a striking wooden sculpture depicting a Maori *tauihu* (canoe prow) carved with images of Tangaroa (god of the sea), the demi-god Maui, and Toi Kai Rakau (one of the earliest Maori to settle in New Zealand).

Five minutes' walk north of here, the **Tairawhiti Museum**, 18 Stout St (Christmas–Jan daily 11am–4pm; Feb–Christmas Mon–Fri 10am–4pm & Sat–Sun 1.30–4pm; donations), sits on the bank of the Waimata River. Frequently changing shows augment extensive displays on East Coast Maori and a strong line in contemporary Maori arts including beautiful *kete* (flax baskets) and greenstone finely carved into *tiki* (pendants). Recent extensions have created a maritime wing that neatly incorporates the original wheelhouse and captain's quarters of the 12,000-tonne *Star of Canada*, which ran aground on the reef off Gisborne's Kaiti Beach in 1912. Most of the ship was scuttled but the bridge was turned into Gisborne's most distinctive house, a role it fulfilled for seventy years before being bequeathed to the city and moved to its present site. The rest of the maritime section is devoted to exhibits on Cook's arrival, the role of shipping, coastal wrecks and a devotional shrine of the local surfing.

Several disused buildings from around the region are clustered outside the museum, notably the six-room 1872 **Wyllie Cottage**, the oldest extant house in town, and the **Sled House**, built on runners at the time of the Hau Hau uprising (see box on p.429) so that it could be hauled away by a team of bullocks at the first sign of unrest.

The less historically minded might prefer a visit to the small **Sunshine Brewery**, 109 Disraeli St (Mon–Sat 9am–6pm), an excellent, award-winning boutique brewhouse that sells its Pilsener-style Gisborne gold and malt stout Black Magic all over town and particularly in Wellington. Brief tours are available and the shop prices are the best around.

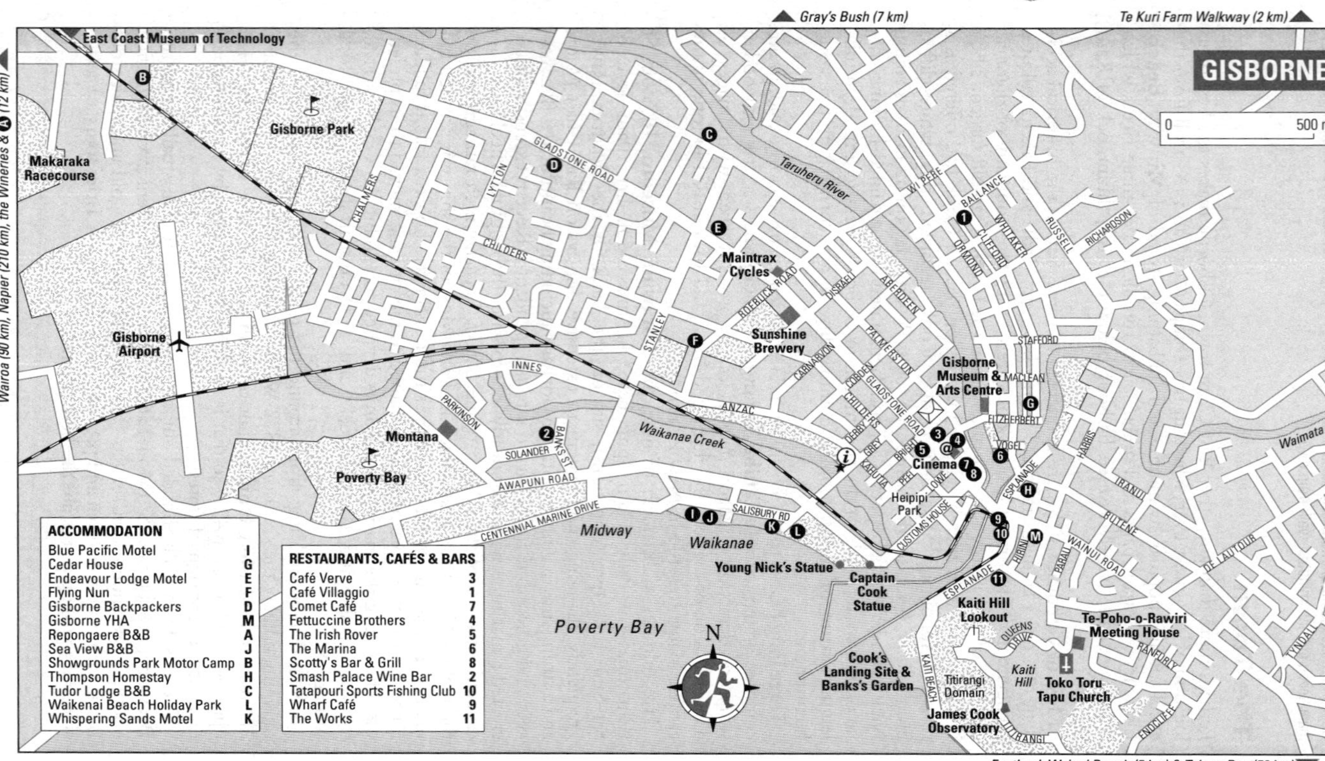
GISBORNE
0 500 m
Gray's Bush (7 km)
Te Kuri Farm Walkway (2 km)
Wairoa (90 km), Napier (210 km), the Wineries & A (12 km)
Eastland, Wainui Beach (5 km) & Tolaga Bay (50 km)
East Coast Museum of Technology
Makaraka Racecourse
Gisborne Park
Gisborne Airport
Montana
Poverty Bay
Maintrax Cycles
Sunshine Brewery
Gisborne Museum & Arts Centre
Cinema
Heipipi Park
Young Nick's Statue
Captain Cook Statue
Cook's Landing Site & Banks's Garden
Kaiti Hill Lookout
Te-Poho-o-Rawiri Meeting House
Toko Toru Tapu Church
Kaiti Hill
Titirangi Domain
James Cook Observatory
Taruheru River
Waimata River
Waikanae Creek
Midway
Waikanae
Poverty Bay
GLADSTONE ROAD
CHALMERS
LYTTON
CHILDERS
STANLEY
INNES
PARKINSON
SOLANDER
BANKS ST
AWAPUNI ROAD
CENTENNIAL MARINE DRIVE
SALISBURY RD
ANZAC
ROEBUCK ROAD
DISRAELI
ABERDEEN
PALMERSTON
CARNARVON
CORDEN
DERBY
GREY
KAHUTIA
BRIGHT
PEEL
LOWE
CUSTOMS HOUSE
WI PERE
BALLANCE
WHITAKER
CLIFFORD
ORMOND
RUSSELL
RICHARDSON
STAFFORD
MACLEAN
FITZHERBERT
VOGEL
ESPLANADE
HARRIS
IRANUI
RUTENE
WAINUI ROAD
DE LAUTOUR
HIRINI
PARAU
QUEENS DRIVE
RANFURLY
TYNDALL
ENDCLIFFE
KAITI BEACH
TITIRANGI
N
ACCOMMODATION
Blue Pacific Motel I
Cedar House G
Endeavour Lodge Motel E
Flying Nun F
Gisborne Backpackers D
Gisborne YHA M
Repongaere B&B A
Sea View B&B J
Showgrounds Park Motor Camp B
Thompson Homestay H
Tudor Lodge B&B C
Waikenai Beach Holiday Park L
Whispering Sands Motel K
RESTAURANTS, CAFÉS & BARS
Café Verve 3
Café Villaggio 1
Comet Café 7
Fettuccine Brothers 4
The Irish Rover 5
The Marina 6
Scotty's Bar & Grill 8
Smash Palace Wine Bar 2
Tatapouri Sports Fishing Club 10
Wharf Café 9
The Works 11

Kaiti Hill and around

On the eastern side of the rivermouth, an obelisk marks **Cook's landing site**, now a couple of hundred metres inland following reclamation for the harbour facilities where mountains of logs now await export. Meanwhile Cook's botanist gets recognition near the obelisk at the waterfront in **Banks' Garden**: a locale full of species – especially low-growing varieties such as ngaio, tutu, karo and puriri – that he and his accomplice Solander collected here and at Anaura Bay and Tolaga Bay as they sailed north. Behind, Titirangi Domain climbs the side of **Kaiti Hill** to the Cook Bicentenary Plaza, designed around another statue of Cook who, after a complicated series of misunderstandings, comes decked out in Italian naval regalia. The highest point of the hill is occupied by the **James Cook Observatory**, which runs public stargazing nights on Tuesdays (Nov–March 8.30pm; April–Oct 7.30pm; $2).

On the eastern side of the hill lies **Te Poho-o-Rawiri Meeting House**, one of the largest in the country. The interior is superb, being almost completely covered in fine ancestor carvings, interspersed with wonderfully varied geometric *tukutuku* (woven panels). At the foot of the two support poles, ancient and intricately carved warrior statues provide a fine counterpoint to the bolder work on the walls. This is one of the most easily accessible working *marae*, but it is still necessary to arrange permission to enter the site (Ⓣ06/868 5364), preferably a day or two beforehand, and a *koha* (donation) is appreciated. Adjacent is the small and decorative **Toko Toru Tapu Church**, though this is seldom open (entry can be arranged by phoning the *marae* number, above).

Town activities

Gisborne offers one of New Zealand's few opportunities for heart-pounding **shark encounters**. Surfit Shark Cage Experience (Ⓣ06/867 2970, Ⓦwww.surfit.co.nz; $165) take small groups about 15km offshore then place two people at a time into a tough metal cage, which is partly lowered into the water where **mako sharks** lurk menacingly. Standing chest deep, you get around half an hour in the water – quite long enough – ducking down with a mask and snorkel or regulator to observe these curious (though not generally aggressive) three-metre-long, eighty-kilo killing machines. There's a fifty-percent refund in the unlikely event of not seeing any sharks, and your whole experience is shot on video, which you can keep for an extra $25.

For something more active, try **surfing lessons** in the generally mild surf of Waikanae Beach with Learn to Surf with Ruth (Ⓣ06/867 5379; $25 per hr, including all gear).

Around Gisborne

Winery visits with free tasting, easy walks and a smattering of specific attractions make a day or so spent around Gisborne an agreeable prospect. If you don't have a car, your best bet is to rent a bike (see p.446) and head out on the flat roads to the wineries before retiring to one of the short walks just north of the city. Alternatively join Trev's Tours (Ⓣ06/863 9815, Ⓔtrevs.tours@voyager.co.nz) for one of their small-group **trips** around the wineries and out to Eastwoodhill Arboretum (6hr; $85) or south to Morere Hot Springs (5hr; $75).

Before setting off for the wineries, walks or water, pay a visit to the **East Coast Museum of Technology**, Main Road, Makaraka, 5km northwest of the city (daily 9.30am–4.30pm; $2), where a former dairy factory has been used to hoard just about every imaginable piece of discarded household, industrial or agricultural junk. Little is labelled, let alone interpreted, but the enthusiasm of the staff is infectious and everyone should find something of interest among the ancient petrol pumps, early photocopiers and VCRs and Coke cans through the years. A couple of kilometres further northwest along SH2 lies the diminutive wooden **Matawhero Presbyterian Church**, the only building left standing by Te Kooti's raids in 1868.

The wineries

Occupying a free-draining alluvial plain, in the lee of the Raukumara Range and blessed with long hours of strong sun with warm summer nights, Poverty Bay wineries have made Gisborne the country's self-professed Chardonnay capital. The region has earned itself a reputation as a viticultural workhorse, churning out vast quantities of Chardonnay, Riesling, Müller-Thurgau and Gewürztraminer grapes to be blended into cheerful wines for everyday glugging. Out in the highly fertile wine country, roadside windbreaks of poplars are a common sight, protecting the vines beyond. Most of the wineries you can visit are small concerns that open according to demand; hours given below are a guideline only, and you'd do well to call in advance.

The national giants of Corban's and Montana account for over eighty per-cent of the regional production, but tours of their factory-style operations are only available to groups by appointment. Still, you might call in to **Montana**, Lytton Road, around 1km west of downtown (daily 9am–5pm; ⓣ06/867 2757), for some free tasting before heading further afield to the more interesting boutique wineries. Many of these are striving to break the Hawke's Bay and Marlborough stranglehold on international sales, which has led some commentators to predict that Gisborne will be the Next Big Thing.

One of the closest and longest-established wineries is **Matawhero**, Riverpoint Road, 8km west of Gisborne (Oct–April Mon–Sat 11am–4pm; rest of year times vary; ⓣ06/868 8366), renowned for its Gewürztraminer and beginning to produce some fine reds. There is more of interest at **Millton Vineyard**, Papatu Road, Manutuke, 2km west (call before visiting ⓣ06/862 8680), which is one of New Zealand's few fully certified organic wineries, and possibly the only one to apply the bio-dynamic principles espoused by Rudolf Steiner to all aspects of wine production. The timing of planting, harvesting and bottling are dictated by the phases of the moon, which combines to produce some delicious wines (especially Riesling, Chenin Blanc and late-harvest dessert wines) that, they claim, can be enjoyed even by those who experience allergic reactions to other wines. Considering the intricacy of such wine making, prices are surprisingly reasonable, so grab a bottle, indulge in a picnic among the vines and a leisurely game of petanque.

One of the few wineries that is open daily all year is **Pouparae Park**, Bushmere Road, 10km west of central Gisborne on Bushmere Road, 4km off the southbound SH2 (ⓣ06/867 7931), where a parkland garden provides a lovely setting for sampling their noted Chardonnay, Merlot and Riesling – all sold at very reasonable prices.

While most wineries concentrate on whites, reds are beginning to make inroads, notably at the youthful **Shalimar Estate Winery**, Ngatapa Road, Patutahi, 15km west of Gisborne (ⓣ06/862 7776; daily 10am–5pm), which is gradually building a reputation for quality reds, and has already won medals for its Merlot which can be sampled for free. Again prices are very reasonable.

Eastwoodhill Arboretum

A bottle of wine tucked under your arm and a groaning picnic hamper is the most conducive way to enjoy New Zealand's largest collection of northern-hemisphere vegetation at **Eastwoodhill Arboretum**, Ngatapa–Rere Road, 35km northwest of Gisborne (daily 9am–5pm; Ⓦwww.eastwoodhill.org.nz; $8). The parched hills surrounding the Poverty Bay plains stand in stark contrast to the arboretum's lush glens and formal lawns. Planting began in 1910, inspired by William Douglas Cook, who had grown to love British gardens and parks. Numerous trails thread through a unique mixture of over 3500 species – magnolias, oaks, spruce, maples, cherries – brought together in an unusual microclimate in which both hot- and cold-climate trees flourish.

Te Kuri Farm Walkway and Gray's Bush

Walks are not Gisborne's strong suit, but there are a couple detailed in DOC leaflets available from the visitor centre. The closest is **Te Kuri Farm Walkway** (5.6km; 2hr; closed during lambing season mid-July to Oct), off Shelley Road, 4km north of the centre of Gisborne. Apart from a lovely panorama over the city from a ridge-top section of pastoral land, this isn't a particularly exciting route – though you do get to walk the land owned by cartoonist Murray Ball, who immortalized this terrain in his archetypal Kiwi cartoon, *Footrot Flats*, which features "the Dog", or Te Kuri. On a hot day, a better bet is the short walk through the cool kahikatea, puriri and nikau woodlands of **Gray's Bush** (30min return), 9km northeast of the city, and the largest remnant of the tall forests that once covered the Poverty Bay flats.

Eating, drinking and nightlife

For its size, Gisborne is surprisingly well supplied with decent **cafés** and **restaurants** to suit all budgets, many of them making good use of their locations on the city's beach, rivers or harbour by means of large glass doors thrown open at any hint of sun. Those same features make the restaurants the best bet for an evening drink, though there are several traditional **pubs** for straightforward beer consumption. A rough-and-ready **farmers' market** is held each Saturday morning (6.30am to around 8.30am) in the park next to the visitor centre, where you can snap up some bargain ingredients in a bustling atmosphere – keep an eye out for some of the subtropical and citrus fruits that grow here all year for the export market. Unusually for New Zealand, where local catches of **fish** are often immediately exported or transported to other parts of the country, excellent prices for fish straight off Gisborne's boats can be had at the Moana Pacific Fisheries shop on The Esplanade and opposite the Tatapouri Sports Fishing Club, the simple reason being that the company owns most of these boats.

Movies are shown at the Odeon **cinema**, 79 Gladstone Rd (Ⓣ06/867 3339).

Cafés and restaurants

Fettuccine Brothers 12 Peel St Ⓣ06/868 5700. Relaxing and long-standing Italian restaurant (with adjacent bar) serving a full range of dishes from pasta ($18) to substantial meat and fish dishes ($24). May–Oct closed Sun.

The Marina Marina Park, Vogel St Ⓣ06/868 5919. One of Gisborne's finest restaurants, with a glass-sided dining room bedecked in crisp white linen and overlooking the confluence of the Taruheru and Waimata rivers. Food is of the modern Kiwi persuasion, along the lines of crayfish followed by venison with roasted-pepper sauce, at around $25 for a main course. Bookings essential for evenings, as well for lunches Dec–Jan.

Café Verve 121 Gladstone Rd. Gisborne's grooviest all-day café and restaurant, with sofas and magazines at the back, internet access, and gorgeous moderately priced food that extends to smoked salmon, enchiladas and a fabulous chicken curry. Licensed & BYO.

Café Villaggio 57 Ballance St. Award-winning casual restaurant set in a suburban Art Deco house and spilling over into the courtyard. A great place for weekend brunch, lunches or simple yet delicious evening meals from around $20. Closed Sun & Mon evenings.

Wharf Café Shed 1, The Esplanade ⓣ06/868 4876. Light and airy harbourside café with a relaxed approach and a varied and well-priced menu: try the chicken fajitas ($15), venison kofta ($17) and knock back a dozen oysters ($18). Book ahead for weekend lunch or dinner.

The Works cnr The Esplanade & Crawford Rd ⓣ06/863 1285. Airy Mediterranean-style café in a former freezing works set back from the wharf, always abuzz with folk in for a coffee and a snack, or with serious diners here for seafood paella or the catch of the day ($24). Bottled wine drinkers have plenty of choice but by-the-glass drinkers only have the house's own somewhat variable range.

Pubs and bars

The Irish Rover 69 Peel St. A place of simple charms and warm atmosphere: Guinness, the natural Gisborne Gold, bar snacks and occasional live bands.

Scotty's Bar & Grill 33 Gladstone Rd. Probably the best bar in town, certainly the classiest and longest established, occupying what was once a big ornate bank. This is a great all-rounder, open daily with good-value food, plenty of outdoor seating, and a DJ or live band on Fri & Sat nights.

Smash Palace Wine Bar 24 Banks St. Wonderfully oddball bar where overalls from the surrounding industrial area rub shoulders with suits in a corrugated-iron barn adorned with all manner of junk, heralded by a bright-yellow Morris Minor at the entrance. The bar occasionally hosts theme evenings in summer. Food basically comprises snack, favourites being flaming pizzas and the nachos that have been flame-toasted with a blow torch.

Tatapouri Sports Fishing Club The Esplanade. When they're not too busy, visitors ($1 day membership) are welcome to this barn-like pub/club right on the wharf. There's veranda seating for the consumption of generous portions of satay, a "wharfie's plate" of seafood, or gourmet burgers (all under $17), while watching the sun set behind the hills beyond the dock.

Gisborne to Wairoa

All roads south from Gisborne involve lengthy travel through vast swathes of farmland, which are sparsely scattered with nowhere villages that offer little incentive to linger. There are two routes: the faster SH2, which sticks close to the coast before veering around Hawke Bay; and the inland SH36, which sees very little traffic – and no public transport.

Following the alternative coastal route of **SH2** from Gisborne along the southern continuation of the Pacific Coast Highway, the Poverty Bay vineyards soon give way to the hill country of the Wharerata State Forest, where the first real diversion is provided by **Morere Hot Springs** (daily: Christmas–Jan 10am–9pm; Feb–Christmas 10am–5pm; $5, private pools an extra $2 for 30min), 60km south of Gisborne. Ancient sea water has been heated and concentrated along the fault line deep underground to form highly saline, iron-rich waters that well up along a small stream as it trickles down through one of the East Coast's last remaining tracts of native coastal forest. Grassy barbecue areas surround the pools and form the nucleus of numerous trails that radiate out through stands of tawa, rimu, totara and matai; a short streamside walk (10min) takes you to the Nikau Plunge Pools, where steel soaking tanks are surrounded by groves of nikau palms.

The adjacent settlement of **MORERE** has a shop and a couple of **places to stay**, both on SH2 as it passes through the village. The appealing *Peacock Lodge* (ⓣ & ⓕ06/837 8824, ⓔpeacocklodge@xtra.co.nz; dorms ❶, rooms ❷; closed June–Aug) is a spacious and broad-verandaed house tucked away amid trees, which is well set up for families and small groups alike, with beds in small dorms and pleasant doubles; there's also accommodation at *Morere Springs Tearooms & Camping Ground* (ⓣ06/837 8792, ⓕ837 8790; camping $10, dorms ❶, cabins ❷).

△ Panekiri Bluff, Lake Waikaremoana

Mahia Peninsula

At Nuhaka, 8km south of Morere, the road flirts briefly with the sea before turning sharp right for Wairoa. A side road spurs east to the pendulous **Mahia Peninsula**, a distinctive high promontory that separates Hawke's Bay from Poverty Bay, linked to the mainland by a narrow sandy isthmus. Surfers make good use of the rougher windward side, while the calmer beaches on the leeward side offer safe bathing and boating for the hundreds of families who descend each summer to swim, fish for snapper and hapuku, dive and generally chill out. Outside the mad month after Christmas it makes a relaxing place to break your journey, or to stretch your legs on the 4km looped track through the **Mahia Peninsula Scenic Reserve**.

At the northern end of the Hawke's Bay side of the isthmus is **Opuatama**, little more than a shop, the pine-surrounded *Blue Bay Holiday Resort* (ⓣ06/837 5867, ⓔbluebay.co.nz; camping $10, kitchen cabins ❸, units ❹), and the simple, hostel-style *Pukeko Lodge*, 69 YMCA Rd (ⓣ06/837 5740, ⓕ837 6453; dorms ❶, rooms ❷).

The peninsula's main settlement of **Mahia Beach** lies at the southern end of the five-kilometre strand, where there are takeaways, a café and a pub, and the well-appointed *Mahia Beach Motels & Holiday Park* (ⓣ06/837 5830, ⓔmahia.beach.motels@xtra.co.nz; camping $12, cabins ❷, units ❹) with spacious camping, simple tourist cabins and flashier motel units. You can also stay just over the hill, closer to the surf beaches, at tiny **Te Mahia**, in the log-built *Cappamore Lodge*, 435 Mahia East Coast Rd (ⓣ06/837 5523, ⓦwww.cottagestays.co.nz/cappamore/cottage.htm; ❺), a self-contained two-storey house.

From Wairoa to Napier

Sleepy **WAIROA**, some 40km west of the Nuhaka junction, hugs the banks of the broad willow-lined Wairoa River a couple of kilometres from its mouth, where ships once entered to load the produce of the dairy and sheep-farming country all around. Today the riverside wharves have all but disappeared, but if you have time between bus connections, stroll along the waterfront past the 1877 kauri-wood **lighthouse** beside the bridge at the town centre, which was relocated here in 1961 from Portland Island, off the southern tip of the Mahia Peninsula.

Nearby, the **Wairoa Museum**, on Marine Parade (Mon–Fri 10am–4pm, Sat 10am–1pm; donation), deserves a brief look for its small but well-presented displays on local history (including the devastating cyclone Bola, which swept through the region in 1988) and the beautifully carved Maori figure dating back to the eighteenth century.

If you are staying a bit longer, try to visit the town's highly decorative **Takitimu Marae**: trips can be organized through the **visitor centre**, centrally located on the corner of SH2 and Queen Street (Nov–March daily 9am–5pm; April–Sept Mon–Fri 9am–5pm; ⓣ & ⓕ06/838 7440, ⓔweavic@xtra.co.nz), which sells but tickets. **Buses** to Waikaremoana (see p.459), and InterCity buses to Gisborne and Napier pick up nearby and are well co-ordinated so you shouldn't need a **place to stay**. If you do, try the *Riverside Motor Camp* at 19 Marine Parade (ⓣ06/838 6301, ⓕ838 6341; tent sites $9, cabins ❷), the basic backpacker beds at the *Clyde Hotel*, Marine Parade (ⓣ & ⓕ06/838 7139; bed ❶, room ❷), or *Vista Motor Lodge*, on SH2 north of the Wairoa bridge (ⓣ06/838 8279, ⓕ838 8277; ❹), which has an on-site **restaurant**.

Travelling by bus, or even by car, there is little to justify stopping in the inland farming country that lines the highway between Wairoa and Napier, though cyclists may want to break this 120km stretch. The most sensible place to do just that is three-quarters of the way at *Glen-View Farm Hostel*, Aropaoanui Road, 2km east off SH2 (Ⓣ06/836 6232, Ⓕ836 6067), a small and well-organized backpackers with tent sites ($9) bargain four-shares (❶) and self-contained rooms (❷), plus a farm shop; a separate homestay section, 2km down the road, features an elaborate breakfast – and there's **riding** ($25 per half day, $40 a day) that includes swimming the horses in the river.

A few kilometres further south, the highway passes the small **Lake Tutira** and its diminutive neighbour, Lake Waikopiro, neither worthy of much attention though if you want a breath of air you could tackle one of three farmland loop walks (1km, 20min; 3.5km, 2hr; and 9km, 5hr; all closed Aug & Sept for lambing season), which start at the roadside car park, the shortest walk encircling Lake Waikopiro and the longest incorporating a lookout over both lakes (see DOC leaflet *Napier–Tutira Highway*; $1). On a hot day you might prefer the shade offered by **White Pine Bush Scenic Reserve**, 10km south, a dense clump of kahikatea, rimu and other podocarps, where loop tracks (650m, 30min; and 3km, 1hr) thread through the bush alongside the Kareaara Stream. From here it is just 25km to central Napier.

Te Urewera National Park

Te Urewera National Park, 65km northwest of Wairoa, straddles the North Island's mountainous backbone and encompasses the largest untouched expanse of native bush outside of Fiordland. Unusually for New Zealand, it is almost completely covered in vegetation; even the highest peaks – some approaching 1500m – barely poke through this dense cloak of primeval forests whose undergrowth is trampled by deer and wild pigs, and whose cascading rivers are alive with trout. One road, SH38, penetrates the interior, but the way to get a true sense of the place is to go tramping. For hardy types, this means the **Lake Waikaremoana Track**, which is among the finest four-day tramps in the country, encircling a steep-sided lake at the southern end of the park. Created little more than two thousand years ago, **Lake Waikaremoana**, the "Sea of Rippling Waters", is the undoubted jewel of the park, its deep clear waters fringed by white sandy beaches and rocky bluffs making it ideal for swimming, diving, fishing and kayaking.

Habitation is very sparse. The Tuhoe people, the "Children of the Mist", still live in the interior of the park (the largest concentration around the tramping base of **Ruatahuna**), but most visitors make straight for **Waikaremoana**, which is barely a settlement at all, just a motor camp and a visitor centre right on the lake shore. Immediately to the south, the *Big Bush Holiday Camp* and the quiet former hydro-electrical development town of **Tuai** provide some additional basic services, but otherwise you're on your own.

Lake Waikaremoana

The magnificent, bush-girt **Lake Waikaremoana** fills a huge scalloped bowl at an altitude of over 585m, precariously held back by the Panekiri and Ngamoko ranges which, at the slightest opportunity, seem ready to part and spill the contents down the pastoral valley towards Wairoa. The lake came into being around 2200 years ago when a huge bank of sandstone boulders was dis-

Te Kooti Rikirangi

Te Kooti Rikirangi was one of the most celebrated of Maori "rebels", a thorn in the side of the colonial government throughout the New Zealand Wars of the late 1860s and early years of the 1870s. Depicted, at least in Pakeha-biased school books, as a ruthless guerrilla leader and the wildest outlaw in Maori history, in truth he was a mild-mannered man with a neatly trimmed beard and moustache rather than the more confrontational *moko* (traditional tattoos). An excellent fighter and brilliant strategist, Te Kooti kept the mountainous spine of the North Island on edge for the best part of a decade, eluding the biggest manhunt in New Zealand's history.

Though not of chiefly rank, Te Kooti could trace his ancestry back to the captains of several *waka* (canoes) that brought the Maori to New Zealand, and was born near Gisborne into a respected family around 1830, though little else is known of his early years. By the middle of the 1860s, he was fighting for the government against the **Hau Hau** (see box on p.429), a fanatical, pseudo-Christian cult that started in Taranaki in 1862. The cult spread to the East Coast where, in 1866, Te Kooti was unjustly accused of being in league with its devotees. Denied the trial he so often demanded, he was subsequently imprisoned on the Chatham Islands, along with 300 of his supposed allies. In 1867, he was brought close to death by a fever, but rose again, claiming a divine revelation and establishing a new religion, **Ringatu** ("the uplifted hand"), which still has some ten thousand believers today. Ringatu took its cues from the Hau Hau, but developed into a uniquely Maori version of Catholicism, drawing heavily on the Old Testament. Some say Te Kooti saw himself as a Moses figure, called to lead his people to freedom, and he was certainly charismatic in his approach – apparently given to dousing his uplifted hand in phosphorus so that it glowed in the dim meeting houses.

After two years on the Chathams, Te Kooti and his fellow prisoners commandeered a ship and engineered a dramatic escape, returning to Poverty Bay. Te Kooti sought the rugged safety of the **Urewera Range**, with the Armed Constabulary in hot pursuit, relentlessly tailing him through snow, mud and heat on horseback and on foot. Nonetheless, Te Kooti conducted successful campaigns, exacting revenge against government troops at Whakatane on the Bay of Plenty, Mohaka in Hawke's Bay and at Rotorua. The government posted a reward of £1000 on his head, but he was always able to stay ahead of the game and it was never claimed. With the end of the New Zealand Wars in 1872, Te Kooti took refuge in the Maori safe haven of the **King Country**. He was eventually pardoned in 1883, and in 1891 was granted a plot of land near Whakatane, where he lived out the last two years of his life.

lodged from the Ngamoko range, blocking the river that once drained the valleys and thereby forming the lake. Maori have a more poetic explanation of the lake's creation, pointing to the work of Hau-Mapuhia, the recalcitrant daughter of Mahu, who was drowned by her father and turned into a *taniwha*, or "water spirit". In a frenzied effort to get to the sea, she charged in every direction, thereby creating the various arms of the lake. As she frantically ran south towards Onepoto, the dawn caught her, turning her to stone at a spot where the lake is said to ripple from time to time, in a watery memory of her titanic struggle.

One of the beauties of the lake is that there is no town nearby, just the DOC-operated Aniwaniwa visitor centre (see below), and a motor camp, both well set-up for helping hikers tackle the Lake Waikaremoana Track (see below). Short visits are repaid with the opportunity to see the **Papakorito Falls**, a twenty-metre-wide curtain of water located 2km east of the visitor centre. To

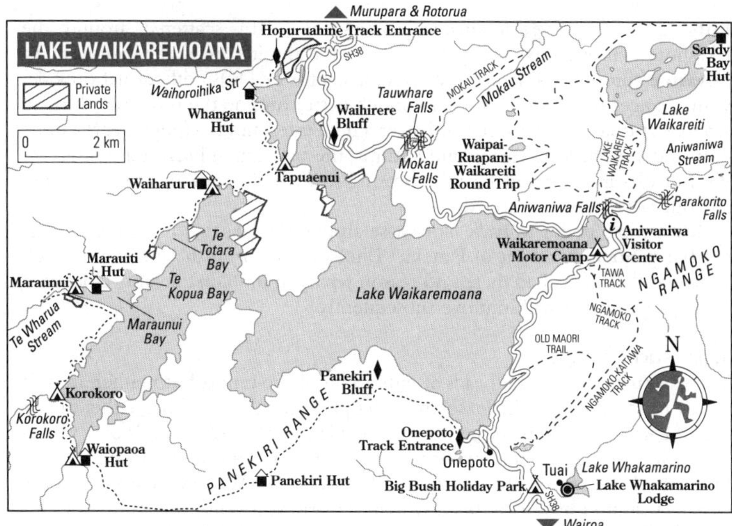

really see and get a feel for the place you'll need to walk, preferably armed with DOC's *Lake Waikaremoana Walks* leaflet ($2), which details the region's shorter hikes such as the stroll to the double-drop **Aniwaniwa Falls** (1km; 15min return), starting from beside the visitor centre, or the **Black Beech Track** (2km; 30min one way), which follows the old highway from the visitor centre to the motor camp. With the best part of a day to spare, take on the **Waipai–Ruapani–Waikareiti Round Trip** (15km; 6hr), which starts 200m north of the visitor centre and winds up through dense beech forest past the grassy-fringed Lake Ruapani to the beautiful and serene **Lake Waikareiti**, where you can rent row-boats ($15 per half day, $40 deposit), though you'll need to plan ahead, as the key is held at Aniwaniwa visitor centre. Return down the Waikareiti Track or head on around to the northern side of the lake (3hr one-way) and stay at **Sandy Bay Hut** (18 bunks; $14).

You can also explore the lake with watercraft rented from the Waikaremoana Motor Camp by two companies, both offering **kayaks** for $35 a half-day and **canoes** for $25.

The Lake Waikaremoana Track

The **Lake Waikaremoana Track** (46km; 3–4 days; 900m ascent) is one of New Zealand's "Great Walks", and undoubtedly ranks among the finest multi-day tramps in New Zealand. It is also the most popular such tramp in the North Island and is often compared with the South Island's Routeburn and Milford tracks, but with the exception of an exhausting climb on the first day, this is a much gentler affair. Well-paced and mostly hugging the lakeshore, the tramp offers plenty of opportunities to fish and swim, as well as to simply admire the majestic scenery and listen to the cacophonous birdlife.

All the **information** you need to walk the track is on DOC's *Lake Waikaremoana Track* leaflet ($1), though **map** enthusiasts may fancy the detailed 1:100,000 *Urewera Parkmap*. Though three days is enough for fit individuals, the walk is normally done in four days, spending nights in the five "Great Walk"

huts ($14) and five designated **campsites** ($10) scattered around the lakeshore. Throughout the year, huts and campsites must be **booked in advance** through the Aniwaniwa visitor centre or DOC offices nationwide; your chances of getting a place are much better outside the busy month or so after Christmas and the week of Easter. The winter months (June–Sept) can be cold and wet, making spring and autumn the best times. Each hut is supplied with drinking water, toilets and a heating stove, but a cooking stove, fuel and all your food must be carried.

Most people prefer to walk clockwise around the lake, getting the challenging but panoramic ascent of Panekiri Bluff over with on the first day, though if the weather looks bad there's no reason why you shouldn't go anti-clockwise in the hope that it will improve subsequently.

Trailhead transport

You can **drive** to the trailheads at either end of the tramp, but neither are safe places to leave your vehicle, so most people leave their clobber either at *Big Bush Motor Camp* (free); in the car park beside the Waikaremoana Motor Camp store (free); or for extra security, inside the motor camp itself ($3 per night). From the latter, **access** to the start and finish of the Waikaremoana Circuit is either by shuttle bus or by boat: whichever way you walk, you can be on the track by 9am, and you need to finish your last day's walk by 2pm.

Two **ferry services** now operate from the Waikaremoana Motor Camp to Onepoto, Hopuruahine: Waikaremoana Guided Tours (☎06/837 3729) and Big Bush Water Taxi (☎06/837 3777). They offer virtually identical services, both running several times a day to the ends of the track and charging $25 for a joint drop-off and pick-up package. Both will also run a **water taxi** service to anywhere else you might want to start or finish enabling you to walk shorter sections of the circuit by means of pre-arranged pick-ups from specified beaches – prices are dependent on numbers, but are broadly comparable with the regular ferries.

The route

When tackled clockwise, the first leg **from Onepoto to Panekiri Hut** (9km; 5hr; 600m ascent) is the toughest; carry plenty of drinking water and start at a shelter by the lakeshore close to SH38. The track climbs steeply past the site of a redoubt set up by soldiers of the Armed Constabulary in pursuit of Te Kooti (see box on p.456) to the Pukenui trig point, from where the track undulates along the ridge top. Steps up a rocky bluff bring you to the Panekiri Hut (36 bunks), magnificently set on the brink of the cliffs that fall away to the lake far below. Even if you've the energy to push on, it would be a shame not to stay here, though camping in this fragile environment is prohibited, so the hut is your only option. Committed campers must press on to Waiopaoa, a whopping nine hours' walk from the start.

From Panekiri Hut to Waiopaoa Hut (7.5km; 3–4hr; 600m descent) you lose the height gained the previous day, slowly at first along the descending ridge, then very rapidly through an often-muddy area where protruding tree roots provide welcome hand-holds. Occasional lake views and the transition from beech forests to rich podocarp woodlands make this an appealing, if tricky, section of track down to the hut (21 bunks) and campsite.

Pressing on **from Waiopaoa Hut to Marauiti Hut** (11km; 4–5hr; 100m ascent), you largely follow the lakeshore, initially across grassland and through kanuka scrub where a side track leads to the impressive 20m Korokoro Falls

(25min return) and, just beyond the junction, the Korokoro campsite (1hr 30min from Waiopaoa Hut). Meanwhile, the main track climbs slightly above the lake past barely accessible bays, eventually reaching the Maraunui campsite and, after climbing the low Whakaneke Spur, descends to the waterside Marauiti Hut (22 bunks). **From Marauiti Hut to Waiharuru Hut** (6km; 2hr; 100m ascent) the track passes the lovely white-sand Te Kopua Bay and climbs an easy saddle, before dropping down to Te Totara Bay and following the lake to Waiharuru Hut (40 bunks) and campsite. It is a short hike **from Waiharuru Hut to Whanganui Hut** (5.3km; 2–3hr; 50m ascent) across a broad neck of land to the Tapuaenui campsite and beyond, following the shore to the pleasantly sited hut (18 bunks).

The last easy section, **from Whanganui Hut to Hopuruahine** (5km; 2–3hr; 50m ascent), skirts the lake and follows grassy flats beside the Hopuruahine River. The trail then crosses a suspension bridge to the access road where there's another camping area (free).

Waikaremoana practicalities

The only **public transport** into the region is run by *Big Bush Holiday Camp* (bookings essential on ⓣ06/837 3777, who operate a daily bus service to the *Holiday Camp* from Wairoa, where it connects with InterCity buses. There's also a service to Waikaremoana from Rotorua (departs 1.30pm Mon, Wed & Fri only). The Rotorua service runs around the eastern side of Lake Waikaremoana past the **Aniwaniwa visitor centre** (daily 8am–4.45pm; ⓣ06/837 3803, ⓔureweraInfo@doc.govt.nz), the main source of information on Lake Waikaremoana and Te Urewera National Park. There are a stack of brochures detailing the numerous walks in the area plus excellent and extensive displays on the geology and ecology of the region, details of local social history, and the opportunity to view Colin McCahon's controversial *Urewera Mural* (see p.460).

The only **accommodation** inside the park is at the well-equipped *Waikaremoana Motor Camp*, on SH38, 2km south of the visitor centre (ⓣ06/837 3826, ⓦwww.lake.co.nz; ❶–❹), with a compact but grassy camping area ($10), a perfectly serviceable bunkhouse, cabins and more luxurious self-contained chalets; showers are available for non-guests at $2 a time. Just outside the park on SH38 16km south of the Aniwaniwa visitor centre, the best bet is the *Big Bush Holiday Park* (ⓣ06/837 3777, ⓦwww.lakewaikaremoana.co.nz; ❶–❸), which is fully set up for track trampers and offers camping ($8), backpacker beds (❶) and some comfortable self-contained units (❸) with TV and a small sunny deck. A further kilometre south in Tuai, former construction workers' quarters are now *Lake Whakamarino Lodge* (ⓣ06/837 3876, ⓦwww.lakelodge.co.nz; rooms ❹, self-contained units ❺), which is rather short on character, despite being wonderfully sited right on the shores of the trout-filled Lake Whakamarino. There are also a couple of DOC **campsites** along SH38: *Mokau Landing* ($4), 11km north of the visitor centre, and *Taita a Makora* ($3), 11km further north.

You'll largely have to fend for yourself when it comes to **eating**, with the only food in the park being the limited range of groceries at the *Waikaremoana Motor Camp*. Tuai's *Big Bush Holiday Park* has reasonably priced meals and decent coffee in its licensed restaurant, and meals are available on request at the *Lake Whakamarino Lodge*.

The Urewera Mural

The Aniwaniwa visitor centre is the unlikely permanent home of one of New Zealand's finest and most (in)famous pieces of modern art, the epic 1976 *Urewera Mural* by Colin McCahon, one of New Zealand's most celebrated artists. A large, dark triptych with boldly delineated hills emblazoned with Maori text, the painting was intended to be non-judgemental, symbolizing Tuhoe stories of time, place and spirit on each of the three panels. It immediately became contentious as some Tuhoe disputed the relevance and historical accuracy of the Maori text McCahon had used, adding to the general feeling that McCahon – a Pakeha with a very limited understanding of the Maori language – was appropriating indigenous property. In the spirit of compromise McCahon changed some elements of the painting before it was hung in the Aniwaniwa visitor centre, but disquiet continued to simmer until June 1997 when the painting was "liberated". After a few months the Tuhoe activist **Te Kaha** was convicted of the theft and fined, but not until after he and fellow activist **Tame Iti** had struck up a friendship with Auckland arts patron Jenny Gibbs, who had stepped in to broker the return of the work. The painting had been damaged during its ordeal, but was subsequently repaired and returned to the Aniwaniwa visitor centre. Meanwhile Tame Iti has fashioned his own arts career, for a time running an art dealership specializing in Maori (specifically Tuhoe) art, and even picking up the brushes himself. At least one of his works is now held at Te Papa in Wellington.

Beyond Lake Waikaremoana: the heart of the park

Beyond Lake Waikaremoana, SH38 twists and turns for over two hours before regaining the tar seal at Murupara, almost 100km northwest of the lake and just an hour (62km) short of Rotorua. The road, which took 45 years to build and wasn't completed until 1930, makes a tortuous journey through the heart of Te Urewera National Park, the ancestral home of the Tuhoe people.

Historically, the Tuhoe had limited contact with Europeans; even today, they live in relative isolation in ramshackle roadside villages such as **RUATAHUNA**, 48km from Waikaremoana, which has the road's only store, takeaway and petrol supplies. Ruatahuna also serves as a base for a couple of little-used tracks into beautiful and remote country north of SH38. These are most often used by anglers and hunters, but are excellent for tramping, too, with backcountry huts ($5) at regular intervals. Two DOC leaflets ($1 each) cover these tramps, the easiest of which is the **Whakatane River Round Trip**, a three-to-five-day walk suitable for most levels of fitness through varied scenery encompassing river valleys, native forest, grassy flats and farmland. For tougher specimens, there's the **Upper Waikare River Guide**, an amalgam of several tracks, many of them following riverbeds (seek local advice on the likelihood of flooding) and enabling various route combinations (2–4 days).

Napier and around

The port city of **NAPIER** is Hawke's Bay's largest, yet with its beautiful seafront position, a Mediterranean climate and a population barely touching 50,000, it is an easy place to come to terms with. Add to that the world's finest collection of small-scale Art Deco buildings, heaps of amusements for kids and a burgeoning café society, and you have one of New Zealand's most likeable regional centres. There are even better reasons to stick around the Napier area, not least for the trip out to the gannet colony at Cape Kidnappers, and to tour the barrel-load of excellent **wineries** on the surrounding plains.

In 1769, James Cook sailed past **Ahuriri**, the current site of Napier, noting the sea-girt Bluff Hill linked to the mainland by two slender shingle banks and backed by a superb saltwater lagoon – the only substantial sheltered mooring between Gisborne and Wellington. Nonetheless, he anchored just to the south, off what came to be known as Cape Kidnappers, on account of a less-than-cordial encounter with the native Ngati Kahungunu people. Some thirty years later, when early whalers followed in Cook's tracks, Ahuriri was all but deserted, the Ngati Kahungunu having been driven out by rivals equipped with guns – the dubious contribution of European settlers in the Bay of Islands. During the uneasy peace of the early colonial years, Maori returned to the Napier area, which weathered the **New Zealand Wars** of the 1860s relatively unscathed and profited from the peace sustained by the guiding hands of men like the missionary printer William Colenso and Land Commissioner Donald McLean, both staunch supporters of sheep farming in Hawke's Bay. The port boomed, but by the early years of the twentieth century all the available land was used up and Napier had begun to stagnate.

Everything changed in two-and-a-half minutes on the morning of February 3, 1931, when the city was rocked by the biggest **earthquake** in New Zealand's recorded history, measuring a massive 7.9 on the Richter scale. More than six hundred aftershocks followed over the next two weeks, hampering efforts to rescue the 258 people who perished throughout Hawke's Bay, 162 of them in Napier alone. The centre of the city was completely devastated: almost all the brick-built shops and offices crumbled into a heap of smouldering rubble; the more flexible wooden buildings survived the initial tremor only to be consumed by the ensuing fire, which was fanned by a stiff sea breeze. The land twisted and buckled, finding a new equilibrium more than two metres higher; the sea drained out of the Ahuriri Lagoon, leaving trawlers high and dry and fish floundering on the mud flats. Three hundred square kilometres of new land were wrested from the grip of the ocean – enough room to site the Hawke's Bay airport, establish new farms and expand the city; cast your eye inland and you can still pick out a stranded line of sea cliffs a couple of kilometres away.

All this happened in the midst of the Great Depression, but Napier grasped the opportunity to start afresh: out went the trams; telephone wires were laid underground; the streets were widened; and buildings had to have cantilevered verandas, obviating the need for unsightly support poles. In the spirit of the times, almost everything was designed according to the precepts of the **Art Deco** movement, the simultaneous reconstruction giving Napier a stylistic uniformity rarely seen – and ranking it alongside Miami Beach as one of the largest collections of Art Deco buildings in the world.

Arrival, information and transport

Flights touch down at Hawke's Bay Airport, 5km north of town on SH2, where they are met by the Super Shuttle (ⓣ06/844 7333), which charges $10 into town; a taxi between two costs about the same. Long-distance **buses** pull in at the Napier Travel Centre, Munroe Street (ⓣ06/834 2720), some ten minutes' walk from the large, modern **visitor centre**, 100 Marine Parade (Mon–Fri 8.30am–5pm, Sat & Sun 9am–5pm, often until 6pm or 7pm in summer; ⓣ06/834 1911, ⓦwww.hawkesbaynz.com). A few steps along the seafront, Napier's former courthouse houses the **DOC office**, 59 Marine Parade (ⓣ06/834 3111, ⓕ834 4869; Mon–Fri 9am–4.15pm), where you can consult tide tables for the Cape Kidnappers walk (see p.469), pick up some free and mildly diverting heritage trail leaflets, and find out about walks into the remote Kaweka and Ruahine ranges to the west. For **internet access** try Cybers Internet Café, 98 Dickens St; the **post office** is on the corner of Hastings and Dickens streets and you can glean local listings from the weekday-only *Hawke's Bay Today* newspaper, especially the Friday listings pull-out.

Getting around Napier's central sights is easily done on foot, which is fortunate as the Nimbus **local bus** services (Mon–Fri only) is of little use except for visits to Hastings, or the Mission Estate Winery (where they drop off within walking distance). To venture further afield, either join a **winery tour**, **rent a car** (try Avis ⓣ06/835 1828; Hertz ⓣ06/835 6169; or Rent-a-Dent ⓣ06/834 1420), or **rent a bike** from Marineland on Marine Parade ($15 a half day), or grab a **taxi** with Napier Taxis (ⓣ835 7777).

Accommodation

Apart from the usual shortage of rooms during the month or so after Christmas, and to a lesser extent during February and March, you should have little trouble finding accommodation in Napier. In Kiwi-seaside fashion, there are dozens of **motels** around town, the greatest concentration being in Westshore, a beachfront suburb a few kilometres from the centre beside SH2 heading north. Right in the thick of things, Marine Parade has both low-cost backpacker **hostels** and classy **B&Bs**, but for homestays look no further than Bluff Hill. Predictably, none of the **campsites** are especially central.

Hotels and motels

Albatross Motel 56 Meeanee Quay, Westshore ⓣ06/835 5991 & 0800/252 287, ⓔalbatrossmotel@xtra.co.nz. Large and good-value motel close to Westshore Beach, with a pool, spa, studio units and self-catering family rooms. ❸

Beach Front Motel 373 Marine Parade ⓣ06/835 5220 & 0800/778 888, ⓔbeachfrontmotel@xtra.co.nz. High standard motel of luxury suites all having balconies, sea views, full kitchen, in-room spa pool or spa bath and breakfast supplied. ❺

The County Hotel 12 Browning St ⓣ06/835 7800 & 0800/843 468, ⓔcountyhotel@xtra.co.nz. Elegant business and tourist hotel in the Edwardian former council offices building, one of the few to survive the earthquake. Rooms all come with en-suite facilities, Sky TV and writing desks. ❽

Gardner Court Motel 16 Nelson Crescent ⓣ06/835 5913 & 0800/000 830, ⓔslmacqueen@xtra.co.nz. Quiet and reasonably central motel with a solar-heated outdoor pool and standard motel rooms at bargain prices. ❹

B&Bs and homestays

Cornucopia Lodge 361 SH5, Eskdale ⓣ06/836 6508, ⓦwww.cornucopia-lodge.com. A little rural luxury amid orchards and vineyards 15km north of Napier (on the road to Taupo), with two en-suite rooms, each with open fire and sunny deck. There's also a fully equipped kitchen for guests' use. A sumptuous breakfast is included, and a three-course dinner and wine costs $70. ❽

Madeira B&B 6 Madeira Rd ⓣ06/835 5185, ⓔjulieball@clear.net.nz. Wonderfully central homestay with just one double room and breakfast on the veranda overlooking the town. ❹

Mon Logis Guesthouse 415 Marine Parade ⓣ06/835 2125, ⓔmonlogis@xtra.co.nz. Classy and sumptuously furnished boutique hotel with a French theme. Some rooms in this lovely two-storey wooden house overlook the sea. The tariff includes a delicious breakfast, but you'll have to stump up $55 for the superb five-course table d'hôte dinner. ❻

Parsons Garden Loft 29 Cameron Rd, Bluff Hill ⓣ06/835 1527. Smallish en-suite room set in the leafy grounds of a fine homestead on Middle Hill, five minutes' steep walk up steps from Dalton Street, beside the Municipal Theatre. A good breakfast is served in the main house. ❹

Sea Breeze B&B 281 Marine Parade ⓣ06/835 8067, ⓔseabreeze.napier@xtra.co.nz. Low-cost B&B with smallish but pleasant rooms, some with sea views, and a self-service continental breakfast. ❹

Spence Homestay 17 Cobden Rd, Bluff Hill ⓣ06/835 9454, ⓔksspence@actrix.gen.nz. En-suite room in a sunny 1880 villa, set in a quiet area and boasting a large attractive garden and grounds. ❺

Treeways 1 Lighthouse Rd, Bluff Hill ⓣ06/835 6567, ⓔmckeeling@clear.net.nz. Homestay in a peaceful warm house amid garden and bush benefiting from good views over the sea, a sunny terrace with spa pool, and home-grown fruit and vegetables. Two en-suite rooms. ❺

Hostels

Aqua Lodge Backpackers 53 Nelson Crescent ⓣ06/835 4523, ⓔaquaback@inhb.co.nz. Home-style hostel with dorms and doubles shoehorned into a suburban house in a quiet area close to the train and bus station. There's a pool, good facilities, free bikes and welcoming hosts. ❶–❷

Archie's Bunker 14 Herschell St ⓣ06/833 7990, ⓔarchiesbunker@xtra.co.nz. Modern office conversion right downtown, with good facilities (including a huge TV and pool lounge) but a bit soulless. The unisex showers (though with separate cubicles) are a little unusual. Bike rental for $10. ❶–❷

Criterion Backpackers 48 Emerson St ⓣ06/835 2059, ⓔcribacpac@yahoo.com. Napier's biggest hostel, right in the centre in an Art Deco former hotel with large communal areas and a friendly atmosphere. Accommodation is in 6- to 8-bed dorms, triples and four-shares, and there are double rooms (one en suite). Free pick-up from bus. ❶–❸

Napier YHA 277 Marine Parade ⓣ06/835 7039, ⓔyhanapr@yha.org.nz. Well-run hostel that rambles across three joined houses right on the waterfront with some sea views. There are four-shares, doubles, singles, twins and a 5-bed family room, and a suntrap at the back with barbecue. ❶–❷

Stables Lodge 370 Hastings St ⓣ & ⓕ06/835 6242, ⓔstables@ihug.co.nz. Small, friendly and relaxed hostel close to the waterfront with stereo, hammocks, a book exchange and good cooking facilities along with a barbecue area in the central courtyard. ❶–❷

Campsites

Bay View Snapper Holiday Park 10 Gill Rd, Bay View ⓣ06/836 7084 & 0800/287 275, ⓔjimc@xtra.co.nz. Beachfront yet sheltered campsite 9km north of Napier, beyond the airport and 200m from a market garden for fresh vegetables. Camping $9, on-site vans ❷, s/c units ❹

Kennedy Park Top 10 Storkey St, off Kennedy Rd ⓣ06/843 9126, ⓦwww.kennedypark.co.nz. Well appointed site that's the closest to town, 3km from the city centre, and with a pool and barbecue area. Camping $10–12, cabins ❷–❸, kitchen cabins ❸–❺, units ❹–❻

Westshore Holiday Camp 1 Main Rd, Westshore ⓣ06/835 9456, ⓔann.david@xtra.co.nz. Located midway along Westshore Beach, 3km north of town, this site is a little less formal than *Kennedy Park*, but still has all the facilities you're likely to need. Camping $9, cabins ❷, flats ❸

The Town

Napier is blessed with a fine location, neatly tucked under the skirts of **Bluff Hill** (Mataruahou), a three-kilometre-long outcrop festooned with the twisting roads of the eponymous and highly desirable suburb. At its eastern summit is **Bluff Hill Domain Lookout** (daily 7am–dusk), offering views of Cape Kidnappers to the west, and right across to the distant Mahia Peninsula in the east.

On Bluff Hill's southern flank, steep roads and even steeper steps switchback down to the grid pattern of the Art Deco **commercial centre** where, at the whim of mid-nineteenth-century Land Commissioner, Alfred Domett, streets were given the names of literary luminaries – Tennyson, Thackeray, Byron, Dickens, Shakespeare, Milton and more. Bisecting it all is the partly-pedestrianized main thoroughfare of Emerson Street, whose terracotta paving and palm trees run from Clive Square, one-time site of a makeshift "Tin Town" while the city was being rebuilt after the earthquake, to the pine-fringed **Marine Parade**. The long strip of grey shingle flanking Marine Parade is Napier's main **beach**, where treacherous undertows and powerful surf make it unsafe for swimming.

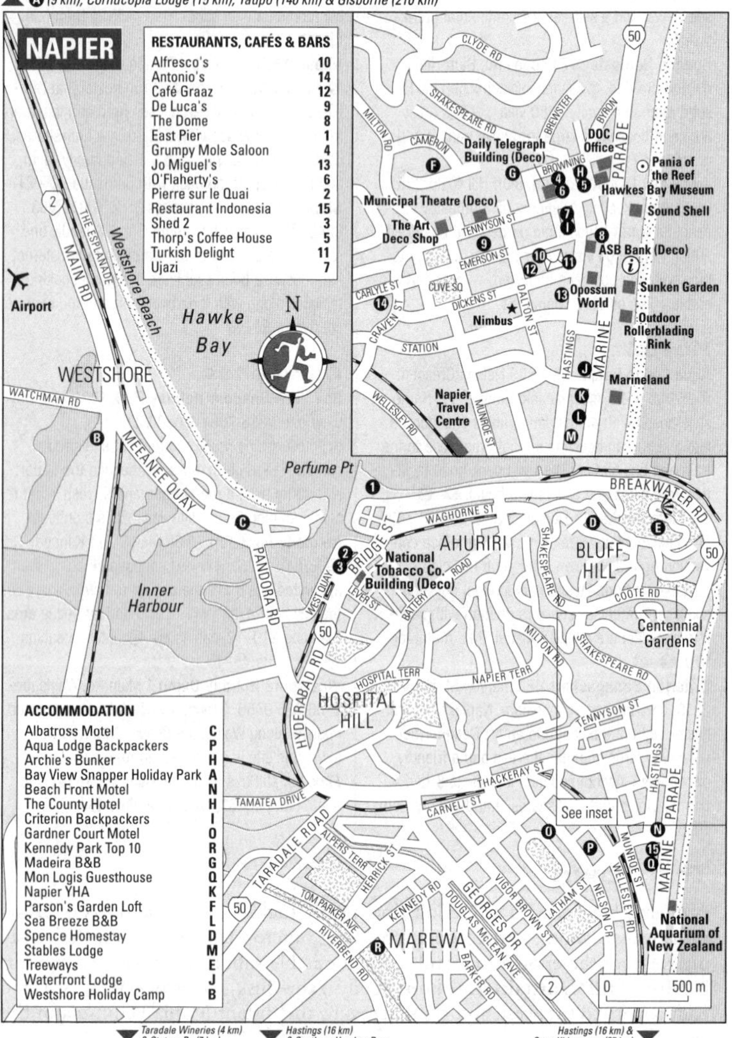

Around the northeastern side of Bluff Hill lies the original settlement site of **Ahuriri**, long since abandoned to factories and car sales yards, but now resurgent, with several of its warehouses being tarted up and a handful of trendy café/bars taking their chances.

The commercial centre: Art Deco Napier

If the dark cloud of the 1931 earthquake had a silver lining, it was the chance it gave Napier to rebuild from scratch, not just with more quake-resistant materials but to completely re-invent itself. Drawing on contemporary themes,

Pania of the Reef

Local Maori tell the tale of **Pania**, a beautiful sea-maiden who, each evening, would swim from the watery realm of Tangaroa, the god of the ocean, to quench her thirst at a freshwater spring in a clump of flax close to the base of Bluff Hill, then return to her people each morning. One evening, she was discovered by a young chief who wooed her and wanted her to remain on land. Eventually they married, but when Pania went to pay a final visit to her kin they forcibly restrained her in the briny depths, and she turned to stone as what is now known as **Pania Reef**. Fishers and divers still claim they can see her with her arms outstretched towards the shore.

Napier fell for **Art Deco** in a big way. A reaction against the organic and naturalistic themes of Art Nouveau, Deco embraced modernity, glorifying progress, the machine age and the Gatsby-style high-life, expressed by means of elaborate friezes featuring Adonis-like men, dancing women and springing gazelles. The onset of the Great Depression at the end of the 1920s pared down these excesses, not least because the key American exponents of the style, Louis Sullivan and Frank Lloyd Wright, were restrained by Chicago and New York statutes which dictated that tall buildings had to be stepped back to let the sun penetrate the dark canyons below. Necessity became the mother of invention, and the recurring theme of ziggurats was introduced.

Napier's version of Art Deco was informed by the privations of this austere era. At the same time, the architects looked for inspiration to California's similarly sun-drenched and earthquake-prone Santa Barbara which, just six years earlier, had suffered the same fate as Napier, and had risen from the ashes. They adopted fountains (a symbol of renewal), sunbursts, chevrons, lightning flashes and stylized fluting, embedding them in highly formalized but asymmetric designs. What emerged was a palimpsest of early-twentieth-century design, combining elements of the Arts and Crafts movement, the Californian Spanish Mission style, Egyptian and Mayan motifs, the stylized floral designs of Art Nouveau, the blockish forms associated with Charles Rennie Mackintosh, and even Maori imagery. For the best part of half a century, Napier's residents went about their lives, unaware of the architectural harmony all around them and merrily daubing everything in grey or muted blue paint. Fortunately this meant that when a few visionaries recognized the city's potential in the mid-1980s and formed the **Art Deco Trust**, everything was still there. The trust continues to promote the preservation of buildings and provides funding for shopkeepers to pick out distinctive architectural detail in pastel colours.

Visitors with only a passing interest in architecture can get a sense of what the fuss is about by wandering along the half-dozen streets in the city centre, notably **Emerson Street**, with its particularly homogeneous run of upper-floor frontages. Worth special attention here is the **ASB Bank**, on the corner of Hastings Street, its exterior adorned with fern shoots and a mask form from the head of a *taiaha* (a long fighting club), while its interior has a fine Maori rafter design. On Tennyson Street, look for the flamboyant **Daily Telegraph** building with stylized fountains capping the pilasters; and the **Municipal Theatre**, built in the late 1930s and exhibiting a strikingly geometric and streamlined form.

The only building to merit a foray outside the centre is the **National Tobacco Company Building** (interior Mon–Fri 9am–5pm only), on the corner of Bridge Street and Osian Street, in Ahuriri, whose entrance is probably the single most frequently-used image of Deco Napier and exhibits a decorative richness seldom seen on industrial buildings. The facade merges Deco asymmetry and the classic juxtaposition of cubic shapes and arches with the softening Art Nouveau motifs of roses and raupo (a kind of Kiwi bulrush).

Along Marine Parade

Napier's Art Deco finery may earn it a place on the world stage, but its defining feature is undoubtedly **Marine Parade**, a 2km-long boulevard lined with stately Norfolk pines and fashioned in the British seaside tradition. Currently faintly elegant and restrained, it is about to undergo a facelift with its string of attractions – chiefly Marineland and the National Aquarium of New Zealand – to be linked by curving walkways and bike and skating routes.

Marine Parade starts by Napier's port at the northern end of town and passes the foot of Bluff Hill, where native and exotic trees have been cultivated in **Centennial Gardens** (unrestricted entry), a former prison quarry backed by a picturesque waterfall cascading down the cliff face.

Pushing south you stroll past the outdoor swimming pool (currently being redeveloped into open-air hot pools), floral clock and the ornamental Tom Parker Fountain, to the bronze cast of the curvaceous **Pania of the Reef**, a siren of Maori legend (see box on p.465).

Opposite, the **Hawke's Bay Museum**, 65 Marine Parade (daily: Dec–March 9am–6pm; April–Nov 10am–4.30pm; $5), contains small but well chosen and competently presented exhibits, notably *taonga* (treasures) of the Ngati Kahungunu, including some exquisite clubs and fish-hooks. Downstairs there's detailed coverage of Hawke's Bay's colonial history; a photo display of the damage wrought by the 1931 earthquake, and a poignant and continuously running thirty-five-minute audiovisual of survivors' stories; and an excellent and manageable trawl through a century of design, from Art Nouveau and Art Deco through to the Philippe Starck-influenced 1990s. There's also a small yet intriguing display about paleontologist Joan Wiffen's 1979 discovery of a Megalosaur's tail bone in a creekbed northeast of Napier. Significantly, this

Art Deco Napier tours and trails

Keen observers will find classic Art Deco everywhere, but for a systematic exploration of Napier's Art Deco revival, begin at **The Art Deco Shop**, 163 Tennyson St (daily 9am–5pm), where you can watch a free twenty-minute introductory video and buy a leaflet for the **self-guided "Art Deco Walk"** ($2), outlining a stroll (1.5km; 1hr 30min to 2hr) through the downtown area. Dedicated Deco buffs meet here for the two-hour **Art Deco Afternoon Walking Tour** (2pm: Oct–June daily; July–Sept Sat, Sun & Wed 2pm; $10), which brings 1930s Napier to life through anecdote-laden patter, and offers access to some of the finer buildings giving you the chance to gaze around the interiors of shops and banks without feeling quite so self-conscious. The shorter **Art Deco Morning Walking Tour** (daily 10am; 1hr; $8) starts at the visitor centre. There's even a **Self-Drive Art Deco Tour** (leaflet $2.50), which presents a broader sweep of the district's distinctive architecture, reverentially trawling through Napier's far-flung Deco buildings, Hastings' Spanish Mission structures, the totally non-Deco Havelock North and the former Taradale Hotel, now a McDonald's but tastefully remodelled after the multinational was successfully petitioned by the Art Deco Trust. Finally, for real Deco fanatics, there's also the self-guided **Marewa Meander** (leaflet $1.50), covering the less-sexy domestic architecture in Napier's principal Art Deco suburb.

proved dinosaurs had existed in New Zealand when it broke away from the supercontinent of Gondwana eighty-five million years ago, despite earlier scientific beliefs that they never lived here.

Assorted seafront constructions line the next piece of the promenade: the curving colonnade of the Veronica Sun Bay and the stage known as the Sound Shell give way to a putting course and some attractive sunken gardens. Opposite, at 157 Marine Parade, **Opossum World** (daily 9am–5pm; free) presents all you ever need to know and more about New Zealand's greatest pest. Well-considered displays recount the struggle against the voracious destroyer of native bush, and a small shop sells all sorts of possum products – including pelts, fur hats and garments knitted from opossum fur blended with merino wool – with the motto that every item bought saves a tree.

Continuing beyond the sunken gardens and popular outdoor **rollerblading/skating** rink you reach **Marineland** (daily 10am–4.30pm; dolphin & seal shows 10.30am & 2pm; $4 to visit between shows, $9 to include the shows, $15 for a behind-the-scenes tour), a small marine zoo that houses a leopard seal, sea lions and penguins – many of them recovering from injuries sustained in the wild. During the outdated shows performing dolphins and seals are put through their paces. In the summer months you should try to book a couple of days in advance (a couple of weeks immediately after Christmas) if you fancy **feeding the dolphins** or an hour-long **swim with the dolphins** in the pool (ⓣ06/834 4027; $45, plus $10 for the near-essential wetsuit); they can usually be persuaded to play ball.

Further along the seafront, past the go-karts and boating lake, lies the **National Aquarium of New Zealand** (daily: Christmas–Jan 9am–9pm; Feb–Easter 9am–7pm; Easter–Christmas 9am–5pm; $12; ⓦwww.nationalaquarium.co.nz). Newly revamped, it is consolidating its position as the finest such establishment in the country, and comes packed with distinct marine environments – Africa, Asia and Australia – plus a substantial New Zealand section that includes an exact replica of a waterfall and rocky shoreline and walkways at different levels allowing you to inspect at close quarters. The most spectacular section is the **ocean tank** (hand-feeding at 2pm), with its Perspex walk-through tunnel giving intimate views of rays and the odd shark. There's more hand-feeding at the **reef tank** at 10am, plus Behind the Scenes tours tours ($20) at 9am and 1pm.

It is not all aquatic and there are interesting sections on New Zealand's reptilian *tuatara*, and a nocturnal **kiwi house**.

Eating, drinking and entertainment

As elsewhere in New Zealand, Napier's dining scene has improved markedly over recent years and, while no match for larger centres, there are enough places to keep you well fed and watered for a few days. It is worth eating at least one lunch at one of the **wineries** around about, getting there either under your own steam or on an organized tour, but there are plenty of **cafés** and **restaurants** scattered around the centre, and several more in the upper price bracket in waterside Ahuriri.

It is rare to find any really exciting entertainment, unless you hit town at **festival time** (see box on p.469), but a couple of the **bars** host live music at weekends and when touring bands pass through. Straightforward drinking happens along Hastings Street, mostly the short stretch between Browning and Emerson streets, where packs of revellers surge between any of half a dozen popular bars.

There are mainstream **movies** at Downtown Cinema 4, at the corner of Station and Munroe streets (Ⓣ06/831 0600), and more arthouse films at Century Cinema, 65 Marine Parade (Ⓣ06/835 9248), in the Hawke's Bay Museum building.

Alfresco's 65 Emerson St. Somewhat barn-like upper-level café and restaurant, which is worth a visit for good-value lunches and evening mains such as venison sausages, Moroccan fish or smoked hoki ($19–21).

Antonio's cnr Carlyle St & Craven St. Unpretentious and good-value eat-in and takeaway pizzeria with some budget pasta dishes. Closed Mon.

Café Graaz 82 Dalton St. Great snack spot, from giant toasted sandwiches to their own specialized cakes, both sweet and savoury. Get stuck into their potato cakes with sour cream and relish or, on the sweeter side, their scroggan, chocolate sludge cake or fudge espresso cake. Closed Sun.

De Luca's 180 Emerson St Ⓣ06/834 1988. Excellent, elegant Italian café-style food and great coffee daytime during weekdays. Extends on Fri nights to unusual dips and antipasto platters, enjoyable with their small selection of local reasonably priced wines and boutique beers; while Sat nights see a set menu of tapas or antipasto for $24 a head. Weekend brunches are exotic affairs, such as kumara hash browns with crème fraîche, or coconut and banana pancakes. They make all their own bread (except the sour dough). Bookings recommended for Sat night; closed Sun.

The Dome/Governors Inn cnr Marine Parade & Emerson St. Prominently sited wood-floored restaurant with attached coffee shop, intimate corner bar and a nightclub; a good haunt for any time of the day or night. Straightforward fare includes black pudding breakfast ($10), lamb pie ($12) and blackberry and apple crumble ($8).

East Pier Hardinge Rd. Modern and breezy waterfront café/bar that's great for just relaxing by the water or dining on ostrich fillet, steak-and-kidney pie or slow-roasted organic lamb, with all mains mostly around $25.

Grumpy Mole Saloon cnr Hastings St & Tennyson St. Napier's most jumping party bar, styled in Wild West mode and offering nightly drinks specials, plus big-screen TV sport and pool tables. On Fri & Sat nights a DJ keeps the place pumping till the small hours. Closed Mon.

Jo Miguels 193 Hastings St. The glazed-tile bar gives an authentically Spanish feel to this tapas bar where there's a daily blackboard of a dozen or so tapas to be washed down with a glass of chilled fino or local wine. Also has pizzas, cocktails and live music at weekends.

Restaurant Indonesia 409 Marine Parade Ⓣ06/835 8303. Compact seafront restaurant decorated with Indonesian prints and fabrics, and dishing up Indonesian mains ($18–22) and a choice of rijstaffel spreads, including a vegetarian version ($28 to $35 a head). Licensed & BYO.

O'Flaherty's 35 Hastings St. Lively Irish bar proffering simple bar food, big-screen TV sport when the rugby's on, and live music every Fri & Sat night.

Pierre sur le Quai 60 West Quay, Ahuriri Ⓣ06/834 0189. The place for that romantic dinner for two, exuding French provincial style and serving delicious dishes such as haloumi tart with harissa ($14) and roast venison leg with thyme jus ($32) followed, of course, by crème brûlée ($9). Closed Sun.

Shed 2 cnr West Quay & Lever St, Ahuriri Ⓣ06/835 2202. Fashionable restaurant and bar in a former wool store that's fine for a beer or gourmet pizza (such as Sichuan chicken with hoisin sauce) but also good for dining on imaginative mains ($20–$25) like sesame-seed and nori-crumbed steak or braised octopus and squid with wasabi/honey dressing. The bar comes alive on weekend evenings.

Thorps Coffee House 40 Hastings St. Excellent eat-in and takeaway build-your-own sandwich place also serving good breakfasts, lunches, cakes, shakes and coffee; the interior features fine Art Deco details. Closed Sun.

Turkish Delight 3 Market St. Excellent value authentic Turkish and Middle Eastern dishes, to eat in or take away. The *boreks* are to die for.

Ujazi Café 28 Tennyson St. Small daytime café with a vaguely alternative and somewhat erratic feel, serving largely vegetarian snacks for breakfast and lunch: quiches, pies, sandwiches and salads, plus scrumptious juices and good strong coffee.

Hawke's Bay festivals

During January and February, Napier and nearby Hastings flip into festive mode. Small-time events take place in January, but the first of the major events is the **Harvest Hawke's Bay** (first weekend in February; ⓦwww.harvesthawkesbay.co.nz), when food and wine lovers from around the country flock to the Hawke's Bay Racing Centre, Prospect Rd, Hastings, for music, food and wine. Proceedings reach fever pitch for the Charity Wine auction, which is followed by a Sunday drive around the wineries. The **Mission Vineyard Concert** usually takes place in early February (the precise dates are dependent on artists' bookings, and announced in November), when an internationally famous vocalist – Kiri Te Kanawa, Ray Charles and Dionne Warwick have attended in recent years – performs outdoors at the Mission Estate Winery to an audience of around 20,000.

No sooner has the Hawke's Bay summer festival wound up, than Napier gears up for the **Art Deco Weekend** (ⓣ06/835 1191, ⓦwww.artdeconapier.com), usually held on the second or third weekend in February and extending to five light-hearted days of merriment, extending to guided walks, open-house tours of domestic Art Deco, bicycle tours, Thirties-dress picnics, champagne breakfasts, dress balls, silent movies and the like.

Cape Kidnappers and the wineries

No visit to Napier or Hastings is complete without spending some time exploring the surroundings: the gannet colony at **Cape Kidnappers** and the forty or so **wineries** around Napier and Hastings. Heading from Napier towards Cape Kidnappers, Marine Parade (SH2) trawls through an industrial sprawl on the outskirts of Napier until 9km south it passes the windswept **Waitangi Mission site**, where a plaque records the establishment of Hawke's Bay's first mission station by William Colenso in 1844. From here it is a couple of kilometres to the village of **Clive**, where a signed turn leads to the beachside settlements ofTe Awanga and Clifton, starting point for trips to Cape Kidnappers.

Cape Kidnappers

After James Cook's ill-starred initial encounter with Maori at Gisborne, he sailed south to the southern limit of Hawke's Bay and anchored off the jagged peninsula known to the Ngati Kahungunu as Te Matua-a-maui, "the fishhook of Maui" – a reference to the origin of the North Island, which was dragged from the oceans by Maui. Here, Cook experienced a second unfortunate meeting. This time Maori traders noticed two young Tahitian interpreters aboard the *Endeavour*; believing them to be held against their will, the traders captured one of them and paddled away. The boy escaped back to the ship, but Cook subsequently marked the point on his chart as **Cape Kidnappers**.

Neither James Cook nor Joseph Banks, both meticulous in recording flora and fauna, mentioned any gannets on the peninsula's final shark-tooth flourish of pinnacles. However, a hundred years later, twenty or so pairs were recorded, and now there are over five thousand pairs – making this the world's largest mainland **gannet colony**. Gannets are big birds, members of the booby family distinguished by their gold-and-black head markings and

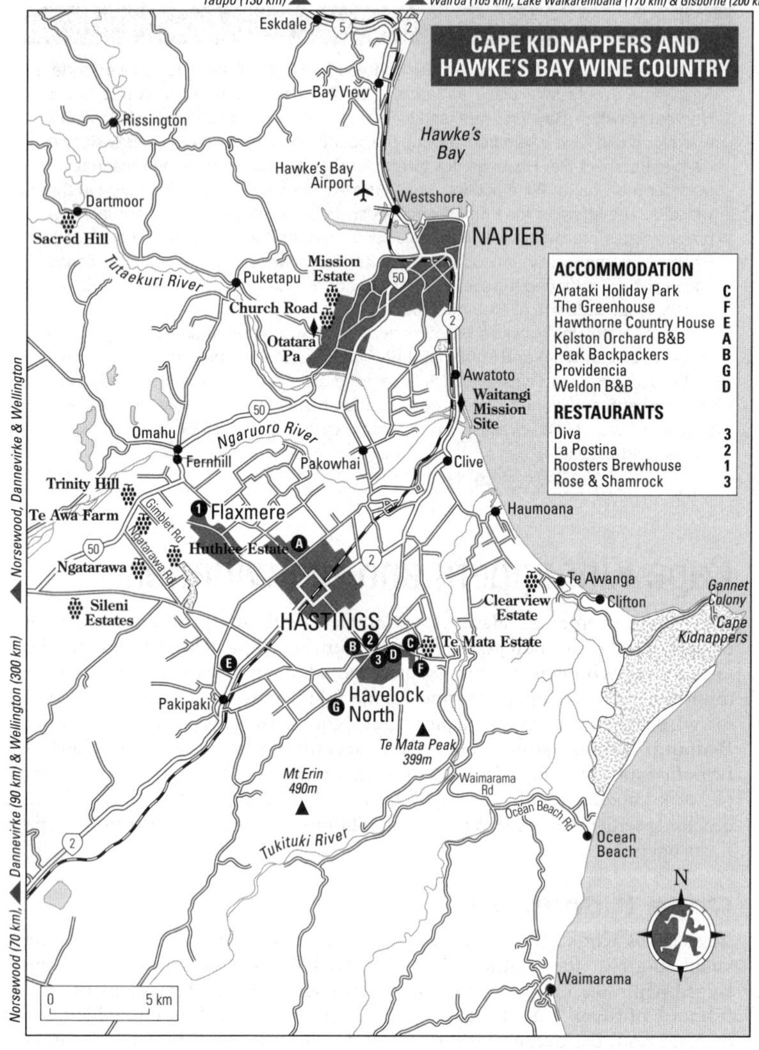

their apparent lack of fear of humans. The birds start arriving at Cape Kidnappers for nesting in June, laying their eggs from early July through to October, with the chicks hatching some six weeks later. Once fledged, at around fifteen weeks, the young gannets embark on their inaugural flight, a marathon and as-yet-unexplained 3000-kilometre journey to Australia, where they spend a couple of years before flying back to spend the rest of their life in New Zealand, returning to their place of birth to breed each year.

Practicalities

During the **breeding season** (June–Oct), the cape is closed to the public, and one colony, The Saddle, is always reserved for scientific study. At other times you can get within a metre or so of the remaining two sites: The Plateau, a few hundred metres back from the saddle, where two thousand chattering pairs nest beak-by-jowl; and the beachside Black Reef, the largest colony, a couple of kilometres back from the tip of the peninsula, where there are a further 3500 pairs.

There are several ways to visit the gannets, all starting from well-signposted points in the adjacent settlements of **Clifton** and **Te Awanga**, 20km southeast of Napier, both reached from the Napier or Hastings visitor centres with Kiwi Shuttle (ⓣ027/593 669; booking essential; $15 return). Most tours are tide-dependent, travelling to the colony along the beach below unstable hundred-metre-high cliffs. The least expensive way to get to the gannets is simply to walk the 11km along the beach from Clifton (roughly 5hr return); no permits are needed, but you'll need to check **tide tables** with DOC or the Hastings or Napier visitor centres and plan to leave between three and four hours after high tide; the useful DOC Guide to Cape Kidnappers ($1) contains a **map** and a few tips. Gannet **trips** come and go, but the traditional and best way is aboard tractor-drawn trailers along the beach with Gannet Beach Adventures (Oct to late-April daily; 4hr; $25; ⓣ06/875 0898 & 0800/426 638, ⓦwww.gannets.com), whose pace and approach give plenty of opportunities to appreciate the geology along the way and observe the birds at close quarters. These end at a DOC shelter, from where you face a twenty-minute uphill slog to The Plateau, where you'll have half an hour to admire the birds. A worthwhile alternative, which takes you right to the gannets with almost no walking, is with Gannet Safaris (ⓣ0800/427232 & 06/875 0893, ⓦwww.gannetsafaris.com; Sept–April daily 9.30am & 1.30pm; $40) which gains access **overland** through Summerlee Station on three-hour trips in air-conditioned 4WD minibuses.

Hawke's Bay wine country

Napier and Hastings are almost entirely encircled by the **Hawke's Bay's wine country**, one of New Zealand's largest and most exalted grape-growing regions threaded by the **Hawke's Bay wine trail**, which wends its way past thirty-odd wineries, most offering free tastings. Many places are now fashioning themselves as "destination wineries" where tasting is almost an adjunct to eating lunch at one of the vineyard restaurants (undoubtedly a Hawke's Bay highlight), enjoying a picnic in the landscaped grounds, maybe looking through a small museum, and even appreciating the architectural style designed to catch the eye of discerning wine tourists.

Hawke's Bay is largely the province of boutique producers, with an unshakeable domestic reputation and an international standing challenged only by the South Island's Marlborough region. One of New Zealand's most classically well-suited areas for viticulture, with a climatic pattern similar to that of the great Bordeaux vineyards, Hawke's Bay produces fine **Chardonnay** and **Cabernet Sauvignon**. As scientific studies unravel the complexity of the local soils and microclimates, growers have begun to diversify into **Merlot**, which has gained a foothold north of Napier along the Esk Valley, while others predict that Hawke's Bay may one day topple Marlborough's **Sauvignon Blanc** primacy. Hawke's Bay is New Zealand's longest-established wine-growing region: vines were first planted in 1851 by French Marist missionaries, ostensibly to produce sacramental wine. The excess was sold, and the commercial aspect of the operation continues today as the Mission Estate Winery. Some fifty-odd years later, other wineries began to spring up, initially favouring the fertile plains, but as tastes became more sophisticated, such sites were forsaken for the open-textured gravel terraces alongside the Tutaekuri, Ngaruroro and Tukituki rivers, which retain the day's heat and are free from moist sea breezes. In this area the vineyards of the **Gimblett Road** area produce increasingly praiseworthy wines.

If you have your own transport, head out with a copy of the *A Guide to the Wineries* leaflet (free from Napier and Hastings visitor centres), which lists wineries open to the public – see box on p.474 for the pick of the bunch – along with their facilities and current opening hours (generally daily 10am–5pm in summer but sometimes closed early in the week). Much of the country covered by the wine trail is also part of the region's **art and food trails**. The free *Hawke's Bay Art Trail* booklet directs you to the workshops and galleries of some of the best painters, sculptors, potters and craftspeople hereabouts; while the *Hawke's Bay Wine Country Food Trail* leaflet (also free) includes a map showing the whereabouts of all manner of places selling quality produce, along with cafés, wineries and restaurants.

If you can't find an abstemious driver, take a **wine tour**, most of which visit four or five wineries over the course of a morning or afternoon. They're all Napier-based but will pick up in Hastings and Havelock North, either free of for a small fee. Vince's Vineyard Tours ($40; Ⓣ06/836 6705) are great fun with an entertaining and knowledgeable guide and a flexible schedule. Other good bets include the popular Bay Tours & Charters (Ⓣ06/843 6953, Ⓦwww.bay-tours.co.nz), who offer a basic four-stop tour (daily 1pm; $30) and a five-stop lunch tour (daily 11.30am; $40, food not included); and the more intimate Vicky's Wine Tours (Ⓣ06/843 9991), who offer a number of morning and afternoon tours ($40–50).

A leisurely alternative is a **bike tour** of half a dozen wineries run by On Yer Bike (Ⓣ06/879 8735, Ⓔinfo@onyerbike.net.nz; $40), who are based 9km south west of Hastings near Ngatara Wines. Reserve a day in advance, and you'll be provided with a bike, a map of the wineries, a mobile phone and a substantial packed lunch and can then make your way around at your own pace. Any wines you buy will be picked up for you, and if you overindulge they'll come and pick you up.

Hastings and around

As little as ten years ago, inland **HASTINGS**, 20km south of Napier, was a rival to its northern kin as Hawke's Bay's premier city, buoyed by the wealth generated by the surrounding farmland and orchards. In recent years, shifting economic patterns, the closure of Hastings' two huge freezing works (abattoirs) and Napier's ascendancy as a tourist destination have put Hastings firmly in second place. However, the city is now playing catch-up and there's a certain reborn civic pride evident in the smartened up central streetscape, new paving, street lighting and a profusion of imaginatively planted flower beds. Unfortunately it doesn't completely disguise the presence of warehouse-style shops in among the far more handsome central buildings that were erected after the same 1931 earthquake that rocked Napier. Hastings was saved from the worst effects of the ensuing fires, which were quenched using the artesian water beneath the city before they could take hold. Nonetheless, the centre had to be rebuilt. As in Napier, **Art Deco** predominates and, though Hastings lacks the flamboyance and overall exuberance of its neighbour, there are some unusually harmonious townscapes along Russell, Eastbourne and Heretaunga streets. Hastings also enthusiastically embraced the **Spanish Mission** style, and two exemplary buildings warrant a brief visit.

Hastings is at the heart of the wonderful Hawke's Bay wine country (see p.471), and most of the vineyards are easier to reach from here than Napier. Long before grapes were big business, Hastings relied on apples, pears and peaches, all still grown in huge quantities. The harvest, which begins in February and lasts three or four months, provides casual **orchard work** for those willing to thin, pick or pack fruit; the hostels (see below) are the best sources of work and up-to-the-minute information.

Hastings' eastern neighbour is the upmarket **Havelock North**, 3km east at the foot of the striking ridge-line of **Te Mata Peak**. There isn't a great deal to it and the only diversion is a drive up the peak, but the cobbled central streets give it a village atmosphere and the proliferation of tranquil **B&Bs** in the vicinity make good bases for exploring the central Hawke's Bay area.

Arrival and information

Passenger trains no longer rumble right through the centre of town, but long-distance **buses** continue to pull up outside the Hastings Travel Centre on Caroline Road. Local bus operator Nimbus (ⓣ06/877 8133) runs to Napier, Havelock North and Flaxmere (Mon–Fri only) from the corner of Eastbourne Street East and Russell Street.

New transport arrangements mean that long-distance buses may soon stop outside the **visitor centre**, cnr Russell & Heretaunga streets (Mon–Fri 8.30am–7pm, Sat & Sun 8.30am–5pm; ⓣ06/873 5526, ⓦwww.hawkesbaynz.com) located inside the Westerman's Building. Here there's **internet access** and **left-luggage lockers**, though these are only accessible during opening hours. There's also internet access at Internet World Cyber Café, 102 Queen St East.

Accommodation

Hastings' **accommodation** is greatly affected by the harvest: from mid-February to May, there is precious little chance of finding a bed at any of the cheaper places, which meet the demand for self-catering and longer stays. If you're hoping to secure a bed for the **fruit-picking season**, plan to arrive early in February and expect to pay around $80 a week for a bunk in a cramped room. Occupancy in the more expensive places is dictated by the normal summer-holiday pattern, and it's advisable to make **reservations** a few days ahead if you'll be here between December and February. Some of the nicest places to stay are scattered through the countryside around Havelock North, where exclusive **B&Bs** and swanky self-catering houses are the mainstay.

Hastings

AJ's Backpackers Lodge 405 Southland Rd ⓣ06/878 2302, ⓔajslodge@xtra.co.nz. Pleasant hostel in an Edwardian villa that has something of the communal feeling of a student flat. It is popular with orchard workers, usually keeps a bed or two for overnighters, has bikes for guests' use, and a couple of boxer dogs. Dorms ❶, rooms ❷

Hastings Backpackers Hostel 505 Lyndon Rd East ⓣ06/876 5888, ⓦwww.medcasa.co.nz. Comfortable house near the centre, with good facilities and very low rates, but full of pickers in the season. Camping $10, dorms ❶, rooms ❷

Hastings Top 10 Holiday Park 610 Windsor Ave ⓣ06/878 6692 & 0508/427 846, ⓔholiday-park@hastingstourism.co.nz. Appealing campsite

Hawke's Bay wineries

With over forty **wineries** in the region, it would be hard to give comprehensive coverage of them all, but listed below are a few favourites, concentrating on those that make good lunch spots or feature some sort of attraction other than the obligatory wine tasting. Napier's closest wineries are 8km to the southwest in the suburb of **Taradale**, en route to a couple more wineries in the western foothills of the Kaweka Range along Dartmoor Road. Closer to Hastings, there are clusters outside **Havelock North**, 9km east of Hastings, and 10km west near **Fernhill** – the fastest-growing wine district in Hawke's Bay.

Church Road Winery 150 Church Rd, Taradale ⓣ06/844 2053. A tolerably interesting wine-making museum ($5), some excellent bottles to sample – notably the Church Road Chardonnay – and a restaurant using fresh local produce, that spills out into the gardens, serving Mediterranean-style dishes at reasonable prices.

Clearview Estate Winery 194 Clifton Rd, Te Awanga ⓣ06/875 0150. Some of New Zealand's most highly rated wines are produced here, in tiny quantities and sold only from the vineyard. You do pay a premium for this sort of attention to detail, but the wines are superb, especially when enjoyed with the restaurant's equally classy southern Mediterranean lunches outside in the restaurant. Can be combined with a visit to Cape Kidnappers (see p.469).

Huthlee Estate 84 Montana Rd, Bridge Pa ⓣ06/879 6234. A small and very welcoming winery west of Hastings where the emphasis is on reds, notably Merlot and Pinot Grigio, but their Sauvignon Blanc has done well, too. They will take you on a free vineyard walk and there's a picnic area, plus petanque.

Mission Estate Winery 198 Church Rd, Taradale ⓣ06/844 6025. Worth a visit for its pivotal position in the development of the Hawke's Bay's wine industry alone, but it hasn't rested on its laurels, offering well organized, free guided tours (Mon–Sat 10.30am & 2pm). There's an à la carte restaurant on site.

Ngatarawa Wines 305 Ngatarawa Rd, Bridge Pa ⓣ06/879 7603. An excellent

on the edge of Windsor Park, with tent sites, a range of modern units and good facilities, though it does get busy over the fruit-picking season. Camping $10, cabins ❷, kitchen cabins ❸, motel units ❹

Kelston Orchard B&B 49 Ormond Rd ⓣ06/879 7301, ⓔkelston.orch@xtra.co.nz. Attractive and extremely relaxing homestay in a big beautiful rose garden attached to an apple orchard about 3km from the town centre. In the house are two twin rooms, sharing a bathroom, and in the garden is a self-contained en-suite double. ❹

Travellers Lodge 606 St Aubyn St West ⓣ06/878 7108, ⓔtravellers.lodge@clear.net.nz. Well-managed hostel in a pair of suburban houses, with a sauna, garden and off-street parking. There is a range of rooms, all with comfy beds, but these are often full from November to May. Dorms ❶, rooms ❷

Woodbine Cottage 1279 Louie St ⓣ06/876 9388, ⓔnshand@xtra.co.nz. B&B in an attractive cottage on the outskirts of Hastings with a large garden, tennis court and pool, and pleasant sunny rooms. ❺

Havelock North and around

Arataki Holiday Park 139 Arataki Rd ⓣ06/877 7479, ⓔarataki.motel.holiday.park@xtra.co.nz. Rurally sited and well-appointed campsite that benefits from being one of the few inexpensive places around here that doesn't take fruit pickers. Camping $10, cabins ❷, kitchen cabins ❸, motel units ❹

The Greenhouse 228 Te Mata Rd ⓣ06/877 4904, ⓔthe.greenhouse@xtra.co.nz. Superbly equipped self-catering cottage, surrounded by beautiful vineyards and sleeping up to four. ❽

Hawthorne Country House 420 SH2, 7km south-west ⓣ06/878 0035, ⓦwww.hawthorne.co.nz. Beautiful and very welcoming B&B in a grand Edwardian villa surrounded by croquet lawns and farmland. Huge en-suite rooms are decorated with

first stop, a small winery with free tastings of quality tipples (notably Chardonnay, Sauvignon Blanc and Cabernet Merlot, as well as highly acclaimed dessert wines from Riesling) in a century-old stable complex with attractive picnic areas and a petanque court.

Sacred Hill Wines 1033 Dartmoor Rd, 20km west of Taradale ⓣ06/844 0138. A lengthy excursion rewarded by a few sips of their albeit superb wine, and a tasty meal served on rustic tables under olive trees (Dec–April only; booking essential).

Sileni Estates 2016 Maraekakaho Rd, Bridge Pa ⓣ06/879 8768. A relative newcomer that has brought a new level of professionalism to the area with landscaped grounds (complete with culinary garden), and striking buildings that house a classy café (mains $15), a fine restaurant (four-course degustation menu $75), a gourmet food store, a culinary school and, of course, a winery with tastings ($5 for seven wines). Their first vintage was in 1998 and they're already gaining an international reputation.

Te Awa Farm Winery 2375 SH50, Fernhill ⓣ06/879 7602. Sited near the famed Gimblett Road, this winery produces exceptional reds (Merlot, Cabernet Merlot and Pinotage) that are more aromatic and livelier than many of their Hawke's Bay contenders; and their Chardonnays are pretty good too; tastings $2 for six. An indoor and outdoor lunchtime restaurant is highly regarded and serves excellent platters and daily specials that are reasonably priced.

Te Mata Estate Winery 349 Te Mata Rd, Havelock North ⓣ06/877 4399. New Zealand's oldest winery on its existing site, now making a fairly small volume of premium hand-made wines, notably their Coleraine blend of Cabernet Sauvignon, Merlot and Cabernet Franc. Free tasting, winery tours at 11am, and the added bonus of architecturally controversial house among the grapes designed by Ian Athfield (see box on p.497).

Trinity Hill Winery 2396 SH50, Fernhill ⓣ06/879 7778. Strikingly modern winery in the Gimblett Road area, where you can taste ($5; refunded with purchase) some of their excellent reds as well as the Chardonnay.

understated elegance and the breakfasts are delicious. ❼

Peak Backpackers 33 Havelock Rd ⓣ06/877 1170, ⓕ877 1175. Small and relaxed hostel close to the centre of Havelock North but with free Hastings pick-up and a weekday bus service outside. Dorms ❶, rooms ❷

Providencia 225 Middle Rd, 3km south of town ⓣ06/877 2300, ⓦwww.providencia.co.nz. Very comfortable rural B&B with one queensize and one kingsize room in a beautifully preserved homestead built in 1903. Delicious breakfasts are served either in the guest lounge or out on the veranda, and there are complimentary drinks on arrival. Also comfy, modern self-catering cottages in the grounds with breakfast supplied. Cottages ❻, queen ❼, king ❽

Weldon B&B 98 Te Mata Rd ⓣ06/877 7551, ⓦwww.weldon.co.nz. Quiet B&B in a French-provincial style home surrounded by mature gardens. Well-appointed rooms all come with fresh flowers and there are great breakfasts. ❺

The Town

After the 1931 earthquake, Hastings looked to the Californian-inspired **Spanish Mission** style of architecture. A couple of key buildings set the tone, with rough-cast stucco walls, arched windows, small balconies, barley-twist columns and heavily overhung roofs clad in terracotta tiles. All the finest examples can be seen in an hour or so, using the self-guided *Heritage of Hastings* walk leaflet (free from the visitor centre), but if time is short, limit your wanderings

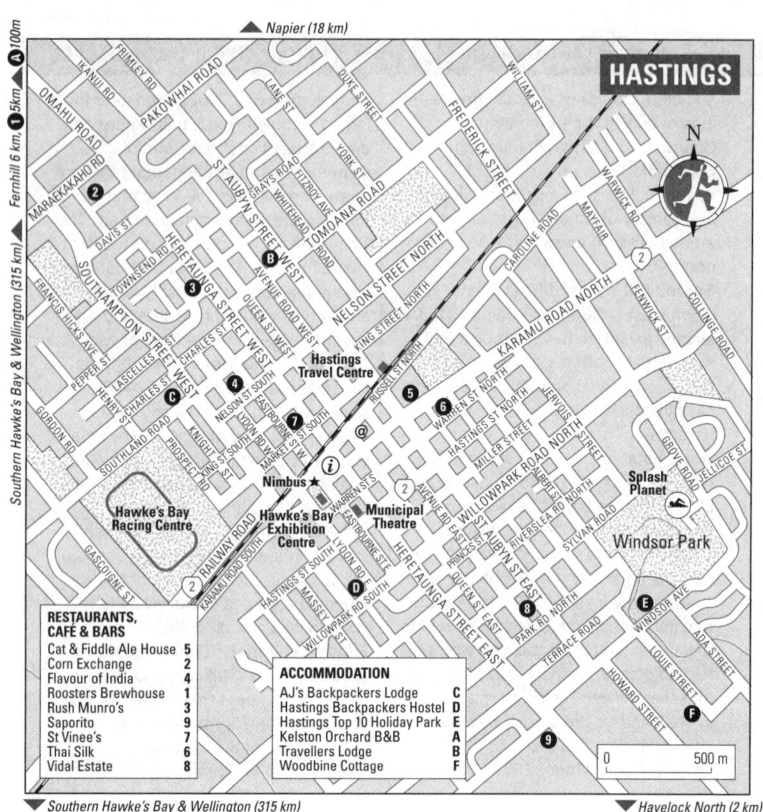

to Heretaunga Street East, where the visitor centre is located inside the **Westerman's Building**, recently restored to show off its gorgeous bronze-work and sumptuous lead lighting. The **Municipal Theatre**, on the corner with Hastings Street, was actually built fifteen years before the earthquake, but was remodelled to create the region's finest Spanish Mission facade. Also worth a quick look is the **Hawke's Bay Exhibition Centre**, opposite the junction of Eastbourne Street and Karamu Road (Mon–Fri 10am–4.30pm, Sat & Sun 11am–4pm; free except for special exhibitions), which hosts all manner of local, national and international art shows, and has a relaxing café with good coffee.

Families may well find themselves at **Splash Planet**, Grove Road (daily 10am–6pm; $22 for the whole park or $69 for a family; ⓣ06/876 9856, ⓦwww.splashplanet.co.nz), the first fully themed waterpark in the country, centred on a replica Disney-like castle and offering a welter of amusements from a double-dipper dual-tube ride and a "Never Ending River Ride" to hot pools ($8 without a parkwide ticket) and boating lake. Togs, towels and arm-bands can be rented.

Foodies in town at the weekend should make for the **Hawke's Bay Farmers Market** (Sun 8.30am–12.30pm), a relatively new venture which has quickly establishing itself at the Hawke's Bay Showgrounds on Kenilworth Road.

Te Mata Peak

Driving from Hastings to Havelock North, the long ridge of limestone bluffs which make up the 399m **Te Mata Peak** looms into view. The ridge is held to be the supine form of a Maori chief, Rongokako, who choked on a rock as he tried to eat through the hill – just one of many Herculean feats with which he attempted to woo the beautiful daughter of a Heretaunga chief. The long and winding Te Mata Peak Road climbs the hill to a wonderful vantage point overlooking the fertile plains, north across Hawke's Bay and Cape Kidnappers, and east to the surf-pounded strands of Ocean Beach and Waimarama, the main swimming **beaches** for Hastings and Havelock North.

The peak is encompassed by the Te Mata Peak Trust Park, entered 3.5km up Te Mata Peak Road, where there is a parking area and a number of **walking tracks** through the hill's patches of parkland. These are outlined in the $1 brochure on the park available at visitor centres and can be combined to create a route through groves of native trees and redwoods, and a wetland area before reaching the summit (2–3hr return).

Overcome with grief at her father's death, Rongokako's own daughter threw herself off the peak – something you can emulate by **tandem paragliding** with Peak Paragliding (ⓣ06/843 4717 & 025/512 886; from $120), an activity that uses the thermals and winds off the Pacific to carry you along the ridge and back for at least fifteen minutes.

Eating and drinking

For a town of its size, Hastings is relatively poorly supplied with good **places to eat**, though a small selection of places in Havelock North bumps up the quota, and lunches at the **wineries** are a great option. Keep an eye out, too, for Hawke's Bay summer festival happenings (see box on p.469).

Drinkers will find a smattering of welcoming places in both towns, with **beer** fans well served at *Roosters Brewhouse* (see below).

Hastings

Cat & Fiddle Ale House 502 Karamu Rd. A traditional English-style pub with a huge range of tap and bottled beers, as well as bargain chips-with-everything meals.

Corn Exchange 118 Maraekakaho Rd. Stylish but unpretentious restaurant and bar converted from an attractive 1940s grain store on the western fringes of the city and serving $10–15 brasserie lunches and $20–25 dinners, or just drinks.

Flavour of India cnr Lyndon Rd & Nelson St ⓣ06/870 9992. Tasty curry dishes served up in a central Hastings house with most mains around the $12 mark. Licensed & BYO.

Roosters Brewhouse 1470 Omahu Rd, 7km west of central Hastings. Small welcoming micro brewery, offering traditional natural brews, best supped in their pleasant café or outdoors at garden tables, while tucking into straightforward hearty dishes at reasonable prices. There's also free tasting of their English ale, lager and dark beers, and you can buy a flagon to take away. Closed Sun.

Rush Munro's 704 Heretaunga St West. A small ice-cream garden and takeaway that's been packing in the locals for some seventy years. Its sumptuous and intensely fruity natural ice cream is fashioned into distinctive, peaked cones. Concoctions of coffee, chocolate and nut are available, but it is hard to beat the traditional fruit flavours – feijoa is particularly scrumptious, though something of an acquired taste. They also sell ice-cream sundaes and take-home packs.

Saporito 1101 Heretaunga St ⓣ06/878 3364. Quality meals to take away; try one of the meat or veg lasagnes ($10) or something from the carvery ($10–13). Closed Sun & Mon.

St Vinee's 108 Market St South. Well-regarded wine bar and café in the centre of Hastings, serving an innovative selection of mid-range mains, plus potato wedges, nachos, venison sausages and light lunches.
Thai Silk 601 Karamu Rd. Standard Thai restaurant, but welcoming and with a good range of traditional Thai dishes cooked to perfection.
Vidal Estate 913 Aubyn St East; book at weekends ⓣ06/876 8105. Popular semi-formal restaurant attached to a winery with the linen and polished glassware set amid huge wine barrels. Lunch dishes (each matched with a Vidal wine) might be duck terrine or mussel and coriander cakes ($16–18), and dinner mains start at $24.

Havelock North

Diva Café & Bar in the Village Court, Napier Rd ⓣ06/877 5149. Casual daytime café and evening restaurant with a blackboard menu of tasty mains from around $20; alfresco dining out the back.
La Postina cnr of Havelock Rd & Napier Rd ⓣ06/877 1714. Classy Mediterranean restaurant with minimal decor, outside seating and a strong local wine list. Expect field-mushroom risotto ($9) followed by the likes of dukkah-encrusted lamb rump on kumara and snow pea mash ($24).
Rose & Shamrock 15 Napier Rd. A fair attempt at an English/Irish pub, with Guinness and a broad range of Irish beers, draught ales, guest beers from Kiwi micro breweries, well-priced bar meals and occasional Irish folk bands.

Southern Hawke's Bay

South of Hastings, the main road (SH2) gives the coast a wide berth, taking you through the relentless sheep stations of **Southern Hawke's Bay**, a region uncluttered by places of genuine interest. Small farming towns stand as fitting memorials to the steadfast pioneers who tamed the region, spending the latter half of the nineteenth century clearing the huge totara trees of Seventy Mile Bush, pushing through communication links, and then establishing sheep runs on the rich plains.

None of the towns are especially interesting and if time is short you'd do as well to push straight on through, but with a little more leisure, the "Scandinavian" settlements of **Norsewood** and **Dannevirke** warrant a brief stop. The New Zealand Wars of the 1860s had discouraged British immigrants and, as new areas were opened up for colonization, the authorities took their search for settlers elsewhere, briefed to find rugged folk with strong ties to the land. In 1872, Danes, Norwegians and a few Swedes answered the call, arriving in Napier ill-prepared for the hardship ahead of them. Their promised plots of land turned out to be tracts of impenetrable bush; the wages paid to construction workers who toiled to build road and rail links barely covered exorbitant food costs; and when the government demanded that the settlers repay their passage, many promptly upped sticks for North America, leaving little trace of their brief sojourn.

Almost all traffic follows SH2, but visitors in search of the esoteric might want to stray along **SH52**, which loops east towards the rugged coastline from dull **Waipukurau**, 50km south of Hastings, re-emerging at Masterton in the Wairarapa (see p.480). Thirty-five kilometres south of Waipukurau (and 6km south of Porangahau), a sign marks the hill known as **Taumatawhakatangihangakoauauotamateaturipukakapikimaungahoronukapokaiwhenuakitanatahu**, which, unsurprisingly, rates as the world's longest place name; roughly, this mouthful translates as "the hill where Tamatea, circumnavigator of the lands, played the flute for his lover".

Whichever way you head south, the coastline is almost entirely inaccessible, apart from at Castlepoint (see p.482), reached by a sixty-five-kilometre road from Masterton.

Norsewood

Some 85km south of Hastings, SH2 enters a cutting which bisects the hilltop village of **NORSEWOOD**, invisible from the highway and easily missed. Predominantly settled by Norwegians, it manages to retain a mildly Scandinavian tenor. Like most southern Hawke's Bay towns, it was carved out of the forest, but in 1888 the bush bit back, and a raging bushfire virtually razed the place. Some regarded the devastation as an act of God precipitated by a local plebiscite that ended temperance – but, as the local paper noted, "the church was burnt down and the pub was saved".

The village is in two parts. Upper Norsewood is basically just one short, quaint and deathly quiet main street (Coronation Street) that runs past a glassed-in boathouse containing the fishing boat *Bindalsfareing*, a gift from the Norwegian government on the occasion of Norsewood's centenary, and a small **visitor centre** staffed by volunteers in a gift shop called The Barn (ⓣ06/374 0991; roughly daily 10am–4pm). Opposite is the **Pioneer Museum** (daily 8.30am–4.30pm; $2), a cottage museum full of reminders of pioneering days housed in an 1888 house. Kiwis are more familiar with Lower Norsewood, 1km to the south, which is mainly strung along Hovding Street and home to Norsewear, a company famed for its hard-wearing woollen garments in rustic Scandinavian designs; the socks in particular last for years. If a chill wind is swooping down from the Ruahine Range, check for bargains in the **factory shop** (Mon–Fri 8.30am–5pm, Sat & Sun 9am–5pm).

Dannevirke

There's no reason for more than the briefest of stops in **DANNEVIRKE**, a small farming town 20km south of Norsewood, that struggles to play up its heritage, with little more than a rather unpleasant modern windmill in Copenhagen Square on the main street to support its cause. Records and artefacts amassed in the **Gallery of History**, Gordon Street (Mon–Fri 9.30am–4pm, Sat & Sun 1.30–4pm; $2), provide comprehensive coverage of the founding of the town in 1872, when the forest was hacked away to create Dannevirke ("Dane's Work") – a name recalling both the ninth-century defensive earthwork constructed across the waist of the Jutland peninsula in their homeland and the task ahead, the forging of a road from Wellington to Napier. Early photos give a sense of the hard life that drove away many of the Danes, their place taken by British migrants lured by the opening of the Napier–Wellington railway in 1884. The few Danes who remained were soon outnumbered; only a flick through the telephone directory or a glance at some of the shops and street signs betray Dannevirke's Scandinavian heritage.

Napier–Wellington **buses** stop in town not far from the **visitor centre**, 156 High St (Mon–Fri 9am–5.30pm, Sat & Sun 10am–2pm; ⓣ06/374 4167), and there's the usual selection of tearooms, plus *State of the Art*, 21 High St, a reputable **café** and espresso bar. Should you want to **stay** the night here, check out the *Dannevirke Holiday Park*, Christian Street (ⓣ06/374 7625; tent sites $10, cabins ❷, flats ❸), which has a heated indoor pool and is beautifully set in a dell surrounded by a few remnants of bush; or the *Viking Lodge Motel*, 180 High St (ⓣ06/374 6669, ⓕ374 6686; ❹).

South of Dannevirke, SH2 runs 25km to Woodville, the junction of SH3, which strikes west through the Manawatu Gorge to Palmerston North (see p.293), and SH2, which continues south into the Wairarapa.

The Wairarapa

Most of the **Wairarapa** is archetypal Kiwi sheep country, with white-flecked green hills etched sharply behind towns that share much in common with the workaday service centres of southern Hawke's Bay. In recent years, however, the southern half of the region has increasingly aligned itself with Wellington, a source of free-spending day-trippers and weekenders just an hour away over the hills.

The Wairarapa is separated from the capital by the Rimutaka Range, a persistent barrier to communication that kept the region relatively isolated for decades, until the spell was broken by the establishment of New Zealand's earliest sheep station close to present-day Martinborough. Soon the rich alluvial lands were selected for development by the **Small Farm Association** (SFA), a brainchild of Joseph Masters, a Derbyshire cooper and a long-time campaigner against the "Wakefield Scheme" of settlement, which promoted the separation of landowner and labourer. Aided and abetted by liberal governor George Grey, Masters founded the progressive association, which had the express aim of giving disenfranchised settlers the opportunity to become smallholders. At Grey's suggestion, SFA representatives sallied forth in 1853, persuading Maori to sell land for the establishment of two towns – Masterton and Greytown.

Initially **Greytown** prospered, and it retains an air of antiquity rare in New Zealand towns, but the routing of the rail line favoured **Masterton**, which soon became the main town, famed chiefly for the annual Golden Shears shearing competition. North of Masterton, the **Mount Bruce National Wildlife Centre** provides a superb opportunity to witness ongoing bird conservation work; to the south, **Featherston** is a base for walks up the bed of the Rimutaka Incline Railway.

The goal of many Wellingtonians and visitors is **Martinborough**, the region's wine capital and far-and-away its most appealing town. Back on the coast, the holiday settlement of **Castlepoint** is the place for swimming, and **Cape Palliser** is an equally good destination for blustery mind-clearing walks and dramatic coastal scenery.

Cross the **Rimutaka Range** towards Wellington and you're into the Hutt Valley, full of commuter-belt communities none of which really warrant a stop until you reach Petone on the outskirts of the capital.

Mount Bruce

The northern half of the Wairarapa is very much a continuation of southern Hawke's Bay, but instead of speeding through this pastoral country, leave a couple of hours aside for the award-winning **Mount Bruce National Wildlife Centre**, in majestic forest 50km south of Woodville (daily 9am–4.30pm; $8; Ⓦwww.mtbruce.doc.govt.nz). This is undoubtedly one of the best places in the country to view endangered native birds and a pioneer in the field of captive-breeding programmes (though much of this happens behind the scenes). Visitors have the chance to see some of the world's rarest birds – kokako, saddleback, kea, kakapo, kiwi and takahe – in spacious aviaries set along a one-kilometre trail through part of the last remnant of the Forty Mile Bush, lowland primeval forest which once covered northern Wairarapa. Beyond the trail several thousand hectares of forest are used for reintroducing birds to the wild. The generous size of the cages on the trail and the thick foliage often make the birds hard to spot, so you'll need to be patient (Jan & Feb are the best times); more immediate gratification comes in the form of a stand of Californian redwoods, a nocturnal kiwi house, reptilian tuatara, and a closed-circuit camera trained on a kokako nest in the breeding season (Oct–March). A continuously running twenty-minute audiovisual in the visitor centre gives a moving account of the decline of birdlife in New Zealand; while at 3pm each day a flock of kaka come to feed, causing quite a stir, and eels are fed at 1.30pm, ducks ten minutes later. Visitors can make use of a designated picnic area or relax in the café, which serves good coffee and snacks, indoors or out on the decking. The centre relies heavily on donations, so give if you can. **Buses** between Palmerston North and Masterton pass the centre, but none at convenient times for a stop-off.

Masterton and around

As the Wairarapa's largest town, workaday **MASTERTON**, crouched at the foot of the Tararua Mountains some 30km south of Mount Bruce, makes a tolerable base for exploring a few minor sights. Time it right and you could even attend the annual **Golden Shears** shearing competition, effectively the Olympiad of all things woolly, held on the three days leading up to the first Saturday in March. Contestants flock from many lands to demonstrate their prowess with the broad-blade handset; a top shearer can remove a fleece in under a minute, though for maximum points it must be done with skill as well as speed and leave a smooth and unblemished, if shivering, beast. Sideshows include wool-pressing and wool-handling competitions, and even a wool-inspired fashion parade. The visitor centre handles tickets which range from $10 for preliminary heats to $25 for the Saturday finals and over $100 for the wind-up dinner and cabaret.

Central Masterton is bounded on its eastern side by the large **Queen Elizabeth Park**, and walking around the formal gardens is a pleasant way to pass a sunny afternoon, but the town's only real sight is **Aratoi**, at the corner of Bruce and Dixon streets, opposite the park entrance (daily 10am–4.30pm; free; ⓦwww.aratoi.co.nz), a recently revamped art and history museum concentrating on the Wairarapa region. There are no permanent exhibits, but the airy modern spaces (including the interior of a church) deserve an hour of your time.

Draped over the hills to the west of town, the **Tararua Forest Park**, while not among New Zealand's tramping hotspots, offers some excellent walking through beech and podocarp forests to the sub-alpine tops, where the weather is notoriously fickle, so it can be dangerous. Serious trampers should consider the **Holdsworth–Jumbo Tramp**, a twelve-hour circuit that can be broken down into two or more manageable days by staying at some of the four **huts** (two at $10 and two at $5) evenly spaced along the route. The track starts at the backcountry-hut style *Holdsworth Lodge* (tent sites $4, lodge $8), 25km west of Masterton at the end of Norfolk Road, off southbound SH2 (accessible only by taxi ⓣ06/378 2555; about $25), where day-trippers can undertake easy riverside walks (1–2hr) and bathe in the cool waters. For details of all these tramps, pay a visit to the Masterton DOC field centre (see below), where you should also buy hut tickets.

Practicalities

Masterton's commercial heart is strung along the parallel Chapel, Queen and Dixon streets. Tranzit **buses** (ⓣ0800/471 227) pull up on Queen Street, between Russell and Smith streets, around 300m from the **visitor centre** at 5

Dixon St (Mon–Fri 9am–5pm & Sat–Sun 10am–4pm; ⓣ06/378 7373, ⓦwww.wairarapanz.com), which backs on to Queen Elizabeth Park. Tranz Metro (ⓣ04/801 7000) run commuter services from Wellington to the **train station**, at the end of Perry Street, a fifteen-minute walk from the centre, or call Masterton Radio Taxis (ⓣ06/378 2555). For trampers, DOC maintain a **field centre** (ⓣ06/378 2061; Mon–Fri 8am–5pm), opposite the aerodrome at the western end of South Road, the continuation of Queen Street.

Masterton's range of **accommodation** is fairly limited. At the budget end try the spacious and attractive *Mawley Park Motor Camp*, 15 Oxford St (ⓣ06/378 6454, ⓔjclarke@contact.net.nz; camping $8, cabins ❷), ten minutes' walk north of the centre; or the *Empire Lodge*, 94 Queen St (ⓣ06/377 1902, ⓕ377 2298; backpacker beds ❶, rooms ❹), which acts as the town's hostel and offers courtesy transport to the bus and train. There's also quality budget B&B accommodation in a central two-storey residence at *Victoria House*, 15 Victoria St (ⓣ06/377 0186, ⓔparker.monks@xtra.co.nz; ❸), and relaxing motel accommodation at the well-appointed *Cornwall Park*, 119 Cornwall St (ⓣ06/378 2939, ⓔcormnwall@wise.net.nz; ❹), in a quiet suburb a five-minute drive from central town, with a pool and spa. Of the numerous homestays, try the excellent hospitality of *Fulton House*, 1 Homebush Rd (ⓣ06/378 9252, ⓦwww.wags.co.nz/fulton; ❺), a pretty house in a beautiful English garden only 2km from the town centre, offering a double room with private bathroom next door.

Masterton's **eating** scene has improved of late, with the introduction of a decent café at Aratoi, though best coffee is still at *Russian Jack's Café*, 78 Queen St (closed Sat & Sun). Budget eating is best at the sedate *Slug and Lettuce*, upstairs at 94 Queen St, an ersatz English pub with bargain steaks ($16) and lasagne-type meals (under $10) plus a good range of snacks such as curry samosas, wontons and chicken satay sticks, though service and food are much better at *Café Cecille* (ⓣ06/370 1166; closed Sun & Mon eve), in Queen Elizabeth Park, a modern café in the genteel former aquarium building with wide verandas where you can dine while watching the miniature train chug by the boating lake. They might be serving a ricotta, tomato and olive tart ($14) followed by baked stonefruit and vanilla-bean ice-cream ($11). There are also good evening meals upstairs at *Bloomfields*, cnr Chapel Street & Lincoln Road (ⓣ06/377 4305; closed Sun), which turns out the likes of pork medallions with figs, mango and mint coulis for around $22.

Drinkers should head for *Burridges*, corner of Queen Street North and Shoe Street, a **micro-brewery** with a choice of three beers made on site, or join the smart young things at *Stellar*, 109 Chapel St, in a former Masonic Lodge and with outside seating. Finally, if you turn up on the last Sunday in February, make for Queen Elizabeth Park (see p.481), where local winemakers and restaurateurs ply their wares as part of the **Wairarapa Wine and Food Festival**.

Castlepoint

The 300km of coastline from Cape Kidnappers, near Napier, south to Cape Palliser is bleak, desolate and almost entirely inaccessible – except for **CASTLEPOINT**, 65km east of Masterton, where early explorers found a welcome break in the "perpendicular line of cliff". A commanding lighthouse presides over the rocky knoll, which is linked to the mainland by a thin hourglass double **beach** that encloses a sheltered pool known as The Basin. Nearby is a small settlement where Wairarapa families retreat for summer fun in the calm **lagoon**, walking to the lighthouse or the cave at its foot, riding the breakers or surfcasting from a huge rock platform. Castlepoint is at its most frenetic around the third or fourth Saturday in March, when there's an informal **horse race** along the beach – a somewhat unorthodox betting set-up requires punters to bet "blind" on numbers before they are allocated to particular horses.

In the absence of a visitor centre, ask for **information** at the Castlepoint Store (Ⓣ06/372 6823). The store holds a list of *baches* which can be rented (some by the night), or you can **stay** here at the *Castlepoint Holiday Park* (Ⓣ06/372 6705, Ⓦwww.castlepoint.co.nz; camping $10, dorm ❶, cabins ❷, kitchen cabins ❸) or the *Castlepoint Motels* (Ⓣ & Ⓕ06/372 6637; units ❹), which has a bunkroom (❶) and a garden cottage (❹). There are no restaurants at Castlepoint, but the store has a daytime **café** and sells **takeaways**.

Carterton

Once you've shaken free of the outskirts of Masterton, a string of small towns guide you towards the Rimutaka Range and over into the Hutt Valley towards Wellington. Staunchly conservative **CARTERTON**, 15km south of Masterton, is mainly known to Kiwis as the unlikely place where Georgina Beyer rose to prominence as New Zealand's first transsexual mayor. In 1999 she resigned the post when she became the world's first transgender member of Parliament. Being Maori and fairly flamboyant, it is perhaps appropriate that she should be associated with the home of the **Paua Shell Factory**, 54 Kent St (Mon–Fri 8am–5pm, Sat & Sun 9am–5pm; free; Ⓦwww.pauashell.co.nz), an Aladdin's Cave of objects fashioned from this beautiful rainbow-swirled seashell. It is a treat for lovers of kitsch souvenirs, with superbly polished examples of the shells themselves retailing for up to $50, but other extraordinary items can be yours to treasure for a much more modest sum. The factory supplies just about every tourist knick-knack shop in the country and, if you can't resist, you can even take a brief, free tour to see how the stuff is made.

Some 5km south of Carterton, a road runs 15km west into the foothills of the Tararua Range to **Waiohine Gorge**, a picturesque chasm that's ideal for picnics and safe swimming.

Greytown

There's a more traditional appeal to **GREYTOWN**, 9km south of Carterton. Laid out in 1853, the town still retains something of its Victorian feel, despite the traffic that now trundles between the rows of two-storey wooden buildings. Until the end of the nineteenth century, this was the Wairarapa's main settlement, but railway planners diverted the new line around the flood-prone environs and set the seal on a gradual decline that was only arrested by the development of profitable orchards and market gardens in the latter half of the twentieth century.

The real appeal here is the selection of **cafés** and **restaurants** along Main Street, notably the excellent and moderately priced *Main Street Deli*, at no. 88 (Ⓣ06/304 9022; licensed & BYO), which provides reason enough to stop in Greytown to stock up on unusual breads and cheeses, or tuck into more substantial fare in the attached café (daytime and Fri & Sat evenings).

If you feel you need to earn your lunch, spend an hour among the re-sited Victorian buildings and stagecoach paraphernalia at the **Cobblestones Museums**, 169 Main St (Mon–Sat 9am–4.30pm, Sun 10am–4.30pm; $2.50); or take a historical **walk** guided by the *Heritage Trails of Wairarapa* booklet ($2) from the volunteer-run **visitor centre** (hours vary) in the Public Services building on Main Street.

Featherston and the Rimutaka Incline

The last of the Wairarapa towns before SH2 climbs west over the Rimutakas is **Featherston**, 13km south of Greytown, where the **visitor centre**, in the Old Courthouse on Fitzherbert Street (daily 10am–3pm; Ⓣ & Ⓕ06/308 8051), stands in front of the town's pride and joy. The **Fell Locomotive Museum** on Lyon Street (Mon–Fri 9.30am–4pm, Sat & Sun 10am–4pm; $2 donation) contains what, to the casual observer, appears to be an ordinary old railway engine. Nevertheless, steam buffs cross the country to this last surviving example of the locos which, for 77 years (until the boring of a new tunnel in 1955), climbed the 265-metre, one-in-fifteen slope of the Rimutaka Incline over the range into the Hutt Valley, gaining purchase by gripping a central rail.

The rails have long been pulled up, but you can follow the trackbed on the **Rimutaka Incline Walkway** (17km; 4–5hr; 265m ascent), which starts 10km south of Featherston at Cross Creek, passes old shunting yards and shuffles through the 576-metre summit tunnel, before descending to Kaitoke. A free leaflet from the visitor centre details the route, provides background information and pinpoints three basic, grassy campsites along the way. Many walk just an hour or two from either end and back, but if you fancy the full trek, contact South Wairarapa Tours (Ⓣ06/308 9352), who will organize pick-ups (cost depends on numbers). There's no public transport to Cross Creek, but Masterton–Wellington buses pass within 1km of the Kaitoke end of the walkway.

Accommodation options in Featherston are pretty limited: there's a big homestead B&B and backpackers combo, *Fareham House*, Underhill Rd (Ⓣ06/308 9074; dorms ❶, backpacker rooms ❷, B&B rooms ❸), in a peaceful rural setting with pool and tennis courts; and the more salubrious *Woodland Holt B&B*, 47 Watt St (Ⓣ06/308 9027, Ⓔwoodland-hold@xtra.co.nz; ❺), where you can get dinner by arrangement ($35). This is probably a good idea since there are few worthwhile **places to eat** in Featherston, though Greytown and Martinborough are both close.

Martinborough

In the last fifteen years tiny **MARTINBOROUGH**, 18km southeast of Featherston, has been transformed from a small and obscure farming town into the centre of a compact wine region synonymous with some of New Zealand's finest red wines. Being within easy striking distance of Wellington, weekends see the arrival of the smart set, ready to lunch at the handful of appealing cafés and restaurants and load up their shiny 4WDs at the two dozen wineries that surround the town. On Mondays much of the town simply shuts down to recover. Go midweek, though, and Martinborough is a beguiling place – so small that you immediately feel at ease and will have a number of excellent wineries within easy strolling distance of the centre (see box opposite).

The town was initially laid out in the 1870s by patriotic landowner John Martin, who named the streets after cities he had visited on his travels and arranged the core in the form of a Union Jack centred on a leafy square. Martinborough languished as a minor agricultural centre for over a century until the first four wineries – Ata Rangi, Dry River, Chifney and Martinborough (all of which produced their first vintages in 1984) – re-invented Martinborough as the coolest, driest and most wind-prone of the

North Island's grape-growing regions. With the aid of shelter belts that slice the horizon, the wineries produce some outstanding **Pinot Noir**, very good **Cabernet Sauvignon** (though it is losing favour as the grapes fail to fully ripen in poor years), crisp and fruity **Sauvignon Blanc** and wonderfully aromatic **Riesling**.

Martinborough is no slouch at promoting its viticultural prowess, and the best time to visit is during one of its **festivals**. The first of the summer is Toast Martinborough (third Sun in Nov), a specifically wine-orientated affair with all the vineyards open, free buses doing the rounds, and top Wellington and local restaurants selling their produce; it is an exclusive event and tickets (sold from first Mon in Oct through Ticketek ⓣ04/384 3840 & ⓣ09/307 5000, www.ticketek.co.nz; $55) are hard to obtain. There's a considerably more egalitarian feel to the two Martinborough Fairs (first Sat in Feb & March), a huge country fête, during which the streets radiating from the central square are lined with stalls selling all manner of arts and crafts.

Outside these times, the best starting point is **Martinborough Wine Centre**, 6 Kitchener St (ⓦwww.martinboroughwinecentre.co.nz), where you can taste wines and plan the rest of your peregrinations around the wineries.

Practicalities

Tranzit Coachlines **buses** (ⓣ0800/471 227), shuttling between Featherston, Masterton and Martinborough, meet the TranzMetro commuter **trains** from

Martinborough wineries

For visitors, Martinborough has the edge over other wine regions in that ten of its wineries are accessible on foot, and a dozen more are easily reached by car or a bike rented locally. The best **guide** is the widely available and free *Martinborough and Wairarapa Wine Trails* brochure, which details the hours and facilities of the 26 wineries that conduct **tastings**, most of which charge a couple of dollars especially if there are reserve wines on offer. Throughout the summer places generally open 10am–4pm at weekends and shorter hours midweek, some of the smaller places closing if they've sold their year's stock. Here's our pick of the wineries to kick-start your explorations.

Ata Rangi Puruatanga Rd ⓣ06/306 9570, ⓦwwwatarangi.co.nz. A great place to start as it's central and increasingly well known for its Pinot Noir and Chardonnay, as well as its Pinot Gris and Rosé.

Martinborough Vineyard Princess St ⓣ06/306 9292, ⓦwww.martinboroughvineyard.co.nz. A Martinborough original and still one of the largest, producing top-quality Pinot Noir and Chardonnay. Picnicking is encouraged.

Muirlea Rise Princess St, across the road from Martinborough Vineyard ⓣ06/306 9332. Top-quality Pinot Noir to go with a ploughman's lunch and lovely coffee.

Nga Waka Kitchener St ⓣ06/306 9832, ⓦwww.nzwine.com/ngawaka. One of the small, young boutique wineries known for their bone-dry whites with elegant fruit.

Palliser Kitchener St ⓣ06/306 9019, ⓦwww.Palliser.co.nz. This pioneering Martinborough winery limits its impact on the environment while producing premium wines – Pinot Noir, Chardonnay, Sauvignon Blanc and Riesling; picnics are encouraged in the pleasant formal garden.

Te Kairanga Martins Rd, 5km southeast ⓣ06/306 9122, ⓦwww.tkwine.co.nz. A consistent award-winner which produces some delicious small-volume reserve wines; tastings are held in a 130-year-old pit-sawn-plank cottage moved to the vineyard from Martinborough. Tours on Sat & Sun at 2pm.

Wellington (Ⓣ0800/843 596; Mon–Fri, plus weekend day-trips in summer) and drop off at the small but informative **visitor centre** on Kitchener Street (daily 10am–4pm; Ⓣ06/306 9043, Ⓔmartinborough @wairarapanz.co.nz). **Internet access** is available at the library on Jellicoe Street.

The range of **accommodation** leans heavily towards mid- and upper-price B&Bs and homestays, most of them in rural surroundings out of town, or self-contained cottages starting at around $100 midweek, $120 at weekends. Those on a budget should try the *Martinborough Camping Ground*, Princess Street (Ⓣ06/306 9336; $10 per site), or the central *Martinborough Motel*, 43 Strasbourg St (Ⓣ06/306 9408, Ⓕ306 8408; ❸). With a bit more cash in your pocket it is worth stepping up to *Oak House*, 45 Kitchener St (Ⓣ06/306 9198, Ⓔchrispolly.oakhouse@xtra.co.nz; ❺), a homestay run by a local winemaker with attractive rooms in a Californian-style bungalow, substantial breakfasts and dinners from $35 with wine. Tempting alternatives include *The Old Manse*, at the corner of Grey and Roberts streets (Ⓣ06/306 8599, Ⓦwww.oldmanse.co.nz; ❻), 1km from town in a wonderful old villa among the vines; the centrally located and stylish straw-bale-built *Straw House*, 24 Cambridge Rd (Ⓣ06/306 8383, Ⓦwww.thestrawhouse.co.nz; ❻); and the sumptuously refurbished two-storey colonial *Martinborough Hotel*, The Square (Ⓣ06/306 9350, Wwww.martinboroughhotel.co.nz; ❽).

Martinborough caters to discerning diners. There are almost a dozen **restaurants**, with smarter and more varied places opening all the time, usually charging city prices; just wander around and see what takes your fancy. Accolades are heaped on the *Martinborough Bistro*, at the Martinborough Hotel, with beautifully prepared and presented dishes drawing on traditional French and modern Mediterranean cuisines at around the $25 mark. *The Flying Fish Café*, at the corner of The Square and Jellicoe Street (closed Mon–Wed in winter; licensed & BYO), is one of the best all-day **cafés** for great coffee, snacks, all-day brunches, light meals and takeaways in an attractive old building with a garden bar; and the local **pub**, the *Pukemanu Tavern*, The Square, sells cheap lunches and dinners in its steakbar restaurant.

Cape Palliser

The low-key cosmopolitanism of Martinborough stands in dramatic contrast to the bleak and windswept coast around **Cape Palliser**, 60km south. The southernmost point on the North Island, the cape was named in honour of James Cook's mentor, Rear Admiral Sir Hugh Palliser. Apart from a few gentle walks and the opportunity to observe fur seals (see below) at close quarters, there's not a lot to do out here but kick back, especially since swimming is unsafe and the weather changeable owing to the proximity of the Tararua Range, but the breeze will soon blow away the cobwebs.

From Martinborough, a sealed road leads 25km south to **Lake Ferry**, a tiny laid-back surfcasting settlement on the sandy shores of Lake Onoke, which once had a ferry service on the coastal route to Wellington before the Rimutaka Road was completed. Here, the *Lake Ferry Hotel* (Ⓣ06/307 7831, Ⓔamtipoki@xtra.co.nz; ❶–❸) – the southernmost of the North Island – has fairly ordinary rooms and backpacker dorms but does excellent **meals** specializing in seafood. Three kilometres to the north, the *Gateway Holiday Park* (Ⓣ06/307 7780, Ⓕ307 7783; camping $9, cabins ❷, self-contained units ❹) has a pool.

From a road junction just before Lake Ferry, the Cape Palliser road twists for 13km through the coastal hills until it meets the sea near the **Putangirua**

Pinnacles, dozens of grey soft-rock spires and fluted cliffs up to 50m high, formed by wind and rain selectively eroding the surrounding silt and gravel. The pinnacles lie within the little-visited Aorangi (Haurangi) Forest Park, and can be reached along an easy streambed path (1hr return) from the roadside Putangirua Scenic Reserve, where there are barbecue areas and a primitive **campsite** ($7); longer walks of up to 5hr are outlined on a map in the car park.

From here, the partly metalled road hugs the rugged, exposed coastline for 15km to **NGAWI**, a small fishing village where all manner of bulldozers grind out their last days, hauling fishing boats up the steep gravel beach. It is five rough kilometres on to the Cape proper, where the only well-established **fur-seal colony** on the North Island lies right beside the road, overlooked by the century-old Cape Palliser **lighthouse**, standing on a knoll 60m above the sea at the top of a long flight of some 250 steps. It is easy enough to get within 20m of the seals, but you should keep your distance from any pups – and their protective parents – and don't get between any seal and the sea.

Travel details

Trains

There are no longer any passenger trains to Hawke's Bay, but Wellington commuter services reach out into the Wairarapa.

From Masterton to: Carterton (2–5 daily; 15min); Featherston (2–5 daily; 40min); Wellington (2–5 daily; 1hr 30min).

Buses

InterCity and Newmans run most of the bus services through the region, with a service connecting Gisborne with all the Hawke's Bay towns, Palmerston North and Wellington; one linking Gisborne to Rotorua via Whakatane; one running from Napier and Hastings to Auckland via Taupo; and another joining Palmerston North, Masterton and Wellington. Tranzit connect Wellington with the main Wairarapa towns.

From Gisborne to: Auckland (1 daily; 9hr); Hastings (1 daily; 5hr); Napier (1 daily; 4hr); Opotiki, via SH2 (1 daily; 2hr); Rotorua (1 daily; 4hr 30min); Wairoa (1 daily; 1hr 25min); Whakatane (1 daily; 3hr).

From Hastings to: Auckland (3 daily; 7hr 30min); Dannevirke (3 daily; 1hr 30min); Gisborne (1 daily; 5hr); Napier (Mon–Fri hourly or better, Sat–Sun 4–5 daily; 30–45min); Norsewood (3 daily; 1hr 10min); Taupo (3 daily; 2hr 30min); Wellington (3 daily; 4hr 45min).

From Masterton to: Carterton (2 daily; 25min); Greytown (2 daily; 40min); Featherston (2 daily; 1hr); Palmerston North (2 daily; 1hr 35min); Wellington (2 daily; 2hr).

From Napier to: Auckland (3 daily; 7hr); Dannevirke (3 daily; 2hr); Gisborne (1 daily; 4hr); Hastings (Mon–Fri hourly or better, Sat–Sun 4–5 daily; 30–45min); Norsewood (3 daily; 1hr 30min); Palmerston North (3 daily; 3hr); Taupo (3 daily; 2hr); Wellington (3 daily; 5hr 15min).

From Wairoa to: Gisborne (1 daily; 1hr 25min); Napier (1 daily; 2hr 30min).

Flights

From Gisborne to: Auckland (3–5 daily; 1hr); Wellington (3–4 daily; 1hr 10min).

From Napier to: Auckland (7–10 daily; 1hr); Wellington (4–5 daily; 55min).

7

Wellington and around

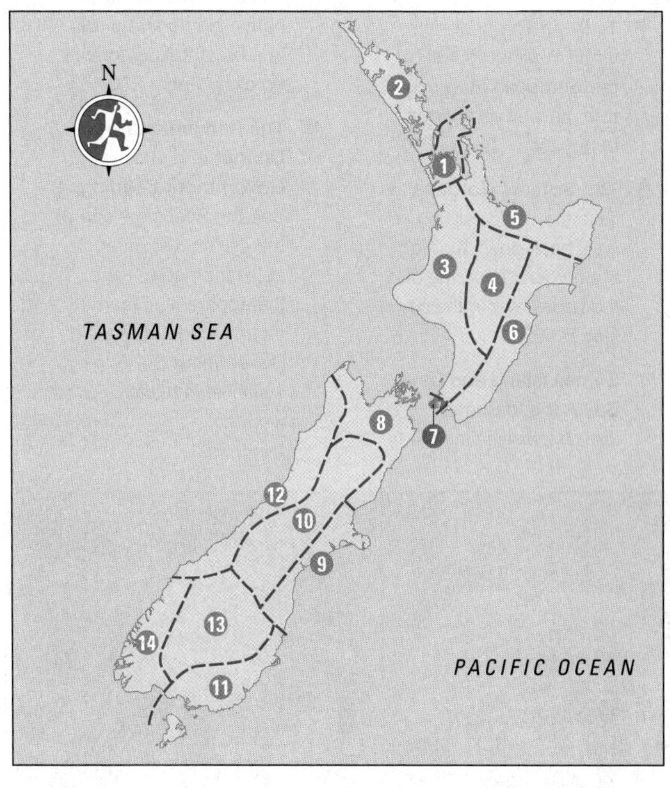

CHAPTER 7

Highlights

* **Cuba Street** Hustle, bustle and divergent styles all come out to play in Cuba Street, where a distinct taste of the city can be had by people watching and browsing in the shops. **See p.497**

* **Te Papa** The best museum in Wellington, full of pre-European Maori culture, as well as a virtual bungy jump. **See p.500**

* **The Botanic Gardens** Take the cable car up and walk back down through the gardens for some of the best views in the city. **See p.502**

* **Somes Island and Days Bay** A trip to Somes Island, a fascinating mixture of wildlife and history, can be augmented by another to Days Bay, where you can admire Logan House. **See p.510**

* **Karori Sanctuary** A superb sanctuary that has been restocked with native plants and birds, in a breathtaking forested alley. **See p.505**

* **The Parliamentary District and Old Government Buildings** See the Beehive – one of the city's most recognizable landmarks – and the apparently cream-stone facade of the Old Government Buildings, which is, in reality, wooden. **See p.503**

7

Wellington and around

Lying at the southwestern tip of the North Island, at the junction of SH1 and SH2, **Wellington** is the capital city of New Zealand and the seat of government. With a population of 400,000, it is also the country's second-largest city and enjoys a scenic setting, wedged between steep hills and the broad harbour of **Port Nicholson**. An engaging and friendly place to explore, Wellington boasts plenty of outdoor activities, a decorative and bustling waterfront, a stimulating combination of historical and modern architecture, and an exuberant café society and nightlife, complemented by a buzzing entertainment and cultural scene. However, Wellington lives up to its nickname of "the windy city", lashed most days by air funnelled through Cook Strait, an effect that's amplified by the city's high-rise buildings, which create wind tunnels. The harbour, on the other hand, remains relatively sheltered and is a perfect spot from which to appreciate the cityscape. With its ferry terminal and airport, Wellington is the principal departure point for the South Island, but the city warrants much more than just a fleeting glimpse. You're best off allowing three to four days to explore the sights concentrated within the central city and to make the most of the harbour, the beaches and bays, and Somes Island.

East of Wellington, where the **Rimutaka Range** separates the Hutt Valley from the Wairarapa (see p.522), a forest park offers several popular bushwalks that make for a pleasant day away from the city, or head to **Lower Hutt** and the excellent gallery, Maori Treasures, where you can learn about Maori artistic tradition on a one hour tour. The remaining meagre attractions of the commuter-belt communities of the Hutt Valley and Porirua, on the other hand, don't really warrant a special trip.

To the north, the Kapiti Coast is a pretty thirty-kilometre stretch of silvery beach scattered with tiny communities full of holiday and retirement homes, bowling greens and golf courses, with the region's most significant attraction just offshore: the long thin Kapiti Island (see p.303), a bird sanctuary that you can visit on an overnight-trip from Paraparaumu Beach (see p.302). Finally, Wellington is well placed for exploration of New Zealand's premier wineries, with Martinborough (see p.484) only a short scenic drive away through the Rimutaka Range to the Wairarapa, and the sunny Marlborough wineries (see p.485) accessible by boat across Cook Strait.

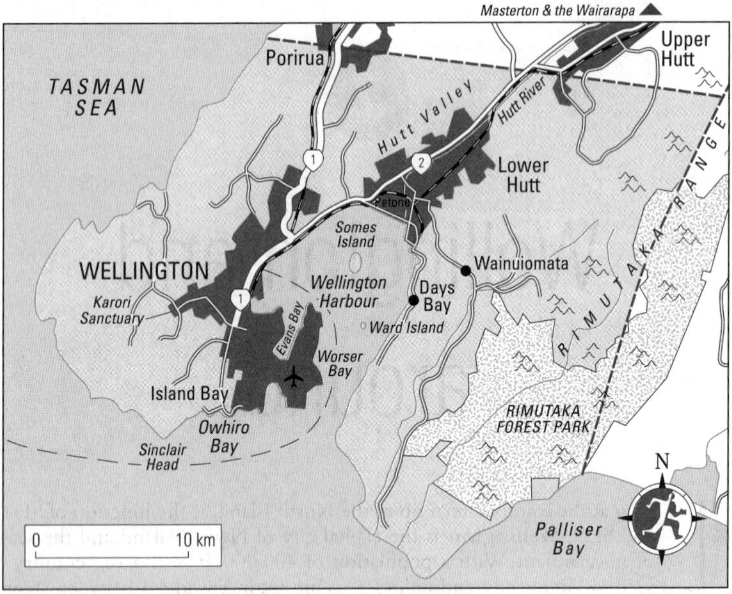

Wellington

The vibrant city of **WELLINGTON** is the cultural, political and commercial capital of New Zealand, though this is not what most Aucklanders would have you believe. A healthy antipathy exists between the two cities, fuelled by Auckland's conviction that it should be capital. Wellington is by no means a pale shadow of Auckland, though, not least because of the high levels of investment in recent years, aimed at making the city worthy of its capital status and more attractive to visitors. Most of the city is built on the foreshore and the precipitous hills overlooking a magnificent harbour, fringed by beaches, marinas and warehouses. The inner city is an energetic mix of historic stone buildings and modern structures, most notably the radical contemporary **architecture** of Ian Athfield, one of New Zealand's best-known architects, while the suburbs are a combination of grand residential villas and unspectacular commercial buildings. The surrounding hills have provided a natural barrier to the unbridled development typical of other New Zealand cities, helping to keep central Wellington an easily walkable area with a definite identity.

Wellington is truly cosmopolitan, offering a huge range of culinary experiences, alongside nightlife and artistic **culture** from all over the world. The most exciting months to visit are February and March, when the city hosts three separate **festivals**: the annual Wellington Fringe Festival, a carnival along the lines of the Edinburgh Festival; the biennial International Festival of the Arts, a month-long celebration that draws the best international acts in opera, theatre and music; and the annual Dragon Boat Festival (in late February), which attracts huge crowds to the inner harbour.

Some history

Maori believe that the first Polynesian navigator, **Kupe**, discovered Wellington Harbour (in 925 AD) and he is said to have camped here for some time on the Miramar Peninsula at the harbour mouth, naming the harbour's islands Matiu (Somes Island) and Makaro (Ward Island) after his daughters. Several *iwi* (tribes) settled around the harbour over the centuries, including the Ngati Tara people, who enjoyed the rich fishing areas and the protection that the bay offered. Both Abel Tasman (in 1642) and Captain Cook (in 1773) were prevented from entering Wellington Harbour by fierce winds and, apart from a few whalers, it was not until 1840 that the first wave of **European settlers** arrived, not long after the New Zealand Company had purchased a large tract of land around the harbour. The first settlement, named Britannia, was established on the northeastern beaches at Petone; shortly after, the Hutt River flooded, forcing the settlers to move around the harbour to a more sheltered site known as Lambton Harbour (where the central city has grown up) and the relatively level land at Thorndon, at that time just north of the shoreline. They renamed the settlement after the Iron Duke and, finding flat land scarce, began **land reclamations** into the harbour in the 1850s, a process that continued at intervals for more than a hundred years.

By the turn of the century the original shoreline of Lambton Harbour had all but disappeared, replaced largely by wharves and harbourside businesses. The growing city, at the hub of coastal shipping, became a thriving import and export centre, and in 1865 it superseded Auckland as the **capital** of New Zealand, largely because of its central location and fine harbour. Wellington has prospered ever since, and these days around seven million tonnes of cargo pass through the wharves each year. Parts of the waterfront no longer needed by the modernized shipping industry have been redeveloped for public use, while along the coast a number of shipwrecks are further testament to the city's maritime history, victims of the region's notorious high winds. Sailing ships of the 1800s were particularly susceptible, but even as late as 1968 a modern roll-on roll-off ferry, the *Wahine*, foundered at the harbour entrance in the worst storm of the century.

Arrival and information

Wellington International Airport is about 5km southeast of the city centre and has one terminal, shared by Qantas and Air New Zealand along with some small domestic airlines. There's a small **visitor centre** in the terminal (open for flight arrivals; ⓣ04/385 5123), as well as left-luggage lockers ($2) and a bureau de change (Mon–Fri 4–7am & 8.30am–5pm, Sat noon–5pm, Sun 8.30am–5pm, also open for night arrivals). A public bus service operates from the airport to the town centre for around $4.50 as well as three shuttle-bus companies, ShuttleExpress (ⓣ0800/579 957), Super Shuttle (ⓣ04/387 8787) and A.P. Shuttles (ⓣ0800/959 595), who run a twenty-four-hour door-to-door service to central Wellington (daily; $8–10 first passenger, $2 per extra person), plus a direct service to Wellington train station (roughly every 30min at peak times, otherwise hourly Mon–Fri; $8–12). A taxi ride from the airport costs roughly the same.

The main **train station** is in downtown Wellington on Bunny Street, just off Waterloo Quay, and is the last destination on the main north–south rail line from Auckland and the branch line from Napier. Newmans and InterCity **buses** also pull in here (at platform 9). Arriving **by car**, SH1 and SH2 merge just north of the city, continuing into the centre, after running briefly along the harbourside and giving excellent views of the city ahead. Most **ferries** from Picton on the South Island arrive at the Interisland Ferry Terminal (information on ⓣ0800/802 802) just off SH1, 2km north of the train station. A free shuttle service operates between the ferry terminal and train station; the Super Shuttle bus (see the airport details above) costs around $5, and a taxi $5–10. The exception is the *Lynx*, which docks at Waterloo Quay, opposite the train station.

For details of **sea and air routes** between Wellington and the South Island, see "Listings", pp.519-520.

Information

As well as the small office at the airport (see p.493), there's the well-stocked and efficient **visitor centre** on the corner of Wakefield Street and Victoria Street (Mon & Wed–Fri 8.30am–5.30pm, Tues 8.30am–5pm, Sat & Sun 9.30am–6.30pm; longer hours in summer according to demand; ⓣ04/802 4860, ⓦwww.WellingtonNZ.com) which shares a glass-fronted section of the Civic Centre with a café and an internet-access business. The info desk sells city maps for $1 and provide a useful free booklet, *Wellington – What's On*, published by Jasons and including a central-city map. The **DOC office** is in the Old Government Buildings at the corner of Lambton Quay and Whitmore Street (ⓣ04/472 7356; ⓣEphewson@doc.govt.nz; Mon–Fri 9am–4.30pm, Sat 10am–3pm), with stacks of information on walks in the Wellington region, including tramps on Kapiti Island and the forest parks around the city; hut passes are also sold here, as are permits to visit Kapiti Island, which some organized trips (see p.303) may require you to get before taking you out there.

City transport

Wellington has a comprehensive **local bus** service that links the inner city to most of the central suburbs. Normal services (Mon–Sat 7am–11pm, Sun 8am–11pm) depart from the train station or the main city bus stop at Courtenay Place, at the intersection with Cambridge Terrace; the limited after-midnight hourly (Sat & Sun 1–3am) departs from Courtenay Place, then from Dixon Street (near Cuba Mall) three minutes later and picks up from all city stops. Frequent **trolley buses** (same hours as local buses) also trundle around the city, resembling the normal buses but running on overhead cables between the eastern end of Courtenay Place and the train station, along Lambton Quay. Whatever type of bus you end up on, **fares** are $2 within the inner city, beyond which a zonal system comes into operation, with fares ranging from around $1.10 to $3.50, and all journeys on the weekend after-midnight service at $3; buy tickets from the driver. "Daytripper" **passes** ($8) are also available from the drivers, giving unlimited travel for a day after 9am and including the cable car to the Botanic Gardens (see p.502). For **train and bus information** on all trains and local buses in the Wellington region, call the Ridewell Service Centre (Mon–Sat 7.30am–8.30pm, Sun 9am–3pm; ⓣ04/801 7000). A free general bus and train guide, plus free route maps and timetables, are also available from the visitor centre and train station (see above and p.493).

Driving around the inner city is simple once you get used to the extensive one-way system and remember to avoid the rush-hour traffic (roughly 7–9am & 4.30–6.30pm), but since it's so easy to get around on foot or by public transport you're best off ditching the rental car at your earliest opportunity and, if crossing to the South Island, picking up a new one there, thus reducing costs on the ferry. Unoccupied **parking** spaces in the inner city are a nightmare to find. Thankfully at weekends you can park at meters and in car parks for up to two hours for free, after which both cost in excess of $3 per hour (see "Listings" on p.519 for location of car parks). The hills around the city are very popular with **mountain-bike** enthusiasts (pick up the $1 leaflet *Off-road Mountain Biking in Wellington City*, containing maps and full descriptions of tracks in the Town Belt), but cycling is also a great way to enjoy the scenic coastal route around the harbour and its bays; most **bike rental** companies (see p.519 for a recommended outfit) will charge at least $25 for half a day.

Accommodation

Your best bet is to plump for **accommodation** in the city centre, close to all the action. There are various excellent hostels, loads of B&Bs (many in beautifully preserved Victorian villas) and hotels, but only a few centrally located motels. Also, and unusually for New Zealand, the city has no **campsite** – instead you have to head all the way out to the Hutt Valley on the harbour's northeastern shore for the *Hutt Park Holiday Park*, 95 Hutt Park Rd, Lower Hutt (ⓣ04/568 5913, ⓔinfo@huttpark.co.nz; tent sites $10, cabins ❷, tourist flats ❹, motel units ❺), about 14km from Wellington's train and bus station, but close to beaches, shops and bush walks.

B&Bs can be a good option centrally but bear in mind that part of the joy of the Wellington experience is to try out some of the excellent and good value breakfasts and brunches available in the cafés and food halls around the city, which means you'll be paying for breakfasts you don't actually want at your accommodation. On the city centre's western fringes, but within easy walking distance of all the attractions, the leafy and characterful suburb of Thorndon contains a couple of delightful B&Bs and a pleasant historic hotel, while the inner-city's eastern border, the suburb of Mount Victoria, offers a range of accommodation within a stone's throw of the busiest part of town.

Availability anywhere in the inner city is limited during the busiest part of the summer (Christmas, Jan & Feb), so it pays to book as far ahead as possible: for the most popular hostels, you need to allow a week or more. **Prices** are a touch above average: in hostels, most dorms are four- to six-bed and rates hover around $21, while doubles and twins go for $45–50. At the other end of the scale, hotels are expensive during the week, but most offer special weekend deals, sometimes shaving off as much as fifty percent. For B&Bs you pay on average at least $20 more than you would elsewhere.

Hotels and motels

Abel Tasman cnr Willis St & Dixon St ⓣ04/385 1304, ⓔhotelnz@xtra.co.nz. What it lacks in character it makes up for by being an extremely central hotel with good weekend discounts and regular rates towards the lower end of the market. ❹–❺

Apollo Lodge Motel 38–49 Majoribanks St ⓣ04/385 1849, ⓔaccommodation@apollolodge.co.nz. Central, medium-sized motel, 400m from Courtenay Place. Most units have fully equipped kitchens. ❺–❻

Carillon Motor Inn 33 Thompson St ⓣ04/384 8795, ⓕ385 7036. Cheaper prices reflect an average location, about a kilometre south of Courtenay Place, and a communal kitchen simply equipped with a microwave and fridge. ❹–❻

Duxton 148 Wakefield St ⓣ0800/475 292, ⓦwww.duxton.com. A gleaming modern corporate hotel on the waterfront near Civic Square, with an à la carte restaurant and brasserie. Marginally cheaper than the the *Intercontinental* (see below), especially at weekends. ❼–❽.

Halswell Lodge 21 Kent Terrace ⓣ04/385 0196, ⓕ385 0503. Comfortable central accommodation in a small hotel/motel with hotel rooms and motel units in a modern well-kept complex, with friendly hosts. ❹–❻

Hotel Intercontinental cnr Grey St & Featherston St ⓣ0800/857 585, ⓔreservations@interconnental.co.nz. The most expensive place in town, this luxurious international hotel in a tower block near Queens Wharf is geared chiefly to businesspeople, but has half-price weekend rates (around $175). Facilities include a gym and a pool, a classy restaurant and an airport limousine service. ❾ upwards

Majoribanks Apartments 38 Majoribanks St ⓣ04/385 8879, ⓔaccommodation@apollolodge.co.nz. Several big, fully self-contained apartments in a modern block close to the heart of the city; off-street parking. ❺–❻

Museum Hotel between Cable and Wakefield sts ⓣ04/385 2809, ⓦwww.museumhotel.co.nz. Big, brash black hotel within spitting distance of the city centre and with some great views from the more expensive harbour-facing side. It lacks real style but makes up for it with reasonable rates for this level of quality. ❼–❽

Shepherd's Arms 285 Tinakori Rd, Thorndon ⓣ0800/393 782, ⓔshepherds@xtra.co.nz. Near the Parliamentary District, this small 1870s hotel (reputedly New Zealand's oldest) with bar and restaurant is tastefully renovated in period style, but also has all mod cons. There's also a self-contained cottage. ❼

Wellington Motels 14 Hobson St ⓣ04/472 0334, ⓔwellington.motels@clear.net.nz. Small, quiet and well-equipped, but only really worthwhile if you want to be close to the Picton ferry terminal. ❺

B&Bs and guesthouses

The Mermaid 1 Epuni St, cnr with Aro St ⓣ & ⓕ04/384 4511, ⓔmermaid@paradise.net.nz. A luxurious guesthouse for women only, set in a restored turn-of-the-century house among bush-covered hills, a ten-minute walk from downtown. Four tastefully furnished rooms (one with private bathroom), each with a view of the garden or hills. Kitchen and lounge. ❹–❻

Talavera 7 Talavera Terrace, Kelburn ⓣ04/471 0555. An 1897 villa on a quiet, leafy hill above the central business district, five minutes' walk from Lambton Quay and on the cable-car route. Sweeping views from a self-contained flat with a veranda. ❻

Tinakori Lodge 182 Tinakori Rd, Thorndon ⓣ04/473 3478, ⓔ100035.3214@compuserve.com. A well-appointed, big Victorian villa, a short walk from the Parliamentary District, with several airy rooms and a conservatory that looks onto a bushland reserve. ❺

Hostels

Cambridge Hotel 28 Cambridge Terrace ⓣ04/385 8829, ⓕ385 2503, ⓔinfo@cambridge-hotel.co.nz. A converted 1930s colonial hotel that has been painted an unfortunate brown on the outside but has been beautifully renovated inside. There are just under 50 rooms for backpackers, from dorms to twins and doubles, as well as space for more conventional hotel guests and long-term stayers, all kept fairly separate. Dorms are six- to eight-bed, and twins and doubles are also available, some of which are ensuite. Dorms ❶, rooms ❹–❺

Downtown Backpackers 1 Bunny St ⓣ04/473 8482, ⓔdb@downtownbackpackers.co.nz. Huge and impersonal hostel occupying a 1930s hotel, opposite the train station but a bit of a walk from the action on Courtenay Place. The doubles are en suite, with made-up beds and some even with TVs (a few with views of the Beehive), though dorms vary from OK to awful. Perks, or recompense (depending upon your point of view), include a courtesy pick-up from the ferry, bargain bar (possibly the cheapest beer in the city) and a café serving low-cost breakfasts and dinners. Dorms ❶, rooms ❷

Lodge in the City 152 Taranaki St ⓣ04/385 8560,ⓔlitcnz@voyager.co.nz. This rambling but central 1950s building – a recent conversion from student lodgings – is gradually being revamped – but is blighted by long-stay residents whose wants and needs are at odds with those of visiting tourists. Cybercafé, Sky TV, bar, free shuttle to the ferry, bus and train are all available, plus a roof garden with good views over the city and a glimpse of the harbour. Dorms ❶, rooms ❷, self-contained units ❹

Wellington City YHA 292 Wakefield St, cnr Cambridge Terrace ⓣ04/801 7280, ⓔyhawgtn@yha.org.nz. The best hostel in town, possibly even the country, that's extremely good value, right in the heart of the city and has great harbour views from the top-floor rooms. All rooms (twins, doubles, and four- or six-shares) are en suite. Book at least a week in advance in summer. New World supermarket opposite; bike storage; car park nearby on Wakefield St; travel desk for all bookings. YHA members only on public holiday weekends. Dorms ❶, rooms ❷–❸

World Wide 291 The Terrace ⓣ0508/888 555, ⓕ802 5590, ⓔwide.world@paradise.net.nz. Bright and cheerful hostel in an attractive house with singles, doubles and twins, some en suite, with dorms planned, and a free public phone for local calls.

Prices include breakfast and a complimentary glass of wine in the evening. Dorms ❶, rooms ❷

Wildlife House Old Dept of Conservation Building, Tory St ☎04/381 3899, ⓦwww.wildlifehouse.co.nz. An excellent new high-rise hostel painted on the outside with zebra stripes and converted inside to provide comfortable and roomy accommodation in dorms, twins and doubles (some en suite) Dorms ❶, Rooms ❷–❸

The City

Wellington's **city centre** is compact and easy to cover on foot, with most of the major attractions within a two-kilometre radius. The heart of the city stretches from the train station in the north to Cambridge and Kent Terraces at the eastern end of Courtenay Place, taking in the waterfront along the way, while the central business district runs along The Terrace and Lambton Quay; the latter is also the principal shopping thoroughfare. The main districts for eating, drinking and entertainment are Courtenay Place, Cuba Street, Willis Street, and down to the waterfront at Queens Wharf. **Cuba Street** is also the "alternative" shopping district with secondhand bookshops, record stores, retro clothes retailers and quirky cafés.

Meanwhile, the main sights are concentrated in four distinct areas: around **Civic Square and the waterfront**; the **Botanic Gardens**; the **Parliamentary District**; and the historic suburb of **Thorndon**. The nearest beach to the city centre is **Oriental Bay**, skirted by an elegant esplanade, Oriental Parade, which is a favourite spot for jogging, walking, swimming, or simply admiring the view of the city and harbour, especially at night. On the hills enclosing the city centre is the **Town Belt** – originally set aside in 1839 by the New Zealand Company for aesthetic and

The architecture of Ian Athfield

The work of New Zealand's most influential and versatile living architect, **Ian Athfield**, generates the kind of love-hate reaction usually associated with the Lloyd's Building in London and the Pompidou Centre in Paris. His principal motif is the juxtaposition of old and new, regular and irregular, as seen in the facade of the **Palmerston North Public Library** (see p.294). However, many of the finest examples of Athfield's work are in his home town of Wellington, where the facade of the **Moore Wilson Building** from 1984 (a food warehouse at the corner of College and Tory streets) explores fractures, while the **Oriental Parade Apartments**, built in 1988 near the start of the Southern Walkway on Oriental Parade (see p.504), have an almost Egyptian facade. Athfield also likes artwork to appear as part of his buildings, as demonstrated by the sculptural forms of the **Wellington Public Library** (see p.500). Perhaps the best example of his work is **Logan House** at Windy Point in Eastbourne, across the bay from Wellington (see p.511), where he has cleverly combined an old structure with a new one, making full use of the natural surroundings and revitalizing a disused building. However, many people's favourite Athfield building is a house-cum-office on a hillside in the northern suburb of **Khandallah** (at 105 Amritsar St; closed to the public). Visible from the Wellington motorway and – at some distance – from the ferry to Days Bay, it seems to grow organically down the hill, showing a respect for the environment and a willingness to engage with it that's often lacking in New Zealand architecture. In contrast, the house adjoining the **Te Mata Estate Winery** in Havelock North (see p.475) is a sly backhanded tribute to the modernists of the 1930s and an expression of the architect's humour, though it still manages to look perfectly placed in its surroundings.

CENTRAL WELLINGTON

ACCOMMODATION

Name	Key
Abel Tasman Hotel	G
Apollo Lodge Motel	M
Cambridge Hotel	N
Carillon Motor Inn	S
Downtown Backpackers	D
Duxton	I
Halswell Lodge	O
Hotel Intercontinental	F
Lodge in the City	R
Majoribanks Apartments	P
The Mermaid	Q
Museum Hotel	J
Shepherd's Arms Hotel	C
Talavera B&B	E
Tinakori Lodge B&B	A
Wellington City YHA	K
Wellington Motels	B
Wildlife House	L
World Wide	H

RESTAURANTS, CAFÉS & BARS

Name	No.	Name	No.
Angkor	25	Krazy Lounge	32
Axolotl	36	The Lido	14
Backbencher Pub	2	The Malthouse	9
Bar Bodega	44	Massala	27
Blue Note	48	Matterhorn	24
Bond St Brewhouse	11	Midnight Espresso	42
Café Brava	39	Molly Malone's	26
The Catch	34	Café Neo	13
Cell Bar	21	Nicholini's	36
Chicago Bar	6	Nikau Gallery Café	10
Chow/Motel	41	The Opera	39
City Limits	15	Paradiso	36
Coyote	33	Q Bar	36
De Luxe	47	Red Eye	19
Dockside	5	Roti Chenai	8
Expressoholic	29	Sahara Café	38
The Fat Ladies' Arms	28	Shed 5	4
Felix	17	The Skyline	7
Fidel's	51	Stamp and Go	46
Fiebigs	1	Strawberry Fare	50
Fishbowl	16	Sushi of Japan	43
Food Court	19	Tupelo	40
Fusion	45	Uncle Chang's	31
The Grand	33	The Vegetarian Café	43
Great India	22	Vista	23
Humming Bird	36	Wellington Sports Bar	34
Icon	20	Wellington Trawling Sea Market	49
Imbibe	37	Wholly Bagels	3, 12
JJ Murphey	30	Zest	35
Kitty O'Shea's	36	Zico	39
Kopi	18		

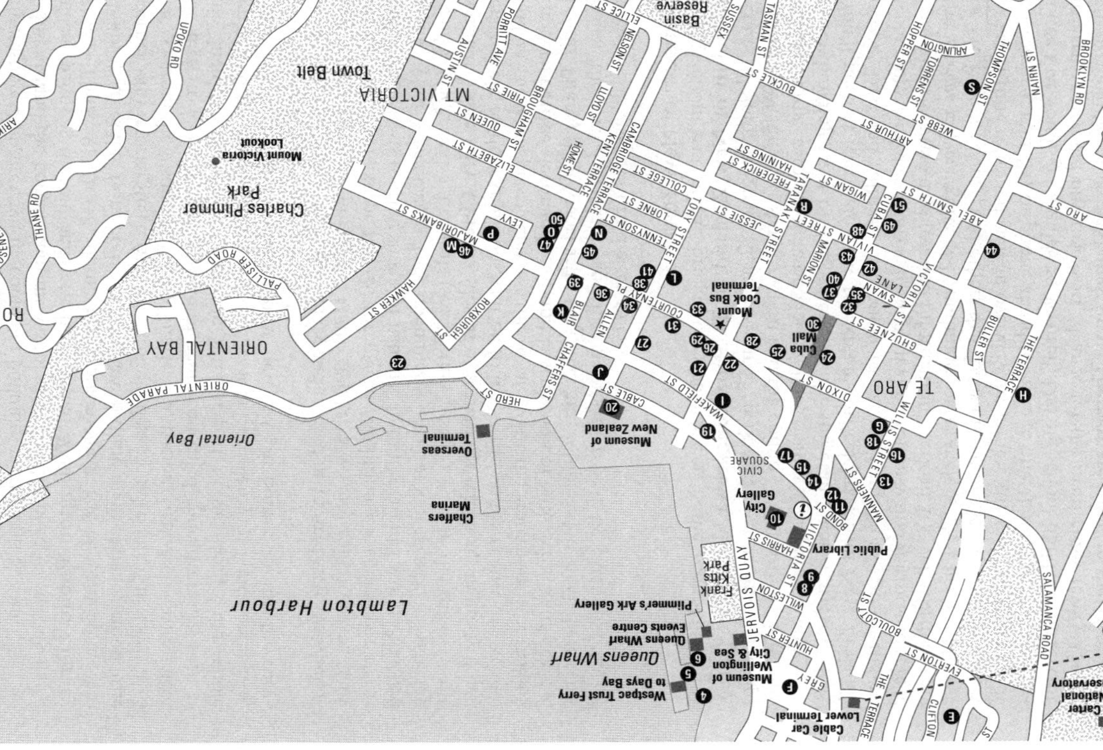
Scorching Bay (10 km)
Wind Turbine (2 km)
0 (200 m)
Lambton Harbour
Oriental Bay
ORIENTAL BAY
ORIENTAL PARADE
ROSENEATH
MT VICTORIA
TE ARO
Charles Plimmer Park
Mount Victoria Lookout
Town Belt
Basin Reserve
Chaffers Marina
Overseas Terminal
Museum of New Zealand
Westpac Trust Ferry to Days Bay
Queens Wharf
Queens Wharf Events Centre
Plimmer's Ark Gallery
Museum of Wellington City & Sea
Frank Kitts Park
City Gallery
Public Library
CIVIC SQUARE
Cuba Mall
Mount Cook Bus Terminal
Cable Car Lower Terminal
Carter National Observatory
JERVOIS QUAY
CARLTON GORE
MAIDA VALE
EVAS BAY PARADE
THE CRESCENT
GRAFTON ROAD
ROSENEATH TERR
TE ANAU RD
ARIKI RD
THANE RD
UPOKO RD
PALLISER ROAD
HAWKER ST
ROXBURGH ST
MAJORIBANKS ST
LEVY
ELIZABETH ST
QUEEN ST
AUSTIN ST
PIRIE ST
PORRITT AVE
BROUGHAM ST
HOME ST
LLOYD ST
NELSON ST
ELLICE ST
KENT TERRACE
CAMBRIDGE TERRACE
HERD ST
CHAFFERS ST
BLAIR
ALLEN
CABLE ST
COURTENAY PL
TENNYSON ST
LORNE ST
COLLEGE ST
TORY STREET
WAKEFIELD ST
JESSIE ST
FREDERICK ST
HAINING ST
TARANAKI STREET
SUSSEX
TASMAN ST
BUCKLE ST
MARION ST
WIGAN ST
VIVIAN STREET
CUBA ST
ARTHUR ST
WEBB ST
HOPPER ST
TORRENS ST
ARLINGTON
THOMPSON ST
NAIRN ST
BROOKLYN RD
ABEL SMITH ST
ARO ST
SWAN LANE
VICTORIA ST
GHUZNEE ST
DIXON ST
BULLER ST
THE TERRACE
WILLIS STREET
MANNERS ST
BOND ST
HARRIS ST
WILLESTON
HUNTER ST
GREY
BOULCOTT ST
EVERTON ST
SALAMANCA ROAD
CLIFTON
ST

recreational purposes, it contains several good walks and many of the city's best lookout points.

Civic Square and the waterfront

The thoroughly modern **Civic Square**, behind the visitor centre, is a good place to start your sightseeing before making the short walk to the waterfront and Wellington's star attraction, the Museum of New Zealand (Te Papa Tongarewa). A popular venue for outdoor events, Civic Square was revamped in the early 1990s by Wellington architect Ian Athfield (see p.497) and is full of interesting sculptures, with a couple of buildings worth a quick visit.

Just around the corner from the visitor centre and flanked by striking metal nikau palms is the big and refreshingly bold **Wellington Public Library** (Mon–Thurs 9.30am–8.30pm, Fri 9.30am–9pm, Sat 9.30am–5pm, Sun 1–4pm), accessible from both Civic Square and the main entrance around the corner on Victoria Street. Another Athfield design and opened in 1991, it's a far cry from the fustiness of most libraries – a spacious high-tech environment of steel, stone and timber. Instead of being concealed, inner workings such as air ducts are exposed to form an integral part of the design, the whole enhanced by strong sculptural forms, colour and plenty of light flooding in. From the upper floor, you get a great view of Civic Square through the curving glass wall.

Across Civic Square from the library and housed in an Art Deco 1939 building is the **City Gallery** (Ⓣ04/801 3952, Ⓦwww.city-gallery.org.nz; daily 10am–5pm; free, except $10–20 for special exhibitions), a contemporary art gallery that hosts touring shows of national and international works. Attached is the stylish *Nikau Gallery Café*, opening onto an outdoor terrace and offering drinks, snacks and light meals (see "Eating", p.513). Also in the gallery is the small arthouse **City Cinema** (details of screenings, which relate pretty much exclusively to the exhibitions, can be found at the visitor centre, the website and in the local press). Linking the square with the waterfront is a striking modern **bridge** decorated with timber sculptures of birds, whales and celestial motifs. The work of Maori artist Para Matchitt, completed in 1993, these symbolize the arrival of Maori and European settlers and, by extension, that of present-day visitors from the sea to city.

Museum of New Zealand

About 500m east of the bridge, on Cable Street, is the monolith of the **Museum of New Zealand**, or **Te Papa Tongarewa** (daily 10am–6pm & Thurs till 9pm; free; map $2, audio tour $5, parking $2 per hr; Ⓦwww.tepapa.govt.nz), Wellington's star attraction and the country's first national museum. A major project (to the tune of $350 million) occupying a purpose-built five-storey building right on the waterfront, the museum opened in early 1998. You'll need at least half a day to explore this celebration of New Zealand's people, land and cultures, all brought to life with ambitious state-of-the-art technology aimed at adults and children alike. You may find it easiest to spread your visit over two days to avoid information overload. It's well worth buying the *Te Papa Explorer* guide ($2), outlining routes such as "Te Papa in a Hurry" or "Te Papa for Kids", and others that focus on nature, Maori culture, history or art. If time is limited gain an overview by joining the **guided tours** (daily 10.15am; 45min; $9) or phone ahead to arrange one, though there's no guarantee that you'll get a guide to yourself. During school holidays you're wise to arrive early and buy tickets in advance for the main **rides** (every 15min; $6–8), including a virtual bungy jump. The best are based in the Time Warp zone on **Level 2**, where, while getting jerked about watching a screen and listening to the sound effects, you are jolted forwards to Wellington 2055 ("Future Rush") or back to a prehistoric New Zealand to witness the extraordinary formation of the land ("Blastback"). Other Level 2 highlights are an interactive section on earthquakes and volcanoes, where you can experience a mild quake in a house, watch Mount Ruapehu erupt on screen and hear the Maori explanation of the causes of such activity; and an interesting "X-Ray Room" housing the skeletons of great sea creatures such as whales, dolphins and seals. **Level 4** is home to an excellent Maori section including a thought-provoking display on the Treaty of Waitangi dominated by a giant replica of this significant document. On the same floor there's also an active *marae* with a modern meeting house painted in rainbow colours, mirrored by a stunning stained-glass window and protected by a sacred boulder of *pounamu* (greenstone). Note that you cannot enter the meeting house unless invited. The remaining levels of the museum contain extensive exhibitions on art, heritage, navigation and Maori history, while out through the ground floor is a native plant adventure garden with its own weeny swing bridge. This is also the home of one of New Zealand's top restaurants, the *Icon* (see p.514), and the museum also has two much simpler cafés.

Museum of Wellington City and Sea, and Queens Wharf

In the opposite direction and on the waterfront north of the visitor centre sits the **Museum of Wellington City and Sea** on Queens Wharf, beside Jervois Quay (daily: Feb–March 9.30am–6pm; rest of year 9.30am–5pm; $5), which unfolds the social and maritime history of Wellington. Occupying a former bond store (customs house), display highlights inside this fine stone building of 1892 include holographic projections, a tall cinema screen featuring one of four short films every thirty minutes. In addition are a twelve-minute special-effects show telling Maori creation legends and a gripping 12-minute film commemorating Wellington's worst disaster to date: the sinking of the inter-island ferry, *T.E. Wahine*, in April 1968, with the loss of 51 lives. Returning from Lyttelton with 734 people on board, the ferry entered the harbour just as one of the most violent storms ever recorded in New Zealand struck up. Rescue attempts were repeatedly thwarted until, finally, the weather calmed enough for passengers to start abandoning ship, only to find there were insufficient lifeboats.

While at **Queens Wharf**, take a few moments to soak up the atmosphere. Bustling and modernized, this T-shaped wharf dating from 1862 is a popular spot for a drink or a bite to eat (see "Eating", p.512) and has a large state-of-the-art Events Centre that functions as a sports stadium and a venue for bands. Past the Events Centre and on the left is **Shed 5**, the oldest building on the waterfront (1886) and, along with **Dockside** next door, one of the last two remaining timber warehouses. In the 1990s they were both sympathetically converted into trendy restaurant bars, quickly becoming two of the most popular watering holes in the city. Also at Queens Wharf is a hugely popular **climbing wall** at Ferg's Rock & Kayak opposite Shed 5 (Ⓣ04/4998878, Ⓦwww.fergskayaks.co.nz; Oct–April Mon–Fri 9am–10pm, Sat & Sun 9am–8pm; May–Aug Mon–Sun 10am–8pm). It's worth popping in to watch the activity and if it inspires you to have a go you're best off either in a pair or group of three so you can relay ($7 per person for 1hr including introductory lesson; equipment and shoes $4). Ferg's Rock & Kayak also hires out **rollerblades** (from $7 per half-day including pads) for use at nearby Kitts Park and all manner of **kayaks** (see p.510) for paddling on the harbour.

Finally, on an historic note, between Queens Wharf and Frank Kitts Park is **Plimmer's Ark Gallery** (24hr; free), a long corridor where the remains of the good ship *Inconstant* are kept in soggy perpetuity. The ship had a colourful career – having sailed from Plymouth to Adelaide with a cargo of female Irish immigrants the entire crew were confined, on arrival, for "disobedience"– ending in disaster when it sank in Wellington Harbour. The hulk was bought by John Plimmer, a Shropshire carpenter, who turned it into a trading store on the wharf – hence Plimmer's Ark – where it became part of his growing empire. Plimmer became known as the Father of Wellington because of his devotion to the growing community (and turning a buck, which helped Wellington commercially), but the boat fell into disrepair and was only rediscovered in 1997 under the Old Bank Arcade, where the bow of the ship is on display. Now it, or bits of it at least, rest in glass cases constantly sprayed with water, to prevent them drying out and disintegrating, surrounded by information boards describing its history and the characters involved.

The Botanic Gardens, cable car and the Carter Observatory

Wellington's **Botanic Gardens** (daily dawn–dusk; free) form a huge swathe of green on peaceful rolling hills high above the city to the west and make for a pleasant hour or two's distraction, containing an observatory, a gorgeous rose garden, a begonia house and an atmospheric Victorian cemetery (pick up the useful free leaflet and map of the gardens from Wellington visitor centre). There are main entrances on Glenmore Street and Upland Road, but the best way to get there is via the short yet scenic **cable-car** ride to Kelburn. The cable car departs every ten minutes from Cable Car Lane, just off Lambton Quay (Mon–Fri 7am–10pm, Sat & Sun 9am–10pm; $1.50 one way, $3 return), climbing an extremely steep incline, making four stops on the way and giving great views over the city and harbour. Operational since 1902, the cable cars were originally driven by steam but succumbed to electricity in 1933; in 1978 the current Swiss system was installed, whereby two shiny red, modern cars, each at either end of a single rope, are propelled by an electric motor at the top station. There's a **lookout** at the top, just inside the Botanic Gardens, offering spectacular views over the city, brought into focus by coin-operated binoculars. At the terminus itself is a small building that, at the time of writing, was to become a museum recording the cable car's history. On the other side of the track, the licensed **Skyline Café** (daily 10am–4pm; see "Eating", p.514) is a great spot to sit with a drink, enjoying views of the city through panoramic windows, or, when the wind abates, from an outside balcony.

Once inside the Botanic Gardens, several paths lead back down to the city, meandering through stands of pohutukawa, remnants of dense native forest and ornamental flower beds. It's a two-minute walk from the Kelburn terminus to the 1941 **Carter National Observatory** (Mon–Fri 10am–4pm, Sat & Sun noon–5pm; free) where during the day you can check out the astronomy displays, computers and telescope, and take in a planetarium show (Mon–Fri noon; Sat & Sun hourly 10am–4pm; $7). Three nights a week you can also view the southern skies: the programme includes a thirty-minute planetarium show, audiovisual presentations, a short talk on astronomy, and, weather permitting, telescope viewing (phone ahead for details ⓣ04/472 8167; Tues, Thurs & Sat from 6.30pm; planetarium show at 6.40pm & second show later in evening; $5). Within sight of the Carter Observatory is the recently renovated 1912 **Thomas King Observatory** (daily 11am–4pm), which still contains its original instruments. One of the first observatories in the Wellington area, it played a vital role in navigation and time-keeping.

The *tour de force* of the gardens and their most visited section is the **Lady Norwood Rose Garden**, on flat ground at the city end, near the Centennial Entrance on Glenmore Street, and also accessible by car, or buses #12, 13 or 21 from Monday to Friday. The fragrant garden blooms throughout the summer, with 300 varieties of roses laid out in a formal wheel shape around a fountain and the whole enclosed by a colonnade of climbing roses. Adjacent is the large **Begonia House** (daily: Oct–March 10am–5pm; April–Sept 10am–4pm; free), which is divided into two areas: the tropical, with an attractive lily pond and a small cage containing carnivorous plants; and the temperate, which has seasonal displays of begonias and gloxinias in summer, changing to cyclamen, orchids and impatiens in winter. Further down from the rose garden, a striking memorial to New Zealand's most lauded politician, Richard Seddon, marks the entrance to **Bolton Street Memorial Park**, an attractive Victorian cemetery where many of the city's early pioneers are buried. Old-fashioned roses clamber over the ageing headstones and twist through ironwork in the shade of mature trees. Established in 1840 as three separate cemeteries (Anglican, Jewish and public), in 1892 the cemetery was closed to all except new burials in existing plots. In the 1960s, amid public outcry, it was abandoned altogether, and over 3500 bodies were exhumed and relocated to make way for the motorway that now bisects it.

From Robertson Way, the main pathway through the memorial park, a footbridge crosses the motorway. It leads to the smaller half of the cemetery, which contains a small chapel (daily 10am–4pm) with a few displays, and comes to an abrupt end where the high-rise buildings of The Terrace back onto it. It's a short walk from here to the Parliamentary District.

The Parliamentary District

Northwest of The Terrace, in the **Parliamentary District**, is Wellington's architectural masterpiece, the **Old Government Buildings** (Mon–Fri 9am–4.30pm, Sat & Sun 10am–3pm; free), at the corner of Lambton Quay and Whitmore Street. At first glance an opulent Italian Renaissance construction of cream stone, it is, in fact, built from wood, its entrances decorated with grand columns and porticoes. Designed by Colonial Architect William Clayton (1823–77) to mark the country's transition from provincial to centralized government, it was the largest building in New Zealand when completed in November 1876, and it remains the second-largest timber building in the world. Built on a small block of reclaimed land, it was physically isolated from the rest of the city and dominated Lambton Harbour. This grandiose building housed government ministers and most of the Wellington-based public service for many years, and Cabinet regularly met in the room immediately above the main entrance from 1876 to 1921. As departments grew, they moved to other buildings and by 1975 only the Education Department remained. Fully restored, it is now the home of Victoria University's Law Faculty. At the entrance is a visitor centre, managed by the DOC, which provides maps for a free self-guided **tour** through part of the building, including the Cabinet Room with its great view of the Beehive (see below). Compared to the exterior, you'll find the interior quite a restrained affair of honey-coloured kauri panelling, except for two carved rimu staircases that are among the finest in the country. Downstairs are photographic displays of the building's construction and mid-1990s restoration, while in the hallway you'll find commemorations for staff of note.

Wildlife walks around Wellington

There are several worthwhile walks around Wellington, the most popular being the **Red Rocks Coastal Walk**, beginning about 7km south of the city centre and tracing a shoreline reserve to an unusual volcanic rock formation. Other, longer tracks pass through sections of the Town Belt. The best of these, and the easiest to reach from the city centre, are the **Southern** and **Northern Walkways**, which are described in leaflets from the visitor centre, each with a helpful map. The Town Belt also contains numerous lesser tracks, but their layout is confusing, so don't attempt them without a map.

Well worth a visit for its several short bush walks and variety of Kiwi plantlife is the **Otari Native Botanic Garden** (or "Otari-Wilton's Bush" as it is sometimes known locally), on steep slopes dissected by the deep Kaiwharawhara streambed. The reserve lies 6km northwest of the city centre, and is best visited on a calm day, since the prevailing northwesterlies can gust to over 96km per hour in exposed places.

Red Rocks Coastal Walk

The easy **Red Rocks Coastal Walk** (4km each way; 2–3hr return) follows a rough track along the coastline from Owhiro Bay to Sinclair Head, passing a quarry and the eponymous **Red Rocks** – well-preserved volcanic pillow lava, formed about 200 million years ago by underwater volcanic eruptions and coloured red by iron oxide. Maori variously attribute the colour to bloodstains from Maui's nose or blood dripping from a paua-shell cut on Kupe's hand, while another account tells how Kupe's daughters cut themselves in mourning, having given up their father for dead. From May to October Sinclair Head is visited by an established colony of New Zealand **fur seals**.

The track starts at the quarry gates at the western end of Ohiro Bay Parade, where there's a car park. To get there by **bus** you have several options: from the central city take the frequent #1 to Island Bay (daily), get off at The Parade at the corner of Reef Street and walk 2.5km to the start of the walk; at peak times, catch #4 instead, which continues to Happy Valley, only 1km from the track. Otherwise, take a #1 or #4 to Wellington Hospital, at the intersection of Adelaide Road and John Street, and change to the #29 (Mon–Sat), getting off at Happy Valley, again about 1km from the start of the track.

The Southern Walkway

The **Southern Walkway** (11km; 4–5hr, or as shorter segments) cuts through the Town Belt to the south of the city centre, between Oriental and Island bays, and is fairly easy going overall, despite a few steep stretches. The walk offers plenty of variety, yielding excellent views of the harbour and central city, shade and tranquillity in the Town Belt forest, and exposed coastline between Houghton and Island bays. Much of the walkway is shaded, richly scented by exotic trees, and covered with pine needles; among the **birds** you might encounter are fantails, grey warblers and wax-eyes. Highlights include the sweeping views from the lookout at the **Mount Victoria** summit (196m) and from **Mount Albert** (178m), the rugged coastline of **Houghton Bay**, and the safe and popular beach at **Island Bay**.

The walk can be undertaken in either direction and is clearly marked by posts bearing orange arrows. To start at the city end, take the #14 Kilbirnie (via Roseneath) **bus** to Oriental Parade (near Ian Athfield's Egyptian-style Oriental Apartments); the walkway entrance is signposted near the *Hotel Raffaele*, at no. 360. To begin at the other end, take the #1 bus to Island Bay and follow the signs from nearby Shorland Park.

Visible across Lambton Quay are the **Parliament Buildings** in use today, a complex of three highly individual structures: the unmistakable **Beehive** (often confused with Parliament House itself, but in fact the executive wing, where ministers and civil servants huddle), the Edwardian Neoclassical

The Northern Walkway

Extending through tranquil sections of the Town Belt to the north of the city centre, the **Northern Walkway** (16km; 4hr, or tackled in sections) offers spectacular views. Stretching from Kelburn to Johnsonville, it covers five distinct areas (Botanic Garden, Tinakori Hill, Trelissick Park, Khandallah Park and Johnsonville Park), which can be accessed from various suburban streets and are served by public transport. Highlights are the **birdlife** on Tinakori Hill (tui, fantails, kingfishers, grey warblers, silver-eyes); regenerating native forest in **Ngaio Gorge** in Trelissick Park; great views across the city and the harbour and over to the Rimutaka and Tararua ranges from a lookout on **Mount Kaukau** (430m); and, in **Johnsonville Park**, a disused road tunnel hewn through solid rock.

From the city end, the track starts at the Botanic Garden lookout at the top of the cable-car terminus, or you can begin instead at the Tinakori Hill section by climbing St Mary Street, off Glenmore Street, and following the orange arrows through woodland. Starting at the far end means taking a **train** to Raroa station (Mon–Sat), or a #49 Johnsonville **bus** (Sun only).

Otari Native Botanic Garden

The **Otari Native Botanic Garden** (daily dawn till dusk; free) offers 80 hectares of mature and regenerating native bush. It's best approached via the main entrance, junction of Wilton Road and Gloucester Street, where you'll find a map of the walks and an unmanned visitor centre (daily 9am–5pm) with simple displays. From here a hundred-metre **Canopy Walk** of sturdy decking high in the trees crosses the streambed far below. Other walks include the **Nature Trail** (30min), a good introduction to the New Zealand forest and its many plants (the track is steep in places and has many steps); the **Circular Walk** (30min) follows the Kaiwharawhara Stream through plant collections, native forest, lawn areas and a picnic site. Three other bush trails push further afield (2 at 40min; 1 at 1hr). The streamside picnic site (with coin-operated BBQs; $0.50) is ten-minutes' walk from the main entrance. To reach the reserve **by bus** take #14; **by car** follow Moleworth Street north from the centre, which becomes Wadestown Road and then Blackbridge. At the junction with Churchill Drive turn left and continue till it becomes Wilton Road, off which is the main entrance.

Karori Sanctuary

The **Karori Sanctuary** (daily 10am–5pm, entry through the visitor centre; ⓣ04/920 9200, ⓦwwwsanctuary.org.nz), Waiapu Road, is a relatively new project, the beginning of an epic multi-million dollar plan to restore purely **native flora and fauna** to 253 hectares secured by a predator fence that keeps all introduced mammals (except man) out. As well as restocking the area with native trees, the trust is introducing kiwi, weka, kaka, tuatara, morepork, tui, bellbird, weta, whitehead and North Island robins to name but a few to the sanctuary from the overspill of the successful conservation and restocking programme on Kapiti Island (see p.303). **Guided tours** cost about $15 and take from one- to three-hours, including a dusk tour (max 12 people) that involves listening to kiwi as well as spotting many other birds (when stocks are higher it will involve seeing kiwi in the wild). Check the website for details of upcoming tours, the profits from which are fed back into the conservation programme.

Parliament House, and the Victorian Gothic **Parliamentary Library**. You can visit all three on a free **guided tour** (departing on the hour Mon–Fri 10am–4pm, Sat 10am–3pm, Sun 1–3pm; 45min) from the visitor centre in the ground-floor foyer of Parliament House, parliamentary meetings and functions

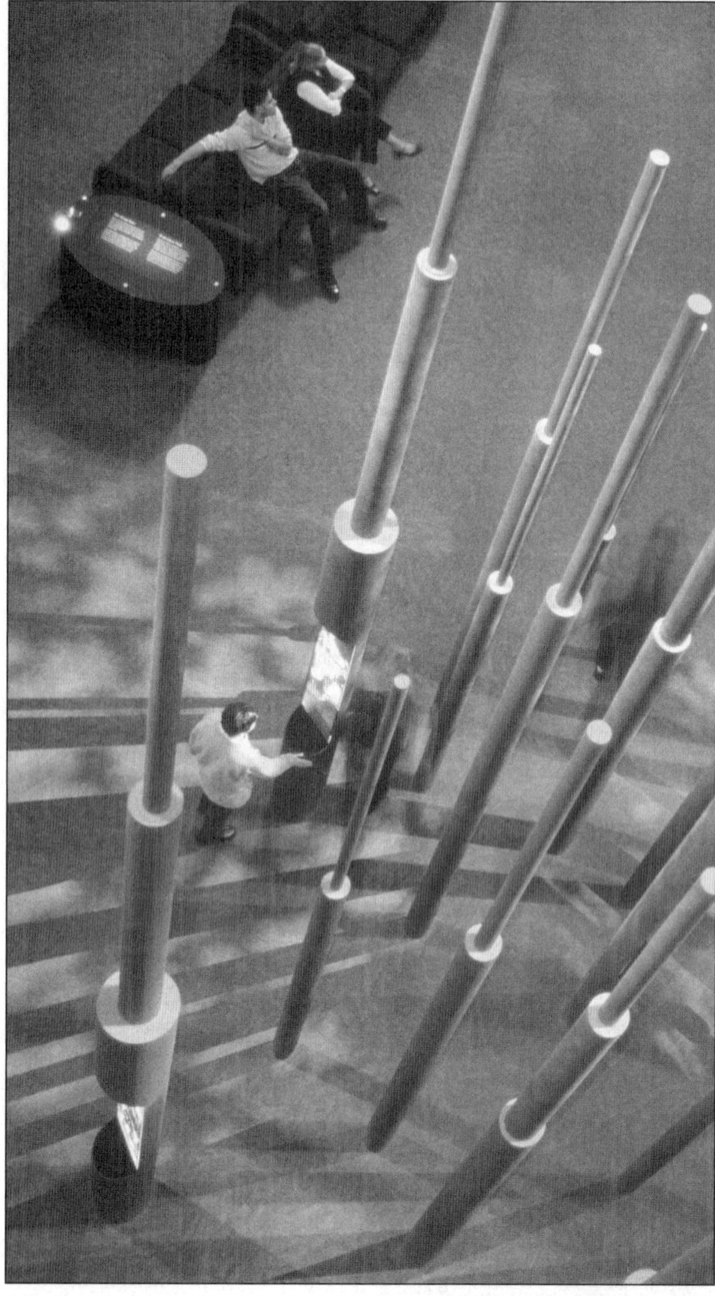

△ Signs of a Nation exhibition, Te Papa

permitting (call ⓣ04/471 9999 or go to ⓦwww.parliament.govt.nz to check). The highly informative and anecdotal tour begins with a short video on the extensive and detailed restoration work that was carried out after a fire in 1992, which began in the library and swept through parts of Parliament House. Incorporated into the restoration is some pretty impressive anti-earthquake work (Parliament House stands a mere 400m from a faultline), which puts it at the cutting edge of earthquake technology. The remainder of the tour highlights some exquisite architecture and a few surprisingly modern areas and artworks juxtaposed with the old, before you enter the library. The latter was built in 1899 by Thomas Turnbull, who was famous for designing churches and endowed the library with a strong Victorian Gothic, ecclesiastical feel. A striking contrast to such European style is found in the **Maori Affairs Select Committee Room** at the front of the building – included in the tour if a committee is not sitting. It's remarkably decorated with specially commissioned carvings and *tukutuku* (woven panels) in the different styles of all the *iwi* (tribes) of New Zealand.

When Parliament is not in session, tours continue into the comfortable-looking Debating Chamber itself, where the first MPs elected by New Zealand's system of proportional representation took their seats on the inauspicious date of Friday, December 13, 1996. On the other side of Parliament House, you briefly enter the foyer of the modernist **Beehive**, designed by British architect Sir Basil Spence, which was started in 1969 and completed in 1982. The story goes that Spence designed this curiosity on a napkin after dinner, having been inspired by the label on a box of matches. The building is apparently impractical and hell to work in. Opposite the Parliament Buildings, on Molesworth Street, is the 1893 **Backbencher Pub**, where MPs go to relax, and worth popping into to admire the decor, sporting satirical cartoons and puppets of various Kiwi politicians.

On your way from the Parliamentary District back toward the city centre, along Bunny St heading toward the harbour foreshore, you'll pass the imposing redbrick Art Deco edifice housing **Wellington Railway Station** (1937), worth a quick look for its sheer scale. Stepping through the unashamedly self-important entrance, framed by two towering stone pillars, you'll find a magnificent marble entry hall, its spectacularly vaulted ceiling decorated with ornate plasterwork.

The National Library and Archives

In the next block north from the pub along Molesworth Street is the **National Library of New Zealand** (Te Puna Matauranga o Aotearoa), on the corner with Aitken Street (Mon–Fri 9am–5pm, Sat 9am–1pm; free), the most comprehensive research library in New Zealand and home of the **Alexander Turnbull Library**, a vast collection of volumes, documents, paintings and so on, mostly relating to New Zealand and the Pacific, which was assembled by a wealthy Wellington merchant and gifted to the Crown in 1918. The ground-floor area has a range of reference books that you can take into a reading room, but the rest of the books are off-limits to the public. Also worth checking out is the library's large **gallery** (Mon–Fri 9am–5pm, Sat 9am–4.30pm, Sun 1–4pm), which regularly hosts free exhibitions, lectures and events (listed in Wednesday's *Evening Post* and Friday's *Dominion*).

Opposite the library is the pink concrete monstrosity of **St Paul's Cathedral**, a curious mix of Byzantine and Santa Fe styles, designed in the 1930s and 40s by Cecil Wood of Christchurch, a renowned ecclesiastical architect. Queen Elizabeth II laid the foundation stone in 1954 but the cathedral was not completed until 1998, replacing Old St Paul's, one street away. The interior is cavernous and you can't escape the powder pink or the concrete, but there are some interesting modern stained-glass windows, and a distinctive organ that was built in London and first installed in Old St Paul's.

A stone's throw away, at the junction of Aitken Street and Mulgrave Street, are the **Archives of New Zealand** (Mon–Fri 9am–5pm, Sat 9am–1pm; free), which exhibit a number of important documents relating to New Zealand's social and constitutional development. On permanent display and sealed into an environmentally controlled display case in the centre of the **Constitution Room** (really a vault) is the original **Treaty of Waitangi**, which barely survived a long spell lost in the bowels of the Old Government Buildings, suffering water damage and the gnawings of rodents before it was rescued in 1908. Other archives on display in the room highlight important milestones on the country's road to independent nationhood. There's a facsimile of an extensive **petition for women's suffrage**, a significant contribution on the way to New Zealand becoming the first country to enfranchise women (look for Kate Sheppard's signature), and **Maori petitions** dating back to 1909, which complain of broken treaty promises. Outside the Constitution Room is a small container of water, to help Maori neutralize *tapu* (ill-effects caused by a taboo action or object) after viewing the treaty. Mounted on a wall nearby is an enlarged copy of the treaty and a map, showing who signed where; the great Maori chief Te Rauparaha signed it twice, in two different locations, each time receiving muskets and blankets. Other galleries display some great Maori carvings and *tukutuku* (woven leather and flax panels), alongside rotating exhibitions of works by well-known Kiwi artists and of material relating to New Zealand history.

Thorndon

From 1866 to 1964, the modest-looking **Old St Paul's**, at the corner of Mulgrave Street and Pipitea Street (Mon–Sat 10am–5pm; free), was the parish church of **Thorndon**. The church's stunning wooden interior was crafted in early English Gothic style (more commonly seen in stone), the native timbers having since darkened with age to a rich mellow hue. The serried ranks of arches, the pews, pulpit and choral area are all highlighted by fabulous stained-glass windows and the sheen of polished brass plaques on the walls. Consecrated in 1866, the church was the major work of an English ecclesiastical architect, Reverend Frederick Thatcher, who designed it for Bishop Selwyn and was vicar here for a few years.

Head north for about ten minutes, crossing the bridge over the motorway into Thorndon, Wellington's oldest suburb, and you'll reach the **Katherine Mansfield Birthplace**, 25 Tinakori Rd (daily 10am–4pm; $5.50). A modest wooden house with a small garden, this was the first childhood home of New Zealand's – and the world's – most famous short-story writer and is described in some of her works, notably "Prelude" and "A Birthday". Stuffed with antiques and ornaments, the house has a cluttered Victorian/Edwardian charm and unusual decor, which was avant-garde for its time, inspired by Japonisme and the Aesthetic Movement. This has been beautifully restored and the walls are bright with colour and reprints of original wallpapers. In the kitchen is a doll's house, reproduced from the story of the same name, while an upstairs room is set aside to recount a history of the author's life and career, with some black-and-white photos of Wellington and the people that shaped her life, and an excellent 45-minute video, *A Woman and a Writer*. Born Kathleen Mansfield Beauchamp in 1888, the writer lived here for five years with her parents, three sisters and beloved grandmother before they moved to a much grander house in what is now the western suburb of Karori. At 19, Katherine left Wellington for Europe, where she spent the rest of her short life, before dying of tuberculosis in France in 1923.

Mount Victoria Lookout and southwest to Brooklyn Hill

To the east of the city centre, the **Mount Victoria Lookout** (196m) is one of the best of Wellington's lookout points, offering sweeping panoramic views, day or night. You can get there by car, by bus (#20; Mon–Fri) or on foot as part of the Southern Walkway (see p.504). If you're driving, follow Hawker Street, off Majoribanks Street, then take Palliser Road, which twists uphill through **Charles Plimmer Park**; on the other side, turn into Thane Road, which snakes up to the lookout. Next to the car park at the top is the **Byrd Memorial**, a triangular construction faced with multicoloured tiles and intended to simulate an Antarctic expedition tent, with the Southern Lights playing across it. The memorial honours the American aviator and Antarctic explorer Richard E. Byrd (1888–1957), who mapped large areas of the Antarctic and was the first man to fly over the South Pole, using New Zealand as a base for his expeditions. From the memorial, there's an impressive view of the city waterfront, the docks and the airport. Up a short flight of steps is the lookout proper, giving magnificent 360-degree views of the surrounding hills, the city and its suburbs, the harbour, Hutt Valley and eastern harbour bays.

You can get another fantastic all-round view of the Wellington region from the further-flung **wind turbine** crowning **Brooklyn Hill** in the southwestern part of the city. The turbine, a sort of giant plane propeller loudly whirring atop a mighty tower (31.5m), has generated power for Wellington since 1993, at its maximum capacity supplying over a hundred homes. On a clear day you can see as far as the Kaikoura Ranges on the South Island. To reach the turbine by car, take Brooklyn Road from the end of Victoria Street, turn left at Ohiro Road, then right at the shopping centre up Todman Street and follow the signposts (the road up to the turbine closes at 8pm Oct–April and 5pm May–Sept). Bus #7 (daily) drops you within walking distance.

Wellington Harbour

The sight of multicoloured sails scudding across the water should be enough to convince you that it's impossible to come to Wellington and ignore the lure of the water. On top of that, **Wellington Harbour** and its reliable winds offer excellent sailing experiences. Take your pick between a harbour cruise, a thrilling hands-on sailing trip, kayaking, and windsurfing.

Another option is to take a ferry to **Somes Island**, a hilly little knoll stranded in the northeastern waters of the harbour. Steeped in history and abounding in wildlife, the island enjoys panoramic views across the harbour. You can combine a day-trip here with a stint at the city's favourite beach of **Days Bay**, one of several beaches around the harbour that Wellingtonians flock to in good weather. For visitors there's really more fun to be had out on the water or exploring the city, but if you must hit the beach try **Scorching Bay**, a crescent of white sand 13km east of the city centre on the main coastal road, which has safe swimming and a play area. At peak times you can take bus #30 all the way there; otherwise, catch bus #11 to Seatoun (daily) and change onto the #26 (Mon–Fri) or #30 (peak times).

The best of the **harbour cruises** are run by Dolphin Sailing Academy, 6 East

View Grove, Normandale (ⓣ025/421 194, ⓦwww.dolphinsailing.co.nz). Up to eight people are taken out on a Nanoose yacht for a short cruise (1hr; $100), where you can either lend a hand or sit back and take in the atmosphere. Wet-weather gear and lifejackets are supplied.

Windsurfing is huge here and a popular spot is Kio Bay, to the east of Oriental Bay and around the point towards Evans Bay (bus #24, Mon–Fri). Near the bus stop is good wave-jumping water. For lessons, try Wildwinds Sail & Surf back at the overseas terminal, off Oriental Parade and beside Chaffers Marina (ⓣ04/384 1010; 2hr; $65 including gear), or Board Riders Windsurf School (ⓣ04/4993655, 021/388 130), who operate for the same rates and will meet you at a prearranged destination (they pick the beach based on the prevailing conditions). You can also explore the harbour by **kayak** from Ferg's Rock 'n' Kayak, Shed 6, Queens Wharf (ⓣ04/499 8898; sit-on-top kayaks $5 per 30min; single kayaks $7 per 30min, $40 per day; double kayaks $25 per hr, $80 per day; a credit card and photo-drivers licence are required as security), who let you loose without a guide as long as there are two or more people. They also run **guided trips** in double kayaks on calm nights, with romantic city-illuminated views, for a minimum of four people including a light supper (3hr; $45, book at least a week in advance).

Somes Island

Once a focal point for Maori canoes navigating their way out into the Pacific, **Somes Island** has long held spiritual significance to Maori. Kupe is said to have named it Matiu, meaning "peace", when he sailed into the harbour in the tenth century. The first Maori to arrive in the Wellington area settled the island and their descendants lived here until the 1830s. Later, European settlers renamed the island after Joseph Somes, then deputy governor of the New Zealand Company which "bought" it. For eighty years it was a quarantine station for animals, and until the 1920s travellers suspected of carrying diseases such as smallpox were also quarantined here; subsequently, German, Italian, Turkish, Mexican and Japanese prisoners of war were kept in camps on the island during both world wars.

Now managed by the DOC, the island is open to the public (daily 8.30am–5pm; free) and permanently staffed by a DOC officer, but your best bet for further information is the city's DOC office in Government Buildings (ⓣ04/472 7356). Work has recently started in earnest to revitalize **native vegetation** and plans are afoot to restore several historic buildings. Currently, the island is home to sheep and various wildlife species including three types of lizard, a breeding colony of about a thousand black-backed gulls and several hundred little blue penguins, and seals are gradually drifting back to its shores. In 1998 about fifty tuatara (New Zealand's small, unique reptile-like creatures with an ancient ancestry) were released, the majority hatched at Victoria University in Wellington, and their population has steadily increased since that time.

A number of **Evening Post Ferry** sailings to Days Bay (see below) stop here (Mon–Fri 1 daily at noon; Sat & Sun 3 daily), enabling you to explore the island for a couple of hours or so before catching a later ferry on to Days Bay. A popular option is to take a picnic lunch onto the island. Note that this is a protected reserve, so smoking is not allowed. From the wharf at the island's northeastern end, a sealed road runs uphill for 500m to the **DOC field centre**, in an old hospital, which has maps of the island (although you're better off picking one up in advance from the city DOC office to save you time here).

Days Bay

There's not much at **Days Bay**, southeast of Somes Island, except for the beach (at the foot of sheer bush-covered hills), a single main road lined with a few holiday homes, a park, and a popular café; and a remarkable house designed by Ian Athfield, visible from the harbour as you approach. The cliffside **Logan House** at Windy Point, 500m from the Days Bay wharf, is best viewed from the main road, which runs in front of it. It was built around and within two big old stone chimneys, whose thick walls are punctured by arrow-slit windows, like medieval towers. Athfield then designed the rest of the house to link with not only the chimneys but also the cliff-face directly behind them, so that the new structure fully interacts with its natural surroundings.

A stone's throw from the wharf, on the main road, is *Cobar*, a large, very popular, glass-fronted bar, restaurant and **café** looking out onto the bay and serving international cuisine and weekend brunches (see "Eating", p.513). From the Days Bay Boatshed beside the wharf (Ⓣ04/562 8150 or by mobile Ⓣ025 409 490; Boxing Day–Mid Feb daily from 10am; Oct–Christmas Day & mid-Feb to April Sat & Sun from 10am), you can **rent** windsurfers and kayaks (both $20 an hour), and canoes ($8 an hour), for use in and around the bay; prices include wetsuits if needed. The nearest shops are at **Eastbourne village**, a kilometre further south along the coast, which also has a few cafés and restaurants.

The **Evening Post Ferry**, a powerful catamaran (Ⓣ04/499 1282, timetable Ⓣ04/499 1273), runs daily to Days Bay (Mon–Fri up to 8 daily 6am–6.30pm, Sat & Sun 5 daily 10.15am–5pm; 30min; $7.50 one way, $15 return or $16.50 if via Somes Island; bikes free), departing from the end of Queens Wharf, behind the *Shed 5* café/bar. You can also get there and back by **bus** (#81 or #83 daily until 6pm, #82 Mon–Fri), or by **bike**, taking the SH2 around the harbour.

Eating

The gastronomic centre of New Zealand, Wellington is reputed to have more restaurants and cafés per head of population than New York City and once you've hacked up and down a few of its streets you'll find it difficult to think of anywhere in the world that has more to offer. It's a cosmopolitan scene, with a plethora of ethnic restaurants catering to all tastes, and new places opening up all the time. Recent years have seen an explosion of Indian, sushi and kebab outlets, especially in Courtenay Place. There's also a thriving **coffee bar** culture, and thankfully the cooler-than-thou attitude once projected by staff in some of these cafés has all but disappeared. As well as all that, Wellingtonians have a penchant for indulgent weekend **brunches**, especially on Sundays, in the cafés, restaurants and bars.

During the day, Wellington's **food courts** offer bargain grazing from an array of international fast-food outlets: the best of these is on Jervois Quay, near the junction with Wakefield St, where a broad selection of various excellent Asian food stalls compete with the famous Maori-run Red-Eye Diner, a monument to cholesterol worship where filling plates of steak, onions, egg and chips, with toast and tea or coffee, will set you back just $8 and a full breakfast will cost only $6. If you fancy an alternative, try the licensed *Gourmet Lane*, in the BNZ Shopping Centre on the corner of Willis Street and Willeston Street (Mon–Thurs 9am–5.30pm, Fri 7am–8pm, Sat 10am–4pm); *James Smith Markets Food Court*, 53 Cuba St (Mon–Thurs 10am–6.30pm, Fri–Sat 10am–late, Sun 6.30am–6.30pm), which also has a bar that's very popular on Fridays; or the *Asian Food Market*, Cable Street, where authentic Indian, Chinese, Malaysian,

Middle Eastern and Bengali food is served at weekends (Fri–Sun 10.30am–6pm), albeit in rather dowdy surroundings.

An excellent specialist **bakery** is *Pandoro*, on the corner of Wakefield and Allen streets (Mon–Fri 7am–6pm, Sat & Sun 7am–3pm), supplying all manner of loaves, as well as bap sandwiches for $5 or under, to eat at one of their two tables, washed down with a coffee. In the evenings, attention shifts to **Queens Wharf** and **Courtenay Place**, offering a choice between waterfront dining or the buzz of the city.

Opening times are given below where establishments are more likely to stick to them; otherwise, hours can be longer or shorter than the usual meal times according to custom.

Cafés and takeaways

Axolotl Café 34 Courtenay Place. Stylish, central, national-award winning café and friendly spot for a snack such as seafood chowder with garlic focaccia or a main course for up to $20, and good weekend brunches (from 3am). Mon–Fri 5pm–3am, Sat & Sun 24hr; licensed.

Café Brava 2 Courtenay Place ☎04/384 1159. Next to the Downstage Theatre, this classical, modern and airy café/bar serves well-priced all-day breakfasts, lunches with Mediterranean flair, and scrumptious Sunday brunches. Daily from 7am, until 3am on weekends & show nights. Book for pre-theatre dining. Licensed.

The Catch 48 Courtenay Place. Inexpensive sushi bar with dishes revolving on the countertop conveyor belt (colour-coded according to price), to take away or eat in; also does side orders and bigger meals ($10–18) from a set menu. Mon–Sat lunch & dinner, Sun dinner only; licensed.

City Limits 122 Wakefield St. Under new management but still the unpretentious and friendly founding father of Wellington's café society, open from early morning until late (Sun till 5pm) and including an Italian- and South African-inspired deli. Big breakfasts and light lunches are served, including wonderful seafood chowder, progressing to a broad dinner menu of well-presented food later in the day. Licensed & BYO.

De Luxe 10 Kent Terrace, beside the Embassy Theatre. Cheap snacks and counter food, most of it vegetarian, served in a hip bar that's popular with the post-cinema and theatre crowd. Excellent sandwiches alongside sushi and samosas, as well as good coffee from their own roasted beans. Daily morning 10am to midnight.

Expressoholic128 Courtenay Place. Seriously hip café, with great home-ground coffee, breakfasts for $8–18 and big portions of soup, filled focaccia, salad and pasta the rest of the day for $12–17. Also plenty of newspapers and magazines for perusing and some backyard seating. Sun–Thurs 8.30am till 12.30am, Fri & Sat 8.30am till 3am; licensed.

Felix cnr Cuba St & Wakefield St. A happening all-day café bar where you can enjoy pasta or udon noodles for under $20, or their famous copper pan breakfast/brunch, of eggs, bacon sausage, toms and hash browns ($15), whilesipping strong coffee and browsing the newspapers.

Fidel's 234 Cuba St. Great value all-day breakfasts, excellent food and snacks (check out the imaginative food stacks (where various constituants are piled upon one another to form a tower) in a fun and cosy den plastered with pics of Fidel Castro. There's a camouflage–netted,partially open-air seating area at the back for smokers. Mon–Fri 7.30am–midnight, Sat & Sun 9am–midnight; licensed.

Fiebigs 55 Mulgrave St, opposite Old St Paul's. Good coffee and fresh seasonal food for breakfast, lunch and dinner at expensive prices, all in a warm and clubby atmosphere or out in the courtyard. Mon–Fri 8am–11pm, Sat from 6pm only, closed Sun; licensed.

Kopi 103 Willis St. Something of an antidote to Wellington coffee-houses. Good-value Malaysian dishes such as roti and chicken korma (from 10am till late) in a cosy café on two floors, with smoking allowed on a small balcony upstairs. Licensed & BYO.

Krazy Lounge cnr Cuba St & Ghuznee St. This convivial, hip café/restaurant serves curries, good soups, pasta and char-grilled mains for $10–20. Mon–Fri 7.30am till the early hours according to custom, Sat & Sun 9am–3pm for food, 6pm–late for coffee, juice and drinks; licensed.

The Lido cnr of Wakefield and Victoria sts, opposite the visitor centre, is a stylish and good-value-for-money café/bar serving solid breakfasts and brunches, inspired lunches – pumpkin and pine nut fritters, kaffir lime chicken – blackboard specials and some zing-inducing coffee. Mon 7.30am–3pm, Tues–Fri 7.30am–10.30pm, Sat & Sun 9am– late. Licensed & BYO.

Matterhorn 106 Cuba St. Smallish bohemian venue so typical of Cuba Street (see Pubs and bars, p.517), a café and a bar/club, specializing in good coffee, cocktails, wines and European bar food, such as pizza, tapas, soups and salads. There's a cool, marquee seating area at the back (see also Clubs and gigs, p.517). Open from noon until the cats go home.

Midnight Espresso 178 Cuba St. A caffeine junkie's heaven, this mellow coffee-house peddles beans for all palates. Sip a cup on its own, with breakfast or alongside a cheap snack (good toasted sandwiches, focaccia and pizza, plus vegetarian and vegan food), while poring over their reading material. Mon–Fri 8.30am–3am, Sat & Sun 9am–3am; licensed.

Café Neo 132 Willis St. Extra-quick service and big servings at great prices in a warm bustling atmosphere for breakfast and lunch. Delicious pancakes are filled with banana and covered in maple syrup, or choose from an array of salads, pasta, and focaccia sandwiches. Closed Sun; licensed & BYO.

Nikau Gallery Café City Gallery, Civic Square. Decently priced café/bar with stylish contemporary fare and a sumptuous setting to match, opening onto an outdoor terrace. Keep an eye out for the kedgeree made with Mapua smoked Warehou, the free-range scrambled eggs and excellent coffee. Mon–Thurs 7am–5pm, Fri 7am–8pm, Sat & Sun 9am–4pm.

Roti Chenai 120 Victoria St ⓣ04/3829807. Tiny, simple South Indian and Malaysian café with an open kitchen in the middle where roti are prepared in front of your eyes, as well as delicious *dosai*, *murtabak*, curries and *rendang*. Lunch 11.30am–3pm, dinner 5pm to midnight according to demand; licensed & BYO.

Sahara Café 39 Courtenay Place ⓣ04/385 6362. Not to be confused with the kebab takeaway next door, this is an intimate venue for quality Middle Eastern dinners at good prices, plus belly dancing and live music on Saturdays. Book ahead at weekends. Licensed & BYO.

Stamp and Go 21 Marjoribanks St. A refreshing addition to the cafe scene is this lively Caribbean-style eat-in and takeaway that specializes in wraps and baps filled with spicy sausage and Jamaican Pepperpot (slow-simmered beef), Jamaican patties, Jerk chicken and char-grilled vegies, salted cod fritters and fresh mango lassi. Tues– Sun 11am–9pm, licensed.

Sushi of Japan 189 Cuba St, one of a national chain that do excellent value sushi and miso soups. Mon–Sat 9am–6pm.

The Vegetarian Café 179 Cuba St. Calming, mostly vegan spot with a broad-ranging menu that includes meals in a bowl ($6–12). Mon–Sat 9am–9pm, Wed 9am–4pm & Sun 9am–3pm; no alcohol allowed.

Wholly Bagels 39 Johnston St. The only place in New Zealand where you can get a decent bagel to take away, freshly made every day and sold on their own or as sandwiches, plus salads from the deli. Mon–Fri 7.30am–3.30pm, Sat 8.30am–3pm.

Zest 146 Cuba St. Funky bistro bar serving well-priced and presented weekday breakfasts, lunches and dinners, weekend brunches (from 10am) and Saturday night dinners, closes 3pm Sunday. Licensed.

Restaurants

Angkor 43 Dixon St ⓣ04/384 9423. An affordable, cool, spacious authentic Cambodian restaurant serving *ang* (lamb marinated in fresh lemon grass, spices and garlic), some delicious curries and spicy grilled dishes complemented by a good range of kiwi wines.

Cobar 12 Main Rd, Days Bay. Virtually opposite the wharf, this stylish bar, restaurant and café specializes in seafood and international cuisine; they also do weekend brunches. Mon–Fri from 11am, Sat & Sun from 10.30am.

Chow/Motel 45 Tory St. Part club, part restaurant, this atmospheric little spot does a broad range of Asian-style tapas – little plates of well-prepared grub from Korea, China, Thailand, Malaysia and Japan. The surroundings are slicker than a lounge lizard's shiny suit and it's not cheap, but it is very stylish and attached to one of the most exclusive clubs in town (see Clubs and gigs, p.517).

Dockside Shed 3, Queens Wharf ⓣ04/499 9900. Classy place-to-be-seen restaurant and bar in a vast converted wooden warehouse with a glass frontage and deck area overlooking the harbour, serving lunch and dinner, plus brunch at weekends. Hot on seafood – try the Dockside Fish and Chips, $20, and other fish dishes for $20–40. Book if you want a window seat and expect to spend money like the water you overlook in the busy deck bar. For an extra lively night (Fri) they also add a DJ into the mix; licensed.

Fusion 18 Cambridge Terrace ⓣ04/384 6968. A relatively new and inexpensive spot with a growing reputation, serving wonderful vegie and Malay curries, seafood fettuccine and tender steaks with fried onions and chips. Mon–Fri dinner & lunch, Sat dinner; BYO only.

Great India 141 Manners St ⓣ04/384 5755. The best dinner restaurant in town for tandoori, biryani or curry (all under $15). Licensed & BYO (corkage $1.50 per person); book for Fri & Sat nights.

Humming Bird 22 Courtenay Place. A restaurant and swish bar serving small tapas-style platters to accompany the huge selection of wines and award-winning cocktails. Occasional live jazz nights. Mon–Fri 11am–3am, Sat & Sun 10am–3pm.

Icon Restaurant Level 2, Museum of New Zealand (see p.500) ⓣ04/801 5300. One of New Zealand's top restaurants, offering an inspired range of good-value dishes for lunch on weekdays (noon–3pm), brunch at weekends (11am–3pm) and dinner daily (6–10pm) in an elegant contemporary setting overlooking the harbour. Dinner mains cost around $25–30, plus side dishes of $5–8 each, and the in-house cellar boasts an excellent selection of wines. The pleasant bar is open all day every day and serves bar snacks from 11am, though none of it is cheap.

Masala 2–12 Allen St ⓣ04/3852012. Snazzy modern Indian with long tables that feels like a big friendly café serving good quality lunches and dinners daily. They do cheap lunch specials with free rice and naan and some hot steamy curries. Licensed.

Nicholini's 26 Courtenay Place, a genuine no-fuss, inexpensive Neapolitan restaurant, small, bustling and full of divine smells and colourful food. Delicious Pork scaloppine, fish marinara, reasonably priced wine and a friendly atmosphere.

Shed 5 Queens Wharf ⓣ04/499 9069. Thriving upmarket café, restaurant and bar that is partner in crime and location with the *Dockside* (see p.513), proffering great seafood in a stylishly converted 1888 woolshed. Lunch, dinner and weekend brunches are served, and prices start at $25 for char-grilled yellow-fin tuna, rising to $35 for West Coast whitebait. Book ahead for the restaurant. Licensed.

The Skyline 1 Upland Rd, Kelburn, near the Botanic Gardens ⓣ04/475 8727. Sweeping views over the city enhance this glass-fronted café, bar and split-level restaurant designed by Ian Athfield. The café (10am–4pm) offers snacks, while the restaurant lays on an expensive but broad selection of seafood, hot and cold meat dishes, vegetarian alternatives, salads and desserts. The main reason to visit is to look over the building and the view. Licensed.

Strawberry Fare 25 Kent Terrace. Good for luxurious desserts at just over $10, washed down by a glass or two of dessert wine. Also serves scrummy breakfasts (around $16); and Mediterranean-style lunches and dinners ($15–20). Closed Mon–Fri 3–5pm; licensed & BYO.

Uncle Chang's 72 Courtenay Place. The best Chinese in town, for lunch and dinner daily. Great rice noodle soups and combination menus for $22–38 per person. Licensed & BYO.

Vista 106 Oriental Parade ⓣ04/385 7724. Famous for fine fish dishes and a welcoming casual atmosphere, they also produce excellent Spanish omelettes, Harrington's black-pudding and bacon brunches, and tempting desserts, all at reasonable prices ($14–26). Brunch Mon–Sun 9am–11pm, dinner Tues–Sat from 6pm til 11pm. Licensed.

Wellington Trawling Sea Market 220 Cuba St. An absurdly long name for the best fish-and-chip shop in the city, eat in or takeaway, which also sells wet fish. Mon,Tues, Sat & Sun 7am–8.30pm, Wed & Thurs 7am–9pm, Fri 7am–10pm.

Zico 8 Courtenay Place ⓣ04/802 5585. Young, exuberant, authentic Italian that won't break the bank, with veal scaloppini, creamy risotto, calamari and delicious tiramasu. Daily for lunch & dinner, licensed.

Drinking, nightlife and entertainment

The capital city has the best **nightlife** in the country and it just keeps getting better, with a huge array of late-night cafés, restaurants, bars and clubs, all within walking distance of each other. New ones constantly join their ranks, while the tired ones just quietly drop off the perch or, after a lick of paint and a name change, reinvent themselves. Wellington's playground is **Courtenay Place** and a few streets just off it (Blair, Cuba, Allen and Dixon streets), extending to Willis Street and Lambton Quay. The scene spreads from there to **Queens Wharf**, ten minutes' walk away, where mostly upmarket bars overlook the harbour. The partying goes on late into the night, and pumps hardest from Thursday to Saturday. The distinction between pubs, **bars** and **clubs** is often blurred, since many of the bars have free live music and dancing in the evenings, especially at weekends. A new addition to the entertainment available along Courtenay Place, for those drunk, foolish or brave enough to want to reacquaint themselves with previous meals, is the **reverse bungy**, a three-seater bench attached to two pieces of elastic that will propel you into the air at 160kmph at a force of 5gs (daily noon–late; $35). Busiest after the pubs close at weekends, the screams of glee (or terror) add an extra layer to the already lively atmosphere along Courtenay Place at the junction with Taranaki Street.

Gay and lesbian Wellington

The scene in Wellington is focused in the inner city, particularly around **Courtenay Place**, and woven into the general café/bar mainstream; and though smaller than that of Auckland, it tends to be less cliquey and judgemental. In the centre, at least, gays openly express affection in public, and gays, lesbians, transgender and bi-folk mix freely together. Fairly low-key for most of the year, the scene takes off during the annual festival, **Deus**, which combines with the **Gay & Lesbian Fair**, a big traditional fair of stalls and live entertainment ending with a big all-night dance party. Anyone's invited as long as they get into the over-the-top spirit of things (any one Sat in Feb/March; around $20; information from ⓔhindley@consumer.org.nz). The annual finals of the national competition **Mr Gay New Zealand** are often held in Wellington in October: check out ⓦwww.mrgaynz.org.nz, or email ⓔinfo@mrgaynz.org.nz.

For **information** on venues and events at other times, check out the national gay **magazine** *Express* ($2.50; ⓦwww.gayexpress.co.nz), available from the YHA and Unity Books (see "Bookshops", p.519); the free *City Voice* (which has a "Queer City" section every 6 weeks); or the national *OUT* magazine. Other contacts are the Gay Switchboard (ⓣ04/385 0674), the Lesbian Line (ⓣ04/499 5567) or Bisexual Women's Group (ⓣ04/385 1162). The Lesbian & Gay Advisory Group also produces a free all-encompassing *Venue Guide* in an A4 folder, available from various venues. Further information is also available from the Lesbian Hotline (ⓣ04/499 5567 & on ⓔwgtnlesbianline@hotmail.com).

The most established Wellington **venues** and **meeting places** include two saunas: Wakefield, 15 Tory St, behind OUT bookshop (ⓣ04/385 4400), and Sanctuary, 39 Dixon St (ⓣ04/384 1565), both among the best sources of information on what's happening. Other choices are *Flipp Brasserie*, RSA Building, 103 Ghuznee St (ⓣ04/385 9493), a café/bar offering continental cuisine to a predominantly business crowd (daily for lunch & dinner, brunch on Sat & Sun; mixed); *Zest Café*, 146 Cuba St (ⓣ04/801 8007); *Evergreen*, 141 Vivian St, an after-hours coffee lounge (from 10pm; mixed/trannies); *Eva Dixon's*, corner of Dixon and Eva streets, which has good coffee; *Paua* on Kent Terrace, a reasonably priced eatery: while for a big dance venue there is the *Pound*, Level One, Oaks Complex, in Dixon St opposite the Sanctuary (see above), as advertised in *The Express* and around town, though entertainment sometimes carries a cover charge; *Checkmate*, on Garret St, and *The Valve*, 154 Vivian St, a bar that turns gay on Wed nights only from 8pm, with Valve Night (ⓣ0800/422 326; *boyznite@badboyz.co.nz*, $5–10 cover charge). There is also a gay swimming club that meets at the Freyberg Pool and Fitness Centre, 139 Oriental Parade (ⓣ04/384 3107); see *The Express* for details.

The non-profit New Zealand Gay and Lesbian Tourism Association, Private Bag MBE P255, Auckland (ⓣ09/379 0776, ⓔsecretariat@nzglta.org.nz), provides **travel information** aimed at gay, lesbian and bisexual visitors. Gaytravel Net in Wellington (ⓣ04/384 1865 & 0800/429 872,ⓦwww.gaytravel.net.nz, ⓔreznzgaytravel.net.nz) can advise on gay, lesbian, trans and bi-friendly **accommodation** and offers a **reservations** service; likewise TWG Ltd (ⓣ04/479 8224, ⓔrobert.twg@clear.net.nz); and Gaylink International Ltd (ⓣ04/384 1877, ⓦwww.gaytravel.net.nz/nz, ⓔoperations@gaylink.co.nz), which is an information/consultancy company for gay and lesbian tourism within New Zealand. A Web site devoted to women's travel and accommodation is at ⓦwww.womenstravel.co.nz. For general gay/lesbian information on New Zealand, check out the Virtual Gay New Zealand Tour on the Internet at ⓔhttp://nz.com/glb/tour.

Neither is Wellington short on **performing arts**, for this is the home of not only four professional theatres but also the Royal New Zealand Ballet, the New Zealand Symphony Orchestra, the Wellington Sinfonia, the Wellington Opera Company and the New Zealand Schools of Dance and Drama. On top of that, there's the month-long **International Festival of the Arts** in March of even-numbered years, which draws the top performers from around the world to the country's biggest cultural event. Celebrating the huge diversity of the arts, performances include classical music, jazz and pop, tragic opera, puppet shows and the Grotesque, cabaret, poetry readings, traditional Maori dance, modern ballet and experimental works – and most of the venues are within easy walking distance of one another. For more information and bookings, call Ⓣ04/473 0149 or email Ⓔnzfestival@festival.co.nz; for bookings only call Ⓣ04/384 3840. Originally part of the Arts festival, the vibrant **Wellington Fringe Festival** (information and bookings Ⓣ0800/226 6548) is now run as a separate event every March, filling the inner city with street and indoor theatre. October sees a two-week **Wellington International Jazz Festival**, bringing some of the world's best performers. As well as official mid-evening concerts there are free performances in restaurants and bars, and improvised sessions in Civic Square, on the waterfront and all over the city. For more information on the jazz festival, check out the visitor centre and free pamphlets and flyers around town.

The best introduction to what's on is the *Wellington – What's On* booklet, free from the visitor centre and from accommodation around the city. There are also weekend **listings** in *The Dominion* and *The Evening Post*, while bland reviews and more useful listings appear in both of the city's free ad-ridden weeklies, *City Voice* and *Capital Times*, which you can pick up at the visitor centre and from racks around town. The visitor centre also provides **CityLine** (Ⓣ04/494 3333, on reply punch in code 1325), which gives a brief rundown of events.

Pubs and bars

Most **pubs** and **bars** are open daily, from around eleven in the morning until around midnight or later. Those closest to the business district, The Terrace and Lambton Quay, tend to be the most expensive.

The Backbencher Pub cnr Molesworth St & Kate Sheppard St, opposite Parliament House. Lively, comfortable pub, a bolt hole for MPs who quench their thirst amid satirical cartoons and *Spitting Image*-style puppets. Bar snacks all day and a well-priced café serving unpretentious fare. At its busiest on Fri night, when there's free live music from 7.30pm.

Bar Bodega 286 Willis St. Great atmosphere is the draw in this small bar aimed at a slightly older drinking crowd, offering an excellent range of boutique beers on tap and doubling as a venue for bands (see p.517).

Cell Bar Beneath *Zibibo* restaurant on Taranaki St. An intimate cocktail lounge (daily 4pm–3am) with live jazz on Thursdays and some excellent value antipasta, cheese, paté or calamari platters. Currently one of the in places.

Coyote 63 Courtenay Place. Urban Mexican-style bar that pulls in the dance crowds on Fri & Sat nights with its own brand of commercial and hard house.

Chicago Queens Wharf, opposite the Events Centre. Huge, bright and brash American-style sports bar with a dance floor, packed on Fri and Sat nights, when DJs crank up the atmosphere with house beats and retro sounds. Reasonably priced snacks are available to soak up all that Bud. Open from 11am until after the witching hour (around midnight).

Fishbowl 156 Willis St, A simple long bar that is extremely friendly and very well run, with a good selection of beers, pool, pinball and a good crowd of regulars, particularly from Thurs onwards. Occasional DJ music (Sat) but mostly just a good place to drink.

The Fat Ladies Arms Dixon St, a renowned, no frills, studenty sort of bar that's good for a drinking session, particularly a loud one.

The Grand 69–71 Courtenay Place. Sophisticated

and always busy nightspot on three levels in a big converted hotel of bare brick walls. Downstairs is an elegant restaurant bar with palm trees; upstairs are two main bars, the first incorporating a balcony over Courtenay Place, a covered garden bar and relaxing sofas (disco on this floor Fri & Sat nights playing mostly chart and dance music); the top floor is a pool bar.

J.J.Murphey & Co 119–121 Cuba St. Unpretentious, comfortable, modern Irish-style bar full of rich dark-wood furniture where cheap food is readily available, there's occasional live music, stout and real Irish whiskey.

Kitty O'Shea's 28 Courtenay Place. Small, often packed Irish bar with a none-too-broad mix of live music every night, including a Mon jam session, and then from Tues to Sun, Irish music, a few originals and a lot of covers bands.

Bond St Brewhouse 12–14 Bond St, off Willis St. Once the *Loaded Hog*, this big, first-floor, lively bar serving naturally brewed beer and reasonable food hasn't really changed much. DJ music and dancing Fri & Sat nights.

Matterhorn 106 Cuba St. A café during the day and a bar/club at night where they have a range of imported beers, excellent cocktails and a long wine list. From noon to the wee hours (see Clubs and gigs, below).

The Malthouse 47 Willis St. Airy yuppy first-floor bar with table service and a pleasant balcony over the street where over thirty high-quality naturally brewed Kiwi beers are on tap at any one time, swilled by a mixture of suits from offices and some discerning ale-heads, especially on Fri evening. Closed Sun May–Aug.

Molly Malone's cnr Taranaki St & Courtenay Place. Hugely atmospheric, loud and in-your-face Irish pub, with foot-tapping live Irish music every evening (jam sessions on Mon night). Upstairs is the quieter *Dubliner* restaurant and bar, serving snacks, $10 lunches, reasonable dinners and weekend brunches, though Sat nights a musician plays up here too.

The Opera cnr Courtenay Place & Blair St. Spacious and slick bar with DJ-led dancing and party atmosphere on Friday and throughout the weekend as well as some pretty creaky live bands on Thursday and Jazz on Friday. Thurs–Sat 11am–5am, otherwise till midnight.

Tupelo 6 Edward St. Intimate chic bar/club just off the beaten track with a European café feel, serving meals earlier in the day, becoming a bar at night. Excellent wine and beer list, including Emerson's real ale and Bookbinder beer. Mon–Tues from 5pm, Wed–Fri from noon, Sat from 6pm.

Clubs and gigs

Live **bands** (usually Kiwi but sometimes international) are a regular fixture, though less so now than a few of years ago. They play in bars, dedicated smaller venues or bigger halls like the Queens Wharf Events Centre (☎04/472 5021) and occasionally in **free concerts** in the waterfront Frank Kitts Park or at the Civic Square. Otherwise the usual scene is similar to most capitals, broad-ranging styles of music, mixed and matched by local or visiting (guest or celebrity) DJs to create a party- and/or club-style atmosphere.

Bar Bodega 286 Willis St. Wellington's longest-running musical institution. Every Kiwi band worth its salt has played here; DJs also visit, and it sometimes hosts dance parties.

The Blue Note cnr Cuba St & Vivian St (☎04/801 5007). Intimate club open every night from 4pm (till 6am Sun–Fri, till 3am Sat) regularly hosting live jazz or acoustic bands; occasional cover charge of $5–15.

Imbibe 3 Swan Lane, off Cuba St. Asian-Italian fusion in an attractive converted 1911 bakery, with good antipasta platters, that turns smooth club after 10pm (Fri & Sat) with mellow DJ music in an intimate space.

La Luna Club Oaks Complex, Dickson St. Popular hideaway for a youngish crowd into pool, hip-hop and light dance music. Bands play regularly and there are two bars.

Matterhorn 106 Cuba St. Smallish bohemian venue (see also Cafés and takeaways, p.513, and Pubs and bars above), specializing in cocktails and wines with a live jazz band (Wed) and DJs into soul, hip-hop, house and dance (Thurs–Sat), and mellower sounds (Sun).

Motel/Chow 45 Tory St. More exclusive than a royal garden party, where ultra-cool sounds (mostly jazz) are played in this leather and wood, Sinatra-style lounge that starts jumping around 10pm. It is notoriously difficult to find: head up Tory St from Courtenay Place and take the first alley on the left. The discreet door is on your left, ring the buzzer beneath the video camera and then wait, and you might get in. Part of the same address is *Chow*, a stylish eatery (see Restaurants, p.513).

Paradiso Behind the *Humming Bird* (see Restaurants, p.514). A busy little club/wine bar with live jazz (Wed & Thurs), and DJs playing dance and house music long into the night (Fri & Sat, closed Sun). They also have one special event each weekend, involving a musical theme or visiting DJ, when they may impose a cover charge of $5–10.

Q Bar Above *Nicholini's* (see Restaurants, p.514). Small, neat lounge-bar open from 8pm nightly with predominantly DJ-led house music every weekend. Over thirty imported beers, unimposing and pleasing place for an evening drink or a bit of a bop.

Studio Nine Upstairs at the *Edward Street Café*, 9 Edward St. Cool dance club that draws the young and hip with DJs playing house, dance, techno, high NRG and jungle. Cover charge $15–20, depending on the DJ; also has rave-style parties some weekends.

Tatou Ground floor, 22 Cambridge Terrace. Upmarket techno bar and dance club attracting smart young professionals to its two bars that stay open until 6am. Gets very busy later on; occasional visiting DJs.

Valve, 154 Vivian St. Small, studenty drinking den and club, open nightly till 3am, with all kinds of music (sometimes live), from jazz and reggae to jungle and techno. Beer for $2 on Tues night; pool and pinball.

Wellington Sports Café cnr Courtenay Place & Tory St. Late-night post-pub dancing in a sports bar. Live music every other Thurs, DJs playing middle-of-the-road dance and chart music Thurs–Sat, and expensive drinks. Mon–Sun 11am–til the last dude leaves.

Classical music, theatre and cinema

The city regularly hosts **orchestral** and other performances, while four professional **theatres** stage Kiwi and international shows. Tickets normally cost $25 upwards (average $35), but the visitor centre sells theatre tickets cheaper depending on availability. In addition to its quota of multiplexes, Wellington also has a smattering of arthouse **cinemas**. The cheapest night to head for the movies is Tuesday, when tickets cost $8–10 all day instead of the usual $12; in some cinemas tickets are also $8–10 for screenings before 5pm Monday to Friday.

You can book **tickets** direct at venues or, for a small fee, through two booking agencies: Ticketek, State Opera House, 111–113 Manners St (ⓣ04/384 3840; Mon–Fri 9am–5.30pm, Sat 9am–4pm), for events throughout the Wellington region; or MFC Ticketing, 111 Wakefield St (ⓣ04/801 4263; Mon–Thurs 9am–5.30pm, Fri 9am–7pm, Sat 10am–1pm), for shows and events held in the city only.

Theatres and concert halls

Bats 1 Kent Terrace ⓣ04/802 4175. Lively theatre concentrating on alternative works.

Circa cnr Taranaki St & Cable St ⓣ04/801 7992. One of the country's liveliest and most innovative professional theatres, which has fostered the skills of some of the best-known Kiwi directors and actors. At either of the two spaces in this brand-new complex (the main house and a 100-seater studio) you can count on intimate, imaginative productions.

The Downstage cnr Courtenay Place & Cambridge Terrace ⓣ04/801 6946. Stages both its own productions and the best touring shows: a mix of mainstream and new drama, dance and comedy, with the emphasis on quality Kiwi work. Cheaper gallery seats available.

Michael Fowler Centre Town Hall, 111 Wakefield St ⓣ04/801 4325. Wellington's major venue for orchestral and other performances. More details at ⓦwww.wcc.govt.nz/wfcc.

State Opera House 111–113 Manners St ⓣ04/384 3840. Hosts opera, ballet and musicals.

Westpac Trust St James 77–83 Courtenay Place ⓣ04/802 4060. A newly refurbished theatre in a fine 1912 building, home to the Royal New Zealand Ballet and host to opera, dance, musicals and plays. It also has a licensed café for pre- and post-performance drinks.

Westpac Trust Stadium Between Aotea Quay and Waterloo Quay. Overlooking the cruise ship terminal is the newish, purpose-built sporting venue for all things rugby and cricket (particularly international matches and the World Rugby Sevens), which also acts as an occasional rock concert venue.

Cinemas

Embassy 10 Kent Terrace ⓣ04/384 7657, ⓦwww.deluxe.co.nz. Mainstream and independent movies on a single giant screen in the city centre. You can take a glass of wine or beer in with you.

Hoyts Manners Mall, Manners St ⓣ04/472 5182, ⓦwww.hoyts.co.nz; and Hoyts Mid City, Manners St ⓣ04/384 3567. Central five-screen complex showing standard general releases.
Paramount 25 Courtenay Place ⓣ04/384 4080, ⓔinfo@deluxe.co.nz. A central venue showing both arthouse and mainstream movies on three screens, which you can watch while sipping a glass of beer or wine.
Rialto Film Centre cnr Cable St & Jervois Quay ⓣ04/385 1864, ⓦwww.rialto.co.nz. Independent and avant-garde productions, plus special screenings of New Zealand films from their archives. The ground floor has regular exhibitions on movies, video and television (Mon–Thurs & Sun noon–5pm, Fri & Sat noon–8pm; entry cost depends on exhibition, though many are free).

Listings

Airlines and flights International airlines include British Airways ⓣ04/472 7327 & 0800/274 847; Cathay Pacific ⓣ0508/800 454; Lufthansa ⓣ0800/945 220; Malaysia Airlines ⓣ0800/777 747; Qantas ⓣ0800/808 767(information & reservations); and Singapore Airlines ⓣ0800/808 909; United Airlines ⓣ04/472 0470. See p.493 for details of the airport and transport between it and the city. Note that there's a tax of $25 if leaving the country. Soundsair Shuttles (ⓣ04/801 0111) fly to Picton (about 20min; $79 one way, $139 return), while Air New Zealand (ⓣ0800737000, ⓦwww.airnz.co.nz) fly daily to Blenheim and Nelson ($64 one way, $97 return). Note that you can only book special-offers across Cook Strait in New Zealand.
American Express Cable Car Centre (through the Body Shop), 280–292 Lambton Quay, ⓣ04/473 7766.
Automobile Association 342–352 Lambton Quay ⓣ04/470 9999.
Banks and foreign exchange ANZ at 215–229 Lambton Quay ⓣ0800/180 925; BNZ at 1 Willis St ⓣ04/474 6000; National Bank of NZ at 60–64 Courtenay Place ⓣ0800/741 100; Thomas Cook bureau de change, 108 Lambton Quay ⓣ04/473 5167; and Travelex NZ Ltd and Western Union, at the airport ⓣ04/801 0130 (same tel for both).
Bike rental Penny Farthing Cycle Shop, 89 Courtenay Place ⓣ04/385 2279. A full day's rental costs $35.
Bookshops The biggest general bookshops are: Books and More, at 310 Lambton Quay ⓣ04/472 9694, and 89 Cuba Mall ⓣ04/384 8179; and Whitcoulls, 312 Lambton Quay ⓣ04/472 1921. Others include Dymocks, 366 Lambton Quay ⓣ04/472 2080; and Unity Books, which has the best range of Kiwi literature, at 57 Willis St ⓣ04/499 4245. For good secondhand and book exchanges try Arty Bee's Books, 17 Courtenay Place ⓣ04/385 1819; Bellamy's, which also stocks tapes and CDs, at 105 Cuba St ⓣ04/384 7770 (there are a few others also worth checking out on Cuba St); and Crossroads, 110 Featherston St ⓣ04/499 5212. There's a gay-interest section at Unity Books, 57 Willis St ⓣ04/499 4245. New Zealand's largest comics shop is Comics Compulsion, 105 Cuba Mall ⓣ04/384 2691.
Buses InterCity (ⓣ04/472 5111 and Newmans (ⓣ04/472 5111) head north to Auckland via the Kapiti Coast and Hamilton; and to Rotorua, Tauranga and the Coromandel. Heading northwest they link with New Plymouth via Palmerston North and Wanganui; and to the northeast they run to Gisborne via Hastings and Napier.
Camping and outdoor equipment Mainly Tramping, 39 Mercer St ⓣ04/473 5353; Kathmandu, 34 Manners St ⓣ04/801 8755; and Ski & Camping, who also provide a repair service for tents, backpacks, stoves and lights, at 181 Wakefield St ⓣ04/801 8704.
Car parks Council car parks: Civic Centre (entry at Harris St; 7am–midnight); Clifton, Shell Lane (entry off The Terrace; 7am–6pm); Jacobs Place (entry off Tory St; 24hr), James Smith (entry on Wakefield St; 24hr); Michael Fowler Centre (entry on Wakefield St; 24hr; suitable for campervans); Lombard Parking Building (entry off Bond St; 24hr). Independent car parks: Capital Carpark, Boulcott St (Mon–Thurs till 9pm, Fri till midnight); Condrens, Wakefield St (secure; $4 overnight till 9am; $7 for 24hr); Midland Carpark, Waring Taylor Street (Mon–Thurs till 7pm, Fri till 10pm, Sat 10am–4pm). Charges are $15 per day Mon–Fri 6am–6pm, free Sat & Sun.
Car rental International operators include: Avis, at the airport ⓣ04/802 1088, ferry terminal ⓣ04/801 8108 & 0800/655 111, and 25 Dixon St ⓣ04/801 8108, ⓔavis.res@xtra.co.nz; Budget, at the airport ⓣ04/388 0987, and 81 Ghuznee St ⓣ04/802 4548 & 0800/283 438, ⓔreservations@budget.co.nz; and Hertz, at the airport ⓣ04/388 7070, and cnr Tory St & Buckle St ⓣ04/384 3809 & 0800/654 321. Mid-range firms include: Ace, 150 Hutt Rd ⓣ04/586 2533 & 0800/535 500; NZ Rent-a-Car, 82 Tory St ⓣ04/384 2745; Nationwide, 37–39 Hutt Rd

ⓣ04/473 1165, ⓔppetersen@xtra.co.nz. Budget rental firms include: Rent-a-Dent, 50 Tacy St, Kilbirnie ⓣ04/387 9931, ⓔwellington@therentalcarcentre.co.nz; Shoestring Rentals, 138 Adelaide Rd, Newtown ⓣ04/389 2983, ⓕ389 2704, ⓔshoestring@carhire.co.nz; and Thrifty, at the airport ⓣ04/388 9494, and in the city ⓣ04/499 5691 & 0800/737 070, ⓔreservations@thrifty.co.nz.

Doctors, hospitals and dentists Call the Free Ambulance (ⓣ04/472 2999) for the nearest on-duty doctor; for 24hr emergency treatment, the After-Hours Medical Centre, 17 Adelaide Rd, Newtown, near Basin Reserve ⓣ04/384 4944. Wellington Hospital is on Riddiford St, Newton ⓣ04/385 5999. For dental care, try Central Dental Surgery, Harbour City Tower, 29 Brandon St ⓣ04/472 6306; or Symes deSilva & Associates, Second Floor, Olympic House, 97 Courtenay Place ⓣ04/801 5551; for emergency dental services, call ⓣ04/472 1394, or check the Yellow Pages under Dentists.

Embassies and consulates Australia, 72 Hobson St, Thorndon ⓣ04/473 6411; Canada, 61 Molesworth St ⓣ04/473 9577; UK, 44 Hill St (ⓣ04/472 6049); USA, 29 Fitzherbert Terrace, Thorndon (ⓣ04/472 2068); for other countries, look in Yellow Pages, under "Diplomatic and consular representatives".

Ferries Standard ferries to Picton depart from the Interisland Ferry Terminal (see p.493); a complimentary bus service runs there from the train station 45min before sailings. Services (daily; 3hr) cost $52 one way (plus $10 per bike or surfboard, $52 per motorbike, and $179 for a car or campervan), but if you book well in advance or take a night or early morning crossing you can save up to half; there are also special rates for day excursions. The more comfortable and faster *Lynx* daily catamaran(ⓣ0800/486 7228; 2hr 15min), which leaves from Waterloo Quay, costs $68 one way (plus $12 per bike, $199 per car or campervan).

Internet Email services are readily available; Wellington Public Library (see below for times) contains a number of terminals; Iworld, 100 Victoria St (daily 9am–late); The Cyber Centre, Level 2, The Breeze Plaza, Manners Mall (Mon–Sat, 9am–7.30pm); Email Shop, 175 Cuba St (daily 9am–6pm); I Café, 18 Manners St, The Oaks, Dixon St and 97-99 Courtenay Place (daily 9am–11pm).

Library Wellington Public Library is on Victoria Street, where it backs onto Civic Square. Mon–Thurs 9.30am–8.30pm, Fri 9.30am–9pm; Sat 9.30am–5pm, Sun 1–4pm.

Market James Smith's Market is a popular flea market on cnr Cuba St & Manners St, second floor. Mon–Thurs, Sat & Sun 10am–6pm, Fri 10am–9pm.

Newspapers The main local daily is *The Dominion*, whose Friday edition has events and entertainment listings, as does *Capital Times*, a free weekly, and *Contact*, another free local rag published every Thurs.

Pharmacy Unichem Eddie Fletcher Pharmacy 204 Lambton Quay ⓣ04/472 0362 (24hr) ; After-Hours Pharmacy, 17 Adelaide Rd, Newtown ⓣ04/385 8810 (Mon–Fri 5–11pm, Sat, Sun & public holidays 9am–11pm); for duty pharmacists check the *Dominion* newspaper (see above).

Police Wellington Central Police Station, cnr Victoria St & Harris St ⓣ04/382 4000.

Post office The main post office is in the train station lobby ⓣ04/496 4951; poste restante mail (addressed to Poste Restante, Wellington Post Office, Wellington Railway Station, Bunny St, Wellington) can be collected Mon–Fri 8.30am–5pm.

Swimming Freyberg Pool and Fitness Centre, 139 Oriental Parade ⓣ04/384 3107 (daily 6am–9pm, Fri till 5.30pm), has a 33-metre indoor pool, plus gym, spas, saunas, steamroom, fitness classes and massage therapy.

Taxis The biggest company, and offering YHA members a $10 fare to the airport, are Wellington Combined Taxis ⓣ04/384 4444 & 0800/384 444; try also Central City Taxis ⓣ04/499 4949; Gold & Black Taxis ⓣ04/388 8888; or Wellington City Cabs ⓣ0800/2580 2580. Authorized stands are located at the train station; on Whitmore St (between Lambton Quay & Featherston St); outside the *James Smith Hotel* on Lambton Quay; off Willis St on the Bond St cnr; outside Woolworths on Dixon St; and at the junction of Willis & Aro streets.

Tours Wally Hammond's Wellington City Scenic Tours(ⓣ04/472 0869) run a bus tour (daily 10am & 2pm; 2hr 30min; $25), departing from the visitor centre and Travelworld Holidaymakers, cnr Mercer St & Victoria St, which shows you all the highlights in a relaxed manner; they also run tours to the Kapiti Coast (half-day from 9am or 1.30pm; $55; min 2 people) and the Wairarapa (full day; $110). Smaller and more expensive trips and luxury excursions, to Martinborough wineries or to Mount Bruce National Wildlife Centre, are offered by Five Star Tours (ⓣ04/479 1356; $130). Excellent quad bike expeditions on Wellington's northern hills are operated by All Track Adventures (ⓣ0800/494 335, ⓔalltrack@xtra.co.nz; 1hr

30min–3hr; $99–149), who don't let you loose until you're fully confident and they can arrange pick-ups from the city. For the Red Rocks seal colony (see p.504), there is a guided 4WD Red Rocks Seal Tours (☎0800/732 5277), which will charge you $50 for, effectively, the privilege of a lift out there and some commentary. Closer to home there are two guided walking tours around the city, and a helicopter sight-seeing operation for the terminally lazy in search of a buzz. Walking tours are organized by Walk Wellington (☎04/384 9590), who charge $20 for their Central City and Waterfront tours, while flights are set up by Helipro (☎04/472 1550, Ⓦwww.helipro.co.nz) who offer a variety of excursions, starting at around $75 for ten minutes.

Trains The Tranz Metro network (☎04/801 7000, after hours ☎04/498 3013) is currently in a precarious state and services may well cease. For the moment, Tranz Metro operate regular daily trains from Wellington to Johnsonville, Paraparaumu, the Hutt Valley and the Wairarapa. The national Tranz Scenic provide a daily link with Auckland, via Palmerston North and Hamilton; and with Napier via Palmerston North and Hastings. The Tranz Rail Travel Centre is at the main train station, Bunny St ☎04/498 3000 & 0800/802 802.

Travel agents Air New Zealand Travel Centre, cnr Lambton Quay & Panama St ☎04/474 8950; and Budget Travel, Cable Car Complex, Lambton Quay ☎04/472 8342. Budget agencies include the travel desk at the YHA, 292 Wakefield St ☎04/801 7280; STA, 130 Cuba St ☎04/385 0561; and Lambton Quay Flight Centre, 182 Lambton Quay (☎04/471 2995).

Around Wellington

Crouched on the northeastern shore of Wellington Harbour, 15km from the city centre, is the Hutt Valley and its satellite towns of **Upper Hutt** and **Lower Hutt**. Bisected by SH2, this is little more than a transit point to the Wairarapa and the Hawke's Bay region further up the east coast, and barely merits the trip – unless you happen to be staying at Wellington's closest campsite (see p.522), which languishes in Lower Hutt. Further around the harbour, some respite from suburbia is provided by the **Rimutaka Forest Park**, prime picnicking and tramping territory for weekending Wellingtonians. For those inclined to more cultural pursuits Lower Hutt offers Maori Treasures, a gallery and tour in the suburb of **Waiwhetu** where there is much to divert the traveller who wants to learn about Maori art and tradition.

The Hutt Valley

Built on the alluvial plains beside the meandering Hutt River are the twin towns of **LOWER HUTT** and **UPPER HUTT**, 15km apart and hemmed in by steep bush-covered hills. Accommodating the overspill from the capital, this urban sprawl stretches from the suburb of **Petone**, site of the first, short-lived European settlement in the Wellington region, up the Hutt Valley to the Tararua Range, 30km north. The area is best explored from Wellington and warrants no more than a day-trip, with only a couple of attractions per se. If you have time on your hands, you could visit the **Dowse Art Museum**, in the Civic Centre, 45 Laings Rd, Lower Hutt (Mon–Fri 10am–4pm, Sat & Sun 11am–5pm; free), a gallery showcasing high-calibre contemporary New Zealand art, with a strong leaning towards jewellery, ceramics, textiles and glass, well displayed in changing exhibitions. The art theme continues 3km southeast in the suburb of **Waiwhetu** at **Maori Treasures**, 58 Guthrie St(☎04/560 4630; 90min tours $45, Mon–Fri 10am–4.30pm; 2hr 20min tours $85, Mon–Fri 12.30pm; pick up from Wellington available), a good-quality Maori art studio, gallery and shop where you can feast your eyes on carvings (wood, greenstone and bone), paintings, basketry, fibre arts, clay works and stone sculpture. On the informative tour you'll learn all about Maori artistic traditions and customs, musical instruments, weapons and story-telling, with a range of hands-on activities such as touching a kiwi-feather cloak and making a flax souvenir.

Three kilometres north of Upper Hutt, the scenic **Akatarawa Road** branches off SH2 and snakes 35km northwest through the Akatarawa Range and sumptuous bushland to Waikanae on the Kapiti Coast (see p.303). Along the way are several roadside picnic and river-swimming spots, before the road climbs a 450-metre pass and descends to Waikanae (see p.301).

Practicalities

By car, exit the SH2 motorway at the Petone off-ramp; **by train**, take one of the regular daily Tranz Metro commuter services from Wellington train station to Waterloo. From the station, the Dowse Art Museum is a 1.5-kilometre walk northwest down Knights Road; the Maori Treasures complex is ten-minutes' walk from the station in the opposite direction, along Guthrie Street off Cambridge Terrace. Eastbourne and Big Red **buses** depart hourly from Courtenay Place to Lower Hutt's Queensgate shopping centre on Knights Road, where there's a small **information** kiosk on the ground floor (Mon–Wed & Fri–Sun 9am–5.30pm, Thurs 9am–7pm), stocking local leaflets and public transport timetables. An official Hutt City visitor centre is at Andrews Avenue (Ⓣ04/560 4715, Mon-Fri 10am–5pm, Sat & Sun 10am–3pm), which covers the entire Wellington region, taking bookings for transport, accommodation and activities.

It's worth exploring the ancient forest, the Rimutaka Incline (see p.484) or swimming holes in the secluded river. You can get here by **bus** with Tranzit Coachlines or InterCity (once daily) from downtown Wellington; or from Masterton (departing Tranzit Coachlines depot on Queen Street twice a day).

Rimutaka Forest Park

Due south of Lower Hutt is the main entrance to the **Rimutaka Forest Park**, popular among city-dwellers for its series of easy short and **day-walks** in the attractive Catchpool Valley; there's also a well-maintained **campsite**, and picnic and barbecue facilities. Some 20km from Wellington along the Coast Road, a signpost marks the park **entrance** (gates open 8am–dusk), from where Catchpool Road winds a further 2km up the valley to the car park, the starting point for most of the walks. Keen walkers/campers will want to get as far as the braided Orongorongo River, from where a startlingly grand landscape begins; you can camp for free along the riverbanks. A regular **bus** service (#80, Mon–Fri) runs between Wellington and Wainuiomata, where you can pick up a taxi at Queen Street for the last 12km to the park entrance. Two hundred metres beyond the park entrance is a well-equipped **DOC field centre** (daily Oct–April 9am–5.30pm; May–Sept Mon–Fri 8am–4.30pm, Sat & Sun 11.30am–4.30pm; Ⓣ04/564 8551), which stocks the useful *Catchpool Valley/Rimutaka Forest Park* leaflet (50¢), detailing walks in the vicinity.

Travel details

Buses

Wellington to: Masterton via the Hutt Valley (4 daily; 2hr); New Plymouth (3 daily; 6hr 30min); Paraparaumu (9 daily; 50min); Porirua (9 daily; 25min).

Trains

Wellington to: Auckland (2 daily; 11hr); Hutt Central/Waterloo (daily every hour; 20 min); Johnsonville, a suburb of Wellington (daily every 30min 6am–11.30pm; 21min); Levin (3 daily; 1hr 34min); Napier (1 daily; 5hr 30min); Otaki (1 daily; 1hr 14min); Palmerston North (3 daily; 2hr 15min)

Ferries

Wellington to: Picton (8–12 daily; 1hr 45min–3hr).

Flights

Wellington to: Auckland (14 daily; 1hr); Bay of Islands (9 daily; 2hr 45min); Blenheim (10 daily; 25min); Christchurch (15 daily; 45min); Dunedin (12 daily; 2hr); Gisborne (8 daily; 1hr 10min); Hamilton (10 daily; 1hr 10min); Hokitika (5 daily; 2hr 15min); Invercargill (7 daily; 2hr 20min); Kaitaia (4 daily; 3hr 25min); Milford Sound (6 daily; 4hr 20min); Motueka (2 daily; 1hr 15min); Mount Cook (5 daily; 2hr 25min); Napier/Hastings (15 daily; 1hr); Nelson (10 daily; 35min); New Plymouth (8 daily; 55min); Palmerston North (10 daily; 35min); Picton (8 daily; 25min); Queenstown (10 daily; 3hr 20min); Rotorua (7 daily; 1hr 15min); Taupo (4 daily; 1hr); Tauranga (11 daily; 2hr 20min); Te Anau (5 daily; 4hr 5min); Timaru (7 daily; 1hr 50min); Wanaka (4 daily; 3hr 5min); Wanganui (4 daily; 45min); Westport (2 daily; 55min); Whakatane (10 daily; 2hr 10min); Whangarei (15 daily; 2hr 30min).

8

Marlborough, Nelson and Kaikoura

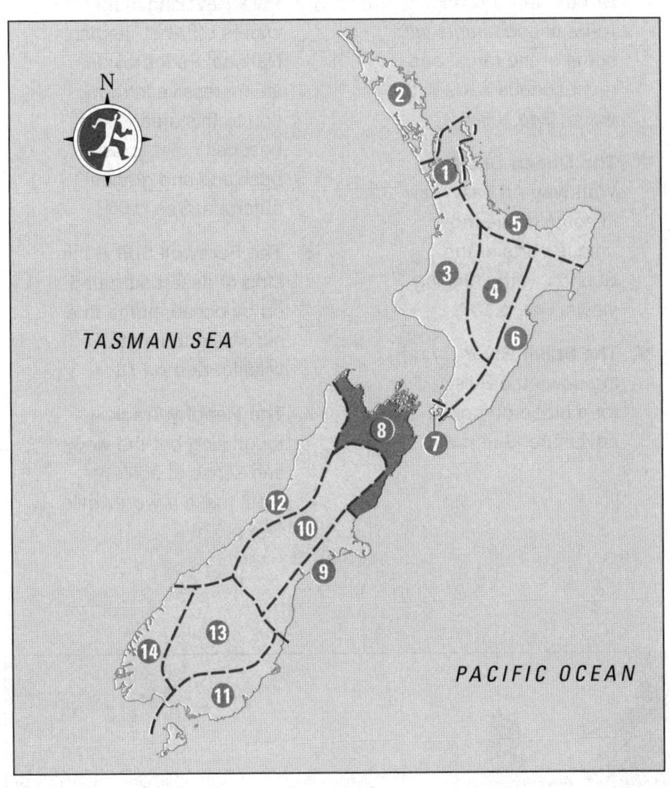

CHAPTER 8

Highlights

* **Marlborough Terranean** A meal at the *Marlborough Terranean* in Picton will rival any culinary experience you have in New Zealand. See p.534

* **Birding in Picton** Face-to-beak encounters with some of the rarest and most curious birds in the world. See p.535

* **The Queen Charlotte Walkway** An easy walk in some of the most unique parts of the Sounds, with stunning views. See p.537

* **The Buller River** Try rafting down the Buller River for a blood pumping adventure. See p.548

* **Beer and wine** No trip to this area is complete without visiting the breweries and wineries of both Nelson and Blenheim. See pp.553 & 586

* **Abel Tasman National Park** Kayaking in the waters off Abel Tasman National Park provides an impressive introduction to this area where beaches meet forest, bushland and granite outcrops. See p.556

* **The Farewell Spit** A thin strip of desert surrounded by ocean, home to a surprising amount of wildlife. See p.573

* **The Heaphy Track** A tough slog but the views and sense of achievement make it worthwhile. See p.576

8

Marlborough, Nelson and Kaikoura

Many people's favourable first impression of the South Island is formed when they travel by boat or plane to its northern end, and is crystallized by the intricacy of The Marlborough Sounds, the sweep of the bays from Nelson as they curl towards Farewell Spit, the splendour of the national parks, mountain lakes and streams, the delights of the wine region and the natural wonders of Kaikoura. In fact, if you had to choose only one area of New Zealand to visit, this would be a strong contender.

Most visitors travel between the North Island and the South Island by ferry, striking land at the town of **Picton** – drab in the winter, lively in the summer and surrounded by the consistently rugged and beautiful **Marlborough Sounds** where bays full of unfathomably deep water lap at tiny beaches and rickety boat jetties, and the land rises steeply to forest or stark pasture. From here, heading west out of the lively city of **Nelson**, you're within easy reach of some of the country's most spectacular walking tracks and dazzling golden beaches. Each of the national parks in the region has a distinct identity: the most famous is the **Abel Tasman National Park**, while the newest is **Kahurangi**, through which the rugged and spectacular **Heaphy Track** forges a route to the West Coast. Hemmed in by these two national parks, **Golden Bay** is an isolated oasis on the far side of a marble mountain with a strange grassy moonscape pockmarked by limestone grottoes - a place chosen by Peter Jackson as a prime location in his epic film **Lord of the Rings**. The curve of the bay culminates in a long sandy bar that juts into the ocean, **Farewell Spit**, an extraordinary and unique habitat. The most neglected of the region's national parks is the **Nelson Lakes**: in the winter a lively and exciting ski area and in the summer a sparsely populated, slumbering territory with access to Alpine lakes, flora and fauna, as well as providing a base for rafting assaults on the Karamea and Buller rivers.

Heading in the opposite direction, east from Picton, you can slurp your merry way through **Marlborough**, the most famous wine-making region in New Zealand, with **Blenheim** and **Renwick** at its heart. The diversity of the region's communities makes for an idiosyncratic outlook, while the rich farmland and coast inspire an easy-going **lifestyle** reminiscent of Mediterranean climes, attracting people from all over the world to settle here and perfect their art, brewing techniques, wine, cooking and hospitality. An alternative to the

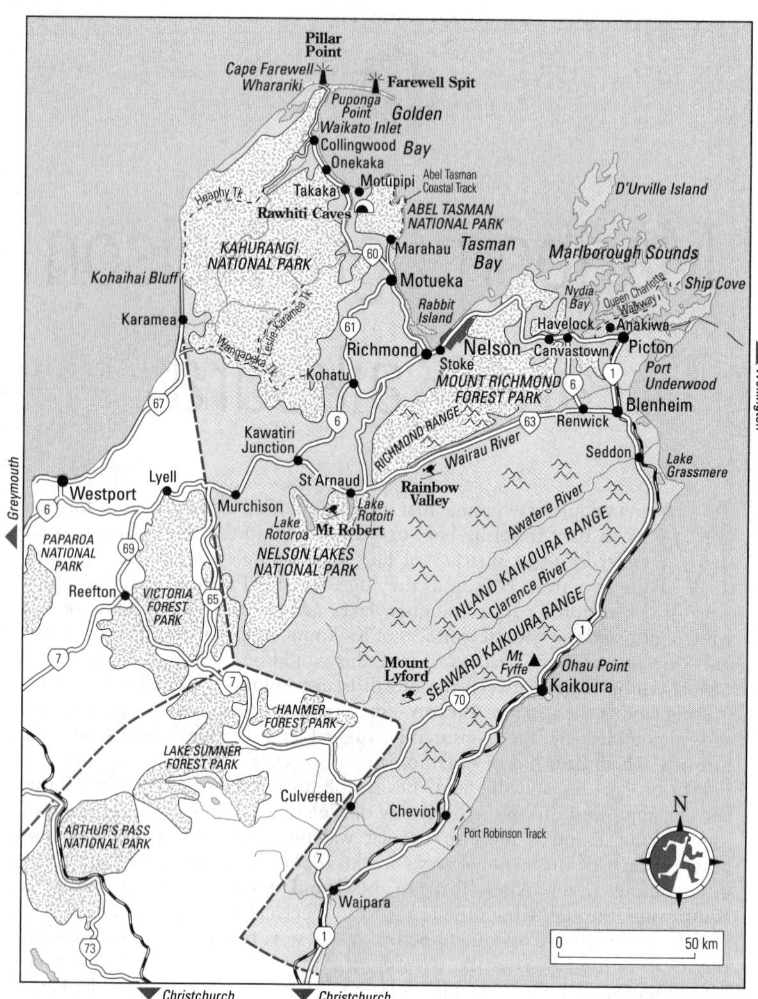

good living available in the area is the chance to spend time with nature, **whale watching** or swimming with **dolphins** in **Kaikoura**, from where there's also the option of a number of challenging skifields – as yet blissfully uncrowded and inexpensive. The **Kaikoura Ranges**, divided into the landward and seaward, provide a spectacular backdrop to travel along the coast, as well as evocative views from some of the highest peaks and most solitary tracks anywhere outside the Southern Alps.

As for the **weather**, Marlborough and Nelson enjoy more sunshine than most other parts of New Zealand in the spring and summer and a mild climate for most of the year; likewise, the Kaikoura region is generally mild, though often windy. Marlborough and Nelson are both extremely popular from Christmas to early February, with the Abel Tasman and Queen Charlotte

walkways both attracting big **crowds**. This means solitude, beach space, bus seats and accommodation are difficult to find and it makes more sense to visit either side of high season if you can. The tourist hot spot in Kaikoura is the town itself and its whale and dolphin excursions which run virtually year-round.

Buses and **boats** provide access to the Nelson region and its coastal national parks, while **trains** and buses from Picton head east through Blenheim, Kaikoura and down the coast to Christchurch.

The Marlborough Sounds

The **Marlborough Sounds** are undeniably picturesque, whetting the appetite for the rest of the South Island and providing a lingering first impression for those travelling by ferry from the North Island. The Sounds' coastline is a stimulating filigree of bays, inlets, islands and peninsulas rising abruptly from the water to rugged, lush green wilderness and cleared farmland. Large parts are only accessible by sea, which also provides the ideal vantage point for witnessing its splendour. The area is part working farms, including salmon or mussel farms, and part given over to some fifty-nine reserve areas – a mixture of islands, sections of coast and land-bound tracts. The Sounds' nexus, **Picton**, is the jumping-off point for the rewarding **Queen Charlotte Walkway**, while close by is the small community of **Havelock**, which is well worth a stop to explore the delightful **Pelorus Sound** before pressing on to Nelson and the Abel Tasman National Park.

Picton and around

Sandwiched between the hills and the sea, **PICTON** is where the **ferries** that ply the Cook Strait dock. Indeed, since the early 1960s, the town's fortunes have been largely determined by the machinations of ferry companies, never more so than in recent years when there has been talk of relocating the ferry terminal to the Blenheim or Nelson areas, though this is unlikely to happen. The European settlement of Picton dates from 1827, when John Guard established a **whaling** station on its shores. Following the New Zealand Company's purchase of the town site for £300 in 1848, Picton flourished, acting as a port and **service town** for the Wairau Plains to the east.

These days Picton has a population of 4500 and acts as little more than a transit town but beneath its workaday surface it serves as a fascinating introduction to the delights of the South Island. Apart from its three **museums** (two focusing on New Zealand's **maritime heritage** and one concerned with Maori and the whaling, gold, logging, fishing and farming interests that have dominated the lives of people who have settled here), the town also boasts a new **aquarium**, some excellent **sea kayaking** trips, access to the underrated **Queen Charlotte Walkway** and one of the most relaxed and enjoyable wildlife adventures around, Dolphin Watch (see p.535), which, despite its name, concentrates mostly on the unique birdlife of the area. As you would expect of a port, Picton also has an immense range of accommodation, some truly average pubs and a couple of fine eating houses, serving up the delicious seafood found in these parts.

Arrival and information

Ferries dock in Picton Harbour, 600m from the town centre, the **train station** is right by the ferry terminal, and **buses** drop off just outside. Koromiko **airport** is 9km from town – Soundsair Buses will run you into the centre for free if you're flying with them, or you can pick up a taxi for around $10 (see "Listings", p.535).

The combined **visitor centre** (daily: Oct–Dec & March–Sept 8.30am–5pm, Jan–Feb 8am–6pm; ⓣ03/573 7477, ⓦwww.picton.gen.nz) and **DOC office** (daily 8.30am–5pm; ⓣ03/520 3002, ⓕ520 3003) is on the foreshore, five minutes' walk from the ferry terminal. They have an enormous amount of information and a gargantuan number of leaflets on the town and the South Island but the pick of the bunch for the immediate area are the *Picton Walkways* leaflet, detailing short walks around town; *Queen Charlotte Walking Track*; the *Art and Craft Trail*, which selects the best of the shops and galleries in the Marlborough region; and *Wines of Marlborough* for a rundown of all the wineries and their locations (all free); or the *Marlborough Sounds* leaflet ($1).

Almost directly opposite the official visitor centre and using a deceptively similar logo is The Station (9am–5pm; ⓣ03/573 8857) in the train station, a private **booking office** for trips, accommodation and onward (though not air) travel – one of many in Picton.

Accommodation

As a major **transit centre**, Picton has a disproportionately large number of accommodation options for its size, ranging from backpacker hostels to swanky hotels, and you should have no difficulty finding somewhere to suit your needs within walking distance of the gangplank for most of the year, although **around Christmas** it makes sense to **book** in advance.

Hotels and motels

Beachcomber Inn 27 Waikawa Rd ⓣ03/573 8900, ⓕ573 8888. A large hotel complex overlooking the harbour with a swimming pool and spacious comfortable rooms; rates are higher for rooms on the upper floors with better views. ❺–❻

Broadway Motel 113 Picton High St ⓣ03/5736563, ⓦwww.broadwaymotel.co.nz. A mixture of revamped old rooms and modern, purpose-designed set units (18 in all) in the centre of town with good views from the 1st floor balcony. ❹–❺

Harbour View Motel 30 Waikawa Rd ⓣ03/573 6259, ⓕ573 6982. Twelve modern, fully self-contained units with views over the harbour. ❹

Jasmine Court 78 Wellington St ⓣ03/573 7110, ⓕ573 7211. Non-smoking throughout, these beautifully kept, luxury motel units are within walking distance of everything and contain all that you might need, including CD players and access to an office with internet access. Unquestionably the best accommodation in the town. ❻–❼

Tourist Court 45 High St ⓣ & ⓕ03/573 6331. Once cheap, well-run, quiet and cheerful, now just cheap. ❸–❹

B&Bs and homestays

Glenora 22 Broadway ⓣ03/573 6966, ⓦglenora.co.nz. A slightly imposing house overlooking part of the town. Besides offering comfortable en-suite rooms and a lovely Swedish-style smorgasbord breakfast, they also run weaving courses (see "Listings", p.535). ❺–❻

The Gables 20 Waikawa Rd ⓣ03/573 6772, ⓦwww.thegables.co.nz. An exceptional B&B run by considerate hosts who offer transport to ferries and planes, and cook up superb and filling breakfasts. Rooms are spacious and have private facilities and there are now two new cottages in which to relax. ❺–❻

North–South Island Transport

Details of **transport** between the **North and South islands** are given in Chapter Seven; see "Listings", p.519.

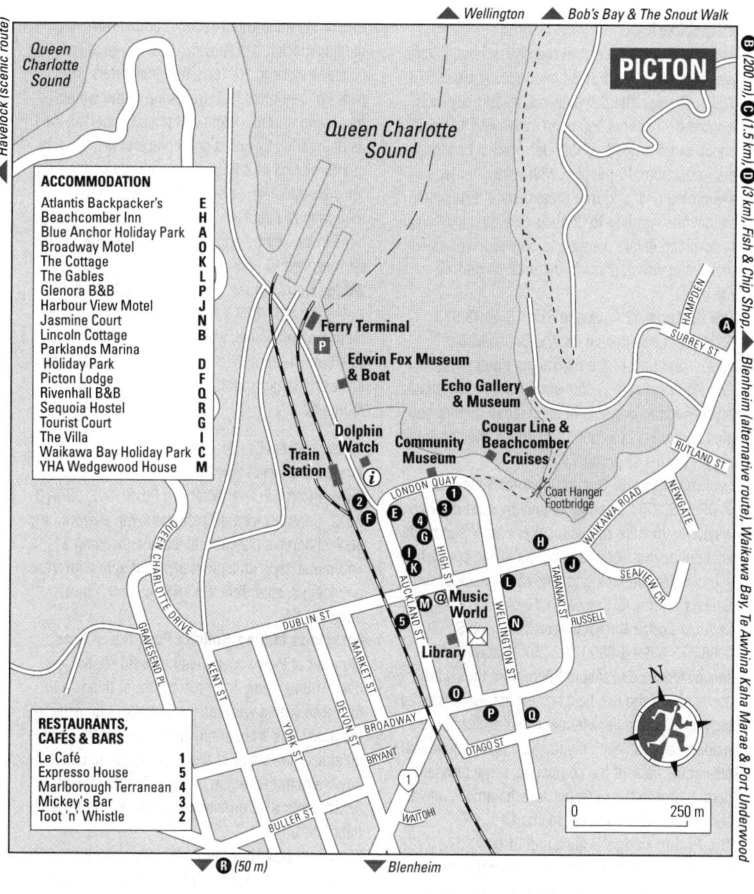

Lazy Fish Guest House In the Sounds Ⓣ03/579 9049. Accessible only by water taxi from Picton (a Cougar drop-off with an open-ended return for $30, 20min; for other alternatives see "Listings" on p.535. This guesthouse offers beautiful views, seclusion and comfort at very reasonable prices. Dorms ❶, rooms ❸

Lincoln Cottage 19 Lincoln St Ⓣ03/573 5285, Ⓦwww.picton.co.nz/lincolncottage. A traditional B&B with two pleasant rooms sharing a terrace and kitchen with the house and a small garden cottage, all about 1.5km from the town centre. Unmissable because of the Art Deco architecture and authentic sky-blue exterior. ❹–❺

Ocean Ridge Holiday Apartments Off the Port Underwood Rd, about 35km from Picton on the way to Blenheim Ⓣ & Ⓕ03/579 9474. Perched high on a hill overlooking Ocean and Robin Hood bays, this homestay enjoys one of the most spectacular settings of any on the South Island. It has its own short walking tracks to the sea's edge and there are superb panoramic views from most of the large, en-suite rooms. There is also a squash court/half basketball court, a separate three-bed holiday apartment and stimulating company (the owners make and sell their own jewellery and pewter work). ❻.

Rivenhall 118 Wellington St Ⓣ03/5737692, Ⓔlaurenson_nan_malcolm@xtra.co.nz. On the left hand side up the hill, this is a charming, historic homestay with big rooms and grand views, particularly from the balcony of the suite, and a warm welcome from the hosts. ❹–❼

Hostels

Atlantis Backpackers In the dive school, Diver's World, cnr Auckland St & London Quay ⓣ03/573 7390, ⓦwww.atlantishostel.co.nz. This centrally located dive school has been converted into a very cheap but cramped, rabbit-warren of a backpackers (maximum 40 people), with a free heated swimming pool and free breakfasts. It's designed for anyone wanting to do their dive qualifications or qualified divers wanting to do various open-water and wreck dives in the area. Dorms ❶, rooms ❷

The Cottage 42 Auckland St ⓣ & ⓕ03/573 6536. Formerly known as *The Bougainvillea Lodge*, and part of the expanding empire that is *The Villa* (see below), this small house provides a much-needed overspill of snug small dorms, doubles and twins in a functional and homey atmosphere. Dorms ❶, rooms ❷

Lochmara Lodge Queen Charlotte Sound ⓣ & ⓕ03/573 4554. Accessible only by boat ($15 each way), this mixture of backpacker and chalet (with kitchen) accommodation is in an idyllic spot where you can just sit back and enjoy the peace of the Sounds. Dorms ❶, chalets ❹–❺

Sequoia Lodge Backpackers 3a Nelson Sq ⓣ & ⓕ03/573 8399 & 0800 222 257, ⓔstay@sequoialodge.co.nz. About 800m from the centre, this is one of the two best hostels in town, with free pick-up from the ferry terminal and excellent home-made free bread each night. There are en-suite doubles at the back of the compound, some pleasant dorm rooms in the main house, a hammock and a barbecue area. Dorms ❶, rooms ❸

The Picton Lodge 3 Auckland St ⓣ03/573 7788, ⓕ573 8418. This purpose-built hostel is the closest to the ferry terminal and railway and noisier as a result, with a range of twins, doubles and dorms. $3 extra for linen and towel. Dorms ❶, rooms ❷

The Villa 34 Auckland St ⓣ & ⓕ03/573 6598. One of the most-often-recommended hostels on the backpackers' grapevine, this 100-year-old house is close to the ferry terminal, offers free pick-up, free breakfast, free soup in the winter, free apple crumble nightly and a spa pool, as well as being friendly and a good place to pick up lots of information on things to see and do in the area (they produce their own seasonal newsletter), though their popularity causes a few space problems in the dorms and kitchens. Dorms ❶, rooms ❷, ensuites ❸

Wedgewood House (YHA Associate Hostel) 10 Dublin St ⓣ03/573 7797. Uninspiring central hostel in a small house, with restricted office hours (8–10am, 1–2pm, 5–6.30pm, 8–10pm), but there are extra, larger rooms next door. Dorms ❶, rooms ❷

Campsites and motor parks

Blue Anchor 70–78 Waikawa Rd ⓣ & ⓕ03/573 7212. Centrally located campsite with a swimming pool, children's playground, cabins (bedding $1) and motel-style units, in a pleasant spot with trees providing shelter. Tent sites ❶, cabins & motel units ❷–❹

Parklands Marina Holiday Park Beach Road, 3km out of Picton along Waikawa Rd ⓣ & ⓕ5736343. Away from the centre of things and for those with a car there is no better campsite in the area. This wonderfully kept, comfortable and quiet site has some of the best-equipped cabins anywhere in the region and two friendly Swiss hosts. Tents $10, on-site caravans ❶, cabins ❷, flats ❸–❹

Waikawa Bay Holiday Park 302 Waikawa Rd ⓣ & ⓕ03/573 7434. Five minutes' drive from the ferry terminal, this large, sheltered site has views over the water. Tent sites $18, cabins & motel units ❷–❸

The Town

The town heads away from the ferry terminal toward the surrounding hills where dense native and introduced forest and foliage provide a green backdrop. Most of Picton's most interesting sights are on or near the foreshore, a pretty area with palms, mini golf and picnic benches overlooking the harbour.

Between the ferry terminal and the town centre is the hulk of the **Edwin Fox** (daily 8.45am–5pm; $5), the sole survivor of the fleets that once brought migrants to New Zealand. You access the shell of the ship from the centre alongside, which contains fascinating displays on what remains of this 1853 ship, constructed from teak and saul timber in India, and its colourful life, as well as the mammoth task of preservation that lies ahead. The *Edwin Fox* operated as a troop carrier in the Crimean War and transported convicts to Australia, before bringing free settlers to New Zealand. In later years, the ship was put to service as a merchant vessel, including a spell helping to establish the frozen meat trade in New Zealand. Towed into Shakespeare Bay (just west of Picton) in 1967, for twenty years the *Edwin Fox* received only the attentions of the weather and vandals until, in 1986, surprisingly still sound below the waterline, the vessel was floated back to Picton Harbour where in 1999 she was finally dry-docked in a purpose–built berth which now has a cover to protect her and her visitors from inclement weather. Beside the Edwin Fox some entrepreneurial types have erected, in a hanger-like construction, the **Aquarium of the Marlborough Sounds** (daily 8.30am–5.30pm, though longer if busy; $10), whose information boards and simple tanks filled with local marine life, including flat fish, rays, sharks, mussels and locally farmed organic salmon, rather undermine the aquarium's grand title. For an extra $10 they'll let you catch a salmon from the tank – a bit like shooting a fish in a barrel – and they'll even gut it so you can take it home for supper. Definitely worth saving for rainy days.

Heading further around the bay, the foreshore area is home to the **Picton Community Museum**, on London Quay (daily 10am–4pm; $3). The main features of the museum are the displays devoted to the Perano Whaling Station, which operated in Queen Charlotte Sound until 1964. There are photographs of the station in its heyday, and a harpoon gun from one of the steamboat chasers as well as some excellent examples of scrimshaw (whale-bone carving). Smaller displays deal with Maori and *pakeha* local history, and there is a finely carved chair inlaid with *paua* (blue-green shell), as well as a large collection of brightly coloured shells from all over the world.

Continuing around the harbour and across the Coat Hanger footbridge, it is a short walk to the unique **Echo Gallery and Museum** (Dec–March daily 10am–5pm, otherwise weekends only; $3), a tribute to the scows and scowmen of New Zealand that's well worth an hour or two of your time. Built in 1905, the *Echo* was a top-sail schooner, with a square bilge scow-type hull, developed to take cargo from the sea upriver to the remote communities of New Zealand. From 1920 she ran river services out of Blenheim, and was the last ship to trade commercially under sail in New Zealand waters, before entering the fray in World War II. Retrieved from a ships' graveyard, she was used by the US Navy as a supply ship for the New Hebrides, Solomon Islands and New Guinea area – a phase in her long history that inspired the 1961 Hollywood film *The Wackiest Ship in the Army*, a copy of which is shown on the shipboard video from time to time. There are also restored home movies of New Zealand scows at work, paintings and photographs around the hull walls and exhibits and explanations of the important role these ships played in the country's development.

The **Shelly Beach/Bob's Bay Track** starts just by the Marlborough Cruising Club, next to the Echo, and extends for a kilometre along the shoreline, passing small, safe-swimming beaches and providing great views across the water to the ferry terminal and up the Queen Charlotte Sound before ending at Bob's Bay. From here the path heads away from the bay for about 500m to **Victoria Domain** for more superb views and meets the track on to **The Snout** (5km; 1hr 15min one way), whose evocative Maori name, *Te Ihumoeone-ihu*, translates as "the nose of the sand worm". At the tip of the promontory, you are rewarded with panoramic views of the Sounds and the ferries.

Just over three kilometres from Picton, at 210 Waikawa Road, is the **Te Awhina Kaha Marae** (☎03/573 7970), a superbly carved meeting house containing some excellent *tukutuku* (Maori panel work made of flax and wood); call ahead to see if there are any activities arranged – hangi are sometimes organized for groups, and you may be able to tag along but this can be expensive.

Eating and entertainment

Picton has one wonderful restaurant and two good cafés, a number of typical New Zealand **tearooms** offering cheap fare near the foreshore and **cafés** serving snacks and coffee, with little to choose between them. With the three notable exceptions already mentioned, the town is a bastion of barely adequate food and uninspired decor.

As for what passes for entertainment in the town, the free weekly *Marlborough Express* newspaper and the bi-monthly *Discovery* magazine contain **entertainment listings**, mostly centred on several large, slightly tacky **pubs** along the waterfront that serve drink and cheap food all day, and occasionally have live music by desperate bands trying to scrape together enough money to escape, north by ferry or south by train or bus.

Le Café 14–16 London Quay. A good quality, moderately priced European-influenced coffee house/bar that has moved to the foreshore where they have more room, a new terrace, internet access and better views. The menu includes the best coffee in town, mouth-watering steak sandwiches with home-made chutney, wild venison, salads with their own famous dressing and, of course, all sorts of seafood at reasonable prices. Occasional live music also peps up the atmosphere. Licensed, daily 8am–10pm or 11pm if busy.

Expresso House 58 Auckland St. Easy to miss is this well-kept Picton secret where the minimalist surroundings are relieved by rimu flooring, New Zealand oak tables and the odd Native American photograph on the walls. Great food includes chicken satay, Thai beef salads, salmon and brie melts, and delicious baked cheesecake; day-time menu under $15, night-time under $22. Daily except Weds 11am–late, closed June and July; Licensed & BYO.

Marlborough Terranean 31 High St ⓣ03/573 7122. Still the tastiest food in town and one of the best restaurants on the South Island, so book. Fine dining in comfortable surroundings with a relaxed jazz-soaked atmosphere, and imaginative dishes such as New Zealand rack of lamb on garlic potato mash with tarragon jus, tenderloin of Marlborough red deer, Schwarzwaelder Rohschinken cured, air-dried ham, fresh fish in a choice of three delicious sauces – and frighteningly good desserts. Evening meals only (main courses $20–30). Licensed.

Mickey's Bar 18 High St. In the winter this place has live entertainment of some sort every month and a DJ every other weekend. The bar is Tex/Mex-style, there's some alfresco seating and a barn-like nightclub out back. In the summer the gaps between events gets smaller and if you fancy a drink or a game of pool this and the *Toot'n Whistle* are about all that's worth a look. Daily 7pm–3am.

Toot'n Whistle Auckland St, next to the *Picton Lodge Backpackers.* Big locals' bar which hasn't altered in ten years despite a succession of new owners. The food is fried in big portions and cheap. Daily 9am–late.

Listings

Airlines Soundsair Shuttles (ⓣ0800/505 0005 & 03/573 6184) operates services to Wellington (see Listings on p.519 for details).

Airport transport Soundsair Buses (ⓣ0800/505 0005), Blenheim Taxis (ⓣ03/578 0225).

Banks Picton has branches of a couple of the major banks (BNZ and Westpack Trust), on High Street.

Bookshops Paper World, 28 High St (Mon–Sat 9am–5pm).

Buses You can book all the buses through the information centre (ⓣ03/5737477) or directly; InterCity (ⓣ09/357 8400) run to Nelson, Blenheim and Christchurch via Kaikoura; Deluxe Travel Line (ⓣ03/578 5467) go to Blenheim; Nightline Buses (ⓣ03/577 2024) serve Nelson and Blenheim. Sounds to Coast (ⓣ03/578 0225) go to St Arnaud on Mon, Wed and Fri. Atomic Shuttles (ⓣ0508/108 359) run to Christchurch. Kiwilink (ⓣ03/577 8332) run services via Blenheim to Nelson and Motueka. All fares are in the region of $10–$15 to Blenheim, $20–$30 to Nelson and $30–$40 to Christchurch.The Rural Mail Service will pick up and drop off people wishing to do the Queen Charlotte Walkway, or just wanting a cheap ride out to a different destination on their route; to book the Havelock or Kenepuri runs ask at the post office or call ⓣ03/574 2433 or ⓣ025/865 241 respectively.

Car rental Most of the major international and Kiwi companies have offices at the Ferry Terminal. Ace ⓣ0800/422373; Avis ⓣ03/573 6363; Avon ⓣ03/573 6009; Budget ⓣ03/573 6081; Hertz ⓣ03/573 7224; New Zealand Rent A Car

Ⓣ03/573 7282; Pegasus Ⓣ03/573 7733; Rent-a-Dent Ⓣ03/573 7787.
Diving Divers World, cnr London Quay & Auckland St (Ⓣ03/573 7323, Ⓦwww.atlantishostel.co.nz), offers gear rental, dive trips and SSI or PADI courses (all from $399). Wreck dives are especially popular and start at around $59.
Medical treatment Picton Medical Centre, 71 High St Ⓣ03/573 6092.
Internet access Picton Library, Mon–Thurs 8am–5pm, Fri 8am–5.30pm, Sat 10am–noon; *Le Café* (see opposite); Music World, 60–65 High St, daily 9am–8pm.
Pharmacy McGuires, 3 High St Mon–Sat 9am–5pm. The free *Marlborough Express* and the *Seaport News* contain lists of after-hours duty pharmacists and emergency services.
Post office The main post office is in the Mariners Mall on High Street Mon–Fri 9am–5pm, Sat 9am–12.30pm.
Taxis Blenheim Taxis Ⓣ03/578 0225; see also "Water taxis" below.
Tours De Luxe Wine Trail (Ⓣ03/578 5467 & 0800/500 511, Ⓦwww.deluxetravel.co.nz) runs a day-trip taking in a number of the better wineries for around $40; The Sounds Connection (Ⓣ03/573 7726 & 0800/742866, Ⓦwww.soundsconnection.co.nz) offers a number of tours and buses to the skifields and Queen Charlotte Walkway. The Rural Mail Service will pick up and drop off people wishing to do the Queen Charlotte Track, or just wanting a cheap ride out to a different destination on their route; to book the Havelock or Kenepuri runs ask at the post office or call Ⓣ03/574 2433, or 025/865 241 respectively.
Trains Tranz Scenic (Ⓣ0800/802 802) runs to Christchurch once a day, with fares starting at $31 one way.
Water sports Sunnyvale Motel, 384 Waikawa Rd (Ⓣ03/573 6800), rents out windsurfers ($25 an hour), kayaks ($50 per half day), laser yachts ($40 per half day), and a catamaran ($50 per half day).
Water taxis Arrow Water Taxis Ⓣ03/573 8229; Beachcomber Fun Cruises Ⓣ03/573 6175; Cougar Line Ⓣ03/573 7925; Endeavour Express Ⓣ03/579 8465; The Sounds Connection Ⓣ03/573 8843 and West Bay Water Transport Ⓣ03/573 5597.
Weaving The House of Glenora, at 22 Broadway (Ⓣ03/573 6966, Ⓕ573 7735) is a weaving school set in a beautiful old house; tuition costs $50–80 a day, and a workshop to learn a certain technique will take 5–7 days.

Exploring the Sounds

The Marlborough Sounds enclose moody, picturesque bays, small deserted sandy beaches, peninsulas of grandeur and great variation, headlands with panoramic views and cloistered islands, while offering shelter from the winds and storms in Cook Strait and solitude for the contemplative fisherman, kayaker or tramper. For a taster of the labyrinthine waterways around Picton, take one of the many **day-cruises** available, but to really appreciate their tranquil beauty, you're far better off **kayaking** round the bays, **tramping** the Queen Charlotte Walkway or getting a ride on one of the **Dolphin Watch Eco Tours**. The relatively calm waters of the Sounds also give the opportunity for **scuba diving**, either checking out the wrecks and rich marine life or just doing an open-water qualification (see Diver's World in "Listings", above).

Cruises and tours

Several companies run pretty similar **cruises** on the Sounds, or you can catch a water taxi to various points and explore on your own (see "Listings", above). Beachcomber Fun Cruises (see "Listings", above) offers a twice-daily short cruise around the bays on their red-coloured ships (2hr; $35), and a daily cruise with a lunch stop at Torea Bay (5hr; $38; lunch not included); however the best trips are the **mailboat runs** (*The Magic Mail Run* on Mon, Tues, Thurs & Fri at 1.30pm; and the *Pelorus Mail Boat*, from Picton via Portage on Tues, Thurs & Fri, 10.15am, or 9.30am from Havelock; 4hr; $58), which alternate between two routes, either calling at bays in the Queen Charlotte Sound, the Regal Salmon Farm and the Perano Whaling Station, or heading into Endeavour Inlet, Resolution Bay and Ship Cove. Another mailboat runs through Pelorus

Sound from Havelock (see p.539); on all the mail trips, tea and coffee are provided, but you must bring your own lunch. Beachcomber is also the only company that can pick you up off the Queen Charlotte Track in Anakiwa. Cougar Line (Ⓣ03/573 7925 & 0800/504 090, Ⓔcougar@voyager.co.nz) offers a similar, but slightly friendlier, variety of one-day **walking trips** with drop-off and pre-arranged pick up in the bays of the Queen Charlotte Sound ($43), as well as good scenic **cruises** (8am, 10am & 1.30pm; 3hr; $43),which all go to Ship Cove. Endeavour Express (Ⓣ03/579 8465) offer a similarly priced, timetabled, service for dropping off at Ships Cove and also pick-ups from the track linking with the *Lynx*, cross-Cook Strait ferry, and they'll also transfer your pack to your next accommodation while you walk the track ($10).

Excellent in their own right and a good compromise between the standard cruises and the close-up approach of kayaking (see below) are the **eco-tours** offered by Dolphin Watch (Ⓣ03/573 8040). From their office next to the visitor centre in Picton, they drive you to Waikawa Bay, about 4km northeast, where you board their small boat at either 8.30am or 1.30pm (connecting with the Cook Strait ferry). The trips focus on Queen Charlotte Sound (half day eco tour; $65 return, $50 one way to Ship Cove, and $80 for a fantastic bird-watching trip), offering the chance of seeing enormous numbers of sea birds, including penguins, before landing at the stunning **Motuara Island**. The island has a superb lookout over Cook Strait – and is home to the South Island bush robin, bellbird, blue penguin and the rare saddleback. All the birds are quite fearless, since they live in a relatively predator-free environment, and will rest and fly startlingly close to you. The tour continues to Ship Cove, where you'll get a rundown on Cook's history and from where you can either return to Picton or stay and tackle the Queen Charlotte Walkway (see opposite).

Kayaking

The exciting and beautiful kayaking to be had in the Sounds is often overlooked as visitors dash across to Abel Tasman National Park. Those who do stay to kayak in the Sounds, however, are rewarded by uncrowded waters and breathtaking views, and of the many **companies** offering kayaking, there are two, Marlborough Sounds Adventure Company and Sea Kayaking Adventure Tours Anakiwa, which stand a paddle's length above the rest. Marlborough Sounds Adventures (Ⓣ03/573 6078, Ⓔmsac@msadventure.co.nz) is the biggest, best organized and most professional, indicated by their membership of the SKOANZ (Sea Kayaking Operators Association of New Zealand). Also being on the front at Picton they are the easiest to find. Their **guided kayak trips** range from one to four days (day-trip $90, including meals; 4 days, 2 days' kayaking and 2 days' walking, plus accommodation $965). Another popular jaunt is their twilight paddle against a background of the sparkling lights of Picton ($50). Marlborough Sounds Adventure Company also offer guided and self-guided track walks and what they call the three-day ultimate adventure, a mixture of walking, kayaking and mountain biking for $410 ($525 with twin or shared accommodation). Smaller, but in many respects just as good, is Sea Kayaking Adventure Tours Anakiwa, at the end of the Queen Charlotte Track, Anakiwa, opposite the track information shelter and 30m up the hill (Ⓣ & Ⓕ03/574 2765, Ⓦwww.marlborough.co.nz/sea-kayak). They have one-day guided tours ($70) as well as walk and paddle options which involve walking the Queen Charlotte, or part of it, and then sea-kayaking back or vice versa. There are also some two- and three-day jaunts ($180–280). Both companies have **rental kayaks** (around $45 per day) for independent paddlers and Sea Kayaking Adventure Tours rent out mountain bikes ($35 per day).

The Queen Charlotte Walkway

The **Queen Charlotte Walkway** (67km; 3 or 4 days; Ⓦwww.qctrack.co.nz) is a spectacular, though often sadly ignored, walk through the Marlborough Sounds from Ship Cove to Anakiwa, the most popular way of doing the track. The Walkway boasts wonderful views of the Queen Charlotte and Kenepuru sounds, passes through dense coastal forest and golden sandy bays, and sometimes lords over it all on skyline ridges. A classified, DOC-administered track, it's broad and relatively easy going – it doubles as a **mountain-biking** track between March and November (allow 2 days), while Punga Cove to Anakiwa is open to bikes all year round. A leaflet outlining the walk and biking dos and don'ts is available from the visitor centre ($1). There is also a DOC Information Shelter at Anakiwa with a card phone if you haven't booked either transport of accommodation.

Queen Charlotte Sound was an important trade route and provided good shelter and bountiful food for **Maori**, who carried canoes over the low saddles of the walkway to avoid long, unnecessary and hazardous sea journeys around the full length of the Sounds. **Captain Cook** stopped at Ship Cove on five occasions and made it his New Zealand base, spending over 100 days there between 1770 and 1777. The shelter and fresh water made it an ideal spot and its plentiful supplies of (what became known as) Cook's scurvy grass were particularly valued for the vitamin C content.

The changing seasons are reflected by splashes of colour: karaka groves are laden with bright yellow berries in the summer; native clematis (puawanga) is festooned with creamy-white **flowers** in the spring; and supplejacks and kohia (Kiwi passion fruit) produce red and orange fruits in the autumn. As a result, there is no shortage of **birds**, with tui and bellbirds in profusion, as well as the ever-friendly fantails and little piebald robins. The forests also contain the owls known as moreporks (so named for their cry, which sounds like a request for "more pork"), while the beaches and crag faces boast an abundance of shags, gannets, terns and shearwaters, as well as the stooping oystercatchers patrolling in pairs. If you're lucky, you may spot a little blue penguin making its way to the fishing grounds in the morning or on its way home in the evening, and on rare occasions you can see the odd kiwi, endangered and embattled but still clinging obdurately to survival.

Access

Most people walk from Ship Cove to Anakiwa: **water taxis** (see also "Listings", p.535) link with Ship Cove and almost anywhere in between it and the tiny Torea Bay, close to Anakiwa, so you can pick and mix sections fairly easily.

Beachcomber Fun Cruises (Ⓣ03/573 6175) will run you anywhere in the Queen Charlotte Sound or Tory Channel and operate a Picton–Torea Bay **ferry** ($16) or Picton–Anakiwa ($19, they are the only company to offer this service); they also cater for day walkers with several drop-off and pick-up itineraries. Cougar Line (Ⓣ03/573 7925 & 0800/504 090) will drop you at Ship Cove and then deliver your pack to each night's accommodation ($48), and also offer day-walk options. Endeavour Express, based in Endeavour Inlet (Ⓣ03/579 8465), have daily departures for Ship Cove (9.30am; $40, pack transfers free; round trip $45), and return trips to Bay of Many Coves and Torea Bay for **day-trippers** ($15–25 each way). One of the quickest water taxi services is West Bay Water Transport offering Torea Bay, Double Cove, Lochmara Bay, Onahau Bay, Waterfall and Mistletoe Bays all for $15 one way, and Tirimoana, The Grove and Momorangi for $20 one way. In addition, **shuttle bus** services between Picton and Anakiwa are offered by Sounds Connection (ⓣ03/573 8843) and, despite what they tell you at the Picton Visitor Centre (ⓣ03/574 2765), there is still a **Rural Mail Bus Run**. They prefer the shuttle to be booked through the visitor centre but you can book direct if it's closed, and the mail run by contacting the postman on duty; just ask at the post office (picking up at 10am; ⓣ03/574 2433 for the Havelock Mail Servce or ⓣ025/865 241 for the Kenepuri run; $8 and $15 respectively). Both charge around $10–$15 per person, although Sounds Connection impose a minimum of four or a charge of $45. If organising your tramping plans with the Picton Visitor Centre you'll be pressured into being picked up by water taxi or bus because it means you return to Picton. To avoid coming back to the town, try the road pick-up from **Anakiwa** that takes you to Havelock. Booked through the YHA in Havelock (see p.540) or Cougar (see p.535), it includes a boat ride to Ship Cove, bus pick-up (from Anakiwa to Havelock) and a night in the YHA there, all for $75.

Marlborough Sounds Adventure Company (ⓣ03/573 6078, ⓕ573 8827) offers a four-day **guided walk** along the Queen Charlotte Walkway ($845, fully inclusive); a cheaper option is to **self-guide** but have all your accommodation and transport needs taken care of ($410). Sea Kayaking Adventure Tours, Anakiwa (ⓣ03/574 2765), can arrange various trips that combine **biking** and walking the track.

Accommodation

Compared with some of the remoter tracks, the Queen Charlotte Walkway has plenty of **places to stay**. The DOC administer seven **campsites** (all $4), which have water and toilets. There are also several privately owned places to stay on or near the track, for which bookings are essential. Most have a range of accommodation, from camping space and **backpacker bunks** to self-contained **resort units** and luxurious rooms; those offering the better deals are listed below.

Anakiwa Backpackers Diagonally opposite the DOC Information Shelter at Anakiwa ⓣ03/574 1388. A clean and simple hostel under new ownership with dorms and two doubles. Dorms ❶, doubles ❷

Blist'd Foot Café, Tiramoana House B&B Excellent, luxury B&B, ideal for relaxing after the track, just ten minutes' walk from the trail end. It's well-run, has stunning views over to Picton and offers a two course dinner for an extra $30. The attached café has wonderful scones and refreshing ice cream. ❺

The Chill Inn 770 Queen Charlotte Dr, Mahakipawa Arm ⓣ03/574 1299. Comfortable backpackers, about halfway between Anakiwa and Havelock, and a good spot to rest up after the track. Dorms ❶, rooms ❸

Furneaux Lodge Endeavour Inlet ⓣ03/579 9411. A swanky lodge with a bar and restaurant and some shared accommodation. Dorms ❶, chalets ❻

Noeline's Homestay Nr Punga Cove ⓣ03/ 579 8375. There's a friendly welcome to this comfortable accommodation in a relaxing atmosphere at the best place to stay in the cove – you may not want to leave. Linen available. ❶

Portage Hotel Kenepuri Sound, ten minutes' walk along the road from Torea Bay ⓣ03/573 4309. A much improved resort hotel with a friendly lounge bar and restaurant. Dorms ❶, rooms ❻–❽

Resolution Bay Cabins Resolution Bay ⓣ03/579 9411. The closest accommodation to Ship Cove (4.5km), in a pretty and atmospheric spot offering swimming, canoes and comfortable rooms in a 1920s-style resort. Dorms ❶ cabins ❸, cottages ❺

Smiths Farm and Holiday Park 4km from the end of the track ⓣ03/574 2806. Not too far to walk and they have camp sites for $9 as well as cabins ❷ and en-suite rooms ❸

Te Mahia Resort Te Mahia Bay, Kenepuri Sound ⓣ03/573 4089. Close to the walkway with a store – and glow-worms – nearby. Dorms ❶, self-contained units ❺

The route

The track passes through some grassy farmland and bleak gorse-covered hills, but both ends of the track are forest reserves with lush greenery, including nikau palms and climbing keikie, right down to the shoreline. There are a number of **detours** off the main track to places of interest, including a short walk from Ship Cove to a pretty forest-shrouded waterfall, a scramble down to the Bay of Many Coves, or a foray to the Antimony Mines (where there are exposed shafts – stick to the marked tracks). The most spectacular **views** are to be had en route to the mines and at Torea Saddle and Kenepuru Saddle.

Beginning at **Ship Cove**, the track climbs steeply away from the shore through largely untouched forest to a lookout with great views of Motuara Island, before dropping down into **Resolution Bay** (4.5km; 2hr), where there's a DOC campsite and other accommodation, or you can press on along an old bridle path over the ridge into **Endeavour Inlet** (15km; 5hr). From here, you have an easy second day, rounding the inlet, climbing to the **Kenepuru Saddle** and returning to the shoreline; there's a campsite in **Camp Bay** (11.5km; 4hr), but you may decide to push on for another four hours to **Bay of Many Coves**, where there is another campsite and cabin accommodation. Otherwise, day three, the longest and most rewarding stretch, takes you from Camp Bay along the ridge that separates the Kenepuru Sound from the Queen Charlotte Sound to **Torea Saddle** (20.5km; 9hr), where you can follow the road to Cowshed Bay for the DOC campsite or stay at the plush *Portage Resort Hotel*. On day four, you can choose a short ridge walk through beech and manuka forest to **Mistletoe Bay** (7.5km; 4hr) or a long slog high above the water, before descending to the DOC campsite at **Davies Bay** and continuing to the road at **Anakiwa** (20km; 9hr).

Havelock and around

The 35km, back-road trip between Picton and **HAVELOCK** is both picturesque and spectacular, sliding past the flat plain at the inland origin of Queen Charlotte Sound and climbing up the hills overlooking Pelorus Sound before descending to SH6 and the settlement itself. Nestled in the heart of the Sound, Havelock forms a thin ribbon along the main road linked to a newly expanded marina that has transformed itself from rough, working jetties to a gleaming haven for, mostly, pleasure boats – though it still pales in comparison with the stunning Pelorus Sound, an exciting maze of sunken seaways with high mountain peaks that can be explored by boat or on foot. About halfway between Picton and Havelock there is a narrow road to the right that heads up towards Portage and much of the accommodation on the Queen Charlotte Track, for those too lazy to walk the walk.

A hundred years ago Havelock was a boom town, revelling in the wealth created by an inland gold rush and rampant logging, before reverting to a sleepy fishing village with a run-down straggle of buildings spread out along the highway and running off down by the wharf. Today it has revived as a result of the travellers who explore the Sound, discovering the fun to be had in these quiet environs. Havelock is the green-lipped mussel capital of the world, and you simply can't leave before you've purchased some choice morsels from the wharf or better still taken some on board at the excellent, award-winning **Mussel Boys Restaurant**. Until his death in 1996, Havelock's other claim to fame was as the home of itinerant author **Barry Crump**. Crumpy, as he was affectionately known, began life as a hunter and bushman, culling deer and pigs in some of New Zealand's roughest country – a way of life he described in a series of humorous, poignant and superbly descriptive novels. The **Havelock Museum** on Main Road, near the Shell Garage (daily 9am–5pm; if locked, ask Mr Skinner, 9 Cook St, at the corner with Peel Street, or call Mrs Jacobson ⓣ03/574 2176; donation), is housed in small cream wooden buildings and is probably only worth the trouble if it's already open. Among the usual collection of bric-a-brac is a wood-milling display and the honour rolls from Havelock School, which feature Ernest Rutherford who went to school here, in the building now occupied by the YHA, from 1886 to 1894, before going on to be the first person to split the atom.

If you are feeling energetic then trudge up the hills behind the town hall along the bush walk (2hrs up, 90min down). The track is well-defined and easy going from the Havelock main road to the waterfall. See "Around Havelock", opposite, for more detail on this.

Practicalities

Buses between Picton and Nelson all stop at Havelock, while local bus and **water-taxi** operators offer services to Kenepuru and Pelorus sounds. Of the two rival **information** outlets here, the Havelock Outdoor Centre, 65a Main Rd (ⓣ03/574 2114 or 574 2144 after hours; daily: May–Oct 9.30am–5pm; Nov–April 8am–6pm), is the best with access to all DOC information, facilities for kayak and boat trip booking and internet access ($2 for 10min). Second choice is Pelorus Enterprises, 60 Main Rd (Dec–March Mon–Fri 8.30am–5pm, Sat & Sun 9am–4pm; April–Nov Mon–Fri 8.30am–5pm, Sat 9am–4pm; ⓣ03/574 2633), where they also book trips and have pretty good local knowledge.

Accommodation options include *Havelock Garden Motel* at 71 Main Rd (ⓣ03/574 2387; ❸–❹), with six fully self-contained units and helpful hosts. On the corner of Main Road and Lawrence Street, *Pelorus Motor Inn* (ⓣ03/574 2961; ❹) has a few simple units without cooking facilities, though you can get a cheap meal in the adjacent *Havelock Hotel* where there are bog-standard colonial hotel rooms (dbl ❷). Centrally located in the characterful old schoolhouse is the much improved *Rutherford YHA Hostel*, 46 Main Rd (ⓣ03/574 2104; tent sites $7, dorms ❶, rooms ❷). Surrounded by large, ancient trees this friendly hostel has bright rooms and the staff are a mine of information on the best trips and things to see. Off the beaten track at **Canvastown**, 10km west of Havelock, and 8km off the main road, is the *Pinedale Motor Camp* (ⓣ03/574 2349; tent sites $8, cabins & units ❷–❹), a delightful spot to relax for a few days, with bushwalks, glow-worms, gold-panning and 1km of river frontage with swimming holes.

Food in Havelock has changed dramatically in recent times, and where once it was difficult to get hold of the glorious green-lipped mussels native to the area, now it couldn't be easier. Without doubt the best place to eat in town is the *Mussel Boys Restaurant*, 73 Main Rd (daily: Nov–March 10am–9pm; April–Oct 11am–6pm; licensed), where they dish up mussels in myriad different sources, excellent chowder and a farmer's platter for those who don't like shellfish. Around the restaurant are details about mussels and a step-by-step guide on the best way to eat them. Other recommendations in town are the simple cuisine in massive portions at the *Havelock Hotel* (see Accommodation), where for under $20 Shirley makes sure you stock up on carbohydrates before attempting any of the local walks. If you're after a simple snack the *Gold'n'Café*, 10m up the road from *Mussel Boys*, does some inspired mussel pies, pizza and other choice morsels, at reasonable prices, throughout the day. Finally for those hankering after an even slower pace there's the *Clansman Bar and Café* at 72 Main Rd where you can have a beer and a variety of Caledonian-inspired meals at a reasonable price. The *Clansman* also operates as an occasional live venue and is the slightly more welcoming of the two main drinking dens, the other being the *Havelock Hotel*, a real locals' haunt.

Exploring Pelorus Sound

One of the best ways to see the Sound is aboard the *Pelorus Mail Boat*, run by Beachcomber Fun Cruises (ⓣ03/572 2114; Tues, Thurs & Fri 9.30am; 7hr; $90), which sets off from Havelock Marina on its leisurely **mail run**, calling at isolated homesteads, a mussel farm and passing countless unspoilt beaches. The same company operates the **French Pass** cruise (8hr; around $69, with a minimum of twenty) along Pelorus Sound past Maud Island, and around to French Pass, at the entrance to the seething channel where the ship of nineteenth-century French explorer D'Urville was spun by tumultuous whirlpools. On both these trips, you need to bring your own lunch and a couple of jumpers out of season. If you're after an alternative then the *MV Mavis* (contact them through Havelock Outdoor Centre) does a scenic cruise to the mussel farms (half-day $49), and the *MV Foxlady* (book at Havelock Outdoor Centre) runs up Kenepuri Sound for about $55 a pasenger.

The best way to get into the nooks and crannies of Pelorus Sound is by **kayak** with the unspoilt, sheltered environment offering wonderful potential for uncrowded exploration. There have long been two competing kayak companies in the town, with little to choose between them. Marlborough Sounds Wilderness Company has excellent guided trips (ⓣ03/574 2610, ⓔsoundswild@xtraco.nz; full day $75, overnight $95, from two to five days $150 per day) and operates from a shed beside the YHA hostel. They also offer freedom rentals for $45 a day. The alternative is Havelock Sea Kayaking Company, bookable through the Havelock Outdoor Centre, who have an almost identical array of trips, rentals, prices and advertising brochures.

Around Havelock

About 1km along SH6, heading east out of Havelock, the road climbs up to the Cullen Point Lookout with great views of the Sounds on clear days. In Havelock itself there's a two-hour **walk** heading up the hill opposite the *Havelock Hotel* and beyond the fire station to the Takorika Ridge Track. Most people only climb the easy bit to the waterfall (about 35min) from where the views over the settlement and into the Sounds are pretty good. If you do go on from here, be warned – the track's a 45-minute, steep slog up to the ridge (1100m), though the panorama from the top rewards your efforts.

Eighteen kilometres west of Havelock on SH6 is the **Pelorus Bridge Scenic Reserve**, which contains superb examples of black beech trees and golden green rimu, as well as kahikatea, miro and the blue-green foliage of matai trees. There's also an abundance of tui, grey warblers and bellbirds as well as many swimming holes along the trout- and salmon-rich, sandy-beached rivers. This fertile area saw a succession of Maori settlements, which prospered until Te Rauparaha conquered the north of the South Island in the 1820s. The misery caused by the war and the encroachment of European settlers drove most of the Maori away – the few that remained produced flax that Te Rauparaha could trade for rifles.

Facilities include a basic DOC **camping** area (ⓣ03/571 6019; tent sites $7, cabins $24) and several walking tracks. The **café** (daily: Nov–March 8.30am–7pm; April–Oct 8.30am–4.30pm) at Pelorus Bridge incorporates a

DOC office and a small **shop**, as well as purveying delicious home-made muffins, pastries, quiches and a selection of light meals.

Most of the **walks** in the reserve are fairly flat, well maintained and well marked: the **Totara** (1.5km return; 30min) and **Circle** (1km return; 30min) routes pass through the low-lying woodland for which the area is famous, while the **Trig K** (2.5km one way; 2hr), after a steady climb to 417m, offers stunning views of the whole area. From the summit you can head straight down or follow the **Beech Ridge Track** (3km; 90min), via two waterfalls, which takes the scenic route back to the start of the Trig K track. Some sources of information mention a track known as the Takarika but ignore them, this track is poorly-marked and you're liable to get lost.

Another rewarding tramp near Havelock is the **Nydia Track** (20km; 2 days), which starts at **Kaiuma Bay**, passes Nydia Bay and finishes at **Duncan Bay**. Following a series of bridle paths, the route makes its way through pasture, shrubland and virgin forest, with great views from the Kaiuma Saddle (387m) and Nydia Saddle (347m), as well as along the head of the bay. Maori called Nydia Bay *Opouri*, which means "place of sadness", because when a *hapu* (one faction of a tribe) was preparing to migrate from the North Island to the Sounds, their leader sacrificed a young boy to Tangora the sea god to ensure a safe journey. When the boy's father found out, he sought *utu* (revenge), storming across to Pelorus Sound and slaughtering the disgraced *hapu*.

Kaiuma Bay is 32km from Havelock by road: turn off SH6 12km west of Havelock onto Daltons Road – a car park at the end marks the beginning of the track. There's a daily (Nov–May) bus from the Outdoor Adventure Centre to the Nydia Track (involving a boat trip) with pre-arranged pick-up at Duncan Bay ($35). The walk on day one from **Kaiuma** Bay to the Nydia Lodge turn-off is 5–6hr, while on day two it's about four hours to the pick up point. **Accommodation** is available at the *Nydia Lodge*, roughly halfway along the track (❶; get the key at the Outdoor Adventure Centre or from the caretaker's house signposted from the lodge), or at *Driftwood Lodge* (Ⓣ03/579 8454; ❶) just beyond *Nydia Lodge* and very cosy.

Nelson and around

In a broad basin between the Arthur and Richmond ranges lies the thriving city of **NELSON**, providing easy access to three national parks and Golden Bay. Add to this the universal appeal of sandy beaches and abundant sunshine, and it will come as no surprise that the Nelson region is one of the most popular destinations in New Zealand, with a mass of great activities and opportunities to indulge in the bounty of the land. The small satellite town of **Richmond**, 14km to the west, holds some of the area's most salubrious guesthouses and serves as a suburban retreat for commuters. Located at the junction of SH6 and SH60, it's also the start of two separate routes: south via the market gardens of Hope, Brightwater, Spring Grove, Wakefield and Belgrove towards Murchison; or northwest via Motueka to the Abel Tasman National Park.

Nelson has the air of a bustling go-ahead city, something which can detract from its **historical pedigree** as one of the oldest settlements in New Zealand – a place where many early European immigrants got their first taste of the South Island. By the middle of the sixteenth century, the Ngati Tumatakokiri occupied most of the Nelson area, providing a reception committee for **Abel**

Tasman's long boats at Murderer's Bay, where they killed four of his sailors. By the time Europeans arrived in earnest, Maori numbers had been decimated by internecine fighting and the nearest *pa* site to Nelson was at Motueka, although this did little to prevent land squabbles, culminating in the **Wairau Affray** in 1843. Despite assurances from Maori chiefs Te Rauparaha and Te Rangihaeata that they would abide by the decision of a land commissioner, the New Zealand Company went ahead regardless, sending surveyors south to the Wairau Plains. A skirmish ensued, during which Te Rangihaeata's wife was shot. The bereaved chief and his men slaughtered twenty-two people in retaliation. The settlers continued their land acquisition undeterred but due to illness and hardship the community was dying on its feet when the arrival of industrious German immigrants saved it from complete dissolution.

Today, basking in one of the sunniest and most scenic areas in the country, Nelson has found a new lease of life as a holiday centre, with its busy **fishing port** and a rich fruit- and vegetable-growing **hinterland** scattered with breweries and wineries. It is also a haven for **artists**, who are drawn by the sunlight, the landscape and the unique raw materials for pottery and ceramic art that lie beneath the rich green grass.

Arrival, information and transport

Flights arrive at Nelson **airport**, 8km west of the centre, and are met by a daily **shuttle** service provided by Super Shuttle Nelson (Ⓣ03/547 5782; $10) or **City Taxis** (Ⓣ03/528 8225; around $15). All **buses** drop you near the centre of the city, within easy walking distance of most accommodation. InterCity pulls in at 27 Bridge St, while the other companies all stop outside the **visitor centre**, on the corner of Trafalgar Street and Halifax Street (daily 8.30am–5pm; Ⓣ03/548 2304, Ⓦwww.nelsonNZ.com). This large and welcoming centre has heaps of leaflets on Nelson and the surrounding region, including guides to the national parks, local studios and workshops; the centre also functions as a booking office for trips, accommodation and onward travel. Inside the visitor centre is the main **DOC office** (same hours) and an additional, less useful DOC Office is located at 186 Bridge St (Ⓣ03/546 9335; Mon–Fri 8am–4pm), in the Munro Building next to the Courthouse.

SBL **buses** (Ⓣ03/548 0285; Mon–Fri 8am–6pm, Sat 8am–12.30pm) run between Nelson and its satellite communities from the terminal on Lower Bridge Street, while numerous smaller **shuttle buses** run further afield to Golden Bay, the Abel Tasman, Kahurangi and Nelson Lakes national parks. Otherwise, you can get around most of the sights in the immediate vicinity with the help of a **rental car** or **bike**, while plenty of **tours** take in the highlights of the city and its surroundings (see "Listings", p.552, for details of all these).

Accommodation

The best places to stay, with a few notable exceptions in the shape of some **outlying B&Bs**, are in Nelson itself, where you have a choice of relaxing **beachside** locations or the bustling **centre** within reach of cultural diversions and nightlife. **Camping**, on the other hand, is not such a good option here, and you'll do better to settle for one of the exceptional **hostels** in the city and save camping for the prettier areas around Motueka, the Abel Tasman National Park or Golden Bay.

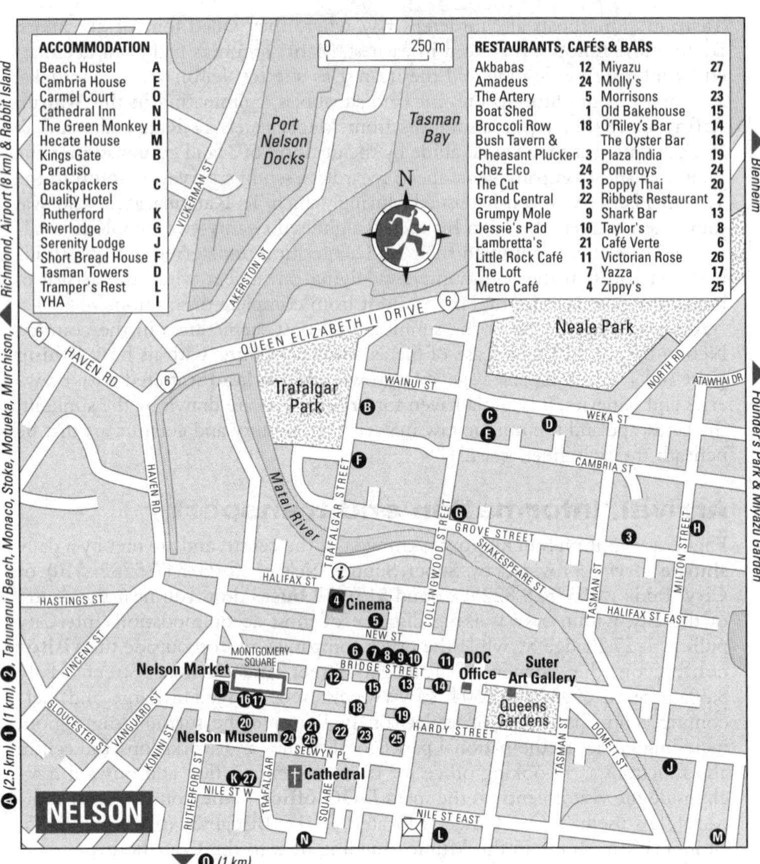

Nelson

Hotels and B&Bs

Cambria House 7 Cambria St ⓣ03/548 4681, ⓕ546 6649. This 140-year-old weatherboard house boasts a lovely back deck and garden, beautiful fireplaces, and a wide choice of breakfasts – all just ten minutes' walk from town on a quiet road. ⑦–⑧

Carmel Court 50 Waimea Rd ⓣ03/548 2234. This motel offers twelve fully self-contained units in a well-kept modern building with off-street parking, but it's a a fifteen- to twenty-minute walk from the main drag. ⑤

Cathedral Inn 369 Trafalgar St South ⓣ03/548 7369, ⓦwww.cathedralinn.co.nz. A superior historic mansion just up the hill behind the cathedral in one of the most peaceful parts of town, and offering elegantly styled, charming rooms and hearty breakfasts. Book ahead. ⑧

Kings Gate 21 Trafalgar Street ⓣ03/546 9108, ⓕ546 6838. Central motel with comfortable well-kept rooms including full kitchens. ⑤

Quality Hotel Rutherford Nile St, near Trafalgar Square ⓣ03/548 2299, ⓔescape@rutherfordhotel.co.nz. An international-style hotel with a number of impressive facilities, including a café, bar and excellent Japanese Restaurant, as well as large, well appointed rooms, some with impressive views. It doesn't hurt to try negotiating during the slacker months of March and April. ⑥

Riverlodge 31 Collingwood St ⓣ & ⓕ03/548 3094. One of the better motels, giving value for money in clean and comfortable rooms. ⑤

Serenity Lodge 380 Hardy St ⓣ03/545 9051, ⓦwww.serenitylodge.co.nz. Luxurious wooden house with suites full of everything you'll ever need and more besides, surrounded by well-kept colourful gardens and ministered by friendly hosts. ❽

Hostels

Beach Hostel 25 Muritai St ⓣ03/548 6817, ⓔnelsonbeachhostel@xtra.co.nz. An intimate hostel by the beach, with free bikes, a lounge with deck and good views, free pick-up from the city and a twice-daily shuttle service, and internet access. Dorms ❶, rooms ❷

The Green Monkey 129 Milton St ⓣ03/545 7421, ⓔthegreenmonkey@xtra.co.nz. An English-owned, converted villa, this boutique hostel is very quiet, well-kept and has a relaxed atmosphere. It has all the usual amenities and is about 1km from the town centre. Book well in advance. Dorms ❶, doubles ❷

Hecate House 181 Nile St East ⓣ03/546 6890, ⓔhecatehouse@xtra.co.nz. A relaxing, tucked–away Californian-style bungalow for women only. The decor is restful and the garden an organic delight. The name, appropriately enough, is that of a Greek god who watched over travellers. Twins or 3-bed dorms ❶, doubles ❸

Paradiso Backpackers 42 Weka St ⓣ03/546 6703, ⓕ546 7533. Based in a large converted 97-year-old house and some purpose-built outbuildings this hostel tends to be claustrophobic in the summer, less so during the rest of the season. Dorms ❶, rooms ❸

Short Bread Cottage 33 Trafalgar St ⓣ03/5466681. Charming, new boutique hostel with just 12 beds, so book ahead. 500m walk from central Nelson. Free pick up and drop off, free bedding, free tea and coffee. Dorms ❶, doubles ❷

Tasman Towers 8–10 Weka St ⓣ03/548 7950, ⓕ548 7897. A purpose-built hostel ten minutes' walk from town that is now under new and very keen management. They have embarked on improving the public areas and creating a warm, friendly atmosphere. Good-sized dining and kitchen areas, a large lounge, and clean spacious rooms make this a sound choice. Dorms ❶, rooms ❷–❸

Trampers Rest 31 Alton St ⓣ03/5457477. A cosy backpackers and wheelpackers haven, with home-style accommodation in comparatively small rooms in a pleasing, no-smoking villa, shared with a real tramping enthusiast. There's a tiny garden with hammock, bike storage and the host is an absolute mine of information. Dorms ❶, doubles ❷

YHA 59 Rutherford St ⓣ03/545 9988, ⓔyhanels@yha.org.nz. This purpose-built hostel in a central location remains the best in town, with a wide range of accommodation, including connecting rooms for families and two disabled-accessible units. One big and one smaller kitchen take the strain and a bike store adds to its appeal, as does internet access, very helpful staff and discounted rates in winter. Dorms ❶, rooms ❷–❸

Richmond and Monaco

Althorpe 13 Dorset St, Richmond ⓣ & ⓕ03/544 8117, ⓔrworley@voyager.co.nz. A pretty B&B in the tranquil neighbourhood of Richmond, with just two neat bedrooms in an 1880s homestead. ❻

The Honest Lawyer 1 Point Road, Monaco ⓣ03/547 8850 & 0800/921 192, ⓦwww.honest-lawyer.co.nz. A surprisingly accurate reconstruction of an English pub in all elements except that it has some luxuriously comfortable en-suite rooms for guests who can't drag themselves away. ❼

Kershaw House 10 Wensley Rd, Richmond ⓣ03/544 0957, ⓕ544 0950. A large, welcoming B&B in a 1929 house in Richmond, which has been authentically restored – a highlight is the gorgeous dark-stained rimu staircase. All rooms are smartly decorated and have private facilities and the owners are German speakers. ❼–❽

Mapledurham 8 Edward St, Richmond ⓣ & ⓕ03/544 4210. The best place to stay out of town, a beautiful rimu villa encircled by a wide, grey-floored veranda and well tended garden. The house is light and airy, dressing gowns are provided, and the breakfasts are superb; dinners are available by arrangement ($45, including wine). ❽

The City and around

The grid pattern streets of Nelson are dominated by the glowering, greystone edifice of the cathedral, perched on a hill with fine views across the harbour and city below. The liveliest **thoroughfares** are Trafalgar Street and Bridge Street, while the **seafront** to the north is strewn with palm trees and parks

Festival mania

The **Wearable Arts Festival** has become an international event, staged every year on September 19–22. This unique, internationally-acclaimed fashion show combines elements of sculpture, performance art, theatre, choreography and dance to create an extraordinary spectacle. The bizarre circus lasts for three nights (tickets around $40–50) and is performed on a sparkling 100m catwalk, with the best of the costumes going on display at the new museum dedicated to the event and its glorious past. Many of the designs use household junk, food, metal, stone, wood – and a surfeit of imagination. An arts festival has also sprung up around the show, spanning three weeks and including jazz sessions, alternative performances and exhibitions.

The **Taste Nelson Festival**, an annual day-long event held at the end of January or early February, espouses much more conservative ambitions. Essentially a celebration of the quality food, beers and wines that are produced in this area, as well as an excuse for local entertainers and bands to strut their funky stuff, the festival attracts over 10,000 gourmands. The **Nelson Jazz Festival**, held from around January 27, also livens up the town around this time of year. The **Sealord Summer Festival**, December 22–February 16, is six weeks of free entertainment, including street performers, weekend concerts and night time outdoor movies. If you're still not all festivalled out then **Hooked on Seafood**, March 23, Vickerham St, Port Nelson, is a demonstration of seafood expertise by chefs working at stalls and dishing up food for passers-by. Food for the brain can be sampled at the **Nelson Arts Festival**, September 13-28, two weeks of arts and entertainment, including a mask festival, sculpture symposium, cabaret, street theatre and writers' readings. Finally, if you want to get down, dirty and funky there's **The Gathering** outdoor party in Golden Bay, December 31–January 3, NZ's largest dance event, with the best electronica and much much more. Tickets cost $130-160.

where you can hear the thrum of cicadas in summer. For respite from the city, there are the long, golden-sand **beaches** and inland a green oasis of shady paths in the central public **gardens**. To get further away from it on a short day-trip, head for **Rabbit Island**, which is accessible at low tide.

Fortunately, the interior of the Anglican **Christ Church Cathedral** is nowhere near as grim as its exterior. Dazzling stained-glass windows illuminate the building, with ten particularly noteworthy examples tucked away in a small chapel to the right of the main altar. The cathedral has had a chequered history, which may account for its ugliness. English architect Frank Peck's original 1924 design was gradually modified over many years due to lack of money; World War II further intervened, and even now the cathedral tower looks as if it's still under construction.

The modern city architecture and well-disguised older buildings of Nelson are enlivened by the temporary presence of the now-famous **Nelson Market** (Sat 7am–1pm), which takes over the Montgomery Square Car Park between Rutherford Street and Trafalgar Street at the back of the YHA, two minutes' walk from the cathedral. Multicoloured stalls are laden with clothes, jewellery, toys, locally made wood carvings, art and crafts. The best of the bunch are the food stalls with mounds of fruit, endless varieties of fresh bread and fish, Thai and vegetarian dishes, preserves, burgers and hot dogs, and coffee and cakes to sustain you while you browse.

The Suter Te Aratoi o Whakatu, a small public art museum, just off Trafalgar Street at 208 Bridge St (daily 10.30am–4.30pm; $2), was built in 1899 as a memorial to Andrew Burn Suter, Bishop of Nelson from 1866 to 1891. One of the finest in the South Island, this small gallery hosts visiting exhibitions and shows relating to the local area, as well as changing displays from the gallery's own and Suter's collections. **Watercolours** predominate – especially those of John Gully, a friend of the bishop whose works here largely depict scenes from the surrounding area – but there are also a number of oil paintings and over a hundred works by **Sir M. Tosswill Woollaston**, a founder of the modernist movement in New Zealand art. Woollaston was one of a group of artists and writers who, during the 1930s and 40s, began exploring notions of a New Zealand culture independent of colonial Britain. Particular significance in the gallery is given to a famous 1909 portrait by Gottfried Lindauer of Huria Matenga, a Maori women who, with her husband and friends, saved many lives from the wreck of the *Delaware* in 1863. Her status is indicated by *moko* (traditional tattoos), feathers, bone, greenstone jewellery and the ceremonial club she holds; in the background is the foundering American ship. The other significant part of the permanent collection is devoted to ceramics and the work of local potters; the Nelson area is rich in raw materials for potters and ceramic artists. The gallery also mounts temporary exhibitions of a range of Maori art, from early more traditional carvings to contemporary work and if that's not enough there's a 159-seat arthouse cinema (see "Drinking, nightlife and entertainment", p.551).

The undoubted new jewel in the Nelson crown is the **World of Wearable Arts and Collectable Cars** (WOW; daily: Dec–March 9am–6.30pm, April–Nov 10am–5pm; $15), a purpose built showcase for the best designs from the Wearable Arts Shows (see "Festival Mania", opposite) combined with some highly desirable shiny automobiles. The fashion show with a difference, first put on by Suzie Moncrieff outside a cobb cottage in 1987, has grown into an international event and now attracts participants from all over the world, the criteria being sculptures or pieces of art that can be worn as clothes – in many cases made from the most unusual materials, like ring-pulls from drinks cans. The WOW gallery displays many of the winning designs plus some of the more inventive entries, in a manner that owes more to glitzy fashion shows and colourful theatre productions than static gallery or museum exhibitions. The vehicles in the Collectable Cars gallery are more run-of-the-mill but the inventive way they are shown adds appeal. To get there take an NSB bus to Stoke, getting off at the *Black Cat* bar, five minutes' walk from the gallery.

Anyone wishing to further indulge their interest in arts and crafts should head for the **Bead Gallery**, 18 Parere St, close to the corner with Vanguard St (Mon–Fri 9am–5pm, Sat 9am–4.30pm, Ⓦ www.beads.co.nz): a small 1920s cottage/shop with a collection of over 2000 beads, including some of the most exotic anywhere in the world ranging from 10¢ to $500. The idea is simple; you can either design your own bead-piece or have one custom made for you depending upon your budget.

Pleasures of a less artistic kind can be found at the **South Pacific Distillery and Bottle Store**, 285 Wakefield Quay (Mon–Sat 9am–6pm), who run a ten-minute tour (Mon–Sat 2.30pm; free): all their spirit products have a "roaring forties" guarantee, which means that they all have forty percent alcohol content. The main reason for visiting is to raid the bottle shop for something suitably potent and uplifting.

Gardens and beaches

Next to the Suter Art Gallery are **Queens Gardens** (daily 8am–dusk; free), hemmed in on three sides by Bridge, Tasman and Hardy streets: a pretty

Victorian garden, with its mature trees and well-populated duck pond. Another tranquil haven can be found in the **Botanic Gardens**, near the corner of Milton Street and Hardy Street East, heading east up Hardy St from the town centre for about 1km, which is full of birds and leads to the **Centre of New Zealand**, the meaningless geographical middle of the nation, appropriately marked. Further out of town are the delightful **Japanese-style Miyazu Gardens** (daily 8am–dusk; free). To get here, continue on from the Botanic Garden down Milton St until you reach Atawhai Drive (about 750m) and then follow Atawhai Drive another 500m passing Founders Park on your way.

This quiet oasis has a traditional tea house, ponds, azaleas, Japanese irises and flowering cherries; the gardens are at their best during December and January. **Founders Park**, 87 Atawhai Drive (daily 10am–4.30pm; $5), 200m back from the gardens, is less impressive, with a collection of old buildings conspiring to produce a somewhat sanitized version of early colonial history, complete with pristine black tarmac roads and a poor-man's-Disney atmosphere. The only place really worth the entrance fee is the organic brewery, where you can sample some tasty locally-brewed ales and lagers.

For an excellent walk with fine views, head west on Haven Road, past the junction with Queen Elizabeth II Drive, and on to Wakefield Quay. Then walk along Rocks Road (SH6) until you reach the **Tahunanui Beach Reserve**, just past the sea wall, some 5km from the city centre. Grassland and drifting dunes back the long, golden beach, which has safe swimming, a fun park, zoo and children's playgrounds – the place swarms around Christmas time. If you don't feel like walking to the reserve, buses run regularly along SH6 from the city.

Some 18km from the reserve (along SH6 and then northwest on SH60), is Nelson's other beach area, **Rabbit Island**, with golden sands backed by trees. This is much less developed, and all the better for it: the views are stunning, and it's picture-book pretty. Access is by the Redwood Road (off SH60, just after the Waimea River Road Bridge), but note that this road is barred at dusk each day.

Stoke

The small satellite town of **STOKE** lying 8km southwest of Nelson on SH6 is linked to the city by suburban buses, and hides a couple of attractions.

One of the best diversions around Nelson is the **Mac's Brewery Tour**, 660 Main Rd (Ⓣ03/547 8097; Mon–Sat: Nov–April 11.15am & 2pm; May–Oct 11.15am; 1hr; $5 tasting), which takes you through the completely natural brewing process: the brewery sits on its own spring, and uses local Motueka Hops. The highlight is the tasting of superior brews – and, inevitably, there's a large shop selling products and souvenirs. Although the beer is still the thing to go for here don't miss out on the wines, a recent addition to the stock range from their own vineyard.

Also in the suburb of Stoke, just off Marsden Road (entrance in Hilliard Street), is **Isel Park** (daily 8am–dusk; free) which contains **Isel House**, dating from 1848 and now owned by the council but not open to the public. Built as a farmhouse for the Marsden family, it is set in woodland of some grandeur.

Activities

A number of companies offer **rafting** trips starting from Nelson, most venturing onto the **Buller River** via Murchison and the Nelson Lakes National Park or onto the **Karamea River** in Kahurangi National Park. Along both rivers, the scenery is breathtaking, the water swift – and the sandflies omnipresent, so don't forget the insect repellent.

The pick of the operators are Ultimate Descents and The Rapid River Adventure Company. Both offer a variety of trips: with Ultimate Descents, based in Murchison (ⓣ03/528 6363 & 0800/748 377, ⓔultimate@rivers.co.nz), itineraries range from day-long excursions on the Buller (Grade III & IV; $105 including lunch) to amazing five-day safaris on the Buller and Karamea (including Grade V; $595 and $675 all inclusive). Their day-trips seem to spend slightly longer on the river than most others, leaving plenty of time for fun with inflatable kayaks and water sledges, as well as for getting your teeth into some serious rafting and a deceptively high cliff jump. A recent addition to the repertoire is "river bugging", the use of purpose-built individual rafts in which you sit and shoot rapids, although not terribly serious ones (3–4hr; $89). Rapid River (ⓣ03/545 7076, ⓕ545 7076) do a good-value day-trip from Nelson ($110, including barbecue lunch) that gets you on the river just after lunch for four hours' rafting on Grade III and IV stretches of the Buller and Gowan rivers, ending at the Owen River Tavern for a well-earned pint.

You won't escape the buffeting on land, either. Just off Cable Bay Road, about ten minutes' drive east of Nelson on SH6, Happy Valley 4WD Motorbike Adventures (ⓣ03/545 0304, ⓕ545 0347) have a number of **quadbikes** and all-terrain vehicles. With over 4000 square kilometres of forest and 40km of track at their disposal, there's an enormous variety to their **safaris**. Climbing the hills, monstrous matai trees along the paths eventually give way to expansive views of Cable Bay and the ocean. Prices range from $25 to $100, and evening forays include glow-worm viewing. The most popular trips are the "Bay View" (2hr; $85), and the barbecue trip (3hr; $115).

About 17km along SH6 west of Nelson through Richmond, the Haycock Road turns off to the historic Clover Road stables, home to Stonehurst Horse trekking (ⓣ03/542 4121, ⓕ542 3823). The majority of the shorter treks (1hr $30, 90min $65, 2hr $65) take place in the foothills of the Richmond ranges and offer great views of the coast and beyond; there are horses to suit all abilities, the routes are challenging but not frightening, there's a full safety briefing and protective head gear's available. Following a slightly more adventurous tack are Western Ranges Horse Treks (ⓣ%03/522 4198, ⓦwww.thehorsetrek.co.nz; half-day $70, day $120, two days $300). To get here from Motueka, turn right at Rothmans clock tower, continue for 30km to Baton Bridge, turn left and carry on for a further 16km.

When you've had your fill of Nelson's earthly pleasures, spice things up with a spot of **parachuting**. Tandem Skydiving (ⓣ03/546 4444 & 0800/422 899; $215 for 9000ft, $260 for 12,000ft; $340 for 15,000ft) operates out of Nelson Airport – or, if the weather is unsuitable there, they adjourn to Motueka. You can even get some pictures of yourself trying to look happy before you plummet from an altitude of 3000m, or for an extra $50, 4000m. Although you may have other things on your mind, the scenery is excellent and the expert parachuting "buddies" are helpful and friendly. Out in Richmond, Nelson Paragliding offers **tandem paragliding** (ⓣ03/544 1182; from $110): a hair-raising drive up the hill to the launch site reveals a spectacular landscape, before you run like hell then glide off into the quiet up draughts for 15–20 minutes of eerily silent flight, surrounded by stunning views. Airborn Paragliding (ⓣ03/548 5520; from $110) is an alternative offering similar trips(ⓣ03/543 2669). Less exciting but useful if you're pushed for time are **scenic flights** with Tasman Bay Aviation (ⓣ & ⓕ03/547 2378), who run trips over Abel Tasman National Park ($155 per hour of plane hire and a minimum of two people),

Kahurangi National Park, the Marlborough Sounds and more local Nelson jaunts.

Eating

The enviable lifestyle of Nelson residents is reflected in the **broad choice** of decent places to eat within easy reach of the town centre. And when you tire of these, there's always fine food and wine in gorgeous settings at the **wineries**. If fast food beckons, try out one of the small **ethnic cafés** which offer everything from sushi to kiwi burgers via kebabs and pasta. Don't forget Nelson's pubs and bars (see opposite) for a quick snack either.

Akbaba's Turkish Kebabs 130 Bridge St. Plenty of cheap kebabs and salads ($5–11) to munch in the courtyard out back, or in booth seating on low floor cushions; Turkish decor and music create a lively and casual atmosphere for lunch and supper (closed Sunday).

Amadeus 284 Trafalgar St. Posh-looking licensed coffee house cum restaurant, with tasty lunches and dinners, where the coffee, cakes and handmade chocolates are to die for and don't cost as much as you might expect. In fact this relaxing Viennese style stop-off is well worth an hour or so of anyone's time. Licensed.

Boat Shed 350 Wakefield Quay ⓣ03/546 9783. Converted for its new role, this boat shed has large windows offering unimpeded and spectacular sunsets over Tasman Bay. Exceptional seafood and a bustling ambience mean that it suffers somewhat from its own popularity. It's definitely worth coming here, but try to avoid the insanely crowded and rushed Friday and Saturday nights. Mains cost $25–35. Licensed.

Broccoli Row 5 Buxton Square ⓣ03/548 9621. Lunches, afternoon snacks and dinners are all served in generous portions at this vegetarian and seafood restaurant, with outdoor dining and blackboard specials ($19–22). Particular favourites are the $8.50 salad bowl with home-made focaccia and the Mediterranean tapas. Mon–Sat 9.30am–10pm; book for dinner at weekends; BYO.

Chez Eelco 296 Trafalgar St. This was the first café/bar in Nelson, and though Eelco decided to hang up his apron a while ago, the next generation took over and continue the European hippy theme, which is starting to look a bit tired. The breakfasts, snacks, lunches and dinners are still good value in largish portions and you can buy cans of his famous, and tasty, mussel chowder from behind the counter. Open till 4pm most days and 11pm Fri & Sat. Licensed and BYO.

The Cut 94 Collingwood St ⓣ03/548 9874. A swish but relaxed café/restaurant in an historic villa with a broad menu including steaks, pan roast pork loin, peppered tuna and at least one veggie option. The wine list is extensive and mains fluctuate around the $25 mark.

Lambretta's 204 Hardy St. Open from 9am daily serving good coffee in the shadow of one eponymous scooter mounted on the wall above the bar and another above the entrance. There are reasonable snacks and main meals with an Italian bent, including the usual pizza and pasta. This place also gets quite lively in the afternoons and evenings and is sometimes the venue for jazz and blues bands. Licensed.

Café Metro Above the cinema, 91 Trafalgar St. A popular stop-off for trendy young things, the waiting cinema crowd and shoppers who've walked far enough. It has a blackboard menu of simple fare and a balcony on which to people watch. You can also take your drink into the film with you. Daily; licensed.

Miyazu Japanese restaurant in the *Quality Rutherford Hotel*, Trafalgar Square ⓣ03/548 2299. Predictably expensive but excellent, dinner only. Authentic preparation and stylish surroundings make this worth a splurge when nothing but sashimi will do. Licensed.

Old Bakehouse 7 Alma Lane, Buxton Square. Quirky decor in an old bakery serving some imaginative lunches and dinners, closed Sunday and Monday, licensed.

Morrisons 244 Hardy St. A café and gallery with tasty brunches, lunches, snacks and pleasing decor; unfortunately the pretensions push the prices up a bit but the local art on view does at least provide a talking point. Licensed.

Plaza India 132 Collingwood St ⓣ03/546 9344. An authentic and reasonably priced Indian restaurant serving tasty lunches and dinners. Eat inside or in the tiled courtyard. Licensed.

Pomeroys 276 Trafalgar St ⓣ03/544 7524. A quiet restaurant and wine bar (plus BYO), with the Vauxhall motor car crest as its logo (Pomeroy started the company). The food is fresh and attractive, starting with imaginative breakfasts, and moving on to filled focaccia for lunch. Blackboard specials for dinner might include Thai chicken curry or local fish dishes. A full meal will set you back between $15 and $28. Daily 9am–10pm.

Poppy Thai 142 Hardy St. Fully licensed, very authentic Thai restaurant where the excellent food and good value make up for its palpable lack of charm and charisma. Mon–Sun for lunch and dinner.

Ribbetts 20 Tahuanui Drive ⓣ03/548 6911. The frog theme always seemed a bit tacky but the restaurant has a business-like charm and serves excellent local produce, prepared with an international slant; main courses cost between $20 and $27. Try the romantic, covered, candle-lit courtyard with wooden tables and stone floors. Daily 10am–3pm & 5.30–10pm; licensed & BYO.

Café Verte 123 Bridge St. Coffee house open daily until the wee hours for breakfast, lunch and dinner and rightly renowned for its kick-ass java, some iffy decor and good value grub. Licensed and BYO.

Yazza Montgomery Sq. A hip little coffee house selling excellent breakfasts, lunches, snacks, coffees and various teas. It's very reasonably priced and turns into an alternative night spot late in the week with various advertised events. Well worth the effort. Licensed.

Zippy's 276 Hardy St. If you're looking for home-baked veggie or wheat-free food, wicked vegan curries, tofu burgers and coffee that bites back, and you can bear the purple and orange walls, then this is the place for you. Mon–Sat 9am–6pm.

Drinking, nightlife and entertainment

While most of its neighbours retire early to sip their cocoa, Nelson stays up all night and has a party – most noticeably at various venues on or near Bridge Street. Pubs and **bars** of all sorts dominate, many with **live music**, karaoke and DJ **nights**; check out the Friday edition of the *Nelson Mail* (80¢) to find out **what's on**.

Attached to The Suter, at 208 Bridge St, is a 159-seat arthouse **cinema**, a comfortable venue for films you're unlikely to see in the mainstream multiplex down the road; screenings are generally on Thursday to Sunday evenings (check the local paper for details). The State Cinema Centre, opposite the central post office, shows the latest releases, and movie munchies and booze are available at the *Metro Café* upstairs.

The Artery In the community Arts Centre, New St (upper half covered by a bright ceramic mural). The alternative, slightly down at heel venue that gets a lot of the more off-the-wall acts and poetry readings as well as some interesting musical events and visiting DJs, advertised in the local press. The Gathering (see Festival Mania) is also organized within these walls. Licensed.

Bush Tavern and Pheasant Plucker 87 Grove St. Moribund English-style pub, with a reputation for good-value bar meals ($7–19) in huge portions. Daily 11am–11pm, with very occasional live music of a dubious nature.

Grand Central Sports Café 223 Hardy St. Open from 10am daily this is supposed to be a hybrid sports bar/café, but it's really just a high-ceilinged drinking and dancing den in the architecturally impressive old Public Trust Building.

Grumpy Mole 141 Bridge St. Always open late with DJs playing top 40 and pop in all the bars including the garden. They have happy hours from 8–10pm, big video screens and a smoking buffalo head over the main bar.

Jessies Pad 145 Bridge St. A laid-back, mostly jazz and blues club with a family-run feel, live music at least three nights a week, including the Monday evening jam when talented locals and passing musicians get together.

The Honest Lawyer 1 Point Rd. A comfortable, country pub with a tree occupying its centre and a beer garden overlooking the beach. They have a wide range of local and foreign beverages, wholesome grub and the odd Irish folk- or cover-band on Tues or Thurs. Daily 11am–11pm. Live music Fri, Sat & Sun.

Little Rock Cafe 165 Bridge St. Very lively and popular dance venue on Fri and Sat when they have a broad-ranging DJ-led party beneath the enormous copper-like globe. Daily 4pm–2.30am.

The Loft Bar 123a Bridge St. Upstairs late night bar and club with a balcony overlooking the excesses of Bridge St. They get a lot of live music and like to play a little hip hop and high NRG from time to time.

Molly's Bridge St. Once a wild west bar that transformed itself into a wild Irish pub, it's now just three dark bars where the Djs play chart and some dance music. Daily 11am–3am.

The Oyster Bar 115 Hardy St. A tiny Californian-style sushi bar where they serve the best gin and tonic in town. Probably the most attractive and welcoming place for a quiet drink, some sushi and cool sounds. Closed Sun and Mon.

Shark Bar 132–136 Bridge St. New and swanky addition to the nightlife in town. A jazz and blues bar that also does DJ-dance parties and has a number of pool tables.

Taylor's 131 Bridge St. Big, bright and garish party bar with live music and a DJ dominated club, massive, noisy and often packed.

Victorian Rose 281 Trafalgar St. Olde English-style pub opposite *Chez Eelco*, which lives off its reputation as a good early evening, live music venue. Latterly the food has definitely gone down hill so avoid it but the jazz sessions on Tuesday evenings are still worth a listen. Daily till 3am but not often worth hanging about after 11pm.

Listings

Automobile Association 45 Halifax St ⓣ03/548 8339.

Bike rental Avanti Pro Cycle Centre (ⓣ03/548 3877) and Natural High (ⓣ03/546 6936) offer bikes at around $20 for half a day, $30 a day.

Buses Abel Tasman Coachlines (ⓣ03/548 0285, ⓔatc@nelsoncoaches.co.nz) leaves Nelson at 7.20am daily for Marahau or Totoranui, via Motueka, connecting with launch services deeper into the park, and operates a service to the head of the Heaphy Track; InterCity (ⓣ03/548 1538) offers daily services to Picton, Blenheim and Christchurch or to Richmond, Motueka, Takaka and Totaranui; Kahurangi Buses (ⓣ03/5259430 & 0800/173 371) goes to Abel Tasman, Golden Bay and the Heaphy; KiwiLink (ⓣ03/577 8332) goes to Blenheim, Golden Bay and the Heaphy, Picton, Totaranui and Havelock; Knightline (ⓣ03/528 7798) runs to Motueka, Blenheim and Picton; Kiwilink (ⓣ03/577 8332) runs from Nelson to Collingwood and the Heaphy, via Takaka (with a Westport, southern end Heaphy Track pick-up), to Kaiteriteri via Motueka, and to Totaranui via Takaka; Lazerline (ⓣ03/388 7652) runs between Christchurch and Nelson via Maruia Springs and Hanmer; Nelson Lakes Transport (ⓣ03/547 5912) runs to the lakes and offers ski transport; Nelson SBCL (ⓣ03/548 3290) runs buses to Stoke, Richmond and small communities thereabouts, as well as to the Abel Tasman National Park; the Rose Express (book through information centres) goes to Picton and Blenheim; and Southern Link Shuttles (ⓣ03/758 3338) goes to Westport, Christchurch, Hanmer, Corner and Reefton. Atomic does daily runs to the Nelson Lakes plus the Abel Tasman National Park, Picton and beyond.

Camping and outdoor equipment Wet-weather clothing and camping gear can be bought from Rollo's BBQ and Camping Centre, 12 Bridge St, or Basecamp, 295 Trafalgar St.

Car rental Avis ⓣ03/547 2727; Budget ⓣ03/547 9586; Hardy Cars ⓣ03/546 1681; Hertz ⓣ03/547 2299; National ⓣ03/548 1618 & 0800/800115; and Rent-a-dent ⓣ03/546 9890. Daily rates start at about $60–70.

Diving gear Scuba gear can be rented from Richmond Sportsworld, 213 Queens St, Nelson.

Internet access Aurora Tech Ltd, 161 Trafalgar St, between New St and Bridge St, daily 9am–10pm; Internet Outpost in the Megabyte Café, 35 Bridge St, Mon–Sat 10am–6pm; and Discount Internet at Boots-off Travel Centre, 53 Bridge St, Mon–Sat, 10am–5pm.

Medical treatment Nelson Public Hospital, Waimea Road ⓣ03/546 1800; main entrance on Kawai Street.

Pharmacy Prices Pharmacy, cnr Hardy & Collingwood St, open nightly till 8pm.

Post office Cnr Trafalgar St and Halifax St, opposite the visitor centre.

Rock climbing Vertical Limits Climbing Wall, 34 Vanguard St, Nelson (ⓣ03/545 7511, ⓦwww.verticallimits.co.nz), have a climbing wall ($15) and do guided day-trips into the stunning limestone scenery ($120).

Taxis and shuttle services Bickley Motors ⓣ03/525 8352; Crown Bus and Shuttle Services ⓣ03/548 0600; NelsonCity Taxis ⓣ03/548 8225; Rural Services ⓣ03/548 6858; Sun City Taxis ⓣ0800/422 666; Super Shuttle Nelson ⓣ03/547 5782 & 0800/438 238; Transport for Trampers ⓣ03/545 1055; and Nelson Lakes Shuttles ⓣ03/521 1023 all offer on-demand services.

Tours Bay Tours (ⓣ03/544 4494 & 0800/229 868) offers arts, crafts and wine tours; J.J.'s Wine Tours (ⓣ03/544 7712) visit local wineries and provide ski transport; Nelson Day Tours (ⓣ025/873 388) do the lot – wine, crafts, city districts, Golden Bay and beaches, while Top of the South Hiking Tours (ⓣ03/548 3813, ⓔtopofthesouth@xtra.co.nz) will take you as far afield as Nelson Lakes, Mt Robert, or Mt Arthur for 3-4hr trekks, if you're moderately fit. Tasman Bay Aviation (see p.549) and The Aero Club (book through the visitor centre, see p.543) operate various airborne tours of the region.

Around Nelson

Most of Nelson's attractions, including the wineries, breweries and galleries for which it is renowned, lie beyond the city and have been made considerably easier to get to by the completion of a bypass round the city's suburbs and the straightening of the road beyond to Motueka.The combination of the soil, natural spring water and climate make this area ideal for the production of **wines** or **beers**, and the attractiveness of the scenery will tempt you to linger and sample a glass of either. If the galleries in town whet your appetite for art, make time to investigate the studios of the enormous number of contemporary artists working in the Nelson region, many of whom exhibit in their own small **galleries**, showcasing ceramics, glass-blowing, woodturning, textiles, sculpture and painting. More details can be found in the *Nelson Potters*, *Winemakers* and *The Coastal Way* leaflets, all free from Nelson visitor centre.

Almost everything worth seeing outside the city of Nelson lies to the south and west: either just off SH6 before it reaches the junction with SH60 or in a slim corridor of land flanking either side of SH60. Nelson Suburban Buses run along SH6, through Richmond and as far as Wakefield, but do not go along SH60; however, **bus tours** run to the wineries and galleries (see "Listings" opposite).

Heading west along SH6, you'll reach the **Craft Habitat Centre** (daily 10am–5pm, some craftspeople arrive late so to see everything visit around 2pm), 12km from Nelson on the southernmost edge of Waimea Inlet, opposite the junction with Champion Road. Turn left off the bypass at the roundabout that leads along Salisbury Road and into Richmond. Set up by Jack Laird and his wife, stalwarts of the Nelson pottery scene, the centre was developed by their son Paul, a potter of unusual, haunting or just absurd pieces inspired by the landscape and animal life. These days he's the only artist of note there and the place is now a bit tired so once you've seen the pottery get back on the road. For something to wash down the great gulp you took when you saw the prices on the pottery, press on through the fruit-growing country to another combined operation, the **Grape Escape**, at the corner of SH60 and McShanes Road (Oct–April daily; May–Sept Wed–Sun 10.30am–4.30pm), where you can sample the respective products of the Richmond Plains Organic Winery and the Te Mania Winery, both of which produce good Sauvignon Blanc and Pinot Noir (free tastings). Also attached are a tacky gift shop and expensive café that are best ignored. Five minutes from here up SH6 is the **Greenhough Winery**, on Patons Road near Richmond (Dec–Feb daily 1am–5pm; Nov–March Sat & Sun 1am–5pm), where you can try fine vintages, or just pick up a crisp Sauvignon Blanc for later.

Högland's Glass Blowing Studio, Korurangi Farm, Lansdowne Road (daily 9am–5.30pm), is signposted from SH60 just after it leaves SH6. In addition to glass-blowing demonstrations, there's a good-value licensed café, live Irish folk music at weekends, a gallery and park-like gardens inhabited by farm animals. The glass-blowers slickly combine art and entertainment, and may even let you blow a glass bubble yourself. The style of the glassware (mostly tableware) is Scandinavian-influenced, which works best in the bigger, bolder pieces with clean lines and bright, unusual colours. Sticking with the Scandinavian theme, the **café** serves excellent lunches and light snacks; try the open sandwiches or the platter of smoked delicacies which is usually enough for two.

The **Seifried Estate Winery**, at the corner of SH60 and Redwood Road, is a smooth operation with an excellent if posh restaurant and shop; tastings take place further up SH60 at Appleby near the Rabbit Island turn-off (daily

△ Waterfall

9am–5pm; wine tasting $3, redeemable against purchase). The **Silkwood** gift shop (daily 10am–5pm), 4km along SH60 from the Seifried Estate Winery, is famed more for its method of construction than its touristy, high-quality but expensive wares. Made of bales of straw plastered over with concrete – a method originally used in the United States in timber-poor areas – the building is virtually fireproof, safe in earthquakes, cool in summer, and warm in the winter. Inside, among the usual tourist tat, is some beautifully designed knitwear made from the wool of the llama, angora and alpaca that graze the property. The **Bronte Gallery**, at the end of Bronte Road East, which veers east off SH60, is recommended for the diversity of its pottery and painting, and for its selection of tableware by internationally recognized practitioner, Darryl Robertson. The highly individual work here provides a useful benchmark for assessing the quality in other outlets; what's more, the gallery enjoys a fine location near the coast, where there are sweeping views across Waimea Inlet to Rabbit Island, as well as some comfy boutique **accommodation** (Ⓣ03/540 2422; ❽).

Mapua Wharf and the Motueka road

Mapua Wharf is at the end of the Arunui Road, which turns off SH60, 34km from Nelson. Overlooking the west end of Rabbit Island and the Waimea Estuary, the wharf was once legendary for producing smoked fish from a quirky jumble of old buildings. These days it has taken on a very different feel with *The Smokehouse*, a polished operation that still produces excellent smoked fish to take away, or eat at its specially created waterside licensed café (Ⓣ03/540 2280; $20–25 per head, considerably more if you have alcohol): there are mussels, a staggering variety of fish and a widely acclaimed fish paté, as well as some of the best smoked salmon in the country, all done to a cured turn over manuka wood after being soaked in a salt and sugar solution. You're best to try lunch times as this spot is now so popular that it's booked up almost every evening. Other additions to the increasingly touristy wharf are an **aquarium**, which isn't as tacky as it looks (daily Oct–April 9.30am–9pm, May–Sept 10.30am–4.30pm; $5), and contains touch-tanks full of fish and some informative video and static exhibits. Much more fun is to be had with Mapua Adventures (Ⓣ03/540 3833, Ⓦwww.MapuaAdventures.co.nz) whose **jetboat** at the wharf does a $55 zoom around Rabbit Island (45min), stopping off along the way to identify some of the rare birds that inhabit the shores. They also do an eco/bird-watching tour (2hr 30min, $150) and a three-adventure combo involving a guided sea kayak paddle from Nelson to Rabbit Island, mountain biking the trails on mercifully flat land and jetboating round the rest of the island before catching a minibus back to Nelson (all day, $120). There are various other options all of which, tide and weather willing, provide a platform from which to explore the area. Last but not least at the wharf is the *Mapua Wharf Café/Bar*, leaning out over the water (Dec-April daily 10am–late, May–Nov Wed–Sun 10am–late), where you can pick up reasonable **food** and better still catch the odd live band in an appealing, often packed, waterside-bar atmosphere. Heading back towards SH60, you'll pass Mapua Village and its *Village Rest*, a licensed café with excellent **coffee** in an impressive modern building and a large deck where you can sup a pint of locally brewed beer. You'll also see the Laughing Fish Studio, 24 Aranui Rd, where extremely bright, mediterranean-style pots catch the eye alongside some imaginative watercolours and acrylics.

On the opposite side of SH60, the Seaton Valley Road heads west and inland to the eccentric **Glover's Vineyard** (daily Oct–April 10am–5pm, closed

May–Sept; tastings $2), a small concern that produces fine reds and whites and boasts especially good Cabernet Sauvignon and Pinot Noir (most costing $18 or more); you can draw your own conclusions from the fact that the owner, a serious wine buff, used to tuck a Wagner CD into every package destined for overseas. The **Nuerdorf Winery** (Mon–Sat Sept–May 10am–5pm, or by appointment ⓣ03/543 2643; free tastings), an altogether more down-to-earth prospect, is further inland. Once you hit the junction with Moutere Highway, join Nuerdorf Road by heading southeast on the highway for 100m and turning right. The winery is in a low-slung wooden building covered by vines with simple outdoor seating in the shade of some tall ancient trees, where a glass of Chardonnay is complemented perfectly by cheese, bread, olives and other simple fare that is served here ($8–12). From Nuerdorf head further inland south along the Moutere Highway as far as Sunrise Valley Road, and follow the signposts for 2km to **Moutere Hills Vineyard** (daily Oct–April 11am–6pm, or by appointment ⓣ03/543 2288) where there's a good café serving large platters and some lovely Sauvignon Blanc, Chardonnay with a bite and good Merlot-Cabernet Franc, all for around $17. On your way back to the main road, if you have time, there is the well-respected **Karhurangi Vineyard** (Dec–Mar daily 10am–5pm, 11am–4pm the rest of the year, except July when it closes). They make powerful vintages from some of Nelson's oldest vines and some splendid olive oil.

Back on SH60, about 2km from Ruby Bay, is **Steve Fullmer's Gallery** (daily 10am–5pm), near the Tasman Store on Baldwin Road. One of the best galleries in the region, this place is worth a browse even if you can't afford any of the remarkable ceramic art or solid tableware. Further up this stretch is the Marriages Road turn off and then the Awa Awa fork that leads to the last vineyard of note, **Denton's** (daily, labour weekend to Easter 11am–5pm), where you can pick up some brisk and fresh white wines and enjoy the view of the lake. The last real point of interest, or weirdness, 10km before you hit Motueka, is **The Jester** (ⓣ03/526 6742, ⓦwww.jesterhouse.co.nz), an inspired café (Dec-Mar daily 9.30am–5pm, April–Nov Wed–Sun 9.30am–4.30pm), where the coffee is strong, the tasty food is all home-baked and the garden is idiosyncratic. You can also **stay** in an enormous red, concrete boot, inside which is an open fire, comfortable lounge and strangely romantic bedroom (B&B; ❸).

Abel Tasman National Park and around

Abel Tasman National Park is a stunningly beautiful area with an international reputation – resulting in large crowds of trampers, kayakers and day-trippers all through the summer. Don't let this put you off though: within the park are beautiful golden sandy beaches lapped by crystal-clear waters and backed by lush green bushland and forest, all interspersed with granite outcrops and inhabited by a multitude of wildlife. The goal of most visitors is the **Abel Tasman Coastal Track**, combining as it does a picturesque mixture of dense coastal bushwalking with gentle climbs to lookouts and walks across idyllic beaches, but this is also a wonderful place to get into a **kayak** and explore the mercurial coastline and rivermouths.

The park's dearth of settlements means that often all you can hear is birdsong and the gently soporific lapping of the waves on the shore. **Motueka** acts as a gateway and service centre for hungry trampers and locals alike, while the peaceful communities at **Kaiteriteri** and **Marahau**, en route to the park entrance, each have a smattering of places to stay. Marahau, virtually at the park gate, is the starting point for most of the kayaking and tramping trips, as well as swimming with seals, though the application to build a large hotel here would, if successful, destroy the unique atmosphere.

Motueka

Famous for plentiful sunshine, and surrounded by fertile plains, **MOTUEKA**, 47km from Nelson, is really just a jumping-off point for more interesting destinations – most notably the Abel Tasman National Park, whose popularity has made this a boomtown. The name Motueka means "land of the Weka", a reference to the abundance of these edible birds by Maori, who lived in the area for over a thousand years growing kumera in the fertile soil and exploiting the plentiful marine life, until the arrival of European settlers in 1842 heralded the demise of the community-based traditional Maori lifestyle in the region.

Arrival, information and accommodation

Most of the **bus** companies pick up and drop off on the corner of High Street and Parker Street. Regular **flights** from Wellington land at the grass airfield on College Street, about 3km south of the centre; Motueka Taxis (ⓣ03/528 1031) will take you into town for around $7, and will ferry you to the more out-of-the-way places.

The **visitor centre**, Wallace St (daily 8am–5pm, though they will stay open longer from Nov–Jan depending upon the crowds; ⓣ03/528 6543, ⓔmzpvin@xtra.co.nz), sells bus tickets, arranges tours and accommodation and will deal with all your Abel Tasman and Heaphy track needs and questions. Pick up a copy of the relevant DOC leaflet (free) here, which has a map and descriptions of points of interest. If you're in training for the Abel Tasman Coastal Track, there's also a *Motueka District Walks* leaflet ($1), describing many day walks in the surrounding area. The **DOC office**, on the corner of High Street and King Edward Street, 2km back toward Nelson from the centre of town (Mon–Fri 8am–4.30pm; ⓣ03/528 9117), also gives out information on the national park, and sells tickets for the track. **Camping** and tramping **gear**

Walks around Motueka

A good spot to view Motueka and the surrounding country is **Mount Arthur and the Tablelands**, and the various walks that cross them, as detailed in the new $1 DOC leaflet, *The Cobb Valley, Mount Arthur and Tablelands*, which suggests a series of excellent tramps and is available from the visitor centre in Motueka. The tracks in these areas are always quiet, because most visitors are in a mad rush to join the crowds at Abel Tasman.

The starting point for many of the best walks is the Flora car park, on the Graham Valley Road, which leads off SH61 south of Motueka. From here there are commanding views of the lowlands, with Mount Arthur dominating the southern skyline. From the car park you can take a walk (1hr each way) to the **Mount Arthur Hut** (Category 2; $10), from where you can continue on to Mount Arthur in another 3 hours, or tackle the summit of Mount Lodestone (1448m; 2hr).

There are similar tracks up the **Cobb Valley** (see Takaka, p.566) a little further northwest, or starting 28km along the Upper Takaka turn-off in Golden Bay; further leaflets are available from the Motueka visitor centre although most of what you'll need is in DOC leaflets (see above). Here too, you can lose yourself in beautiful, forested high country, with panoramic views above the tree line.

can be **rented** from Coppins, 255 High St, and Twin Oaks, 25 Parker St.

Accommodation options are getting better. *Abel Tasman Motel and Lodge*, 45 High St (Ⓣ03/528 6688 & 0800/845 678; ❹), offers six basic, clean but slightly rough-around-the-edges looking units. Also on offer are the well-kept units at the *Equestrian Motel*, Tudor St (Ⓣ03/528 9369, Ⓦwww.equestrianlodgethequietplace.co.nz; ❺), which back on to a pool and grass courtyard. Other central places are the exceptionally comfortable, spacious and well-run *Baker's Lodge*, 4 Poole St (Ⓣ03/528 0102, Ⓔbakers@motueka.co.nz, dorms ❶, doubles ❷–❸), where you can enjoy homebaked mini muffins each evening. Also worth a look are the *White Elephant Hostel*, 55 Whakarewa St (Ⓣ03/528 6208, Ⓦwhite.elephant.clear.co.nz, dorms ❶, doubles ❷–❸), and *Twin Oaks*, 25 Parker St, about 1km from the town centre (Ⓣ03/528 7882; dorms ❶, rooms ❷–❸), which also rents out camping and tramping equipment for the Abel Tasman and Heaphy tracks. The nearest **campsite** is *Fearon's Bush Camp*, 10 Fearon St (Ⓣ03/528 7189; tent sites $10, pwrd $11.50, various cabins and motel units ❷–❹), a verdant site with plenty of trees for shelter and clean, well kept facilities just a 1km walk from the town centre.

The Town

Motueka is strung along SH60, with quieter streets fanning out from the main highway. The quay and seafront run parallel to SH60 about five minutes' walk down old Wharf Road or along Tudor and Harbour streets.

One of the most interesting diversions in town is provided by a short walk down to the **Motueka Quay**, where the ghost of this once-busy port lingers among the scant remains of the old jetty and store houses. Here, just 1500m down the Old Wharf Road, the hulk of the *Janie Seddon* – named after the daughter of Richard Seddon, premier of New Zealand from 1893 until his death in 1906 – is disgracefully left to rust. Built in Scotland in 1901, then purchased by the New Zealand government and used as a pilot vessel in Wellington, the ship served in both world wars, patrolling the waters of Cook Strait and Wellington Harbour. In 1946 she was bought by the Motueka Trawling Company, but local regulations outlawing steam-powered craft made her redundant, and she was ignominiously beached near the old wharf in 1955.

The tiny **Motueka Museum** (daily 10am–3pm; $2) delves into the area's history through copious black-and-white photographs and a few Maori artefacts relating to the area, as well as the *94 Motueka Carvings*, four skilfully carved friezes depicting the livelihoods that have traditionally sustained Tasman Bay.

Eating and drinking

Despite its modest size, Motueka has a number of restaurants, cafés and bars, catering to the enthusiastic appetites of fresh-air freaks.

Bakehouse Café and Pizzeria 21 Wallace St. The best place to get a pizza or anything remotely Italian. Everything is home baked and tasty and they have superb Havana coffee. Licensed.

The Grain and Grape 218 High St. A pub/café serving breakfast, brunch and light meals for lunch and dinner with large, moderately priced portions and a long bar. Try the carrot cake. Licensed.

Gothic Gourmet High St. A café/bar in the neo-Gothic setting of a former church. Food is of a reasonable quality, with imaginative French and Italian touches at decent prices. Lunch & dinner daily; licensed.

Hot Mama's 105 High St. A bright interior, patio garden and simple furniture create an attractive and intimate ambience in which to enjoy a good coffee or a drink – and occasional appearances by touring New Zealand folk, jazz, acoustic and rock acts. The coolest and probably best spot in town for entertainment but the food has decidedly gone off. Daily 8am–late; licensed.

Muses Café Beside the Museum Building, High St. Open daily till 5.30pm, this charming little spot has the best coffee in town, some reasonably priced breakfasts and lunches and tasty snacks. Try the smoked fish chowder.

T.O.A.D. (Trading On Another Dimension) Hall 502 High St, 3km from the town centre, on the Nelson side. An organic fruit-and-veg vendor serving delicious home-made ice-cream, good coffee and luscious home-baked cakes.

Kaiteriteri

Passing briefly through the famous local hop fields on either side of SH60, the beach road, 6km off the highway, heads towards the southern end of the Abel Tasman National Park and the tiny resort settlement of **KAITERITERI**, some 15km from Motueka and overlooking Tasman Bay. On your way into the settlement is a flying fox wire ride, allegedly the longest in New Zealand (daily 9am–7pm; $25). A better reason to come here is to connect up with **Kaiteriteri Kayaks** or a **water taxi**, both of which run trips up the coast into the Abel Tasman National Park, a welcome relief from the busy embarkation point in Marahau (see "Trailhead Transport" p.565, and "Arrival", p.562). You'll find both the kayaking trips and various water taxis operate from temporary shelters on either the beach or foreshore, which has pleasant views of the bay and offers a safe and easy entry point to the water.

There are few **places worth staying**, unless you bring a tent, and even fewer places to eat. One of the best for both is the *Kimi Ora Holiday and Health Resort*, a hillside complex on Martin Farm Road, signposted from the beach road (ⓣ03/527/8027, ⓕ527 8134; ❹–❻, depending on season). Set in a pine forest with views of the bay, this is a comfortable place to stay, or to indulge in the various fitness or therapy sessions they run. The *Kimi Ora Café*, in the resort's wood-lined dining room, serves healthy, fixed-menu vegetarian **lunches** and **dinners** for $30, rounded off by a range of coffees, teas and juices. Next to the beach is the *Kaiteriteri Motor Camp* (ⓣ03/527 8010, ⓕ527 8031; tent sites $10, cabins ❷–❸, bedding $5 per person) with a shop, and fish-and-chip takeaway. There's safe bathing, water sports, walking and some good views of the quiet and beautiful bay.

Marahau

About 6km further long the beach road from Kaiteriteri, **MARAHAU** is poised right at the southern entrance to the Abel Tasman National Park and is more tourist-orientated, acting as the base for many operators of tours and water taxis into the park. The proposed scheme to build a massive new hotel here will pretty much destroy any charm the place had, attracting many more visitors to the area and threatening the local eco system.

The beach road runs through the settlement before petering out at the park entrance, where a dirt track, Harvey Road, swerves left to a couple of **places to stay**, neither of which is worth more than an overnight sojourn: *The Barn Backpackers and Campground* (ⓣ03/527 8043; tent sites $10, dorms ❶, rooms ❷) offers limited camping and backpacker accommodation, plus secure parking ($4 a night), but is extremely miserable in the wet if you're under canvas. A mere minute's walk from the park entrance is *Old MacDonald's Farm* (ⓣ03/527 8288, ⓕ527 8289; tent sites $10, dorms ❶, cottages ❷, caravans ❷; day visitors $2), a large, tranquil, family-run campsite with cottages and caravans, all a slight improvement on the opposition. You share the grounds with llamas, alpacas and a host of other animals, there's secure parking ($4 a night), a well–stocked shop and gear storage, and an open-air-seating fish-and-chip shop in the summer months. Back down the beach road from the park entrance is the Marahau Valley Road, where about 200m along is *Abel Tasman B&B* (☎03/527 8181; ❹), the best and most comfortable spot close to the park, offering a friendly welcome, seriously good cooking and the only place worthy of a long visit near to the kayaking and boat operators.

The **park entrance** is marked by an unmanned DOC display shelter with an intentions book and search-and-rescue cards. Next to the centre is the only real **café** in the area, *Park Café* (Sept–May daily 8am–late; licensed), which is legendary among walkers coming out of the park at this point and serves fine, wholesome food and excellent coffee to an appreciative crowd; try the home-made cakes, particularly the blueberry crumble, or check out the blackboard for specials. From here, a long boardwalk across marshland leads into/from the national park.

Abel Tasman National Park

The **Abel Tasman National Park** covers a relatively small area, its boundaries running along the coast from Marahau, about 60km from Nelson, north up to Wainui Bay at the eastern end of Golden Bay, and inland to cover parts of Takaka Hill. Reliable road **access** extends only as far as the park entrances – a road enters the park from Pohara in the north, becomes a single-track dirt surface and then forks, one prong going to Totaranui (the safer route), the other to Awaroa. Some buses head to Totaranui but it's too dangerous in bad weather for private or hire cars that are not 4WD, so to get into the park itself you must either walk, take a boat/kayak or a plane. The main bases for forays into the coastal areas of the park are **Motueka**, **Kaiteriteri** and **Marahau** in the south, and **Golden Bay** in the north (from Takaka, see p.568). The **entrance** to the northernmost parts of the park is via **Totaranui** – little more than limited accommodation options and a lovely beach, from where water-taxi operators head back to their Marahau and Kaiteriteri bases, stopping in the bays on the way home – or you can stay at *Awaroa Lodge and Café* in the heart of the park and explore either direction in comfort. If you're kayaking you'll probably start at Marahau. However, with ever greater crowds, the kayaking companies have had to devise new trips to keep the kayaks from forming a brightly coloured traffic jam just off the park shores, so now there are many more options at either end of the park and from Kaiteriteri. On most trips you'll work your way north before either cruising or walking back; if you're tramping you'll find it doesn't make too much difference which way you go as long as you miss the tides – consult the tide tables or visitor/DOC centre staff to find out which direction gives you the most time to cross the inlets and bays. That said, many of the operators and the information centres will try to persuade you to take a water taxi to Totaranui and then walk back, after a detour to the Whariwharangi Hut and Separation Point.

Something in the water

The organism that causes **giardia** is present in much of the **water supply** of the Abel Tasman National Park and many other streams in this area. Basics, p.25, outlines precautions you should take to minimize the risk of infection. Some huts and accommodation in the park are now equipped with water purification systems but it pays to check this in advance, and ignore any claims that the water will leave you with no ill effects.

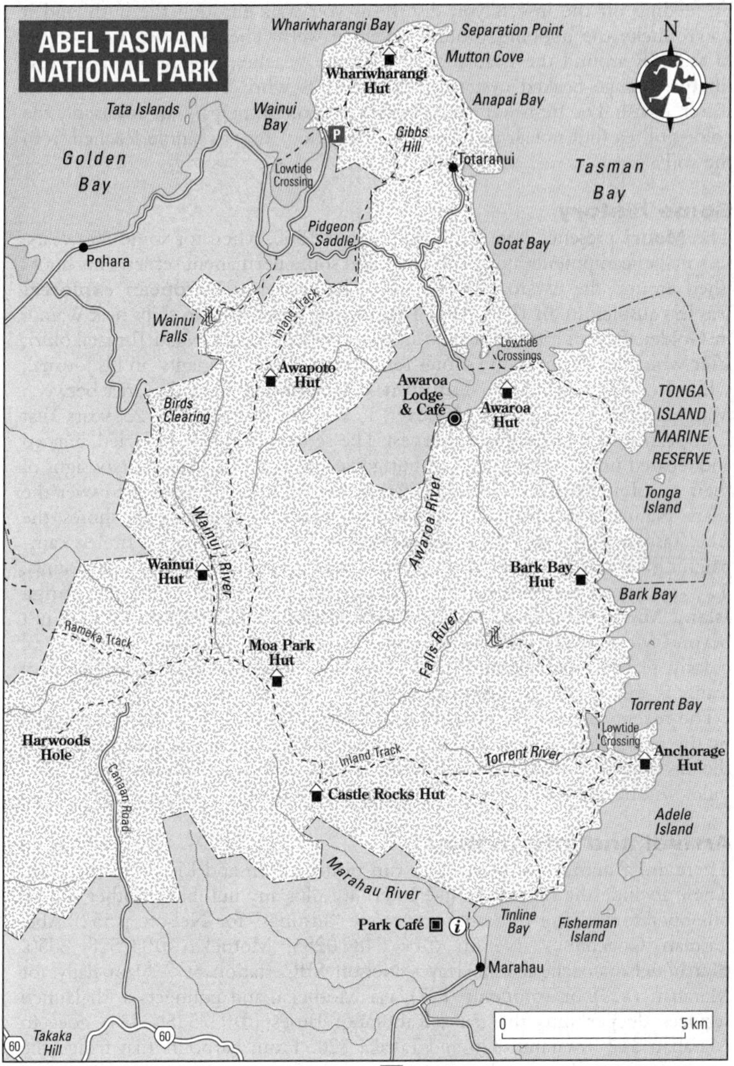

ABEL TASMAN NATIONAL PARK

With a range of habitats from sea level to 1000m, Abel Tasman is full of rich and varied **plant life**. In the damp and torpid gullies, shrubs dominate, but elsewhere several species of beech tree hold sway. Kanuka tolerates the wild and windy areas and manuka thrives on land that has been subject to repeated burnings – as this has, at the hands of both Maori and European settlers. At higher altitudes, there is a proliferation of silver and red beech mixed with rata, miro and totara. **Birds** you might encounter include tui, native pigeons, bell-birds (their presence betrayed by their distinctive call), fantails that flutter close by, feeding off the insects you disturb as you walk through the bush, and if you're lucky the bobbing, ground-dwelling weka. There's also a large variety of seabirds around the headlands and on the beaches, ranging from the distinctive orange-beaked oystercatchers to shags who dive to great depths in search of fish. The fresh waterways burbling through the park are invariably the colour of tea (but not drinkable – see box, p.560), due to tannin leached from the soil.

Some history

The **Maori** presence here dates from about 1500, when for some 500 years, seasonal encampments along this coast and some permanent settlements flourished around the Awaroa Rivermouth. The arrival of **European explorers** was less auspicious. In 1642, **Abel Tasman** anchored his two ships near Wainui in Golden Bay and lost four men in a skirmish with the Ngati Tumatakokiri, after which he departed the shores remarking "There be giants" in his journal; while in 1827, Frenchman **Dumont d'Urville** explored the area between Marahau and Torrent Bay. However, it was not for another 23 years that European settlement began in earnest. The settlers chopped, quarried, burned and cleared until nothing was left but gorse and bracken. Happily, few signs of their invasion remain and the vegetation has vigorously regenerated over the years. Named after the first European explorer to experience its shores, the Abel Tasman National Park was **gazetted** in 1942, following the tireless campaigning of one **Perrine Moncrieff**, a determined woman by all accounts. The sanctity of the park and its wildlife is preserved offshore by the **Tonga Island Marine Reserve**, created in 1993; it extends from Awaroa Head to just beyond Mosquito Bay and includes the island which is famous for its fur seal colony, seabirds and plentiful fish. The DOC Tonga Island Marine Reserve leaflet is well worth the investment of $1.

The recent increases in **visitors** have up to now been fairly easily absorbed by the park, even in summer, but if restrictions are not put in place soon then the environment of the park will suffer and the unique experience it now provides will be spoiled.

Arrival and information

There are a number of **buses** that run from Nelson and Picton to the park. These include the big names like InterCity, plus any number of other shuttle bus operators plying the same route (see "Listings" for Nelson, p.552). Abel Tasman Coachlines (Nelson ⓣ03/548 0285, Motueka ⓣ03/528 8850, ⓔatc@nelsoncoaches.co.nz) leaves Nelson SBC station at 7.20am daily for Marahau ($23) or Totoranui ($37), via Motueka, and connects with launch services deeper into the park; Kahurangi Buses (ⓣ03/525 9434) goes to Marahau $12, Totaranui $26 and Takaka $20. From harbours that fringe the park, **water taxis** can take you to remoter areas (for details, see "Trailhead Transport" on p.565).

The **visitor centres** at Nelson, Motueka and Takaka will all book boats, kayaks, track tickets (huts get booked up at least a week in advance in the summer), transport and accommodation; there are also **unmanned** DOC **display shelters** at the Marahau and Totaranui **park entrances**, with general information about the park, tide times and safety precautions – including intentions books or search-and-rescue cards you should fill in before entering and after leaving the park.

Exploring the park

Most people are keen to stick to the park's **coastline**, with its long golden beaches, clear water, spectacular outcrops and the constant temptation to snorkel in some of the idyllic bays. **Tramping** is one of the most popular ways of getting to grips with the park, and the Coastal Track, in particular, provides easy access to a wilderness area of great beauty and variety (see "The Abel Tasman Track" on p.564 for details). For those who don't wish to walk independently there are now **guided walks** through the park, stopping at comfortable accommodation along the way with all food and transport needs taken care of, at a price (see overleaf).

If you have a few days to spare in the park there are various **accommodation** options; the *Awaroa Lodge and Café* (ⓣ03/528 8758; units ❹–❼), nestled in Awaroa Bay, has a number of well-designed comfortable units and ensuites. The lodge is accessible from Takaka by car/bus or boat and short walk, by plane from Motueka and Nelson, by boat from Marahau, Kaiteriteri and Tarakohe Harbour – and, of course, on foot via the Coastal Track. There are now two boats to stay on, just off the foreshore, both offering a free ferry to their decks: the *MV Etosha* (ⓣ0800/386 742, B&B cabins single share ❷; double ❹; lunch $7-15; dinner $17), and the *Aquabackpackers* (ⓣ0800/430 744, ⓦwww.aquapackers.co.nz; ❸ half board), who work with Abel Tasman Kayaks, moored in Anchorage Bay. Each is an adequate boat conversion with space on deck to lounge around and distinctly less space below decks to sleep in, but the quiet of the park at night and sound of the lapping sea make it worthwhile. Note, however, that it can get pretty choppy out there if the wind is up.

In terms of **food** in the park, the *Awaroa Lodge and Café* (daily 7.30am–8pm) sees a good-humoured, incongruous mix of passing trampers, stopping for a snack, hard-earned drink, excellent meals and a spot by the enormous fireplace.

One of the best ways to explore the park's remoter shores is by **sea kayak**. In spite of the increasing number of operators plying their trade (during the height of the summer over one hundred kayaks may be on the water at any one time), the incredibly clear waters and possibility of being accompanied by seals or, more rarely, dolphins ensure this is still a unique experience. Most operators leave from Marahau and head up what is known as the "mad mile", after which the flotilla feel evaporates as each company goes off to do its own thing.

The two most established operators from the southern end of the park both offer excellent trips and you'll benefit from their experience in the park. Based in Marahua and situated next door to one another, they are Abel Tasman Kayaks (ⓣ03/527 8022 & 0800/527 8022, ⓔatk@kayaktours.co.nz) and Ocean River Adventure Company (ⓣ03/527 8266 & 0800/732 529**).** Not far behind them in terms of experience and the range of trips on offer are Southern Exposure Sea Kayaking, Moss Road Marahau (ⓣ03/527 8424, ⓦwww.southern-exposure.co.nz); Kaiteriteri Kayaks, Sandy Bay Road, Kaiteriteri (ⓣ03/527 8383, ⓦwww.seakayak.co.nz); The Sea Kayaking Company, 506 High St, Motueka (ⓣ03/528 7251, ⓦwww.seakayaknz.co.nz); Natural High, 52 Rutherford St, Nelson (ⓣ03/546 6936, ⓦwww.naturalhigh.co.nz); Kahu Kayaks, 147 Old Coach Rd, Mahana (ⓣ03/543 2727); and Planet Earth Adventures (ⓣ03/525 9095), running from the northern end of the national park, near Takaka. All these companies offer a similar range of one- to five-day trips, guided or freedom rental, and all do a good job at around the same price: guided trips $50 for a half day, $99 for a full day, two days from $190–240, three $150–285 and so on, while rentals average out at about $45–50 a day. They offer various kayak and walk options as well, but remember rentals only go to experienced, water-confident kayakers, so with all the equipment there is also a rigorous safety check and compulsory instruction (around $60 for one day).

Abel Tasman Enterprises (Ⓣ03/528 7801, Ⓔinfo@abeltasman.co.nz), part of which is Abel Tasman Coachlines (see "Arrival and information", p.562), offers **sightseeing** trips, scenic **cruises**, a **water taxi** service, and three- and five-day **guided walks** including stopovers at the comfortable *Awaroa Lodge*, where the excellent food re-energizes you for the next day's exertions. A five -day guided walk is $1200, three-day $800, while cruises and taxis beginning from Kaiteriteri to Tinline Bay are $5, Torrent Bay $16, Bark Bay $19, Awaroa $26 and Totaranui $30. They can also arrange multi–day kayak and walk trips.

This is also one of the best places in New Zealand to **swim with seals**, and Abel Tasman Seal Swim, Marahau Valley Road, Marahau, who also operates an extensive **water taxi** service (Ⓣ & Ⓕ03/527 8136 and Ⓣ0800/527 8136, Ⓔsealswim@ihug.co.nz; Oct–April, 8.45am & 12.30pm; 3–4hr; book at least 5 days ahead; $79), can provide all the gear as well as a safe, professional and unforgettable excursion. Swimming with seals can be a lot more fun than swimming with dolphins simply because seals are often more curious and, having greater manoeuvrability, are capable of tying a mere human in knots in no time. Underwater visibility in the area is usually crystal, and the operators try to minimize the impact on the seals by insisting that you wait for the seals to come and swim with you rather than just leaping in and splashing about among them. The water taxi and scenic trip service with a tour the full length of the park costs around $40.

The least expensive of the scenic cruise/water taxi operators is the ever expanding Aqua Taxi (Ⓣ03/527 8083 & 0800/278 282, Ⓔaquataxi@xtra.co.nz) who run their trips from Marahau to coincide with incoming buses. They are fast and efficient using a powerful Naiad that can get into the shore a lot closer than most boats, and provide a commentated scenic cruise that takes in the split apple rock ($40).

The Abel Tasman Track

Though, strictly speaking, it encompasses both the less crowded and more arduous **Inland Track** as well as the tremendously popular **Coastal Track**, the **Abel Tasman Track** generally refers just to the latter. Part of the attraction of this coastal route is that it is, along with the Queen Charlotte Walkway (see p.537), the **easiest** of New Zealand's Great Walks, and lack of fitness is no impediment: the track is clear and easy to follow, entry and exit to the beach sections clearly marked and you are never more than four hours from a hut or campsite. This ease of access means that from December to the end of February there is an endless stream of hikers heading along the route.

The **route** traverses broad golden beaches lapped by emerald waters, punctuated by granite pillars silhouetted against the horizon and zigzagging gentle climbs through valleys. As well as the two major tracks, there are a number of shorter **day walks** with access by road or from the major tracks; leaflets (50¢–$1) on all of these are available at local visitor centres.

Accommodation

The best way to do either the coastal or the inland track is to walk independently and stay in the DOC huts or at the campsites, including the *Totaranui Campground*. Owing to the track's enormous popularity, the DOC recently imposed a **booking system** with the intention of controlling numbers and stopping the trampers' race that used to occur as people shot along the track in an effort to make sure of a bunk. There's now a two-night limit on each hut and campsite throughout the year, and from October 1 to April 30 you have to pre-book by buying a Summer Season Pass (hut $14 per night, $7 rest of the year; campsite $7 per night). You can do this by post from the Motueka Visitor Centre, Wallace St, Motueka, by phone or fax (Ⓣ03/528 0005, Ⓕ03/528 6563), or by visiting one of the local visitor or DOC centres. Even with this system the large number of park campsites mean the track still gets pretty busy at the height of the summer, and it's better to walk it in early spring, mid-autumn, or perhaps even the beginning of winter, when you'll appreciate it more.

Along the **Coastal Track**, the four **DOC Great Walk huts** are spaced around four hours' walk apart, and have heating, showers and recently upgraded toilets, but no cooking facilities so you have to carry a stove; bunks are basic but comfortable, and you need a sleeping bag. The other option is camping: there are 21 designated **campsites** along the coastal route either on or near the beaches or the DOC huts (whose facilities you can use); all sites have a water supply and toilets, but it means carrying more gear and you'll need an ocean of sandfly repellent. Finally, for a treat midway along the track drop in at the *Awaroa Lodge and Café* (see p.563) for a well-deserved beer and feed while you're overnighting at the *Awaroa Hut* (see p.566).

Camping is not permitted on the **Inland Track**, but there are four back-country huts ($10) spaced no more than five hours' walk apart, and there is rarely competition for beds. Water supplies and toilets are provided, but you'll need to take a cooking stove.

Trailhead transport

The Coastal and Inland tracks share the same starting and finishing points, running between **Marahau** in the south and **Totaranui** or Wainui in the north, all of which are well served by transport.

Buses run to the Marahau or Totaranui entrances to the park from Nelson, Motueka and Takaka (see "Arrival" on p.562 for details). Several **water taxis** offer drop-off and pick-up services to and from Totaranui for trampers and casual walkers, calling at the bays en route to cater for those who don't want to walk the whole track. They all charge roughly the same (for details of operators see "Exploring the park" on p.563) as competition is stiff. **From Kaiteriteri**, Abel Tasman National Enterprises run a motorized catamaran, and Abel Tasman Water Taxis (Ⓣ03/528 7497 & 0800/423 397) operate smaller, quicker naiads to Totaranui**,** while from Marahau the choice is between the zippy Abel Tasman Seafaris Aqua Taxi or Abel Tasman Seal Swim, who both offer an excellent and speedy service.

The Coastal Track

Consult the visitor/DOC centre or a local tide table when planning your trip along the **Coastal Track** (51km; 2–5 days) because crossing the Awaroa Inlet and Torrent Bay are **tide-dependent**; there is no alternative at Awaroa and the inland diversion at Torrent Bay adds at least one hour to the walk. If you are walking into or out of the park from the north, watch the tide at Wainui Bay where you can save a bit of time. Tide times will help you decide which way you're going to do the track – if there are low tides in the afternoon you'll probably want to head south, if they're in the morning, north. Before setting off you should also arrange your transport drop-offs and pick-ups (see "Exploring the park" on p.563).

From **Marahau to Anchorage Hut** (11.5km; 4hr), the track follows a wooden causeway and crosses the Marahau estuary to the open country around

Tinline Bay before rounding a point overlooking Fisherman and Adele islands just off the coast. As the track winds in and out of gullies, the surroundings are obscured by beech forest and tall kanuka trees until you emerge into Anchorage Bay, with its hut and campsite. On the second day, **Anchorage Bay to Bark Bay Hut** (9.5km; 3hr), you have to cross Torrent Bay at low tide, before climbing out of the bay through pine trees and meandering through valleys and a gorgeous inlet before reaching the Falls Rivermouth and the Bark Bay hut, beside the Bark Bay estuary. Day three is a gentle stroll from **Bark Bay Hut to Awaroa Hut** (11.5km; 4hr), overlooking the Tonga Marine Reserve and Tonga Island. The track climbs to the Tonga Saddle before descending to the Awaroa Inlet and the hut, with a campsite alongside; *Awaroa Lodge and Café* is also within easy walking distance.

From Awaroa Hut, you must cross the Awaroa estuary (2hr either side of low tide) and head along Goat Bay and up to a lookout above Skinner Point before reaching **Totaranui** (5.5km; 1hr 30min), where there is an extensive campsite, or you can press on over and around rocky headlands as far as Mutton Cove, where the track leaves the coast and climbs to another saddle before descending to **Whariwharangi Hut** (7.5km; 2hr) and campsite. From here it's possible to take a short hike to **Separation Point**, where there is a fur seal colony and a good lookout, or to tackle the strenuous climb up **Gibbs Hill** for even better views. The last day, **from Whariwharangi Hut to Wainui** (5.5km; 1hr 30min), involves crossing Wainui Bay (2hr either side of low tide) or following the road around the bay. If you follow the road, you can also take in the short climb up to the Wainui Falls which heads off the road at the base of Wainui Bay, where the lowtide crossing reaches the western shore.

The Inland Track

The considerably less popular **Inland Track** (42km; 3–5 days) is a more strenuous walk, and should only be attempted by well-equipped and moderately fit trampers – if you fit the bill you might want to combine it with the coastal track to make a six- to seven-day loop. The route climbs from sea level to **Evans Ridge** past many granite outcrops and views of the coast: highlights include the Pigeon Saddle, the moorlands of Moa Park and the moon-like Canaan landscape; you can also link up with the Rameka Track on Takaka Hill and the Harwoods Hole track (see opposite) along the way.

Starting the walk **from Marahau** in the south, the Inland Track splits away from the Coastal Track at Tinline Bay, following a steady climb through regenerating forest to the **Castle Rocks Hut** (11.5km; 4hr 30min), which is perched near rocky outcrops and has great views of the Marahau Valley and Tasman Bay. From **Castle Rocks to Moa Park Hut** (3.5km; 2hr) is a steeper climb, followed by an undulating section over tussock. The walk from **Moa Park** to the **Awapoto Hut** (14.5km; 6–7hr) involves trekking along Evans Ridge and descending to the hut, while the last day is an easy stroll, after you've topped the **Pigeon Saddle**, to the **Wainui carpark** (10km; 3hr 30min), with a short, but worthwhile, optional detour involving climbing to the summit of **Gibbs Hill** (1hr round trip), from where you get some of the most expansive views across the park, and meet up with the select few Coastal Track walkers who had the energy to make the arduous climb from Totaranui.

Takaka Hill

From Motueka, SH60 climbs **Takaka Hill**, providing the only **road access to Golden Bay** – and glorious views of the seascape from Nelson north to

D'Urville Island. Skirting the inland border of the Abel Tasman National Park, it is possible to explore the hill's fascinating geology from either the Inland Track (see previous page) or from the highway.

The first diversion off SH60, 20km out of Motueka, is the **Ngarua Caves** (Sept–June daily 10am–4pm, guided tours on the hour; 35min; $11, cash only), reached by a short bumpy track. A celebration of tackiness, the caves contain numerous examples of stalactites and stalagmites, including some with musical accompaniments and grand illuminated formations such as the Wedding Cathedral. Tour guides also point out bones from moas and regale you with an informative commentary on the caves' history and geology.

A kilometre or so further along SH60 from the caves turn-off is the entrance to the unsealed 12-kilometre Canaan Road, at the end of which is the starting point of the forty-minute walk to **Harwoods Hole**, a huge vertical shaft 183m deep (don't get too close to the edge), and a fantastic place to explore and survey the surroundings. The walk begins in an enchanted forest landscape, then follows a dry rock-strewn riverbed through eerie country before reaching a viewpoint atop the cliff walls of Gorge Creek, where forests, coastline and sea are all laid out before you. Back on the Canaan Road, you can join the clearly signposted **Rameka Track** (5km; 3hr one way) for more punishment. This follows one of the earliest surveyed routes into the Takaka Valley, from Canaan to central Takaka, with superb views of the granite outcrops and the surrounding country. From here, SH60 twists its way across the mountain before descending in a series of steep, tight, eye-opening switchbacks that eventually straighten out as you roll down into Golden Bay.

If you get **hungry** when you go over the hill or fancy a break before attempting the switch-back descent into Golden Bay then try *Jade Cottage* (Oct–June: daily 9am–5pm, closed the rest of the year), well-signposted beside the road and offering excellent coffee, home-made cakes and snacks. From the veranda there are spectacular views to the east – on a clear day extending beyond Motueka – while inside the cottage gallery the delicate and precise bird paintings of Janet Marshal grace the café walls (prints and cards are also available).

Golden Bay

Occupying the northwestern tip of the South Island, **GOLDEN BAY** curves gracefully from the northern fringes of the Abel Tasman National Park to the encircling arm of **Farewell Spit**, all backed by the magnificence of the Kahurangi National Park. A relatively flat area hemmed in by towering mountains on three sides and with waves lapping at its exposed fourth side, its inaccessibility has kept it almost pristine. The coastline is washed by clear, sparkling water, creating excellent conditions for windsurfing, while its hinterland is home to the country's largest freshwater springs, **Waihoro pupu Springs**, as well as a number of other curious geological phenomena.

Historically, the bay was also the point where Abel Tasman struck land, guaranteeing his place in history as the first European to encounter New Zealand and the local Maori. Today's bayside communities are small, their growth still hindered by **isolation** – the road over Takaka Hill is twisting and can be treacherous, and there is no access from the West Coast Track, save for a long footslog on the Heaphy Track. This perhaps explains the air of **independence**, self-reliance and stoic forbearance and also why the bay has become so attractive to alternative lifestylers and many artists, some of whom produce work of real merit. Sunny, beautiful and full of fascinating sights, Golden Bay is well worth a few days of your time, as it was for the film crew and actors from *The Lord of the Rings*, with a number of scenes from the films using the dramatic landscape as backdrops.

Takaka and around

The small town of **TAKAKA** is situated on SH60, cradled by the sweep of the bay. East of the town and linked to it by road are **Pohara Beach**, where there's safe swimming, and Tarakohe Harbour and Wainui Bay, both providing access to the northern end of the Abel Tasman National Park (see p.560). South of Takaka, **Waihoro pupu Springs** emerge from their underground lair, while to the north yawns a considerable stretch of beautiful bay, running parallel to SH60 as it rolls into Collingwood and Farewell Spit.

Arrival and information

These days only charter flights from Nelson or Wellington land here and if you are on one of these, they should run you the 5km from the **airport** into town. Most **bus** companies drop off outside the information centre on Willow Street (see below). Local shuttle buses will get you to most of the major destinations in Golden Bay, but you can also rent cars or bikes (see "Listings", p.571).

On Willow Street, just south of the main part of town, the **visitor centre** (daily 9am–5pm; ⓣ03/525 9136, ⓦwww.nelsonNZ.com) acts as a booking centre for the national parks and tracks, and stocks a number of leaflets detailing local attractions, including a useful one on the Waihoro pupu Springs, and local walks. The **DOC office** on Commercial Street shuns public attention for the most part so you'll need to rely on the visitor centre and a good map if you're planning a back country tramp. Another useful source of information relating to the whole bay is *The G.B. Weekly*, a 50¢ newspaper containing events, places to visit, entertainment listings and general tittle-tattle.

Accommodation

Golden Bay is a popular holiday spot with both Kiwis and foreign visitors; as a result there is a lot of good quality accommodation in and around Takaka though it can be pricey.

Anatoki Lodge Motels 87 Commercial St ⓣ03/525 8047, ⓔanatoki@xtra.co.nz. Modern, fully self-contained units close to the centre of town, with great service and helpful staff. ❺–❻

Autumn Farm Lodge Turn right at the hospital sign 3km before Takaka, the lodge is 200m up on the left ⓣ03/525 9013, ⓦwww.autumnfarm.com. Very comfortable, charming gay-friendly accommodation in a six hectare plot with a laidback atmosphere; those in rooms get breakfast included. Camping $10, rooms ❶–❸

Golden Bay Lodge and Garden Tukurua, signposted off SH60 17km north of Takaka ⓣ03/525 9275. Two fully self-contained units plus two B&B rooms overlooking a lovely garden and the sea, with easy beach access. ❺–❻

Golden Bay Motel 132 Commercial St ⓣ03/525 9428, ⓕ525 8362. A pretty, well-kept little motel with off-street parking and spacious rooms. ❹

The Nook Between Takaka (9km) & Pohara (1km) on the way to the Abel Tasman Park with a pick–up service from Takaka by arrangement ⓣ03/525 8501, ⓔnook@clear.net.nz. A friendly if a touch too cosy backpackers that's too far from town for people without their own transport. The bonus is the lovely, bordering on luxurious, straw-and-plaster extension, used as two doubles or rented as a self-contained unit. Dorms ❶, doubles ❷–❹, units ❺

Rose Cottage Motel and B&B On SH60, 5km from Takaka heading towards Takaka Hill ⓣ03/525 9048, ⓕ525 9048. Three beautifully maintained motel units set in a large, lovingly tended garden, plus a homestay option, all with friendly and helpful hosts. Very good value. ❹

Sans Souci Inn Richmond Rd, Pohara Beach,

10km east ⓣ & ⓕ03/525 8663, ⓔreto@sanssouciinn.co.nz. Endearing B&B in a building reflecting the Mediterranean atmosphere of the bay, constructed of mudbricks, with sods as the roofing material, and distinctive floor tiles. Toilets are self-composting and occupy a block that effortlessly combines sanitation and horticulture. There's an excellent fixed-menu restaurant in the compound (see p.570). Breakfast costs $8–12, dinner $21–24, depending on the dish that night, remember to book. ❹–❺

Shambhala Onekaka,16km north on SH60 ⓣ03/525 8463, ⓕ525 9734. Quirky accommodation near the *Mussel Inn* (pick-up can arranged). Dorms are in the main house, or there are spacious twins and doubles rooms with good views in a separate block, with solar-heated showers and self-composting toilets. There is easy beach access so you can go out and gather your own mussels, or stay home and munch on a lentil pie or muffin. The only drawbacks are overcrowding in the summer, small kitchens and a plethora of extra charges. Prices seem flexible so it's worth haggling. Camping $15, dorms ❶, rooms ❷

The Town and around

Despite being the bay's largest settlement, the town itself is a low and architecturally barren affair where three roads, SH60 (Commercial Street as it passes through town), Motupipi Road and Meihana Street, form a triangle.

Close to the centre of town on Commercial Street, the restored old post office (1899) now houses the **Golden Bay Gallery** (Oct–April, daily 10am–4pm; May–Sept closed Sun; free) which balances art and crafts. In amongst the usual detritus are wonderful silk paintings by Sage Cox, Philly Hall's stunning water colours and some unusual, but over-priced, sculptures and clocks. The adjacent **Golden Bay Museum** (entry through the Gallery; $2) is well worth a look even if it's only for the breathtakingly detailed diorama depicting Abel Tasman's ill-fated trip to Wainui Bay in 1642. The rest of the museum houses Maori artefacts, some fascinating geological and natural history material, as well as the usual mish-mash of bits and bobs rooted out of attics or accumulated during travels abroad (usually to wars).

The **Rawhiti Caves**, reached via a ten-minute drive along Motupipi Road and over the Motupipi Bridge towards Pohara Beach and then a fifty-minute walk from the car park, were given to a national trust in 2000, and visitors now have the choice of entering and having a look at them free of charge, or paying the Kahurangi Guided Walking company an exorbitant $25 (ⓣ525 7177 pick-up from the info centre). Either way DOC have restricted the parts of the caves you can see, though it's still worth the walk to see the pendulous stalactites that hang from the caves' wide mouth, stained by the earth and rain to hues of dirty brown and brightened by the rich green of the moss that covers some of them. You can still descend partway into the caves to see the fascinating formations, including transparent stone straws full of water, a discarded billy can now encased in rock deposited from the dripping ceiling and rock pools containing perfectly round stone "marbles". If you're really lucky you might run into the original guide – who does shifts at the museum – and who, in the right mood, might give a reprise of her original tour.

Where Motupipi Road meets the Clifton Crossroads, turn right to reach the wonderful **Grove Scenic Reserve** (unrestricted access; free), a mystical place in grey-green that could have been transplanted straight from Arthurian legend, where massive rata trees sprout from odd and deformed limestone outcrops. A ten-minute walk from the car park takes you to a narrow slot between two enormous vertical cliffs where a lookout reveals the flat expanse leading to the beaches of Pohara – and the real world. On the opposite side of the Abel Tasman Drive near Three Oaks, Scott Road leads to Labyrinth Lane and after a short, well-signposted jaunt heads on to **Labyrinth Rocks Park** (daily noon–5pm; $6). This is a maze-like commercial concern with a variety of curiously-shaped limestone features and impressive mosses and trees, and a large number of plastic spiders, gnomes and dinosaurs left in curious places. The spot is well worth the entry fee, containing as it does 2km of easy tracks; a useful map is provided and there's a small canteen.

Back on the Pohara Road, heading west towards the scattered houses of Pohara Beach and Wainui Bay, about 9km from the Clifton Crossroads, you'll see signs for the unsealed 500-metre road to **Wainui Falls**. The falls themselves are a forty-minute return walk from the road, heading up through dense bush and criss-crossing the river on several bridges, with the roar of the falls growing ever louder. Nikau palms shade the banks of the river, and a curtain of spray swathes the rather lovely falls – a great place to just sit and dream.

About five minutes' drive (5km) out of Takaka on SH60 towards Collingwood is **Whaihoro pupu Springs Scenic Reserve** (unrestricted access; free), New Zealand's largest freshwater springs set in a reserve of old gold workings, regenerating forest and a vestige of mature forest. There are at least sixteen springs here, with two major vents in the main springs, one major and several minor vents at Dancing Sands (where the sands, pushed by the surging water, literally dance), and about twelve springs in the Fish Creek. The water that emerges from the main springs is cold and the visibility excellent, making for superb viewing of the rich variety of brightly coloured plants beneath the surface – which can be seen by means of a large reverse periscope on one of the boardwalks. Restricted scuba diving goes on in the springs but they are of cultural significance so DOC are trying to persuade people not to, a task not helped by the River Inn which hires out wet suits for a snorkelling/drifting river swim that begins near the falls.

Eating and entertainment

There's a surprising number of good places to **eat** in Takaka, most clustered on Commercial Street. If you're self-catering though, don't miss the Golden Salami, on a right turn after the Clifton signpost, off the Abel Tasman Drive 7km from Takaka and signposted from there about 1km, which produces a variety of delicious, totally natural salami from their own aggressively healthy Sussex beasts and some other secret ingredients. **Drinking** and music tends to be confined to the big old hotels/pubs, the *Whole Meal Café* or *Mussel Inn* some way out of town. If you are in Takaka and stuck for something to do try the atmospheric local **cinema**, Commercial St (☎03/525 8453 or *The G.B. Weekly* for programme details), where the seating includes bean bags and there are cups of tea to sip during the films.

The Big Fat Moon 1 Commercial St. All-day buffet menu (from $5) of delicious inexpensive Asian dishes from Indonesian rotis to Chinese foo-yungs, plus a more formal menu in the evenings. BYO.

The Dangerous Kitchen 48 Commercial St (☎03/525 8686 for takeaway orders). Peculiarly named though perfectly serviceable little café that specializes mostly in pizzas and good coffee. Summer daily 8am–late; winter Mon–Sat 8am–7pm, Sun 3–7pm.

Milliways 90 Commercial St. A café/wine bar (10am–late), posh restaurant using good quality ingredients but expensive.

Mussel Inn Off SH60, 16km north of Takaka. Do not miss this place – whether you want to eat, enjoy wine or ale (they brew their own), sit and read, play chess or soak up the lively atmosphere of a live band. The wooden building is adorned with local art and some clumpy but comfortable wooden furniture. You can always get a simple, fresh and wholesome meal; try a plate of the local mussels for around $10. Daily: Sept–March 11am till the last person leaves; April–Aug Thurs–Sun 5pm till the last one leaves.

River Inn 3km from Takaka centre on the road to the Pupu Springs. Not exactly salubrious but good for live bands and an edgy night out.

Sans Souci Inn see p.569. This simple restaurant has a daily set menu which can include hot smoked fish or beef fillet with spätzle (traditional

Swiss pasta) and a veggie option each night. There's also a choice of sumptuous freshly made desserts. Licensed; bookings essential and dinner starts at 7pm.

Selecta Bar 46 Commercial St. Choose a salad, an excellent gourmet pie or a thick sandwich from this wee organic grocers and finish it off with a real fruit ice-cream. Daily 9am–5pm.

Whole Meal Café In the arcade on Commercial St. Good bread, pizzas and pastries, all served with a variety of colourful and healthy salads, delicious cakes and excellent coffee. Well worth stopping in though currently the regular evening menu is always variations on the curry theme, from $14 small to $18 large. In the evenings there's sometimes live music and the building is being expanded to make more room for a venue. Daily: summer 7.30am–9pm; winter 8am–9pm. Licensed.

Listings

Airlines There are only charter flights operating into the bay.

Bike rental Quiet Revolution, 7 Commercial St (☎03/525 9555), rents out mountain bikes for $25 a day and can recommend the best routes for trips. Not open weekends.

Buses Bickleys, 98 Commercial St (☎03/525 8352), serves Collingwood and also offers a Heaphy Track service, as do Kahurangi Buses and Abel Tasman Coaches (see "Listings" for Nelson, p.552).

Car rental ID Orange, Motupipi St (☎03/525 9991), has two cars for hire.

Internet Access The Gazebo, 7 Hiawatha Lane, 5min walk from the town centre; Mon–Fri 6–10pm, Sat & Sun 2–10pm.

Paragliding Tasman Tandems operates out of Motueka (☎03/528 9283) and offers fun flights for $120.

Collingwood and around

As you might expect from somewhere that marks the end of the road for SH60, **COLLINGWOOD** is a quiet kind of a town, with one store, a couple of cafés, a friendly pub, a petrol station and a tiny museum. However, its proximity to the Heaphy Track, which traverses Kahurangi National Park (see p.575), and to the wilderness of Farewell Spit, places it firmly on the tourist circuit.

The Town

Over the years, many of the town's older wooden edifices have been burned down, leaving only a few buildings of note on Tasman Street, where the small **Collingwood Museum** (daily 9am–6pm; donation) is devoted to the history of the early settlers and the impact of gold mining on the area. The museum also contains exhibits relating to Collingwood's ambitions to be the capital of New Zealand, with plans of the proposed streets and submissions as to why this tiny community, literally at the end of the line, should be the country's principal city.

Collingwood's surroundings, however, offer endless opportunities for meandering around country galleries situated on its winding roads. About halfway between Takaka and Collingwood on SH60 is **Onekaka Arts**, a gallery containing hand-crafted jewellery and scrimshaw (whale bone carving), created by Peter Meares (☎03/525 7366 for opening times). Eight kilometres southeast of Collingwood on SH60, winding behind Para Para Beach, is Lookout Road, where you'll find **Decorator Pots** (Dec–April daily 9am–5pm), a gallery and potters' studio situated in manicured gardens with great views. The gallery section displays conservative but high-quality stoneware and porcelain. About 2km north on SH60, just after the Para Para Estuary before you enter Collingwood, are signs to **Estuary Arts** (Dec–April Wed–Sun 10am–5pm). Run by Rosie Little and Bruce Hamlin, this is one of the best pottery galleries in the bay, with brightly coloured tableware of striking and bold design, and a

Tours on and near the Spit

Collingwood is the only place where you can take a tour to **Farewell Spit**. The most famous and longest-running of the two operations is The Original Farewell Spit Safari, Tasman St (Ⓣ & Ⓕ03/524 8257, Ⓔenquiries@farewellspit.co.nz), which bounces around in characterful ex-army trucks adapted to this unique environment, as well as a bunch of specially converted newer and more plush vehicles. The pick of their trips are the **Lighthouse Safari** and the **Gannet Colony** (daily, departure times dependent on tides; 6hr 30min; $65 & $85 respectively, lunch $10). Starting in Collingwood, a bright commentary, peppered with local lore, enlivens the ride to Puponga and across the sands of the spit to the historic lighthouse at Bush End Point. During the day, you'll see vast numbers of birds, seals, fossils and the skeletons of wrecked ships, climb an enormous sand dune and visit a massive gannet colony towards the end of the spit.

Farewell Spit Nature Tours, Tasman St (Ⓣ03/524 8188, Ⓦwww.farewell-spit.co.nz), operates two tours. Their **Nature Tour** (year round; 7hr; $75, including lunch) uses a modern air-conditioned bus; they don't venture as far as the gannet colony, but do go to Pillar Point Lighthouse, where you are treated to a panoramic view of Golden Bay and Cape Farewell.

Two kilometres along the road to Wharariki Beach from Puponga is the excellent Cape Farewell Horse Treks (Ⓣ & Ⓕ03/524 8031, Ⓔhorsetrekking@xtra.co.nz), offering some of the most visually spectacular **horse riding** in the South Island – with Mount Beale on one side, views of Farewell Spit, and the Burnett Range forging away down the West Coast. Although they don't actually go onto the spit this is a good way of becoming familiar with the area. There are a broad range of well-organized trips: Pillar Point (90 min; $35); Triangle Valley (2hr; $35), Wharariki Beach (3hr; $55); overnight to Pakawau, along beaches and to Kahurangi and the lighthouse ($150); and any number of other trips from one to seven days (a 3 day trip is $450). The company provides everything you need, including a horse suited to your temperament and abilities (they have 23 beasts to choose from); these days they also offer some pretty special, out-of-the-way accommodation (see "Practicalities", p.574).

gallery of some of Rosie's evocative paintings as well as a lovely setting high on a hill overlooking the bush and parts of the bay.

Southwest of Collingwood, on the road to Rockville (1km before the Rockville Museum), and on the way to the Heaphy Track, is the turn-off for a striking natural sculpture: two plinths of limestone on either side of the road support bulbous overhangs – dubbed the **Devil's Boots** for their resemblance to two feet protruding from the ground with tree and shrubs growing on their soles. Just before the boots the road forks, and if you take the uphill prong for about 1km you'll end up at the **Te Anaroa Caves**, where informal guided tours take you over the slippery surfaces to some stunning limestone formations. Make sure your footwear is both sturdy and waterproof (Ⓣ03/524 8131, its advisable to book in advance; $15).

North to Wharariki Beach

Travelling the 29km to Farewell Spit on SH60, take a detour west to the distinctive **Wharariki Beach**. A twenty-minute walk from the car park at the road end, the beach provides a startling introduction to the rigours of the West Coast; exposed to the harsh winds and waves, Wharariki is backed by striking cliffs gouged with caves. Rock bridges and towering arches are stranded just offshore, while deep dunes have blocked rivermouths, forming briny lakes and islands where fur seals and birds have made a home. The beach is a superb place to swim, explore, watch seals in the rock pools at half-tide and lounge around. Head back towards the car park and join the northeasterly cliff path, which leads after 3km to the **Pillar Point Lighthouse**, perched on the shoulder of the spit, with far-reaching views down the West Coast and over the bay.

Farewell Spit

Farewell Spit stretches out to the very tip of the South Island, with access through Puponga Farm Park, 29km from Collingwood – although the only way you can explore the spit up close and personal is with one of the two licensed tour operators (see box opposite). The 25km-long spit is a **nature reserve** of international importance, providing a variety of habitats for birds: saltmarsh, open mudflat, freshwater and brackish lakes and bare dunes. Formed by debris sluiced out of West Coast rivers in flood and then carried by coastal currents, an uninterrupted desert of sand inches its way into the ocean and curls back towards Golden Bay, whose shores capture much of the windblown sand from the spit's exposed side.

The Farewell Spit **visitor centre and café**, 26km north of Collingwood (Sept–June daily 9am–5pm, closed July & Aug; ⓣ03/524 8454, ⓕ524 8259), is in the Puponga Farm Park, on a hill overlooking the spit. The centre has displays and some evocative photographs that recount the history of the area and the sad story of a mass whale-stranding in 1991, and has leaflets on local walking tracks. You can also enjoy the spit from a distance in the viewing room (with mounted pay binoculars), or the **café**, which offers giant muffins, cakes, good coffee, smoothies, creamy seafood soup, toasted sandwiches, other snacks and quality main meals to accompany its views.

Clustered around the base of the spit is a complex of middens over 50m wide and running for almost 1km, composed mostly of burned shell and evidencing **Maori settlement** over a period of at least 700 years. Puponga Point was the site of a defended *pa*, with the ditches and house terraces clearly visible, and at Whau Creek there are deep pits and extensive midden spilling down to the stream, indicating a *kainga*, or undefended living area. In 1846 explorer Charles Heaphy reported seeing *waka* (Maori canoes) heading to the ocean beach and down the West Coast, and in 1867 Edmund Davidson collected two *waka*, adorned with elaborate artistic designs. The spit was named by Captain Cook in 1770. The original **Farewell Spit Lighthouse** was erected in 1870, from materials carried along the spit, and trees were transplanted to the area to provide shelter for the keepers' dwellings.

The most important feature of the spit these days is the **wildlife** it supports. It's a twitcher's paradise, with over ninety **bird species** recorded, ranging from keas to spoonbills; each year thousands of waders, including the bartailed godwit, wrybill, long-billed curlew and mongolian dotteral, fly the 12,000km from Siberia to escape the fearsome Arctic winter. The spit harbours breeding colonies of Caspian terns and gannets, but you might also spot hawks, wekas and skuas, as well as large numbers of black swans. However, the spit also seems to exert a negative influence on some wildlife, as shown by the frequency with which whales beach themselves here: it appears that their navigational system is confused by the unusual shape of the coastline. If you follow one of the tracks on the spit, you might well come across the wasting carcass of a stranded pilot whale – a sobering sight amid such wild beauty.

There are some interesting, longish **walks** on the spit, restricted to the landward end away from the vehicle tracks and the far end of the sand spit. Starting from the visitor centre, the outer beach track is 2.5km and the inner beach track about 4km; both provide good views of the spit and its wading bird population and offer an undiluted experience of this rather odd landscape.

Practicalities

Buses from Nelson, Motueka and Takaka drop-off in the centre of Collingwood, near the **general store** on Tasman Street (Mon–Sat 9am–6pm), while the **petrol station** (Mon–Fri 7.20am–6pm) is on Haven Road (SH60) as you enter or leave town.

There are a few **places to stay** in town and others en route to Farewell Spit and the Kahurangi National Park. *Beachcomber Motel*, Elizabeth Street (ⓣ03/524 8499, ⓕ524 8599; ❸–❺), backs onto the river estuary with lovely views and clean, self-contained units. Also near the estuary is *Collingwood Motor Camp*, William Street, at the junction with Tasman Street (ⓣ03/524 8149; tent sites $9, cabins ❶–❸), a pretty, sheltered site just two minutes' walk from the shops and pub. One of the best homestays in Golden Bay is the *Collingwood Homestead*, just off Elizabeth Street, entry road beside the garage (ⓣ03/524 8079, ⓕ524 8979; ❸), a beautiful, 1904 colonial-style homestead with spacious comfortable rooms, excellent breakfasts and dinner by arrangement ($45 including wine). There's the chance to sit on the balcony or in the gazebo and watch the birds in the exemplary garden, but to stay you'll need to book at least a couple of weeks in advance at the height of the season. Halfway between Collingwood and Pakawau, at a stop on the Kahurangi bus route, is *The Innlet* (ⓣ03/524 8040, ⓔjhearn@xtra.co.nz; dorms ❶, rooms & self-contained cottages ❷–❹), on Waikato Inlet, which now offers a wide variety of wonderfully characterful accommodation and a series of worthwhile inexpensive guided trips to underground rivers or kayaking to nearby lakes. Walking and caving trips are $55, while river kayaking trips start at $85 and involve exploring the tidal rainforest. A little further along the same road, at a bus stop on the beach side, is *Pakawau Beach Park* (ⓣ03/524 8327, ⓕ524 8509; camping $10, 12 with power, cabins ❷–❸ & motel units ❺) under improved management and with excellent value cabins by the beach, opposite the *Old School House Café*, a shop and some sit-on kayaks for rent (1hr; $10). Still further away but well worth the effort is the romantic hideaway of *Cape Farewell Horse Treks* (see box on p.572), who have designed and built a self-contained cabin that sleeps two ($75) in regenerating bush near a babbling brook. There's no electricity, gaslight, cooking facilities or shower, just solitude and the sound of birds and running water.

The only place worth getting a **drink** in town is the *Collingwood Tavern and Bistro* (daily 10am–late), opposite the Old Post Office on Tasman Street, which is also a reasonable place to eat. Close to the pub, *Collingwood Café* serves rather dull straightforward **food** every day but undoubtedly the best place to eat in Collingwood, and one of the best in Golden Bay, is the licensed *Courthouse Café*, based in the atmospheric 1901 courthouse at the corner of Gibbs Road and Elizabeth Street (ⓣ03/524 8572 for bookings; Oct–Feb daily 8am–late; March–Sept 10am–late, closed Mon). They serve excellent coffee, good cakes and have a reasonably priced but imaginative menu on the blackboard, including pan-fried monkfish and lots of veggie options. At Pakawau Bay, on the way to Farewell Spit, *The Old School House Café Restaurant* (daily 11am–11pm; licensed) dishes up snacks (all day) and simple food in a quiet and relaxed atmosphere, concentrating on locally grown fresh veggies, fish, shellfish and lamb ($19–22).

Kahurangi National Park

The huge expanse of **Kahurangi National Park**, only designated in 1996, covers 40,000 square kilometres of the northwestern South Island; appropriately enough, its name means "treasured possession". The park enfolds the exposed western side of the Wakamarama Range, which are among the wettest mountains in the country and include the peaks of Mount Owen and Mount Arthur. A remote and beautiful place (presently with relatively few other visitors to detract from your enjoyment), the best way to appreciate its extraordinary landscape is on foot. In fact, this is the only way to get to much of the park and most people come here to walk the **tracks**, primarily the **Heaphy Track**, though its lesser-tramped cousins offer equal rewards and more solitude. The best bases for visiting the Kahurangi National Park are **Collingwood** or **Takaka**, from where buses run to the head of the Heaphy Track. **Motueka** also provides access to the Tablelands, Mount Arthur and the Leslie–Karamea Track from the Flora Saddle car park, while the Anatoki River Valley can be reached from **Takaka**.

Geologically this is an incredibly diverse area, comprised of sedimentary rocks faulted and uplifted from an ancient sea, as well as limestone and marble riddled with deep caves, bluffs, natural bridges and arches, sink holes and strange outcrops. Over half of New Zealand's native **plant species** are represented in the park, as are most of its alpine species, while the remote interior is a haven for birds and **animals**, including rare carnivorous snails and giant cave spiders.

Around 800 years ago, the area was well travelled by **Maori**, as they made their way to central westland in search of *pounamu* (greenstone) for weapons, ornaments and tools. From Aorere, they traversed the Gouland Downs, crossed the Heaphy rivermouth and headed down the coast, constantly at risk of being swept away. The first **Europeans** to arrive were the Australian sealing gangs in the 1820s, who within twenty years had almost wiped out the entire seal population. In 1856 the first **gold rush** ignited interest in the area and although it had petered out three years later, prospectors tarried on at the Aorere Gold Fields (now a reserve) and deeper into the interior. Ironically, now the area is protected it faces its greatest test as millions of **possums**, which invaded the area in the late 1960s, obliviously munch their way through the native plants and devastate the snail population.

Exploring the park

There are a number of **walking** tracks in the park, the most famous being the **Heaphy Track**, all of which offer a taste of this unusual and still relatively unknown area. **Information** on the park and all the walks and activities are available at visitor centres in Takaka, Motueka and Nelson. Local shuttle buses provide **trailhead transport**, and Abel Tasman Coachlines (Nelson SBL), Abel Tasman Coaches, Kahurangi Buses and Bickley Motors Ltd run regular services to the park (see "Listings" for Takaka, p.571, and Nelson, p.552).

Two quite arduous but rewarding and uncrowded tracks are the **Wangapeka Track** (60km; 4–5 days), usually walked from Little Wanganui, just south of Karamea on the West Coast (see p.803 for details), and the **Leslie-Karamea Track** (90km; 5–7 days; 1795m ascent), which links the Wangapeka Track with Mount Arthur and the Tablelands above Motueka. The Leslie-Karamea Track starts at the Flora Saddle car park near Motueka (see p.557) and heads south along the Leslie and Karamea rivers and through beech forest before joining the Wangapeka Track near the Luna Hut. There are seven main huts (all back country; $5–10) along the track, which is quite rough in places and should only be attempted by reasonably fit and well equipped trampers. A map of the track ($1) is available from DOC offices and visitor centres.

If you're not inclined to tramp the park on your own, then check out the guided walks organized by **Kahurangi Guided Walks** (Ⓣ & Ⓕ03/525 7177; $30–720) on the Heaphy, Mount Arthur, Wangapeka Track or in Golden Bay.

The Heaphy Track

Crossing the Kahurangi National Park from Golden Bay to Kohaihai Bluff on the West Coast (or vice versa), the **Heaphy Track** (77km; 4–6 days) is one of New Zealand's Great Walks, renowned for the beauty and diversity of landscapes it covers, taking in the confluence of the boiling Brown and Aorere rivers, broad tussock downs and forests, and emerging on the rugged West Coast. The track is named after Charles Heaphy who, with Thomas Brunner, became the first Europeans to walk the route in 1846, accompanied by their Maori guide Kehu. As with the Abel Tasman Coastal Walk, DOC have plans to limit the number of people on this track by restricting the number of hut passes and the length of time trampers can spend in them, although they have increased the number of campsites.

Access and accommodation

A **map** of the track ($1) is available from visitor centres and DOC offices, whom you should advise of your intentions – and of your safe return. Along the route, there are seven **huts** (Great Walk huts; $15), with heating, water and toilets, and ten designated **campsites** ($7–8). Before setting off, you must purchase a hut or camp **pass** from DOC offices, visitor centres, some hostels and travel agents in Nelson, Motueka, Karamea and Westport, though this does not guarantee a bunk and there is a two-night limit in each hut. It's a tough track so go well-equipped and be prepared for sudden changes of weather and a hail of sandflies. There is nowhere along the track to pick up **supplies** so you must take all provisions with you – and carry out all your rubbish.

Trailhead transport

The Heaphy Track is particularly awkward in one respect: if you leave your gear or vehicle at one end, you'll have to re-walk the track or undertake a long journey by road to the place you started. Abel Tasman Coaches (Ⓣ03/528 8850, Ⓔatc@nelsoncoaches.co.nz; $44) operates a service from Nelson and Motueka, stopping at most points along the way; Kahurangi Buses (Ⓣ0800/173 371) leave Nelson and go to Motueka, Golden Bay and the Heaphy ($42); Kiwilink (Ⓣ03/577 8332) run to the track head from Nelson ($109), Motueka, Takaka and Collingwood and will also pick up at the other end; while Bickley Motors Ltd run from Takaka to the Heaphy at 10.15am daily for $22. There's also the option of leaving your car at the Takaka airport, bussing to the head of the track and then getting flown back from Karamea to Takaka, via Collingwood, to pick up your car by either Abel Tasman Aviation (Ⓣ03/782 6617; from $90) and Tasman Bay Aviation (Ⓣ03/547 2378; $135).

The route

The Golden Bay entrance to the **eastern end** of the Heaphy Track is near **Browns Hut**, at the end of the road that runs (28km) from Collingwood past Bainham; the **West Coast entrance** is at Kohaihai Bluff, 10km north of Karamea.

If you are walking the track from east to west, the hardest day is the first, from **Browns Hut to Perry Saddle Hut** (16km; 5hr), by way of the Flanagans Corner viewpoint – at 915m, the highest point on the track. It's then a very easy walk across the Perry Saddle through tussock clearings to the valley before crossing limestone arches to **Goulands Hut** (7.5km; 2hr). From here, cross the Gouland Downs, an undulating area of flax and tussock, to **Saxon Hut** (12.5km; 3hr 30min). From Saxon Hut to **Mackay Hut** (11km; 3hr) involves crossing grassy flatlands, winding in and out of small streams as they tip over into the Heaphy River below. If you have the energy, it is worth pressing on to **Lewis Hut** (12km; 3–4hr), a haven for nikau palms – and less welcome sandflies. Next day can be a long slog to the **Kohaihai Rivermouth** (24km; 8hr), but it's more enjoyable to take your time and stop at the **Heaphy Hut** (8km; 2–3hr), near where you can explore the exciting Heaphy rivermouth: its narrow outlet funnels river water into a torrid sea, resulting in a maelstrom of sea and fresh water. The final day (16km; 5hr) is a gentle walk through forest down the coast until you reach Crayfish Point, where you can cross the beach if you are within two hours of low tide; otherwise, take the high-tide track. Once you reach Scott's Beach, you have only to climb over **Kohaihai Bluff** to find the car park on the other side – and hopefully your pre-arranged pick-up from Karamea (see p.803).

Nelson Lakes National Park and around

Around 118km southwest of Nelson, the **Nelson Lakes National Park** encompasses tranquil mountains, beech forest and mirror-like lakes, with spectacular tramping in summer and skiing in winter. The park is best known, though, for its two glacial lakes, **Rotoroa** ("long lake") and **Rotoiti** ("little lake"). Lake Rotoiti is very popular among anglers, kayakers and yachties, and is surrounded by mountains, beech forest and flax, all criss-crossed with fine walks. The vast expanse of deep blue water that is Lake Rotoroa is rather more rarefied, its enclosing mountains becoming barren and grey at its southern extremity. The park's sub-alpine rivers, lakes, forests and hills are full of bird life, but it has offered little solace to humans: Maori passed through the area and caught eels in the lakes, but the best efforts of European settlers and gold prospectors yielded meagre returns.

The main bases for forays into the park are **St Arnaud**, a tiny community on SH63, just over 100km southwest of Blenheim and 25km from Kawatiri Junction on the road between Nelson and Murchison (SH6); or **Murchison** itself, 35km further southwest, a little larger and more varied.

Once clear of Murchison, SH6 romps alongside the Buller River through the Buller Gorge to the **West Coast** town of Westport, a route covered in Chapter Twelve (see p.796). If you're heading for the **east**, you can retrace your route along SH6, then cut across to Blenheim, 162 scenic kilometres away on SH63.

St Arnaud

ST ARNAUD is a spec of a place poised on the north shore of Lake Rotoiti, which provides accommodation and food for visitors to the Nelson Lakes National Park, its population of around a hundred swelling with trampers and skiers in season. Little more than a jumble of two-storey buildings on either side of the road, the settlement has little to detain you, but if you're after some background on the region, the visitor centre (see overleaf) shows a fifteen-minute video on the Buller River and its unique ecosystem, which supports giant eels, a variety of bird life (including the endangered blue duck) and abundant brown trout. Displays in the centre provide information on Rakaihautu (who according to Maori stories was the particularly powerful chief and magician who created the lakes), as well as on the National Park and its vegetation, including manuka and kanuka trees, the leaves of which were used by Cook and other early visitors to supplement their dwindling stocks of tea, giving them their common name of tea trees.

St Arnaud practicalities

Most **shuttle buses** (Atomic, Kahurangi, Nelson Lakes Shuttles, Nelson Lakes Transport, Coast Shuttles and West Coast) drop you right in St Arnaud, but InterCity and White Star **coaches** between Nelson and Murchison drop you at Kawatiri Junction, from where you'll need to pick up a Blenheim-bound bus along SH63, or call Nelson Lakes Shuttles (Ⓣ03/521 1887; $15 oneway, with a minimum for the shuttle of $30).

The commercial hub of St Arnaud is the **service station** and **store** (daily 7.30am–6.30pm), which also acts as a post office and takeaway (closes at 6pm). The **DOC office**, on View Road overlooking Kerr Bay (Ⓣ03/521 1806, Ⓕ521 1896; Mon–Sun 8am–4.30pm), is guarded by a red Maori statue depicting Rakaihauta, creator of the lakes. The centre has copious information on the region, including walks and mountaineering around Nelson Lakes – and the exceptional caves to be explored around Mount Owen, used as a location in *Lord of the Rings* (the caves should only be explored with the co-operation of the local caving club, contact through the visitor centre); they also book hut tickets and trips, offer advice and provide intentions or search-and-rescue cards as necessary. There is also a short audio/visual display ($1) on the Nelson Lakes and Buller River (on demand). Finally there are two websites relating to the area: Ⓦwww.webnz.com/nelson/lakes and Ⓦwww.doc.govt.co.nz/Marlborough, which also have information on the Rainbow ski field.

A range of **accommodation** is available in modern wooden buildings just off the main road (SH60) at *Alpine Chalet and Lodge* (Ⓣ & Ⓕ03/521 1869, Ⓔenquiries@alpinelodge.co.nz; dorms ❶, rooms ❸–❻); facilities include a licensed restaurant, bar, café and spa pool. There are also *The Yellow House* and *St Arnaud Log Chalets*, 150m from the service station (Ⓣ & Ⓕ03/521 1887; dorms ❶, rooms ❷, chalets ❹): the former is a small hostel with doubles, twins and shared rooms, kitchen, TV and a wealth of information, while the *St Arnaud Log Chalets* are a few delightful, spacious, fully self-contained chalets next door. Around 30km out of town on SH6, near Kawatiri Junction, and signposted from the road, is *Hu ha Backpackers* (Ⓣ03/546 9413; dorms ❶, rooms ❷), an old cottage on a farm which makes a good spot for cyclists, trampers or those who just want to get away from it all; inexpensive breakfast and dinner can be ordered. Finally, there are two DOC **campsites** (Ⓣ03/521 1806; $8), both overlooking the lake, at Kerr Bay and West Bay, with kitchens, toilets and pay showers.

Aside from the rather tasteless fish and chips and **snacks** to be had at the service station takeaway (where they also sell fishing licences which might be a better option), the only other place to eat in St Arnaud is at the *Alpine Chalet and Lodge* (see above), whose licensed **restaurant** offers breakfast and dinner (daily 8–9.30am & 6.30–9pm), or you can opt for the bar/café complex on the other side of the courtyard for cheaper meals (daily 5.30–9pm) of burgers, soups, salads and grills.

Lake practicalities

Lake Rotoiti is the more accessible of the two la along a short road very close to the settlement of St A Road to Lake Rotoroa, which veers off SH6 between N just after the St Arnaud turn-off, is unsealed; near the end of **Rotoroa Ranger Station** (☎ 03/523 9369; Mon–Fri 8am–n Sat & Sun 9am–noon & 1–5pm) offers good advice and literature Nelson Lakes Shuttles (☎03/521 1887) run on demand to Mount R park, Lake Rotoroa, Kawatiri Junction, Howard Valley and Wairau Valley minimum, $20pp).

There are **water taxi** services on both lakes; minimum charges roughly equivalent to four one-way fares apply to all their services. Lake Rotoroa Water Taxis (☎03/523 9199) ply the length of the lake ($75 minimum, $25pp), giving you a chance for a good look around. Lake Rotoiti Water Taxis (☎03/521 1894) run to the head of Lake Rotoiti ($60 minimum, $15pp), and between Kerr Bay and West Bay ($32 minimum, $8pp). Alternatively, you can take a scenic cruise around Lake Rotoiti in one of the taxi vessels (1hr 30min; $60 minimum, $15pp); the company also rents out **kayaks**, canoes, row boats ($20 half day, $40 per day).

There are a few short walks by **Lake Rotoroa**, but although the lake is pretty, there is not much here apart from a few wily fish and some ridiculously expensive accommodation – the exclusive preserve of dedicated anglers and stressed-out executives. The *Lake Rotoroa Lodge*, at the northern lakeside (☎03/523 9121, Ⓕ523 9028; ⑨) and based in a 1920s building garlanded with US and New Zealand flags, is typical.

Mountain biking

There are a number of mountain-biking possibilities around the national park, including the spectacular **Rainbow Road** (1–2 days; impassable in winter) that connects St Arnaud to Hanmer Springs, 112km to the southeast. The road crosses some private land, for which keys and permission must be arranged at the DOC offices at either end. The highest point on the route is **Island Saddle** (1347m), with panoramic views of the Tarndale Lakes, Lake Tennyson

Skiing in Mount Robert and Rainbow Valley

The two skifields close to St Arnaud are very different in character. At both, the **season** usually runs from June to October, and Nelson Lakes Shuttles (☎03/521 1887), Nelson Lakes Transport (☎03/547 5912) and JJ's Ski Transport (☎03/544 7081) operate **shuttle services** out to both fields ($20 minimum, $10pp) for the duration. The **Mount Robert Skifield** (☎03/548 8336), 15km from St Arnaud, is a small ski area that remains quiet due to the ninety-minute walk to the field from the car park and the variable snow fall, though a helicopter provides lifts at weekends (on demand; $40, minimum 4; $15 for packs and skis). Downhill and cross-country skiers enjoy good powdery snow – and two lodges, which provide refreshment. Gear rental is available in St Arnaud village (☎03/521 1850), and lift passes cost $20 per day.

The much more commercial **Rainbow Valley Ski Area** (☎03/521 1861 & 0800/754 724, Ⓦsnow.co.nz/rainbow), 32km from St Arnaud, has an enormous variety of runs catering for a wide variety of skiing and snowboarding abilities, with lessons and equipment rental if needed. Access is via a toll road ($10), and the car park is very close to the lifts ($44 daily).

commodation en route, there are ... and Island Gully ($5) and a campsite ... ly and toilets ($5); be sure to boil or ... is the old 4WD track between Lakes ... some steep climbs and great views, ... **Mt Robert Road**, for the really com- ... **Road**, for the rank amateur. For more ... *a Moutain Bike Trails* ($2) leaflet in the

... ne area, with 270km of track wending its ... y huts. The lakes area also provides access ... of which – the tramp to the Angelus Hut ... are particularly recommended. These are alpin... ed with good boots, and warm and waterproof clothing, as we... nt DOC maps and leaflets, and hut tickets from the DOC office in St Arnaud. Both tracks start from the upper Mount Robert car park, which can be reached by bus with Nelson Lakes Shuttles (☎03/521 1023).

Around Lake Rotoroa

Just before the Rotoroa Bridge on Braeburn Road, close to Lake Rotoroa, is the start of a short section of the **Braeburn Track** (8km; 2hr), which heads along the western shore of the lake, passing through the dense green podocarp forest that surrounds it. The lake's eastern shore is traced by the rather overgrown **Lakeside Track** (28km; 2 days), which heads through the forest to the Sabine Rivermouth at the southern end of the lake and then scrambles up to the backcountry **Sabine Hut** ($10), where you'll have to stay overnight before heading back down.

Around Lake Rotoiti

Better walking can be had on the network of tracks that explore the edge of **Lake Rotoiti**, and then head into forests and up the surrounding hills. There are a number of **leaflets** detailing the various tracks in the area as well as the geology and wildlife, available from the DOC office in St Arnaud (50¢–$1).

Four of the best **shorter walks** are the Peninsula Nature Walk, St Arnaud Range Track, Bellbird Track and Whiskey Falls Track; you can even avoid backtracking by taking a water taxi across the lake and then walking back. The **Peninsula Walk** (2km; 1hr 30min) is a nature trail around the peninsula that divides Kerr Bay from West Bay, and makes an easy and rewarding introduction to the area. Slightly more strenuous is the **St Arnaud Range Track** (18km return; 6hr; 1650m ascent), also beginning at Kerr Bay, before climbing through beech forest, with spectacular views of the lake and mountain once you emerge from the bushline. At the car park by Kerr Bay are signs to indicate the Lakehead Track and a variety of others cut fairly recently, the best and least strenuous of which is the **Bellbird Track** (a twenty-minutes' stroll). This forms a short circle briefly joining the Honey Dew Walk (1hr) – so named because it contains a large number of beech, the hairy bark of which is coated with a clear, sweet honey – and passing the entrance to the Loop Track, that slips up and down through the bush and forest for about ten minutes. The Bellbird Track is best appreciated in the early evening when the large numbers of bellbirds and tui are particularly noisy and frisky. For more walking you can begin on the Mount Robert Road on the western shore of the lake; a 5-kilometre lakeside track leads to the **Whiskey Falls Track** (4hr return, including lakeside section). Almost always shrouded in mist and fringed by moss and hanging ferns, the falls are forty metres high and particularly grand after heavy rain.

To the Angelus Hut

The best route to the recently upgraded **Angelus Hut** (14km; 7–8hr), if the weather is fine, is by way of **Robert Ridge**, which involves walking up the face of Mount Robert to 1411m, then tracing the broad ridge, overlooking the whole area. Head southwest across the Julius Saddle, sticking to the ridge until the beautiful Angelus basin with its welcoming hut unfolds before you. The Angelus Lake is really an alpine tarn, a legacy of glaciers that retreated over 10,000 years ago, leaving the characteristic steep-sided valley walls, bluff-ringed creeks, sharp ridges and water-filled basins. From the Angelus Hut, the easiest route is southeast along the **Cascade Track** (14km; 5hr), which descends beside a stream before heading back to Lake Rotoiti, via either the Lakehead Hut on the eastern shore or the Coldwater Hut on the western shore. The longer and tougher option is to head southwest toward Mount Cedric and the Sabine Hut and then follow the **Speargrass Track** (22km; 9hr) back to the Mount Robert car park. From the Mount Robert car park, you can either walk back to St Arnaud (5km) or pre-arrange a pick-up with one of the shuttle bus services.

The Travers-Sabine Circuit

Not mentioned in the same breath as New Zealand's Great Walks (and, as a consequence, delightfully uncrowded), the **Travers-Sabine Circuit** (80km; 4–7 days) is none the less spectacular for its lowly status.

The track probes deep into remote areas of lakes, fields of tussock and 2000-metre mountains, of which the highlight is the Travers Saddle (1780m) and a deep bowl fed by a 20-metre cascade and subject to freezing conditions at any time of year. At the height of summer, the track verges are briefly emblazoned with yellow buttercups, white daisies, sundew and harebells. According to Maori legend, the area's fecundity and peppering of lakes is due to Rakaihautu, a famous chief who travelled the great mountains with his *ko* (digging stick), digging enormous holes that he filled with water and food for those that followed. The circuit requires a good level of **fitness**, though it is fairly easy to follow, with bridges over most streams. You must obtain **hut tickets** at the DOC office in St Arnaud (all the huts have been recently upgraded) before commencing the walk, as well as stocking up on food, water and the requisite **maps** – the DOC's *Sabine-Travers Circuit* ($1) leaflet is quite adequate, but the more detailed and expensive TopoMaps are also available. There are nine huts along the track and **camping** is allowed – but fires aren't, so carry a stove and fuel.

Murchison and around

MURCHISON, 35km further along SH6 from Kawatiri Junction, is a service centre for local farmers and beloved of shooting, hunting and fishing types due to its proximity to the Matakitaki and Buller rivers. Once a feasible, if no frills, base from which to explore some of the old gold workings and the Nelson Lakes, raft the Buller River (see p.790), or just tramp some of the impressive walks in the area, the town has now become, on a small scale, a travellers' haven and as a result all the services have greatly improved.

Only a few colonial hotels stand as testimony to Murchison's glory days. **Gold** was found in the Murchison district in 1862, though the workings were in remote and rugged areas and difficult to reach. Prospectors flocked to Murchison from Nelson and Collingwood, paddling up the Buller River in Maori canoes to reach the goldfields; the last gold rush was in 1915.

The town itself has a fair bit to offer the passing visitor. It's home of **Ultimate Descents**, 51 Fairfax St (ⓣ03/523 9899 & 0800 RIVERS, ⓔultimate@rivers.co.nz), who run excellent **rafting** and inflatable **kayaking** trips on the Buller, Wairoa and Karamea, from one day to five ($489–$750; see p.790); and their competition, White Water Action Rafting Tours, a smaller outfit, Main Road, Murchison, behind the Information Centre (ⓣ0800100582, ⓦwww.whitewateraction.co.nz), who offer similar trips at similar prices as well as guided bush walks, gold panning, trout fishing and canoe cruises.

Less arduous is a brief peek at the **Murchison Museum**, on Fairfax Street (daily 10am–4pm; donation requested), where the collection is spread between two adjacent buildings; if they're locked, get the key from the petrol station opposite the café. Part of the collection and archives are in the old (1911) post office with newspaper clippings, photographs and various oddities, while the rest is in a wooden, barn-like building which houses the obligatory ancient telephone exchange and, from the gold-rush era, a collection of Chinese pottery, plus opium bottles that once granted temporary oblivion to Chinese gold diggers. Other interesting parts of the collection include an antique flintlock musket from Afghanistan – and Bob Bunn's bike. Bob was a formidable pioneer, who for many years was a forward in the Murchison rugby team alongside his similarly broad-shouldered brother. He sold his last timber mill when he was 82 and died eight years later. He is remembered as "a rugged individualist and colourful personality, known for his down-to-earth philosophy of life, his strong political views, and love of cycling" (hence the bike).

Around Murchison

Murchison is surrounded by mountains and river valleys, in a district dominated by rugged escarpments, bush-clad ranges, lakes and many rivers. A good way to explore the area is by **bike** (as Bob Bunn did), which can be rented from Pedal Power, 27 Grey St, just off SH6 (ⓣ03/523 9425; $25 a day). A town information leaflet (free) details several mountain-bike trails (16–85km) and is available at the visitor centre; all routes begin and end in Murchison. If you want to try your hand at **gold-panning**, pick up the *Recreational Gold Panning* leaflet (50¢ from the visitor centre): this lists the likely places to strike it rich – Lyell Creek, Ariki Falls and the Howard Valley – and advises on technique.

The **Skyline Walk** (6km return; 2hr; leaflet from visitor centre, 50¢) makes a pleasant diversion. The route starts from the car park 500m past the bridge crossing the Matakitaki River, at the junction of SH6 and Matakitaki West Bank Road. Climbing up through the native forest to the skyline ridge above Murchison, the walk yields views of the township and the confluence of the Buller, Matakitaki, Maruia and Matiri rivers.

Practicalities

Bisected by SH6 (Waller Street or Main Road, as it passes through), everything of note in the town hugs either this main thoroughfare or Fairfax Street which meets it at a right-angle in town. **Buses** drop off outside the visitor centre on Main Road, close to the green-roofed *Midwest Café* on Fairfax Street, or in the car park of *Beechwoods* (see below for both), putting you within an easy walk of anywhere in the town. The volunteer-run **visitor centre**, Main Road

(Oct–May only, daily 10am–6pm; ⓣ & ⓕ03/523 9350), has a number of leaflets on walks and other activities in the Murchison area; they can also book bus tickets, from Atomic and Laserline, to other destinations (Intercity buses must be booked in *Beechwoods*). Like many small towns Murchison lost its bank and ATM but managed to hang on to a **post office**, on the opposite corner of Main Road (SH60) and Fairfax Street.

The *Commercial Hotel*, on the corner of Main Road and Fairfax (ⓣ03/523 9696, ⓕ523 9848; ❸–❹), is a classic Kiwi **hotel**: the basic rooms have linen and towels supplied and all guest accommodation is away from the pub, so there's no noise problem. On Hotham Street, clearly signposted about 1km from town, *Mataki Motel* (ⓣ03/523 9088; ❸) is old but clean and quiet; some units have full kitchen, others make do with a kettle and toaster. Slightly more up market is the *Penman* **motel**, 78 Fairfax St (ⓣ & ⓕ03/523 9278; ❹), or *Kiwi Park*, Fairfax St (ⓣ03/523 9248, ⓔkiwipark@xtra.co.nz; camping $8, cabins, cottages and motel units ❷–❺), which has a broad range of accommodation only 1km from the town centre. For **backpacker accommodation** try the newly built Lazy Cow, 37 Walker St (ⓣ03/523 3945, ⓔmdwright @xtra.co.nz; dorm ❶, doubles and twins ❷) which is a small comfortable hostel with a twin, double and small dorm. A kilometre east of town on SH6, the *Riverview Holiday Park* (ⓣ03/523 9315; tent sites $12, cabins ❷, tourist flats ❸, motel units ❹) is a delightful, bird–filled, shady **campsite** by the gurgling Buller River.

As for **eating**, the fixed-in-time, barn-like *Beechwoods Restaurant* (daily 6.30–9.30pm; licensed), on SH6 near the bridge over the Maitakitaki River, serves salads, burgers, snacks, fish and steaks at inflated prices. Similar, but cheaper fried food can be had at the *Midwest Cafe* (daily 7am–9.30pm) on Fairfax Street – look for the dull-green roof – a large store/cafeteria-style eatery, or the *Hampden Hotel*, corner of Fairfax and Walker streets, which has a bistro/cafe (daily 7–9pm) and a more down-to-earth bar meal menu (10am–late). For a good bistro meal head for the revamped *Commercial Hotel*, while the licensed *River Cafe* (in the Ultimate Descents Centre) does some imaginative and reasonably priced snack food (9am–6pm), as well as more substantial main meals for $15-25.

Blenheim and around

There are two ways to travel the 27km from Picton to **BLENHEIM:** either the scenic **coastal route**, which takes in the sights of old whaling stations via Port Underwood, as the road winds tightly up and down the bluffs; or the more **direct route** along SH1, which passes one or two wineries and other sights, including the small community of **Korimiko**, where a garage beside the road sells ridiculously cheap, locally smoked salmon. Just up the road and by its side, in the same town, is one of New Zealand's premier cheese factories, with a wide variety available for tasting and purchase. If travelling from the **Nelson Lakes** there is only one road to follow, the long scenic SH63 which accompanies the Wairau River as far as **Renwick** and then darts right through the centre of the wine region before penetrating Blenheim via Renwick.

Blenheim, with a population of 24,000, is a rural **service town** for all the farming and wine-growing activity on the **Wairua Plains**, where the river valleys of Awatere and Wairau rivers create rich land in the shelter of the **Richmond Range**. Like the plains it stands on, Blenheim is a well-mani-

cured, slightly sterile town, which just about makes a passable base for visiting the internationally renowned **wineries** of the **Marlborough** region.

Arrival, information and accommodation

The **train station** is on Sinclair Street, about five minutes' stroll from Seymour Square and the centre of town; **buses** also drop off just outside the station. The **airport** is 7km south of town, and flights are met by Airport Super Shuttle (☎03/572 9910; about $10). There is now a visitor centre war in the town between the information centre at 2 High St in an unmissable converted petrol station (Nov–April daily 9am–5.30pm or later depending on the number of visitors; May–Oct Mon–Fri 9am–5.30pm, Sat & Sun 9am–2pm; ☎03/578 9904, ©blm_info@clear.net.nz) and the Railway Station, a recently converted centre run by Destination Marlborough. The former is more likely to give you useful information while the latter will try to sell you something. In the old petrol station you can get a large number of useful leaflets, including maps and details of the wineries and art and craft galleries in the area, and it has well-informed, helpful staff and a film processing service.

Marlborough festivals

If Blenheim ever really springs into life it is on the back of the wine region upon which it relies so heavily. The second Saturday in February can usually be counted on as an up-beat time, when 10,000 people flock into town for the annual **Marlborough Wine and Food Festival** ($32, includes a glass for slurping, noon–8pm). The festival takes the form of a vast field full of tents offering local wines and food for purchase, with live music and general revelry; in the week leading up to the festival, Blenheim is thronged with people meandering between arts and crafts demonstrations, exhibitions, markets and special events.

Deluxe Travel Line run **buses** ($6) to the festival site from the town and the airport, as well as from Picton ($14), while The Suburban Bus Company run day-tours from Nelson ($40). There are also shuttle services from Renwick and Spring Creek. The Interislander and Topcat ferry companies also offer good excursion rates at festival time.

Another festival with a culinary flavour – and some would say a little less pretension – at this time of year is the **Blues, Brews and BBQ Festival** (first Sat in Feb) which resides at the Blenheim A&P Showground. It's a combination of musicians and brewers parading their wares from all over the country, mixed in a heady cocktail with some good old-fashioned kiwi snags, kebabs and burgers, as well as some more adventurous fare. Well worth a look if you're in the party mood.

Accommodation

Blenheim and the wine region surrounding it attract gourmet travellers, and they are catered for by **luxury** homestays and **B&Bs** (out of town near the wineries), as well as a stunning **hotel** in town. There are, however, a handful of backpackers in Blenheim and Renwick.

Blenheim

The Grapevine Backpackers 29 Park Terrace ⓣ03/578 6062. In the rather unusual setting of an old maternity home on the banks of the Opawa River, 500m from the centre of town, with free bikes and a friendly welcome. Dorms ❶, rooms ❷

Hotel D'Urville 52 Queen St ⓣ03/577 9945, ⓔhoteldurville@clear.net.nz. This former bank right in the centre of town has been turned into a world-class, highly individual hotel and restaurant, with each room thematically and colourfully decorated. The best, and some say the only, place to stay in town and a good place to eat and party. ❽–❾

Koanui Backpackers 33 Main St ⓣ & ⓕ03/578 7487. A short walk from the visitor centre, this small but cheery hostel has recently been much improved. Dorms ❶, rooms ❷

The Marlborough Hotel 20 Nelson St ⓣ03/577 7333, ⓦwww.the-marlborough.co.nz. Modern, luxury accommodation with Mediterranean decor that somehow fails to capture the spirit, with two restaurants, a bar and large airy rooms. ❻

The wine region

Charmwood Farmstay Cnr Murrays Rd & Rapaura Rd ⓣ03/570 5409, ⓕ574 5110. This beef farm is a homely, welcoming place to stay, with large rooms and hearty breakfasts of home-grown produce. ❺

Cranbrook Cottage Bottom of Giffords Rd, off Rapaura Rd, about 9km from town ⓣ03/572 8606, ⓕ572 8707. Handy for the wineries, this superb self-contained picture-book cottage has the added bonus of breakfast delivered to your door from the main house. Romantic and quiet, it's almost too good. ❻–❼

Old Saint Mary's Convent Rapaura Rd, close to the junction with Hammerich's Rd ⓣ & ⓕ03/570 5700, ⓔold.st/marys@convent.co.nz. A delightful and stylish, wood-dominated historic house with individually decorated rooms, a billiard room, library and charming Dutch hosts. ❽

Uno Piu 75 Murphys Rd ⓣ & ⓕ03/578 2235, ⓔunopiu@iname.com. Run by Gino, an ultra-friendly, former Italian-restaurant owner, who makes this homestay magical. It's hard to imagine being better looked after anywhere else in the country: the food is great and the accommodation comfortable. You'll have to book in advance. ❼ **Watson's Way Backpackers** 56 High St, Renwick Ⓣ & Ⓕ03/572 8228. A very comfortable spot in the shade of large trees in a wonderful garden, with a public tennis court over the fence, snug rooms, two en-suite doubles, easy access to the wineries, free bikes, a safari bath, barbecue and very helpful owners who can't do enough for you. Tents $10, dorms ❶, rooms ❷

The Town

Blenheim is pretty much devoid of either tourist attractions or charm and most people pass through quickly or use it as a base from which to visit the wineries, even though Renwick is more convenient. The town retains few of its early buildings, but a stroll following the route in the *Sideways and Byways* leaflet from the visitor centre unearths some vestiges. In the centre of the town is pretty **Seymour Square** with its flowerbeds and distinctive stone clock tower, a popular lunch spot in fine weather and a useful landmark. About ten minutes' walk north from Seymour Square across Nelson Street (SH6) is **Pollard Park** (7am–dusk, main entrance on Parker St), a charming park area with rose gardens, rhododendrons, native rock garden and ponds, as well as a number of tennis courts, a nine-hole golf course and croquet green catering to more active pursuits.

Some 2.5km south of the town centre, off New Renwick Road, is **Brayshaw Park** (Sat 10am–4pm, Sun 10am–1pm; $2 for museum), a lacklustre reconstruction of an early settlers' community, with many of the historic buildings moved brick by brick from their original sites. The open-air museum also has a formidable collection of vintage farm machinery and vehicles, plus various accoutrements of pioneering life, including an array of textiles and an audio visual display to ram home the point. At the opposite end of town (north), on SH1, is a small 1860s **Cobb Cottage** (Sat 10am–4pm, Sun 1–4pm; donation requested), which has been restored to house yet more displays on the lives of early settlers.

The wineries

Most of the wineries of note are at the other end of SH6 from Blenheim, dotted around **Renwick** – a small, unremarkable town 10km west which has a decent brewery – or strung along the highway heading to Nelson. A couple more vineyards are out on a limb on SH1 between Blenheim and Picton and the remainder tend to be on or adjacent to the southwestern end of Rapaura Road. The region, sheltered by the protective hills of the Richmond Range, records approximately 2400 hours of grape-ripening sunshine a year and is famous for its Sauvignon Blanc, but also produces good Chardonnay, a high-quality Methode Champenoise and some good reds. The area is famous these days too for producing some golden, light and delicious olive oil. All the vineyards are set up for visitors with **tastings** (either free or for a small charge, which is often deducted from any subsequent purchases), cellar-door sales, gardens and **restaurants** where you can relax and enjoy some excellent food. All will ship cases overseas – a popular practice is to accumulate bottles from various wineries, filling a case and then arranging shipment at the last winery you visit, but it's not cheap. In recent years the area has been the centre of attention for wine writers, TV programmes and all manner of hype and as a result it's less friendly than it once was and a good deal more expensive, with many of the winery cafés and restaurants being leased from the vineyards by people who produce food of vastly varying quality. A lot of vineyard owners have also courted infamy by embarking on wholesale trees

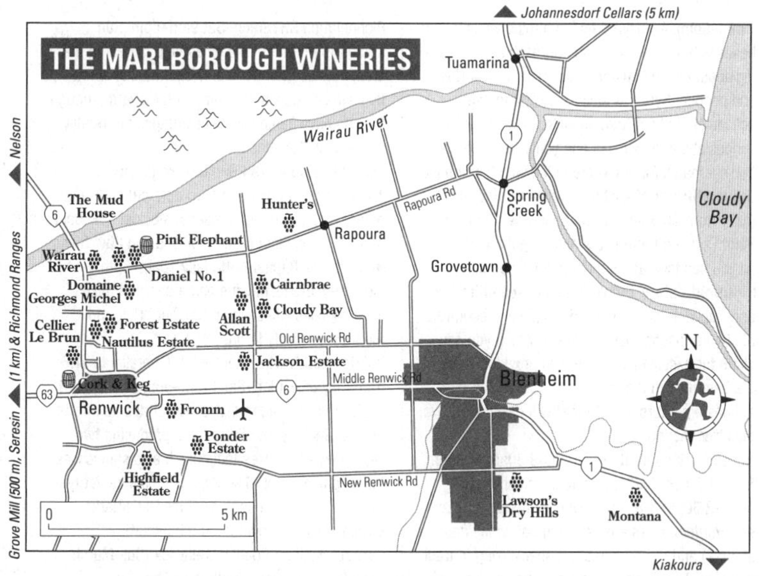

clearance – creating a flat dull landscape of just vines – while others are unpopular for being wealthy new arrivals in the area since the wine boom. Despite the internal politics, or perhaps because of it, this is an enthralling area to find out about, buy or just drink wine and the excellent restaurants that do exist make up for the awful ones.

Maps and descriptions of the wineries are available at the visitor centre in Blenheim (including the snazzy *Wines of Marlborough Map*; $2), but don't be tempted to cram too many into a day; most are more suited to leisurely vineyard tastings than whistle-stop tours. The main transport to the wineries is with **organized tours**, which may also appeal to drivers keen to avoid the pitfalls of too many sips. **Rental bikes** are also a possibility (see "Listings", p.590, for details of both), though the wineries are fairly spread out; so the people renting out bikes have got used to picking them up when the original rider's been too appreciative to cycle home. If wine's not your bag try the **Art and Craft Trail** leaflet from the visitor centre (free) – it's not on a par with Nelson but will kill an afternoon – or alternatively you can visit the local fruit growers or one of the two breweries.

Cellier Le Brun Terrace Road, on the outskirts of Renwick (daily 9am–5pm). Producer of extremely high-quality Daniel Le Brun Methode Champenoise offers free non-vintage tastings, reasonably priced bottles and a small café full of simple but wholesome food.

Cairnbrae Jackson's Rd (daily 9am–5pm). First vintage in 1992, now highly respected and still at reasonable prices.

Cloudy Bay Jacksons Rd (daily 10am–4.30pm). An internationally famous winery offering free tastings and tours around the vineyard.

Daniel No1 Rapaura Rd (daily 10am–4pm, tastings free). Daniel Le Brun has bought another vineyard and is once again making the best Methode Champenoise in the area; it may be pricey but it's worth it.

Domaine Georges Michel Vintage Lane, off Rapaura Rd (daily: Oct–March 9.30am–5pm, April–Sept 10am–4pm). A heavy French influence ensuring lime crisp Sav' Blanc and some sharp Chardonnay.

Fromm Godfrey Rd, SH6 nr Renwick (Mid-De
Feb Tues–Sat 11am–5pm, otherwise S

11am–5pm). A vineyard that is turning winemakers heads with a very hands-on approach and producing about ninety percent red: excellent Pinot Noir, and peppery Syrah as well as a Riesling with echoes of the best German efforts. Visit if you're serious about the subject and you'll taste a product that's a match for anywhere in the world, at a price.

Grove Mill Cnr of Waihopai Valley Rd and SH63 (daily from 10.30am–5pm), good Sav' Blanc and Pinot Gris and there is a small art gallery attached so you can look at something while you sip.

Highfield Estate Brookby Rd, between Blenheim and Renwick (daily 10am–5pm). Easily recognizable by its Tuscan-inspired tower, which you can climb for excellent views. It also provides some of the best food in the region, with tapas and antipasto platters for $25 that will easily feed two, plus free tastings.

Hunter's Rapaura Rd (Mon–Sat 9.30am–4.30pm, Sun 11.30am–3.30pm, restaurant daily noon–2.30pm & 6–9pm). One of the bigger players, *Hunters* offers a broad range of wines (tastings $2) and a fine restaurant specializing in traditional haute cuisine, leavened by Italian snacks such as antipasto and focaccia.

Johannesdorf Cellars Koromiko, 20km north of Blenheim on SH1 (Tues–Fri 10am–4.30pm, Sat & Sun 11am–4.30pm). Famous for its historic underground cellars carved out of the face of the hill (30min tours) and its good-quality cellar door tastings (free) and sales.

Lawson's Dry Hills Alabama Rd, southeast of Blenheim on the way to SH1 (daily 10am–5pm). A relaxed vineyard offering free tastings all year round and provider of the wine for Kaikoura Winery (see p.594). They specialize in Gewürztraminer and Sav' Blanc and have a very good restaurant.

Montana Marlborough Winery 5km south of Blenheim on SH1 (Mon–Sat 9am–5pm, Sun 11am–4pm). One of the oldest and largest in the area, now operating a highly commercial operation, which takes away some of the charm, though they do have some excellent vintages not readily available in the shops.

The Mud House 193 Rapaura Rd (daily 10am–4pm). A mixture of two different vineyards output plus a café and preserve stockist. The best of the wine is Pinot Noir, Pinot Gris and Sav' Blanc.

Nautilus 12 Rapaura Rd (daily 10am–5pm, tastings free). Excellent wine and a board of mixed local cheeses will soak up the Pinot Noir and Merlot very nicely for just $10.

Ponder Estate New Renwick Rd, parallel to SH6 (Oct–May only, Mon–Sat 11am–5pm). A comparatively small operation that concentrates its efforts on pressing superb olive oil and producing two very good wines (free tastings). It also showcases the oil paintings of Mike Ponder, which depict typical New Zealand scenes, with his trademark splash of red somewhere in the picture.

Seresin Bedford Road, nr Renwick (Oct–March daily 10am–4.30pm; April–Sept Mon–Fri 10am–4.30pm). The passion of an NZ-born photographer based in the UK who wants to make the vineyard organic. Despite the emphasis on "design" they make some gentle Pinot Gris and some lovely Reserve Chardonnay.

Wairau River Wines Rapaura Rd (daily 10am–5pm). At the foot of the Richmond Range, this splendid rammed earth and rimu timber construction by the river deals with the wine from three wineries, *Wairau River*, *Shingle Peak* and *Foxes Island*. They offer free tastings and very good quality lunches and snacks, including spicy Thai-style mussels and Manuka smoked salmon salad.

The breweries

If at any point you get turned-off by the wineries and all the hot air that circulates about them then a truly refreshing alternative can be found in either of the two quite wonderful breweries in the area: both offer tastings and brewery door sales.

Cork and Keg Inkerman St, Renwick (daily 11am–late). Comfortable English-style pub that brews its own beer and cider and serves inexpensive bar meals, including OK pork pies. The beer has got better over the years and they now make ...ellent natural brews, including dark, ... English hurricane and some ... an ex-merchant-navy ... stone hearth and tra- ...ts and dominoes, plus fun BYO curry nights.

Pink Elephant Opposite Vintage Lane on Rapaura Rd (Wed–Sun 11am–5pm). This inelegant brewery is where another ex-Englishman really does the business with malt, sugars and hops. Using traditional brewing techniques and a lively sense of humour that extends to the names of the beers, Roger Pink makes some of the best beer in New Zealand. Well worth a visit.

The Richmond Range

Twenty-six kilometres southwest of Blenheim, the **Richmond Range** of mountains is well supplied with **walks** and Scenic Recreation Areas. The DOC leaflets *Central Marlborough Recreation Areas* (50¢ from the visitor centre) and *Mount Richmond Route Guide* ($1) are useful guides to the facilities and trails. For further information you can also try the DOC Field Centre in Renwick High Street (Mon–Fri 9am–12.30pm & 1.30–5pm).

Mount Richmond itself is 1760m high, with expansive views from its summit, taking in the entire Wairau Valley, the Kaikoura and St Arnaud ranges. Easily accessible from the Top Valley and Timms Creek routes, it's possible to tackle the summit on a day-trip from the wineries. The **Top Valley route** (7.5km; 3hr 30min one way) is ideal for a single-minded assault on the **summit**, whereas **Timms Creek** (10km; 4hr 30min) provides access to the backcountry **Mount Richmond Hut** ($5) and longer, more ambitious tramps into the park. Both routes **start** from the **Northbank Road** (16km from Blenheim on SH6) and, if you don't have your own car, you'll need to arrange **drop-off** and **pick-up** with a local shuttle company, such as Deluxe Travel Line (☎03/578 5467), or talk to the visitor centre in Blenheim.

Of numerous other walks in the area, the **Wakamarina Track** (details in the DOC's *Wakamarina Track* leaflet, 50¢) is a useful short cut for trampers and mountain bikers, crossing the Richmond Range from the Wairau Valley to the Wakamarina Valley near Havelock. There are three backcountry **huts** along the track ($5), which is best walked or ridden from south to north: trampers should allow two days to cover the 12-kilometre track; bikers should be able to manage it in a day.

Eating, drinking and entertainment

It used to be possible to do a lot of eating and drinking quite painlessly at the **wineries**, but since many of them now lease out their food operations they're not as reliable as of old (see winery listings, pp.587–8). Blenheim itself has a few restaurants worth exploring, although in some cases they overcharge due to the proximity of the grape growers. **Entertainment listings** can be found in the Friday edition of the daily *Marlborough Express* (70¢).

Bacchus 3 Main St. Long gone are the cowboy boots and chilli burgers, replaced by a suave restaurant serving good quality kiwi favourites with a European touch. Dinner only from 6pm, daily and licensed.

Elbow Room 2 Scott St. An absolute delight and real favourite with locals and travellers alike. You can have stonking coffee, delicious cakes and some finely presented light meals. Licensed, daily 9.30am to late.

First Lane Café Deli 1c Main St. Simple, wholesome and home-made food with good coffee and lots of veggie options. Cheap, BYO and with a good choice of deli food if you haven't time to stop. Mon–Fri 8am–5pm, Sat 9am–2pm.

Whitehaven Restaurant and Wine Bar 1 Dodson St ☎03/577 6634. Stylish mid-range restaurant and wine tasting cellar, specializing in fresh, high-quality New Zealand produce – simple lamb, steak and fish dishes, rounded off with rich desserts and excellent wines – served in a comfortable and atmospheric building. Daily 11.30am–3pm, 6–9pm, or 10am–5pm for tastings.

Hotel D'Urville 52 Queen St. Classy and lively restaurant, with a separate wine bar, that has a Cajun and Mediterranean bent. Try Marlborough mussels steamed in white wine, black bean, tomato and garlic broth, d'Urville Chowder, or gravadlax of salmon, all for around $16. Breakfast, lunch & dinner.

Paddy Barry's Irish Pub 51 Scott St. An unassuming exterior hides the dark wood and lively atmosphere of a popular local boozer, with a Guinness pump to justify the name and reasonably priced bar snacks of pies, hotpots, salads, platters and burgers ($7–20). Occasional live music and regular dedicated drinking at weekends.

Paysanne 1st floor, The Forum, High St. A stylish

café/wine bar with views of the shopping locals. Serves good cakes and coffee during the day and some excellent main meals from $16, including very passable pizza. Occasional live music in the evening but essentially a place to chill.

Peppercorns 73 Queen St. Small deli cum eatery where they serve the best gourmet pies in town as well as some tasty paninis, calzone, quiches and coffee.

Redwood Bakkerij 75 Cleghorn St & 69 Queen St. Odd name, great bread and pastries and their own very distinctive and reasonably priced ice cream. Mon–Fri 8.30am–4.30pm, Sat 9am–1pm.

Rocco's 5 Dodson St ⓣ03/578 6940. The undoubted pick of the bunch under new management and keeping the standards unfeasibly high. An authentic and enjoyable Italian restaurant, which makes its own fresh pasta daily. For a blow-out, order the awesome chicken Kiev alla Rocco – chicken breast filled with ham, garlic butter and cheese, all wrapped in a veal schnitzel. Daily, evenings only, from 5.30pm. Licensed.

Tuscanny's 36 Scott St. A spacious and airy bar with live music every two weeks ranging from jazz to rock. The food is unpretentious but filling and has no Tuscan influences, the name came from the colour the decorators painted the bar.

Listings

Airlines Soundsair (ⓣ04/388 2594) operates daily scheduled flights to Wellington.

Airport bus Airport Super Shuttle ⓣ03/578 9910.

AA (Automobile Association) 23 Maxwell Rd ⓣ03/578 3399.

Bike rental Blenheim Hire Centre, Redwood St (ⓣ03/578 1111), and Spokemans Cycles, Queen St (ⓣ03/578 0433), both charge around $30 a day.

Car rental Hertz ⓣ03/578 0402; Rent-a-dent ⓣ03/577 8347.

Cinema The Cinema 3 Kinross St (ⓣ03/577 5559), next to the swimming complex.

Medical treatment Medical Centre, 24 George St (ⓣ03/578 2174), about 100m from junction with Queen St.

Post office Central post office, cnr Scott St & Main St (Mon–Fri 9am–5pm, Sat 9am–1pm).

Taxis Blenheim Taxis ⓣ03/578 0225; Red Band Taxis ⓣ03/577 2072.

Tours De Luxe Travel Line (ⓣ03/578 5467, ⓦwww.deluxetravel.co.nz) does wine tours for around $45; Highlight Tours (ⓣ03/578 9904) plies the wine and beer trails, and will arrange gardens, arts and crafts itineraries on demand; Marlborough Travel Centre (ⓣ03/577 9997, ⓦwww.marlborough.co.nz) offers a number of day-trips and cruises ($45–80) in the Sounds, the surrounding hills or just to the wineries, as well as taking onward travel bookings; and Molesworth Backcountry Tours (ⓣ03/575 7525 & 0800/104 532) does wine trails and nature trips, including a trek up to Molesworth and multi-day trips on to Hanmer (from $45–$375).

Trains The travel centre (ⓣ03/577 8811) in the station has a booking office for onward travel or excursions, as does the visitor centre.

Kaikoura and around

State Highway 1 ploughs south from Blenheim to Kaikoura, with the spectacular coast on one side and the brooding Seaward Kaikoura Range on the other. Not long after you pass through the small community of **Clarence**, about 25km from Kaikoura, is the **Ohau Point Seal Colony**, the largest on the South Island and a popular stopping point. Although you can see the seals from the road, a signposted lay-by and designated lookout points beside the road and down the steps provide safer viewing. The Mangmanu Beach on the way into Kaikoura offers excellent **surfing** for advanced and experienced boarders only, while the beach opposite the *Peketa Camp Ground*, 7km south of town, has good surfing for those not quite so adept.

KAIKOURA, perched on the east coast almost midway between Blenheim (129km away) and Christchurch (180km south), is famous for its whalewatch and swimming with dolphins, but it is also a good spot for sea kayaking, birdwatching, shark experiences and tramping on the peninsula and in the **Kaikoura Ranges**, as well as the underrated pleasures of swimming with seals.

If you happen to be in the area in the **winter**, the newest and one of the most diverse of New Zealand's skiing areas at **Mount Lyford** is worth investigating.

Kaikoura was named by an ancient **Maori** explorer who stopped to eat crayfish and found it so good he called the place *kai* (food) *koura* (crayfish). Maori legend also accounts for the extraordinary coastline around Kaikoura. A young deity, Marokura, was given the job of finishing the region: first he built the Kaikoura peninsula and a second smaller peninsula (Haumuri Bluff), then he set about creating the huge troughs in the sea between the two peninsulas, where the cold waters of the south would mix with the warm waters of the north and east. Tuterakiwhanoa (the god), realizing the depth of Marokura's accomplishment, said that the place would be a gift (*koha*) to all those who see its hidden beauty – and it is still known to local Maori as Te Koha O Marokura.

The first **Europeans** to settle in the area were whalers, followed relatively

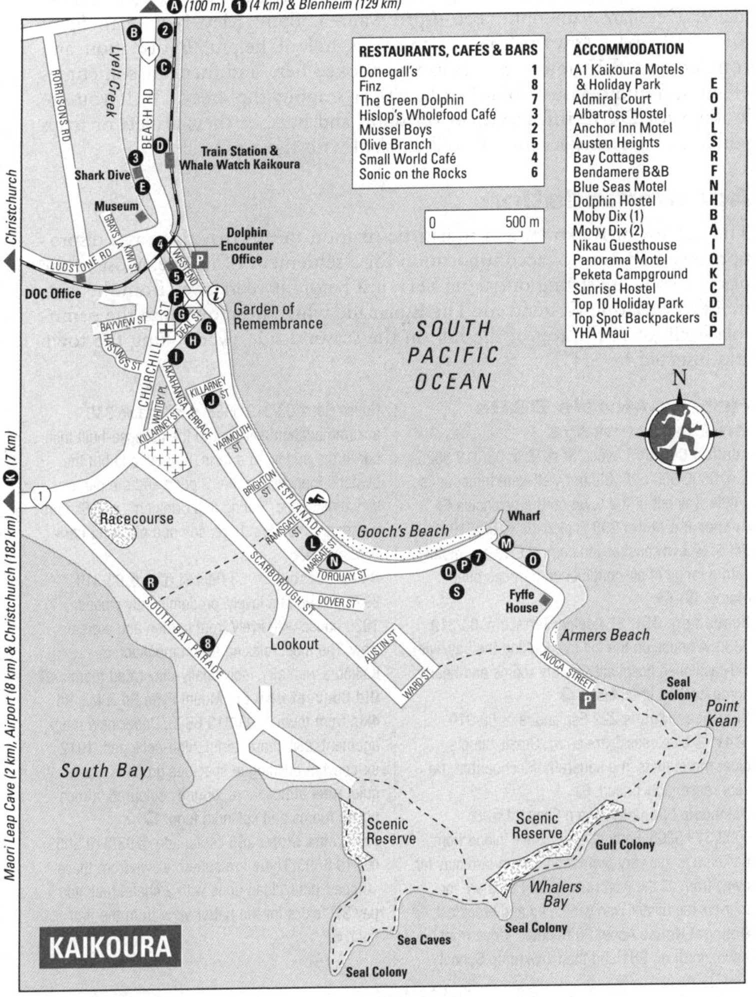

quickly by farmers. The trials and tribulations of their existence are recorded in the Kaikoura Museum and the more evocative Fyffe House. Recent history has been kind to the town, the Maori-owned whalewatch and various tourist spin-offs having brought relative prosperity which continues to grow.

Arrival and information

All the **buses** and shuttle services drop off on Westend Parade, in the town car park near the visitor centre. The Trans Coastal **train** between Picton and Christchurch arrives at the station on Whaleway Station Road, while flights land at the grass Peketa **airfield**, about 8km from the centre of town and served by Kaikoura Taxis (Ⓣ03/319 6214; $10). Most places in town are within walking distance, though as the town now spreads out along SH1 you may find a bike or taxi useful when you're weary.

The large **visitor centre**, a log cabin–like construction on Westend Parade (daily: Dec–Jan 9am–6pm; Feb–April 9am–5.30pm; May–Nov 9am–5pm; Ⓣ03/319 5641, Ⓦwww.kaikoura.co.nz), is full of helpful information and competent staff. Various activities can be booked here, and there are sometimes video and audio visual/multi-media displays about the area ($3). If you are looking for **DOC information** on walks and huts, or their leaflets or maps you'll find the visitor centre is well-stocked with those as well.

Accommodation

The success of Kaikoura as a tourist destination means that there is a disproportionate amount of accommodation for a settlement of its size. Most of the places to stay are strung out along SH1, just before it veers away from the centre of town, along Westend and The Esplanade which head out onto the peninsula itself, or at the top of the hill on the seaward side overlooking the town and bisected by SH1.

Hotels, Motels B&Bs and homestays

Admiral Court 16 Avoca St Ⓣ & Ⓕ03/319 5525 & Ⓣ0800/555 525. Old but well-kept motel units a little way out of the town on the peninsula. ❺

Anchor Inn Motel 208 Esplanade Ⓣ03/319 5426, Ⓦwww.anchor-inn.co.nz. Luxurious motel with a range of air-conditioned purpose built rooms. ❻–❽

Bendamere B&B 37 Adelphi Terrace Ⓣ03/319 5830. A house on the hill overlooking the bay, with old-fashioned hospitality, comfy rooms and hearty home-cooked breakfasts. ❹

Blue Seas Motels 222 Esplanade Ⓣ03/319 5441, Ⓔblue.seas@xtra.co.nz. Small, simple, older motel units in a square horseshoe that are very reasonably priced. ❹

Dillondale Farmstay Stag'n'Spey Rd Ⓣ & Ⓕ03/319 5205. Forty minutes' drive inland from Kaikoura is this very professionally run farmstay far away from all the world's worries. Rates are for four-course dinner with wine, bed and breakfast. ❼

Donegal House About 20 minutes' drive from town, north on SH1 and then 1.5km up School House Rd Ⓣ03/319 5083. Comfortable B&B accommodation adjacent to the purpose-built Irish bar in the middle of a farm. Sounds odd but the owner's friendly, the food's good and the bar is welcoming (see "Eating and drinking", p.596). Late nights are the norm here, so not a place for early bedtimes. ❺

Nikau Guesthouse 53 Deal St Ⓣ & Ⓕ03/319 6973. Based in a lovely, predominantly wooden, 1925 house with lively front garden and a great view. The most relaxing accommodation in Kaikoura with airy, individually-decorated rooms. ❺

Old Convent B&B Cnr Mount Fyffe Rd & Mill Rd, 4km from town Ⓣ03/319 6603. Under new management, this characterful, high-ceilinged, 1912 ex-convent building in spacious grounds has a quiet rural atmosphere, brightly coloured, atmospheric rooms and splendid food. ❼

Panorama Motel 266 Esplanade Ⓣ03/319 5053, Ⓕ319 6605. There are superb views from these stripped-pine, clean units with a chalet feel; you'll pay $10 extra for the better view from the first floor. ❺

Hostels, campsites and motor parks

A1 Kaikoura Holiday Park 11 Beach Rd ⓣ & ⓕ03/319 5999, ⓔkaimotel@voyager.nz. Close to the bridge and the train station, this motor park offers a variety of accommodation from motel units through five different types of cabin, to backpacker bunks and campsites, all on a smart site that backs onto the river. Tent sites $10, tourist cabins ❷, tourist flats ❸, motels ❹

Alabatross Hostel 1 Toruquay St ⓣ03/319 6090. A friendly, spacious converted post office and telephone exchange with a small kitchen and an exceptional Turkish-style dorm, a smokers room and BBQ. Dorms ❶, rooms ❷

Dolphin Lodge Hostel 15 Deal St ⓣ03/319 5842, ⓔdolphinlodge@xtra.co.nz. Boutique hostel with lovely gardens overlooking the sea and pleasant little rooms. Dorms ❶, twins and doubles ❷

Bay Cottages 29 South Parade ⓣ03/319 5506, ⓔbaycottages@xtra.co.nz. The best accommodation in the area: five purpose-built, well-equipped, self-contained units in a quiet spot at a silly price. The owner is exceptionally friendly and takes guests out crayfishing for breakfast in the morning. The only disadvantage is being in South Bay away from the majority of eating houses. ❸

Sunrise Lodge 74 Beach Rd ⓣ03/319 7444. Neatly constructed purpose-built boutique hostel with a fully equipped kitchen and comfortable, if a bit basic, rooms. Dorms ❶, rooms ❷–❸

Dusky Lodge 67 Beach Rd ⓣ03/319 5959. Bought by Jack, owner of *Moby Dix* and a Kiwi Experience drop-off. A decent size, modern hostel with internet access and free bikes for scooting into town. On the downside it's popular with the rowdy Kiwi Experience. Dorms ❶, rooms ❷

Maui YHA 270 Esplanade ⓣ03/319 5931. Much improved by a recent refurbishment, this is the best hostel in the town: spacious with excellent facilities, a great view over the beach and up the coast, and internet access. Dorms ❶, rooms ❷–❸

Moby Dix's Backpackers 65 Beach Rd ⓣ & ⓕ03/319 6699. A large, brightly decorated and professionally run hostel about ten minutes' walk along SH1 from the centre of town. Dorms ❶, rooms ❷

Peketa Camping Ground 7km south of Kaikoura ⓣ & ⓕ03/319 6299. A beachside campsite ($8.50) of great peace with cabins and a shop. Very popular with surfers who make use of the excellent waves on the doorstep. Cabins ❶ for one, ❷ for two.

Top 10 Holiday Park 34 Beach Rd ⓣ & ⓕ03/319 5362. Handy for the train station, this award-winning park with trees and upgraded amenities offers a range of accommodation, including cabins and motels. Tent sites $10, cabins ❷–❸, tourist flat ❸, motel ❹

Top Spot Backpackers 22 Deal St ⓣ03/319 5540, ⓕ319 6587. Tucked away 200m up a signposted track (the Lydia Washington Walkway) starting by the library, this very friendly and well-run hostel boasts good views over Kaikoura and the coast, a log-burning fire, mountain bikes, BBQ and sundeck and offers seal swimming trips. Dorms ❶, rooms ❷–❸

The Town and the peninsula

Considering its ever-growing status as a tourist destination there is little to be said for the town itself; most visitors are dead-set on seeing whales or swimming with dolphins, and other activities are simply ways of filling in the time until their turn comes.

Some distraction is provided by the newly extended **Kaikoura Museum** (also known as "the treasures of the Nga Taonga"), at 14 Ludstone Rd (Mon–Fri 12.30–4.30pm, Sat & Sun 2–4pm; $3). The exhibits cover the period from the early moa hunters, through the various groups that have occupied the land since. The Nga Tahu harvested the wealth of the land and seas until they were decimated by Te Rauparaha in about 1830. Whaling was established shortly after, in 1843, and immigrants came into the area to fish and farm. The museum contains a large number of argillite and greenstone artefacts, as well as a daunting collection of old photos. The other things of great interest, considering the predominance of whale watching in the area, are bits of the fossilized remains of a Plesiosaur and a Mosasaur, two monstrous sea creatures of the Cretaceous period, kept near the front of the museum in a large glass case.

Out on the peninsula, at 62 Avoca St, **Fyffe House** (daily 10am–6pm, excellent 30min guided tours; $5) is well worth a visit as an old whaler's cottage and the town's oldest building, occupying a great site with views up and down the coast. Fyffe House began as part of the Waiopuka Whaling Station (and still rests on its original whalebone foundations), which was founded by Robert Fyffe in 1842. Originally an unprepossessing two-room cooper's cottage, it was extended by George Fyffe in 1860, and looks now much as it did then.

On the opposite side of the road is a single chimney, a testament to the existence of the old customs house, which looks remarkable perched in front of the upright layer-cake rock strata that lead to the sea. The road itself follows the edge of the peninsula round to a car park where fur **seals** from the local colony (4km from the visitor centre) lounge on the flat, sea–worn rocks watching the plentiful bird life, gulls, shags, and black oystercatchers, who in turn explore the rock pools full of rich tidal detritus.

While on the peninsula, you may be tempted to follow the **Kaikoura Peninsula Walkway** (11km full length; 4hr 30min; leaflet available from visitor centre, $1), which takes you right round the peninsula, past Fyffe House and the seal colony and on (either by the cliff tops or at their base) to Point Kean, East Head and Whalers Bay, before continuing back to the town by joining South Bay Road and then the footpath over the hill, before the road reaches SH1. Kaikoura Peninsula is made of limestone and siltstone laid beneath the sea sixty million years ago, with a backdrop of rugged mountains and abundant wildlife. The shoreline section of the walkway from Point Kean, just beyond Fyffe House, to South Bay is particularly fine, revealing gaping sea caves, folded limestone rocks in thin layers and stacks at Atia Point. The walk from the peninsula carpark to Whalers Bay Lookout should take no more than half an hour one way. This stretch is also a favoured haunt of red-billed and black-backed gulls, oystercatchers, herons and shags, as well as a number of fur seals, rejoicing in being away from the crowds back at the car park.

Out of town is **Maori Leap Cave**, 2km south of Kaikoura on SH1 (Ⓣ03/319 5023; 35min tours daily at 10.30am, 11.30am, 12.30pm, 1.30pm, 2.30pm & 3.30pm; $8.50), which contains some remarkable limestone formations. Stalagmites and stalactites sprout from the floor and ceiling of the cave, and translucent stone straws seem to defy gravity by maintaining their internal water level. There are also examples of cave coral and algae that survive in the dank cave by turning darkness into energy – a kind of skewed photosynthesis. There are two rival explanations for the cave's name: one has it that a Maori warrior jumped to his death from the hills above the cave after he was captured by another tribe; the other has two thwarted lovers from different tribes plunging to their deaths.

Just 100m or so further south is the turning for the steep climb to **Kaikoura Wine Company** (daily 10am–5.30pm; tastings $3, redeemable against purchase), perched on the steep sided hill that overlooks SH1 and South Bay. At first it looks an unlikely place for a winery but with specially designed cellars beneath the local rock and fantastic scenic views, spice is added to the tour (on the hour; $7.50, including tasting), complemented by winery tastings of good unoaked Chardonnay. Currently wines are imported from the likes of *Lawson's* in Marlborough, but the intention is to make organic home-grown soon.

Finally, new to the area are **Maori Tours** (Ⓣ03/319 5567, Ⓔmaori-tourskk@xtra.co.nz), who offer a selection of trips organized and guided by an ex-whale watch boat driver and give a real taste of Maori culture and the genuine hospitality it demands. Tours are half or full day, take in various local sights, story telling, explanations of cultural differences and involve the learning of a song (3hr, $55).

Marine life and sea kayaking

Off the Kaikoura Peninsula is a complex network of trenches and troughs, forming an underwater canyon system, with unusually deep water very close to the coastline. This provides a rich habitat, constantly replenished from the Antarctic, which supports an enormous amount and variety of marine life.

One of the main reasons people come to Kaikoura is for a chance to see gigantic sperm **whales** (all year), migratory humpback whales (Jun–July) and Orca (Dec–Feb) at relatively close quarters. The Maori-owned and operated Whale Watch Kaikoura (Ⓣ03/319 5045 & 0800/655 121, Ⓔres@whale-watch.co.nz) runs up to five sailings daily (Dec–Feb 5am, 7.30am, 10am, 12.30pm & 3pm; March, April, Sept & Oct 5.30am, 7.30am, 10am & 12.30pm; May–Aug 7.30am, 10am & 12.30pm; 2hr 30min; $99.50), using modern wave piercing catamarans and more conventional boats. These days they also have an excellent introductory video and safety demonstration. Be warned, though, that trips are cancelled if **bad weather** threatens, so if you don't want to miss out, give yourself a couple of days in Kaikoura. And don't forget your camera.

The other way of seeing whales at Kaikoura is from the air, but you'll need a good pair of binoculars. Wings Over Whales (Ⓣ03/319 6580 & 0800/226 629) and Kaikoura Helicopters (Ⓣ03/319 6609) offer a number of scenic and whale-spotting flights lasting from twenty to forty-five minutes with prices dependent upon whether you go fixed-wing, usually cheaper, or in the whirlybird. Thirty minutes in a plane is $135, while twenty-five in a helicopter is $150. Slightly better value for money, although it doesn't involve spotting whales, is **Pilot a Plane** (Ⓣ & Ⓕ03/319 6579), a chance to take the controls and pilot the plane yourself for thirty minutes. Even without the scenery this would be an adrenaline buzz but in Kaikoura it's a special experience (from $79).

The other main reason people visit Kaikoura is to frolic with **dolphins**. Dolphin Encounter (Ⓣ03/319 6777, Ⓔinfo@dolphin.co.nz) do three trips a day (6am, 9am & 1pm; $95 to swim, $48 to watch; book at least two weeks in advance). Many people find being in the water with the dolphins a vaguely spiritual experience. You'll get most out of the experience if you're a reasonably confident swimmer; the more you duck-dive and generally splash around, the more eager the dolphins will be to investigate. One thing they find attractive is listening to you humming through your snorkel, any tune will do; they also love pregnant women. Whatever you do, don't get too carried away: dolphins have a penchant for swimming in ever-decreasing circles until lesser beings are quite dizzy and disorientated, so keep an eye on the boat. These days Dolphin Encounter also offer bird watching (3 trips daily; 2–3hr; $60) – on a good trip you'll see shags, mollymawks, gannets, petrels and a couple of varieties of albatross, but be warned, the sharks' livers used to attract the birds have an evil stench and if you get downwind of it you may lose your breakfast to the sea.

Swimming with seals can be a lot of fun: seals tend to be more curious than dolphins, often coming closer to check you out. New seal-swim operators are constantly entering the fray, so check out the latest deals when you arrive. Among the most reputable outfits are Graeme's Seal Swim (Ⓣ03/319 6182) and Top Spot Kaikoura (Ⓣ03/319 5540). Run by two brothers who are very professional, friendly and knowledgeable, Graeme's offers two-hour trips between November and April ($40, underwater cameras provided on request), as do Top Spot Kaikoura (also $40). Both trips involve a beach entry and a fair bit of swimming so it helps if you've snorkelled before.

Another way to see the wildlife is **sea kayaking** with Matt Foy, a member of SKOANZ (Ⓣ03/319 7118 & 0800/728223, Ⓔkaikourapedalcab@hotmail.com; half-day trips $60; twilight excursions $60). He offers evocative trips from South Bay or the town end and spends time appreciating the scenic beauty of the peninsula as well as enjoying the bays, birds and occasionally seals that can otherwise only be seen from the peninsula walkway.

The most recent addition to the plethora of water-based activities in Kaikoura is the **Kaikoura Shark Dive** (☎03/319 6777; Dec–Easter; 2 trips a day; 3hr; about 10min in the cage; $120), a novel experience that will certainly get the blood pumping. A lot is made of the danger but you'll be in a shark cage so unless you use your limbs to attract the sharks you'll be OK and you should see either or both of the Blue or Mako sharks.

Eating and drinking

The least expensive way to sample the local **crayfish** is to buy them ready-boiled from one of the shacks and caravans advertising their wares alongside SH1 north of town. You can buy good quality **fresh fish** from the Pacifica Seafoods (Kaikoura) Ltd, near the *Pier Hotel*. There are also a number of chip shops in town producing excellent fried-fish **takeaways**; try the *Continental* on Beach Road. Another good place to stop off is the *Coastline Dairy and Bakery*, 38 Westend (daily 6am–6pm) where they make gorgeous-smelling fresh bread. The **restaurants** and **cafés** in town are all a bit pricey, safe in the knowledge that you're not exactly spoilt for choice, particularly near the town centre, but there are notable exceptions where the cooking is good, the prices fair and the atmosphere pleasing.

Donegal's About 20 minutes' drive from town, north on SH1 and then 1.5km up School House Rd. Recently extended to look more like a family house in the old country, this local legend has an extended menu to cater for a broad palette and it's an odds-on favourite that there'll be some sort of boozy bash most nights. Daily 11am–whenever.

Finz South Bay Parade ☎03/319 6688. An excellent fine-dining restaurant and bar offering a broad range of well-prepared and wonderfully presented evening dishes made from local ingredients with New World panache, also the best seafood in town. Daily 5pm onwards.

Green Dolphin 12 Avoca St. A pleasant if slightly pretentious little café on the peninsula, serving good seafood and grills in a formal atmosphere (mains $25–40), with a reasonable wine list. Licensed & BYO. Daily 6–10pm.

Hislop's Wholefood Café 33 Beach Rd ☎03/319 6971. Excellent café serving teas and coffees, and all-organic meals including excellent daily fresh-baked bread to eat in with their lovely chowder or to take away. Licensed.

Mussel Boys 80 Beach Rd, cnr Beach Rd (SH1) & Edmund Ave. The delightful cousin of the Havelock restaurant (though this one's more popular as an evening eatery) where you can get wonderful mussels, a variety of other seafood delights and thick tasty chowder, washed down with wines from the Kaikoura vineyard at reasonable prices. Nov–March daily 11am–9pm, April–Oct 11.30am–8.30pm.

The Olive Branch 54 Westend. A comfortable upmarket eatery and wine bar offering panini, mussels and fish all prepared imaginatively with either an Asian influence or a soupçon of French style. Daily 10am–late.

Small World Café Cnr Westend & SH1. Atmospheric and relaxing coffee house, serving the best java in town and some juicy Souvlaki, chicken and falafel. This place also acts as alternative night spot and venue when there's a good travelling band or DJ around.

Sonic on the Rocks Café Westend & The Esplanade, opposite the visitor centre. Lively modern café/bar which seems to have lost its way. Poor, simple, budget food aside this is still a bit of a nightspot using its funky design to attract revellers for drinking and occasional live or DJ music. Summer 11am–late, off-season 5pm–late.

Listings

Bike rental Westend Motors 48–52 Westend Parade ☎03/319 5065. $20 a day.

Buses In addition to the services of the major companies, Atomic Shuttles (☎03/322 8883) runs

to Christchurch and Picton via Blenheim; Intercity (☎03/578 7102) runs to Blenheim, Picton and Christchurch; and Southern Link Shuttles (☎03/358 8355) runs to Picton and Christchurch.
Car rental BP, Westend Parade ☎03/319 5036.
Medical Treatment Kaikoura Hospital and Doctors Surgery, Deal St, 50m from cnr Churchill St ☎03/319 5040.
Pharmacy Kaikoura Pharmacy, 37 Westend Parade (Mon–Sat 9am–1pm).
Post office Next door to the pharmacy (Mon–Fri 9am–5pm, Sat 9am–1pm).
Taxis Kaikoura Taxis (☎03/319 6214) operates taxi services, sightseeing and trailhead transport.
Tours/local shuttles Aitkens Picnic Tours (☎03/319 5091) caters to your preferences; while TJs Tours (☎03/319 6803) runs day-trips and shuttle services as well as a land tour of points of interest around town, including the seal colony. Accacia Downs Lake and Eco Tours (☎03/319 7174, ©rodkirk@xtra.co.nz), offers a great trip for any bird lovers. It takes in Lake Rotorua, a 300-acre piece of water near the airport, where among much other birdlife you can see a cormorant colony ($50 for the day tour, $55 for the BBQ tour).

Around Kaikoura

The Seaward **Kaikoura Ranges** and Mount Fyffe completely dominate the town, creating a bleak atmosphere. Leaflets (50¢–$1, from the visitor centre in Kaikoura) outline some of the **walks** in the ranges.

Mount Fyffe is 1602m high and rewards the climber with views across the Seaward Kaikoura Ranges, Banks Peninsula to the south and up to the North Island. The path to the summit (18km return; 8hr) starts about 8km from Kaikoura: head along Postmans Road to the head of the Hinau Track, where there is parking and information. It is also possible to access the Inland Kaikoura Range and the huts of the **Clarence River Conservation Area** from Kaikoura, a journey of about 25km. Head south out of Kaikoura on SH1, then turn inland on the Kaikoura–Waiau Road to the reserve car park at the Kahutara Bridge. The Clarence River Conservation Area offers the opportunity to explore some uncrowded walking tracks in an area with some of the highest mountains outside the Southern Alps and some stunning geological formations. Should you decide to explore, go well-equipped as the weather in this area can change in an instant.

If this sounds too rugged, the privately owned **Kaikoura Coastal Track** (43km; 3 days) offers an excellent way to explore the area. The track begins 50km south of Kaikoura on SH1, where there's secure parking; Kaikoura Taxis

Mount Lyford Skifields

The **Mount Lyford Skifields** (June to mid-Oct, 9am–4pm; general information ☎03/315 6178, premium-rated snowphone 0900/34 444) are 60km from Kaikoura on the road to Waiau (SH70). The newest and smallest of New Zealand's ski areas, Mount Lyford caters for a broad range of abilities and is rarely crowded. There are two separate fields: **Stella** is ideal for advanced skiers and snowboarders, and **Terako** has a variety of intermediate and beginner runs, as well as some more ambitious routes in the Terako Basin. **Access** is along 4km of unsealed road (toll $5–10) off SH70, or by Mount Lyford Transport ski bus from Kaikoura (about $30 return; ☎03/319 6182). **Lift facilities** are limited to one fixed grip and two rope tows; heli-skiing is also an option, as is cross-country. Field charges are $35 per day, there's a learners' package for $55, and ski rental is available ($10–25 per day).

Mount Lyford Village, 3.5km from the field, has comfortable **accommodation** at the *Mount Terako Lodge* (☎03/315 6677; B&B ❺) and *Graeme Chambers Mount Lyford Lodge* (☎03/319 6182; dorms ❶, rooms ❸), while the *Chamois Café* serves snacks and meals at high-altitude prices.

(☎03/319 6214) and TJ's Tours (☎03/319 6803) will also run you out to the **trailhead**. The trail climbs through farmland and native bush across the Hawkeswood Range and along beaches, with spectacular views of the Seaward Kaikoura mountains and the Southern Alps, ending at *The Staging Post* (see below), where transport can be arranged to your next destination. **Accommodation** is in warm, clean cottages with fully equipped kitchens, baths and showers as well as fresh farm produce, milk, bread and home-cooked meals by arrangement. You must **book in advance** (☎03/319 2715; ❺, including 3 nights' accommodation), and only a limited number are allowed to walk the track at any one time, although these days it's also open to mountain bikers. If you want a gentle transition back to civilization after your walk, hole up for a day or two at *The Staging Post*, 2111 Parnassus Rd, Hawkeswood (☎03/319 2898; tent sites $7, dorms ❶, cabins ❷–❸). This idiosyncratic place right at the end of the coastal track on a large sheep station reflects the personality of its ancient and amusing owner, and is well worth a look even if you don't intend to stay.

South from Kaikoura

Continuing south on SH1, the coastal landscape eventually dissolves into a relatively flat extension of the Canterbury Plains, with little to delay you before you hit the eastern suburbs of Christchurch that face out on to **Pegasus Bay** – a bite out of the coastline bounded by the **Hurunui River** and Banks Peninsula, more than a hundred kilometres further south. The main community along the way is the small town of **Cheviot**, 70km from Kaikoura and 115km from Christchurch, but there's little reason to linger unless you're an angler keen to test your mettle on the cunning trout and salmon in the nearby Hurunui and Waiau rivers or an ardent tramper bound for the Port Robinson Track.

Cheviot and around

Like the other towns between Kaikoura and Christchurch, **CHEVIOT** suffers by comparison with those two destinations and has little to delay the discerning visitor for more than an hour or two. SH1 becomes Main Street as it makes its way through the town.

If you're here at a weekend, look in on the **Cheviot Museum**, 6 Main Street (Sat 10am–noon, Sun 2–4pm, or by arrangement with Mr Cropp ☎03/319 8536 or Mr Page ☎03/319 8764; donation requested), which provides some interesting insights into the origins of the town and its surroundings. The three dominant collections consist of a large number of moa bones; a display devoted to George Forbes, local lad made good, who rose to become prime minister between 1930 and 1935; and a daunting collection of documents relating to land redistribution. Forged in the hills around Cheviot, this policy marked a turning point for land tenure in New Zealand. In 1893 Sir John McKenzie bought, on behalf of the government, the Cheviot Estate (about 34,000 hectares of good land), following a dispute about the valuation of the land and the tax that the Robinson family would have to pay on it. McKenzie then parcelled the land into small farms and holdings, so the same land could support 650 people, rather than just 80 – a process that was to be replicated across New Zealand, breaking up the enormous landholdings of a few rich and powerful men (as recounted in John Wilson's book, *Cheviot: Kingdom to Country*).

Gore Bay

To dispel driving fatigue or museum ennui, take a walk by the sea at **Gore Bay**, about 8km from Cheviot and well signposted. There's a lovely beach with safe swimming and, at the east end of the bay, adjoining the road, a scenic reserve that shelters dramatic examples of badland erosion. At the southern end of the reserve, siltstone cliffs called **The Cathedrals** have been eroded into huge stalagmite-like fingers that resemble the pipes of a cathedral organ. Also within the reserve is a 2.5km loop track between Cathedral Gully and Tweedie Gully, with a few steep sections that make it ill-advised outside the summer months.

A more rewarding track is the coastal trail from Gore Bay to Port Robinson and then on to the mouth of the Hurunui River, **The Port Robinson Track**. The whole route takes seven hours return, but most of the highlights – the "cathedrals", spectacular bluffs, Port Robinson, Gibson's Point and the lighthouse – are encountered during the **Gore Bay to Manuka Bay** sector, a three-hour round-trip. Beginning at the southern end of the Gore Bay Scenic Reserve, the sector ends on the south side of Gibson's Point, where the track passes the dead end of the road that leads back to Port Robinson and then Gore Bay. The first part of the walkway is along the beach beneath the bluffs, which must be accomplished at low tide; if you miss the tide, the walk can be joined from the Gore Bay Road, turning down to the Port Robinson boat ramps and then round the point and lighthouse. Self-sufficient trampers might want to take advantage of the extremely basic DOC **campsites** ($5) at Gore Bay and the mouth of the **Hurunui River**, though most will be content to explore briefly and then press on to the more tangible rewards of Christchurch or Hanmer. Note that the track is closed in October due to lambing and may be closed by the DOC between December and March if they feel there is a fire hazard.

The road to Waipara

The road veers away from the coast until it reaches **Waipara**, weaving among gently rolling hills that alternate between green and golden brown depending upon the time of year, and obscure the Pacific Ocean from view. At the tiny hamlet of Waipara, SH1 divides into two, climbing inland towards Hanmer Springs as the Lewis Pass Road/SH7, or continuing as SH1 down the coast to Christchurch.

Travel details

Buses

From Blenheim to: Christchurch (5–6 daily; 4hr 55min); Nelson (6 daily; 1hr 50min); Picton (10–11 daily; 30min); St Arnaud (1–2 daily; 1hr).
From Murchison to: Blenheim (1 daily; 4hr 40min); Nelson (2 daily; 2hr 25min); Westport (2 daily; 1hr 30min).
From Nelson to: Greymouth (2–3 daily; 6hr); Kawatiri Junction, for Nelson Lakes (1 daily; 1hr 5min); Motueka (5–6 daily; 1hr 10min); Murchison (2 daily; 2hr 25min); Picton (5–6 daily; 2hr 10min); Takaka (2–3 daily; 4hr).
From Picton to: Blenheim (10–11 daily; 30min); Christchurch (3–4 daily; 5hr 25min); Kaikoura (3–4 daily; 2hr 15min); Nelson (5–6 daily; 2hr 10min).

Trains

From Picton to: Blenheim (1 daily; 35min); Christchurch (1 daily; 5hr 25min); Kaikoura (1 daily; 2hr 20min).

Ferries

From Picton to: Wellington (8 daily; 2hr 15 min–3hr 15min).

Flights

From Blenheim to: Auckland (17 daily; 1hr 55min); Christchurch (31 daily; 1hr 40min); Wellington (35 daily; 25min); Westport (2 daily; 2hr 5min).
From Kaikoura to: Christchurch (1–2 daily; 1hr 20min); Wellington (1–2 daily; 1hr).
From Motueka to: Takaka (2 daily; 30min); Wellington (2 daily; 45min).
From Nelson to: Auckland (33 daily; 2hr); Blenheim (9–10 daily; 55min); Christchurch (18 daily; 1hr); Queenstown (6 daily; 3hr 20min); Wellington (21 daily; 25min); Westport (2 daily; 2hr 20min).
From Picton to: Wellington (7–9 daily; 25min).

9

Christchurch and south to Otago

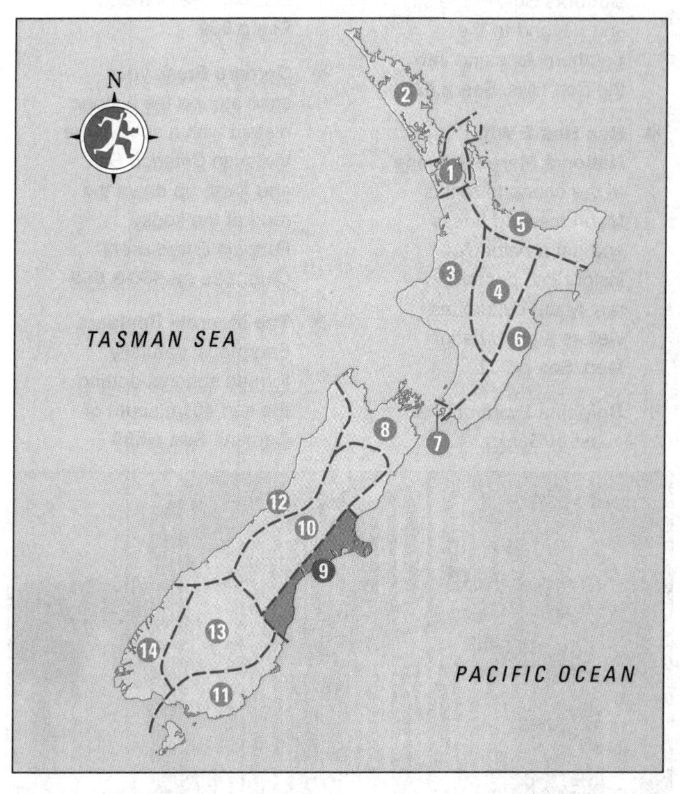

CHAPTER 9

Highlights

* **The Arts Centre, Christchurch** Head down to the markets and food stalls around the Arts Centre to check out arts, crafts and great ethnic food. **See p.616**
* **The Christchurch Gondola** Survey the city and beyond to the Southern Alps and into the Port Hills. **See p.622**
* **Nga Hau E Wha National Marae** See one of the concerts at this Maori meeting house and get a palpable insight into contemporary Maori culture, as well as a good *hangi* feed. **See p.632**
* **Dolphins** Swim off the coast of Banks Peninsula, with the rare native Hector's dolphins. **See p.652**
* **Maori rock art** Maori rock art dates back hundreds of years and offers a window into the culture that existed before European settlement. **See p.659**
* **Oamaru** Break your stroll around the historic district with a spell in the Victorian *Criterion Bar*, and finish up down the road at the kooky *Penguin Entertainers Club*. **See pp.668 & 669**
* **The Moeraki Boulders** Enormous, naturally formed spheres dotting the surf 40km south of Oamaru. **See p.669**

9

Christchurch and south to Otago

Encompassing some stunning and varied scenery, the South Island's east coast perhaps comes closer to most visitors' expectations of New Zealand than any other part of the country. The main hub of the region is New Zealand's third city, **Christchurch**, stretched out between the Pacific Ocean and the agriculturally rich flatlands of the Canterbury Plains, and with the Southern Alps acting as a distant backdrop to the west. A relaxed, green city where parks and gardens rub shoulders with some fine Victorian architecture, it boasts its fair share of urban thrills, provided largely by the cafés, bars and pubs which crowd a busy downtown area. It's also a seaside resort in its own right, with **beach suburbs** like New Brighton and Sumner within easy reach of the centre.

Immediately southeast of Christchurch rise the **Port Hills**, providing welcome relief from the flat Canterbury Plains. Beyond them, **Banks Peninsula** is a popular escape for city residents, its coastline indented by numerous bays and harbours. Perched above these harbours are the two main communities of the peninsula, the brusque port of **Lyttelton** and the attractive, if slightly twee, town of **Akaroa**.

South of Banks Peninsula the main road and rail lines forge across the Canterbury Plains, a patchwork quilt of rich fields and vineyards bordered by long shingle beaches littered with driftwood. Further south the countryside again changes character, with undulating coastal hills and crumbling cliffs announcing the altogether more rugged terrain of **North Otago**. The historic settlements dotted along the coast are a testament to the wealth that farming and mineral extraction brought to the region. The main centres here are the lively port of **Timaru**, close to a series of **Maori rock paintings** that indicate the region has a longer history than the imposed European feel would have you believe; and the quieter **Oamaru**, with an engaging nineteenth-century centre and some captivating **penguin colonies** just outside town. Beyond here routes lead on towards Dunedin and the south, passing the unearthly **Moeraki boulders**, perfect spherical rocks formed by a combination of subterranean pressure and erosion.

Trains trundle up and down the east coast as rarely as once a day, but otherwise **transport** in the region is pretty straightforward, with numerous buses and shuttle buses plying the main routes out of Christchurch.

Christchurch

Capital of the Canterbury region and the largest city on the South Island, **CHRISTCHURCH** (population just over 300,000) exudes a palpable air of gentility and a connectedness with the mother country. After all, it was perceived as an outpost of Anglicanism by its first settlers, was named after an Oxford college, and has some of the feel of a traditional English university

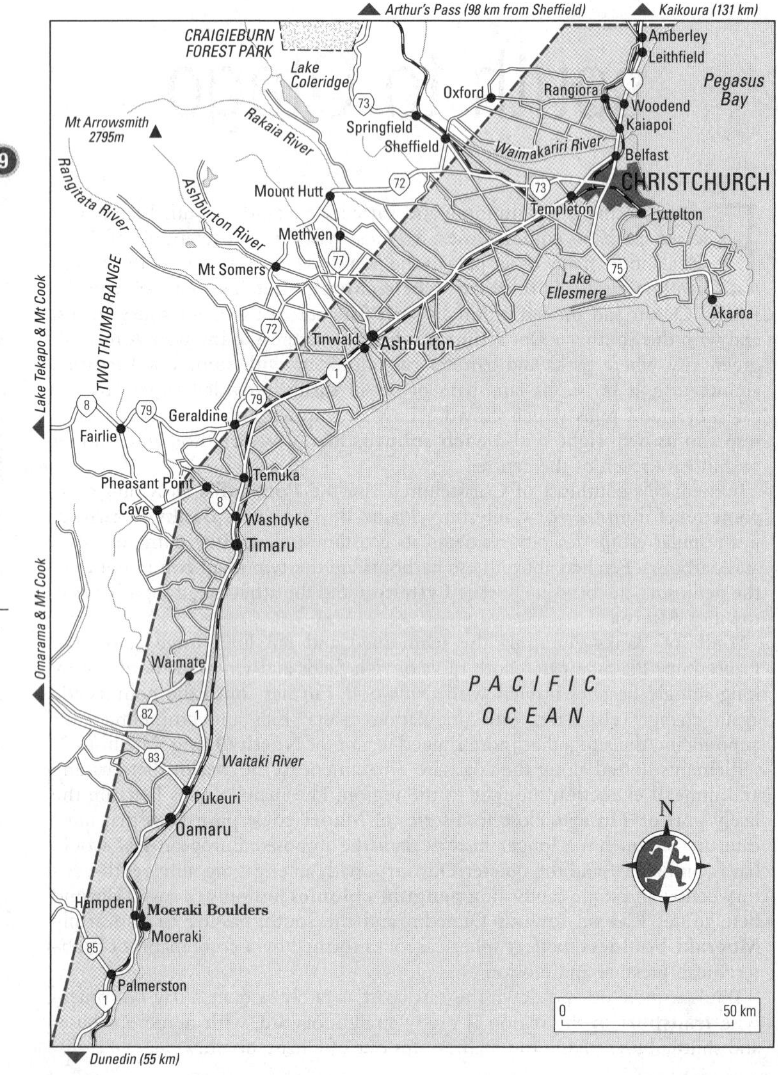

town, with its neo-Gothic architecture and gently winding river. To some degree it pursues an archetype – the boys at Christ's College still wear striped blazers, and punts course along the Avon – but the Englishness is largely skin deep. Modern Christchurch is also a lively melting pot of cultures, with a continental café scene and a distinct, ever-changing Kiwi identity of its own. Indeed, those who regard Christchurch as a quiet place in which to sleep off jet lag or take a break from the long journey across the South Island will be pleasantly surprised by the city's contemporary face. In recent years its traditional conservatism has gained a more youthful, bohemian edge, with an explosion of lively **bars and restaurants** (the city boasts per capita a greater number than Auckland), the emergence of underground **nightlife**, and a burgeoning of the visual arts, theatre, music and street entertainment. Such urban pursuits are nicely balanced by the Pacific Ocean suburbs of New Brighton and Sumner, both of which boast excellent **beaches**.

Straddling the main road and rail routes running down the east coast, Christchurch is used by many tourists as a base from which to explore the South Island, with the steep, angular terrain of **Banks Peninsula** and the **vineyards** of the Canterbury Plains proving the most popular out-of-town destinations. Many of the **outdoor activities** for which New Zealand is famous are accessible from here, with a plethora of city-based companies offering trips involving rafting, paragliding, ballooning and mountain biking in the surrounding countryside (see "Listings", p.633). The city is also within a two-hour drive of several good **skifields** to the west, making it possible to combine a day on the pistes with an evening in Christchurch's numerous watering holes. Indeed the place's only real drawback is its cost: compared with the rest of the South Island, Christchurch is an expensive place to spend any length of time.

Some history

Located in what was historically a dry and windswept area populated only sparsely by Maori, Christchurch came into being as the result of a programmatic policy of colonization by the **Canterbury Association**. Formed in 1849 by members of Christ Church College Oxford, and with the Archbishop of Canterbury at its head, the association had the utopian aim of creating a new Jerusalem in New Zealand: a middle class, Anglican community in which the moralizing culture of Victorian England could prosper. The site of the city was chosen by the association's surveyor Captain Joseph Thomas, who was quick to recognize the agricultural potential of the surrounding plain. A few Europeans were already farming the area (notably the Scottish Deans brothers, who had arrived here in 1843; see p.619), although the main centre of white settlement at the time was the port of Lyttelton to the southeast, a base for whalers since the 1830s. It was at Lyttelton that four ships containing nearly 800 settlers arrived in 1850, bound for the new city of Christchurch – by this stage little more than an agglomeration of wooden shacks. Descent from those who came on the "four ships" still carries enormous social cachet among members of the Christchurch elite. The earliest settlers weren't all Anglicans by any means, and the millenarian aspirations upon which the city was founded soon faded as people got on with the exhausting business of carving out a new life in unfamiliar terrain. Nevertheless, the association's ideals had a profound effect on the cultural identity of the city. The elegant neo-Gothic architecture which still characterizes Christchurch's public buildings oozes with the self-confidence of these nineteenth-century pioneers, while the symmetry of the city's grid-iron street plan hints at the order the planners hoped to impose upon the community.

Arrival and information

Christchurch Airport, 10km northwest of the city centre, stays open day and night so you may well find yourself arriving at the international terminal at some ungodly hour. Fortunately there's an ATM, plus a foreign exchange booth and a **visitor centre** (daily 7.30am–8pm; Ⓣ03/353 7774, Ⓕ353 7754). In addition, there's a freephone board in the arrivals hall for accommodation and car rental bookings, and many Christchurch hotels will provide a free pick-up service from here if you've already booked a room. Failing that, there is one airport hotel (see box on p.608). The domestic terminal is next door and also has a visitor centre (Mon–Sat 6.30am–8pm, Sun 7.30am–8pm; same phone), beside which is a **left luggage** office (daily 6am–11pm; $1 per hour or $8 per day). Checked items can be retrieved out of hours by contacting security.

City buses (see "City transport" opposite) connect the airport with the central bus station just off Cathedral Square (corner of Colombo and Lichfield streets) every 30 minutes on weekdays (6.45am–9.15pm), and every hour at weekends (Sat 8am–9pm, Sun 8am–7pm; $4–5); while various **shuttle** buses (see "Listings" for numbers) operate a door-to-door service (roughly every 20–30 minutes, although departures depend on demand; $10–16) linking the airport with the Christchurch destination of your choice. There are **taxi ranks** in front of the airport terminal building (otherwise ring Blue Star on Ⓣ03/379 9799 or Gold Band on Ⓣ03/379 5795), with the ride into town costing around $30.

Trains arrive at Addington Street Station at the southwestern tip of Hagley Park, just over 2km from Cathedral Square. You can pick up a **shuttle bus** ($5–8) or **taxi** ($12–19) from the station into the centre, although **city buses** don't serve the train station directly – you have to walk 400m down the station access road to Blenheim Road to pick up the bus into town.

Most of the long-distance **bus** companies conveniently drop off at the major hostels and some hotels around town as well as near the visitor centre (see below) usually for no extra charge provided you are staying in the central area bounded by the so-called "Four Avenues" – Moorhouse, Fitzgerald, Bealey and Deans. Cathedral Square itself is within easy walking distance of most of the hostels, major hotels and some of the B&Bs and motels.

Information

The principal visitor centre for Christchurch and the surrounding area is the **Christchurch & Canterbury Visitor Centre**, in the former Post Office on the south side of Cathedral Square (Nov–March Mon–Fri 8.30am–6pm, Sat & Sun 8.30am–5pm; April–Oct Mon–Fri 8.30am–5pm, Sat & Sun 8.30am–4pm; Ⓣ03/379 9629, Ⓦwww.christchurchnz.net, Ⓔinfo@christchurchnz.net). You can book all forms of transport as well as trips and activities here; be sure to pick up the free *Christchurch City Centre Walks* leaflet, which provides a good introduction to local history, as well as the *Tramway* map, which details the main stops on this popular sightseers' route (see "City transport" below). The visitor centre is also the place to find out which of the city's many excellent **festivals** (see "Listings" on p.633) is currently in progress. As with visitor centres all over the country, they only promote places who pay to join the organization. For many of the same and some additional options, including a few smaller companies, pop down the street to Trailblazers, 86 Worcester St (Oct–April 9am–6pm, May–Sept 10am–6pm; ⓣ03/366 6033, ⓔtrailblazer@caverock.co.nz), a **booking service** with stacks of helpful advice and bike rental (see "Listings", p.633).

The **DOC** (Department of Conservation) **office** is 1km northwest of Cathedral Square at 133 Victoria St (Mon–Fri 8.30am–4.30pm; ⓣ03/379 9758), and stocks specific information on wildlife and walking routes, as well as booking Great Walks throughout the South Island.

City transport

You can easily see most of what Christchurch has to offer **on foot**, resorting to public transport for the odd trip out to the suburbs or to get from one side of the centre to another.

Bus services are operated by several companies all co-ordinated by Canride who operate a massive new **bus station** on the corner of Colombo and Lichfield streets as well as an **infoline** (Mon–Sat 6.30am–10.30pm, Sun 9am–9pm; ⓣ03/366 8855, ⓦwww.crc.govt.nz). Tickets for short rides cost $1, most journeys (even to New Brighton and Sumner) are $2, while Lyttelton and the airport cost around $4 one way; multi-trip tickets give twelve rides for the price of ten. All routes run from 6am in the morning until about midnight (slightly longer in the case of more popular routes). In addition there's the free **Shuttle**, a distinctive yellow bus which runs from the Town Hall, through the Square, down Colombo Street to Moorhouse Avenue and back on a 10–15min cycle (Mon–Thurs 8am–10.30pm, Fri 8am–midnight, Sat 9am–midnight, Sun 10am–8pm).

Perhaps the best way of familiarizing yourself with the central city area is to hop on the **Tramway** (daily: Nov–March 9am–9pm; April–Oct 9am–6pm), which weaves a 2.5km circuit past many of the central sights, including the Arts Centre and Cathedral Square. The tramway was only installed a few years back, but the rolling stock is largely made up of lovingly restored 1905 originals. You can get on or off at any stop, depending upon the time limit of your ticket: a one-hour ticket costs $6 and an all-day ticket $7. Thrown in with the price is a rudimentary commentary that will at least identify landmarks and help you get your bearings.

Driving in Christchurch is pretty straightforward providing you avoid morning and evening rush hours. Most central parking spaces are metered from Monday to Saturday between 7am and 6pm (otherwise free). If you have to drive into town, there's free parking in the centre of Hagley Park (Armagh Street entrance).

Given the city's relatively quiet roads, **cycling** is an ideal way of appreciating some of the more out-of-the-way suburbs. Expect to pay around $25–30 a day for **bike rental** (see "Listings", p.633, for details of outlets). Finally, a sedate way of seeing some of the prettier parts of the city is by **punt** up and down the River Avon (daily 9am–dusk; $12–15 per person; book through the visitor centre); the water-level perspective is a refreshing one.

Accommodation

As the largest city in the South Island and a major port of entry, Christchurch has one of New Zealand's broadest ranges of accommodation, and although prices are by no means extortionate, they're understandably higher than in the South Island's smaller towns and cities.

Most of the **business hotels** and backpacker **hostels** are situated within the city centre, as are a number of the better **B&Bs**, though there are also several fine B&Bs out in the leafier suburbs. Probably the best value for money is found at the hostels, none too far away from the action and most offering good deals on rooms and ensuites. The majority of the **luxury hotels** are close to Victoria Square, with **motels** strung out along Papanui Road to the north-west, and on Riccarton Road which runs west from Hagley Park. Predictably, **campsites** are scattered outside the city centre, mostly within walking distance of a bus stop. For those who want to wake up close to the sea, there's a variety of accommodation in the **suburbs** facing the Pacific Ocean: New Brighton and Sumner are the best places to aim for – they're about 8km east of the centre and reached by buses #5, #6 and #29 (for New Brighton); and #30 and #31 (for Sumner).

With Christchurch operating a 24-hour airport, most places are well used to accommodating **late arrivals** and early departures: when making a reservation it pays to double check the dates, especially if you're arriving around midnight.

Hotels and motels

Central Christchurch has plenty of large, flashy **hotels** often with rooms overlooking Hagley Park, the Cathedral Square or Victoria Square. On the whole, these represent the most expensive option, and there are cheaper **motel** rooms not far away. The best hunting ground is around fifteen minutes' walk north-west of the Square: upwards of a dozen highly competitive places line **Papanui Road** which leads to the classy suburb of Merivale. Alternatively, try **Riccarton Road**, again just outside the Four Avenues and only twenty minutes' walk from the city through Hagley Park; or head out to beachside New Brighton (see box, p.623). Rates are pretty competitive, so you shouldn't have any trouble finding a studio for around $80, and many establishments offer **special deals** for weekend and long-term stays.

City centre

Akron Motel 87 Bealey Ave ⓣ03/366 1633, ⓔakron.motel@xtra.co.nz. A small motel in a quiet area set back off the road with plain but functional units, some of which open out onto a small garden, about ten minutes' walk from Cathedral Square. ❹–❺

Cashel Court Motel 457 Cashel St ⓣ & ⓕ03/389 2768. Very reasonably priced motel, fifteen minutes' walk from the city centre and with an outdoor pool. Small but comfortable. ❹

Chateau on the Park 189 Deans Ave ⓣ0800/808 999, ⓦwww.chateau-park.co.nz. Two-hundred-room hotel, memorable for its lovely

Airport accommodation

With efficient shuttle services into the city, and establishments geared towards late arrivals and early departures, you are unlikely to need **airport accommodation.** If pushed you can stay five minutes' walk from the terminal at the *Sudima Hotel Grand Chancellor*, corner Memorial Avenue and Orchard Road (ⓣ0800/100 876, ⓦwww.sudimahotel.co.nz; ❼), a modern business hotel with assorted restaurants and bars. It's quite pleasant if you can land a poolside room.

surroundings on the edge of Hagley Park, with an outdoor pool, restaurants and cocktail bar. Fifteen minutes' walk from the Square. ❻

Holiday Inn 356 Oxford Terrace ⓣ03/379 1180 & 0800/801 111, ⓦ www.holiday-inn.com. Lovely business hotel on the edge of the CBD but beside the Avon River and with relaxing courtyard gardens. High-standard rooms and all the expected facilities including indoor pool, restaurant and bar. ❻

Parkroyal cnr Kilmore St & Durham St ⓣ03/365 7799 & 0800/801 111, ⓔreservations @christchurch.parkroyal.co.nz. This spectacular hotel is an outstanding modern architectural feature of the city – a sort of Maya temple with a glass atrium. Overlooking Victoria Square, it has a magnificent lobby and foyer, but disappointing rooms. There are three bars and three restaurants, and it's well worth dropping in for a drink or afternoon tea even if you're not staying here. ❾

Tudor Court Motel 57 Bealey Ave ⓣ0800/488 367 & 03/379 1465, ⓦwww.tudorcourtmotel .co.nz. Very small motel in a peaceful environment with simple units. Twelve minutes' walk to Cathedral Square. ❹–❺

Papanui Road

Adelphi 49 Papanui Rd, Merivale ⓣ03/355 6037 & 0800/335 560, ⓔadelphi@xtra.co.nz. Good-value motel a kilometre from the city centre, with spacious units, spa and playground around a courtyard car park. The rooms are a bit frumpy, but are clean, functional and have cooking facilities. ❹

Colonial Inn Motel 43 Papanui Rd, Merivale ⓣ03/355 9139 & 0800/111 232, ⓔcolonialinn @xtra.co.nz. A modern well-appointed motel about fifteen minutes' walk from Cathedral Square. Clean and comfortable units. ❹–❺

Diplomat Motel 127 Papanui Rd, Merivale ⓣ03/355 6009, ⓔdiplomatchch@xtra.co.nz. Situated in the heart of Merivale, 2km from Cathedral Square and 8km from the airport, this smart motel has large self-contained units with separate kitchens, where the extra few dollars is justified by a nice outdoor pool and spa. ❺

Strathern Motor Lodge 54 Papanui Rd, Merivale ⓣ & ⓕ03/355 4411, ⓦwww.strathern.com. Spacious and well-presented modern units all with a full kitchen, and one with its own spabath, located fifteen minutes' walk from Cathedral Square with its own spa pool. Excellent value. ❺–❻

Riccarton Road

Aalton Motel 19 Riccarton Rd ⓣ0800/422 586 & 03/3486700,ⓦwww.aalton.co.nz. Very spacious, slightly ageing rooms represent good value and there's an indoor spa and poorly sited outdoor pool that's just about OK for a cooling dip. Close to Hagley Park and with Sky TV. ❹–❺

Annabelle Court Motel 42 Riccarton Rd ⓣ03/341 1189, ⓕ341 3030. Attractive modern motel with spacious and well appointed units, some with spa baths. Studios ❹, spa units ❺

B&Bs and guesthouses

As elsewhere in New Zealand, the standard of **bed and breakfast** accommodation in Christchurch is very high. There's a sprinkling of excellent B&Bs in the centre and in the nearby, easily reached suburbs, and another concentration of places in the seaside communities of New Brighton and Sumner. All represent good value for money, and are invariably comfortable and friendly.

City centre

Croydon House 63 Armagh St ⓣ0800/276 936, ⓦwww.croydon.co.nz. Very pleasant and well-run B&B with smallish modernized rooms in the main house and a couple of lovely cottages in the compact but appealing garden. There's a guest lounge with TV and chess, 24hr tea and coffee, and a cooked breakfast is served. Ensuites and cottages. ❺–❻

Dorothy's 2 Latimer Square ⓣ03/365 6034, ⓦwww.dorothys.co.nz. Boutique hotel with five lovingly restored en-suite rooms and an appreciable gay following. There's a generous continental breakfast plus a fine on-site restaurant serving á la carte inside or alfresco; the *Rainbow Bar* follows a *Wizard of Oz* theme. ❻–❼

Hambledon 103 Bealey Ave ⓣ03/379 0723,ⓦwww.hambledon.co.nz. Luxurious B&B with a rich Victorian theme in one of the city's oldest and grandest houses, built in 1856 for one of the early city fathers – but for all that it has a homey feel with family photos and a hotchpotch of furniture and decoration. Choose from an array of spacious suites inside the house, or a delightful Victorian cottage in the grounds. Complimentary port and sherry, and delicious breakfasts. ❼–❾

Home-Lea 195 Bealey Ave Ⓣ03/379 9977, Ⓔhomelea@xtra.co.nz. Comfortable and recently refurbished B&B in a two-storeyed wooden house, built in the 1900s and ten minutes' walk from the city centre. There's a quiet family atmosphere, the cosy bedrooms mostly have TVs, and continental breakfast is served. Rooms ❹ , ensuites ❺

Orari 42 Gloucester St Ⓣ03/365 6569, Ⓦwww.orari.net.nz. Sumptuous and elegantly styled B&B just steps from the Arts Centre. The bright, sunny rooms all have TVs, phones and either ensuites or private bathrooms. Delicious breakfasts. ❻–❼

Windsor 52 Armagh St Ⓣ0800/366 1503, Ⓦwww.windsorhotel.co.nz. A traditional guest-house with upwards of fifty rooms in a century-old former student hall of residence. Nothing flash, but the rooms are comfortable and mostly quiet, the staff friendly and the cooked breakfast keeps you going all day. They also offer a winter special of a two-course meal at the *Oxford on Avon* for half price and an all-day tram transport pass. ❺–❻

Outside the Four Avenues

Charlotte Jane B&B 110 Papanui Rd Ⓣ03/355 1028, Ⓦwww.charlotte-jane.co.nz. Just 50m from Bealey Avenue, this is a cross between an extremely posh B&B and a boutique hotel, named after one of the four ships – the first (allegedly) – that brought colonists to the area. The accommodation was built in 1890 as a family home cum school, and the property has been lovingly renovated into one of the most desirable places to stay in the city. Beautiful wood-panelled rooms, twelve ensuites, breakfast when you want it and an atmospheric little restaurant attached (dinner only), with a wine cellar. ❽–❾

Elm Tree House 236 Papanui Rd, Merivale Ⓣ03/355 9731, Ⓦwww.elmtreehouse.co.nz. A very appealing and welcoming B&B fashioned out of a listed historic building in Merivale, just 2km from the Cathedral Square. Largely built from dark native timbers with fussy decor eschewed in favour of clean lines and plain colours. All rooms are en suite, there is a spa bath, an ancient Wurlitzer jukebox, a conservatory for evening drinks, and a hearty breakfast. Evening meals by arrangement ($40). ❼–❽

Fendalton House 50 Clifford Ave, Fendalton Ⓣ0800/374 298, Ⓦwww.fendaltonhouse.co.nz. Lovely upmarket homestay located in leafy Fendalton – a pleasant 25min walk from the city through Mona Vale and Hagley Park. There are three spacious ensuites, a spa and an outdoor swimming pool. ❻–❼

Highway Lodge 121 Papanui Rd, Merivale Ⓣ & Ⓕ03/355 5418, Ⓔhighway.lodge@xtra.co.nz. Beautiful Tudor-style home about ten minutes' walk from the city centre, close to restaurants, shops and Hagley Park, with clean, well-equipped en-suite rooms. ❹

Hostels

At last count there were around twenty **backpacker hostels** in Christchurch, most within the Four Avenues, or just beyond, and many of which represent excellent value for money. We've picked the best of the modern quieter hostels, the party oriented downtown places where a night on the tiles is pretty much the norm and sleep is something of a luxury, and those a few blocks out with gardens and a homely atmosphere (something Christchurch specializes in). **Prices** don't vary a great deal, generally just over $20 for dorm beds and around $50 for doubles and twins, a little more for doubles with sheets and towels. None of the hostels listed here have tent sites.

If you are arriving during the peak summer season, try to book accommodation a few days in advance to be sure of getting a bed; most hostels are prepared for late plane arrivals, and many have long-term storage for bike boxes and gear you won't need while in the South Island.

Ballies 50 Cathedral Sq ⓔballie@xtra.co.nz. Recently renovated backpacker rooms and some more expensive boutique hotel accommodation all above a lively bar. ❶–❺

Chester Street 148 Chester St East ⓣ03/377 1897, ⓔchesterst@free.net.nz. The city's smallest hostel (12 beds); very homely and more like a shared house with a few backpacker beds, and provision for longer-term stays for workers. Rooms are three-share or made-up doubles. ❶–❸

Christchurch City Central YHA 273 Manchester St ⓣ03/379 9535, ⓔyhachch@yha.org.nz. Only three minutes' walk from Cathedral Square, purpose-built place, with lots of newly added high-quality rooms, two kitchens, two common rooms and well-informed staff that run the travel, events and booking office. If you're staying in the older wing go for one of the exterior doubles, as some in the centre of the building are cramped and airless. Good discounts on various trips and transport. Sheets and towels available. ❶–❸

Dorset House 1 Dorset St ⓣ & ⓕ03/366 8268, ⓦwww.dorsethouse.co.nz. Renovated, small and spacious hostel in an 1871 house located in a quiet area and firmly pitched at the upper end of the backpacker market, with firm beds (no bunks) and sheets and duvets. There's Sky TV in a huge lounge fitted with stained glass windows, off-street parking and free tea and coffee. ❶–❸

Dreamland 21 Packe St ⓣ03/366 3519, ⓔdreamland@clear.net.nz. Peaceful homely hostel occupying two suburban houses just outside the Four Avenues, but still only fifteen minutes' walk from the Square. Each house is self-contained so there's plenty of lounge and cooking space. All beds come with sheets and duvets, there are bikes for hire, free pick-up on arrival and internet access. ❶–❷

Foley Towers 208 Kilmore St ⓣ03/366 9720, ⓔfoley.towers@backpack.co.nz. Despite its fairly big size, this hostel manages to maintain an intimate B&B feel, occupying an old house with cosy rooms and a lovely garden. Dorms ❶, rooms ❷

Frauenreisehaus Women's Hostel 272 Barbadoes St ⓣ03/366 2585, ⓕ366 2589. Wonderfully relaxed and superbly well-equipped women-only hostel in an old and fairly central wooden house. Much loved by those looking for scented candles, mood music, fresh herbs, spring water direct from the garden and non-violent videos. Spacious rooms have beds rather than bunks; there's also a games room, free local calls, free laundry and internet access. Dorms ❶, twins ❷

New Excelsior cnr Manchester St & High St ⓣ0800/666 237,ⓦwww.newexcelsior.co.nz. The management of this hostel was about to change at the time of writing, but this central, large former hotel should still be a fairly boisterous spot, above a café and bar, with an outdoor revamped deck, small kitchen and lounge areas. Dorms ❶, rooms ❷–❸

The Old Countryhouse 437 Gloucester St ⓣ03/381 5504. If you are prepared to be fifteen minutes' walk from the Square (bus #30) then this lovingly restored suburban house has to be one of Christchurch's finest small hostels. It's all polished wood and bold decor, the dorms are spacious and the kitchen well equipped. Dorms ❷, rooms ❷–❸

Rolleston House YHA 5 Worcester Blvd ⓣ03/366 6564, ⓔyhachrl@yha.org.nz. The best-located accommodation in Christchurch: opposite the Arts Centre and full of character. Plenty of dorms but a limited number of doubles, so book ahead for a room: the office is open daily 8–10am & 3–10pm. Dorms ❶, rooms ❷

Star on the Square 56 Cathedral Sq ⓣ03/982 2225, ⓦwww.startimes.co.nz. Brand new hostel with an enormous number of beds, right at the centre of the city, in an historic (1880) building. Three kitchens, a balcony and barbecue, a lounge bar on the ground floor, and an Indian restaurant. Everything is new, the rooms are fresh and it's a good spot from which to explore the city. Dorms ❶, rooms ❷, ensuites ❸

Vagabond Backpackers 232 Worcester St ⓣ03/379 9677. Very friendly place with only 25 beds, some in a wooden building at the back of the house; all are well kept, quiet, clean and recently redecorated – the kitchen even has a dishwasher. There's off-street parking, barbecue and a lovely garden area. Dorms ❶, rooms ❷–❸

YMCA 12 Hereford St ⓣ0508/962 224, ⓔchchymca@ymca.org.nz. This is state-of-the-art as far as YMCA accommodation goes. Singles, doubles and apartments, many en suite, and equipped with telephone, tea and coffee facilities, and TV. Near the Arts Centre and five minutes' walk from Cathedral Square. Fitness centre, gym, squash courts, climbing wall, sauna and canteen. ❶–❹

Campsites

Given the low cost of hostel accommodation in Christchurch, **camping** saves little money, and most of the sites are in any case some distance away from the city centre. There are some well-equipped motor camps within the city limits which are fine for campervans, offer tent sites and have good deals on cabins, but they tend to have a holiday-camp atmosphere.

All Seasons Holiday Park 5 Kidbrooke St, off Linwood Ave, Linwood ⓣ03/384 9490, ⓕ384 9843. This modern park has a swimming pool, spa pool and large children's playground. Easy access to the beach (good for windsurfing), Linwood shopping centre and Sumner, and only ten minutes' drive from the city centre. Tents $9; cabins and tourist flats ❷–❸

Amber Park 308 Blenheim Rd, Upper Riccarton ⓣ & ⓕ03/348 3327, ⓦwww.holidayparks.co.nz/amber. Spacious, grassy site with all the expected features just 4km south of the city (bus #21 stops right outside), and handy for the train station, Addington Raceway and Canterbury University. Tent sites $10 and cabins ❷–❸

Meadow Park 39 Meadow St, St Albans ⓣ03/352 9176, ⓦwww.meadowpark.co.nz. Situated 4km north of Cathedral Square on SH74 (and reached by bus route #1/4) this campsite, close to supermarkets and restaurants, covers a large area and has a full range of facilities. Tent sites $11, on-site vans & cabins & cottages ❷–❸, flats & motels ❹

The City

The city centre, together with many of its more compelling sights, is encased within the **Four Avenues** of Moorhouse, Fitzgerald, Bealey and Deans. They define a useful border round the downtown area, in the very centre of which is **Cathedral Square**. Scattered in the streets around the square are the city's most attractive buildings, while over on the western edge of the four avenues lies **Hagley Park**, a focal point for leisure activities at weekends. Laid out in a grid pattern, Christchurch is very much a low-rise city, with the cathedral spire serving as a useful landmark. The architecture is predominantly nineteenth-century Gothic, a style which still informs many of the more modern buildings. Beyond the Four Avenues you pass into suburban districts like Riccarton, Fendalton, Merivale and St Albans, each characterized by one- and two-storey residential housing and beautifully kept gardens. Further west lie the coastal suburbs of New Brighton and Sumner, which provide access to the Pacific Ocean beaches.

Within the Four Avenues

Christchurch is dominated by its **Cathedral** (Nov–March Mon–Fri 8.30am–7pm, Sat & Sun 9am–5pm; April–Oct Mon–Fri 8.30am–5pm; free: $5 for guided tours Mon–Fri 11am & 2pm, Sat 11am, Sun 11.30am) and the square that surrounds it. You can climb the 134-step claustrophobic staircase of the 63-metre spire ($4) for the best panoramic views of the city. Designed by George Gilbert Scott, the cathedral was begun in the 1860s and completed in 1904 – a Gothic revival Anglican church with a cool and spacious interior. On the left-hand side from the main entrance, look out for the Maori contribution of *tukutuku* panels made of leather and rimu wood, celebrating the Maori proverb: "What is the most important thing in life? It is people, people, people". Visitors and worshippers contributed many of the stitches. To sample the marvellous acoustics of the building, drop by for choral evensong (Tues & Wed 5.15pm for the full choir, Fri 4pm for boys' choir only); note that this doesn't take place during school holidays, principally Christmas to early February.

Christchurch's grid of streets spreads out from **Cathedral Square** (or just "the Square") – a large, open, paved (and in places slippery) area typically abuzz with lunching office workers, skateboarders and tourists. You'll find yourself passing through several times a day if only to catch a bus or taxi. The visitor centre occupies the **Old Post Office** on the southeast corner of the square, an Italianate building constructed in 1879 which, together with the Palladian-style former **Government Building** (1901), provides a pleasing contrast to the predominantly Gothic architecture on show elsewhere. The **Statue of Robert Godley**, the founding father of Christchurch and agent of the Canterbury Association, stands opposite the **Memorial of the Four Ships** outside the old post office, which shows the vessels sent by the Canterbury Association in 1850 to create a model Anglican community here.

Adjacent, and in the same building, you'll find the **Southern Encounter Aquarium** (daily 9am–4.30pm; $10), a fishy extension of Orana Wildlife Park (see p.620), that mimics many of the damper habitats of the South Island. Although it's on a small scale, many native saltwater and freshwater species of fish are represented, with hands-in touch tanks fashioned after rock pools consigning a number of wee creatures to a life of being picked up and fondled, plus artificial eel and salmon runs and a mock-up of a fly fishing lodge. Your visit is rounded off by three short films – all with dramatic commentaries and swelling music – and if you time it right you can watch **feeding** (eels and salmon are fed at 1pm), or a diver getting wet in the big marine tank (3pm).

Opposite the aquarium and visitor centre is a new **sculpture** in the shape of a monstrous ice-cream cone, coloured silver on the outside and metallic blue on the inside, with various patterns, some leaf-like, cut out of its higher reaches. It attracted little interest among either tourists or locals until September 11, 2001, when it became a focal point for flowers, messages and public grief. Since then, it has taken a place of affection in most locals' hearts and is now climbed quite regularly by people with something to protest about.

Another less permanent occupant of the square is the **Wizard** (Ⓦwww.wizard.gen.nz, usually Mon–Fri 1–1.45pm in summer), a local eccentric and former English lecturer who has been lambasting bemused audiences with muddle-brained but occasionally interesting rantings for over a quarter of a century. After arriving via red VW Beetle (made from two front ends welded together), he pontificates on the nature of the world, god and women. If his philosophy particularly appeals then try out his book, *My Life as a Miracle*, on sale at the visitor centre.

The area south of Cathedral Square has the greatest concentration of shops, restaurants and bars, and you'll continually find yourself back here in the evening. There are no sights to speak of as such, but one area to make for is High Street, lined with the more off-beat music and clothes shops as well as the cooler end of the café scene. Parts of this area (particularly along Lichfield Street) can be pretty seedy at night, but it is seldom intimidating. One area worth avoiding is just one block east of the square, between Worcester and Gloucester streets, passed through by the trams and known, for its bombed-out look, as "Little Lebanon".

North of Cathedral Square

A grid of shopping streets and precincts spreads north from the Square, the most interesting section being around **New Regent Street** two minutes' walk east along Gloucester Street. Built in 1932, and home to some of the city's more interesting upmarket cafés and stores, it's one of Christchurch's most attractive streets, with pastel-coloured buildings and trellised balconies recalling

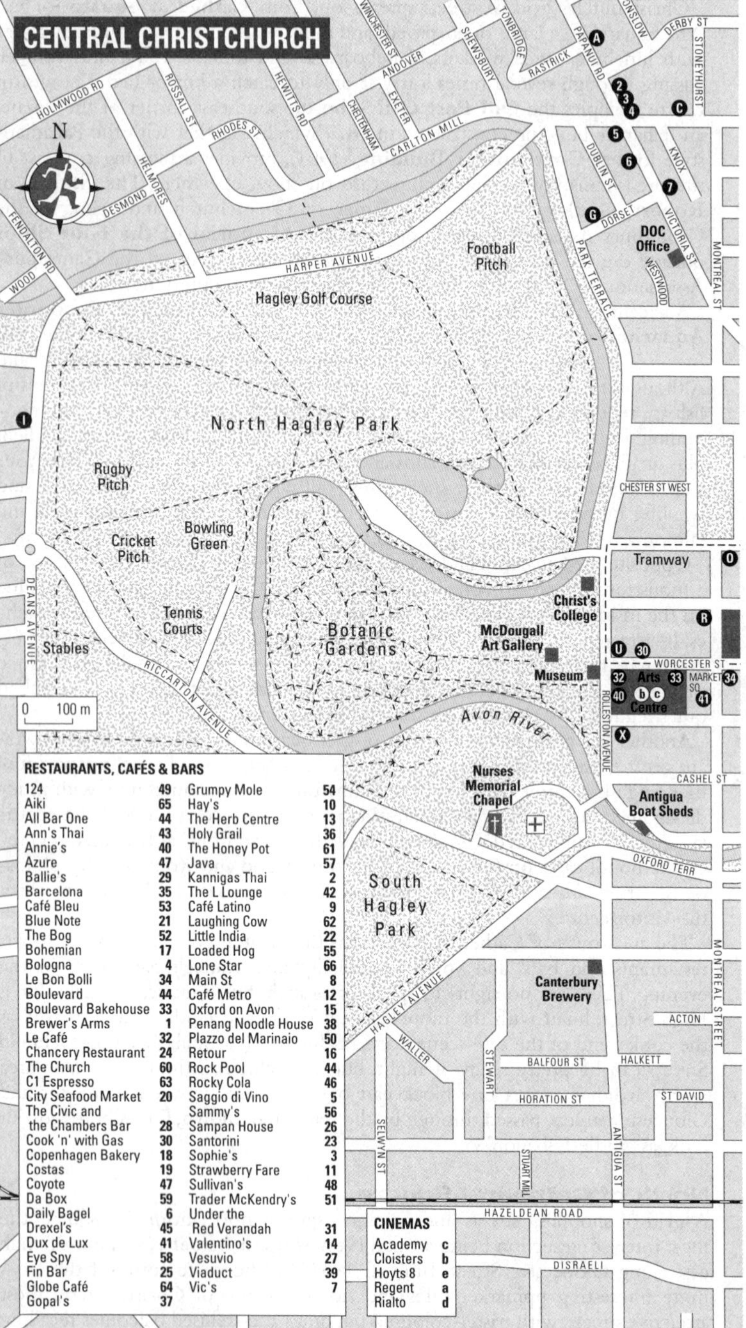

CENTRAL CHRISTCHURCH
(1 km)
HOLMWOOD RD
ROSSALL ST
HEWITTS RD
WINCHESTER ST
ANDOVER
SHEWSBURY
TONBRIDGE
RASTRICK
PAPANUI RD
CONSLOW
DERBY ST
STONEYHURST
RHODES ST
CHELTENHAM
EXETER
CARLTON MILL
HELMORES
DESMOND
FENDALTON RD
WOOD
DUBLIN ST
KNOX
DORSET
VICTORIA ST
DOC Office
WESTWOOD
PARK TERRACE
MONTREAL ST
Football Pitch
HARPER AVENUE
Hagley Golf Course
North Hagley Park
Rugby Pitch
Cricket Pitch
Bowling Green
Tennis Courts
Stables
DEANS AVENUE
RICCARTON AVENUE
Botanic Gardens
CHESTER ST WEST
Tramway
Christ's College
McDougall Art Gallery
Museum
WORCESTER ST
Arts Centre
MARKET SQ
ROLLESTON AVENUE
Avon River
0 100 m
CASHEL ST
Nurses Memorial Chapel
Antigua Boat Sheds
OXFORD TERR
South Hagley Park
Canterbury Brewery
HAGLEY AVENUE
WALLER
STEWART
ACTON
MONTREAL STREET
BALFOUR ST
HALKETT
HORATION ST
ST DAVID
SELWYN ST
STUART MILL
ANTIGUA ST
Train Station
HAZELDEAN ROAD
DISRAELI
RESTAURANTS, CAFÉS & BARS
124 49
Aiki 65
All Bar One 44
Ann's Thai 43
Annie's 40
Azure 47
Ballie's 29
Barcelona 35
Café Bleu 53
Blue Note 21
The Bog 52
Bohemian 17
Bologna 4
Le Bon Bolli 34
Boulevard 44
Boulevard Bakehouse 33
Brewer's Arms 1
Le Café 32
Chancery Restaurant 24
The Church 60
C1 Espresso 63
City Seafood Market 20
The Civic and the Chambers Bar 28
Cook 'n' with Gas 30
Copenhagen Bakery 18
Costas 19
Coyote 47
Da Box 59
Daily Bagel 6
Drexel's 45
Dux de Lux 41
Eye Spy 58
Fin Bar 25
Globe Café 64
Gopal's 37
Grumpy Mole 54
Hay's 10
The Herb Centre 13
Holy Grail 36
The Honey Pot 61
Java 57
Kannigas Thai 2
The L Lounge 42
Café Latino 9
Laughing Cow 62
Little India 22
Loaded Hog 55
Lone Star 66
Main St 8
Café Metro 12
Oxford on Avon 15
Penang Noodle House 38
Plazzo del Marinaio 50
Retour 16
Rock Pool 44
Rocky Cola 46
Saggio di Vino 5
Sammy's 56
Sampan House 26
Santorini 23
Sophie's 3
Strawberry Fare 11
Sullivan's 48
Trader McKendry's 51
Under the Red Verandah 31
Valentino's 14
Vesuvio 27
Viaduct 39
Vic's 7
CINEMAS
Academy c
Cloisters b
Hoyts 8 e
Regent a
Rialto d

ACCOMMODATION

Akron Motel	D
Ballie's	T
Charlotte Jane B&B	A
Chateau on the Park	I
Chester Street Backpackers	L
Christchurch City Centre YHA	P
Croydon House	N
Dorothy's	W
Dorset House	G
Dreamland	B
Foley Towers	K
Fravenreisehaus	M
Hambledon	E
Holiday Inn	H
Home-Lea	F
New Excelsior	Y
Old Country House	Q
Orari	R
Parkroyal	J
Rolleston House YHA	U
Star on the Square	S
Tudor Court Motel	C
Windsor	O
Vagabond	V
YMCA	X

SPRINGFIELD RD
DURHAM ST NORTH
CALEDONIAN RD
SHERBORNE ST
BISHOP ST RD
PACKE ST
BEALEY AVENUE
After Hours Surgery
DOLLANS
OTLEY ST
MELROSE ST
MOA PL
PEACOCK ST
BEVERIDGE ST
CONFERENCE
GRACEFIELD
AIREDALE
ABERDEEN ST
ELY ST
ULSTER
MANCHESTER STREET
MADRAS STREET
COLOMBO ST
SALISBURY STREET
Victorian Clock Tower
PETERBOROUGH LA
PETERBOROUGH STREET
Convention Centre
Johnson's Grocers
Casino
KILMORE STREET
Town Hall
DURHAM STREET
CHESTER ST WEST
CAMBRIDGE TERR
OXFORD TERR
CHESTER STREET
DAWSON
CRAMNER SQUARE
Centennial Pool
ARMAGH STREET
Provincial Government Buildings
Library
Theatre Royal
NEW REGENT ST
GLOUCESTER STREET
Bus Info Centre
CHANCERY LA
Intercity Bus Stop
LATIMER SQUARE
WORCESTER STREET
BARBADOES STREET
Site of new Christchurch Art Gallery
CATHEDRAL SQ
Cathedral
Aquarium
HEREFORD STREET
LIVERPOOL
WOOLSACK
AA Office
CASHEL STREET
OXFORD TERR
CAMBRIDGE TERR
BEDFORD ROW
CLARKSON
FITZGERALD AVENUE
LICHFIELD STREET
St Michael's & All Angels
HIGH ST
POPLAR
ASH
GILMOUR
DUKE
TUAM STREET
MOLLETT ST
COLOMBO STREET
ST ASAPH STREET
ALFRED
WELLES ST
SOUTHWARK
WILLIAMS
FERRY RD
WALKER ST
WINCHCOMBE
QUILL
ALLEN ST
COVENTRY
ATLAS
ROPE
Cathedral of the Blessed Sacrament (RC)
WILMER ST
AVCESTER
DUNDAS ST
EATON
BATH ST
MORTIMER
MOORHOUSE AVENUE
IVERSON
CARLYLE
WALTHAM RD
CASS
SANDYFORD
BYRON

O (200m)
31 (400m)

the Spanish Mission style of architecture which flourished in eighteenth-century California and New Mexico.

One block west, the well-manicured Victoria Square is bounded to the north by the languid Avon River and Christchurch's starkly modern **Town Hall** (daily 9am–5pm), an angular piece of minimalist design linked by footbridge to the equally radical, glass-fronted Convention Centre on the opposite side of Kilmore Street. As Christchurch's premier entertainment venue, the town hall harbours a magnificent 2300-seat auditorium – an impressive sight even when empty. It also contains the Women's Suffrage Commemorative Wall Hanging, commissioned in 1992 to commemorate Women's Suffrage Year and depicting aspects of women's lives over the last hundred years. You can enjoy views of Victoria Square from the *Town Hall Restaurant*, a good place to stop for coffee. Epicureans should nip around the corner to the venerable **Johnson's Grocers**, 787 Colombo St, a treasure trove stacked to the rafters with just about every packaged gourmet product imaginable.

Following the river a few steps to the southwest you find the **Provincial Government Buildings**, corner of Durham Street and Armagh Street (Mon–Sat 10.30am–3pm, also Oct–May Sun 2–4pm; donation requested), built between 1858 and 1865. These are the only provincial government buildings left in New Zealand and are widely regarded as the masterpiece of Christchurch's most renowned early architect, **Benjamin W. Mountfort**. Built in Gothic style with medieval-influenced ornamentation, the older wooden portion of the chambers has a fine flagstone-paved corridor. The stone council chamber, the high-Victorian Great Hall (1869), is magnificently decorated with an intricate ceiling and elaborate stonework. Masks of the two craftsmen responsible for all this finery appear in the stonework: on the east wall near the fireplace on the ground floor and on the east wall of the public gallery.

Heading northwest from here along Victoria Street, the Victorian **clock tower** houses a clock originally imported from England in 1860 to adorn the government buildings. Also on Victoria Street, at no. 30, Christchurch's **casino** is open 24 hours all year round and contains the usual array of bars, table games and a flood of one-armed bandits. You have to be smartly dressed and aged over 18 to get in.

The Arts Centre

Ten minutes' walk west from Cathedral Square along Worcester Street brings you to the Gothic revivalist **Arts Centre**, built in 1874 as the University of Canterbury and Christchurch Girls' and Boys' High Schools. The university decamped to suburban Ilam in 1975 and, after a period of uncertainty, the Arts Centre, with its restaurants, food stalls, shops and galleries, moved in. Look above each entranceway for an inscription indicating the subject – biology, zoology, etc – once studied in that particular part of the building. Today the leafy courtyards and grassy quadrangles make a great place to watch the world go by: it is especially active at weekends when the Market Square on the east side is turned over to a lively **craft market**, complete with buskers and musicians. Much of what's on sale is made in the Arts Centre's stores and workshops dotted throughout the building. To the rear of the arts centre, via the *Dux de Lux* pub and courtyard, a collection of ethnic food stalls (Sat & Sun 10am–5pm) offer Czech, Lebanese, Thai, Korean, Chinese and a planet-load of other national dishes dirt cheap. The arts centre also houses a number of restaurants, a cinema and the Court Theatre (see p.632); the **information centre** (Ⓣ03/366 0989, Ⓦwww.artscentre.org.nz;

daily 9am–5.30pm) provides useful information and access to the much-improved and expanded displays on **Ernest Rutherford**, including a new upstairs gallery and the basement laboratory used for post-graduate research by the Nobel Prize winning atom-splitter. Join the 45-minute **guided tours** (Mon–Fri 11am; $5), led by the town crier, to learn more about the buildings, fashioned in volcanic "bluestone" and Oamaru limestone by Benjamin W. Mountfort, who also designed the Christchurch Museum, Christ's College and the Provincial Chambers.

Hagley Park and around

Across Rolleston Avenue from the Arts Centre lies **Hagley Park** which, it is whispered by the mischievous priest of St Michael's, was put here in order to protect the solidly Anglican districts within the Four Avenues from the Presbyterians in the suburbs beyond. The park contains the spectacular Botanic Gardens, the McDougall Art Gallery, a golf course, sports centre and playing fields. At weekends you can find what seems like the entire population of Christchurch here, merely strolling around or playing hockey, tennis, cricket, netball, rugby or golf.

If there's one place that totally lives up to Christchurch's Garden City moniker it has to be the **Botanic Gardens** (Rolleston Ave gate; daily 7am until 1hr before sunset; conservatories 10.15am–4pm; free), an astonishing collection of indigenous and exotic plants and trees that's unrivalled on the South Island. Throughout summer and autumn the perennials here give a constant and dazzling display of colour. There is also a herb garden, containing a variety of culinary and medical plants; a rose garden with over 250 types of roses; and the Cockayne Memorial Garden, an area of native bush named after one of New Zealand's greatest botanists. Several conservatories, the largest of which is the galleried Cuningham House, contain tropical and indoor plants. Most of all, though, it is just a great place to hang out on a sunny day with picnicking families, studying students and couples flattening the grass.

Conducted **tours** of the gardens in tractor-pulled carts (Sept–April 10.15am–4pm, May–Aug 11am–3pm; $6) depart from the main entrance by the museum on Rolleston Ave. There are also guided walking tours departing from the *Gardens Restaurant* at the northern end of the gardens, of which the most intriguing is the **Te Puna Ora** (book in advance in summer ⓣ03/377 2025; $6), an unusual storytelling tour which incorporates Maori and European myths and legends, as well as pure invention. The gardens are enclosed by a meander of the River Avon and you can explore by water either in a **punt** ($12.50 per person for 30min) or by paddleboats ($12 per half hour) or canoe ($6 per hour); all available from Antigua Boat Sheds, 2 Cambridge Terrace (ⓣ03/366 5885).

The lovely old building just to the right of the Rolleston Avenue gate formerly housed the Robert McDougall Art Gallery (since relocated to a new gallery a couple of blocks east of the park – see below – and probably reopened in the lifetime of this book). Completed in 1932 after designs by Gisborne architect Edward Armstrong, the building's classical Oamaru stone exteriors blend perfectly into their green surroundings. Since closing it has been the subject of various proposals, but nothing has been settled as yet. The **Christchurch Art Gallery**, at the corner of Montreal and Gloucester streets, is due to open in 2003 and will house the McDougall Gallery's collection of more than four thousand paintings, sculptures, prints, drawings and craft objects, many by New Zealand artists and many others by incoming Europeans. The building itself, a massive, impressive modernist conglomeration of glass, steel, concrete and wood sitting within a block of the Avon River, will provide an excellent alternative to the other major Christchurch attractions.

Immediately north of the Rolleston Avenue entrance to Hagley Park you'll find the **Canterbury Museum** (daily: Oct to mid-March 9am–5.30pm; mid-March to Sept 9am–5pm; donation appreciated), a neo-Gothic structure founded in 1870 and initially directed by archeologist Julius Haast (who gave his name to the Haast Pass, see p.840). One of the best exhibits is the "Exploration of Antarctica", covering the many expeditions that have used New Zealand as their jumping-off point. The exhibits of Maori treasures have undergone a fair bit of restructuring and are also well worth a look. Other rooms deal with Moa hunters, European settlers, native birds and mammals, fossils and geology. On the top floor the café is a good spot for a snack and a drink.

Adjacent, **Christ's College** is the city's most elite private school. You can visit the hallowed halls on ninety-minute **guided tours** (Oct to mid-March Mon–Fri 10.30am, 2.30pm & 7pm; $10), which include the college's oldest building, Big School (1863), and the Memorial Dining Hall designed by Cecil Wood in 1925.

On the southern borders of Hagley Park stand the Christchurch Hospital and, a little further on, the **Nurses' Memorial Chapel** (Mon–Sat 1–4pm, Sun 10am–4pm; free). Designed by J.G. Collins (who also worked with his father on the Arts Centre), it was constructed after the death of three Christchurch-trained nurses aboard the troopship *Marquette*, torpedoed in 1915. The walls are Oamaru stone with terracotta bricks and the roof is tiled in green slate, but the best feature is the extensively timbered interior. Windows and doors are framed with matai (native black pine), and the simply patterned floors made of blackwood and oak, with redwood sarking and an elaborate oak panel behind the altar. There are nine stained-glass windows, including four by the English glass artist Veronica Whall, all with an uneven texture and a variety of colours set off by the otherwise dark, low-ceilinged interior.

Heading east back into town, along Oxford Terrace, you'll pass the lovely **St Michael and All Angels Church**, overlooking the river (Oct–April Mon–Fri 10am–5pm, Sat & Sun 2–5pm; guided tours on demand; April–Oct open for regular church services only). The church was designed by William F. Crisp and completed in 1875, combining elements of both the French and English medieval Gothic styles. Much of the architectural ingenuity that went into the building can be glimpsed in the impressive, dark-wood interior: the structure is made of matai timber on stone foundations, and supported by monumental pillars carved from single trees. The pine darkens as it grows older, so it is possible to spot new additions by gauging the blackness of the surrounding wood. The stained-glass windows covering both east and west wings are particularly beautiful, their bright colours contrasting with the dark hues of the surrounding timber. Look out also for the **Te Tapenakara o te Ariki** ("The Tabernacle of the Lord") hung from the ceiling over the central aisle, traditionally a container used by Maori chiefs to store *taonga* (treasure such as ceremonial feathers). This one was dedicated by the Bishop of Aotearoa for use as a Christian vessel to contain consecrated bread, and depicts symbols from both Maori and Christian tradition. The rather dainty belfry standing outside the church was designed by Mountfort in 1861, and houses a bell from one of the first four migrant ships. Historically it served as a timepiece for the settlers and was rung on the hour.

Two blocks south of St Michael's, St Asaph Street leads back towards Hagley Park, passing the **Canterbury Brewery Heritage Centre** at no. 30. Fifty-minute guided tours (reservations advised ⓣ3/379 4940; Mon–Thurs 10am; $8) give you a brief history of brewing in the region, a glimpse of the working brewery itself, and the usual reward at the end.

Beyond the Four Avenues

Inspired by a couple of hours spent in the Botanic Gardens, you might fancy a stroll across North Hagley Park to their logical extension, the beautiful precincts of **Mona Vale** at 63 Fendalton Rd (ⓣ03/348 9659, grounds open daily Oct–March 8am–7.30pm; April–Sept 8.30am–5.30pm; free). Originally part of the Deans' estate (see below), the site became the property of the city in 1969 and is now tended by the Canterbury Horticultural Society. The gardens have majestic displays of roses, dahlias, fuchsias and irises, as well as magnolias, rhododendrons and herbaceous perennials. The Bath House has been converted for use as a greenhouse and the old homestead is open for lunch daily. You can rent a punt at the old homestead and enjoy the gardens from the river ($15 per person for 30min).

You could hardly make a greater botanical leap than to wander ten minutes to the southwest to the suburb of Riccarton and **Deans Bush** (daily dawn–dusk; free), an area of native forest containing several 500-year-old kahikatea trees. The survival of this valuable area of forest is largely due to Scottish brothers William and John Deans, who came to farm the area in 1843 and somehow resisted the temptation to put all their property to immediate agricultural use. Today a concrete path navigates the bush, with signs pointing out the species that still grow here. By the northern entrance off Kahu Road, the gracious, Victorian **Riccarton House** (Mon–Thurs 2–4pm, Sunday 2–5pm, ⓣ03/348 5119) hides the black pine **Deans Cottage** (daily 9am–5pm), the oldest structure on the Canterbury plain, built by the Deans brothers upon their arrival in 1843. This tiny affair is furnished as it would have been until the deaths of William (1851) and his brother (1854).

Beyond Deans Bush, Memorial Avenue runs northwest to the airport where there are one or two attractions worth seeing. Much the most interesting is the **International Antarctic Centre**, Orchard Road (ⓦwww.iceberg.co.nz; daily: Oct–March 9am–8pm; April–Sept 9am–5.30pm; $16), a well-presented and dynamic exhibit concentrating on New Zealand's involvement on the cold continent. Since the mid-1950s, Christchurch airport has been the base of the US Antarctic programme which sponsors over 140 flights a year to their base at McMurdo Sound, and the neighbouring New Zealand outpost at Scott Base. There's stacks here on Antarctic exploration and the fragile polar ecosystem with continuous video presentations, daily digital photos emailed from the ice depicting life at Scott Base, recordings of the current weather conditions, traditional and interactive displays and innovations such as the Snow & Ice Experience where you can don a down jacket and experience a snowy environment at –5°C, cooled further by a fan giving a wind chill of –25°C. Antarctic enthusiasts should leave time for the hourly **Hägglunds Ride** ($20, combined ticket including the museum $32), a 45-minute jaunt in a genuine five-tonne tracked buggy. The centre also has the *60° South Cafe and Bar* and one of the country's more imaginative gift shops. True fans of all things Antarctic can even pick up a free *Antarctic Heritage Trail* leaflet detailing connected sites around Christchurch and Lyttelton.

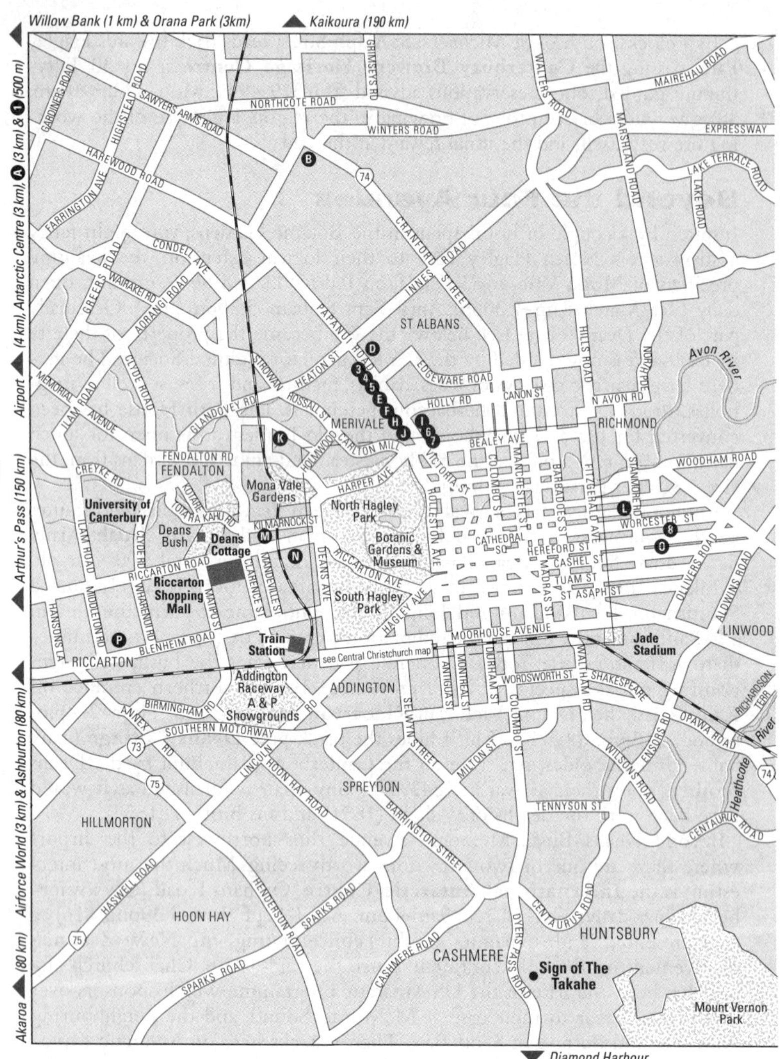

Drivers can skirt around the northern perimeter of the airport – follow Russley Road then McLeans Island Road – to **Orana Park**, within the McLeans Island Recreational Area (daily 10am–5pm; $12, shuttle-bus pick-up from the city $15; ⓣ03/332 6012), a well-organized zoological park containing a wide variety of native and imported animals. Volunteer guides are on hand, and highlights include endangered New Zealand bird species like kiwi and tuatara, and the chance to observe the feeding of lions and tigers from a treetop viewing balcony.

Although nowhere near as exciting as Orana Park, the smaller and more inti-

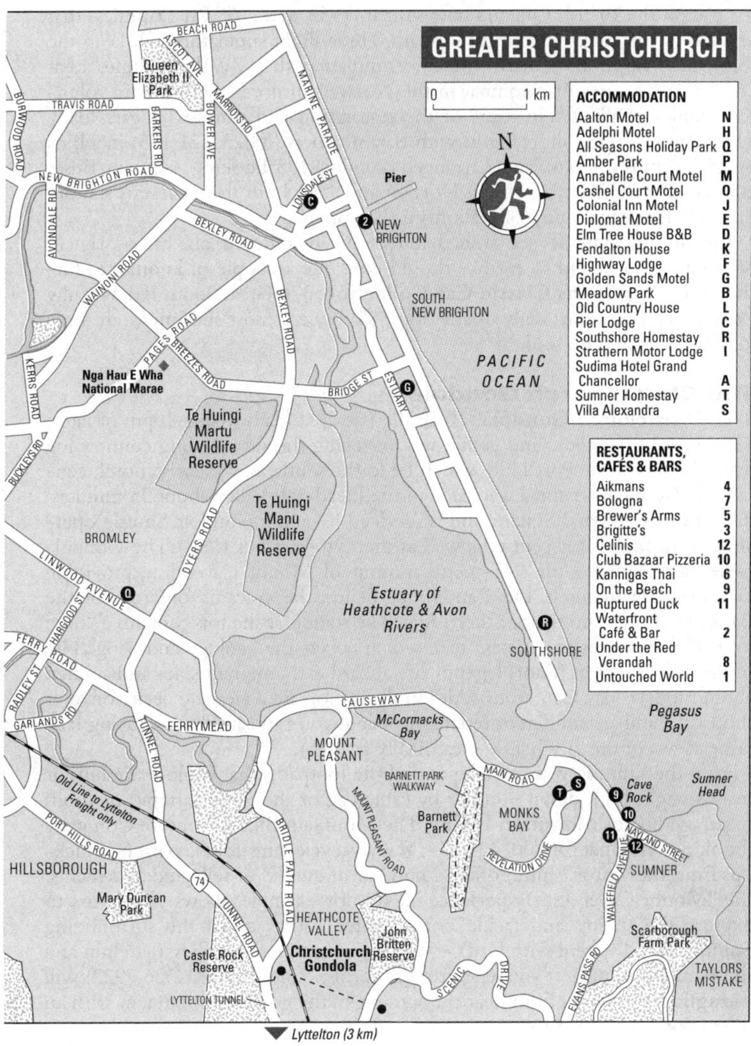

mate **Willowbank Wildlife Reserve**, 60 Hussey Rd (daily 10am–10pm; $14, ⓣ03/359 6226), has some good displays of native birds including a kiwi house (11.30am–10pm). To get there, ride bus #1/4 from Cathedral Square as far as the junction of Harewood Road and Gardiners Road, then walk northeast up Gardiners Road for five minutes or so before turning right into Hussey Road.

Around twenty minutes' drive southwest of Hagley Park and accessible via Blenheim Road and Great South Road is **Air Force World** (ⓣ03/343 9532, ⓦwww.afw.co.nz; daily 10am–5pm; $10), located beside the former RNZAF base at Wigram. Among the two dozen aircraft you'll see the Dakota converted for use on the British Queen's state visit in 1953, and a WWII Dauntless that crashed in the Pacific islands of Vanuatu. Three flight simulators will keep the (big) kids happy, particularly the one simulating the WWII Mosquito as it engages in very realistic combat in the Norwegian fjords. Enthusiastic volunteer guides conduct free tours of the restoration and storage hangars (daily 11am, 1pm & 3pm); short flights with Barnstormers (ⓣ025/321 135) in a Pitts Special stunt plane can also be arranged (20min; $195; booking essential). Buses #81 & 82 to Lincoln or #5 to Hornby and #51, both from the bus station, drop off about five minutes' walk from the entrance.

Anyone desperate to see a shed full of nicely restored old cars – Jaguar, Mercedes, Lancia and so forth – should continue a couple of kilometres further out to **Dr Heins Classic Car Collection**, 376 Great South Rd, Hornby (ⓦwww.classics.co.nz; daily 10am–5pm; $5), where most specimens are only kept on display until sold.

The Christchurch Gondola

The **Christchurch Gondola**, 10 Bridle Path Rd (daily 10am–10pm or later; $16 return), is a scenic and gentle way of seeing the surrounding countryside from the top of the Port Hills, which lie to the southeast of Christchurch centre. The Gondola terminal is located in the Heathcote Valley about 25 minutes' drive from Cathedral Square, and is serviced by a free Gondola Shuttle operating from the visitor centre, as well as the Lyttelton bus (#28). The Gondola cable cars climb to the 945-metre summit of Mount Cavendish, providing views of Christchurch, the Canterbury Plains, the volcanic outcrops of the Banks Peninsula and the Southern Alps. The station at the top contains a "time tunnel" museum (same hours; free), which covers the geology and geography of the area as well as Maori legends, life aboard early migrant ships and a video about modern-day Canterbury. Also in the station are a viewing deck, souvenir shop, café, and an indifferent restaurant where you can eat while enjoying fantastic views of the city below – especially at night.

From the summit, you can take one of the footpaths that explore the hills or head straight back down – either by cable car, or the more intrepid methods of paragliding or **mountain biking**. The Mountain Bike Adventure Company (bookings essential ⓣ0800/424 534; ⓦwww.cycle-hire-tours.co.nz; free pick-ups from the visitor centre) offers a number of guided or self-guided descents: the "Mount Cavendish Experience" ($40), for example, allows two hours to explore the station and tackle one of three routes down the surrounding Summit Road system with bird's-eye views of Sumner's beaches, Lyttelton and the Banks Peninsula. If you're after more thrills, Nimbus (ⓣ03/326 7922) will **paraglide** you down from near the summit of the gondola, in tandem with an instructor, for about $100.

Christchurch's beaches

As the summer sun bakes the city streets it's very tempting to head for the beach, and Christchurch has plenty on offer; all accessed by frequent buses, and with a choice of places to stay and eat if you fancy spending some time out there.

Around eight kilometres east of the centre, a long swathe of sand runs from Waimari Beach south along a spit to the mouth of the Avon estuary – the whole area is a great place to swim or simply lounge on a towel. The centre of activity is **New Brighton** (bus #5, #6 or #29 from the city), locally famed in the 1970s and early 1980s for its Saturday shopping in the days when nowhere

Accommodation at the beaches

Christchurch is a very manageable city and staying in the centre is by no means unpleasant, but there is something about waking up close to the beach. Staying in the city's waterside suburbs of New Brighton and Sumner is an appealing prospect particularly if you've got your own vehicle, though city buses are frequent.

All the following establishments are marked on the map on p.620.

Golden Sands Motel 121 Estuary Rd, South New Brighton ⓣ03/388 7996, ⓕ388 2221. A small, clean and tidy motel with six units containing kitchens and TVs. There's a pool, kids' playground and you're only 500m from the beach. ❹

Pier Lodge 97 Lonsdale St, New Brighton ⓣ & ⓕ03/388 3388. A large friendly low-cost guesthouse with eight plain bedrooms, three shared bathrooms and a separate kitchen and dining room for guests. There's a big garden, petanque court and tea and coffee available all day. B&B ❸–❹

Southshore Homestay 71a Rockinghorse Rd, Southshore ⓣ03/388 4067. Pleasant homestay with two clean and cosy bedrooms, located just south of New Brighton on a spit between estuary and sea. Twenty minutes' drive from Cathedral Square. Dinner on request ($25). ❺

Sumner Homestay Panorama Rd, Clifton Hill, Sumner ⓣ03/326 5755, ⓔpanoramahomestay @xtra.co.nz. Comfortable accommodation in one double room, with use of a separate guest lounge and a stunning terraced garden. Dinner by arrangement ($25–30). Three minutes' drive from the beach. ❺

Villa Alexandra, 1 Kinsey Terrace, Clifton Hill, Sumner ⓣ03/326 6291, ⓔvilla-Alexandra@xtra.co.nz An excellent-value, spacious villa overlooking Sumner Bay with a sunny veranda and turret, offering a couple of bedrooms and one loft apartment all en suite or with private bathroom. Welcoming hosts prepare meals using garden vegetables and their own free-range eggs (dinner $25, plus wine). ❹–❺

else was open at weekends. Its tenor has slipped a good deal since then, but New Brighton is resplendent with its long concrete **pier**, built seemingly just for the scores of anglers hanging over the sides. Cafés around the base of the pier plus a good stretch of sand make this the place to hang out.

Marine Parade runs north from here, close to **Queen Elizabeth II Park**, an impressive stadium built for the 1974 Commonwealth Games sited at the corner of Travis Road and Bower Avenue, about 500m inland. The complex contains an Olympic-sized swimming pool (Mon–Fri 6am–9pm, Sat & Sun 7am–6pm; $3) and is worth a look around as it is currently being revamped.

South of New Brighton, a spit of land provides shelter for the waters of the Avon and Heathcote river estuary, which is backed by the quiet suburb of **Bromley** and the Te Huingi Manu and Te Huingi Martu **wildlife reserves** (daily dawn-dusk; free), great spots for bird watchers. The estuary basin is excellent for windsurfing and dinghy sailing.

Redcliffs and Sumner

On the whole, you are better off on the southern side of the river estuary where Redcliffs, and particularly Sumner (both accessed by bus #30 or #31 from Cathedral Square), have developed into tight beachside communities with plenty going on and a number of good places to stay and eat.

Redcliffs is significant mainly as the starting point for the five-kilometre-long **Barnett Park Walkway** (1hr 45min round-trip), which begins at a car

△ Yellow-eyed penguin

Walks around Sumner

The *Christchurch Scenic Walk, Nicholson Park and Scarborough* leaflet (free from Christchurch visitor centre) describes a series of **short walks** (each around 15min) that can also be combined to form a **longer route** (2.5km; 1hr 30min).

Mouldeys Track starts just inland from the beach at the junction of Nayland Street and Herberden Avenue. After a short, sharp climb with the sea to the northwest and the head rising to the southeast, the path continues for about fifteen minutes before being crossed by a track to the Boat Shed. Head down this for a great view of Pegasus Bay, stretching away to the northwest (the bay is named after the *Pegasus*, in which Captain Chase sailed the coast looking for sealing grounds), and then join the **Boat Shed to Sumner Head Track**. This ploughs uphill again for about fifteen minutes, skirting the cliff edge and giving increasingly spectacular views.

From **Sumner Head** you can see the Kaikoura Peninsula in the west, and Godley Head and Banks Peninsula to the east. At this point you have two alternatives for reaching the botanical reserve of **Nicholson Park**: either head straight inland along a clay track to the park ten minutes away; or, more interestingly, continue around the cliffs, climbing quite steeply, for views down the eastern side of the head (20min). On entering Nicholson park the latter track leads onto a small point, from which you can see **Whitewash Head** (so named because of the large number of seabirds that nest on its cliffs), and the **Giants Nose**, a small finger of land behind which is the bay named **Taylor's Mistake**, where according to local lore, a captain named Taylor ran aground after mistaking the bay for the entrance to Lyttelton Harbour.

park just off Main Road. A well-formed track climbs through grassland onto rock outcrops, with steps giving access to a large rock shelter and several caves. The walkway then bisects a copse of native bush and passes a seasonal waterfall, before crossing a creek and descending via bluffs past **Paradise Cave**, home of a Maori family in the 1890s.

As you follow the coast around from Redcliffs you pass the river mouth, and estuary beaches become sea beaches, the best being at **Sumner**, a Norfolk Pine-backed strip of craft shops, restaurants, cafés, wine bars, surf shacks and a cinema, all fronting a broad patch of golden sand. Named after Dr J.B. Sumner, Archbishop of Canterbury and president of the Canterbury Association in the 1850s, it's now one of Christchurch's more desirable suburbs and a popular destination on summer weekends. The highlight of the beach is **Cave Rock**, a geological anomaly of honeycombed rock – its underside is peppered with little caves like an enormous Swiss cheese – which you can walk through at low tide. You can also clamber up the rock to reach the lifeguard's lookout point on top. More or less opposite Cave Rock on the other side of Main Road is a small, untidy and much-graffitied **moa cave**, where bones from these now-extinct flightless birds were discovered. Most interesting of all, though, are a series of short walks to and around Sumner Head (see box above) – a must if you lack the time to explore the Banks Peninsula further south.

Eating

Christchurch has the largest number and widest range of **restaurants** in the South Island, with yet more opening every week and more culinary styles added to the old favourites. Particularly popular now are sushi houses, Thai restaurants and, increasingly, Indian food, alongside an abundance of extremely good kiwi cuisine that mixes styles from Europe and Asia. To whet your appetite, buy a copy of the comprehensive *Classic Canterbury Dining Out Guide* from the visitor centre ($4.95). Top-quality gourmet cuisine is increasingly well represented, and now nicely balances the selection of ethnic restaurants on offer. There's also a growing number of fun, themed establishments featuring live music, and for a more down-to-earth atmosphere, many of the city's **pubs** serve hearty food to soak up their brews.

With more and more **cafés** and **bars** offering substantial food, distinctions between eating and drinking venues are increasingly blurred, and many of the establishments listed under "Drinking" (p.360) are perfectly good places in which to enjoy a main meal, as well as a bit of a bop afterwards. For something different, you could always try the Tramway transport system, who operate a **dinner tram** (☎03/3667511), a mobile restaurant operating from 7.30pm offering local delicacies as well as a broader selection of New Zealand cuisine at $99 for five courses and drinks.

All the places listed below are **open daily**, unless otherwise stated. We've also noted any unusual opening hours.

Central Christchurch

For **eating** there is little reason to venture beyond the Four Avenues; in fact you'll find most of what you need in the grid of downtown streets close to Cathedral Square, notably along Colombo Street, Cashel Street, Manchester Street and High Street. One area which deserves special mention is Oxford Terrace between Cashel and Gloucester streets, which has become known as "The Strip" and bears a run of restaurant/bars that all spill out onto pavement seating with views across the street to the River Avon. There's plenty of good dining, and as the evening wears on the lights go down, the music is cranked up and booze flows freely. The clubbing set usually pops in for a couple of hours around 10.30pm before drifting off to livelier dancefloors.

Cafés and takeaways

Bohemian Café Bar 256 Oxford Terrace ☎03/366 2563. Slightly out of the way, quiet and just across the road from the river is this open-fronted eatery-cum-bar that provides the ideal spot for weekend brunch. They also do breakfast, lunch and dinner, good coffee and have a series of tempting specials on blackboards, like honey-grilled salmon and peppers on pasta with a peach-wine sauce. Prices range between $5 and $25 and it's not the cheapest place to drink, but the setting makes it worthwhile.

Boulevard Bakehouse in the Arts Centre, Worcester St. A delightfully simple place where you can get a good brie-and-salad-filled bagel, sit outside and watch the world go by; also serves breakfast, lunch and snacks, including muffins and organic focaccia ($5–10). Open Mon–Thurs & Sun 8am–9pm, Fri & Sat 8am–11pm.

City Seafood Market 277 Manchester St. An extraordinary range of reasonably priced fresh fish, including the best fish and chips in the centre of the city (takeaway only). Mon–Thurs 9am–7pm, Fri 9am–8pm, Sat 9am–1pm.

Le Café in the Arts Centre, Worcester St ☎03/366 7722. This very popular café is open from 7am to midnight daily – except Friday and Saturday, when it stays open until 2am. Pop in anytime for breakfast specials, club sandwiches ($12), a selection from their broad-ranging main menu (all dishes are under $18), including fruit crumble ($7) and excellent coffee. BYO & Licensed.

Café Metro cnr Colombo St & Kilmore St. One of the best cafés in this part of town, right by the town hall with great coffee, a good range of quiches, pies, muffins and cakes, and a varied stack of up-to-date mags to read.

C1 Espresso 150 High St. Tardis-like, red-brick, young and funky café where you get filling gourmet sandwiches (around $10), omelettes, bagels, pizza, flat breads, smoothies and dynamite coffee, all of which can be enjoyed as you browse their selection of mags and papers. Old rucksacks hang from a metal rack, there's a mishmash of furniture and boomy music.

Copenhagen Bakery Armagh St, diagonally opposite *Costas* (below). Consistently one of the best bakers in town, with good Danish crusty bread, muffins, biscuits and cakes. Mon–Fri only.

Costas Souvlaki Bar 150 Armagh St (Mon–Sat 11am–8pm). Unpretentious and cheap little kebab, falafel, greek salad and, obviously souvlaki cafe that has been around since time began.

The Daily Bagel 179a Victoria St. Tiny shop with three tables and a few seats under an awning outside that serves authentic bagels with New York-inspired fillings and superb coffee. Mon–Fri 7.30am–3.30pm, Sat 8am–3pm & Sun 10am–3pm.

Drexel's 106 Hereford St. Surprisingly comfortable American-style breakfast and lunch diner serving the likes of omelettes ($13), chicken fajitas ($14) and a full stack of pancakes ($8). Reservations advisable for Saturday and Sunday brunch ☎03/379 8089.

The Globe Café 171 High St. Wonderful coffee spot and lunchtime hangout for students from the Jazz school across the road, which turns into a slightly more sophisticated eatery on Fridays after 5.30pm. The spacious interior and pavement seating are both great for people-watching over something from their huge selection of teas, or tucking into all manner of panini, salads, quiches and stunning cakes. The evening menu varies taking a particular country as the theme and producing its signature dishes. Licensed.

The Laughing Cow cnr Colombo and Mollet sts. An alcohol-free, strictly vegetarian café run by some commercially very switched-on Hare Krishnas and serving good-quality food at rock-bottom prices (all you can eat $5). Open for lunch Mon–Fri 11am–4pm.

The Herb Centre 225 Kilmore St. Daytime eat-in and take-out café specializing in vegetarian and vegan cuisine served up with a range of caffeine-free drinks or organic coffee. For the dedicated, there's Piko Healthfoods, two doors up at no. 229, which sells great bread and self-catering supplies and has a good earthy noticeboard. Closed Sun.

Java cnr High St & Lichfield St. Young and very groovy coffee bar with options on the strongest coffee in town and very loud music at the more challenging end of the spectrum. Low-cost meals start with breakfast and continue with hot snacks, salads, sandwiches, specialty burgers ($5–12) and cakes until the small hours. A mezzanine floor for smokers. Open 24hr at weekends.

Under the Red Verandah 502 Worcester St. Delightful suburban, daytime café fifteen minutes' walk east of the centre, but worth the effort for its predominantly vegetarian fare – pumpkin and corn cakes, bacon and kumara frittata, organic breads and good coffee served in the bare-boards interior or out in the sunny courtyard. Closed Sun & Mon.

Vic's Café and Bakery 132 Victoria St. Bakers of the best organic bread in the city; also purveyors of exceptionally good-value and tasty meals throughout the day. BYOB. Sun–Tues 7am–5pm and Wed–Sat 7am–10pm.

Restaurants

Aiki 599 Gloucester St. A Japanese organic kitchen producing authentic, seemingly simple but highly stylized and very tasty food at middle-of-the-range prices, daily for lunch and dinner. No bookings. Licensed.

Annie's The Arts Centre ☎03/365 0566. Superb wine bar and restaurant within the polished wood-floor confines of the Arts Centre and spilling outside into the courtyard. Lunches ($13–16) might include a summer frittata or Cajun baked chicken, though if there are a few of you order the antipasto plate ($20), groaning with mussels, squid, smoked salmon and salami. Dinner mains are usually $23–30 and include aubergine tofu ratatouille and baked Canterbury ostrich. Licensed.

Ann's Thai Restaurant and Bar 165 Hereford St ☎03/379 9843. Classic Thai cooking in a simple, clean-lined café-style restaurant with a pleasant little bar and broad wine list. Try the spicy salad or the roast duck.

Azure 128 Oxford Terrace. Bustling moderate to expensive restaurant and bar that is very much part of "The Strip", serving Mediterranean-inspired dishes on Oxford Terrace or inside. Occasional live jazz, plus a DJ at weekends.

Blue Note 22 New Regent St ☎03/379 9674. Restaurant and bar where diners spill out onto the pedestrianized street as they tuck into $18–25 mains such as warm lamb and feta with cashews and salad or chicken stuffed with leek and feta accompanied by zingy new-world wines. Live jazz two nights a week. Mon–Sat 11am til late. Licensed.

Café Latino 830b Colombo St ☎03/366 9264. A little café (actually more of a restaurant) in its infancy, where you can sample dishes from Mexico, Chile, Venezuala, Argentina and Hondouras plus a range of Caribbean fare, all at good prices in a friendly and relaxed atmosphere. A real shot in the arm. Open Tues–Sun dinner only, Fri for lunch as well. Licensed & BYO.

Chancery 98 Gloucester Rd ☎03/379 4317. Traditional, no-nonsense New Zealand restaurant – and that really does mean roast lamb, fried fish or steaks served with potatoes or chips, roast kumara (sweet potato) and possibly another vegetable, all at good-value prices and in tacky surroundings. Licensed.

Cook'n' with Gas 23 Worcester St. Award-winning, intimate restaurant based in an historic villa, opposite the Arts Centre, using fresh, exclusively NZ ingredients. Mon–Sat dinner only.

Dux de Lux cnr Hereford St & Montreal St. Excellent restaurant and microbrewery (see p.630) that's one of the most popular places in town, with outdoor and indoor seating and a longstanding reputation for superb seafood and vegetarian meals at moderate prices. Licensed.

Hay's Café 63 Victoria St ⓣ03/379 7501. A must for lamb aficionados, though the fairly spartan interior gives little indication of the exceptional quality and presentation of the succulent dishes prepared using lambs reared on the owners' Banks Peninsula property. Mains around $25–30; closed Mon lunch and Sun. Licensed & BYO.

The Honey Pot 114 Lichfield St (no bookings). Brilliant restaurant and all-day café with funky decor and rustic wooden tables, where you can enjoy all-day breakfasts, pizzas on nan bread, char-grilled marinated lamb, fantastic steaks and imaginatively presented veggies, daily 8am–late. Licensed.

Le Bon Bolli cnr Worcester St & Montreal St ⓣ03/374 9444. Don't let the modern brick exterior fool you – inside you could imagine you're in France. Lunchtime attracts the business crowd to dine in the café downstairs. Upstairs is more formal (booking essential) with beautifully presented French cuisine such as duck in orange sauce ($32). Licensed.

Little Indian cnr of Gloucester & New Regent St. Café-style, reliable Indian restaurant, part of a chain, with quite expensive but still authentic curries and an extensive veggie menu, from $16–26. Best value are the set menus, for lunch and dinner. Licensed.

Main Street Café & Bar 840 Colombo St ⓣ03/365 0421. Very good vegetarian restaurant with a wide selection of dishes (some vegan) served in huge portions at low prices. Come with a big appetite and the capacity for $2 bottomless coffee. Licensed.

Oxford on Avon 794 Colombo St ⓣ03/379 7148. Pub on the banks of the Avon, famed for its enormous portions of unimaginative nosh. Always busy with the food-bargain hunters and open for breakfast, lunch and dinner. The bar serves the usual stock of native beers.

Plazzo del Marinaio's 108 Hereford St (2nd floor of Shades Mall) ⓣ03/365 5911. If you've been saving up for a week then this is the place to treat yourself to some of the best seafood and steaks, plus the finest wine, port, brandy and malt whisky. The extent of the lavish indulgence means you'll be lucky to get change from $100 for two. Open daily for lunch and dinner.

Penang Noodle House 172a Manchester St ⓣ03/377 2638. Cheap, cheerful and authentic, with a menu that never strays over $16. Try the pan-fried noodles with any two mains or one of the noodle soups and/or the specials. Lunch Mon–Sat only, dinner daily.

Retour cnr Cambridge Terrace & Manchester St ⓣ03/365 2888. Beautifully located restaurant in a glass-sided bandstand on the banks of the Avon. The award-winning European chefs melt influences from the world over with fresh and wholesome local ingredients to create a real eating experience to remember (mains $20–40). Dinner only. Licensed & BYO.

Saggio di Vino 185 Victoria St ⓣ03/379 4006. Classy tile-floored Italian restaurant where dishes such as chicken and artichoke salad ($24) or fresh grouper fillet ($25) can be accompanied by something from an extensive award-winning wine cellar; all available by the glass. Servings are not overly generous but what there is is delicious. Dinner nightly; lunch Thurs & Fri. Licensed.

Santorini Greek Ouzeri cnr Gloucester St & Cambridge Terrace ⓣ03/379 6975. A taste of the Greek islands, with live Bouzouki Tues–Sat evenings only; licensed.

Sophies 8 Papanui Rd ⓣ03/355 2133. Pound for dollar the best-value steakhouse in the city, run by Sophie Ellerm, a larger-than-life woman of tremendous energy and even greater eccentricity. Almost everything on the menu has steak in it somewhere, and comes in portions fit to make John Wayne bust, all dished up in surroundings that reflect their owner. Open daily for breakfast, lunch and dinner; licensed.

Untouched World 155 Roydvale Ave. The ultimate shopping and eating experience from one of New Zealand's home grown and growing icons. Untouched World produce fantastic natural, multipurpose designer clothing as well as beautifully presented food and wine in this one-stop outlet/café. Lunch and dinner; licensed.

Valentino's 813 Colombo St ⓣ03/377 1886. Specializing in Italian pasta, pizza and grilled dishes, this is a no-nonsense, highly popular spot, particularly busy towards the end of the week. Dinner daily; lunch weekdays only; licensed.

Papanui Road and Merivale

There's little culinary reason to leave the city centre and head out to the suburbs, but if you are staying along Papanui Road or in the northern reaches of the city, then there are some handy and reputable places to dine nearby.

All the following places are marked on the map on p.620.

Aikmans 154 Aikmans Rd, Merivale. A moderately priced café/bar with a laid-back atmosphere, and serving all-day breakfast, and a broad range of salads, pasta dishes and curries for lunch and dinner. More of a bar as the evening wears on. Licensed.

Bologna 6 Papanui Rd ⓣ03/379 7497. Tiny country Italian restaurant with a short menu of traditional and gourmet pizzas plus pasta dishes and Italian desserts, all served without fuss at modest prices. There's a bottle store across the road – handy since it is BYO only.

Brigitte's Espresso/Wine Bar Hawkesbury Building, Aikmans Rd, Merivale. Conveniently located opposite *Aikmans*, this is a another relaxed place with an open courtyard at the back, and good-quality Mediterranean and Kiwi-style food as well as some wonderful New Zealand–Thai combinations, all at moderate prices. Licensed.

Kannigas Thai 18a Papanui Rd ⓣ03/355 6228. Great Thai food served in fairly soulless surroundings at low prices – try the chicken pad Thai ($12) or ginger prawn and rice ($15). BYO.

New Brighton and Sumner

You won't starve during your day at the beach. With one notable exception, New Brighton makes do with cheap-and-cheerful beachfront cafés and takeaways, but Sumner is well endowed with notable places to dine and drink. You might even want to come out here for the evening, especially considering the #31 bus back to the city runs until gone 11pm.

All the following places are marked on the map on p.620.

Celini's 32 Nyland Rd, Sumner ⓣ03/326 6720. Bright, bustling and modestly priced café serving a wide range of dishes from Indonesian sweet beef curry and Akaroa smoked salmon salad to Mediterranean vegetable-stuffed pita, smoothies and coffee. Licensed and BYO wine only.

Club Bazaar Pizzeria 15 Wakefield Ave, Sumner ⓣ03/326 6155. Bar and elaborate balcony where you can sample cheap pasta dishes and pretty acceptable pizzas in a distinctive atmosphere of Kiwi nostalgia. Licensed.

On the Beach 25 The Esplanade, Sumner ⓣ03/326 7090. Excellent seafood lunches and dinners served up on the veranda or inside this light and spacious restaurant built out over the sand beside Cave Rock. Prices reflect the location, with mains starting around the $25 mark. Licensed.

Ruptured Duck 4 Wakefield Ave, Sumner ⓣ03/326 5488. Pizza palace where a large polystyrene duck watches your every mouthful of such popular favourites as Moroccan lamb and capsicums or pork with kumara – toppings that are an acquired taste but have a cult following. Licensed & BYO wine only.

Waterfront Café & Bar Marine Parade at the foot of the pier, New Brighton ⓣ03/388 4483. New café that's become *the* place for coffee, lunches and dinners such as salmon ravioli ($15) or stir-fried seafood, including mussels ($14). Sit inside or out, sheltered from the onshore breeze by glass panels. Licensed.

Drinking, nightlife and entertainment

Gone are the days when evenings in Christchurch revolved around decaying, male-dominated Edwardian pubs. The modern city harbours enough traditional hostelries, late-night cafés and throbbing music bars to suit most tastes, and many of these offer more than just booze: live music, resident DJs and good food are increasingly taken for granted. After about 10pm the restaurants of

"The Strip" metamorphose into rowdy bars and clubs: just follow the crowds.

Serious music and drama are centred on venues like the Town Hall and the Arts Centre, while less cerebral entertainment is offered by a concentration of downtown clubs and a clutch of city-centre cinemas. Entertainment **listings** are published in Christchurch's daily newspaper *The Press* (the "What's On" section on Fridays is best for live music and clubbing), and in the free monthly magazines *Volume* and *Presto*.

Drinking

Most drinking venues are to be found within the Four Avenues, with Colombo and Cashel streets harbouring a particularly dense concentration of watering holes. This is probably the best place to stroll at weekends, when a variety of establishments use loud music and late licences to pull in the crowds. In addition to the The Strip's establishments (*Viaduct*, *The L Lounge*, *All Bar One*, *Azure*, *Coyote*, and *124*), a few people also count *Vesuvio* as part of this litany of merriment – it's just a block away from *Viaduct*.

Pubs and bars

All Bar One 130 Oxford Terrace. Occasional live music between these oh-so-orange walls, but mostly DJs playing hip hop, dance, 1980s retro and more mainstream chart sounds. Open till late Fri & Sat.

Azure 128 Oxford Terrace. DJs create a lively atmosphere at weekends with progressive, house and hardcore sounds, while the rest of the week it's a very mild-mannered bar.

Eye Spy Lichfield St. A late-night bar full of mellow music and intimate DJ action Thurs–Sat. Known mainly for its stylish decor, padded walls, lovely cocktails and a higher-rolling crowd.

Ballies 50 Cathedral Sq. Lively, much improved and recently renovated old Irish-style bar with live local jazz and rock bands.

Barcelona cnr of Oxford Terrace and Worcester St. Part of The Strip, serving half-decent food during the day and early evening and then becoming a bit more alcohol- and dance-oriented particularly on Friday and Saturday nights.

The Bog 82 Cashel Mall. Rowdy Irish bar with draught stouts and bitters plus live music Wed–Sat evenings and jam sessions on Tues. Has *The Vault* above it.

The Boulevard 76 Hereford St, cnr with Oxford Terrace. Part of The Strip, with after-dark DJ fun from 10pm and some passable grub up to that point. Open from 8am till late daily.

Brewers Arms 177 Papanui Rd, Merivale. Northwest of the centre, this is a suburban pub with horse brasses, a range of beers, and English-style pub food in large portions at moderate prices. Open from 11am until late.

Café Bleu 88 Cashel St. All-day café that becomes a drinking and dancing venue at the end of the week. DJs play mostly pop music and they occasionally have live jazz early in the evenings on Fri and Sat.

The Chambers Bar in *The Civic*, 186 Manchester St. Pleasing and spacious bar with live music most evenings, while *The Civic* acts as a venue for dance parties, bigger-draw live acts and latin dancing on Mon, Tues and Thurs.

Coyote 126 Oxford Terrace. The heart of "The Strip" (see above) which, around 10pm, becomes one of the main gathering places before a night's clubbing with a mixture of commercial chart-toppers and house music. Still no excuse for the imitation adobe walls and fake beams.

Dux de Lux cnr Hereford St & Montreal St. Ever popular restaurant (see p.628) that doubles as a great bar with several award-winning beers brewed on the premises. Live music Thurs–Sat and no cover charge.

Fin Bar Gloucester St. Traditional Irish pub with occasional live music.

Grumpy Mole cnr of Cashel St & Manchester St. Long, cowboy-style, saloon bar, with pool table and big-screen TV.

Holy Grail 88 Worcester St. A sports bar by day and a DJ-orchestrated dance spot at night with chart hits and retro 70s, 80s and 90s to keep the 900-plus that pack this barn-like den interested. Separate restaurant and quietish corners to be found.

Loaded Hog cnr Manchester St & Cashel St. Comfortable but ever-busy city-centre boozer with ales brewed on the premises, and good bar meals in the $10–15 range served all day and substantial breakfasts at weekends. Jazz on Tues, latin dancing on Thurs and DJs Fri and Sat.

Main Street Café & Bar 840 Colombo St

☎03/365 0421. Ever popular bar attached to the vegetarian café of the same name (see p.628) with a huge range of imported and local beers.

124 124 Oxford Terrace. Recently revamped, old "Strip" favourite which is trying to smarten up its act and go for the serious dining and drinking dollars while benefiting from being next to the places all the pretty people go to.

Rocky Cola Café Bar 154 Manchester St. Usually a beer-drinkers' paradise with added DJs, dance music, karaoke-style singing on Wed, open mike on Thurs, backpackers' drink offers and plain old loud and lively on Fri–Sat.

Rock Pool 85 Hereford St. A broad spectrum of imported beers, cocktails and 22 pool tables to choose from, as well as a PA rarely turned below ear-splitting level. Daily 9am till late.

Sullivan's 150–152 Manchester St. Noisy NZ–Irish bar with pictures of the old country, gallons of beer, live Irish-style bands from Wed–Sat, and late-night dancing towards the end of the week.

Trader McKendry's 179 Cashel St, on the corner with Manchester St and opposite the *Loaded Hog*. Big, boisterous pub with wooden floors, arcade games and big TVs. DJs Thurs–Sat and the occasional live band.

Vesuvio 182 Oxford Terrace ☎03/365 4183. East and west come together at this European-style café and cool night bar, where all the food is made using fresh local ingredients. After 10.30pm items on the menu are reduced to half price and you are entertained by opera on Sun & Mon, jazz Tues–Fri and jazz, blues and Djs on Sat. As well as an extensive wine list they also have 60 single malts.

Viaduct 136 Oxford Terrace. A plush-looking restaurant and bar with progressive, house and mellower sounds on Friday and Saturday nights, and a cocktail-type atmosphere the rest of the week.

Clubs and gigs

Christchurch may not be the clubbing capital of the southern hemisphere, but there's a sprinkling of places within the Four Avenues offering a range of dance-music styles. Some of these are full-on **club venues**, although there's a growing number of bars which transform themselves into dancing venues at weekends by drafting in a DJ or two. There's a surfeit of bars offering **live music**, although most places content themselves with a meagre diet of cover bands or minor local rock acts. If you want to just stroll around and see where the crowds are going, make for Lichfield Street, home to a heady mix of cutting-edge dance clubs and seedy massage parlours.

There's a **club information** line (☎03/363 5000) giving a rundown of what's on from night to night.

BASE 674 Colombo St ☎03/377 7149. Dark and sweaty, high-energy club with guest DJs mainly spinning platters from the UK dance scene. Open until late Thurs–Sat. Cover charge $3–10.

Civic 186 Manchester St ☎03/374 9966. Popular, large clubbing venue offering a range of themed nights (eg funk, hip-hop, rare groove, house, techno), some headline live acts and latin dancing on three weeknights; check listings in *The Press* to see what's on. 10pm–6am.

The Church 110 Lichfield St – look for the grey gargoyles perched on the concrete awning. The newest, brashest and biggest club in town, with massive dance floors, big bars and quieter hideaways for a young energetic crowd to whom dance is religion. From 9pm till whenever.

Da Box 112a Lichfield St, up the stairs beside *The Church* (see above). A small dark club with a good bar and DJ music ranging from retro funk to house via fever. Very busy with a discerning crowd.

Lone Star 26 Manchester St. A jumping bar and nightspot that also serves an eclectic mix of Southwestern and Cajun food.

Ministry 88–90 Lichfield St ☎03/379 2910. One of the biggest and liveliest of the clubs, with two dance floors; deep, dark and with a thumping drum'n'base till very late.

Occidental Pub and Chats Club Hereford St, opposite Latimer Square. Buzzing spot with live bands on Fridays & Saturdays and dance music.

Platinum 76 Lichfield St ☎03/377 7891. Well-respected, gay cellar bar with an even mix of men and women. Thumping dance music In the main room and a quieter cocktail bar out the back.

Sammy's Jazz Review 14 Bedford Row. Live jazz in hepcat surroundings from 5pm till late Mon–Sat. Good Kiwi food to boot, and the electric-blue glass revolving door will fascinate.

Concerts, theatre, cinema and spectator sports

Apart from in Rotorua, the best chance you'll get to sample a Maori concert (and savour a *hangi*) is here in Christchurch at the **Nga Hau E Wha National Marae**, 250 Pages Rd (Marae of the Four Winds; ⓣ0800/456 898 or ⓣ388 7685, ⓦwww.nationalmarae.co.nz), which was set up in 1990 to symbolize the meeting of people from all points of the compass. The meeting house, one of the largest in New Zealand, is named Aoraki after Mount Cook (see box on p.704), and the carved posts (*poupou*) depict ancient and contemporary ancestors, acting as memory aids encouraging the continuation of oral tradition. A unique feature is the appearance of two European ancestors (one of which is Captain Cook), intended to symbolize the coming together of the two peoples (for more on Maoritanga, see Contexts). Provided they get enough advance bookings, there's a choice of two events: the "Night of Maori Magic" (daily 6.45pm; $60) follows pretty much along the lines of the Rotorua-style concert and *hangi* but includes a detailed look around the *marae* with a full explanation of the protocol and tribal history; the "Maori Tour and Concert" (daily 7.55pm; $27.50), is the same except that there's no *hangi*. Free transport is laid on for those with reservations.

The shining star in Christchurch's **drama** firmament is the Arts Centre's Court Theatre, 20 Worcester Boulevard (bookings ⓣ0800/333100 & 03/366 6992, ⓦwww.courttheatre.org.nz), home to one of New Zealand's longest-standing and most highly reputed professional theatre companies. Their current and upcoming performances are well advertised around town and in *The Press*. Touring shows frequently play in the James Hay Theatre at the Town Hall on Victoria Square (box office ⓣ03/366 8899), which also has a programme of **classical music** and ballet in the main auditorium.

Concerts by touring **jazz** and **rock** acts take place either at the Arts Centre or at the Theatre Royal on Gloucester Street (ⓣ03/366 6326), a fine old Edwardian venue which attracts the glitzier, more mainstream acts. You can catch a host of local jazz and rock performers playing in some of the bars and clubs listed under "Drinking" and "Clubs and gigs", on pp.630-631. There is also a varied programme of music events in Hagley Park throughout the summer (ⓣ03/371 1495, ⓦwww.summertimes.org.nz).

If it is first-run international **movies** you are after, head for the city-centre multiplexes: the Regent, 94 Worcester St (ⓣ 03/366 0140), right by Cathedral Square; Hoyts 8, Moorhouse Ave (ⓣ03/366 6367), at the southern end of Manchester Street; and the Rialto, 250 Moorhouse Ave (ⓣ03/374 9404) on the corner of Durham Street. **Arthouse** movies are shown at the Academy and Cloisters cinemas (ⓣ03/366 0167, ⓦwww.artfilms.co.nz) in the Arts Centre.

Jade Stadium, southeast of the centre near the junction of Moorhouse Avenue and Ferry Road, is the main venue for the big spectator **sports**, hosting **cricket** in the summer and **rugby** on weekends throughout the autumn and winter. **Information** and **tickets** can be obtained from the stadium itself (ⓣ03/366 2961) or from Canterbury All Sports (ⓣ03/366 9688).

Listings

Airlines Air New Zealand, 702 Colombo St, Triangle Centre ⓣ0800/737 000, flight arrivals and departures ⓣ 03/374 7100; British Airways (see Qantas); Japan Air Lines, Level 11 ⓣ03/366

5879; Jordanian Airlines, 391 Manchester St ⓣ03/365 3910; Mount Cook Airlines, 91 Worcester St ⓣ0800/737 000; Lufthansa, International Ariport ⓣ0800 945 220; Qantas, Level 18, Price Waterhouse Building, 119 Armagh St ⓣ0800/808 767 & 03/379 6504; Singapore Airlines, Level 3, Forsyth Barr Building, cnr Armagh St & Colombo St ⓣ0800/808 909.

American Express 773 Colombo St (Mon–Fri 9am–5pm, plus Dec–Feb Sat 9am–noon) ⓣ03/365 7366.

Automobile Association 210 Hereford St ⓣ03/379 1280.

Ballooning Up Up And Away (ⓣ03/355 7141, ⓦwww.ballooning.co.nz) offers peaceful and eye-bulging hour-long balloon flights over Christchurch for around $170-220. Aoraki Balloons (ⓣ03/302 8172, www.nzballooning.co.nz) also offer good trips from $199–540.

Banks and exchange Most banks have branches and ATMs on or near Colombo St and Hereford St. Foreign exchange is best conducted at American Express (see above); Thomas Cook (see p.634); Asia Pacific World Travel, cnr Hereford St & Manchester St (ⓣ03/379 5722); and Travelex, 730a Colombo St (ⓣ 03/365 4194).

Bike rental The most convenient bike rental is from Trailblazers, 86 Worcester St, by the Square (ⓣ03/366 6033; $6 per hr, $26 per day), though you can also call City Cycle Hire (ⓣ0800/343 848) who deliver bikes to your accommodation or to the visitor centre. Note that Trailblazers also do long-term rentals with touring bikes equipped with panniers going for around $250 for 4wks.

Bookshops The majors, Whitcoulls and Dymock's, are both in Cashel Street Mall. Another good high-street bookshop is Scorpio Books, 79 Hereford St; Liberty Books, 151 High St, is good for second-hand paperbacks; while Map World, 173 Gloucester St, has the best range of walking maps and street plans. Bookshops are generally open Mon–Thur 8am–3pm, Fri & Sat 9am–4pm.

Car rental There are dozens of car rental places in Christchurch and yet from January to March you may have trouble landing anything if you don't book ahead; for more on car hire, see "Basics", p.33. Of the majors, Avis, Budget, Hertz and Thrifty are all at the airport, while smaller agencies often deliver. The following are the majors plus some reputable local agencies: Ace, 237 Lichfield St (ⓣ0800/202 029 & 03/366 3222, ⓕ377 4610); Avis, 26 Lichfield St (ⓣ03/379 6133); Avon, 166 St Asaph St (ⓣ 03/379 3822); Better, 226 St Asaph St (ⓣ0800/269 696 & 03/365 2979, ⓕ365 6725); Budget, cnr Oxford Terrace & Lichfield St (ⓣ03/366 0072, ⓕ365 7194); Hertz, 46 Lichfield St (ⓣ03/366 0549, airport ⓣ03/358 6730); McDonalds, 156 Tuam St (ⓣ0800/164 165 & 03/366 0929, ⓕ366 0927); National, 134 Victoria St (ⓣ03/366 5574, ⓕ366 5027); Nationwide, 524 Wairakei Rd (ⓣ03/359 2013, ⓕ359 2085); Pegasus, 127 Peterborough St (ⓣ03/365 1100, ⓕ365 1104); Renny's Rentals, 341 Madras St (ⓣ03/366 6790 & 0800/944 466); Scotties, 288 Lincoln Rd (ⓣ0800/736 825 & 03/338 0997, ⓕ338 0992); Thrifty, at the airport (ⓣ03/358 7533); U-Save, 12 Holt Place (ⓣ03/358 2299).

Emergency services ⓣ111.

Festivals The local city council enthusiastically backs a number of summer festivals, most of them much better than you'd expect to find elsewhere. Look out particularly for the Jazz Festival (mid-Oct); the World Buskers Festival (late Jan), which is lots of fun and free and mostly takes place around the Arts Centre and in front of the *Dux De Lux*; and the Festival of Romance (early to mid-Feb,) on the lead up to Valentine's Day. Check at the information centre for more details.

Horse riding Heathcote Valley Riding School, 131 Bridle Path Rd, 500m from the Gondola terminal (ⓣ03/384 1971), offer hour-long treks for around $30 per person for a minimum of four people.

Internet access Christchurch is littered with places offering internet access, but none are bigger and more centrally sited than Vadal (daily 8am–10pm, ⓔvadal@xtra.co.nz) on the north side of Cathedral Square, with fast connections, low prices and cheap international phone calls as well as a left luggage facility. Other places to try are: Cyber Café, 127 Gloucester St (Mon–Fri 8am–10pm, Sat & Sun 9am–8pm); Cyber Pass Internet Café, 27 Chancery Lane, near the Square (Mon–Fri 9am–9pm, Sat & Sun 11am–4pm); and E-Caf, 28 Worcester St, above the Boulevard Bakehouse (daily 8am–midnight); Netopia, 728 Colombo St, daily 10.30am–late; and finally Net Zone, 78 Worcester St, daily 9am–10pm.

Left Luggage Vadal (see "Internet accesss" above) store luggage from $3 a day per item.

Library Christchurch Central Library, Gloucester St (Mon–Fri 10am–9pm, Sat 10am–4pm, Sun 1–4pm).

Medical treatment In emergencies call ⓣ111. Biggest of the hospitals is Christchurch Hospital, cnr Oxford Terrace & Riccarton Ave (ⓣ03/364 0640; emergency dept ⓣ03/364 0270). For a doctor at any time call The 24 Hour Surgery, cnr Bealey Ave & Colombo St (ⓣ03/365 7777, no appointment necessary).

Mountain biking The Mountain Bike Adventure Company (ⓣ0800/424 534) offers a range of trips, from just over an hour to a full day rattling around the hills ($45–70).

Paragliding Nimbus Paragliding (Ⓣ03/328 8383) offer 20-minute tandem flights from around $100 per person; pick-ups available.
Pharmacies Urgent Pharmacy, 931 Colombo St, cnr Bealey Ave (Ⓣ03/366 4439), stays open daily until 11pm.
Police Central Police Station Ⓣ03/379 3999.
Post office The main post office on Cathedral Square (Ⓣ03/353 1814) has poste restante facilities.
Shuttle buses For airport and train station transfers, shuttle buses offer a cheaper alternative to taxis. Try Super Shuttle (Ⓣ03/365 5655), City Shuttles (Ⓣ03/343 0399) or Falcon Shuttles (Ⓣ0800/859 898), who all run from Cathedral Square to the airport ($15 for one, $8 each for three). They'll also pick you up from your accommodation. If you're catching a morning flight you should book your transfer the evening before.
Taxis Blue Star (Ⓣ03/379 9799); Gold Band (Ⓣ03/379 5795); City Maxi (Ⓣ03/343 0399); and Arrow Taxis (Ⓣ03/379 9999; they also have a cab to accommodate disabled customers).
Thomas Cook cnr Armagh St & Colombo St (Ⓣ03/379 6600; Mon–Thurs 8.30am–6pm, Fri 8.30am–8pm, Sat & Sun 10am–4pm).
Tours Guided walking tours (Ⓣ03/342 7634; daily: Oct–April 10am & 1pm; May–Sept 1pm; 2hr; $8), led by local volunteers who really know their stuff, start from a kiosk in Cathedral Square near the cathedral entrance. Christchurch Sightseeing Tours (Ⓣ0508/669 660, Ⓦwww.christchurchtours.co.nz) offer 3 tours and combinations which save $5–10: City Gardens (mid-Sept to early Dec & mid-Jan to March Tues–Sat 9.30am–12.30pm; $25) visits 4 of their roster of 20 gardens each day; Heritage Homes (Wed & Sat 1.30–4.30pm; $25) calls at 3 homes not normally open to the public; and Sightseeing (mid-Sept to mid-April daily 9am & 1.30pm, mid-April to mid-Sept 1.30pm) spends 3–4hr touring the vicinity including Mona Vale, Sumner, Lyttelton and the Summit Road. Christchurch Wildlife Cruises (Ⓣ0800/436 574, Ⓦwww.blackcat.co.nz) runs 2hr Hector's dolphin spotting cruises on Lyttelton Harbour (Nov–March 10am & 2.30pm; April–Oct 2.30pm only; $39). They depart from Lyttelton Marina at Magazine Bay, but there's a free shuttle running from the Christchurch visitor centre half an hour before the boat departure. For tours of the wineries, see box on p.636.
Train information Ⓣ0800/802 802.
Travel agencies Your best bets are Destinations Travel, 485 Papanui Rd (Ⓣ03/352 2612); Flight Centre, 761 Colombo St (Ⓣ03/377 1441); Guthrey United Travel, 126 Cashel St (Ⓣ03/379 3560); and STA, 90 Cashel St (Ⓣ03/379 9098), or Student University Building, Canterbury University (Ⓣ03/348 6372).
Whitewater rafting Easily the best trip in these parts is with Rangitata Rafts (Ⓣ0800/251 251, Ⓦwww.rangitata.rafts.co.nz) who run the Grade IV+ gorge section of the Rangitata River between September and May ($115). It is a full day out from Christchurch with around 3hr on the water.

Around Christchurch

Far too many travellers head straight from Christchurch towards the mountains to the west or Otago to the south, thereby missing out on the many attractions on the city's own doorstep. North of Christchurch are the rich agricultural flatlands of the northern Canterbury Plains, a pleasantly rural area which harbours the sleepy town of **Kaiapoi**, and the vineyards and wineries included in the **Canterbury Wine Trail**, a popular tourist itinerary among more bibulous visitors. However, the city's main vacation area is **Banks Peninsula**, southeast of Christchurch, an imposing lump of largely volcanic rock penetrated by fiord-like fingers of deep water. At the peninsula's northern end, **Lyttelton** is a hard-edged international cargo port which controls access to the bays and coves of a large inlet known as **Lyttelton Harbour**. Further south, chintzy, French-influenced **Akaroa** is a classic seaside resort, enduringly popular with weekending city folk. There are some excellent **walking** opportunities in the **Port Hills** between Lyttelton and Christchurch, and around **Mount Bradley** and **Mount Herbert** south of Lyttelton Harbour.

Moving on from Christchurch

Straddling the main road and rail routes down the east coast, Christchurch provides easy air, road and rail access to most parts of the South Island.

The quickest way of getting around the South Island is **by air**, with flights to Dunedin, Hokitika, Invercargill, Mount Cook, Nelson, Queenstown and Timaru, with other destinations reached via Wellington. See Travel Agencies, opposite, for bookings.

By comparison, **trains** (☎0800/692 378) represent a much cheaper but relatively time-consuming way of getting around, with only one passenger train heading north to Picton at the northern end of the South Island and one along the most popular stretch of rail in New Zealand, from Christchurch on the TranzAlpine to Greymouth – a Kiwi classic which crosses the Canterbury Plains then climbs the Southern Alps to Arthur's Pass before descending to the West Coast. So spectacular is this journey that many people treat it as a day out from Christchurch: for more details see box p.685.

Most inter-city journeys are best attempted by **bus** or **shuttle bus**, which are reasonably frequent to major destinations, though it is worth bearing in mind that journeys from, say, Christchurch to Nelson or Queenstown are likely to take up most of the day. Almost all companies now operate a door-to-door policy picking up and dropping off at the visitor centres, main hostels, some hotels and airports where applicable. Usually there's no additional cost, though there is sometimes a charge if you are being picked up outside Christchurch's central Four Avenues area. The main exception to this rule is the nationwide InterCity/Newmans, whose services currently depart from the junction of Gloucester and Manchester streets. These companies run the following services:

Akaroa Shuttles ☎0800/500 929: to Akaroa.
Alpine Coaches ☎ 0800/274 888: to Greymouth and Hokitika via Arthur's Pass.
Atomic Shuttles ☎ 03/322 8883: north to Kaikoura, Blenheim, and Picton; south to Ashburton, Timaru, Oamaru and Dunedin; west to Greymouth, then down the West Coast to Queenstown; and inland through Geraldine and Twizel to Wanaka and Queenstown.
Catch-a-bus ☎ 03/363 1122: south to Ashburton, Timaru, Oamaru and Dunedin then inland to Wanaka and Te Anau.
Coast to Coast ☎ 0800/142 622: to Greymouth and Hokitika via Arthur's Pass.
EastWest ☎ 0800/500 251: to Westport via Hanmer Springs and Reefton.
InterCity/Newmans ☎03/379 9020: north to Kaikoura, Blenheim, Picton and Nelson; south to Ashburton, Timaru, Oamaru, Dunedin and Invercargill; west to Arthur's Pass and Greymouth with connections to Westport, Hokitika and the Glaciers; and inland to Methven, Mount Cook, Wanaka and Queenstown.
Lazerline ☎ 03/388 7652: to Nelson via Hanmer Springs and Murchison.
Methven Travel ☎ 03/302 8106: to Methven.
South Island Connections ☎ 03/366 6633: south to Ashburton, Timaru, Oamaru and Dunedin; and north to Kaikoura, Blenheim, and Picton.
Southern Link Shuttles ☎ 03/358 8355: north to Kaikoura, Blenheim and Picton; and inland to Wanaka and Queenstown via Geraldine and Twizel, Nelson, Hanmer Springs and Murchison.
Supa Kut Price Shuttles ☎03/377 7782: to Dunedin via Ashburton, Timaru and Oamaru.

Kaiapoi, Lyttelton and Akaroa are all served **by bus** from Christchurch, although once you stray beyond these centres you'll be largely on your own.

The Canterbury wine trail

Canterbury is now the country's fourth largest wine producing region, with the cool, temperate climate lending itself to Chardonnay, Riesling and especially Pinot Noir. There are two main areas: the immediate vicinity of Christchurch has upwards of a dozen wineries within twenty minutes' drive of the city; while the go-ahead Waipara area, an hour's drive to the north, has another large and rapidly increasing concentration. Many are beautifully situated and there are plenty of opportunities to sample **fine wines** and **gourmet food**. For well written descriptions of the wineries and their historical context, pick up a copy of the *Canterbury Wine Trail* leaflet (free from Christchurch visitor centre), by A.K. Grant, one of New Zealand's leading wine writers.

North of Christchurch

North of Christchurch, SH1 heads straight and true along the coast. As you leave the city suburbs, you pass one or two vineyards (see "Canterbury Wine Trail" box above) and a lot of the patchwork-quilt fields so typical of the Canterbury Plains. With flat farm country to its west and Pegasus Bay to its east, the road bisects a series of tiny communities such as **Kaiapoi**, many containing camping facilities for holidaymakers wishing to gaze at the bay or fish the waters.

Kaiapoi and beyond

Nineteen kilometres north of Christchurch, SH1 crosses the braided Waimakariri River, and rolls into the small town of **KAIAPOI**. Once a flourishing port with a reputation for producing high-quality woollen goods, Kaiapoi faded into insignificance after it had been bypassed by the railway. It's now a satellite town for Christchurch commuters, who constitute about sixty percent of the town's population, and has little of note – unless you are an angler keen to flick the rivers for trout or salmon. The best thing to do in Kaiapoi is take a trip on the 80-year-old **MV Tuhoe**, a twin-masted, steam-powered schooner which is moored in the Kaiapoi River near the William Street Bridge. Most weekends, weather and tides permitting, the *Tuhoe* still chugs, albeit slowly, down the Kaiapoi until it merges with the Waimakariri River and the sea (1hr 20min; $10, buy tickets an hour before sailings at Williams Street Bridge kiosk ⓣ03/327 8721). Tide and sailing times are published in Saturday's edition of *The Press*.

About 32km further north at the junction of SH1 and SH7 is **Waipara**, a town with six **wineries** within a 3km radius, each producing excellent, inexpensive white wines (tastings available on request 11am–5pm; expect to pay $3–6). From Waipara you can either head along SH1, a pretty unexciting haul towards Cheviot on the way to Kaikoura, or turn inland along the SH7 Lewis Pass Road towards Hanmer Springs.

Banks Peninsula

Flying into Christchurch only the least observant could fail to be struck by the dramatic contrast between the flat plains of Canterbury and the rugged, fissured topography of **Banks Peninsula**, a volcanic thumb sticking out into the Canterbury Bight. When James Cook sailed by in 1769 he erroneously charted it as an island and named it after his botanist Joseph Banks. His error was only one of time, as this basalt lump initially formed as an island, one only joined to the land as silt sluiced down the rivers of the eastern flanks of the Southern Alps has accumulated to form the plains.

The fertile **volcanic** soil of the peninsula's valleys sprouted totara, matai and kahikatea trees which, along with the abundant shellfish in the bays, attracted early Maori around a thousand years ago. The trees soon succumbed to the fire stick, a process accelerated with the arrival of European timber milling interests. The lumber yards ground to a halt when the trees ran out in the late 1880s and the peninsula is now largely bald, with large areas of tussock grass on the rolling hills, and tiny pockets of regenerating native bush.

Today, the two massive drowned craters which form Banks Peninsula are key to the commerce of the region. Lyttelton Harbour protects and nurtures the port town of **Lyttelton**, disembarkation point for many of the fledgling provinces' migrants and now the South Island's major port. It is a workaday town, but interesting for its historic timeball station, harbour cruises and a couple of entertaining places to eat and drink. The various pleasure trips including swimming with dolphins. There's also an altogether more refined and prestigious tone to the town of **Akaroa**; picturesque and French-influenced on account of its first of batch settlers who arrived from France at the same time as northern Maori and the British were signing the Treaty of Waitangi. Elsewhere on the peninsula, a network of narrow, twisting roads – not least the ridge-crest-hugging Summit Road – wind along the crater rims and dive down to gorgeous, quiet bays once alive with whalers, sealers and shipbuilders, but now seldom visited except during the peak of summer.

Despite the denuded and parched nature of much of the landscape, Banks Peninsula is very popular for relatively easy scenic **walks**, with panoramic views, geological features (such as ancient lava flows, or the dykes caused when fissures filled up with molten rock), relics from the earliest Maori and European settlers, and great beaches. A number of tracks cross private land and there are folk offering their services to deliver your pack to your destination. As befits a city playground, the peninsula is also well endowed with country-style accommodation, especially B&Bs and farmstays, and, particularly in Akaroa, fine restaurants.

The peninsula merits at least a day-trip from Christchurch. With more time on your hands, you could enjoyably spend two to three days exploring the quieter nooks and crannies. From Christchurch, the main route to Akaroa is the **SH75**, via Lake Ellesmere and Little River, but a more picturesque route follows the **Summit Road** from Sumner via Lyttelton, along the Port Hills and ridges of the peninsula. **Buses** from Christchurch serve only the main towns of Lyttelton and Akaroa, and to reach the smaller communities tucked into the bays you'll need your own transport, whether motorized or pedal-powered (see Christchurch listings, p.633, for car and bike rental details). If you're planning on cycling, bear in mind that the peninsula is extremely hilly, and the routes linking the summit road with the various bays below can be very steep. A good alternative is to join the Akaroa mail run (see p.652), as the long-suffering mail van winds in and out of the tiny bays.

Although the peninsula is prone to **sea mists** and storms, both the Port Hills and the peaks across the neck of the peninsula shelter it from the winds that blaze across the Canterbury Plains. The climate tends to be very warm in the summer and extremely cold in the winter but the **weather** is noted for its unpredictability, so it's worth carrying rain gear at any time of year.

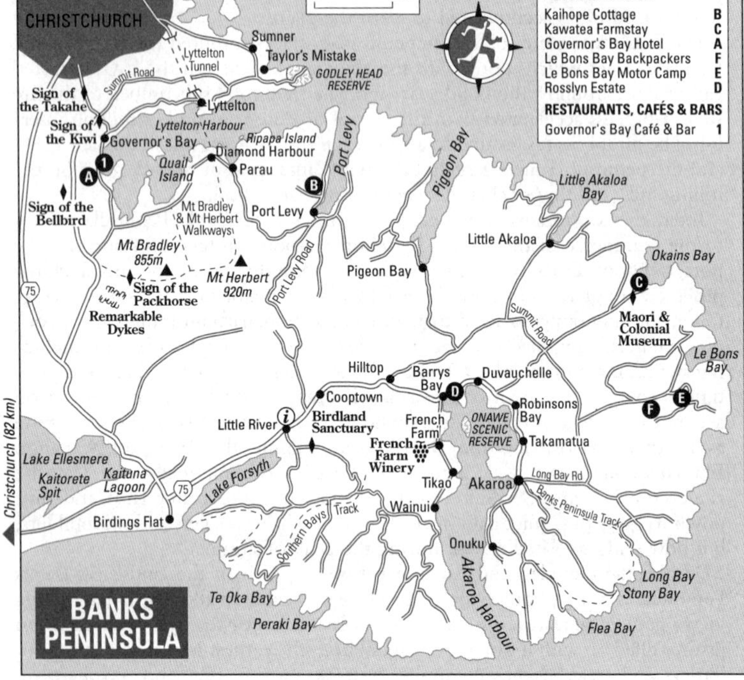

Lyttelton

Just 12km from Christchurch city centre, **LYTTELTON** is a world apart, hemmed in by the rocky walls of the drowned volcanic crater that forms **Lyttelton Harbour**. Attractive though its setting is, Lyttelton is foremost a port, one where countless European migrants disembarked to start their new lives. It still retains a raffish air: rowdy clanking from the docks, rumbustious waterfront bars, and plenty of overheard snippets of Polish, Russian and Filipino. Boats servicing the New Zealand and US bases in Antarctica leave from here, and there are even a few dozen cruise ships calling each year, though the passengers are bussed off to Christchurch as soon as they arrive.

The town itself overlooks the docks and quays, climbing up the Port Hills behind and spreading southwest along the coast toward Governors Bay. Running parallel to the waterfront, the main road of Norwich Quay is fringed by a series of down-at-heel pubs designed to attract dockers, ships' crews and lorry drivers. The web of streets behind are primarily residential, although it's here that the best bars, restaurants, shops and accommodation possibilities are to be found.

Arrival, information and accommodation

The quickest way from Christchurch to Lyttelton is through the 4km Lyttelton Tunnel, which ejects you right in the heart of town, just twenty minutes after leaving Christchurch. The #28 **bus** from Cathedral Square leaves about every half hour (35min; $3.60 return) and can drop you right by the **visitor centre**, 20 Oxford St (daily 9am–5pm; ⓣ03/328 9093, ⓔlyttinfo@ihug.co.nz). The staff will hand out a leaflet describing a self-guided **walk** around Lyttelton's many historic sites and help you learn what lurks behind Lyttelton's workaday facade.

Accommodation right in Lyttelton is somewhat limited, though there is an excellent backpackers and a couple of B&Bs. Most of the best places are some way out of town around Lyttelton harbour, along with the only campsite that is remotely close.

Cavendish House B&B 10 Ross Terrace ⓣ03/328 9505, ⓔgsorell@xtra.co.nz. Set high in the hills with great views over the town and the port is this luxurious B&B, occupying an Edwardian villa, with two en-suite guest rooms. It was named after one of the original members of the Canterbury association and boasts the sort of care visitors in those days would have been thrilled to receive. ⑥

Dockside 22 Sumner Rd ⓣ03/328 7344. Central, self-catering B&B apartment with a sunny en-suite room and a deck with panoramic harbour views. Continental breakfast included. ④

Governors Bay Café and Bar 79 Main Road, on the other side of the bay facing Lyttleton ⓣ03/329 9825. Simple self-catering accommodation next to the café with panoramic views. ④–⑤

Governors Bay Hotel Main Road, opposite the café above ⓣ03/329 9433. A large colonial hotel that has been entirely renovated and offers some simple rooms above the bar and restaurant but mostly concentrates on food, beer and entertainment. ③

Orchard House Governors Bay ⓣ03/329 9622. Pleasant accommodation 8km from Lyttelton in a small, address-free settlement (phone ahead if you need directions). The house offers views of the harbour and surrounding farmland; the double room has French doors that open onto a deck where breakfast is served, weather permitting. ⑤

Parau Bay Holiday Park Diamond Harbour ⓣ03/329 4702, ⓕ329 4212. Pleasant campsite situated among tall sheltering trees and across the road from the bay, 2km from Diamond Harbour and half an hour's drive from Lyttelton. There are cabins, a bunkhouse, a shop, pool and a kitchen. Tent sites $10 per pitch, dorms ①, cabins ③

Randolph House B&B 49 Sumner Rd ⓣ03/328 8877, ⓔrandolph@netaccess.co.nz. Set in a nineteenth-century wooden villa, this guesthouse has a double attic bedroom, plus other comfortable rooms with shared facilities, grand views over the harbour and tasty breakfasts. ⑤

Tunnel Vision Backpackers 44 London St ⓣ & ⓕ03/328 7576. Without doubt the best place to stay in Lyttelton, this is a brightly decorated, well-maintained, first-class backpackers, occupying a renovated old hotel in a central location, right by the town's more interesting bars, cafés and restaurants. Added bonuses are an outside deck, free tea and coffee and a good selection of double and twin rooms, some with harbour views. Dorms ①, rooms ②

The Town

There is one attraction above all others for which Lyttelton is famous – the **Timeball Station**, Reserve Terrace (Wed–Sun 10am–5pm; $2.50), a steep 1km climb up Sumner Road from the centre. Built by prisoners in 1876, it looks for all the world like a Gothic tower that has carelessly lost its castle. It is clearly visible from all over town and harbour, and for over fifty years mariners recalibrated their on-board chronometers – critical for accurate navigation – on the descent of a large black ball down the pole on the roof. Radio signals replaced the timeball in 1934 and the station fell into disrepair, but progressive restoration since the 1970s has left it in immaculate condition. Once again, the ball is hoisted up its pole every day at precisely 12.57pm, then on the stroke of 1pm (to the nearest half-second) it begins its descent. Inside the station are a number of exhibits explaining the importance of the timeball to navigational techniques, plus the oily mechanism itself. The view from the roof is superb, and you can see the battered zinc ball close up.

Another intriguing attraction is **Lyttelton Museum**, Norwich Quay (Tues, Thurs, Sat & Sun 2–4pm; donations appreciated), a former Seaman's Institute

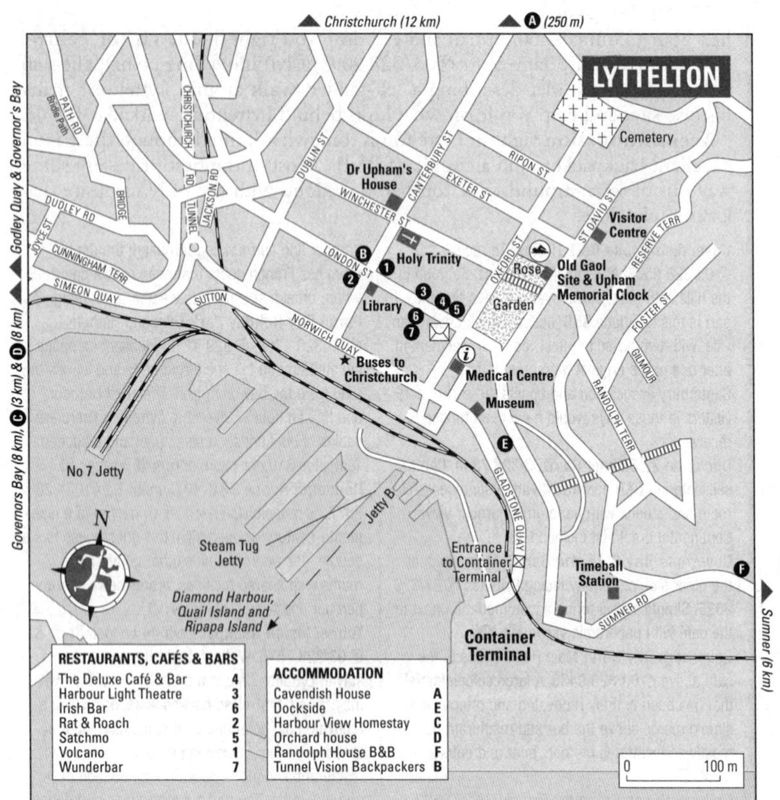

where you are greeted by a penguin. The nautical flavour lingers in a display of ancient telescopes, which straightfacedly informs visitors that the size and elaborateness of a sailor's telescope denoted his rank. Other exhibits reflect the town's history, while the Antarctic display spotlights Scott and Shackleton, both of whose expeditions set out from Lyttelton. Other curious artefacts have been salvaged from the small shelters built during the nineteenth century on various islands off the New Zealand shore, which were supplied with provisions to cater for unfortunate shipwrecked souls. Overall, the museum has the air of a long-neglected attic filled with a mishmash of collectables, among which are occasional jewels such as a fossilized crab and watercolours of early Lyttelton personalities.

Opposite the museum is the wooden **Lyttelton Signal Box**, relocated here from the mouth of the Moorhouse Rail Tunnel through to Christchurch, and tagged by a 1902 halfpenny (above the entrance) marking the date of the box's construction.

Docked at the wharf opposite Norwich Quay, over the Overhead Bridge, is the black **Steam Tug Lyttelton** (available for charter Oct–March), the older of only two steam tugs still operating in the country. Built in Glasgow by the Ferguson brothers in 1907, this beautiful antique boat is maintained in full working order by an impassioned bunch of volunteers. If you climb aboard, one of the volunteers will escort you on an unofficial and extremely informative tour, which includes a museum occupying the captain's cabin, officers' quarters, saloon and other cabins. The boiler room is particularly impressive: all sparkling brass and oily pistons, it was at the cutting edge of technology in its heyday, with steam-power-assisted steering. On Sundays, throughout most of the year, the tug also fires up for some thrilling round-trip **cruises** (booking required ☎03/322 8911; 2.30pm, 1hr 30min; $12), steaming all the way to the head of the harbour.

Prettiest of the town's churches is the 1860 **Holy Trinity Anglican Church**, on the corner of Winchester Street and Canterbury Street, which was originally earmarked as the Cathedral of the Diocese, a status never afforded it once building started in Christchurch. Diagonally opposite stands **Dr Upham's** 1907 house: for over fifty years the two-storey house served as the home for this saintly doctor, remembered for his devotion to the lepers of Quail Island, his refusal to accept money from patients who could not afford to pay, and his penchant for walking the town accompanied by his faithful hound. The good doctor is also commemorated at the end of Winchester Street by the **Upham Memorial Clock**, which stands in the Rose Garden on the site of the old jail – the remains of a couple of the cells can be seen on the northern side of the gardens. Built in 1851, the jail became the South Island's major penal institution, even accommodating sheep rustler James McKenzie (see box p.702) for a time. Above the jail site is the Old Cemetery, full of gravestones dating back to the earliest settlers, except for the seven who were hanged at the jail between 1868 and 1918 – they did not merit a stone.

Eating and drinking

Lyttelton has a well-founded reputation for quality food and a nightlife that's way livelier than you'd expect for such a small town. In fact, a trip to Lyttelton is justified solely on the intention to dine at the *Volcano Café* and then troop over the road to sample the pleasures of the *Wunderbar*.

The Deluxe Café & Bar 18 London St. Polished wooden furnishings and floors provide a relaxing setting for high-quality moderately priced lunches and dinners.

Governors Bay Café and Bar 79 Main Road ☎03/329 9825. On the other side of the bay facing Lyttleton is this little gem perched upon a hill overlooking the water and surrounding hills. The food here is simple, inexpensive, home-baked and available from about 10am daily, and later into the evenings on Thurs, Fri & Sat. They also have rooms available (see "Accommodation" above).

Governors Bay Hotel Main Road, opposite the café, above ☎03/329 9433. A large colonial hotel that has been entirely renovated and contains a wonderful long wooden bar and veranda seating where you can enjoy the straightforward but tasty fare, including fish and chips and Irish Stew. They also have a slightly more upmarket restaurant and rooms available (see "Accommodation").

Harbour Light Theatre and Bar 22 London St. Old theatre that still hosts some pretty lively gigs, usually advertised on the door or in the local press, with a functional little bar that opens when someone's playing.

Irish Bar 17a London St. This long, thin, would-be Irish bar opens its doors to the hungry and the thirsty daily 9am–late, and provides live music or a DJ for those with itchy feet on Fri and Sat nights.

Rat and Roach 47 London St. A characterful little bar serving coffee and booze and famous for its massive burgers, blackboard specials and live Irish music on Fri and Sat. Open daily from noon to 3am-ish.

Satchmo 8 London St. Casual restaurant and bar with a good line in salads, gourmet pizzas (from $12) and pasta dishes ($14) served in a peaceful garden or inside with background jazz. Licensed.

Volcano 42 London St ☎03/328 7077. A Lyttelton institution fashioned out of a former fish-and-chip shop with bright, eclectic decor and meals served on Formica tables all with fresh flowers. Cuisine draws on Cajun, Mexican, Spanish and Italian influences, with all sorts of home-made treats in substantial portions (mains $20–25). Licensed and BYO.

Wunderbar London St. An idiosyncratic late-night drinking-hole and club with decor ranging from crushed velour to a gruesome doll's-head light-shade. There's pool, table football and a wonderful deck overlooking the harbour that's great for a peaceful drink if you can't take the clamour within. Entertainment ranges from 1940s and 50s cabaret nights, through poetry, live bands, stand-up comics, club and disco music, to film noir evenings. Mon–Fri 5pm–late, Sat & Sun 3pm–even later. Entry is down steps beside the supermarket, and up an iron fire escape.

Around Lyttelton Harbour

Lyttelton would be nothing without its harbour, and it would be a shame to spend time here without venturing onto it to gain a sense of its maritime importance. Boats reached Lyttelton through "the heads", best seen from Godley Head – a moody, grass- and rock-covered promontory with steep sea cliffs offering excellent views. On the water, the main destinations are the small community of **Diamond Harbour**, and two islands: **Quail Island** in the centre of Lyttelton Harbour and the tiny **Ripapa Island** just east of Diamond Harbour. Both are havens for birds, as well as offering solitude and superb views; for access to the islands, see the box below.

Godley Head

At the northernmost tip of the harbour, **Godley Head** stands guard – a spectacular piece of land with high cliffs and excellent views, administered by the DOC. Follow the signs east out of Lyttelton to the Summit Road, which takes you out onto Godley Head (about 10km) and the **Godley Head Reserve**, a delightfully scenic spot for walks and picnics. The walkway network is extensive, in places stumbling across installations left behind after World War II, including dark warren-like tunnels and searchlight emplacements perched like birds' nests on the cliffs. From here, you can also walk down to the tiny coastal settlements of Boulder Bay and Taylors (see box on p.625).

Diamond Harbour

In bright sunlight the harbour sparkles like a million gems at **Diamond Harbour**, directly across the water from Lyttelton. Black Cat Cruises (see box below) operate passenger **ferries** (sailings every 1–2hr: Mon–Fri 6.15am–6.50pm, Sat & Sun 6.55am–7.10pm; $3.60 each way) across the harbour making a handy shortcut to Camp Bay, the Mount Herbert Walkway and the rest of Banks Peninsula. Arriving at the Diamond Harbour wharf you can generate a thirst with a 500-metre walk uphill, then slake it at either the *Country Store*, which does coffee, muffins and toasted sandwiches, or at **Godley**

Lyttelton harbour cruises

A variety of **cruises** depart from Lyttelton offering a splendid sea-level perspective on the harbour. If you can do without a commentary or simply want more time to explore, check out the regular ferry services to Diamond Harbour and Quail Island (see above) run by Black Cat Cruises (☎03/328 9807) who depart from Jetty B opposite Norwich Quay: most sailings link with the #28 bus from Christchurch. Black Cat also offer a Wildlife Cruise (2.30pm daily; $39), departing from jetty B, which includes the prospect of seeing Hector's dolphins up close. **Hector's dolphins** are also the target of The Dolphin Adventure run by Canterbury Sea Tours (☎03/326 5607) who offer informative morning (2hr; around $40) and afternoon (3hr 30min; around $70) trips around the harbour.

House, a popular vantage point with gardens and lawns overlooking Diamond Harbour which have attracted visitors from Christchurch and beyond for more than a hundred years. The house has been taken over by the conference market in recent years, but on summer weekends you can still buy a beer or lunch and sprawl out on the grass. If you want to stay over this way there's the *Parau Bay Holiday Park* (see p.639) at Parau 2km east.

Quail and Ripapa islands

Set in mid-harbour, **Quail Island** was known by the local Maori as *Otamahau* because it was the place where children collected seabirds' eggs. It was used as a leper colony between 1907 and 1925 (when the afflicted were transported to Fiji), Shackleton and Scott quarantined their dogs here before venturing to the South Pole, and the wrecks of several ships can sometimes be spied at low tide. These days it's a venue for day-trips, swimming and walking; it makes a relaxing and fascinating place to spend a day: pack provisions, plenty of drinking water (there's none on the island) and rain gear. Travel with Black Cat Cruises (Mon–Fri 1.30pm, pick-up at 4.40pm; Sat & Sun sailings 9.30am and 1.30pm, pick-up at either 1.40pm or 4.40pm; $9 return), and pick up the *Quail Island Walkway* leaflet ($0.50) from the Christchurch DOC office or the Lyttelton visitor centre, which details two circular **walking tracks** (1hr & 2hr 30min), both starting from the island's wharf.

Historically the defensibility of **Ripapa Island**, just off the southern shore of the Harbour near Diamond Harbour, has been its key feature. Successively a Maori *pa*, then the site of an 1880s fort built as a measure against a feared Russian invasion that never materialized, it later became a prison camp for Count Felix Von Luckner, a German "sea raider". The island now enjoys some peace as a historic reserve administered by the DOC, which can only be visited on **guided tours** run by Black Cat (bookings essential, minimum of six people per sailing; ferry departs jetty B at 1pm; $15).

Christchurch to Akaroa: SH75

With ample time on your hands and a taste for exploration consider approaching Banks Peninsula on the Summit Road (see box on p.646), which winds around the crater rim of Lyttelton Harbour then around the northern bays before finally dropping you down to Akaroa. A much faster and most convenient way of covering the 85km run **from Christchurch to Akaroa** is on SH75 which heads south from the city before curling southeast along the southern shore of the peninsula, then over the hills to Akaroa: it takes around an hour and a half, though there are reasons to pause along the way.

Lake Ellesmere and Little River

Around 30km from Christchurch SH75 tracks the water's edge of **Lake Ellesmere** (*Waihora*), a vast expanse of fresh water separated from the Pacific Ocean by the 30km-long Kaitorete spit, which juts southeastwards from Banks Peninsula to rejoin the mainland. It's a picturesque area popular with fishermen, although other visitors will probably content themselves with the fine views of the lake to be had from the road. At the base of the spit is **Birdlings Flat**, a narrow shingle bank that has traditionally been a rich source of food for local Maori, who were granted protected fishing rights here in 1896; the accumulated shingle of the sheltering bank also provides a fossicking ground for greenstone and gems. Birdlings Flat separates the sea from **Lake Forsyth** (*Wairewa*), a long finger of water skirted by SH75 on the way to the tiny

The Southern Bays Track

The spectacular **Southern Bays Track** (mid-Oct to May only), in the southwestern corner of Banks Peninsula, is a three-day (two-night) outing across private land, similar in character to the Banks Peninsula Track, but much more physically demanding, with many climbs and one **gruelling** ascent from sea level to 800m. The track crosses beaches, native bush, cliff tops and tussock, with the possibility of sighting shag colonies, seals and dolphins in between long vistas across to the Canterbury Plains and the Southern Alps.

There are three options, but all walkers spend both nights in comfortable road-accessible cottages equipped with hot showers, flush toilets, mattresses and cooking equipment. Those with confidence and strong legs can take the cheapest option – the so-called **Freedom Walk** ($98), where you carry your own food, sleeping bag and personal effects, and have to prepare your own meals. Less rugged individuals might prefer the **Freedom Walk – Packs Carried** ($98 per person plus a flat $110 for up to four people's packs), where your overnight gear is delivered to each cottage and the end of the walk. The most leisurely option is the **Guided Walk** ($680) where you just walk: everything is done for you, including making up the beds and cooking the meals.

Numbers are strictly limited, so advance bookings are pretty much essential; and there is a $10 fee to have your car delivered to the end of the track and safely stored: a wise course of action. Everyone needs good boots and wet-weather gear; Freedom walkers will also want a sleeping bag and enough food for three days.

community of **LITTLE RIVER**, 53km from Christchurch, primarily of interest for the excellent café, bar and bakery of the *Little River Store*, and the **Old Railway and Craft Station** on Main Road, which houses a small **visitor centre** (Oct–April daily 9am–5pm; May–Sept daily 10am–4pm; ⓣ03/325 1255). There's also a reminder of the area's Maori heritage – a statue of Tangatahara, the famous chief of the ultimately unsuccessful defence of the Onawe Peninsula, which stands in the town, alongside a lengthy Maori inscription describing many of his battles. Just before you enter town a sign on the right guides you to the **Birdlands Sanctuary,** Okuti Valley Road, 6km from Little River (ⓦwww.birdlands-sanctuary.co.nz; Oct–April daily 9am–5pm; May–Sept Mon–Sat 9am–4pm; $8), a private venture dedicated to the preservation of New Zealand bird life, with a variety of paths running through different habitats. The kids will be happy hand-feeding the peacocks, ducks and pigeons; others may prefer a stroll through the bush along boardwalks to viewing platforms where bellbirds come to feed off the nectar supplied.

Little River is also the base for the circular **Southern Bays Track** (see box above). If you need somewhere to gather your strength for the Southern Bays Walkway or a place to rest up afterwards, try the *Birdland Sanctuary Holiday Park* right by the sanctuary (ⓣ03/325 1141; tents $11, cabins ❸). It's one of the prettiest **campsites** on the peninsula, with cooking facilities and a small shop.

Barry's Bay

From Little River, SH75 starts climbing the hills which separate Akaroa Harbour from the rest of Banks Peninsula. The road tops out at the *Hilltop Tavern* from where there is a great view of what is still to come, including the steep descent to **BARRY'S BAY**, right at the head of Akaroa Harbour. This is home to the settlers' original dairy factory, **Barry's Bay Cheese**, SH75 (ⓣ03/304 5809; Mon–Fri 8.30am–5pm, Sat & Sun 9.30am–5pm), a bit of a tourist trap visited by all the coaches, though it is worth nipping in for free samples of their produce, much of which is pretty decent. Accounts of early cheese-making go back as far as 1844, when chessets (the traditional cheese moulds still in use today) were brought from Europe. Ironically, Banks Peninsula was one of the first areas in New Zealand to start producing and exporting cheese to Europe because the clean pastures produced such pure milk. All their cheeses are sold on the premises: try the cheddar, Barry's Bay Sharp, Havarti, Akaroa Mellow or Port Cooper, with one of the locally made chutneys or mustards on a piece of fresh bread for lunch.

Rosslyn Estate, just off SH75 (Ⓣ & Ⓕ03/304 5804, Ⓔrosslyn@xtra.co.nz; ❺-❻), is a reasonable **B&B**, occupying a large 1860s country house with two luxurious en-suite rooms that contain queen-sized beds. There are extensive grounds for exploring, as well as home-baking on arrival and evening meals on request ($25).

French Farm

If you are interested in more formally presented cuisine, turn down the south fork off SH75 at Barry's Bay and head for **FRENCH FARM**. According to Maori tradition, the heights of French Farm were home to the *patupaiarehe* ("children of the mist"), whose chants can be heard on misty days or in the evenings. Of a more practical nature, the settlers in Akaroa used this fertile and sheltered area to establish orchards and vegetable plots to grow produce that would not otherwise have been available to them.

Some of the latter-day products of these plots can be sampled at the excellent **French Farm Winery and Restaurant**, French Farm Valley Road (Ⓣ03/304 5784, Ⓦwww.frenchfarm.co.nz; tasting daily 10am–5pm), a French-style villa set among native trees. They've now been producing wines for over seven years and have gained something of a reputation for their chardonnay and pinot noir ($1 per tasting, refunded with purchase). But the place is best known for its food and a better approach is to come for lunch or dinner and sample a glass with a meal at one of the two restaurants: the main restaurant garners the greatest acclaim with Pacific Rim cuisine served under an arbour (mains $25–30; daily 10am–5pm for lunch and wine tastings), *La Pizza* is less formal and serves excellent and large wood-fired examples ($19; til 8pm only) along with grills and great gelato, again served outside.

Back on SH75 at Barry's Bay, it is only 12km to Akaroa, first passing a turn-off for the **Onawe Peninsula Scenic Reserve** (daily dawn–dusk), a peninsula that juts out into Akaroa Harbour, which once offered a highly defensible sanctuary for local Maori. Remains of the *pa* fortifications, deep ditches and ramparts are still distinguishable, despite years of farming. From there you pass through the tiny but pretty settlements of Duvauchelle, Robinson's Bay and Takamatua – originally known as German Bay after the first settlers who arrived with Akaroa's French.

Akaroa

The small waterside town of **AKAROA** ("Long Bay"), 82km from Christchurch on the eastern shores of Akaroa Harbour, comes billed as New Zealand's **French settlement**. Certainly the initial settlers came from France, and some of their architecture survives and the street names they chose have stuck, but that's about as French as it gets. Nonetheless, the town milks the connection with a number of French-ish restaurants, some French-sounding boutique B&Bs and a tricolour fluttering over the spot where the first settlers landed.

Still, it is a pretty place with attractive scenery all around, a smattering of low key activities to keep you occupied – including the **Banks Peninsula Track**,

The Summit Road and bush walks from it

Drivers – and particularly **cyclists** – should consider passing up the fast and relatively straight SH75 from Christchurch to Akaroa, in favour of the **Summit Road**, actually a sequence of connecting backroads which forms a giant S-shaped circuit around the peninsula's two crater harbours. Designed with pedestrians and wagons in mind, it keeps as close as possible to the ridge tops marking an undulating course – with few sustained ascents – and offering stupendous views all around. For cyclists, **traffic** is fairly sparse, but what there is tends to hare around blind corners, so keep your wits about you. Armed with the *Summit Road Map* ($6 from the Christchurch visitor centre) you can pinpoint the sights and identify trailheads for some of the fine short walks listed – nearly forty in all.

The Summit Road was the consuming passion of the public-spirited **Harry Ell**. He dreamed of building a highway with **walking tracks** and fourteen rest stations along the summit of the Port Hills and right around the peninsula. The project got under way at the turn of the twentieth century, and when Ell died in 1934 only four rest stations (mostly named after native birds) had been built. The first, sited at what was the southern limit of Christchurch trams (now bus #2), the junction of Dyers Pass Road and Takahe Drive, was the **Sign of the Takahe** – a Gothic-style house distinguished by enormous kauri beams, salvaged from a bridge that once spanned the Hurunui River. This house is now a café and evening restaurant, so for the price of a coffee you can still take a look at some unique friezes fashioned from old packing cases and stone quarried from the peninsula, which are kept in a memorial room. Look out for the heraldic embellishments relating to early governors of New Zealand, coats of arms of local families and shields portraying significant events in British history. From the Sign of the Takahe, Dyer's Pass Road runs 4km uphill to the Summit Road and the second rest station, the **Sign of the Kiwi**, now a reasonable café. This is perhaps the best place to start following the Summit Road. However, enthusiasts needing a sense of completeness should start at the true beginning by Godley Head, near the Lyttelton Harbour entrance.

From the *Sign of the Kiwi* the Summit Road follows the ridgetops 9km southwest to the single remaining room of the third of Ell's structures, the **Sign of the Bellbird**, a stone picnic shelter with exceptional views. The last of the rest stations, the **Sign of the Packhorse**, is a trampers' hut off the Summit Road which can also be accessed on the **Mount Bradley Walkway** (13km return; 6hr). This starts from the Summit Road near Gebbie's Pass and heads through open country past the **Remarkable Dykes** – fissures created by the heat of volcanic activity, forming a receptacle for molten rock. As the molten rock cooled and solidified, it proved more resistant to erosion than the surrounding material, thereby creating the protruding ridges which were subsequently dubbed "dykes". The Walkway then skirts Mount Bradley through very old native bush and heads down to Diamond Harbour.

All Harry Ell's rest stations can also be reached as part of the worthwhile **Crater Rim Walkway** (18.5km; 4hr), a magical path along a part of the crater of the extinct Lyttelton volcano; the DOC's *Crater Rim Walkway* leaflet ($1) has a detailed map and further information

The Summit Road completes its circuit of Lyttelton Harbour by dropping down to Diamond Harbour and over to Port Levy, a tiny valley with a beach that once supported the largest Maori population in Canterbury. The Summit Road returns to follow the ridgetops, occasionally throwing spurs down the valleys to secluded coves such as **Pigeon Bay**, the lovely **Okains Bay** (see p.654) and **Le Bons Bay** (see also p.654) before descending to Akaroa.

which starts and finishes nearby (see box on p.651) – and, most of all, a very relaxed air well suited to gentle strolls followed by quality cuisine and a comfy bed. These factors combine to make Akaroa a popular Kiwi holiday destination; a full two-thirds of its houses are *baches*, leaving only around 750 permanent residents.

Once the domain of the Ngai Tahu paramount chief, Temaiharanui, the site of Akaroa attracted the attention of some of Canterbury's earliest migrants. In 1838 a French Commander, Jean Langlois, purchased what he believed to be the entire peninsula for goods to the value of 1000 French francs, and returned to France to encourage settlers to sail with Captain Lavaud and populate a new French colony. However, while the French were making their way to New Zealand, the British sent Captain William Hobson to assume the role of lieutenant-governor over all the land that could be purchased; and just six days before Lavaud sailed into the harbour, the British flag was raised in Akaroa. Lavaud's passengers decided to stay, which meant that the first formal settlement under **British sovereignty** was comprised of sixty-three French – and six Germans who had come along for the ride.

You can treat Akaroa as a day-trip from Christchurch, although you'll only have time to scratch the surface of this beguiling spot; far better to spend a night or two in order to appreciate the town and its surrounds.

Arrival and information

Buses run by Akaroa Shuttle (book 24hr ahead and check times, which can vary ⓣ0800/500 929 & 03/304 7609; Dec–March 3 daily, 9am, 10.30am and 2pm from Christchurch, returning at 3.35 and 4.30pm from Akaroa; April–Nov 1 daily, 10am from Christchurch, returning at 4pm from Akaroa; $17 one way, $30 day return) and French Connection (☎03/366 4556; Mon–Sat departing 8.30am; $15 one way) leave the Christchurch visitor centre for the 1hr 30min run to Akaroa. They drop off outside the **visitor centre**, 80 rue Lavaud (daily 10am–5pm; ⓣ & ⓕ03/304 8600, ⓦwww.akaroa.com), which shares a building with the **post office**. There's a stack of free brochures here, but you may also want to obtain various walks leaflets ($0.50 each) and the *Akaroa Historic Village Walk* booklet ($3.50). The *Turenne* café across the street (see "Eating and drinking" p.653) has limited **internet access**, as does the library on rue Jolie. There is a BNZ **bank** (Mon–Fri 9.30am–4.30pm) opposite the visitor centre on Rue Lavaud.

Accommodation

There is a wide choice of **accommodation** in and around Akaroa: although much of it caters to the weekend getaway set and is relatively expensive, there are some lovely B&Bs which have the edge over the motels in terms of home comforts and atmosphere. The cheapest option is offered by backpacker hostels – two in town, one in Onuku (see all below) and a fourth at Le Bons Bay (see p.654).

Akaroa Holiday Park Morgan's Rd, off the Old Coach Rd ⓣ & ⓕ03/304 7471. Sprawling across a terraced hillside overlooking the harbour and the main street running through town, this site has modern facilities, including a swimming pool. Tents $9; powered sites $10; cabins, on-site vans and tourist flats ❷–❸

Akaroa Village Inn 81 Beach Rd ⓣ03/304 7421 & 0800/695 2000, ⓦwww.akaroa.co.nz. One of the prettiest hotels in Akaroa, situated in the heart of town opposite the main wharf and built on the site of the first residential hotel, which dated from 1842. The current incarnation is French-inspired, with iron lacework on the first-floor balconies, and has a swimming pool and a spa. There are attractive motel-style studio rooms as well as luxurious two-bedroom apartments ideal for two couples or families. Studios ❹, apartments ❻–❽

Bella-Vista 21b Watson St ⓣ & ⓕ03/304 7137. Comfortable family home containing two double rooms and a single, all with shared facilities. Continental breakfast is served, and there are great views from the veranda. ❹–❺
La Belle Villa 113 rue Jolie ⓣ & ⓕ03/304 7084. B&B in a lovely wooden house with spacious light rooms, a large swimming pool and alfresco breakfasts in summer. ❹–❺
Blythcliffe 37 rue Balguerie ⓣ & ⓕ03/304 7003, ⓦwww.nz-holiday.co.nz/blythcliffe. One of Akaroa's finest B&Bs in a grand old house – equipped with a full-size billiard table – surrounded by semi-formal gardens and bush. There are a couple of lovely rooms with private bathrooms and a delightful garden cottage. Rooms ❻, cottage ❻–❼
Bon Accord Backpackers 57 rue Lavaud ⓣ03/304 7782. Small hostel fashioned from two tiny houses knocked into one, with just eight bunks (in three rooms) and one double. Off-street parking. Dorms ❶, room ❷
Chez La Mer Backpackers rue Lavaud ⓣ & ⓕ03/304 7024, ⓔchez_la_mer@ckear.net.nz. Historic building dating back to 1871, and offering high-quality budget accommodation in a homely environment with a nice garden out the back. The staff are helpful, offer free use of bikes and some useful hand-drawn maps of local walks and points of interest. Dorms ❶, en-suite doubles ❷
Grand Hotel 6 rue Lavaud ⓣ03/304 7011, ⓕ304 7304. Basic singles and doubles, with shared facilities, above a refurbished 1860 pub with bottle shop, restaurant and beer garden.❶ per person, dbls ❸
Kahikatea Wainui Valley Road, nr Akaroa ⓣ03/304 7400, ⓦwww.kahikatea.com. If you want to treat yourself and you've got some dosh ($295 a night) to spare then try this ultra-friendly and well-run B&B/homestay where the level of care is exceptional, the food delicious, the accommodation luxurious, and the views are stunning. ❾
Lavaud House B&B 83 rue Lavaud ⓣ & ⓕ03/304 7121. Historic home overlooking the main swimming beach, with fresh flowers and antique furniture in every room. A comfortable and friendly place, with four bedrooms and a choice of cooked or continental breakfast. ❺–❻
Linten B&B 68 Rue Balguerie ⓣ03/304 7501. Dating back to 1881 and known locally as the *Giant's House*, this place owned by sculptor Josie Martin is a working testament to her abstract art, with every room, the garden and even the drive to the garage becoming a canvas on which she can display her talents. As a result this lovely old house has an added charm and even if you're not staying here it's worth a visit just ot look over the place (Wed–Sun 1.30–4.30pm). Rooms are large and colourful, the bathrooms highly individual and the whole deal is no more than three minutes' walk from the town centre. ❺
Maison des Fleurs 6 Church St ⓣ & ⓕ03/304 7804. Boutique accommodation in a two-storey cottage (you get all of it), recently built from peninsula-milled timbers. It's superbly appointed along allergy-free lines – no polyurethane varnishes, natural fibre beds and so on – plus there's a sunny balcony, wood stove for winter, and always a heap of fresh flowers, complimentary port and current magazines. ❽
Mount Vernon Lodge and Stables 500m uphill from the waterfront on rue Balguerie ⓣ03/304 7180. A bit of a climb, but well worth the effort for excellent accommodation in purpose-built wooden self-contained chalets, motel units, and budget beds in a dorm hut, all built on a hillside overlooking Akaroa and the bay. Other perks are a swimming pool, nature walks and a courtesy bus to and from the town centre. Dorms $15, dbls $50, chalets & motel units ❹–❺
Onuku Farm Hostel 6km south of town on the Onuku road ⓣ03/304 7612. Beside the bay, this secluded and quiet spot on a sheep farm has accommodation in the main house or in very cheap summer-only huts. Closed June–Aug. Tents $10, dorms ❶6, rooms ❷
La Rive Motel 1 rue Lavaud ⓣ & ⓕ03/304 7651, ⓣ0800/247 651. Large, curiously shaped motel (its open-sided, two-storey conical tower is an allusion to French chateau architecture) in a tranquil garden setting, with a white picket fence at the front and eight units, all containing full kitchens and TVs. ❹
Tree Crop Farm 2km up rue Grehan ⓣ03/304 7158. Romantic retreat in one of three rustic huts (two without electricity) set on a private farm (see p.650), where they believe in "hot bush baths under the stars and late, late breakfasts on the veranda". Bath robes are provided so you can stroll to your outdoor bath (heated for you after dark), and there is afternoon tea and brunch provided. ❻

The Town

Akaroa is strung along the shore in a long, easily walkable ribbon. In fact the best way to get acquainted with the place is by following the **Akaroa Historic**

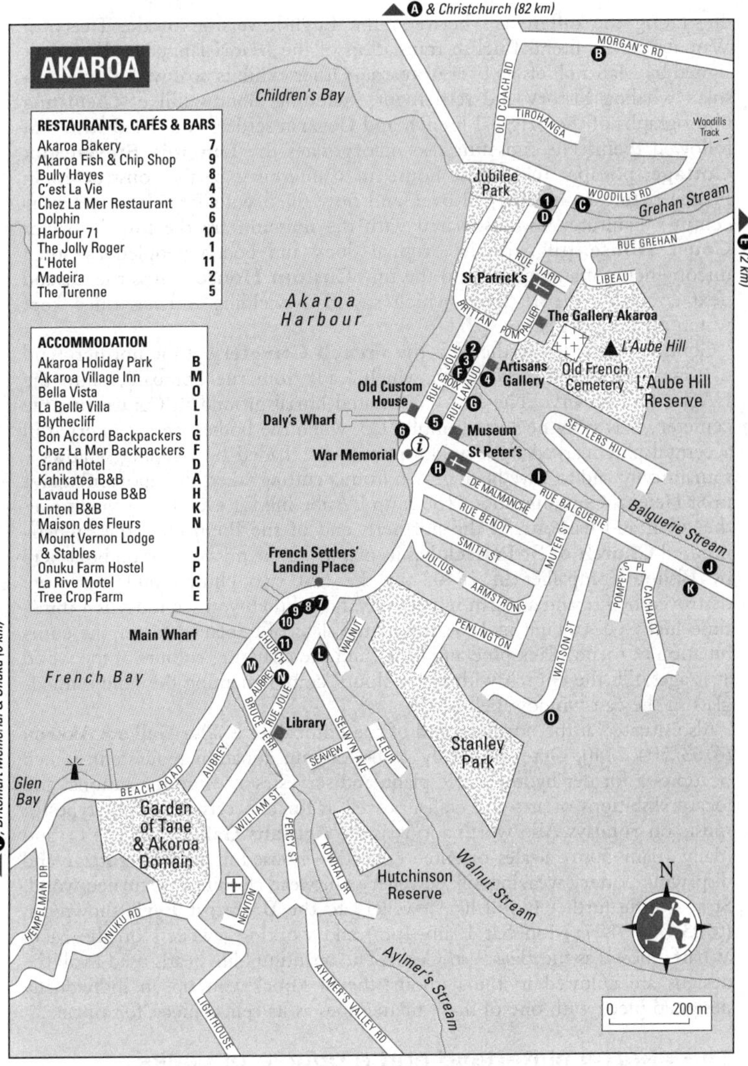

Village Walk (booklet available from the visitor centre; $3.50), which pinpoints buildings of interest and architectural note.

Opposite the visitor centre, the **Akaroa Museum**, corner rue Lavaud and rue Balguerie (daily: Oct–April 10.30am–4.30pm; May–Nov 10.30am–4pm; $3.50), stands head and shoulders above most small-town museums. You might only spend half an hour or so inside but will come away with a good sense of Akaroa's place in New Zealand history. Several interesting Maori artefacts and a twenty-minute film account of the remarkable and sometimes violent history of Maori settlement on the peninsula are backed up by a display illustrating the differences between the English version of the Treaty of Waitangi and a literal English translation of the Maori-language document signed by Maori chiefs all over Aotearoa. Other exhibits deal with the peninsula's whaling history and settlement, including albums full of fascinating photographs of the original French and German settlers and the British that followed them. The museum also incorporates the **Langlois–Eteveneaux Cottage**, possibly the oldest house in Canterbury, partly constructed in France before being shipped over, and now filled with French nineteenth-century furniture. Also associated with the museum are the town's former **Court House**, still with its original dock and bench peopled by some unconvincing mannequins, and the tiny **Custom House**, across rue Lavaud next to Daly's Wharf, from which spy-glass-wielding officials once kept watch on the port below.

Continuing the Gallic theme is the **French Cemetery** at the northern end of town, reached by a footpath which leads from rue Pompallier into the L'Aube Hill Reserve. The first consecrated burial ground in Canterbury, the cemetery was sadly neglected until 1925, when the bodies were reinterred in a central plot marked by a single monument, shaded by weeping willows – romantically said to have been grown from a cutting taken at Napoleon's grave in St Helena. Continue about 150m up L'Aube hill for even better views over the town and harbour. At the northern end of rue Pompallier, the French-inspired **Church of St Patrick** has its origins in the mission station built here by Bishop Pompallier in 1840, but the first two church buildings were destroyed by fire and a storm respectively. The church you see today is a third-time-lucky effort, built in 1864 from large slabs of unplaned totara; the combination of totara, black pine and kauri, and the changing colours of the wood as it ages, fills the church with rich colours, complementing the bold stained-glass in the east window, behind the altar.

Also situated at the northern end of rue Pompallier is **The Gallery Akaroa** (Ⓣ03/304 7140; Oct–April daily 1.30–4.30pm; donation requested), which occupies a former hydroelectric plant, and serves as a venue for national and local exhibitions of arts and crafts, as well as for concerts of various types of music on Sundays. Also worth a look is the **Artisans Gallery**, 45 rue Lavaud (daily 10am–5pm), a sales-oriented collection housed in an 1877 cottage and displaying pottery, weaving, silk, jewellery, knitwear, clothing and turned wood. Stray a little further if you like jewellery to the **Brereton Eyris** showroom (Ⓣ03/304 7877; Mon–Sat 10am–4pm) and working jewellers on the Main Wharf, known as the *Blue Pearl Centre*. The beautiful blue pearls used in all the designs are cultured in the harbour; they'll knock you up an individually designed piece with one of these mementoes as its centre piece, for a price.

The Akaroa hinterland and a couple of walks

Drivers, and those who fancy more than just a gentle walk around town, can head out into the immediate surroundings of Akaroa. One destination that divides opinions is **Tree Crop Farm**, 2km up rue Grehan (daily 9am–5pm; $2), a private lifestyle farm centred on a garden area with a kind of managed overgrown look. Fans love to amble along the farm tracks and through the gardens reading aphorisms written everywhere imaginable. They're initially entertaining – "the best plastic surgery is to cut up your credit cards", "old age isn't bad when you consider the alternative" – but soon become tiresome, especially when you are sat on deep sheepskins on the veranda and everyone around you is quoting them to each other. A small café serves berry juices and exotic

The Banks Peninsula Track

One of the most popular tracks in the area is the **Banks Peninsula Track**, a thirty-five kilometre private track which traverses spectacular volcanic coastline, verdant farmland, exposed headlands and sandy beaches, as well as the Hinewai Nature Reserve (a marine reserve around the southeastern bays of the peninsula), before reaching the end of the track at Mount Vernon Lodge just east of Akaroa. The track is open from Oct 1 to April 30 and typically takes four days to walk (though there is a two-day option for robust hikers). Either way, a reasonable level of **fitness** is required, but because you're guaranteed a bunk at each hut you can walk at your own pace. The **fee** ($150 4-day option; $100 2-day option) includes transport to the start from Akaroa and accommodation along the way; though you'll need to bring a good pair of boots, sleeping bag and all-weather gear. You should also carry provisions for at least the first two days, although it is possible to augment your **supplies** with fresh farm produce at Stony Bay and snacks at Otanerito Beach. You can also have your pack carried in for you on the first day, or transported out on the fourth ($60 and $40 respectively).

Only twelve people are allowed to start the track each day on the 4-dayer, and four people on the 2-dayer, so **bookings** should be made well in advance through Banks Peninsula Track, PO Box 50, Akaroa (ⓣ03/304 7612, ⓦwww.bankstrack.co.nz).

The route

The trail starts at Onuku, 5km south of Akaroa, and the first night is spent in **Onuku hut** at the start of the track. There's usually enough time on the following day to explore neighbouring trails before embarking on the first stage of the walk proper from **Onuku to Flea Bay** (11km, 3hr 30min), passing three small waterfalls and providing views of the peninsula's east coast. Accommodation at Flea Bay is in a charming 130-year-old cottage with a veranda overlooking the beach, and comes complete with electric stove, lights and hot showers. The second day, **Flea Bay to Stony Bay** (8km; 2hr 30min) is an exposed hike along coastal cliffs, with a seal colony providing lunchtime distraction around the halfway point. The night is spent in one of the huts-cum-cottages in Stony Bay, where there's also a modest family museum, a bath under the stars, a small shop selling bread, tinned food and beer, and a few short tracks exploring the bay. The walk from **Stony Bay to Otanerito Bay** (6km; 2hr) takes care of the third day, with overnight accommodation provided in a farmhouse just 50m from a great swimming beach, run by New Zealand author Fiona Farrell and her partner. The fourth and final day's walk heads inland, from **Otanerito Bay to Mount Vernon Lodge** (10km; 3hr; 600m ascent), passing two waterfalls and providing a last glimpse of the ocean before descending to the calmer waters of Akaroa Harbour.

coffee drinks at relatively high prices, and there is accommodation (see p.648) in simple but nicely furnished huts.

Sticking to the waterside, there is an interesting walk (or drive) along **Beach Road to Onuku** (5km one way; 1hr 15min), taking in some of the historical sights. You first head towards Glen Bay and the nineteenth-century red-and-white wooden **lighthouse**, which used to stand at Akaroa Head to guide ships into the harbour before being moved to its current location in 1980. Continuing towards Akaroa Head for about fifteen minutes, you'll come to **Red House Bay**, the scene of a bloody massacre in 1830, when the great northern chief Te Rauparaha bribed (with flax) the captain of the British brig *Elizabeth* to conceal Maori warriors about the vessel and invite Te Rauparaha's unsuspecting enemies (led by Temaiharanui) on board, where they were

Akaroa activities

Two main companies are eager to take you out **swimming with dolphins**, both also offering spectator-only rates effectively turning the trip into a **harbour cruise**. The big deal here is that you get to swim with **Hector's dolphins**, the world's smallest breed of dolphins, usually 1.2–1.4 metres in length.

The biggest operation is Black Cat's "Dolphins Up Close", Main Wharf, Beach Rd (ⓣ0800/436 574, ⓦwww.canterburycat.co.nz, ⓔccat@voyager.co.nz; ticket office daily 10am–4pm), who run a large modern catamaran (Nov–April 6am, 9am & noon; June–Oct noon; $80, spectators $33) which cruises to the mouth of the harbour and back via a rookery, a beautiful high-walled volcanic sea cave, colonies of spotted shags and cormorants, Penguin Caves (where blue penguins can sometimes be spotted) and a fish-feeding stop in Lucas Bay. Trips take around two hours and if you don't see any dolphins you can go again free of charge until you do. The longer alternative is Dolphin Experience, 61 Beach Rd (ⓣ0508/365 744, ⓕ304 7726), a more personal experience (daily: Nov–April 6am, 9am & 3pm; May–Oct noon; $75, spectator only on outer bay trips $35, inner bay $30) taking up to three hours. If you don't get to swim with the dolphins you can return at any time for a second try at $39. **Seal Viewing** is available with Akaroa Seal Colony Safari (ⓣ & ⓕ03/304 7255, ⓔdouble.l@xtra.co.nz), who run air-conditioned 4WD coaches to view fur seals from Goat Point on the eastern tip of the peninsula. Tours (daily 9.30am & 1pm; $50) last over two hours and are limited to six people.

Dolphin Experience also run a fully commentated three-hour **Out of the Harbour Cruise** (daily 2.30pm; $35), while Coastline Adventures will take you out on their wonderfully atmospheric *Fox II* (ⓣ03/384 9238; daily 9.30am & 12.30pm; around $60), a wooden boat built in 1922 and powered by its original engine. The cruise takes a good look round Akaroa Harbour and the outer bays.Bluefin Charters also do cruises in the bay (ⓣ03/304 7866; dolphin-watching for around $35 a head). Directly opposite the Dolphin Experience office on Beach Rd is Akaroa Kayaks (ⓣ03/304 8758), who will rent out their boats ($25 half-day, $35 full-day) to people with a high level of **kayaking** competence. Although the bay is sheltered, it's not worth trying to fool them if you've not done much paddling before because it can quickly get windy and the waters rough.

Otherwise, Bluefin Charters (ⓣ03/304 7866) run three-hour harbour **fishing trips** ($45) and specialize in small-boat sea fishing charters ($80 per half day, $130 full day), as well as a harbour cruise designed to include a bit of dolphin-watching ($35 per head). **Horse riding** can be organized with Horse Trekking Akaroa, Mount Vernon Lodge and Stables, rue Balguerie (ⓣ03/304 7180), who offer various guided treks depending on the amount of time you want to be in the saddle over hilly country ($20 per hour). **Off-road riding** is offered by 4 Wheel Bike Safaris (ⓣ03/304 7866), who run two-hour cross country trips on 4WD bikes ($79) leaving from the Akaroa Heritage Park on Long Bay Road, 3km from town (sturdy shoes required); while Cloud Nine (ⓣ03/385 4739) will take you **parasailing**, towed behind a boat on the harbour for around $8, though they only operate during the school holidays. Lastly, you can join the **Akaroa mail run** (booking essential ⓣ03/304 7207; summer only Mon–Sat 8.20am; 4hr 30min; $20) which follows a 140-kilometre rural delivery run, serving the eastern bays of the peninsula, including Okains and Le Bons Bays.

slaughtered. Te Rauparaha and his men then feasted on the victims on the beach. The final part of the walk takes you to **ONUKU**, 5km from Akaroa, where you'll find the **Onuku Marae** and a tiny church, established in 1876–78. Onuku is even quieter than Akaroa: roughly translated, the name means "coming and going though never staying long" – and, sure enough, there's little to keep you here, except maybe more walks and the prospect of a bed for the night at the *Onuku Farm Hostel* (see p.648).

If you lack the time or inclination to tackle the **Banks Peninsula Track** (see box on p.651), there are some equally rewarding shorter walks. The best is the **Round the Mountain Walk** (10km; 4hr return) which circumnavigates the hills above Akaroa via the Purple Peak Road – the route is shown on a hand-drawn photocopied map, available for $0.50 from the visitor centre. For something a little longer, try the **Akaroa–Le Bons Bay walking track** (booking essential ⓣ03/304 8533; 16km; 5hr each way) which heads east over the hills to the *Le Bons Bay Motor Camp* (see p.654) where you spend the night, ready to return the next day (or later). It crosses private land, but no fees are charged if you stay at the motorcamp; pack transport can also be arranged.

Eating and drinking

With an eager tourist market and its **French heritage**, Akaroa is a very good place to eat, making it popular with people from Christchurch, who think nothing of driving 85km for their evening meal. This does tend to push up prices a little and means that more **expensive** establishments predominate, although there are the usual takeaways and cheaper cafés to fall back on. The reliance on the summer **tourist trade** also means that many places cut back their hours, or even close completely, during winter.

Akaroa Bakery 51 Beach Rd. Excellent fresh-baked bread, plus a small café serving sandwiches, pies, cakes, pizza and bottomless cups of coffee. Daily from early morning to 5pm.

Akaroa Fish and Chip Shop Beach Road, near the harbour. Takeaway "Fush 'n' Chups"(though they do have some picnic tables out the front), considered by many to be the best in the region. Daily lunch & dinner.

Bully Hayes 57 Beach Rd ⓣ03/304 7533. Named after a famous local con-man, this place serves reliable, moderately priced dishes of standard kiwi fare, including roast lamb, steaks and seafood. Open for lunch and dinner. Licensed.

C'est La Vie 33 rue Lavaud ⓣ03/304 7314. Probably Akaroa's best restaurant: an exceptional, intimate dinner-only establishment with relaxing live music. The fine French cuisine uses organically grown ingredients and fresh seafood, all rounded off with delicate pastries. Main courses such as canard à l'orange and escargots in herb butter are about $25–30. BYO only.

Dolphin 6 rue Balguerie ⓣ03/304 7658. Fresh and well-presented lunches and dinners, with mains from about $22, served in comfortable nautical surroundings with some outside seating on the waterfront. Open for lunch and dinner. Licensed.

Harbour 71 71 Beach Rd ⓣ03/304 7656. Moderately priced lunches from the deli and bistro dinners, including pizza and wine evenings on Fridays. Try the salmon or scallops, or the filet beef with balsamic red onion jus. Licensed.

L'Hotel 75 Beach Rd. Airy café and wine bar with outdoor seating and harbour views, serving, unusually for Akaroa, modern Italian cuisine that won't break the bank, augmented by a broad selection of beers and spirits. Open for lunch and dinner.

Waeckerle's in the *Grand Hotel*, 6 rue Lavaud. Pleasant and reasonably priced lunch and dinner venue, with particularly tasty fish dishes and a few bar snacks. Mains $15–25. Licensed.

Madeira rue Lavaud. Spirited Kiwi pub always jumping at weekends.

The Turenne 74 rue Lavaud. Great daytime café with seats outside and internet access within. There's a range of breakfasts, superb muffins and savouries such as gado-gado flan and pumpkin and mushroom pie, and bottomless coffee.

Around Akaroa

Unless you have reached Akaroa by means of the Summit Road, you'll have missed some of the best Banks Peninsula has to offer. Fortunately it is easy enough to drive over the hills to gems such as **Le Bons Bay** and **Okains Bay**, though getting around the twisty roads will take you longer than you'd expect.

Le Bons Bay

As SH75 enters Akaroa from the north, Long Bay Road rises off into the hills giving access to the Summit Road and the verdant **LE BONS BAY**, 20km from Akaroa. It is a small peaceful community with a number of holiday homes ranged behind a gorgeous sandy **beach**, framed on two sides by cliffs, that provides safe swimming. One satisfying way to get here is via the Akaroa–Le Bons Bay walking track (see p.653) which winds up at the *Le Bons Bay Motor Camp*, 15 Valley Rd (Ⓣ & Ⓕ03/304 8533, Ⓔlebonsholiday@xtra.co.nz; tents $9.50, powered sites $10, on-site vans ❶, cabins ❷), a well-kept and picturesque **campsite** by a stream, with a store, swimming pool, organized horse trekking, and mountain-bike rental.

The only other accommodation in the area is the wonderful family-run *Le Bons Bay* **backpackers** (Ⓣ03/304 8582; closed June–Sept; dorms ❶, rooms ❷), a cosy 120-year-old house situated 5km back from the beach, far enough up the bay to provide spectacular views. It is a great place to relax for a few days, lounging on the veranda or in the garden hammock, popping down to the beach to fish or gather shellfish which might be used in the communal evening dinner ($10, and well worth it), or taking long walks down the valley or across the hilltops. The owners run daily low-key **boat trips** (1hr 30min; $20) to see penguins, dolphins, shags and seals. Breakfast is free, and you should call to arrange pick-up from Akaroa.

Okains Bay

The next bay north from Le Bons Bay is **OKAINS BAY**, some 30km from Akaroa, a popular holiday and picnic area with a tiny permanent population. No public buses come this far, so those without their own transport will have to use one of the Akaroa mail runs (see p.652). The beach and the placid lagoon formed by the **Opara Stream** are excellent for swimming and boating, but the real reason to visit is a remarkable museum containing one of the best collections of Maori artefacts in the South Island. The **Okains Bay Maori and Colonial Museum** (daily 10am–5pm; $5), on the only road going into the bay, was originally the private collection of a Maori-obsessed local man, and is housed in the old cheese factory. Within the same compound, several outbuildings contain the more traditional exhibitions relating to European settlement, including a "slab" stable and cottage – simply constructed from large slabs of totara wood. Among the thought-provoking Maori exhibits are a god stick dating back to 1400, a war canoe from 1867 and various weapons, as well as a valuable *hei tiki* (a pendant with a design based on the human form) recovered in England and brought back to Okains Bay. Beside the Maori exhibition building, there is also a beautiful meeting house (it's *tapu* or sacred, although visitors are allowed to look around it), with fine symbolic figures carved by master craftsman John Rua.

Also on the only road descending to Okains Bay, the very welcoming *Kawatea Farmstay* (Ⓣ & Ⓕ03/304 8621; $120; dinner on request, ❺) is a 90-year-old **homestead** set in lush gardens bordered by 5km of scenic coastline and offering three rooms decorated with native timbers and stained glass. At the end of this road is the *Okains Bay Domain* **campsite**, just behind the beach (office 200m back up the road; tents $5.50, dorm $8, on-site caravan $30), which offers a choice of sites or bargain beds in the pavilion which has a fridge, stove and showers. Be sure to bring supplies with you as there is nowhere to eat in the bay.

Pigeon Bay and Port Levy

The two largest bays on the northern side of Banks Peninsula are further west, closer to Lyttelton Harbour and reached by yet more narrow and steep lanes. Neither warrant a special visit though both are of some historical interest: **Pigeon Bay** was an important timber milling and shipbuilding settlement in the nineteenth century when the peninsula had trees; and **Port Levy** once held the largest Maori community in Canterbury. The main reason to come now is to rest up for a couple of days at Port Levy's lovely and historic *Kaihope Cottage* (Ⓣ03/329 4690, Ⓔrbarnett@clear.net.nz; ❸), situated on part of a deer and sheep farm, but right by the sea. The two-bedroom cottage sleeps six and is fully self-contained: bring bedding and food.

South to Otago

Heading south from Christchurch both the principal road, SH1, and the rail line forge across the **Canterbury Plains** in an unrelenting straight line, bisecting small service towns catering for the farms on the rich flat land. The **Southern Alps** flank the route to the west and in clear weather provide awesome views. In the main though, it is a monotonous landscape broken only by the broad gravel beds of braided rivers, usually little more than a trickle spanned by kilometre-long bridges, though they can overspill their broad gravelly banks after heavy rain. The first of the bridges, the 1.8km-long structure spanning the Rakaia River 58km from Christchurch, was the longest in the southern hemisphere at the time of its construction in 1939. It leads into the tiny salmon-fishing and sheep-shearing settlement of **Rakaia**, where a minor road called Thompson's Track heads inland to link with SH77, which in turn grants access to Methven, Mount Hutt and Mount Somers, on the western fringes of the Canterbury Plains. A further 27km south is the larger though equally quiet settlement of **Ashburton**, where SH77 joins SH1.

As the road (and the parallel rail line) passes the pottery town of **Temuka** and reaches the southern end of the Canterbury Plains, looming hills force it back to the shoreline at **Timaru**, a small city with a busy port and a fading holiday resort. Timaru is also the point where SH8 strikes inland towards Fairlie, Lake Tekapo and Mount Cook. From here on, the trip south is a visual treat, with rolling hills inland and spectacular sea views, and yet another opportunity to cut inland. This time it is SH82 and SH83, which head along opposite banks of the Waitaki River – noted for its excellent whitebait, sea-run trout and quinnat salmon fishing – en route to Omarama, Mount Cook and Wanaka.

The coastal highway and railway continue south to the architecturally harmonious city of **Oamaru**, and the unique and fascinating **Moeraki Boulders**. You are also heading into **penguin** country with several opportunities to stop off and spy blue and yellow-eyed penguins. From Moeraki there is little to delay you on your progress toward Dunedin, except maybe the small crossroads town of **Palmerston**, where SH85, "The Pigroot" to **Central Otago**, leaves SH1, providing another opportunity to forsake the coast and follow a historical pathway to the goldfields inland.

Ashburton

The long, thin and stubbornly suburban town of **ASHBURTON** lies 87km southeast of Christchurch, perched on the north bank of the Ashburton River, with an extension, **Tinwald**, across the bridge on the opposite bank. Built on a long defunct ceramics industry and maintained as a service town for the local farms, Ashburton is off the itinerary for most visitors, but if you are heading along SH1 you'll be passing through and may care to stop and examine the smattering of minor sights.

Breaking up the dreary huddle of the town centre the **Ashburton Domain** (daily 8am–dusk), facing West Street, is fringed by stately hundred-year-old European trees and contains expertly manicured gardens and an artificial lake, created from the water race of an old mill. Just north of the Domain is the **Ashford Craft Village**, at 429 West St (daily 9am–4.30pm), which comprises a café, antique shop, the Eastside Gallery, and a massive collection of spinning wheels, looms and accessories, all of which are for sale – though bargains are few and far between.

The **Historic Museum and Art Gallery**, 248 Cameron St (Tues–Fri 10am–4pm, Sat & Sun 1–4pm; donation requested), is a cool and airy place with temporary art exhibitions upstairs. The neat museum has an informative display on braided rivers and the bird life they support, such as the endangered black-fronted tern and the wrybill plover, which breeds only in this region. The most interesting of the town's other four small museums is the **Museum of Woodworking and Ornamental Woodturning**, tucked away at 103 Alford Forest Rd (Tues–Sat ⓣ03/308 6611; donation). Housed in a woodturner's workshop, it contains a substantial collection of antique ornamental lathes, with plenty of intricately turned pieces on display. Ashburton's other museums – the Plains Vintage Railway Museum (ⓣ03/308 9621), the Ashburton Aviation Museum (ⓣ03/308 3262) and the Vintage Car Museum (ⓣ03/308 3392) – are primarily for enthusiasts and are only open limited hours or by arrangement.

Practicalities

InterCity and assorted shuttle **buses** pause outside the **visitor centre**, corner of East Street and Burnett Street (ⓣ & ⓕ03/308 1064, ⓔashinfo@actrix.co.nz; Mon–Fri 9am–4.30pm, Sat 10am–3pm, Sun 10am–1pm), which stocks a free local map and timetable information for local buses and shuttles. The **post office**, 390–408 East St (ⓣ03/308 3184), has poste restante facilities.

Ashburton has an adequate range of **accommodation**, with many places either clustered at the south end of East Street, or across the river in Tinwald. In winter many cater to skiers from the Mount Somers and Mount Hutt fields just a short drive away. **Campers** and budget travellers should head for *Coronation Park*, 778 East St, adjacent to the Domain (ⓣ03/308 6603; tents $10, dorms ❶, on-site vans & units ❷–❹), though you might prefer the relative comforts of the nearby *Academy Lodge Motel*, 782 East St (ⓣ03/308 5503; ❹), or the more homely environment at *Renfrew Country Homestay*, Mitcham Rd, on the edge of town (ⓣ03/308 5559, ⓔrenfrew1@xtra.co.nz; ❹). A little further out, try the pretty and secluded *Carradale Farmstay*, Ferriman's Rd, Lagmhor, 8km west of Tinwald (ⓣ03/308 6577, ⓕ308 6548; ❺), which presents the opportunity to join in farm activities and offers dinner by arrangement ($25).

Ashburton has a few decent **places to eat**. For good coffee, lunches and light evening meals, the place to go is *Kelly's Café and Bar* on East Street, though later on you might be tempted by *Cactus Jacks*, 209 Wills St, off East Street, one of the liveliest places in town, serving a New Zealand version of Tex-Mex at moderate prices. *Tuscany*, opposite the visitor centre, is a café/bar offering resonably priced snacks and meals as well as booze and coffee (daily 11.30am–10pm). The finest dining in town goes on at *Jester's*, 9 Mona Square (Ⓣ03/308 9983; closed Sun; licensed), occupying a pretty two-storey wooden house and offering upmarket evening dining and more modest daytime fare.

Temuka

The small town of **TEMUKA**, 60km south of Ashburton on SH1, takes its name from the Maori for "fierce oven", and a large number of Maori earth ovens have been found in the area. It continues to live up to its reputation today with the presence of kilns for the ceramic factories built by immigrants from the "Potteries" area around Stoke-on-Trent in England. Within New Zealand, Temuka has become synonymous with **pottery**, and you can visit the Temuka Pottery shop (Mon–Fri 9am–5.30pm, Sat & Sun 10am–4pm) on SH1 at the junction of Domain Avenue. Once a byword for dowdy patterns and colours, they've smartened their image in recent years, and if you are inspired enough to want to look around the factory, make sure you are here for the hour-long **factory tour** (Ⓣ03/615 9551 for information; Wed 1.30pm; free).

Across Dominion Avenue you'll find the old court house containing the **Temuka Museum** (Oct–June Fri–Sun 2–4pm, otherwise enquire at the library; donation requested) which has a fair bit on the pottery industry but, oddly, nothing on Temuka's favourite son, aviator **Richard Pearse** – locally held to be the first man to achieve powered flight in 1902, some months in advance of the Wright brothers. Pearse's plane was technically far ahead of that of his rivals, but Pearse himself did not believe his first powered flight was sufficiently controlled or sustained to justify his townsfolk's claim. He managed a rather desperate 100m, followed by an ignominious landing in gorse bushes. He was a lifelong tinkerer and inventor, although the true gauge of Pearse's genius was his idea for an aircraft that could fly and hover like a modern Harrier jump jet. There's a memorial to Pearse at the site of the legendary flight, about 13km from Temuka on the way to Waitohi; and further reminders of his achievements in the South Canterbury Museum at Timaru (see p.661).

Practicalities

Most buses will drop off and pick up in Temuka, and onward travel can be arranged at the **visitor centre**, which is situated in the library, 72 King St (Mon–Thurs 9am–5.30pm, Fri 9am–8pm; Ⓣ03/615 9537, Ⓕ615 9538). There is really little reason not to continue on to Timaru or beyond, but you'll find **accommodation** at the clean and comfortable *Benny's Motel*, 272 King St (Ⓣ03/615 7886, Ⓕ615 7936; ❹), or the *Temuka Holiday Park*, 1 Ferguson Drive (Ⓣ03/615 7241; tents $9, cabins ❷), a spacious, well-looked-after site in the Domain, five minutes' walk from King Street.

You'll find a number of **pubs** and bars along King Street and one or two **restaurants**, but none of them beats the ultra-friendly *Benny's* **café/bar** at no. 134 (daily 11.45am–2pm & 5.30pm–late), which has good coffee, cheap and imaginative food including vegetarian options, plus wine and a tempting dessert menu.

Timaru

The small port city of **TIMARU**, 18km south of Temuka, is one of the South Island's larger provincial centres, weighing in with 28,000 residents. At the end of a straight and flat two-hour drive from Christchurch, the city's gently rolling hills mark a subtle change and provide the setting for an austere streetscape partly built of volcanic "bluestone" – the local council insisted on stone and brick constructions after a devastating fire in 1868. With the possible exceptions of the **Aigantighe Art Gallery** and the **South Canterbury Museum**, there is no vastly compelling reason to stop here; though if you are looking to rest up somewhere pleasant that doesn't have much in the way of tempting demands on your cash supply, then you may just have found your spot.

The name Timaru comes from *Te Maru*, **Maori** for "place of shelter", as it provided the only haven for *waka* paddling between Banks Peninsula and Oamaru. In 1837 European settlement was initiated by Joseph Price, who set up a **whaling** station south of the present city at Patiti Point. A large part of today's commercial and pastoral development was initiated by Yorkshiremen **George and Robert Rhodes**, who established the first cattle station on the South Island in 1839 and founded Rhodes Town not long after, just north of the existing settlement of Government Town – the towns gradually grew together and merged to form Timaru. Despite an influx of European migrants aboard the *Strathallan* in 1859, it was some years before a safe harbour was established on the rocky coast. A welcome by-product of the land reclamation that created the harbour in 1877 was the fine sandy beach of Caroline Bay. For a time, Timaru became a popular seaside resort, and its annual **summer carnival**, starting at Christmas and running for three weeks, is still well worth dropping in on.

Arrival and information

Timaru's own domestic-only **airport** is just 1km from the town; a shuttle from the airport is $10. The **train station** on Station Street in the centre of the city is the principal drop-off and pick-up point for all trains and most buses; the Reservation Centre inside the station (Ⓣ03/688 3594) sells bus and train tickets for onward travel. Many buses drop you at your chosen accommodation, and a few stop outside the delightful **visitor centre**, 2 Lower George St (Mon–Fri 8.30am–5pm, Sat & Sun 10am–3pm; Ⓣ03/688 6163, Ⓦwww.southisland.co.nz), which provides free maps of South Canterbury and Timaru, and leaflets for several historic walks about town. You probably won't need Timaru's **local bus service**, which is run by CRC, with a flat rate of $1 for all journeys around the city and suburbs, including unlimited transfers within a four-hour period.

Accommodation

There's is a wide range of **accommodation**, generally in good supply except for the Christmas to mid-January period when you should book well in advance. Most places are fairly central, with motels lining Stafford Street to the north and B&Bs more widely distributed.

Anchor Motel & Timaru Backpackers 42–44 Evans St Ⓣ & Ⓕ03/684 5076. Extremely friendly and central, if slightly run-down, 1960s two-storey building with off-street parking and eight comfortable units, some of which get put to use as part of *Timaru Backpackers*, run jointly with the *Anchor* to provide highly flexible accommodation – dorms, motel units, homestays and a variety of double and single rooms – along with a nice veranda that catches the afternoon sun. Free tea and coffee. Dorms ❶, rooms ❷–❸

Benvenue Hotel 16–22 Evans St Ⓣ0800/104

049, Ⓔ benvenue@voyager.co.nz. Set on a hill with a good view of the bay and the town, this hotel has refurbished rooms, a bar, restaurant and heated indoor pool and spa. ❺–❻

Grosvenor Hotel 26 Cains Terrace Ⓣ 03/688 3129 & 0800/106 102, Ⓔ grosvenortimaru@xtra,co.nz. The most lavish centrally located accommodation, this imposing white-stone and red-roofed 1875 building was once known as the "Grand Old Lady of the South". It has fifty comfortable rooms, and even if you're not staying here, it's worth a look and a drink in one of the bars. ❺

Margaret & Nevis Jones 16 Selwyn St Ⓣ & Ⓕ 03/688 1400. A lovely late-1920s house with lush gardens and its own grass tennis court. Rooms are either en suite or have private facilities, it is only fifteen minutes' walk from town and they pick up and drop off. ❹

Mountain View 200m along Talbots Rd off SH1, 3km from Timaru Ⓣ 03/688 1070, Ⓕ 688 1069, Ⓔ mvhomestay@xtra.co.nz. Small farm B&B offering homely rooms with private bathrooms and a cooked breakfast. Dinner by arrangement ($20); venison a speciality. ❹

Okare B&B Wai-iti Rd, on the right and 20m after you turn off SH1 Ⓣ 03/688 0316, Ⓔ okare@xtra.co.nz. Relaxed and comfortable, boutique B&B run by a lovely couple who offer three ensuites (one double, one twin and another double with a separate bathroom) in their spacious 1909 house of mansion-like proportions, with heart rimu floors, a balcony and excellent breakfasts. ❺

Panorama Motor Lodge 52 Bay Hill Ⓣ 03/688 0097, Ⓦ www.panorama.net.nz. Excellent, striking and very hospitable motel with big spacious units, and all the usual facilities plus a sauna, spa baths, gym and off-street parking, plus truly stunning views over Caroline Bay. Within walking distance of some of the best restaurants in town. ❺

Seabreeze 28 The Bay Hill Ⓣ 0800/443 443, Ⓔ seabreezetim@xtra.co.nz. Comfortable, well-appointed and quiet motel close to town, Caroline Bay and a couple of good restaurants. ❺

Selwyn Holiday Park 8 Glen St Ⓣ 03/684 7690 & 0800/242 121, Ⓕ 688 1004. Slightly pricey but high-standard holiday park close to the golf links and within walking distance of Maori Park. Tent sites $20, cabins ❷, tourist flats ❸, motel units ❹

Tighnafeile House 62 Wai-iti Road Ⓣ 03/684 3333, Ⓔ taighnafeile-house@timaru.co.nz. Boutique lodge in a grand 1911 house close to the art gallery. Rooms are all sumptuously decorated – even the garage has a carpet. ❽

The City

Timaru undulates over low hills, all roads eventually bringing you down to the reclaimed land of the harbour and the park-backed golden sweep of Caroline Bay, a good spot for the kids even if the beach is overlooked by the port. Nearby, at the southern end of Stafford Street, is the central business district. Here you'll find the train station and, opposite, the visitor centre, now in part

Rock art

Around five hundred years ago, Maori moa hunters visited the South Canterbury and North Otago coastal plain, leaving a record of their sojourn on the walls and ceilings of open-sided limestone rock shelters. There are more than three hundred **rock drawings** around Timaru, Geraldine and Fairlie: the faded charcoal and red ochre drawings depict a variety of stylized human, bird and mythological figures and patterns. Some of the best cave drawings can be seen in the region's museums (notably the North Otago Museum in Oamaru, see p.666). Those remaining in situ are often hard to make out, but the best examples are at Risk Shelter, Acacia Downs, Blackler's Cave and Hazelburn Shelter, all on Three Mile Bush Road, which can be reached by driving northwest from Timaru along SH8 to Pleasant Point (15km distant), then continuing west along the Ohipi River.

Even equipped with your own wheels, and the free *Pleasant Point Ward Map* from the Timaru visitor centre, the paintings can be hard to find, and access is often across **private land**. The best bet is to call at the Timaru visitor centre so that they can arrange for permission before you set out: they will also help you plan your route.

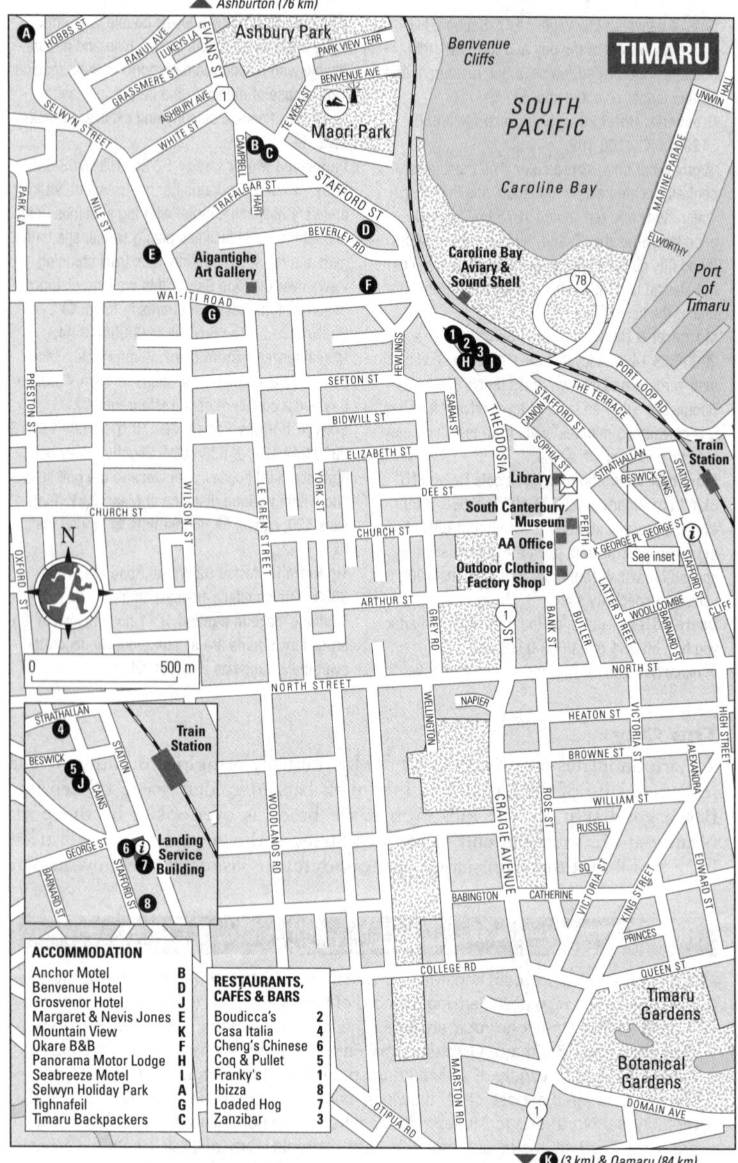

of the 1870 Landing Service Building, built of volcanic "bluestone" and originally used to store goods unloaded from the small boats that were winched up onto a shingle beach in front – roughly where the railway lines are now. The building is shared by *The Loaded Hog* restaurant and bar (see p.662), and hosts occasional historic maritime displays, accessible through the visitor centre.

A couple of hundred metres uphill, the **South Canterbury Museum**, Perth St (Tues–Fri 10am–4.30pm, Sat & Sun 1.30–4.30pm; donation appreciated), has recently expanded into new premises allowing more scope to display well-labelled local Maori artefacts, some good examples of **scrimshaw** (intricate etchings on whale teeth and bone) and other memorabilia from the whaling station that occupied Patiti Point in the late 1830s and early 1840s. Look out, too, for the wonderful **E.P. Seally collection** – drawers crammed full of butterflies, moths, eggs, minerals and rare colourful shells. A nineteenth-century naturalist, Seally collected hundreds of butterflies and moths from all over the world, each one conscientiously labelled, including the *Morpho Cypris*, a beautiful blue from Brazil; the smaller electric-aquamarine *Morpho Adonis*; and the (now sadly silent) yodelling cicada. Hanging over the main hall of the museum, and best viewed from the first-floor balcony, is a reconstruction of the 1902 **aircraft** used by Richard Pearse in his attempt to notch up the first powered flight in the world (see p.657).

Probably the best way to pass an hour or two is to visit the **Aigantighe Art Gallery**, 49 Wai-iti Rd (ⓣ03/688 4424; Tues–Fri 10am–4pm, Sat & Sun noon–4pm; donation appreciated), constructed around a venerable Timaru house known as *Aigantighe* (Gaelic for "at home") in the days before it became a gallery. Original features of the house have been preserved and provide a suitable setting for a rotating permanent collection founded on donations and bequests from Timaru's wealthier families – some works date back to the seventeenth century. A vigorous purchasing policy has produced an enviable collection of works by South Canterbury artists including relatively minor, but often intimate and personal, works by native son Colin McCahon. Other artists to look out for are Frances Hodgkins, and the prolific Austen Deans, whose luminous landscapes interpret the local countryside as well as any.

In 1990 Kiwi, Japanese and Zimbabwean sculptors came here as part of a symposium and carved thirteen works from soft Mount Somers Stone (see p.697). These have weathered nicely and now sit harmoniously in the gallery's small but impressive **sculpture garden**, a great place for a picnic (bring your own). Look particularly for *Baboon*, nearest the house, carved with power tools by a Zimbabwean who had only ever hand carved. The nodules in the animal's hand represent the seeds of knowledge gained by the experience. Call the gallery for details of temporary exhibitions.

Hector's dolphins have always swum around off the coast at Timaru and Timaru Marine Cruises (ⓣ03/686 9365) have permission to run **dolphin watching** trips (around $35 per head and taken by the harbour master, who fits in the trips around his other duties, so be flexible) from the corner of Port Loop Road and Ritchie Street. On a fine day, you could also spend a quiet hour ambling around the **Botanical Gardens**, Queen Street (daily 8am–dusk; free), or strolling along the low cliffs north of Caroline Bay past the wooden 1878 **Blackett's Lighthouse** to Dashing Rocks. Wet days are better spent on the ninety-minute tour and sampling at the **DB Brewery**, Sheffield Street, Washdyke, 2km north of town on SH1 (ⓣ03/688 2059; Mon–Thurs 10.30am; free; no sandals).

Finally, for those with a desire to see a traditional craft revived in a truly modern and totally eccentric way go and visit **The Artisan**, formerly known as Gareth James, a bare-foot blacksmith living and working in **Pleasant Point**, just 12km from Timaru. His shop and forge (5 Maitland Rd, close to the historic railway; ⓦwww.iron.co.nz) are open daily (10am–5pm,) and he'll give you a casual tour or you can join a more formal one, and (for a price) he'll make you a memento then and there or you can choose some of his ready-made handiwork. You'll need either a car to get here, or to take one of the very rare public buses or see if a shuttle will drop you off on the way to Fairlie (see p.701).

Eating, drinking and entertainment

Timaru's **restaurants**, though numerous, don't offer great variety in terms of decor or ambitious cuisine, but you'll find the usual cache of fish-and-chip shops, as well as a couple of Italian and Asian eateries: the best of the bunch are listed below.

Things hot up in Timaru for the three post-Christmas weeks of the **summer carnival**, when there's a circus, a fair, and free concerts in Caroline Bay. Otherwise, Timaru is a pretty quiet place; if there is anything going on in town, then the **entertainment** listings in the daily *Timaru Herald* (particularly the Friday and Saturday editions) will provide details. You can catch first-run Hollywood **movies** at Movie Max 3, corner of Canon and Sophia streets (☎03/684 6987).

Boudicca's 64 The Bay Hill. Good-quality, stylish café/bar specializing in Middle Eastern and Kiwi cuisine. A kebab, salad and a variety of sauces, including delicious sweet chilli, will set you back less than $10, and there's felafel and other meat-free options, as well as mouth-watering, home-made desserts, fresh fish and big steaks. Mon–Fri 11am–9pm, Sat & Sun 10am–late; licensed.

Casa Italia Ristorante 2 Strathallan St ☎03/684 5528. Located in the atmospheric Victorian Customs House, this is probably Timaru's finest restaurant. The Italian chef reliably turns out authentic cuisine with pasta made on the premises ($17), superb risotto, pizza ($18) and *segundi piatti* around the $25–30 mark. Leave room for the chocolate mousse ($8). Evenings daily; licensed.

Cheng's Chinese Restaurant 12 George St. Excellent set menus, good fish dishes, and great chow mein, with main meals hovering in the $12–25 range. Open daily for lunch and dinner; licensed.

Coq and Pullet 209 Stafford St. Daytime café and deli opening early for breakfast, and offering panini, gourmet pies and reasonable coffee. Closed Sun.

Franky's 68–70 The Bay Hill. The third of a highly popular trio of good-quality restaurants, adjacent to one another, overlooking Caroline Bay. The food here is fresh and colourful, combining some old Kiwi favourites, like lambs liver and bacon with onions, gravy and chips, with more exotic dishes like chicken korma or a hot vegetable curry. Nothing is frighteningly expensive and like their two competitors they are licensed and do weekend brunches.

Ibizza 129 Stafford St, in the old national bank. Not much of a place but what passes for a dance club in these parts (Wed–Sun), with a late licence, table football and local and visiting DJs. Whatever you do, don't confuse them with *The Odyssey Night Club*, next door, which is *not* recommended.

Loaded Hog Landing Service Building on George St, adjacent to the visitor centre. Former brewpub that now gets its supply from a sister operation in Christchurch, this cavernous establishment occupies a wonderful stone grain store. The blackboard menu features $5 lunch specials and mains such as their famous beer-battered fish, using the Hog's Weiss beer ($12.50). Touring bands tend to play here (usually Thurs–Sun till 3am).

Zanzibar 56 The Bay Hill. Bustling, modern bar and restaurant with good views over the port and Caroline Bay, serving hearty helpings ranging from Thai fish cakes ($13) to beer-battered blue cod ($14). Licensed.

Listings

Automobile Association 26 Church St ☎03/688 4189.

Bike rental The Cyclery, 98 Stafford St (☎03/688 8892), rents bikes from $20 a day.

Car rental 6 Sefton St ☎03/684 7179.

Internet Bay City Internet, 47a Stafford St (☎03/688 6554; Mon–Fri 9am–6pm, Sat 10am–1pm) and Computer Shop Timaru 2000, 329 Stafford St (☎03/684 9333; Mon–Fri 9am–5.30pm, Sat 9am–noon).

Library Timaru District Library, Sophia St (Mon, Wed & Fri 9.30am–8pm, Tues & Thurs 9.30am–6pm, Sat 10am–noon, Sun 1–4pm).

Medical treatment Call ☎03/684 8209 for a

duty doctor. Timaru Hospital is on Queen St (☎03/684 4000); or you could try the Medical Clinic, 5 Dee St (weekdays 24hr, Sat & Sun 9am–noon, 4–6pm; ☎03/684 8209).

Post office The post office in Books and More, 19 Strathallan St (☎03/686 6040), has poste restante facilities.

Pharmacies Faulks & Jordan, 234 Strafford St; Central Pharmacy, 266 Strafford St. Details of duty pharmacies are listed in the *Timaru Herald*.

Shuttle buses Shuttle bus companies operating Timaru–Christchurch, Timaru–Dunedin and Timaru–Twizel routes include Atomic Shuttles (☎03/322 8883); Budget Shuttles (☎021/344 780; also run an airport service for $10); Catch-a-bus (☎03/489 4641); and Supa Kut Price Shuttles (☎0800/662 772).

Taxis Budget (☎03/688 8779) and Timaru Taxis (☎03/688 8899) both offer a 24hr service.

Oamaru

The former port town of **OAMARU**, 85km south of Timaru on SH1, is one of New Zealand's more alluring (and undersold) provincial cities, making it a relaxed place to spend a day or two. Perhaps its most immediate appeal is the presence of two **penguin colonies** on the outskirts of town, which provide an unmissable opportunity to observe both the diminutive blue penguins and their larger yellow-eyed cousins. The town itself has attractions too, not least the well-preserved core of nineteenth-century buildings of its central **historic district**, built of the distinctive cream-coloured local limestone, which earned Oamaru the title "The Whitestone City". At the turn of the twentieth century it had a reputation as being the most attractive city in the South Island, and with the ongoing restoration it may well regain that status. For the moment, several grand edifices have yet to be restored, but it only seems a matter of time before the buildings will be taken over by cafés and chi-chi galleries, as has happened with sections of the rest of the area already.

The limestone outcrops throughout the area once provided shelter for Maori and later the raw material for ambitious European builders. As a commercial centre for goldrush prospectors, and shored up by quarrying, timber and farming industries, Oamaru grew in wealth, giving shape to its prosperity in the elegant stone buildings that today grace the town centre. The port opened for **migration** in 1874, with three hundred ships arriving that year and a further four hundred between 1876 and 1878, although many foundered on the hostile coastline and wrecks littered the late nineteenth-century shore. After this boom period the fortunes of the town declined, and it's only in recent years that the town has begun to come alive again.

The writer Janet Frame (see Contexts, p.1004) spent some of her childhood in Oamaru and lived here on and off in later years. Fans of her work may want to follow the **Janet Frame Trail** (a leaflet is available from the visitor centre, see below) which concentrates on locations used in varying degrees of disguise in her books – the former subscription library in the Athenaeum that featured in *Faces In The Water*, or the rubbish dump that formed the symbolic centre of *Owls Do Cry* – although such sights are hardly essential for the uncommitted.

Arrival and information

Buses drop off at the corner of Eden and Thames streets, while the dilapidated **train station** is just northeast of the centre on Humber Street. You can walk just about everywhere from here, but if you have heavy bags you can always call for a **taxi** (☎03/434 1234).

The **visitor centre**, 1 Thames St (Nov–Easter Mon–Fri 9am–6pm, Sat & Sun 10am–5pm; Easter–Oct Mon–Fri 9am–5pm, Sat & Sun 10am–4pm; ☎03/434

1656, ⓦwww.tourismwaitaki.co.nz), is less than ten minutes' walk from the train station and bus stop. Enthusiastic staff dish out some useful leaflets, including *Historic Oamaru*, which focuses on the historic district, and *Heritage Trails of North Otago* ($1), which includes details of the Janet Frame Trail.

If you can manage it, the times to be here are from November to January when penguins are in greatest numbers, or over the third weekend in November when the streets of the historic district become a race track for penny-farthings, cheered on by local residents in Victorian attire and accompanied by a fair.

Accommodation

Most of the accommodation is on, or near, Thames Street. If your budget will stretch to it, try one of the homestays, which reflect Oamaru's charm.

Hotels and motels

Alpine Motel 285 Thames St Ⓣ03/434 5038 & 0800/272 710, Ⓕ434 6301. Modern building close to the town centre, with ten spacious studio units, some with full kitchens. ❸–❹

Brydone Hotel 115 Thames St Ⓣ0800/279 366, Ⓕ434 5719. Magnificent old building of Oamaru stone with an ornate Italian facade, dating from 1880. Extensively renovated and redecorated, this is one of the smarter places in town. ❺

Criterion Tyne St Ⓣ03/434 6247. Charming boutique accommodation and a solid breakfast. ❺

Heritage Court Motel 346 Thames St Ⓣ03/437 2200, Ⓕ437 2600. One of the newer and more upmarket motels: modern, clean, spacious and comfortable units, with cooking facilities and in-house video.❹–❺

Midway Motel 289 Thames St Ⓣ & Ⓕ03/434 5388, Ⓣ0800/447 744. Opposite the fire station and close to the centre of town, this budget establishment has units with full cooking facilities. ❹

B&Bs and homestays

Anne Mieke Guesthouse 47 Tees St Ⓣ03/434 8051, Ⓕ434 8050. A large suburban house offering B&B close to the town centre and the blue penguin viewing area. Each room has its own washbasin, bathrooms are shared and the rooms at the back of the house have views of the bay. ❸

Jenny and Gerald's Homestay 11 Stour St Ⓣ03/434 9628. About twenty minutes' walk from the bus stop, this attractive 1920s house contains an ornate staircase, a pleasant double with private facilities, and two singles, one with private, the other shared, facilities. Jenny and Gerald are very friendly and share an interest in local history, as well as running Slightly Foxed, a secondhand bookshop. Dinner ($30) by arrangement. ❺

Pen-y-Bryn Lodge 41 Towey St Ⓣ03/434 7939, ⓦwww.penybryn.co.nz. One of the finer lodges in these parts; a splendid restored Victorian home on a hill overlooking the town, graced with hand-crafted floor-to-ceiling fireplaces, a billiard room, richly carved bookcases and a Florentine-style dining room of rimu timber and English oak. The large and luxurious rooms all have private facilities. Rates are $250 per person (May–Sept $175) and include a sumptuous four-course meal and breakfast. ❾

Tara Springhill Rd Ⓣ & Ⓕ03/434 8187, Ⓔsmith.tara@xtra.co.nz. Worth considering if you have your own transport, this rural homestay is set among rose gardens, native trees and farmland around 10km west of town off Weston Ngapara Road. They have just one twin room with a private bathroom. Good food, including free-range eggs, home-made bread and home-grown veg. Dinner ($30) by arrangement. ❹

Hostels and campsites

The Hall–Coastal Backpackers All Day Bay, 18km south of Oamaru near Kakanui Ⓣ03/439 5411, Ⓕ439 5242. Hugely relaxing rural backpackers well off the beaten track but within easy walk of a good beach and some coastal wetlands. Doubles and dorms are in a couple of separate buildings each with lounge and log-burning stove; they've got free laundry on request and free use of bike, boogie boards and canoes; and there are $10 evening meals available. Oamaru pick-ups for booked guests, and Magic and Atomic both pass the gate. Dorms ❶, rooms ❷

Oamaru Gardens Holiday Park Chelmer St Ⓣ0800/280 202, Ⓕ434 7666. In a lovely sheltered setting, this site offers pitches, tourist flats and cabins. Tents $10, cabins & flats ❷

Red Kettle YHA cnr Reed St & Cross St Ⓣ & Ⓕ03/434 5008. Small, pleasant and well-managed hostel close to the town centre with small dorms, a couple of twin-bunk rooms and a couple of twins. Dorms ❶, rooms ❷

Swaggers 25 Wansbeck St Ⓣ03/434 9999, Ⓔswaggers@es.co.nz. Small, homely hostel in a suburban house with twins, four-shares and one five-bunk dorm. Dorms ❶, twins ❷

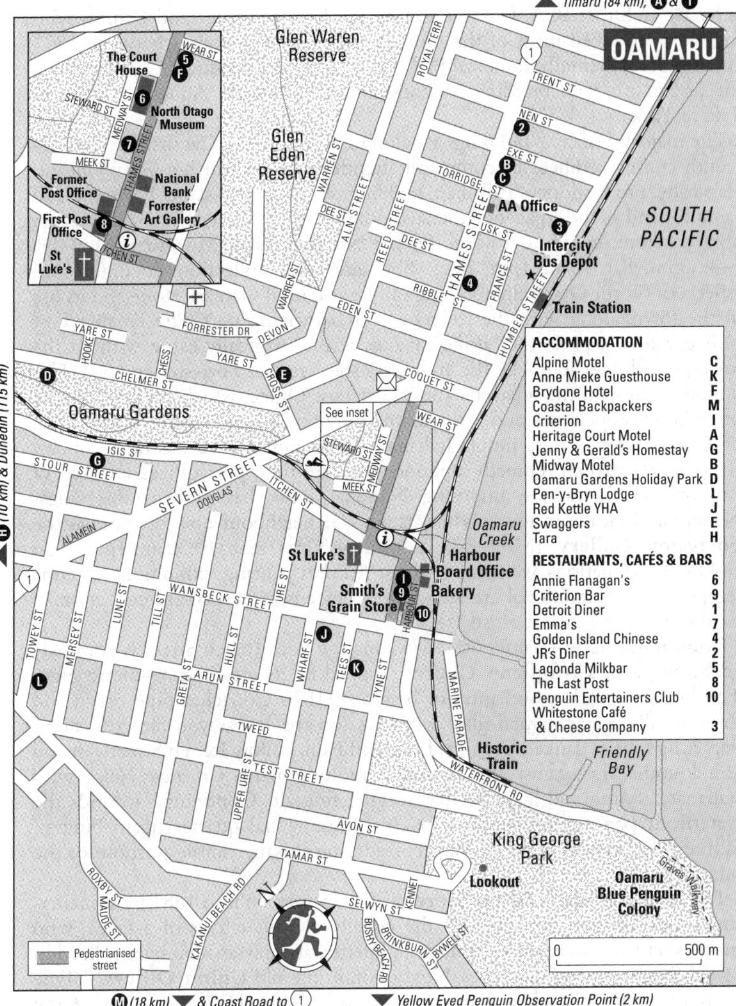

The Historic District

Thames Street and the knot of streets around Tyne, Itchen and Harbour streets define Oamaru's Historic District, a dense cluster of grand civic and mercantile buildings that sets the town centre apart from any other in the land. The key is Oamaru stone, which hardens with exposure to the elements but, when freshly quarried, is what is known in the trade as a "free stone", easily cut and worked with conventional metal hand tools. While keeping the prevailing Neoclassical fashion firmly in mind, the architects' imaginations ran riot, and the craftsmen were given free rein to produce deeply fluted pilasters, finely detailed pediments and elegant Corinthian pillars topped with veritable forests of acanthus leaves. Oamaru was given much of its character by architect R.A. Lawson and by the firm Forrester and Lemon who together produced most of the more accomplished buildings between 1871 and 1883. Incidentally, the local Parkside Quarry still produces Oamaru stone for use in modern buildings; witness the new Waitaki Aquatic Centre in Takaro Park

The majority of civic buildings are along Thames Street. The first of the nineteenth-century edifices to command attention is the Courthouse, an elegant, classically proportioned Palladian building showing the same Forrester and Lemon hand as the adjacent Athenaeum building, that served as a subscription library before providing a home for the **North Otago Museum** (Mon–Fri 1–4.30pm, Sat 10am–1pm; free). This absorbing collection documents all aspects of North Otago life focusing on the origin of Oamaru stone and its use in the town, along with the town's role as a thriving port. The Former Post Office, a few steps further along Thames Street, originally came without the tower, which was added by the architect's son, Thomas Forrester, in 1903. This building replaced the adjacent 1864 First Post Office, which predates all the other Whitestone work and is the town's only remaining example of the work of W.H. Clayton, whose simple Italianate design houses a very good restaurant and bar (see p.668). Directly opposite the one-time post offices are two of Lawson's buildings: the imposing National Bank has perhaps the purest Neoclassical facade in town; while its grander neighbour now operates as the **Forrester Gallery** (Mon–Fri 10.30am–4.30pm, Sat 10.30am–1pm, Sun 1–4.30pm; donations welcome), which features touring exhibitions of contemporary and traditional art, alongside an extensive permanent collection of works by New Zealand artists.

Continuing along Thames Street, its junction with Itchen Street is dominated by **St Luke's Anglican Church**, topped by its looming 39-metre spire. The beautiful dark-wood interior boasts an 1876 Conacher pipe organ and three locally made stained-glass windows (on the left as you face the altar), depicting Christ flanked by saints Luke and Paul. Follow Itchen Street east and you'll come up against the infinitely more profane *Criterion Hotel*, with Italianate styling and a quaint bar serving fine ale. Continuing towards the waterfront you enter Oamaru's original commercial quarter, again built of Whitestone and often flamboyant considering the mercantile purpose of the buildings.

The elegant **Smiths Grain Store** on Tyne Street, built in 1881 by stonemason James Johnson, now houses the equally elegant efforts of a tailor, who makes Victorian-style shirts, blouses and petticoats, ably assisted by a collection of old Singer sewing machines. Next door, in the old **Union Offices**, 7 Tyne St, is a traditional bookbinder's workshop (ⓣ03/434 9277; Mon–Fri 2–6pm; free), where you can watch fine bookmaking, binding and repair work and see examples of old printing and letterpress machines. A block east of here on the waterfront, Harbour Street boasts the sadly neglected Venetian Renaissance-style Harbour Board Office, built in 1876 and one of the first public buildings designed by the prolific Forrester and Lemon. At the opposite end of Harbour Street is the striking Loan and Mercantile Warehouse which, when it was built in 1882, was the largest grain store in New Zealand. Look out for the ornamental rope design garlanding the second storey.

On weekends and public holidays you can gaze at the backs of some of these buildings from the **Oamaru Historic Steam Train** (ⓣ03/434 5634; every 30min 11am–4pm; $5 return), if it is working, which it does for most of the summer and when the volunteers can get round to repairing it in the winter, from a platform beside the visitor centre on Itchen Street a few hundred metres along the waterfront. The engines and carriages have been lovingly restored by a friendly bunch of fanatics, who also care for the blue penguins that nest in the engine shed at the end of the line.

The Oamaru Gardens

Five minutes' walk west of Thames Street along either Severn Street or Itchen Street lies the manicured natural beauty of the **Oamaru Gardens** (daily dawn–dusk, glasshouses 9am–4pm; free). These are among the most stunning gardens in New Zealand, dating back to 1876 and indicative of the wealth the town once enjoyed. The main Severn Street entrance leads to the spectacular Craig Fountain, built from Italian marble and surrounded by packed flowerbeds. Further on is the hundred-year-old Victorian summerhouse, full of bright blooms from around the world, with an extensive collection of cacti in a nearby purpose-built glasshouse. Flanking Oamaru Creek as it flows through the gardens are a rhododendron dell and two large ponds, while a splendid red Japanese bridge spans the creek to reach the Chinese and Fragrant Gardens. Most popular with younger visitors, though, is an enclosure at the far end of the gardens, full of wallabies and alpacas.

The penguin colonies

Oamaru is unique in having both yellow-eyed and blue **penguin colonies** within walking distance of the town centre. It is usually possible to see both colonies in one evening, since the yellow-eyes tend to come ashore earlier than the blues, but check at the visitor centre for expected arrival times. There are some important **guidelines** you must observe when viewing penguins, since these are timid creatures and are easily distressed. Flash photography is banned; you should keep quiet and still; and do not encroach within ten metres of the birds. Once disturbed, the penguins may not return to their nests for several hours, even if they have chicks to feed.

First up, about fifteen minutes' walk southeast of the town centre along Waterfront Road, is the **Blue Penguin Colony** (best visited just before dusk but check for exact times at the visitor centre; around $10). There has recently been a massive investment here to upgrade the facilities and the experience, with a dedicated visitor centre on the site, containing, among all the usual bits and pieces, a series of videos on blue penguins and an infra-red 24-hour monitor in one of the nest boxes. The old viewing platforms have been done away

Blue penguins

Blue Penguins, the smallest of their kind, are found around the coasts of New Zealand, and along the shores of southern Australia, where they are known as fairy penguins. White on their chests and bellies, they have a thick head-to-tail streak along their back in iridescent indigo-blue. Breeding takes place from May to January, and the parents take it in turns to stay with the egg during the 36-day incubation period. The newly hatched chick is protected for the first two or three weeks before both parents go out to sea to meet the increasing demand for food, returning full of krill, squid and crustaceans, which they regurgitate into the chick's mouth. At eight weeks the chicks begin to fledge, but 70 percent will die in the first year; the juveniles that do survive usually return to their birthplace. At the end of the breeding season the birds fatten up before coming ashore to moult: over the next three weeks their feathers are not waterproof enough for them to take to the sea and they lose up to half their bodyweight.

with and replaced by a grandstand capable of seating 350 people, although there is good evidence to suggest that his will not adversely affect the penguins. If you come during the breeding season (June–Dec), you'll see chicks – and hear them calling to their parents out at sea, hunting for food. When the parents return around dusk, travelling in groups (known as rafts), they climb the steep harbour banks and cross in front of the grandstand to their nests. Outside the breeding season the penguins indulge in much less to-ing and fro-ing, but provide an engaging spectacle nevertheless. In the peak season (Nov–Jan) you might hope to see a hundred penguins in a night, though this might drop to a dozen or so in March, June and August.

This stretch of coast is also home to the much larger **yellow-eyed penguins**, which nest in smaller numbers but keep more sociable hours, usually coming ashore in late afternoon or early evening (best Oct–Feb). They mainly arrive on **Bushy Beach**, reached by road 2km along Bushy Beach Road, or on foot via the **Graves Walkway** (closed at the time of writing because of storm damage but due to reopen; 1.25km; 30min each way) which starts just past the blue penguin colony. The path curves round a headland at the end of Oamaru Harbour and continues to a point overlooking the small cove of Boatman's Harbour. This is worth exploring at low tide when **lava pillows** about 50cm in diameter are exposed in the cliff wall. These were formed millions of years ago when molten lava encased hard fossil-bearing limestone, producing a honeycomb effect with each cell defined by a rim of black lava. The walkway ends overlooking Bushy Beach, where a hide enables you to see the yellow-eyed penguins making their way across the beach. An alternative to watching the penguins from the hide is to join Jim Caldwell's **Yellow-eyed Penguin Tour** (2.5hr), which set out from the hide via the Bushy Beach car park about before dark (Oct–April; $7.50, check with the visitor centre for exact time). Jim's been working with the penguins for years and can fill you in on anything you want to know, with the added advantage that he's allowed to take you onto the beach and within about 5m of the birds.

Eating, drinking and entertainment

Oamaru isn't over-endowed with good places to eat and drink, though you'll do well enough for a night or two, and a range of pockets are catered for. You shouldn't have to stray too far from the central Thames Street to find what you want.

Annie Flanagan's 84 Thames St. An Irish bar Oamaru-style with the usual range of draught Guinness and Kilkenny plus live music on Saturday nights and a pretty decent selection of stews, curries, soups, steaks and sandwiches mostly around the $10–15 mark.

Criterion Bar *Criterion Hotel*, Tyne St. The strong Victorian feeling of the wooden bar is carried over into an ancient till and some old-fashioned, good beer, including London Porter and Emersons traditional ale. They also do good pork pies, bacon butties, fish and chips and bangers and mash.

Detroit Diner on SH1, next to the Waitaki Truck Stop 4.5km north of the centre. Retro American-style diner serving breakfasts, snacks, grills and scallops for only $15 a plate. Solid and cheap, this place is much favoured by truckies. Daily 7am–10pm.

Emma's Café 30 Thames St. Hip café serving great coffee, bagels, wholemeal croissants, muffins and lemon syrup cakes. Work by local artists decorates the walls. Mon–Sat 10am–6pm.

Golden Island Chinese Restaurant 243 Thames St. Dependable and inexpensive Chinese with a good range of set menus for couples or groups, and some generous vegetarian dishes. Daily 5–9pm or later; licensed & BYO.

JR's Diner 301 Thames St. Eat-in and takeaway snack shack, serving burgers, fish and chips, steak and superior Chinese food at cheap prices ($8–12). Daily 11am–10pm. BYO & licensed.

Lagonda Milkbar 193 Thames St, cnr Eden St. One of the better greasy spoons in town, open for breakfast, lunch and early dinner. Also operates as the InterCity booking office and has internet access.

Penguin Entertainers Club off Harbour St ⓦwww.penguinclub.co.nz. Oamaru's premier back-alley fun house and perhaps the coolest place in town. Friday nights are jam nights (from 9pm, $2 non-members) and watch out for the advertised gigs ($10 cover charge) by visiting artists from all over New Zealand. The club is now so legendary that just about everybody of note, and anyone who will be of note, plays here. Also hosts poetry, theatre, and more. From the *Criterion Hotel*, walk down Harbour St, turn left down an unprepossessing alley at the sign "WFC In", beside the Willets Furniture Company, and follow the alley to steps and a small door on the righthand side, near the waterfront, where a sign of a penguin with sun glasses resides above said door.

The Last Post in the First Post Office building, Thames St. Upmarket bar/restaurant with a beer garden. Snacks and cocktails, as well as good lunch and dinner menus. Sun–Thurs 11am–10pm, Fri & Sat 11am–midnight.

Whitestone Cheese Café, cnr of Torridge and Humber streets. Small café associated with the Whitestone Cheese Company, great simply for a coffee and cake but mainly the place for sampling their excellent cheeses with some of the local wine. Particularly good are the Farmhouse, a semi-soft cheese with a lemongrass aroma and nutty taste, the Brie, which has a hint of mushroom, the strong Airedale and the Windsor Blue, a creamy soft cheese – all made on the premises. Mon–Fri 9am–5pm, Sat & Sun 10am–4pm.

Listings

Car rental Smash Palace Rentals, 1 Meek St (ⓣ03/434 1965), rents newer cars for $55 per day, or some old ones for as little as $25.

Cinema The Old Oamaru Opera House, cnr Medway St & Thames St (ⓣ03/434 1070), shows movies; screenings are advertised in the visitor centre, on a noticeboard outside the library, and in the newspapers.

Library Oamaru Public Library, next door to the North Otago Museum on Thames St (Mon–Thurs 9.30am–5.30pm, Fri 9.30am–8pm, Sat 10am–12.30pm).

Medical treatment Oamaru Hospital, 8 Stewart St (ⓣ03/433 0290). In emergencies call ☎111.

Newspaper The Mon–Fri only *Oamaru Mail* ($0.60)has entertainment listings and emergency numbers.

Post office The post office, 2 Severn St (ⓣ03/434 78840), has poste restante facilities.

Tours Book through the visitor centre for informative, guided walking tours of the town (1hr; $7.50).

South to Moeraki - and the Moeraki Boulders

SH1 heads south from Oamaru and constitutes the quickest way to the Moeraki boulders and Dunedin, though a more appealing alternative is to take the quieter backroads for the first 20km – follow Kakanui Beach Road. This route reaches the coast at Kakanui and continues 3km to All Day Bay, the peaceful location of *Hall-Coastal Backpackers* (see p.664), then winds back to the main highway.

Forty kilometres south of Oamaru on SH1, a car park and restaurant-cum-**visitor centre** (daily: Oct–April 8am–6pm; May–Nov 9am–5pm; ⓣ03/439 4827) overlooks the beach occupied by the strangely compelling **Moeraki Boulders**, visited on a short private trail ($2 in the honesty box at any hour). Large, grey and almost perfectly spherical, the boulders (some of which reach 2m in diameter) lie partially submerged in the sandy beach and by the wash of high tide. Their smooth skins hide honeycomb centres, which are revealed in some of the broken specimens. Despite appearances, the boulders did not fall from the sky, nor were they washed up by the sea, but rather lay deep in the mudstone cliffs behind the beach. As the sea eroded the cliffs, out fell the smooth boulders, and their distinctive surface pattern was formed as further erosion exposed a network of veins. The boulders were originally formed around a central core of carbonate of lime crystals which attracted minerals from their surroundings – a process that started sixty million years ago, when muddy sediment containing shell and plant fragments accumulated on the sea floor. The masses formed range in size from small pellets to large round rocks, some with a small void in the middle. There were a large number of these boulders in the area, but the smaller ones have all been souvenired over the years, leaving only those too heavy to shift.

Maori named the boulders *Te Kai-hinaki* (food baskets), believing them to have been washed ashore from the wreck of a canoe whose occupants were seeking *pounamu*. The seaward reef near Shag Point (see below) was the hull of the canoe, and just beyond it stands a prominent rock, the vessel's petrified navigator. Some of the Moeraki Boulders were *hinaki* (baskets), the more spherical were water-carrying gourds and the irregular-shaped rocks farther down the beach were *kumara* (sweet potatoes) from the canoe's food store. The survivors among the crew, Nga Tamariki, Puketapu and Pakihiwi Tahi, were transformed at daybreak into hills overlooking the beach.

Once you've had a good look at the boulders it's worth walking along the beach to the Moeraki Point whalers' lookout, where there's a view south down the coast to the lighthouse, and the likelihood of seeing Hector's dolphins, which often surf in the breakers off the beach. If you're in the area in the winter (June–Aug), you might chance upon some of the thin, silvery frost fish which beach themselves along the shoreline on frosty nights for no apparent reason.

Moeraki village

You can eat tolerably well in the restaurant/bar at the boulders' visitor centre which has great views of the ocean and boulders, but if you want to stay hereabouts your only options are in the sleepy fishing village of **MOERAKI**, 1km to the south along SH1 then 1.5km down a side road, which makes a tranquil place to break your journey.

On the right-hand side of the road just before you enter the village is the **Kotahitanga** ("One People") **Church**, built in 1862 and containing beautiful stained-glass windows, crafted in Birmingham in 1891. Considered unusual for its (at the time rather daring) portrayal of Maori alongside Jesus and Mary, the left light of the window is a portrait based on a photograph of Te Matiaha Tiramoreh of Moeraki, a respected leader of the Ngai Tahu who died in 1881. Sadly the church is only open for services (third Sunday of the month at 2pm), though you might get a glimpse of the stained glass through cracks in the church's frosted windows.

Of the **accommodation** available in the village, the *Moeraki Motel* (Ⓣ & Ⓕ03/439 4862; cottages ❷, units ❸), on the only road entering the village, is a friendly place located close to a beach with six cottages and four two-storey units facing the bay, all with fully equipped kitchens. There's also the *Moeraki Motor Camp* (Ⓣ & Ⓕ03/439 4759; tent sites $9.50, cabins ❷–❸), situated on a hill farther into the village, with cooking facilities (camp kitchens and outdoor barbecues) and a store.

Smaller shuttle bus companies will drop you in the village, although services run by the major companies merely drop off at the point where the side road into the village leaves SH1.

Shag Point

A number of smaller, odd-shaped boulders can be found at **Shag Point**, 10km south along SH1 and 2.5km in from the highway (or an 11km walk along Katiki beach if you're feeling energetic). The beach near the point is sometimes visited by fur seals (Oct–March) and yellow-eyed penguins, which usually come ashore between 3.30pm and nightfall – there's a small hide with a little wooden bench overlooking the beach where you can keep watch.

Palmerston

The lumber town of **PALMERSTON**, 22km south of Moeraki, marks the junction of two routes: SH1 running 55km south to Dunedin; and the "Pigroot" (SH85) inland to the Maniototo and the historic goldfield heartland of Central Otago. There's little reason to stop long in Palmerston, though on even the briefest visit you'll notice the **monument** atop Puketapu Hill. It was erected in recognition of John McKenzie, a Scottish shepherd who, in the 1870s, rose to high office and pushed through the Land Settlement Act which effectively laid the groundwork for modern farming by breaking up the vast holdings of absentee landlords and making them available to new immigrants. To take in the extensive view from the monument, follow signs to Goodwood Road from the central junction.

Palmerston's culinary offerings are hardly an enticement to stop, though the *Postmark Café*, on the main street, is OK for a cuppa and something basic to **eat**. Simple **accommodation** is covered by *Pioneer Motels*, 56 Tiverton St (Ⓣ03/465 1234; ❸), with self-contained units, and *Pleasant Valley Motor Camp*, 3km south of town on SH1 (Ⓣ03/465 1370; tent sites $10, dorms ❶, cabins ❷), which has been converted from an old sanatorium. For something considerably more luxurious, call for directions to *Centrewood*, Bobby's Head Road (Ⓣ & Ⓕ03/465 1977, Ⓦwww.friars.co.nz/hosts/centrewood), a high-ceilinged 1904 homestead set amid English rose gardens well away from the road in the coastal hills and close to beaches frequented by seals and yellow-eyed penguins. The approach is low-key, but there is an effortless grace to the single suite of rooms let either as one room, a room and exclusive use of the vast lounge with polished rimu floors and a small billiard table, or the lounge and both bedrooms (sleeping up to four; $250 per couple). Evening meals ($40 and up) include wine and can be taken with the family who are descended from physicist Ernest Rutherford (see p.617), and keep a small collection of mementoes.

The main South Island train route runs from Picton through Blenheim and Kaikoura to Christchurch: there's just one train a day in each direction. The coastal bus route from Christchurch to Dunedin is the most hotly contested in the South Island with over half a dozen companies offering a range of schedules and very competitive prices. The inland run from Christchurch to Queenstown is another hot ticket, but services running inland from the coast are sporadic to say the least: InterCity (Ⓣ03/379 9020), Atomic Shuttle (Ⓣ03/322 8883) and Southern Link Shuttles (Ⓣ03/358 8355) have the broadest networks.

Travel details

Buses

From Ashburton to Geraldine (2 daily; 40min); Timaru (9–11 daily; 1hr); Twizel (2 daily; 3hr 40min).

From Christchurch to: Akaroa (1–2 daily; 2hr 50min); Arthur's Pass (3 daily; 2hr 10min); Ashburton (10–12 daily; 1hr–1hr 20min); Blenheim (7 daily; 4hr 30min–5hr); Dunedin (9–11 daily; 5–6hr); Geraldine (3–4 daily; 1hr 30–2hr);

Greymouth (3 daily; 5hr); Hanmer Springs (1–2 daily; 2hr 30min); Invercargill, via Dunedin (9–11 daily; 5–6hrs); Kaikoura (7–8 daily; 2hr 45min); Lyttelton (every 30min 8.10am–11.25pm; 35min); Methven (3 daily; 1hr 15min); Mount Cook (1 daily; 5hr 20min); Nelson (3 daily; 7–8hr); Oamaru (9–11 daily; 3hr 30min–4hr 30min); Picton (7 daily; 5hr–5hr 30min); Timaru (9–11 daily; 2hr 30min); Twizel (5–6 daily; 3hr 30min–7hr); Queenstown (6–7 daily; 7–9hr); Wanaka (3–4 daily; 6hr 20min–9hr 20min).

From Oamaru to: Dunedin (9–11 daily; 2hr 15min); Mount Cook (3 weekly; 2hr 30min); Twizel (1 daily; 2hr 15min).

From Timaru to: Dunedin (9–11 daily; 3hrs 30mins); Oamaru (9–11 daily; 1hr 20min); Mount Cook (3 weekly; 3hr 30min); Twizel (1 daily; 2hr 15min).

Flights

From Christchurch to: Auckland (14 daily; 1hr 20min); Blenheim (1–2 daily; 50min); Dunedin (4–5 daily; 1hr); Invercargill (4 daily; 1hr 15min); Mount Cook (1–2 daily, 45min); Napier (2–3 daily; 1hr 30–2hr); Nelson (2–6 daily; 50min); Queenstown (3–5 daily; 50min); Rotorua (2 daily, 1hr 15min); Wellington (10–13 daily; 45min).

10

The Central South Island

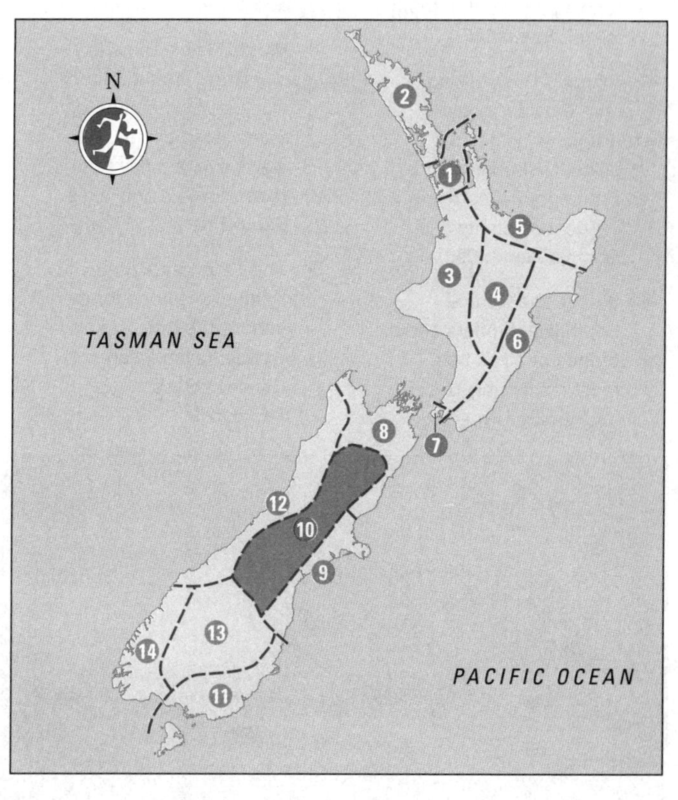

CHAPTER 10

Highlights

✱ **Hot springs** A dip in the waters at Hanmer or Springs Junction is the perfect way to unwind. **See p.677**

✱ **The Tranzalpine Express** Take one of the world's top rail journeys, running across the South Island. **See p.685**

✱ **Arthur's Pass** Hiking here provides a jaw-dropping insight into a uniquely beautiful landscape populated by indigenous plants and animals. **See p.690**

✱ **Skiing** The Central South Island offers some of the country's best, most reasonably priced and least-crowded skiing, within reach of the coffee-house culture of Christchurch. **See p.703**

✱ **Lake Tekapo** A glorious photogenic lake with clear uninterrupted views of the southern hemisphere stars at night. **See p.704**

✱ **Mount Cook** The short day walks around Mount Cook repay the effort of some steep climbs, with views over alpine mountains, glaciers and lakes. **See p.710**

✱ **The Elephant Rocks** Unique limestone formations in the weird and wonderful landscape of Dansey's Pass. **See p.721**

10

The Central South Island

The **Central South Island** is one of the most varied and intriguing areas in New Zealand, with extensive pasturelands, dense native forests, and a history rich in tales of human endeavour. The defining feature of the region, however, is the rugged mountain ridge of the **Southern Alps**, which runs from north to south forming the South Island's central spine. The middle portion of this ridge, which culminates in Australasia's highest peak, **Mount Cook**, presents an almost insurmountable barrier to travel between east and west coasts. The foothills of the Alps harbour rare and sometimes unique alpine plants and wildlife, including the famous Mount Cook Lilies, the largest white mountain daisies in the world, the most mischievous of birds, and the only alpine parrot in the world, the kea. A logistical nightmare to Maori and European settlers alike, the region is typical pioneer country, and the communities themselves (often named after the explorers and surveyors that opened the region up; Arthur's Pass and Lewis Pass being two prominent examples) are simple places, tinged with the toughness and idiosyncrasies of the early settlers.

The rugged nature of the terrain ensures that it's impossible to traverse the region on a north–south axis, and access to the area is determined by routes approaching the mountains from the east and west coasts. The most northerly of these routes is the **Lewis Pass Road**, which conveys traffic from the Canterbury Plains north of Christchurch to Westport on the west coast, passing the spa resort of **Hanmer Springs** on the way. Hanmer is a tranquil place surrounded by striking forested hill and mountain scenery, and a good base from which to visit the neighbouring Hanmer Springs Ski Area, as well as **Hanmer Forest** and **Maruia Springs** further west. South of here, another major cross-mountain route served by both road and rail links Christchurch with the western seaboard town of Greymouth via **Arthur's Pass**, historically an important trade route connecting the coalfields of the west coast with the port of Lyttelton. It's now much travelled by tourists, with the Christchurch–Greymouth **TranzAlpine Express** providing one of the world's most spectacular rail journeys. It's also one of the better places for day walks and longer treks, with hundreds of miles of walks available in the **Arthur's Pass National Park**.

South of Christchurch, roads lead up from the southern Canterbury Plains

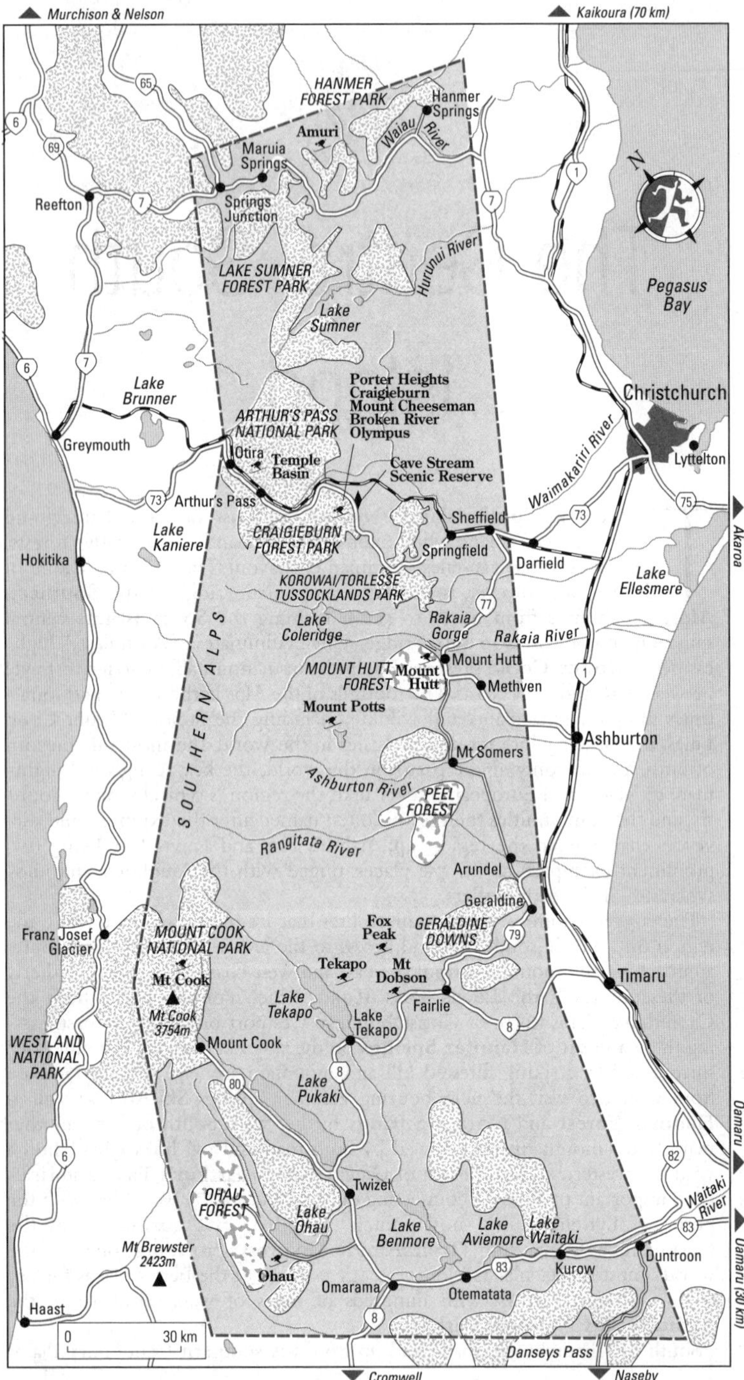

Murchison & Nelson
Kaikoura (70 km)
HANMER FOREST PARK
Hanmer Springs
Amuri
Maruia Springs
Waiau River
Reefton
Springs Junction
Hurunui River
LAKE SUMNER FOREST PARK
Lake Sumner
Pegasus Bay
Lake Brunner
Porter Heights
Craigieburn
Mount Cheeseman
Broken River
Olympus
Christchurch
ARTHUR'S PASS NATIONAL PARK
Greymouth
Otira
Temple Basin
Cave Stream Scenic Reserve
Waimakariri River
Lyttelton
Arthur's Pass
Sheffield
Akaroa
Lake Kaniere
CRAIGIEBURN FOREST PARK
Springfield
Hokitika
Darfield
KOROWAI/TORLESSE TUSSOCKLANDS PARK
Lake Ellesmere
Lake Coleridge
Rakaia Gorge
Rakaia River
SOUTHERN ALPS
MOUNT HUTT FOREST
Mount Hutt
Methven
Mount Potts
Ashburton
Mt Somers
Ashburton River
PEEL FOREST
Rangitata River
Arundel
Geraldine
Fox Peak
GERALDINE DOWNS
Franz Josef Glacier
MOUNT COOK NATIONAL PARK
Tekapo
Mt Dobson
Timaru
Mt Cook
Lake Tekapo
Fairlie
Mt Cook 3754m
WESTLAND NATIONAL PARK
Mount Cook
Lake Pukaki
Oamaru
Twizel
Waitaki River
OHAU FOREST
Lake Ohau
Lake Benmore
Lake Aviemore
Lake Waitaki
Oamaru (30 km)
Mt Brewster 2423m
Kurow
Duntroon
Ohau
Omarama
Otematata
Haast
0 30 km
Danseys Pass
Cromwell
Naseby

towards the small but lively foothill settlements of **Methven**, **Mount Hutt** and **Mount Somers**, which together make up one of the most exciting ski areas on the South Island. It's a popular destination for adventure seekers in summer too, with whitewater rafting, kayaking, paragliding, climbing and ballooning proving the main attractions. South of here, the attractive town of **Geraldine** provides access to the Geraldine Downs, for many the most England-like landscape on the South Island; while **Farlie** stands at the borders of the **McKenzie Country**, an area renowned for massive sheep runs and the beautiful blues of its glacier-fed lakes, **Tekapo** and **Pukaki** – both of which shimmer beneath the Southern Alps' most imperious peak, Mount Cook.

Mount Cook Village, huddling at the foot of the mountains, is the starting point of numerous walks, but because of a push toward the more lucrative luxury tourist market it is no longer the best base from which to explore the national park due to a limited range of accommodation. Routes south from Mount Cook towards Otago pass through **Twizel**, an odd settlement that after thirty years of existence is now developing a more pronounced identity, as a cheaper and more varied base from which to explore the Mount Cook region. Further south is the the rural backwater of **Omarama** – not so much a town, more a series of buildings around a busy crossroads commanding access to the scenic **Waitaki Valley** route east to Oamaru and the coast, the sweeping and spectacular SH8, heading to SH8A and **Wanaka**, or joining SH6 to **Queenstown** at **Cromwell**.

Upland areas of the South Island typically have a wide-ranging and very variable **climate**, with long hot summers, cold crisp winters, and over four metres of rainfall annually. Road **transport** around the area is plentiful, with most towns and settlements easily accessible by coach and shuttle bus, while the single rail track from coast to coast, via Arthur's Pass, provides a viable and entertaining alternative.

Hanmer Springs and Lewis Pass

Most northerly of the cross-mountain routes, the **Lewis Pass Road** (SH7) follows the course of a track that provided both Maori and early *pakeha* (European settlers) with a necessary link between the east and west coasts. For those travelling from the east coast the route starts at the town of Waipara, 80km north of Canterbury, where the SH7 leaves the coastal plain and begins its gradual climb between foothills of the Southern Alps. Lying just off this route in a side valley, the spa resort of **Hanmer Springs** acts as a base for summer walks and adventure activities, and as a convenient resting place for winter sports enthusiasts who enjoy the nearby **Hanmer Springs Ski Area**. It also offers the best range of accommodation hereabouts, a wooded mountain hinterland, and one of the top ten golf courses in the country. Some 60km further west, the **Lewis Pass** itself is set amidst some exhilarating subalpine terrain and deep forest; while **Maruia Springs**, just beyond the summit of the pass, is another elegant, though minute, resort in which to soak in soothing thermal waters. There is a variety of public **transport** into the region, with several daily buses making the trip from Christchurch direct to Hanmer Springs, and other services heading from Christchurch over the pass to Westport on the West Coast.

Hanmer Springs

About 140km north of Christchurch, a side road leaves SH7 to head north towards the quaint spa resort of **HANMER SPRINGS**, some 10km distant. Just after the turn-off from SH7, you'll cross the spectacular **Waiau Ferry Bridge**, designed by John Blackett. This was considered a major feat of engineering at the time of its opening in 1887, and the locals threw such a party that the site of the hospitality tent became known as Champagne Flat. The bridge now witnesses the tortured expressions of bungy jumpers as they hurl themselves from a specially constructed platform midway across the span. Hanmer Springs itself is pleasantly situated at the edge of a broad, fertile agricultural plain, with steep, forested hills above. Sadly apart from the highly developed thermal pools, the hotel- and motel-riddled, mall-infested resort has little to offer. However, it does give access to some entertaining river trips and the **Hanmer Forest Park**, where the walks are particularly attractive in autumn when the birch, poplar, sycamore and rowan trees are rich in golden hues.

Arrival and information

There are a number of buses to Hanmer – including the Hanmer Connection (☎03/315 7575 & 0800 377 378), who operate a daily service from Christchurch, either as a day-trip (2hr each way; $45 return) or a one-way shuttle ($25). Hanmer Connection also run a linking service with Kaikoura ($30) that connects with buses running up or down the east coast. East West Coachline Service (☎0800 142 622) drops off in Hanmer as part of their Christchurch–Westport service, Lazerline Coaches (☎ 03/315 7128) as part of

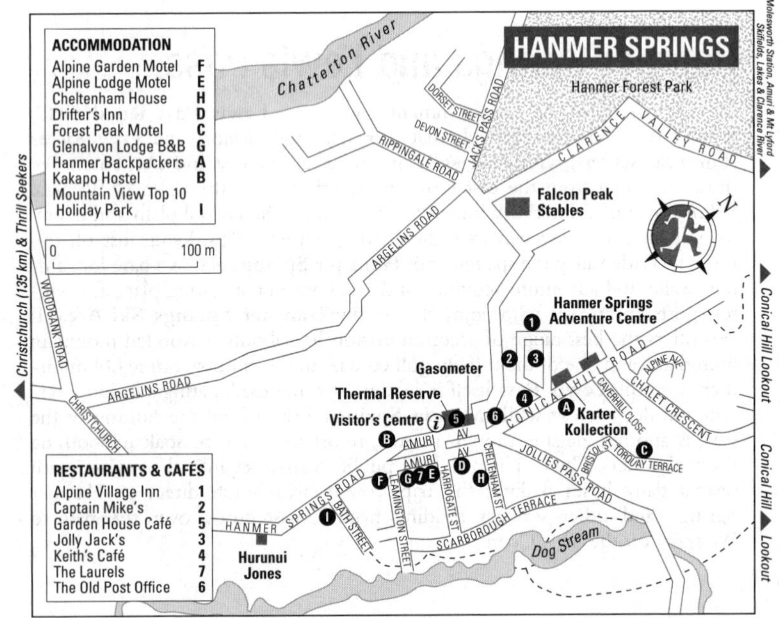

its Christchurch–Nelson service, and InterCity Coaches as part of its Christchurch–Kaikoura service – all deposit passengers near the visitor centre, and have a fare structure in a similar bracket to Hanmer Connection.

The **visitor centre** on Amuri Avenue, next to the Thermal Reserve baths (daily 10am–5pm; ⓣ03/315 7128, ⓦwww.hurunui.com), has helpful staff and handles all DOC enquiries; upstairs are illuminating displays on the Hurunui region's natural assets and journeys through the area by Maori, cattle drovers and the remarkable Park brothers who canoed across the main divide via Harper's Pass. Despite an excessive amount of accommodation development Hanmer has only two small **supermarkets**, but at least now it has an ATM (9am–9pm), and one bank (Mon & Fri 10am–2pm), so it's still a good idea to bring cash and supplies.

Accommodation

Hanmer's reputation amongst Kiwis as an elegant little resort has attracted a disproportionate amount of hotel and motel development meaning that accommodation tends to be on the expensive side, although there's a modest sprinkling of backpacker-style dorms and inexpensive cabins. The town is busiest at the height of summer and during school holidays, when it's wise to book ahead.

Alpine Garden Motel 3 Leamington St ⓣ03/315 7332, ⓔ alpinegarden@xtra.co.nz. Clean, comfortable, self-contained units, in a quiet setting three minutes' walk from the thermal pools. ❹–❺

Alpine Lodge Motel 1 Harrogate St, crnr of Amuri Ave ⓣ03/315 7311 & 0800 993 377, ⓔreservations@alpinelodgemotel.co.nz. Opposite the thermal pools these chalet units are comfortable and well equipped. ❹–❼

Cheltenham House 13 Cheltenham St ⓣ03/315 7545, ⓦ www.cheltenham.co.nz. Just two minutes from the visitor centre, this is the best B&B in town. There are four large, light rooms set in a lovingly and tastefully renovated 1930s house and two cottages in the well-tended, three-quarter-acre garden. ❻

Drifters Inn cnr Amuri Ave and Harrogate St ⓣ 03/315 7554, ⓦwww.driftersinn.co.nz. The best deal in this price range, this is a centrally located motel-cum-boutique-hotel, diagonally opposite the thermal pools. You'll get neat comfortable rooms and use of several communal areas. Prices include a continental breakfast. ❹–❻

Forest Peak Motel 4 Torquay Terrace ⓣ & ⓕ 03/315 7132. Ten minutes' walk from the visitor centre, this motel has ten clean comfortable units (some with open fires) and three attractive pine cabins. ❹–❻

Glenalvon Lodge B&B 29 Amuri Ave, diagonally opposite the visitor centre ⓣ03/315 7475, ⓔ glenalvon@xtra.co.nz. Luxury accommodation in two B&B rooms in the main house or eight well-kept, motel-like units out the back. ❹–❻

Hanmer Backpackers 41 Conical Hill Rd ⓣ03/315 7196. One of the few budget options close to the resort centre, offering mostly shared rooms, with two doubles. Not for the claustrophobic. Dorms ❶, rooms ❷

Kakapo Hostel 14 Amuri Av ⓣ03/315 7472, ⓔstay–kakapo@xtra.co.nz. This was just another tiny hostel at the time of visiting, but the massive new (YHA-affiliated) replacement under construction next door will, when finished, outclass every other hostel in town. Dorms ❶, rooms ❷–❸

Mountain View Top 10 Holiday Park cnr Amuri Ave & Bath St ⓣ03/315 7113, ⓔmtviews.hanmer@clear.net.nz. A range of tourist flats and cabin accommodation, in a large well-kept area. Tent sites $9, cabins & units ❷–❸

The Resort

The main street is Amuri Avenue, which forks into Conical Hill Road heading north and Jollies Pass Road heading northeast. Amuri Avenue is divided into two carriageways by a central, tree-shaded reservation that gives this small town a quiet, sheltered feel.

The **Thermal Springs**, on Amuri Avenue (daily 10am–9pm; $8, $15 private pools, $5 extra for hydraslide), were discovered in 1859 by William Jones while he searched for stray cattle. The springs are fed by rainwater that seeps down through fractures in the rocks of the Hanmer Mountains, accumulating in an underground reservoir some 2km beneath the Hanmer Plain. After absorbing some minerals and being warmed up by heat radiated from the earth's core, the water rises to the surface via fissures in the greywacke rock. Hanmer became famous in the 1870s for the relaxing and curative powers attributed to its waters, and since then the springs have undergone massive development, thereby losing their Victorian charm. The modern pool complex contains various sized, artificially landscaped thermal pools full of light-blue springwater, as well as a standard chlorinated 25m swimming pool. There's also a toddlers' pool, a series of play pools including a hydraslide, volcano lava pools, a gym, health and beauty centre and the licensed *Garden House Café* (ⓣ03/315 7115; daily 10am–9pm), which provides snacks, lunches and some tasty dinners, including excellent pizza.

Hanmer's other "attractions" aren't much to shout about. The small, privately owned **Karter Kollection Museum** (daily 8.30am–5.30pm, opening hours sometimes vary; $2), about two minutes' walk from the Thermal Springs on Conical Hill, contains a mish-mash of odds and ends that barely justifies the price of admission, unless the weather is awful and you are desperate. Last and most decidedly least, meanwhile, is **Hurunui Jones**, Amuri Avenue (about 1km from the visitor centre; daily: Nov–March 9.30am–6.30pm, April–Oct 10am–4.30pm; $5.50), a maze with obstacles that is supposed to pay homage to the adventurous archeological discovery scenes in *Indiana Jones* movies but merely looks like a cheap imitation; young children will probably enjoy it, though.

Hanmer Forest Park

By far the best and least expensive entertainment to be had around Hanmer is exploring the forest. Ranged around the resort to the north and east, the **Hanmer Forest Park** can be reached by walking along Jacks Pass Road, Conical Hill Road, Jollies Pass Road or by following McIntyre Road out to Mullens Road and the Mount Isobel Stream. The park was created in 1901 using convict labour to plant a wide variety of exotic trees, which are now protected from logging. An easy **Forest Walk** (2.5km; 1hr), accessible from Jollies Pass Road, leads through some of the oldest of the sycamore, oak and silver birch, while another comfortable and rewarding trail is the **Woodland Walk** (2km; 45min), accessible from Jollies Pass Road, featuring a stream, flax wetland and ponds teeming with birds. For the more adventurous there are moderately strenuous treks to **Conical Hill** (1.5km; 150m ascent; 1hr), accessible

The Hanmer Springs Ski area

Hanmer Springs is a good place from which to enjoy the **Hanmer Springs Ski Area** (ⓣ03/315 7233, ⓔhbc@clear.net.nz), a forty-minute drive from Hanmer up the Clarence Valley Road (free for skiers, but sightseers have to pay a $10 toll) on the slopes of Mount St Patrick and the St James Ranges. **Transport** from Hanmer can be arranged with Rainbow Adventures (on request; $19 return; ⓣ03/315 7233). All the field tows cost $34 per day, and conditions tend to favour snowboarding and intermediate skiers; **equipment** can be rented from Hanmer Springs Adventure Centre, 20 Conical Hill Rd, Hanmer (ⓣ03/315 7233). At the field there is also a centrally heated day lodge, with stoves, toasted sandwiches and tea and coffee.

The **Mount Lyford Skifield**, 60km to the northeast, is also accessible from Hanmer via SH1.

△ Arthur's Pass

from the Conical Hill Road (or as an extension to the Woodland Walk), which offers a panoramic view; and the **Waterfall Track** (2.5km; 400m ascent; 3hr), leading to the 41m-high Dog Stream Waterfall, connected to town by the **Upper Dog Stream Track** (3km; 2hr), accessible from Pawson Road off Jollies Pass Road. These walks are detailed in the excellent DOC leaflet, *Hanmer Forest Recreation* ($1), which highlights eighteen different trails in the forest, ranging in timescale from an hour to a full day. The leaflet also contains an information sheet on Molesworth Station (see below).

Hanmer Forest is also renowned for **mountain biking** and hosts trail-bike races twice a year over September and October, and April and May. **Bike rental** ($30 per day) and **guided trips** (4hr; $65) are available at Dust 'n' Dirt, 20 Conical Hill Rd (☎03/315 7233), and you can pick up a bike-track map from the visitor centre (10¢). One of the most popular routes follows an old Maori and then European packhorse route to Blenheim (191km), via **Molesworth Station**, one of New Zealand's largest farms: a DOC leaflet, *Molesworth* ($1), sets out information about the **scenic drive/bike ride**, and the cattle station's history. The section through the station is 56km (2hr by car, cycling times vary from 3hr 30min to 6hr), and, as this is still a working farm, is only open from December 28 to February 11. You must register at either the *Molesworth Cob Cottage* at the northern end of the trail or the *Archeron Guesthouse* at the southern end, both of which offer camping facilities. There is no camping elsewhere on the station. The quiet and atmospheric station road traverses rugged terrain prone to landslips, washouts and snow; note that caravans, campervans and buses are banned.

Activities

Thrillseekers, an adventure centre next to the spectacular Waiau Ferry Bridge (☎03/315 7046, Ⓦwww.thrillseekers.co.nz), enjoys a near-monopoly on local water-based activities. These include scenic **rafting** trips on the Waiau River (grade 2–3, $65); **jetboat** rides through the steep-sided gorges of the Waiau River (20min $49, 30min $69; 90min raft and jet combo, $115), and **bungy jumps** ($99 per jump), from the Waiau Ferry Bridge. **Horse riding** in the area is run by Falcon Peak Stables, Jacks Pass Road (☎03/315 7444; 1hr $35, half day $70, full day $150, Twilight Trail $70) which caters for people of all abilities and experience. More serious riders should contact Alpine Horse Safaris, based on Waitohi Downs near Hawarden, off SH7 about 60km south of Hanmer, which organizes some of the best **horse safaris** in the region (☎03/314 4293; 2hr–10days; $35–$1200). Longer trips include all food and accommodation, but must be booked at least a month in advance.

As an alternative to pedal power, check out **Backtrax 4xwheel Motorbike Safaris** (book via Dust'n'Dirt, above, or directly on ☎03/315 7684 or 0800/422 258, Ⓦwww.backtrax.co.nz), which offers a River Valley Ramble (2hr 30min; $98) and an Alpine spectacular (4hr; $169), involving tackling backcountry tracks up to some spectacular views, with a guide. Dust'n'Dirt (see above) also rents out **mopeds**, good for transport into the forest or up the road to Maruia Springs (1hr; $28), and **fishing** gear (2 days; $28).

Eating and drinking

Considering Hanmer is a highly regarded Kiwi holiday resort which has recently seen an epidemic of hotel and motel building, it offers few options in terms of value-for-money – or indeed characterful – **eating**. The friendliest place to dine is *Keith's Café*, on Amuri Avenue (daily 9am–8.30pm; licensed), a rustic-looking spot offering a wide range of mountainous, inexpensive snacks and meals including full cooked breakfasts and main meals for under $20. The best fine dining in town is at the *The Old Post Office*, Jacks Pass Road (☎03/315 7461; daily 6.30–11pm; licensed), a stylish, imaginative restaurant with $25-plus main courses and a surprisingly reasonable wine list. The only other fine dining establishment is *The Laurels Café and Bart*, 31 Amuri Av (☎03/315 7788; licensed), with excellent dinners and a long-as-your-arm dessert list. Otherwise the *Garden Café*, in the Thermal Springs (see p.679), is not bad, while for the very best in fish and chips try the award-winning *Captain Mike's Fish and Chip Shop*, Shop D, Hanmer Mall (Tues–Sun noon-9pm). Just opposite *Captain Mike's* in the mall, the relatively new *Jollie Jack's* dishes up pork, pasta, salads, steaks and fish at reasonable prices. Those in need of a **drink** should make for the bar of the *Alpine Village Inn*, a locals' haunt behind the mall and beside the public car park, where they also serve very basic bar food at economy rates and occasionally have some form of live entertainment.

West to Lewis Pass

West of the Hanmer Springs turn-off, SH7 continues on its climb towards the **Lewis Pass** 65km away. The high country around the pass was never actually settled by Maori, although it lay on a trail they tramped in search of *pounamu* (greenstone). Later, European pastoralists sought an easier route between east and west coasts, and in 1860, the surveyors Christopher Maling and Henry Lewis stumbled upon the pass. In 1866 a bridle track linking Hanmer Plain with Murchison was finished, and by 1936 a spectacular highway suitable for motor vehicles was finally opened.

The land between Hanmer and the squat hills of the **Boyle Bluffs**, which herald the **Doubtful River Valley** (a one-time gold diggers' route), is a rugged area of low-yielding grassland, with broom (a blazing yellow in the summer), spiky matagouri, manuka and kanuka taking hold where the farms have failed. As you approach the pass, red and silver beech forest begins to predominate. Shortly after the tiny cluster of houses that is the settlement of **BOYLE**, 50km out from Hanmer, you will come across **Sylvia Flat**, part of the Lewis Pass National Reserve, where it is possible to park and follow a track beside the Lewis River for about 50m to pools where warm water bubbles up through the rocks, mixing with the cold river water to create refreshing thermal pools. Be warned this area is difficult to find when the water levels of the river are high and the DOC, for some reason best known to themselves, have removed the signpost from the roadside. The 907-metre-high **Lewis Pass** itself is just 15km further on, and offers views along the high-sided Cannibal Gorge (see above) towards the Spenser Mountains.

Maruia Springs and Springs Junction

Eight kilometres beyond Lewis Pass, **MARUIA SPRINGS** is another thermal spa resort, grouped around a swanky bath complex with **hot pools** (daily 9am–9pm; $7 communal pool areas; $20 private baths) overlooking the Maruia River. The outside pools contain waters whose colours range from black to milky white, depending on the level of minerals they contain. The steaming waters are allegedly good for arthritis – but not so good for jewellery, which gets badly tarnished by the sulphurous fumes. **Accommodation** at the *Maruia Springs Resort* (☎03/523 8840, ⓔenquiries@maruia.co.nz; tent sites $20, units $95-140) ranges from camping to simple en-suite units; guests are entitled to free and unlimited use of the springs. Within the complex there's also the *Hot Rocks* **café/bar** and the Japanese-style *Shuzan Restaurant*.

Twenty kilometres west of Maruia Springs, there's a parting of the ways at **SPRINGS JUNCTION**, with the SH7 continuing west towards Reefton and the SH65 forging northwards to Murchison. Springs Junction itself has little to recommend it except an unmanned **DOC Information Centre** and walks; and essential services such as a petrol station and village shop.

Arthur's Pass and around

Another classic east–west route across the Southern Alps is the one linking Christchurch with Greymouth via **Arthur's Pass**. Traversed by both a highly scenic rail line and the equally breathtaking SH73, the route is easily accessible from Christchurch, making it a popular excursion for city-based travellers eager for a quick taste of the high country and winter sports enthusiasts who wish to take advantage of the many and varied ski fields.

The pass gets its name from civil engineer **Arthur Dobson**, who "discovered" it after hearing about it from local Maori who, for hundreds of years, used the route – from the West Coast to the Canterbury Plains – to trade, sometimes *pounamu*, or as a highway for raiding parties. Dobson surveyed the pass in 1864, and by 1866 horse-drawn coaches were using it to serve the Westland goldfields. The railway was built in 1923, coinciding with the booming interest in alpine tourism worldwide.

From Christchurch to Arthur's Pass

Whether travelling by road or rail, the trip from Christchurch to the pass is an adventure encompassing great geographical contrasts, beginning in the agriculturally rich Canterbury Plains and ending in an earthquake-shaken village 737m above sea level. The actual summit of the pass is at 912m, 4km to the west of Arthur's Pass village, marked by a large obelisk inscribed with the name Arthur Dudley Dobson, and is the start of many rewarding walks.

Initially both road and rail follow the course of the shingle-lined Waimakariri River, passing though a series of low-lying farm communities before begin-

St James Walkway

You can either start the **St James Walkway Subalpine Track** (66km; 5 days; 271m ascent; outlined in a DOC leaflet of the same name (50¢), the *Lewis Pass* leaflet (50¢), or the travel map of the area ($13.50); all available from Hanmer Springs and Reefton visitor centres), 4km along SH7 from the Hanmer Springs turn-off, just south of the confluence of the Boyle and Lewis rivers at the Boyle Shelter car park, or at the Lewis Pass picnic area and car park, about 16km further up SH7. The better way is north to south, Lewis Pass to the Boyle and Lewis rivers, beginning with the descent to the **Cannibal Gorge Bridge**, an excellent short walk for the less adventurous (2km, 80min).

There are a number of **bus services** between Lewis Pass and Boyle, so you can get back to your car from either end of the track. This is a subalpine region, so go well-equipped with **all-weather gear** and a plentiful supply of **food**. Accommodation is provided by five DOC **huts** (20 bunks; $10), all with wood stoves, firewood, intentions book and walkway map. A mixture of riverside walk, forest, farmland, descents, climbs and tussock, this is a strenuous tramp: the hardest day involves an ascent to the highest point, Anne Saddle (1136m), with spectacular views to the Rokeby and Boyle Flat huts to the south and the Anne Hut to the north.

The TranzAlpine Express

The **TranzAlpine Express** (4hr 10min; $81 one way, $109 day return) from Christchurch to Greymouth leaves Christchurch train station at 9am every morning and returns by 6.35pm. The train has large viewing windows and comfortable seats, with an open-sided observation car to aid photographers. Complimentary morning or afternoon tea is served, and snacks are available at only slightly inflated prices.

The scenic, 231km, coast-to-coast journey rises from an altitude of 3m above sea level at Christchurch to 737m at Arthur's Pass (the railway tunnels beneath the 920m summit of the pass), passing through nineteen tunnels and crossing numerous viaducts spanning picturesque braided rivers. This area is noted for its relatively high rainfall of 0.5m a year, and purple lupins festoon the railway embankments, interspersed with yellow broom and beech forest beyond the crest of the pass. If you travel in December you will also see red and white rata in bloom, but the trip is at its romantic, snow-cloaked best in the winter months (June–Aug).

The route traverses the Canterbury Plain as far as Springfield, after which you start to see the mountains, and reaches the halfway point around Craigieburn, where the piped commentary used to give way to a TranzAlpine Rail pop song of Lloyd-Webber-like horror. There's a pause at Arthur's Pass itself to add an extra locomotive, after which the train dives through the 8.5km-long Otira Tunnel. Descending to the west coast, you'll be treated to impressive views of Lake Brunner before trundling into Greymouth (see p.714), having covered in less than five hours a journey that took the horse-drawn coaches of Cobb and Company two days – and shortened the average life expectancy of the draught horses to a mere eighteen months.

ning the gradual climb away from the neatly organized fields of the plains. The route ascends gently to **Springfield**, 70km out of Christchurch, at which point the river and the rail line veer away to the northwest, while the road continues climbing steadily past the sources of several rivers and streams to the 923m **Porter's Pass**, at the northern end of Lake Lyndon. As the route winds through increasingly dramatic gorges it passes the **Korowai/Torlesse Tussocklands Park** (New Zealand's first tussock grassland conservation area), the Porter Heights Skifield (see p.691), lakes **Pearson**, **Grasmere** and **Sarah** to the north, which are directly opposite **Craigieburn Forest Park**, and the **Craigieburn**, **Mount Cheeseman**, **Broken River**, and Mount Olympus skifields (see p.691). About 6km beyond Lake Grasmere is the small settlement of **Cass**, where the tarmac and track routes rejoin and once again accompany the Waimakariri River along its winding progress through the Southern Alps. On reaching **Bealey**, at the northern foot of the mountain of the same name (1823m), the river once again bids farewell before heading south to its source on the mountain, while the road and railway line push on to Arthur's Pass, in the centre of the national park, with 2271m **Mount Rolleston** to its southern side, and both 1705m **Mount Pfeifer** and the **Temple Basin Skifield** (see p.691) to its northwest. Just after Arthur's Pass the railway dives through the long glum **Otira Gorge Tunnel** while the road climbs beyond the settlement and then descends through the recently constructed **Otira Viaduct**, a spectacular engineering marvel that greatly improves the road's safety. Just above the viaduct, on the Arthur's Pass side, is a lookout point where you can snap some spectacular photographs of the road and, in one spot, the roof which keeps the cascade of mountain water off its surface. After that both road and rail slip quickly down toward the pounding seas of the West Coast.

Springfield

Although it doesn't look much, **SPRINGFIELD**, 70km from Christchurch, is the first place worth stopping, especially if you fancy a high-speed boat trip down the **Waimakariri Gorge** to blow away the cobwebs. Waimak Alpine Jet, on Rubicon Road, off the Kowahi Bush Road (ⓣ03/318 4881; 30min $55, 1hr $85), operates fourteen-seater jetboats on demand all year round. The gorge is narrow, and the river water as clear as gin, with many waterfalls making for a safe, spectacular and beautiful ride.

In town on the northwest side of SH73 (Main Road) is the local domain where you can easily spend a relaxing twenty minutes exploring the pleasing **monument** to Springfield's best-loved son, Rewi Alley. Named after Rewi Maniapoto, the Maori leader who shouted at the battle of Orakau, *Kaore e manu te tongo. Ake! Ake!* ("We will never make peace. Never! Never!"), Alley displayed similar resilience throughout his fascinating life. After World War I he worked as a missionary in China, setting up small manufacturing co-operatives during the hazardous Japanese occupation. He went on to found schools, help with oil development, translate Chinese poetry, write poetry and prose of his own and act as an unofficial ambassador for China, despite his misgivings about the direction of the post-war communist regime and his increasing isolation within the country. The peaceful, Chinese-style garden memorial includes rock and water features, Rewi's abridged biography and a memorial to his remarkable mother, Clara, a leader in the New Zealand women's suffrage movement.

If you feel like breaking your journey, Springfield offers one of the friendliest and most comfortable affiliate YHA **hostels** on the South Island – *Smylie's* opposite the domain (ⓣ03/318 4740, ⓕ318 4780; dorms ❶, rooms ❸, motel units ❹). Busiest in the winter when it operates as a ski lodge, *Smylie's* has great facilities, a refreshing Japanese influence (Japanese baths, winter only) and cosy rooms. For sustenance or a refreshing **drink** try the *Old Springfield Pub* on Main Street, offering a selection of ales, reasonably priced rustic snacks and substantial main courses.

Korowai/Torlesse Tussocklands Park

About 10km after Springfield, continuing west along SH73 to Porter's Pass, the highway neatly bisects the **Korowai/Torless Tussocklands Park**, New Zealand's first tussock grasslands conservation park and covering 21,000 hectares. This is a key site for the protection of the unique and quickly disappearing eastern Southern Island high country landscape and ecosystems typified by great swathes of treeless grassland covering mountainous knolls and ridges, seen in relief against the snow-capped Torlesse and Big Ben mountain ranges. The region is filled with endangered shrubs, unusual plants and animals adapted to the unstable screes and rock ridges with flowers like vegetable sheep, Haast's scree buttercup, scree lobelia, mountain daisy, and animals such as the native grasshopper, weta, butterflies and kea. The park is named after the Maori word *korowai* meaning cloak – a symbol of togetherness and prestige – and surveyor Charles Torlesse, who was the first *pakeha* led to the summit of these mountains by Maori in 1849 to view the "romantic and chaotic mass of mountains to the westward".

Approaching Porter's Pass along the highway, the extraordinary **Torlesse Gap**, a narrow fissure of 20m width and 40m depth, between the Red and Castle Hill peaks, looms on the horizon, drawing the eye because of the otherwise rolling nature of the ridgeline. It's best seen from the Cave Stream Reserve – locally it is also known as Gunsight Gap, at a height of 1700m, though if viewed from Springfield the ridgeline can resemble the outline of a woman lying on her back with the the gap defining her neck. Although there are no marked tracks in the park there are several routes that are not too difficult to follow, like the climb from **Porter's Pass** (beside the road) to **Foggy Peak** (1733m). Various huts are dotted throughout the park but if you are going to explore it on foot check in with the DOC and make sure you have provisions and a good map.

Another way into the park is to turn left off SH73 after Porter's Pass and head towards Lake Lyndon, between Mount Lyndon and the Big Ben Range.

Kura Tawhiti (Castle Hill Reserve)

About 30km west of Springfield, SH73 passes through the well-signposted **Kura Tawhiti** (Castle Hill Reserve), where there are a number of walks among the rising tussock-covered hills and limestone outcrops. One of the most interesting is a twenty-minute stroll that starts from the old cattle station/main entrance (2km south of Castle Hill Village) and heads among large, grey, Stonehenge-like rocky outcrops protruding from mounds of grass and gorse. This rather surreal landscape also offers excellent rock-climbing and good photo opportunities. The lumpy tussock is brightened by mountain daisies and Castle Hill buttercups in the summer.

Cave Stream Scenic Reserve

A bare wild area in the same vein as Kura Tawhiti (see above), **Cave Stream Scenic Reserve** nestles among limestone outcrops with views of the Craigieburn and Torlesse ranges. Access is from SH73 6km west of Kura Tawhiti where a dirt, oval car park and a number of DOC information boards announce this rare opportunity to explore a limestone cave by blackwater hiking (362m; 1hr, mostly wading with a 3m ladder climb). Cave art, artefacts, signs of seasonal camps and the discovery of a wooden framed flax backpack, over 500 years old (now in the Canterbury Museum, see p.617), indicate that Maori once visited the area extensively. The cave itself contains bones, suggesting it was a burial site; it also provides a home for large harvestman spider-like insects and young eels who wriggle along the walls. This is an exciting, if wet, underground adventure (though the cave often hosts school outings so don't get too worried). If you venture ahead then dress warmly, take torches with spare batteries (there's no light in the cave) and make sure you have something dry to change into afterwards. The **walk/wade** itself involves entering at the downstream end where you'll cross a deep pool (waist high; if the water is higher, fast flowing, foaming and discoloured do not attempt the walk) before gradually climbing upstream. There are only two obstacles: a 1.5m rockfall about halfway and a 3m waterfall at the very end. The latter you'll negotiate by crawling along a short, narrow ledge and up a ladder of iron rungs embedded in the rock.

Craigieburn Forest Park

The **Craigieburn Forest Park** lies on the eastern ranges of the Southern Alps, about 15km beyond Kura Tawhiti, on the opposite side of SH73 from the Cave Stream Reserve and 42km before Arthur's Pass. It is chock-a-block with good walking tracks, longer tramps and climbing opportunities in the more rugged country further west. The park is dominated by dense, moss-covered mountain beech forest, alpine scrub and tussock grasslands, which are peppered with scarlet native mistletoe flowers from December to February. A variety of native birds streak and squawk through the forest, including bellbird, rifleman, silver eye and kea (alpine parrot), and between October and February, long-tailed and shining cuckoos join the throng. The nearby **Craigieburn skifield**, within the boundaries of the forest park, is one of the most exciting in the vicinity of Arthur's Pass – see box on p.691 for details.

In a signposted car park just off SH73 by Cave Stream is the **Craigieburn Picnic Area** and a walkers' **shelter** with fixed maps of the local tramps. The *Craigieburn Forest Park Day Walks* leaflet (from local visitor centres; $1) details eleven of the best short and day walks in the park. From the picnic area the path up to and around the **Lyndon Saddle** (4km; 3–4hr) is worthwhile, but if you do nothing else take the **Hut Creek Walk** (2km; 1hr) beginning outside the Environmental Education Centre of New Zealand (not open to the public) at the top of the winding, dirt road 3km further on from the picnic site and SH73, or accessible from the Broken River Skifield Road which jags away from SH73 1km south of the picnic area turn-off. The track itself winds down to the creek and continues through mountain beeches, emerging onto a slope of native hebe, dracophyllum (whose leaves shade from green to a reddish-brown in spring and autumn), cassinia and matagouri and allows great views from the lookout. The whole walk boasts an abundance of very watchable kea – but beware of the kleptomanic tendencies of these highly intelligent birds. To tack on a pleasant extra twenty minutes try the nature trail that also begins at the centre.

If you want to break your journey before the final assault on the pass, head for the *Flock Hill Lodge* (ⓣ03/318 8196, ⓦwww.flockhill.co.nz, dorms ❶, linen $5 extra, rooms ❺–❻), 110km from Christchurch, which has a range of units in beautiful grounds and a small café/restaurant. A further 28km on is the solitary *Historic Bealey Hotel* (ⓣ03/318 9277, ⓔbealeyhotel@xtra.co.nz; dorms ❶, motel units ❹), just 12km short of Arthur's Pass Village. Easily spotted because of a large concrete replica *moa* perched on top of the knoll out front, the hotel hunkers between gnarled escarpment faces by a flat broad riverbed. The reason for the *moa* is that a previous owner claimed to have seen one long after they were extinct, massively boosting trade and then decamping with the proceeds. Once a stop-off point for the Cobb Coaches that travelled to and from the west coast, the hotel now provides clean and simple backpacker and motel-style accommodation, beer and reasonable **food** in the *Klondyke* bar, and more filling fare in its bistro and restaurant.

Arthur's Pass Village

ARTHUR'S PASS VILLAGE nestles in one of many steep-sided, forest-covered U-shaped valleys and forms a thin low-rise straggle along the main road (SH73), with power and telecommunication pylons as a fringe. The area receives over five metres of rainfall a year, and the village invariably hunches beneath mist or clouds: there's often a moody contrast between the white clouds that hover halfway up the valley wall, and the rich green trees and vegetation of the valley floor and slopes. Another common sight in and around the village in the early evening are the kea, whose lolloping sideways gait, scavenging tendencies and inexhaustible curiosity give much entertainment. If you're enjoying a sandwich you'll hear the ruffle of swift passing feathers and see the flash of red beneath their wings as they join you, but although they are mischievous and adorable you must never feed them: many human foods basically poison them.

The Arthur's Pass settlement came about in the early 1900s to provide shelter for tunnel diggers and rail workers, and nowadays ekes a living from the tourists visiting the surrounding **national park**. It's a superb base for walking and climbing, with the nearby **Temple Basin skifield** (see box on p.691) providing good skiing and snowboarding opportunities in the winter.

Practicalities

Regular coast-to-coast **buses** (Coast to Coast ⓣ0800/800 847, Alpine Coach and Courier ⓣ025/342 460) stop in the centre of the settlement on the main street, while the TranzAlpine **train** (see p.685) pulls in close by. Being no more than a thin ribbon of buildings beside the highway the village is best explored on foot.

There is an excellent **DOC office** and **visitor centre**, on the main street, diagonally opposite the public shelter (daily: June–Oct 9am–4pm, Nov–May 8am–5pm; 24hr unmanned information area with search-and-rescue cards; ⓣ03/318 9211, ⓕ318 9210, ⓦwww.canterburypages.co.nz or www.softrock.co.nz), with numerous walks leaflets and background information on the whole of New Zealand. The visitor centre also has extensive displays on wildlife, plants, geology and local history, and a video about the trail blazed by the stage coaches and the railway is played on request ($1). The only public phones are just outside the YHA. There's a rarely open **post office** (in a shed), a **petrol station** and a couple of stores in the village, but no banks although the bottleshop/store does take EFTPOS.

Accommodation

There's a reasonable choice of good-value accommodation in the village, although places fill up quickly during the high season (early Dec to late Feb), when it's a good idea to book in advance. If there's no room at the inn, you could always try the *Historic Bealey Hotel*, 12km to the east, or the *Flock Hill Lodge*, 40km east, toward Christchurch (see opposite).

Alpine Motel on SH73 as you enter the village across Rough Creek, almost immediately on your left ⓣ03/318 9233. Basic motel units with private facilities, and simpler rooms at slightly cheaper rates. ❹

The Chalet west end of the village on the main road ⓣ & ⓕ03/318 9236, ⓔbohny@voyager.co.nz. A relatively large alpine chalet offering B&B in ten rooms with central heating and TVs. There's also an iffy restaurant and a bar where you can get a beer. ❻

DOC Campsite next to Arthur's Pass Public Shelter and backing on to the railway. Basic site with cold water and toilets. Tent sites $4.

Mountain House Backpackers & Cottages on the main road through the village, opposite the YHA and next door to the Outdoor Education Centre ⓣ03/318 9258, ⓦwww.trampers.co.nz.

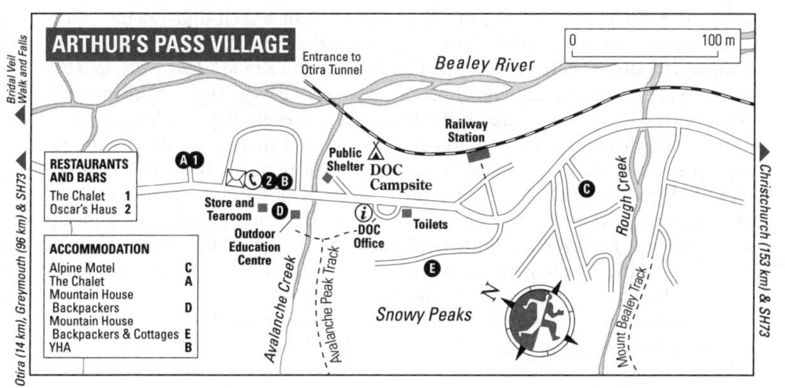

Clean bunkrooms, plus some doubles and twins, and a large common room and kitchen, run in tandem with the area's best accommodation – a row of spacious, self-contained, cottages with two to three bedrooms, high on the hill over the village. Tent sites $10, dorms ❶, rooms ❷, whole cottage ❻

Sir Arthur Dudley Dodson YHA on the main street, next to the phone box ☎03/318 9230. Occupying a prime spot in the village, the country's first purpose-built hostel boasts helpful and informed staff, a large firewood-warmed common room with a polished native timber floor, a bike shed and gear storage. As the best-value central accommodation, this tends to get full, so book ahead. Tent sites $10, dorms ❶, rooms ❷

Eating and drinking

The village is small so **eating and drinking** options are pretty much limited to *Oscar's Haus* (daily: June–Oct 10am–4pm, Nov–May 10am–10pm, kitchen closes 8.45pm, earlier if business is slow), a licensed café on the main street which serves freshly baked, differently flavoured muffins daily and some café-snack meals (including some veggie dishes), costing $12.50–20, as well as a selection of local arts and gifts. *The Chalet* (see "Accommodation" above), is only worth visiting for its **bar**. Otherwise, the village's one **shop**, the *Arthur's Pass Store and Tearooms* (daily 8am–7.30pm, although hours vary), sells basic supplies, acts as a bottle store/off-licence (with prices reflecting the captive nature of the market) and sells snacks and fish and chips. There is no ATM.

Arthur's Pass National Park

Despite the spectacular views you get from the pass itself, you really need to take one of the many day (or longer) walks to get a feel for this remarkable alpine landscape. The 720 square kilometres surrounding the pass were designated the **Arthur's Pass National Park** in 1929, and have exerted a powerful attraction over walkers and climbers ever since. The park encompasses much of the alpine flora unique to New Zealand, including the rich crimson of the southern rata trees and also highlights the contrast between the tussock grasslands and scrub of the eastern South Island and the broad-leaved evergreen podocarp forest of the wetter west.

Although easily accessible, the park can still be a hazardous place: take simple precautions and use your common sense. The weather is highly changeable and often wet, so be sure to bring warm and waterproof clothing, sturdy footwear, a supply of drinking water and (even on the shortest walks) some energy-giving food. If you're embarking on tramps of a day or longer, inform the DOC office in Arthur's Pass Village, or fill in the relevant search-and-rescue action card (available at the DOC/visitor centre in Arthur's Pass), before setting out.

Suggested **short walks** are detailed in the *Walks in Arthur's Pass National Park* leaflet ($1), stocked by the DOC office in Arthur's Pass Village, and there is an entire series of exhaustive national park guides covering day and longer walks (50¢ each); all these leaflets work best when used in conjunction with the appropriate topographical maps. Among the most popular short walks are the **Devil's Punch Bowl** (2km; 1hr return), an all-weather climb and descent to the base of a 131-metre waterfall, crossing two footbridges and zigzagging up steps, and the **Bridal Veil Nature Walk** (2.5km; 1hr 30min return), which ascends a gentle gradient through mountain beeches then crosses the Bridal Veil Creek before returning along the road.

Longer and more strenuous is the climb to **Avalanche Peak** (5km return; 6–7hr; 1000m ascent), which offers wonderful views of the surrounding

Skifields around Arthur's Pass

There are five skifields in the area around Arthur's Pass, each offering accommodation and equipment rental unless otherwise stated. Although there is not an enormous variety of runs they are unusual and challenging with some spectacular views, as well as reliable snow and relatively deserted slopes. To find out more about skiing here and in the rest of New Zealand visit ⓦwww.snow.co.nz which also has information on snow conditions. The fields are described from east to west, heading along SH73 from Christchurch. Many people choose to access the skifields from Christchurch, but if you want to cut down on travelling stay at *Smylie's* in Springfield (see p.686) or in Arthur's Pass.

Only 96km west of Christchurch is **Porter Heights**, just off SH73 via a 6km unsealed road (ⓣ03/379 7087, ⓔski@porterheights.co.nz), which boasts the longest single run in the southern hemisphere. Lift passes cost $47 per day and learners' lift $30 per day.

Just over 100km out of Christchurch along SH73 another 6km-long side road leads to the **Craigieburn Valley skifield** (ⓣ & ⓕ03/365 2514), a challenging area whose extreme slopes (a 609m vertical drop) make it the best-kept secret in the southern hemisphere. It's only really suitable for intermediate and advanced skiers and boarders. Lift passes about $38 per day.

The **Mount Cheeseman skifield**, 112km from Christchurch along SH73, is an exceedingly well appointed club field (ⓣ03/358 9249 or 379 5315, ⓔcheeseman@ch.cyberxpress.co.nz) with good facilities and a friendly atmosphere. There's a good variety of runs for intermediates, and a wilderness skiing option for those with experience. Lift passes are $42 per day.

The **Broken River skifield** (ⓣ03/318 7270) lies 120km out from Christchurch, at the end of a 6km access road through native beech from SH73. It's a very well equipped field, offering night skiing and good snowboard terrain. Lift passes are $35 a day. Accommodation huts ❷, instruction package $25 an hour. The ski area is only about 15min walk from the car park and there's a free goods lift.

Mount Olympus (ⓣ & ⓕ03/318 5840, ⓔmtolympus@xtra.co.nz), 128km from Christchurch, is in the Craigieburn range, set at the end of a road off SH73 only accessible by 4WD. This is a small field with deserted slopes suitable for all ability levels. Lift passes are $35 per day, learner's tow $10 but there's no equipment rental on site (arrange this in Christchurch or at one of the other nearby fields).

Temple Basin (ⓣ03/377 7788 or 318 9258, ⓔski@temple.org.nz), is 4km west (45min walk) from Arthur's Pass Village and 300m on from the Dobson Memorial. It's a superb spot for snowboarding with a 430m drop, floodlit for night-skiing and has a variety of runs for all abilities. Lift passes cost $34 a day plus free goods lift.

mountains, but should only be attempted in reasonable weather. The best way is going up the Avalanche Peak track and then making a circuit of it by returning on the **Scotts Track** (total walking time 6–7hr).

For $5 you can obtain a set of leaflets listing eleven **longer tracks** (ranging from 2 to 5 days) from the DOC office in Arthur's Pass Village, which should be used in conjunction with the *Arthur's Pass National Park Map*. One of the most demanding is the **Harman Pass to Kelly Saddle** (55km; 4–5 days), a rewarding trip mostly along unmarked tracks and involving the crossing of unbridged rivers. Prospective trampers need to be fit and well-equipped; all the huts along the way are backcountry ones ($5–10) but still quite comfortable, and the best views are to be had from the ridges near Kelly Saddle. One of the slightly easier tracks that doesn't skimp on great views is **Casey Saddle to Binser Saddle** (40km; 2 days), a pleasant tramp crossing easy saddles on well-defined tracks through open beech forest, staying overnight in Casey Hut (16 bunks; $10). For those well-equipped and interested, the **Mingha Deception** (25km; 2 days) is the route of the arduous Coast to Coast triathlon following marked and unmarked areas, and river crossings (there are no bridges so watch the water levels). If you're feeling particularly fit and travelling in the summer add on the 500m side trip to Lake Mavis, a high mountain tarn with some lovely views. You can use either the Goat Pass Hut (20 bunks; $10, with a radio link to Arthur's Pass Visitor Centre for emergencies) or the Upper Deception Hut (6 bunks; $5) and ponder how mad you'd have to be to run the route competitively.

For those feeling even more energetic, there is good **rock climbing** at Castle Hill (see p.687) and at the Temple and Speight buttresses on Mount Rolleston.

For something a little different from the walks listed above, Irie Tours, based in Castle Hills Village near Temple Basin Skifield (☎03/318 7669; precise directions on where to meet are given when you phone), offers so-called Alpine Canyoning trips for the relatively fit adventure-seeker. Each excursion involves a series of **abseils** and scrambles and some pretty good scenery ($140). The owner will also take you **rock climbing** for $125, on a nature walk for $65, or lend you a wetsuit and lead you through Cave Stream (see p.687) for $70.

The South Canterbury foothills

Easily accessible from the east coast and its main artery, SH1, the **South Canterbury foothills** are often ignored by travellers hurrying westwards from Christchurch to Mount Cook (see p.704). Marking the transition from the flat Canterbury Plains to the more rugged and spectacular Southern Alps, the area is primarily known for the skifields grouped around the winter resort town of **Methven**, which serves the slopes of **Mount Hutt** and provides a jumping-off point for more distant pistes at Erewhon, now renamed **Mount Potts**. Things are relatively quiet here in summer, but there's a wealth of natural attractions in the region, with the **Mount Hutt Forest**, the **Rakaia Gorge** and **walks** around **Mount Somers** rewarding travellers who make the effort to stop. Further south, inland from Timaru, the tiny communities of **Geraldine** and **Fairlie** link the east coast with the mountains and provide bases from which to enjoy either skifields or summer adventure activities. Fairlie is promoted as the "Gateway to the **McKenzie Country**", an area of farmland mixed with tussock and stands of forest, which gives hints of the high country to the west.

Main **routes** into the area from the east coast are the SH72 from near Sheffield on the Arthur's Pass Road, SH77 from Ashburton south of Christchurch, and SH8 from Timaru. **Buses** from Christchurch and Ashburton represent the main means of getting here by public transport, even though services may be limited to one or two per day.

Methven

Thirty-four kilometres northwest of Ashburton on SH77, **METHVEN** is the capital of a bustling winter sports area known as the "Snowfed Republic". Scotsman Robert Patton bought land in the area in 1869 and named Methven after his home town. The Scottish influence may also have had some bearing on the building of an outstanding 18-hole golf course, which keeps the thousand-strong population and many visitors entertained once the winter snows have receded.

Being close to Mount Hutt, Mount Potts (Erewhon) and Mount Somers,

Methven makes a good base for some skiing or tramping amid spectacular scenery. Activity operators also offer ballooning, horse riding and jetboating, but the **ski season** (May–Oct) is essentially what everyone lives for. In summer the town is much quieter, so much so that many of the restaurants and hotels close down for several months.

Arrival and information

Buses stop on Main Road (SH77), outside the visitor centre which includes the Methven Travel Centre and Adventure Shop (Ⓣ03/302 8106), where you can buy tickets, and arrange **car rental** (from around $60 per day) or local minibus tours. They also run a shuttle to Christchurch ($26 one way). The town itself is easily explored on foot, and a constantly changing array of companies offer minibus **transport to the skifields** (expect to pay around $22 return); the visitor centre has details of current operators.

The friendly and helpful staff at the **visitor centre**, on Main Road, opposite Bank Street and next to the BNZ Bank (daily: Nov–March 9am–5pm, May–Oct 7.30am–8pm; Ⓣ03/302 8955, Ⓦnz-holiday.co.nz/methven), will reserve and have lots of information about Methven, the skifields, and guided **walks** in the vicinity. The town also has a small shopping centre, off Main Road, including banks, a post shop and several **ski shops** (specializing in gear rental and repairs), the best of which is Big Al's.

Accommodation

During the winter there is a wide variety of accommodation in Methven; in summer much of it disappears, but then so do most of the visitors. The advantage of being here in the summer is the scope it gives you for haggling.

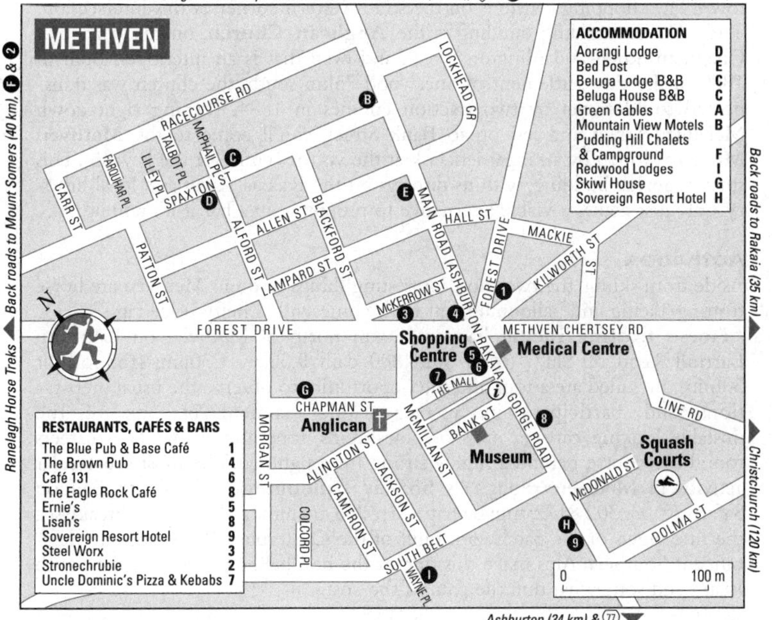

Aorangi Lodge 38 Spaxton St ⓣ03/302 8482, ⓔaorangi.lodge@xtra.co.nz. Excellent single-storey simple wooden building with twin, double, triple and quad rooms; some doubles are en suite, other rooms share facilities. Free and hearty continental breakfast, with a cooked breakfast $11 extra. ❸
Bed Post 177 Main Rd ⓣ & ⓕ03/302 8508. Offers 20 beds in twins, doubles and shared rooms, plus cooking facilities and motel units. Dorms ❶, rooms ❷, motel units ❸
Beluga Lodge and Beluga House B&Bs 40 Allen St ⓣ03/302 8290, ⓕ302 9290. Luxurious accommodation, much loved by skiers, in two well-kept houses which have retained their original charm and are surrounded by tranquil gardens. Bathrooms are separate but not shared, robes are provided, and home-made bread accompanies a breakfast of your choice. ❼
Green Gables 3km north of Methven on SH77 ⓣ03/302 8308. A peaceful rural B&B partly surrounded by a deer farm. Accommodation consists of one en-suite double, and a double and single with shared facilities. Breakfasts are generous, and dinner is available by arrangement ($30). ❺–❻
Pudding Hill Chalets and Campground SH72 ⓣ03/302 8416. Five kilometres northwest of town, this upmarket site offers spas and saunas, a drying room, restaurant and well-kept cabins. Very busy in winter, but prices are negotiable in summer. Tent sites $10, ski lodges ❶–❸, apartments ❸–❻
Redwood Lodges 5 Wayne Place ⓣ03/301 8964, ⓦwww.snowboardNZ.com. Comfortable, budget, communal accommodation for both winter and summer. Dorms ❶, rooms ❷
Skiwi House 30 Chapman St ⓣ03/302 8772. Cosy singles, doubles and bunk rooms, a TV lounge, kitchen and drying facilities in a white weatherboard house around a 5-min walk from the centre. Dorms ❶, rooms ❷
Sovereign Resort Hotel Rakaia Gorge Rd ⓣ03/302 8724, ⓕ302 8870. A modern hotel set in extensive grounds, with good views from its 46 rooms. Guest facilities include a spa, heated outdoor pool, 9-hole golf course, plush restaurant, ski drying room and nightclub with entertainment on Wed, Fri & Sat. ❻–❼

The Town

A small and uninspiring place, widely scattered across the plain, Methven has two main streets: the Ashburton–Rakaia Gorge Road (aka Main Street; or SH77), which heads north to Mount Hutt and south to Ashburton; and the Forest Drive/Chertsey Road (SH72), which bisects SH77 in the centre of town. The shopping centre is on the southwestern corner of this intersection. The only outstanding building is the **Anglican Church**, on the corner of Chapman Street and Alington Street, and even that is an interloper. Built in 1880 in the tiny settlement of Sherwood 75km south, the church was transported to Methven by two traction engines in 1884. Turning right down McMillan Street and left on to Bank Street, you'll come to the **Methven Museum** (open by arrangement, ask at the visitor centre for the key; $5). This small redbrick building, with its displays on the Rakaia River and local history, only just makes a viable alternative to propping up a bar if it's raining.

Activities

Aside from skiing, the two most interesting things to do in Methven are horse trotting/racing and ballooning, but both come with a hefty price tag.

Horse trotting/racing happens 20km north of Methven on Lauriston Barrhill Road, off SH77 (ⓣ03/302 4800; daily 9.30am–1.30pm; $155 for 2hr 30min). Included are a tour and the opportunity to observe the usual preparations and participate in a race, riding tandem in one of the unstable-looking carts (a mess of poles, reins, rope and string) as it careers round the course behind a highly strung thoroughbred. The most spectacular activity in Methven, though, is **hot-air ballooning** with Aoraki Balloon Safaris (ⓣ03/302 8172; sunrise trip 4hr; $255, including champagne breakfast): the fine views of the patchwork quilt of the Canterbury Plains and the magnificent Southern Alps make this one of the best balloon flights on the South Island and somewhat dull the pain of the cost.

If you're an energetic (and very wealthy) skier or snowboarder, Methven Heli-ski (ⓣ03/302 8108; $700 per person, 3–5 passengers) offers a rather drastic way of finding unsullied snow – by **helicopter**. The company usually operate five runs, with professional guides; and in summer, they switch to helicopter drop-offs for trampers and mountain bikers. Wetter, noisier but cheaper is a **jetboat ride** with Rakaia Gorge Scenic Jets (ⓣ03/318 6515, ⓕ318 6512), whose tours range from twenty to fifty minutes, with a standard trip weighing in at about $65 per person. Slightly more edifying is to let them take you to the end of the **Rakaia Gorge** ($20 per person, min of 2) and then walk back. The gorge offers a delightful and easy walk – take a picnic and it's a great way to spend an afternoon.

Eating and drinking

There are some snug little cafés and coffee houses serving thick, steaming soups to winter sportsmen or low-fat Italian salads and panini to the summer crowds, along with a smattering of pleasant if not overly lively bars. Some establishments open only in the winter but prices lean to the higher side no matter what the season. All of the places listed below are open year round.

The Blue Pub & Base Café *Methven Hotel*, cnr Kilworth St & Barkers Rd. The 1918 hotel has long been more of a drinkers' den than somewhere for a civilized meal, though the new café goes some way to compensate, with its deli sandwiches, soups and cakes. Both places are crowded in winter, when entertainment is often laid on, although in summer things are fairly quiet.

The Brown Pub opposite *The Blue Pub* in the old *Canterbury Hotel*. Passable and very cheap bar meals in this locals' drinking hole, which also boasts a bottle shop and basic accommodation.

Café 131 131 Main Rd. Lags behind the *Base Café* in popularity because it is slightly more expensive, but serves some tasty light meals including delicious gourmet smoked-chicken salads and veggie samosas, plus full breakfasts for under $15. The coffee and brandy cake with cream is dreamy. Daily: winter 7.30am–5pm, summer 9am–4pm; licensed.

Ernie's next to *Uncle Dominic's* (see below). An unusual licensed pizza, kebab and Mexican restaurant, with a takeaway service, that makes up for its lack in authenticity with enormous enthusiasm and sensible prices. Open daily for dinner only.

Lisah's Main Rd, above the *Eagle Rock Café*. Arguably the best value dinners in town. Daily from 5pm; licensed.

Sovereign Resort in the *Sovereign Resort Hotel*, Rakaia Gorge Rd ⓣ03/302 8724. Plush hotel restaurant with correspondingly high prices.

Steel Worx 36 Forest Drive. Seasonal restaurant and bar that's the nearest thing the town has got to a lively modern take on nightlife. DJs in the back and a (summer) beer garden with a stage area for live music, as well as pleasant gourmet food that won't break the bank.

Uncle Dominics's Pizza and Kebabs 253 Forest Drive, inside the main shopping centre. Surprisingly good pizzas and kebabs, at reasonable prices, to eat in or take away. Summer lunches and evenings, weekends only, winter daily; BYO.

Around Methven

Many winter sports enthusiasts choose to stay in Methven because of its easy access to the surrounding skifields. **Mount Hutt**, 26km to the northeast on SH72, is the nearest and most convenient, although **Mount Potts (Erewhon)**, 75km to the west and serviced by the nearby settlement of **Mount Somers,** is also within striking range. The tiny settlements at both Mount Hutt and Mount Somers are little more than feeding stations for the skiers in the winter, and have a ghost-town feel for the rest of the year, although they border on regions of outstanding natural beauty. Around Mount Hutt to the north and west, the **Mount Hutt Forest** provides an opportunity to explore the native flora. Fourteen kilometres southeast of

Methven is the **Rakaia Gorge** (see opposite), offering riverside walks and the chance to fish for salmon or trout.

Finally, those seeking an adrenaline rush might like the **Mount Hutt Bungy**, at the Mount Hutt car park, near the triple lift. Here you can throw yourself out into thin air off Kea Rock, attached to a piece of elastic, for around $150.

Mount Hutt Forest

Fourteen kilometres northwest of Methven and accessible via SH77 is the **Mount Hutt Forest**, which covers 444 square kilometres of tall trees on the eastern flanks of the Southern Alps, adjoining the **Awa Awa Rata Reserve** and **Pudding Hill Scenic Reserve**. Mountain beech is the dominant native species of tree, while snow tussock above the scrub line provides a home for a variety of native and introduced birds.

Free leaflets are available about the forest and reserves from local visitor centres, describing the flora and fauna as well as the many **walking tracks** you can explore – most of which can be accessed from the McLennans Bush Road entrance to all three reserves (reached by heading north from Methven on SH77 and turning left onto McLennans Bush Road after about 15km). It is worth taking a little extra time to examine the Mount Hutt flora during the spring and summer: of the **alpine plants** of New Zealand, 94 percent grow only in New Zealand, of which 130 species can only be found on Mount Hutt. One such is the unique vegetable *Sheep Raoulia eximia*, which forms huge grey mounds that look not unlike sheep lying down, from a distance. There's also the *Ranunculus haastii*, a beautiful species of buttercup with blue-grey leaves and luminous yellow flowers, and ten species of mountain daisies, *Celmisias*, which form huge cushions of flowers.

Rakaia Gorge

Along the northern stretches of the Rakaia River, 14km from Methven, is the **Rakaia Gorge**, a steep-sided defile created by an ancient lava flow and now lined in many places with regenerating forest. The **Maori** account of the gorge's formation tells how a *taniwha* (water spirit) lived nearby, hunting and eating *moa* and *weka*; his possessions, because of his status as a spirit, were *tapu*. One cold day he went to find a hot spring, and while he was away the northwest wind demon flattened his property. To prevent this happening again, the *taniwha* collected large boulders and stones from the mountains to

Mount Hutt Skifield

Twenty-six kilometres northeast of Methven, just off SH72, **Mount Hutt** is widely regarded as the best and most developed skifield in the southern hemisphere, with a vertical rise of 655m and a longest run of 2km. It also enjoys the longest season and offers a broad range of skiing and snowboarding conditions. A daily lift pass costs $68. Beginners can take advantage of a one-day starter pack, a five-day package, or the many learn-to-snowboard packages (around $40 per hour in a group session, including board rental). Leopard Coachlines run **buses** to and from Methven and Christchurch every day, dropping off in the morning and picking up in the afternoon (ⓣ03/332 5000, $26 from Methven), and a variety of shuttle buses run between the skifield and Methven or Mount Hutt village. There's a Mount Hutt skifield information line (ⓣ03/302 8811), or you can find out more at ⓦwww/nzski.com, or email ⓔadmin@mthutt.co.nz.

block the course of the demon, and in so doing narrowed the Rakaia River so that it flowed between the rocky walls. The spirit became so warm because of his exertions that the heat from his body melted the snow and ice on the mountains, and his perspiration fell on the rocks and formed crystals in the riverbed.

Just off SH72, an information shelter has maps of the area and a list of activities, next to the head of the **Rakaia Gorge Walkway** (15km; 3–4hr return). The path leads through several forest stands and spectacular geological areas, past hardened lava flows of rhyolite, pitchstone and andesite, to the upper gorge lookout. The Rakaia River is worth a look simply because it is a typical example of a braided river, a form found all down the east of the South Island.

Mount Somers and around

On SH72, 35km from Mount Hutt, at the junction of the road to Mount Potts (Erewhon) Skifield (see box below) is the small settlement of **MOUNT SOMERS**. The town itself has little to offer, although those keen on geology and local history might want to look in on the **Foothills Museum**, housed in a shabby weatherboard shed in the Mount Somers Domain (open by arrangement, ⓣ03/303 9860; donation requested). The truly obsessed, meanwhile, can check out the **Staveley Geological and Historical Centre** in the Springburn School Building (itself dating back 125 years), where there are displays on the unique geology of the mountain; it's located in the tiny Staveley Village 42km from Ashburton and between the town and Mount Somers.

However the **Mount Somers Recreation and Conservation Area**, roughly 10km north of town on Flynn's Road, has some fine tramps (see the *Mount Somers Recreation and Conservation Area* leaflet in local visitor centres and DOC offices; $1); and along the road towards Mount Potts (Erewhon) a proliferation of lakes provide superb scenery, trout-fishing and, on **Lake Clearwater**, excellent windsurfing (details from the Methven visitor centre). If you don't fancy exploring the area independently, you could join Tussock and Beech Encounters (ⓣ03/303 0880, ⓦwww.nature.net.nz) for one- to three-day eco-tours ($140–420 including transport, DOC fees, accommodation and food, though finding your own way to Staveley will save you $40), which are informative, entertaining and convivial. They also operate tours to other areas in the South Canterbury Foothills and are experts on the climbs around Mt Somers.

Mount Potts (Erewhon) Skifield

The **Mount Potts** previously known as Erewhon and **Skifield** (ⓣ03/309 0960, ⓦwww.mtpotts.co.nz), 40km west of Mount Somers, has the highest elevation on the South Island and remains a small-scale affair. Its change of name represents an attempt to market it as an exclusive, international-play-person field following lodge renovations and the introduction of a **snowcat** and **heli-ski** operation. The cat holds a maximum of 11 people and only 22 will be allowed on the field at any time; the helicopter element is not restricted to the field and can drop off in 60,000 acres of virgin snow. A massive price hike has accompanied the new regime: cat passes cost $290 a day, a five-run helicopter day will set you back around $2230. Alternatively a week-long "powder pig" deal on the cat costs the same, including accommodation.

Walks around Mount Somers

The landscape around Mount Somers differs from its surroundings as it's formed from volcanic rhyolite rock, which is harder than greywacke and shows fault lines, exposing columns and fractures of darker andesitic material. As a result the terrain is generally more rugged, with outcrops of rock poking out from patches of regenerating beech forest and large areas of low-fertility soil subject to heavy rainfall turning to bog. Due to these conditions you'll find bog pine, snow totara, toatoa and mountain flax as well as (though less often) the rare Whio (blue duck). The *Mount Somers Conservation Area* leaflet ($1, from visitor centres) describes in detail the geology and the history of the region, and also gives information on the 17km **Mount Somers Subalpine Walkway**, which passes abandoned coal mines, volcanic formations and a deep river canyon. The walk can be done in ten hours, although it's often treated as a leisurely two-day affair, with the *Mount Somers Hut* (see below) providing overnight accommodation. To get to the start of the track head along the Ashburton Gorge Road for 11km to Erewhon where a signpost directs you 3km along an old tramway route to **Coalminers Flat Carpark**. From the picnic area, follow the nature walk to the signposted junction and follow the poles from there to the plateau lip, from which you can make your own way to the beacon on the gently rolling top. This can be accomplished more quickly by beginning at **Sharplins Falls Carpark**, off SH72 via Staveley, and heading up via Hookey Knob. Once at the summit (1687m) you can then either head back the way you've come or make for either the *Mount Somers Hut* or the *Pinnacles Hut* (back country; $5). If you decide to stay on the mountain try to take in the north face and climb to Slaughter House Gully (named in the days when red deer roamed the area and were hunted in large numbers), near the *Pinnacles Hut* and One Tree Ridge. Remember that the rolling country on top of the hills is subject to fog and can be very disorienting so never climb these mountains without a topographical map, a compass and a clear idea of your route.

There are also a number of excellent **shorter walks**, taking from ten minutes to half a day, from either car park, all of which are well worth the effort.

Practicalities

InterCity **buses** drop off in the centre of the tiny Mount Somers community, where the best **accommodation** in the area is provided by the pleasant tree-filled campsite of *Mount Somers Holiday Park*, Hoods Road, 1km off SH72 (ⓣ03/303 9719; tent sites $18, cabins ❷).

The finest **food** in the region and in the top ten on the South Island is to be had at *Stronechrubie*, just south of Mount Somers on SH72 (bookings essential ⓣ03/303 9814; summer Wed–Sun 6.30–11pm, winter daily; licensed), where the Swiss chef uses fresh local ingredients and only the best meat to produce mouthwatering dishes. Try the rack of lamb (under $30), or filleted grouper on a bed of marinated mushrooms (under $25), and for dessert don't miss the McRae's whisky cake and whisky sabayon. If you can't tear yourself away after dinner (or can't move), *Stronechrubie* also has five standard **rooms** and three family rooms, all with kitchens, wicker furniture and views of the mountain (same phone number; ❹).

Geraldine and around

The quiet, pretty town of **GERALDINE** lies 45km south of Mount Somers via SH72, and 15km west of the main coastal highway (SH1) along SH79. Set on the Geraldine Downs – gently rolling hills standing out in sharp relief against the craggy, snow-capped Southern Alps – the town is at the centre of a prosperous farming community. Geraldine has a surprising number of **craft shops** – some even interesting – and **galleries**; when you've exhausted the town's limited attractions, the walkways and brilliant rafting trips of **Peel Forest** beckon and are within easy reach. Also of note is the Kakahu Bush Reserve, where well-marked walks will reveal an area of alluring natural beauty and some unusual rock formations.

Arrival and information

Buses drop off at *Oakes Restaurant* on the junction of Talbot Street with SH79, while InterCity services drop off at Orari, 15km away on SH1, where they're met by a shuttle bus into town (Geraldine Community Mini Buses; ⓣ03/693 1007; $4.50). Geraldine's **visitor centre**, 32 Talbot St (Oct–April Mon–Fri 8.30am–5pm, Sat & Sun 10am–4pm; May–Sept daily 10am–2pm; ⓣ03/693 1006, ⓔinformation@geraldine.co.nz), is run by helpful staff who provide a full booking service, all the DOC leaflets for the area and have a broad range of local knowledge. They can also guide you to the nearest place to get any DOC passes.

Accommodation

There's a small concentration of accommodation in Geraldine, none of it too expensive, and it's rarely a problem getting a bed for the night.

The Crossing Woodbury Rd ⓣ03/693 9689, ⓕ693 9789. This beautiful old English-style manor with a shady veranda houses a fully licensed restaurant and four en-suite guest rooms, each individually and lavishly decorated. Continental breakfast included. ❼

Crown Hotel 31 Talbot St ⓣ03/693 8458, ⓕ693 9565. Upmarket pub with eight clean and airy rooms, all with en-suite bathrooms. ❹

Forest View Homestay 128 Talbot St ⓣ 03/693 9928, ⓔforest.view@xtra.co.nz. A 10-min walk from the town centre, this cosy homestay offers two doubles and shared facilities, with two-course dinners by arrangement ($20). ❹

Geraldine Backpackers The Old Presbytery, 13 Jolie St ⓣ03/693 9644. Revamped, clean and well-kept dorm accommodation in a historic building opposite the Talbot Forest Reserve, with helpful hosts and a warm and friendly atmosphere. ❶

Geraldine Motel 97 Talbot St ⓣ03/693 8501. Six pleasant fully equipped units close to the town centre. Complimentary newspaper in the morning. ❹

Geraldine Motor Camp Hislop St ⓣ03/693 8147. Surrounded by sheltering trees, this spacious site is inside Geraldine Domain. Tent sites $9 per person, cabins and units ❷–❸

The Town

In town, the tiny **Geraldine Historical Museum**, on Cox Street (Mon–Sat 9.30am–midday & 1.30–3.30pm, Sun 2–4pm; donation), has little of outstanding interest but is housed in a rather quaint blue-and-white stone building with an attractive garden. More extensive is the **Geraldine Vintage Car and Machinery Club**, 174 Talbot St (Nov–Feb daily 10am–4pm; March–Oct Sat & Sun only 10am–4pm; $5), which houses a surprising collection of old cars, tractors and planes, mostly well-kept but with a few not quite so well-loved.

To check out Geraldine's wealth of **artists, galleries and craft shops**, pick up the *Geraldine District Arts and Crafts Guide* or the *Geraldine* leaflet from the visitor centre. Stained Glass Windows, 177 Talbot St (Mon–Thurs 9.30am–4.30pm), where you can browse among the colourful lampshades and stained-glass work, is well worth visiting. Equally good to explore is The Giant Jersey, 10 Wilson St (Mon–Fri 9am–5pm, Sat & Sun 10am–5pm), where amongst the usual display of jumpers you'll find the *Guinness Book of Records'*

World's Largest Jersey (weighing 5.5kilos). There's also an array of heraldic mosaics and scenes of the Bayeux Tapestry (34m in length), made from tiny pieces of spring steel broken from knitting machines. The tapestries, creations of immense fiddliness, can never be repeated as the supply of machines, from which the pieces came, is exhausted. Once you've finished staring yourself bug-eyed at the tapestries you can then drive yourself batty by trying out a few of the owner's homegrown, cypher-like alphametics and magic number cubes, after which you'll probably need some fresh air.

Just 1km from the town centre, at the end of Hislop Street, **Talbot Forest Scenic Reserve** is the last remnant of a once extensive native forest, with the largest radiata pine in the world and plenty of other mature native trees including matai, kahikatea and totara. It's a peaceful place to spend an hour or two with a picnic.

Eating and drinking

Given Geraldine's small size, you wouldn't expect to find a wide range of culinary choice in town, but there's something to satisfy most appetites all along Talbot St.

Berry Barn Bakery and Café 66 Talbot St. The usual coach party stop-off where savouries, pies, chips and cakes are all served in cheap and cheerful surroundings. Next to *Barker's Winery*. Daily 6am–5pm.

The Easy Way 76F Talbot St, near the *Berry Barn*. Large stylish café/bar with imaginative food at half-decent prices and some hot, steaming curries. Daily 10am–late; licensed.

The Oaks 72 Talbot St, cnr Cox St. Bacon, eggs and chips for $11, great hash browns and the usual café fare. Daily 9am–6pm.

Papillon Chinese Restaurant, Tea Rooms and Takeaway 40 Talbot St. A peculiar mix of East-meets-New-Zealand café: Chinese food, fish, burgers and chips. Closed Mon & Tues; licensed & BYO.

Plum's Café 44 Talbot St ☎03/693 9770. Good-quality food, home baking and a wood-burning stove. Delicious lunches daily, dinners Fri & Sat; licensed & BYO.

Riverside Café 45C Talbot St, set back from the main road near the police station. Nice enough little spot, with verandas overlooking the river, offering excellent quiches, strong coffee and passable snacks. Daily 9am–5pm.

Talbot Forest Cheese 76G Talbot St, near *The Easy Way*. A pleasant deli selling highly individual cheeses which go well with some pickle from the *Berry Barn*. Daily 9am–5.30pm.

Totara Bar and Restaurant *Crown Hotel*, 31 Talbot St ☎03/693 8458. A large restaurant serving reasonably priced Kiwi nosh. The bar is one of two reasonable places in town for a drink.

The Village Inn 41 Talbot St. A broad selection of reasonably priced and fairly imaginative food for lunch or dinner in a comfortable bar setting, or on the outdoor terrace. Geraldine's other good place for a drink.

Around Geraldine

One of the more beautiful places in the area is **Peel Forest Park**, enclosing a vast expanse of forest, scrub and alpine vegetation 19km northwest of Geraldine. To get there, head north on the SH72 as far as Arundel, before turning west onto the Cooper's Creek/Peel Forest Road. You'll pass through the hamlet of **PEEL FOREST** about 1.5km short of the reserve entrance, a useful spot for stocking up on supplies and picking up information from the **Peel Forest Store, Post Office and Petrol Station** (☎03/696 3567; Mon–Thurs 8am–7pm, Fri & Sat 8am–7.30pm, Sun 9am–7pm), which serves as a visitor centre, campsite booking office, bottle store, takeaway and tea rooms. It also displays various DOC leaflets on the area, although the commercial operation tends to take precedence.

A free leaflet (available at the DOC office) describes the **Peel Forest Tracks**, twelve walking tracks ranging from 45 minutes to six hours. Of these, the best are the **Acland Falls Walking Track** (1.5km; 45min one way), a steep climb followed by a short streamside walk to a fourteen-metre-high waterfall, and **Allan's Track** (4km; 2–3hr round-trip), a steady ascent past the head of Mils Stream and through podocarp forest which can be extended by joining the **Deer Spur Track** (5km; 2hr return), a steep but well-defined route which climbs above the bushline to a sparkling mountain tarn at an altitude of about 900m. Take time while you walk to admire the huge, ancient totara trees, rata and ferns, and to watch the antics of the fantails and tomtits – these little birds often hover around, feeding on the insects disturbed by trampers and picnickers.

The park is also the home of one of the best **whitewater-rafting** operators in New Zealand, Rangitata Rafts (Ⓣ0800/251 251, Ⓦwww.rafts.co.nz) at Peel Forest River Base, about 14km north of Peel Forest Store. The raft company offers **camping** ($10 per site), very basic bunk **accommodation** in its lodge (dorm ❶, double or twin ❷, breakfast $5), and, of course, fantastic rafting **trips on the Rangitata River** (May–Sept daily at 11.30am; 3hr; $130 including lunch & dinner, but not pick-up, by arrangement, from Geraldine or Christchurch). The whole operation is very professional and bucketloads of fun: a maximum of six rafts take to the river at once, with a full briefing beforehand and one guide for every nine passengers. The first part of the rafting is Grade I, which gives you a chance to get used to the self-baling boats before the thrilling trip through the high-sided Rangitata Gorge, where you traverse Grade I–V rapids; there's also an optional ten-metre cliff jump near the end. Afterwards, your ordeal by water is rounded off with welcome hot showers and a barbecue dinner.

There is also an Outdoor Pursuits Centre based 100m north of the Peel Forest Store (Ⓣ03/696 3800), which offers a sit-on (as opposed to sit-in) **kayaking trip** (half-day; $95), along the Rangitata or Orari rivers, paddling up to Grade II, all equipment provided.

A worthwhile trip out of Geraldine is to travel 15km west on SH79 to Hall Road and then follow it for 2km until you hit the **Kakahu Bush Reserve**, which offers a series of excellent walks (10min–2hr), taking in a marble gorge, mushroom rocks, an impressive limestone escarpment, a 30-metre pinnacle with a balancing boulder, a balancing rock (a tall finger on top of a hidden pinnacle), and some wonderful views from the Pinnacles Lookout.

Finally, at the Bélanger-Taylor Glass Blowing Studio (Ⓣ03/693 9041) you can see the delicate and intricate **glass working** in progress (ring first), and a home-made kiln. The beautiful bright plates, mosaics and jewellery produced by this French-Canadian artist are extremely expensive however. Take SH79 toward Fairlie and after about 5km turn onto Te Moana Road; follow this until it becomes a dirt road and then watch out for the signs to the studio on your right.

Fairlie and around

Heading west from Geraldine towards the wilds of the McKenzie Country and the mountains around Mount Cook, you first pass through the small town of **FAIRLIE**. Defined by its position at the junction of the two main routes that strike inland from the east coast to Lake Tekapo – SH79 from Rangitata via Geraldine and SH8 from Timaru – Fairlie is a quintessential crossroads town, with a resident population of only six hundred. Originally called Fairlie Creek, the name was shortened after the telegraph office opened in 1892, the creek having long since dried up. The rail link with Timaru closed in 1960, and the town has pretty much remained in stasis ever since. Your best bet is to look around quickly, and then move on.

Within reach of Fairlie are the **skifields** of Mount Dobson and Fox Peak (see box, p.691).

Arrival, information and accommodation

Daily InterCity **buses** stop near the centre of town on Main Street, from where everything's easily reached on foot. One ad hoc **visitor centre** is housed in The Sunflower Centre, just down the street at no. 31 (daily 8.30am–6pm; ⓣ03/685 8258), where there's a fair stock of leaflets but they're more interested in selling veggie burgers ($5) than helping tourists so you're better off going to the Resource Centre, corner of Riddle and Talbot streets (Mon–Fri 10am–4pm). **Accommodation** options in Fairlie aren't particularly exciting or varied, but the town is rarely busy, so you shouldn't have too much trouble finding a bed.

Aorangi Motel 26 Denmark St ⓣ & ⓕ03/685 8340, ⓦwww.aorangi.co.nz. This is the most central motel, with seven spacious self-contained units, plus a spa. ❸–❹

Fairlie Lodge 16 School Rd ⓣ & fax 03/685 8452. Well-cared-for motel offering a very friendly welcome, clean, small units with their own facilities, microwaves, TVs and toasters. ❸

Fontmell Farmstay 3km southwest of Fairlie on Nixons Rd ⓣ03/685 8379. Comfortable B&B accommodation in an English-style homestead, surrounded by pastureland and woods. There are two doubles and one single room with shared bathrooms. ❹

Pinewood Motel 27 Mount Cook Rd ⓣ03/685 8599, ⓔpinewoodmotels@xtra.co.nz. Modern motel with airy, self-contained units close to the town centre. ❹

Mount Dobson Motel 6km west of Fairlie on SH8 ⓣ03/685 8819 & 0800/362 766. A quiet motel with large units next door to the *Silverstream Hotel* (which serves meals) and bottle shop, and 5km from the Toll Gate to Mount Dobson and Fox Peak skifields. Ski bus pick-ups arranged. ❸–❹

The Town

The centre of the town is marked by the junction of Allandale Road (SH79) and Main Street (SH8), which becomes Mount Cook Road as it heads west out of town. The most interesting sight is the **Mabel Binney Cottage and Vintage Machinery Museum** (daily 8am–5pm; $2 turnstile), on Mount

James McKenzie

A Kiwi folk hero, **James McKenzie** lends his name to the crescent of flat land between Fairlie and Kurow (to the south on SH83) known as **McKenzie Country**. A Scottish immigrant of uncertain background, McKenzie was arrested in 1855 for being a sheep stealer on a grand scale. He stole over 1000 in all, most of them from the Rhodes brothers' Levels Run station near Timaru (see p.658), grazing them in the basin of rich high-country pastureland which now bears his name. McKenzie escaped from prison three times during the first year of his five-year sentence, and was finally released on condition that he leave the country never to return, which he subsequently did.

It's nowadays difficult to fathom why exactly McKenzie became such an important and popular figure in New Zealand lore. He was certainly a prodigious thief, somehow controlling a vast flock of rustled animals with the assistance of a single dog, Friday – a hound fondly remembered as the prototype for the many hard-working sheep dogs held in deep affection by South Islanders. McKenzie is also regarded as one of the great pioneers, opening up an area of hitherto undiscovered grazing land that contained some of the best sheep runs in the country. There is a poem in honour of the great man and his dog in the visitor shelter at Lake Pukaki near the turn-off to Mount Cook.

Cook Road, where three buildings are set back from the road with a Sampson wind pump (a tower surmounted by a wind-turned fan) out front. The display in the cottage remembers the first European settlers, and there's an extensive collection of early photographs. The museum is stuffed with farm machinery, wagons and traction engines. The third building on the site is the old railway station, which was moved here in 1968.

For a little exercise, wander along the **Fairlie Walkway** (3km; 40min one way). Beginning below the Allendale Road Bridge over the Opihi River, the walkway follows the willow-shaded riverbank past open pastureland and through trees to emerge near Talbot Road. **Guided walks** further afield are offered by Off the Beaten Track (☎03/685 8272; $15 per hour; (10am–4pm), run by local tramper Louise Wynn.

En route to Lake Tekapo or Mount Cook, you could also stop by the **Three Springs Historic Sheep Station** (☎03/685 8174; daily 10am–4pm, closed April–Nov; tours by arrangement, $5), 5km west of Fairlie on SH8. Built from local limestone, the woolshed (where the shearing took place) is a magnificent example of early settler farm architecture, while the stable contains displays highlighting the station's history.

Eating and drinking

There's a surprisingly good choice of eateries in Fairlie offering a fair range of culinary styles.

BB Stop 81 Main St. Variations on a theme of meat, fish, chips and vegetables, followed by a touch of luxury in the form of Irish coffee. Burgers and light meals under $10, full meals $10–17. Daily 8.30am–10.30pm; licensed & BYO.

Old Library Café 6 Allendale Rd. Originally built in 1914, this café is charming and very comfortable. The menu offers chef's specials, light meals and snacks; there are always T-bone steaks and veggie choices. Prices are moderate. Daily 10am–late; licensed.

The Sunflower Centre 31 Main St. A wholefood café and health-food shop, offering inexpensive meals and snacks, including soups and falafel, but be warned – the veggie burgers are enormous ($5). Daily 8.30am–6pm; no licence or BYO.

Wild Olive 64–68 Main St. Open early every day for snacks and cheap breakfasts, herbal teas, good coffee and pies, as well as larger meals for lunch in the winter and lunch and dinner in the summer. Licensed and BYO.

Mount Dobson and Alpure/Fox Peak skifields

Mount Dobson Skifield (☎03/685 8039, ⓔmtdobson@xtra.co.nz) is located in a 3km treeless basin 26km north of Fairlie, up a 15km unsealed road off SH8. The mountain is known for its powder snow, long hours of sunshine, uncrowded fields and suitability for all levels of skiing and snowboarding. Equipment rental is available, and there is a lodge serving hot pies and drinks. Lift passes cost $42 per day, beginners' packages $50 including lift passes (equipment rental is extra), and snowboard rental weighs in at around $30 per day; a full snowboard package is $58. The nearest accommodation is in Fairlie. There are shuttle buses from Fairlie in season; for details call ☎03/693 9656.

The Alpure/Fox Peak Skifield (☎03/685 8539, snow phone ☎ 03/688 0044) is 30km northeast of Fairlie, with access from near the Mount Dobson access road, at the end of a 15km unsealed track. Although a small field it covers a good variety of terrain, catering for all abilities. There are now no lifts at the field; like Mount Potts (see p.697), it has been converted to a snow-cat-only field and so costs a whopping $175 a day. There are no ski-rental facilities and no accommodation, but refreshments are available. For information on Fairlie–Alpure/Fox Peak shuttle buses contact ☎03/688 1870.

Mount Cook and around

From Fairlie SH8 shoots, lupin- and broom-flanked in the summer, westward through the sheep-chomped grasslands of the McKenzie Country into the Mount Cook area, considered by many – including Peter Jackson, director of *Lord of the Rings* – to be the most spectacular section of the Southern Alps. Dominating the region to the northwest, the 3764-metre **Mount Cook** is the highest point in New Zealand. Known as Ao-raki by Maori, who passed through the area on their way east or west in search of trade, war and *pounamu*, it was named Mount Cook by Captain J.L. Stokes of HMS *Acheron* in 1851, although its summit wasn't conquered until 1894.

Mount Cook's permanent cover of snow and ice contrast vividly with the turquoise, glacier-fed **lakes Tekapo and Pukaki**, which stretch beneath its eastern flanks. Both lakes offer abundant fishing, water skiing and ice skating, although it's Lake Tekapo that has the bulk of the tourist facilities. Lake Pukaki is quiet in comparison, even though the view of Mount Cook across its still waters is one of the most memorable in New Zealand. Main access to the mountainous terrain around Mount Cook itself is provided by **Mount Cook Village**, which grew at the base of the mountain purely to cater for nineteenth-century tourists, who were brought here by horse-drawn coaches from Fairlie. You can walk from Mount Cook Village to the glaciers lurking beneath Mount Cook's flanks, most important of which is the 27km-long **Tasman Glacier**, running parallel to the Main Divide and fed by icefalls tumbling from the heavily glaciated peaks. Another good base from which to explore the area is **Twizel**, 70km south on the road to Cromwell and Queenstown, an unexciting modern town, which nevertheless rewards visitors with a glimpse of the extremely rare **Black Stilt**, wading birds that are protected in a reserve nearby. From **Omarama** 30km south of Twizel, SH83 runs eastwards down the **Waitaki Gorge** to Oamaru, providing a quick link between the Mount Cook area and the east coast. Public transport into the region is meagre but adequate, with Mount Cook Village served by daily **buses** from both Christchurch and Ashburton on the east coast, and three daily services from Queenstown to the south. In addition, Christchurch–Queenstown buses pass through Tekapo, Twizel and Omarama.

Lake Tekapo and around

About 42km from Fairlie on SH8, via Burke's Pass, is **Lake Tekapo** and **LAKE TEKAPO VILLAGE** – little more than a roadside ribbon of buildings, with a population of just 400. It's a popular tour-bus stop for obligatory

How Mount Cook (Ao-raki) came to be

Both the **sky father** (Raki) and the **earth mother** (Papa-tua-nuku) already had children by previous unions. After their marriage, some of the sky father's children came to inspect their father's new wife. Four brothers, Ao-raki, Raki-roa, Raki-rua and Raraki-roa, circled around the earth mother in a **canoe** called Te Waka-a-Aoraki, but once they left her shores, disaster befell them. Running aground on a reef, the canoe was turned to stone. The four occupants climbed to the higher western side of the petrified canoe, where they too were turned to stone: **Ao-raki** became Mount Cook, and his three younger brothers formed flanking peaks. Ao-raki towers over his brother mountains in height, age and spiritual status, as an Atua (Maori god).

photo-snapping, and shopping in the string of outlets whose stock leans towards high-priced tourist tat. In the last couple of years the settlement has spread towards the lakeshore, with new accommodation, eateries and tourist outlets adding nothing to its charm. To make the best of the place, stay overnight and enjoy the scenery and sunset free of the mob, then move on.

At an altitude of 707m, the area is reputed to have the clearest air in the southern hemisphere, and on a good day views really do have sharp edges and vibrant colours, making this is one of the best places from which to photograph the Southern Alps. The most striking thing about the **lake** itself is its colour: the light reflected from microscopic rock particles suspended in glacial meltwater lends its waters a vibrant turquoise hue. Fed by the **Godley** and **Cass** rivers, the lake covers 83 square kilometres and spills into the **Tekapo River**, which tumbles across the McKenzie Basin.

Arrival and information

Every other day **buses** complete the journey between Timaru and Twizel and drop off at Lake Tekapo Village, while each day at least one of the many bus and **shuttle bus** operators (InterCity, Atomic, Southern Link and so on) call in as part of the Christchurch–Queenstown route also plied by Kiwi Discovery Express and Magic. Timetables and fares for all these services are available from the visitor centre, where you can make bookings and buy tickets.

Buses pull into an area off SH8, opposite the main shops, and you can walk to all the accommodation and worthwhile sights from there. The **visitor centre** is in Kiwi Treasures, a souvenir outlet in the middle of the settlement, beside *Robin's Café* (ⓣ03/680 6686; daily: April–Oct 8am–6pm, Nov–March 8am–8pm). Staff have an assortment of leaflets but are usually busy introducing tourists to the joys of retail therapy.

Accommodation

Most accommodation in this tourist-oriented village is on the expensive side, and the few budget options tend to be oversubscribed – it's a good idea to book ahead. Meanwhile new investors are building more and more motels by the lake and gradually destroying what little character the village once had.

The Chalets 14 Pioneer Drive ⓣ03/680 6774. Six individually decorated, self-contained motel units overlooking the lake and well away from the highway, run by a friendly Swiss couple who also rent out holiday homes for four people and will do breakfasts. ❺–❻

Godley Resort Hotel in the centre of the village by the Tekapo River Bridge (ⓣ03/680 6848, ⓦwww.tekapo.co.nz. The original inn building is 33 years old, though several new sections have been added since: old hotel rooms are cheaper than new ones, and motel units are cheaper still. The complex incorporates a variety of restaurants and shops, and various activities are arranged for guests. Lake views are costly so unless your legs are broken go for a room without. Prices might be worth negotiating if things seem quiet. ❻–❽

Lake Tekapo Motel and Motor Camp Lakeside Drive ⓣ03/680 6825, ⓕ680 6824. Situated among trees at the southern end of Tekapo, this is a large, well-equipped campsite. Tent sites $10, cabins, tourist cabins and motel ❷–❺

Tailor-made-Tekapo Backpackers 9–11 Aorangi Crescent ⓣ03/680 6700. Off SH8, five minutes' walk from the bus stop and shops, this friendly hostel has 30 bunks, plus an organic vegetable garden and a telescope – the clear mountain air makes for great stargazing. Dorm ❶, rooms ❷

Tekapo YHA Simpson Lane, just west of the village ⓣ03/680 6857, ⓔinfo@yha.org.nz. This lakeside hostel is the settlement's best place to stay and boasts one of the finest locations of any hostel in New Zealand ; the common room has a floor-to-ceiling window so make the most of the magnificent view. Doubles and twin rooms, as well as bunks. Dorms ❶, rooms ❷–❸

The Village and around

The name Tekapo derives from the Maori *taka* ("sleeping mat") and *Po* ("night"), suggesting that this place has long been used as a stopover between destinations. Although surrounded by heart-stopping scenery, there is little to the settlement itself – though you should pause long enough to look inside the tiny **Church of the Good Shepherd**, on Pioneer Drive. Overlooking the lake from a small raised platform, the stone church was built as a memorial to the pioneers of the McKenzie Country in 1935. Behind the rough-hewn Oamaru stone altar, a square window perfectly frames the lake and the surrounding hills and mountains; in the stillness of this simple church, the sunset can be quite a moving experience. About 50m east of the church is the perky-looking **Collie Dog Monument**, erected in 1966 by the sheep farmers of the McKenzie Country as a mark of their deep respect and affection for the dogs that make it possible to graze this harsh terrain.

Of a number of good **walks** in the area, the best is to **Mount John Lookout** (10km; ascent 300m; 3hr return), starting just past the motor camp on Lakeside Drive and climbing through a larch forest, full of birds, to a loop track which circles the summit of Mount John, with views of the McKenzie Basin, Lake Tekapo and the Southern Alps. You can either return the way you came or continue on the loop path and back along the lakeshore to your starting point, well worth the extra hour it adds. The *Lake Tekapo Walkway* leaflet gives a rundown of five alternative routes and is available from the local visitor centres ($1).

The air is so clear that organized **star gazing** (☎03/680 6565; starting between 7 & 9pm depending on season; $35) can be an educational and visually stimulating treat, but only when tour operator Hide (pronounced Ha–day) guides the trip himself. Other pursuits include skiing at the Tekapo Skifield, **ice skating** at the rink (May–Aug only) on Lakeside Drive, and guided **horse treks** through spectacular scenery (30min–2hr; $15–50; ☎03/680 6882).

Finally, determined sightseers short of time can join Air Safaris on SH8, about 6km west of Tekapo (free transfers arranged for customers), for a "Grand Traverse of Mount Cook". This **scenic flight** swoops across the Main Divide to the west coast, providing views of the Franz Josef and Fox glaciers, the Hooker and Muller glaciers, and, of course, Mount Cook (☎03/680 6880, bookable from the Tekapo office ☎0800/806 880; hourly, weather permitting; 50min; $230).

Eating and drinking

Catering to a relatively captive market, most of the cafés and restaurants in Tekapo are quite pricey; if you're on a tight budget, your best bet is probably a picnic by the lake. Otherwise, the main street through the village has the *Reflections Restaurant* in the *Tekapo Tavern* (daily 9am–late) offering simple bar food and a good place for a beer with DJ-orchestrated music on Friday and Saturday evenings, while best for filling cheap grub is the *Tekapo Bakery and Coffee Shop*, producing its own bread and pies and serving an all-day $10 breakfast (daily: Nov–March 6am–8pm, April–Oct 6am–6pm). *Jade Palace* (daily 11.30am–2pm & 5–9pm; licensed) is a modern, airy Chinese **restaurant** with very tasty set menus for under $30 a head. The pick of the restaurants in the *Godley Alpine Inn* complex, right in the centre of the village by the Tekapo River Bridge, is the highly expensive *Kohan* (evenings only; licensed), specializing in subtle Japanese cuisine. Other alternatives on the main drag are *Robin's Café* (daily 7am–8pm; licensed), serving wholesome lamb chops and steaks, pizza and fish, with an adjacent takeaway, and *The Observatory Café* (daily:

Oct–April 8.30am–late, May–Aug 8.30am–5pm; licensed), a sort of tearoom-cum-restaurant/bar with passable food at barely digestible prices.

Towards Lake Pukaki

Southwest from Tekapo, SH8 heads towards **Lake Pukaki** some 47km distant, where SH80 branches off northwards towards Mount Cook Village. There's an **Information Shelter** made of local boulders at the road junction, boasting several useful and interesting displays on Maori and *pakeha* history, a poem to McKenzie and his dog (see box on p.702) and a beautiful view of the lake – a massive blue-green expanse of water where winds sometimes whip up white-capped waves. It's also the starting point for a worthwhile **scenic drive**, which heads up the eastern side of the lake via Hangman Drive and Tasman Downs Road, offering over 40km of scenic lake and mountain views, before eventually petering out at the base of 2035m **Mount Burnett**.

Mount Cook Village

The road from the Lake Pukaki junction to Mount Cook heads north along the west bank of the lake for 55km, squeezed between the shore and an area of gorse- and tussock-covered hills. Thirty kilometres from the junction you'll pass **Peter's Lookout**, a popular viewing point on the lake side of the road and then the *Glentanner Park*, a campsite and cabins with its own restaurant and a helicopter pad (see p.708).

On hot days, an atmospheric white mist rises from the plain at the base of the mountain, as you approach the diffuse huddle of buildings that make up **MOUNT COOK VILLAGE**. At a height of 760m, this ugly, low-slung settlement is dominated by **The Hermitage**, an alpine-style hotel at the end of the valley that leads to the mountain; there's been a hostelry here since 1886, though the current incarnation was built in 1958 and extended in 2001, its new $10 million wing providing luxury rooms for visiting coach tourists and well-heeled travellers. Mount Cook is something of a company town, since the same people who own *The Hermitage* own just about everything else – and most of the summer population of 500 work for them. This means that most of the accommodation and eateries, the hideously expensive and complicated petrol station and the ill-stocked shop are pitched at rich overnighters, while the more budget-oriented accommodation and food are of uniformly poor quality (although there's hope that a good independent café/restaurant will open in 2003). For this reason, many people now stay, despite the inconvenience, in Tekapo or Twizel, and explore the park from there. Rain frequently shrouds the village, but the scenery round about more than compensates.

Practicalities

All the major operators run **buses** to Mount Cook from Christchurch via Tekapo, or from Queenstown to the southwest. There are additional services from Twizel and Tekapo, and most stop at Glentanner along the way. These days, as well as the usual suspects, you can get a Cook Connection (☎025/583 211; $45 one way) bus from either Timaru or Oamaru and a High Country Shuttle (☎0800/435 050; $35 & $40 respectively) from Queenstown or Wanaka. All the buses drop off in the car park near *The Hermitage*, from where everything is within walking distance, or at the *YHA*. Mount Cook **airport**, 3km south of the village, is currently served by regular daily flights from Auckland, Christchurch, Queenstown, Rotorua, Taupo, Te Anau, Wanaka and Wellington.

The **DOC office and visitor centre** (daily: April–Sept 8.30am–5pm, Oct–Nov 8.30am–6pm, Dec–March 8.30am–6.30pm; ⓣ03/435 1186, ⓔmountcookvc@doc.govt.nz), located between the *The Hermitage*'s hotel and the motel buildings, is the best and friendliest place for information and advice on walks and activities. It stocks everything from leaflets to detailed maps and a number of lavish gifts for the less discerning. There are also displays of Mount Cook memorabilia, and a **video** recounting Maori legends, the glacial history of the mountain, and a survey of the people who have, over the years, attempted to climb it (from 8.30am, English version on the hour; 20min; $3). Two hundred metres southeast of the centre is the unmanned **petrol station** – you'll need an EFTPOS card and pin number to use it, or phone the hotel desk and pay them $5 extra to do it for you. The post office is in the new *Hermitage* gift shop where they also sell meagre, overpriced supplies. You can get more reasonably priced foodstuffs at the YHA shop, though for anything fresh you'll need to go to Twizel. Banking transactions can be completed at *The Hermitage*, and the *Hermitage*-owned bars take EFTPOS and credit cards. Alpine Guides, adjacent to the single petrol pump (daily 8am–5pm; ⓦwww.alpineguides.co.nz), offer experienced **climbing guides** and stock equipment, while *The Hermitage* rents out **mountain bikes** at typically exorbitant hourly rates.

Accommodation

There is a lot of accommodation in Mount Cook, almost all of it owned by *The Hermitage*. The YHA hostel, the Alpine Club's *Unwin Hut* and the campground are the last bastions of independence and the sole budget options, which means booking early during the peak season (Oct–April & July–Sept). Conversely, the village is deserted between April and June, a window between the summer tourist and winter skiing seasons, when it is generally possible to negotiate tariffs at the various forms of *Hermitage* accommodation.

Glentanner Park 20km south on SH8 ⓣ03/435 1855, ⓕ435 1854. Well-equipped, *Hermitage*-owned site with shop, recently renovated restaurant, camping, new dorm-like accommodation and cabins in a wide open space, with panoramic views of the mountains and the Tasman Valley. Tent sites $ 9, dorms ❶, cabins ❷–❹

The Hermitage on the northwestern border of the village ⓣ03/435 1809, ⓔhermitage.mtcook@xtra.co.nz. This rambling wooden structure topped by a greeny-blue roof has several grades of room, all with a balcony, though not always a view. The complex also includes seven heated and self-contained A-frame chalets (often booked out by Kiwi Experience), 32 motel units and the *Glencoe Lodge*, as well as the new tower-block-style luxury wing where all the highly expensive rooms (prices reach $450) have views of the mountain, when it's visible. ❻–❾

Mount Cook YHA Hostel cnr Bowen Drive & Kitchener Drive ⓣ & ⓕ03/435 1820, ⓔyhamtck@yha.org.nz. Excellent hostel with 66 beds in a wooden building and modern, well-kept facilities. Free videos are shown in the evenings, there are free saunas between 7 & 9.30pm, pizzas for just $5.50, and a well-stocked shop. It's nearly always full so book well in advance. Office hours: 8–10.30am, 12–3pm & 5.30–9pm. Dorms ❶, rooms ❸

Unwin Hut near the airport turn-off, 4km from the village ⓣ 03/433 1102. An Alpine Club hut that's open to travellers, offering basic bunk-room accommodation and the use of a massive common area with kitchen. Dorms ❶

White Horse Hill Camping Area a 30min walk north from the village at the start of the Hooker Track (no advance bookings). A serene and informal camping area with stony ground, flush toilets and running water (which is not treated and so should be boiled for 3min before use); camping spots are indicated by markers. Tent sites $5.

Eating and drinking

The Hermitage will provide **picnics** for all comers (ask in the lobby; under $30, 24hr notice required), with a free cooler bag thrown in, and within the hotel complex itself there are three excellent, well-staffed, highly priced fine-dining

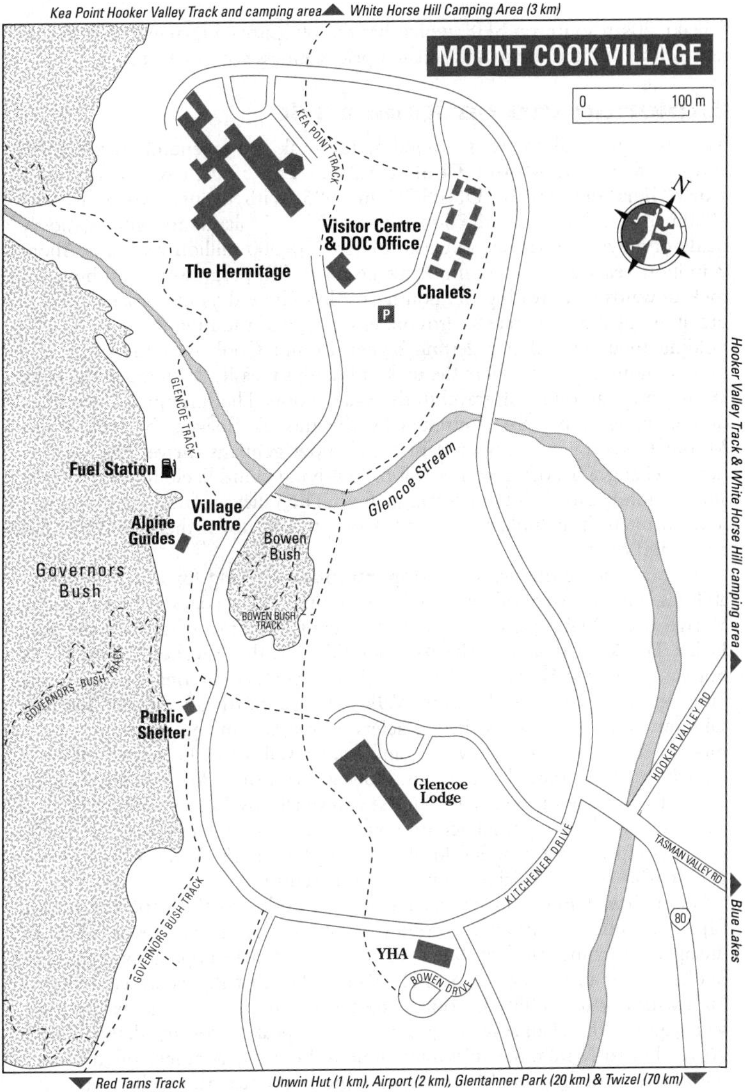

Kea Point Hooker Valley Track and camping area ▲ White Horse Hill Camping Area (3 km)

MOUNT COOK VILLAGE

0 100 m

KEA POINT TRACK
Visitor Centre & DOC Office
The Hermitage
Chalets
P
GLENCOE TRACK
Fuel Station
Village Centre
Alpine Guides
Glencoe Stream
Bowen Bush
BOWEN BUSH TRACK
Governors Bush
GOVERNORS BUSH TRACK
Public Shelter
Glencoe Lodge
HOOKER VALLEY RD
TASMAN VALLEY RD
KITCHENER DRIVE
80
GOVERNORS BUSH TRACK
YHA
BOWEN DRIVE
Hooker Valley Track & White Horse Hill camping area ▶
▶ Blue Lakes

▼ Red Tarns Track
Unwin Hut (1 km), Airport (2 km), Glentanner Park (20 km) & Twizel (70 km) ▼

and buffet restaurants and a slightly cheaper balcony coffee shop, with mini-market. The lower echelons are catered for by the **bar and bottleshop** in *Glencoe Lodge*, where the bog-standard pub fare only becomes appetizing when you consider the cost of the alternatives.

There are **bars** in the hotel complex, with views of the mountain, so bite the bullet and sup a couple of expensive beers as the sun goes down. The only other eating or drinking alternative is *Glentanner Park*, on the shores of Lake

Pukaki, 20km south on SH8, which has the obligatory big-windowed restaurant, with a limited menu and inflated prices. Guess who owns it.

Exploring the national park

The 700 square kilometres surrounding the peak and extending to the north and east forms the **Mount Cook National Park**, which was designated a **world heritage site** by UNESCO in 1986. With twenty-two peaks over 3000m, the park contains the lion's share of New Zealand's mountains, mostly made of greywacke laid in an ocean trench 250–300 million years ago. About 2 million years ago the Alpine Fault began to lift, progressively pushing the rock upwards and creating the Southern Alps. These days the process continues at about the same rate as erosion, ensuring that the mountains are at least holding their own, if not getting bigger. Mount Cook is at the heart of a unique mountain area, where the rock of the Alps is easily shattered in the cold, leaving huge amounts of gravel in the valley floors. The inhospitable ice fields of the upper slopes are contrasted by the tussock-cloaked foothills, where Mount Cook Lilies, summer daisies and snow gentians thrive. The weather here is changeable, often with a pall of low-lying cloud liable to turn to rain, and the mountain air is lung-searingly fresh. The valleys around the mountains tend to retain heat (unless the winds blow straight down them) and can feel airless and oppressive.

There are numerous **walking opportunities** catering for a wide range of abilities, with a variety of scenic trails beginning on the edges of Mount Cook Village itself. Main routes into the mountains from the village are the **Kea Point Track** northwest to the **Mueller Glacier**, the **Hooker Valley Track** northwards to the **Hooker Glacier** (although you can no longer climb to the Hooker Hut), and the **Tasman Valley Road** northeast to the **Tasman Glacier**. Walking as far as these glaciers is well within the capability of any moderately fit recreational walker, and longer walks for the more ambitious branch out from these basic routes. However you shouldn't actually walk on the surface of any of the glaciers unless you've already had experience of such walks and you've sought advice on conditions from the local DOC, or you're in the company of a qualified local guide. A *Walks in the Mount Cook National Park* **leaflet** ($1) is available from the visitor centre.

Although walking is an unbeatable way of exploring the park, the **scenic flights** on offer can provide you with glimpses of areas that you could never dream of reaching on foot. Such flights are extremely popular, and must be booked as far in advance as possible. Remember that flights are cancelled in high winds or if visibility is poor – and the weather can change by the hour, so if you get the chance to go, jump at it. The peak season for flights is from November to March, but in winter (June & July) the weather's often clearer, with better visibility. The Mount Cook region's **ski season** (see box, opposite) lasts from July to September, and the steep, inaccessible slopes (you're delivered to them by helicopter) present an exciting challenge to experienced skiers. Another alternative is **helihiking**, which involves hopping on a helicopter and getting delivered three-quarters of the way along one of the walks, climbing to a summit and then walking back. If none of this appeals then one of the most entertaining experiences is a **boat ride** (see p.713) up the Tasman Lake, which gets you within touching distance of the terminal moraine and the honeycomb ice of the Tasman Glacier.

Mount Cook ski areas

The **skiing and snowboarding** around Mount Cook tend towards the exhilarating, although the experience doesn't come cheap. None of the steep runs is served by ski lift, so helicopters provide access during the **season** (July–Sept), thereby ensuring high prices and preserving the resort's status as a rather exclusive preserve. There are no runs suitable for beginners. Access to the fields is generally provided by Alpine Guides (Ⓣ03/435 1834, Ⓦwww.heliskiing.co.nz); enthusiastic and adept skiers can "Ski the Tasman", with two guided 10km runs on the Tasman glacier for $650, while all-day skiing with helicopter transfers to a range of different runs starts at around $710 and advances into orbit, with equipment rental extra.

Walks

Walks range from gentle day-hikes to arduous and spectacular alpine treks that take several days. Tramping **information** is available from the DOC office in Mount Cook Village. Most of the trails are suitable for well-equipped independent walkers and unless you want to spend a fortune, stick to walks you're comfortable with. If you must have a little help on the way, Cloud 9 Heli-hiking (Ⓣ03/435 1077, Ⓔglacier007@xtra.co.nz) will take you up Mount Dark and guide you back down on foot for $148 (see "Helihiking", p.712). Alpine Guides (see above) also offer experienced climbing **guides**, although it concentrates on 7–10 day walking options.

The DOC leaflet *Walks in Mount Cook National Park* ($1) describes the national park and lists twelve excellent **shorter walks** (10min–5hr), all of which can be extended by those with relevant experience. Each of the walks starts in Mount Cook Village and heads out along the banks of one of the two glacier-fed rivers, the Hooker River and the Tasman River. Of these, the most popular is the superb **Hooker Valley Track** (9km; 3hr 30min return). Crossing two swingbridges at the top and bottom of the Mueller Lake, the track climbs opposite the western side of Mount Cook, past the site of the original hermitage (a stone fireplace remains) and the viewpoint at the Alpine Memorial, ending at the Hooker Lake. If you want to continue and are fit and well-equipped, you can head back to the footbridge at the source of the Mueller Lake and make for the **Ball Shelter** (14km; ascent 300m; 6hr; $10), spend the night and walk down to the Blue Lakes (9km; 3hr) and then return on the Freedom Bus (check its timetable) or walk along the Tasman Valley Road back to the village (about 7km; 2.5hr).

The **Mueller Glacier**, nestling 5km northeast of Mount Cook Village beneath the hanging glaciers and icefalls of Mount Sefton, is reached by the **Kea Point Track** (3hr return), which starts just north of the DOC office and ends at a lookout over the Mueller Lake. Again, a more gruelling alternative is available to those who first check on weather conditions with the DOC, in the shape of the **Mueller Hut Track** (5km; 5hr one way), which requires moderate fitness. The route leaves the Kea Point Track just before its arrival at the glacier, climbing steeply westwards up the **Sealy Tarn Track** along a route marked by cairns. From the tarns the route to the hut is marked by the less romantic but more useful orange triangles (every 200m). The final assault is up a loose gravel slope to a skyline ridge, from which you head south towards the 1800m **Mueller Hut** (28 bunks; $18). The views are quite startling and you are engulfed by almost perfect silence, interrupted only by the murmur of running water and the twittering of birds.

The trail to the **Tasman Glacier** starts from the Blue Lakes car park, 3km north of the village up the Tasman Valley Road, and leads to the **Glacier Lookout** (500m; 20min one way; 100m ascent). The glacier is 600m deep at its thickest, 3km across at its widest, and moves at a rate of 20cm a day. A gentleman called Sir Harry Wigley landed an Auster aircraft on the glacier in 1955, paving the way for today's squadrons of tourist flights. One last excellent walk which is achievable for the lazier traveller is the **Red Tarns Track** (2km; ascent 300m; 3hr return), a steep but short climb to two tarns named after the red pondweed that grows in them. From the tarns you have an uninterrupted panoramic view of Mount Cook, the village and along the Tasman Valley which is well worth the sweat.

Helihiking

Guided **helihikes** (Snow Feast $241, Mount Dark $148) offer travellers the opportunity of getting high up into the Alps by helicopter, and completing tracks without having to do the hard work of walking up the initial few thou-

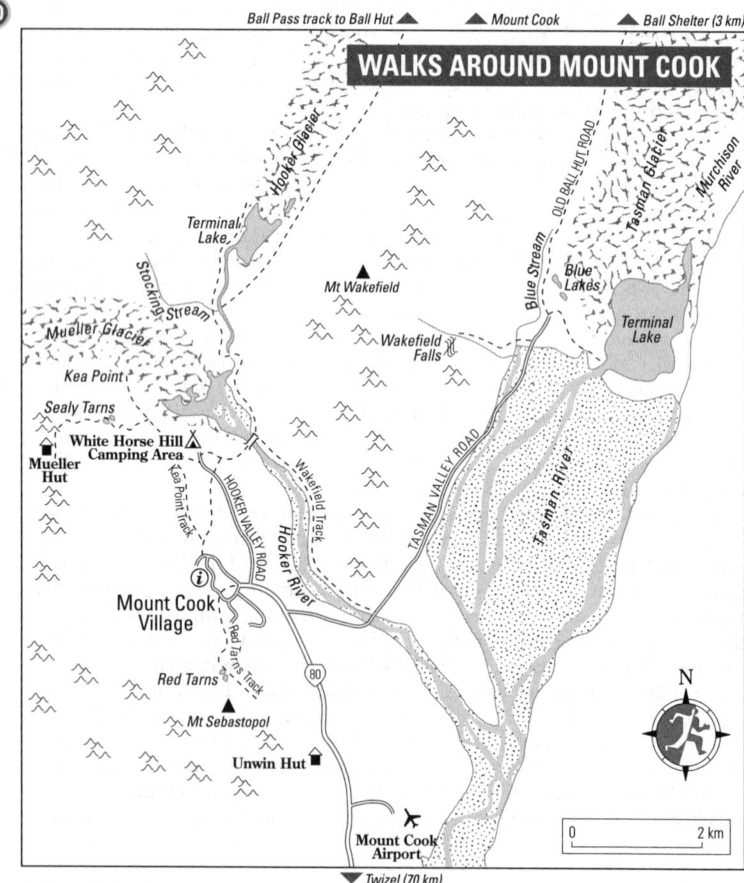

sand feet. On either trip you only need to climb a little bit and then the remainder of the time is spent going downhill. This both reduces the fitness levels required and enables you to see some of the area's more spectacular but otherwise inaccessible sights. However, you must still have good equipment (they provide poles and food) and although going downhill is easier, it's still fairly energetic and even pretty knackering after a while.

Boat trips

One of the most fun trips available, and less expensive than flights or multi-day guided walks, is the Glacier Explorer – a short walk (25min) to and then ride up the Tasman Glacier in moulded plastic boats (Ⓣ & Ⓕ03/435 1077, Ⓔglacier007@xtra.co.nz; Oct–May daily at 10am, noon & 2pm; 3hr; $85). It's worth booking in advance for this eerie **boat ride** on the glacial lake where icebergs, recently detached from the glacier itself, drift around. The lake is grey in colour, a result of the large amount of ground-down rock, or rock flour, that mixes with the water and reflects the light. As you approach the glacier you'll be able to watch various-sized chunks of ice fall off and get the chance to examine it up close, revealing a mixture of beautiful honeycombed ice cells and the detritus that has been picked up and carried along its course. The guides are a mine of information and stories, and the three hours will pass quickly providing you had the good sense to wrap up warmly.

Scenic flights

All the **scenic flights** from the Mount Cook Airfield are operated by Mount Cook Ski Planes (Ⓣ03/435 1026 & 0800/800 702, Ⓕ435 1886, Ⓦwww.skiplanes.co.nz). Other helicopter and sightseeing trips run from Glentanner Park or the other local airfields (see below). These allow you to see the tops of the mountains and the steepness of the valley walls, and to appreciate the length and mass of the glaciers, and in some instances land on them for a quick walk around. By far the most exhilarating landings and take-offs are in the fixed wing aircraft, when the value of prayer becomes evident.

Helicopters

The **helicopter trips** on offer in the vicinity of Mount Cook operate from *Glentanner Park* campsite/accommodation complex, 20km south of the village, and are run by The Helicopter Line (Ⓣ03/435 1801 & 0800/650 651, Ⓕ435 1802), part of the same network that owns the Mount Cook Ski Planes.

There are three flights on offer: the "Mountains High" flight over the village, circumnavigation of Mount Cook, traverse of the Southern Alps, snow landing, and views of the glaciers (45min; $350); "Alpine Explorer" cruise over the Ben Ohau Mountains, views of Mount Cook and the glaciers and a snow landing on the Richardson Glacier (30min; $225); and the "Alpine Vista" swoop over the Ben Ohua Range, snow landing and panoramic views (20min; $165). Each is an exciting and bumpy ride, hovering alongside the valley walls and peaks, or viewing the tumbling blocks of the Hochstetter Icefall and landing on the snow of the glacier when the weather allows, and when it's all over you'll get a commemorative glossy booklet.

Alternative helicopter trips run from Twizel with Glacier Southern Lakes Helicopters, opposite the *Mackenzie Country Inn* (Ⓣ03/435 0370, Ⓔgslhtwiz@es.co.nz). On offer are five trips ranging from $155 to $455 along similar lines to those from *Glentanner Park* but covering greater distances, with the longer you spend in the air adding to the amount you pay.

Planes

Mount Cook Ski Planes, based at the Mount Cook airfield, offer the best four fixed-wing scenic adventures, the ultimate of which is the longest ("The Grand Circle"; 55min; $350), which circles Mount Cook, crosses (briefly) the Main Divide, then lands and takes off from the Tasman Glacier in a heart-stoppingly short distance. The glaciers are silent once the plane engine splutters off and wandering around on the footprint-free snow is almost as exhilarating as the landing and take-off, though wear sunglasses to avoid going a little snow blind. Of the three shorter flights on offer, one lands on a glacier and the others offer alternative routes around and between the Alps. The company also (under the umbrella of Air Safaris) offers scenic flights from nearby Glentanner, Tekapo, Twizel or Omarama, with various flight plans including a whizz round the Mount Cook summit – although you'll be starting slightly further away from the mountains and consequently spending less time over them. It's best to go from Mount Cook airfield if you can, so only book one of the alternatives if it is impossible to do so there or you'd like a quick look at the mountains but have no intention of travelling to Mount Cook Village itself. There are also fly-overs and scenic flights available from the West Coast.

Twizel and around

Seventy kilometres from Mount Cook, retracing your route on SH80 then veering south on SH8 at Lake Pukaki junction, you'll come upon **TWIZEL**, which sits on the west side of the main highway. A tree-bounded island surrounded by seas of pasture with a backdrop of alpine scenery, it's often windy, dry and cold in the winter, and dry and hot in summer.

The modest settlement began life in 1966 as a staff hostel for people working on the local hydroelectric scheme (see box on p.720), and was supposed to have been bulldozed flat after the project was finished. Some think this might have been a kinder fate but now the functional settlement has come into its own, offering some of the best budget accommodation, shopping, eating and drinking (though for the last two only at *Hunters Bar and Restaurant*), within reach of Mount Cook. It also boasts a decent and worthwhile side-trip to the **Kaki (Black Stilt) Aviary**, 3km from town, which aims to save these rare wading birds from extinction. You can also try **helibiking**, a new addition to the long list of things you can do with a helicopter in this area, or content yourself with exploring the heavily forested banks, tall grassy hills and mountains surrounding **Lake Ohau**, where various tramps provide views over the broad turquoise lake.

Arrival and information

A variety of **shuttles** and **coaches** stop off in Twizel including Cook Connection (Ⓣ025 583 211), from either Mount Cook, Timaru or Oamaru, High Country Shuttles (Ⓣ0800/435 050), and Intercity from almost everywhere, including Queenstown and Wanaka. They tend to disgorge at the **DOC office** car park, or the one outside the council buildings, just behind the town's central shopping mall. It is here that you'll find the **visitor centre**, Twizel Info (daily: Oct–April 9am–7pm; May–Sept 10am–4pm; Ⓣ03/435 3124, Ⓦwww.twizel.com), which has a good stock of leaflets, friendly, knowledgeable staff who can book most things for you, and a gift shop and radio station on site. For further information try the free monthly *McKenzie Mail*, an insight into the community's collective psyche. The town's accommodation is all within walking distance of either point of arrival; for exploring further afield,

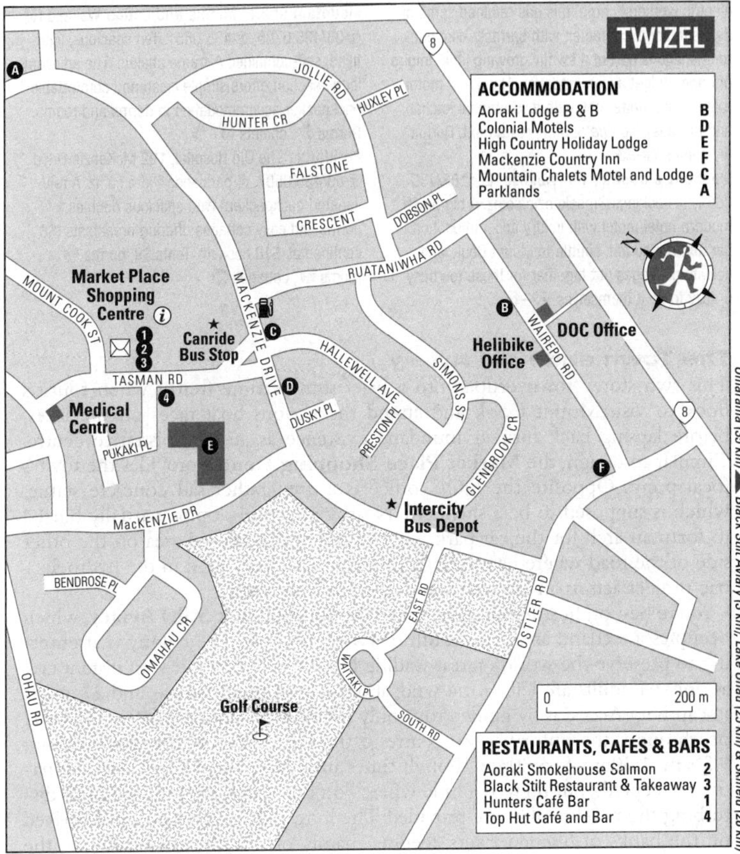

Mackenzie Country Inn, Warepo Road, offers **bike rental** ($10 a day). There is a **petrol station** on McKenzie Drive, and the Market Place mall in the centre of town has a supermarket, restaurants and a **bank** and a **post office**.

Accommodation

Being only half an hour's drive from Mount Cook, Twizel's accommodation is some of the best value around but it pays to **book ahead** around Christmas, New Year, the second week in February and Easter, when the town is packed with holidaying New Zealanders.

Aoraki Lodge B&B 32 McKenzie Drive ⓣ03/435 0300, ⓔaorakilodge@xtra.co.nz. A luxurious spot with bedecked, individual rooms, wheelchair access, en-suite bathrooms, the use of a large comfortable lounge and tastebud-tingling breakfasts and dinners (3-course dinner from $30; BYO). ❺

Colonial Motels 36–38 McKenzie Drive ⓣ03/435 0100, ⓕ435 0499. Superior ground-floor units with full kitchens and facilities, and conveniently close to shops and restaurants. ❺–❻

High Country Holiday Lodge McKenzie Drive ⓣ03/435 0671, ⓕ435 0747. The former hydroelectric workers' camp, this has retained some of its institutional character, with barracks-like bunk rooms, and is part of a swiftly growing little empire offering budget accommodation. Hotel and motel rooms are a better bet, with a communal kitchen and there is also *The Summit* restaurant. Dorms ❶, rooms ❷–❹

Mackenzie Country Inn Wairepo Rd ⓣ03/435 0869, ⓔbookings@mackenzie.co.nz. A big brash modern hotel/motel with luxury accommodation, bar and restaurant, shuttle to Mount Cook, and activity packages put together for those too busy or lazy to do it themselves. ❻–❼

Mountain Chalet Motels and Lodge Wairepo Rd ⓣ03/435 0785, ⓕ435 0551. Ten spacious, light-filled, self-contained A-frame chalets. The adjacent lodge section offers simple clean and comfortable backpacker accommodation in dorms and rooms. Dorms ❶, chalets ❹–❺

Parklands The Old Hospital, 122 McKenzie Drive ⓣ03/435 0507, ⓔparklands@xtra.co.nz. A rejuvenated backpackers with spacious doubles, dorms and cosy cottages offering breakfasts ($8 continental, $10 cooked). Tents $9, dorms ❶, rooms ❷, cottages ❹

The Town and Kaki Aviary

This two-storey town erupts into a brief summertime frenzy when tourists flock to visit Mount Cook and attend the various boat races on the lakes, before lapsing back into its mundane existence as an administrative centre. Circular in design, the **Market Place Shopping Centre** provides the town's focal point. Opposite the DOC office is a grey, rather sad concrete statue, which is supposed to be a shepherd. Nearby, a section of pipe partially buried to form an arch for the car park gives notice of the grassed area on the other side of the road where heavy earth-moving machinery used in the hydroelectric project acts as an attraction and children's play area.

You're best off heading straight out to the **Kaki (Black Stilt) Aviary**, which occupies a wetland area 3km south of Twizel on SH8. The colony is attempting to preserve the world's rarest wading bird from extinction – an urgent task as only 61 adults are left in the wild, about half of them female, and 27 adults in captivity. Access is by guided tour only (book in advance on ⓣ03/435 0802 or through the information centre ⓣ03/435 3124, ⓔinfo@twizel.com; 9.30am, 1.30pm & 5.30pm, though times may vary; 1hr; $12.50, extra donations accepted), but there is a hide where you can watch the birds without disturbing them; binoculars are provided. The long-red-legged kaki once thrived on the banks of braided rivers, feeding mainly on mayfly and exhibiting the endearing post-coital behaviour of walking cross-billed as if indulging in upright pillow talk. All this changed due to habitat loss as a result of introduced plant species, the Waitaki hydroelectric project and the introduction of mammalian predators such as cats, ferrets, rats and stoats.

The centre operates by incubating clutches from all the wild and captive kaki pairs, hatching the eggs in captivity and raising the chicks to three or nine months before releasing them into the wild. At present there's a relief-inducing eighty-plus percent survival rate. Given that the majority of your $12.50 tour fee goes into the project you can both enjoy the education and get to feel good about it, unlike those individuals who have missed the point and with powerful binoculars look at the kaki from the road. If you want to know more about the kaki or other braided-river species and their habitat then get copies of the informative *Conservation of Braided River Birds*, *Braided River Care Code* and *Project River Recovery* leaflets, available in DOC offices and visitor centres.

Activities

What Twizel lacks in charm its surroundings make up for, and there are plenty of ways to get out there. If you're a fit and experienced **trail biker**, or just a willing one without a history of heart problems, then Heli Bike (ⓣ03/435

0626 & 0800/435 424, Ⓦwww.helibike.com) will fly you and the bikes somewhere spectacular and guide you on the pedal back. Routes take in such diverse places as the Benmore Range, beginning about 5km south of Twizel; Omahau Hill, 15km southwest of town; and the easier Pyramid Circuit (daily on demand, 2–4hr; $90–145; bikes and other gear all available for rent). Heli Bike also organizes the annual Helibike Challenge (second Sat in Feb) which is generally an excuse for groups to spend a day riding for fun, although there's always someone who takes it seriously. Also held in the second week of February, and well worth catching if you're around, is the biannual **Wings Over Water** event, a combination of speedboat and helicopter displays on (and over) Lake Ruataniwha.

A more sedate way to enjoy the area is to follow some of the picturesque walks around lakes Aviemore, Ohau and Tekapo set out in the DOC leaflet *Day Walks of the McKenzie Basin and Waitaki Valley* ($1), while if you are intending to **climb** any of the peaks in the area, contact Shaun Norman (Ⓣ03/435 0622), a skilled and experienced guide who also offers introductory, intermediate and advanced mountaineering instruction. There are also Mount Cook **scenic flights** operating from Twizel (see p.713 for details) and **skiing** at Mount Cook or Ohau (see p.718). Finally, and most absurdly, there's **golfcross**, a game using golf clubs, small oval balls and rugby posts (instead of holes). The whole thing started out as a joke but now there's a course across the lake from *Glentanner Park* and people are paying $9 each to have a go, though, as yet, no one has finished a game in under a day.

Eating and drinking

Unfortunately **Twizel's** lack of charm extends to most of its **eating and drinking** options, which tend to be uninspiring – with the notable exception of *Hunters Café Bar*.

Aoraki Smokehouse Salmon 3 Market Place, adjacent to *Hunters*. A small shop selling locally smoked salmon and one or two other delicacies. The fish is some of the best you'll taste in the country. Mon–Sat from 9.30am-4.30pm.

Black Stilt Restaurant and Takeaway 25 Market Place. A regular milk bar serving bacon and eggs ($10), light lunches and burgers ($5–15), and main meals (up to $16). Mon–Sat all day, Sun dinner only.

Hunters Café Bar 2 Market Place Ⓣ 03/435 0303. The best place to eat and party in town, with a weak spot for McKenzie Country-themed decoration, such as corrugated iron, a bit of barbed wire and wood. Generous well-prepared lunches and dinners ($6–20) include beer-battered fish, locally farmed salmon, meatballs with fettuccine, steaks and merino lamb kebabs, rounded off with good coffee. The buzzy atmosphere is helped along by occasional live music and theme nights, not to mention cocktails such as McKenzie's Dog. Daily 11am–late, happy hours 5–6pm and 10–11pm.

The Top Hut Café and Bar 13 Tasman Rd. Pub and glorified takeaway with chairs if you want to eat in, serving things with chips and now part of the High Country lodge empire. They've divided the building and added on a Chinese restaurant which is a touch more formal.

Lake Ohau

West of Twizel and around 25km along a narrow service road and over a few cattle stops, **Lake Ohau** is famed for its forest, river and **skifield** (see box overleaf). Renowned for the purity of its water, the lake surrounds boast some distinctive natural features, such as kettles (small depressions left when blocks of glacial ice melt, causing sediment above to subside), and the terracing on its banks that reflects the light of summer sunsets. Although it lacks the colour of Lake Tekapo, it is popular for fishing and kayaking, as are the Dobson and Hopkins rivers that flow into the lake's northern end (contact Twizel's visitor centres for details of boat rental). Ohau ("the place of the wind") was a seasonal food gathering stop-off for Maori making their way to and from the West Coast via Brodrick Pass and was the scene of many battles between rival *iwi*.

The **Ohau Forests** lie northwest from the lake, their stands of mountain beech and subalpine scrub criss-crossed by numerous tracks; the *Ohau Conservation Area* ($1), available from the visitor centres in Twizel, details various walks (30min–4hr). The forests flank wide valleys cut by once surging rivers (now a little more gentle unless in flood) and separated by narrow mountain ranges, with short tussock grasslands predominating around the lakes and lowlands. It's a pretty area but lacks any real points of interest so unless you're planning to head up to the backcountry huts to get away from it all you'll probably find more worthwhile entertainment and sights around Mount Cook or along the well-beaten roads running south.

As you enter the community near the lake you'll soon realize it is made up almost entirely of holiday homes, has no amenities and that the only **accommodation** is camping, the huts or at the lodge. If you become enamoured with the lake and forests, or simply want to stay and ski or tramp, *Lake Ohau Lodge*, on the southwestern shore of the lake, a 25km drive from SH8 along the Lake Ohau Road (Ⓣ & fax 03/438 9885; dorms ❶, rooms & chalets ❸–❺, camping $9), offers a wide variety of **accommodation**. Breakfast and dinner are available here, too. The huts on the tramps are all backcountry with a few bunks and nothing else ($5 a night).

Omarama and around

A crossroads town at the heart of the Waitaki Valley, on the edge of the McKenzie Basin, **OMARAMA** lies 30km south of Twizel. Sitting at the junction of SH8, which continues south to Cromwell, and SH83 to Oamaru, it is also on the main tourist route between Christchurch and Queenstown, via Mount Cook. The town itself has little to offer, with the nearby **Clay Cliffs Scenic Reserve** and the excursions offered by the local **gliding** club providing the main reasons to stop.

Arrival, information and accommodation

Regular **buses** plying the Timau–Twizel–Oamaru loop stop in Omarama, as do services from Queenstown and Wanaka and the major national bus companies, all dropping off at or near (InterCity drop off at the *Merino Café* diagonally opposite) the **visitor centre** on SH83, about 50m from the junction

Ohau skifield

Ohau Skifield, about 42km southwest of Twizel, off SH8 (Ⓣ03/438 9885, Ⓦwww.ohau.co.nz; July–Oct), is a small high-country (1033m) field with powder snow and uncrowded slopes which, as a part of the Main Divide, has reliable snowfall. There are several slopes catering for all standards of skier and snowboarder, with the added bonus of spectacular views of Lake Ohau and the longest T-bar in New Zealand. The *Lake Ohau Lodge* (see above) provides **accommodation** near the field, while the **Ohau Ski Lodge** on the field has no accommodation but does offer log burners, a sun deck with panoramic views, café and shop. **Equipment rental** is available at the field and lift passes cost $40 per day, with access provided by **bus** from the Lake Ohau Lodge ($20 return); otherwise, transport can be arranged by phoning the skifield information number (see above). Learners' **packages**, with gear rental and passes thrown in, start at $35 for ninety minutes.

(where there is a stone merino sheep) with SH8 in the Caltex Garage on the south side of the road (daily 7am–8pm; ⓣ03/438 9544), which provides leaflets and advice, accommodation reservations and bus or trip bookings.

As befits a passing-through kind of town, **accommodation** in Omarama is more geared to stopovers than to kicking back for a few days. The most conducive place is *Buscot Station*, about 8km north of Omarama on SH8 (they'll arrange pick-ups if you book ahead; ⓣ03/438 9646; dorms ❶, rooms ❷), a merino sheep farm where **backpacker** accommodation is provided in the old shearers' quarters, surrounded by a beautifully kept garden. Otherwise, you're faced with the usual choice of **campsite**, motel, or the local pub. *Omarama Holiday Park*, at the junction of SH8 and SH83 (ⓣ03/438 9875; tent sites $20 for two, on-site vans & cabins ❷), is an expansive site with sheltering trees and modern well-kept facilities. A rambling low-slung building on SH83, 50m away from the junction with SH8, the *Omarama Hotel* (ⓣ03/438 9713; B&B ❹) has clean basic **rooms** – a good bet so long as you don't mind some noise from the bar beside. Finally there's the *Ahuriri Motel*, on the corner of SH83 and Ahuriri Drive, 500m from the junction with SH8 (ⓣ03/438 9451; ❹–❺), with clean **motel** units in a rejuvenated building.

The Town and around

The name Omarama is Maori, and roughly translates as "place of light", but the town is short and squat with a population of just 300 – maybe it's the wrong kind of light. The settlement is mostly used as a way-station for picking up supplies, but there's one curiosity worth visiting if you're here in summer. Situated 4km back up SH8 towards Twizel then west for 15km up the Quailburn and then Henburn roads, the **Clay Cliffs Scenic Reserve** (ⓣ03/438 9780; $5 per person in the honesty box) is a combination of bare pinnacles and angular ridges separated by narrow ravines and canyons. The braided Ahuriri River provides a picturesque backdrop to this eerie landscape of badland erosion – created when a 100m uplift caused by the Ostler Fault exposed gravels, which became differentially weathered.

The Maori name for the clay cliffs is *Paritea*, meaning white or light-coloured cliff, and they were so named by Araiteuru, who brought the *kumara* sweet potatoes from Hawaiki. The cliffs provided natural shelter for moa hunters, with several earth ovens indicative of early Maori settlement. If the weather is very wet don't risk going up to the reserve in your own vehicle – you may never get it back. If you're still keen then join a guided tour run by Omarama Safari Tours (ⓣ03/438 9547; 1hr 30min; $30).

The northwesterly winds that blow across the basin make Omarama a fine spot for **gliding**, and Alpine Soaring (ⓣ03/438 9600; 20–40min; $89–$175) takes advantage of the reliable wind and flat surrounds to provide spectacular flights in two-seater gliders. The land and rivers around Omarama are also prime territory for hunting chamois and red deer, and fly fishing for trout and salmon. The fish and the venison are delicious, but no one seems to know what to do with the chamois – except hang their heads on walls. Bookings for fly fishing can be made through Omarama visitor centre; licences are $13 for 24hr.

Eating and drinking

Possibly because the town's restaurants and cafés cater for coach parties, the food is generally rather bland. The only place really worth visiting is the *Clay Cliffs Estate* (ⓣ03/438 9654; closed in June (11am–5pm for tastings, 11.30am–3pm for lunch, 6–10.30pm for dinner), a stylish **cafébar** and **vineyard** 1km along SH8 from the junction with SH83. A lakeside hacienda with a 1960s American sheriff's car under a weeping willow by the man-made pond, it serves good-quality, eclectic lunches and dinners ($7–$28) – highlights include great seafood chowder and grilled lamb with roast garlic and mint – as well as some very drinkable wine (tastings $2, redeemable against any purchase).

The Lindis Pass and the Waitaki Valley

Travelling on from Omarama on SH8 towards Wanaka, Cromwell and Queenstown (see Chapter 13), you'll cross the **Lindis Pass**, a rewarding scenic drive on narrow roads through predominantly tussock and grassland, though in bad weather it can feel distinctly foreboding.

The **route to Oamaru** on the east coast is an easier drive, following SH83 as it passes through a string of small settlements, which are surprisingly evenly spaced along the **Waitaki Valley**. The valley itself has been irrevocably changed by a mammoth hydroelectric scheme and the lakes it created (see box below).

The first settlement you come to, 26km from Omamara, is **OTEMATATA**, with little to offer except the *Otematata Lakes Hotel* (Ⓣ & Ⓕ03/438 7899; ③), which overlooks Lake Aviemore and provides accommodation, dining and a bar. **KUROW**, 30km further along SH83, is regarded as a fisherman's paradise. Twin wooden bridges (dating from 1880) span the salmon- and trout-filled Waitaki River, and there are a few limestone buildings of some minor grandeur in the settlement itself. One such is the old church which is now also a **visitor centre** (daily 10am–4pm; no tel), on the corner of Bledisoe and Wynard streets. Another 19km on, at the side of the road, you'll see the remains of some highly accessible Maori **rock paintings** (see box, p.659) sheltered beneath a bird-infested rock overhang. Another 4km on is **DUNTROON**, full of Gothic revival architecture, the *Duntroon Tavern* (good for cheap snacks), and a new

The Waitaki Valley Hydroelectric Scheme

The **Waitaki Hydroelectric Scheme** is made up of twelve power stations, built between 1925 and 1981, and currently provides nearly one-third of the nation's power. The scheme has its origins in the work of the engineer Peter Seton Hay, who in 1904 submitted a report to the New Zealand government indicating the extraordinary hydro-electric potential of the country, in particular the headwater lakes of the Waitaki river: Tekapo, Pukaki and Ohau. Construction of the Waitaki Power Station began some 24 years later. Most awesome of the stations are the Benmore, Aviemore and Waitaki, all ranged along the Waitaki River **east of Omarama**.

The nearest to Omarama, 15km away on SH83, is the earth-built **Benmore Dam** (Ⓣ03/438 9212; daily 10.30am–4.30pm; tours can be arranged by the Omarama Visitor Centre, in the Caltex Station, and run Tues, Thurs, & Sun at 11am, 1pm & 3pm, or by request; closed May–Sept; 1hr 15min; $5). The tours take you around the control room and generators, past lots of gushing water and views from the top of the dam. The scale of the dam is quite breathtaking, and you can walk or drive to the top; there is also a loop track with distant views of Mount Cook. **Aviemore Dam**, between Otematata and Kurow, supports SH83, and lay-bys on either side enable you to admire its construction. Alongside the dam is a trout- and salmon-spawning canal, with the lake glinting aquamarine against the mountains. About 20km south of Aviemore Dam on SH83, **Waitaki Power Station** is the oldest station on the river, with good views from a platform just beyond the dam, near an immense grey 17-tonne turbine used in 1941 to drive the generators.

Fossil Centre (Mon–Sat 10am–4pm) whose primary exhibit, "The Valley of the Disappearing Whale", tells the story of the fossilized whale skeleton recently discovered in Dansey's Pass, and provides the visitors with a chance to go and see it in the hills: a brochure ($8), with photos and maps, is available here. Following this celebrated old road, built in prospecting days, out towards **Naseby** provides another chance to cut across to the goldfields area and is a gentler route than the Lindis Pass. Just off the road, after about 1.5km, a winding narrow road climbs for 4km to the weird limestone formations of **Elephant Rocks**, popular with rock-climbers and abseilers; the difficulty ranges from beginner to medium but it's advisable to have had some experience and be well-equipped. The unmissable stand-alone rocks look like a small herd of elephants, in shape and colour, making their way through a grassy bowl. They were formed by hard limestone subjected to chemical erosion similar to the tor process that occurs in schist, where vertical cracks have eroded the stone around them with the remaining harder rocks becoming solid pachyderms. Back in Duntroon, a road beside the alarmingly cream church leads, after 6.5km, to the poorly signed **Earthquakes**, a collapsed cave where you can walk up the gently sloping roof and peer through dark crevices to the floor many feet below, flanked by the cave walls, which in place extend a sheer 20m above you.

Pressing on from Duntroon, the junction with the main east-coast highway (SH1) is just 35km away, and Oamaru is a further 8km south.

Travel details

Trains

Arthur's Pass to: Christchurch (1 daily; 2hr 5min); Greymouth (1 daily; 2hr 5min).
Christchurch to: Arthur's Pass (1 daily; 2hr 5min).

Buses

Arthur's Pass to: Christchurch (2 daily; 2hr 10min); Greymouth (2 daily; 2hr).
Ashburton to: Fairlie (1 daily; 1hr); Geraldine (1 daily; 50min); Methven (1 daily; 45min); Mount Cook (1 daily; 3hr 10min).
Christchurch to: Arthur's Pass (2 daily; 2hr 10min); Fairlie (1 daily; 3hr 15min); Geraldine (1 daily; 2hr 5min); Hanmer Springs (2 daily; 2hr); Methven (2 daily; 1hr 30min); Mount Cook (1 daily; 5hr 30min); Tekapo (1 daily; 4hr 10min).
Fairlie to: Christchurch (1 daily; 3hr 15min); Tekapo (2 daily; 1hr); Timaru (1 daily; 50min).
Geraldine to: Christchurch (1 daily; 2hr 5min); Fairlie (2 daily; 35min).
Hanmer Springs to: Christchurch (2 daily; 2hr); Murchison (1 daily; 2hr 30min).
Methven to: Christchurch (2 daily; 1hr 30min); Geraldine (2 daily; 1hr 30min).
Mount Cook to: Ashburton (1 daily; 3hr 10min); Christchurch (1 daily; 5hr 30min); Queenstown (3 daily; 4hr); Tekapo (2 daily; 1hr 20min); Twizel (2 daily; 1hr).
Oamarama to: Oamaru (1 daily; 2hr); Queenstown (2 daily; 2hr 20min); Twizel (3 daily; 35min).
Tekapo to: Christchurch (1 daily; 4hr 10min); Fairlie (2 daily; 1hr); Mount Cook (2 daily; 1hr 20min); Twizel (2 daily; 3hr).
Twizel to: Mount Cook (2 daily; 1hr); Omarama (3 daily; 35 min).

Flights

Note that after recent cuts in Air New Zealand, these services may be reduced.
Mount Cook to: Auckland (1 daily; 2hr 55min); Christchurch (1 daily; 45min); Queenstown (4 daily; 40min); Rotorua (1 daily; 3hr 25min); Taupo (1 daily; 5hr); Te Anau (1 daily; 1hr 25min); Wanaka (2 daily; 1hr 20min); Wellington (8 daily; 1hr).

11

Dunedin to Stewart Island

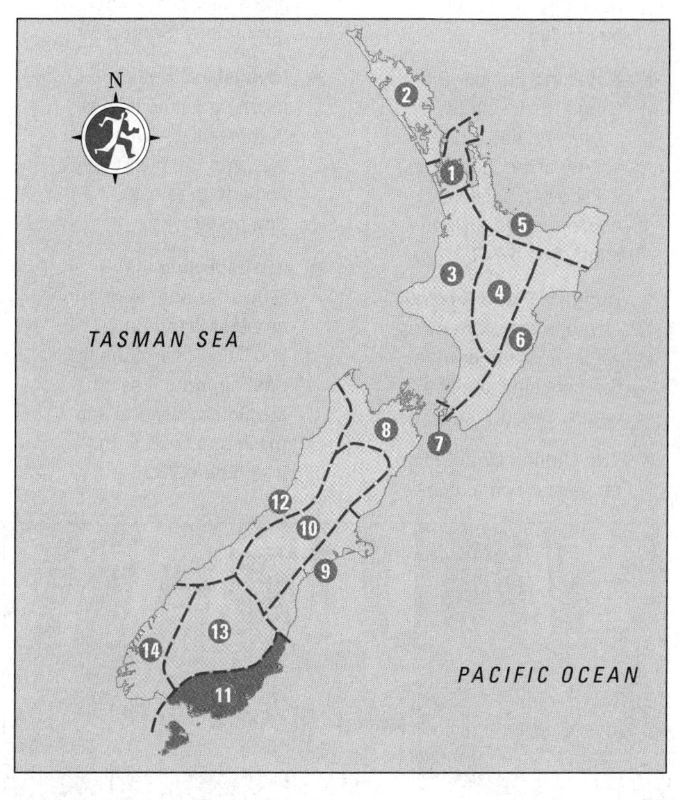

CHAPTER 11 **Highlights**

* **Dunedin Public Art Gallery** An airy and beautifully designed gallery. **See p.734**
* **The Otago Museum** A fascinating insight into the southern end of the South Island and the people who inhabit it. **See p.735**
* **Kayaking** Explore the Otago Peninsula by kayak and see a rich variety of landscape and wildlife in a sheltered and evocative environment. **See p.747**
* **Penguin Place** A unique environment of trenches where you, rather than the penguins, are in the cages. **See p.750**
* **The Catlins Coast** Flora, fauna and some stunning natural features combine to make this one of New Zealand's most photogenic locations. **See p.757**
* **Curio Bay** See Hectors dolphins surf in the waves, a petrified forest and a yellow-eyed penguin colony. **See p.763**
* **Ulva Island** Not so much bird watching as bird meeting – when you step into the bush, they come to greet you. **See p.780**
* **Kiwi-spotting** Off Stewart Island, in or around Mason Bay, you'll find one of the best opportunities on the South Island to see these rare birds in the wild. **See p.782**

Dunedin to Stewart Island

The southeastern corner of the South Island contains some of the least-visited parts of New Zealand, yet, hidden away here are a couple of real gems. The first is the darkly attractive city of **Dunedin**, lying 400km south of Christchurch on SH1. Once the commercial and cultural centre of the country, this harbourside city was made prosperous by the discovery of **gold** in the craggy mountains of Otago's hinterland in 1861. Today Dunedin is New Zealand's fourth-largest city, and still a seat of learning and culture, influenced by its university and strong Scottish tradition. From here down to Stewart Island, local accents are marked by a distinctive Scots "burr", the only true regional variation in the country. Within easy reach of the city is the inviting **Otago Peninsula**, an important wildlife haven where you can observe at close range a variety of marine life and seabirds, including penguins and even rarer albatross. South of Dunedin stretches the second highlight, the wild **Catlins Coast**, a large protected reserve reaching towards New Zealand's southernmost city of Invercargill. This is a magical, virtually forgotten region, home to several rare species and offering dramatically varied scenery, from hills covered with dense native forest to a shoreline vigorously indented with rocky bays, long sweeps of sand and unusual geological formations.

On the South Island's southern tip and bordered by rich pastureland lies **Invercargill**. Servicing Southland's prosperous farming communities and New Zealand's export industry, it acts as the springboard to the country's third island, the comparatively small **Stewart Island**. Attracting as yet only limited numbers, the island is a growing tourist destination, its blanket of virgin rainforest offering a tramper's paradise. Others come for the abundant birdlife, particularly on **Ulva Island**, and to unwind in the restful setting, have a drink in New Zealand's southernmost pub, or to spot kiwi in the wild, on the only organized trip of its kind in the world.

Generally, the best time to visit the region is during the **summer** months (Oct–April), when you're most likely to enjoy warm, though changeable, weather, with mid-summer temperatures averaging around 19°C in Dunedin. You'll also catch the best of the wildlife, coinciding with the breeding season of many species. Kiwis from more northern parts take great delight in condemning the **climate** of the southern South Island, describing a permanently harsh, cold and rain-lashed landscape – but this is an exaggeration. It's true, though, that the further south you go, the wetter it gets. The Catlins and Invercargill get their highest rainfall in the spring (Sept–Oct), while Stewart Island has showers most days in between bursts of sunshine.

Getting around is a straightforward business, with regular bus services linking all the major towns as well as crossing the island to Queenstown and the West Coast. Stewart Island is served by ferries and planes from Invercargill.

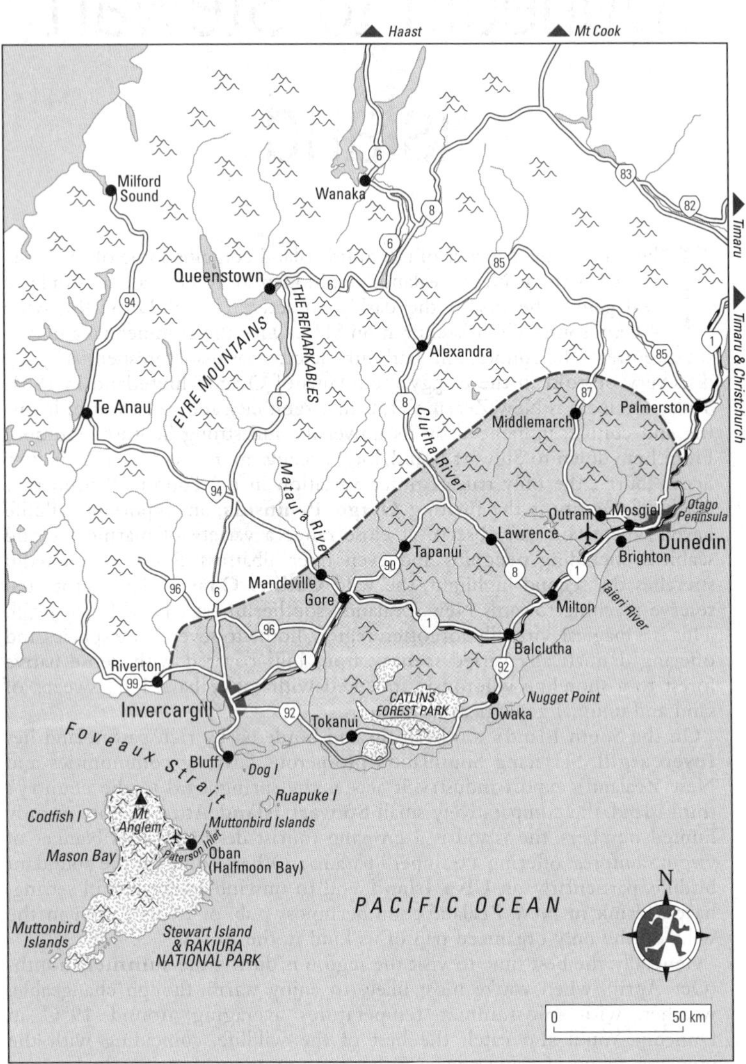

To do the region justice you need to ease into the slower pace of life, allowing a minimum of three days for Dunedin and the Otago Peninsula, two or more days in the Catlins and at least a couple on Stewart Island.

Dunedin

If any city were the living embodiment of a black-and-white Bergman film then it would be **DUNEDIN**, with many Gothic-Revival buildings and imposing, relatively closely packed villas climbing its numerous slopes. On a lighter note it is manageable in size despite the hills, blessed with numerous parks and gardens, a temperate, if changeable, climate, and pleasant beaches. Known as the "Edinburgh of the South", its name is a Gaelic translation of its Scottish counterpart, and it shares the same street and suburb names. Despite a compact city centre, Dunedin's official boundaries stretch far beyond its confining hills to accommodate a total population of around 120,000.

The city is home to **Otago University**, the first such institution in New Zealand, founded in 1871 and still occupying a substantial area near the city centre. The presence of eighteen thousand students contributes to a lively **arts scene**, helping to consolidate Dunedin's long-held reputation as a cultural and intellectual centre, but also contributes to the slightly tatty nature of certain areas where there are concentrations of student housing.

To see the city at its busiest, visit during term time (mid-Feb to mid-June & July–Nov) when the **nightlife**, in particular, takes off, with students packing the bars, pubs and clubs, which foster Dunedin's thriving local music scene, known as the "Dunedin Sound". There are also a number of **festivals** during the year, including two internationally recognized film festivals (April & July); The Great New Zealand Craft Show (the country's largest professional show of its kind; late Sept to early Oct); the two-week-long Dunedin Festival, celebrating the region (February); and Scottish Week, commemorating the city's cultural roots (March). Springtime sees Dunedin ablaze with colour as the myriad rhododendrons for which it is famous burst into bloom, duly celebrated by **Rhododendron Week**, a moveable visual feast dependent upon the weather (late Oct to early Nov).

Dunedin's **architecture** is another defining characteristic, dating from the city's foundation in 1848 and, in particular, the boom years of the 1860s gold rush. Its streets brim with elegant and carefully preserved Victorian and Edwardian buildings: mansions and villas (many with whimsical, sometimes foreboding towers and turrets), rows of terraced houses, churches with spires, an ornate cathedral and huge neo-Gothic piles. A variety of local stone was used in the construction, ranging from bluestone (a hard, dark volcanic stone quarried near the city) to a pleasing creamy limestone originating in the coastal Oamaru to the north.

The jewel in Dunedin's crown, though, is its long sheltered **harbour**, site of two working ports and home to a rich variety of wildlife. Dunedin sits at the head of the bay, all but encircled by rugged hills, formed ten million years ago by a series of volcanic eruptions. Jutting out from the city to form one of the harbour's shores is the **Otago Peninsula** (see p.747), which most people visit on a day-trip from the city to view the rare and varied wildlife at its tip and take in a few sights along the way. Halfway along the bay's opposite shore lies the small and once-thriving **Port Chalmers** (see p.754), which still attracts a few container ships and supports a tiny community, and is worth a quick look. Dunedin is also a major jumping-off point for the Otago Goldfields, which lie on the way to Queenstown but also make a good day-trip out from the city.

Some history

By the time the first wave of Scottish immigrants arrived at the site of modern-day Dunedin, the area was rich in Maori history. Since about 1100 AD, **Maori** had fished the rich coastal waters of nearby bays, travelling inland to hunt moa, duck and freshwater fish, and initiating trade in *pounamu* (greenstone) with other Maori based further north. Eventually they formed a settlement on both sides of the harbour, calling it Otakou (pronounced "O-tar-go") and naming the headland at the harbour's entrance after their great chieftain, Taiaroa. Today a well-developed *marae* occupies the Otakou site. Towards the end of the eighteenth century, the area became the scene of a prolonged feud between three related chiefs of the Ngai Tahu tribe, and a general state of conflict lasted many years. The carnage caused by warfare, however, was nothing compared with the havoc wreaked by European diseases brought by the early nineteenth-century **whalers and sealers**, attracted to the only safe anchorage along this stretch of coast. By 1848 the depredations of measles and influenza had reduced the once-considerable Otakou population to a meagre 110. In the end, intermarriage between Maori and whalers bolstered numbers and formed a resilient cultural mix.

In 1840, the New Zealand Company selected the Dunedin area as a suitable site for a planned **Scottish settlement**. Despite the Treaty of Waitangi (designed to preserve the Crown's right of pre-emption), the company was allowed to deal directly with Maori, who were finally persuaded to sell 1620 square kilometres for a meagre sum. On July 31, 1844, the deed was signed on the site of what later became Port Chalmers. In 1848, the migrant ships *John Wickliffe* and *Philip Laing* arrived, led by Captain William Cargill and the Reverend Thomas Burns, nephew of the Scottish poet, Robert Burns. Most of the 344 passengers were staunch Scots Presbyterians, but they were soon in the minority, as the following year another seven hundred people joined them, among them English and Irish. However, Scottish fervour was sufficient to stamp a distinct character on the growing town, bequeathing some fine churches, as well as a passionate enthusiasm for education.

In 1861, a lone Australian prospector discovered **gold** at a creek near modern-day Lawrence, about 100km from Dunedin, in Central Otago. Within three months, gold fever struck and diggers poured in from Australia. As a port of entry, Dunedin suddenly found itself at the forefront of an international gold rush and, requiring a larger port area, it expanded onto land reclaimed from the tidal flats. In six months, its population doubled in size; within three years it trebled again, becoming New Zealand's most important city. This was Dunedin's period of unbridled construction, with the new-found wealth used to establish the university, Otago Boys' High School as well as Otago Girls' High School. By the 1870s gold mania had largely subsided, but Otago sustained economic primacy through **shipping**, railway development and the efforts of thousands who stayed on to farm. Decline set in during the early years of the twentieth century, when the opening of the Panama Canal in 1914 re-routed British and European trans-Atlantic shipping away from the great colonial-era port of Otago Harbour to the country's northernmost city, Auckland. In the 1980s, however, the improvement in world gold prices and the development of equipment enabling large-scale recovery of gold from low-yielding soils re-established **mining** in the hinterland. Today you can visit massive mining operations, including the one at Macraes, an hour's drive from Dunedin (see p.919).

Arrival, information and city transport

Dunedin **airport** is served by domestic flights from Auckland, Christchurch, Queenstown, Invercargill and Wellington, as well as international flights direct from Sydney, Melbourne and Brisbane. The airport is located 30km south of the city centre, just off SH1. Several shuttle bus companies operate from the airport to the city centre (from $10), meeting each flight and dropping off at accommodation along the way. A taxi ride to the city centre will set you back about $40. You can change money at the airport **bureau de change** in the main terminal building (only open for international flights), which offers the same rate of exchange as the city's banks. Note that no bureaux de change are open in Dunedin at weekends, but the visitor centre can change money for you with a five percent commission.

The **train station** (ⓣ03/477 4449) is centrally located in Anzac Square, off Stuart Street, a major stop on the Tranz Scenic Southerner Christchurch–Invercargill route. All long-distance bus and shuttle bookings are made here. The long-distance InterCity **buses** drop off in the city centre at 205 St Andrew St. Two of the South Island's shuttle bus companies – Atomic and Southern Link – terminate at the train station; South Island Connections terminate at the visitor centre (see below).

Information

You can't miss Dunedin's **visitor centre** (mid-Dec to mid-April Mon–Fri 8.30am–6pm, Sat & Sun 9am–6pm; mid-April to mid-Dec Mon–Fri 8.30am–5pm, Sat & Sun 9am–5pm; ⓣ03/474 3300, ⓦwww.CityofDunedin.com & ⓦwww.dunedinNZ.com) in the grand stone Municipal Chambers that dominate the Octagon, an eight-sided grassland area at the centre of the city. The extremely helpful and well informed staff will book transport (InterCity, train and ferry; for long-distance shuttles book at the train station), accommodation and tours, and the centre is well stocked with leaflets and maps, including the excellent free *A–Z Central Otago* and *Southland* booklets which list most things of interest in the area, and the *Walk the City* leaflet ($2.50) which details points of interest along a gentle stroll round central Dunedin. The **DOC** office is at 77 Lower Stuart St, first floor (Mon–Fri 8.30am–5pm; ⓣ03/477 0677), and has plenty of information on Otago, Fiordland and Mount Aspiring. They also sell hut tickets and passes for the Routeburn and Milford tracks. For free **internet access** try the *Arc Cyber Café*, 135 High St (daily until late; see p.742).

For entertainment and events **listings**, the most comprehensive source is the free weekly publication *Fink*, a complete guide to music, exhibitions and movies in Dunedin (see also ⓦwww.fink.net.nz). Chiefly aimed at students, it's available all over the city. The parochial *Otago Daily Times* also has a listings section, best in the Friday and Saturday editions.

City transport

A number of different companies operate an efficient **bus** system throughout the city – you can pick up free timetables and route maps from the Dunedin City Council on the ground floor of the Civic Centre on the corner of the Octagon and George Street. Most services run Monday to Saturday and on public holidays (except Christmas Day, Good Friday and Easter Sunday), from around 7.30am to 11pm, and some services operate on Sunday from 1pm to 5pm. Buses are identified by their route, for example, Octagon–Maori Hill, rather than by numbers. **Fares** are calculated according to the number of zones crossed, with a single one-zone ticket costing $1.10, increasing by about 50¢ per extra zone; the central city is all contained within zone one, and maps of the other zones are available from the info centre. Concessions are available at off-peak times on inner-city routes. If you're staying a couple of days or longer, it's a good idea to buy a **Multi-trip Ticket**, which gives ten or more journeys for a ten-percent discount. Most bus drivers sell these tickets direct or you can get them during business hours from the City Council in the Civic Centre.

There are several **taxi** ranks in the city centre (see p.746 for locations and details of taxi companies). If you're **driving**, note that strict parking restrictions are enforced in the city centre with meter parking operating Monday to Saturday (see p.746 for details of car parks). A one-way system operates through the inner city, connecting the northern and southern sections of SH1 and affecting Cumberland, Castle, Great King and Crawford streets.

Accommodation

There's a broad choice of accommodation in Dunedin, most of it in or near the city centre. The **hotels** are located in the heart of town, but, with a couple of exceptions, are bland affairs designed to attract business people. Several **motels** line George Street, with others dotted around the city, while the best **B&Bs and homestays** are in the hillside suburbs 2–5km from the centre. The handful of **hostels** are generally good value and closer to the city centre. The three well equipped **campsites** are no more than three kilometres out of town and two are on bus routes. As in all New Zealand's major cities, **booking ahead** in summer is advisable, wherever you're staying. A small but varied amount of accommodation is also available on the **Otago Peninsula** (see p.747), should you prefer to stay there and travel in to the city.

Hotels

Bentley's 137 St Andrew St ⓣ03/477 0572, ⓔbentleys.hotel@xtra.co.nz. A fairly luxurious, modern place, right in the heart of the city, offering double rooms, a couple of studios and a family unit, all with private facilities. There's an airy restaurant, a bar and café on the premises, while next door is the lively *Rosie O'Grady's* bar, owned by the hotel. ❺–❼

Leviathan 24 Queens Gardens, cnr Cumberland St ⓣ03/477 3160, ⓔleviathan@xtra.co.nz. The most atmospheric hotel in Dunedin, and the best value. Built in 1884, it's grand yet comfortable in the style of a classic railway hotel, and just a short stroll from both the Octagon and the train station. Accommodation ranges from spacious suites and self-contained studios to standard and budget en-suites. There are also a bar and high-quality, moderately priced licensed restaurant, plus a courtesy bus. Off-street parking. ❹–❻

Manor Inn 310 Princes St ⓣ03/477 1455, ⓔmanorinns@xtra.co.nz. A corporate crowd frequents this central but characterless hotel, where thoroughly modern rooms hide behind an ornate nineteenth-century facade. On-site café, two restaurants and a fully-equipped gym. ❺–❻

Southern Cross cnr Princes St & High St ⓣ03/477 0752, ⓔreservations@southern-crosshotel.co.nz. Huge hotel in the heart of the business district, five minutes' walk from the Octagon. Three fully licensed restaurants and two bars, a fitness centre, Sky TV and off-street parking. ❻–❽

Motels

Allan Court 590 George St, cnr Union St ⓣ03/477 7526, ⓔallan.court@earthlight.co.nz. Central, modern, upmarket and comfortable, with cookers in all units and a choice of breakfasts for an extra charge. In-house video and guest laundry. ❺

Cargills Motor Inn 678 George St, near cnr St David St ⓣ03/477 7983, ⓔcargills@es.co.nz. Adjacent to the business district and university, this stylish place offers a peaceful garden setting and a variety of well-appointed rooms equipped with minibars and fridges. The on-site licensed *Garden Restaurant* serves Kiwi and international cuisine. ❺–❼

Chequers 119 Musselburgh Rise ⓣ & ⓕ03/455 0778. Good-value motel in quiet surroundings, five minutes' drive from the centre and close to the peninsula. Its large units are ideally suited to families and there's a playground on the premises. ❸

858 George St Motel 858 George St ⓣ & ⓕ03/474 0047, ⓔreservations@858georgestreetmotel.co.nz. Unusual, new and well-executed design by Dunedin architects, based on Victorian houses divided into big luxurious units. ❺–❻

Farrys 575 George St ⓣ03/477 9333, ⓔfarrysmotel.co.nz. An excellent family motel next to the main shopping area offering one-, two- and three-bedroom units, all fully self-contained, plus a free laundry and small playground.❺–❻

97 Motel 97 Moray Place ⓣ03/477 2050, reservations only ⓣ0800/909 797, ⓔbookings@97motel.co.nz The best-located, friendliest motel in town, with spacious, gleaming units, each equipped with a microwave. ❺

Sahara 619 George St ⓣ03/477 6662, ⓕ479 2551. A motel section round the back of the guesthouse of the same name (see below), with ten standard self-contained units.❹

B&Bs and homestays

Albatross Inn 770 George St ⓣ & ⓕ03/477 2727, ⓔalbatross.inn@xtra.co.nz. Extremely hospitable Edwardian house of character close to the university and city centre, where rooms are en suite or have private bathrooms; some have their own kitchenette and dining facilities. ❺–❻

Fletcher Lodge 276 High St ⓣ0800/843 563, ⓔlodge@es.co.nz. Extremely luxurious and central B&B in a calm English baronial-style home built in 1924 for a leading Kiwi industrialist, Sir James Fletcher, with an established secluded garden. The living room is richly oak-panelled, everything is kept spotless and all rooms are en suite. There's also off-street parking and a laundry service. ❻–❼

Gowrie House 7 Gowry Place, Roslyn ⓣ03/477 2103, ⓕ477 9169. Excellent rural and city views from this small, cosy, turn-of-the-century house set on a hill five minutes' drive from the centre and on the Octagon to Maori Hill/Prospect Park bus route. Two double rooms, both light and airy with big windows and shared facilities. ❺

Hulmes Court 52 Tennyson St ⓣ0800/448 563, ⓔnormwood@earthlight.co.nz. One of the oldest homes in Dunedin, a big rambling affair built in the 1860s with plenty of character, just off the Octagon yet quiet. Rooms are big and individually themed, two of them en suite and two sharing bathrooms; off-street parking, free bus and rail pick-up, free mountain bikes, free email link. ❹–❺

Lisburn House 15 Lisburn Ave, Caversham ⓣ03/455 8888, ⓔstay@lisburnhouse.co.nz. Luxurious and beautifully preserved Victorian-Gothic house run by very friendly hosts, in a suburb ten minutes' drive south of the city. Each of the three distinctly styled and spacious rooms has a four-poster bed, fine linen, fresh flowers and a private bathroom. Not suitable for children. ❻–❼

Magnolia House 18 Grendon St, Maori Hill ⓣ & ⓕ03/467 5999. A spacious Victorian villa, set in a large garden in the leafy suburb of Maori Hill, 2km north of the Octagon (courtesy car available). Three well appointed doubles with shared facilities, and two house cats. ❹–❺

Sahara Guesthouse & Motel 619 George St ⓣ03/477 6662, ⓕ479 2551. Spacious, central 1863 guesthouse where most rooms have shared facilities. TV lounge, off-street parking. ❹

Hostels

Adventurer Backpacker Lodge 37 Dowling St ⓣ & ⓕ03/477 7367 & ⓣ0800/422 257. A convivial, newish hostel in the heart of the city, with dorms ranging from 2-bed to 9-bed and a few singles, doubles and twins; off-street parking. Dorms ❶, rooms ❷

Chalet Backpackers 296 High St ⓣ03/479 2075 & 0800/242 538, ⓕ479 2050. Central, comfortable hostel with a great atmosphere and excellent kitchen and dining facilities. Four-bed dorms, plus single and double rooms. Pool room, free bikes and free pick-up. Dorms ❶, rooms ❷

Elm Lodge 74 Elm Row ⓣ03/477 1872, bookings ⓣ0800/356 563, ⓔELM_WILDLIFE_TOUR@compuserve.com. An airy, clean, 1930s house on a hill near the centre. The dorms are 4- or 6-bed. Free linen and pick-up service. Dorms ❶, rooms ❷

Manor House 28 Manor Place ⓣ03/477 0484 &

0800/477 0484, Ⓔ mail@manorhousebackpackers.co.nz. Well-equipped and beautifully kept colonial house on a hill fifteen minutes' walk south of the Octagon. Dorms are 4-bed to 8-bed; free pick-up service. Dorms ❶, rooms ❷

Stafford Gables YHA 71 Stafford St Ⓣ & Ⓕ 03/474 1919, Ⓔ yhadndn@yha.org.nz. Characterful, if a bit run down, YHA in a large, turn-of-the-century homestead ten minutes' walk from the Octagon. The best bit is the roof garden with excellent views over the city. The dorms are 3- to 7-bed, double and twin rooms are generally large, some doubles come with balconies and there are also family rooms.Office hours from 8am–2pm and 4–9pm. Free linen. Dorms ❶, rooms ❷–❸

Campsites and motorparks

Aaron Lodge Motel & Holiday Park 162 Kaikorai Valley Rd Ⓣ 03/476 4725, Ⓔ aaron.lodge@xtra.co.nz. A sheltered, fairly spacious and well-tended site, in hills 2.5km west of the city centre. Facilities include a spa pool and playground. Tent sites $11, powered sites $12, cabins ❷, flats ❸, motel units ❹.

Dunedin Holiday Park 41 Victoria Rd Ⓣ & Ⓕ 03/455 4690. Lying alongside St Kilda Beach, this well-appointed park is five minutes' drive from the city centre and served by the Octagon to St Kilda bus. Standard and more comfortable en-suite cabins. There's a seven-day camp store. Tent sites $9, powered sites $12, cabins ❷, en-suite units ❸, tourist flats ❸

Leith Valley Touring Park 103 Malvern St Ⓣ 03/467 9936, Ⓕ 467 9502. A small, pleasant campsite beside a creek at the foot of bush-clad hills, 3km north from the centre. The site is served by the Octagon to Garden Village bus on weekdays and there's a 24hr grocery within walking distance. Tent sites $10, on-site vans ❷, flats ❸

The City

Day or night, the hub of Dunedin's activity is the **Octagon**, a green, tree-filled space in the heart of the city, bordered by historic buildings and circled by Moray Place. Restaurants, offices, banks, bars, clubs and most of the sights are concentrated around it, and the **shopping district** stretches immediately north and south along George Street and Princes Street. Further north lies the **university area** and the expanse of the **Botanic Garden**. To the east is the head of **Otago Harbour**, a sheltered inlet 22km long and no wider than a river in places. The waters are shared by windsurfers, yachts and sightseeing boats, and occasionally dolphins and whales. Two sandy **beaches** lie a short bus ride south from the city centre in the suburbs of St Clair and St Kilda. For an overview of the city, head for the **lookout points** on the hills around Dunedin (see box on p.736) or take a double-decker **bus tour** with Citisights (Ⓣ 03/477 5577; 1hr 30min; around $15), which departs from the visitor centre at 10am and 3.30pm daily.

The Octagon

The **Octagon** was originally laid out in 1846 by Charles Kettle, the Chief Surveyor of the New Zealand Company, who subsequently died in a typhoid epidemic that swept the city during the 1862 gold rush. Today, following a substantial face-lift in the 1980s, it's a mixture of modern and beautifully preserved buildings overlooking grassland and trees, presided over by a statue of Robert Burns, a potent symbol of Dunedin's Scottish origins and literary associations. Every Friday (10am–4pm; also Sat Oct–April & daily in Dec; closed Dec 26–Jan10), the area spills over with **market** stalls selling locally made crafts, such as stained glass, pottery, woodwork and jewellery, while live bands provide free entertainment.

Dominating the Octagon is the **Municipal Chambers** building, a grand, classical structure with a clock tower, which originally opened in 1880. Constructed from limestone dramatically offset against volcanic bluestone, it's a fine example of a recurring combination of materials that's seen throughout

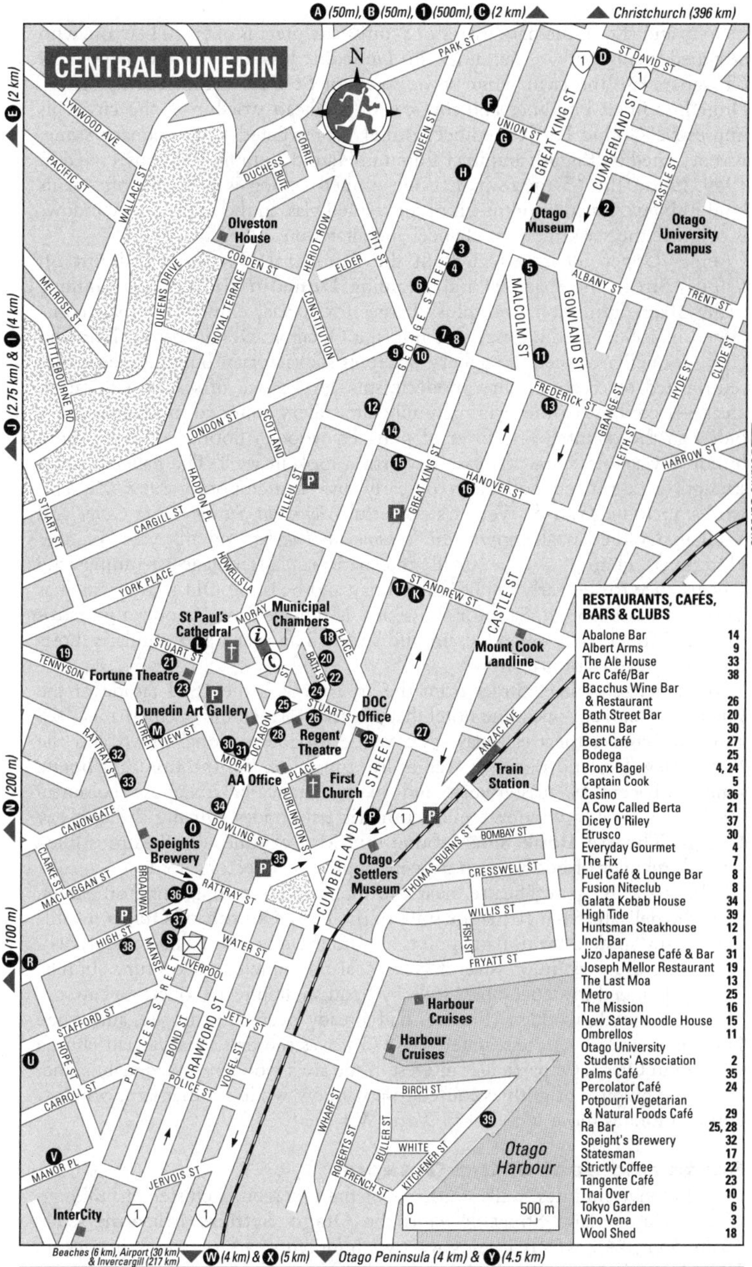

CENTRAL DUNEDIN

RESTAURANTS, CAFÉS, BARS & CLUBS

Name	No.
Abalone Bar	14
Albert Arms	9
The Ale House	33
Arc Café/Bar	38
Bacchus Wine Bar & Restaurant	26
Bath Street Bar	20
Bennu Bar	30
Best Café	27
Bodega	25
Bronx Bagel	4, 24
Captain Cook	5
Casino	36
A Cow Called Berta	21
Dicey O'Riley	37
Etrusco	30
Everyday Gourmet	4
The Fix	7
Fuel Café & Lounge Bar	8
Fusion Niteclub	8
Galata Kebab House	34
High Tide	39
Huntsman Steakhouse	12
Inch Bar	1
Jizo Japanese Café & Bar	31
Joseph Mellor Restaurant	19
The Last Moa	13
Metro	25
The Mission	16
New Satay Noodle House	15
Ombrellos	11
Otago University Students' Association	2
Palms Café	35
Percolator Café	24
Potpourri Vegetarian & Natural Foods Café	29
Ra Bar	25, 28
Speight's Brewery	32
Statesman	17
Strictly Coffee	22
Tangente Café	23
Thai Over	10
Tokyo Garden	6
Vino Vena	3
Wool Shed	18

Beaches (6 km), Airport (30 km) & Invercargill (217 km) W (4 km) & X (5 km) Otago Peninsula (4 km) & Y (4.5 km)

ACCOMMODATION

Name	Key
858 George St Motel	A
97 Motel	L
Aaron Lodge Motel & Holiday Park	I
Adventurer Backpacker Lodge	O
Albatross Inn	B
Allan Court	G
Bentley's	K
Cargills Motor Inn	D
Chalet Backpackers	T
Chequers	Y
Dunedin Holiday Park	W
Elm Lodge	N
Farrys	H
Fletcher Lodge	R
Gowrie House	J
Hulmes Court	M
Leith Valley Touring Park	C
Leviathan	P
Lisburn House	X
Magnolia House	E
Manor House	V
Manor Inn	S
Sahara Guesthouse & Motel	F
Southern Cross	Q
Stafford Gables YHA	U

the city and also of the handiwork of Scottish architect Robert A. Lawson, who designed many public buildings in Dunedin. Just behind the Municipal Chambers rise the twin white stone spires of **St Paul's Cathedral**, one of Dunedin's finest buildings and the seat of Anglican worship in the city. This impressive Gothic Revival edifice, entirely constructed from Oamaru stone, was designed by English architect Edmund Harold Sedding and consecrated in 1919. Inside, the 65-metre-high stone-vaulted ceiling is the only one of its kind in New Zealand, and much of the stained glass in the impressive windows is original; the stark modern chancel and altar were added in 1971.

Across Upper Stuart Street from the Municipal Chambers and just off Princes Street, the spacious and gleaming **Dunedin Public Art Gallery** (daily 10am–5pm; donation, plus charges for special exhibitions) was completed in 1996, breathing new life into the Octagon. Designed by a Dunedin City Council architect, the gallery occupies six Victorian buildings, elegantly refurbished to create an airy, modern, split-level space of several exhibition areas – a contrast to the original public art gallery, founded in 1884 and the oldest in the country. The foyer of polished wooden floors, ironwork and a hundred-year-old spiral staircase is worth a look in itself. The gallery's main strength is a rotated collection of early and contemporary New Zealand works, including Van der Velden's powerful *Mountain Stream Otira Gorge* and William Goldie's well-known *All 'e same t'e Pakeha*, and many by Frances Hodgkins. There's also a small international assemblage spanning the Renaissance to the early twentieth century and boasting Old Masters such as Turner, Gainsborough, Salvator Rosa, and Machiavelli; and modern maestros such as Monet, Rousseau, Derain and Tissot. The space also regularly hosts temporary international shows.

South, across Princes Street from the art gallery, is the 1874 facade of the **Regent Theatre**, a one-time hotel that was transformed into a cinema in 1928 and, later, into a theatre. Today it's a venue for international shows and the Royal New Zealand Ballet, as well as live music (see p.745). Inside, elaborate nineteenth-century plasterwork and marble staircases juxtapose colourful 1920s stained-glass windows and geometric balustrades. During the one-day **Regent Theatre Book Sale** (around mid-May or June) the theatre is filled with all manner of books, from 50-cent copies to collector's items.

Behind the Regent Theatre, near the intersection with Burlington Street, soars the delicate, 54-metre stone spire of the **First Church of Otago**, a landmark easily spotted from many points around the city. The edifice, widely recognized as the most impressive of New Zealand's nineteenth-century churches, was designed in neo-Gothic style by Scottish architect Robert A. Lawson. Two other small, wooden churches had already occupied this site, and when Lawson's version was consecrated in 1873 it was the first Presbyterian church to open in Otago. Of particular interest inside are a wooden gabled ceiling and, above the pulpit, a brightly coloured rose window, while another large window commemorates those who fell in World War I.

South and east of the Octagon

Less than five minutes' walk southeast of the Octagon, a cluster of buildings at 220 Cumberland Street contains the **Otago Settlers Museum** (daily 10am–5pm; $4), which catalogues two hundred years of social history in Dunedin and Otago, drawing from an exhaustive collection of artefacts, paintings and photographs. Highlights include the chance to sit on a penny-farthing; a restored double-ended Fairlie steam engine; and the "Portrait Gallery", whose walls are plastered with black-and-white photographs of the region's early settler families. Also worth a look is "Window on a Chinese Past", providing an insight into the lives of the legions of Chinese who left their families behind to seek a fortune in the Otago Goldfields, many of them staying for years.

A stone's throw away from the museum, near the junction of Castle Street and Anzac Avenue, **Dunedin Railway Station** is an imposing building, faced with pale Oamaru stone. Opened in 1906, the station was designed by George A.Troup, and constructed on reclaimed swampland, which made it an extraordinary feat of engineering for its day. The exterior, complete with towers, turrets and minarets, is grand enough, but the real surprise lies inside. The main foyer, which has been preserved in its original state, gleams with majolica wall tiles made especially for New Zealand Rail by Royal Doulton, in gentle tones of green, yellow and cream. A fine, classical, china frieze of cherubs and foliage encircles the room, and elaborate tilework decorates the ticket booths. The mosaic floor celebrates the steam engine and consists of more than 700,000 tiny squares of Royal Doulton porcelain. Upstairs on the balcony, a stained-glass window at each end depicts an approaching train, whose headlights gleam, no matter from which angle you look at them. Also on the first floor of the building is the **New Zealand Sports Hall of Fame** (daily 10am–4pm; $5), a collection of memorabilia relating to those New Zealand sports people lucky or talented enough to have been inducted, and intended purely for the committed sports anorak.

Further east beyond the train station is the **Hocken Library** at 90 Anzac Ave, near the junction with Parry Street (Mon–Fri 9.30am–5pm, Tues also 6–9pm, Sat 9am–noon; free), an extensive university research library that opened on campus in 1910, before moving here in the late 1990s. Its impressive collection of books, manuscripts, paintings and photographs relating to New Zealand and the Pacific was originally assembled by Dr Thomas Morland Hocken, a Dunedin physician and one of the country's first historians. Details of exhibitions held in the library gallery (Mon–Fri 9.30am–5pm, Sat 9am–noon, Sun check on ⓣ03/479 1100 ext 8873; free) are regularly advertised in the *Otago Daily Times*.

After an injection of more than one million dollars to jazz it up, the **Speights Brewery**, one of New Zealand's oldest and smallest breweries, at 200 Rattray St (tours booked on ⓣ03/477 7697; Mon–Sat at 10am, 11.45am, 2pm & Mon–Thurs 7pm as well; about 1hr; $12), is well worth a look. The entry is near the drinking fountain – whose sweet-tasting water is pumped directly from the brewery bore, the same as that used to brew the beer and popular with locals who fill up water bottles and containers here – beneath the tall, brick chimney stack topped by a barrel crafted from stone and visible from across the city. The tour guides take you on an essentially light-hearted journey through the alchemy of traditional brewing, and there's the chance to sniff some of the raw materials, watch some mildly giggle-inducing re-runs of the famous *Southern Man* ad campaign, hear an awful, especially written, *Southern Man* song and last, but by no means least, the chance to sample four of the ales in wee glasses.

North of the Octagon

A few minutes' walk north of the Octagon, at 419 Great King St, is the recently rejuvenated and much improved **Otago Museum** (daily 10am–5pm; $5, guided tour $10; and a short lecture presentation on a specified subject at 2pm each day), an extensive (it has almost doubled in size) and entertaining museum on three floors. You can easily spend half a day here, ambling through the

Walks in the Dunedin area

From the city, a variety of walks (1–3hr) lead up to and along the skyline ridges surrounding the harbour, giving spectacular views of tussock-covered hilltops, fine bushland, river valleys and beaches. The DOC publishes factsheets describing each walk, for $1 (or $5 for a folder on the Dunedin area) from the DOC office or visitor centre. Dunedin's weather is notoriously changeable, so equip yourself with warm clothing and wet-weather gear, just in case.

If these suggestions whet your appetite for tramping, see "Walks on Otago Peninsula" (p.752) for more routes in the vicinity.

Signal Hill

A fairly gentle walk up **Signal Hill** (6km return; 1hr ascent, 30min descent), a scenic reserve just north of the Botanic Garden, culminates in a magnificent view over Dunedin, the upper harbour and the sea. At the top (393m), the Centennial Lookout sports two powerful bronze figures symbolizing the past and the future, a commemoration of one hundred years of British sovereignty (1840–1940) following the signing of the Treaty of Waitangi. Embedded in the podium is a tribute to Scotland: a chunk of the rock upon which Edinburgh Castle was built.

To reach the hill from the city centre, follow Great King Street to the northern edge of the Botanic Garden and turn right along Opoho Road for 1.25km. Signal Hill Road, which is the fourth on the left, leads to the top of the hill. The Opoho bus from outside the Savoy Building in Princes Street will take you up and over Signal Hill, and there's a stop at the top.

Tunnel Beach

One of the best walks – **Tunnel Beach** (1.5km return; 1hr) – is also the shortest and least strenuous, yet offers breathtaking coastal views of creamy sandstone cliffs and islets weathered into curious shapes. Untouched by lava flows, it gives a glimpse of Dunedin's geology before the volcanic eruptions that changed the landscape. A steep path drops through bush and pasture to impressive sandstone clifftops and a magnificent sea-arch. Additionally, at low tide, you can walk down the steps of a short tunnel carved through the cliff in the 1870s, which leads to a pretty sandy

special exhibitions gallery (containing travelling shows and one-off displays), the fascinating Southern Land, Southern People gallery, displays of Maori and Pacific Islands anthropology, New Zealand natural history, archeological finds, decorative arts from all over the world – including a gently swaying perspex slab, by a local artist, that dangles between the balconies of the central atrium – and, most amusing of all, the regressive Animal Attic, a deeply Victorian amalgamation of macabre skeletons and stuffed beasts literally strung up among the skylights where some wit has secreted a monkey and a couple of chickens, and painted the chook (chicken) droppings on the rafters beneath them. On level one is also Discovery World, an interactive science museum-within-a-musuem that will cost you an extra $6 – money not worth spending unless you're aged between six and eleven. You can round off a visit by taking advantage of an indoor picnic area, or munch out at the musuem café.

Olveston

At 42 Royal Terrace, ten minutes' walk northwest of the Octagon, lies Dunedin's showpiece historic home of **Olveston** (booking essential ⓣ03/477 3320; guided tours only: daily 9.30am, 10.45am, noon, 1.30pm, 2.45pm & 4pm; 1hr; $12). Contained within the walls of this fine Edwardian house is a

beach on the other side with sandstone buttresses towering above – a pleasant spot for a picnic. The walk crosses private land and is closed during the lambing season (Sept & Oct).

The route starts from the car park at the end of Green Island Bush Road, some 16km from the centre on the city's southwestern outskirts. The Corstophine bus from the corner of the Octagon and Princes Street will drop you within a kilometre of the start of the walk – get off at Stanhope Crescent.

Mount Cargill

Unrivalled panoramic views of the Dunedin area are the reward for making it to the windy summit of **Mount Cargill** on the city's northeastern outskirts. There are in fact three peaks – Cargill, Holmes and Zion – which to the Maori represent the petrified head and feet of an early Otakou princess. European settlers named the dominant peak after their lay leader, Captain William Cargill.

You can either drive to the summit car park – twenty-minutes from the city centre along Pine Hill Road – and just tackle the network of easy tracks around the summit area, or walk the whole track from Bethunes Gully picnic ground, about 7.5km northeast of the Botanic Gardens (8km return; 3hr). This skirts the mountain's northern flank and climbs steadily to 550m before sidling around to the saddle and onto the summit. To reach the picnic ground by bus catch the Normanby bus from outside the Savoy Building in Princes Street and get off at the junction of North Road and Norwood Street. From here it's about 2km northeast along Norwood Street to the picnic ground.

On the slopes of nearby Mount Holmes, an intriguing ancient rock formation called the **Organ Pipes** can be reached on foot, either from the Mount Cargill summit – following the peaks and saddles of Cargill, Buttar and Holmes (3km return; 90min) – or from a steep track starting at the car park on Old Mount Cargill Road (3km return; 1hr), on the mountain's eastern side (not accessible by public transport). Either way, the route passes through colourful remnant forest to a series of rock columns, formed about ten million years ago by molten lava that cracked as it cooled.

treasure trove of art and exquisite antiques collected from all over the world by one family and left just as they were when the last of the lineage passed away. The collection was gradually assembled by a wealthy, Jewish mercantile family, the Theomins, who lived here from 1906 and were passionately interested in travel, art and music. On her death in 1966, the longest-surviving member of the family, Dorothy, bequeathed the house and its contents to the City of Dunedin.

Built in 1904–1906 for David Theomin and his wife, Marie, the Jacobean-style house itself is reminiscent of the English Arts and Crafts Movement. London architect Sir Ernest George filled the house with extraordinary decorative detail, incorporating such features as polished wooden floors, stained-glass windows, wood panelling, fine brass fittings and stairways leading to mezzanine galleries. A particularly striking piece of craftsmanship is the oak staircase in the Grand Hall, made in England and constructed without the use of nails. The house was also a masterpiece of modernity for its time, being among the first to be fitted with the conveniences of central heating, heated towel rails and an in-house telephone system.

The University

Less than ten minutes' walk north of the city centre lies New Zealand's oldest university, founded by Scottish settlers in 1869. Based on the design of Glasgow University, the **University of Otago** quickly expanded into a complex of imposing Gothic bluestone buildings, foremost among them the registry building on Leith Street with its Gothic **clock tower**, an academic icon and one of the most-photographed landmarks in Dunedin. Today the campus covers several blocks between Albany and Dundas streets in one direction, and Cumberland and Clyde streets in the other, and is set in spacious grounds with the Water of Leith, a small river, winding through it. The **Student Enquiries Office** (Mon–Fri 9.30am–4.30pm) in the registry building has simple free campus maps for visitors, and a stroll through the campus from Union Street to Leith Street will take you past the key buildings.

The **Hocken Building**, on the corner of Castle Street and Union Street, once housed the impressive Hocken Library, which opened here in 1910 before moving in the late 1990s to Anzac Avenue.

The Botanic Garden

Established in 1863 at the far northern end of the inner city, the well-tended **Dunedin Botanic Garden** (sunrise–sunset; free) lies at the foot of Signal Hill. The hilly Upper Garden contains an expansive Rhododendron Dell, where well-established specimens grow among native bush, flowering trees and plants. This is the star attraction during the city's annual **Rhododendron Week** in the third week of October. On the hills there's also an arboretum, a native plant collection and a modern aviary complex, home to native birds such as kea and kaka, as well as exotic birds from all over the world. The flat Lower Garden features exotic trees, Winter Garden conservatories (daily 10am–4pm), an Alpine House (daily 9am–4pm), a rose garden and a well-equipped playground. A volunteer-run information centre (daily 10am–4pm) lies between the tea kiosk and the Winter Garden, stocked with maps and displays on the Botanic Garden. The garden's tea kiosk (daily 9.30am–4.30pm) serves inexpensive snacks and meals. Access to the Lower Gardens car park is from Cumberland Street, while the Upper Gardens car park is on Lovelock Avenue.

Baldwin Street

Dunedin has the dubious honour of containing the steepest street in the world. In the northern part of town, off North Road, **Baldwin Street** has a maximum gradient of 1 in 2.9, an angle of over 38°. You can walk up to the top in about five minutes, but the views aren't anything special. During the annual "Gutbuster" event in mid-February (part of the Dunedin Festival) contestants run to the top and back down again – the current record is around two minutes. Cashing in on the gradient, a shop now resides in the former post office, 282 Great North Rd (daily 8.30am–6pm), just around the corner from the hill and dating back to 1914, where you can buy a much needed drink, a T-shirt or certificate marking your achievement.

Baldwin Street is a short **bus** ride from the city centre: take the Normanby bus from outside the Savoy Building in Princes Street to North Road, which drops you near the Gardens Shopping Centre. Head north along North Road for fifteen minutes; Baldwin Street is the tenth street past the shopping centre.

Dunedin's beaches

Four kilometres south of the city centre, the suburbs of St Kilda and St Clair culminate in a long wild sweep of creamy sand enclosed by two volcanic head-

△ Lonnekers Beach, Stewart Island

lands (served by buses from the corner of the Octagon and Princes Street). **St Clair Beach** is excellent for surfing and is patrolled by lifeguards during the summer. For swimming in calmer waters, there's a large, outdoor, heated saltwater pool beside the rocky point at the western end of the beach (normally Oct–March Mon–Sat 6am–7pm, Sun 8am–7pm, but being renovated at the time of writing, so check with the visitor centre). About halfway along the strip, St Clair merges with **St Kilda Beach**, which is reasonably safe for swimming as long as you keep between the flags; it is also patrolled in summer. At the beach's eastern end, a headland separates St Kilda from the smaller **Tomahawk Beach** (not safe for swimming), often dotted with horses and buggies preparing for trotting races at low tide. The best swimming beach in Otago is only 15km south of Dunedin, at **Brighton Bay** (Brighton bus from New World supermarket in Cumberland Street), a combination of sand and rocky outcrops.

Taieri Gorge Railway

One of the world's most dramatic rail lines and a feat of Victorian engineering, the **Taieri Gorge Railway** stretches 77km from Dunedin inland to the high country of Otago, penetrating rugged mountain scenery that is only accessible by train. Once free of the city and its environs, the track follows the Taieri Gorge, deeply carved into the schist rock. Constructed between 1879 and 1921, the line extended 235km to the old gold town of Cromwell in its heyday, carrying supplies from Dunedin and transporting farm produce, fruit and livestock back to the port and points north. The journey is rewarding at any time of year, from the snow in winter to the searing heat of summer, and rainy days encourage the waterfalls.

Today, as well as offering **day-trips** from the city, the rail line is a good way of heading further inland to the Central Otago Goldfields, or even as far as Queenstown by linking with a bus. Bear in mind, though, that on day-trips the return journey can be rather dull. The train departs from Dunedin Railway Station and you need to book well ahead to be sure of a seat (Ⓣ03/477 4449, Ⓦwww.taieri.co.nz). The train itself is comfortable and air-conditioned, made up of a mix of modern steel carriages with large panoramic windows, and nostalgic, refurbished 1920s wooden cars. Storage space is available for backpacks and bicycles (bikes travel free), and there's a licensed snack bar on board. Ask ahead and you might even be able to ride with the driver for a spell.

The most frequent trip is to **Pukerangi** – a peaceful spot 58km from the city near the highest point of the track (250m), where you spend ten minutes – arriving back in Dunedin four hours later (April–Sept daily 12.30pm; Oct–March daily 2.30pm, plus end Dec–March extra morning service selected days 9.30am & Jan–March extra morning service Sun 9.30am; $57 return). On Sundays in summer the train continues a further 19km to the old gold town of **Middlemarch** in the fertile Strath Taieri Plains, a five-hour round trip (Oct–Feb; $65 return). You can stay overnight around Pukerangi where there are various whitewater-rafting and horse-trekking activities (details from Dunedin Railway Station). In addition, the abandoned line between Middlemarch and Clyde, deep in the gold country, has been developed for walking and mountain biking. The so-called **Otago Central Rail Trail** is a spectacular and none-too-difficult, 150-kilometre trip for anyone who can ride a bike, and by far the best way to complete the trail (3–6 days, depending on your speed and stamina; bike hire is available in Dunedin – see "Listings" p.746 – or in Alexandra, see p.913). The route can be completed in either direction and includes sixty modified rail bridges and viaducts (several span over 100m), beautiful valleys, long agricultural plains – this is Graham Sydney country, one of New Zealand's most celebrated landscape painters – and various welcoming and excellent accommodation options (for more on which see under Alexandra, p.913). Day-trips taking in portions of the trail, departing from the central goldfields, are also available

To get to Alexandra or Queenstown from the Taieri Gorge Railway, you'll need an Otago Central Connection ticket (Ⓣbook at least 24hr in advance through the rail service, see above; $95 or $110 one way repectively). The bus meets the train at Middlemarch and follows a scenic route via the Maniototo Plain through Alexandra before tackling the remaining, much less interesting 86km to Queenstown. This journey can, of course, be done in reverse; or you can book a flight connection from Pukerangi (check details with Dunedin Railway Station).

Eating

In a city that's undeniably enthusiastic about food, with cuisine from around the world, you'll never be at a loss for somewhere to satisfy your appetite, plus you'll seldom need to stray far from the **city centre**. Many eateries are strung along George Street, particularly from the junction with Hanover Street for two blocks, heading away from the Octagon; others are concentrated on or around the Octagon. You'll find there's an excellent range, across the board from classic espresso cafés to fine dining restaurants, but many places close on Sundays. Recent years have also seen an explosion in ethnic cafés and take-aways, in answer to the city's large student population. Some of the city's **pubs** also serve reasonably priced food (see p.744). Useful spots for **stocking up** are *Tangente Café and Bakery* for organic bread, the *Everyday Gourmet* deli (for both these venues see p.742-3) and *Night 'n' Day*, a 24-hour food store that's a Dunedin institution, located on the corner of George and Regent streets and handy after the pubs have closed for sandwiches, pies and snacks. Eating places on the **Otago Peninsula** are listed separately on p.753. Unless otherwise stated, those listed below are open daily and BYO relates to bottled wine only, usually carrying a small corkage charge.

Restaurants

Bacchus Wine Bar & Restaurant 1st floor, 12 The Octagon, cnr Lower Stuart St Ⓣ03/474 0824. A great vantage point overlooking the Octagon from a prestigious historic building. Over fifty wines, accompanied by moderately priced lunches ($9–12) and dinners ($20–26). Popular office workers' lunch spot Mon–Fri; dinner Mon–Sat.

A Cow Called Berta 199 Stuart St Ⓣ03/477 2993. Reasonably priced Swiss-style country dinners of simple strong flavours based on French cuisine, in the cosy yet classy ambience of a converted Victorian terraced house. Closed Sun; licensed.

The Curry Box 442 George St Ⓣ03/477 4713. Café-style restaurant dishing up good curries, tandoori breads, chicken balti, rogan josh and a whole lot more, including the usual vegetarian suspects. It won't cost a mint for dinner, Mon–Sat, and the lunch specials are spicy and filling, Mon–Fri. No alcohol.

Etrusco 1st floor, Savoy Building, 8a Moray Place, cnr George St Ⓣ03/477 3737. Authentic Italian fare presented in an airy and lovingly restored building. Moderate prices and friendly service. Dinner only from 5.30pm. Good wine list, also BYO.

High Tide 29 Kitchener St Ⓣ03/477 9784. A quietly romantic and friendly waterside hideaway for evening meals, complemented by great views over the harbour and peninsula. The moderately priced menu consists of imaginative seafood, vegetarian and meat dishes, as well as home-made soups and desserts. Tues–Sat from 6pm; licensed.

The Huntsman Steakhouse 311 George St. Great steaks for around $25 and including salad from a huge selection; dinner only and closed Sun. Licensed & BYO.

Joseph Mellor Restaurant 1st floor, Otago Polytechnic, cnr York Place & Tennyson St, entrance directly opposite Kavanagh College Ⓣ03/479 6172. Unbelievably cheap, high-quality

French/New Zealand cuisine prepared by world-class chefs and their students in a bustling restaurant with one of the best city views in Dunedin. Book a few days ahead. Open March–Oct Tues–Thurs only noon–1.30pm & 6.30–9pm; licensed and BYO.

Ombrellos 10 Clarendon St, off Frederick St ⓣ03/477 8773. An attractive Mediterranean-style courtyard café/bar in the heart of the university area. Open all day, offering breakfast through to dinner (mostly around $15–20) and an affordable wine list. Closed Mon, plus Sun evening; bar open 4pm–late with occasional live music.

Palms Café 18 Queens Gardens ⓣ03/477 6534. Something of an institution among locals and any visitor who has been lucky enough to eat here once – everyone enjoys its leisurely pace and genteel atmosphere, so be sure to book ahead. From a turn-of the-century setting (complete with enormous windows and high ceiling), you can feast your eyes on the greenery of Queens Gardens, while tucking into hearty vegetarian, seafood and meat dishes. Two-course special for $15 (Mon–Fri 5.30–6.30pm) and a moderately priced, à la carte menu ($20–26), including Jim's Southern Haggis and seared lamb Otago-style. Dinner only; licensed & BYO.

Thai Over 388 George St. Authenitc Thai food in a modern, bright and open café-style space, where you can sample *larb gai*, *tom kar* and *tom yum*, green, yellow and red curries and peanut sauce with satay and stir fry. Open daily for lunch and dinner; licensed.

Tokyo Garden 351 George St ⓣ03/474 5993; not to be confused with *Tokyo House* a few doors up. Easily affordable Japanese food in simple surroundings for lunch (except Sun; great specials for under $10) and dinner (daily) to eat in or take away, washed down with *sake* ($4). Licensed & BYO.

Cafés and snack bars

Arc Café/Bar 135 High St. Excellent, big and groovy cyber café/bar serving well-priced gourmet vegetarian and vegan snacks. In a separate clubby section at the back live bands or DJs play most nights, and top Dunedin acts Fri & Sat (principal venue for the Dunedin Sound; see box opposite). Free internet access plus eye-opening coffee and a good range of herbal teas; licensed.

Best Café 30 Stuart St. A local legend, despite the spartan decor and unprepossessing appearance, where you are liable to be greeted by the sort of smile last seen on a recently deceased blue cod. Probably the best spot in the city for traditional fish and chips, served in a time warp in this location for over fifty years, with bread and butter and the constant background yap of the television. Mon–Sat 11.30am–7pm.

Bronx Bagel cnr Stuart St & Bath St. A simple little eat-in and takeaway American-style deli, where a variety of authentically boiled schmear-filled bagels are knocked off. The coffee is effective, and the doors are open daily from 8am.

Everyday Gourmet 466 George St. A cosy deli-cum-café stuffed with specialist cheeses, salami, fine meat pies and other imported speciality foods. Also bagels, substantial sandwiches, take-home meals, great Anzac biscuits and excellent coffee. Closed Sun.

The Fix 15 Frederick St. Small, favourite student-haunt for cheap but very good coffee and juices, with a garden terrace where you can eat your own food. Mon–Fri 7.30am–5pm.

Fuel Café 21 Frederick St. The closest café to the university and a big student zone, open till late Thurs–Sat, and jam-packed from Feb to Oct. It's well known for its breakfasts and generous portions of great food – including vegetarian and vegan – though it reverts to snacks late at night. There's also the *Lounge Bar* and *Fusion Niteclub* at the back (see p.744). Daily from 9.30am, closes around 6pm Mon–Thurs. Licensed.

Galata Kebab House 126 Princes St. Authentic, cheap Turkish food to eat in or take away, offering the usual mix of vegetarian dishes, falafels and kebabs, from 11am till late. Licensed & BYO.

Jizo Japanese Café and Bar Savoy Building, 56 Princes St. Inexpensive sushi, rice dishes, miso and noodle soups to take away or eat in at this small, split-level café. Lunch and dinner Mon–Sat; licensed & BYO.

New Satay Noodle House 16 Hanover St. A cheap-and-cheerful all-day spot for noodle soups, satay and Thai dishes from 11am. All the Asian students come here.

Otago University Students Association Cumberland St, opposite the Otago Museum. Mixing with the students on their home turf is not as naff as it sounds: the atmosphere is lively and you can find out about some good gigs and under-publicized events. On the righthand side, as you pass through the arch heading for the quadrangle, is a food court with several different outlets serving passable and cheap food. There's also a late-night spot called *The Link* which is open till 11pm during term time. Jan–Nov daily 8am–8pm; licensed.

Percolator Café 142 Stuart St. A well-established inexpensive espresso bar just down from the Octagon, open from 9am till the early hours Fri & Sat, till 10pm the rest of the week. Brunch served

Sat & Sun morning, plus full lunch and dinner menu.

Potpourri Vegetarian and Natural Foods Café 97 Lower Stuart St, near Moray Place. Established veggie venue got up to look like a church. Wholemeal baking, a big salad bar and great frozen yoghurt to eat in or take away. Closed Sun; no alcohol and no smoking.

Strictly Coffee 23 Bath St. The best coffee in town, some might even say on the coast, sold in an elegantly simple café, and also available for you to take away by the packet load. They also do a variety of homemade cakes and some simple sandwiches. Mon–Fri 8am–5pm.

Tangente Café and Bakery 111 Moray Place. Mellow spot next to the Fortune Theatre above the Octagon, using organic grains and flours, cold-pressed oils, free-range eggs and filtered water to produce gourmet snacks and meals from breakfast onwards. Try a home-baked organic bread cup – a bowl made of bread filled with the concoction of your choice – while browsing their magazines. Dinner, Fri & Sat nights only, makes for a popular pre- or post-theatre stop; licensed & BYO.

Vino Vena 484 George St ⓣ03/479 0110. Swish Italian-style spot on the first floor and set back from the main road, where you can sip some very smooth coffee and taste some delightful smoked Warehou with poached eggs and hollandaise sauce, linguini with smoked salmon or pansotti with pumpkin lasagna, all for under $25. Sun–Wed 7am–5pm, Thurs–Sat 7am–late; licensed.

Drinking, nightlife and entertainment

As the evening draws in, Dunedin shifts into a higher gear, especially during term time or one of its many festivals. Drinking is taken seriously here and there's no shortage of **pubs** and **bars**, many of them student hangouts where local **bands** play at weekends, plus some of the **cafés** double up as bars or clubs (see above). You can also catch live bands at the Empire, 396 Princes St (ⓣ03/477 8826), and the city is well served with **theatres**, **cinemas** (both arthouse and mainstream) and **concert halls**. For information on what's on, pick up a free copy of *Fink* or check the "Entertainments" section of the *Otago Daily Times*. The ornate **casino**, in a beautifully restored 1883 building,

The Dunedin Sound

In the late 1970s and early 1980s an idiosyncratic style of rock music began to emerge from Dunedin's local pub scene, and it was quickly tagged the **Dunedin Sound.** Isolated from the commercial mainstream – the Kiwi music market constitutes a mere three million or so people – the bands indulged in songwriting for the sheer hell of it, which perhaps explains their originality and why so many of the early songs have stood the test of time. Spurred on by local record labels Flying Nun (now based in Auckland) and Xpressway, the bands developed over a number of albums and in relative obscurity until several – notably the Chills, The Clean, Straitjacket Fits and the Verlaines – started to find a receptive audience in Europe and the States. The 1990s brought inventive new bands like Mink, Mestar, Cloudboy and HDU, while a strong body of singer-songwriters also proliferated at the city's premier music venue, *Arc Café/Bar* – among them Dunedin Sound pioneers David Kilgour and Martin Phillips. By this time the city enjoyed international status, prompting the *Chicago Tribune* in 1992 to call Dunedin the "Rock Capital of The World". At the end of 1999 it was announced that Otago University was introducing a degree in rock music under Verlaines singer-songwriter Graeme Downes. For the latest on the Dunedin Sound, check out *Fink*, the free entertainment pamphlet available all around town, including the visitor centre (or see ⓦwww.fink.net.nz), which keeps track of Dunedin's bands, singers and songwriters. **Records, CDs & Tapes** can be found at Records Records, 213 Stuart St (Mon–Fri 10.30am–5pm, Sat 10.30–1pm), a new- and secondhand-music shop for local and international records, tapes and CDs; it's particularly strong on Kiwi music.

is worth a look even if you don't want to play. The local **micro-brewery** is Emerson's (not open to the public), which produces six beers – London Porter (a dark old English style), 1812 India Pale Ale, Organic Pilsner, Hefe Weissbier (Bavarian-style cloudy wheat beer), Bookbinder (a full, hop-flavoured English-style beer) and Dunkelweizen (dark wheat) – plus two or three seasonal brews a year. For a taste head for the *Arc Café/Bar* (see p.742), the *Inch Bar* or the *London Lounge* at the *Albert Arms*, as listed below. Bear in mind that on Sunday many bars open at around 5pm, close early or don't open at all. Also worth remembering is that during term time, everywhere's usually busy, but when the students go home for the holidays some of the dance floors can look pretty sad.

Pubs, bars and clubs

Abalone 1st Floor, 44 Hanover St, cnr George St, above the BNZ Bank ⓣ0800/222 2256. Slick, yuppie bar-cum-restaurant with modern metal furnishings, terracotta flooring and lots of glass. Moderately priced drinks and seething with people at weekends. The food's pretty good too, a mix of traditional Kiwi and fusion, with generous proportions and local ingredients).

Albert Arms cnr George St & London St. Sedate, tartan-decorated pub with live Irish music on Mon, jazz or blues Tues and kiwi rock Wed. Bar snacks such as doorstep toasted sandwiches downstairs, while upstairs the *London Lounge* serves Emerson's beer on tap and good bistro fare (including steaks and roasts). Downstairs closes 7.30pm Sun.

The Ale House 200 Ratray St ⓣ03/471 9050. Very popular, relatively new, Speight's-owned, traditional-looking pub with excellent brews and very good quality food, even if under all the wood and antique memorabilia it's just a glorified sports bar with big screen TV, that borrows heavily on the *Loaded Hog* theme of urban/arable chic. Open daily from 11.30am.

Bath Street Bar 1 Bath St (between the Octagon & Moray Place). Intimate and stylish studenty nightclub tucked away on a quiet road just below George St, where DJs play underground stuff. Cover charge $3 Thurs–Sat (and extra for special events); open from 10pm till around 5.30am; closed Mon.

Bennu Bar 12 Moray Place. Young professionals are drawn to this elegant venue in one of Dunedin's finest buildings, decorated with a skylight right over the bar, and palm trees. Mon–Fri from 11.30am, Sat from noon & Sun from 5pm.

Bodega 12 The Octagon. Cool café/bar with live jazz every other Thurs, in-house local DJ music or alternatively PA sounds, and some decent food from 8am daily.

Captain Cook cnr Albany St & Great King St. A favourite student pub, reputed to have the highest turnover of beer in New Zealand and can be seedy. The downstairs bar has pool tables, cheap bar snacks, a pleasant garden bar and a happy half-hour every day 5–6.30pm. Upstairs has a DJ and disco (Thurs–Sat till 3am), with no cover charge. Open till 10pm Sun.

Dicey Oriley 131 High St. Big Irish pub that serves inoffensive bar meals at lunch and in the evenings, though it's better known for being open late, with live Irish-ish music every Fri, and the enormous amount of booze that is consumed on the premises.

Dunedin Casino cnr Princes St & High St. Men need to wear a collared shirt and no trainers or jeans are allowed in this ornate restoration of what was the *Grand Hotel* of 1883. You don't have to play the tables or slot machines to enjoy the gold-leaf plasterwork, a drink or a meal at their *Grand Bar and Café*. Sun–Thurs 11am–3am, Fri & Sat 11am–4am.

Fusion Niteclub & The Lounge Bar at *Fuel Café*, 21 Frederick St ⓦwww.fuelcafe.co.nz. The university's closest club and bar, so they keep on pumping. The relaxed *Lounge Bar* has sofas and pool tables (open from 6pm), and *Fusion* has live bands and DJs (open from 8pm, but kicks off at 10pm). Wed is $2-a-pint night and every second Sat from Feb to Oct is gay night ("Powder"). It's comfortable, a bit grungy and the music usually includes house, drum'n'bass, trance, progressive jungle and new live bands. Closed Sun & Mon.

Inch Bar 8 Bank St. Tiny hip watering hole with plenty of special beers on tap (including the locally brewed Emerson's) and a wide range of imported brands. Bar snacks available. Open daily from 5pm.

The Last Moa 157 Frederick St. A student institution and pick-up joint, with dance floor (till 1am Fri & Sat) and occasional live acts.

Metro 153 Stuart St. A brightly coloured café/bar that serves passable brunches, lunches and evening meals, good wines, beers and cocktails and accompanies them with live jazz and DJs (usually borrowed from the Bath Street Bar), especially on Fri & Sat.

The Mission 65 Hanover St, cnr Great King St Hanover St. Situated in an old, brick and stone church – which adds to a Gothic feel – is this perpetually youthful DJ-orchestrated dance venue. House, techno and occasional chart music keep the place pumping. 9pm onwards.

Ra Bar 21 The Octagon. An airy all-day street bar and café right in the thick of things, attracting the city's professionals, which explains the snooty staff. Reasonable light food and weekend all-day brunches (from 9.30am).

Statesman 91 St Andrew St A big party pub where popular Kiwi rock bands play Thurs, Fri & Sat nights. Open till 3am Fri & Sat.

Woolshed 318 Moray Place. A long, thin bar stretching back from the road that looks like it's been decorated with the leftovers from a number of clearance sales, and offering some simple, wholesome blackboard specials for lunch and supper. Invariably there are live bands or loud music and a good atmosphere, concentrated mostly around the end of the week.

Theatre, cinema, classical music and sports

The Ticketek office in the Regent Theatre in The Octagon takes bookings for a selection of national and local events (ⓣ03/477 8597, ⓦwww.ticketek.co.nz; Mon–Fri 8.30am–5pm, Sat 10.30am–1pm) for a small handling fee on credit card bookings. Alternatively book through the venue.

The Fortune Theatre at 231 Stuart St (box office ⓣ03/477 8323; tickets around $25; closed Jan), in the Neo-Gothic converted Trinity Methodist Church, divides its programme between new works by Kiwi playwrights, fringe theatre, popular Broadway-style **plays** and occasional musicals. The Regent, 17 The Octagon (ⓣ03/477 8597), is the city's largest and most ornate theatre, hosting musicals, ballets, touring plays and performances by popular singers, comedians and groups. The small, intimate Globe, 104 London St (ⓣ03/477 3274), features contemporary plays, classical drama and experimental works. You can catch more fringe on campus at Allen Hall on Clyde Street (ⓣ03/479 8896), the showcase for the university's drama students.

Mainstream **films** are shown at Hoyts, a six-cinema multiplex at 33 The Octagon (ⓣ03/477 7019), and at the Rialto, 11 Moray Place (ⓣ03/474 2200), while there are international arthouse screenings at the delightful and tiny Metro, housed on the ground floor of the 1920s Town Hall on Moray Place (discounted tickets Mon–Fri before 5pm). This is the smallest public cinema in New Zealand (56 seats), and it's essential to book ahead by leaving a message on their answer machine (ⓣ03/474 3350); collect tickets ten minutes before screening time.

Regular **concerts** are given by the New Zealand Symphony Orchestra, the Dunedin Sinfonia (a semi-professional orchestra), and chamber music groups at the Town Hall or the Glenroy Auditorium at the Dunedin Centre (ⓣ03/477 4477). The Dunedin Opera Company stages two or three productions a year at the Trust Bank Theatre, 100 King Edward St (ⓣ03/455 4962), and regular public recitals are held by the music department of the University of Otago (see posters around town or ⓣ03/479 1100 during office hours).

Rugby matches are usually held every second weekend at the Carisbrook Stadium on Burns Street during the season (roughly the end of Feb to end of Oct; tickets can be booked through Otago Rugby Football Union ⓣ03/455 1191). A free schedule of games for the season is available from Otago Rugby Football Union, 28 Burns St, Caversham, Dunedin.

Listings

Airlines Air New Zealand, The Octagon ☎03/479 6594.

Airport transport Airport Direct Shuttle Service ☎03/471 4101; Airport Shuttle City Taxis ☎03/477 1771; Call-a-Cab Shuttle ☎03/477 7800 & 0800/477 800; Dunedin Airport Shuttle ☎03/477 6611; and Super Shuttle ☎03/456 0073 & 0800 365 5655. Shuttles charge $40 for one person, $20 per head for two, and $15 for three.

Automobile Association Shopping Centre, Moray Place, near cnr Burlington St (☎03/477 5945, Ⓕ477 9760), for road maps and travel products. Emergency breakdown service ☎0800/500 222. Road reports ☎0900/33222.

Banks and foreign exchange The major banks are clustered on George Street, most of them with ATMs, and some also line Princes Street. Thomas Cook is at cnr St Andrew St & George St (☎03/477 7204; Mon–Fri 8.30am–5pm, Sat 10am–12.30pm).

Bike rental R & R Sport, 70 Stuart St (☎03/474 1211) has mountain bikes for $25–30 a day; The Cycle Surgery, 67 Stuart St (☎03/477 7473) offers repairs, and rents bikes for $25 per day; Browns Avanti Pro Cycle Centre, Lower Stuart St (☎03/477 7259) has good-quality mountain bikes for short- and long-term rental ($25 per day), with helmets and locks, and does repairs.

Bookshops University Bookshop, 378 Great King St, opposite the Otago Museum (☎03/477 6976, Ⓔubs@xtra.co.nz; Mon–Fri 8.30am–5.30pm, Sat 9.30am–1.30pm), is a comprehensive independent bookshop on two floors, stocking a broad range of New Zealand and international fiction and non-fiction – bargains upstairs; Hyndman's, Civic Centre, 17 George St (just down from the visitor centre; ☎03/477 0174), stocks books on New Zealand, fiction, children's books and stationery. ☎

Buses National bus companies: InterCity Coachlines, 205 St Andrew St (coach terminal ☎03/477 8860, reservations ☎03/474 9600 or book through Dunedin visitor centre), links Dunedin with Christchurch, Queenstown, Te Anau, Wanaka and Invercargill. Local shuttle buses: Atomic Shuttles (to and from Christchurch and Queenstown; book through the train station ☎03/477 4449); and Southern Link Shuttles (to and from Christchurch, Wanaka, Queenstown and Kaikoura; ☎03/358 8355). All run from the train station.

Camping and outdoor equipment R & R Sport, 70 Stuart St, has the biggest range of camping, skiing, cycling and all sporting equipment; also mountain bike and pack rental. The Wilderness Shop, 101 Stuart St, has mountaineering, skiing and kayaking gear for rent and for sale; also tramping and alpine gear for sale. Wild Planet, 120 Lower Stuart St (☎03/471 8555), offer a variety of outdoor gear.

Car parks City centre ($0.50 per 30min): off Upper Moray Place, opposite View St; Lower Moray Place, near Stuart St; Filleul St, between St Andrew & Hanover; Great King St, between St Andrew & Hanover; Anzac Ave, at junction with Castle St; Crawford St, at junction with Castle St, and another between Water & Liverpool; High St, near junction with Broadway.

Car rental ☎☎ Budget, 330 Moray Place (☎03/474 0428) and Dunedin Airport (☎03/486 2660); Hertz, 121 Crawford St (☎03/477 7385 & 0800/654 321); Reliable Rentals, no office in Dunedin – they deliver to you (☎03/488 3975), for cars and minibuses; Rhodes, 124 St Andrew St (☎03/477 9950), for cars, vans, minibuses and 4WDs; and Thrifty, 223 Hillside Rd (☎03/477 7087). Cheapest of all are Rent-a-Dent, 212 Crawford St (☎03/477 7822), for cars, station wagons, vans and minibuses; and Jackies, 23 Cumberland St (☎03/477 7848).

Dentist Raymond J. George, 7th floor, National Mutual Building, cnr The Octagon & George St (☎03/477 7993, after hours ☎025/331 570.

Library Dunedin Public Library, cnr John St & Stewart St (☎03/474 3690; Mon–Fri 9.30am–8pm, Sat 10am–4pm), has excellent facilities, newspapers and internet access.

Medical treatment Dunedin Hospital, 201 Great King St (☎03/474 0999). For general practice medical care, try Bell Hill Health Centre, 399 Moray Place (☎03/477 9183; Mon–Fri 8.30am–6pm). After-hours' doctors are available at 95 Hanover St (☎03/479 2900).

Pharmacy After-hours service at Urgent Pharmacy, 95 Hanover St (☎03/477 6344; Mon–Fri 6–10pm, Sat, Sun & public holidays 10am–10pm).

Police In an emergency call ☎111.

Post office Dunedin Post Shop, John Wickliffe Plaza, 243 Princes St; Moray Place Post Shop, 233 Moray Place. Poste restante held at Dunedin Post Shop (Mon–Fri 8.30am–5.30pm, Sat 8.30am–noon).

Taxis You'll find taxi ranks in the Octagon, between George St & Stuart St; on St Andrew St, between George St & Filleul St; and on Frederick St, between George St & Filleul St. Radio cabs include United (☎03/455 5282), Otago Taxis

(Ⓣ03/477 3333), City Taxis (Ⓣ03/477 1771; 24hr service) and Dunedin Taxis (Ⓣ03/477 7777 & 0800/505 010).

Tours The visitor centre has information on the vast array of tours from Dunedin. Citibus Newton (Ⓣ03/477 5577) runs good city tours (daily 10am & 3.30pm; 1hr 30min, $35) and trips out to the Otago Peninsula (2hr 15min, $30); while the Otago Peninsula Express (book through the visitor centre) minibus runs to various points on the peninsula. More luxurious city tours can be had from Heritage Tours (booked through the visitor centre, see p.729; $85), who offer limousine trips from outside the visitor centre. Harbour and wildlife cruises on the *Monarch* leave from Dunedin Wharf, cnr Wharf St & Fryatt St (Ⓣ03/477 4276, Ⓔmonarch@ wildlife.co.nz; 5hr, from $58; or 1hr from Wellers Rock on the peninsula, $27), giving close-up views of royal albatross, seals, penguins, cormorants and waders on the peninsula. See box on p.759 for details of tours of the Catlins. Monarch will also drop people off so that they can go on a Penguin Colony tour and then be picked up by the boat for $85. Trojan Riding (Ⓣ03/465 7013, Ⓦwww.trojanriding.co.nz) offer well-structured horse-riding treks along the coast at Karitane.

Travel agents Amo & Holmes Travel, 233 Stuart St Ⓣ477 2233 & 0800/877 2233, Ⓕ479 0678; STA, 32 Albany St Ⓣ03/474 0146; Thomas Cook, cnr St Andrew St & George St Ⓣ03/477 7204; and Winston Darling, 138 Princes St Ⓣ03/474 5483.

The Otago Peninsula

Jutting out to the east of Dunedin and dividing its harbour from the Pacific Ocean, the **OTAGO PENINSULA** is a lightly populated undulating area of natural beauty and exceptional wildlife. Its grass-covered hills afford excellent views of the harbour, the open sea and the spread of Dunedin against its dramatic backdrop of hills. Served by well-kept roads, the peninsula is easily accessible from the city, the trip from one end to the other taking an hour by car. You'll need to allow at least a day, though, to take in the sights and wildlife.

The chief reason for visiting the peninsula is to appreciate, at close range, the intriguing variety and abundance of **marine wildlife** that is drawn to its shores year round. At its tip is the small headland of **Taiaroa Head**, a protected area where several colonies of mammals and sea birds congregate. Unique among these is the majestic **royal albatross**, which breeds here in the only mainland colony of albatross in the world. Also concentrated on the headland's shores are **penguins** (little blue and the rare yellow-eyed) and **southern fur seals**, while the cliffs are home to other sea birds including three species of **shag**, **muttonbirds** (sooty shearwaters) and various species of gull. The peninsula's other beaches and inlets play host to a great variety of wading and waterfowl and, occasionally, New Zealand **sea lions** (while offshore, orca and other **whales** can sometimes be spotted.

Although there's ample opportunity to see much of the wildlife without having to pay for the privilege, it's well worth forking out for one or more of the several official **wildlife tours**, since they are informative and take you up close, yet cause minimal disturbance to the animals.

On the way to Taiaroa Head there are a handful of other sights, including the large woodland gardens and walks of **Glenfalloch**, particularly renowned for their rhododendrons, azaleas and camellias; the bizarre **Larnach Castle**, which is little more than an overblown folly; **Fletcher House**, a delightfully restored small Edwardian villa; and the excellent Marine Studies Centre **aquarium**. A number of **scenic walks** cross both public and private land to spectacular views and unusual land formations created by lava flows.

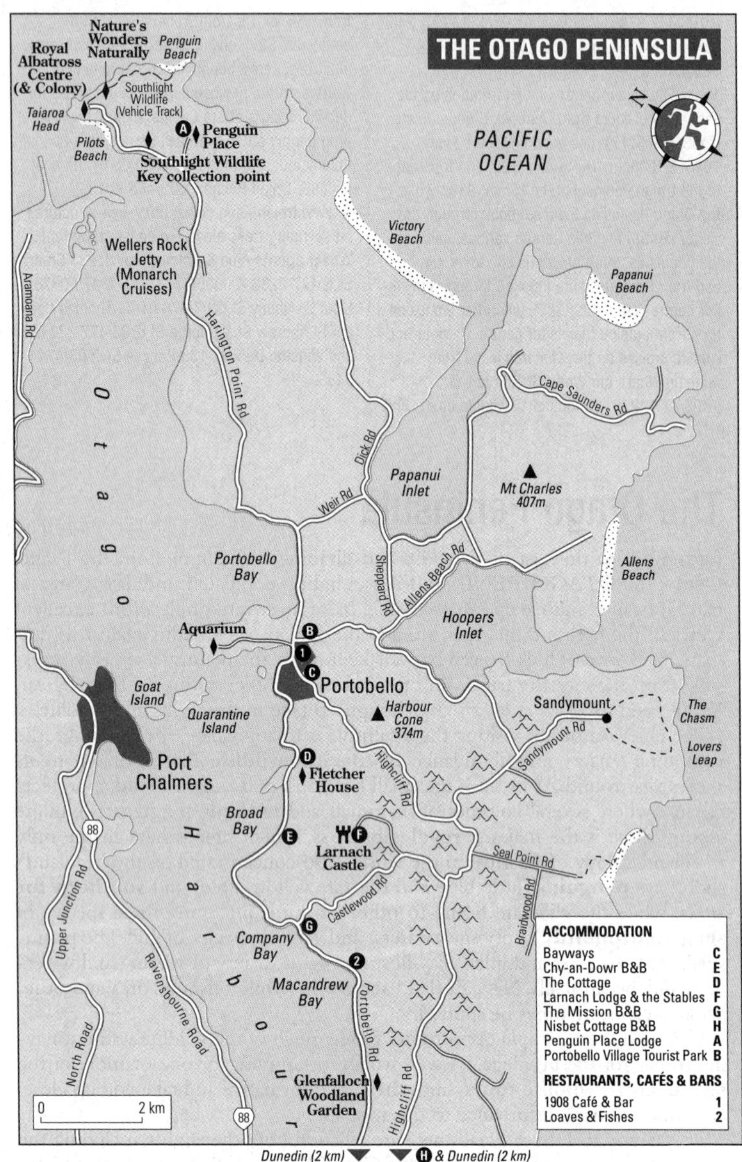

Around Taiaroa Head

The peninsula's marine wildlife is mostly concentrated around **Taiaroa Head**, where a rich and constant food source is created by cold waters forced up by the continental shelf. Other than taking a tour, the best opportunities for seeing animals are on the beaches and inlets on either side of the headland. Southern fur seals can be seen at **Pilots Beach**, on the western side (follow the main road to the shore as it snakes past the Royal Albatross Centre) and from the **cliff tops** on the eastern side of the headland. Pilots Beach is also home to a small colony of little blue penguins, which are best visited around dusk but be sure to keep your distance and stay quiet or they'll turn tail. A short signposted walk from the Royal Albatross Centre car park to a **cliff-edge viewing area** unfolds spectacular scenes of a spotted shag colony, while royal albatross in flight can be spied all year round from anywhere on the headland.

When **observing wildlife**, respect the animals by staying well away from them (at least 5m), and keeping quiet and still. **Penguins** are especially timid and easily frightened by people getting too close. They will be reluctant to come ashore (even if they have chicks to feed) if you are on or near the beach and visible. In summer, stay well away from them and keep to the track as they're extremely vulnerable to stress while nesting and moulting. Never get between a **seal** and the sea; these animals can be aggressive and move surprisingly quickly.

The Royal Albatross Centre

Serving as the gateway to the only mainland colony of albatross in the world, the **Royal Albatross Centre** (daily: Nov–April 9am–7pm; May–Oct 10am–4pm; free) at Taiaroa Head is 33km from Dunedin's city centre. Its galleries contain displays on local wildlife and history, and there's a comfortable café with panoramic windows. The centre's excellent **guided tours** (daily except Sept 17–Nov 23; booking essential on ⓣ03/478 0499 or through the Dunedin visitor centre; $24–30) include an introductory film and talk, plenty of time to view the birds from an enclosed area in the reserve (binoculars provided) and an optional but uninspiring visit to the labyrinthine tunnels of Fort Taiaroa beneath the nature reserve.

At Taiaroa Head, adult birds arrive for the new season in September. Courting and mating takes place in October and eggs are laid and incubated from November to December. The chicks hatch in January and February. The **best months** for viewing are between April and August, when parent birds leave the nests and return towards the end of the day to feed their chicks. By

The royal albatross

The majestic and mysterious **albatross**, one of the largest seabirds in the world, has long been the subject of reverence and superstition. A solitary creature that regularly circumnavigates the globe, the albatross spends most of its life in flight or at sea, and is traditionally held to be the embodiment of a dead sea captain's soul, condemned to wander the oceans for ever.

The largest of all the albatrosses is the **royal albatross** – a stunning sight, with an impressive **wing span** of up to 3.5 metres. They travel up to 190,000km a year, at speeds of 120kph, and have a **life expectancy** of 45 years. The albatross mates for life, but male and female separate to fly in opposite directions around the world, returning to the same **breeding** grounds once every two years, and arriving within a couple of days of one another. The female lays one egg (weighing up to 500g) per breeding season, and the parents share incubation duty over a period of eleven weeks. Once the chick has hatched, the parents take turns feeding it and guarding it against stoats, ferrets, wild cats and rats. Almost a year from the start of the breeding cycle, the fledgling takes flight and the parents leave the colony and return to sea.

The yellow-eyed penguin (hoiho)

Considered the most ancient of all living penguins, the **yellow-eyed penguin**, or *hoiho*, evolved in forests free of predators. Found only in southern New Zealand, it is an endangered species, numbering around four thousand birds, due to introduced predators (ferrets, stoats and cats), the loss of its forested habitat, disturbance by humans and livestock, and recurring food shortages. The small mainland population of just a few hundred occupies nesting areas dotted along the wild southeast coast of the South Island (from Oamaru to the Catlins); other smaller colonies inhabit the coastal forest margins of Stewart Island and offshore islets, and New Zealand's sub Antarctic islands of Auckland and Campbell.

Male and female adults are identical in colouring, with pink webbed feet and a bright yellow band that encircles the head, sweeping over their pale yellow eyes. Standing around 65cm high and weighing 5–8kg, they have a **life expectancy** of up to twenty years. Their **diet** consists of squid and small fish, and hunting takes them up to 40km offshore and to depths of 100m.

Maori gave this rare penguin the name of **hoiho**, meaning "the noise shouter", because of the distinctive high-pitched calls (an exuberant trilling) it makes at night when greeting its mate at the nest. Unlike other penguins, the yellow-eyed does not migrate after its first year, but stays close to its home beach, making daily fishing trips and returning as daylight fails.

The penguins' **breeding season** lasts for 28 weeks, from mid-August to early March. Eggs are laid between mid-September and mid-October, and both parents share in the duties of incubation, a period lasting about 43 days. The eggs hatch in November and for the next six weeks the chicks are constantly guarded against predators. By the time the down-covered chicks are six or seven weeks old, their rapid growth gives them voracious appetites and both parents must fish daily to satisfy them. The fledglings enter the sea for the first time in late February or early March and journey up to 500km north to winter feeding grounds. Fewer than fifteen percent of fledged chicks reach breeding age, but those that do return to the colony of their birth.

September the chicks and adults are ready to depart and new breeding pairs start to arrive.

Penguin-viewing

Only one company on the peninsula run tours, which concentrate solely on the yellow-eyed penguins. The best months for viewing are mid-August to early March.

The most concentrated carefully-controlled and extremely informative guided tours are run by an award-winning penguin-conservation project at **Penguin Place**, on McGrouther's Farm, Harington Point Road, 3.5km before the albatross colony (book ahead on ⓣ03/478 0286 or through Dunedin visitor centre; daily; 90min; $27). Here you are given the rare privilege of entering a protected nesting area of around 200 birds through a unique system of hides and tunnels. The best months to visit here are between early November and May, but at any time of year, cold wet days make for especially good viewing. Tours begin with a talk about penguins and their conservation, before a guide takes you to the beachside colony, where well-camouflaged trenches and hides among the dunes allow an extraordinary proximity to the penguins and excellent photographic opportunities. Proceeds from the tours are used to fund the conservation work and a unit that looks after injured penguins. If you want to stay overnight, budget accommodation is available on the farm (see

"Accommodation and Eating," p.753). Running in conjunction with Penguin Place are Twilight Wildlife Conservation Tours (Ⓣ03/474 3300, Ⓕ454 3117; groups of 15 maximum; 6–7hrs; around $75–100) who offer fascinating trips onto the peninsula for those interested in New Zealand's natural history and its conservation, covering either the albatross colony or viewing the majestic birds from the *Monarch* (see Dunedin "Listings", p.747), the penguin colony, and a large variety of other sights and wildlife.

One of the most original and characterful tours on the heads is offered by a tourist mouthful, **Nature's Wonders Naturally** (Ⓣ0800/246 446, Ⓕ478 0714; 1hr; $30), who operate from opposite the albatross colony. They offer personalized adventure conservation tours, which involve a lively ride around the head on specially constructed tracks in specially modified 8WD argoes (a type of plastic, multi-wheeled-drive vehicle). The tours, run with unstinting good humour and exhausting enthusiasm, take in penguin-viewing areas, New Zealand fur seals, sea lions as well as old World War II sights. Although you might wonder what the animals will make of these odd, noisy little vehicles speeding around this working sheep farm, it doesn't seem to stop them going about their business.

Another good way to get a look at the penguins, the albatross and the other animals on the peninsula is from a sea kayak with **Wild Earth Adventures** (Ⓣ03/473 6535, Ⓦwww.wildearth.com), who operate out of Dunedin and run three paddling tours round the peninsula (Taiaroa Ocean Tours, $139; Ocean Discovery Tour, $69; Eco-marine Tour, $69; all 4–5hr), all of which are well worth the effort if you have the time and money. Kayaking beside the peninsula is a magical experience and provides a different perspective on both the coast and the wildlife.

The rest of the peninsula

Lying between Dunedin and Taiaroa Head are four sights worthy of a brief diversion, most of them strung along the harbourside on Portobello Road. Eleven kilometres from Dunedin, the peaceful **Glenfalloch Woodland Garden**, at 430 Portobello Rd (daily dawn–dusk; donations requested), contains 120 square kilometres of rambling mature garden and bush, surrounding a homestead built in 1871. The garden is at its best between mid-September and mid-October, when it is resplendent with rhododendrons, azaleas and camellias and, to a lesser extent, magnolias, fuchsias and roses. Near the entrance, a licensed café (daily 10am–4.30pm) serves snacks and drinks, and also stocks leaflets on the peninsula.

Set high on a hill above the harbour, 16km from the centre of Dunedin and signposted off Castlewood Road, is a bizarre nineteenth-century Gothic Revival building. The so-called **Larnach Castle** (daily 9am–5pm; grounds only $6, grounds and castle $12) was the sumptuous residence of William Larnach, an Australian banker politician, who spent a fortune on its construction and decoration. Completed in 1871, it was designed by Scotsman R.A. Lawson, architect of the First Church and the Municipal Chambers in Dunedin. Most impressive is the sheer scale of the project. The very best local and overseas craftsmen were employed to build the family home entirely by hand, using materials shipped from all over the world, including glass and marble from Italy and tiles from England. On arrival, these were punted across the harbour and then laboriously dragged up the hill by ox-drawn sleds. Today the castle is owned by a family who renovated it to provide accommodation (see p.753) in two of the castle's buildings. Without your own transport, you'll have to take the Portobello **bus** either to Company Bay, from where it's a five-kilometre (signposted) walk, uphill all the way, or to Broad Bay, from where you'll have an even steeper but shorter walk (2km).

Back on the coast, about halfway along the peninsula, **The Fletcher House**, 727 Portobello Rd, Broad Bay (daily 11am–4pm; April to mid-Oct Sat, Sun & public holidays only; $3), is an attractive small Edwardian villa, lovingly restored to its original state and furnished in period style. Built entirely of native wood in 1909, it was the family home of the Broad Bay storekeeper. Inside the house, the absence of restricting ropes allows you to appreciate fully the furniture and fine woodwork, including the tongue-and-groove panelling in the small kitchen and richly coloured rimu ceilings and floors.

Further east, at Portobello, Hatchery Road leads 2km along a headland to the Marine Studies Centre **Aquarium** (daily noon–4.30pm; $7, or $14 per family), the best ticket on the peninsula for anyone wanting to find out more about marine life here and around New Zealand. The fun part is sticking your hands into the several shallow "touch tanks" to feel the small sea creatures. As part of a marine laboratory run by the University of Otago, this is an efficient venture, and staff are always available to answer questions. Visitors are also invited to participate in **fish feeding** (Sat 2–3pm; Dec–Feb also Wed 2–3pm).

Practicalities

With your own transport, access to the peninsula from Dunedin is easy, either via the snaky **Portobello Road**, which hugs the western shoreline overlooking the harbour, or the inland **Highcliff Road**, which heads up and over the hills. Dunedin visitor centre supplies a handy free map of the peninsula. The public **bus** (Mon–Sat) from Cumberland Street in Dunedin runs halfway along the peninsula, as far as Portobello (35min), from where it's still another 14km to Taiaroa Head. Several **guided-tour buses** depart daily from Dunedin visitor centre ($35–60, return; all booked through the visitor centre or direct), the best being the guided Elm Wildlife Tours (ⓣ03/474 1872, ⓔtours@elmwildlifetours.co.nz; up to 6hr, $43, plus optional extra $23 to visit the albatross colony). A straightforward **shuttle** also operates: the Otago Explorer goes to Larnach Castle only (ⓣ03/474 3300 & 0800/322 240; $30 return, including a guided tour of the castle). There are also daily harbour wildlife **cruises** on board the *Monarch*; see p.747 for details.

Walks on Otago Peninsula

A free map from the Dunedin visitor centre or DOC office, *Otago Peninsula Tracks*, briefly describes several walks on the peninsula. Bear in mind that they cover hill country and that though most tracks are well defined, some are pretty steep. Also, the weather here can turn cold or wet very quickly, even on the sunniest days.

The most rewarding walks include the easy loop track to **Lovers Leap and the Chasm** (3km; 1hr; closed Aug–Oct) which crosses farmland to sheer cliffs dropping 200m to the sea, with collapsed sea caves and rock faces of layered volcanic lava flows visible. The track begins from the end of Sandymount Road, a 25-minute drive from the centre of Dunedin. Also good is the track along **Sandfly Bay** (3km; 80min) which leads to sweeping dunes visited by yellow-eyed penguins and, occasionally, New Zealand sea lions (see box on p.762). There's a penguin hide at the far end of beach. This walk begins at the end of Seal Point Road, a twenty-minute drive from the city.

The Dunedin visitor centre can also help with accommodation, and stocks plenty of leaflets about the peninsula, including maps of various walking tracks.

Accommodation and eating

There's a limited amount of accommodation on the peninsula, and you'll find it pricier than in Dunedin. **Camping** is permitted only at the small *Portobello Village Tourist Park*, 27 Hereweka St, Portobello (ⓣ & ⓕ03/478 0359, ⓔpeninsula@es.co.nz; ❸), which has on-site caravans and cabins, as well as tent sites ($9) and powered sites ($10).

Budget accommodation is available at Taiaroa Head at the simple *Penguin Place Lodge*, McGrouther's Farm, Harington Point Rd (ⓣ03/478 0286, ⓔpenguin.place@clear.net.nz; single ❶, double or twin ❷, plus $5 linen hire), 3.5km before the albatross colony, with single, double and twin rooms, shared showers and kitchen; and at Company Bay at *The Mission B&B*, Mission Cove (ⓣ03/476 1321, ⓔcummings@deepsouth.co.nz; ❺), a former nurses' home with double and twin rooms, two guest bathrooms, a large garden and harbour views.

Mid-range options include three fully self-contained **motel** units with sundecks and harbour views at *Bayways Motel*, 697 Highcliff Rd, Portobello (ⓣ03/478 0181, ⓕ478 0382; ❹); a cosy, turn-of-the-century harbourside **cottage** aptly called *The Cottage*, 748 Portobello Rd, Broad Bay (ⓣ03/478 0073, ⓔthecottage@xtra.co.nz; ❺), with one double en suite; and the *Chy-an-Dowr* **B&B**, 687 Portobello Rd, Broad Bay (ⓣ & ⓕ03/478 0306, ⓔhermanvv@xtra.co.nz; ❺–❻), a spacious harbourside house midway along the peninsula, with three doubles (two en suite, one with separate but private bath) and a sunroom giving a panoramic view of the harbour. Further out there's also the tranquil 1930s *Nisbet Cottage B&B*, 6a Elliffe Place, Shiel Hill (ⓣ03/454 5169, ⓔwingsok@es.co.nz; ❺–❻), ten minutes' drive from central Dunedin (also served by Shiel Hill bus), offering great hill views and en-suite double and twin rooms.

Alternatively you can choose to stay in a couple of buildings in the grounds of Larnach Castle (ⓣ03/476 1616, ⓔlarnach@larnachcastle.co.nz), but you pay a premium for the tranquil garden setting high above the harbour. The converted *Stables* (❸) contains six basic rooms (sharing bathrooms), while the *Larnach Lodge* (❻–❼), refurbished to imitate a two-storey colonial farm building, has twelve en-suite rooms, each individually decorated in period style. All guests get a free tour of the castle during opening hours and you can also book for dinner in the castle's dining room (around $45 per head plus wine).

Eating is limited to simple takeaway snacks at the *MacAndrew Bay Store*, 497 Portobello Rd (ⓣ03/476 1107), a simple café/visitor centre at Portobello on Harington Point Rd and two reasonable waterfront venues, both cashing in on the harbour views and rustling up seafood, meat and vegetarian dishes. Closest to the city is the modern, glass-fronted *Loaves and Fishes*, 494 Portobello Rd, MacAndrew Bay (ⓣ03/476 1081), which is open daily for dinner (plus lunch on Friday and Sunday) and combines a bar, expensive licensed restaurant and cheaper café. Further along, in Portobello, the elegant *1908 Café & Bar*, 7 Harington Point Rd (ⓣ03/478 0801; licensed & BYO – bottled wine only), serves pricey lunches and dinners daily in summer (June–Aug lunches by prior arrangement only & dinner days vary; phone ahead) in a converted turn-of-the-century house, enhanced by excellent views of the harbour and city against a backdrop of hills. The varied menu includes enormous desserts.

Port Chalmers

If you have half a day left after exploring Dunedin and the Otago Peninsula, the small, attractive historic town and modern container port of **PORT CHALMERS**, on a tiny peninsula 12km along the western shore from Dunedin, is worth a trip. You'll be rewarded by magnificent harbour views offset by bush-covered hills, a short coastal walk, fine nineteenth-century buildings and a thriving artistic community.

The site was chosen in 1844 as the port to serve the proposed Scottish settlement of New Edinburgh, later called Dunedin. The first settlers arrived on the *John Wickliffe* in March 1848 and named the port after the Reverend Dr Thomas Chalmers, who had led the split between the Presbyterian and Free churches of Scotland. Development was slow until the Otago **gold rush** of the 1860s, which heralded a boom for Port Chalmers. Later, it served as the embarkation point for several **Antarctic expeditions**, including those of Captain Scott, who set out from here in 1901 and again, ill-fatedly, in 1910. The first trial shipment of **frozen meat** to Britain was sent from Port Chalmers and today the export of wool, meat and timber is its chief business.

The Town

The main street, **George Street**, connects the docks with SH88 and is lined with several old stone buildings containing shops, galleries, a few cafés and a bank. Most of the town crawls up hills on either side, where two churches dominate. On Mount Street stands the tall stone spire and clock tower of **Iona Church**, completed in 1883 and once Presbyterian but now United (Presbyterian Methodist), and on the opposite side, on Grey Street, sits the squat Anglican **Holy Trinity** (1874), designed by Scottish architect R.A. Lawson and built from local bluestone (volcanic rock).

On the George Street waterfront, you'll find the small, rather atmospheric **Museum**, in the old post office building. Run by volunteers, its hours vary considerably (Oct–March daily; April–Sept by arrangement only; donations requested; ⓣ03/472 8233). Brimming with maritime artefacts and some local settler history, museum highlights include a history of navigational equipment with splendid models and photographs. Downstairs is a large working electric model of a **gold dredge**, built in 1900 by a boilermaker apprentice. Staff can fill you in on local walking trails, and can also arrange escorted historical walks along the nearby beaches.

On the corner of Grey and George streets is the private studio (not open to the public) of artist **Ralph Hotere**, one of New Zealand's best-known abstract artists. The rest of George Street is lined with **art galleries** and **craft shops**. Port Chalmers Aero Club (Thurs–Sun; free), at no. 10, a delightful 1884 building, shows contemporary works by local artists displayed over several floors and has a **café** downstairs serving cheap lunches and snacks. Next door, occupying an old bank, The Crafty Banker (Thurs–Sun) is a pleasant gallery and craft shop, while further up the hill, Portfolio (Thurs–Sun or by appointment ⓣ03/472 7856) has a good selection of rugs, kilims and objets d'art.

For a spectacular panorama of the harbour and Otago Peninsula, a **coastal walk** (4km; 45min–1hr) starts from Wickliffe Terrace, at the junction with George Street. After crossing the rail line, the road takes you past Mussel Bay to the commanding headland. Continuing around the coast, home to a wide variety of sea birds including terns, oystercatchers, shags, gulls, herons and ducks, you reach Back Beach, and can return to George Street via a log-storage area or detour up to Flagstaff Lookout, above the headland.

Practicalities

By **car** from Dunedin, it's a ten-minute scenic harbourside drive along SH88, or you can take the longer scenic route, following Mount Cargill and Upper Junction roads. From the north on SH1, take the road to Port Chalmers from Waitati. **Buses** from Dunedin to Port Chalmers leave from Stand 4 opposite Countdown supermarket in Cumberland Street, dropping you off in George Street about 25 minutes later (Mon–Sat).

Eating options are limited to cafés and takeaways, the best being *Café Giardino* at the Aero Club, 10 George St, which serves cheap soups, sandwiches, bagels and quiches, and *Port Stables Bar & Café*, 56 George St, in tastefully converted stables with a pool table and a roaring fire in winter. You'll find scenic picnic spots along Peninsula Beach Road, just around from the harbour.

South from Dunedin: Balclutha and the Catlins Coast

The dramatic, rugged coastal route linking Dunedin and Invercargill, part of the **Southern Scenic Route** that continues on to Fiordland, is one of the least travelled highways in New Zealand, and traverses some of the country's wildest scenery along the **Catlins Coast**. Within this significant region is the largest area of native forest on the east coast of the South Island, most of it protected as the **Catlins Forest Park**, and consisting of rimu, rata, kamahi and silver beech. Roaring southeasterlies and the remorseless sea have shaped the coastline here into plunging cliffs, windswept headlands, white sand beaches, rocky bays and gaping caves, much of this accessible on a number of short bushwalks. Not surprisingly, this relatively untouched area abounds with **wildlife**, including several rare species of marine bird and mammal, and the whole region rings with birdsong most of the year, though the **birds** are at their most active during June to August when breeding. The Catlins have something to offer at any time of the year, but from mid-November to mid-December you benefit from spring/summer weather and avoid the busy season during and after Christmas. The only major stop-off point between Dunedin and the Catlins Coast is **Balclutha**, which is a good place to stock up before entering the wilderness beyond. At Balclutha, SH1 turns inland, skirting the Catlins region before turning south to Invercargill at the town of **Gore**, a centre for brown-trout fishing.

Maori hunters once thrived in the Catlins region, one of the last refuges of the flightless moa, but by 1700 they had moved on, to be supplanted by European **whalers and sealers** in the 1830s. Two decades later, having decimated whale and seal stocks, they too moved on. Meanwhile, in 1840, Captain Edward Cattlin arrived to investigate the navigability of the river that bears his (misspelled) name. He purchased a tract of land from the chief of the Ngai Tahu and soon after, boatloads of **loggers** began to arrive, lured by the great podocarp forests. Cleared valleys were settled, bush millers supplied Dunedin with much of the wood needed for housing and, in 1872, more timber was exported from the Catlins than anywhere else in New Zealand. From 1879, the rail line from Balclutha began to extend into the region, bringing with it sawmills, schools and farms. Milling continued into the 1930s, but gradually dwindled and today's tiny settlements are shrunken remnants of the once-prosperous logging industry.

Although the 126-kilometre stretch of road through the Catlins should present no problems for vehicles, be aware that a twenty-kilometre section is **unsealed**, as are smaller roads edging out to the sea. For this reason, none of the major bus companies operates through the Catlins and there is no train either. Without your own transport, or if you just want to make a day-trip, you can take one of several **guided tours** (see box on p.759), which operate from Dunedin, Balclutha and Invercargill.

Balclutha

Located on SH1, 80km southwest of Dunedin and 185km from Invercargill, **BALCLUTHA** lies amid rich pastures in the heart of South Otago. Nicknamed "Big River Town", Balclutha occupies both banks of the mighty **Clutha River**, with the town centre on the southern shore linked to SH1 by an unmissable, arched concrete bridge. The river was once a source of alluvial gold but today is used to generate hydroelectricity. Anglers are lured to Balclutha by the river's substantial stocks of brown trout and salmon; for non-fishing folk, there are few attractions in the small township apart from a laid-back **jetboat** trip on the river, and the main reason to stop is to pick up information and supplies for the trip south.

If you can't resist getting on the water, Blue Mountain Jet (Ⓣ03/415 9268) offer a range of **jetboat** tours (from 20min for $30 to 1hr at $55), filling you in on the local ecology and history. There's plenty of birdlife and they'll show you an 1896 paddle steamer that operates as a ferry, these days propelled by the current and a system of rudders and pulleys. The jetboat is also available for **fishing** charters (half day $350, full day $600) and the company runs a B&B ($80).

All **buses** except InterCity stop outside the visitor centre (see below) – InterCity pull up outside the *Café Italio* on John Street – and the centrally located **train station** is at the junction of Scotland Street and Baxter Street. Balclutha's well-organized and helpful **Clutha visitor centre** is beside the bridge at 4 Clyde St (Nov–March Mon–Fri 8.30am–5pm, Sat & Sun 9.30am–3pm; April–Oct Mon–Fri 8.30am–5pm, Sat & Sun 10am–2pm; Ⓣ03/418 0388, Ⓔclutha.vin@cluthadc.govt.nz) and has plenty of information on the Catlins and Gore, including the excellent *Southern Scenic Route Map* ($1), and a series of leaflets on walks in the Clutha district ($0.50 each). You'll find **internet access** at Sound Trax record store, 36 Clyde St (Mon–Fri 9am–6pm, Sat 9am–4pm).

There's a small selection of **accommodation** in town. The best campsite is the small *Naish Park Motor Camp*, 56 Charlotte St (Ⓣ03/418 0088), five minutes' walk from the town centre and set in pleasant parkland with excellent modern facilities. There are plenty of tent sites ($9 per person), powered sites ($9 per person), one on-site caravan (❶) and five cabins (❷–❸). The only **hostel** is the basic *Balclutha Backpackers*, 20 Stewart St (mobile Ⓣ021/139 3248; ❶), a converted 1950s convent but far better are the **motels,** including the friendly *Helensborough Motor Inn*, 23 Essex St (Ⓣ & Ⓕ03/418 1948, reservations only 0800/113 355; ❹–❺), north of the bridge, with fully self-contained units; and *Rosebank Lodge*, 265 Clyde St (Ⓣ03/418 1490, Ⓕ418 1493; ❹), a quiet

The **western continuation** of the **Southern Scenic Route**, from Invercargill to Te Anau via Tuatapere, is covered in the *Fiordland* chapter.

complex with eighteen units, three bars, a restaurant, spa and sauna. Twelve kilometres north of Balclutha is the luxurious *Garvan Homestead B&B* (Ⓣ03/417 8407, Ⓕ417 8429; ❺), a large tudor-style retreat in rambling gardens with a good licensed restaurant.

Places to eat are strung along Clyde Street. *The Captain's*, a centrally located and pleasant pub, at no. 13, serves reasonable and well-priced bar food, from snacks to steaks, and there's a good Chinese, *Gins*, at no. 27 (closed Tues; BYO). The moderately priced à la carte restaurant at *Rosebank Lodge* is the best place for something special.

The Catlins Coast

The best way to enjoy the **CATLINS COAST** is to take it slowly, absorbing its unique atmosphere over at least a couple of days. There's plenty to see at any time of year, but if you visit during the week you'll avoid most of the summer day-trippers from Dunedin. From Nugget Point in South Otago (just southeast of Balclutha) to Waipapa Point in Southland (60km northeast of Invercargill), the wild scenery stretches unbroken, with dense rainforest succumbing to open scrub as you cut through deep valleys and past rocky bays, inlets and estuaries. The coast is home to **penguins** (both little blues and yellow-eyed), **dolphins**, several types of sea bird and, at certain times of year, migrating **whales**. Elephant **seals**, fur seals, and increasingly, the rare New Zealand **sea lion** are found on the sandy beaches and grassy areas, and within the mossy depths of the forest are abundant **birds**: tui, resonant bellbirds, fantails, grey warblers and colourful tree-top dwellers such as kakariki and mohau.

The most awe-inspiring natural features scattered along the way are **Nugget Point**, a rugged, windswept promontory favoured by fur seals and sea lions; the **Purakaunui Falls**, among the most photographed in New Zealand; the impressive **Cathedral Caves**, their high "ceilings" and deep chambers carved out of the cliffs by the sheer force of the sea; and **Curio Bay**, where an intriguing forest has been captured in stone.

The main settlement is **Owaka** (Place of the Canoe), a farming town 38km from Balclutha and inhabited by less than two hundred people. It has a small selection of accommodation, services and shops, including a pub, supermarket, store/diner/backpackers, pharmacy and a 24-hour medical centre. Elsewhere, there are general stores at **Kaka Point**, **Papatowai** and at **Curio Bay** Camping Ground. **Petrol** stations are few and far between, so fill up before you set off, then at Kaka Point, Owaka, Papatowai or Tokanui (pumps close at around 5pm). Note that there are **no banks** within the Catlins. Bear in mind, too, that **theft from cars** is on the increase in the region, especially in the remoter spots, so don't leave valuables in the car and be sure to lock it.

Kaka Point to Owaka

First stop inside the Catlins is **Kaka Point**, a tiny beachside community 22km from Balclutha (turn off SH92 at Romahapa). There's a general store beside a pub and restaurant of dubious distinction, a petrol station and postshop, as well as an extremely well-appointed hillside **motel**, *Nugget View & Kaka Point Motel* (Ⓣ03/412 8602, Ⓔnugview@catlins.co.nz; ❸–❺), whose spacious units all have decking and ocean views. The motel also runs **boat trips** around Nugget Point (weather permitting) and fishing trips. Another friendly spot offering charming, self-contained accommodation by the beach is *Nugget Lodge*

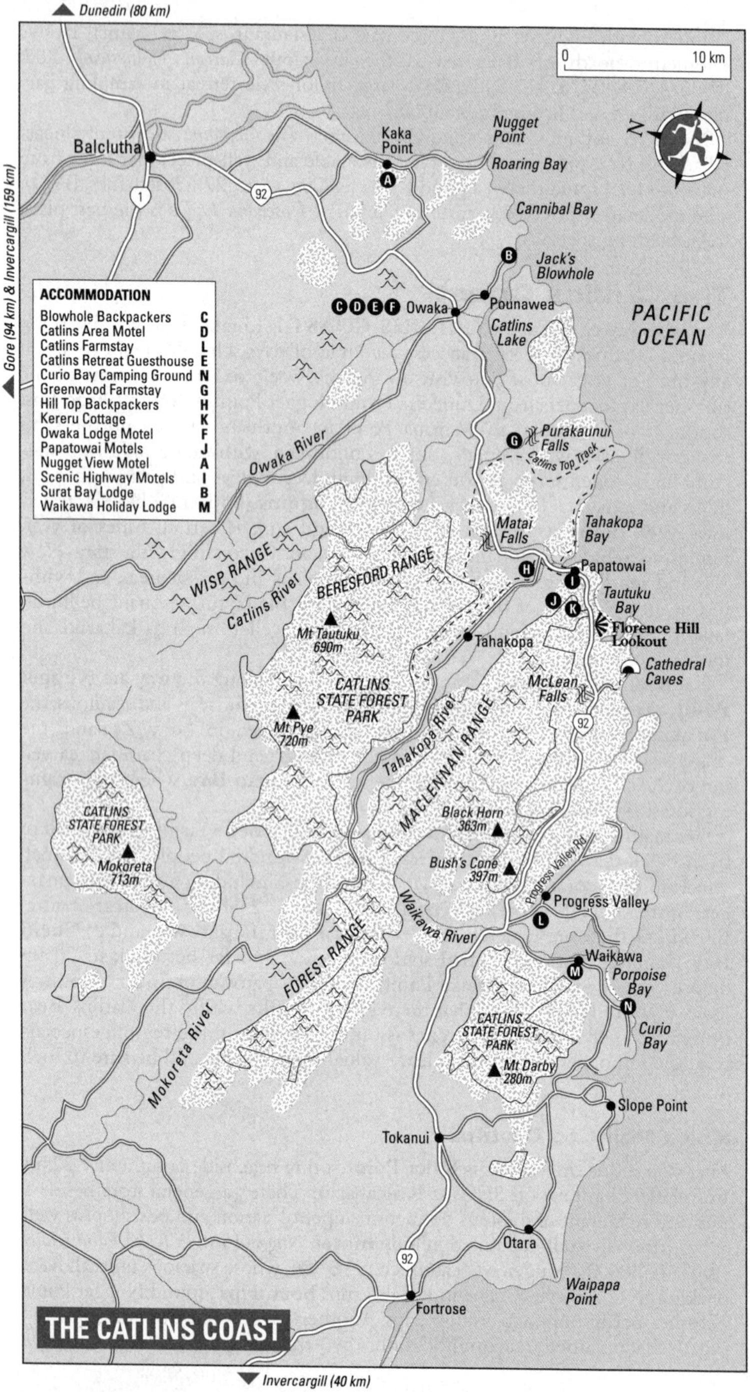

THE CATLINS COAST

Dunedin (80 km)

Gore (94 km) & Invercargill (159 km)

Invercargill (40 km)

0 10 km

N

ACCOMMODATION

Blowhole Backpackers	C
Catlins Area Motel	D
Catlins Farmstay	L
Catlins Retreat Guesthouse	E
Curio Bay Camping Ground	N
Greenwood Farmstay	G
Hill Top Backpackers	H
Kereru Cottage	K
Owaka Lodge Motel	F
Papatowai Motels	J
Nugget View Motel	A
Scenic Highway Motels	I
Surat Bay Lodge	B
Waikawa Holiday Lodge	M

Balclutha
1
92
Kaka Point
A
Nugget Point
Roaring Bay
Cannibal Bay
B
Jack's Blowhole
C D E F Owaka
Pounawea
Catlins Lake
PACIFIC OCEAN
Owaka River
G
Purakaunui Falls
Catlins Top Track
Matai Falls
Tahakopa Bay
WISP RANGE
Catlins River
BERESFORD RANGE
H
Papatowai
I
J
K
Tautuku Bay
Florence Hill Lookout
Cathedral Caves
Mt Tautuku 690m
Tahakopa
CATLINS STATE FOREST PARK
McLean Falls
Mt Pye 720m
92
Tahakopa River
MACLENNAN RANGE
CATLINS STATE FOREST PARK
Mokoreta 713m
Black Horn 363m
Bush's Cone 397m
Progress Valley Rd
Progress Valley
L
Waikawa River
FOREST RANGE
Waikawa
M
Porpoise Bay
N
Curio Bay
Mokoreta River
CATLINS STATE FOREST PARK
Mt Darby 280m
Slope Point
Tokanui
Otara
92
Waipapa Point
Fortrose

Tours of the Catlins

If you don't have your own transport, **guided tours** are really the only way of exploring the Catlins; trips start from Dunedin, Balclutha and Invercargill.

Highly recommended is an inspirational **eco-tour** run by **Catlins Wildlife Trackers** (☎03/415 8613, ⓦwww.catlins-ecotours.co.nz; advance bookings essential), sharing in-depth knowledge about the local ecology, history and geology. The organizers are committed to conservation and offer an intimate two- or four-day tour ($270 & $540 respectively) for groups of up to eight, which explores remote beaches and rich rainforest from their secluded coastal home deep in the Catlins at Papatowai. You can drive there or be picked up from Balclutha on Mon, Wed & Sat mornings. All meals, accommodation, transport and equipment are provided and a shuttle service to and from Dunedin can be arranged for an extra fee or through Clutha visitor centre (see p.756). You stay in their tranquil house – overlooking native forest, an estuary, beach and ocean – in a separate section containing double and twin rooms sharing a bathroom.

A no-frills guided minibus tour, **Catlins Coastal Link**, shuttles from Dunedin to Invercargill along SH1 via Gore, returning the same or next day via the Catlins and allowing plenty of time off the bus for bush and beach walks, wildlife encounters and the major scenic sights. The tour is extremely friendly and relaxed and you can also get on or off where you like and pick up a later bus. Buses depart in both directions (daily mid-Nov to April only, book ahead through visitor centres; Dunedin one-day return $90, 2-day return $110, Invercargill–Dunedin one way via the Catlins $80; an optional popular extra on all trips is an overnight farmstay including a full day on a working sheep, beef and deer farm, $195 including the travel). The tour also links in with shuttles from Te Anau and Queenstown.

The Bottom Bus (☎03/442 9708), which supplements the Kiwi Experience bus trips in Southland, but in small personal buses without the reckless booze-bus approach, runs from Dunedin through the Catlins to Invercargill on its clockwise loop to Riverton, Te Anau and Queenstown, returning to Dunedin (3 days minimum; $160 for whole trip or other flexible options). You can travel sections of this journey if you don't want a ticket for the whole thing, and jump on along the way; departures from Dunedin are on Mon, Wed, Thurs, Sat & Sun mornings (Dunedin–Invercargill $79).

A more intimate day-trip from Balclutha, Kaka Point or Owaka, or one-way overnight trip from Invercargill to Dunedin, can be had with **Catlins Natural Wonders** (☎0800 353 941, ⓦwww.catlinsnatural.co.nz & ⓦwwwcatlins-nz.com), who take groups of up to nine and allow plenty of time for walking. On Nov 8–April 10, day-trips from Balclutha, Kaka Point and Owaka ($85, $80 & $60, respectively) run on Mon–Wed & Sat and offer an optional yellow-eyed penguin viewing in the evening for an extra $36; tours from Invercargill to Dunedin leave Thursday ($175 plus accommodation of your choice; or an overnight package deal including supper, B&B and yellow-eyed penguin viewing for $295). During the rest of the year tours run on demand, and during school termtime (check dates with visitor centres) the bus runs a shuttle service in both directions between Balclutha and Dunedin on Fri & Sun ($15).

(☎03/4128783, ⓦwww.nuggetlodge.co.nz, ❺), run by a wildlife photographer and ranger who share their enthusiasm for the area with their visitors. The beach's golden sands are patrolled by lifeguards in summer, making Kaka Point a good spot for swimming as well as surfing. Just behind the township a fine scenic reserve of native forest is accessible on an easy loop track (2.5km; 30min; signposted from the top of Marine Terrace).

Nine kilometres further down the coast, accessed by road and a short track, is **Nugget Point**, a steep-sided, windswept promontory rising 133m above the sea. Just offshore lie jagged stacks of rock (the nuggets), whose layers have been tilted over time. A lighthouse dating from 1870 still operates here and from the high-level track beside it you can see southern fur seals, elephant seals (on the only mainland breeding site in the world, Oct–March), penguins and a variety of seabirds, including gannets, spoonbills and three species of shag. Around the corner a track leads to a hide overlooking the sandy beach, **Roaring Bay**, from where you can watch yellow-eyed penguins (see box on p.750) as they leave their nests at sunrise and descend the steep grassy cliffs to the sea or as they return two hours before dark. Their progress is slow, so you need plenty of patience, and binoculars are handy. To reach the next bay south, **Cannibal Bay**, you hit the road again, backtracking from Nugget Point a few kilometres to the turn-off to inland Otekura, before zipping back to the coast (about 20km in all). Rare New Zealand sea lions (see box on p.762) haul out onto the long crescent of sand – it's worth walking along the beach for a closer look (from a distance they look like logs) but keep at least five metres away from them and back off quickly if they rear up and roar.

As you approach the farming town of **OWAKA**, you'll see totara growing in abundance. On the main street is the tiny **Catlins Museum** (Dec–Feb daily 1–4pm; March–Nov Sun 1.30–4.30pm or by arrangement ⓣ03/415 8490; $1 donation), focusing on local pioneer history, early settlement, sawmills, dairy factories and shipwrecks. Well-run **horse treks** in the unspoilt tussock hills are given by Valley View Horse Treks (ⓣ03/415 8239, ⓔlattajf@es.co.nz; minimum of 2 people; 2hr, $85). The **Catlins visitor centre**, located in the diner on Main Road (March–Oct Mon, Wed & Fri 10am–3pm; Nov–Feb daily 10am–5pm ; ⓣ03/415 8371) has plenty of leaflets and tide tables to help you plan for a couple of the sights only accessible at low tide, and there's also an unmanned **DOC Field Centre** at 20 Ryley St (pick up the key from the visitor centre), with good displays of Catlins history, marine habitats, flora and fauna. Places to **stay** comprise the very comfy *Blowhole Backpackers*, on Main Road (ⓣ03/415 8830; dorm $18, room $45); the fresh, friendly and elegant *Catlins Retreat Guesthouse*, 27 Main Rd (ⓣ03/415 8830; ❹), owned by the same people and opposite the *Blowhole*; the *Catlins Area Motel*, corner Clark and Ryley streets (ⓣ & ⓕ03/415 8821, ⓔcatlinsareamotel@hotmail.com; ❹–❺); and *Owaka Lodge Motel*, 12 Ryley St (ⓣ03/415 8728; ❹), which has four fully self-contained modern units. Tucked away in a peaceful spot at the coast five kilometres from Owaka is the well-kept *Surat Bay Lodge*, Surat Bay Road, Newhaven (ⓣ & ⓕ03/415 8099, ⓔsuratbay@actrix.gen.nz; dorm ❶, rooms ❷), overlooking the Catlins Estuary, with free pick-up from Owaka and kayaks for rent. If you want something to eat in town then the choice is between *The Lumberjack*, 3 Saunders St, near the T-junction, which serves the most high-class lunches and dinners in the Catlins at a price (Nov–March daily noon–2pm & 6pm–late; April–Oct Wed–Sun only); the *Owaka Pub*, 21 Ryley St, where the food is great value and less pretentious, mostly arriving with chips attached (Nov–Feb daily 5.30–9pm; Mar–Oct Thurs–Sat only); and the *Catlins Diner* (daily 9am–7pm), serving basic take-away and eat-in food.

Owaka to Papatowai

This section contains an impressive **blowhole** and two sets of striking **waterfalls**, close to one another. **Jack's Blowhole** (closed Sept & Oct due to lambing), signposted 6km from Owaka, was created when the roof of a subterranean cave fell in and is pretty spectacular at high tide. It lies about 13km from

The Catlins Top Track and Beach to Beech walks

The longest and most varied walk in the region is **Catlins Top Track** (26km; 9–10hr $10; 2 days, $25 including overnight stay), which delivers the best views, true tranquillity, fascinating geology and a great variety of flora and fauna. It begins and ends at Papatowai, in the heart of the Catlins, crossing sweeping beaches and privately owned bush and farmland. You need to be moderately fit and most people walk it in two days rather than rushing.

The first day takes about six hours, starting with a walk along one of the finest open beaches in the Catlins, then following an old coach road and climbing to weathered sandstone cliffs and the night's accommodation beyond. The second day takes half the time and is very different: you pass through bush containing ancient trees and emerge at the walk's highest point (just over 300m) to spectacular views before following a former railway line to the McLennan River and then continue to the pre-arranged pick up point.

Numbers are limited to six overnight walkers, who stay in a converted 1960s trolley bus high up on a spectacular viewpoint, which has one double bed and four single bunks, electric lighting, a gas camping stove with cutlery and dishes, a wood-burning stove for heat in winter, and its own water supply. There's even a separate loo with a view. You need your own food, drinking water and sleeping bag, but the organizers, **Catlins Wildlife Trackers** (Ⓣ0800/228 5467, www.catlins-ecotours.co.nz), deliver your pack to the bus for $20 per group. All walkers are given an excellent booklet that details each section of the walk accompanied by a map. Catlins Wildlife Trackers can help with accommodation, or take your pick from a range at Papatowai (see below); they also provide a pick-up service from Balclutha (Mon, Wed & Sat at 10am), but only for those on their guided tours.

Catlines Wildlife Trackers also offer the **Beach to Beech walk**, a two-day trek (Nov–March Thurs & Fri; 26km, 8 people maximum; $275 including overnight accommodation, all food and transport back to starting point) for the moderately fit with only light packs. The walk begins at Papatowai Beach and heads over private land and through beech forest up the beautiful old rail route in the McLennan Valley before stopping the night in *Mohua Lodge*. The following day takes a gentle tramp through the Catlins River Valley, spotting wildlife and listening to stories about the area before halting at Wisp. Thereafter the bus picks you up and heads back to Papatowai where you can pick up your vehicle, stay or grab a shuttle.

the main road and you have to walk the last two kilometres along a track (30min). The renowned three-tiered **Purakaunui Falls** lie in a scenic reserve of silver beech and podocarp, signposted off the main road 17km from Owaka. There's a picnic area here and an easy track (10min) through the forest to a viewing platform. Just before the falls, *Greenwood Farmstay* (Ⓣ & Ⓕ03/415 8259, Ⓔgreenwoodfarm@xtra.co.nz; ❹), a beautifully kept house on a sheep, cattle and deer farm, offers accommodation and dinner on request. Two kilometres south of the Purakaunui turn-off are the exquisite **Matai Falls**, best viewed late in the morning. The track to the falls (10min) cuts through regenerating podocarp forest, including fuchsia trees.

Across the estuary of the McLennan River, the small settlement of **PAPATOWAI** offers a general store (Mon–Fri 9am–5pm, Sat 10am–1pm), several forest and beach walks, a craft gallery, and an excellent **eco-tour** with the Catlins Wildlife Trackers (book well ahead, see box on p.759) and the start of the **Catlins Top Track** (2 days; see box above). In a cheerful old bus beside the main road The Lost Gypsy Gallery (hours vary, closed June–Aug; cash only) sells reasonably priced Kiwi crafts such as jewellery, handmade flax paper and decorative tiles, mainly from the southern South Island. There are also a few good **places to stay**: the wonderful *Hill Top Backpackers* (ⓣ03/415 8028; ❶), on a farm off the Tahakopa Road, just before the bridge near Papatowai, occupies a delightful, well-kept cottage with astounding panoramic views; in town, *Papatowai Motels* (ⓣ & ⓕ03/415 8147; ❸–❹), next to the general store, has three newish units with fully equipped kitchens; the modern self-contained *Kereru Cottage* (book through Catlins Wildlife Trackers; ⓣ & ⓕ03/415 8613, ⓔcatlinw@es.co.nz; ❻, $20 each per extra person) offers great ocean and estuary views and a queen-sized en-suite bedroom, plus bunks and a sofabed; the same people offer a homestay (❹, dinner $20 each) with double and twin rooms; and at the beach, there's a self-contained cottage (ⓣ03/415 8259; ❹).

The New Zealand sea lion and Hector's dolphin

Two extremely rare species – the **New Zealand or Hooker's sea lion** (*Phocarctos hookeri*) and **Hector's dolphin** (*Cephalarhynchus hectori*) – are found only in New Zealand waters. The former mostly live at the subantarctic Auckland Islands, 460km south of the South Island, but a small amount of breeding also takes place at the Otago Peninsula, the Catlins Coast and Stewart Island. The large, adult male sea lions are black to dark brown, have a mane over their shoulders, weigh up to 400kg and reach lengths of over 3m. Adult females are buff to silvery grey and much smaller – less than half the weight and just under 2m. Barracuda, red cod, octopus, skate and, in spring, paddle crabs together make up their diet, and although Hooker's sea lions usually dive less than 200m for four or five minutes, they're capable of achieving depths of up to 500m. Pups are born on the beach, then moved by the mother at about six weeks to grassy swards, shrubland or forest, and suckled for up to a year.

Sea lions prefer to haul out on sandy beaches and in summer spend much of the day flicking sand over themselves to keep cool. Unlike seals they don't fear people. If you encounter one on land, give it a wide berth of at least five metres (30m during breeding, Dec–Feb) and if it rears up and roars, back off quickly – they can move surprisingly swiftly. When swimming or diving near haul-out sites, be aware that the sea lions can be boisterous and don't antagonize or attempt to feed them.

The Hector's dolphin, with its distinctive black and white markings, is the smallest dolphin in the world and also one of the rarest (population 3000–4000). It's only found in New Zealand inshore waters – mostly around the coast of the South Island – with eastern concentrations around Banks Peninsula, Te Waewae Bay and Porpoise Bay, plus western communities between Farewell Spit and Haast. In summer they prefer shallow waters within 1km of the shore to catch mullet, arrowsquid, red cod, stargazers and crabs; they seldom venture beyond 8km in winter. Unusually perhaps, female dolphins are slightly larger than the males, growing to 1.2–1.4m and weighing 40–50kg. The main birthing season is from November to mid-February, and calves stay with their mothers for up to two years.

In Porpoise Bay – where the dolphin population is tiny (about twenty residents with occasional visits by others) and, in summer and autumn, regularly enters the surf zone or even comes within 10m of the beach – the following DOC **rules** apply: never approach a dolphin; always enter the water at least 50m away from any dolphin or pod, and always on the Curio Bay (southern) side; never surround, follow or pass through a pod; no boat or kayak should spend more than forty minutes within the 5 knot zone; don't touch a dolphin; don't feed them. In addition, under the Marine Mammals Protection Regulations of 1992 it is illegal to disturb or harass a marine mammal, or swim with juvenile dolphins or pods containing juvenile dolphins.

Papatowai to Waipapa Point

From Papatowai the road seal runs out and stays that way for a further 20km or so to Waikawa, the road narrow and winding in places.

Just south of Papatowai is **Tautuku Bay**, a magnificent crescent beach of pale sand backed by extensive forest, with a great view point, Florence Hill Lookout, on the main road, offering a complete panorama of the bay, forest and coastline. The grandest and most accessible of about fifteen caves along this part of the coast are the **Cathedral Caves** ($2 per person or $5 per car), signposted 36km south of Owaka. The caves are formed by two connecting caverns with massively high walls created by furious sea action against the cliffs. They can only be entered one hour before or after low tide; times are published by the DOC at Owaka and are also posted on the gate by the carpark at the turn-off from the highway. There's a picnic area and it's a pleasant, easy forty-minute walk to the caves. A kilometre or so further along the main road is the turn-off (along Rewcastle Road) to the spectacular **McLean Falls**, at the end of a 30-minute forest walk. At the fishing village of **WAIKAWA**, 40km from Papatowai, an old church houses a dolphin and penguin information centre and a coffee shop (Oct–April daily 9am–7pm). In summer and autumn (Nov–April), the world's rarest dolphins **'Hector's dolphins'** come close to the shore at nearby **PORPOISE BAY** to rear their young. This is the only place in the world where dolphins live permanently so close to shore, and there are about twenty resident, with others coming and going near the long arc of golden sands. Dolphin Magic Cruises (Ⓣ0800/377 581, Ⓔdolphinmagic@xtra.co.nz) operate sensitive, regular, one-hour **dolphin encounter trips** for small groups from Waikawa Jetty to the sheltered waters of Porpoise Bay ($50 per person); on their twilight cruise (2hr 30min, $75) you'll also see some spectacular geology and colonies of seals and yellow-eyed penguins. Since the dolphins are extremely shy and easily upset, swimming is not allowed on any of their trips. Whether on an organized trip or on your own it is important not to pester the dolphins in any way, either from the shore or in the water, as this has a significant impact on their feeding, which in turn affects their already threatened breeding rate (see box above). The dolphin information centre has a key to the nearby **Waikawa District Museum** (pick it up from the information centre), whose chief attraction in a higgledy-piggledy exhibition is a display on seafarers and logging. Opposite the information centre is a **place to stay**, *Waikawa Holiday Lodge* (Ⓣ03/246 8552; dorm ❶, rooms ❷), a clean friendly hostel in a renovated cottage with a four-bed dorm, a twin and a double.

Sections of the road linking Waikawa and **CURIO BAY**, next door to Porpoise Bay, have been surfaced, so it is no longer quite such a cringe-making trip for anyone with a hire car. Curio Bay is home to an international treasure, a fine example of a Jurassic **fossil forest** that's clearly visible at low tide. Over 180 million years ago, when most of New Zealand still lay beneath the sea, this would have been a broad, forested floodplain. Today, the seashore, composed of several layers of forest buried under blankets of volcanic mud and ash, is littered with fossilized tree stumps and fallen logs. **Hector's dolphins** often cavort in the surf here, but take note of the beach signs that warn you to keep your distance (see box above). **Yellow-eyed penguins** can be viewed on the Porpoise Bay side, from the top of McClogan's Loop, but again keep your distance (at least 10m) and stay hidden; most activity is at sunrise and towards the end of the day, and if they spy you they will not come ashore in the evenings, thus depriving their young of an eagerly awaited meal. The region's prime **campsite**, the *Curio Bay Camping Ground & Store* (Ⓣ03/246 8897; tent sites $4, powered sites

$7.50, on-site vans ❷), is located here, spread across a peninsula between Curio Bay and Porpoise Bay, with wonderful views on all sides, a store, and sites sheltered by long grass and shrubs – though at the time of writing the camp's future was in question, with Southland District Council and Tourism Southland apparently keen, to the consternation of the locals, to hand it over to outside investors for development. Just fifteen-minutes' drive northeast of Curio Bay is the welcoming *Catlins Farmstay*, Progress Valley Road (ⓣ03/246 8843, ⓔcatlinsfarmstay@xtra.co.nz; ❻), a comfortable **homestead** on a large, secluded sheep, deer and cattle farm, offering an en-suite queen room, a twin and a double, as well as providing home-cooked meals ($35 per head for a three-course dinner). Two kilometres away, the farm also owns a four-bed **backpacker cabin** (❶), hidden away in the bush and equipped with a pot-bellied stove and cooker, but no electricity; you need your own sleeping bag.

From Curio Bay your best bet is to press on along the unsealed road towards Otara, past the turn-off to **Slope Point**, the southernmost point in the South Island (accessed several kilometres off the main road and through private land) and aim instead for **Waipapa Point**, 22km beyond Curio Bay. In 1881 this was the site of New Zealand's worst civilian shipwreck (a lighthouse was erected three years later) when 131 lives were lost on *SS Tararua*; nowadays it's the haunt of **fur seals** and **sea lions** that bask on the golden beach and rocky platform. If you want to **stay** out near Slope Point there are two backpackers, the better of which is *Pope's Place*, next door to the *Slope Point Backpackers* (both ⓣ & ⓕ03/24668420; dorms ❶, rooms ❷) in the middle of nowhere, with pet sheep but little else to occupy you. Back on the main road, once past the windswept trees of Fortrose, it's a clear run of 60km along a bland inland stretch of SH92 to Invercargill.

Gore

Seventy-one kilometres west of Balclutha on SH1 is **GORE**, a pleasant enough transit point at the intersection of routes from Dunedin to Te Anau and Invercargill. Dominated by the Hokonui Hills, Gore spans the Mataura River ("reddish swirling water"), which is renowned for its plentiful brown trout. Apart from breaking your journey for a night or grabbing a bite to eat, there's little reason to linger unless you're heavily into fishing or country music. This is the **brown trout** capital of the world (celebrated by an enormous fish statue in the town centre), and New Zealand's centre of **country music**. For eight days during late May and early June, this normally quiet rural town is the scene of the **Gold Guitar Awards**, during which hundreds of would-be country stars and a few established performers congregate to celebrate their art.

One attraction in town worth a brief visit is a combined museum and visitor centre, the **Hokonui Heritage Centre**, on the corner of Norfolk Street and Hokonui Drive (Mon–Fri 9am–5pm, Sat & Sun Oct–March 10am–4pm, April–Sept 1–4pm), where the **Historic Museum** (same times as visitor centre; donation requested) concentrates on local history through the usual kinds of memorabilia. More entertaining, however, is the **Hokonui Moonshine Museum** (Mon–Fri 9am–4.30pm, Sat & Sun Oct–March 10am–3.30pm, April–Sept 1–3.30pm; $5), detailing decades of illicit whisky distillation deep in the local bush-covered hills, which began in 1836 and reached a peak during Prohibition at the turn of the century. Among notable distillers were the Scottish McRae family, who settled in this area during the 1870s. Despite the best efforts of police and customs, the only people caught in the act were the Kirk brothers, whose cow shed and stills are on display. If you're here during the **fishing** season (Oct–April), and want to pit your wits against a wily brown trout you'll need a licence from the visitor centre (around $15 for 24hr). Tackle can be rented from B&B Sports, 65 Main St. Seventeen kilometres northwest of Gore on SH94 lies the Old Mandeville Airfield, home of **vintage aircraft** – a Tiger Moth, Fox Moth, Dominie and Dragonfly – which still take to the air in 20-minute **joyrides** including a few mind-blowing acrobatics, at probably the best prices in New Zealand (Croydon Air Services ⓣ03/208 9755, ⓔcroydon.aircraft@esi.co.nz; $59–$70, or more negotiable for longer trips, also depending on number of passengers). You're welcome to have a look around the hangar, where renovation is constantly in progress on all sorts of aircraft, and there's a restaurant/bar here, too (see below). The eighth weekend of every year sees the **Mandeville Fly-in**, a two-day celebration of vintage and modern aircraft, classic cars, joyrides and so on (for more details contact the Gore visitor centre).

Practicalities

Gore lies on the major **bus** route between the two cities. Buses drop off at the **visitor centre** on Hokonui Drive (Mon–Fri 9am–5pm, Sat & Sun Oct–March 10am–4pm, April–Sept 1–4pm; ⓣ & ⓕ03/208 9908, ⓔgoreinfo@esi.co.nz), opposite the giant trout, where you can book accommodation and transport and pick up information on the town and surrounding area.

Accommodation

Croydon Lodge Motor Inn cnr SH94 & Waimea St ⓣ03/208 9029, ⓔthelodge@esi.co.nz. A modern hotel-cum-motel with two bars and restaurants, set in extensive grounds, including a golf course, on the outskirts of town. ❹

Dellmount Woolwich Street, East Gore ⓣ & ⓕ03/208 1771. A super-friendly B&B-cum-farmstay on a small Arabian horse stud 2km from Gore town centre on the banks of the Mataura River. Dinner on request $20. ❹

Esplanade Motels 35 Railway Esplanade ⓣ & ⓕ03/208 0888, ⓣ0800/285 050. Comfortable, spacious, well-maintained units in a compound run by friendly hosts, about 1.5km walk from the centre of town. ❹

Gore Motor Camp 35 Broughton St ⓣ & ⓕ03/208 4919. Well-run and fairly central campsite with tent sites for $11, powered sites $11, and cabins. ❷

Fire Station Backpackers 19 Hokonui Drive ⓣ & ⓕ03/208 1925, ⓔsiandvic@esi.co.nz. Small, clean hostel with dorms, doubles and twins. Dorms ❶, rooms ❷

Riverlea Motel 46–48 Hokonui Drive ⓣ & ⓕ03/208 3130, ⓔriverleamotel@xtra.co.nz. Snazzy and slightly more expensive, but worth it for the well-equipped, plush white units and breakfast on request. ❹–❺

Eating

Croydon Lodge Hotel cnr SH94 & Waimea St. There are two licensed restaurants in this hotel on the outskirts of town, serving moderately priced lunchtime grills, à la carte dinners and a popular Sunday-night smorgasbord.

Da Vinci's Medway St, next door to *Howl at the Moon* ⓣ0800/727 476. Cheap and cheerful café-style pizza house where you can eat in or take away. Mon 4.30–8.30pm, Tues–Fri 11.30am–2pm & 4–11.30pm, Sat 11.30am–11.30pm, Sun 11.30am–10pm.

Gables Villa 81 Hokonui Dr ⓣ03/208 8142. Award-winning, classy, intimate licensed restaurant ten minutes' walk from the town centre serving good-quality food presented imaginatively, including feta soufflé, lamb short loin with mushroom and saffron risotto, scallops, tandoori kebabs and much much more ($14–30 for mains). Mon–Sun from 5.30pm.

Howl at the Moon 2 Main St. Airy all-day café/bar with a subdued, Kiwi cowboy feel, serving a good range of snacks and bigger meals for under $25. The bar hots up Fri & Sat nights.

The Moth Restaurant and Bar Old Mandeville Airfield, 17km northwest of Gore on SH94 ⓣ03/208 9662. Good-quality food and coffee at reasonable prices in a sumptuous, airy 1920s-style restaurant and bar kitted out with nostalgic aircraft mementoes, Lunch from noon, dinner from 6pm, & open all day for coffee and drinks. Closed Mon. Licensed.

Table Talk 70 Main St. Friendly café popular with the locals, offering a broad range of coffees, teas, big muffins and sumptuous cakes, all-day lunches and breakfasts, and internet access. Closed Sun.

Invercargill and around

For most visitors, the southern city of **INVERCARGILL** is little more than a transit point for some of New Zealand's most remote regions. Southland's thriving economic and cultural centre, with a population of around 50,000, it was settled in the mid-1850s, and has, like Dunedin, a predominantly Scottish character. Here the legacy is evident in streets named after Highland rivers, and a few fine old stone buildings in the city centre, ornately carved from white Oamaru stone transported from the east coast, beyond Dunedin.

Regularly lashed by harsh winds and rain yet occasionally blessed with bright days, Invercargill sprawls over an exposed, broad expanse of flat land at the head of an estuary, the monotony compounded by a low skyline, but much relieved by the city's huge parks and its friendly people. Jutting out into the Foveaux Strait beyond, and partially enclosing the estuary, is a small peninsula, the departure point for ferries to Stewart Island and worth a half-day visit for a handful of sights and a couple of short coastal walks. At its tip sits the busy yet run-down island port of **Bluff**, linked to the city by a southbound finger of SH1. Across the choppy Foveaux Strait is the island retreat of **Stewart Island** (see p.773), twenty minutes away by plane and one hour by ferry.

Arrival, information and city transport

Invercargill's **airport** is 2.5km northeast from the city centre and receives domestic flights from New Zealand's main cities as well as Stewart Island. Spitfire Shuttles ($7) and taxis ($10–15) provide transport into town. Arriving by **bus**, InterCity will drop you at the defunct train station and most of the shuttles (Atomic, Walker Motors and Catch a Bus) stop at the visitor centre, while Knightrider shuttles from Christchurch pull up at their depot on Tay Street. The city is laid out in a grid system of wide streets that is easy to negotiate by **car**. The main highways entering the city, SH1 from the east (Tay Street) and SH6 from the north (Dee Street), meet at right angles in the city centre. See "Listings", p.771, for locations of car parks.

The city's excellent **visitor centre** is in the foyer of the Southland Museum and Art Gallery, Victoria Avenue (May–Nov Mon–Fri 9am–5pm, Sat & Sun 10am–5pm; Dec–April Mon–Fri 9am–7pm, Sat & Sun 10am–7pm; ⓣ03/214 6243 or 214 9133, ⓦwww.invercargill.org.nz), and stocks free street maps and leaflets on Invercargill and Southland in general, plus Stewart Island and Fiordland. It also serves as a booking agency for travel, accommodation, activities and attractions all over the country. The **DOC office**, in the State Insurance Building, Level 7, on Don Street, near the junction with Dee Street (Mon–Fri 9am–4.30pm; ⓣ03/214 4589), is the best place to go for information on walks and wildlife in the Catlins, Stewart Island and Fiordland. For local events listings, check out *The Southland Times* or the *Southlands Events Calendar*, available from the visitor centre. You can also get **internet access** at the visitor centre, or try Gordon Data Services, 124 Dee St (Mon–Fri 10am–5.30pm, Sat 10am–noon).

There are ten **city bus routes**, most of them circular (Mon–Fri 7.10am–5.45pm, Sat 9.15am–1.45pm or earlier; timetables available from the visitor centre; information ⓣ03/218 7108). One-way fares to the inner and outer suburbs cost $1.20.

Accommodation

Accommodation prices this far south are very reasonable, and there's a good choice in the centre close to the transport links, mostly on or near Tay Street. Motels are plentiful and good quality, starting at around $65. Bluff also has a couple of places to stay if you want to avoid Invercargill altogether on your way to or from Stewart Island.

Admiral Court Motel 327 Tay St ⓣ 03/217 1117, ⓕ217 4447. Ten spotless, fully self-contained units with extras including breakfast delivered to your door and transport to and from the airport, train and bus stations. ❹–❺

Awamoa Cottage B&B 110 Leet St ⓣ & ⓕ03/214 3164, ⓔmgmiller@southnet.co.nz. Extremely central B&B/homestay offering double rooms that share a guest bathroom.❹

Balmoral Lodge 265 Tay St ⓣ03/217 6109, ⓔbalmorallodge@xtra.co.nz. Just outside the centre, this upmarket motel has 27 luxurious units with queen-sized beds. Breakfast available. ❺

Birchwood Manor 189 Tay St ⓣ03/218 8881, ⓔbirch@birchwood.co.nz. A well-run new complex with 35 spacious units just beyond the city centre. Spa baths; supermarket opposite; courtesy vehicle to and from public transport. ❺

Coachman's Motel Inn 705 Tay St, cnr Rockdale Rd ⓣ03/217 6046, ⓔtwilkes@southnet.co.nz. Motel about 3km from the city centre, also with tent sites ($8), powered sites($8) and cabins (❷–❸). ❹

Gala Lodge 177 Gala St ⓣ03/218 8884, ⓔcharlie.ireland@xtra.co.nz. A welcoming, large and central homestay overlooking Queens Park, with extensive gardens and a double and a twin room sharing a bathroom; courtesy car. ❹

Gerrards cnr Esk St & Leven St ⓣ03/218 3406, ⓕ218 3003. Nostalgic hotel right in the heart of the city, offering well-appointed budget rooms, B&B and suites; also a pleasant bar and licensed restaurant. B&B ❺, rooms only ❹

Heritage Court Motel 44 Thomson St ⓣ03/214 7911, ⓔheritagemotels@clear.net.nz. The most reasonably priced motel just outside the centre in a quiet sunny spot near Queens Park and the visitor centre. ❹

Lorneville Lodge 352 Lorne Dacre Rd, RD6, 8km east from Invercargill ⓣ03/235 8031, ⓔlornepark@xtra.co.nz. An attractive combined campsite and B&B on a 7-hectare farm, offering tent and powered sites ($9.50) and vans, cabins, flats and units (❸–❹). The B&B offers two doubles and a twin, sharing a guest bathroom. ❹

Montecillo Motel and B&B 240 Spey St ⓣ03/218 2503, ⓕ218 2506. Central accommodation with good-value motel units and B&B in the airy en-suite rooms of a 100-year-old hotel. Motel ❹, B&B ❺

The Oak Door 22 Taiepa Rd, Otatara ⓣ & ⓕ03/213 0633, ⓔblstuart@xtra.co.nz. A modern, airy B&B in a tranquil bush setting, three minutes' drive west of the centre, close to Oreti Beach. ❺

Riverside Guesthouse 70 Filleul St ⓣ03/218 9207, ⓔtheriverside@xtra.co.nz. Small hostel and B&B in a quiet setting 1.5km from the centre, with river views from the pretty garden. There are a 4-bed dorm, a single, a double with its own bathroom, and a simple cabin for two in the garden; free river kayaks. Dorm ❶, cabin ❷, room ❷, B&B ❸

Southern Comfort 30 Thomson St ⓣ03/218 3838. One of the better of the city's hostels, this beautifully kept Art Nouveau villa is set among manicured lawns. Pleasant, clean dorms and double rooms, an excellent kitchen, large dining room and free bikes. Dorms ❶, rooms ❷

Tuatara Backpackers 30/32 Dee St ⓣ03/214 0954, ⓔtuataralodge@xtra.co.nz. In the very centre of town, new, recently decorated, friendly and spacious, with all the amenities you could wish for, including good security, and undoubtedly the best hostel in the vicinity as a result. Dorms ❶, rooms ❷, en suites ❸

YHA 122 North Rd, cnr Bullar St, Waikiwi ⓣ03/215 9344, ⓕ215 9382). Under new management, this is a friendly, simple yet clean hostel in a quiet suburb 3.5km north of the centre, on the bus route (Mon–Fri & Sat morning), with dorms (2- to 8-bed), twins, doubles and family rooms. It's occasionally occupied by school groups, so book ahead. Dorms ❶, rooms ❷

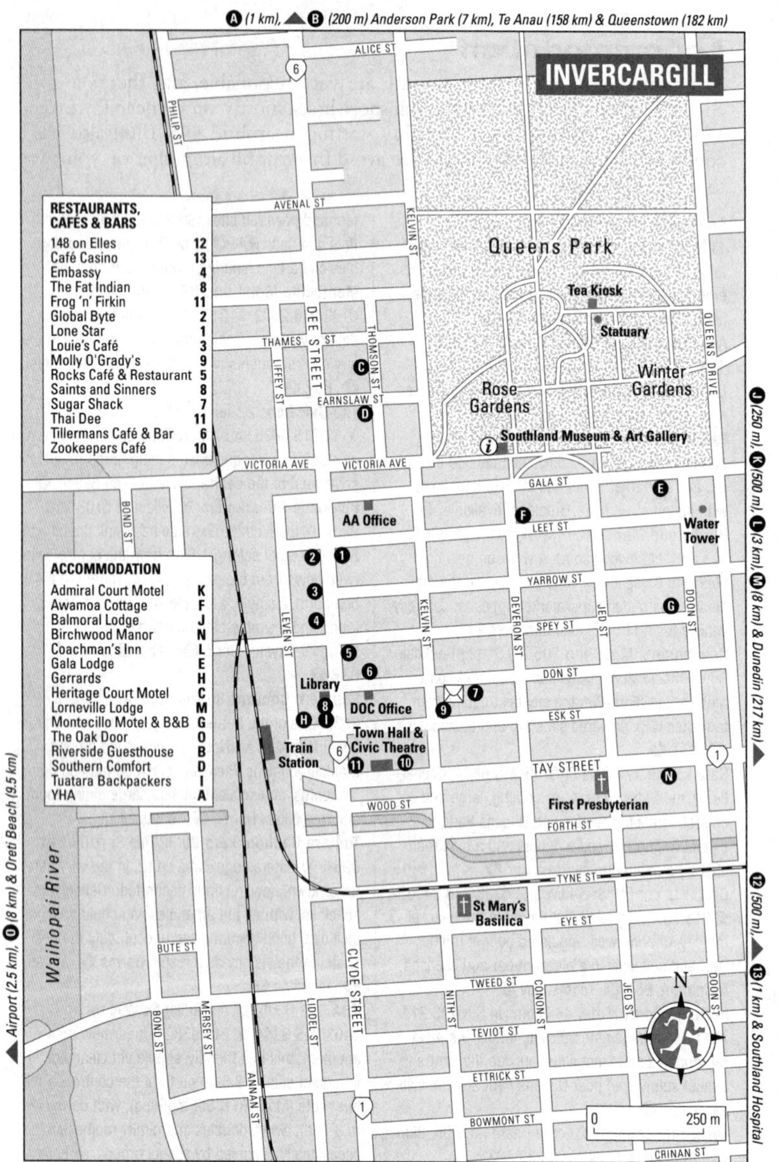

The City

The best place for an overview of the city is from the top of the forty-metre-high brick **water tower** (1889), centrally located at the junction of Doon Street and Leet Street (Sun & public holidays 1.30–4.30pm; outside these times collect a key from next door; $1). Invercargill's chief attraction is the large **Southland Museum and Art Gallery**, at the southern entrance to Queens Park on Victoria Avenue (Mon–Fri 9am–5pm, Sat & Sun 10am–5pm; $2 donation requested). Capped with a big white pyramid, the building houses a well laid out collection, over two storeys. Upstairs, the extensive and imaginative "Beyond the Roaring Forties" focuses on New Zealand's **subantarctic islands**, the tiny windswept clusters lying thousands of kilometres apart between New Zealand and the Antarctic. These are the only obstacles in the path of the westerly gales that rage through these latitudes, earning them the names Roaring Forties and Furious Fifties. In a region mostly made up of ocean, the islands provide a vital breeding ground for marine wildlife, including albatross. A 25-minute audio-visual show (Mon–Fri 11.30am & 3.30pm, Sat & Sun 11am, noon, 2pm, 3pm & 4pm; $2) introduces the history, flora, fauna and marine life of this extraordinarily exposed part of the world. Displays cover shipwrecks through the ages, wildlife, climate and so on. Downstairs, there's coverage of a successful breeding programme of **tuatara**, reptilian relics from the dinosaur age found nowhere else in the world. You can observe several of the small, well-camouflaged tuatara in simulated natural environments, but you'll need to peer hard to spot them (they usually come out of hiding on sunny days in the early afternoon). The remainder of the museum covers Southland's history, both human and natural, with exhibits ranging from moa bones to Maori artefacts and Victoriana. The simple **art gallery** displays international and national works, with exhibitions changing every few weeks.

The huge public gardens of **Queens Park** stretch north behind the museum from Gala Street and have been a public reserve since 1869. Today there are showhouses, a formal rose garden, a rhododendron dell, a walk-through aviary, a small animal park and a statuary, as well as an eighteen-hole golf course, various sports grounds and **Splash Palace** – a multi-million-dollar aquatic centre with a fifty-metre sports pool and hydroslide. The park's main entrance is on Queens Drive; other entrances (with car parks) are located off Gala Street and Victoria Avenue, while there's pedestrian-only access from Kelvin and Herbert streets.

Back in the city centre, Tay Street has some distinctive **architecture**. At the junction with Jed Street is the so-called **First Presbyterian Church** of 1915 (in fact the second, built after the First Church of Otago, in Dunedin), which is kept locked. Designed by architect John T. Mair, in Romanesque style, it has impressive ornamental brickwork, fashioned into a mosaic. Near the corner with Deveron Street stands the magnificent **Town Hall and Civic Theatre**. The Town Hall was completed in 1906 and is a fine example of neo-Renaissance style with its plasterwork, pediments and ornamental parapets carved from white Oamaru stone. Two streets south, on Tyne Street and near the junction with Nith Street, the striking Roman Catholic **St Mary's Basilica** was designed by F.W. Petre, its brick exterior concealing a sumptuous interior lining of Oamaru stone, unfortunately only visible when the church is open for services. Its elegant copper dome can be spotted for miles around, but the best vantage point is from the gardens flanking the Otepuni Stream on the other side of the road.

Anderson Park and Oreti Beach

On the outskirts of Invercargill, 7km north of the city centre, are the beautifully preserved grounds and stately home of **Anderson Park**. Donated to the city in 1951, the house contains an atmospheric **gallery** (daily 9.30–5pm; by donation except during special exhibitions) set amid extensive **grounds**, also open to the public (free). The Georgian-style mansion was built in 1925 as the family home of a local businessman. Designed by Christchurch architect Cecil Wood, it was constructed from reinforced concrete and set against a backdrop of forest. The delightful gallery displays a permanent collection of traditional and contemporary New Zealand art. During the month of October, a spring exhibition of recent Kiwi art replaces the permanent collection, and there are recitals each Sunday, when classical music drifts around the gardens. Behind the gallery, **The Maori House**, also built in the early 1920s, was used for dances, its doorway and porch decorated with carvings by Tene Waitere, a renowned Rotorua carver. Anderson Park is a three-kilometre drive along McIvor Road, via North Road/SH6, or during daylight hours through Donovan Park, off Bainfield Road. There is no bus service out to here; a taxi will cost you about $15–20 one way.

Oreti Beach, 9.5km west of the city centre, is a beautiful broad expanse of fine sand, sweeping 30km right around to the seaside resort of Riverton to the west, and giving great views of Stewart Island and Bluff. In summer, it's popular for swimming (surf patrols operate), yachting and water-skiing, but there are sometimes shark alerts, and windy days cause violent sandstorms. Use the entrance off Dunns Road (the others are pretty rough going); there's no bus service to the beach.

Eating and drinking

The explosion of café society in New Zealand is now well entrenched in once backward Invercargill. Most of the eating places are concentrated on Dee Street, with a few on Tay Street. A strength is the local **seafood**, including excellent blue cod and Bluff oysters (April–Nov). Another local delicacy is **muttonbird**, though the oily and rather fishy flavour is something of an acquired taste.

Serious **drinking** doesn't generally start until Thursday night, but there are an ever-increasing number of good boozers and happening dance venues open most nights.

148 on Elles 148 Elles Rd ☎03/216 1000. An elegant and upmarket dinner restaurant, serving local seafood, steak, venison and ostrich, at a price, in a restored 1912 building. Open 6pm–late. Licensed.

Café Casino 200 Elles Rd, beside the *Strathern Inn*. Cheap, big-portioned meals at this straightforward café/bar beside the "casino" (a room full of one-armed bandits), serving breakfast for less than $5 and steak for under $10. A reasonably priced à la carte restaurant is attached. Both open Mon–Fri 10am–10pm, Sat & Sun noon–10pm; licensed.

The Fat Indian Picadilly Lane, 38 Dee St ☎03/218 9933. Along with *Louie's* one of the best licensed restaurants in town. Modern decor, friendly and prompt service, and best of all, authentic Indian-via-the-north-of-England grub. BYO wine only.

Global Byte Café 150 Dee St. Open until around 5pm this modern, shiny internet café serves snacks and good breakfasts.

Lone Star cnr Leet St & Dee St. Tex-Mex dinner venue in a big old building with a bar at one end and café at the other. One of *the* dance spots in town, with a DJ on Thurs–Sat nights.

Louie's Café & Tapas Bar 142 Dee St ☎03/214 2913. A dinner café and popular bar run by the same owner as *Tillermans* (see below), serving well-priced good-quality food, from seared ostrich fillet to chicken carbonara (mains $15–25). Closed Mon; licensed.

Rocks Café & Restaurant Courtville Place, 101 Dee St ☎03/218 7597. A small and trendy, exclusive and award-winning café-cum-wine bar where voices and background music reverberate off brick walls and terracotta-tiled floors. Food is expensive, with lunches around $15, and dinners from around the $20 mark on upwards. Licensed.

Thai Dee 9 Dee St ☎03/214 5112. Modern, licensed and authentic Thai restaurant where the food strikes an exotic balance between salty, spicy, sweet and sour, with many Kiwi variations on Thai favourites. Mon–Sat for lunch, daily for dinner.

Tillermans Café & Bar (or **The Café**) 16 Don St ⓣ03/218 9240. This excellent-value local institution offers high-quality cosmopolitan food (lunch for under $15, dinner for under $28). The atmosphere is relaxed, and large vibrant paintings adorn the brick walls. Upstairs is a popular bar with pool tables, a focal point for live music on Sat nights. Closed Mon & Tues evenings, Sat lunch and all day Sun; licensed.

Zookeeper's Café 50 Tay St. Very popular, zany, inexpensive, split-level café and bar easily identified by the corrugated ironwork elephant on the outside roof. Open 10am till late, they serve brunch, bar food, snacks (great seafood chowder) and meals from a wide-ranging menu with generous portions – nothing over $20. Best for brunch and lunch, coffee or a drink.

Entertainment

Local bands play at several of the city's hotels on Friday and Saturday nights (check *The Southland Times* for details) and occasionally at local bars. There are also a handful of **nightclubs**, listed below, of varying quality but always full of enthusiasm, energy or alcohol-fuelled lunacy, particularly during term time.

For details of productions at the Civic Theatre in Tay Street, check *The Southland Times* **arts** page on Tuesday. Details on occasional shows at the Southland Museum can be gleaned from the visitor centre or reception at Invercargill City Council on Esk Street (ⓣ03/218 1959). The five-screen Movieland **cinema** at 29 Dee St (ⓣ03/214 1110) has reduced ticket prices ($7 instead of $10) on Tuesday and any weekday before 5pm.

Clubs

Embassy Theatre 112 Dee St ⓣ03/214 0050. Onetime hotel and then a cinema, this spectacular (inside at least) old building is now a dance venue, hosting live bands, comedy, poetry readings and DJ-led grooving with big-screen videos, so check out the posters or local listings for upcoming events.

Frog 'n' Firkin Café & Bar Dee St, next door to the cinema. Serving good, economical pub food for lunch and dinner. and transforming into a popular dance spot Thurs–Sat (with DJs playing mostly chart stuff, and sometimes a live band beforehand on Friday night); open till 3am at weekends.

Molly Ogrady's 16 Kelburn St. Open from 11am until late, this first-floor pub has DJs on Friday and Saturday and a live band once a month, as well as a comedy night every second Thurs of the month.

Saints & Sinners 34 Dee St. DJs playing mostly dance music, plus occasional live music, student nights, "who dares wins" roulette wheel (whereby if you have the winning number and then do the dare to get some free booze or the like), party games and really kicks off around midnight, when anybody with inhibitions has forgotten them. Gold coin cover charge.

Sugar Stack 77 Don St. Garish night club and late-night bar with lots of DJs but rarely anything live. The play list is mostly middle of the road and chart-oriented, with banks of video screens to entertain the 300-plus crowd.

Tillermans see above under "Eating and drinking". Relaxed venue with a pleasant bar, which concentrates on live music on a Saturday night.

Listings

Airlines Air New Zealand ⓣ03/215 0000 & 0800/737 000; ⓣ Stewart Island Flights ⓣ03/218 9129, ⓦwww.stewart Island Flights.com

Automobile Association 47 Gala St ⓣ03/218 9033.

Bike rental ⓣBig on Bikes, 2 Dee St (ⓣ03/214 4697), $10–15 a day depending upon the state of the bike; Wensley's Cycles, cnr Tay St & Nith St (ⓣ03/218 6206), $$10–25 a day.

Buses InterCity (ⓣ03/214 0598) operate daily from the train station to Dunedin, Christchurch, Queenstown & Te Anau. Shuttle bus services include Atomic Shuttles (ⓣ03/218 9000 or 24hr reservation line 216 0714) to Gore, Queenstown and Wanaka, and to Dunedin and Christchurch; Catch-a-Bus (ⓣ03/ⓣ214 5652) to Dunedin; and Spitfire Shuttle Service (ⓣ03/214 1851) to Te Anau, via the Southern Scenic Route. Campbelltown Passenger Service (ⓣ03/212 7404) run regular buses to the airport, and to Bluff for the ferry to Stewart Island.

Car parks There's plenty of 1hr parking on the streets. Council car parks (24hr) are located in Don St, Deveron St & Esk St.

Car rental The multinational firms have branches in the city and Avis, Budget, Hertz & Thrifty have desks at the airport: Avis, 73 Airport Ave (℗03/218 7019); Budget, 79 Airport Av (℗03/218 7012); Hertz, 92 Airport Ave (℗03/218 2837). Cheaper alternatives include: Crawford Rentals, 166 Clyde St (℗03/218 3870); Inner City Rentals, cnr Clyde St & Tweed St (℗03/214 0457); Rent-a-Dent, 99 Airport Ave (℗03/214 4820); and Riverside Rentals, cnr Bay Rd & North Rd (℗03/215 9030)℗.

Ferry The Foveaux Express (℗03/212 7660; $84 return) departs Bluff for Stewart Island Sept–April Mon–Sun 9.30am & 5pm; May–Aug Mon–Fri 9.30am & 4pm, Sat 9.30am, Sun 4pm.

Library Invercargill Public Library is at 50 Dee St (Mon–Fri 9am–8.30pm, Sat 10am–1pm; ℗03/218 7025).

Medical treatment Southland Hospital, on Kew Rd (℗03/218 1949), has a 24hr accident and emergency department. For illness and minor accidents outside surgery hours, contact the Urgent Doctor Service at 100 Don St (℗03/218 8821; Mon–Fri 5–10pm; Sat, Sun & public holidays 24hr).

Pharmacy Inside the Countdown supermarket (daily Mon–Fri 8.30am–10pm, Sat & Sun 9am–7pm); Ascot Pharmacy, 702 Tay St (℗03/217 7696; Mon–Sat 9am till late).

Police The central police station is at 117 Don St (℗03/214 4039).

Post office The main post office is at 51 Don St, near the junction with Kelvin St (Mon–Fri 8.30am–5pm, Sat 10am–1pm).

Taxis Blue Star ℗03/218 6079; ℗City Cabs ℗03/214 4478; and Rakiura Rides ℗03/213 1081.

Tours Invercargill Passenger Transport (℗03/218 2320) run a two-hour city tour ($30 per person) taking in the Southland Museum, Queens Park, Anderson Park and a few historic landmarks. They also offer 3hr trips to Bluff ($40). Guided tours to the Catlins are operated by Catlins Natural Wonders (see box on p.759). Scenic flights to Stewart Island can be arranged with South East Air (℗03/214 5522) and Southland Air Charter (℗03/218 6171).

Bluff

Twenty-seven kilometres south of Invercargill, perching at the tip of a peninsula, is the small run-down fishing town of **BLUFF** and its man-made port. Offering great views across Foveaux Strait, Bluff is the departure point of the **Stewart Island ferry**, and you may choose to avoid Invercargill altogether and stay here in the local B&B or hotel. You won't need more than half a day to get a good look at the place, but without a car this involves a good deal of walking as the town spreads along the shoreline for about 6km.

Bluff is the oldest European town in New Zealand, having been continuously settled since 1824. These days it's still struggling to recover from the 1980s recession, and has an increasingly tired feel about it. The **harbour**, however, flourishes, exporting Southland's meat, timber, aluminium, fish and wool, and importing a variety of goods from overseas. In addition the Foveaux Strait yields a highly sought-after delicacy – the **Bluff oyster**. This deepwater shellfish has a sweet and succulent taste, and is usually dredged from the end of March until November, depending on stocks, then processed in oyster sheds at Bluff before being sent all over the country. Between June and August you can watch them being processed at Johnson's Oyster Factory (daily 8am–5pm; free; bookings ℗03/212 8665) and buy them direct at factory prices. An annual festival celebrates these slimy little bivalve molluscs on the first Saturday of May, with cook-offs, oyster opening competitions and street entertainment (contact the Invercargill visitor centre on p.766, or log on to ⓦwww.bluff.co.nz, for details). Across the harbour, at Tiwai Point, is the sprawl of a giant **aluminium smelter**, Southland's biggest employer. The smelter (℗03/218 5999; Mon–Fri 10am) is accessible by road from Invercargill, lying 25km south; phone ahead if you simply must have a free tour.

Bluff's small **Maritime Museum** (Mon–Fri 10am–4.30pm, Sat & Sun 1–5pm; $2), on Foreshore Road as you enter town from Invercargill, has historical displays focusing on whaling, the harbour development, oyster harvesting and shipwrecks. Pride of place is given to a vast triple-expansion steam engine, taken from a steam tug, *Monica*, which spent most of its life working the harbour. Back on the main road, you'll pass the ferry wharf and, three streets further, on the corner with Henderson Street, the kitsch **Paua Shell House** (daily 9am–5pm; donation). This was the home of Fred and Myrtle, a couple who, until Myrtle's death in 2000, spent years amassing a collection of shells from all over the world – most noticeably iridescent paua shells gathered from local beaches, which are plastered all over their living-room walls, creating a wall-to-wall shimmer in blue and green.

From here it's another 1.5km to the end of the road, and **Stirling Point**, which feels rather like the end of the earth, with its jokey signpost marking the distance to major international cities. The views are impressive and, on a clear day, you can see as far as Stewart Island, 35km away. From the car park at the end of the road you can set out on a couple of easy walks: the **Foveaux Walkway** (6.6km; 2hr one way) and, branching off it, the **Glory Track** (3.8km; 1hr return). The first is an exposed walk skirting Bluff Hill's rugged coastline, with some magnificent views, before cutting back across open farmland to the main road at the other end of town, near the old freezing works. The second is a loop track, mixing forest and coastal scenery. Short sections of the Glory Track are very steep, but the surface is sealed.

The turning to another good viewpoint, **Bluff Hill Lookout**, leaves the main road in town at Lee Street, opposite the ferry wharf. From here it's a three-kilometre drive, or a ninety-minute walk, to the car park and viewing platform beyond. From 267m up you get a 360-degree view of Stewart Island and the other, smaller islands in Foveaux Strait, Southland's estuaries and the harbour. The sunsets here are astonishing.

Practicalities

Bluff is a twenty-minute drive down SH1 from central Invercargill. Local **buses** run a regular daily service between the city and Bluff ($10, same-day return $20), to connect with the ferry. For details on sailings to Stewart Island, see below.

Good **accommodation** in Bluff is limited to the *Foveaux Hotel*, 40 Gore St (ⓣ03/212 7196; ❹, breakfast included), which has four en-suite rooms and three sharing bathrooms, plus an in-house bar; the four en-suite B&B rooms above the *Land's End Wine Bar and Café* at Stirling Point (ⓣ & ⓕ03/212 7575; ❺); and the self-contained cottage for two at *The Tanti*, 230 Marine Parade (ⓣ03/212 8886, ⓔthetanti@southnet.co.nz; ❷–❸). The *Land's End*, perched high on the hill, also serves meals including breakfasts, lunches, teas and dinners daily, with specialities including pan-fried blue cod ($16.50) and oysters. Beside the *Land's End* is the *Drunken Sailor*, set high on the hill with good views out over the water and some reasonable sea-food snacks and main meals for lunch (daily) and dinner (Fri–Sun only; licensed).

Stewart Island

New Zealand's third main island is the small, rugged triangle of **STEWART ISLAND**, separated from the mainland by Foveaux Strait and until recently largely ignored by tourists. These days the island has proved to be more of a draw, having been designated the **Rakiura National Park**, a status greatly enhancing the pulling power of this otherwise fairly inaccessible place –

although it's still quite expensive to get to and to stay on, most of the island is uninhabited and covered in dense native bush and coastal podocarp rainforest, and the climate though temperate is unpredictable. Once you arrive, though, there is some serious wilderness tramping to be had, along with great sunsets (hence the island's Maori name of Rakiura, meaning "Land of the Glowing Skies"), but the chief reasons for coming here are to visit **Ulva Island**, a protected predator-free haven for native New Zealand birds only eight minutes away by water taxi, and to go kiwi-spotting in the wild, either on your own at **Mason Bay** or on a guided trip that needs to be booked six months ahead in summer, when the island becomes crowded with tourists. Sea kayaking on the vast flooded valley of **Paterson Inlet** is proving another popular option, and in addition, Stewart Island boasts one of New Zealand's Great Walks, **The Rakiura Track** (3 days) – not to be confused with the island's mud-ridden **North–West Circuit Track** (10–12 days), only suited to the most experienced (and masochistic) tramper.

Inhabited by Maori from the thirteenth century and erroneously recorded as a peninsula by Captain Cook in 1770, the island was named after William Stewart, the first officer on a sealing vessel that visited in 1809. The island is characterized by bush-fringed bays, sandy coves, windswept beaches and a rugged interior of tall rimu forest and granite outcrops. The only settlement is tiny **Oban**, its bland hotch potch of old and new buildings huddling around Halfmoon Bay and creeping up the hill towards the airfield, cut into the bird-filled bush.

The mainstay of the economy was once rimu milling, with three thousand people living on the island in the boomtime of the early 1930s as opposed to about 300–400 these days, but the main industries today are **fishing** (crayfish, blue cod and paua) and **fish farming** (salmon and mussels) in Big Glory Bay. Bear in mind that there are no **banks** or **bureaux de change** on Stewart Island, although most businesses take credit cards and visitors with New Zealand bank accounts can use EFTPOS at most businesses; some will also exchange foreign currency.

Island practicalities

The easiest and quickest way (20min) to get to the island is by **plane**, with Stewart Island Flights, three times daily from Invercargill Airport (Ⓣ03/218 9129, Ⓦwww.stewartislandflights.com; $80 one way, $145 return). Shuttle-bus transfers between central Oban and the airfield are included in the price of your ticket. Note that a strict **luggage allowance** of 10kg per person applies and camping gas canisters are not allowed. The airline company also offer, in conjunction with Seaview Water Taxis, one of the best chances of seeing a **kiwi** in the wild: instead of being dropped off at the Stewart Island Airport (a long strip of tarmac) they will land on the beach at Mason Bay. From there you can either walk back to the DOC Freshwater Hut (4hr) and then get picked up by the water taxi and deposited in Oban, or stay overnight at Mason Bay (vastly increasing your chances of seeing a kiwi in the wild) and then walk back to Freshwater for an afternoon pick-up. The plane to Mason Bay and from Oban airport back to Invercargill is $155.

The *Foveaux Express*, alternating between a sixty-five-seater and a hundred-seater catamaran **ferry**, leaves regularly from Bluff (Ⓣ03/212 7660; $47 one way, $84 return), usually taking one hour to cross the choppy Foveaux Strait, and docks at the wharf in Oban, a stone's throw from the town centre. It has a reputation of trying the stomachs of even the hardiest sailors, a factor embraced

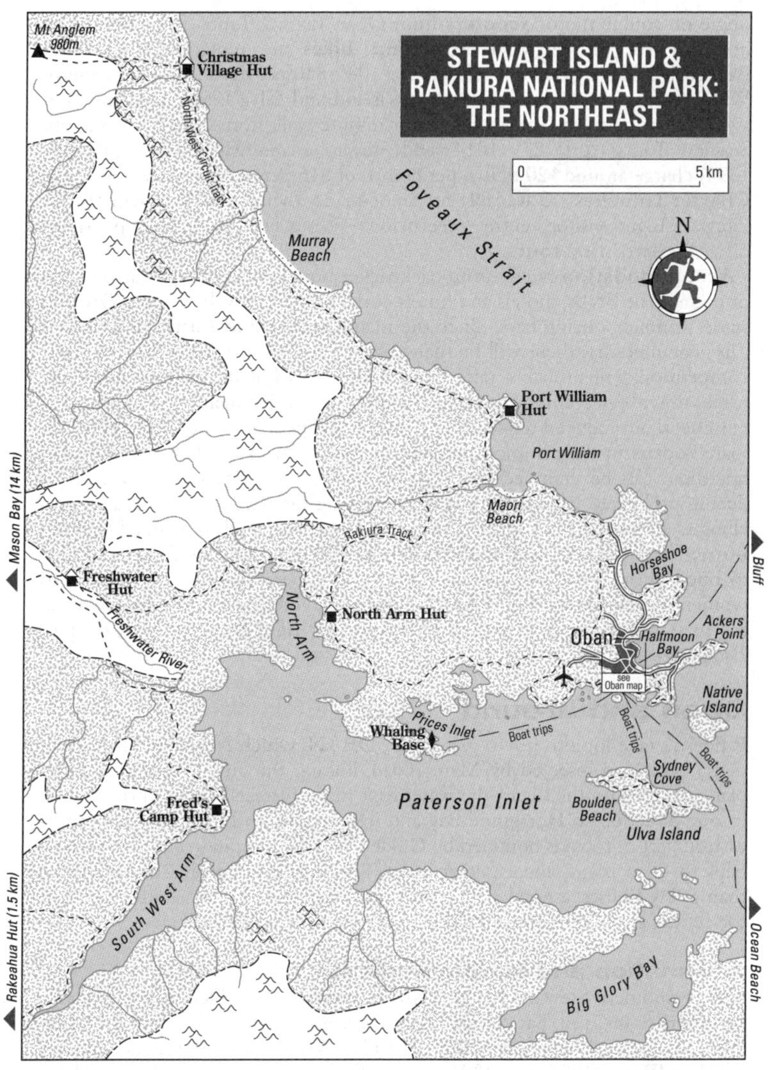

by the company who sell T-shirts stating "I braved the *Foveaux Express*."

Since it's easy to walk around the inhabited part of the island, you're unlikely to need much road transport once you've arrived, although Oban Taxis & Tours (☎03/219 1456) operate a daily **shuttle service** and have four **rental cars** ($50 a half day, $70 full day, guided tours $20 extra). Alternatively, try Sam Sampson for shuttle hire and guided bus trips, based at Stewart Island Travel on Main Road in Oban (☎03/219 1269, after 5pm 219 1456). You can also rent single or double motor **scooters** from Oban Taxis & Tours (from $18/25 an hour, or $60/65 per day). **Mountain bikes** are rented out by Innes Backpackers on Argyle Street (ⓣ03/219 1080; $10 per day including helmets). **Water taxis** operate between Stewart Island and Ulva Island, eight minutes away, departing from Golden Bay, a ten-minute walk from central Oban; both Seaview Tours (ⓣ03/219 1014) and Stewart Island Water Taxi (ⓣ03/219 1394) charge around $20 return per person or $16 per person for two or more. **Charter launches** are available for tailor-made diving, fishing or nature trips (Stewart Island visitor centre – see below – has a list); see box on p.781 for other Stewart Island **tours**.

Accommodation ranges from backpacker hostels and self-contained cabins or cottages to B&Bs, motels and hotels, some of them in Oban (see p.776) and some in neighbouring bays. Since the island has become a national park you can guarantee that there will be many more options to come and that greater competition will probably raise current standards but do little to bring the prices down – accommodation here is more expensive than on the mainland, but check out reduced off-season prices. Several people on the island **rent** out spare **rooms** in their homes (different to the well-run B&Bs we have listed), but these can be cramped and claustrophobic, becoming especially difficult during prolonged bad weather. If you're staying for a week or more, and travelling as a couple or in a group, then consider renting a self-contained **holiday home** from Stewart Island Holiday Homes (see opposite). It's always advisable to book ahead, especially during summer, in general. A word of warning to women travellers: repeated reports on the grapevine suggest you should avoid the massage "therapy" advertised at *Andy & Jo's B&B* and steer clear of *Innes Backpackers*.

Oban and around

It doesn't take long to get to grips with **OBAN**, which is enclosed by hills of dense bush and bisected by Main Road, linking the airfield with the other principal road on the island, the waterfront Elgin Terrace. This, in turn, extends in one direction to Horseshoe Bay and in the other to Leask Bay. The south-eastern part of town is bounded by Golden Bay, the jumping-off point for boat trips to Ulva Island and Paterson Inlet. The township consists of little more than a few houses, a hotel with a pub (very much the social centre), the visitor centre, a tiny museum, a couple of stores and a couple of cafés.

Information and accommodation

The combined Stewart Island **visitor centre** (late Dec to end March Mon–Fri 8am–7pm, Sat & Sun 9am–7pm; rest of the year Mon–Fri 8am–5pm, Sat & Sun 10am–noon; ⓣ03/219 1218, ⓦwww.stewartisland.co.nz) and **DOC office** (ⓣ03/219 1130) is centrally located on Main Road and has excellent displays on the island's tracks and natural history. Staff are helpful and have free maps of Oban and neighbouring bays, and can advise on and book accommodation, boat trips, water taxis, kayaking, bus tours, guided walks, island flora and fauna, tracks and transport; they also sell hut passes for the two major Stewart Island tracks. There's a stock of free videos about Stewart Island that you can watch at the visitor centre, the best being *Beyond the Mainland* (a general overview; 45min), *The Underworld of Paterson Inlet* (focusing on the marine life; 15min) and *The Other Side* (a tongue in cheek TV programme about out-of-the-way places and their inhabitants; 45min). The best thing to pick up here is DOC's *Explore an Island Paradise, Ulva Island Guide*, which provides all the information you could possibly want while wandering the deserted tracks ($1). The other main **booking agencies** for the above mentioned activities are Stewart Island Travel on Main Road (☎03/219 1269), who have taken over Oban Taxis & Tours on Main Road (☎03/219 1456), the Stewart Island Flights office on Elgin Terrace (☎03/219 1090), and the Adventure Centre in the ferry office on the wharf (☎03/219 1134), who all charge the same as booking direct. The **post office** is in the Stewart Island Flights depot, Elgin St on the waterfront, near the junction with Ayr Street (daily: Oct–March 7.30am–6pm; April–Sept 7.30am–5pm), where stamps are still cancelled by hand. For **internet access** try *Justcafé* on Main Road (see p.779) and the hotel.

Accommodation

Dave's Place Horseshoe Bay Rd ☎03/219 1427, ⓔchrisdillon@clear.net.nz; no advance bookings. A small, friendly backpackers in relaxed surroundings 200m from the wharf, with TV, microwave and fridge. Dorms ❶, own sleeping bag essential.

Ferndale Campsite Horseshoe Bay Rd ☎03/219 1176. The only official campsite on the island and just 200m north of the wharf. Facilities include coin-operated showers, a covered cooking area with hotplates and a washing machine. Tent sites $8.

Deep Bay Cabin Deep Bay ☎03/219 1219, ⓔewanjengell@xtra.co.nz. Snug private self-contained wooden cabin hidden in the bush with four bunks, kitchen and shower. Roughly a 20min walk from town and a great spot for resting after the longer tracks. There's a pot-bellied stove in winter. ❷, $15 per extra person, min $40.

Goomes B&B Elgin Terrace ☎03/219 1057. Five minutes' walk from the *South Sea Hotel*, this bright and comfy B&B offers two en-suite rooms with great sea views; free pick-up. ❺

The Nest B&B Lonnekers Beach ☎03/219 1310, ⓔthenest@es.co.nz. Two kilometres from the wharf (free pick-ups), this big, pretty house perched on a hill overlooking Halfmoon Bay and Lonnekers Beach has plenty of character. Two double rooms with shared facilities. ❻

Port of Call Jensen Bay ☎ & ⓕ03/219 1394, ⓔinfo@portofcall.co.nz. Relaxing upmarket B&B in a big, secluded, beautifully designed sun-filled contemporary house overlooking the bay, 30min walk from Oban centre, though there is a free pick-up. The twin ensuite has sea views. ❽

Rakiura Lodge Motel Horseshoe Bay Rd ☎03/219 1096. Great views over Halfmoon Bay from a hill just outside Oban, 2.5km from the wharf (a 25-minute walk, or $8 taxi ride). Five well-maintained units sleeping four to six. Courtesy transfers. ❺

Room with a View Kamahi Rd ☎03/219 1552, ⓔsoyabean@xtra.co.nz. Comfortable self-contained en-suite unit on a hill near the wharf, with sea views. ❹

Stewart Island Backpackers cnr Ayr St & Dundee St ☎03/219 1114, ⓔshearwater@stewart-island.co.nz. Central, large and basic, this hotel is divided into 20 rooms (mostly doubles and some 3-bed) sharing bathrooms, and a backpacker section of 4-bed dorms, twins and doubles. Everyone shares the cramped kitchen and sizeable lounge, but redesigning plans are afoot. A BBQ area and breakfast are available. Rooms with linen cost a stonking $14 extra.❶–❹

South Sea Hotel cnr Main Rd & Elgin Terrace ☎03/219 1059, ⓔsouthsea@stewart-island.co.nz. Clean rooms – some with sea views – above the waterfront pub in a hundred-year-old building. It can be a little noisy, especially in Room 6 right above the bar. Facilities include a TV lounge; there are also nine new, spacious motel studio units behind the hotel. ❹–❺

Stewart Island Holiday Homes Elgin Terrace ☎03/219 1057. Two modern, fully self-contained holiday homes on a hill overlooking the harbour and surrounded by bush, run by the owners of *Goomes B&B*. Each has four bedrooms with good sea views and two private bathrooms; courtesy car for transfers. ❺, $25 per extra person.

Stewart Island Retreat Horseshoe Bay ☎ & ⓕ03/219 1071, ⓔretreat@southnet.co.nz. An ideal place to unwind, 6km from Oban wharf (free pick-up), is this spacious and comfortable B&B on the shore of the bay. Large rooms with shared facilities; excellent dinners and packed lunches by arrangement. ❻

The View Nichol Rd (☎03/219 1328). Friendly, warm, spacious and clean, this backpackers is just 500m from the wharf, its double rooms just nudging into this code. Dorm ❶, rooms ❷

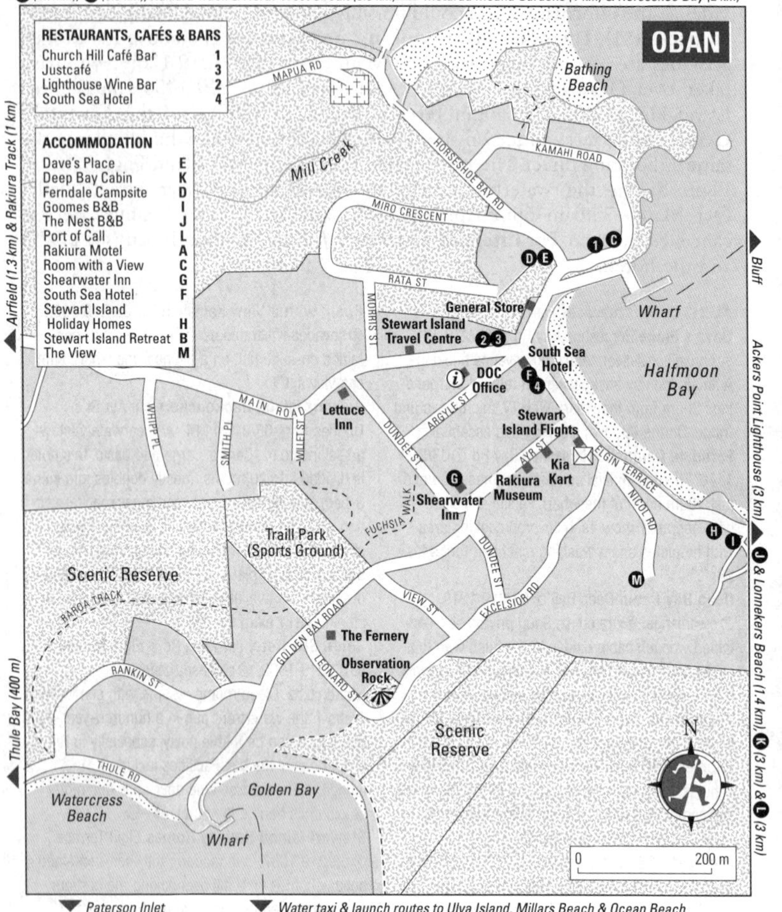

The town

Oban's sights are fairly limited: a compact, recently extended museum, a small craft shop, a tiny theatre and a few short walks. The **Rakiura Museum** on Ayr Street (Mon–Sat 10am–noon, Sun noon–2pm; donation) is worth a few minutes, with its adequately displayed artefacts imparting some local history. The small Maori collection boasts a rare necklace of dolphin teeth, while the whaling display has two individual giant teeth from a sperm whale. Less than ten minutes' walk up the hill along **Ayr Street**, until it becomes Golden Bay Road, you'll find The Fernery shop near the summit (Ⓣ03/219 1453; Oct–March daily 10.30am–5.30pm; winter by arrangement only), a cornucopia of souvenirs and gifts, all inspired by the island and handmade by New Zealand artists and craftspeople. One place that's well worth a look is the home-grown Glowing Sky, up **Main Road** and on the left, a relatively new designer clothing company that produce hand-printed T-shirts and other club wear with their own highly individual and desirable designs – many influenced by nature or inspired by Maori design – at reasonable prices (☎03/219 1249, www.glowingsky.co.nz).

Oban's short **walks** are listed in the $1 DOC pamphlet *Day Walks*, and the main ones are also marked on the maps available at the visitor centre. One takes you up to a lookout point and another through bird-filled bush. Definitely worthwhile is the stroll up to the hilltop vantage point of **Observation Rock** (15min). From here the panorama laid out below (best seen at sunset) includes Golden Bay and the island's highest point, Mount Anglem, on one side, and Horseshoe Bay on the other, as well as the expanse of Paterson Inlet, broken by the long strip of Ulva Island and the blobs of other islets. To reach the summit, follow Ayr Street and Golden Bay Road to just past The Fernery (see above), from where Observation Rock is signposted up Leonard Street and along a short forest track on the left to the lookout point. Return to town the same way or by entering Traill Park, opposite The Fernery, to follow the Fuchsia walk (see below). Or, instead of returning, you can continue away from town on the Raroa Walk from Traill Park (see below).

For a taste of some stunning bush, first dominated by fuchsia, then by rimu, follow the signposted **Fuchsia Walk,** which begins at Dundee Street and emerges five minutes later up the hill at Traill Park. In summer the foliage rings with the birdsong of tui, bellbirds and pigeons. From the end of the Fuchsia Walk, you can return via Golden Bay Road or follow the **Raroa Walk** down through fine rimu forest to Watercress Bay (15min). Thule Road and Golden Bay Road lead back to town from the bay (1km; 30min).

Eating and drinking

Oban has only a few places to eat and even these close early some evenings, particularly in the winter if they open at all, but generally the choice and opening times have improved considerably in the last two years and will continue to do so now that the place is part of a national park. If you're cooking for yourself, you can buy basic foodstuffs, fruit and vegetables at the Ship to Shore **general store** near the wharf (end Oct to end Feb Mon–Fri 8am–6.30pm, Sat 9am–6pm, Sun 10am–4pm; rest of the year Mon–Fri 8am–5.30pm, Sat 10am–4pm, Sun 10am–3pm) and *Lettuce Inn* up the hill on Main Road (Mon, Wed & Fri noon–7pm, Tues–Thurs 9am–6pm, Sat & Sun 10am–6pm), though the house is currently up for sale and the business may not continue, both of whose prices compare well with those on the mainland. The *Ship to Shore* also sells salted muttonbirds ($5, an acquired tasted but worth at least a try). Fresh fish and crayfish can be bought from Southern Seafoods at Horseshoe Bay (☎03/219 1389), or direct from the locals who will sell you a boiled cray, but you don't approach the boats as it's illegal for them to sell direct due to health and safety regulations.

There are only a couple of decent **cafés** in Oban. The tiny *Justcafé*, up from the hotel on Main Road, has good coffee and snacks such as smoked salmon and cream-cheese sandwiches, plus pack lunches ($10) and internet access (daily 9am–6pm; June–Sept 11am–3pm). The best place to eat in town (and on the island) is the licensed *Church Hill Café Bar & Restaurant*, just up Church Hill from the wharf, which has fine views of Halfmoon Bay from an airy late 1800s house, good-value lunches and dinners, and specializes in local seafood (book for dinner ☎03/219 1323; Oct–April daily from 10am, rest of the year sometimes limited to Thurs–Sat); it also runs a courtesy vehicle to get you to and from your accommodation. The *South Sea Hotel* has a simple **restaurant** offering lunches and early evening meals (closes 8pm) at rather inflated prices. It also operates as a café but still at off-the-scale costs. Perhaps the best-value eating in town is the *Kai Kart* (noon–2pm, & 6–9pm or later), in fact the old *Pie Kart* from Gore, a glorified caravan shipped to the deep disappointment of the late-night drinkers of Gore, who used to frequent it while wending their way home. It serves fresh fish, mussels, steak and chips, sausages, eggs, burgers and all the like at low prices, to take away or eat at the adjacent bench. However, if pizza is more your style then try the *Lighthouse Wine Bar and Pizzeria*, 10 Main Rd (☎03/219 1208), if you're ever lucky enough to catch it open. Just outside Oban, at Horseshoe Bay, the tiny café adjoining the *Stewart Island Retreat* serves coffee and cake, and with prior arrangement will provide lunch-boxes ($10).

Drinking is confined to the two bars at the *South Sea Hotel*, the focus of most social activity in these parts. The local ale, once brewed on the island but now produced in Invercargill, is the powerful and aptly named Roaring Forties.

Around Oban

North of Halfmoon Bay, twenty-minutes' walk along Horseshoe Bay Road, are the attractive and secluded **Moturau Moana public gardens**, which were donated to the island in 1940. Picnic tables, barbecues and a viewing platform looking out across the bay to Oban are set amid lawns, native plants and dense virgin forest.

One of the more interesting historical sites on the island is an abandoned Norwegian whaling base near **Millars Beach** at Prices Inlet, about 6.5km west of Oban. The only access is by boat, so you'll need to take the guided tour with Seabuzz Glass-Bottom Boat (see box opposite) or charter a water taxi or launch from Golden Bay (15min; around $40 return). From Millars Beach, an easy twenty-minute coastal walk heads north from the beachside picnic shelter through native bush to the whaling base. Several eerie relics remain from 1923–33, when a fleet of Antarctic whaling ships was repaired here, and the beach is littered with objects left behind: old drums, cables, giant iron propellers, a boiler out in the water and, at the far end, a wrecked sailing ship deliberately sunk by the whaling company to create a wharf.

A good **coastal walk**, the Harrold Bay to Ackers Point Lighthouse track (1.25km; 20min), starts at the end of Leask Bay Road, 2.5km east of the post office along the waterfront, and gives you the chance to see little **blue penguins** and **muttonbirds** returning to their nests at dusk (Nov–Feb). The entire track has recently been gravelled making it much easier going and more fun for the less committed hikers. Near the start of the track, you can follow a brief diversion to Harrold Bay, the site of a simple stone house built in 1835, making it one of the oldest European buildings in New Zealand. The main track continues through coastal forest to a lighthouse and lookout point from where you can watch the penguins arduously climbing to their nests hidden in the bush. You'll need a flashlight to find your way around after dusk, but it's important to keep the beam pointed to the ground to avoid disturbing the birds, which are easily distressed.

Ulva Island and Paterson Inlet

Well worth a visit for its astonishing bird life, pleasant walks, beaches and rich natural vegetation is the open sanctuary of **Ulva Island**, the largest of several islands in **Paterson Inlet**, a flooded valley cutting deep into Stewart Island. **Water taxis** ply out here regularly from the wharf at Golden Bay ($16–20

Tours on and around Stewart Island

General **tours of the island** are run by the irrepressible Sam on Billy the Bus; a naturalist and historian, he imparts his intimate knowledge of local history, flora and fauna and the islanders' way of life on a short tour leaving from Stewart Island Travel on Main Road (book ahead on ⓣ03/219 1269, ⓕ219 1355; most days at 11.30am & 2.30pm; 1hr 30min; around $16). Also worthwhile are his longer afternoon excursions, which include guided walks (2hr 30min; $25). Tours to the old whaling base at **Millars Beach**, only accessible by boat, are given by Seabuzz Glass-Bottom Boat & Watertaxi (ⓣ03/219 1282; $30).

Guided tours of **Ulva Island** and its plant- and birdlife can be arranged as part of a summer visitor programme, which involves a DOC volunteer showing you the tracks and filling you in on the wildlife, plantlife and history of the island (Jan & Feb; $35 half day; includes transport to the island), while Thorfinn Charters (ⓣ03/219 1210) include Ulva Island in their afternoon tour of Paterson Inlet ($50). To visit on your own, take a water taxi, or go with Mareno Excursions (ⓣ03/219 1023), who can drop you off after either a half- ($45) or full-day ($65) scenic or fishing trip in Paterson Inlet. Moana Charters (ⓣ03/219 1202) offer a similar half-day boat excursion ($50 per person), which includes stops for fishing and a visit to salmon farms on the way to the island, where you're dropped off and collected later.

The self-guided option is more fun and fulfilling if you have the *Explore an Island Paradise, Ulva Island Guide*, which tells you everything you need to know about the island and its feathered inhabitants, including the rare and recently introduced Yellow Head (Mohua). As part of the realization that Ulva Island is an upcoming attraction, DOC have upgraded the tracks to make for easier walking for the expected increased number of visitors.

A good alternative to the island tour is the twilight **kiwi-spotting trip** which takes you to a remote area to see the Stewart Island brown kiwi (a sub-species of the mainland birds) in the wild. Bravo Adventure Cruises (book 6 months ahead – it's a small boat and fills up quickly – in summer on ⓣ & ⓕ03/219 1144, or contact the Stewart Island visitor centre, see p.776; around $60) run four-hour trips every other night, leaving from the wharf in Halfmoon Bay around dusk. You'll need warm clothing, sturdy footwear and a flashlight, as the outing entails a short boat trip and a brief uphill bushwalk in the dark to a windswept beach, where the kiwi feast on tiny crustaceans. Great care is taken to avoid disturbing these timid birds.

Further kiwi spotting opportunities can be had at Mason Bay, accessible on scenic **flights** ($155) arranged with Stewart Island Flights (see p.771), who will drop you off for sightseeing and tramping there and other inaccessible parts of the island; if yo decide to go down this route, don't go crashing about in the bush with torches: just pick a spot and wait for them to come to you. They also offer overflights.

return) and you should allow a full day (bring a packed lunch) to explore the several gentle tracks around the island; see box above for details of **guided tours**.

Clearly visible from Oban, the long, low island has largely escaped the effects of introduced predators and is full of birdsong. Thriving in its dense vegetation are weka, bellbirds, oystercatchers, kaka, yellow- and red-crowned parakeets, tui, fantails and pigeons, who fearlessly approach visitors out of curiosity. Plant life includes many species of fern and orchid, and the forest floor is covered in mosses and liverworts. Tracks begin from the wharf at **Post Office Bay** (where there's a no-longer-functioning hundred-year-old post office, a remnant from the days when the island was the hub of the community) and there's a pleasant picnic shelter on the beach at **Sydney Cove** nearby. Note that camping overnight is not allowed.

The best way to explore the sheltered waters of Paterson Inlet without getting wet is on the Seabuzz Glass-Bottom Boat (see p.781; 1hr, daily at 11am depending on weather; about $30), which allows **underwater viewing**. The adventurous will want a more thorough exploration by **sea kayaking**, and scattered around the inlet's margins are several navigable rivers and four **DOC huts** where you can stay overnight (arrange in advance with the DOC field centre in Oban; see p.760). Frequent visitors to these waters are bottle-nosed dolphins and fur seals, while the tidal flats attract wading birds, including herons, oystercatchers, godwits and the New Zealand dotterel. Bear in mind that the waters around Stewart Island can be changeable and May to August brings the most settled weather; only extremely experienced kayakers should venture into these waters unaccompanied. Completely Southern Sea Kayaks (ⓣ03/219 1275), based at Thule Bay, rent kayaks ($50 per person per day), and their guided trips cost $60 for a half day, $80 full day.

Mason Bay

If you want to visit **Mason Bay** and stay overnight in the trampers' hut to have a chance of viewing kiwi in the wild, or see both the east and west coasts of Stewart Island without completing either of the major tracks, you can do all this by combining a scenic flight (see p.772) and a water-taxi ride (see p.776). The two companies work together to provide flexible trips, so you can fly in or out from the east coast (Halfmoon Bay) to Mason Bay on the west, or fly in and walk an easy flat section of the North–West Circuit with ever-changing views to the hut at Freshwater Landing (14km, 3–4hr) to pick up a water taxi, or vice versa (around $200 total transport cost, 2 people min; huts $5 per person); the trip is weather dependent.

The Rakiura Track and North-West Circuit

You need to be well equipped for Stewart Island's two major walks, both of which fan out from Oban. As the weather is changeable, often mixing sunshine and rain within an hour, take several layers of clothing for warmth, good waterproofs (including gaiters) and don't forget sandfly repellent. The DOC office has a helpful video and leaflets ($1 each) on the tracks, and you must buy hut or campsite passes before you set out. You'll need a Great Walks pass for the Rakiura Track and for part of the North–West Circuit. Both tracks are usually deserted except for the Christmas period.

One of New Zealand's Great Walks, the **Rakiura Track** (29km, plus a further 7km of road walking to complete the circuit; 3 days) makes an excellent introduction to the island's history, forest and birdlife. Starting and ending in Oban, the circuit can be walked in either direction, and at any time of the year, since boardwalk covers most of the track's boggy sections. Staying within the bushline, the track follows the open coast, before climbing over a three-hundred-metre forested ridge and traversing the shores of Paterson Inlet. The highlight is a lookout tower on the summit ridge, which provides excellent views of Paterson Inlet and beyond to the Tin Range. The two huts en route (30 bunks; $8 per person) are equipped with mattresses, wood stoves for heating only, running water and toilets, but you'll need your own stove. Camping is allowed at three designated areas ($6 per person) along the way – Maori Beach, Port William and Sawdust Bay – and sites have water supply and toilets.

Only the hardiest and most experienced tramper should consider attempting the **North–West Circuit** (130km; 10–12 days; pass $38, includes a night in either Port William or North Arm and 9 nights in other huts) around the island's northern arm. Mud on the tracks is the main problem, usually widespread and often deep and thick. The North-West Circuit has ten huts, which are spaced at intervals suited to an average day's tramping, most of them on the coast, but there are no campsites. The track itself alternates between open coast and forested hill country, offering highlights of a side trip to the 980-metre summit of Mount Anglem (5.5km; 6hr return) and the chance to see kiwi in the wild at Mason Bay.

Travel details

Trains

From Dunedin to: Middlemarch (2 daily; 2hrs; Pukerangi (2 Daily, 2.5hrs).

Buses

From Dunedin to: Alexandra (4 daily; 3hr); Balclutha (6 daily; 1hr 35min); Cromwell (4 daily; 3hr 30min); Gore (6 daily; 2hr 35min); Invercargill (6 daily; 3hr 10min); Lawrence (4 daily; 1hr 30min); Oamaru (5 daily; 1hr 30min); Queenstown (4 daily; 4hr 25min); Te Anau (4 daily; 4h 30min).
From Invercargill to: Balclutha (2 daily; half day); Dunedin (6 daily; 3hrs 10 mins); Gore (2 daily; 55min); Queenstown (4 daily; 2hr 40min); Te Anau (2 daily; 2hr 25min).

Ferries

From Invercargill to: Stewart Island (2 daily; 1hr).
From Stewart Island to: Invercargill (2 daily; 1hr).

Planes

From Dunedin to: Auckland (12 daily; 2hr 40min); Blenheim (9 daily; 3hr 5min); Christchurch (10 daily; 45 min); Gisborne (6 daily; 3hr 15min); Hamilton (7 daily; 2hr 30min); Hokitika (4 daily; 1hr 45min); Invercargill (2 daily; 30min); Kaitaia (3 daily, 4hr 20min); Napier/Hastings (6 daily; 3hr); Nelson (12 daily; 2hr); New Plymouth (5 daily; 4hr); Palmerston North (7 daily; 2hr 40min); Rotorua (7 daily; 3hr 50min); Taupo (4 daily; 3hr 50min); Tauranga (9 daily; 3hr); Wanganui (3 daily; 3hr); Wellington (12 daily; 1hr 10min); Westport (2 daily; 3hr); Whakatane (6 daily; 4hr 5min); Whangarei (8 daily; 3hr 45min).
From Invercargill to: Auckland (8 daily; 3hr 30min); Blenheim (6 daily; 4hr); Christchurch (8 daily; 1hr 40min); Dunedin (3 daily; 30min); Gisborne (4 daily; 5hr); Hamilton (4 daily; 7hr); Hokitika (4 daily; 6hr); Kataia (2 daily; 4hr 40min); Napier/Hastings (4 daily; 4hr 30min); Nelson (7 daily; 4hr 30min); New Plymouth (4 daily; 4hr); Palmerston North (6 daily; 3hr 25min); Rotorua (4 daily; 4hr 25min); Stewart Island (3 daily; 20min); Taupo (6 daily; 3hr 45min); Tauranga (8 daily; 3hr 30min); Wanganui (3 daily; 4hr); Wellington (8 daily; 2hr); Westport (2 daily; 7hr); Whakatane (5 daily; 8hr); Whangarei (5 daily; 4hr 30min).
From Stewart Island to: Invercargill (3 daily; 20min).

12

The West Coast

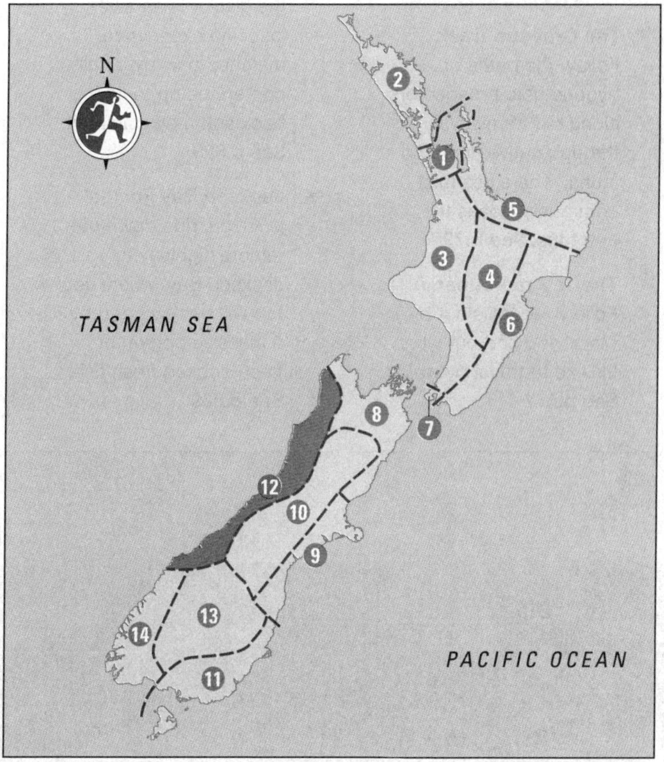
N
TASMAN SEA
PACIFIC OCEAN
1
2
3
4
5
6
7
8
9
10
11
12
13
14

CHAPTER 12 **Highlights**

* **The Buller Gorge** Cross the gorge on one of the longest swing bridges in New Zealand and fly back the other way, Superman-style. See p.790

* **The Croesus Track** Follow the paths of bygone gold prospectors along old tramways through native flora and fauna, where sea mist commonly cloaks the tree tops. See p.796

* **The Te Ara Pounamu** Follow the trails cut by Maori and find out what it's like to travel by *waka*. See p.817

* **White water rafting** Try rafting out of Greymouth to give you a real buzz. See p.817

* **The Franz Josef glacier** A walk up to the head of the glacier is an awe-inspiring experience, matched only by a helicopter ride up to its back and a hike along it. See p.829

* **Jackson Bay** For real isolation, ride down the remote highway to Jackson Bay, where your trip will be rewarded by a massive portion of fresh-cooked fresh fish. See p.839

12

The West Coast

The Southern Alps run down the backbone of the South Island, both defining and isolating **the West Coast**. A narrow, rugged and largely untamed coastal strip of turbulent rivers, lush bushland and crystal lakes that's seldom more than 30km wide, it comes fringed by astonishing surf-pounded beaches backed by the odd tiny shack or, more frequently, nothing at all. What really sets "the Coast" apart is the interaction of settlers with their environment. **Coasters**, many descended from early gold and coal miners, have long been proud of their ability to coexist with the wild primeval landscape – a trait mythologized in their reputation for independent-mindedness and intemperate beer-drinking, no doubt fuelled by a heavy admixture of Irish drawn to the 1860s gold rushes. Stories abound of late-night drinking sessions in pubs way past their closing times, and overall, your fondest memories of the West Coast might well be chance encounters one evening in the pub, rather than the sights.

Cook sailed up this way in 1770, when he described the Coast as "an inhospitable shore, unworthy of observation, except for its ridge of naked and barren rocks covered with snow. As far as the eye could reach the prospect was wild, craggy and desolate". Little here then for early **European explorers** such as Thomas Brunner and Charles Heaphy, who made forays in 1846–47, led by Kehu, a Maori guide. They returned without finding the cultivable land they sought, and after a shorter trip in 1861 Henry Harper, the first Bishop of Christchurch, wrote, "I doubt if such a wilderness will ever be colonized except through the discovery of **gold**". Prophetic words: within two years reports were circulating of flecks of gold in West Coast rivers and a year later Greymouth and Hokitika were experiencing full-on gold rushes. The boom was soon over, but mining continued into the twentieth century, with huge dredges littering the landscape, looking like beached galleons as they worked their way up the gravel riverbeds, scuttling through spent tailings.

As gold was worked out, longer-lasting **coal** took its place, laying the foundation for more permanent towns. Many of these have since foundered (although the West Coast still produces a third of the country's coal) and a shrinking economy has tapped the resourcefulness of the people – you'll still find individual miners hacking away at a single coal seam or running a sawmill in the bush single-handed (for some years now the timber industry has formed a large part of the west coast economy), alongside people taking advantage of the abundant open space and low land prices and nurturing a thriving **alternative culture** – you may well spot the smoke stack of some purple bus sticking out from behind the trees. In the last fifteen years or so, however, every-

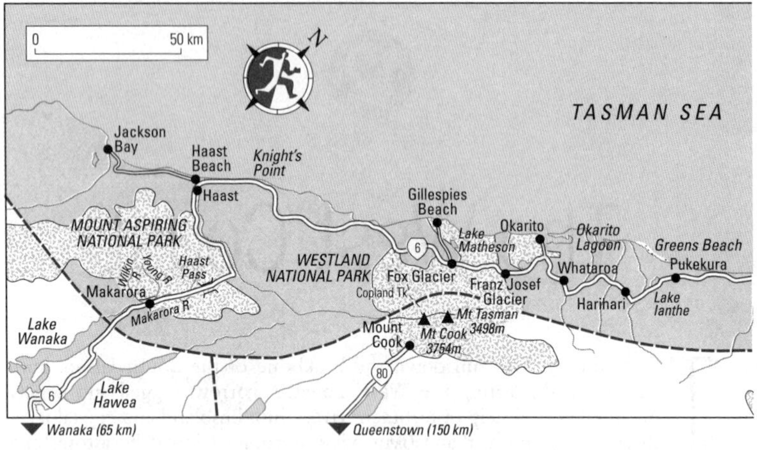

thing has been turned upside down by the challenge of increasing **tourism** and a greater awareness of the Coast's fragile **ecosystems**, a situation that has given rise to tension between the Coasters and the government, particularly regarding native timber felling and its detrimental effect on the unique environment.

While the Coasters see the lucrative industry of harvesting native timber as a pragmatic way of stemming unemployment in the area and a gradual, associated decline in the local population, the government have attempted to discourage the practice in the hope of preserving this distinct environment, through legal action and by subsidising eco-friendly tourism and business. The debate will no doubt rage for some time, but if the big milling interests win then the area will never be the same again (see "Westland's endangered forests", p.791).

No discussion of the West Coast would be complete without mention of the torrential **rainfall**, which falls with tropical intensity for days at a time; every rock springs a waterfall and the bush becomes vibrant with colour. Such soakings have a detrimental effect on the soil, retarding decomposition and producing a peat-like top layer with all the minerals leached out. The result is **pakihi**, scrubby, impoverished and poor-looking paddocks that characterize much of the West Coast's cleared land. But the abundant sunshine that alternates with the downpours produces excellent conditions for **marijuana**-growing, a significant component of the local economy. Enthusiasm for dope-growing is matched only by the springtime rush to catch **whitebait**, when fishers line the tidal riverbanks on rising tides trying to net this epicurean holy grail of Kiwi angling.

The boom-and-bust nature of the West Coast's gold- and coal-mining past produced scores of ghost towns, but also spawned its three largest towns – the harbour town of **Westport**, and the former ports of **Greymouth** and **Hokitika**. The real pleasure of the West Coast, though, lies in smaller places more closely tied to the countryside, where the Coasters' indomitable spirit shines through: places such as **Karamea**, on the southern limit of the Kahurangi National Park, the strike town of **Blackball** at the foot of the Croesus Track on the Paparoa Range, the gold town of **Ross** and windswept

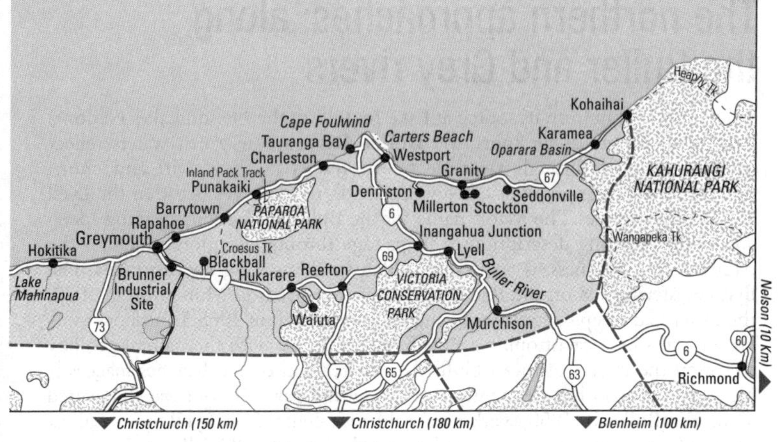

Okarito. With the exception of a couple of decent museums and a handful of sights, the West Coast's appeal is in its scenic beauty. The **Oparara Basin**, near Karamea, and the **Paparoa National Park**, south of Westport, exhibit some of the country's finest limestone formations, including huge arched spans and the famous Pancake Rocks, while in the Westland National Park the frosty white tongues of the **Franz Josef** and **Fox glaciers** career down the flanks of the Southern Alps into dense emerald bush almost to sea level.

Most people visit from November to April, and you might expect that a place with such a damp reputation is a bad place to visit in **winter**, but temperatures are not as low as you might think and the greater number of clear days make for cloud-free viewing. Pesky sandflies are also less active in the winter. The West Coast never feels crowded but in the off-season you'll have even more room to move and accommodation will be cheaper; the downside is that **whitewater rafting**, **caving** and scenic **flights**, which require minimum numbers to operate, may be harder to arrange.

The simplest way to get around the West Coast is with your own **vehicle**. Likewise, **cycling** isn't such a chore: the coast road is undulating but the distances between towns aren't off-putting and you can always find somewhere to camp in between. Public transport, on the other hand, is fairly restrictive. **Trains** only penetrate as far as Greymouth; **bus services** are infrequent and, though they call at all the major towns, they won't get you to most of the walks. Having said that, with patience and a degree of forward planning it is possible to see much of interest, especially if you are prepared to walk a little. The major bus route along the coast is provided by InterCity (in Christchurch ⓣ03/379 9020), running once a day in each direction with an overnight stop in either Franz Josef or Fox Glacier. For service frequencies and journey times, consult "Travel Details" on p.842.

Some of the best deals are West Coast **travel passes** offered by several companies including the backpacker tour-bus operators, Kiwi Experience and Magic Bus, which both run southbound services several times a week (see Basics, p.31).

The northern approaches: along the Buller and Grey rivers

Stretching 169km from its source at Lake Rotoiti in the Nelson Lakes National Park to its mouth at Westport, the **Buller River**'s blue-green waters reflect sunlight dappled through riverside beech forests as they swirl and churn through one of the grandest of New Zealand's river gorges between the Lyell and Brunner ranges. The Maori name for the Buller is *Kawatiri*, meaning "deep and swift", a fitting description of its passage through a region which, in the national consciousness, is associated with two devastating **earthquakes**. The first, registering 7.8 on the Richter Scale, was centred on Murchison in 1929; the other had its epicentre near Inungahua and struck in 1968. Landslides associated with these catastrophic events have combined with the natural geology to soften the curves of rocky bluffs that shelter white-sand beaches inaccessible from the road but frequently used by rafting parties. Gold was discovered along the Buller in 1858, sparking a gold rush centred on **Lyell**, now a ghost town whose outlying remains can be visited on the **Lyell Walkway**.

The Buller is traced by SH6 from Kawatiri Junction to Westport through Inungahua Junction, where Greymouth-bound travellers turn south towards Reefton. From Reefton, SH7 hugs the **Grey River**, a far less dramatic watercourse than the Buller, as it flows through a wide valley to the east of the granite tops of the Paparoa Range past more evidence of long-dead gold and coal industries, principally at laidback **Blackball** and the **Brunner Industrial Site**.

The Buller Gorge

SH6 from Nelson passes through Murchison (see p.581) and follows the Buller River 11km to **O'Sullivan's Bridge** where you turn right to remain on SH6 as it enters the Upper Buller Scenic Reserve. After 6km, the road passes the **Buller Gorge Swing Bridge** (Ⓣ03/548 2193, Ⓦwww.BullerGorge.co.nz; $5), the longest example of the swaying pedestrian footbridges known in New Zealand as swingbridges; crossing high above the Buller River, the 110-metre span has a fun 160-metre-long **flying fox** (a two person chair that dangles from a wire and rushes downhill from one side of the river to the other), on which you can ride back, prone (Superman-style) or sitting, for $25. Based around the bridge and the flying fox, on the far side of the swift flowing water, is a heritage park with a variety of **bush walks** (ranging from 15min to over 2hr) taking in a waterfall, where White's Creek joins the river, the White's Creek faultline, epicentre of the 1929 earthquake, and the miner's workings that took advantage of the 4.5-metre rise in the ground caused by the quake. You can also pan for gold or if you've a mind push on into the bush to lookouts and the Ariki Falls (1hr round trip) all for the cost of crossing the bridge; a waterproof map is provided, which must be returned. For those wishing to add another thrill to the package there is also an exciting **jetboat** ride ($65; 30min) up river to the Ariki Falls and then spinning round back to the bridge along the gorge.

Fifteen kilometres on, a lay-by provides the **View of Earthquake Slip** which, thirty-odd years after the Inungahua earthquake, is gradually being recolonized but still bears the scars of the huge landslide that completely dammed the Buller River for several days. Following a four-kilometre bend in the river, the road passes the grassy site of **Lyell**, a former gold-mining town named after the great geologist Charles Lyell. The town sat high above the Buller on flats beside Lyell Creek and, in its 1890s heyday, supported five hotels, two banks, two churches and even its own newspaper, all serving a population of three thousand spread between here, Gibbstown and Zalatown, further up the Lyell Creek. Fires and the gradual decline in gold mining saw off all three settlements, but a few mementoes remain, and can be visited via the short but fairly strenuous **Lyell Walkway**, which passes terraces where huts once stood, the sobering slabs that stand askew in the cemetery (15min return), and the ten-hammer Croesus quartz stamping battery (1hr 30min return). The roadside site of the former township itself is now a peaceful DOC **campsite** ($5).

The next town, 17km to the west, is **INUNGAHUA JUNCTION**, which is little more than a service station attached to a café and grocery shop, an excuse for a brief stop only, unless you want to stay at the very cheap *Inwoods Farm Backpackers* (☎03/789 0205; closed July & Aug; ❶), a house with no more than four in a room, signposted 400m down Inwoods Road which spurs off beside the fun general store with excellent free-range eggs.

West of Inungahua Junction the river approaches Westport through the **Lower Buller Gorge**, the narrowest and most dramatic section. The road hugs the cliff-face in places, most notably at **Hawks Crag**, where the rock has been hewn to form a large overhang – the fact that the water level rose several metres above this carved-out section during a 1926 flood will give you some idea of the volume of water that can surge down the gorge.

Westland's endangered forest

If gold and coal built the West Coast's foundations, then the **timber industry** supports the structure. Ever since timber was felled for sluicing flumes and pit props, Coasters have relied on the seemingly limitless forests for their livelihood. As coal and gold were worked out, miners became loggers, felling trees which take from three hundred to six hundred years to mature and which, according to fossil records of pollen, have been around for 100 million years.

Few expressed any concern for the plight of Westland's magnificent stands of **beech** and **podocarp** until the 1970s, when the magnitude of the threat to the forests became clear. Environmental groups rallied around a campaign to save the Maruia Valley, east of Reefton, which became a touchstone for forest conservation, but it wasn't until the 1986 **West Coast Accord** between the government, local authorities, conservationists and the timber industry that some sort of truce prevailed. In recent years most of the forests have been selectively logged, often using helicopters to pluck out the mature trees without destroying those nearby. While it preserves the appearance of the forest, this is little comfort for New Zealand's endangered **birds** – particularly kaka, kakariki (yellow-crowned parakeet), morepork (native owl) and rifleman – and long-tailed **bats**, all of which nest in holes in older trees.

With the benefit of hindsight, many considered the accord far too weak: felling of the south Westland rimu forests stopped in 1994, but continued apace in Buller until the election of the left-leaning Labour–Alliance coalition government in 1999. Though torn between their commitment to jobs and to the environment, Labour leader Helen Clark honoured her election pledge and almost immediately banned the logging of beech forests by the State-owned Timberlands company. Precious West Coast jobs were immediately lost, the continued viability of several communities remains threatened, and thousands felt betrayed in this traditionally Labour-voting part of the world. The future may look brighter for the forests, but Coasters will probably become increasingly reliant on tourism for their survival.

Reefton and around

Located beside the Inungahua River at the intersection of roads from Westport, Greymouth and Christchurch, **REEFTON**, as its name suggests, owes its existence to rich gold-bearing quartz reefs. These were exploited so heavily in the 1870s that Reefton was considered by some "the most brisk and businesslike place in the colony". This frenzy of financial speculation put Reefton in the vanguard, and it became the first place in New Zealand, and one of the first in the world, to install electric street lighting powered by a hydroelectric generator. Such forward-looking activity soon abated and, despite decades as an important coal-mining town, Reefton weathered poorly. However, things are now looking up: a couple of interesting galleries and even a very good café opening in recent years, together with a couple of pleasant strolls on the outskirts of town, mean you may want to tarry a while. After a couple of hours, though, you'll probably want to explore the Victoria Conservation Park to the north or press on down the Grey Valley.

Specific points of interest around town are linked by two walks, both the subject of brochures available from the visitor centre (see "Practicalities", below). The elegiac **Historic Walk** (40min) meanders around Reefton's grid of streets, bidding farewell to the dilapidated exteriors of once-grand buildings – the Masonic Lodge, the School of Mines and the Court House – all ripe for preservation. The pleasant **Powerhouse Walk** (40min) also recalls a more illustrious past but succeeds in being more uplifting, perhaps because of its course along the Inungahua River. In the centre of town, on the corner of Walsh and Broadway, is an old **miner's cottage** and smithie (daily 9.30am–4.30pm, closed bank holiday weekends; donation), with four different local curators who all have something to offer, will fire up the forge and answer any questions to the best of their ability. It'll take about ten minutes to see all there is.

The water race for Reefton's original hydroelectric scheme was diverted 2km from Blacks Point, where the **Blacks Point Museum**, SH7 towards Springs Junction (Ⓣ03/732 8808; Oct–April Thurs & Fri 9am–noon & 1–4pm, Sat & Sun 1–4pm; $2), occupies a former Wesleyan Chapel. The museum charts the district's cultural and mining history through engaging photos and a large collection of lamps, moustache cups, clunky old typewriters and the like. Outside, parts from two ancient stamper batteries have been knitted together to form one five-hammer battery hydro-driven by a Pelton wheel; the whole ensemble is cranked into action on Sunday afternoons and during school holidays. **Walks** along mining trails through the regenerating bush to the mine shafts and stamping batteries of the Murray Creek Goldfield start from behind the museum and range from half an hour to a day; pick up the informative *Walks in the Murray Creek Goldfield* leaflet from the visitor centre or museum.

Coal- and gold-mining heritage combines with a vast area of bushland in the **Victoria Conservation Park**, which cloaks the ranges right around the western side of Reefton. The park is well off the traditional tourist itinerary and is consequently little-visited, making it all the more appealing for wilderness freaks. Day-walks are possible, but most require overnight stays in DOC huts; the visitor centre in Reefton can fill you in on all the options.

Practicalities

Buses all stop on Broadway, Reefton's main street, within sight of the helpful combined **visitor centre** and **DOC office**, 67–69 Broadway (daily: Dec–Feb 8.30am–6pm; Mar–Sept 8.30am–4.30pm; Sept–Nov 8.30am–5.30pm;

Ⓣ03/732 8391, Ⓕ732 9661), which has **internet access**, a small purpose-built goldmine (50 cents), rents out gold pans for $2 a day and bikes for $25 a day.

Almost all Reefton's **accommodation** is on, or just off, Broadway; the cheapest place is *Reefton Backpackers*, 64 Shiel St (Ⓣ & Ⓕ03/732 8383; beds ❶, rooms ❷), a spacious, though run down house with just a few beds in each room and self-catering facilities, all managed from the lotto shop on Broadway. Alternatively there's the *Old Bread Shop Backpackers*, 155 Buller Road (Ⓣ03/732 8420; dorms ❶), a small well-run hostel of just eleven beds. The best place in town is *Reef Cottage B&B*, 51–55 Broadway, beside the *Reef Café* (Ⓣ0800/770 440, Ⓣ & Ⓕ03/732 8440, Ⓔereefton@clear.net.nz; ❹–❺), where they offer beautiful, individually decorated Victorian- and 1920s-style ensuites and a friendly welcome. **Motels** units are available in the *Bellbird*, 93 Broadway (Ⓣ03/732 8444; ❹), and at the *Reeftom Auto Lodge*, 74 Broadway (Ⓣ03/732 8406, ❸–❹); while **campers** should make for the *Reefton Domain Motor Camp*, 1 Ross St, at the top of Broadway (Ⓣ03/732 8477; tents $8, powered sites ❶ for two, cabins ❷), where there's good swimming in the Inungahua River, or head 10km south down the Grey Valley to the DOC's *Slab Creek* campsite ($5).

Culinary relief from the usual rural tearoom hell comes in the form of *The Reef Café* (daily: Dec–March 8am–7pm; April–Nov 8am–5pm; see above), a bright and comfortable **spot** serving muffins, sandwiches, pasta, soup, good coffee and specializing in particularly luscious desserts (menu ranges from $5–15, BYO). For something more substantial try *Alfresco Outside Eatery*, on Upper Broadway (Ⓣ03/732 8513), with light meals, good coffee and lovely pizza served at lunch, and in evenings during the summer. If you're after a fry-up or something a bit more calorific then the *Dawson's on Broadway* and *Electric Light Café*, both in the *Reefton Auto Lodge* (see above), will provide you with fish and chips, steak, full breakfasts and of course a pint, as will the *Inaugahua Arms*, 172 Buller St, a straight-up pub with large portions of good fish to tempt you and karaoke to drive you away.

The Grey Valley

Southwest of Reefton, SH7 follows the Grey Valley, cut off from the Tasman Sea by the rugged Paparoa Range and hemmed in by the Southern Alps. From both sides, the bush is gradually reclaiming the mine workings that characterized the region for a century. Nothing has stepped in to replace them, and the small communities tick over, a few eking a living from inquisitive tourists keen to explore the former mining towns of **Waiuta** and **Blackball**, and to walk the **Croesus Track**.

Waiuta

The first diversion of any consequence lies 21km south of Reefton where **Hukarere** marks the junction for **WAIUTA**, a ghost town seventeen partly-sealed kilometres east. This was the last of the West Coast's great gold towns, attaining a population of 6000 in the 1930s.

The end came for Waiuta when a mine shaft collapsed in 1951, burying large deposits of gold-bearing reef-quartz 879m down, where it was uneconomic to extract them. Miners left for jobs on the coast, much of the equipment was bought by Australian mining companies – many houses were even carted off – but the town wasn't completely abandoned; four or the remaining five cottages are occupied and there are several more buildings scattered around, including the original post office. The rolling country pocked by waste heaps is slowly being colonized by pioneer species like gorse and bramble, but the cypresses and poplars that once delineated gardens and the fruit trees that filled them remain; the rugby field, whippet track, croquet lawns and swimming pool are faring less well.

The whole place is wonderfully atmospheric for just mooching around, guided by the invaluable *Waiuta* leaflet (available from Reefton visitor centre) and strategically placed interpretive panels. You can see the lot in a couple of hours, but Waiuta is an ideal **place to stay** for well-equipped campers, who can pitch their tent just about anywhere. For the less hardy, there's the open-plan thirty-bunk *Waiuta Lodge* (book through the Reefton visitor centre; ❶), with a fully equipped kitchen, TV and video and a public phone. There's no other accommodation, no public transport and nowhere to buy food, so come prepared.

Blackball

Both the Grey River and SH7 meander through inconsequential small towns until they reach **Stillwater**, 11km short of Greymouth, where side roads lead to Blackball and Lake Brunner.

Refugees from the blistering pace of Greymouth gravitate to languid **BLACKBALL**, a former gold- and coal-mining village spread across a plateau at the foot of the Paparoa Range, 11km northeast of Stillwater. Here, commuters, neo-hippies and gnarled folk still hunting and prospecting in the bush seem to coexist fairly harmoniously. Blackball owes its existence to alluvial gold discovered in Blackball Creek in 1864, but gold returns diminished by the early twentieth century and it was left to coal, also mined from 1893, to save the day. Coal supported Blackball until the mine's closure in 1964, along the way staking the town's place in New Zealand's history as the birthplace of the **labour movement**.

During the first three decades of the twentieth century, the whole of the Grey Valley was a hotbed of doctrinaire socialism, as organizers moved among the towns, pressing unbending mine managers to address the atrocious working conditions. Anger finally came to a head, resulting in the crippling 1908 "cribtime strike", when Pat Hickey, Bob Semple and Paddy Webb requested an extension of their "crib" (lunch) break from fifteen to thirty minutes. Management's refusal sparked an illegal ten-week strike – the longest in New Zealand's history – during which the workers' families (already suffering enormous sacrifice and deprivation) were fined £75 for their action. None had the money to pay and although the bailiffs tried to auction their possessions, the workers banded together, refusing to bid – one then bought all the goods for a fraction of their worth and redistributed them to their original owners. It is this spirit which eventually won the day: the workers returned to the mine and crib time was extended, but the £75 was extracted from subsequent wages.

The struggle led to the formation of the Miners' Federation, which later transformed itself into the Federation of Labour, the country's principal trade union organization. Eric Beardsley's historical novel *Blackball 08* (see "Books" in Contexts) gives an accurate and passionate portrayal of the 1908 strike, but the most powerful evocation of the labour spirit is in the TV room at *Formerly the Blackball Hilton* (see below), with its relics and press cuttings from the strike and red flags bearing rousing slogans.

Ironically, these days Blackball's tranquillity is the main draw, abetted by excellent walking through the gold workings of Blackball Creek and up onto the wind-blasted tops of the Paparoa Range along the **Croesus Track** (see box on p.796). If you fancy using four legs rather than shanks's pony, try Clayton Horseriding (☎03/732 3551; from $45), who offer some pleasant short and half-day trips.

Practicalities

Blackball's social life revolves around the welcoming and wonderfully low-key *Formerly The Blackball Hilton*, Hart Street (ⓣ0800/425 225, ⓦwww.blackball-hilton.co.nz; tents $9, dorms ❶, rooms ❸), the last of the mining-era **hotels** which opened as the *Dominion* in 1910 and subsequently operated as the *Hilton* – ostensibly named for the former mine manager remembered in Hilton Street nearby – until challenged by the international hotel chain of the same name. Apart from lively drinking with quirky local characters, the hotel offers accommodation, breakfast, lunch and dinner, a hot tub for guests, gold panning in local rivers ($3 pan rental), horse riding (half-day; $45) and a hatful of suggestions for walks and exploration. Self-caterers can feast on venison sausages, salamis, cooked and preserved meats and other bits and pieces from the excellent *Blackball Salami Co.* across the road; everyone else is limited to no-nonsense bar **meals** at the hotel and **takeaways** from the local dairy.

There is no public transport but the hotel can often organize a ride from Greymouth.

Lake Brunner

From Stillwater another sealed road runs 25km southeast to Lake Brunner (Moana Kotuku), a filled glacial hollow celebrated for its trout fishing; you can pick up a hire rod at the general store at the motor camp (see below), and a licence at the local garage. It's also good for warm summer swimming. Although not brimming with things to do there is the two-kilometre **Velenski Walkway**, which meanders through unspoilt native bush beside the Arthur River nearby. Note that the lake is also accessible off SH73 between Greymouth and Arthur's Pass.

The only facilities are a couple of kilometres further on at the lakeside village of **MOANA**, where the TranzAlpine **train** makes a regular newspaper stop on Saturdays and will halt on request at other times. Accommodation extends to the improved *Moana Hotel*, Ahau Street (ⓣ & ⓕ03/738 0083; cabins ❶, rooms ❸, units ❹–❺), and the well-run neighbouring *Lake Brunner Motor Camp* (ⓣ & ⓕ03/738 0600; tents $8, powered sites $10, cabins ❷). The *Stationhouse Café & Bar*, Koe Street (ⓣ03/738 0158, BYO wine only but worth it because their wine list is a work of creative accountancy), has the best **eating** around about, with lunches from $15, dinners from $22 and excellent lake views.

Brunner Industrial Site

Back on SH7, a couple of kilometres past Stillwater, a tall brick Tyneside chimney marks the **Brunner Industrial Site** (unrestricted access). Roadside information panels mark the path to a fine old suspension bridge (now relegated to foot traffic only), which crosses the swirling river to the few remaining buildings and the largely intact ruins of distinctive beehive coking ovens.

On his explorations in the late 1840s, Thomas Brunner noted the seam of riverside coal. By 1885, the mine site was producing twice as much coal as any other mine in the country and exporting firebricks throughout Australasia, but in 1896 New Zealand's worst mining disaster (with 69 dead) heralded its decline. The site was finally abandoned in the 1940s, and only exhumed from dense bush in the early 1980s. Half an hour wandering around the foundations and the fifty-minute bushwalk to some of the old mine sites evoke a long-gone era.

The Croesus Track

The DOC's informative *Croesus and Moonlight Walks* pamphlet shows adequate detail for walkers. The NZMS's 1:50,000 *Ahaura Topomap* is the one for map enthusiasts.

Prospectors seeking new claims gradually pushed their way up the Blackball Creek, cutting paths to get their reef-quartz rock down to stamping batteries and to get supplies back up to their shelters in the bush. The scant remains of decades of toil now provide the principal interest on the **Croesus Track**, the first half easily explored in a day from Blackball, the whole track over the 1200m Paparoa Range to Barrytown on the coast north of Greymouth taking two relatively gentle days or one eight-hour slog.

Access and accommodation

The track **starts** at Smoke-Ho car park, at the end of a rough but passable road 5km north of Blackball, and **finishes** opposite the Barrytown Tavern on SH6, where southbound and northbound buses pass twice daily. There are two **huts** along the track: the **free Garden Gully Hut, with two sack bunks and an open fire, and the Cec Clarke Hut (24 bunks; $10)**, with panoramic views, pots and a good coal-burning stove; the adjacent Top Hut is now abandoned.

The Track

Much of the track was designed to accommodate tramways and the requirements of a gentle, steady grade characterize today's track. The route wends through hardwood and native podocarps interspersed with ferns and mosses and vines, gradually giving way to hardier silver beech and eventually alpine tussock and herbfields above the tree line. Sea mist commonly cloaks the tops during the middle of the day.

The trail from **Smoke-Ho** begins along a well-graded track, gradually descending to cross Smoke-Ho Creek then rising gently to a clearing (reached in half an hour), from where a ten-minute return path leads to the former site of the **Minerva Battery**. Immediately after the clearing, the path crosses Clarke Creek on a new wire bridge above the remains of an old wooden bridge. Another half hour on, a side track leads to two more clearings that once contained **Perotti's Mill** (10min return) and the **Croesus Battery** (50min return), respectively. After almost an hour, another side path leads to the primitive **Garden Gully Hut** (5min return) and the **Garden Gully Battery** (40min return). The main track turns sharply west before reaching the **Cec Clarke Hut** on the tree line in around an hour: fill your water bottles here, there is no supply beyond. The top of the ridge near Mount Ryall (1220m) lies two undulating hours beyond, a little more if you run off to climb **Croesus Knob** (1204m) along the way. If it isn't cloaked in cloud, the broad ridge offers wonderful views down to the coast, which is reached in under three hours by a steep but well marked path that dives down into the bush.

An alternative for experienced and fit trampers is to follow a loop that joins the Croesus Track with **The Moonlight Track**, detailed in the DOC's *Croesus and Moonlight Walks* leaflet.

Westport and around

WESTPORT runs Greymouth close for the dubious honour of being the West Coast's most dispiriting town, a drab low-slung place of wide streets and slim opportunities which nevertheless warrants a visit for the nearby sights, principally the seal colony of **Cape Foulwind** and the former coal towns of the **Rochford Plateau** to the north. Besides, as this is a principal transport interchange, you may well end up spending a couple of nights here, which is made tolerable by reasonable accommodation, some decent restaurants and pubs – and a few adventure activities to keep you entertained.

Westport was the first of the West Coast towns, established by one **Reuben Waite** in 1861 as a single store beside the mouth of the Buller River. He made his living provisioning the few Buller Gorge prospectors in return for gold, but when the miners moved on to richer pickings in Otago, Waite upped sticks and headed south to help found Greymouth. Westport turned to the more dependable coal and, while the mining towns to the north were becoming established, engineers channelled the river to scour out a **port**, which fast became the largest coal port in the country but now lies idle. Westport battles on, with a respectable-sized fishing fleet and the odd ship laden with the produce of New Zealand's largest cement works at Cape Foulwind, which is fuelled by coal from open-cast Stockton, the only large mine left.

Arrival, information and transport

Almost everything of consequence in Westport happens around Palmerston Street. The helpful **visitor centre**, 1 Brougham St (daily: Christmas–Jan 9am–7pm; rest of year 9am–5pm; ⓣ03/789 6658, ⓦwww.westport.org.nz), is just off Palmerston Street, a few steps from the **DOC office**, at 72 Russell St (Mon–Fri 9am–noon & 1–5pm; ⓣ03/788 8008); though only the visitor centre handles Heaphy Track **hut tickets**, so god help you, or get them through another outlet. There's **internet access** at the library opposite the visitor centre (Mon–Thurs 10am–5pm, Fri 10am–6.30pm, Sat 10.30am–1.30pm).

Bus stops are scattered around town. Atomic stops outside the visitor centre; Cunningham's Coaches from Karamea pull up at their depot at 179 Palmerston St; and InterCity stop outside the Caltex service station at 197 Palmerston St. The **airport**, with a direct flight (Sun–Fri) to Wellington, is 8km south of the centre (Buller Taxis ⓣ03/789 6900; around $12). Westport is compact enough for you to **get around** on foot, though to reach the nearby attractions you'll need your own transport or a taxi. Alternatively you could try Burning Mine Adventures (ⓣ0800 343 337, ⓦwww.burning-mine.co.nz) who run **tours** to Stockton open-cast mine ($55), and do track connections and tailor-made tours. **Bike rental** is available from Becker's Sports World, 204 Palmerston St ($15 a day; ⓣ03/789 8787).

Accommodation

Accommodation is surprisingly abundant in Westport, so it isn't usually hard to find somewhere to stay. **Backpackers** are well catered for, and there's a cluster of decent **motels** along The Esplanade, though the choice of more luxurious places is limited.

Bazil's 54 Russell St ⓣ0800/303 741, ⓔbazils.backpackers@xtra.co.nz. An attractive, airy house converted to backpacker accommodation, with a pleasant garden, some nice modern doubles and twins, bike rental for $25 a day. Blighted slightly by being the favoured destination of Kiwi Experience buses, the occupants of which descend upon the place en masse. Tents $10, dorms ❶, rooms ❷ and a $10 key deposit.

Bella Vista & Cedar Motels 314 Palmerston St ⓣ0800/493 787 ⓔbella.vista.westport@xtra.co.nz. Excellent new motel on the main street, with nicely decorated units that have satellite TV. The cheapest are small and have limited cooking facilities, but larger ones are much more spacious and well-equipped, and some even have spa baths. ❹

Beaconstone Eco Lodge 17km south of Westport, nr Charlston ⓣ0274/310 491. Great-value and welcoming backpacker lodge, with a few doubles and one triple. Eco-friendly features include composting toilets and solar power, and it's set in 120 acres of native bush in which are various trails. One of the best places to stay on this part of the coast. Dorms ❶, dbls ❷

The Happy Wanderer 56 Russell St ⓣ03/789 8627, ⓔhappy-wanderer@xtra.co.nz. Large, comfortable and sprawling associate YHA hostel that has rooms in three buildings, the dorms all having TV, toilet, shower and their own kitchen. Many of the newer doubles are particularly luxuriant. Cooked and continental breakfasts are available, and non-guests can make use of the showers ($3). Tents $8, van hook-ups $12 dorms ❶, rooms ❷

Havanlee 76 Queen St ⓣ03/789 8502, ⓔhavanlee76@hotmail.com. One comfortable twin and one double, with shared facilities, in a very friendly homestay where you're plied with a continental breakfast each morning and helpful information. ❹

Robyn's Nest 42 Romilly St ⓣ03/789 6565, ⓕ789 8015. Renovated, spacious old house with comfortable lounge and gardens and a good variety of rooms. Tent sites $8, dorms ❶, rooms ❷

River View Lodge Buller Gorge Rd, 7km south of Westport ⓣ0800/184 656, ⓦwww.rurallodge.co.nz. Attractive lodge overlooking the Buller River with four en-suite rooms each with a veranda. Three-course dinners by arrangement ($40, which also gets you a glass of wine). ❻

Seal Colony Tourist Park Marine Parade, Carters Beach, 5km west ⓣ03/789 8002, ⓕ789 6732. Spacious, fully equipped site with some very comfortable motel units fronting onto a broad beach on the way to Cape Foulwind. Tent and powered sites $11, cabins ❷, motel units ❹

Trip Inn 72 Queen St ⓣ03/789 7367, ⓔtrip-inn@clear.net.nz. Small dorms, doubles and some family units in a big old rambling backpackers that discourages the backpacker tour buses. There's a barbecue area and all the usual features, including plenty of videos, though no quiet lounge. Tents $10, dorms ❶, rooms ❷

Westport Holiday Park 31–37 Domett St ⓣ03/789 7043, ⓕ789 7199. Smallish, low-key site partly hemmed in by native bush and ten minutes' walk from the town centre. Tents $9, powered sites $10, dorms ❶, chalets ❷, on site vans ❷, en-suite chalets ❷–❸

Westport Motels 32 The Esplanade ⓣ & ⓕ03/789 7575, ⓣ0800/805 909. Older but very reasonable prices are downtown motel units, all well-appointed and complete with modern kitchens; cooked ($12) or continental ($9) breakfast is also served. ❹

The Town and around

Anyone with even the vaguest interest in Westport's coal-mining past should visit **Coaltown**, Queen Street (daily: Christmas–Jan 8.30am–5pm; Oct–Christmas & Feb–June 9am–4.30pm; July–Sept 9am–4pm; $6), an imaginatively presented museum concentrating on the Buller coalfield. Scenes of the workings in their heyday pack an interesting video, which complements remnants salvaged from the site – a coal wagon on tracks angled, as it was in situ, at an unsettling forty degrees, and a huge braking drum – and a mock-up of a mine tunnel, complete with musty smells and clanking sound effects. Fascinating photos of the inclined tramways in operation, a scale model of the plateau and a collection of miners' hats and lamps round out this engaging exhibition. The museum also tries to fulfil the role of a pioneer museum, with less compelling exhibits on gold dredging, the Buller earthquakes, brewing and the town's maritime history.

Before leaving town, try the preservative- and chemical-free beers made by the co-operatively run **Miner's Brewery**, 10 Lyndhurst St (ⓣ & ⓕ03/789 6201; Mon–Fri 10am–5.30pm, Sat 10am–5.30pm, tours 11.30am & 3.30am; $5), which distributes its beers throughout the West Coast and Marlborough. They'll give you a quick tour (Mon–Sat 11.30am & 1.30pm), let you sample their beers – a draught, a dark and the organic "Green Fern" lager – and sell you some to take away.

Once again we have Captain Cook, battling heavy weather in March 1770, to thank for the naming of Westport's most dramatic and evocatively titled stretch of coastline, **Cape Foulwind**, 12km west of town. Cook's name has stuck, and also lends itself to the undulating four-kilometre **Cape Foulwind Walkway**, which runs over exposed headlands, airing superb coastal views. It

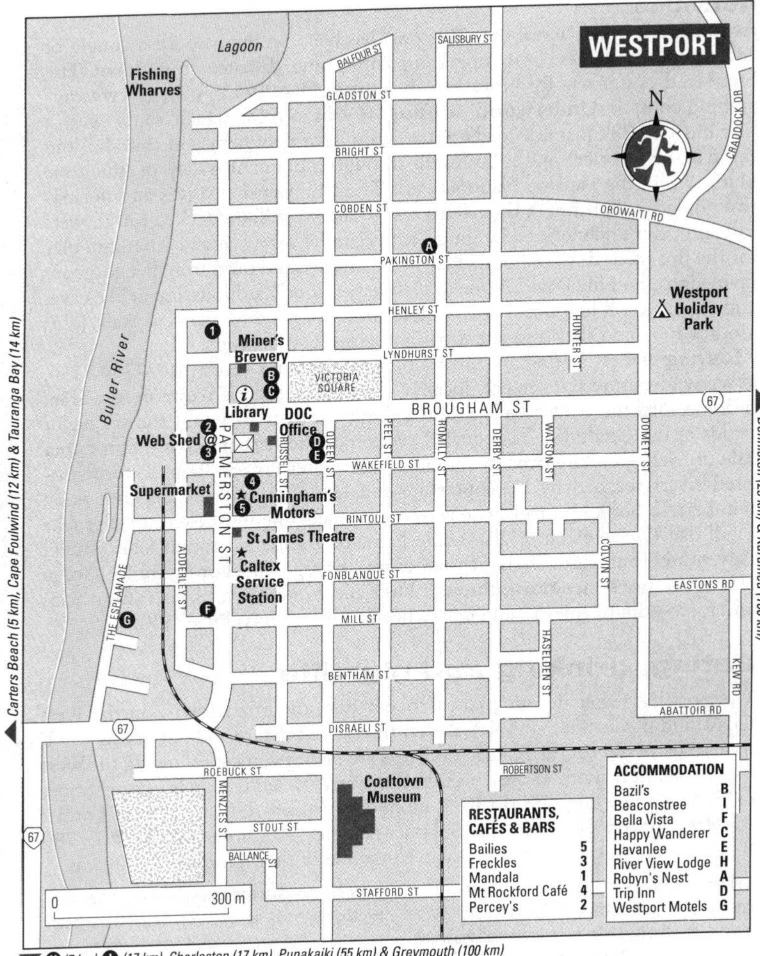

is perfect for sunset ambling between the old lighthouse, a replica of Abel Tasman's astrolabe and the **Tauranga Bay Seal Colony**, where platforms overlook New Zealand's most northerly breeding colony of fur seals. The seals are at their most active and numerous from October to January, often numbering three hundred or more, a sign of the welcome recovery from the decimation of 150 years of sealing.

The quickest access to the seals is from the sandy but treacherous beach of Tauranga Bay, accessible by road and at the southern end of the walkway, ten minutes along from the seals. To save retracing your steps all the way back, look for a marker around the halfway point, indicating an alternative route around the foot of the cliffs. Burning Mine Adventures (☎03/789 7277) run two-hour **tours** to the seal colony for around $30.

Activities

As the largest town hereabouts, Westport has become the base for a couple of adventure companies, both operating trips some distance from town. The bread-and-butter trip for Norwest Adventures (ⓣ0800/116 686, ⓦwww.caverafting.com) is **Underworld Rafting** (4–5hr; $105), which starts with a minibus trip 28km south to the Charleston Tavern (where you can also join the trip; same price) and a bushwalk through a dramatic valley of limestone bluffs within the Paparoa National Park. The trip proper involves an informative guided walk through the Metro cave system; you'll be decked out in wetsuit and caver's helmet, and lugging a rubber inner tube, which comes into play for the final drift down a flooded glow-worm cave and out through a gorgeous ravine into the Nile River. None of it is tremendously arduous; if you like caves and water, you'll like this. For the more timid there's a Metro cave walk (3hr; around $60), and they also run a trip for experienced cavers.

Rafting and jetboating are run by Buller Adventure Tours (ⓣ03/789 7286, ⓦwww.adventuretours.co.nz), located some 8km east of Westport on SH6, heading into the Buller Gorge. Throughout the year they run the six major rapids of the Grade IV "earthquake" section of the **Buller River**, 4km either side of Lyell, spending over two hours on the water for $85. Trips to more isolated rivers reached by helicopter are run less often and are dependent on numbers, so booking in advance is recommended. The most exciting trips take a full day (Dec–March; $125), while helirafting starts at around $245. Buller Adventure Tours also offer **jetboat rides** through the Lower Buller Gorge (1hr; $60), **horse trekking** through bush and along a river beach (from $45) and forty-minute rides in an eight-wheeled all-terrain vehicle ($30).

Eating, drinking and nightlife

Westport has fewer decent **places to eat** than the other towns on the West Coast, and if you want anything flasher than tearoom fare and pub meals you'll have to drive out to *The Bay House*. **Pubs** are plentiful, most following the West Coast tradition, with those towards the northern end of Palmerston Street exhibiting a raw edge. **Nightlife** is limited to occasional bands at *Bailies* or *Mt Rockford* and **movies** at the fine St James cinema, 193 Palmerston St (ⓣ03/789 8936), where in the interval you can slurp one of their glorious ice creams.

Bailies 187 Palmerston St. Westport's best attempt at an Irish pub – only Guinness, pint glasses and the odd folk-music tape distinguishing it from the others. Pretty lively though, and with decent bar lunches, a cook-it-yourself barbecue, and occasional live music at weekends. Popular with the Kiwi Experience bus.

Freckles 216 Palmerston St. Simple breakfasts, hearty sandwiches, quiches and cakes, and a few tasty treats such as Thai beef burgers ($8). Closed Sun.

Mandala 110 Palmerston St ⓣ03/789 7931. Just a notch up from your average tearoom but a decent enough spot for burgers and toasted sandwiches, pizzas in the evenings and some good coffee. Licensed; book for dinner.

Mt Rockford Café and Bar 18 Wakefield St ⓣ03/789 7640. Known locally as the *Red Dog Saloon* and stocking locally brewed ale as well as other international and domestic beers is this stylish addition to an otherwise pretty moribund local café/bar scene. Sophisticated decor, veranda tables, bar snacks, excellent full meals including cajun fillets and green-lipped mussels, and late-night entertainment with DJ-led music and occasional groups on tour. Fast becoming the most popular local spot.

Percy's 198 Palmerston St ⓣ03/789 6648. Swanky little licensed café open for snacks, lunch and dinner, offering steaks, venison, veggie stacks and heavenly bananas mixed with caramel, rum, pecan nuts and vanilla ice cream.

The Bay House Tauranga Bay ⓣ03/789 7133. Superb restaurant, café out towards the seal colony at the southern end of the Cape Foulwind Walkway. Coffee, lunch and excellent dinners (around $26) – such as fillet of beef with potato and parsnip rosti, locally caught turbot, at least one veggie option and wonderful desserts – are served in the cosy interior or on the terrace, where you can watch the surfers on the bay. Lunch and dinner daily plus weekend brunch. Licensed.

Around Westport

Westport's role as a service town was entirely dependent on trade from the coal-mining towns to the north, towns often sited in such inhospitable spots that fresh vegetables were hard to grow and sheep were almost impossible to raise. Foremost among them was **Denniston**, for years New Zealand's most productive coalfield, located high on the Rochford Plateau. Coal hasn't been mined here in any quantity for thirty years; houses have been carted away and the bush is rapidly engulfing what remains of the mining machinery. It makes an intriguing place to explore for half a day, or longer if you want to tackle the **Denniston Incline Walk**. All the other deep mines have gone the same way, leaving a legacy of inclines, tramways and rusting machinery that can be visited on a number of walks, the **Charming Creek Walk** being the best.

Denniston

The Karamea Road runs north from Westport 15km to Waimangaroa, the junction for a steep 9km road that wends its way 600m up to the lonely Rochford Plateau and the semi-ghost-town of **DENNISTON**, the finest and best-preserved example of once-numerous isolated mining communities. The old schoolhouse here has been turned into a small **museum** (Sun only 10am–3pm; free; check opening on ⓣ03/789 9755), containing historical photos and old mining machinery, which also acts as the local information centre. On a fine day the views across the coastal plain down to Westport and north towards Karamea are impressive, but even the vaguest suggestion of bad weather brings a blanket of cloud and damp fog down over the town, adding a suitably ethereal quality to this desolate landscape. At its peak, around 1910, the plateau supported three mining villages, Denniston, Coalbrookdale and Burnetts Face, which were home to over 2500 people, served by a post office, three hotels and numerous shops. After limping by on a skeleton staff for several years, the last coal was extracted in 1995, leaving the post office, a fire station, half a dozen scattered houses, twenty-two people and a treasure trove of industrial archeology centred on a gaunt winding derrick.

The Coalbrookdale Seam was first discovered by one John Rochford in 1859, and the plateau was soon humming with activity, though the difficult access slowed development until the construction of the **Denniston Self-acting Incline** in 1879. Regarded as something of an engineering marvel in its time, and still impressive today, this gravity-powered tramway was the steepest rail-wagon incline in the world, lowering coal-filled wagons 518m over 1.7km, while hauling up empty wagons. Throughout its 88-year lifespan, over a thousand tonnes of coal a day would rattle at a prodigious 70km an hour down to Conn's Creek, where they would be marshalled onto rail tracks for the trip into Westport. Initially everything destined for Denniston – goods, machinery and people – also came up the incline but after four people were flung to their death from careering wagons, a path was constructed in 1884 and sixteen years later the road was put in, finally easing some of the hardship of living up on the plateau. Considering how recently the mines were abandoned, there is surprisingly little left, save for foundations of mine workings and the remains of a few horse-drawn tramways – the greatest pleasure is in just rambling about (exercising some care not to disappear down mine shafts).

Fit and ambitious visitors to Denniston can approach on the **Denniston**

Walk (2km; 2–3hr; 520m ascent), starting at Conn's Creek, 2km inland from Waimangaroa. The route follows the 1884 path roughly parallel to the incline, but the most interesting section is close to the top and can more easily be reached from Denniston. From Denniston to Middle Brake (1hr 30min return), the incline can still be seen among the bush, as can the midway point where wagons where disconnected from one hauling cable and connected to another for the lower half of the journey.

Minor roads continue beyond Denniston to the sites of Burnetts Face and Coalbrookdale, neither of which have much to detain you, but you can pass a day exploring the backroads and walkways then repair to *The Railway Tavern* in Waimangaroa to admire the photos of Denniston, and, if you're hungry, chow down on the cheap pub grub - fish and chips, bacon, eggs and chips, and so on.

North of Waimangaroa

The road north of Waimangaroa passes a turn-off running 1km to the **Britannia Track** (3hr each way), which leads to the Britannia Battery and other remnants of the gold-mining era. **Granity**, 6km further on, has the excellent all-day *Drifters Cafe and Bar*, 97 Torea St, on SH67, decorated with beach junk and relics of yesteryear and operating as a fully fledged dairy during the day. There's always a relaxed atmosphere, and the menu features good coffee, breakfasts, whitebait, veggie options, homemade cakes and a lively bar, with live music weekly in the summer. If the place really appeals you can **stay** at the backpackers across the street; the *Granity Sands*, 94 Torea St (☎03/782 8558), offers simple accommodation backing on to the beach (dorms ❶, rooms ❷). Granity also marks another junction, this time of a road that sweeps up the range to **MILLERTON**, an old coal town with a few houses still inhabited, and **Stockton**, the site of a vast open-cast mine, which is still worked and therefore inaccessible. It's worth going as far as the **Millerton Incline Railway Walk** (10min loop), a pleasant, gently graded stroll which starts 3km off the main highway and passes the 4.7km-long Millerton Incline; though less impressive than Denniston, this one is easier to visit.

At **Ngakawau**, 2km north of Granity, the coal depot signals the start of the lovely **Charming Creek Walk** (4km; 2hr one way; 100m ascent), which follows an old railway that was used for timber and coal extraction between 1914 and 1958. The first half hour is the least diverting, but things improve dramatically after the S-shaped Irishman's Tunnel, with great views of the boulder-strewn river below and, after a swingbridge river crossing, the Mangatini Falls. From here to the picnic stop by the remains of Watson's Mill is the most interesting section of the walk and is commonly the furthest people get (2–3hr return). The walk finishes among the manuka and gorse scrub and post-industrial wasteland of Charming Creek Mine, which is also accessible by 12km of mostly dirt road through the hamlet of Seddonville, just beside the Mokihinui River.

Ngakawau merges imperceptibly with **Hector**, notably mainly for *The Old Slaughterhouse*, SH67 2km north of the village (☎03/782 8333; dorms ❶, rooms ❷), a small **hostel** in a lovely wooden house perched on the hillside with wonderful views and access either on foot or by a 4WD buggy which meets you if arranged in advance. If you decide to walk up, take the easier, unmarked, walking track, on your right after about 50m, up to the house. The owner has carved an excellent bush walk out of the forest behind his property, which just happens to be within walking distance of beach where Hector's dolphins regularly play in the surf.

There's more accommodation and some good meals 15km further north at

The Cow Shed (Ⓣ03/782 1826, Ⓦwww.gentleannie.co.nz), a very relaxed place beautifully sited near the mouth of the Mokihinui River, beside Gentle Annie Beach; turn left off the highway on the Karamea side of the bridge and head 3km west of SH67 on an unsealed road. Fresh, wholesome and moderately priced meals – waffles, smoothies, stir fries, steak and fish mains – are served throughout the day in a much-converted cow shed or outside in the extensive grounds. **Accommodation** ranges from camping ($8) and dorm beds (dorms ❶), to spacious and well-equipped self-catering cottages (❸–❹) all with either sea or river views.

Karamea and the Oparara Basin

The northwestern corner of the South Island competes with Fiordland as the least developed and most inaccessible region in the country, a fact sanctioned by the formation of the **Kahurangi National Park** in 1996. The second-largest park in the country, it embraces a vast wilderness of spectacular hill country supporting alpine meadows, the high Matiri ("Thousand Acre") Plateau, fifteen river catchment areas, New Zealand's finest karst landscape, dramatic windswept beaches and a coastal strip warm enough to support extensive stands of nikau palms. Charles Heaphy and Thomas Brunner surveyed the region in 1846, paving the way for European and Chinese goldminers, who came a couple of decades later and sporadically took thin pickings as late as the Depression years of the 1930s. Pioneers followed, establishing themselves at **Karamea**, now the base for visiting the fine limestone country in the southern half of the park – and the first sign of civilization for walkers coming off the Heaphy Track (see p.576); other activities in the area are concentrated in the **Oparara Basin** and the final straight of the track.

The road north from Westport initially runs parallel to the coast, pinched between the pounding Tasman breakers and bush-clad hills as it passes through meagre hamlets with barely a shop or a pub. The journey takes roughly two hours if you don't stop, though there are plenty of opportunities to do so, not least at the coal towns around Westport (see p.796). North of the **Mokihinui River**, the road leaves the coastal strip, twisting and climbing over **Karamea Bluff** before descending again into a rich apron of dairying land. Rainfall begins to drop off and humidity picks up, promoting more subtropical vegetation, characterized by marauding cabbage trees and coastal nikau palms. At the foot of the bluff, **Little Wanganui** marks the turn-off for the start of the **Wangapeka Track** (60km; 4–5 days), which traverses the southern half of the Kahurangi National Park to Matariki, 50km west of Nelson. Though it lacks the coastal scenery of the more famous Heaphy Track, it easily compensates with dramatic mountain terrain. Trampers searching for something quieter than the Heaphy should pick up the DOC's *Wangapeka Track* leaflet (50¢), and be prepared for backcountry huts; *The Last Resort* in Karamea (see "Practicalities", overleaf) and several companies in Nelson, Motueka and Takaka run transport to the trailheads.

Karamea

Diminutive **KARAMEA**, 100km north of Westport, is one of those places where doing nothing seems just right. This peaceful and isolated spot is virtually at the end of the road; to continue any distance north, you'd have to go on foot along the Heaphy Track. At the same time there is no shortage of things to do in the vicinity, the southern section of the Kahurangi National Park easily justifying a day or two of exploration.

Back in 1874, when land grants lured pioneers to a dense and isolated patch of bush at the mouth of the Karamea River, this was very much **frontier territory**, with the port providing the only link with the outside world. Settlers on the south shore of the Karamea River eked a living from **gold** and **flax**, but after a couple of fruitless years realized that the poorly drained pakihi wouldn't support them. Haunted by ill fortune, they moved upstream and north of the river to the current town site which, sure enough, soon after their move, was devastated by **floods**. Determinedly they pushed on, opening up the first road to Westport just in time for the upheavals of the 1929 Murchison **earthquake**, which altered the river flow and permanently ruined the harbour. Life hasn't been much better since: one sawmill remains, but **tourism** is increasingly the town's lifeblood.

Only devoted fans could spend more than ten minutes among the pioneering and sawmilling paraphernalia inside the **Karamea Centennial Museum**, SH67 (Ⓣ03/782 6652; Christmas–Feb Mon & Tues & Thurs–Sat 10.30am–4pm; other times by arrangement; $2). Otherwise there's **swimming** and **fishing** in the Karamea River, or **rafting** further upstream run by *The Last Resort* (see "Practicalities", below); they negotiate the relatively gentle lower reaches (2hr; $30) and heliraft some magnificent Grade IV–V water far inland (1 day; $240, minimum of 6 people). There are various other rafting companies who will have a crack on the Karamea, Buller Adventure Tours (see "Activities", p.800) and Ultimate Descents, who work in with *The Last Resort* (see "Practicalities", p.805). More modest waters can be tackled in canoes rented from the *Karamea Holiday Park* (see overleaf; $7 first hour, $16, 4 hrs), who will also run you up to the start of the Karamea Gorge and pick you up once you've canoed down ($20) to the Karamea Bridge, as do Karamea Express (Ⓣ03/782 6916; min 4). If that sounds a little too damp and dangerous, and safety levels do vary based on the amount of rainfall and water rushing down the river, then hire a mountain bike from *The Last Resort* ($5 per hr).

Practicalities

Two scheduled **bus** services ply the Westport–Karamea route: Cunningham's Coaches (in Westport Ⓣ03/789 7177) run to Westport in the morning (Mon–Fri only; $15 one way, bikes $5), returning in the afternoon; Karamea Express (Nov–Easter Mon–Sat; Easter–Oct Mon–Fri; $15 one way; call *The Last Resort* – see below) also run to Westport in the morning and set off around 11.30am for the return journey. Both buses connect with ongoing services in Westport. Minibus **charter services** at fairly competitive prices are run by Karamea Motors (Ⓣ03/782 6757). Karamea Express also serves the **Heaphy Track** end at Kohaihai with a daily run (Nov–Easter daily, on demand outside the season; $5 one way for five or more passengers), as do Cunninghams, who also run to the Wangapeka ($30, or $5 per person with 6 people, on demand). The track, which is generally walked from north to south, is covered on p.576.

The **visitor centre** at Market Cross, 2km east of the centre (Jan–April daily 9am–5pm; May–Dec Mon–Fri 9am–5pm & Sat 9am–1pm; Ⓣ & Ⓕ03/782 6654, Ⓦwww.karamea.co.nz), has information about exploring the local area, **internet access**, and issues **hut passes** for the Heaphy and Wangapeka tracks, as do *The Last Resort* and the *Karamea Tavern*.

In recent years Karamea has begun to gear itself towards tourism and there are now quite a few **places to stay**. The widest selection of rooms is at *The*

Last Resort, unmissable on SH67 (ⓣ0800/505 042, elast.resort@xtra.co.nz; dorms ❶, rooms ❸–❹, cottages ❻), based around a lovely central complex consisting of turf-roofed buildings and low-profile salvaged-timber constructions containing backpacker dorms and doubles, comfortable en-suite hotel rooms, a small gym and spa ($5 per half-hour). They've lost the plot somewhat with the newer additions: plain and functional motel units and two-bedroom cottages. For **motels** you are much better off at the brand-new *Bridge Farm Motels*, SH67, 700m south of the visitor centre (ⓣ0800/527 263, ⓔebrdg-farm@voyager.co.nz; ❹), with spacious units and a free continental breakfast; or the much-improved *Karamea Village Hotel*, SH67 (ⓣ03/782 6800; kitchen cabins ❷, en-suite units ❹, motel units ❺), with a range of well appointed accommodation. There are $5 **dorm beds** at the *Karamea Domain* (no phone, enquire at adjacent caravan; tent sites $5, dorms ❶); and a more organized **campsite** 3km south of town on the south side of the Karamea River at the *Karamea Holiday Park* (ⓣ03/782 6758, ⓕ782 6738; tents $8, powered sites $18 per site, cabins ❷, motels ❸), a neat and well-kept site with ageing cabins and motel units.

The only **places to eat** are: the *Saracens Café*, opposite the visitor centre, which serves coffee, pies, enormous sausage rolls and sandwiches in a craft gallery; the *Karamea Village Hotel*, which dishes up straightforward bar meals and takeaways; and *The Last Resort*, with pub snacks and meals at the *LR Café & Bar* (licensed), and a main restaurant, where you can get good-quality meat and fish for under $24.

The Oparara Basin and Kohaihai

Kahurangi's finest limestone formations lie east of the Karamea–Kohaihai Road in the **Oparara Basin**, a compact area of **karst** topography characterized by numerous sinkholes, underground streams, caves and bridges created over millennia by the action of slightly acidic streams on the heavily jointed rock. This is home to New Zealand's largest native **spider**, the gradungular spider (found only in caves in the Karamea and Collingwood area, where it feeds off blowflies and cave crickets), and to a rare species of ancient and primitive carnivorous **snail** that grows up to 70mm across and feeds on earthworms. Tannin-stained rivers course gently over bleached-white boulders and, in faster-flowing sections, the rare whio or blue duck swims for its supper. Even if your interest in geology is fleeting, the Oparara Basin makes a superb place for an afternoon **swim** or a **picnic** by one of the rivers.

Ten kilometres north of Karamea, North Beach marks the turn-off for the steep and narrow 16km dirt road to the **Honeycomb Caves**, only discovered in the 1970s and a valuable key to understanding New Zealand's fauna. The lime-rich sediment on the cave floor has helped preserve the ancient skeletons of birds, most of them killed when they fell through holes in the cave roof. Bones of over fifty species have been found here including those of the Haast Eagle, the largest eagle ever known with a wingspan of up to four metres. In total there are 15km of passages through the cave system, some of which are visited on the excellent and educational **Honeycomb Caves Tour** (ⓣ03/782 6617; 5hr; $60 including light lunch; run by *The Last Resort* in Karamea), which includes the adjacent **Crazy Paving and Box Canyon caves**, good for spider-spotting, where, as is common in limestone areas, the watercourses alter frequently, leaving behind dry caves. The tour is the only way you can get into the caves, but if you are exploring under your own steam you can join the tour group at the entrance (2hr; $30), so long as you book in advance. If you don't fancy the caves but want transport to the Oparara Basin area, they'll carry you for $30 return, provided they have space. DOC are not keen on people going into the Honeycomb caves without a guide, but if you want to explore the Crazy Paving and Box Canyon Caves (about 30min return) be sure to take a torch, and watch out for slippery floors and the fossils on the ceilings.

The two most spectacular examples of limestone architecture lie at the end of beautiful, short bushwalks signposted from a car park 3km back down the road towards Karamea. The largest is the **Oparara Arch** (40min return), a vast two-tiered bridge 45m high, 40m wide and over 200m long, which appears magically out of the bush but defies any attempt at successful photography. The **Little Arch** (1hr return) is more easily captured on film but harder to reach, requiring a short fixed-rope descent and a good deal of mud, though the untouched, high-canopy native forest and a magnificent cavern make it all worthwhile. A short path to the deep black reflections in **Mirror Tarn** (20min return) spurs off the road nearby.

Kohaihai

Visitors with no aspirations to tramp the full length of Heaphy Track can sample the final few coastal kilometres from the mouth of the Kohaihai River, 17km north of Karamea, where there is good river (but not sea) swimming, a basic DOC **campsite** ($5) and an abundance of sandflies. In the heat of the day, you're much better off across the river in the cool of the **Nikau Walk** (40min loop), which winds through a wonderfully shaded grove dense with nikau palms, tree ferns and magnificent gnarled old rata dripping in epiphytes. When it cools off, either continue along the Heaphy to **Scott's Beach** (1hr 30min return), or stick to the southern side of the Kohaihai River and the **Zig-Zag Track** (35min return), which switchbacks up to an expansive lookout.

Paparoa National Park and around

South of Westport lies the Paparoa Range, a 1500m granite and gneiss ridge inlaid with limestone that separates the dramatic coastal strip from the valleys of the Grey and Inungahua rivers. In 1987, the limestone country of the South Island's western flank was designated the **Paparoa National Park**, still one of the country's smallest and least-known parks. The highlight is undoubtedly the **Pancake Rocks**, where crashing waves have forced spectacular blowholes through a stratified, pancake-like stack of weathered limestone. But to skip the rest would be to miss out on a mysterious world of disappearing rivers, sinkholes, caves and limestone bluffs best seen on the **Inland Pack Track**, but also accessible on shorter walks up river valleys close to Punakaiki.

Fertile limestone soils always support distinctive flora and fauna, a trait exaggerated here by the Tasman Convergence, a current warmed in the Coral Sea off Queensland, Australia. Striking this stretch of coast, the current creates a balmy microclimate favoured by the **Westland black petrel** and insects such as the **Captain Cook cicada**, the largest and noisiest of native cicadas.

The mild climate provided a sustaining bounty for **Maori**, who often stopped here while travelling the coast in search of *pounamu* (greenstone). Early **European explorers** followed suit seeking agricultural land. Charles Heaphy, Thomas Brunner and two Maori guides came through in 1846, finding little to detain them, but within twenty years this stretch of coast was alive with **gold**

△ Franz-Josef Glacier

prospectors at work on the quartz veins at **Charleston** and **Brighton**, the former barely hanging on, the latter long gone.

Visitor interest is centred on **Punakaiki**, close by the Pancake Rocks, where bus passengers get a quick glimpse and others pause for the obligatory photos. A couple of days spent here will be well rewarded with a stack of wonderful walks, horse riding, canoeing up delightful limestone gorges and just slobbing about.

Westport to Punakaiki

South of Westport, SH67 crosses the Buller River and picks up SH6, the main West Coast road. There's little reason to stop before you reach the **Little Totara River** and *Multi-Kulti*, known locally as *Jack's Place* (ⓣ03/789 6501, ⓔjack.schubert@xtra.co.nz; ❷–❸), 20km south of the junction. This small **accommodation**, **café** and bar serves an array of meals and snacks – Thai curry, Greek salad, fruit shakes – and sandwiches on excellent sourdough rye bread, which is also sold by the loaf. Many of the ingredients are from the garden and are organic. The whole set-up is pretty laid-back, with a couple of colourful and very cheap **rooms** ($50), free **camping** if you are eating here, a sauna, swimming in the creek and loads of great bush walking. A couple of kilometres further along SH6 is **Mitchells Gully Gold Mine** (open intermittently 10am–3 or 4pm; $5; call ⓣ03/789 6553 to check hours), a family-run mine working dating back to 1866, which has been reopened mainly to demonstrate the time-honoured methods used to extract fine gold held in a cement-like mass of oxidized ironsand. Along with a predictable collection of mining paraphernalia, you can see a restored overshot wheel driving a stamping battery, and water races and tunnels still in use.

The most intensive mining went on 3km to the south at **CHARLESTON**, then a rollicking boom town of around 18,000 people, but now with a mere thirty residents. The dozens of **hotels** that thrived on the gold spoils have collapsed or been burned down, leaving only the modern *Charleston Tavern*, which dishes up suitably modern fare of nachos and grills. There really isn't much to be seen here, though there are a couple of short coastal walks and free primitive **camping** beside the lovely little Constant Bay. Other accommodation consists of the modest *Charleston Motel* (ⓣ & ⓕ03/789 7599; ❸), the *Charleston Motor Camp* (ⓣ & ⓕ03/789 6773; tents $10, powered sites $10, cabins ❷) and the fantastic *Beaconstone* (see p.797).

Some 20km south of Charleston, the Fox River marks the site of the classic boom-and-bust town of **Brighton**, which experienced just four months of frantic activity in 1867, temporarily eclipsing Charleston for gold exports. Immediately to the south rise the 50m cliffs of Te Miko – tagged Perpendicular Point by Charles Heaphy, who in 1846 recorded climbing the cliff on two stages of ladders constructed of shaky and rotten rata vines while his dog was hoisted on a rope. The vines were later replaced by a chain ladder, but Te Miko remained an impenetrable barrier to pack animals until 1866, when the combined needs of traders and the new Westport–Greymouth telegraph line prompted the forging of the **Inland Pack Track**, a path now followed by the tramp of the same name (see box on p.810).

The coast road, finally completed in 1927, now climbs over Te Miko, passing the **Iraiahuwhero Point Lookout**, with stupendous coastal views extending to the Te Miko cliff and layered rocks similar to those at Punakaiki, 6km ahead.

Punakaiki and the Pancake Rocks

The **Pancake Rocks** and blowholes at **PUNAKAIKI** are often all visitors see of the Paparoa National Park, as they tumble off the bus outside the visitor centre opposite the ten-minute paved track which leads from the road to Dolomite Point. Here layers of limestone have been weathered to resemble an immense stack of giant pancakes created by **stylobedding**, a chemical process in which the pressure of overlying sediments creates alternating durable and weaker bands. Subsequent uplift and weathering has accentuated this effect to create wonderfully photogenic formations. The edifice is undermined by huge sea caverns where the surf surges in, sending spumes of brine spouting up through vast **blowholes** – but only when all the elements combine in the right way, so although the rocks are magnificent in calm conditions, at high tide with a good swell from the south or southwest their performance is stunning.

More shapely examples of Paparoa's karst landscape are on show on a number of walks. The **Punakaiki Cavern Track** (5min return), 500m north, leads into a glow-worm cave (torch essential), and 2km beyond that, the **Truman Track** (30min return) runs down from the highway to a small beach hemmed in by wave-sculpted rock platforms.

No matter how slight your interest in birds, you could hardly fail to be impressed by the sight of **Westland black petrels** bundling through the trees at dusk to the world's only breeding colony of this, the largest of the burrow-nesting petrels. These relatives of the albatross glide effortlessly at sea, where they live most of their lives, but are less gainly when they leave their offshore rafts to crash land at their burrows. Birds arrive nightly from March to December, but activity reaches fever pitch from April to June, when the single egg is laid and hatched. Call Paparoa Nature Tours in advance for dawn and dusk **guided visits** (Ⓣ03/731 1826, or in Christchurch Ⓣ03/322 7898; April–late Dec daily; 2hr; around $35), using a viewing platform right in the middle of a sub-colony.

Kiwa Sea Adventures run excellent nature trips (Ⓣ025 /377 199, after hours Ⓣ768 7765; Dec–Feb daily; 2–3hr; $100), taking to the ocean in search of Hector's, dusky and common dolphins with a maximum of five onboard. They make no promises, but usually find something and offer the opportunity to go **dolphin swimming**. More conventional swimming spots are rare along the West Coast but relatively abundant here, with good **river swimming** in the Pororari and Punakaiki rivers, and **sea bathing** at the southern end of Pororari Beach, a section also good for point-break **surfing**.

Keeping with aquatic pursuits, Punakaiki Canoe Hire (Ⓣ03/731 1870) rent out **kayaks** ($15 for the first hour, $40 per day) from their base beside the Pororari River. There's also excellent **horse riding** through bush and along the beach with Paparoa Horse Treks (Ⓣ03/731 1839), who charge $60 for a couple of hours; and a range of **caving** and **environmental tours** with Green Kiwi Tours (Ⓣ03/731 1141 & 0800/474 733, Ⓦ www.greenkiwitours.co.nz), starting at around $30 for a two-hour trip.

Practicalities

North- and south-bound **buses** run by InterCity and Atomic stop for around half an hour outside the Punakaiki visitor centre, giving enough time for a quick look at the Pancake Rocks across the road. Both InterCity services pass in the middle of the day, but the northbound Atomic service arrives at 8.30am making it possible to treat Punakaiki as a day-trip from Greymouth with eight free hours before the south-bound Atomic comes through at 4.30pm. The area

Paparoa walks and the Inland Pack Track

The 1:50,000 Paparoa National Park map covers the region in great detail, but the DOC's Inland Pack Track leaflet (50¢) provides enough information for that tramp. The best way to truly appreciate the dramatic limestone scenery of the Paparoas is on the **Inland Pack Track** (27km; 1–3 days). Most of the terrain is easy going with only one pass to negotiate, but there are no bridges for river crossings, and while the water barely gets above your knees in dry periods, you need to be aware of the possibility of flash floods. With less time or greater demand for comfort, some of the best can be seen on two day-walks. The delightful **Punakaiki–Pororari Rivers Loop** (12km; 4–5hr; 100m ascent) follows the initial stretch of the Inland Pack Track as far as the Pororari River, which is then followed downstream between some magnificent limestone cliffs to return to Punakaiki. The **Fox River Caves Track** (12km; 4–5hr; 100m ascent) traces the last few kilometres of the Inland Pack Track from the Fox Rivermouth as far as the caves and returns the same way.

Practicalities

The Inland Pack Track can be walked in either direction, though by going from south to north you eliminate the risk of missing the critical turn-off up Fossil Creek. There are no huts along the way and you're advised to carry a **tent**. This isn't absolutely necessary, as trampers can shelter under the rock **bivvy** known as The Ballroom at the end of a long first day; by carrying full **camping gear**, though, you get protection from bugs, earn the freedom to break the walk into more manageable chunks and, perhaps most importantly, avoid a wet night in the open if the rivers flood. Choose a spot well away from flood risk areas and take care off the main track, as there are unmarked sinkholes. **Campfires** are permitted, but the DOC recommends carrying a stove, particularly for stays at The Ballroom (see below), where most of the usable wood has already been burned. All tracks can become difficult or even hazardous in some weather conditions, so check the latest **weather forecast**, available from the visitor centre in Punakaiki, where you should fill out an **intentions form**, remembering to check in on your return.

Drivers should leave their vehicle at the end of the walk and either hitch or catch one of the infrequent **buses** to get to the start. Alternatively, base yourself in Punakaiki and call *The Rocks* **homestay** (ⓣ03/731 1141) who run a drop-off and pick-up service for around $25 per run (max 4 people.)

The Inland Pack Track

The starting point of the Inland Pack Track is 1km south of the Punakaiki visitor centre

continues to grow in popularity because it's now on the major bus routes mentioned above, and as result a large, wooden hotel and restaurant now make an unwholesome imposition at the base of the hill.

The extensive DOC-run **Paparoa National Park visitor centre** (daily: Dec–Easter 9am–6pm; Easter–Nov 9am–4pm; ⓣ03/731 1895, ⓔpunakaikivc@doc.govt.nz), has excellent displays on all aspects of the park, information on activities, walking maps and leaflets and extremely helpful staff.

Punakaiki's accommodation, with the exception of the exclusive new hotel, designed primarily for wealthy coach tourists and representing a bit of a blot on the landscape, has formed two clusters: the first is by the Pororari Beach close to the rivermouth, around 800m north of the visitor centre; the second is a further kilometre north, right by the Truman Track. There are two **hostels**, both of which are are excellent. By the sea there's the relaxed and vibrantly painted *Punakaiki Beach Hostel*, Webb Street (ⓣ0800/726 225, ⓔpunakaiki.beachhostel@xtra.co.nz; dorms ❶, rooms ❷, motel unit ❹), where guests can buy freshly

at the end of a 1.5-kilometre track that follows the south bank of the Punakaiki River to a car park. From **Punakaiki River to Pororari River** (3.5km; 2hr 30min; 120m ascent, 100m descent), the track crosses to the right bank then cuts northeast, gradually rising to a low saddle then descending to the Pororari River, which is forded a couple of hundred metres upstream. From **Pororari River to Bullock Creek** (6km; 2hr; 100m ascent) it stays pretty level with views inland to the Paparoa Range before reaching Bullock Creek, which should be forded with some care – in flood conditions a wall of water courses down the creek's usually dry lower section. Camping is possible on the DOC-owned farm by the Bullock Creek crossing. From **Bullock Creek to Dilemma Creek** (8km; 2hr 30min; 100m ascent, 100m descent), the farm track soon becomes a path, skirting swampland then climbing to a ridge. Descend gradually to Fossil Creek, where you wade downstream from pool to pool, occasionally clambering over fallen tree trunks. After half an hour of this, Fossil Creek meets the main tributary of the Fox River, Dilemma Creek, by a small sign – keep your eyes peeled. Heading **downstream to Fox River** (2km; 1hr; gradual descent) is the most dramatic section of the trip but potentially the most dangerous, with 18 fords to cross between gravel banks in the bed of Dilemma Creek: if you have any doubts about the first crossing, turn back, as they only get worse. The lower river carves out a deep canyon between gleaming white vertical cliffs and, if you can find a patch of sun, this makes a great place to rest awhile. The track resumes by a sign on the left bank just above the confluence with the Fox River; a steep bluff on the right makes a useful landmark.

Even if you don't plan to stay, the vast limestone overhang of **The Ballroom** (1km; 30min each way; negligible ascent) is worth a look. A signposted track crosses to the right bank of the Fox River below the confluence, then crosses several more times higher up. There's no chance you'll miss the 100m-long lip, which could easily provide shelter for a hundred or more campers; a long-drop toilet has been installed and a huge fire pit has developed. Return the same way to **the confluence**, from where the track **to the Fox Rivermouth** (5km; 2hr; 100m descent) follows the left bank. A short distance along, a sign points across the river to the **Fox River Caves** (30min); the safest and most impressive of the caverns is the upper leftmost of the three. Meanwhile, the Inland Pack Track crosses to the car park by the Fox Rivermouth, some 12km by road from your starting point; the southbound InterCity **bus** currently passes around noon, or you can walk back along SH6.

baked wholemeal bread, surf the Net and use the outdoor spa pool. Up the road, *Te Nikau Retreat*, Hartmount Place (Ⓣ03/731 1111, Ⓕ731 1154; dorms ❶, rooms ❷, en-suite doubles ❸), must rank as one of the most relaxing backpackers in the country, carved out of bush that's peppered with nikau palms and occasionally reveals a building with small dorms, rooms and rustic huts for couples. Again, fresh bread and muffins are sold, and there's internet access.

There are comfortable **motel** units at *Punakaiki Cottage Motels*, Mabel Street (Ⓣ03/731 1008, Ⓕ731 1118; ❺), with some overlooking the breakers; though you might prefer to **homestay** at *The Rocks*, Hartmount Place (Ⓣ03/731 1141, Ⓦwww.minidata.co.nz/therocks; ❺–❻), a comfortable and welcoming spot with three rooms (all with private facilities and two with sea views), and dinners available on request (around $30). The same folk manage the **self-catering** *Te Puna Retreat*, Hartmount Place (❻), a well-appointed and nicely designed modern home surrounded by bush and sleeping four. **Campers** should make for the spacious and grassy, DOC-run *Punakaiki Motor Camp*, SH6 (Ⓣ03/731

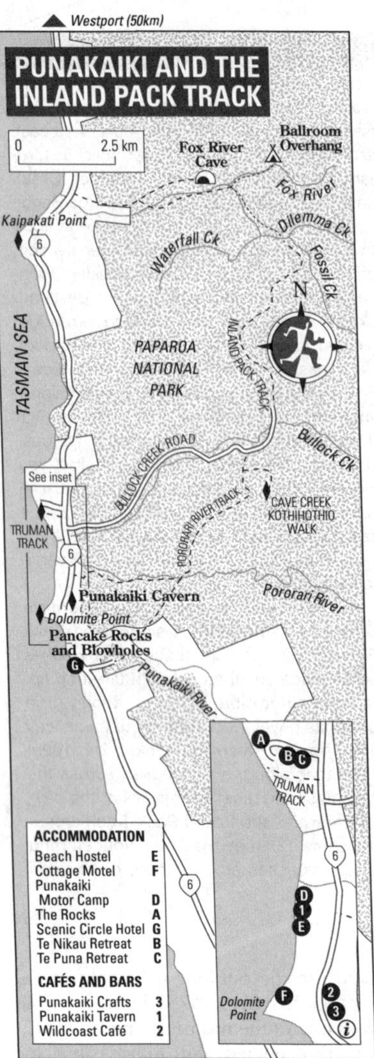

1894, ⓕ731 1897; tents $8.50, powered sites $10, cabins & units ❷–❸).

Daytime **eating** options are limited to the coffee shop at *Punakaiki Crafts*, by the visitor centre, where you can sit on the deck under nikau palms and munch counter-food and boutique organic chocolate; and the appealing though expensive *Wild Coast Café* (licensed & BYO) next door, which serves "blow-hole" breakfasts (a mass of bacon, eggs and hash browns), bagel brunches, panini, salads and snack foods until around sunset. The best value grub around comes in the form of the bar meals at the *Punakaiki Tavern & Bistro*, near the campsite, which can be eaten out in the garden; they offer gourmet pies, veggie quiche, fisherman's baskets, steaks, burgers and snacks in a cowboy-style roadhouse setting. If you're **self-catering**, you'll do well to bring supplies from Westport or Greymouth.

Punakaiki to Greymouth

The road from Punakaiki to Greymouth is a spectacular drive, sometimes pushed onto the sea-cliffs by intrusive ramparts of the Paparoa Range, but there's little to stop for until you get close to Greymouth. The former gold town of **BARRYTOWN**, 16km south of Punakaiki, is no more than a scattered shock of houses and the *Barrytown Tavern* (ⓣ03/731 1812; dorms ❶, motel units ❷–❸), which has a self-catering kitchen but also offers cheap meals of locally caught fish; the tavern is principally used by those who stagger in from the **Croesus Track** (see p.796), though you might want to stop by for the occasional live music at weekends. One of the more reasons that people head for this place, however, is the unusual *Barrytown Buffalo* **restaurant** (daily 11.30am–late; licensed), perched on a hill overlooking the ocean and 1.5km from Barrytown as you head towards Greymouth: an eatery that specializes in serving up water buffalo, who also wander about in the paddocks adjacent to the restaurant, in various forms (excellent steaks, stews, salami and so on), as well as a few fish options; diners watch other water buffalo wander the extensive grounds. A little further south, there's also the simple *Hexagon* backpackers, Golden Sands Road (Ⓣ03/731 1827; dorms ❶, rooms ❷), a nice little **hostel** with beds in a glassed-in hexagon, and a couple of lovely cabins, one featuring a sunhouse with cacti and a grapevine. Guests can help themselves to organic produce from the garden.

The next settlement of any consequence is **RAPAHOE**, which boasts about the safest bathing beach on the coast and has a reputation for gemstones among those in the know. Seven Mile Creek meets the sea here, by the beginning of the **Point Elizabeth Track** (5km; 3hr return; 100m ascent), a lovely and little-used walk along former gold-miners' trails and through dense bush that ends 5km north of Greymouth at the end of Domett Esplanade, though you can go just as far as the excellent vantage of Point Elizabeth (2hr return). If you want to stay near here, try the basic *Rapahoe Beach Motor Camp*, 10 Hawken St (Ⓣ & Ⓕ03/762 7025; tents $8, on-site vans & cabins ❷), a space filled with large clumps of flat-leafed spear grass, like big cacti, within a stone's throw of the roaring surf, which has a swimming pool and volleyball court, and is only a short stagger from the local pub.

Greymouth and around

The Grey River forces its way through a break in the coastal Rapahoe Range and over the treacherous sand bar to the sea at workaday **GREYMOUTH**, which ranks as the West Coast's largest town but still claims under ten thousand residents. Greymouth is hardly going to be a highlight on most visitors' itineraries, though there's a pleasant enough walk along the riverwall a couple of kilometres out to **Blaketown Beach** and a few worthwhile **adventure activities**. Best to do what you need to and move on, especially in winter when you might be plagued by **The Barber**, a razor-sharp cold wind that whistles down the Grey Valley and envelops the town in a thick icy fog.

The town began to take shape during the early years of the **gold rush** on land purchased in 1860 by James Mackay, who bought most of Westland from the Poutini Ngai Tahu people for 300 gold sovereigns. The deal was finalized on the site of their Mawhera *pa*, where the river bridge across to the suburb of Cobden now stands; a plaque beneath the bridge marks the spot. Several respectably grand buildings from the prosperous later decades of the nineteenth century pepper Greymouth's gridplan streets but there's nothing to give the place any defining character except for the river, which is deceptively calm and languid through most of the summer, but awesome after heavy rains. Devastating **floods** swept through Greymouth in 1887, 1905, 1936, 1977 and 1988; since the last great flood, the Greymouth Flood Protection Scheme, completed in 1990, has successfully held back most of the waters.

Arrival, information and transport

The stylish way to arrive in Greymouth is on the daily TranzAlpine **train** from Christchurch (see box on p.685), which pulls in at the station on Mackay Street and is met by InterCity **buses** (tickets from the visitor centre or the agency inside the station; Ⓣ03/768 7080) running south to Hokitika and Franz Josef, and north to Westport and Nelson. Greymouth is also served by **shuttle buses** from Christchurch, Nelson, Picton, Hokitika and Queenstown. Greymouth's nearest **airport** is at Hokitika; Greymouth Taxis (ⓣ03/768 7078) charge about $20 each way and will meet planes.

The **visitor centre**, inside the Regent Cinema on the corner of Mackay Street and Herbert Street (Nov–Easter Mon–Fri 8.30am–7pm, Sat & Sun 9am–7pm; Easter–Oct Mon–Fri 9am–5.30pm, Sat & Sun 10am–4pm; hours may vary according to demand; ⓣ03/768 5101, ⓦwww.westcoastbookings.co.nz), will provide a free street map, but little else of value. **Bike rental** is available from Scenicland Dolphin Adventure Tours (ⓣ0800/929 991) for around $25–30 a day, and several other competitive outlets nearby. You might also want to check out **tours** to the Pancake Rocks (9am & 2.15pm; 2hr 30min; $40–50) run by Kea Tours (ⓣ0800/532 868, ⓦwww.minidata.co.nz/kea).

Folk planning to rent a car in Christchurch are increasingly riding the TranzAlpine then picking up a rental in Greymouth; Avis and Budget both have **car rental** offices at the train station, though you may find it cheaper to go with one of several local outfits for long-term rentals, who often charge little or no fee for rentals dropped off in Queenstown or Christchurch. Try Value Rentals (ⓣ03/762 7503, ⓕ762 7500), NZ Rent a Car (ⓣ03/768 379, ⓔgreenfield@minidata.co.nz) or Auto Rentals (ⓣ03/768 4002, ⓕ768 9002).

Accommodation

Visitor demands seldom put much pressure on Greymouth's modest collection of **places to stay**, except during the Coast to Coast Race (around the second weekend in Feb; see box on p.816), when everything is packed to the gills. At other times there is a fair choice of hostels, moderately priced motels and a couple of comfortable B&Bs.

Ardwyn House 48 Chapel St ⓣ03/768 6107, ⓕ768 5177. Appealing and very welcoming homestay in a comfortable 1920s house, surrounded by a quiet garden and close to the town centre. No ensuites, but expansive views across the town from many rooms. ❹

Greymouth Seaside Holiday Park 2 Chesterfield St ⓣ03/768 6618, ⓕ768 5873. The more central of the two motor parks, right by the beach and with very good facilities. Tent and powered sites $11, cabins ❷–❸, motel units ❹

Global Village Backpackers 42–54 Cowper St ⓣ0508/542 636, ⓔlsp@minidata.co.nz. Light and spacious hostel, notable for its various African decorations, a result of the owner's travels, backing onto a river leading to an estuary and parkland, and with bikes and kayaks (to use on the adjacent tidal stream). Dorms, rooms ❷

Noah's Ark Backpackers 16 Chapel St ⓣ0800/662 472, ⓔnoahsark@minidata.co.nz. Large and comfortable hostel occupying a two-storey villa originally built as a monastery, with great verandas, a spacious lounge, Sky TV and internet access. Rooms and dorms are all lavishly decorated with a different animal theme. Dorms ❶, rooms ❷

Oak Lodge SH6, 4km north of town ⓣ03/768 6832, ⓦwww.oaklodge.co.nz. Swanky modern B&B with olde-worlde styled rooms set among gardens enhanced by a nice outdoor pool, spa and tennis court. Lavish breakfasts are served with freshly baked bread. ❺–❻

Revingtons Hotel Tainui St ⓣ03/768 7055, ⓦwww.revingtons.co.nz. Spanish Revival-style hotel built in the 1930s with improved, comfortable backpacker rooms, dorms, twins and doubles, above various bars and food outlets. Dorms ❶, rooms ❷

Sanford's Guest Lodge 62 Albert St ⓣ & ⓕ03/768 5605. Excellent-value small hotel with simple, fresh and airy rooms, complete with colour TV and the option of a continental or cooked breakfast. ❷–❸

Willowbank Pacifica Lodge SH6, 3km north of town ⓣ0800/668 355, ⓕ03/768 6022. Sprawling motel with a good range of modern and older en-suite rooms and use of a small indoor swimming pool and spa. ❺

YHA Kainga-ra 15 Alexander St ⓣ03/768 4951, ⓔyhagymth@yha.org.nz. Much improved, relaxed, low-key and central hostel, once for Catholic priests, with all the usual facilities, including a well-informed booking facility, a selection of dorms, twins and doubles, and sea views over the town. Dorms ❶, rooms ❷

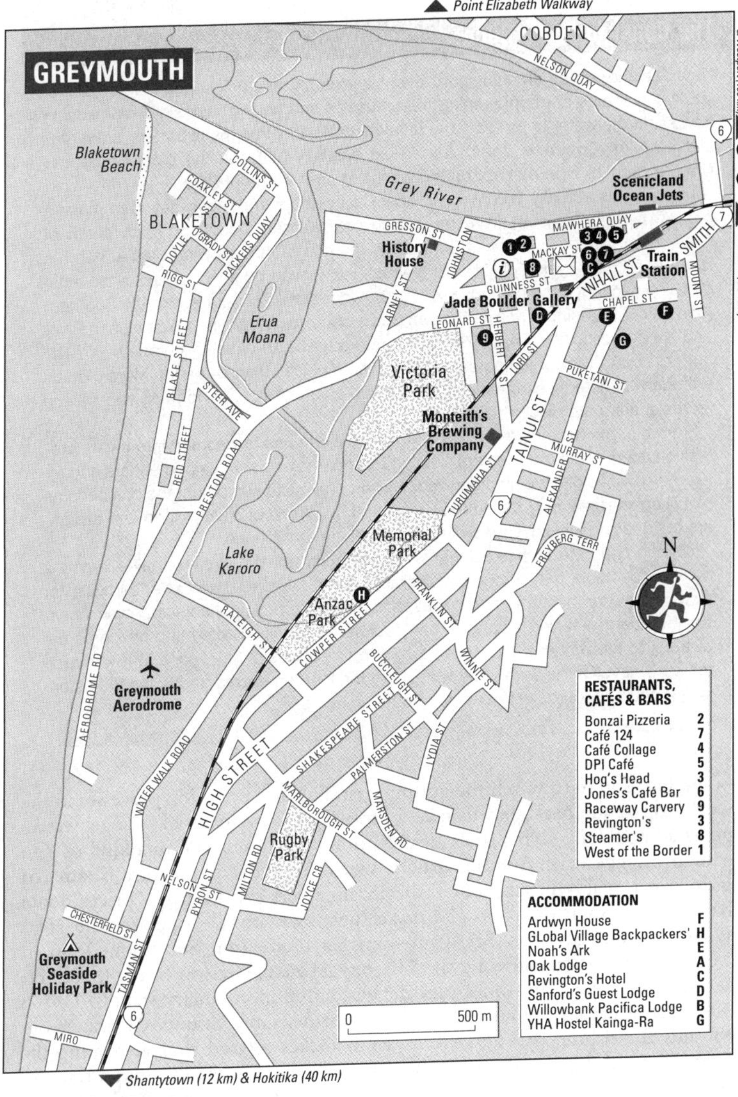

The Town and around

It is impossible to wander for long around central Greymouth without stumbling on one outlet or another flogging greenstone carving of one sort or another, at various prices, of varying quality and from various different locations – not all of them in New Zealand. The **Jade Boulder Gallery**, 1 Guinness St (daily: Nov–March 9am–9pm; April–Oct 9am–5pm), is a sales outlet for a vast range of carved greenstone pieces. Even if you have no intention

The Coast to Coast Race

New Zealand is mad on multisport. Every weekend from early spring to late autumn you'll see scores of people toning their muscles and honing their skills on bikes, in kayaks, in the water or on foot. The ultimate goal of all true multisporters is the gruelling 239km **Coast to Coast Race** held annually between the West Coast and Christchurch in mid-February on the weekend after Waitangi Day.

The event is actually two races in one. Competitors in the two-day race make a pre-dawn Saturday start from the beach near Kumara Junction, 15km south of Greymouth, aiming to finish at Sumner by the end of the following day. A 3km run leads to a 60km cycle uphill to Otira where jelly-kneed contenders tackle the most gruelling section, a run up and down the boulder-strewn creek beds of the Southern Alps before kayaking for several hours down Canterbury's braided Waimakariri River and then cycling the final stretch. A hundred elite tri-athletes compete in "The Longest Day", the same course in a time frame of less than 24 hours. Mere mortals – though admittedly extremely fit ones – can also compete by forming two-person teams sharing the disciplines.

From humble beginnings in 1983 the whole event has blossomed into a very professional affair with competitors training for months and serious contenders engaging the services of a highly organized support crew. The equipment too has become highly specialized; only the lightest and most high-tech of bikes will do and designers build racing kayaks especially for Waimakariri conditions.

Women compete in increasingly large numbers, but the event remains largely a macho spectacle that draws considerable press interest – with one journalist for every seven competitors – and correspondingly generous sponsorship. As an incentive to record-breaking a vehicle manufacturer is usually coaxed into offering a car or truck to the winner if they break a certain time. Several have gone to Kiwi superathlete, Steve Gurney, who has won six of the last ten events and holds the astonishing course record, just over ten and a half hours.

of buying, pop in to watch the cutting, grinding and polishing processes in the workshop at the back, and to take a look at the raw material – huge, water-polished boulders – lying strategically around the showroom in a kind of Zen garden arrangement. Another gallery worth a gander is the tiny **Shade of Jade**, a reasonably priced spot – the local carvers can keep the prices down because they own the shop and make their own stock – opposite the *Hog's Head*, 16 Tainui St (Mon–Fri 10am–4pm, Sat 10am–2pm, Sun noon–2pm).

Greymouth's local museum, the **History House**, Gresson Street (Mon–Fri 10am–4pm, Sat & Sun times vary depending upon voluntary staff; ⓣ03/768 4028; $3), is harder to find. Hidden in the former Grey County Chambers out towards the fishing harbour, the museum makes a good shot at relating the Grey District's history through piles of maritime memorabilia and a stack of photos depicting the town's heyday. The townspeople's long struggle to combat the floods is also given thorough and diverting treatment.

Rainy and sweltering days both provide equally good excuses to join the tastings and brewery tours at **Monteith's Brewing Company**, corner of Turumaha Street and Herbert Street (ⓣ03/768 4149, ext 1; Mon–Thurs 10am, 11.30am & 2pm; $5), where age-old recipes have recently been revived to produce some deep-brown, flavoursome brews popular all down the Coast. Sample them at the end of a brief tour.

Greymouth also makes a good base for the **Point Elizabeth Track** (see p.685), beginning over the river north of the suburb of Cobden and returning from Rapahoe by one of the twice-daily buses. If you're looking for a short walk and somewhere to watch the sun go down, try the ten-minute **Lions Walk**, starting up Weld Street in Cobden and meandering through the bush to a panoramic viewpoint over the city and the Southern Alps.

Shantytown

The replica 1880s West Coast gold-mining settlement of **Shantytown** (daily 8.30am–5pm; entry and train ride $8.80, plus gold panning $11.20, plus lunch $26.40), 8km south of Greymouth and 4km off the main highway, is unashamedly a tourist trap, frequented by a near-constant stream of visitors who pile off tour buses. Although mostly constructed since the early 1970s, the complex incorporates rescued older buildings: the 1902 Coronation Hall from Ross, an 1865 church originally from No Town in the Grey Valley, and a hotel cobbled together from parts. With the exception of the pristine church, though, even these have been insensitively restored, with scant regard for authenticity. The most interesting buildings to wander through are the printing shop, with its faded billboards advertising the latest films; the wonderful 1837 Colombian Press, which found its way here from Philadelphia via London, Auckland and Napier; the hospital, identical to one built in Greymouth; and the Gem Hall, with its collection of minerals. At the replica train station, your entry ticket entitles you to a 2-kilometre round-trip ride behind the 1887 steam engine *Kaitangata*, calling at a mine site and sawmill, where boards are cut on summer days and, of course, sage prospectors will help you pan for "colour" in salted tanks. As if that weren't more than enough schmalz, a mock hotel serves sandwiches, bar meals and beer in saloon surroundings.

No public **transport** runs to the site, but Kea Tours (see p.814) finish their Goldstrike Tour (2 daily; 2hr 30min; $32) around various gold rush sites at Shantytown.

Activities

If you'd rather tackle something more thrilling, Wild West Adventures (ⓣ0800/223 456, ⓦwww.nzholidayheaven.co.nz) can oblige. Their Dragons Cave Rafting (5hr; $105) is a challenging **caving** trip into the Taniwha cave system; wetsuits and cavers' lamps are the order of the day for muddy scrambling down a fairly steep underground streambed, floating along deep sections on inner tubes and, for the adventurous, squeezing through some tight sections. Their far more restrained Chasms Underworld Whitewater Tunnel Rafting ($125) has elements of its racier cousin, with a short spell underground in proper rafts, plus time spent above ground in a **4WD**, learning about the history and wildlife of the region. They also have gentler trips, including one for those hopping off and then back on the TranzAlpine Express (3hr; $95) and a **jungle/rainforest trip** in an imitation *waka* (Maori canoe)as well as a series of **walking** and/or **rafting trips** lasting up to six days (from $100) under the title of Te Ara Pounamu (The Greenstone Pathway).

Few of the dramatically steep rivers spilling out of the alpine wilderness inland from Greymouth and Hokitika have any road access, and hardly any had been kayaked or rafted until recent years when helicopters were co-opted to reach them. Now, Hot Rock Rafting (ⓣ0800/223 456, ⓕ03/768 9149) will take you **whitewater rafting** on one of the local rivers: the Grade III Taipo ($135), just south of Greymouth, includes 4WD access and gets you around an hour and a half on the water; the Grade IV Wanganui ($185), south of Hokitika, includes helicopter access and gives you four hours on the water, including time spent in some riverside hot pools; and the scary Grade V Perth ($265), inland from Whataroa, is another heliraft trip with six hours of boating.

Equally pleasurable whitewater-rafting trips are run by Eco-Rafting out of the *DPI Café*, 106 Mawhera Quay (Ⓣ03/768 4005, Ⓦwww.ecorafting.co.nz), such as half-day trips on the tame Grade II Arthur River ($70), or helirafting day-trips on the Perth, Whitcombe and Hokitika rivers (from $210), as well as trips on the Buller (full day; $120), the upper Grey (full day; $120), two to three day trips from $300–450, helirafting and grade IV on the Hokitika ($195), the Whataroa ($230) and the Perth, grade V ($250).

Dolphin- and **seal-watching** trips (1hr 30min; around $70) are run by Scenicland Dolphin Adventure Tours (Ⓣ0800/929 991, Ⓦwww.dolphin-tours.co.nz), who use their nippy jetboat to chance the Grey Bar and head up the coast in search of Hector's dolphins. They'll also take you **sea kayaking** (4–6hr; around $90) in areas often frequented by dolphins, or down-river kayaking (2hr; $80) on relatively gentle sections of the Grey River.

Eating and drinking

You'll soon exhaust Greymouth's scope for **eating and drinking**, but there are enough places serving tasty and hearty dishes to last the night or two you're likely to stay.

Bonzai Pizzeria 31 Mackay St. Cheerful licensed restaurant with tearoom staples through the day, including some good pastries and quiches and a broad range of reasonably priced and tasty pizzas served daytime and evening.

Café 124 Mackay St. New café with a fine range of light meals and a good brunch menu, muffins and good coffee served inside or at outdoor seating suitably sheltered from the West Coast weather. Licensed.

Café Collage 115 Mackay St Ⓣ03/768 5497. Greymouth's best and priciest food is served upstairs in this wooden-floored Art Deco room. The varied menu might include fish of the day, roast beef and butter chicken. Book in summer and at weekends; closed Sun & Mon.

DPI Café 106 Mawhera Quay. Licensed café serving snacks and excellent coffee, with internet access, regular gigs, and Djs every other weekend.

Hog's Head 9 Tainui St. A licensed steak house serving enormous slabs of meat and reasonable chowder.

Jones's Café Bar 37 Tainui St. Reliable spot for coffee and cake or filling and moderately priced full meals in the roast meat and boiled veg tradition.

Raceway Carvery *Union Hotel*, 20 Herbert St. Huge plates of grilled and roast meat for under $15, and bargain all-you-can-eat barbecues nightly in summer.

Revington's Tainui St. Multiple bars, including a big-screen TV sports bar, Djs every Friday, and loads of eating options, including pizza, pies, steaks and seafood, with more upmarket lamb and veggie dishes in the restaurant.

Steamers Carvery 58 Mackay St. High-quality, low-priced licensed carvery that also has a full menu.

West of the Border 19 Mackay St. A Kiwi-style Tex-Mex dinner restaurant serving groaning plates of barbecued chicken, buffalo wings, Cajun fish fillets and the like for $20–28.

Hokitika and around

South from Greymouth, SH6 hugs a desolate stretch of coast that's fine for long moody beachcombing walks, but there's little of abiding interest until **HOKITIKA**, 40km away. On initial acquaintance "Hoki", as it is known to its friends, appears only marginally more interesting than Greymouth – its jumble of mundane modern buildings interspersed with edifices from the town's golden days mouldering away, though some have recently been tidied up. Still, it is a long way to the next place of any size, and its proximity to the beach and good bushwalks, and a couple of quality restaurants, give it the edge.

Like the other West Coast towns, Hokitika owes its existence to the **gold rushes** of the 1860s. Within months of the initial discoveries near Greymouth in 1864, fields had been opened up on the tributaries of the Hokitika River, and Australian diggers from Ballarat and Bendigo and Irish hopefuls all flogged over narrow passes from Canterbury to get their share. Hokitika boomed and within two years it had a population of 6000 (compared with today's 4000), streets packed with hotels, and a steady export of over a tonne of gold a month, mainly direct to Melbourne. Despite a treacherous bar at the Hokitika Rivermouth, the **port** briefly became the country's busiest, with ships tied up four deep along Gibson Wharf. As gold became harder to find and more sluicing water was needed, the enterprise eventually became uneconomic and was replaced by dairying and the timber industry. The **railway** started to transport the region's produce and the port closed in 1954, only to be smartened up in the 1990s as the focus for the town's Heritage Trail.

Arrival and information

Although a rail line comes as far as Hokitika, there are no passenger services. Coast to Coast run from Christchurch and terminate here, InterCity offer a southbound **bus** service in the afternoon as far as Fox Glacier, while Atomic come through in the morning making for Queenstown. All stop outside the Hokitika Travel Centre, 65 Tancred St (Ⓣ03/755 8134), and all except InterCity also stop at the visitor centre: both places sell tickets. Air New Zealand Link **fly** daily to Hokitika from Christchurch, arriving 2km east of the centre.

Hokitika's **visitor centre**, on the corner of Hamilton Street and Tancred Street (Dec–March daily 8.30am–6pm; April–Nov Mon–Fri 9am–5pm, Sat & Sun 10am–2pm; Ⓣ03/755 6166, Ⓦwww.westlanddc.govt.nz), is staffed by helpful folk and should provide you with all you need to know on your short sojourn in the town. Just a few paces away, the **DOC office**, on Sewell Street (Mon–Fri 8am–4.30pm; Ⓣ03/755 8301), is stocked with leaflets on local walks. **Internet access** is available at Aim West Spots Shop, 20 Weld St, and at the public library.

While here, you may need to make some preparations for the long drive south. Though there are EFTPOS facilities in Franz Josef, Fox Glacier and elsewhere, the **banks** and ATMs here are the last before Wanaka, more than 400km away over the Haast Pass. **Cyclists** can obtain spares at the well-stocked Hokitika Cycles and Sports, 33 Tancred St (Ⓣ03/755 8662).

Accommodation

Apart from during the Wildfoods Festival (second weekend in March), **accommodation** is seldom hard to find.

Black Sands Motor Lodge 252 Revell St Ⓣ0800/755 222, Ⓦwww.blacksands.co.nz. Spacious motel offering a range of comfortable units ten minutes' walk from the centre, plus swimming pool, spa, kids' playground and internet access. ❹

Blue Spur Lodge Cement Lead Rd Ⓣ & Ⓕ03/755 8445, Ⓔbluespur@xtra.co.nz. Spacious, modern and airy pine house, plus a new house with lovely en-suite doubles, all in a tranquil setting 5km from town and close to bushwalks; they do free pick-ups from town and offer free use of bikes. They'll also drop off and pick up at trailheads, and rent out kayaking and fly-fishing gear at very reasonable rates. Dorms ❶, rooms ❷–❸

Hokitika Holiday Park 242 Stafford St Ⓣ03/755 8172, Ⓔholidaypark@hokitika.com. Hokitika's only campsite, neither spacious nor very appealing though it does have a good kids' playground. Tent & powered sites $8–9.50, cabins & motels ❷–❸

Jade Court Motor Lodge 85 Fitzherbert St Ⓣ0800/755 885, Ⓦwww.jadecourt.co.nz. Modern and very well-equipped motel five minutes' walk from town with in-house video and pleasant gardens. Some rooms have private spa baths and all come with coffee plungers. ❹–❺

Kapitea Country Lodge and Cottage Chesterield Rd (SH6), Kapitea Creek Ⓣ03/755 6805, kapitea.co.nz. Twenty minutes from both Hokitika and Greymouth, this purpose-built lodge overlooking the beach and the highway has beautifully decorated rooms, all the facilities you'd expect to find in a hotel, great breakfasts and sumptuous dinners with wine (both extra). There's also a self-contained cottage, a perfect hideaway for up to 4 people. Lodge ⑧–⑨, cottage ⑥ (min 2 nights).

Shining Star 11 Richards Drive ⓣ0800/744 6464, ⓦwww.nzcentre.co.nz/hokitika. Close to the beach with campervan hook-ups and eight attractive log cabins mostly with good self-catering facilities. Hook-ups $20, self-contained cabins ④–⑤

Teichelmann's B&B 20 Hamilton St ⓣ0800/743 742, ⓔteichel@xtra.co.nz. Comfortable, well-appointed and central B&B, with friendly hosts and a hearty continental breakfast. ⑤–⑥

Villa Polenza Brickfield Rd ⓣ0800/241 801, ⓦwww.friars.co.nz/hosts/polenza.htm. Luxurious bed and breakfast in a gorgeous Italianate mansion set on a plateau high above Hoki where you can watch the sun set amid lavender on Cape Cod chairs or bathe under the stars in a pair of tubs. Everything is very stylishly modern, with swathes of bold colour and well-chosen designer furniture. ⑧–⑨

The Town

Hokitika's leading role in the West Coast gold rushes rightly occupies much of the **West Coast Historical Museum**, entered through the visitor centre (daily: Dec–Easter 9.30am–5pm; Easter–Nov Mon–Fri 9.30am–4pm, Sat & Sun 10am–2pm; $5, gold panning $5 extra) and which, along with greenstone

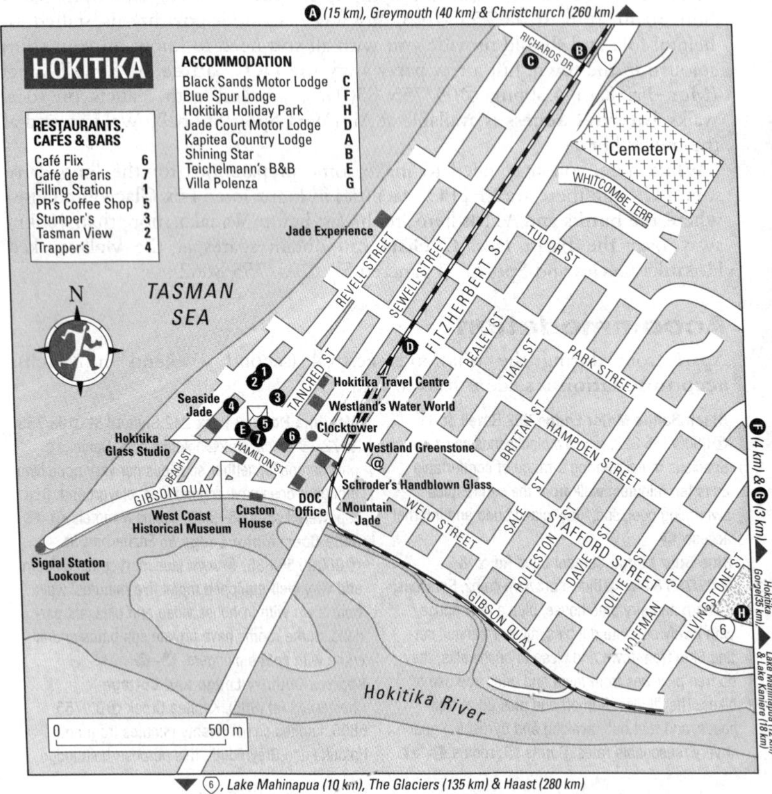

Greenstone

Maori revere **pounamu** (hard nephrite jade) and **tangiwai** (the softer, translucent bowenite), usually collectively known as **greenstone**. In Aotearoa's pre-European culture, it took the place of durable metals for both practical, warfaring and decorative uses: adzes and chisels were used for carving, *mere* (clubs) were used for hand-to-hand combat, and pendants were fashioned for jewellery. Charles Heaphy observed a group of Maori producing a *mere* in 1846, and noted the process by which they "saw the slab with a piece of mica slate, wet, and afterwards polish it with a fine sandy limestone which they obtain in the vicinity. The hole is drilled with a pointed stick with a piece of Pahutanui flint. The process does not appear so tedious as has been supposed; a month sufficing, apparently, for the completion". In Maori, the entire South Island is known as **Te Wahi Pounamu**, "the place of greenstone", reflecting the importance of its sole sources, the belt from Greymouth through the rich Arahura River area near Hokitika south to Anita Bay on Milford Sound – where the beautifully dappled tangiwai occurs – and the Wakatipu region behind Queenstown. When the Poutini Ngai Tahu arranged to sell most of Westland to James Mackay in 1860, the Arahura River, their main source of pounamu, was specifically excluded.

Its value has barely diminished. Mineral claims are jealously guarded, the export of raw greenstone is prohibited and no extraction is allowed from national parks; penalties include fines of up to $200,000 and two years in jail. **Price** is heavily dependent on quality, but rates of $50,000 a tonne are not unknown in the raw state – and the sky's the limit when the stone is fashioned into sculpture and jewellery. Many of the cheaper specimens are quite crude, but pricier pieces (and we're talking a minimum of $100 for something aesthetically pleasing, and closer to $1000 for anything really classy) exhibit accomplished Maori designs executed to perfection; at the other end of the scale, simple pendants can be picked up for as little as $10. **Hokitika** is the main venue for greenstone shoppers: bear in mind that the larger **shops** and **galleries** are firmly locked into the tour-bus circuit so prices (and quality) are consequently high. They are fine for learning something about the quality of the stone and competence of the artwork, though it is worth checking out the smaller places which often have more competitive deals. Specific **recommendations** are given overleaf.

and pioneering life, forms the focus for an interesting audio-visual presentation every half hour. The photos of the submerged horrors of the Hokitika River bar and the pleasures of the hundred or so bars of another kind that once lined Tancred Street are highlights among a predictable collection of fire-fighting and shipping paraphernalia.

With interest suitably kindled, grab the free **Hokitika Heritage Trail** leaflet, which details the remaining landmarks from the town's past, including the centrepiece **clock tower** commemorating the Boer War, a statue of **Richard Seddon**, local boy made good to become prime minister from 1893 to 1906, and the Gibson Quay area. This former riverside dock has been tarted up in recent years and makes a pleasant place for an evening stroll from the 1897 **Custom House**, past an ugly concrete memorial to ships lost on the bar, to the spit-end **Signal Station Lookout**, where coloured flags and raised balls used to help guide ships into the rivermouth. The Heritage Trail also crosses the river to a plaque marking the site of the Southside Aerodrome where, in 1934, one Bert Mercer started New Zealand's first licensed air service to the glaciers, using a de Havilland Fox Moth, a replica of which stands outside Hokitika Airport.

Only those with kids to entertain and fans of immense fat eels will get much out of the revamped **Westland's Water World**, Sewell Street (daily: 9am–5pm; around $10), which concentrates on Westland's river and sea fish and gives you a chance to catch your own salmon from indoor tanks. Owned by the same people and brought from Lake Brunner is the (misleadingly) renamed **National Kiwi Centre**, 86 Revell St (daily 9am–7pm; around $6), which boasts kiwis in nocturnal displays and audio visual displays. The centre, to its credit, does donate some money to Massey University's research on diets for captive kiwi breeding. There's a lot more watery fun to be had going **white-water rafting** with one of the Greymouth-based companies (see p.817), who both do pick-ups in Hoki.

Hokitika is crafts mad. Everywhere you look there is someone trying to sell you carved wood, blown glass, woven wool or a greenstone pendant, preferably with gold embellishments; and if you are in buying mode, there are quality pieces to be found. **Greenstone** (see box on p.821) is big business, and the shops with the best ranges are Tectonic Jade, 41 Weld St, and Westland Greenstone Ltd, 22 Tancred St; both lay on stone-cutting and shaping demonstrations and through them you can contact Gordon Wells (also on ⓣ03/755 7612) who can arrange for you to design and carve your own, simple, jade piece ($80 over two days). Hokitika Jade Country, at the corner of Hamilton and Tancred streets, and the Traditional Jade Company, 2 Tancred Street, are worth a look for pendants at middling prices. **Glass blowing** is another long-standing Hoki tradition, and there are currently two exponents, both with working artisans on show: the Hokitika Glass Studio, 25 Tancred Street, is the more venerable; while Schroders Handblown Glass, 41 Weld St, goes for more contemporary designs.

The Hokitika year ticks by peacefully until the annual **Wildfoods Festival**, on the second Saturday in March (ⓣ03/755 8322, ⓔwildfoods@westland-dc.govt.nz; $15 at the gate, or $12.50 in advance). The town quadruples its population for this celebration of bush tucker, which takes place around Cass Square, where up to fifty stalls sell such delicacies as stir-fried possum, golden-fried huhu grubs, marinated goat kebabs and smoked eel wontons, all washed down with home-brewed beer and South Island wine. The gorging is followed by an evening hoe-down, the Wildfoods Barn Dance ($10).

Lastly, Wilderness Wings, out at the airport (ⓣ03/755 8118), do a number of **scenic flights** (from $235), principally around Mount Cook and the glaciers.

Eating and drinking and entertainment

In *Trapper's* and the *Café de Paris*, Hokitika is fortunate in having a couple of the best **restaurants** on the Coast – reason enough to make this an overnight stop before heading south. Neither are prohibitively expensive but if you are counting the pennies there are several cheaper cafés maintaining high standards. The most pleasant places to **drink** are the restaurants, though Hokitika has its share of beer barns. Evening entertainment is limited to a stroll to an attractive glow-worm dell about a kilometre north of the centre beside SH6; and the Regent **cinema**, 15 Weld St.

Café de Paris 19 Tancred St ⓣ03/755 8933. This fine restaurant is tastefully decorated and has a relaxed atmosphere that doesn't rule out a daytime snack. An extensive selection of moderately priced breakfasts gives way to bistro lunches and more formal evening dining with a Mediterranean theme (from around $21 for a main course). Licensed & BYO; booking advisable in the evenings.

Café Flix 15 Weld St. Great lunch and coffee spot in the same building as the Regent cinema, and open in the evenings when the projector is turning, serving breakfast, muffins, cakes and excellent coffee all day and imaginative pizzas on cinema nights.

Filling Station 111 Revell St. Daily, worthwhile coffee bar and good place to pick up omelettes, crepes, sandwiches, salads and soups.

PR's Coffee Shop 39 Tancred St. Popular and well-priced all-day café serving light lunches, dinners, cakes and coffees. Licensed.

Stumpers 2 Weld St, cnr of Weld and Revell sts. Newly opened modern swish sports bar and daytime café with live bands and some passable grub.

Tasman View 111 Revell St ⓣ03/755 8344. Predominantly seafood restaurant with great sea views, mains from around $26 and a good-value smorgasbord on Friday evenings, as well as à la carte on Sat & Sun. Licensed.

Trapper's 79 Revell St ⓣ03/755 5133. Book ahead and then concentrate on the unusual food: crocodile, chamois, possum and sautéed kea dishes are all cooked in imaginative ways and priced around $25; also try the trademark ostrich, kangaroo, wild boar and, in season, whitebait (which costs a little more)and the wonderful other fish and occasional veggie options. Licensed.

Around Hokitika

Some of the best bush scenery and the finest **walks** hereabouts lie among the Taharoa Forest, where the dairying hinterland turns into the foothills of the Southern Alps some 30km inland along Stafford Street. Minor roads make a good seventy-kilometre scenic drive (shown in detail on the DOC's *Central West Coast* leaflet, available from the visitor centre for $1), passing the fishing, water skiing and tramping territory of **Lake Kaniere**, a glacial lake 18km from Hokitika with several picnic sites and primitive camping ($5) along the eastern side. The most popular walk is the **Kaniere Water Race Walkway** (9km one way; 3hr; 100m ascent), which starts from the lake's northern end and follows a channel that used to supply water to the goldfields, through stands of regenerating rimu. Close by is the **Lake Kaniere Walkway** (13km one way; 3–4hr; flat), which traces the western lake margin by way of the basic Lawyer's Delight Hut – more of a lunch stop than a place to stay. The eastern-shore road passes the attractive **Dorothy Falls** and continues to a spur leading to the **Hokitika Gorge**, 35km from Hoki, where a short path leads to a swingbridge over the tranquil Hokitika River as it eases through a deep gorge.

Immediately south of Hokitika, SH6 runs inland for 15km before meeting the old coastal Rautapu Road near Lake Mahinapua. Take the old road to visit the **Lake Mahinapua Recreation Reserve**, from where there are a number of short walks plus the easy **Mahinapua Walkway** (16km return; 4hr; mainly flat), detailed in a free leaflet available from the Hokitika DOC office. Gentle paddle-boat **cruises** along the Mahinapua Creek to the lake (ⓣ03/755 7239; Dec–April 2pm; 90min; excellent value at $25) start 5km south of Hokitika.

From Hokitika to the glaciers

The main highway leaves the coast **south of Hokitika** and snuggles in close to the Southern Alps for most of the 135km to the glacier at Franz Josef, the next town of any size. The journey through pakihi and stands of selectively logged native bush is broken by a series of tiny insignificant settlements such as **Ross**, **Pukekura** and **Harihari**), none of which warrant stopping long, except perhaps **Okarito**, where you'll find yourself seduced by the charms of its lagoon.

Ross

The tiny village of **ROSS**, 30km south of Hokitika at the base of the bush-clad Mount Greenland, lies right on top of one of New Zealand's richest alluvial **goldfields**. The mining company is still chewing away at the large hole on the edge of town and would dearly love to get at the gold-bearing gravels underneath. The government have given consent provided all the townspeople agree to move off the land: around half are adamant they'll stay.

Once all the claims had been staked along the West Coast's original gold river, the Greenstone River near Hokitika, prospectors descended on the **Totara River** and soon there were over 3000 people here, digging down into the rich gravel layers of ancient riverbeds. By the early twentieth century, waterlogging and the lack of power for pumping put an end to a lengthy boom time, but just as things were winding up in 1909 a couple of diggers prospecting less than 500m from the current visitor centre turned up the largest gold nugget ever found in New Zealand, the 3.1-kilo "**Honourable Roddy**", named after the then Minister of Mines. The nugget was eventually bought by the government and given as a coronation gift in 1910 to Britain's George V, who melted it down to make royal tableware. A replica of the fist-sized lump of gold resides in the 1885 **Miner's Cottage**, Bold Street (daily 9am–4pm; free), surrounded by gold-rush photos.

A DOC leaflet (from the visitor centre – see below) details a popular short stroll, the **Water Race Walk**, which passes the remains of fluming designed to supply water for gravel washing. For any other walks in the area check with the visitor centre, if you are really twitchy before journeying on to your next destination. While you are in town, there's more **jade** worth seeing directly opposite the visitor centre at 23 St James St, where the Jade Studio (daily noon–5pm) is one of the best small galleries in the region offering highly individual "3D philisophical statements in jade carving" by Steve Maitland.

Practicalities

The **visitor centre**, 4 Aylmer St (daily 9am–4.30pm; ⓣ03/755 4077), presents an interesting **multi-media** show (free) on the 1865 gold rush and subsequent sawmilling and farming history, and stocks DOC leaflets on local walks (50¢ each).

The best **accommodation** in town is at the *Bellbird Bush B&B*, 4 Sale St (ⓣ03/755 4058, ⓔp.v.b@actrix.co.nz; ❹), about 200m off SH6, which offers a separate unit with a good view and a continental breakfast. Otherwise, you're limited to the *Historic Empire Hotel*, 19 Aylmer St (ⓣ03/755 4005, ⓔraz-empross@paradise.net.nz; tent sites $8, cabins ❶, rooms ❸), which has spacious verandaed doubles (some en suite), four-person cabins and tent and campervan sites, and the basic but functional *Ross Motel*, Gibson Street (ⓣ & ⓕ03/755 4022; ❸–❹). If there's nobody at the motel, ask at the *Ross Price Cutter General Store*. For sustenance, the *Empire Hotel* does good bar **snacks** and **meals**, and the *Roddy Nugget Café* does tearoom staples and has what passes for a restaurant in this town.

Pukekura

The roadside south of Ross is dotted with places that process sphagnum moss, which grows readily around here and is much appreciated by Japanese and Taiwanese orchid growers for its absorptive properties. The moss is also noted for being sterile and was used during the two world wars for swabs. The industry is covered in some detail at the **Bushman's Museum** (Dec–March 9am–6pm; April–Nov 9am–5pm; $2), inside the **Bushman's Centre** (free), marked by a giant sandfly at the hamlet of **PUKEKURA**, 25km south of Ross. The centre takes a light-hearted approach to showing how people make a living from the forest through timber milling and possum trapping, as well as housing several huge eels. You can also try your hand at knife- and axe-throwing if there's at least six of you. The best way to experience the museum is on a guided tour ($4) only available for groups (again, 6 min): tag along with one of the backpacker tour buses which stop by if you can't make up the numbers. You can **stay** also across the road at the welcoming *Wildfoods Restaurant and Pub* (ⓣ03/755 4008; dorms ❶, rooms ❷–❸), in the house or in a cabin; they also have artificial hot pools out back. The bar has a pool table amongst all the rough-hewn country decor, and they serve filling breakfasts, billy-tea steaks, wild boar sandwiches, rabbit, possum, hare and chamois, most of which aren't part of the traditional Kiwi diet.

The rest areas around beautiful **Lake Ianthe**, 4km south, make good picnic stops, but exploring the region in any more depth is for the committed only. An unsealed road winds 10km through the Lake Ianthe Forest to the exposed **Greens Beach**, from where it is an hour and a half's walk south to a seal colony.

Harihari

Lake Ianthe feeds a tributary of the Whanganui River, crossed just before the village of **HARIHARI**, 20km further south. Harihari's chief claim to fame is its proximity to the marshy landing site of **Guy Menzies**' aircraft when he flew from his home town of Sydney to New Zealand in 1931, becoming the first to do the trip solo, only three years after Charles Kingsford Smith and his team made the original crossing; he bettered Kingsford Smith's time by two and a half hours. Menzies' plane, the *Southern Cross Junior*, crash-landed in the La Fontaine swamp, leaving Menzies strapped in upside down in the mud. There's little reason to actually stop in Harihari but you might want to turn onto Wanganui Flat Road and drive 20km coastwards to the start of the **Harihari Coastal Walkway** (8km; 2–3hr; negligible ascent), which follows a track used by miners heading south in the 1870s. The route runs through kahikatea forest to a spectacular piece of coastline, a sandy beach and the Doughboy Lookout, with great views of the Southern Alps.

Harihari **accommodation** is limited to a couple of places on the main road (SH6): the old but pleasant and cycle-friendly *Tomasi Motel* (ⓣ0800/753 3116; cabins ❷, motel rooms ❸) and the Harihari Motor Inn (ⓣ0800/833 026, ⓔhhmi@xtra.co.nz; dorms ❶, rooms ❹), which also has a caravan site ($20 per site) and a spa; and the excellent *Wapiti Park Homestead* (ⓣ & ⓕ03/753 3074, ⓔwhapitipark@countrylodge.co.nz; ❻), a farmstay on the southern exit from town. Most **eating** happens at the *Harihari Motor Inn*, where there are good bar meals, or at the *Glenalmond* tearooms (noon–8.30pm) on SH6.

Whataroa

From November to February, New Zealand's entire population of the graceful white heron (*kotuku*) arrives to breed at the Waitangiroto Sanctuary, by the northern end of the Okarito Lagoon. The sanctuary is near **WHATAROA**, 35km south of Harihari, but access is strictly controlled and the only way to visit is with the DOC-sanctioned **White Heron Sanctuary Tours** (booking advised ⓣ0800/523 456, ⓦwww.whiteherontours.co.nz; Nov–Feb 3–7 daily;

2.5hr; around $99), which include a twenty-minute bus journey, a twenty-minute jetboat ride on the narrow Waitangitaona River, and half an hour observing the birds from a well-placed hide. Outside the heron season, there's still plenty to be seen on their Rainforest Nature and Jetboating Tours (all year; $89), essentially the same route but concentrating on what's appropriate to that season – tui and bellbirds feeding on flowering kowhai from August to October for example. Southwestland Horsetreks (Ⓣ021/575 243 & 0800/575 243) run **horse riding** from the *Sleepy Hollow* B&B (see below), ranging from an hour's worth for $35 to three-and-a-half hours for $50 for a river swim, or, more invitingly, an ironically named pub crawl that only involves one bar. In the town itself it's worth having a look in the Kotuku Gallery, which contains some local, one-off greenstone, bone and wood carvings and some hand-woven flax items, all at reasonable prices.

The White Heron Sanctuary Tours office on the main highway acts as the local **visitor centre** (no set hours; Ⓣ03/753 4120) and also has **motel** units (❹) and cabins (❷). For **B&B** try *Sleepy Hollow*, SH6 (Ⓣ03/753 4139, Ⓔhollow@xtra.co.nz; ❺), which has comfortable rooms with a guest-share bathroom; or the *Whataroa Hotel* (Ⓣ03/753 4076; ❸–❹), which also has B&B, as well as a bit of wasteland out the back for campervans ($15). The *Whataroa Hotel* serves evening **meals** and is the focal point of the town, while the *White Heron Tearooms* caters to daytime snackers.

Okarito

In 1642, Abel Tasman became the first European to set eyes on Aotearoa at **OKARITO**, a hamlet scattered around the southern side of its eponymous lagoon and reached by a 13-kilometre side-road, 15km south of Whataroa. Two centuries later, the discovery of gold sparked an eighteen-month boom that saw fifty stores and hotels spring up along the lagoon's shores. Timber milling and flax production stood in once the gold had gone but the community foundered, leaving a few holiday homes, around twenty permanent residents, and a lovely beach and lagoon used as the setting for much of Keri Hulme's Booker Prize-winning novel, *The Bone People*.

The best of the **Okarito Lagoon** is hard to fully appreciate from the shore, but Okarito Nature Tours (Ⓣ & Ⓕ03/753 4014, Ⓦwww.okarito.co.nz) run excellent-value and well-organized **kayaking trips**, generally self-guided using double sea kayaks and with emergency back-up in the unlikely event you strike difficulties. On the two-hour trip ($35), you get to paddle around the sheltered lagoon, and you'll venture further on the full-day trip ($55), but best of all is the overnight trip ($85), where you camp at a remote beach. Also excellent value is the kayak with white herons trip (2hrs $30) and guided trips (on demand, min of two; $65). Some experience is needed for all the trips, and all are tide-dependent: call ahead to check times. Worth a look for its interpretation of the local ecology are gentle two-hour **guided boat trips** (usually 9am; $55) around the lagoon, which can be booked through Okarito Nature Tours but are run by a separate group.

Boating aside, Okarito seems to draw people in, mainly just to laze about and take long strolls along deserted beaches, the most popular being the **Okarito Trig Walk** (1hr 30min return; 200m ascent) at the southern end of town, which climbs to a headland with fabulous mountain and coastal views. An extension to the Trig Walk, the **Coastal Track Walk** (3hr return from Okarito, negligible ascent), should only be tackled on a receding tide.

Practicalities

There's no fancy accommodation here, but a good range of budget places. A memorial commemorating Tasman's sighting stands next to the associate YHA, The Strand (Ⓣ03/753 4124; ❶), a simple two-room affair – one of the oldest hostels in New Zealand at over 100 years of age – in the former schoolhouse, with twelve bunks with bedding and a spacious and well-appointed kitchen/living area. A little along the street is the quirky *Royal Motel & Hostel* (Ⓣ03/753 4080, Ⓔroyalokarito@hotmail.com; dorms ❶, motel units and huts ❷–❸), a hostel without dorms comprising one motel unit, a house with a double and a twin, and a nice self-contained hut; fishing gear is available, there are sometimes locally grown vegetables to be had and backpackers get breakfast. There's also a shady campsite ($5; no powered sites) with showers that take 50¢ coins; handy since the YHA has no showers. Note that Okarito has no shop or café, so bring provisions with you. If you fancy staying for a few days, consider renting one of the houses along the main street (typically ❹). Most of the owners live out of town, but someone local usually looks after the place: ask around when you arrive.

Back on SH6 just south of the Okarito junction, there's a fine DOC **campsite** ($5) at Lake Mapourika.

The glaciers

Around 150km south of Hokitika, two blinding white rivers of ice force their way down towards the thick rainforest of the coastal plain – ample justification for inclusion of this region in Te Wahipounamu, the South West New Zealand World Heritage Area. The glaciers are stunning viewed from a distance, but are even more impressive close up, generating a palpable connectedness between the coast and the highest peaks of the Southern Alps, a sensation heightened by being able to walk on the glaciers on guided trips. Within a handful of kilometres the terrain drops from over 3000m to near sea level, bringing with it **Franz Josef glacier** and **Fox glacier**, the two largest and most impressive of the sixty-odd glaciers that creak off the South Island's icy backbone, together forming the centrepiece of the rugged **Westland National Park**. Legend tells of the beautiful Hinehukatere who so loved the mountains that she encouraged her lover, Tawe, to climb alongside her. He fell to his death and Hinehukatere cried so copiously that her tears formed the glaciers, known to Maori as Ka Riomata o Hinehukatere – "The Tears of the Avalanche Girl".

The park is equally characterized by the West Coast's prodigious **precipitation**, which here reaches its greatest expression, with five metres being the typical yearly dump. These conditions, combined with the rakish angle of the western slopes of the Southern Alps, produce some of the world's fastest-moving glaciers; stand at the foot for half an hour or so and you're bound to see a piece peel off. But these phenomenal speeds haven't been enough to com-

The glacial name game

To avoid confusion between the **villages** and the **glaciers** from which they derive their names, we've used a capital "G" for the Franz Josef Glacier (Waiau) **village**, and a lower-case "g" for the Franz Josef **glacier**; the same goes for the village of Fox Glacier (Weheka), which lies close to the foot of the Fox glacier.

Glaciers for beginners

The existence of a **glacier** is always a balancing act between competing forces: snowfall at the **névé**, high in the mountains, battles with rapid melting at the **terminal** lower down the valley, the victor determining whether the glacier will advance or retreat. Snowfall metres thick gradually compacts to form clear **blue ice**, which accumulates to the point when it starts to flow downhill under its own weight. Friction against the valley walls slows the sides while ice in the centre charges headlong down the valley, giving the characteristic scalloped effect on the surface, which is especially pronounced on such vigorous glaciers as Franz Josef and Fox. Where a riverbed steepens, the river forms a rapid: under similar conditions, glaciers break up into an **ice fall**, full of towering blocks of ice known as **seracs**, separated by **crevasses**.

Visitors familiar with grubby glaciers in the European Alps or American Rockies will expect the surface to be mottled with **rock debris** which has fallen off the valley walls onto the surface; however, the glaciers here descend so steeply that the cover doesn't have time to build up and they remain pristine and white. Rock still gets carried down with the glacier though, and when the glacier retreats, this is deposited as **terminal moraine**. Occasionally retreating glaciers leave behind huge chunks of ice which, on melting, form **kettle lakes**.

The most telling evidence of past glacial movements is the location of the **trim line** on the valley wall, caused by the glacier stripping away all vegetation. At Fox and Franz Josef, the advance associated with the Little Ice Age around 1750 left a very visible trim line high up the valley wall, separating mature rata from scrub.

pletely counteract melting, and both glaciers have receded over 3km since Cook saw them at their greatest recent extent, soon after the Little Ice Age of 1750. In 1985 the process reversed, but after fifteen years of bucking the world trend by advancing, the glaciers look to be backtracking once again.

Art critic and arbiter of public taste in Victorian England, John Ruskin, once postulated that glaciers retreat "on account of the vulgarity of tourists", and Franz Josef and Fox had certainly turned their tail when contemporary travellers battled their way down the coast to observe these wonders of nature, initially named "Victoria" and "Albert" respectively. In 1865, geologist Julius von Haast renamed Franz Josef after the Austro-Hungarian Emperor, and following a visit by prime minister William Fox in 1872, the other glacier was bestowed with his name.

Activity in the glaciers focuses on two small **villages**, which survive almost entirely on tourist traffic. Both lie close to the base of their respective glacier and are near the start of numerous walks, and both offer a comparably wide variety of plane and helicopter **flights** and **guided glacier walks** (see box on p.833). Franz Josef has marginally better facilities, while Fox Glacier is the quieter, with a more rural aspect; with your own transport, it makes sense to base yourself in one of the two villages and explore both glaciers from there.

The ever increasing number of tourists flocking to see the West Coast means that both villages at times resemble building sites, as locals rush to put up or extend tourist accommodation, which they are woefully short of during the summer. The knock-on effect, despite extra government investment, is the gradual (or sometimes spectacularly quick) overloading of the area's **infrastructure**, particularly electricity and plumbing, and a lack of readily available services like emergency rooms and pharmacies. Though not serious, it's worth remembering to stock up on any medicine you might need and make sure you have batteries for your torches.

Franz Josef Glacier

Historically there has been little to choose between the two glacier villages, but in recent years **FRANZ JOSEF GLACIER** has edged ahead, with a wider range of places to stay and an improving culinary scene. The Franz Josef glacier almost licks the fringes of the village, the Southern Alps tower above and developers have done what they can with steeply pitched roofs and pine panelling, but the village somehow lacks alpine character, perhaps owing to the encircling rain-soaked bush. It is an appealing place though, and small enough to make you feel almost like a local if you stay for more than a night or two – something that's easily done, considering the number of fine walks hereabouts and the proximity of the glaciers.

Arrival and information

Daily InterCity **buses** in both directions arrive in the evening (around 8.30pm) and leave the following morning (around noon): the southbound bus drops off around Franz Josef then continues to Fox Glacier; in the morning it picks up in both villages and continues south. The northbound bus does the reverse, dropping off in Fox Glacier first. Atomic buses in both directions come through in the middle of the day on their Greymouth–Queenstown run.

First stop in Franz Josef should be the excellent combined **DOC office** and **visitor centre** on SH6 (daily: Nov–April 8.30am–6pm; May–Oct 9am–5pm; Ⓣ03/752 0796, Ⓔvctemp@doc.govt.nz), which has stacks of leaflets on walks in the area and first-class displays on every aspect of glaciation and the region's geology. Every half hour they show a documentary film ($3) discussing the whole South West New Zealand World Heritage Area with limited coverage of the glaciers. The centre also gets up-to-the-minute **weather reports** so check with them before starting any of the walks.

Pretty much everything else you are likely to need is within a couple of hundred metres along, or just off, SH6. There are no banks or cash machines either here or in Fox Glacier, but several places have **EFTPOS** facilities and most places accept credit cards. There's fast and efficient **internet access** in the building used by Franz Josef Glacier Guides and the Helicopter Line, at the *Café Franz Josef* and at Ferg's Kayaks (see p.831); and **bike rental** from Ice Flow Arts (Ⓣ03/752 0144; $6 per hr, $35 per day) right by the *Blue Ice Café*.

Accommodation

As a consequence of the bus schedules and the tendency for folk to spend at least two nights here, accommodation is very tight throughout the summer. Between December and March, you should aim to make **reservations** at least a week in advance. The better backpacker places are all clustered at one end of Cron Street, just along from a couple of good motels; guesthouses are a better bet than the large motor lodges.

A1 Rata Grove Motel 25 Cron St Ⓣ0800/101 933, Ⓔratagrove@xtra.co.nz. Central and fairly modern motel with kitchen-less studios and spacious fully equipped self-catering units. ❸–❺

Chateau Franz 8 Cron St Ⓣ0800/472 8568, Ⓕ752 0738. Easy-going though in decline, with an occasionally rowdy atmosphere, a wide selection of videos and an iffy pool table. The caravans out back offer some of the cheapest doubles in town. Tents $10, dorms ❶, rooms ❷

Franz Josef Holiday Park & Black Sheep Backpackers Lodge 1km south on SH6 Ⓣ03/752 0766, Ⓔfjhp@ihug.co.nz. Big riverside complex with a large and well-appointed backpackers that's tied into the Kiwi Experience tour buses. Plenty of camping and a wide selection of tourist cottages, self-contained tourist flats, and high-quality modern motel units. There's also internet access, outdoor games, a life-size chess set and a café. Tents and powered sites $9–10,

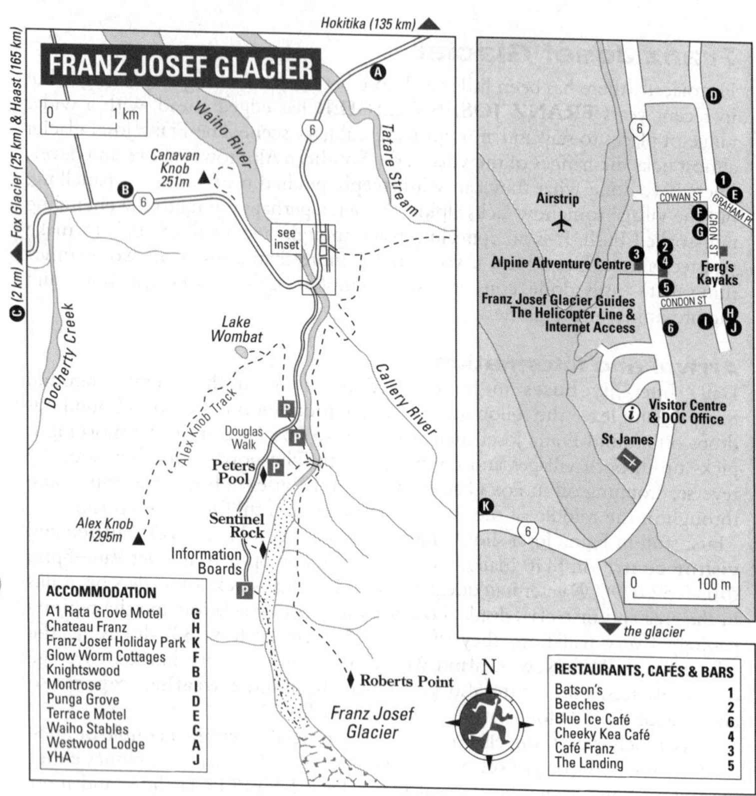

dorms ❶, rooms ❷, cottages ❷, flats ❸–❹, motels ❹

Glow Worm Cottages 27 Cron St ⓣ0800/151 027, ⓕ03/752 0173. Small and homely hostel with a spacious well-equipped kitchen, 6-bed dorms, four-shares with their own bathrooms and comfy doubles, some of them en suite. Dorms ❶, rooms ❷–❹

Knightswood SH2, 3km south of town ⓣ03/752 0059, ⓕ752 0061. Comfortable en-suite B&B rooms in a spacious modern native-timber house surrounded by bush and a deer farm. Hearty breakfasts put you in good stead for glacier hiking. ❻

Montrose Lodge 9 Cron St ⓣ & ⓕ03/752 0750, ⓣ0800/66 877, ⓔemontroselodge@hotmail.com. A well run and reasonably spacious backpackers in a re-sited house recently expanded with a large section containing good dorms and made-up doubles. Plenty of common space, videos, internet access and a spa. Dorms ❶, rooms ❷–❸

Punga Grove Motor Lodge Cron St ⓣ0800/437 269, ⓦwww.pungagrove.co.nz. Very well-kept combination motel and campervan park set on the edge of town but feeling more like it's in the bush. Those needing a roof have a choice of spacious cabin units with kitchens, atmospheric tree houses with kitchens and appealing log cabins with ensuites and a brand new backpacker lodge. There's internet access, a spa pool and you can have breakfast ($9) delivered to your room. Powered sites $15, dorms ❶ cabins ❸–❺, motels ❺–❻

Terrace Motel Cowan St ⓣ0800/837 7223, ⓔterrace.motel@xtra.co.nz. High-quality motel with all mod cons, close to the centre of town. ❹–❻

Waiho Stables Country Stay Docherty Creek, 6km south ⓣ03/752 0747, ⓦwww.waiho.co.nz. Boutique country stay with a strong environmental slant in very peaceful setting. Modern wood-panelled rooms come with bathroom and full continental breakfast, and a vegetarian BYO dinner is available for around $30. ❾

Westwood Lodge 2km north on SH6 Ⓣ & Ⓕ03/752 0111, Ⓔwestwood@xtra.co.nz. The best Franz Josef has to offer: a spacious, comfortable guesthouse with a cosy alpine lodge feel, well-appointed en-suite rooms, a full-size billiard room and a buffet continental or cooked breakfast, as well as dinner. ❾

YHA 2–4 Cron St Ⓣ03/752 0754, Ⓔyhafzjo@yha.org.nz. After a large investment this is now the best budget accommodation in the area. Completely renovated, larger, very modern, well-run, airy hostel with a spacious kitchen, clean comfortable rooms, dorms, twins and doubles, a sculptured reception and booking office and shop, and disabled access. Dorms ❶, rooms ❷–❸

Walks and activities around town

Top of everyone's list of **walks** is the one from the information kiosk and car park, 5km south of the village, to the face of the Franz Josef glacier (4km return; 1hr 20min; flat), a roped-off and ever-changing wall of ice beside an ice cave – the visibility of which depends upon the weather conditions and under no circumstances should be entered – where the Waiho River issues from beneath the glacier. The rough track crosses gravel beds left behind by past glacial retreats, giving you plenty of opportunity to observe the glacier-scoured hump of Sentinel Rock just downstream, small kettle lakes, the trim line high up the valley walls and a fault line cutting right across the valley (marked by deep gullies opposite each other).

Worthwhile walks off this access road include one to **Sentinel Rock** (20min return), the circular **Douglas Walk** (1hr) past Peter's Pool, a serene lake left by a retreat in the late eighteenth century, and the **Alex Knob Track** (12km; 8hr return; 1000m ascent), which climbs high above the glacier through several vegetation zones and offers fine views up the valley. The first few metres of the Douglas Walk are shared with the spectacular **Roberts Point Track** (9km; 5hr return; 600m ascent) which climbs up through dripping rainforest on the opposite (northern) side of the valley, high above the glacier. Slippery stream crossings and occasional rockface ladders make this an entertaining though not especially strenuous walk. The only way to actually walk on the glacier surface is with a guide (see box on p.833).

The shortest walk from town follows SH6 for a couple of hundred metres south to **St James Church**, which once framed the glacier in the altar window. The ice retreated from view in 1953, and the church itself nearly did the same in 1995, when the flooded Waiho River scoured away the alluvial bank and left the church precariously poised on a cliff. The authorities have since constructed protective stop banks which also serve to ensure the town doesn't get flooded: the glacier's advance in recent years has pushed forward so much gravel that the riverbed is now higher than most of the town.

Glacier hikes tend to go in most weathers, but on misty and **wet days** you may well find that scenic flights and helihikes are called off and alternatives are limited. There's always the twenty-minute *Flowing West* wide-screen film (3–5 showings daily; $10) at the Alpine Adventure Centre, an over-produced journey around the region with all the spirit of a failed fizzy-drink commercial. A better bet might be to take a lowland interpretive **minibus tour** with Kamahi Tours (Ⓣ03/752 0793): they run to the glacier car park (1hr; $5); to the glacier terminal (2hr 30min; around $25); to Lake Matheson (3hr; $45) and to Okarito (2–3hr; $40). **Off-road tours** in an eight-wheeled amphibious buggy are run by Wildtrax (Ⓣ03/752 0793; 2hr 30min; $60) who'll show you the bush and coastal wetlands.

One of the best activities in the area is a **guided kayaking** with Ferg's Kayaks, The Red Bus, Cron St (Ⓣ03/752 0230, Ⓦwww,glacierkayaks.com), with relaxing and informative trips on the rain-forest fringed Lake Mapourika (Flower of the Dawn). Trips run in the morning, afternoon and early evening, last about 3.5hrs (2.5hrs on the water; $45), offer an insight into the local plant- and bird-life, loads of photographic opportunities and are, surprisingly, enormously enjoyable even when it's raining.

Eating and drinking

With the opening of an innovative **restaurant** or two in recent years, a couple of days in Franz Josef doesn't mean culinary deprivation, and there's even a central **bar**. The relatively remote location keeps prices high though, and even if you are self-catering you can expect to pay over the odds for a limited stock of **groceries**.

Batson's cnr Cowan St & Cron St. The most down to earth of Franz Josef's pubs, with a convivial if intimate atmosphere, good beer, a pool table and a range of bistro meals for $12–$20, including some tasty pizzas; justifiably a favourite with the locals.

Beeches SH6. Easy-going café and restaurant with a good line in coffee sandwiches, paninis, muffins and salads during the day and steaks ($23), westcoast beef ($22), salmon fillet ($25) or even whitebait fritters ($30; seasonal) in the evening. Licensed.

Blue Ice café SH6. Modern and airy addition to the Franz Josef scene, with café-style all-day dining, and the best coffee in town. In the evening the restaurant serves imaginative and tasty mains for around $25 and a range of gourmet pizzas from $15, which can also be ordered to take away or eaten in the upstairs bar where the free pool table and rowdy music draws in a lively, sometimes backpacker heavy, crowd nightly; another local favourite.

Café Franz in the Alpine Centre, is a new addition with tasty all day snacks, some tempting, well-presented evening meals (around $25); licensed.

Cheeky Kea Café SH6. Cheerful and inexpensive BYO café serving a middle-of-the-road selection of grills, burgers, steaks, chicken, fish, sandwiches and lots of chips. BYO.

The Glass House *Franz Josef Glacier Hotel*, SH6 ⓣ03/752 0729. Formal dining in a cavernous restaurant that lacks atmosphere but serves good food – tuna fillets with charred pepper and lime, or West Coast beef in thyme jus – for around $28.

The Landing cnr of SH6 and Condon St. All day licensed café and bar serving samosa, wonton, spring rolls, mussels, pasta ($7–15) and more substantial fare in the evenings, like the veggie filo samosa, baked venison, steaks and fish ($17–27); also good for wine and coffee.

Fox Glacier

FOX GLACIER, 25km south of Franz Josef, lies scattered over an outwash plain of the Fox and Cook rivers, and supports the local farming community, as well as sightseers. Everything of interest is near SH6 or Cook Flat Road, which passes the scenic Lake Matheson on the way to the former gold settlement and seal colony at Gillespies Beach. The foot of the Fox glacier lies around 8km away.

Arrival and information

The village of Fox Glacier experiences the same **bus** schedule as Franz Josef (see p.829) and consequently has similar problems with accommodation through the summer months. If you come unstuck, seek help at the combined **DOC office** and **visitor centre**, SH6 (May, June, Sept & Oct daily 8.30am–4.30pm; Nov–March Mon–Sat 8.30am–6pm; closed for lunch from noon–1pm, Sun restricted hours; July & Aug Mon–Fri 8.30am–4.30pm; ⓣ03/751 0807, ⓕ751 0858) which, besides providing information about the region, has displays concentrating on lowland forests.

Glacier flights and guided walks

The range of flights, glacier walks and activities available from Franz Josef Glacier and Fox Glacier are almost identical.

Flightseeing

On any fine day the skies above both villages are abuzz with choppers and light planes. Safety demands that specific **flight paths** must be followed, limiting what can be offered and forcing companies to compete on price; ask for youth, student, senior or just-for-the-sake-of-it **discounts**, most readily given if you can band together in a group of four to six and present yourselves as a ready-to-go plane or chopper load: YHA card holders are entitled to a 20 percent discount with the Helicopter Line. **Plane** flights tend to be longer for the same money, but apart from the Mount Cook Airline ski planes, only the **helicopters** land, usually on a snow saddle high above the glacier where the rotors are left running – hardly a serene setting. Of the **plane operators**, Air Safaris (Ⓣ0800/723 274, Ⓦwww.airsafaris.co.nz) run overflights of both glaciers (30min; around $200), circuits of Mount Cook (50min; $230), and Mount Cook Airline (Ⓣ03/752 0714 & 0800/800 702) do the same flights for similar prices and also do snow-landing flights (conditions permitting; 40–60min; $210–280), **Helicopter operators** Fox and Franz Josef Heliservices (Ⓣ0800/800 793, Ⓔfox_heli@xtra.co.nz), Glacier Southern Lakes Helicopters (Ⓣ03/752 0755, Ⓕ752 0778) and The Helicopter Line (Ⓣ03/ 752 0767 & 0800/807 767, Ⓔhinfo@helicopter.co.nz) all charge similar prices for flights, including snow landings: one glacier (20min; $155), two glaciers (30min; $210), and two glaciers plus Mount Cook (40min; $300).

Walking on glaciers

Two companies are licensed to take visitors on **Franz Josef glacier walks**. The longest established are Franz Josef Glacier Guides, SH6 (Ⓣ0800/484 337, Ⓦwww.franzjosefglacier.co.nz), who undertake a **half-day trip** (daily 9.15am & 2pm; around $45) that involves a trudge across the braided riverbed below the glacier in hobnail boots then an hour or so on the ice, snaking up ample ice steps cut by your guide. Although you're steadied by a fixed rope, it can be unnerving balancing beside deep blue crevasses – vertigo sufferers beware. For a more tangible sense of adventure, fork out for the full-day **icefall climb** (daily 9.15am; $80) which gives around five hours on the ice, with an ice axe and specially designed flexible crampons that are easy to master for additional purchase on far smaller ice steps. Currently the fashion is for **helihiking** (2hr 30min; $230), which combines a short helicopter flight with a couple of hours on a fascinating section of ice caves, pinnacles and seracs that you couldn't hope to reach on foot in a day: well worth saving up for. Try to be clear about your aspirations and abilities and you can be matched up with a party of like-minded folk. The Guiding Company (Ⓣ0800/800 102, Ⓦwww.nzguides.com) offer an almost identical selection of trips, plus ice climbing ($175) – an instructional roped-up day in plastic boots with crampons and ice tools on steep ice.

Glacier walking is perhaps more rewarding on the **Fox Glacier**, where entry is from the side, giving more immediate access to crevasses and seracs. Alpine Guides (Ⓣ0800/111 600, Ⓦwww.foxguides.co.nz) lead half-day walks (9.15am & 1.45pm; $42), with around an hour on the ice, and do **longer trips** (6hr total; $70), giving around three hours on the ice. For serious ice addicts, there are even **Ice Climbing Instruction Days** ($185) and a **helihike**, all day; $385. finally if all this leaves you unruffled then try a **tandem skydive** (Ⓣ03/751 0080; $225–255 depending on how high you want to jump from).

Accommodation

Fox Glacier's range of places to stay is more limited than Franz Josef's but is generally pretty good and well priced; **booking** as far ahead as you can is a good idea if you are determined to stay in the village.

Fox Glacier Holiday Park Cook Flat Rd ⓣ03/751 0821, ⓦwww.holidayparks.co.nz/fox. Spacious campsite with standard facilities with tent sites, a bunkhouse and a range of cabins and flats. Camping $20, dorms ❶, cabins & flats ❷–❸

Fox Glacier Inn Sullivan's Rd ⓣ03/751 0044, ⓔfoxglacierbackpacker@xtra.co.nz. New backpackers that's greatly improved as a result of extensive expansion, with a broad range of room options, a booking centre, bar and café. Dorms ❶, made-up rooms ❷–❹

Fox Glacier Lodge and Campervan Park SH6 ⓣ & ⓕ03/751 0888, ⓦwww.holidayparks.co.nz/foxglacier. The fanciest place right in town in a pine-lined alpine chalet with attractively furnished en-suite rooms (some

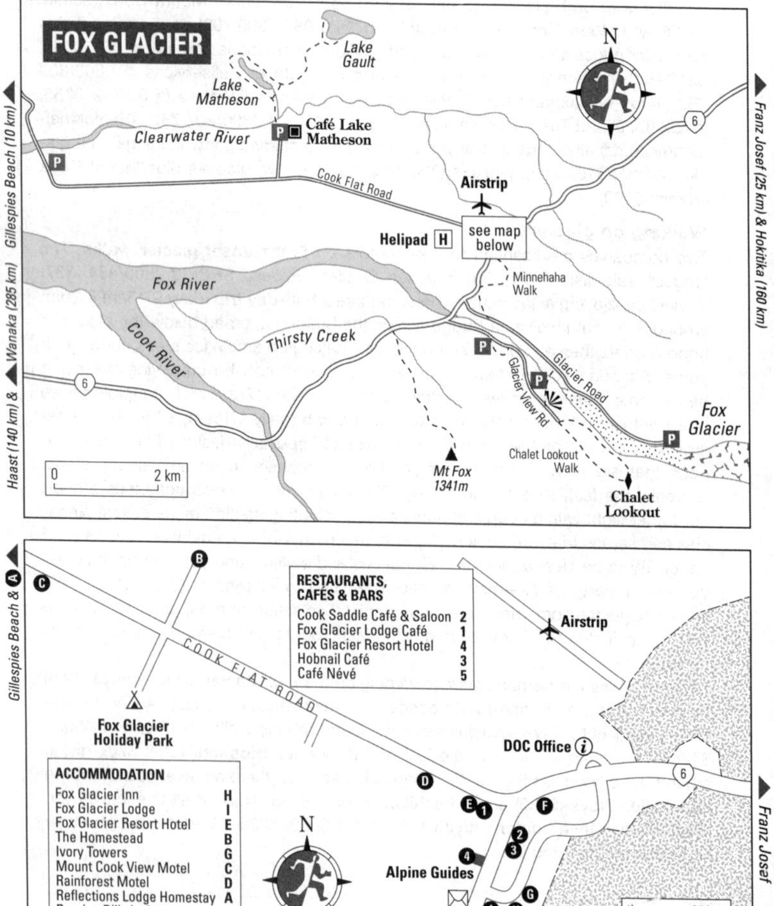

with spa baths) all sharing communal cooking facilities and lounge area plus a wine bar/restaurant. A buffet breakfast is included, and there are campervan hook-ups outside but no tent sites. Bikes can be rented for around $20 a day. Hook-ups $11, rooms ❺

Fox Glacier Resort Hotel Cook Flat Rd ⓣ0800/369 800, ⓔinfo@resorts.co.nz. Ageing hotel with faded but still elegant public areas and widely varying rooms, ranging from economy twins to modern ensuites. Dorms ❶, rooms ❸–❻

The Homestead Cook Flat Rd (ⓣ03/751 0835, ⓕ751 0805). Friendly homestay in a lovely old house within walking distance of town, with views of Mount Cook and attractive ensuites. ❺

Ivory Towers Sullivan's Rd ⓣ & ⓕ03/751 0838, ⓣ0800/151 027, ⓔivorytowers@xtra.co.nz. Friendly, clean and colourfully decorated hostel, most dorms having beds rather than bunks and some rooms (all with sheets) sharing a separate lounge area. The kitchen is spacious, there's a spa, and bikes can be rented for $20 a day. Dorms ❶, rooms ❷–❸

Mount Cook View Motel Cook Flat Rd ⓣ & ⓕ03/751 0814, ⓣ0800/828 814. High-standard motel with characterful older units and spacious, luxurious newer units, some with spa baths. ❺–❻

Rainforest Motel Cook Flat Rd ⓣ0800/520 000, ⓔrainforest@xtra.co.nz. Log cabin exteriors belie the clean interior lines of smallish but attractive studio units and larger one-bedroom units. ❺

Reflection Lodge Homestay Cook Flat Road ⓣ03/751 0707), 1.5km from the highway running through town. So named because of the reflection of the mountains in the large garden pond, this neat homestay offers reasonably-priced accommodation in comfortable and friendly surroundings. ❺–❻

Roaring Billy Lodge SH6 (ⓣ & ⓕ03/751 0815, ⓣ0800/352 121, ⓔbilly@xtra.co.nz. Friendly homestay in the centre of Fox Glacier with simple rooms and a comfortable lounge area; venison sausages are occasionally on offer for breakfast. The owner also runs nature-guiding trips to order. ❹–❺

Walks

It would be a shame to miss the Fox glacier just because you have already seen the Franz Josef glacier: the **approach walks** are quite different and their characters are very distinct, the Fox valley being less sheer but with more impressive rock falls. The approach, imaginatively named Glacier Road, crosses the wide bed left by glacial retreats and is occasionally re-routed as "dead" ice under the roadway gradually melts. From the car park, 8km from the town, a track leads to the foot of the glacier in half an hour, crossing a couple of small streams en route. Part way back along Glacier Road, **River Walk** (2km; 30min) crosses a historic swingbridge to the Glacier Valley Viewpoint on Glacier View Road, which runs along the south side of the Fox River. From here, the **Chalet Lookout Walk** (4km; 1hr 15min return) climbs moderately for stupendous glacier and mountain views.

It's difficult to imagine a New Zealand calendar or picture book without a photo of Mount Cook and Mount Tasman mirrored in **Lake Matheson**, 6km west of town along Cook Flat Road. A well signposted lakeside boardwalk through lovely native bush encircles the lake, which was formed by an iceberg left behind when the Fox Glacier retreated 14,000 years ago. It takes around an hour and gives everyone, but particularly those who venture out before breakfast, a chance for that perfect image. The *Café Lake Matheson*, by the Lake Matheson car park, is beautifully sited and pleasant enough.

Continue 15km along Cook Flat Road to reach **Gillespies Beach**, a former gold-mining settlement where a small cemetery, the remains of a dredge and piles of tailings can be seen. Several **walks** fan out from there, the most celebrated taking you in a long run north, parallel with the beach, on to the beach before Gillespies Point, then heading inland to cross Quinlin Creek before reaching Galway Beach and a colony of **fur seals**; aim to leave a couple of hours before low tide (consult the visitor centre for times), allowing about four hours for the round trip.

Back in Fox, fill an empty half hour with a stroll around the flat **Minnehaha Walk** (1km; 20min loop), which winds through lush bush that's cool and shady on a summer day, or dank and brooding in the rain.

Eating and drinking

For its diminutive size, Fox Glacier does a reasonable job of catering to hungry walkers coming off the glacier-side paths, with a small selection of reasonably priced **cafés**, a restaurant and a couple of lively **bars**.

Café Névé SH6. Fox's best café serving excellent food and coffee throughout the day – try the smoked chicken and brie salad, BLT on Turkish flatbread, Thai fish cakes, salmon and cheese plate, more traditional evening main courses, or gourmet pizzas that come in three sizes ($15–20). Dinner mains cost around $26 and there is a broad range of wines available by the glass. Licensed.

Cook Saddle Café and Saloon SH6. Hearty drinking in a mountain-lodge atmosphere, solid bar meals all day and occasional live music.

Fox Glacier Lodge SH6 (see p.834). Presentable café, wine bar with an open fire, good platters, some fine dining options (around $26);daily from 2pm, closed July.

Fox Glacier Resort Hotel Cook Flat Rd. Upmarket restaurant following the Kiwi taste for Mediterranean and Pacific Rim cuisine, adjacent to a noisy and fairly scruffy public bar.

The Hobnail Café SH6. Adequate café in the same building as Alpine Guides, with a standard range of pies, sandwiches, cakes and coffee in alpine-chalet surroundings.

South Westland and Makarora

South from the glaciers, the West Coast feels remoter still. There wasn't even a road through here until 1965 and the final section of tarmac wasn't laid on the Haast Pass until 1995. SH6 mostly runs inland, passing the start of the ambitious **Copland Track** (see box below), through kahikatea and rimu forests as far as **Knight's Point**, where it returns to the coast along the edge of the Haast Coastal Plain, with its stunning **coastal dune systems** sheltering lakes and some fine stands of kahikatea. The plain continues south past the scattered township of **Haast** to the site of the short-lived colonial settlement of **Jackson Bay**. From Haast, SH6 veers inland over the Haast Pass to the former timber town of **Makarora**, not strictly part of the West Coast but moist enough to share some of the same characteristics and a base for the excellent **Gillespie Pass** Tramp.

South to Haast

Many visitors do the run from the glaciers to Wanaka or Queenstown in one day, missing out on some fine country that makes up for its relative lack of comforts with its sheer sense of remoteness. Facilities aren't completely absent: the majority of the accommodation and eating places are clustered around Haast, but there are a few pitstops along the way. One place you might like to break your journey is **Bruce Bay**, 46km south of Fox Glacier, where the road briefly parallels a long driftwood-strewn beach perfect for an atmospheric stroll. Some 15km further south, the road crosses the **Paringa River**, where a plaque marks the southern limit of Thomas Brunner's 1846–48 explorations. He recorded in his diary the desire to "once more see the face of a white man, and hear my native tongue". Nearby, the *Salmon Farm* makes a good place to break (which is probably why so many coaches stop here) for an expensive snack or light lunch sat on a wooden deck overlooking salmon-rearing ponds.

Welcome Flat Hot Springs and the Copland Track

The three-to-four-day **Copland Track** over the spectacular 2150m Copland Pass has long been regarded as the pinnacle of tramping achievement, on the cusp of real mountaineering. It requires competent use of an ice axe and crampons but is currently highly dangerous on account of unstable rock rubble beside the Hooker Glacier on the Mount Cook side. Guided crossings are currently suspended, though DOC continues to issue an instruction leaflet (50c) and Alpine Guides in Fox Glacier and Mount Cook will rent out equipment. Conditions do change though, so ask locally; and note that the track is usually hiked from Mount Cook to the West Coast. At present, the best compromise is to tackle just the sector from the foot of the **Copland Valley to the thermal pools** (17km; 6–7hr; 400m ascent), near the back-country **Welcome Flat Hut** ($10; 30 bunks). It is pleasant bushwalking all the way and the open-air pools are a wonderful incentive. The track starts by a car park just off SH6, 26km south of Fox Glacier, and follows the right bank all the way to Welcome Flat, crossing numerous streams by hopping from rock to rock or wading. If the creeks are high, as they commonly are, you may have to use the flood bridges, which will add an hour or so; after really heavy rain, the track becomes impassable.

A better bet is to pick up some delicious hot- or cold-smoked salmon to take away. There's less appealing dining to be had 7km beyond at the *Lake Paringa café* though you might wish to stay at the associated *Lake Paringa Motels* (ⓣ03/751 0894, ⓕ751 0050; studios ❹, units ❺), located on the northern shores of **Lake Paringa** and equipped with a dinghy and fishing tackle for guests' use. They also sell fishing licences, handy if you are planning to fish for Quinnat salmon (Oct–March) and brown trout (all year) from the DOC's simple but beautifully sited Lake Paringa **campsite** ($5), a further kilometre to the south.

Around 18km south of Lake Paringa, the **Monro Beach Walk** (5km; 1hr 30min return) leads through lovely forest to one of the best places for spotting rare **Fiordland crested penguins** – mainly during the breeding season (July–Dec), but also occasionally in February, when they come ashore to moult. Nature lovers with ample wallets can gain a deeper appreciation of the fragile ecosystems of south Westland by staying nearby at the exclusive *Wilderness Lodge Lake Moeraki* (ⓣ03/750 0881, ⓦwww.wildernesslodge.co.nz; ❾) where, for around $250 per person per day, you get lodge **accommodation**, all meals, free canoe use and all manner of guided nature walks and safaris.

The highway finally returns to the coast 5km on at **Knight's Point**, where a roadside marker commemorates the linking of Westland and Otago by road in 1965; a dog belonging to one of the surveyors lends his name to this dramatic bluff fringed by magnificent seascapes where, with binoculars, seals can often be picked out on the rocks below. Ahead lies the **Haast Coastal Plain**, which kicks off at the tea-coloured **Ship Creek**, where a picnic area and information panels by a beautiful long surf-pounded beach mark the start of two lovely walks: the twenty-minute **Kahikatea Swamp Forest Walk** up the river through kahikatea forest to a lookout and the **Mataketake Dune Lake Walk** (2km; 30min return) along the coast to the dune-trapped Lake Mataketake.

From Ship Creek it is only another 15km to the 700m-long Haast River Bridge, the longest single-lane bridge in the country, immediately before Haast Junction.

Haast

HAAST is initially a confusing place, with three communities all taking the name: Haast Junction, at the intersection of SH6 and the minor road to Jackson Bay, Haast Beach, 4km along the Jackson Bay Road (see opposite) and Haast Township, the largest settlement 2km along SH6 towards the Haast Pass and Wanaka.

The first stop is Haast Junction, site of the distinctive **Haast World Heritage Centre** (daily: mid-Nov to mid-April 9am–6pm; rest of year 9am–4.30pm; ⓣ03/750 0809), which serves as the local visitor centre but is much more, with highly informative displays on all aspects of the local environment, and the short *Edge of Wilderness* film shown every half hour ($3). Time spent in here may well induce you to spend longer in what they are at pains to point out is part of the Southwest New Zealand World Heritage Area. To explore deeper into this region, consider joining a **jetboat safari** with Waiatoto River Safaris (ⓣ0800/865382 & 03/750 0001, ⓦwww.riversafaris.co.nz; daily on demand; $99), a two-hour ride from the coast into the heart of the mountains with the emphasis firmly on appreciation of the area's history and scenery. Alternatively, try Heliadventures Haast (ⓣ03/750 0866), who offer scenic flights priced on where you want to go and how many of you want to go there.

With the jetboat trip in mind, you may well want to stay over: you'll find everything you need on Pauareka Road, and remember that over the summer you should **book ahead** for a room. There's comfortable and welcoming **accommodation** at *Wilderness Backpackers* (ⓣ & ⓕ03/750 0029, ⓣ0800/750 029; dorms ❶, rooms ❷–❸), with four-bed dorms, doubles and twins, some made-up and with ensuites. Motel accommodation and probably the best rooms of any nature are provided next door at the excellent and extremely friendly *Heritage Park Lodge* (ⓣ0800/526 252, ⓔheritageparklodge@xtra.co.nz; ❹–❻), which has modern, comfortable studios with TV and video, and some units with self-catering facilities. If these are full, you may need to fall back on the YHA associated *Haast Highway Accommodation* (ⓣ03/750 0703, ⓕ750 0718; dorms ❶, rooms ❷), which has powered sites for vans ($15), and the linked *Aspiring Court Motel* (ⓣ03/750 0777, ⓕ750 0718; studio ❸, unit ❺). **Campers** may be allowed to pitch a tent at the *Haast Highway Accommodation* ($10), but if it is raining or the manager decides the hostel facilities are already stretched you'll be forced to either travel 17km to the *Haast Beach Holiday Park* (see below), or use a little discreet imagination.

Visitors planning to self-cater should note that the supplies at the single small supermarket are limited and fairly expensive. Three places serve **meals**, but the only one worth recommending is *Smithy's Tavern* which offers standard fish and chips, steak and chips, a humungous mixed grill, some half decent sea food and perhaps a pasta dish in large portions for $15–20. The tavern is also the favoured watering hole of most of the locals, from far and near, so can prove quite entertaining on a busy weekend evening.

The road to Jackson Bay

A real sense of isolation soon sets in on the 50km dead-end road south to the fishing village of Jackson Bay, a long thin strip of tarmac hemmed in by verdant prehistoric bush and tall trees. A modest number of inquisitive tourists make it down this way, to discover a place hanging on by its fingernails. Leaving Haast Junction, the canopies of windswept roadside trees are bunched together like cauliflower heads down to and beyond **Haast Beach**, 4km south, where

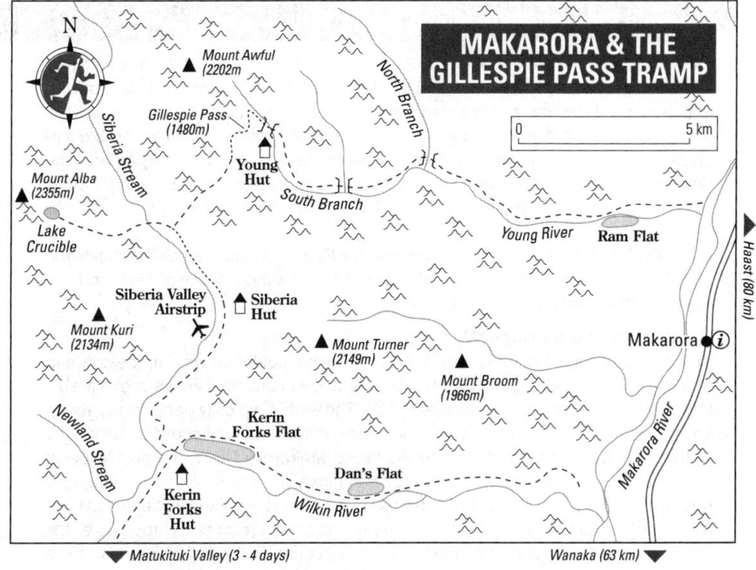

there's a small shop, petrol and the decent *Acacia & Erewhon Motel* (Ⓣ03/750 0803, Ⓕ750 0817; studios ❸, chalets ❺–❻). The one-time Maori fishing and greenstone-gathering settlement of **Okuru**, 10km further south, dates back to around 1300, and now comprises a strip of beach housing set back from a wild coastline. Just beyond, some 15km south of Haast Junction, the decent *Haast Beach Holiday Park* (Ⓣ & Ⓕ03/750 0860; tents $10, dorms ❶, cabins ❷, motel units ❹–❺) stands opposite the **Hapuku Estuary Walk** (20min loop), which follows a raised boardwalk over a brackish lagoon and through kowhai forest that gleams brilliant yellow in October and November. Old sand dunes support rimu and kahikatea forest, and there are occasional views out to the **Open Bay Islands**, noted by Cook in 1770 and later gainfully employed as a sealing base away from the sandflies of the coast. They are now a **wildlife sanctuary** and a major breeding colony for fur seals and Fiordland crested penguins.

The road continues 35km to **Jackson Bay** (Okahu), a former sealing station tucked in the curve of Jackson Head, which protects it from the worst of the westerlies. In 1875 it was chosen as the site for a "Special Settlement", a significant port and commercial centre to rival Greymouth and Hokitika. Assisted migrants – Scandinavians, Germans, Poles, Italians, English and Irish – were expected to carve a living from tiny land allocations, with limited and irregular supplies. Sodden by rain, crops rotted, and people were soon leaving in droves; a few stalwarts stayed, their descendants providing the core of today's residents, who eke out a meagre living from lobster and tuna fishing.

If you can bear the sandflies, try the **Wharekai Te Kau Walk** (40min return) across the low isthmus behind Jackson Head, the **Smoothwater Track** (3hr return), with great coastal views on the way to the Smoothwater River, or the longer **Stafford Bay Walk** (8–10hr return), with the possibility of a night at the Stafford Bay Hut (Category 3; $5). Details and tide tables are available from the Haast World Heritage Centre.

Gillespie Pass: the Wilkin and Young Valleys circuit

This tramp over the 1490m **Gillespie Pass** links the upper valley of the **Young River** with that of the **Siberia Stream** and the **Wilkin River**. The scenery is superb, the match of any of the more celebrated valleys further south, but is tramped by a fraction of the folk on the Routeburn or the Greenstone tracks; perhaps the biggest gripe for the tramping purist is the disturbance caused by **planes** flying into the Siberia Valley. The tramp can be divided up into smaller chunks, using Siberia Experience's planes and jetboats (see p.842), but the full circuit (60km) takes three days.

The DOC's *Tramping Guide to the Makarora Region* ($2.50) has all the detail you need for this walk, though the 1:150,000 *Mount Aspiring National Park* and the 1:50,000 *Wilkin* **maps** are useful.

Access and accommodation

All the **huts** ($10) in the Wilkin and Young valleys are equipped with mattresses and heating (but not cooking) stoves; hut **tickets** and annual hut **passes** are available from the DOC office in Makarora (see p.842). The walk is typically done up the Young Valley and down the Wilkin – the way we've described it here. **Access** at both ends of the walk is a question of **wading** the broad **Makarora River**. If it hasn't rained substantially in the last five days and you can pick your spot well (the river changes course frequently, so ask locally), you'll barely be in up to your knees, but if you have any doubt, band together with other trampers and get a **jetboat** to drop you at the confluence of the Young and Makarora rivers (around $20 per person); it's also a good idea to arrange a **pick-up** by jetboat ($42) or plane (around $75, depending on the number of people) from Kerin Forks at the far end of the walk, unless you want to take your chances with river crossings or a stand-by flight out of Siberia Valley. The DOC leaflet indicates which operators are providing access and pick-up services at any given time of the year.

The route

The walk proper starts on the northern bank of the confluence of the Young and Makarora rivers; from Makarora, walk 3km upstream, find a good crossing place upstream of the confluence then walk down the right bank of the Makarora to the bush-side marker. From the **confluence to Young Hut** (15km; 7–9hr; 700m ascent), the easy-to-follow track traces the left bank through beech forest then, after a fork, follows the left bank of the South Branch, climbing steeply with some difficulty over

There are no **facilities** in Jackson Bay except for *The Cray Pot*, a kind of diner on wheels where you can get extremely cheap, fantastic fresh-cooked, fresh fish and chips, big mugs of tea and various meat options, away from the sandflies while gazing at the sea-tossed fishing boats through fake leadlight windows and listening to the roar of the surf. Occasionally, you'll even see hungry local hunters dropped off at the beach by helicopter.

Haast Pass and Makarora

From Haast it is nearly 150km over the **Haast Pass** (at 563m, the lowest road crossing of the Southern Alps) to Wanaka – a journey from the verdant rain-soaked forests of the West Coast into the parched, rolling grasslands of Central Otago. Ngai Tahu used the route as a greenstone trading route and probably introduced it to gold prospector Charles Cameron, who became the first *pakeha* to cross in 1863; he was closely followed by the more influential **Julius Von Haast**, who immodestly named it after himself. The pass was finally opened as

a bad slip. It eases after a while and the track continues, sometimes indistinctly, through ever more stunted bush and occasional clearings to the tree line. Collect firewood here – you're now less than half an hour from the Young Hut (20 bunks), which is wonderfully sited on the right bank in a magnificent avalanche-scoured rock cirque crowned by 2202m Mount Awful, apparently named in wonder rather than horror.

Suitably rested, you've another fairly strenuous day ahead from **Young Hut to Siberia Hut** (9km; 6–7hr; 500m ascent, 800m descent) over the Gillespie Pass. Keep to the right bank until you reach a rock cairn, which marks the start of a steep and lengthy ascent, following snow poles to a saddle; it'll take two or three hours to reach this fabulous, barren spot with views across the snow-capped northern peaks of the Mount Aspiring National Park. Grassy slopes marked by more snow poles lead steeply down to Gillespie Stream, which is followed to its confluence with the Siberia Stream, from where it's a gentle, undulating hour downstream to Siberia Hut (20 bunks), though keen types might tag on a side-trip to **Lake Crucible** (4hr return) before cantering down to the hut. Those with more modest aspirations can spend two nights at Siberia Hut and do the **Lake Crucible side trip** (13km; 6–7hr return; 500m ascent) on the spare day. From the Siberia Hut, retrace your steps to the confluence of the Siberia and Gillespie streams, ford the Gillespie Stream and continue along the left bank of the Siberia Stream a short distance until you see Crucible Stream cascading in a deep gash on the far side. Ford Siberia Stream and ascend through the bush on the right bank of the stream. It is hard going, and route-finding among the alpine meadows higher up can be difficult but the deep, alpine lake tucked under the skirts of Mount Alba and choked with small icebergs is ample reward.

Planes fly in and out of the **Siberia Valley airstrip**, and you can take your chance on "backloading" **flights out** ($25). To continue tramping from **Siberia Hut to Kerin Forks** (6km; 2–3hr; 100m ascent, 300m descent), enter the bush at the southern end of Siberia Flats on the left bank of Siberia Stream and descend away from the stream then zigzag steeply down to the Wilkin River and the **Kerin Forks Hut** (10 bunks), where many trampers arrange to be met by a jetboat. If it has rained heavily, fording the Makarora lower down will be impossible, so don't forgo the jetboat lightly. The alternative is to walk from **Kerin Forks to Makarora** (17km; 6–7hr; 100m ascent, 200m descent), following the Wilkin River's left bank, then crossing the Makarora upstream of the confluence.

a vehicular road as far as Haast in 1960, linked through to Fox Glacier in 1965 and completely sealed in 1995.

The road starts beside the broad **Haast River** which, as the road climbs, narrows into a series of churning cascades. Numerous short and well signposted walks, mostly to waterfalls on tributaries, spur off at intervals. The most celebrated include the **Thunder Creek Falls** (10min), the roadside **Fantail Falls**, and the **Blue Pools Walk** (30min return), where a stream issues from a narrow gorge. Though there are few specific sights, it is a great area to linger a while, **camping** in one of the DOC's toilets-and-water sites (all $5 per person) along the way: first up is Pleasant Flat, 45km from Haast, followed by Davis Flat, 3km over the Pass, and Cameron Flat, just 3km beyond that and 14km short of Makarora.

Makarora

The hamlet of **MAKARORA** lies roughly midway between Haast and Wanaka, on the northern fringe of the Mount Aspiring National Park. If you're aching for the relative comforts of Wanaka and Queenstown there's little reason to stop, but keen trampers with a few days to spare should consider tackling Gillespie Pass.

In the nineteenth century the dense **forests** all about and the proximity of Lake Wanaka made Makarora the perfect spot for marshalling cut logs across the lake and coaxing them down the Clutha River southeast to the fledgling North Otago **gold towns** of Clyde and Cromwell. The creation of the national park in 1964 paved the way for Makarora's increasing importance as the main northern access point to a region of majestic beauty, alpine vegetation and dense beech-filled valleys.

About all you'll find here is a motor camp, a shop and a **DOC office** (Dec–March daily 8am–5pm; April–Nov Mon–Fri 8am–noon & 1–5pm; ⓣ03/443 8365, ⓕ443 8374), the place to go for information and hut tickets for tramps. The main justification for stopping here is to head out on the Gillespie Pass tramp (see box on p.840) or to join Southern Alps Air's **Siberia Experience** (ⓣ0800 345 666, ⓕ443 8292; mid-Oct to mid-April; 4hr; ❻), an excellent combination of flying into the remote Siberia Valley, three hours of tramping to the Wilkin River and jetboating back to Makarora; the same operator also offers overflights of Mount Aspiring (around $160, min 3 people), and just about anywhere else if they can get the numbers. The **jetboating** can also be tackled separately with Wilkin River Jet (ⓣ0800/538 945 & 03/443 8351; 1hr; $55), as good value a jetboat ride as you'll find anywhere in New Zealand. Finally, if the Gillespie Pass seems a little daunting, there are a couple of **shorter walks** close to Makarora, the **Makarora Bush Nature Walk** (20min), which starts near the visitor centre and, branching off this, the **Mount Shrimpton Track** (5km return, 4–5hr, 900m ascent), which climbs very steeply up through silver beech to the bushline, then to a knob overlooking the Makarora Valley.

InterCity and Atomic buses pass through, and backpacker **buses** stop overnight at Makarora; everyone **stays** at the *Makarora Tourist Centre*, SH6 (ⓣ03/443 8372, ⓕ443 1082; tent sites $9, dorms ❶, chalets ❸–❺), a collection of self-catering and simple A-frame chalets in a clearing. It is all very peaceful and there's a pool, making it a good place to hole up for a day or two, provided you are well supplied – the tearooms are only open daily May–Sept 9am–4pm, Oct–April 8.30am–4.30pm, and the shop has fairly limited supplies. The only alternative is *Larrivee Homestead*, SH6 (ⓣ03/443 9177, *andrea_larrivee@hotmail.com*; ❺), a lovely house hidden behind the DOC office, with B&B in the main house and a cheaper cottage, plus dinners for $30.

Continuing towards Wanaka, the only place you are likely to want to break your journey is *Kidds Bush*, a DOC **campsite** ($4) beside Lake Hawea, 6km down a side road off SH6 at The Neck, where lakes Wanaka and Hawea almost meet.

Travel details

The only passenger **train** services to the West Coast are from Christchurch over Arthur's Pass to Greymouth. An InterCity **bus** makes the journey from Christchurch over Arthur's pass, meets the train at Greymouth and continues north via Punakaiki and Westport, arriving in Nelson in the early evening. Another InterCity service also meets the train in Greymouth and heads south through Hokitika to Franz Josef Glacier and Fox Glacier. The following morning, this bus picks up in both glacier villages and continues south via the Haast Pass and Wanaka to Queenstown. Smaller **minibus**

operators run feeder services to the main West Coast towns, running one or two services a day in each direction, and sometimes give a small fare saving over the InterCity. The most useful of these are Atomic Shuttles, who run a service from Picton to Greymouth via Blenheim, Nelson, Reefton, Westport and Punakaiki; another (summer only) from Picton to Greymouth via Reefton; and a particularly useful one south from Greymouth to Queenstown which leaves early and completes the journey in one day. All these feeder services run in both directions. The visitor centres have the latest details and handle bookings.

Trains

From Greymouth to: Arthur's Pass (1 daily; 2hr); Christchurch (1 daily; 4hr 30min).

Buses

From Fox Glacier to: Franz Josef (1 daily; 45min); Hokitika (1 daily; 2hr 45min); Makarora (2 daily; 4hr); Wanaka (2 daily; 5hr 15min).
From Franz Josef Glacier to: Fox Glacier (2 daily; 45min); Haast (2 daily; 3hr); Hokitika (1 daily; 2hr); Makarora (2 daily; 4hr 30min); Queenstown (2 daily; 8hr); Wanaka (2 daily; 6hr).
From Greymouth to: Arthur's Pass (3 daily; 1-2hr); Blenheim (1-2 daily; 4hr 45min-9hr); Christchurch (3 daily; 5hr); Fox Glacier (2 daily; 3hr 30min-4hr 30min); Franz Josef (2 daily; 3-4hr); Hokitika (2 daily; 30–45min); Murchison (mid-Nov to April 1-2 daily, May to mid-Nov 3 weekly; 3hr–3hr 30min); Punakaiki (2 daily; 40min); Reefton (mid-Nov to April 1-2 daily, May to mid-Nov 3 weekly; 1hr); St Arnaud (mid-Nov to April 1-2 daily, May to mid-Nov 3 weekly; 3hr 45min); Westport (2 daily; 1hr 40min–2hr).
From Hokitika to: Arthur's Pass (3 daily; 2hr); Christchurch (3 daily; 5-6hr); Franz Josef (2 daily; 2hr 30min-3hr); Greymouth (2 daily; 30-45min); Ross (2 daily; 25min); Whataroa (2 daily; 1hr 30min).
From Westport to: Christchurch (2 daily; 4hr 40min–7hr); Greymouth (2 daily; 1hr 40min–2hr); Karamea (2 daily; 1hr 30min); Murchison (3 daily; 1hr 15min–1hr 30min); Nelson (2 daily; 3hr 40min–4hr); Punakaiki (2 daily; 1hr); Reefton (2 daily; 1hr–1hr 15min).

Flights

From Hokitika to: Christchurch (2–3 daily; 35min).
From Westport to: Wellington (1 daily; 50min).

13

Queenstown, Wanaka and the Gold Country

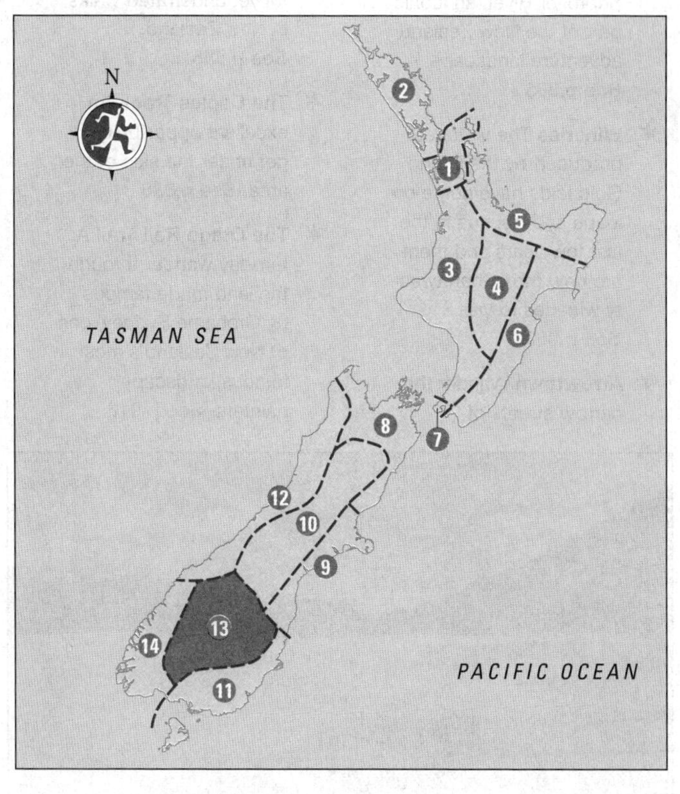

CHAPTER 13 # Highlights

* **Pipeline Bungy** Combine bungy, jetboat and whitewater-rafting outings to keep your adrenaline running for at least a day. **See p.862**

* **Shotover River** Take a jetboat ride on the Shotover River, an iconic part of the New Zealand adventure landscape. **See p.863**

* **Wineries** The vintages produced by the Otago Goldfields have come on leaps and bounds in the last few years and there are now more than twenty wineries to visit. **See p.863**

* **Arrowtown** Wander the narrow streets of Arrowtown and sample a pie from the bakery or a beer from one of the bars, the ideal antidote to the pace of Queenstown. **See p.872**

* **The Routeburn Track** One of the most beautiful yet underrated walks in New Zealand. **See p.885**

* **The Caples Track** An excellent opportunity to get under the skin of the area. **See p.886**

* **The Otago Rail Trail** A ten-day wander through the land made famous by Grahame Sydney, one of New Zealand's most famous landscape painters. **See p.916**

13

Queenstown, Wanaka and the Gold Country

Wedged between the sodden beech forests of Fiordland, the fertile plains of south Canterbury, the city of Dunedin and the sheep country of Southland lies Central Otago, a region encompassing **Queenstown**, **Wanaka** and the surrounding **gold country**. Rolling, deserted hills to the east give way to the sharper profiles of the mountains around Queenstown and Wanaka, which rub shoulders with the final glaciated flourish of the Southern Alps. Meltwater and heavy rains course out of the mountains into the seventy-kilometre lightning bolt of **Lake Wakatipu**, which in turn drains through the Kawarau River, carving a rapid-strewn path through the Kawarau Gorge. Along the way it picks up the waters of the Shotover River from the goldfields of Skippers and Arrowtown. To the north the pristine, glassy lakes of Wanaka and Hawea feed the **Clutha River**, which joins forces with the Kawarau at Cromwell and high-tails it to the coast through the heartland of the Otago gold country.

Queenstown is a jewel of sorts, looking across Lake Wakatipu to the craggy heights of the Remarkables range, and it is also New Zealand's self-proclaimed adventure capital, offering the chance to indulge in just about every adrenalin-fuelled activity imaginable: numerous competing operators have honed bungy jumping, jetboating, rafting and paragliding into well-packaged, forcefully marketed products – although they're no less exciting for all that. All this wonderful scenery and adventure has gained something of an international profile of late providing some of the background for a couple of major feature films – Peter Jackson's *Lord of the Rings* trilogy and Martin Campbell's *The Vertical Limit* – and the extreme adventure docusoap *Adventure Central*. The cumulative effect of these various elements means that Queenstown can have the atmosphere of a theme park.

Whether this appeals to you or not, you'll soon be looking for a break, something easily done in neighbouring **Arrowtown**, an extremely popular day-trip destination from Queenstown which wears its gold heritage well. Visit the intriguing remains of a former Chinese settlement and take a day-long walk to the defunct gold mines around the nearby ghost town of **Macetown**.

Perhaps the perfect antidote to the rigours and flash of Queenstown is the great outdoors, and some of the country's most exalted multi-day tramps start

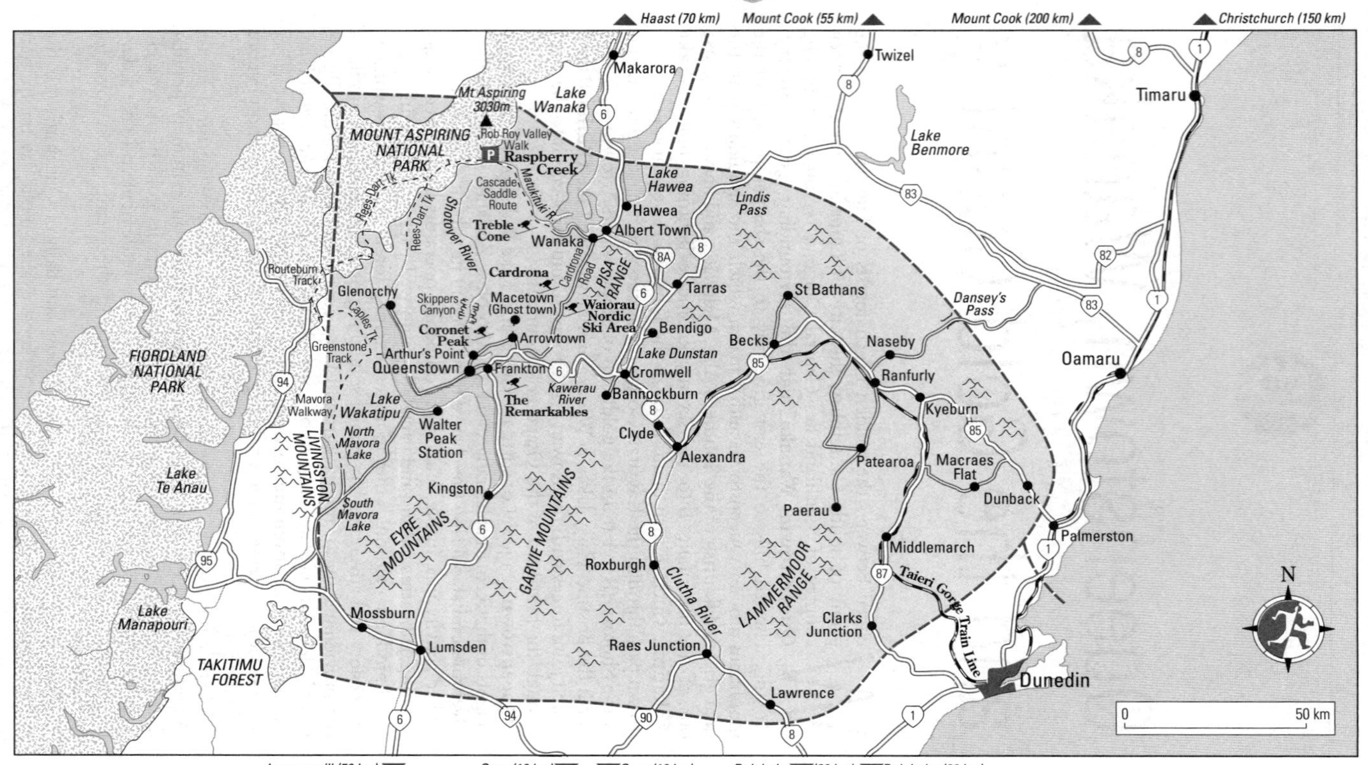
Haast (70 km)
Mount Cook (55 km)
Mount Cook (200 km)
Christchurch (150 km)
Makarora
Twizel
Timaru
Mt Aspiring 3030m
Lake Wanaka
MOUNT ASPIRING NATIONAL PARK
Rob Roy Valley Walk
Raspberry Creek
Lake Benmore
Lake Hawea
Lindis Pass
Cascade Saddle Route
Matukituki R.
Rees-Dart Tk
Shotover River
Hawea
Treble Cone
Albert Town
Wanaka
Cardrona Road
PISA RANGE
Routeburn Track
Cardrona
Tarras
St Bathans
Dansey's Pass
Glenorchy
Caples Tk
Skippers Canyon
Macetown (Ghost town)
Waiorau Nordic Ski Area
Coronet Peak
Arrowtown
Bendigo
Becks
Naseby
Oamaru
Greenstone Track
Arthur's Point
Queenstown
Frankton
Lake Dunstan
Cromwell
Ranfurly
FIORDLAND NATIONAL PARK
Kawerau River
Bannockburn
Mavora Walkway
Lake Wakatipu
Walter Peak Station
The Remarkables
Kyeburn
North Mavora Lake
Clyde
LIVINGSTON MOUNTAINS
Alexandra
Patearoa
Macraes Flat
Lake Te Anau
Kingston
Dunback
South Mavora Lake
GARVIE MOUNTAINS
Paerau
EYRE MOUNTAINS
Palmerston
Middlemarch
Roxburgh
Taieri Gorge Train Line
Clutha River
LAMMERMOOR RANGE
N
Lake Manapouri
Mossburn
Clarks Junction
Lumsden
Raes Junction
TAKITIMU FOREST
Dunedin
Lawrence
0
50 km
Invercargill (50 km)
Gore (10 km)
Gore (10 km)
Balclutha (30 km)
Balclutha (30 km)

from the nearby town of **Glenorchy** at the head of Lake Wakatipu. Well-organized track transport will drop you at the trailheads of the magnificent **Routeburn Track**, the match of any in the country; the less challenging **Caples** and **Greenstone** tracks, which can be combined with the Routeburn to make a satisfying five-day circuit; and the rugged **Rees–Dart Track**, which opens up the arduous Cascade Saddle Route towards Mount Aspiring.

The glacially scoured, three-sided pinnacle of "the Matterhorn of the South" forms the centrepiece of the **Mount Aspiring National Park**. This permanently snow-capped alpine high country is linked by the Matukituki valley to the peaceful resort of **Wanaka**, slung around the placid waters of its eponymous lake. Wanaka's laid-back atmosphere stands in marked contrast to the frenetic bustle of Queenstown, though there's no shortage of operators keen to take you canyoning, stunt flying, rock climbing or on any number of other pursuits.

Queenstown and Wanaka lie on the fringe of the **Otago Goldfields**, which stretch east towards the coast at Dunedin. Most of the gold has long since gone and the area is largely deserted, but there are numerous interesting reminders of New Zealand's gold-rush days, including old workings set amidst rugged scenery. Queenstown and Arrowtown were two of the biggest gold towns, but to the east lie the more modest centres of **Cromwell**, **Alexandra** and **Roxburgh**, scattered along the banks of the Clutha River which once provided Maori with the easiest path to the *pounamu* fields of the West Coast. Gold miners subsequently used the same paths, fanning out to found tiny and now moribund towns such as **Bannockburn**, **St Bathan's** and **Naseby**, the most enjoyable places in which to idle among the mouldering boomtime remains.

From June to October the region's focus switches to **skiing**, with Queenstown acting as a base for the downhill resorts of Coronet Peak and the Remarkables, while Wanaka serves the Cardrona and Treble Cone fields, as well as the **Waiorau** Nordic field.

Getting around the region is easily done on the reasonably frequent buses linking the main towns, supplemented by shuttle buses to trailheads, and minibuses transporting you from your hotel out to the various adventure activities. For more detailed coverage of route frequencies and times, consult "Travel details" on p.921.

Queenstown

QUEENSTOWN, the country's main centre for adventure sports, is in many ways a victim of it own popularity, at times feeling like an overcrowded theme park where things are just too money-conscious. One of New Zealand's most commercialized year-round resorts, it has capitalized to an enormous degree on being set beside the beautiful, deep-blue Lake Wakatipu and hemmed in by craggy mountains, but a haphazard attitude to local planning and massive building programmes has allowed hotels to appear on the foreshore and more and more lavish residences – some owned by Hollywood film stars, including Sam Neill – to climb into the hills, spreading out toward Arrowtown. However, the place still retains a semblance of its original character, thanks in part to the inventive renovation the centre received after being heavily flooded in the late 1990s, and the knock-on effect of the extensive re- and new-building has been to markedly increase the number of shopping, eating and drinking options. And its commercial popularity isn't a total drawback, possessing as it does some excellent restaurants and some of the flashiest (and most highly priced) accommodation outside of Auckland, Wellington or Christchurch.

With all this in mind, Queestown is best taken in small doses, either as a base from which to plan lengthy forays into the surrounding countryside, or as a venue for sampling one of the many outdoor activities on offer. The most prominent of these is undoubtedly **bungy jumping**. The town's environs now boast four of the world's most gloriously scenic bungy sites, visited either in isolation or as part of a multi-thrill package, perhaps including **whitewater rafting** and **jetboating** on the Shotover River, or a helicopter flight into the dilapidated former gold workings of **Skippers Canyon**.

Visitors after a more sedate time are equally spoilt for choice, with **lake cruises** on the elegant TSS *Earnslaw*, the last of the lake steamers; the **gondola ride** to Bob's Peak, which commands magnificent vistas over Queenstown and The Remarkables range; and a choice of **wine tours** around some of the world's most southerly wineries. Formal lakeshore gardens and hillside viewpoints provide the focus for easy local **walks**, with the heartier multi-day tramps all starting at Glenorchy (p.878) at the head of the lake.

Even the frantic summers are nothing in comparison to winter, when Kiwi and international skiers descend on **Coronet Peak** and **The Remarkables**, two fine ski fields within half an hour of Queenstown which are at their peak during the annual **Queenstown Winter Carnival** towards the end of July.

Arrival, information and city transport

Buses all arrive in the centre of Queenstown at The Top of the Mall, the intersection of the Mall and Camp Street, from where it's less than fifteen minutes' walk to most hotels and hostels; better still, most of the smaller bus companies will drop you off outside your chosen accommodation. Kiwi Discovery stop outside their office at 37 Camp St, but also do pick-ups and drop-offs around Queenstown – as do Atomic Shuttle, Southern Link Shuttles, Southern Explore, Magic Bus and Kiwi Experience.

Queenstown's **airport** is just outside Frankton, 7km northeast of central Queenstown; the Shopper Bus runs roughly hourly (9am–3.30pm; 15min; around $3.50), and the Super Shuttle (around $10 for one, cheaper for two) meets most flights. **Taxis** (Ⓣ03/442 6666 or 442 7788) charge around $20 for the ride into town. Most of the major car rental companies also have offices at the airport, and there's a small visitor centre that stays open for all incoming flights.

Information

Queenstown's main downtown area is concentrated around Rees Street, Shotover Street, Camp Street and the pedestrianized Mall, which runs from the Main Town Wharf eastwards to Ballarat Street. The crossroads formed by Camp and Shotover streets, and along Shotover Street itself, is awash with visitor centres-cum-booking offices for local and national activities as well as for travel. The official **visitor centre**, on the corner of Camp Street and Shotover Street (daily: Nov–April 7am–7pm; May–Oct 7am–6pm; Ⓣ03/442 4100, Ⓔqvc@xtra.co.nz), is not much different from any of these more commercially oriented operations, processing questions and bookings as quickly as a jet- boat up a gorge, though it does offer slightly less partisan advice than the other dozen or so booking agents masquerading as information centres in order to push their own tours and products. For more on booking adventure activities, see p.861. The best place for **online information** is at Ⓦwww.itag.co.nz, and

Itag also produce an activities magazine (both winter and summer) with a list of things to do and up to the minute prices (free).

The best unbiased information on walks in the area comes from the **DOC office** at 37 Shotover St (Dec–April daily 9am–6pm; May–Jun Mon–Sat 9am–4pm; July–Sept closed; Oct–Nov 9am–4pm; usually closed every 12.30-1.30pm but times can vary by half an hour; ⓣ03/442 7933, ⓕ442 7932), which is stacked with leaflets on DOC activities and operates a Great Walks Booking Desk (July–April daily 9am–4.30pm) for aspiring Routeburn, Kepler and Milford track walkers.

City transport

Pretty much everywhere you are likely to want to go in central Queenstown can be reached **on foot**. Most of the activities – bungy jumping, whitewater rafting and the like – take place out of town, although all operators run courtesy buses from the centre of town to the site, usually picking up from accommodation en route. There's a **taxi rank** on Camp Street at The Top of the Mall and one on Shotover Street, or call ⓣ03/442 6666 or 442 7788.

The only useful bus services are those to Arrowtown (see p.873) and the Shopper Bus, from The Top of the Mall (ⓣ03/442 6647; daily departures every 1–2hr 8.15am–5.15pm), which runs out to Frankton and the airport.

More personalized transport comes in the form of **rental cars** and **bikes**, which are available from several outlets around town (see "Listings", p.871). It pays to shop around – especially for one-day or overnight rentals to Milford Sound, which can work out to be real bargains, with companies sometimes offering a group of four a car plus petrol and a Milford cruise for around $70 per person, but it's a very long, tiring drive.

Drivers will have no problem negotiating Queenstown's streets, but may fall foul of stringent **parking restrictions**. Parking meters in the central streets (checked daily until 9pm) cover several spaces and it is easy to inadvertently pay for someone else's vehicle; there's usually some free parking to be found within a few hundred metres in any case.

Accommodation

Queenstown has the widest selection of **places to stay** in this corner of New Zealand, but such is the demand in the middle of summer and at the height of the ski season that rooms can be hard to come by and prices are correspondingly high.

With a few exceptions, all the accommodation is packed into a compact area less than fifteen minutes' walk from the centre of town. Good deals are sometimes offered by the big **hotels** in what passes for Queenstown's off season (essentially April, May & Nov) but in general you'll do better in smaller places, particularly the **B&Bs**, **homestays** and **lodges** of which there are some fine examples. Families, groups and keen self-caterers might consider **motels**, which match the Kiwi standard but tend to charge a little more than in less popular resorts. The best budget deals are to be found at the many **hostels** and backpackers, which compete fiercely for trade. Considering their number (over fifteen at last count), few of them are up to the standards found elsewhere: they generally offer a similar range of services – free activity booking, free luggage storage and the like – for much the same rates. The Queenstown district also has abundant **campsites** with attendant cabins, though only a couple of these are within walking distance of town.

If a less frantic atmosphere – and lower prices – appeal, it's also worth considering **Arrowtown** as a base for exploring the Queenstown area – see pp.873-875 for reviews of places to stay in the vicinity – or **Glenorchy** (see p.879).

Hotels

A-Line Hotel 27 Stanley St ⓣ0800/807 700, ⓔaline@es.co.nz. A cluster of nicely furnished rooms in A-frames with good lake views. This place is firmly on the tour bus circuit, but some discreet haggling when business is slow can bring rates down considerably. ❺

Aspen on Queenstown 155 Fernhill Rd ⓣ03/442 7688 & 0800/427 688, ⓔaspen@xtra.co.nz. A sprawling hotel with a small indoor pool and great lake views. The abundantly equipped rooms and apartments are overpriced in high season but can be an off-peak bargain – especially the very comfortable two-bedroom apartments, whose rates drop by as much as a third. The hotel is 2km from the centre of Queenstown, so phone ahead. Hotel rooms $120–140, apartments ❻–❾

Hurley's cnr Frankton Rd & Melbourne St ⓣ03/442 5999 & 0800/589 879, ⓦwww.hurleys.co.nz. Tasteful, luxuriously appointed apartments and studios close to the centre of Queenstown, each equipped with a full kitchen, TV, CD and cassette player, spa baths and with free access to two saunas and a full gym. Studios ❽, apartments ❻–❾

Motels

Alpha Lodge 62 Frankton Rd ⓣ03/442 6095, ⓕ442 8010. Good value, low-cost motel close to town with all basic amenities and a range of budget and studio units. ❹–❺

Alpine Sun Motel 18 Hallenstein St ⓣ03/442 8482, ⓔalpine.sun@xtra.co.nz. Good-value basic motel units with Sky TV, kitchenettes, spa and off-road parking. ❹

Alpine Village Motor Inn 633 Frankton Rd ⓣ03/442 7795, ⓕ442 7738. Large place midway to Frankton (the Shopper Bus passes by) and frequented by tour groups. Most rooms and chalets come with views of the Remarkables, and all have the run of two restaurants, a tennis court and the jacuzzi. ❹–❺

Amity Lodge 7 Melbourne St ⓣ0800/556 000, ⓔamity@queenstown.co.nz. Modern and well-maintained one-bedroom units, all fully self-contained and with microwaves. ❹–❻

Four Seasons Motel 12 Stanley St ⓣ03/442 8953, ⓕ442 7233. Reasonable downtown motel with off-street parking, good kitchens, mountain views, an outdoor swimming pool and a spa. ❺–❻

Goldfields Motel 57 Frankton Rd ⓣ0800/344 272, ⓕ442 6179, ⓦnz.com/queenstown/goldfields. A range of decent chalets all equipped with TV and fridge. ❹

The Lodges 8 Lake Esplanade ⓣ03/442 7552, ⓦnz.com/queenstown/thelodges. Top-quality lakeside studio units and three-bedroom apartments with full kitchens, laundry and parking. Good value for groups of four or more. ❻–❾

B&Bs and homestays

Bush Creek Health Retreat 21 Bowen St ⓣ03/442 7260, ⓕ442 7250. This wonderfully secluded house 1km from central Queenstown is surrounded by beautiful organic gardens tended by Ileen Mutch, a renowned iridologist and holistic healer. A relaxing and rejuvenating place to stay. ❸–❺

Dairy Guesthouse 10 Isle St ⓣ0800/333 393, ⓦwww.thedairy.co.nz. Very fine central B&B lodge tastefully decorated with historic Queenstown prints, ethnic rugs and kilims, and with very comfortable en-suite rooms. Complimentary wine on arrival sets the relaxed atmosphere; breakfast is served in the former dairy that gives the place its name. ❽–❾

Hulbert House 68 Ballarat St ⓣ & ⓕ03/442 8767, ⓦwww.heritageinns.co.nz/hulbert.house. In a rambling century-old Victorian villa built on the hill behind Queenstown Bay, this opulent but tasteful B&B has a large library, idyllic gardens and great breakfasts. ❽–❾

Little Paradise Lodge Meilejohn Bay, 28km along Glenorchy Rd ⓣ & ⓕ03/442 6196. An idyllic homestay on a mostly self-sufficient lifestyle block close to the lake and with good walking and fishing nearby. Almost everything is made from logs cut or stone hewn by the Swiss owner and part-time forester, Thomas, including the non-chlorinated swimming pool fed by its own stream and complete with water lilies. Accommodation is in standard rooms and a charming en-suite chalet. You can cook for yourself and there is free use of kayaks, a dinghy and fishing gear. ❺

Remarkables Lodge SH6, 14km from Queenstown ⓣ & ⓕ03/442 2720, ⓦnz.com/queenstown/remarkableslodge. This is in the premier league of Kiwi boutique lodges and its exquisite meals are as much a part of the experience as the super-comfortable rooms, spacious and beautifully decorated lounge, outdoor pool, spa, tennis court and croquet lawn. Secluded at the foot of the Remarkables (exactly 3.4km south of the ski field approach road), there are walks into the foothills just beyond the helipad. Rates are around $700 per person including breakfast, pre-dinner drinks and dinner. ❾

The Stable 17 Brisbane St ⓣ03/442 9251, ⓔgi-mac@queenstown.co.nz. Cosy and popular home-stay stacked with books and housed in a former stable. Cooked or continental breakfasts are served, as are dinners ($35) if ordered in advance. ❻

Turner Lodge 2 Turner St ⓣ03/442 9432, ⓦnz-accommodation.co.nz/stay/turnerlodge. Central, relaxed and modern place that operates as a comfortable homestay serving a cooked breakfast, and has three additional rooms which are let on a self-catering basis, sharing kitchen facilities, a lounge and a sun deck. Room ❹–❺

Hostels

Alpine Lodge 13 Gorge Rd ⓣ03/442 7220, ⓕ442 7038. Small, welcoming and central hostel which can be a little cramped when full. Ask about the self-contained unit that's sometimes let separately to groups. Dorms ❶, rooms ❷

Black Sheep 13 Frankton Rd ⓣ03/442 7289, ⓕ442 7361. Converted motel that's spacious enough to cope with the backpacker tour-bus crowd who frequently pack out the four- to ten-bed dorms. Can be rowdy, but everything is very well organized, there's a barbecue out back near the spa pool and you can book just about everything at the 24hr reception; there's a $1 charge per night for storing luggage. Dorms ❶, rooms ❷

Bumbles 2 Brunswick St, cnr Lake Esplanade ⓣ0800/428 625. Among the best hostels in town and justly popular; well-sited across the road from the lakefront and with recently renovated communal areas including a large kitchen, central lounge, barbecue area and plenty of washing facilities. Dorms ❶, twins ❷, made-up doubles ❸

Butterfli Lodge 62 Thompson St ⓣ03/442 6367, ⓦwww.butterfli.co.nz. A small house overlooking the lake that provides a friendly atmosphere and cosy accommodation for a limited number of people. Book early. Dorms ❶, rooms ❸

Deco Backpackers 52 Main St ⓣ03/442 7384, ⓕ442 6258. Small and peaceful hostel in an Art Deco-style house. It's a bit of an uphill trudge from town but worth the effort. Dorms ❶, rooms ❷

McFee's Waterfront Hotel 48a Shotover St ⓣ03/442 7400, ⓕ442 7403. Large hostel with good communal areas overlooking the lake; accommodation is in four-bed dorms, budget doubles with TV, and flashier en-suite rooms. Dorms ❶, rooms ❸–❹

Pinewood Lodge 48 Hamilton Rd ⓣ03/442 8273, ⓕ442 9470. Scattered collection of new and older renovated buildings (all surrounded by lawns) jointly making up one of Queenstown's nicer backpackers, located on the edge of town ten minutes' walk from the centre. Good facilities all round including a spa bath ($5 per half-hour) and bike rental (around $25 per day). Tents $11, dorms ❶, rooms ❷–❸

Scallywags 27 Lomond Crescent ⓣ03/442 7083, ⓕ442 5885. Pitched as an upmarket backpackers' hostel, this suburban house is a ten-minute walk up from town (you can cut through the motor park). It has stupendous views and a very laid-back muck-in atmosphere, with use of a kitchen and free tea and coffee. Dorms ❶, rooms (including towels & bedding) ❸

YHA 88 Lake Esplanade ⓣ03/442 8413, ⓔyhaqutn@yha.org.nz. Always bustling, particularly in the ski season, this is one of New Zealand's flagship YHAs, ten minutes' walk along the waterfront from town. Accommodation is in spacious, mostly six-bed dorms and new doubles, many with good lake views. Dorms ❶, rooms ❷–❸

Campsites and motorparks

Arthur's Point Holiday Park close to the Shotover Jet site at Arthur's Point ⓣ & ⓕ03/442 9306, ⓔtop10.queenstown@xtra.co.nz. Smallish, quiet and fully equipped site with a small pool. Tent and powered sites $9.50, standard cabins ❷, kitchen cabins ❸, motels ❺

Creeksyde Campervan Park 54 Robins Rd ⓣ03/442 9447, ⓕ442 6621, ⓔcreekside@camp.co.nz. This highly organized and spotlessly clean site ten minutes' walk from town is primarily aimed at campervanners, though there are tent sites. A central building houses a spa bathroom ($5 per half-hour for two), sauna ($10), ski store and drying rooms. Tents & powered sites $12.50, motels ❷–❸

Kawarau Falls Lakeside Holiday Park 7km north of Queenstown on SH6, near Frankton airport ⓣ03/442 3510, ⓦwww.campsite.co.nz. Very attractive lakeside campsite that's ideal for exploring the region. Excellent facilities extend to spacious tent sites, a backpacker-style lodge and three different grades of cabins, some with their own facilities. In peak season, the Shopper Bus comes to within 500m; within 1km out of season. Tents & powered sites $10, dorms ❶, cabins ❷–❹

Lake View Queenstown Motor Park Man St ⓣ0800/482 735, ⓔinfo@motorpark.co.nz. Enormous site that sprawls over the base of Bob's

Peak and seems to swallow just about all of Queenstown's campers. Facilities are extensive and accommodation runs the gamut from grassy tent sites ($11) to self-contained motel units, but it can hardly be considered peaceful. ❷–❺

Twelve-Mile Creek Reserve 5km south of Queenstown, off the Glenorchy road (no phone). DOC campsite with facilities limited to basic toilets and water. Tent sites $5.

The Town and around

The best all-round views of the Queenstown region and Lake Wakatipu are undoubtedly those from **Bob's Peak**, which rises up immediately behind the town and can be reached on one of Queenstown's gentler rides. The four-minute **Skyline Gondola**, Brecon Street (daily 9am–midnight; $14 return), deposits you at the Skyline Complex, where a fair proportion of passengers are herded into **Kiwi Magic** (daily 10am–8pm; 30min; $8), a well-produced and engagingly corny promotional film that's beginning to show its age, not least because the lead, comedian Billy T. James, died a decade ago. Everyone else either peels off to The Ledge bungy and/or swing (see p.863), the Luge (see p.856) or makes straight for the viewing balcony, getting their bearings off The Remarkables and Cecil and Walter peaks beyond Lake Wakatipu. The *Skyline*

Walks around Queenstown

All the hard-sell on adventure activities in Queenstown can become a bit oppressive, and a few hours away from town can be wonderfully therapeutic. The majority of the walks outlined below – listed in ascending order of difficulty – are well covered by the DOC's *Queenstown Walks and Trails* leaflet ($1), which also includes a sketch map. Serious multi-day tramps in the region are centred on Wanaka and Glenorchy (see p.889 and p.878, respectively).

One Mile Creek Walkway (1hr 30min return; 6km; 50m ascent). Fairly easy walk through a gully filled with beech forest and following a 1924 pipeline from Queenstown's first hydroelectric scheme. The route starts on the lakefront by the Fernhill roundabout, and offers a good opportunity to acquaint yourself with fuchsia, lancewood and native birds – principally fantails, bellbirds and tui.

Queenstown Hill Track (2–3hr return; 5km; 600m ascent). Starting from the top of York Street, this is a fairly steep climb up through mostly exotic trees to panoramic views from the 907m Queenstown Hill.

Frankton Arm Track (1hr–1hr 30min one way; 7km; flat). This easy path is ideal for an early-morning or sunset stroll. Start from Peninsula Street in Queenstown, follow the lakeside to Frankton, and continue a further 2km round to the Kawarau River outlet.

Ben Lomond Summit Track (6–8hr return; 11km; 1400m ascent). A full-day, there-and-back tramp scaling the 1748m Ben Lomond, one of the highest mountains in the region and consequently subject to inclement weather, especially in winter when the track can be snow-covered. Start by the One Mile Creek Walk or use the Skyline Gondola and walk up past the paragliding launch site to join the track, which climbs through alpine tussock to reveal expansive views. Gentler slopes approach Ben Lomond Saddle, from where it's a steep final haul to the summit.

Ben Lomond–Moonlight Track (8–10hr one way; 16km; 1400m ascent). A demanding and occasionally difficult-to-follow route which combines the ascent to Ben Lomond Saddle (see above) with a poled sub-alpine route to the site of the former gold town of Sefferstown and the eastern section of the Moonlight Track to Arthur's Point. Organize someone to pick you up at Arthur's Point or be prepared for a 5km slog back to Queenstown.

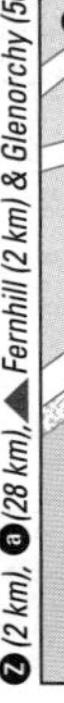

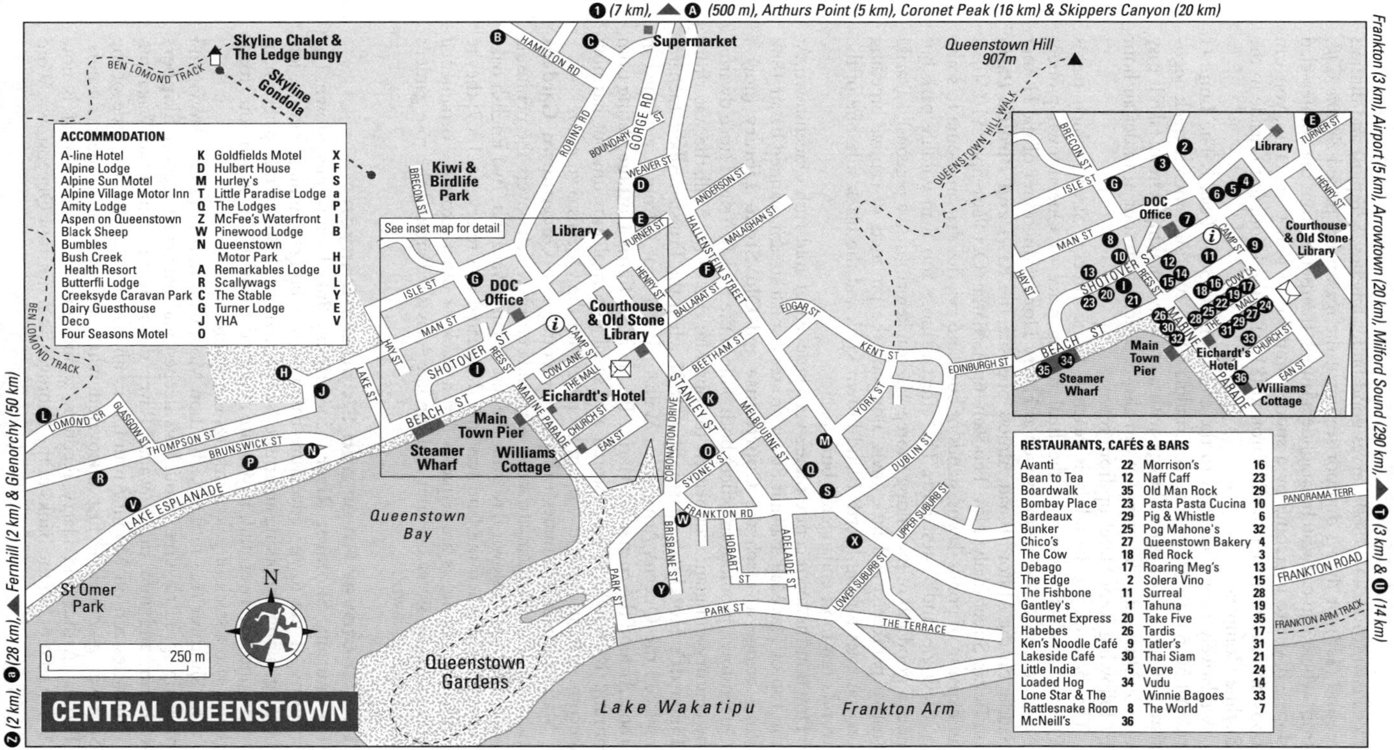
CENTRAL QUEENSTOWN
1 (7 km), A (500 m), Arthurs Point (5 km), Coronet Peak (16 km) & Skippers Canyon (20 km)
Frankton (3 km), Airport (5 km), Arrowtown (20 km), Milford Sound (290 km), T (3 km) & U (14 km)
Z (2 km), a (28 km), Fernhill (2 km) & Glenorchy (50 km)
Skyline Chalet & The Ledge bungy
Skyline Gondola
Ben Lomond Track
Queenstown Hill 907m
Queenstown Hill Walk
Supermarket
Kiwi & Birdlife Park
See inset map for detail
Library
DOC Office
Courthouse & Old Stone Library
Eichardt's Hotel
Main Town Pier
Steamer Wharf
Williams Cottage
Queenstown Bay
Queenstown Gardens
St Omer Park
Lake Wakatipu
Frankton Arm
Frankton Arm Track
Hamilton Rd
Robins Rd
Gorge Rd
Boundary St
Weaver St
Anderson St
Malaghan St
Hallenstein Street
Turner St
Henry St
Ballarat St
Brecon St
Isle St
Man St
Hay St
Shotover St
Rees St
Camp St
Cow Lane
The Mall
Church St
Ean St
Marine Parade
Beach St
Lake St
Lomond Cr
Glasgow St
Thompson St
Brunswick St
Lake Esplanade
Coronation Drive
Stanley St
Beetham St
Melbourne St
Edgar St
Kent St
York St
Dublin St
Edinburgh St
Sydney St
Frankton Rd
Brisbane St
Hobart St
Adelaide St
Park St
Upper Suburb St
Lower Suburb St
The Terrace
Panorama Terr.
Frankton Road
N
0 250 m
ACCOMMODATION
A-line Hotel K
Alpine Lodge D
Alpine Sun Motel M
Alpine Village Motor Inn T
Amity Lodge Q
Aspen on Queenstown Z
Black Sheep W
Bumbles N
Bush Creek Health Resort A
Butterfli Lodge R
Creeksyde Caravan Park C
Dairy Guesthouse G
Deco J
Four Seasons Motel O
Goldfields Motel X
Hulbert House F
Hurley's S
Little Paradise Lodge a
The Lodges P
McFee's Waterfront I
Pinewood Lodge B
Queenstown Motor Park H
Remarkables Lodge U
Scallywags L
The Stable Y
Turner Lodge E
YHA V
RESTAURANTS, CAFÉS & BARS
Avanti 22
Bean to Tea 12
Boardwalk 35
Bombay Place 23
Bardeaux 29
Bunker 25
Chico's 27
The Cow 18
Debago 17
The Edge 2
The Fishbone 11
Gantley's 1
Gourmet Express 20
Habebes 26
Ken's Noodle Café 9
Lakeside Café 30
Little India 5
Loaded Hog 34
Lone Star & The Rattlesnake Room 8
McNeill's 36
Morrison's 16
Naff Caff 23
Old Man Rock 29
Pasta Pasta Cucina 10
Pig & Whistle 6
Pog Mahone's 32
Queenstown Bakery 4
Red Rock 3
Roaring Meg's 13
Solera Vino 15
Surreal 28
Tahuna 19
Take Five 35
Tardis 17
Tatler's 31
Thai Siam 21
Verve 24
Vudu 14
Winnie Bagoes 33
The World 7

Restaurant (☎03/442 7860) serves good buffet lunches ($28 plus) and dinners around ($38), or there's outdoor seating at the reasonably priced *Skyline Café*, from where you can watch paragliders launch themselves from the conifer-clad slopes. If you're overcome by a sudden impulse to join their ranks, you can book an introductory paraglide around ($155) at the booth just outside in the Skyline Complex.

A relatively recent addition to the attractions at Bob's Peak is The **Luge** (1 ride $4.50, 5 rides $16, 5 rides & Gondola $26), a twisting concrete track negotiated on a wheeled plastic buggy with a primitive braking system: take it easy on your first run. The complex can also be reached on foot in under an hour by following Kent Street up from town.

The base of the Gondola is reached along Brecon Street, which passes Queenstown's **cemetery** – the final resting place of Queenstown pioneer Nicholas von Tunzelmann, as well as Henry Homer, discoverer of the Homer Saddle on the Milford Road. Almost opposite, the **Kiwi and Birdlife Park**, on Bevan Street (daily: Nov–Feb 9am–6pm; March–Oct 9am–5pm; $10.50), is an expanse of ponds, lawns, stands of bush and aviaries that are home to some of New Zealand's rarest birds. The effect is more zoo than wildlife park but does a good job of presenting morepork, kea, kereru (native pigeons), kakariki (native parakeets) and little owls, alongside the products of captive breeding programmes for the North Island brown kiwi, and the black stilt, one of the world's ten most endangered bird species.

Down in the town centre there's very little left of gold-rush Queenstown. At the Top of The Mall, Ballarat Street crosses a small stream spanned by an 1882 stone bridge to reach the **Courthouse** and **Old Stone Library** (now a Queenstown promotions office) both built in the mid 1870s and since dwarfed by century-old giant sequoias. At the opposite end of the Mall, the waterfront **Eichardt's Hotel** dates partly from 1871 when the Prussian Albert Eichardt replaced the Queen's Arms, a bar William Rees created from a woolshed in 1862. Around the corner on Marine Parade is **Williams Cottage**, dating from around 1866, which was restored as a small historical museum but has now become a high-class gift shop, in keeping with the Queenstown ethos.

Marine Parade continues east past the cottages to **Queenstown Gardens** (unrestricted entry), an attractive parkland retreat which covers the peninsula separating Queenstown Bay from the rest of Lake Wakatipu. Two English oaks were planted when the land was first designated as a reserve in 1867; they're still going strong, as are sequoias and a stack of other exotics – ornamental cherry, maple, sweet chestnut and the like – lavished around the rose gardens and bowling lawns.

The Shotover River and Skippers Canyon

The churning **Shotover River** is inextricably linked with Queenstown. The majority of the town's adventure-based trips – bungy jumping, rafting, jet-boating, mountain biking and more (see "Activities", p.862) – take place on, in or around the river and, if you are prepared to drive the treacherous road, there's also a stack of gold workings to explore.

The Shotover rises in the Richardson Mountains north of Queenstown and picks up speed to surge through its deepest and narrowest section, **Skippers Canyon**, and into the Kawarau River downstream from Lake Wakatipu. Tributaries run off Mount Aurum, beneath which is the mother lode of the Shotover goldfields – first discovered when a couple of pioneer shearers, Thomas Arthur and Harry Redfern, found gold in 1862 at what is now Arthur's Point, on the banks of the Shotover 5km north of Queenstown. Word spread that prospectors were extracting the equivalent of over ten kilos a day, and within months thousands were flocking from throughout New Zealand and Australia to work what was soon dubbed "The Richest River in the World". The river-edge gravels had been all but worked out by 1864, necessitating ever more sophisticated extraction techniques. With the introduction of gravity-fed water chutes, mechanical sieves and floating dredges, the construction of a decent road became crucial. From 1863, Chinese navvies spent over twenty years hacking away with pick and shovel at the Skippers Road; those who stuck out the harsh conditions began building quarters more substantial than the standard-issue canvas tents. Meanwhile, entrepreneurially minded pioneers began to exploit the boom, building 27 hotels along the 40km of road, and selling fresh fruit and vegetables at extortionate prices to miners as often as not suffering from scurvy. By the turn of the century the river was worked out, though a few stayed on; even today there are a couple of die-hards who make part of their living from gold panning and sluicing. Occasionally they get some extra company, and the heavy rains which caused substantial flooding in Queenstown in November 1999 sluiced down enough to tempt quite a few. As the townsfolk were mopping up and repairing their homes, and the turbid waters were clearing, happy hunters were out with their shovels. For a few days there it wasn't unusual to pan $600 worth in a couple of hours, hardly a fortune, but a good haul nonetheless.

The extremely narrow and winding **Skippers Road** is best left to experienced drivers. Locals who know the road like the back of their hand tend to hare around, leaving little space for oncoming traffic; besides, rental cars aren't insured for Skippers. Being driven into either the Pipeline bungy sites or the start points for the Skippers Canyon Jet and Shotover rafting trips (see p.864 for more on all of these) gives you a good chance to see the valley. By far the best way, though, is on a four-hour **tour** with Skippers Grand Canyon (Ⓣ03/442 5455, Ⓦwww.grandcanyon.co.nz), who take in most of the highlights, and also produce a useful, and widely available, free leaflet and map ($45; $59 including afternoon tea, $105 including a 16km jetboat journey; $199 including a helicopter flight).

The Skippers Road, which follows the Shotover River only in its upper reaches, branches off Coronet Peak Road 12km north of Queenstown. It is approached along Malaghans Road through **Arthur's Point**, 5km north of Queenstown, marked by the historic *Arthur's Point Hotel*, the only one of the Skippers Road hotels still operating, adjacent to where Thomas Arthur first struck gold. Half a kilometre on, the Edith Cavell Bridge spans a gorge where the Shotover Jet performs its antics, its upstream progress limited by the Mother-in-Law rapid and the 1911 **Oxenbridge Tunnel**. After three years of drilling, this 200m-long bore – designed to absorb the flow of the Shotover while the gold-bearing riverbed was worked – reaped meagre rewards, returning only 2.5kg of gold.

Skippers Road soon begins to shadow the river, negotiating Pinchers Bluff, where Chinese and European navvies cut the road from a near-vertical cliff face. Upstream, the 1901 **Skippers Bridge** was the first high-level one built – and consequently survived the winter floods which had swept away all past efforts. For the first time, the township of Skippers had reliable access, though this did little to prevent the exodus that saw a population of 1500 dwindle to nothing once the gold ran out. The old schoolhouse has been restored and there are the ruins of a few more buildings scattered around, but otherwise it is a bleak, haunted place. You can **camp** here at a toilets-and-water site for around four bucks.

The wineries

Grapes have been grown commercially in the **Central Otago** district – essentially Wanaka, Queenstown and the Clutha Valley – only since the 1980s, but local winemakers have already garnered a shelf-full of awards. Widely billed as "the world's most southerly wine-growing region", the vineyards lie close to the 45th Parallel – in country which detractors pooh-poohed as too cold and generally unsuitable for wine production, despite the fact that the Rhône Valley lies on a similar latitude. A continental climate of hot dry summers and long cold winters prevails, which tends to result in low yields and high production costs, forcing wineries to go for quality boutique wines sold at prices which might seem high ($15–30) until you taste them.

The steep schist and gravel slopes on the southern banks of the **Kawarau River** were first recognized as potential vineyard sites as early as 1864, when French miner Jean Désiré Feraud, by now bored of his gold claim at Frenchman's Point near Clyde, planted grapes from cuttings brought over from Australia. His wines won awards at shows in Australia (though standards were none too exacting at the time), but by the early 1880s he'd decamped to Dunedin. No more grapes were grown commercially until 1976, when the Rippon vineyard was planted outside Wanaka (see p.894). It was another five years before the Kawarau Gorge, with its long summer days of intense light followed by cool nights, was recognized as ideally suited to the cultivation of Pinot Gris, Riesling and particularly Pinot Noir grapes. As an added bonus, the dry conditions inhibit growth of fungus and mildew; the dreaded phylloxera has been kept at bay so far and, to keep it that way, strict protocols exist about bringing vines into the district. Recent vintages (especially 1998 and 1999) have been very good, the 2000 crop was not expected to do wonders, but 2001 turned out to be an excellent year with several international-award winning wines.

Altogether, over twenty wineries are open for tasting throughout Central Otago, a handful of them on the southern slopes above the Kawarau Gorge, around 20km northeast of Queenstown, where SH6 is flanked by sections of lifestyle and commercial grape growing. The closest is the charming **Chard Farm Winery** (Ⓦwww.chardfarm.co.nz; daily 11am–5pm), reached down a precipitous dirt road off SH6 opposite the Kawarau bungy bridge. They don't conduct tours but do offer free tasting of current vintages, most notably the Chardonnay, Pinot Noir and Pinot Gris, though the Gewurztraminer and range of bubblies can be good too. **Gibbston Valley Winery** lies 700m further northeast towards Cromwell and is more business-like and more visitors-oriented, with a **Wine Cave Tour** (hourly 10am–4pm; 30min; $9.50, refundable with a six-bottle purchase) which explores cellars burrowed into the hillside. This is not especially impressive, but the tour includes an informed and generous tasting session – highlights are the citrusy Riesling and the award-winning Pinot Noir. If you fancy a tasting but not the tour then it will set you back $4, refundable on purchases of three bottles or more. All the wines are sold in the shop and the highly regarded vineyard restaurant, which is open for lunches and snacks throughout the day. Another vineyard worth a sniff is the **Peregrine Winery**, roughly 4.5km on from Gibbston Valley, a small winery on the left hand side of the road where tastings of the excellent Sav' Blanc and Pinot Gris are free of charge (daily 10am–5pm) and where cellar-door sales are highly tempting. Two other wineries of growing reputation and with a reputation for growing are **Waitiri Creek** (Ⓣ025 281 8037) and **Mount Edward** (Ⓣ03/442 6113), both of which can be visited by appointment only.

All or some of these vineyards are included on conducted **wine tours**: the

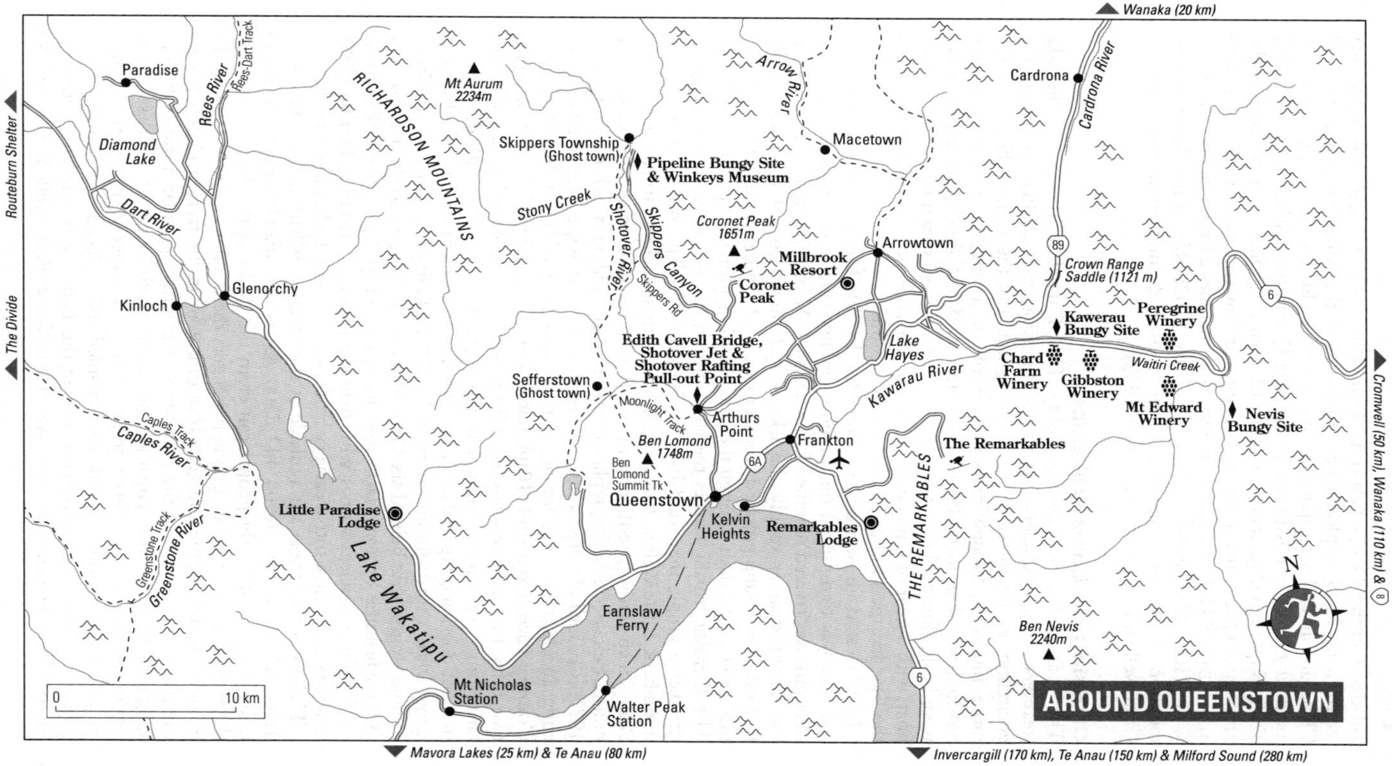

AROUND QUEENSTOWN

Wanaka (20 km)
Routeburn Shelter
The Divide
Cromwell (50 km), Wanaka (110 km) & 8
Mavora Lakes (25 km) & Te Anau (80 km)
Invercargill (170 km), Te Anau (150 km) & Milford Sound (280 km)

Paradise
Diamond Lake
Rees River
Rees-Dart Track
Dart River
Glenorchy
Kinloch
RICHARDSON MOUNTAINS
Mt Aurum 2234m
Skippers Township (Ghost town)
Pipeline Bungy Site & Winkeys Museum
Stony Creek
Shotover River
Skippers Canyon
Skippers Rd
Coronet Peak 1651m
Coronet Peak
Millbrook Resort
Arrow River
Macetown
Arrowtown
Cardrona
Cardrona River
89
Crown Range Saddle (1121 m)
6
Kawerau Bungy Site
Peregrine Winery
Chard Farm Winery
Gibbston Winery
Waitiri Creek
Mt Edward Winery
Nevis Bungy Site
Lake Hayes
Kawarau River
Edith Cavell Bridge, Shotover Jet & Shotover Rafting Pull-out Point
Sefferstown (Ghost town)
Moonlight Track
Arthurs Point
Frankton
6A
The Remarkables
THE REMARKABLES
Ben Lomond 1748m
Ben Lomond Summit Tk
Queenstown
Kelvin Heights
Remarkables Lodge
Caples Track
Caples River
Greenstone Track
Greenstone River
Little Paradise Lodge
Lake Wakatipu
Earnslaw Ferry
Mt Nicholas Station
Walter Peak Station
Ben Nevis 2240m
N
0
10 km

full-day Central Otago Gourmet Tour (Ⓣ03/442 6622, Ⓔbookings@cowt.co.nz; daily; $149) explores these and some of the wineries at Cromwell and Clyde and includes sampling at five wineries plus cheese tasting and a fine lunch at *Oliver's* in Clyde (see p.912); the Queenstown Wine Trail (Ⓣ03/442 3799, Ⓔqwinetrail@xtra.co.nz; daily 12.30pm; 5hr; $65) restricts itself to the immediate Queenstown area with tastings at four wineries; the Awsome Wine Tour (Ⓣ03/442 2905; 12.15pm; 5hrs; $85) includes a local cheesery, while It's Wine Time (Ⓣ0508/946 384; 9am; full day; $162) offers a fine lunch, not to mention the various tours that come from, and concentrate more on, the Cromwell and Clyde vineyards (see p.910).

Cruising on Lake Wakatipu

The coal-fired twin-screw steamship **TSS Earnslaw**, the last of the lake steamers, is one of Queenstown's most enduring images. Wherever you are, the encircling mountains echo the haunting sound of the steam whistle, and the more mundane, though reassuring, throb of its engine, as this beautifully restored relic slogs manfully out from Steamer Wharf. Before the lakeside roads were built, almost all commerce in and out of Queenstown was conducted by boat, with a fleet of four steamers serving the large sheep stations at the top of the lake and the southern railhead at Kingston.

Prefabricated in sections in Dunedin by McRae and McGregor's, the *Earnslaw* was transported on the now defunct railway to Kingston, where its steel hull was riveted together. Launched in 1912, the 51-metre-long craft was the largest steamer to ply the lake – and surely one of the most stately. Burnished brass and polished wood crown its gleaming white hull, and its vertical prow cuts a dash through the lake, reaching a top speed of thirteen knots. The *Earnslaw* usually crosses the lake and returns five or six trips throughout the day: a simple there-and-back **cruise** costs $34. This doesn't allow you to disembark at the Walter Peak homestead, a tourist enclave carved out of Walter Peak Sheep Station, nestling in the southwestern crook of Lake Wakatipu. The house itself, a convincing replica of an original building which burnt down in 1977, is beautifully sited among lawns that sweep down to the lakeshore, creating an elegant setting for tea and scones as part of the Walter Peak High Country Farm Excursion (10am, noon, 4pm daily; 3.5hr; $52). This combines two forty-minute lake crossings with a visit to the colonel's house after the farm tour – an entertaining if sanitized vignette of farm life, with demonstrations of dog handling and shearing. The farm tour element can be substituted either with a forty-minute horse ride ($99 including the crossing), or forty-minute wagon ride behind six Clydesdales in the Wagons to the Past package ($99). Mealtime options (farm tour only) extend to the Barbecue Excursion ($67), which replaces scones with snags (sausages); or Evening Dining ($88), where you can tuck into a carvery buffet served up in the homestead ballroom.

Tickets for all these are available at the Steamer Wharf and the Fiordland Travel Visitor Centre (Ⓣ03/442 7500, Ⓦwww.fiordlandtravel.co.nz): up to three hundred and fifty people can cram the decks of the *Earnslaw*, though there are usually far fewer, giving passengers the freedom to peer down at the gleaming steam engine and get a blast of hot air in the face, or cluster around the piano at the back of the boat for a surprisingly popular music-hall sing-song that can make the return journey seem much longer. If real desperation sets in the onboard café serves some excellent (if expensive) pies and alcohol. In June each year the *Earnslaw* is overhauled and replaced by a launch.

There are other ways to get a ride on the *Earnslaw*: if you have your own motorbike or bicycle, take a one-way trip to Walter Peak (adult $25, motorbike

$10, bicycle free), where you'll have the freedom of the remote and unsealed 80km road up the Von River to SH94 at Burwood, 27km east of Te Anau.

Activities

Queenstown has a vast array of operators running every conceivable type of adventure trip. Many essentially run their companies by mobile phone and don't operate an office as such, though most are directly associated with one of the **information** and **booking offices** that line Shotover Street. In practice, you can book just about any trip from any of these, or directly from your

Winter in Queenstown

Two substantial ski fields – **Coronet Peak** and **the Remarkables** – within easy striking distance of numerous quality hotels, good restaurants and plenty of après-ski combine to make Queenstown New Zealand's **premier ski destination**. Both fields have interchangeable lift tickets, giving you the freedom to pick your mountain. The highlight of the season is the week-long **Queenstown Winter Carnival**, usually around the third week in July, which, as well as all the conventional ski events, has dog racing on snow and a great line-up of entertainment. Of the various other events, the Remarkables' family-oriented **Spring Ski Carnival**, in the first week of the September school holidays, is one of the best. The main fount of knowledge is ⓦwww.nzski.com – the Web site for both of Queenstown's ski fields as well as Mount Hutt – which has contact details, sno-cams and all the latest pricing and rental availability info. Day passes are specific to each field, but there are **multi-day tickets** valid at all three (3-day around $190, 5-day $290, 8-day $430).

Neither field has **accommodation** on site, but frequent shuttle buses run to and from Queenstown ($25–35), where the supply is plentiful – except during school holidays. See "Listings", p.872, for details of **ski rental**.

Coronet Peak

Coronet Peak (ⓣ03/442 4620, ⓔservice@coronetpeak.co.nz), 18km north of Queenstown, opened in 1947, making it New Zealand's first real ski destination. The field boasts sophisticated snow-making equipment which extends its season into spring, when cobalt blue skies and stunning scenery earn it an enviable reputation. Its range of **runs** for skiers of all abilities, and over 400 vertical metres of skiing, only add to its popularity – get here early to avoid long waits for the tows. Throughout the season, which typically starts in early June and sometimes makes it into October, **buses** from Queenstown shuttle back and forth along the sealed access road (no toll). **Passes** for daytime skiing (9am–4pm) currently cost $68 a day; from mid-July to mid-September there's also floodlit night skiing (4–10pm) for $35 per session.

The Remarkables

The Remarkables (ⓣ03/442 4615, ⓔservice@theremarkables.co.nz), 20km east of Queenstown, is one of the newer commercial fields, occupying three mountain basins tucked in behind the wrinkled face of the Remarkables. It is most renowned as learner and intermediate terrain but there are also good runs for advanced skiers, plus some excellent country for off-piste ski touring. Current **day pass** rates are $65. Though the bottom of the tows is 500m higher than at Coronet Peak, more snow is required to cover the tussock, giving a slightly shorter season (late June to early Oct). At 320m, the total vertical descent from the tows is also less than at Coronet, but you gain an extra 120m by taking the Homeward Run – a long stretch of powder with sparkling scenery – to the 14km unsealed **access road** (no toll), where frequent buses shuttle you back up to the chairlift.

hotel or hostel. Prices don't usually vary, but it may be worth asking for **discounts** –YHA, backpacker and so forth – if you think you might be eligible. Almost all the booking offices are open daily, usually to around 9pm in summer, 8pm in winter. Two of the most useful are **The Station**, at the corner of Camp and Shotover streets (Ⓣ03/442 5252 & 0800/367 874, Ⓦwww.queenstown-nz.co.nz), A.J. Hackett's nerve centre and the main pick-up spot for Hackett bungy and the Shotover Jet; and the **Information & Track Centre**, 37 Shotover St (Ⓣ03/442 9708, Ⓦwww.infotrack.co.nz), a backpacker-oriented booking office, offering useful track advice when the DOC office is closed, and the main stopping point for Kiwi Experience. Also on the opposite corner of Shotover and Camp streets is the **Queenstown Information Centre** (Ⓣ03/442 7319, Ⓦwww.queenstowninfo.co.nz), who operate a booking service, as do **The Skippers Grand Canyon Office**, Shotover St (Ⓣ03/442 5455, Ⓦwww.grandcanyon.co.nz), and **Fiordland Travel**, Shotover St (Ⓣ03/442 7500, Ⓦwww.fiordlandtravel.co.nz).

Most activities in Queenstown are more expensive than elsewhere in the country, so to get the most action for the least money, check out one of the numerous **combination deals** knitting together two to five of the main activities and tending to focus on either the Shotover or the Kawarau rivers. A basic triple combination such as the **Skippers Grand Slam** (5hr; $255) includes the Pipeline Bungy, Flying Fox, Skippers Canyon Jet and best of all a T-shirt, though you can take it one stage further and add in a 3.5hr raft trip ($344). Alternatively, the **Awesome Foursome** (6hr) bundles all the top-money activities: a helicopter ride into Skippers Canyon, rafting the Shotover, joining the Shotover Jet, and tackling either the Pipeline Bungy or the Nevis Bungy for around ($400). Decide what you want to do and there'll probably be a combo to suit.

Photos of your jump, jetboat ride or rafting trip are pretty much de rigueur, so you'll frequently encounter **photographers** demanding a cheesy grin; the results are available for purchase within a couple of hours. A lot of people like to pay extra for a video or photo of themselves patently terrified while pretending not to be, while a few others buy T-shirts proclaiming their exploits and wear them proudly round town.

Bungy jumping

Even visitors who never had any intention of parting with a large wad of money to dangle on the end of a thick strand of latex rubber find themselves **bungy jumping** in Queenstown. A combination of peer-group pressure, magnificent scenery and hard-sell promotion eventually gets to most people and, let's face it, historic bridges high above remote rivers beat a crane over a supermarket car park any day.

The original, most famous and most frequently jumped of the bungy venues is A.J. Hackett's 43m **Kawarau Suspension Bridge** beside SH6, 23km north-east of Queenstown (Ⓣ03/442 4007 & 0800/286 495, Ⓦwww.ajhackett.com; daily 9am–5pm; $125). The price includes a certificate, T-shirt and transport if required: $39 gets you a short video recording your fifteen seconds of fame. At busy times the whole scene resembles a rather ghoulish production line, as bungy initiates are trundled out, and tour buses disgorge spectators to fill several viewing platforms. This is the only Queenstown bungy site where you can get dunked in the river.

Some say that it is only the first metre that counts, but when it comes down to it, size matters. A.J. Hackett know this and have pulled out all the stops with the whopping 134m **Nevis Highwire Bungy** (contact Kawarau Bungy, above; $159) – the highest in New Zealand – where jumpers launch from a partly glass-bottomed gondola strung way out over the Nevis River, a tributary of the Kawarau some 32km from Queenstown. Access is by 4WD through private property so spectators will have to fork out $35 to watch their buddies, though this does give you a ride out to the launch gondola and a wonderful view.

Same-day second jumpers often gravitate to the 47-metre **Ledge** (summer generally 3–7pm; winter 5–9pm; $125, including T-shirt and gondola ride), from the top of the Skyline Gondola, where it feels like you are diving out over Queenstown. Unlike the other sites, you can opt for a body harness allowing you to do running jumps, and if they aren't too busy you may be able to jump with all manner of "toys" (surf boards, bikes and the like) to add an extra dimension to your jump. Night jumps in winter make for yet another variation for the committed. Be aware, though, that jumping with a body harness greatly increases your chances of being smacked in the face by the bungy when it pulls taught, which can prove very nasty indeed.

Jumping at any of these three sites gives you the option of a cheaper **second jump** ($52 at Kawarau or The Ledge; $110 at Nevis) if taken within 24 hours; and all three can be combined in the half-day "Thrillogy" (around $250, no T-shirts included) with one jump from each site. Hackett's fourth site, the seldom-used 71-metre **Skippers Canyon Bridge**, 25km up Skippers Canyon, is occasionally pressed into service, particularly for the summer-only Full Moon Bungy (around $169 including T-shirt), which only happens on full moons and involves a 4WD trip into Skippers Canyon, a barbecue, a night under canvas and a moonlit jump.

Until late in 1999, the real knee-trembler had been the 102m **Pipeline Bungy** (☎03/442 5455; 9am–dusk; $150 including T-shirt, same-day repeat jumps $60, video around $50), spanning the Shotover in Skippers Canyon, where the jumping platform is atop a reconstructed 1864 sluice-water pipeline. With all the attention moving to the Nevis Highwire Bungy, the Pipeline has been somewhat sidelined, but it is still a fine jump, using the same length bungy cable as the Nevis, with much more of a ground rush, and definitely worth considering on its own or as part of a combination deal.

Jetboating

Second in the adrenalin hierarchy of Queenstown activities is **jetboating**, and half a dozen operators would love to relieve you of seventy bucks or so for a quick spin. Aside from the excellent and scenic trips on the Dart River (based in Glenorchy, but also offering Queenstown pick-ups – see p.880), only two rivers are negotiated directly from Queenstown: the **Kawarau**, usually reached by a fifteen-minute buzz across the Frankton Arm of Lake Wakatipu; and the **Shotover**, accessed either at Arthur's Point, 5km north of Queenstown, or from the Skippers Canyon Road. Jetboat trips fall into two main categories – those dedicated solely to thrills, spills and close encounters with canyon walls; and those which take a more traditional approach, exploiting the boats' ability to negotiate shallow, braided rivers.

The most celebrated of all the jetboat trips is undoubtedly the **Shotover Jet** (☎03/442 8570; daily 9am–5pm; $79; 30min), a slick operation and the only company to run thrill-a-second trips down Shotover Canyon downstream from the Edith Cavell Bridge. Battered boats attest to a lifetime of close shaves with rocks and canyon walls. Though more expensive than most other trips, this is undoubtedly the most thrilling, and half an hour of 360-degree turns and periodic dousings is quite enough. Courtesy minibuses run from The Station throughout the day.

The only other company with exclusive use of a section of the Shotover is the **Skippers Canyon Jet** (☎03/442 5455; $99), with three trips every day in the upper section of Skippers Canyon. Small, nimble jetboats are used to negotiate the rapids and tight turns, offering occasional glimpses of the canyon's gold-mining heritage, such as the rusting hulk of an abandoned dredge, long-disused bridge supports and twisted metal sheets which once diverted the water around gold-bearing gravels, and there's the chance to pause briefly and watch the horrified faces and hear the unconvincing yells of bravado of the pipeline bungy jumpers.

The remainder of the companies work the braided sections of the Kawarau and lower Shotover, from either Queenstown or Frankton, and parts of the Kawarau Gorge near the mining centre. None are as well known as the Shotover Jet, as interesting as the Skippers Canyon Jet, or as scenic as the Dart River trips, with little to choose between them, but if hanging on for dear life as the boat spins and gets close to gorge walls or river rocks gets you going then all offer a pretty equal thrill quotient. Also bear in mind that even the slightest rise in fuel prices seems to have an effect on the prices of these trips, though strangely when the prices fall nothing changes.

Rafting

The majority of jetboat operators stick to fairly flat water, leaving the rough stuff for **whitewater rafting**. The same two rivers – the Kawarau and the Shotover – are commercially rafted from Queenstown. The most reliable of the two is a 7km section of the large-volume **Kawarau River**, negotiating four Grade III–IV rapids (exciting but not truly frightening; see "Basics", p.56, for details of river grading) and culminating in the potentially nasty Chinese Dog Leg, said to be the longest commercially rafted rapid in New Zealand. Being lake-fed, its flow is relatively steady, though it peaks in spring and drops substantially towards the end of summer.

In contrast, the fourteen-kilometre rafted section of the Grade III–IV **Shotover River** flows straight out of the mountains and its level fluctuates considerably, thereby affecting its raftability. In winter the lack of sunlight reaching the depths of the canyon makes it too cold for most people (though some companies do run shorter and more expensive helicopter-access trips), while in late summer the flow can be too insubstantial to safely raft some rapids. If one operator deems the river to be unsafe for rafting, then no trips are run – the upshot of an agreement reached after seven deaths had occurred on the river since 1990. During subsequent investigations, the whole industry was condemned for its appalling standards of **safety** and training. Standards have undoubtedly improved – and, of course, thousands of people do these trips every year without incident – but you should bear in mind that rafting, in common with other adrenalin-charged sports, always entails a degree of risk. The Shotover in particular is a demanding river: revelling in names such as Mother Rapid and The Toilet, the rapids reach their apotheosis in the Mother-in-Law rapid, often bypassed at low water by diverting through the 170-metre Oxenbridge Tunnel (see p.857).

Trips on the Kawarau River take around four hours with a little over an hour on the water; those on the Shotover last an hour longer, with most of the extra time given over to more rafting. Rationalization during the late 1990s means there are essentially just three Queenstown rafting companies, operating on both rivers and offering pretty much the same **package**, ferrying punters by bus to an out-of-town base where they kit you out in a wetsuit and provide showers afterwards. **Prices** vary considerably, but expect to pay around $120 for Kawarau trips and $130–170 to ride the Shotover. Note that rafting is usually limited to those over **thirteen years of age**. **Booking** tends to be done directly with the main operators: Queenstown Rafting Co. (Ⓣ03/442 9792), who also run trips booked through Challenge Rafting (Ⓣ03/442 7319); Extreme Green Rafting (Ⓣ03/442 8517); and Queenstown Rafting (Ⓣ03/442 9792).

For those preferring a gentler rafting experience, Extreme Green run the Grade I–II Upper Shotover (around $150) after flying in to a backcountry station; and Family Adventures (Ⓣ03/442 5112) drive into the Skippers Canyon then raft the same stretch of river with oar-rafts, so you don't even need to paddle ($170).

River surfing, whitewater sledging and canyoning

Through the summer months (roughly mid-Sept to mid-May) the rafted section of the Kawarau River has traditionally been a playground for the parallel sports of whitewater sledging and river surfing. Unfortunately, the floods of November 1999 have altered the riverbed and taken some of the edge off the experience by forcing operators to move to a less thrilling section of river lower downstream; though this may change in time. In both cases, small groups are equipped with a board or sledge, a padded wetsuit, a helmet and fins, then led downstream and encouraged to view their independence and freedom of movement as virtues rather than hazards. Given that you're about to be bashed about in various rivers, and that conditions change very rapidly, it's important to note that these activities are for strong confident swimmers only.

River surfing involves floating downstream, grasping a foam boogie board and surfing as many as possible of the rapids' standing waves. While rafters bob around high up on their inflatable perches with little water contact, river surfers get right in the thick of it: what look like ripples to rafters become huge waves and the serious rapids can be thoroughly daunting, as froth engulfs you on all sides. Three- to four-hour trips are run by two companies (generally mid-Oct to April, both offering roughly the same with 1hr 30min in the water: Serious Fun (Ⓣ0800/737 468; $119 including T-shirt) who run the bouncy section twice, and Mad Dog River Boarding (Ⓣ03/442 9708; $119) who do a single longer run adding in rope swings and jet-skiing along the flat section.

Largely the same techniques are used in **whitewater sledging**. Suited primarily to shallow, rocky rivers, this involves grasping the handles of a foam or plastic "sledge" and snuggling arms and upper body down into a streamlined shape. The extra buoyancy gives a better roller-coaster ride over the waves and greater manoeuvrability for catching eddies, though surfing is more difficult, and rocks close to the surface will bang your legs. Trips are run by Wanaka-based Frogz Have More Fun (Ⓣ0800/338 737; $109 from Queenstown; 1hr on the water).

If either of these sports appeal then you'll probably also fancy **canyoning** with 12 Mile Delta (Ⓣ0800/22 696, Ⓦwww.xiimile.co.nz) or Deep Canyon (Ⓣ03/443 7922, Ⓔdeepcanyon@xtra.co.nz), who take small groups down verdant narrow canyons walking in streams, swimming across pools, sliding down rocks and jumping off cliffs all suitably protected by wetsuit, helmet and climbing harness. For $105 you get three hours away from Queenstown, around half that time in the water (morning and afternoon), while for $175 you get into the Matukituki Valley for a full day trip.

Paragliding, hang-gliding, skydiving, fly-by-wire, live-wire, and scenic flights

A fine day with a little breeze is all it needs to fill the skies above Queenstown with people paragliding. Upwards of a dozen operators take folk **tandem paragliding** from the prime jump site, Bob's Peak, immediately above town and reached by the Skyline Gondola. In recent years they've all banded together and operate a system not unlike a taxi rank; so all you do is pay your way up the Skyline Gondola then stand in line until it is your turn. By handing over $160 you then get the next paraglider in the queue for your jump, which typically lasts ten to fifteen minutes. How many acrobatic manoeuvres are executed is largely down to you, your jump guide and the conditions. If you don't see anyone in the air during the main 9am–5pm operating times then the conditions aren't right and you don't need to trouble yourself with the Gondola ride.

There's more of a bird-like quality to **tandem hang-gliding**, where you and your instructor are harnessed in a prone position under the wing of a hang-glider and execute a number of progressively steep turns as you soar down from Coronet Peak to the Flight Park on Malaghans Road 700 metres below. Skytrek Hang Gliding (ⓣ03/442 6311; around $160 for 12–15min in the air) are the longest-standing operator running several flights a day throughout the year, sometimes launching from The Remarkables. They pick up from Queenstown and also offer a develop-yourself roll of shots taken from a wing-tip camera ($20).

Paragliding while being towed behind a boat goes by the name of **parasailing**, an activity offered by Parafly, Main Town Pier (ⓣ03/442 8507; Aug–May daily 9am–5pm), who run a large motorboat saddled with a small helipad. For $69 each, you (and a buddy if you wish) are winched out on a rope until you reach a height of 100m above the lake surface and, after ten minutes admiring the scenery, winched back in again, theoretically still dry.

A touch more down to earth are the excellent **Live Wire** adventure-climbing, nerve-jangling challenges including a suspended climbing wall, a trapeze jump, cable bridges and rope obstacles that are set up to freak you out and buoy you up (ⓣ03/441 6711, ⓦwww.livewire.com). The theory is simple: take several team- and confidence-building adventure activities that gradually become more difficult and/or scary and that look as though they originated as part of an army assault course, suspend them 10m off the ground, with views over a cliff-drop to the river so that they look a lot higher, and get (always safety harnessed) punters to do them for $80. It is terrifying, safe fun and does put you in the mood for bungy and/or sky-diving adventures.

Queenstown is an expensive place to go **tandem skydiving** but the scenery does go some way in compensation. Ultimate JumpSkydive Tandem (around $250; ⓣ021/325 961) take twenty minutes to reach an altitude of 2500m, from where you get around 25 seconds' freefall over Lake Wakatipu, landing by the foot of the Remarkables some five minutes later. Another airborne possibility includes a 25-minute spin in a Pitt Special **stunt plane** with Actionflite (ⓣ03/442 9708; $215).

The majority of Queenstown visitors who take scenic **helicopter flights** do so as part of a combination deal alongside rafting or bungy jumping, though if you have the cash to spare you might want to try landing at the top of the Remarkables (20min; $150) with Southern Lakes Helicopters (ⓣ03/442 3016), or a similar trip with the other main operator, The Helicopter Line (ⓣ03/442 3034 & 0800/500 575).

There's yet one more way to get airborne, and a novel one currently only offered in New Zealand, the **Fly By Wire** adventure ride (ⓣ025/300 474,

△ Post Office, Arrowtown

Ⓦwww.flybywire.co.nz; $145). Boasting definite petrolhead appeal, this involves piloting a kind of miniature plane which is tethered by a hundred-metre leash to a fixed point on a wire strung between two hills. Loaded with a seven-minute charge of fuel, there's free rein to circle around, gaining height (up to almost 100m) and swooping down, potentially reaching 170km per hour. Once the fuel cuts out you drift back to earth. Trips from Queenstown out to the site (on private property) run 2–3 times daily, and videos of your flight are available (around $30).

Horse riding, off-road driving and mountain biking

Superb scenery makes Queenstown a great place to go **horse riding**. Good-value trips are run from Shotover Stables on Malaghans Road, 7km north of town (Ⓣ03/442 7486); their treks ($55; 1hr 30min) emphasize local history, exploring gold-mining relics down by the Shotover riverbed and often visiting the old mining tunnel on St Kilda Hill. Alternatively there are a couple of horse-riding companies running out of Glenorchy (see p.878).

If you feel more comfortable with horsepower rather than just a nag then try guided **off-road driving**, with either four or two wheels, with Off Road Adventure Bikes (Ⓣ03/442 7858, Ⓦwww.offroad.co.nz; $119 guided trip), and enjoy their back country trip (2hrs to a half day) up the back of Queenstown Hill. For those wishing to relinquish control completely there are a number of 4WD vehicles on offer where the driver/guides take a gentler more informative approach to the countryside: Goldseekers Tours (Ⓣ03/442 5949; $85); Nomad Safaris (Ⓣ03/442 6699; $75–120); Skippers Canyon Herritage Tours (Ⓣ03/442 5949; $82); and Skippers Grand Canyon (see above).

The remaining option is to take the strain yourself with Gravity Action (book through Backpacking Specialists Ⓣ03/442 8178; mid-Nov to March) who run exhilarating **mountain-biking** trips ($69, with over 2hr in the saddle), descending almost 600m down a narrow track which, until a better road was pushed through in 1888, was the only route into Skippers Canyon. Alternatively there's Vertigo Heli Adventures (Ⓣ03/442 6393, Ⓦwww.heli-adventures.co.nz; $195), who use rotor blades to get up big hills and then bike down. For something less adrenalin-fuelled, consider Queenstown-based Adventure Biking (Ⓣ03/442 9708), who lead mountain-bike trips to the historic gold towns of Seferstown (3–4hr; around $50) and Macetown (4–5hr; around $65). For any other variations on the adventure and touring theme check Listings (see p.872).

Eating

You can eat well in Queenstown. Some restaurants try, and usually fail, to be all things to all people, but those that concentrate on one cuisine shine, with **prices** to match. An increasing number of places are making the most of Queenstown's summer climate, spilling out onto the pedestrianized streets or stretching out along the waterfront, where you can sit and watch the *Earnslaw* glide in. **Breakfast** and **snack** places generally close by 6pm, though some serve early **dinners**, while restaurants often double up as bars as the evening wears on. A lot of national and international food outlets are attracted to the area but, almost without exception, they are worth avoiding in favour of the home grown eateries and bars.

With the opening of Queenstown's first large **supermarket**, just five minutes' walk along Gorge Road from town, grocery prices came more-or-less into line with city prices.

Breakfasts, cafés and snacks

Bean to Tea 42A Shotover St. Greek-style friezes decorate this café, open daily for breakfast, lunch and afternoon tea, and serving good strong beverages and tasty snacks at reasonable prices, including homemade muesli, quiches and salads.
Gourmet Express Bay Centre, Shotover St. About the nearest you'll get in New Zealand to a genuine American diner, with pancakes, French toast, all-day breakfasts, burgers and sandwiches at reasonable prices. Open daily & licensed.
Habebes Wakatipu Arcade, Beach St. Hole-in-the-wall vegetarian and Lebanese daytime café serving Queenstown's best felafel, tabouleh and Kiwi variations on Middle Eastern dishes, as well as juicy lamb and chicken kebabs,daily.
Ken's Noodle Café 37 Camp St. Small and hectic east Asian joint serving an inexpensive menu of miso soup, tempura and a stack of noodle dishes daily until 9pm.
Lakeside Café Wakatipu Arcade, Beach St. Lively breakfast and lunch spot with excellent muffins, sandwiches, soups and cakes served in bright folk-art surroundings or outdoors by the lake.
Naff Caff 1/66 Shotover St. A relaxed daytime café that's great for hanging out over some of the best coffee in town, notably the "mega mucho" strong cappuccino, and stick-shaped tea-bags. There's also a good range of muffins and Danishes for breakfast and, at lunch, they do pies, quiches,paninis and salmon and cream-cheese bagels, and there's an open-air terrace at the back.
Old Man Rock 15 The Mall, beneath *Chico's* (see "Bars and Clubs", p.870). Café/bar with good-quality food and great coffee. Turns into a club in the evenings.
Queenstown Bakery 15 Shotover St. Not so much known for its fantastic baking as the fact that it's open 24hr in the summer and feeds the post-club crowd with cheap pies, cakes, breakfasts and all the usual moreish fare.
Take 5 Steamer Wharf, at the end away from the centre of town, Beach St. The best coffee in town, excellent juices, fine toasted bagels and sandwiches, and newspapers and mag's galore in this tiny little all-day café.
Vudu 23 Beach St. One of Queenstown's groovier cafés with booths, comfy chairs and loads of recent magazines to while away half an hour, which is usually about the time it takes to get served. The place is strong on inexpensive breakfasts, quiches, panini, scrumptious muffins and good coffee, plus more substantial fare like chicken wraps, steak sandwiches and pasta.

Restaurants

Avanti 20 The Mall. Cheery Italian place whose reasonable food at modest prices ($18–32 for main courses) guarantees popularity, especially on Wednesday seafood nights. Gourmet pizzas and bowls of pasta go for $15–25.
Boardwalk 1st Floor, Steamer Wharf ☎03/442 5630. Swanky, expensive restaurant that often caters to very distinguished guests. It serves some of the freshest seafood in town, imaginatively prepared and often with delicate Asian touches. Dress smartly and expect to pay $27–35 for mains and then mortgage your kidneys for a bottle from their extensive wine list.
Bombay Place 68 Shotover St, beside *Naff Caff* ☎03/441 2886. Excellent little authentic Indian lunch and dinner restaurant serving all the usual suspects, plus some wonderful veggie options, at rock bottom prices. BYO and Licensed.
Bunker Cow Lane ☎03/441 8030. Behind the signless exterior is this very exclusive, stylish and swish fine-dining restaurant, with a funky upsatirs cocktail bar (see "Bars and Clubs", p.870). The food covers a broad range of influences and is not cheap, but it is beautifully presented and made from the best ingredients. Try the salmon wrapped in prosciutto , mescalin tossed chicken or a mezze platter, all just about under $32, and sample some of their sophisticated wine list to wash down the bill.
The Cow Cow Lane. Reasonably priced ($1&–25 a head) and popular pizzeria that fails to live up to its exalted reputation. A small range of fairly mainstream dishes are served in a cosy stone house; be prepared to share a table. BYO & licensed.
The Fishbone Bar and Grill 7 Beach St. Has been around for a long time, is deservedly famous and manages to combine two disciplines, as a high-class, quirky and fun fish-restaurant and a work-a-day fish-and-chip takeaway, favoured by all the locals in the area. Open for lunch and dinner, this restaurant offers the tastiest fish and the best value in town. BYO ($2 corkage) and licensed.
Gantley's Malaghans Rd, Arthur's Point ☎03/442 8999. Fancy, award-winning restaurant serving beautifully cooked modern Kiwi food with French leanings in an 1863 former inn 7km north of Queenstown. Mains start at $25 and the wine list is extensive. Reservations are essential, and courtesy transport from Queenstown is laid on.
Little India Bistro & Tandoori 11 Shotover St ☎03/442 5335. Tastefully decorated restaurant drawing influences from all over the sub-continent. Enormous banquets with spiciness adjusted to your taste are available ($24–30 per head), as are takeaways and home delivery. Licensed.

Lone Star Café and Bar 14 Brecon St. Cajun, Southern and Mexican dishes of immense proportions ($25–30) are served in a rowdy "saloon"; see opposite).

McNeill's Cottage Brewery Restaurant 14 Church St. Micro-brewery built into an 1880s stone building selling its own brews and a selection of wines as well as offering some excellent and cheap pizza and pasta dishes.

Tatler 5 The Mall ☎03/442 8372. Despite the name change this is still one of Queenstown's most fashionable and cosmopolitan restaurant/bars, serving crispy duck, Thai curry and lamb shanks as well as some sticky desserts. Eat early if you want to avoid the inevitable smoke and clamour as the place transforms itself into a lively jazz and wine bar (see opposite).

Tahuna 17 The Mall. Restaurant-cum-wine bar with a splendid array of breakfasts, brunches, lunches and dinners, from salmon cakes and poached eggs to garlic prawns, blue cod and traditional Greek salads, and none of it overly expensive.

Pasta Pasta Cucina 6 Brecon St ☎03/442 6762. Simply decorated Italian restaurant serving wonderful crisp pizza from the *manuka*-fired oven and great pasta dishes, try the smoked-chicken pizza with chilli and garlic oil, tomatoes and egg for lunch and dinner. Desserts and coffee are equally superb. Takeaway service too. Licensed.

Roaring Meg's 57 Shotover St ☎03/442 9676. Candlelit dining in an original Skippers gold-miners' cottage reconstructed here in 1922. The lamb is excellent, as is the smoked salmon and the *osso bucco* venison. Mains $25–30. Licensed.

Solera Vino 25 Beach St ☎03/442 6082. This small, licensed, elegant fine dining restaurant (on the first floor) is open daily from 6pm. The food is exceptional with a distinct French influence (around $30 mains), and a wine list as long as baguette.

Thai Siam 43 Beach St ☎03/442 4815. Straightforward Thai restaurant serving tasty food in simple surroundings at low prices. Try *tom yum* or *tom kar* soups ($14) or any of their fried rice, curry or noodle dishes ($11–17). Licensed and BYO.

Winnie Bagoes 7–9 The Mall. Excellent gourmet pizzas and pasta, good à la carte and blackboard menu, all at reasonable prices (see also "Bars and Clubs", p.871).

Drinking and nightlife

Despite its high profile and large number of visitors, Queenstown is still essentially a small town. Touring bands are relatively rare, there isn't much in the way of highbrow culture but at least the **clubs** have improved and can be great fun; though some are still bordering on backpacker cattle markets, while others remain just cheesy. That said, there is no shortage of lively **places to drink**, many doubling as restaurants early in the evening, when there are often a couple of **happy hours** to help get things going. The free *Mountain Scene* newspaper, found all over town, gives up-to-date **listings**, including the **movies** shown at the Embassy Cinema, 11 The Mall (infoline ☎03/442 9990). For full listings throughout any given week check out *The Source* (free), available in any bar or info centre, a booklet that provides cinema programmes and listings of what's on and what's best in the clubs and bars.

About the only regular entertainment is the **Maori Concert and Feast**, 1 Memorial St (Wed–Sat; reservations essential ☎03/442 8878; around $45, concert only $20), a five-course *hangi* buffet followed by an hour-long cabaret-style concert that takes a tongue-in-cheek romp through potted Maori mythology, the *haka*, *poi* dances and stick games. Yes, it is as corny as it sounds, but if you enter into the spirit of the thing, it can be fun.

Bars and clubs

Bardeaux 5 Eureka Arcade, daily 5pm–late. A funky little cocktail bar, intimate with big sofas, a broad selection of excellent whisky, wine and occasional jazz and blues bands.

Bunker Cow Lane ☎03/441 8030. A funky, stylish, upsatirs cocktail bar with cool music, open very late.

Chico's 15 The Mall ☎03/442 8439. One of the latest of all Queenstown's late bars, this joint starts to jump when the others close around 2am. Some form of live music most nights.

Debajo Cow Lane. A Catholic-icon-filled Spanish bar sitting uneasily beneath the *HMS* Britannia (an English-style pub), this could almost be Majorca.

Open until 5am with DJ music, mostly funky house and sexy grooves, some killer cocktails, a real lounge feel and some affordable snacks.
The Edge cnr Camp St & Robins Rd. Club that's often jumping to top forty and mainstream dance tunes. Very cheesy but fun.
The Loaded Hog Steamer Wharf, Beach Road. Typical of the national chain: good beer, well-priced, wholesome food, quirky decor, and Djs on Friday and Saturday evenings.
McNeill's Cottage Brewery Restaurant 14 Church St. Micro-brewery built into an 1880s stone building and usually selling at least three beers –a lager, a malty bitter and a dark stout-like brew – in the cosy bar or outside. They also serve a good selection of wines by the glass and run a happy hour (5–7pm), featuring their own brews at $3.50 per pint, as well as hosting an acoustic rock or blues session every Friday night.
Tatler 5 The Mall.Lively, cool, late-night jazz bar, with a balcony, that attracts people who want to be looked at, and serves some lovely wine, at a price.
Morrison's Stratton House, Beach St, next to the *Hard Rock Café* and above the restaurant. Lively new-ish bar with Irish beers, imported lagers and a 5–7pm happy hour.
Old Man Rock 15 The Mall, beneath *Chico's* (see above). Café/bar with good quality food and live music every second week.
Pig and Whistle Camp St, beside the post office. Traditional-style drink and good-value bar-meal flogger, with a DJ-run disco on Friday and Saturday nights.
Pog Mahone's 14 Rees St. Queenstown's established Irish bar, typically crowded with folk clamouring for draught Guinness and loosely-Irish bar meals. It is even fuller for the live Irish music and Celtic rock on acid, usually Fri, Sat and Sun.
Red Rock 48 Camp St ☎03/442 6850. Popular town bar with hints of a ski-lodge atmosphere and a good range of beers, a happy hour 7–8pm, and local rock and indie bands once a month (though at the height of the season they tend to play a little more often).
The Rattlesnake Room 14 Brecon St ☎03/442 9995. Part of the *Lone Star* complex (see "Eating", opposite), this upstairs bar is a rowdy spot for an early-evening drink with a happy hour (4–7pm), pool tables, and DJs Wed–Sun nights.
Surreal 7 Rees St. Early evening restaurant that soon transforms into a harder-edged club with Djs and occasional live music. The preferred sounds are house, techno, and big beat, which kick off after about 10.30pm.
Tardis cnr Cow Lane and Skyline Arcade. A little bar with a big heart serving drinks from 11am and then building to progressive DJ-cranked high NRG, free-style, jungle, drum'n'bass, as well as more simplistic dance music in the evenings (until 4am).
Winnie Bagoes 7–9 The Mall. Italian eating joint (see "Restaurants", opposite) with jazz or other bands, pool tables and thumping DJ-inspired music, which means it progressively becomes less restaurant-like later.
The World 27 Shotover St. One of the livelier clubs with a dedicated budget clientele here for the happy hours and adventure give-aways.

Listings

Airlines Air New Zealand Travel Centre, 41 Shotover St ☎03/441 1900.
Banks and exchange All major banks have a branch and ATM around the centre. Best bets for exchange services are Thomas Cook, in the AJ Hacket Building, cnr Camp St & The Mall (☎03/442 6403; daily: Oct–May 8am–8pm; June–Sept 8am–7pm); and the ANZ Bank, 81 Beach St (☎0800 180 921; daily 9am–9pm); Travelex, in the main visitor centre (same hours), also have reasonable rates.
Bike rental Outside Sports, cnr The Mall & Camp St (☎03/442 8883; 9am–9pm), rents out suspension-equipped mountain bikes with track information for $45–75 a day and $35–45 a half day – and also serves as a meeting place for keen off-roaders. More straightforward bikes go for $35 a day, or you can rent one-person scooters ($49 a day, $39 a half day), which require only a car licence and are fine for most purposes, but deemed unsuitable for Skippers Road. Bikes, tandems and scooters are also available from Queenstown Bike Hire, 25 Beach St (☎03/442 6039), at similar prices.
Buses Atomic Shuttles (☎03/442 8178) run to Christchurch, Dunedin and up the Coast to Greymouth; Catch-a-Bus (☎03/471 4103) operate a door-to-door service to Dunedin; InterCity (☎03/442 5628) operate the most extensive services to all major destinations; Kiwi Discovery (☎03/442 7340) run a fast service to Christchurch and minibuses to the major trailheads and Milford Sound; Kiwi Experience (☎03/442 9708) add a special Milford Sound run to their backpacker tour-bus setup; Magic Bus (☎03/442 8178) run through Queenstown en route from the West Coast to Dunedin; Southern Link Shuttles (☎03/442 8178) run to Dunedin, Christchurch and Picton;

Super Shuttle (ⓣ03/442 9803) meets planes from Queenstown's airport; and Wanaka Connexions (ⓣ0800/879 926) run the most direct service to Wanaka.

Camping and outdoor equipment At the Small Planet Recycling Co, 17 Shotover St (ⓣ03/442 6393; daily 10am–6pm), you can pick up used gear, including snowboards, ski gear, wetsuits, bikes, camping and tramping gear and books – all at good prices and with competitive buy-back deals. If you've got something to get rid of, they'll hawk it for 20 percent commission. See also "Ski rental", below.

Car rental Typical summer rates from the major firms start at $90 a day, rising to around $150 for 4WD vehicles. Smaller companies generally offer better deals, with rates for cars of $45–70 a day for week-long rentals, and around $80 per day for 4WD vehicles with snow chains included. Even in high summer you should be able to get something for $50 a day with unlimited kilometres, though for short rentals (for example a 2-day rental to go to Milford Sound) $70 a day is more likely. Apex, 18 Shotover St (ⓣ0800/531 111, 03/441 0107); Budget, cnr Camp St & Shotover St (ⓣ03/442 9274) and the airport (ⓣ03/442 3450); NZ Rent a Car, cnr Camp St & Shotover St (ⓣ03/442 7465); Queenstown Car Rental, 18 Shotover St (ⓣ03/442 9220); Reg's Rentals, 23 Beach St (ⓣ03/442 6039); Rent-a-Dent, 48 Shotover St (ⓣ03/442 9922 & 0800/736 823).

Guided walks Arrowtown Lodge and Hiking Co (ⓣ03/442 1101, ⓕ442 1108, ⓦwww.arrowtown-lodge.co.nz) run a series of guided walks around the Queenstown, Glenorchy and Arrowtown areas, ranging from gentle scenic and historic walks (short half day; $50) to reasonably energetic alpine tramps (full day; $150).

Internet access Fierce competition means good rates, fast connections and long opening hours, often until 10pm or later. Places to look out for are *E Café*, 50 Shotover St; *Budget Communications*, 2nd floor, O'Connell's Mall (ⓔbudgetc@xtra.co.nz); *Internet Outpost*, 27 Shotover St (ⓔoutpost.queenstown@xtra.co.nz); and *Queenstown's Visitor Bureau*, 26 Shotover St 7.30am–midnight.

Library cnr Shotover St & Gorge Rd.

Medical treatment Queenstown Medical Centre, cnr Stanley St & Shotover St (ⓣ03/442 7301, 442 3053 for after-hours doctor), and Lakes District Hospital, 20 Douglas St, Frankton (ⓣ03/442 3053).

Pharmacy Wilkinsons Pharmacy, The Mall (ⓣ03/442 7313), is open daily from 8.30am to 10pm.

Police 11 Camp St (ⓣ03/442 7900).

Post office The main post office, cnr Camp St Ballarat St (Mon–Fri 9am–5pm) has poste restante facilities.

Scenic flights Air Fiordland ⓣ03/442 3404; Air Wakatipu ⓣ03/442 3048, ⓔqueenstown@flying.co.nz; Milford Sound Scenic Flights ⓣ03/442 3065 & 0800/101 767.

Ski rental Outside Sports, cnr The Mall & Camp St & (ⓣ03/442 8883), rent skis, boots and poles from $28 per day for the basic kit to $45 for top-quality gear; snowboards go for $30 a day, as does telemark equipment. The excellent Brown's, 39 Shotover St & 4 Brecon St (ⓣ03/442 4003) offer similar rates on new gear, deliver to your hotel and also do overnight tuning.

Taxis Alpine Taxi ⓣ03/442 6666 & 0800/730 066; and Queenstown Taxis ⓣ03/442 7788 & 0800/477 888.

Thomas Cook Inside The Station, cnr Camp St & Shotover St ⓣ03/442 6403.

Tours and booking agencies In Queenstown, the frenzied tour industry means that pretty much anywhere in the southern half of the South Island is fair game for a flight or a bus trip. Stewart Island and Mount Cook are both possibilities for visitors in a massive hurry, but those with a little more time on their hands will find trips to the Milford Sound area or a mosey around the old gold towns more rewarding.

Arrowtown and Macetown

The former gold-rush settlement of **ARROWTOWN** seems perched on the brink of tour-bus hell as day-trippers from Queenstown, 23km to the south-east, swarm around the sheepskin, greenstone and gold of its souvenir shops. But Arrowtown manages to retain the spirit of a living community, with the grocers' shops, pubs and post office fitfully coexisting alongside the gift-wrapped centre. The best way to appreciate Arrowtown is to linger on after the crowds have gone, leaving behind a peaceful farming town at the confluence of the Arrow River and Bush Creek. The sheltering hills give Arrowtown parched summers and snowy winters, thrown into sharp relief by autumn, when the deciduous trees planted by the mining community cast golden shadows on a central knot of picturesque miners' cottages.

Arrowtown's permanent population is only around 1200 but in summer, when holiday homes are full and tourists arrive in force, it comes close to regaining its 7000-strong peak attained during the **gold rush**. There is some debate as to whether American William Fox was actually the first to discover alluvial gold in the Arrow River in 1862, but there is no doubt that he dominated proceedings hereabouts, managing to keep the find secret while he recovered over 100kg of gold. Jealous prospectors tried to follow him to the lode, but he gave them the slip, on one occasion leaving his tent and provisions behind in the middle of the night. The town subsequently bore his name until Foxes gave way to Arrowtown. The eponymous river became known as the richest for its size in the world – a reputation which drew Chinese miners (for more on which, see the box on p.874), who lived in the now partly restored **Arrowtown Chinese Settlement**, and enticed prospectors to the surrounding hills, where brothers Charley and John Mace set up **Macetown**, now an appealing ghost town.

As prospectors pushed further up the Arrow and Bush Creek, they began to populate **the valleys**; scattered communities sprang up along the banks, but were abandoned just as suddenly, leaving telltale poplar, rowan and willows to be reclaimed by nature. Where settlers' cottages once stood, **fruit** trees have colonized the riverbanks, and in autumn apples, pears and plums weigh down the branches, and bushes of blackberry, blackcurrant, gooseberry, raspberry and elderberry become rampant. There are few specific sights, but you can easily spend a lazy afternoon gorging on fruit and trying to identify the overgrown sites of houses. The surrounding hills are speckled with **rose bushes**: according to folklore, these were planted by miners seeking vitamin C (rosehips are one of the richest sources); others contend that they were planted primarily for their root systems, which could be fashioned into briar pipes.

Arrival and information

Two **buses** run from Queenstown to Arrowtown, both departing from The Top of the Mall on Camp Street in Queenstown and stopping outside the library on Buckingham Street in Arrowtown. The scheduled Arrow Express (Ⓣ03/442 1900; 3–5 daily; 25min; $10 one way, $18 return) runs mostly via Frankton and Queenstown airport, though some services go via the Shotover Jet and Millbrook Resort. The Double Decker Bus Tour uses a red London bus to operate Queenstown-based **tours** (Ⓣ03/442 6067; daily 10am & 2pm; 2hr 30min; $27), visiting the Kawarau bungy bridge en route and spending an hour in Arrowtown.

Arrowtown's **visitor centre** is inside the foyer of the Lakes District Museum at 49 Buckingham St (daily 8.30am–5pm, except from May-Oct when it's 9am–5pm; Ⓣ03/442 1824, Ⓔmuseum@queenstown.co.nz), where you can pick up an *Historic Arrowtown* booklet ($2.50), and the informative *Arrowtown Chinese Settlement* booklet ($2.50). Bike rental is available from Arrowtown Wines and Spirits on Ramshaw Lane ($25 per half day)

Accommodation

To see Arrowtown at its best, you really need to **stay** the night; happily, there's plenty of accommodation, much of it especially affordable for lone travellers, with single rooms just over half the price of doubles.

Arrowtown's hidden Chinese history

The initial wave of miners who came to Arrowtown in the early 1860s were fortune-seekers intent on a fast buck. When gold was discovered on the West Coast, most of them hot-footed it to Greymouth or Hokitika, leaving a much-depleted community that lacked the economic wherewithal to support the businesses which had mushroomed around the mining communities.

The solution, as it had been ten years earlier on the Victorian goldfields of Bendigo and Ballarat in Australia, was to import **Chinese labour**. The first Chinese, who principally came from the Canton delta region of Kwangtung (now known as Guangdong), arrived in Otago in 1866, their number reaching 5000 by 1870. The community settled along Bush Creek, its **segregation** from the main settlement symptomatic of the inherent racism of the time – something which also manifested itself in working practices that forced the Chinese to pick over abandoned mining claims and work the tailings of European miners. Even Chinese employed on municipal projects such as the Presbyterian church were paid only half the wages paid to Europeans doing the same job.

A ray of light is cast amid the prevailing bigotry by contemporary newspaper reports, which suggest that many citizens found the Chinese conduct of their business "upright and straightforward" and their demeanour "orderly and sober" – perhaps surprisingly in what was an almost entirely male community. Most came with starry-eyed dreams of earning their fortune and returning home so, initially at least, few brought their families; a process of chain **migration** later brought wives, children and then members of the extended family. Few realized their dreams, but around ninety percent did return home, many in a box, driven into an early grave by overwork and poor living conditions. Many more were driven out in the early 1880s when recession brought racial jealousies to a head, resulting in the enactment of a punitive poll tax on foreign residents. There was little workable gold by this time and those Chinese who stayed mostly became market gardeners or merchants and drifted away, mainly to Auckland, though the Arrowtown community remained viable into the 1920s. Once the Chinese had left or died, the Bush Creek settlement was **abandoned** and largely destroyed by repeated flooding.

Hotels and motels

Golden View Motel 48 Adamson Drive Ⓣ & Ⓕ03/442 1833, reservations Ⓣ0800/246 538, Ⓔgoldenview@southnet.co.nz. Fairly standard motel with well-equipped rooms, an outdoor pool and mountain bikes to rent at modest rates. ❹

Millbrook Resort Malaghans Rd, on the outskirts of town Ⓣ03/441 7000 & 0800/800 604, Ⓦnz.com/queenstown/millbrook. A highly-rated 18-hole golf course, several bars and restaurants, and luxury accommodation in suites and chalets make this one of New Zealand's more exclusive resort complexes – and account for its popularity with Queenstown tour groups. ❾

Settlers Motel 22 Hertford St Ⓣ03/442 1734 & 0800/803 801,Ⓔettlersmotel@clear.net.nz. A lace-and-Laura Ashley place that has earned numerous plaudits. Studios and one- and two-bedroom units are all fitted out to a high standard, with decorations based on traditional pioneer motifs. ❹–❺

Viking Lodge Motel 21 Inverness Crescent Ⓣ & Ⓕ03/442 1765, reservations 0800/181 900, Ⓔviking@inq.co.nz. One of Arrowtown's best-value motels, featuring an outdoor pool and a cluster of one- and two-bedroom A-frame chalets with well-equipped kitchens and VCRs. ❹

B&Bs and homestays

Anne & Arthur Gormack 18 Stafford St Ⓣ03/442 1747, Ⓔa.gormack@xtra.co.nz. Comfortable, well-appointed rooms in a spacious modern homestay five minutes' walk from the town centre. Has a pool and badminton court, plus long views over the Arrow Basin. ❺

Arrowtown Lodge 7 Anglesea St Ⓣ03/442 1101, Ⓦwww.arrowtownlodge.co.nz. Four modern, comfortable and tastefully furnished cottages built from recycled nineteenth-century mud-bricks, each with en-suite bathroom and mountain views. Breakfast is served out on the sunny deck, and can be followed by guided walks (see Queenstown "Listings", p.872). There's also free Internet access and laundry. ❺–❻

Polly-Anna Cottage 43 Bedford St ⓣ03/442 1347. Homestay in a tidily restored hundred-year-old miner's cottage with a sun deck and manicured lawns; close to the centre. ❹

Speargrass Lodge Speargrass Flat Rd, 5km from Arrowtown ⓣ03/442 1417, ⓔspeargrass@xtra.co.nz. One of the most attractive, spacious and luxurious country B&Bs around, surrounded by landscaped lawns and mature exotic trees. Simply decorated rooms are all en suite and there's free use of mountain bikes and a dinghy on nearby Lake Hayes. Breakfast is included. ❻

Hostels and campsites

Arrowtown Holiday Park 11 Suffolk St ⓣ & ⓕ03/442 1876. Marginally the handiest and largest of the town's two campsites with showers and laundry available to non-guests ($3 each) and a tennis court. Tent/powered sites $10, standard cabins ❷, tourist flats ❸–❹

Hippo Hideaway 24 McMillan Rd, Arthurs Point ⓣ03/442 5785, half way between Queenstown and Arrowtown. A simple, friendly little get-away-from-it-all bolt hole. You'll need your own transport and to take some food, but otherwise it's ideal. Dorms ❶, rooms ❷–❸

Royal Oak Hotel 46 Buckingham St ⓣ03/442 1700. Old hotel in the centre of town with the cheapest beds in town in simple rooms sharing facilities, along with some singles.❶–❸

The Town

Twin rows of sycamores and oaks planted in 1867 have grown to overshadow the tiny miners' cottages along the photogenic **Avenue of Trees**, Arrowtown's most recognizable image. Most of the sixty or so cottages were built towards the end of the nineteenth century and they're unusually small and close together, the chronic lack of timber undoubtedly being a factor.

A visit to the informative nearby Lakes District Museum (see below) is probably the best preparation for a stroll around the **Arrowtown Chinese Settlement** (part of the Otago Goldfields Park; unrestricted entry). This string of heavily restored buildings hugging a narrow willow-draped section of Bush Creek at the western end of Buckingham Street is easily the best-preserved of New Zealand's Chinese communities, and provides an insight into a fascinating, if shameful, episode in the country's history (see box opposite). Many of the buildings were originally built as temporary retreats from peripatetic prospecting and to provide shelter during the harsh winters, only becoming permanent homes as miners aged. With tin, sod and timber the principal building materials, little was left standing when an archeological dig was begun in 1983, and most of the dwellings languish in a state of graceful decay. Some schist, mortar and corrugated-iron buildings fared rather better and five of these have been restored. The best is **Ah-Lum's Store**, built in typical Canton delta style in 1883 for Wong Hop Lee and leased from 1909 to 1927 to Ah-Lum, one of the pillars of the Chinese community in its later years. By this time integration was making inroads: Ah-Lum sold European as well as Chinese goods, and operated an opium den and bank. Wood panelling divides the store into low-roofed rooms with mezzanine areas above, perhaps used for opium smoking. Beyond that it is mostly stone plinths and chimney breasts fleetingly brought back to life by interpretation panels.

Artefacts found during the 1983 Chinese Settlement dig are displayed inside the former BNZ building of 1875 that now operates as the **Lakes District Museum**, 49 Buckingham St (daily 9am–5pm; $4), a bits and bobs museum which nevertheless succeeds in bringing local history to life. Not surprisingly, it mainly covers the lives of the gold-miners and their families, with a particular emphasis on the Chinese community and the archeological excavations. There's also a feature on opium smoking, which remained legal in New

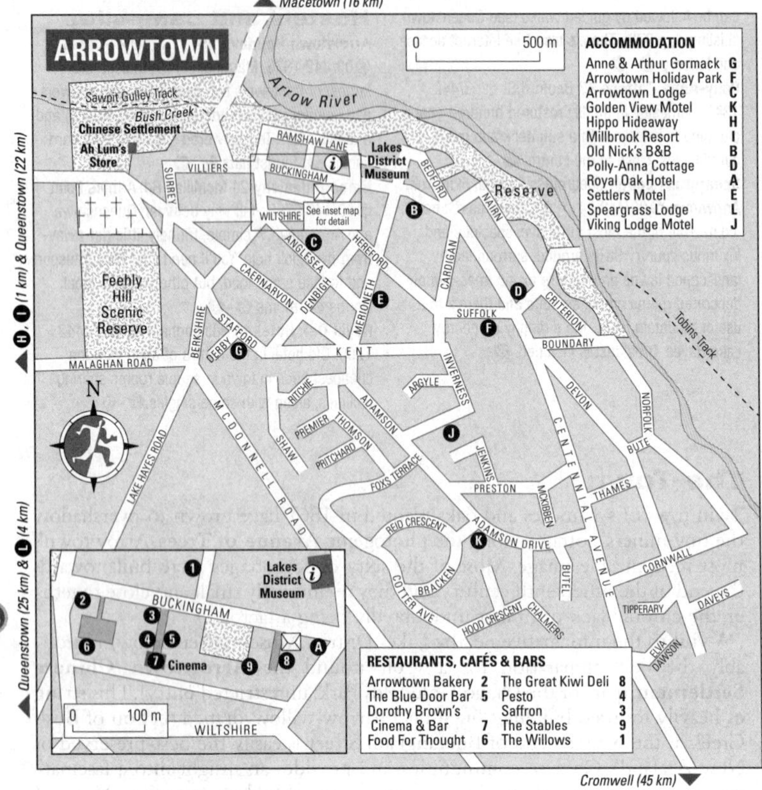

Zealand until 1901, some twenty years after games of chance – *fantan* and *pakapoo* – were proscribed. Technophiles also get a look in, with displays on the quartz-reef mining used at Macetown and on the country's earliest hydro scheme, which once supplied mining communities in Skippers and Macetown with power. Down in the basement are displays on the old brewery, a bakery, a print room with a hot metal press and a school room, which all add a little more of the community feel to the whole venture.

Around Arrowtown: Macetown

As gold fever swept through Otago in the early 1860s, prospectors fanned out, clawing their way up every creek and gully in search of a flash in the pan. In 1862, alluvial gold was found at Twelve Mile, sparking the rush to what later became known as **Macetown** (part of the Otago Goldfields Park; unrestricted entry), now a ghost town of three buildings and a popular destination for mountain bikers, horse trekkers and trampers (see box opposite). On first acquaintance, it isn't a massively exciting place, but the grassy plateau makes a great free camping spot, sheltered by low stone walls and willow, sycamore and apple trees. The only facilities are long-drop toilets and river water, but walking in here with tent and provisions, and spending a day or two exploring the

The Arrowtown–Macetown Circuit

The sixteen-kilometre 4WD road up the Arrow Creek from Arrowtown to Macetown is the district's premier biking and trekking route, but walkers have the edge by being able to include the road as part of the fairly strenuous, full-day **Arrowtown–Macetown Circuit** (8hr; 32km).

The walk is best done in the months from **Christmas to Easter**, after the winter snows have melted and the swollen Arrow River has subsided a little, making the 22 river crossings on the Arrow Creek a little easier – though even in summer, access can be problematic after rain. The *Macetown and the Arrow Gorge* booklet makes a good companion for the route, interpreting sights along the way.

The walk starts by the confluence of the Arrow River and Bush Creek, following the northern bank of the latter westwards, then skirting the base of German Hill and branching up Sawtooth Gully. The gully emerges through open hill country to Eichardt's Flat, a terrace named after a local farmer and brother of the Queenstown hotelier. At this point, about an hour out of Arrowtown, you can pursue the **Sawpit Gully variation** east down Sawpit Gully to meet the Arrow River road and Arrowtown, thus making a two- to three-hour circuit.

From the Sawpit Gully junction, the Macetown path contours gradually around to the **Big Hill** saddle, with its expansive views back to Lake Hayes and the Remarkables. The route then drops steeply towards Eight Mile Creek, the path becoming indistinct – marked by infrequent poles – as it traverses soggy and potentially ankle-twisting country. After three or four hours, you stumble across the Arrow Creek road, just a couple of kilometres short of **Macetown**.

When you've had your fill of Macetown, follow the Arrow Creek road back to Arrowtown, occasionally diverting on to paths that run parallel to the road for respite from the dust.

old mines and grubstake claims, is the best way to experience the place's unique atmosphere.

Macetown's story is one of boom and bust: at its peak, it boasted a couple of hotels, a post office and a school; but when the gold ran out, it couldn't fall back on farming in the way that Arrowtown and Queenstown did and, like Skippers, it died. All that remains of the town itself are a couple of stone buildings – the restored schoolmaster's house and the bakery – and a smattering of wooden shacks. The surrounding creeks and gullies are littered with the twisted and rusting remains of gold batteries, making a fruitful hunting ground for industrial archeology fans; the area is covered in some detail in the *Macetown and the Arrow Gorge* booklet ($4, available from the Lakes District Museum in Arrowtown).

Macetown is a full-day (or overnight, if you want to camp among the ruins) outing either on foot (see box, opposite), by **mountain bike** (you'll need to rent one from Queenstown unless you have your own), or on a **4WD** trip with Outback Tours (☎03/442 7386; 4–5hr; $75).

Eating and entertainment

In the last few years, Arrowtown's culinary scene has almost caught up with Queenstown, not so much in numbers but in variation and quality on offer. Further afield there is also refined dining at the *Gibbston Valley Winery and Cheesery*, 14km away on SH6 (☎03/442 6910), whose fine restaurant is open for lunch and dinner; or you could splash out at one of the swanky restaurants in the *Millbrook Resort* complex on Malaghans Road (☎03/441 7000), a few kilometres outside Arrowtown.

Finally, if your visit is during the week leading up to Easter, you can partake in the **Autumn Festival** (enquiries to the visitor centre), with all manner of historic walks, street theatre and hoe-downs, much of it free.

Arrowtown Bakery in the Ballarat Arcade on Buckingham St. Fantastic bakery that produces a prodigious range of wonderful and unusual pies and wonderful breads, from Italian and sourdough to gluten-free and organic; try their "football", a kind of soft-bread calzone. Stop in at the café for lamb-and-kumera, duck-and-orange or oyster pies, some of their delicious ice cream or just a sandwich (daily 8am–5pm).

The Blue Door Bar owned by the same people and up the lane from *Saffron* (see below). Stylish, intimate and really very cool little bar in a 130year old cellar that once belonged to the general store. The bar has a cocktail feel but is informal and occasionally presents live, jazz, blues, Caribbean and Latin music, backed up by a smooth P.A. system with silky sounds.

Dorothy Brown's Cinema and Bar behind *Pesto and Saffron* and *The Blue Door Bar*, up a flight of steps ☎03/442 1968, ⓦwww.dorothybrowns.com. A charming small-scale cinema with stupendously comfortable seats, where some unusual and wonderful films get an airing, while the tiny attached bar dishes up booze and plates of cheese and olives. Quirky and almost too good to be true.

Food For Thought 4 Buckingham St. Small coffee shop and bar, tucked back off the street with courtyard seating and internet access. They do a nice line in breakfasts, including a Mexican burrito, all-day snacks and lunches.

The Great Kiwi Deli 44 Buckingham St. A deli cum all-day café with organic coffee and locally produced ingredients in the sandwiches, salads and juices. Lots of eat-in or takeaway options plus gluten free choices and BBQ grills on summer evenings. Licensed.

Saffron and Pesto 18 Buckingham St. Sam Neill, the film star, rates the *Saffron* half of this award-winning dual operation catering to all tastes as one of the best eating places on the South Island, and when you step upon their polished wood floors you'll have no difficulty seeing why. Equally suited to a coffee at the pavement tables, a lunchtime antipasto plate for two ($30), or fantastic classy meals. The evening meals, like duck curry, in *Saffron*, are worth every expensive penny, while the pasta and pizza dishes in the *Pesto* part of the operation are tasty and wholesome. Try the seasonal seafood and pasta, gourmet pizza, spiral pasta with gorgonzola, ham, rocket and onion and much much more. Licensed.

The Stables 28 Buckingham St ☎03/442 1818. Beautiful old stone building with outdoor seating where you can feast on classy bistro-style dishes, such as Thai chicken or stuffed capsicum, or just nip along for a Devonshire tea. Closed Mon.

The Willows Ramshaw Lane. A glorified New Zealand tea room with all that is good and bad in such an institution, but with the added bonus of a bookshop. Licensed, and doling out pizza, quiche, soup, cakes and coffee, all at decent prices.

Glenorchy and the major tramps

The tiny town of **GLENORCHY**, at the head of Lake Wakatipu 50km north-west of Queenstown, is quiet and supremely picturesque, making it a perfect retreat for a couple of days. For the majority of visitors, though, this still isn't remote enough, and for them Glenorchy is simply a staging post en route to some of the finest **tramping** New Zealand has to offer – a circuit of the Rees and Dart Rivers, the Routeburn Track and the Greenstone and Caples **tracks**.

Glenorchy and around

The Glenorchy region's fantastic scenery owes a debt to beds of ancient sea-floor sediments laid down some 220–270 million years ago and metamorphosed into the grey-green schists and *pounamu* (greenstone) of the Forbes and Humboldt mountains. The western and northern flanks of the Forbes Mountains were shaped by the Dart Glacier, now a relatively short tongue of ice which, at its peak 18,000 years ago, formed the root of the huge glacial system that gouged out the floor of Lake Wakatipu.

In pre-European times the plain beside the combined delta of the Rees (*Oware*) and Dart (*Oturu*) rivers was known as **Kotapahau**, "the place of revenge killing", a reference perhaps to fights between rival *hapu* over the esteemed *pounamu* littering an area centred on the bed of the Dart River. There's still greenstone up there, but most is protected within the bounds of the Mount Aspiring National Park, including a huge, 25-tonne boulder estimated to be worth some $15 million.

The first **Europeans** to penetrate the area were gold prospectors, government surveyors, and nearby runholders in search of fresh grazing. James McKerrow finished the first reconnaissance survey in 1863, about the same time as a party of five miners led by Patrick Caples made their way up the Dart River. The fledgling community of Glenorchy served these disparate groups, along with teams of sawmillers and workers from a mine extracting sheelite, a mineral used in the manufacture of armaments. Despite the lack of road access to Glenorchy, **tourists** began to arrive early this century, cruising across Lake Wakatipu on the TSS *Earnslaw*, before being decanted into charabancs for the 20km jolt north to the Arcadia homestead at **Paradise**. Disappointingly drawing its name from the locally abundant paradise ducks rather than its idyllic qualities, Paradise has nevertheless been deemed stunning enough to emulate the Rockies or the European Alps in numerous movies.

The **road from Queenstown** was eventually pushed through in 1962, opening up a fine lakeside drive that passes **Bob's Cove**, the best place to observe the lake's seiche, an ill-understood phenomenon which causes the lake level to cycle by around 150mm every five minutes. Glenorchy has remained defiantly rural, and while there has been a marked increase in tourist traffic since the road was finally sealed all the way through in 1997, the few tourist-oriented ventures barely disturb the bucolic atmosphere.

Arrival and information

Summer-only backpacker **buses** ply the Queenstown–Glenorchy route, charging around $15 for the one-hour run. Most frequent are those run by Backpacker Express (ⓣ03/442 9939, ⓦwww.glenorchyinfocentre.co.nz; 3–5 daily), though there are competing, and often cheaper, buses run by Upper Lake Wakatipu Tours (ⓣ03/442 9986).

The Backpacker Express is operated from the grounds of the *Glenorchy Holiday Park*, at 2 Oban St (ⓣ03/442 7178), which is also the one of the best sources of general **information** and the place to go for post-tramp **transport bookings**. Alternatively try the **DOC-run Glenorchy Visitor Centre**, at the corner of Mull and Oban streets (ⓣ03/442 9937, glenorchyvc@doc.govt.nz; Mon–Fri 9am–4.30pm, with a 1hr lunch break, in the summer Sat 10am–noon), which is also useful for the lowdown on tramping information.

Accommodation

After the rigours of the tramp, Glenorchy is a welcome sight and, considering its size, there is a reasonable range of accommodation to suit most budgets.

Glenorchy Holiday Park & Backpackers Oban St ⓣ03/442 7178, ⓔglenpark@queenstown.co.nz. This well-organized campsite is the cheapest place in town, with spacious tent ($8) and powered sites ($9), plus bunks, basic double or twin cabins and a self-contained unit. Non-residents can shower here for $3. Dorms ❶, cabins ❷, villa ❹

Glenorchy Hotel cnr Mull St & Argyll St ⓣ03/442 9902, ⓔglenorchy.hotel@xtra.co.nz. Good backpacker-style dorms, with communal kitchen and lounge, are hidden behind this hotel. From

November to April, plain double rooms – but with great views up the Dart Valley – are also available. Dorms without bedding ❶, rooms ❸–❹

Glen Roydon Outdoor Lodge cnr Mull St & Argyll St ⓣ & ⓕ03/442 9968. Good modern rooms with a nod to ski-lodge style, all sharing the comfortable guest lounge with its open fire, TV and videos. ❺

Mt Earnslaw Motels 87/89 Oban St ⓣ03/442 6993, ⓦwww.earnslaw.bizland.com. Well-kept, clean and spacious cabin-style units with a comfortable and homey feel run by very friendly and helpful people. This is Glenorchy's only motel, right in the heart of town. ❺

The Town and nearby activities

Glenorchy, though in recent years it has grown to meet the ever-increasing number of tourists, still doesn't amount to much – a petrol station, a post office, a couple of pubs and cafés, some accommodation and a grocery shop. To get a feel for the area and its geography, follow the 2km loop of the **Glenorchy Walkway** from the wharf at the end of Islay Street along the edge of Lake Wakatipu and through the wetlands around the town's lagoon, a pleasant way to soak up the mountain scenery at either end of the day. In town itself is the somewhat out of the ordinary Glenorchy Fur Products, Mull St (ⓦwww.glenorchy-fur.co.nz; Mon–Fri 9am–3pm), which produces all manner of sometimes surprising items from the fur and hide of one of New Zealand's biggest environmental pests, the possum.

Almost all the non-tramping visitors are here for the excellent **jetboating** trips up the **Dart River**, a two-hour journey which fully utilizes the jetboat's shallow-water capabilities, picking routes through braided river beds and finally entering a short gorge before turning round at Sandy Bluff on the edge of the Mount Aspiring National Park. The usual jetboating antics are duly performed, but the real star is the magnificent scenery, featuring snowcapped mountains and dense bush, which is most easily appreciated from the middle of the river. The highlight is the brief stop to walk (or jetboat if conditions are right) in to **Rockburn Chasm**, where a small tributary of the Dart has carved out a narrow, twisting canyon filled with calm, clear water. Dart River Safari (ⓣ03/442 4933 & 442 9992, ⓦwww.dartriver.co.nz) runs two or three daily trips from Glenorchy (2hr; $145) and Queenstown (5–6hr; $159). Their Backroad Safari (same prices) involves a ride in a 4WD coach, a twenty-minute bushwalk then the downstream jetboat ride.

Better still, combine the upstream section of the Dart River Safari with **canoeing** back downstream in Fun Yaks (ⓣ0800/386 925 & 03/442 9992, ⓦwww.funyaks.com), two- or three-person inflatable canoes carried upriver in the jetboats, then paddled down. Suitable even for absolute beginners, this is a gentle trip with no rapids and very little likelihood of an enforced swim. Trips run on demand, take nine hours return from Queenstown (6hr from Glenorchy) and cost $195 from either town, including lunch. Dart River Safari is part of the slick Shotover Jet operation, with all the production-line tourism and merchandising that that entails. If you'd prefer something a little more personal, go with Dart Wilderness Adventures (ⓣ03/442 9939, ⓔinfo@glenorchyinfocentre.co.nz), who currently charge $129 from Glenorchy for a similar jetboat run up to Sandy Bluff and back.

If you're not here for the major tramps, and still fancy a hike, consider just walking the first couple of hours of the Routeburn from Routeburn Shelter, or tackle the **Lake Sylvan Walk** (5km; 1hr 30min; negligible ascent), which starts at a signposted car park 3km before Routeburn Shelter. It largely crosses gravel river terraces supporting beech and totara forest then loops around the Lake Sylvan, turned brown from its feeder streams leaching through the soil.

Eating

There's pretty decent daytime and evening **eating** at the *Glenorchy Café* on Mull Street (daily), which serves homemade pies, doorstep deli sandwiches, light meals, coffee and booze, as well as offering an extensive dinner menu of steaks, pizzas, lamb and salmon, all in a cosy, if eccentric, wood-panelled café, or on the rustic seating outside. They also host a jam session every Thursday night for locals and anyone else who can strum a guitar. Hungry and thirsty trampers can also gravitate toward the *Glenorchy Hotel*, which serves a good selection of Kiwi staples, with bar snacks from $10 and main dishes from $15. Lunches and dinners are more formal, though not much, across the road at the *Roydon Restaurant and Café* in the *Glen Royden Lodge*, where substantial mains cost $18–26, or you can snack on homemade pies, quiches, cookies and assorted treats.

The widest selection of **tramping food** is to be found in Queenstown, where prices are also slightly lower, but you can always pick up some last-minute supplies from the store at the *Glenorchy Holiday Park*.

The major tramps

The fame of the **Routeburn Track** is eclipsed only by that of its westerly neighbour, the Milford Track (see p.943). Many justly claim that the Routeburn is superior, citing its more varied scenery, longer time spent above the bushline away from sandflies, and better spacing of huts. It can't be denied that the Routeburn is one of New Zealand's finest walks, straddling the spine of the Humboldt Mountains and providing access to many of the southwestern wilderness's most archetypal features: forested valleys with rich bird life and plunging waterfalls are combined with river flats, lakes and spectacular mountain scenery. In the past the Routeburn was treated as a cheaper and less regimented alternative to the Milford Track, but overcrowding and the consequent introduction of a booking system have redressed the balance. The nature of the terrain means that the Routeburn is usually promoted as a moderate tramp, though the short distance between huts eases the strain considerably. Fit hikers might consider doing it in two reasonably long days, though that doesn't leave much time for soaking up the scenery and wallowing in the relative solitude. To return by road from the end of the Routeburn to the start is something approaching 300km, so to avoid a lot of backtracking, anyone with an extra day or two to spare should consider returning to Glenorchy by hiking either the Greenstone or Caples tracks.

Both the **Greenstone and Caples tracks** are easy tramps, following gently graded, parallel river valleys where the wilderness experience is moderated by grazing cattle from the high-country stations along the Lake Wakatipu shore. The Greenstone occupies the broader, U-shaped valley carved out by one arm of the huge Hollyford Glacier, but despite the grandeur of the surrounding mountain scenery, it is sometimes criticized for being dull. Its detractors prefer the track over the sub-alpine McKellar Saddle and down the Caples Valley, where the river is bigger and the narrow base of the valley forces the path closer to it.

As the Routeburn reaches maximum capacity, the **Rees–Dart Track** is now being primed for wider usage; in parts the path is being graded, the track is being re-routed to avoid a hairy stepladder and the huts are slowly being improved. Nonetheless, it remains the toughest of the major tramps in the area, covering some fairly rugged terrain and requiring six to eight hours of effort each day. It follows the standard Kiwi tramp formula of climbing one river valley, crossing

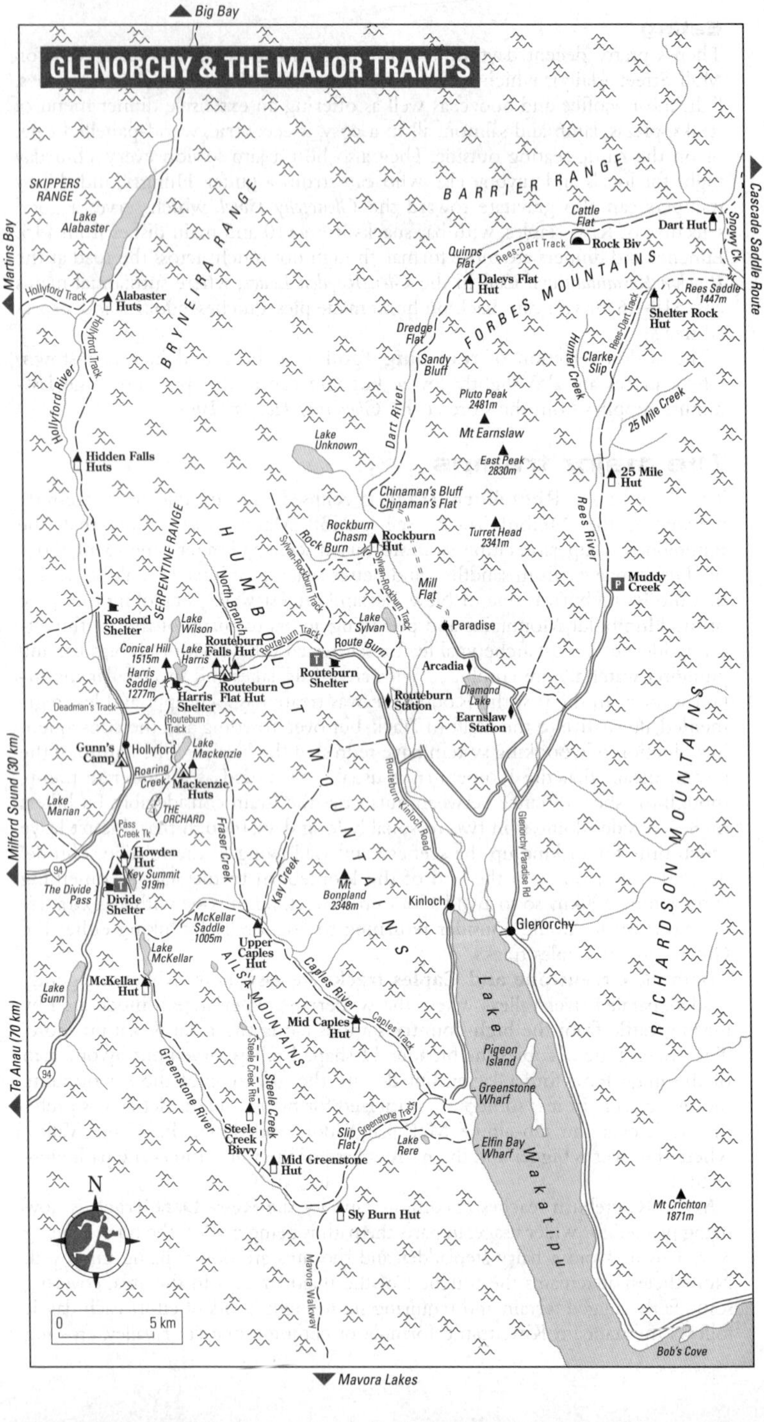

GLENORCHY & THE MAJOR TRAMPS

Big Bay
Martins Bay
Cascade Saddle Route
Milford Sound (30 km)
Te Anau (70 km)
Mavora Lakes

SKIPPERS RANGE
Lake Alabaster
Hollyford Track
Alabaster Huts
Hollyford River
Hollyford Track
BRYNEIRA RANGE
BARRIER RANGE
Cattle Flat
Rock Biv
Dart Hut
Snowy Ck
Rees-Dart Track
Quinns Flat
Daleys Flat Hut
FORBES MOUNTAINS
Rees Saddle 1447m
Shelter Rock Hut
Rees-Dart Track
Dredge Flat
Sandy Bluff
Hunter Creek
Clarke Slip
Pluto Peak 2481m
Dart River
Mt Earnslaw
25 Mile Creek
Lake Unknown
East Peak 2830m
25 Mile Hut
Hidden Falls Huts
Chinaman's Bluff
Chinaman's Flat
Rees River
SERPENTINE RANGE
HUMBOLDT MOUNTAINS
Sylvan-Rockburn Track
Rockburn Chasm
Rockburn Hut
Turret Head 2341m
Rock Burn
Sylvan-Rockburn Track
Mill Flat
Muddy Creek
North Branch
Lake Sylvan
Roadend Shelter
Lake Wilson
Paradise
Conical Hill 1515m
Lake Harris
Routeburn Falls Hut
Routeburn Track
Route Burn
Harris Saddle 1277m
Routeburn Shelter
Arcadia
Harris Shelter
Routeburn Flat Hut
Diamond Lake
Routeburn Station
Deadman's Track
Routeburn Track
Earnslaw Station
Gunn's Camp
Hollyford
Lake Mackenzie
Roaring Creek
Mackenzie Huts
Routeburn Kinloch Road
Glenorchy Paradise Rd
RICHARDSON MOUNTAINS
Lake Marian
THE ORCHARD
Pass Creek Tk
Fraser Creek
Howden Hut
94
Key Summit 919m
Kay Creek
Mt Bonpland 2348m
The Divide Pass
Divide Shelter
Kinloch
McKellar Saddle 1005m
Glenorchy
Upper Caples Hut
Lake McKellar
AILSA MOUNTAINS
Caples River
Lake Gunn
McKellar Hut
Lake Wakatipu
Mid Caples Hut
Caples Track
Pigeon Island
Steele Creek Rte
Steele Creek
94
Greenstone River
Greenstone Wharf
Steele Creek Bivvy
Slip Flat
Greenstone Track
Lake Rere
Elfin Bay Wharf
Mid Greenstone Hut
Sly Burn Hut
Mt Crichton 1871m
N
Mavora Walkway
0 5 km
Bob's Cove

the pass and descending into another, but adds an excellent side-trip to the Cascade Saddle and the choice of a jetboat or inflatable kayak trip to complete the final day.

In **winter** the Routeburn takes on a different character and becomes a much more serious undertaking. The track is often snowbound and extremely slippery, the risk of avalanche is high and the huts are unheated. Return day-trips from Routeburn Shelter to Routeburn Falls Hut and from The Divide to the Lake Mackenzie Hut are much better bets. The lower-level Greenstone and Caples tracks also make a less daunting prospect – not least because the huts are heated by wood-burning stoves which can be used throughout the year – though the McKellar Saddle is often snow-covered. Only experienced, knowledgeable and well-equipped trampers should venture onto the Rees–Dart Track in the winter.

Practicalities

Tramping **information** is best sought at the **DOC office** on Glenorchy's Oban Street (Nov–April daily 9am–4.30pm; May–Oct Mon–Fri 9am–4.30pm; ⓣ03/442 9937, ⓔgreatwalksbooking@doc.govt.nz), where you can fill in intentions forms (not required for the Routeburn), get the latest weather forecast, gen up on track conditions and either rent ($5, plus $10 deposit) or buy ($15-20) maps.

DOC's leaflets on *The Routeburn Track* ($1; free with hut booking – see p.879) and *The Greenstone and Caples Tracks* ($1), together with the 1:75,000 *Routeburn/Greenstone Trackmap,* cover these three walks. For real route-finding, the detailed 1:50,000 *Eglinton Topomap* is better, though you can also make do (at least for the Routeburn) with the 1:150,000 *Mount Aspiring National Park* map. For the Rees–Dart Track, again the 1:150,000 *Mount Aspiring National Park* **map**, along with the DOC's *Rees–Dart* leaflet ($1), make good background material, but aren't really adequate for proper route-finding; the considerably more detailed 1:50,000 *Tutoko* and *Earnslaw* Topomaps are far better.

Remember that any mention of the **left** or **right bank** refers to their position when facing downstream.

Trailhead transport

During the summer tramping season, there is little difficulty with transport to or from either end of the tracks. Most walkers use Glenorchy as a base, where a couple of small **bus companies** (Backpacker Express ⓣ03/442 9939; Upper Lake Wakatipu Tours ⓣ03/442 9986) compete for trailhead business. Routes are divided into sectors – Queenstown to Glenorchy; Glenorchy to the start of the Routeburn; Greenstone car park to Glenorchy; Glenorchy to the start of the Rees-Dart – and all cost $15. The only exceptions are the time-saving 4WD run to 25-mile Hut at the start of the Rees-Dart (around $20) and the run from Chinaman's Bluff to Glenorchy (around $20) at the end of the Rees-Dart.

Trampers wanting to be dropped off or picked up at The Divide (the western end of the Routeburn) can hop on buses plying between Te Anau and Milford Sound (ask visitor centres or the companies above for schedules); in addition, Fiordland Tracknet (ⓣ03/249 7777, ⓔtracknet@destinationnz.com) operate a thrice daily loop service from mid-October to mid-May, leaving Te Anau (7.30am, 9.30am & 1pm) before calling at The Divide (8.30am, 11am & 2.15pm), Milford Sound (9.15am, 11.45am & 3pm), The Divide (10.15am, 3.45pm & 5.45pm), and returning to Te Anau (noon, 5pm & 7pm). From The Divide you can expect to pay around $25 to Te Anau, $50 to Queenstown, and $20 to Milford Sound.

To save backtracking, trampers can also arrange to have their bags sent on to Te Anau for a small fee through the Backpacker Express people.

Hut and campsite bookings

The **Routeburn Track** has a compulsory system of booking **accommodation passes** for all four Great Walk huts and two campsites for the duration of the tramping season (Nov–April). It's a reasonably flexible system, allowing people to walk in either direction, retrace their steps and stay up to two nights in a particular hut. Numbers are limited, so you'll need to book as far ahead as possible – three weeks if you can be adaptable, three months if you need a specific departure date or are part of a large group. This does have the huge advantage of guaranteeing you a bed, so you don't have to get up at the crack of dawn and almost sprint to the next hut to be sure of a bunk. The huts have all recently been tidied up and improved and are all equipped with flush toilets, running water (which must be treated, filtered or boiled), heaters and gas rings, but you'll need to carry your own pans and plates. The cost is $35 per person per night; everyone gets a twenty percent discount during the first ten days of the season, and families get that same discount throughout the season. A limited number of simple **campsites** (with long-drop toilets and water; $12) exist close to the Routeburn Flats and Mackenzie Huts; campers are not allowed to use hut facilities.

Credit-card phone or mail **bookings** are taken from July 1 for the following season: contact the Great Walks Booking Desk in Te Anau or, from November, the DOC visitor centres in Glenorchy or Queenstown. Accommodation passes can be collected from Te Anau or Glenorchy the day before you start and up to 2pm on your day of departure: those without accommodation passes will be charged $50 a night. If the track is closed due to bad weather or track conditions, full refunds are given – but new bookings can only be made if there is space. Changes can be made to existing bookings ($5 per alteration) either before you start or with the wardens at each hut, but again only if there is space. **Outside the season** the Mackenzie and Howden huts revert to backcountry status and, like the campsites, cost $5 a night. Routeburn Falls and Flats huts are $10 as they have heating. Bookings are not required and annual hut passes are valid.

The **Greenstone and Caples tracks** are far less popular, and bookings are not necessary at any time of year. Each trail has two $10 huts, but none of them have gas rings. One warden patrols each valley and may be inclined to sell you hut tickets, although you should really buy them in advance unless you have an annual hut pass (see "Basics", p.553). Free camping is allowed in both valleys along the fringes of the bush (but not on the open flats), but you are encouraged to camp close to (but at least 50m away from) the huts and use their outside facilities – long-drop toilets and water – for which you'll pay half the hut fee.

The three **Rees–Dart** huts (all $10) currently cannot be booked in advance. Trampers should carry an annual hut pass or two hut tickets per night.

Guided walks

Routeburn aspirants who aren't confident about their level of fitness or who prefer not to lug heavy backpacks should consider joining a **guided walk**. The pace is fairly leisurely and walkers have to carry only their personal effects (no food or camping equipment); daily hikes are still typically 5–6 hours, occasionally on rough terrain, so anyone unused to hill walking should still do a good deal of preparatory hiking.

Accommodation is in clean, plain huts which are by no means luxurious, but do have hot showers, duvets on the bunks, and you'll be served cooked breakfasts and three-course dinners with wine. All you have to do is walk – but there's a **price** to pay for all this pampering: the **Routeburn Guided Walk**, PO Box 568, Queenstown (ⓣ03/442 8200, ⓕ442 6072; Nov–April), including return transport from Queenstown and three days' walking with two nights' accommodation in huts, costs around $950; while the **Grand Traverse**, a five-day, six-night walk combining the Routeburn and Greenstone tracks, will set you back about $1250.

> **Route times**
> Note that all **times** and **distances** given in the following accounts are **one way**, unless otherwise stated.

The Routeburn Track

Most people walk the **Routeburn Track** (33km; 2–3 days) westwards from Glenorchy towards The Divide; it can also be combined with the Greenstone and Caples tracks to make three- to five-day loops. The Routeburn isn't for everyone, though. The terrain is sometimes rough and the paths steep, but anyone of moderate fitness who can carry a backpack for five or six hours a day should have little trouble. That said, the track passes through sub-alpine country and snowfall and flooding can sometimes close it, even in summer.

The first day on the Routeburn is an easy one. Trailhead buses offer mid-morning and mid-afternoon start times, both leaving enough time to reach either Routeburn Flats or Routeburn Falls huts, and the earlier one giving ample opportunity to explore the North Branch of Route Burn. From **Routeburn Shelter to Routeburn Flats Hut** (7km; 2–3hr; 250m ascent) the route follows Route Burn steadily uphill on a metre-wide track, though it's never strenuous and has an even shingle surface. Because Route Burn is a tributary of the Dart River, you are following a side valley and will have experienced a wide variety of scenery – river flats, waterfalls and open beech forest – by the time you reach the Routeburn Flats Hut. The nearby Routeburn Flats campsite is superbly sited on the edge of wide alluvial flats at the end of a short path a couple of hundred metres beyond the hut. Only a few tents are permitted so there is plenty of space to spread out, and campers can make use of an open fireplace and a small shelter, the run-off from which provides water for cooking. Hut users are better off making the first day a little longer and tackling the next leg, **Routeburn Flats Hut to Routeburn Falls Hut** (2km; 1hr–1hr 30min; 300m ascent), which is considerably steeper and rougher, but the extra exertion is rewarded by a stay at the well-sited Routeburn Falls Hut, perched on the bushline above a precipice with eastward views looking back to Routeburn Flats and Sugar Loaf (1320m).

The second day is the longest, continuing from **Routeburn Falls Hut to McKenzie Hut** (11km; 4–7hr; 300m ascent, 250m descent) on the most exposed section of the track. Most of the day is spent above the bushline among the sub-alpine snow tussock of the Harris Saddle (1277m) and passing through bog country, where sundews, bladderworts and orchids thrive. You might even catch sight of chamois clambering on the rocks to either side of the saddle. The track climbs gradually enough to the Harris Saddle Shelter (2–3hr), which offers respite from the wind and has toilets; on a clear day, drop your pack here and climb up to the summit of **Conical Hill** (1515m; 2km return; at least 1hr; 240m ascent) for superb views down into the Hollyford Valley and along it to Martin's Bay and the Tasman Sea. Continuing from the Harris Saddle Shelter you cross from the Mount Aspiring National Park into the Fiordland National Park and skirt high along the edge of the Hollyford Valley, before switchbacking down through silver beech, fuchsia and ribbonwood to Mackenzie Hut. The bush beside the hut hides a campsite, a cramped affair that comes as a big disappointment after the Routeburn Flats site.

From **Lake McKenzie Hut to Howden Hut** (8km; 3–4hr; 400m descent), the track continues along the mountainside through a grassy patch of ribbonwood known as The Orchard and past the cascading Earland Falls to the Howden Hut at the junction of three tracks. The Greenstone and Caples tracks (handy for turning the tramp into a five-day Glenorchy-based circuit) head south, while the Routeburn continues from **Howden Hut to The Divide** (2.5km; 1hr–1hr 30min; 50m net descent), initially climbing for fifteen minutes to a point where you can make a half-hour excursion to Key Summit for views of three major river systems, the Hollyford, the Eglinton and the Greenstone. From the **Key Summit** (919m) turn-off, the track descends through silver beech to the car park and shelter at The Divide.

The Greenstone Track

Trampers starting on the **Greenstone Track** (35km; 2–3 days) at The Divide first cover the short section to Howden Hut (described in reverse, above), then walk south from **Howden Hut to McKellar Hut** (6km; 2hr–2hr 30min; 50m descent), passing (after 20min) a free primitive **campsite** where fires can be lit. The Greenstone continues beside Lake McKellar to McKellar Hut ($10; 20 bunks), just outside the Fiordland National Park.

The easy track from **McKellar Hut to Mid-Greenstone Hut** (12km; 4–6hr; 100m descent) starts by crossing the Greenstone River and follows the left bank down a broad, grazed valley mostly along river flats and through the lower slopes of the beech forests. A swingbridge then crosses Steele Creek, and the track continues for another half-hour to the Mid-Greenstone Hut ($10; 12 bunks), located on the edge of a grassy expanse.

It is eminently possible to finish the Greenstone in a day from here, though you might want to walk from **Mid-Greenstone Hut to Sly Burn Hut** (5km; 1hr–1hr 30min; 30m descent) and use the hut ($5; 8 bunks) as a base for exploring the gentle **Mavora Walkway** to the south, taking two to three days through open tussock country and beech forest to Mavora Lakes (see p.889); a couple of Category 3 huts provide accommodation en route.

From **Sly Burn Hut to Greenstone car park** (10km; 3–5hr; 100m descent), the track follows the left bank as the valley narrows and the river heads into a long gorge. The river soon meets the Caples River, an enticing series of deep pools that make great swimming holes. A swingbridge gives access to the left bank of the Caples River and the Caples Track; turn right to Greenstone Wharf (20–30min), or left to Mid Caples Hut (see opposite).

The Caples Track

The Caples Track (27km; 2 days) follows the Greenstone Track from **The Divide to Howden Hut** and then the first half of the section from Howden Hut to McKellar Hut, turning off an hour south of Howden Hut and beginning the very steep bush-clad zig-zag up the **McKellar Saddle** (1005m). Try to assess your capabilities beforehand as many find the walk from The Divide to Upper Caples Hut (11km; 5–7hr; 550m ascent, 600m descent) too much for one day, but are obliged to push on, as camping is neither pleasant on the saddle's bogland nor permitted on what is very fragile open tussock. The descent mostly follows snow poles, crossing and recrossing the infant Caples River before regaining beech forest and the **Upper Caples Hut** ($10; 20 bunks).

Greenstone Wharf is within a day's walk of here, though you can break it up into two sections: from **Upper Caples Hut to Mid Caples Hut** (7km; 2hr–2hr 30min; 50m descent) you cross easy grassland, finishing up by a short but dramatic gorge right outside the Mid Caples Hut ($10; 12 bunks); then from **Mid Caples Hut to Greenstone Wharf** car park (9km; 2–3hr; 150m descent) the path crosses the gorge and follows the left bank, continuing alongside the bush edge and crossing grassy clearings before arriving at the junction with the Greenstone Track, from where it is only twenty minutes to Greenstone Wharf.

The Rees-Dart Track

The standard approach to the Rees–Dart Track is to walk up the Rees and down the Dart, an anticlockwise circuit which leaves open the option of finishing off with either a Fun Yak or a jetboat ride (see p.863). The track from **Muddy Creek car park to Shelter Rock Hut** (16km; 6–8hr; 450m ascent) follows a 4WD track across grass and gravel flats on the left bank of the braided lower Rees and requires a couple of foot-soaking stream crossings. You can save yourself the trouble (and a couple of hours hiking) by getting Backpacker Express (see p.879) to drop at the end of the 4WD track, 6km beyond the Muddy Creek car park, and close to the simple Twenty-five Mile Hut, which is owned by Otago Tramping Club but can be used (pay $3 to the DOC in Glenorchy). Press on across Twenty-five Mile Creek and over more river flats for another hour or so, with Hunter Creek and the peaks of the Forbes Mountains straight ahead. Just past the confluence of Hunter Creek, the Rees valley steepens appreciably and becomes cloaked in beech forests. Soon after, the track crosses a swingbridge to the right bank and climbs above river level, eventually coming out on the grassy flats of Clarke Slip. The track is bush-bound again up to just below the tree line, where it passes the site of the old Shelter Rock Hut then continues for a kilometre until you hit tussock country. One final crossing of the Rees River, now a large stream, takes you back to the left bank and the new Shelter Rock Hut ($10; 20 bunks).

The second day, from **Shelter Rock Hut to Dart Hut** (7km; 4–6hr; 500m ascent, 500m descent), is the shortest but one of the toughest, scaling the 1447m Rees Saddle. Stick to the left bank of the Rees over sub-alpine scrub and gravel banks for a couple of kilometres before crossing the river and gradually climbing up to a tussock basin and the saddle. Descend rapidly and then more steadily across snow grass following the left bank of Snowy Creek, which churns down a narrow gorge to your right. A kilometre or so later the track crosses a swingbridge to the right bank, commencing a loose and rocky descent past a long series of cascades to another crossing of Snowy Creek, just above its confluence with the Dart River. Grassy areas on the right bank provide camping spots and the Dart Hut ($10; 20 bunks) sits on the left bank; this is the pinch point for Rees–Dart accommodation, with tramper numbers swelled by those staying two nights to explore the Cascade Saddle route (see "Walks in the Matukituki Valley" box on p.904).

The track from **Dart Hut to Daleys Flat Hut** (16km; 6–8hr; 430m descent) initially climbs high above the river and stays there for 3km, passing through beech forest before dropping to Cattle Flat, 5km of grassed alluvial ridges traced by a winding and energy-sapping but easy-to-follow route. At the end of Cattle Flat the track returns to the bush and runs roughly parallel to the river until it reaches the beautiful grassy expanse of Quinns Flat (perfect in the late afternoon light), where the track turns inland. Within half an hour you reach the sandfly-ridden **Daleys Flat Hut** ($10; 20 bunks), redeemed by its pleasant location on the edge of a clearing.

Trampers planning to pick up a jetboat or Fun Yak to Glenorchy at 10.30am will need to leave around 8am for the **Daleys Flat Hut to Sandy Bluff** section (7km; 2hr–2hr 30min; 100m ascent, 110m descent). The walk skips through the bush for around 4km until Dredge Flat, where you make your own track, looking for markers on the left that indicate where you re-enter the bush. The track then climbs steeply up Sandy Bluff to reach a belvedere high above the river before dropping down to river level and the jetboat pick-up point.

If you are determined to walk all the way, you'll find the section from **Sandy Bluff to Chinaman's Bluff** (12km; 3hr; negligible descent) fairly easy, crossing the flats south of Sandy Bluff and following the river to Chinaman's Bluff. Pick-ups from here can be arranged, though you can continue on foot from **Chinaman's Bluff to Paradise car park** (6km; 2hr; negligible descent) through Dan's Paddock and along either the 4WD track or a more direct walking track.

Kingston and the road to Fiordland

Most people travel from Queenstown to Fiordland by road, making the 170km journey to Te Anau in under three hours. It is an attractive if unspectacular route that follows the lakeshore road, hugging the foot of the Remarkables then striking out across open Otago and Southland farming country.

As the Dart glacier retreated at the end of the last ice age, Lake Wakatipu formed behind the terminal moraine at what is now **KINGSTON**, a scattered community 46km south of Queenstown on SH6. The lake's waters formed the Mataura Valley to the south, but successive terminal moraines raised the lake level to the point at which it was able to carve out a new passage down the bed of the Kawarau, out of the Frankton Arm. In the 1860s the Mataura Valley provided a perfect route from the populated coast to new gold fields on the Shotover and Arrow rivers. Kingston became a major transit centre, accommodating up to five thousand people while they waited for boats across the lake or bullock carts to transport their spoils to Dunedin or Invercargill. By 1878, the railroad had reached Kingston, and the prefabricated parts for ever-larger steamers could be brought in and assembled on the lakeshore. The 1936 completion of the lakeside road to Queenstown drove the last nail into the coffin of the steamer freight trade, and goods trains went the same way, but the line has managed to struggle on thanks to the **Kingston Flyer** tourist train, Kent Street (ⓣ03/248 8848, ⓔdgarnett@tranzrail.co.nz; daily Oct–April 10.15am & 3.45pm; $20 one way, $25 return). Initially it plied the 60km to Lumsden and was much eulogized in those halcyon days before Kiwi tourism went ballistic, but since 1982 the cut-down forty-minutes-each-way service only runs 15km to the nowhere town of Fairlight. Gleaming black steam engines haul creaky but sumptuous turn-of-the-century first-class carriages with embossed steel ceilings and brass gas lamps: arrive early to avoid being shunted down to the less exalted second-class seats, which are charged at the same rate.

The only **accommodation** in Kingston, and for some distance either side, is at the roadside *Kingston Stream Holiday Camp*, 10 Kent St (ⓣ & ⓕ03/248 8501; tent & powered sites $10, dorms ❶, cabins–motel units ❸–❹).

Beyond Kingston there's little to delay your progress to Te Anau. Just short of the dull Southland farming town of **Lumsden**, a signposted short-cut diverts you to **Mossburn** and SH94. Some 14km west of Mossburn a narrow road cuts north towards **Mavora Lakes**, a very popular summertime retreat that recently formed part of the backdrop to the *Lord of the Rings*; the southern lake is reserved for quiet pursuits like fishing and canoeing while the larger North Mavora Lake hosts rowdy boats. Trails through the surrounding beech forests make great mountain-biking territory, and trampers can head north along the Mavora Walkway (see p.886) and link up with the Greenstone Track (see p.886).

Back on SH94 you soon enter the Red Tussock Conservation Area, named for a type of grass essential to the livelihood of the takahe (see Contexts, p.994), and before long you'll find yourself in Te Anau, perched on the brink of Fiordland (see p.927).

Wanaka

WANAKA, only 55 air kilometres northeast of Queenstown but an hour and a half by the main road, once languished in the shadow of its brasher southern sibling, though it offers a similar combination of beautiful surroundings and robust adventure activities, but of late it has been catching up due to a massive development makeover and is regarded by many as the next Queenstown, albeit a more refined version. Situated at the point where the hummocky, poplar-studded hills of Central Otago rub up against the dramatic peaks of the Mount Aspiring National Park, it commands a wonderful spot on the shores of the willow-girt Lake Wanaka, with the jagged summits of the Southern Alps as often as not mirrored in its waters.

Founded in the 1860s as a service centre for the local run-holders and itinerant gold miners, the town didn't really take off until the prosperous middle years of the twentieth century, when camping and caravanning Kiwis discovered its warm, dry summer climate and easy-going pace. Today it is gradually picking up speed, but Wanaka remains a small and eminently manageable place, with the tenor of a village and an overwhelming feeling of light and spaciousness. It continues to promote itself as an adventure destination in its own right, and it's an excellent place in which to relax for a couple of days and eat well in some fine cafés and restaurants.

A half day spent exploring Wanaka's intriguing **maze** and absorbing **museums** will leave plenty of time to go kayaking, jetboating, rock climbing, horse riding or, best of all, canyoning. Wanaka is also the perfect base from which to explore the surrounding region, notably the Mount Aspiring National Park and the Cardrona Valley. During the winter months, Wanaka's relative calm is shattered by the arrival of **skiers and snowboarders** eager to explore the downhill ski fields of Treble Cone and Cardrona, and the Nordic terrain at Waiorau.

Arrival, information and transport

Daily direct **buses** from Christchurch, Dunedin, Queenstown and Franz Josef all arrive centrally: InterCity stop outside The Paper Place, 84 Ardmore St (Ⓣ03/443 7885), while Catch-a-Bus, Atomic and Southern Link Shuttles pull up in front of United Travel, 99 Ardmore St (Ⓣ03/443 7414, Ⓕ443 9434). You'll usually have to book in advance through these agencies or direct with the company, particularly for the Catch-a-Bus, Atomic and Southern Link services, which will generally drop off and pick up at your hotel if they're not too busy. Wanaka Connexions (Ⓣ0800/879 926 & 03/443 9122) run a door-to-door service between Wanaka and Queenstown ($25 one way, $50 return) using the direct but windy Cardrona Road.

The best source of general and tramping **information** is the **Wanaka visitor centre** (Nov–April daily 8.30am–6pm; May–Oct Mon–Fri 9am–5pm; Ⓣ03/443 1233, Ⓦwww.lakewanaka.co.nz), who share a lakeside building with Lakeland Adventures at 99 Ardmore St (see below), or the DOC's **Mount Aspiring National Park visitor centre** (Mon–Fri 8am–5pm, Sat 9.30am–4.30pm, closed for a 1hr lunch break in the winter; Ⓣ03/443 7660, Ⓕ443 8777), 500m east of central Wanaka on SH84 at the corner of Ballantyne Road. The centre contains some interesting displays on local wildlife, an audio visual display (8min) in the company of a variety of tatty looking stuffed birds and plenty of up-to-the-minute info on the longer tracks. The Lakeland Adventures, 99 Ardmore St (Ⓣ03/443 8174 & 0800/684 468, Ⓕ443 8589; opening times same as Wanaka visitor centre), acts as the booking agent and central radio contact for many of the adventure travel companies both here and in Queenstown, and books flights to Milford and elsewhere and rents kayaks and boats for a paddle on the lake. There are several **banks** around town, with foreign-exchange facilities and ATMs.

Wanaka is so compact that you can **walk** everywhere in the centre, and most accommodation is less than fifteen minutes' away on foot. Longer excursions are best made with **bicycles** or **cars** rented from several shops around town (see "Listings", p.900); for short trips into the surroundings, there's always Wanaka Taxis (Ⓣ03/443 7999).

Accommodation

For such a diminutive town, Wanaka has a splendid and ever-expanding range of accommodation, and **rates** are generally a fair bit lower than in Queenstown. You should have no problem finding a place to suit, except during the peak months of January and August, when **booking** is essential – and some establishments respond to the surge in demand by raising their rates.

Hotels and motels

Altamont Lodge Mount Aspiring Rd, 2km west of Wanaka Ⓣ03/443 8864 & 0800/429 590. The perfect ski lodge, with a pine-panelled alpine atmosphere, communal cooking and lounge areas, drying rooms, and ski-tuning facilities. Rooms are functional but attractive, with shared bathrooms and good rates for singles, reduced if you use your own bedding. The spa pool is open only during the winter season, but the tennis court is available year round. ❷–❸

Aspiring Lodge cnr Dungarvon St & Dunmore St Ⓣ0800/269 367, Ⓔaspiring@voyager.co.nz. Spacious and attractive wood-panelled studio units and executive suites, with full kitchens and drying room for ski gear. Continental and cooked breakfasts available. Studios ❹, apartments ❺–❻

Bay View Motel Mount Aspiring Rd Ⓣ0800/229 843, Ⓦwww.bayviewwanaka.co.nz. Well-appointed motel with lake and mountain views, a spa pool, and a pleasant site well back from the road, just over 1km west of Wanaka up the Matukituki Valley. ❺

Cardrona Hotel 26km along the sealed section of the Cardrona road south towards Queenstown Ⓣ & Ⓕ03/443 8153, Ⓔinfo@cardrona-hotel.co.nz. Characterful, restored gold-rush hotel. Decent bathless doubles are in a new extension and are very popular with skiers from the nearby Cardrona and Waiorau slopes. ❹

Lakeview Motel 68 Lismore St Ⓣ & Ⓕ03/443 7029, Ⓔbassgc@xtra.co.nz. Well-placed en-suite studios, and slightly pricier but better-value larger units – all high above town with tremendous views. ❹

Manuka Crescent Motel 51 Manuka Crescent Ⓣ0800/626 852, Ⓦwww.manukacrescentmotel.co.nz. Pleasant, good-value motel with a mix of modern and older units and a small pool. Twenty minutes' walk from town, but there's a courtesy minibus. Breakfasts available. ❺–❻

Matterhorn South Lodge 56 Brownston St ⓣ03/443 1119, ⓔmatterhorn@xtra.co.nz. This upmarket section adjoining the hostel of the same name has modern, nicely furnished en-suite rooms with TV and fridge, and access to an excellent kitchen and comfortable lounge area. ❸

Wanaka Motel 73 Helwick St ⓣ & ⓕ03/443 7545. Spacious two-bedroom units with huge lounges, a full-size kitchen and all mod cons. ❹

B&Bs and homestays

Aspiring Images 26 Norman St ⓣ03/443 8358, ⓦwww.nzhomestay.co.nz/russell.html. Comfortable suburban homestay, with nice rooms, each with a terrace, and there are mountain bikes for exploring the town. ❺

Renmore House B&B 44 Upton St ⓣ03/443 6566, ⓦwww.renmore-house.com. Large purpose-built house in which the swish accommodation, a double and twin with ensuites, overlooks a lovingly tended garden. This is a quiet spot no more than two minutes' walk to the lake edge with friendly hosts and a 3 course dinner on request ($35). ❼

River Run Halliday Rd, 7km east of Wanaka ⓣ03/443 9049, ⓦwww.riverrun.co.nz. Stylish lodge gloriously sited on ancient river flats with trails leading down to the Clutha River. The house, thoughtfully designed by the owners, contains five individually designed and beautifully appointed en-suite rooms as well as sunny verandas and a communal dining area where most guests stay for three-course meals of the highest quality ($80). Rates include breakfast and pre-dinner drinks, and the cheaper rooms only just fall into this top price bracket. ❾

Te Wanaka Lodge 23 Brownston St ⓣ0800/926 252, ⓦwww.tewanaka.co.nz. One of the finer B&B inns in central Wanaka, with twelve luxurious and quiet en-suite rooms, communal TV, and a cedar hot tub during winter. The sumptuous buffet breakfast is a mellow affair centred on a huge dining table. ❼

Tirohanga 102 Lismore St ⓣ03/443 8302, ⓔtiro-hanga@xtra.co.nz. Friendly homestay with stupendous views across the lake to Mount Roy. Sleep in either the modest twin room or the self-contained unit and eat a light breakfast with the family. Evening meals available. ❺

Wanaka Springs 21 Warren St ⓣ03/443 8421, ⓦwww.wanakasprings.com. As far as central luxury accommodation goes, this takes the biscuit. About five minutes' walk from the lake, a purpose-built boutique lodge with a mixture of top-notch, ensuites, twins and doubles decorated individually in tasteful swank. There are also comfortable communal areas, free liqueurs, all the facilities you could wish for, a spa pool in a charming native garden and well-informed and helpful hosts. ❽–❾

Hostels

Bullock Creek Lodge 46 Brownston St ⓣ & ⓕ443 1265, ⓔbullockcreeklodge@clear.net.nz. Former motel that's been turned into a first-rate hostel with en-suite and TV-equipped rooms pressed into service as four-shares, twins and doubles. There's a comfortable and spacious cooking and lounge area with a deck that catches the afternoon sun, and also a fully self-contained apartment. Beds ❶, rooms ❷, apartment ❸

Cliffords 21 Brownston St ⓣ & ⓕ3/443 6560, ⓔpeterwilliamson@bigfoot.com. The place to go if you are looking for the cheapest beds in town. Fairly functional backpacker beds in single or double rooms with sheets provided, a communal lounge, kitchen and bathroom. Located at the back of a large town hotel of the same name. Dorms ❶, rooms ❷

Matterhorn South see"Hotels and Motels", above. Small but appealing hostel right in the centre of town with en-suite four-shares, cheaper 5- and 7-bed dorms, plus doubles, and a log fire surrounded by scatter cushions. Dorms ❶, rooms ❷

Mountainview Backpackers 71 Brownston St ⓣ & ⓕ03/443 9010, ⓦwww.mountainview@mad-mail.com. New, small and fairly cosy hostel with cheery dorms and doubles that come with a free continental breakfast with home-made bread. There're also tent sites, free storage, barbecue and free use of basic bikes. Tents $12, dorms ❶, rooms ❷

Purple Cow 94 Brownston St ⓣ0800/772 277, ⓔstay@purplecow.co.nz. Large and spacious hostel in a former hotel with maximum 6-bed dorms, many in separate former motel rooms with their own lounge, bathroom and TV; and plenty of doubles (some with en suites). Sit and gaze at the fabulous lake view through the big picture windows or play pool and table tennis in the large lounge. Bike rental ($18 a day), kayak rental ($40 a day), frequent bargain barbecues in the evening and Internet access. Dorms ❶, rooms ❷–❸

Wanaka Bakpaka 117 Lakeside Rd ⓣ03/443 7837, ⓔwanakabakpaka@xtra.co.nz. Low-key hostel five minutes' walk from town and with great lake and mountain views, a peaceful atmosphere, summer barbecues and rental of canoes ($18 a day), sea kayaks ($24 a day) and bikes ($25 a day). Cabins & dorms ❶, rooms ❷-❸

YHA 181 Upton St ⓣ & ⓕ03/443 7405, ⓔyhawnka@yha.org.nz. Decent hostel ten minutes' walk from the centre with small dorms, cheap bike rental ($25 per day), and a good garden in which you can camp ($10). Dorms ❶, rooms ❷–❸

Campsites and motorparks

Albert Town Recreation Reserve 6km northeast of Wanaka on SH6. Open, informal camping area, with water and toilets, on the banks of the swift-flowing Clutha River. $4

Glendhu Bay Motor Camp Mount Aspiring Rd, 15km west of Wanaka ⓣ03/443 7243, ⓔglendhucamp@xtra.co.nz. Popular lakeshore family campsite with fabulous views across to Mount Aspiring, boat-launching facilities, canoe and bike rental. Tents $9, powered sites $11, bunks ❶, cabins ❷–❸

Outlet Motor Camp Lake Outlet Rd, 6km from Wanaka ⓣ03/442 7478, ⓕ443 7471. Beautifully sited campground at the point where Lake Wanaka becomes the Clutha River and in a great position for strolls along the lake or river frontage. Tent and powered sites $10, on-site vans ❷

Top 10 Pleasant Lodge Holiday Park 217 Mount Aspiring Rd, 3km west of Wanaka ⓣ & ⓕ03/443 7360, ⓦwww.nzsouth.co.nz/pleasant-lodge. Sprawling, family-oriented site with tent sites ($10), a range of cabins and heaps of amenities, including mountain-bike rental. Cabins ❷, tourist apartments ❸, motel units ❹

Wanaka Lake View Holiday Park 212 Brownston St ⓣ03/443 7883, ⓕ443 9086. The most convenient of the campsites, ten minutes' walk from central Wanaka, with $10 tent sites and all the usual facilities including rooms in a new lodge which has bathrooms and kitchen under the same roof. Lodge and cabins ❸–❹, tourist flats ❹

The Town

The solid lump of Mount Iron rises immediately east of town, pointing the way to **Stuart Landsborough's Puzzling World**, almost 2km away on SH84 (daily 8.30am–5.30pm; $9). Star attraction is "The Great Maze", a complex wooden structure comprising 1500m of dead-end passageways packed into a dense labyrinth, with overhead bridges linking the four sections. Should you choose to accept it, your mission is to reach all four corner towers, either in any order (30min–1hr) or in a specific sequence (at least 1hr), then to find your way out again; if it all goes horribly wrong, you can cheat by using escape doors. Put aside a couple of hours to appreciate this prototype for the Eighties maze-building boom that swept New Zealand and Japan – where Stuart Landsborough briefly enjoyed a fanatical following. The ticket price includes entry to the "Hologram Hall", full of the usual numbing circus of 3-D images, and the "Tilted House", which revels in tricks of perspective produced by the floor being fifteen degrees off the horizontal. Zip through these to get to the "Hall of Following Faces", a large octagonal room with seven of the sides made up by arrays of moulded images of famous people – Churchill, Einstein, Van Gogh, Lincoln, etc. As you walk around the faces appear to watch your every move in true Mona Lisa fashion. Also worth noting is that none of the figures have ears, which apparently hinder the illusion. Of the various other things involving messing with your eyes, the great Games Room presents a TV, a computer and monocular vision, through which you can see yourself looking massive at one end of the display and tiny at the other. Leave half an hour aside for the café, where you can play with the puzzles scattered over the tables.

Wanaka's airport, 7km east of Puzzling World on SH6, is the base for a number of aerial activities (see "Activities", p.897) and the **New Zealand Fighter Pilots Museum** (daily: Christmas–Jan 9am–6pm; rest of year 9am–4pm; $8), which honours Kiwi pilots and ground crew who fought in the two world wars. This homage to the New Zealand contingent contains hagiographic profiles of the men and blow-by-blow descriptions of the major battles and cam-

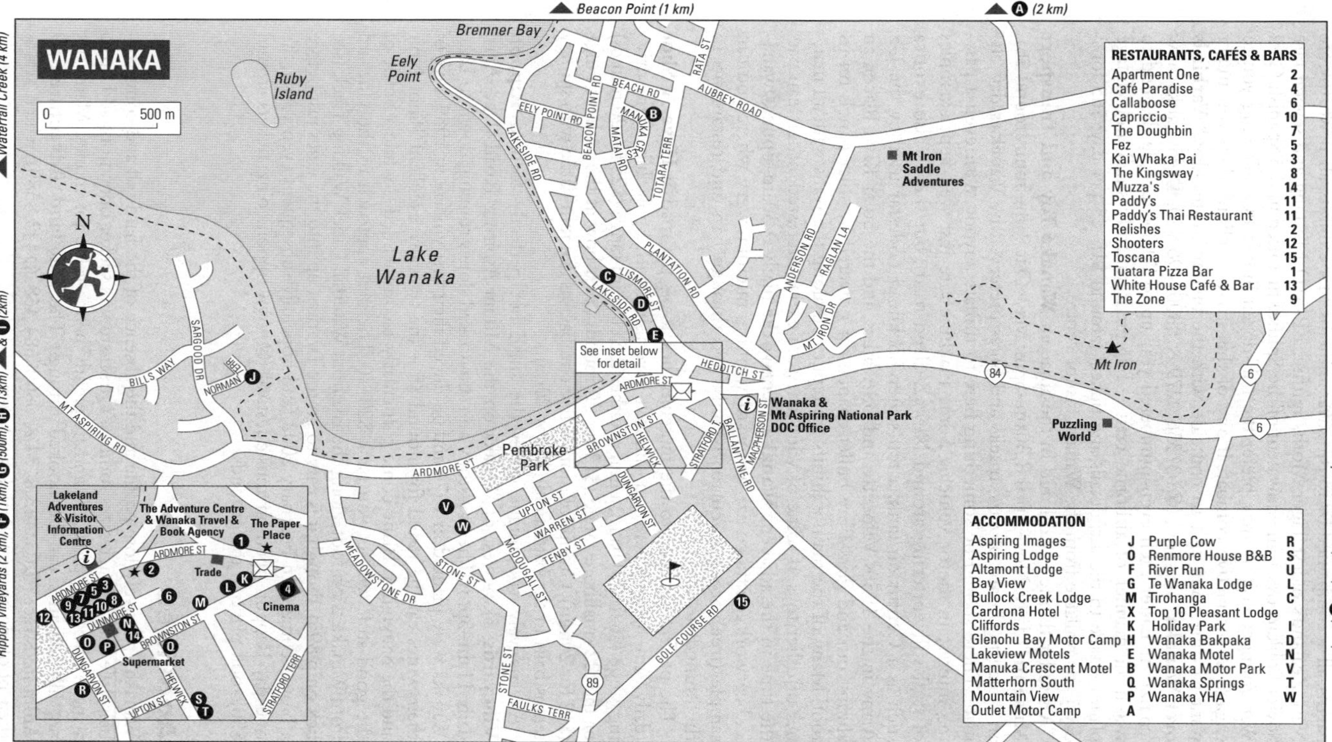

WANAKA
0 500 m
N
Beacon Point (1 km)
A (2 km)
Albert Town (1 km), Hawea (10 km) & Haast Pass (80 km)
Queenstown (115 km), Airport, Fighter Pilots', Transport Museums (6 km) & U (4km)
Cardrona (26 km), X (25km) & Queenstown (70 km)
Mt Aspiring National Park (50 km), Treble Cone (20 km), Glendhu Bay (14 km), Rippon Vineyards (2 km), F (1km), G (500m), H (13km) & I (2km)
Waterfall Creek (4 km)
Bremner Bay
Eely Point
Ruby Island
Lake Wanaka
Mt Iron
Mt Iron Saddle Adventures
Puzzling World
Wanaka & Mt Aspiring National Park DOC Office
Pembroke Park
See inset below for detail
BEACH RD
EELY POINT RD
BEACON POINT RD
MANUKA CRES
MATAI RD
TOTARA TERR
RATA ST
AUBREY ROAD
LAKESIDE RD
PLANTATION RD
LISMORE ST
ANDERSON RD
RAGLAN LA
MT IRON DR
HEDDITCH ST
ARDMORE ST
BROWNSTON ST
HELWICK
STRATFORD T
BALLANTYNE RD
MACPHERSON ST
DUNGARVON ST
UPTON ST
WARREN ST
TENBY ST
McDOUGALL ST
STONE ST
MEADOWSTONE DR
FAULKS TERR
GOLF COURSE RD
SARGOOD DR
BILLS WAY
NORMAN TERR
MT ASPIRING RD
84
6
89
RESTAURANTS, CAFÉS & BARS
Apartment One 2
Café Paradise 4
Callaboose 6
Capriccio 10
The Doughbin 7
Fez 5
Kai Whaka Pai 3
The Kingsway 8
Muzza's 14
Paddy's 11
Paddy's Thai Restaurant 11
Relishes 2
Shooters 12
Toscana 15
Tuatara Pizza Bar 1
White House Café & Bar 13
The Zone 9
ACCOMMODATION
Aspiring Images J
Aspiring Lodge O
Altamont Lodge F
Bay View G
Bullock Creek Lodge M
Cardrona Hotel X
Cliffords K
Glenohu Bay Motor Camp H
Lakeview Motels E
Manuka Crescent Motel B
Matterhorn South Q
Mountain View P
Outlet Motor Camp A
Purple Cow R
Renmore House B&B S
River Run U
Te Wanaka Lodge L
Tirohanga C
Top 10 Pleasant Lodge Holiday Park I
Wanaka Bakpaka D
Wanaka Motel N
Wanaka Motor Park V
Wanaka Springs T
Wanaka YHA W
Lakeland Adventures & Visitor Information Centre
The Adventure Centre & Wanaka Travel & Book Agency
The Paper Place
Trade
Cinema
Supermarket
DUNMORE ST
UPTON ST
STRATFORD TERR

paigns, all accompanied by rousing war anthems. Star exhibits, all airworthy, are New Zealand's oldest Tiger Moth, Spitfire, a P-51D Mustang and several rare Soviet Polikarpovs – an equivalent of the Spitfire first used in the Spanish Civil War. Younger visitors may prefer the half-dozen linked PCs allowing you to engage in interactive combat. If any of this strikes a chord, then you might want to time your visit to coincide with the biennial, three-day "**Warbirds over Wanaka**" air show (Ⓣ03/356 0279 & 0800/496 920, Ⓔwow@skyshow.co.nz). At Easter each even-numbered year up to 70,000 people descend to watch all manner of airborne craft – but predominantly small and vintage planes – take to the air; details and tickets (around $15–25 per day; $65 for 3 days) are available from the Wanaka visitor centre.

A similar theme is explored in the adjacent **Wanaka Toy and Transport Museum** (daily: Nov–April 8.30am–6pm; May–Oct 9am–5pm; around $6), an engaging hoard of cars, trucks and bikes preserved by Wanaka's dry climate. There should be something here to titillate anyone with even a passing interest in motor vehicles. Some machines are just well-kept examples of stuff still puttering around New Zealand roads, but there's also exotica such as a Centurion tank, a ten-seater Lockhead Lodestar used by the US Army in the 1950s, Velocette and BSA bikes, and the Solar Kiwi Racer, an aluminium and glass-fibre bullet-shaped car powered by solar panels on its roof. Many of the main exhibits are replicated along the walls with all manner of other toys. If some of your party are extra-interested, others can pass the time in the adjacent **Wanaka Beerworks** (daily 9.30am–6pm; Ⓔwanaka.beerworks@xtra.co.nz), an award-winning microbrewery where you can sample (free) products currently only sold through bars and restaurants in the immediate area.

The perfect antidote to the museums lies across the road at **Have A Shot** (daily 9am–6pm), where you can, well, have a shot with a golf club on the driving range ($6 for 50 balls), a gun at either the claybird range ($25 for 20 rounds) or the .22 smallbore range ($12 for 30 rounds), or a bow at the archery range ($12 for 20min). Groups of more active combatants can join battle with spongy tennis balls in the battlefield ($6 for 20min).

Alternatively you might prefer the small but perfectly formed **Rippon Vineyards**, 3km west of Wanaka on the Mount Aspiring Road (Dec–April daily 11am–5pm). The dry, stony and sun-soaked slopes running down to Lake Wanaka were planted in 1974 and produced their first vintage in 1989. Five of their wines can be tasted for around $5 – the typically excellent Pinot Noir and the Sauvignon Blanc come particularly recommended – while a bottle of the good stuff will set you back $20–40. The best approach to the vineyard from Wanaka is on foot, along the lakefront Waterfall Creek Walking Track (see box on p.895), though it is easy to go too far: turn up into the vines just before a brown cottage. In February 2002 (and hopefully subsequent even years), the one-day Rippon open-air music festival (Ⓦwww.rippon.co.nz; tickets around $50) took place in the grounds.

Activities

Wanaka's relatively low profile and the absence of the hard sell and conveyor-belt style that characterizes some of Queenstown's slicker operations add up to a more relaxed approach – and frequently better value for money. Many, but not all, activities can be booked through The **Lakeland Adventures**, 99 Ardmore Street (Ⓣ03/443 8174 & 0800/684 468, Ⓕ443 8589), which acts as their booking agent and pick-up point.

Walks around Wanaka

Visitors shy of the beard-and-Gore-Tex walks in the Mount Aspiring National Park to the west might reap greater rewards from these more modest expeditions. No special gear is required, just robust shoes, wet-weather gear and sun protection.

Mount Iron

The most accessible of Wanaka's hilltop walks is up the 527m **Mount Iron** (2km; 1–2hr; 240m ascent), a glacially sculpted outcrop, its western and northern slopes ground smooth by the glacier that scoured its southern face. The path through farmland and the bird-filled kanuka woodland of the Mount Iron Scenic Reserve starts 1.5km east of Wanaka on SH84, climbing the steep southern face to the summit. Here you can enjoy magnificent panoramic views of Wanaka and the nearby lakes, before following the path down the east face of Mount Iron towards the entrance to Puzzling World (see p.892).

Mount Roy

Mount Roy Walking Track (16km; 4–6hr; 1100m ascent) is a much more ambitious prospect, winding up to the 1581m summit of Roy's Peak for wonderful views over Lake Wanaka and surrounding glaciers and mountains. The path starts 7km west of Wanaka on the Mount Aspiring Road, but is closed during the lambing season (Oct to mid-Nov).

Diamond Lake Walking Track

The long vistas from Mount Iron and Mount Roy are only really challenged by those on the **Diamond Lake Walking Track** (7km; 2hr 30min; 400m ascent), a community project which requests a $2 donation. From the car park 18km west of Wanaka on the Mount Aspiring Road there are a couple of short variations – but to get the views, you'll need to tackle the 775m summit of Rocky Hill.

Beacon Point–Clutha Outlet Circuit

This is a long but undemanding riverbank and lakeside walk which starts from Wanaka and follows the shore to **Eely Point** (15min), a sheltered bay popular for boating and picnics. Beyond Eely Point is Bremner Bay and the continuation of the waterfront path to **Beacon Point** (a further 30min). Either return the same way or continue along Beacon Point Road to the Outlet Motor Camp and pick up the **Outlet Track**, which runs 4km to Alison Avenue, then down to SH6 not far from the Albert Town bridge. By following SH6 this can be turned into a loop back to Wanaka (16km in all), passing Puzzling World (see p.892) and the base of Mount Iron (see above). The map in the DOC's *Wanaka Walks and Trails* leaflet ($1) makes the route a little clearer.

Waterfall Creek to Damper Bay

The westbound equivalent of the Beacon Point–Clutha Outlet Circuit leaves Roy's Bay along the **Waterfall Creek and Damper Bay Track** (5km one way; 1hr; negligible ascent), heading through Wanaka Station Park and past Rippon Vineyard to Waterfall Creek (35min). It continues along lakeside terraces to a high point on the Wanaka side of Damper Bay.

Canyoning

If abseiling down thirty-metre waterfalls and sliding down eighty-degree polished rock chutes into deep green pools appeals, then **canyoning** should fit the bill. You don't need any special experience, just a sense of adventure and water confidence – once you start into the canyon, there is only one way out. Deep Canyon (book through Lakeland Adventures Ⓔ deepcanyon@xtra.co.nz; mid-Nov to April or May) take up to five canyoners with each guide, who secures all abseils with safety ropes and provides enough warm, protective clothing to ease the sense of vulnerability. First-timers usually tackle **Emerald Creek** ($175 for a full day), a narrow fissure where fern-draped verdure envelops you, in complete contrast to the parched landscape of the surrounding Matukituki valley. Half-time tea and biscuits are served on a huge slab wedged high above a cascade, and the day is rounded off with a fine picnic and strong camp-brewed coffee. Other canyons in the vicinity are roped into service for second trips including the 400m-high **Twin Falls**; prices depend on numbers and guide:client ratio.

Rock climbing and mountaineering

Wanaka's dry, sunny climate is ideal for **rock climbing**. Tuition and guiding are offered by Wanaka Rock Climbing (contact The Adventure Centre), who run full-day top-roping, seconding and abseiling courses for two to four people ($149 each), inclusive of all transport and equipment. For the more experienced they offer one-on-one guided climbing (around $225 a day); or you can get out onto the Matukituki valley schist and gneiss unsupervised with a copy of *Wanaka Rock* ($14, available from Good Sports – see p.900). On a wet day visit Wanaka Gym, 155 Tenby St, which houses a fairly basic bouldering wall; call ⓣ03/443 9418 for opening hours.

If the idea of performing gymnastics on roadside crags tends to pale beside the prospect of getting up into the ice and snow of the Southern Alps, then you can always try one of the expensive but professional all-inclusive **mountaineering** packages offered by Mount Aspiring Guides (ⓣ03/443 9422, ⓔaspguide@xtra.co.nz). Their Summit Week ($2000 per person) sees two of you and one guide exploring the upper reaches of the Southern Alps (often around Fox glacier where ice climbing skills are honed) and bagging a number of peaks. Specific ascents include Mount Cook (Oct to mid-Jan; $3985), Mount Tasman (Oct–May; $3850), and Mount Aspiring (Oct–May) which has a four-day helicopter access option or a six-day walk in variation (both $2042). All these require a high degree of fitness and some mountain experience. Private mountain guiding will set you back around $300–500 per person per day depending on the trip, plus the cost of equipment rental, hut fees, transport and food.

Biking, riding and off-road trips

Wanaka abounds with shops renting out all-terrain bikes, but for a day's guided **mountain biking**, join Alpine Biking (The Adventure Centre or ⓣ03/443 8943) who specialize in **helibiking**, whisking you up to Treble Cone (Nov–April; 3–5hr; $235) or Mount Alpha (all year; 3–5hr; $235) for up to 1600 vertical metres of downhill track. They also run a 4WD-supported biking day-trip (Nov–May; 6hr; $165); and you can head to Cardrona ski field where, during January, they fire up a chairlift and turn some of the trails into a bike park (lifts $15 half day; bike rental $40).

Saddles of a different cut are employed by Lake Wanaka Saddle Adventures (ⓣ03/443 7777), which runs **horse-riding** treks (2hr; around $55) over farmland and through kanuka forest on the easy northern slopes of Mount Iron from their stables on Anderson Road, five minutes' drive northeast of Wanaka. More experienced riders can undertake a ride across open country ($50). A wider range of rides are offered by Backcountry Saddle Expeditions (ⓣ03/443 8151, ⓔbackcountry.saddle.expeditions@xtra.co.nz; 2hr–2 days; $45–130) from their stables 25km south of Wanaka in the Cardrona Valley; they'll pick you up from Wanaka if you book in advance.

To explore some of the less accessible parts of Wanaka and its environs, try the **4WD tours** organized by Edgewater Adventures, 59a Brownston St (Ⓣ & Ⓕ03/443 8422, Ⓔewa@clear.net.nz; 2hr 30min; $95); or the **quad-bike tours** with Criffel Peak Safaris (Ⓣ03/443 1711, Ⓔcriffelpeak.safaris@xtra.co.nz) which start with a three-hour meander around a high-country deer farm (around $95), and range up to a tour of nineteenth-century gold diggings (3hr ; $130).

Photographic tours

Budding photographers may fancy personalized **photographic tours** run by Aspiring Images (Ⓣ03/443 8358, Ⓔgrussell@xtra.co.nz; around $80 per half day, maximum 4 people), who tour the prime viewpoints and provide professional cameras, or Clean Green Images, Ballantyne Rd (Ⓣ03/443 7951, Ⓦwww.cleangreen.co.nz) who run nature tours with a photographic bent.

Flights, skydiving and paragliding

Magnificent scenery, clear skies and competitive prices make Wanaka an excellent place to get airborne. Bi-Plane Adventures (Ⓣ03/443 1000) will pick up in town and run you out to Wanaka airport for any of a number of one-pilot-one-passenger **scenic and stunt flights**. Cheapest (both $170) are the twenty-minute joyride in the open-cockpit 1920s Tiger Moth biplane and fifteen minutes in a closed-cockpit Pitts Special, which is designed specifically for aerobatics. For adrenalin junkies with money to burn there's also the 1940s-designed Mustang, which combines aerobatic agility with neck-snapping acceleration (20min; $2000). More mundance scenic flights are run by Wanaka Flighseeing (Ⓣ03/443 8770, Ⓔinfo@flightseeing.co.nz; $145–295) over Mt Aspiring or Milford Sound, and Aspiring Air (Ⓣ0800 100 943, Ⓦwww.nzflights.com; $90–295), over anything from Wanaka to Mt Cook. A twenty-minute scenic flight can be combined with a thirty-second freefall on a **tandem skydive** with Tandem Skydive Wanaka, Wanaka Airport (Ⓣ03/443 7207 & 025/796 877; $225).

A less fraught approach to viewing the tremendous scenery is to go **tandem paragliding**, a kind of scenic flight and paraglide all in one with Lucky Montana's Flying Circus (Ⓣ0800/247 287; around $155). You and your tandem guide are attached water-skiing-style to the back of a boat as you take off from the town beach and gradually gain around 600m over 15 minutes as the boat recedes to a dot below. You then detach from the tow line and begin the normal tandem paraglide turns and wing-overs back to the beach. If you'd rather take the controls you can learn **paragliding** with Wanaka Paragliding (Ⓣ03/443 9193), who offer various learn-to-fly courses from a basic introduction (1–3 days; $168), to the full solo rating ($600 plus equipment rental).

Flights to Milford (see p.946) from Wanaka tend to be a few dollars more expensive than those from Queenstown, but you're in the air longer and fly over a wider range of scenery including Mount Aspiring, the Olivine Ice Plateau and the inaccessible lakes of Alabaster, McKerrow and Tutoko. Most local accommodation receives daily bulletins on Milford weather and flight conditions. Both Aspiring Air (Ⓣ03/443 7943 & 0800/100 943) and Alpine Scenic Flights (Ⓣ03/443 8787 & 0800/435 444) do an extensive range of flights, the most popular being a combination flight and Milford Sound cruise (4hr; $295).

Cruises and boat activities

With a beautiful lake, a number of decent rivers and a friendly, low-key approach, there's plenty of opportunity for getting wet in style. Lakeland Adventures, Main Wharf (ⓣ03/443 7495), lay on all manner of waterborne activities, the most leisurely being the hour-long **lake cruise** ($50) around Ruby Island, Glendhu Bay, Pigeon Island and the lake outlet, and half-day trips landing on Pigeon Island and making the short walk to Arethusa Pool, a lake within a lake (3hrs;$120). For thrills and spills, try the fifty-minute **jetboat rides** onto the upper reaches of the Clutha with Clutha River Jet, Main Wharf (same phone; $65). Just along the beach Sail, Kayak Lake Wanaka (ⓣ03/443 9180) rent yachts, catamarans, **windsurfers** and **sea kayaks** by the day or hour. *Wanaka Springs* (see accommodation; ⓦwww.lakewanakacruises.co.nz) have also branched out into the gentle luxury and picnic cruise market with a standard trip weighing in at around $55 for two hours.

From October to April, Alpine Kayak Guides (ⓣ03/443 9023, ⓦwww.alpinekayaks.co.nz) will take you on a number of different full-day **kayaking** trips on the Matukituki, Clutha or Hawea rivers (all Grade II; $120). Independent paddlers may also be able to rent kayaks, depending on their abilities and intended river. A far cry from Queenstown's boisterous Kawarau and Shotover rivers, the **rafting trips** run by Pioneer Rafting (ⓣ03/443 1246; Sept–April; half day around$115, full day $160) are pitched at families, the emphasis being on appreciating the scenery, swimming and gold panning as you drift down the Upper Clutha or follow the historic timber-rafting route down the Makarora in oar-rigged rafts. No-holds-barred thrill-seekers need look no further than **whitewater sledging** with Frogz Have More Fun (ⓣ0800/338 737), who mainly sledge the seven-kilometre stretch of the Kawarau River with its four major rapids (Grade II–IV; 1hr 30min on the water; $109). The season runs from November to April, though by late summer the low water levels mean that the rapids have lost much of their might.

Fishing

Wanaka and Hawea lakes and the rivers flowing into them are popular territory for brown and rainbow **trout fishing**. There's a maximum bag of six fish per day and you'll require the sport fishing licence (around $15–20 a day, $30 a week), obtainable from the visitor centre or the DOC office. Unless you really know your bait, you'll have a better chance of catching your supper with Lakeland Adventures; charter rates start at $200 for two hours on a six-metre cabin cruiser (maximum 4 passengers), or they'll rent you a rod, reel and lures for about $15 a day and a four-metre runabout carrying five adults for $40–50 an hour.

Eating and drinking

The sophisticated tastes and open wallets of Wanaka's skiers, combined with a healthy influx of summer tourists, have together fostered an abundance of very good places to eat. The town's drinking dens are less appealing, but you can always take refuge in the restaurant bars. Unless you strike lucky and catch a band passing through, the only entertainment is the wonderful Paradiso **cinema**, corner of Ardmore Street and Ballantyne Road (ⓣ03/443 1505; closed Mon; $10), an off-beat place where you sit in beat-up old sofas, armchairs, cushions and even a Morris Minor installed along one side. Unless there is a general consensus to press on through, there will be an interval when everyone tucks into cookies, ice-cream, coffee or booze from the on-site café (see below). Films range from quality Hollywood to arthouse.

Apartment One Lounge Bar 1st floor, 99 Ardmore St, entry from the car park and concrete steps at the back of the building. Well-kept secret that's difficult to find but well worth looking for, as it has a balcony that looks out over the lake and is undoubtedly the cruisiest, loungiest, most fun drinking den for miles in any direction. Usually open from 4pm, with occasional DJ sounds, a simple selection of antipasto platters and mellow background music, this is the perfect place to enjoy the sun going down.

Café Paradiso cnr Ardmore St & Ballantyne Rd. Groovy little café attached to its cinema namesake with Formica tables and piles of old *Empire* magazines to keep you occupied over muffins, sandwiches, pasta dishes, some excellent main courses, coffee that's freshly roasted in the basement, cookies and home-made ice-cream that's free of additives and wondrously fruity. Licensed.

Callaboose 2 Dunmore St ☎03/443 6262. Restaurant-cum-bar that is both classy and informal, with reasonably priced lunch and brunch menus, including door-step sandwiches, giving way to some excellent, more expensive, mains in the evening which feature lamb shanks, steaks, fish and some lovely pumpkin pansotti. The bar attached is loungy with live piano most evenings.

Capriccio 123 Ardmore St ☎03/443 8579. A little gem of an Italian-style restaurant, which branches out into Thai and Kiwi flavours, with filling pasta dishes for lunch and more sophisticated evening meals for around $27. Go for anything with fish in it. Licensed.

The Doughbin Pembroke Mall. Home-style bakery with good cakes and pies, including vegetarian versions, from 6am–6pm and offering late menu, through a serving hatch round the side, for the hungry drinkers and clubbers from midnight-4am..

Fez Pembroke Mall, next to *The Doughbin*. Fantastic and authentic little Turkish kebab house, serving cheap but delightful lamb and shish kebabs, falafel, *iskenders*, strong coffee and wonderful sweet deserts from 9am–midnight.

Kai Whakapai cnr Ardmore St & Helwick St. Undoubtedly Wanaka's essential daytime eating spot and a hot favourite with the locals, who come here for Danish pastries and croissants for breakfast, damn fine coffee and fabulous meals in gargantuan proportions through the day. Expect the likes of smoked chicken and avocado salad ($15), salmon ravioli ($25) and pizzas big enough for two ($25). Closed Sun evening; BYO & licensed.

The Kingsway 21 Helwick St. Nearly the coolest bar in town, cavernous and airy with a pool table, the local Beerworks draught on tap, and music that gets cranked up as the evening wears on.

Muzza's cnr Brownston & Helwick Sts ☎03/443 7296. Restaurant and bar with unimaginative decor but good-value straightforward meals such as roast lamb ($15) and blue cod ($21). Licensed.

Paddy's cnr of Pembroke Mall and Dungarvon St. A drinkers pub from 4pm until the wee hours with eclectic live music most nights and jam sessions on Tues and Sun. Very busy at weekends with a happy hour (5–6pm) and various drink deals. When the music kicks in at about 9.30pm they get rid of the ingenious pool table to make a dance floor.

Paddy's Thai Restaurant 21 Dunmore St ☎03/443 7640. Next door to *Paddy's* pub and owned by the same people, but don't let the name fool you, this is a surprising and authentic Kiwi/Thai cross, producing spicy salads, *thom ka*, crispy stir-fries, thick red curries, and a 500g pure NZ steak with all the trimmings. Licensed.

Relishes 99 Ardmore St. Pretension-free, swish dinner-only BYO and licensed restaurant that has been around long enough to become an institution. Wonderful pasta dishes for under $20, excellent mussels and scallops, buttered chicken masala and mouth-watering deserts.

Shooters cnr of Ardmore and Dungarvon sts. Big, uncharacterful drinkers bar, just across the road from the lake, with loud, chart-oriented DJ-mixed tunes on Friday and Saturday.

Trade 71 Ardmore St ☎03/443 6722. Yet another of the new upmarket restaurants offering day-long snacks, brunches and lunches, and then sumptuous evening meals, with chargrilled ribeyes, lamb racks and a wine list that starts at $16 and then gets silly.

Toscana 76 Golf Course Rd ☎03/443 1255. Authentic and moderately priced Italian restaurant in a modern Tuscan cottage-style building with a wonderful view over the town and lake, and a terracotta patio flanked by fig trees. Expect antipasto ($20), and spinach and ricotta cannelloni ($19). Dinner nightly, lunch summer only. Licensed.

Tuatara Pizza Bar 72 Ardmore St. Licensed eat-in and take-out evening-only pizzeria – but more renowned for its pool table and lively bar, from 6pm onwards.

White House Café & Bar 33 Dunmore St ☎03/443 9595. One of Wanaka's best: a classy yet casual restaurant in a flamboyantly nautical blue and white open-plan house with a sunny patio (or a raging fire in winter). The cuisine is Mediterranean with strong Mahgrebi and Middle Eastern leanings, accompanied by wonderful fresh breads and great strong coffee. Mains are around $16–30, and can be washed down with something from the extensive wine list, all available by the glass. The desserts are sensational. Licensed.

The Zone Pembroke Mall. One of the coolest places for a cup of coffee, a full breakfast or something from the à la carte menu that contains many vegetarian and/or organic options. They mix Pacific Rim, Kiwiana, Mexican and anything else they fancy to come up with some taste-bud twanging combinations at reasonable prices, as well as offering some thick smoothies and funky music. Licensed.

Listings

Bike rental Good Sports, Dunmore St (℗03/443 7966), rent some very flash machines for $50 a day, though there are others at $30 & $25. Mountain Bikes Unlimited, 99 Ardmore St (℗03/443 7882), also rent out the latest off-road machines for around $35 a day ($20 per half day) during the summer season, complete with a local map indicating prime mountain-biking routes. Less exalted specimens are available across the road at Lakeland Adventures, Main Wharf (℗03/443 7495), for $10 an hour or $30 a day. The bargain deal is from the YHA, 181 Upton St (℗ & Ⓕ03/443 7405), which rents out basic bikes for $25 a day to all-comers.
Buses Atomic (℗03/442 8178) run to Christchurch, Dunedin, Invercargill and Greymouth; Catch-a-Bus (℗03/471 4103) runs to Dunedin; InterCity (℗03/442 5628) stop in Wanaka on the Queenstown to Franz Josef and Queenstown to Christchurch runs, and go to Dunedin; and Southern Link Shuttles (℗03/358 8355) run to Christchurch.
Camping and outdoor equipment Good Sports, Dunmore St (℗03/443 7966), rents out fishing tackle ($10 a day), hiker tents ($10 a day), alpine tents ($15 a day) and just about everything else imaginable for use in the outdoors.
Car rental Aspiring Car Rentals (℗03/443 7883) have cars for around $65 a day, with unlimited kilometres and insurance, but don't allow drop-offs; Queenstown-based Apex (℗0800/531 111) do allow one-way rentals and rates start at $60 a day.
Internet Fast machines and lively musical accompaniment at *Wanaka Web*, upstairs at 3 Helwick St ℗03/443 7429, *from_wanaka@hotmail.com*; daily 9am (roughly) to 9pm.
Medical treatment Wanaka Medical Centre, 39 Russell St ℗03/443 7811.
Pharmacy Wanaka Pharmacy, 33 Helwick St ℗03/443 8000.
Police Helwick St ℗03/4437272.
Post office The post office at 39 Ardmore St (℗03/443 8211) has poste restante facilities.
Ski rental Harris Mountain Heliskiing, 99 Ardmore St (℗0800/684 468), and Racers Edge, 99 Ardmore St (℗03/443 7882), rent out skis and snowboards for $25–42 per day, and also run a ski tuning and repair service – as does Good Sports on Dunmore St (℗03/443 7966).
Taxis Wanaka Taxis (℗03/443 7999).

Around Wanaka

Wanaka is the only town of any size within a huge area of western Central Otago, and the only resort with easy access to tramps in the **Mount Aspiring National Park**. Consequently, it's a popular base for exploring the surrounding countryside, principally the open and mountainous areas to the north and west, the Haast Pass road over to the West Coast (see p.790), and the tortuous **Cardrona Road**, the most direct route to Queenstown, passing through the **Cardrona Valley** at perilous altitudes.

The Cardrona Valley

Though designated a state highway (SH89), the **Crown Range Road** through the **Cardrona Valley** from Wanaka to Queenstown is one of New Zealand's highest public roads, reaching an **altitude** of 1120m, and many consider it little more than a track: caravans are banned and car-rental agencies forbid travel over one unsealed twenty-kilometre section. On a fine day, however, its twists and precipitous drops present no more of a problem than any other dirt road in New Zealand. The effort expended is rewarded by a shorter if slower alternative route from Wanaka to Queenstown – 70km as against 120km by SH6 – and a drive past the detritus of the valley's gold-mining heyday. Note that work is underway to tarmac the whole thing; a project due for completion by 2002.

Rumours of William Fox's unwitting discovery of gold in the Arrow River at Arrowtown in 1862 sparked a frenzy of activity. Prospectors spread far and wide, quickly moving north along the Crown Range and stumbling into the Cardrona Valley, where **gold** was discovered later that year. Five years on, the Europeans legged it to the new fields on the West Coast, leaving the dregs to Chinese immigrants, who themselves had drifted away by 1870.

From Wanaka the road is currently sealed for the first 26km, past the Cardrona and Waiorau Nordic ski area access roads (see "Winter in Wanaka" box on p.902) to the few cottages and long-forgotten cemetery that make up the hamlet of **Cardrona**. Here, the *Cardrona Hotel* (see "Accommodation", p.890) stands in a state of arrested decay. Built in 1868, it survived the floods of 1878 that destroyed most of the old town, battling on until 1961. After years of neglect it was reopened in 1984, with its original facade and a completely renovated interior opening onto a great beer garden; it's now a popular watering hole for skiers in winter, and a good spot for bar and restaurant meals ($10–20) at any time.

South from here, the surfaced section ends, heralding 20km of twisting dirt road through grassy flanks of bald, mica-studded hills to a great viewpoint overlooking Queenstown and Lake Wakatipu. Here the tarmac resumes, just in time for the steep switchback down towards SH6 and Queenstown.

The Matukituki Valley and Mount Aspiring National Park

The **Matukituki Valley** is very much Wanaka's outdoor playground, a 60km tentacle reaching from the parched Otago landscapes around Lake Wanaka to the steep alpine skirts of Mount Aspiring, which at 3030m is New Zealand's highest mountain outside the Mount Cook National Park. Extensive high-country stations run sheep on the riverside meadows, briefly glimpsed by skiers bound for Treble Cone, rock climbers making for the roadside crags, Matukituki-bound kayakers, and trampers and mountaineers hot-footing it to the **Mount Aspiring National Park**.

The park, first mooted in 1935 but not created until 1964, is one of the country's largest, extending from the Haast Pass (where there are tramps around Makarora) in the north, to the head of Lake Wakatipu (where the Rees–Dart Track and parts of the Routeburn track fall within its bounds) in the south. The pyramidal Mount Aspiring undoubtedly forms the centrepiece of the park, rising with classical beauty over the ice-smoothed, broad valleys and creaking glaciers. It was first climbed in 1909 using heavy hemp rope and none of the modern climbing hardware used by today's mountaineers, who still treat the mountain as one of the grails of Kiwi mountaineering ambition. Travelling along Mount Aspiring Road beside the Matukituki River, the peak hoves into view just outside Wanaka, and remains tantalizingly present all the way to the **Raspberry Creek**, where a car park and public toilets mark the start of a number of magnificent tramps (see box on p.904–905) into the heart of the park.

Winter in Wanaka

May signifies the end of the summer season, and Wanaka immediately starts gearing up for **winter**. Mountain-bike rental shops switch to ski rental (see "Listings", p.900), watersports instructors don their salopettes, pot-bellied stoves replace parasols at restaurants, and frequent shuttle buses run up to the ski fields, calling at the hotels, hostels and sports shops along the way. Reports on snow conditions can be heard on the local radio at around 6.45am, and shops around town post up the morning's report in their windows – you can't miss them. If you plan to drive up to the ski fields, you'll need tyre chains, which can be rented at petrol stations in Wanaka.

Cardrona

Cardrona Ski Resort (Ⓣ03/443 7341, Ⓦwww.cardrona.co.nz) sprawls over three basins on the southeastern slopes of the 1934-metre Mount Cardrona, the 12km unsealed access road branching off 24km south of Wanaka and just short of the hamlet of Cardrona. Predominantly a family-oriented field – they run a junior ski school and a crèche – Cardrona is noted for dry snow and an abundance of gentle **runs** ideally suited to beginners and intermediates (including snowboarders). Currently there are two quads, a double chair and learner tows, giving a maximum vertical descent of 390m and, though there is little extreme terrain, snowboarders have the run of four half-pipes. As you would expect, there's a full programme of lessons, ski packages and gear rental, plus full restaurant and bar facilities. Beginners can spend the day on the learner field for less than half the $60 adult **lift pass**. Through most of the long season (June to early October), you'll need snow chains to negotiate the access road ($12 a day) which drops you at the base facilities halfway up the field. Non-drivers can get **buses** from Wanaka, and from Queenstown, an hour and a half away.

Cardrona is unique in offering **accommodation** actually on the mountain – in luxury, fully self-contained three-bedroom apartments sleeping six for around $400 (Ⓣ03/443 7341).

Treble Cone

More experienced skiers tend to frequent the excellent steep slopes of **Treble Cone** (Ⓣ03/443 7443, Ⓦwww.new-zealand.com/treblecone), 20km west of Wanaka, where additional snow-making equipment has extended the season, which now lasts from mid-June to early October. Its appeal lies in open uncrowded slopes, spectacularly located high above Lake Wanaka, and a full 610 vertical metres of skiing, served by New Zealand's first detachable six-seater chair, a couple of T-bars and a learner tow. The **terrain** is very varied with moguls, powder runs, gully runs and

Buses operated by Mount Aspiring Express (Ⓣ03/443 8422; around $25 one way, $45 return), and Alpine Shuttles (Ⓣ03/443 7966, Ⓔinfo@good-sports.co.nz; similar prices) run 55km along Mount Aspiring Road to the national park's main trailhead at Raspberry Creek. Both also run a charter service, which gives you greater flexibility and works out cheaper if you can get at least five people together.

Towards the West Coast: Lake Hawea and Hawea

Mountain-backed **Lake Hawea**, immediately east of Lake Wanaka, receives a fraction of the attention of its western neighbour. With its milky, azure waters this might seem surprising, but much of its appeal was shorn away in 1958 with

plenty of natural and created half-pipes; the limited extent of wide, groomed slopes makes it hard work for beginners, but snowboarders will have a ball. Day **lift passes** go for $61 and there's a first-timer's package (skiers $50, boarders $60) including a lower lift pass, rental and instruction.

Lessons, gear rental and food are all on tap, and the field is easily reached along a 7km toll-free access road. Morning **buses** leave from Wanaka, and a shuttle bus takes skiers from the start of the access road on Mount Aspiring Road up to the tows.

Waiorau

With so many Kiwi skiers committed to downhill, it comes as a surprise to discover the **Waiorau Snow Farm** (ⓣ03/443 7542), a Nordic ski area across the valley from Cardrona, some 24km south of Wanaka, then 13km up a winding dirt road. At around $25 for access to the field and $20 for ski rental, it is a relatively inexpensive way to get on the snow; and Nordic skiing – essentially tramping on skis – is beginning to catch on. From July to September, exponents negotiate the 55km of marked and groomed Nordic trails designed to cater to beginners and experts in both the Nordic and telemark disciplines. The ski school caters to all levels with improvers' clinics and children's programmes run throughout the season, though more frequently at weekends.

Heli-skiing

No one is going to fool you into believing that **heli-skiing** is cheap, but there's no other way of getting to runs of up to 1200 vertical metres across virgin snow on any of six mountain ranges. From June to October, Harris Mountains Heli-skiing (ⓣ03/442 6722, ⓦwww.new-zealand.com/hmh), New Zealand's biggest heli-skiing operator, offers almost 400 different runs on 150 peaks – mainly in the Harris Mountains between Queenstown's Crown Range and Wanaka's Mount Aspiring National Park.

Strong intermediate and **advanced skiers** generally get the most out of the experience, though those with more limited skills can still participate provided they meet the minimum standard determined by an ability questionnaire. **Conditions** are more critical than at the ski fields, but on average there's heli-skiing on seventy percent of days during winter, typically in four- to five-day weather windows separated by storms. Of the multitude of packages, the most popular have to be a three-run day ($595),"The Classic" ($655), with four runs in a day, and "Maximum Vertical" ($830), comprising seven runs for advanced skiers only; **bookings** should be made well in advance and accompanied by a substantial deposit (around 40 percent).

the completion of a small dam, which raised the lake level by twenty metres, in the process drowning the lake's beaches and gently shelving shoreline. Nevertheless, the lake is still popular with anglers intent on bagging landlocked rainbow and brown trout, and salmon. Otherwise there is little reason to spend time here – except to recharge your batteries in the peace and quiet of **HAWEA**, a village that clings to the lake's southern shore 15km northeast of Wanaka. The Lake Hawea Store (Mon–Sat 8am–7pm, Sun 9am–7pm), right in the centre of the village, sells one-day fishing licences ($13) and can put you in touch with local angling experts; expect to pay $300–400 a day for fly-fishing guides.

If you stay, you'll find **camping** and basic **accommodation** in the cabins of the spacious, leafy *Lake Hawea Motor Camp*, SH6 (ⓣ & ⓕ03/443 1767; tent sites $10, cabins & flats ❷–❹) right by the lakeshore. The *Lake Hawea Motor*

Walks in the Matukituki Valley

The DOC's *Matukituki Valley Tracks* and *Rees–Dart Track* leaflets ($1 each) are recommended for these walks, along with the 1:150,000 *Mount Aspiring National Park* map which has a 1:80,000 detail on the back that's perfect for the Cascade Saddle Route.

These walks can be tackled by relatively fit and experienced trampers; all times and distances given are one way, and remember that any reference to the left or right bank of a river assumes you're facing downstream. The climatic differences in the park are extreme, and the half-metre of rain that falls each year in the Matukituki Valley is no indication of the six metres that fall on the western side of the park; as ever, go prepared.

Several huts in this area are owned by the New Zealand Alpine Club (NZAC) but are open to all.

Raspberry Creek to Aspiring Hut

The popular day walk from **Raspberry Creek to Aspiring Hut** (9km; 2hr 30min–3hr; 100m ascent) starts along a 4WD track which climbs gently from the Raspberry Creek car park beside the western branch of the Matukituki River, only heading away from the river to avoid bluffs en route to Downs Creek, from where you get fabulous views up to the Rob Roy Glacier and Mount Avalanche. Bridal Veil Falls is only a brief distraction before **Cascade Hut** (NZAC; 4 bunks; $10), which is usually locked but does take overspill if the other hut is full. You can gain access through the DOC in Wanaka, but it is barely worth the trouble as it is followed thirty minutes later by the relatively luxurious stone-built **Aspiring Hut** (NZAC; 44 bunks; Nov–April $18 with gas; May–Oct $10 without), a common base camp for mountaineers off to the peaks around Mount Aspiring, which is wonderfully framed by the hut's picture windows.

Rob Roy Valley

The **Rob Roy Valley Walk** (6km; 2hr 30min; 400m ascent) is shorter and steeper than the walk to *Aspiring Hut* but just as spectacular, striking through some magnificent alpine scenery, snowfields and glaciers. From the Raspberry Creek car park, follow the right bank of the Matukituki for fifteen minutes to a swingbridge; cross to the left bank of the Rob Roy stream, which cuts through a small gorge into the beech forest. Gradually the woods give way to alpine vegetation – and the Rob Roy glacier nosing down into the head of the valley.

Aspiring Hut to the head of the valley

An excellent day out from *Aspiring Hut* involves exploring the headwaters of the Matukituki River to the north. The **Aspiring Hut to Pearl Flat** (4km; 1hr 30min; 100m ascent) stretch follows the still-broad river as it weaves in and out of the bush to Pearl Flat. From **Pearl Flat to the head of the valley** (3.5km; 1hr 30min; 250m ascent) the path follows the right bank, crosses a huge avalanche chute off the side

Inn, 1 Capell Ave (Ⓣ03/443 1224, Ⓕ443 1024; dorms ❶, motel units ❺–❻), is optimally sited for uninterrupted lake and mountain views; the backpacker-style lodge has pleasant four-bunk dorms complete with bedding, and self-catering facilities. The best of the **B&Bs** is at 4 Bodkin St (Ⓣ03/443 1343; ❹), where a couple of balconied rooms tucked atop a craft-filled A-frame boast fine mountain views.

Eating is best done in the B&Bs if that's where you are staying; otherwise, make for the substantial bar meals and beer garden at the *Lake Hawea Hotel* or the takeaway and small café at the Lake Hawea Store.

of Mount Barff and climbs high above the river through cottonwood and into open country. Scott Rock Bivvy, marked on some maps, is little more than a sheltering rock 50m east of the river and reached by a bridge.

An alternative, initially following the same route, goes from **Aspiring Hut to French Ridge Hut** (9km; 4hr; 1000m ascent); the new **French Ridge Hut** (NZAC; 20 bunks; $10) has great mountain views but is usually only below the snowline from December to March.

Cascade Saddle Route

The most challenging and most satisfying of the local tramps connects the Matukituki Valley to the Rees–Dart Circuit centred on Glenorchy (see p.878), via the arduous **Cascade Saddle Route** (4–5 days one way), a magnificent alpine crossing with fine panoramic views of the Dart Glacier and the Barrier Range. Long stretches of exposed high country and a finishing point 150km (by road) from the start mean that the route is not one to be undertaken lightly, though it is usually possible to send your excess gear ahead to Queenstown with Wanaka Connexions (☎0800/879 926), who charge around $10 per bag. Cascade Saddle can only be negotiated without specialized mountaineering equipment for around four months a year (typically Dec–March), and requires sound route-finding skills, totally waterproof clothing and a compass, while a tent gives you the option of breaking the longest day by spending a night in the alpine meadows at the saddle.

The first part of the route follows the track from **Raspberry Creek to Aspiring Hut** (9km; 2hr 30min–3hr; 100m ascent - see description opposite). From **Aspiring Hut to Dart Hut** (13km; 8–11hr; 1350m ascent) views of Mount Aspiring improve as you rise above the tree line onto the steep tussock and snowgrass ridge above. The route is now marked by orange snow poles which lead you to a steel pylon (1835m) that marks the top of the ridge, down to Cascade Creek and across it before climbing gently to the meadows around Cascade Saddle (1500m); four to six hours so far. Non-campers will have to press on another four or five hours to the somewhat oversubscribed *Dart Hut*, some 500m lower down, along the upper **Dart Valley**. The initial steep descent beside snow poles is treacherous when wet, but on a warm afternoon enjoys expansive views towards the mouth of the rubble-topped Dart Glacier, where chunks of ice periodically crash into the milky river that surges beneath it. In 1914, the terminus of the glacier had crept to within a kilometre of *Dart Hut*, but it is retreating an average of 50m a year and could all but disappear within eighty years. After following lateral moraine, rounding bluffs and fording streams, you eventually reach the **Dart Hut** ($10; 20 bunks), from where it is two days to Glenorchy, following either the Dart or Rees river valleys. The loading on the *Dart Hut*'s meagre twenty bunks is a bit of a push at peak periods but DOC hope to expand it.

The Central Otago goldfields

Though Queenstown's gold-rush heritage has largely been swamped by adventure tourism, the mining past remains a significant part of the main attraction of the **Central Otago goldfields**, an historically rich region which has begun to adapt and evolve into a tourist destination of moody splendour covering much of the country east of the Queenstown–Wanaka axis to the coast at Dunedin. This barren, rugged and peculiarly beautiful high-country hinterland is where, from the 1860s to the end of the century, gold was panned from the streambeds, dredged from the deeper rivers, and eventually mined and blasted

Gold from dirt

The classic image of the felt-hatted old-timer **panning** merrily beside a stream is only part of the story of gold extraction, but it's a true enough depiction of the first couple of years of the Otago gold rush. Initially all a miner needed was a pick and shovel, a pan, and preferably a special wooden box known as a "rocker" for washing the alluvial gravel. Periodic droughts lowered the river levels to reveal unworked banks, but as the easily accessible gravel beds were worked out, all manner of ingenious schemes were devised to gain access to fresh raw material. The most common technique was to divert the river, and some far-fetched schemes were hatched, especially on the Shotover River: steel sheets were driven into the river beds with some success, landslides induced to temporarily dam the flow, and a tunnel was bored through a bluff.

When pickings got thinner miners turned their attentions to the more tightly packed banks of the gorges. Hillside dams were constructed and water was piped under pressure to **sluicing** guns that blasted the auriferous gravel free, ready for processing either by traditional hand-panning or its mechanical equivalent, where "riffle plates" caught the fine gravel and carpet-like matting trapped the fine flakes of gold. Eventually the scale of these operations put individual miners out of business and many pressed on to fresh fields.

To get at otherwise inaccessible gravel stock, larger companies began building **gold dredges**, great clanking behemoths anchored to the riverbanks but floating free on the river. Buckets scooped out the river bottom, then the dredge processed the gravel and spat the "tailings" out of the back to pile up along the riversides.

Otago's alluvial gold starts its life underground embedded in reefs of quartz, and when economic returns from the rivers waned, miners sought the mother lode. **Reef quartz mining** required a considerable investment in machinery and whole towns sprang up to tunnel, hack out the ore and haul it on sledges to the stamper batteries. Here, a series of water-driven (and later steam-powered) hammers would pulverize the rock, which was then passed over copper plates smeared with mercury, and onto gold-catching blankets, before the remains were washed into the berdan – a special kind of cast-iron bowl. Gold was then separated from the mercury, a process subsequently made more efficient with the use of cyanide.

from the land. Small-time panners still extract a little "colour" from the streams and a few commercial mines still operate, but for the most part the gold has turned its back on the country it built. The landscape is now littered with abandoned mines, perilous shafts and scattered bits of mysterious-looking machinery, while shingle banks in the rivers occasionally reveal the remains of huge dredges, or the detritus of hare-brained schemes to divert the waters and reveal the gold-bearing riverbed.

Towns that boomed in the 1860s were mostly moribund by the early years of the twentieth century, but a few either struggled on as way-stations between the coast and the farmlands of the interior, or developed into prosperous service towns for the stone-fruit orchards which thrive in the region's crisp, dry winters and searingly hot summers. A shortage of water to irrigate these fertile lands was subsequently addressed by building a couple of controversial hydro dams on the Clutha River, drowning many of the orchards in the process. The result of the very particular weather conditions and now readily available irrigation has meant that the region is burgeoning into a **wine region** of unique flavours and enormous potential (see p.858).

Many of the significant locales in the gold country fall under the auspices of the DOC's **Otago Goldfields Park**, which encompasses a score of diverse sites scattered throughout the region – all of which are listed in the free *Otago Goldfields Heritage Highway* leaflet, available from local visitor centres. When out exploring, take **precautions**: deep shafts and heavy machinery are potentially hazardous, so at recognized sites, keep to marked paths and heed safety barriers; elsewhere tread extremely carefully.

The reconstructed nineteenth-century boom town at **Cromwell** probably won't delay you long, but the town is a good jumping-off point for the former mining settlements of **Bannockburn** and **Bendigo**. Cromwell's Lake Dunstan is actually a reservoir backed up behind a dam, adjacent to the peaceful town of **Clyde**, now an attractive knot of restaurants and guest houses. **Alexandra** acts mainly as a service town at the fork of two roads penetrating deep into the less-visited part of the gold county: SH85 heads northeast onto the **Maniototo** Plain, skirting the dilapidated former gold towns of **St Bathan's** and **Naseby** on the way to workaday **Ranfurly**, and the only accessible working mine at **Macreas Flat**; while SH8 dives southeast towards the coast through dull **Roxburgh** and **Lawrence**, where the gold rush initially started.

Major **bus** and shuttle companies run fairly regular services along SH8 between Queenstown and Dunedin, and Catch-A-Bus (Ⓣ03/471 4103) run a once-daily service from Wanaka through the Maniototo, but to really explore this region you need your own vehicle.

Some history

New Zealand's greatest gold rush kicked off in 1861 when Gabriel Read, an Australian who had previously worked the Californian fields, unearthed flakes of the precious metal beside the Tuapeka River, south of Lawrence. Within weeks Dunedin had all but emptied and thousands were camping out on the **Tuapeka Goldfield** around Gabriels Gully. The excitement at Tuapeka soon fizzled out, although by the winter of 1862 Californian prospectors Horatio Hartley and Christopher Reilly teased their first flakes out of the Clutha River, bagging a 40kg haul in three months. This sparked off an even greater gold rush, this time centred on Cromwell, which mushroomed as wagon trains made their way over the rough muddy trails from the coast into the interior. Tent cities sprang up, soon to be replaced by more permanent buildings as merchants moved in founding banks, hotels, shops, bars and brothels. Later in 1862, Thomas Arthur and Harry Redfern struck lucky at what is now Arthur's Point on the Shotover River, sparking a mass exodus for the fresh fields of what soon became known as "the richest river in the world". Miners flooded into Skipper's Canyon, but a few months later some of the heat was taken from its banks by discoveries on the Fox River near Arrowtown, the last of the major gold towns to be built and still the best preserved. Within a few years, returns had dwindled and many headed off to investigate reports of richer finds on the West Coast. As fortunes waned and traders saw their profits diminishing, Chinese miners were co-opted to pick over the tailings (discarded bits of rock and gravel) left behind by Europeans, and were occasionally allowed to work unwanted claims.

Though the boom and bust cycle was as rapid here as in gold country elsewhere, some form of mining continued for the best part of forty years, and the profits fuelled a South Island economy which, for a time at least, dominated New Zealand's exchequer. Dunedin's economy boomed, and the golden bounty funded the majority of that city's grand civic buildings.

Many claims were eventually abandoned not for lack of gold but because of harsh winters, famine, war, a dip in the gold price, lack of sluicing water, or just disinterest. Although returns are far from spectacular, there are still people out there eking out a living from gold mining; stakes are still claimed and you'll find small- and medium-scale operations all over the province. There's very little appliance of science and despite a fair bit of sophisticated machinery, these are very much backyard operations where instinct counts for much and fancy mining theories not at all. Bigger capital-intensive companies occasionally gauge the area's potential, and as one mining engineer pithily put it, "there's still a shitload of gold out there".

Cromwell and around

East of Arrowtown, SH6 runs for 40km through the scenic Kawarau Gorge, past the Goldfields Mining Centre (see p.910), to **CROMWELL**, a dull, flat little service town with its gold-mining roots waterlogged below the shimmering surface of the **Lake Dunstan** reservoir. Formed by the Clyde Dam 20km downstream (see p.911), Lake Dunstan swamped much of Cromwell's historic core, and the present-day town centre is uninspiringly modern. Civic boosters hope that the crisp, dry climate, ever-increasing number of wineries, fruit orchards, water-borne leisure activities and the fact that it's on Otago Central Rail Trail (see p.916) will lure visitors, and very slowly it is beginning to happen, as many travellers make a bid to escape the theme-park feel of Queenstown. Cromwell is a marginally viable base from which to explore the gold diggings hereabouts and a good few young wineries producing impressive vintages, but in truth you're better off staying in one of the other more characterful settlements hereabouts.

Soon after Hartley and Reilly's 1862 discovery of **gold** beside the Clutha River, a settlement sprouted at "The Junction" at the fork of the Kawarau and Clutha rivers. Local stories tell that it was later renamed when a government survey party dubbed it Cromwell to spite local Irish immigrant workers. Miners low on provisions planted the first fruit trees in the region, little expecting that Cromwell would become the centre of the Otago orchard belt. Its location, further from the sea than any other town in New Zealand, dictates an extreme temperature range – hot and arid in summer with still, cool, dry winters – making it perfect for growing dripping, toothsome **stone fruit**, and ideal for vines.

Tour buses disgorge their load at the half-dozen fruit stalls beside SH8, which skirts Cromwell passing the giant glass fibre fruity confection by The Mall. The combined visitor centre (see below) and **museum** (donations welcome) is packed full of gold-mining memorabilia, together with material on the construction of Clyde Dam. Free leaflets outline the self-guided **Cromwell Tour**, mind-numbingly dull but for the section around **Old Cromwell Town** (unrestricted entry), a kind of historic reserve on Melmore Terrace, where Lake Dunstan now laps the increasing number of spruced-up old shopfronts that are part of the town's effort to lure tourists away from the usual travellers trails. In the mid-1970s when the Clyde Dam was planned and the death knell sounded for the heart of old Cromwell, the preservation instinct kicked in, but in the wrong gear and a perfect opportunity to preserve an 1870s town was missed. Instead, a dozen buildings due to be submerged were dismantled stone by stone and have now been rebuilt on the water's edge and house tacky tourist shops.

Aquatic activities are still in their infancy here, though you can take a **lake cruise** with Dunstan Charters (1hr, min of 2 people; $15; ⓣ03/445 0203), from the wharf by Cromwell Old Town, opposite *Jolly's Grape and Grain Café*. Alternatively you can try Eco Experience on Lake Dunstan (ⓣ03/445 0711, ⓔEcoExperience@xtra,co,nz; around 3hr; $160 for the first 2 people and then

$60 per passenger, max of 4; binoculars provided), run from Villa Amo (see "practicalities", below), who offer **bird-watching trips** up to the eerie and ensnaring waterlogged-forest at the north-eastern tip of Lake Dunstan. Cruising the lake are about fifty different species of bird and there is also the possibility of trying to catch a fish for tea (rods provided). If the **fishing** side interests more than the bird-watching then Dick Marquand is your enthusiastic and knowledgeable man; he's been involved in preserving rare species in the area for DOC and in finding ways to lure the brown trout into his boat for years (Ⓣ03/445 1745, Ⓦwww.troutfishingservices.co.nz; $160 for 2hrs, $300 half day, $600 full day).

If you happen to be in the area in early March you might be lucky enough to catch the historic **Cavalcade**, which marks the first Cobb & Co Coaches that made there way around the area, and is an occasion when locals climb upon wagons and horses and undertake a wilderness ride over a couple of days to a fun celebration in Middlemarch (see p.919), the best bit for the uncommitted. It's worth seeing though it's not for inexperieinced riders and requires considerable forward planning to take part (Ⓦwww.nzsouth.co.nz/goldfields).

Practicalities

Queenstown- or Wanaka-bound **bus** travellers may well have to change in Cromwell, using the stop outside the petrol station on Murray Terrace right by The Mall, Cromwell's civic centre and home to the **visitor centre** (daily 10am–4pm; Ⓣ03/445 0212, Ⓕ445 1319), which provides an abundance of leaflets on the gold region.

The cheapest **place to stay** is at the *Cromwell Holiday Park*, 1 Alpha St (Ⓣ03/445 0164, Ⓔcromwell.holiday.prk@xtra.co.nz), which has tent sites for $20, and a range of cabins, flats and motel units (❷–❹). Across town, there's the low-cost *Anderson Park Motel*, Gair Avenue (Ⓣ03/445 0321, Ⓕ445 1523; ❸–❹), and for a few dollars more you can stay by the water at *Gateway Motel*, 45 Alpha St (Ⓣ03/445 0385, Ⓕ445 1855; ❹). The only homestay in town is at *Cottage Gardens*, 3 Alpha St (Ⓣ & Ⓕ03/445 0628, Ⓔeco@xtra.co.nz; ❹), surrounded by an orchard, but on Shine Lane at Pisa Moorings, just a five-kilometre ride along SH6 from Cromwell, is *Villa Amo* (Ⓣ03/445 0711, ⒺVillaAmo@xtra.co.nz), friendly and with two doubles (❻) in a large and airy house sitting right on the lake foreshore.

The Mall has several places for reasonable **meals**, one of the best of which is *The Plough*, 71 The Mall, a pub-cum-restaurant with a good selection of reasonably priced meals, though *The Ferryman Family Restaurant and Bar and Victorian Arms Hotel* (Ⓣ03/445 0607) on Melrose Terrace in "Old Cromwell Town" has most atmosphere. Also worth a look while by the lake front is *Jolly's Grape and Grain Café*, a pleasant little cafe in the old grain store where you can pick up big mugs of coffee, sandwiches and muffins while staring at the lake. For simple requirements, or to pick up stuff for a picnic by the lake, try the *Cromwell Bakery*, 73 The Mall, where you can get excellent bread and pies from the friendly Dutch baker.

Around Cromwell

A hefty heave of a small stone from Cromwell (about 4km on SH6) is Jones' Fruit Orchards and Rose Garden. This well-run successful orchard offers the opportunity to try the local apples, preserves, veggies and other fruits, relatively cheaply, or for the hour-long orchard tour ($7) which takes in the 2000-flowers-strong rose garden. A more appropriate response to the lack of diversions in Cromwell is to get out and explore the remains of the gold-country diggings. Hype is reserved for the **Goldfields Mining Centre** (Ⓣ03/445 1038, Ⓔgoldfields@xtra.co.nz; daily 9am–5.30pm; $14), approached by footbridge over the brooding Kawarau 7km west of Cromwell on SH6. The extensive site, with its jazzed-up café, is strangely attractive and occupies a longstanding though not especially lucrative alluvial mining site where ground-sluicing eventually gave way to Californian-style water jets used to loosen the shingle beds. Museum pieces are stationed on a thirty-minute self-guided tour, but while this was an authentic site, and is surrounded by engaging country, there is an overriding staginess about the mining displays themselves. The stamper battery has been brought in, a turbine was recovered from the river before Lake Dunstan filled and the Chinese Village was constructed as a film set in the early 1990s. As well as the usual opportunity to extract a flake or two you can sample the only Otago-based jetboat ride that actually negotiates rapids: **Goldfields Jet** (Ⓣ0800/111 038, Ⓦwww.goldfieldsmining.com; $69) run forty-minute trips on the Kawarau just below the site. A short distance upstream from the Goldfields site the small **Roaring Meg** power station marks both an important rapid run by sledgers and river surfers, and the "natural bridge", a point where the river narrows into a twisting gorge below cliffs which almost touch. Maori moa hunters and nineteenth-century gold men used the narrows as their main crossing point until ferries and bridges were constructed elsewhere.

Dedicated ruin-hounds should call in at the visitor centre in Cromwell and pick up the *Cromwell and District: Guide to Walks and Outings* leaflet, and any number of other historical pamphlets that detail minor gold sites within a few minutes' drive of Cromwell. Pioneering spirits can head out to remote clusters of cottage foundations such as those in the Carrick Range or the Nevis Valley (both south of Cromwell), but for most the best bet is **BANNOCKBURN**, a scattered hamlet 9km southwest of Cromwell that has the *Bannockburn Domain Motor Camp* (Ⓣ03/445 1450; tents $10), the *Cairnmuir Camp* (Ⓣ & Ⓕ03/445 1956; $10), down by Lake Dunstan, and the award-winning, cheap grub of the *Bannockburn Hotel*. Once home to two thousand people, this tortured landscape now serves to illustrate the effect of gold-mining operations on the landscape. A two-hour **self-guided trail**, with information boards and markers (unrestricted entry except for Aug 20–Oct 20, the lambing season) starts 1.5km along Felton road and weaves around huts, tail-races, sluicing and tunnelling operations following numbered stakes.

In the last decade, the warm, north-facing slopes towards the end of **Felton Road**, between Cromwell and Bannockburn, have been planted with grapes; their fermented end product is available for sampling at nine of this part of Central Otago's **wineries,** all within a short distance of one another (though there are a further twelve wineries throughout the gold country). The following vineyards are particularly worthwhile: Felton Road (Oct–April daily 10am–5pm; May–Oct Mon–Fri 10am–5pm; tours by arrangement; Ⓣ03/445 0885, Ⓦwww. feltonroad.com), recently taken over by new owners, has tasting for $4 and a very business-like attitude but produces some excellent Pinot Noir, while Olssens (daily 10am–4pm; Ⓣ03/445 1716, Ⓦwww.olssens.co.nz) are a bit more relaxed. You can taste (also $4 but refundable against purchase) then buy a bottle, or glass, or two of their wonderful Pinot Noir and Pinot Gris, and sit outside consuming a Vineyard Platter ($10–20), or a picnic you've brought with you. Mount Difficulty, Felton Road (Sept–May 10am–5.30pm; Jun–Aug Mon–Sat same hours; Ⓣ03/445 3445, Ⓦwww.mtdifficulty.co.nz), is a simpler affair with tastings (free) and cellar door sales of their lovely Chardonnay and Pinot Noir.

Similarly excellent vino is available at the Bannockburn Heights' **café**, where they serve tasty and imaginative food and do tastings ($5 a rack and redeemable against purchase) of Akarua wines, situated adjacent to the café on Cairnmuir Rd (☎03/445 3211; daily 10am–9pm), and if you are sick of wine, you can also get a taste of the locally brewed beer. Finally it's also worth dropping in at the Carrick Winery, also on Cairnmuir Rd (daily 10am–5pm except May–Sept, 11am–4pm; ☎03/445 3840), where the wine is crisp and bright. If you'd like someone else to take the strain of negotiating a selection of all the vineyards in the region then contact Grape Escape (☎03/449 2696, 021 449 269) who run **tours** (designed to fit in with time and budget available) in a 1971 Bedford School Bus, a characterful vehicle that just about sums up the whole show (min 4, max 12).

If venturing slightly further afield, consider the quartz-mining district of **BENDIGO**, 15km north of Cromwell towards the Lindis Pass, and its acolytes Logantown and Welshtown. None comprises much more than a few scattered remains and deep **mine shafts**, but a (careful) amble among the ruins makes a fine way to pass a summer evening.

Clyde

SH8 cuts southeast from Cromwell through 20km of the bleak and windswept **Cromwell Gorge**, hugging the banks of Lake Dunstan through what used to be New Zealand's most fertile apricot-growing country. The orchards are now all submerged below the waters of the lake, which are held back by the dam at **CLYDE**. The tiny associated town, peacefully situated off the main highway, languished for a number of years but is newly resurgent as a sybaritic retreat. Notwithstanding a few minor museums, being a part of the Otago Central Rail Trail (see p.916) and three vineyards clustered along the Dunstan Rd, there is nothing much to distract you from lounging around some excellent places to stay and dining in a small but perfectly formed cluster of great cafés and restaurants.

Clyde's streets are lined with ornate stone buildings and simple cottages left over from the gold-mining days of the 1860s. Originally known as Dunstan, the town sprang up just downriver from the spot where Hartley and Reilly made their big find in 1862. As tens of thousands of fortune-seekers flooded in from Dunedin and Lawrence, it quickly became the centre of the Dunstan goldfields, but by 1864 waning fortunes and swift river currents forced out the miners in favour of river dredges.

Since the mid-1980s, the town has been dominated by the giant grey hydro-electric **Clyde Dam**, 1km north of town on SH8, which generates five percent of New Zealand's power and provides water for irrigation. Initially controversial, the dam is nevertheless considered something of an engineering marvel, with special "slip joints" providing the dam wall with flexibility in case of earth tremors.

Clyde's other attractions are limited to the panoramic views from the **Clyde Lookout** hill (500m from town; 30min walk) and three small but well-kept museums within easy walking distance of one another. The 1864 stone courthouse on Blyth Street now operates as the **Clyde Museum** (Tues–Sun 2–4pm or by arrangement; $2), worth a peek for its intriguing coverage of Clyde's Great Gold Robbery of 1870. One George Rennie made off with £13,000 in bullion and banknotes, but his horse was so weighed down with the gold that he left a trail of bags hidden behind rocks at intervals. Unfortunately the co-conspirator for whom this trail had been intended had already ratted on

Rennie to the police, and the ill-fated villain was easily tracked down and arrested. The **Briar Herb Factory Complex**, corner of Fraser Street and Fache Street (Tues–Sun 2–4pm; $2), was established in the 1930s as New Zealand's first herb factory, and thrived for several decades, making use of the common thyme which still grows wild hereabouts, with entire hillsides flowering purple throughout November. The factory closed in the 1970s but lives on as an exhibition space, housing well-maintained displays of drying trays, presses and home-made machines used for processing the herbs. Other parts of the factory are given over to horse-drawn vehicles, a rabbiter's hut and an early hospital full of ghoulish medical instruments. The former Clyde Railway Station next door houses the **Station Museum** (Sat & Sun 2–4pm; $1), enabling rail fanatics to pore over its varied collection of well-kept locomotives. Also worth a look is the **Clyde Cemetery** which as well as being inordinately pretty has a number of ornate and occasionally amusing gravestones.

Practicalities

Pre-booked InterCity and various shuttle **buses** stop in Clyde on demand, pulling up on the main Sunderland Street, which is where you'll find the majority of the good **places to stay** and eat. Those on a tight budget will want to **stay** at *Hartley Arms*, 25 Sunderland St (Ⓣ & Ⓕ03/449 2700, Ⓔhartleyarms@xtra.co.nz; dorms ❶, room ❷), a small and cosy backpackers partly built into Clyde's original gold assay office. Dorms have four bunks and there are doubles made up with sheets and towels. With a fuller wallet, stay at the relaxing and extremely atmospheric *Olivers Lodge & Restaurant*, 34 Sunderland St (Ⓣ03/449 2860, Ⓕ449 2862; ❺–❻), which has a range of individually styled luxury rooms – one with a huge bathroom fashioned like a Turkish bath – in rustic rural-style buildings that were once part of a large general store catering for the gold-miners. Alternatively there's *Dunstan House*, 29 Sunderland St (Ⓣ03/449 2295, Ⓔdunstanhouse@xtra.co.nz; ❹–❼), a boutique B&B in a fine house dating from 1865, which offers spacious comfortable rooms and a wrap-around veranda on the first floor, and whose staff have a number of interesting historical tales to relate about previous guests; and *Clyde Holiday and Sporting Complex*, Whitby Street (Ⓣ03/449 2713; tent & powered sites $10, vans and cabin ❷–❸), a pleasant **campsite**, surrounding a cricket ground with a fully self-contained cabin and several on-site caravans, plus a swimming pool and book exchange.

Lunch on a fine day is best taken in the gardens at *Olivers*, which also has an excellent and characterful, award-winning **restaurant** serving breakfast and wholesome lunches (both around $9–16) and dinners ($21–30; book ahead especially at weekends), featuring the likes of lamb and kumara gateau in red wine and thyme jus. Once unchallenged, *Olivers* cuisine is now at least matched by that at *Blues Café and Bar*, 31 Sunderland St (closed Mon–Wed; licensed), which dishes up wonderful Louisiana Cajun and Creole plates – many named after the legendary blues players that also provide the decorative theme. Tuck into Creole chilli crabs ($20) or Muddy Waters mussels ($10) selected from menus encased in old record covers. This is also the best place to listen to jazz and blues from Friday through to Sunday and there's sometimes comedy, on Saturday nights. *Dunstan House* (see above) also dishes up some pretty tasty fare from its Mediterranean/Italian menu (licensed and BYO) and does tastings for the Alexandra Wine Company ($2). Cheaper pub-style snacks can be obtained 300m away at the attractive *Post Office Café*, on the corner of Blyth and Matau streets, built into the former 1865 post office and with a bar serving a delicious ale, Post Office Dark, their own label of vino and some excellent blackboard and BBQ specials, inside or in the garden bar out the back. They also have occasional live entertainment. Last of the eateries-cum-boozers is the *Dunstan Hotel*, a large, recently refurbished bar where you can pick up cheap bar meals from the blackboard menu and occasionally witness live country, Irish-style and rock bands mashing some old favourites.

Alexandra and around

A large white clockface – visible from as far away as 5km – looms out of the cliff which backs **ALEXANDRA** (affectionately known as Alex), 10km southeast of Clyde. Alexandra sprang up during the 1862 gold rush, and flourished for four frenzied years before settling into decline, although the gold-dredging boom at the end of the century breathed some life back into the town. Now, a prosperous service town for the fruit-growing heartland of Central Otago, it's the largest place for some distance, and its modest clutch of sights and stark mountain scenery may well persuade you to stop, particularly if your visit coincides with the longstanding **Alexandra Blossom Festival**, held on the fourth weekend in September.

A huge waterwheel marks Alexandra's main point of interest, the **Alexandra Museum and Art Gallery** on the corner of Walton Street and Thomson Street (Mon–Fri 10am–4pm, Sat 10am–2pm; donation), which houses exhibitions on the glory years of the 1890s, along with an entertaining display on the sorry tale of rabbits, which were introduced into the area in 1909 and did what rabbits do – so well that they soon became a major menace throughout the South Island. To combat the problem, the town holds an Easter Bunny Shoot every year, and hunters from all over New Zealand congregate on Good Friday to slaughter as many as they can.

In the early years, the only way across the Manuherikia River was by unstable punt, but in 1879 the town built the **Shaky Bridge**, a suspension **footbridge** – originally wide enough for wagons but since narrowed – now crossed to reach a **lookout point** (1.5km; 30min one way) high above the town on Tucker Hill, which affords great views of the whole area.

With its long hours of hot sun, the region is now gaining a reputation for its wines. **Black Ridge Vineyard**, Conroys Road, in an unlikely setting amid black schist 6km southwest of Alex (Ⓣ 03/449 2059; daily 10am–5pm; free tasting), produces award-winning wines from the world's most southerly vineyard, and **William Hill Vineyard**, 2km west of Alex on Dunstan Road (Ⓣ03/448 8436; tastings Sat & Sun 11am–5pm, sales daily Nov–April), also produces high-quality whites; pick up the free *Central Otago Wine Trail* leaflet from the visitor centre (see below), which locates and briefly describes the region's wineries.

Activities

Alex makes a good base from which to explore some impressive mountain ranges and the Roxburgh Gorge, either on a guided tour or under your own steam. This is a great area for **mountain biking**, with plenty of trails to tackle on your own or with a trail guide recommended by the visitor centre. You can rent a mountain bike from MCS Services, 21 Shannon St (Ⓣ03/448 8048, Ⓔinfo@goldrush.co.nz), or Henderson Cycles, 17 Limerick St (Ⓣ03/448 8917); both charge around $15 for a half day, $30 for a full day. MCS Services will also provide excellent **bikes** for the Otago Rail Trail (see p.916), and offer guided and rental **kayaks trips**, usually run from Alexandra to Roxburgh Dam, costing about $50. There are also combination kayak/mountain biking options.

Several other operators run **tours** from Alex into the surrounding mountain ranges: you can go **horse trekking** in the thyme-scented hills of the Dunstan Trail (1hr; $20), with longer treks by arrangement (ⓣ03/449 2445 evenings or 7.30–8am); or try a fantastic **4WD safari** up the Dunstan Mountains, the Old Man Range or other remote gold-mining areas, with John Douglas (ⓣ03/448 7474, or through the visitor centre; around $35 for half day, $90 full day), who has an extraordinary range of knowledge about the area and its plant- and bird-life and takes you to places that are unusual and spectacular. Alternatively, the reasonably fit can try a one-day guided trip paddling a **Canadian canoe** down the Roxburgh Gorge and mountain biking back, with MCS Services, Central Outdoor Adventures (see "bikes", above; Oct–April; 3 people max, around $90 per person). During the winter months there's ice skating on local lakes, cross-country skiing and trips by snow **skidoo** into the mountains (for more information, contact the visitor centre).

Practicalities

InterCity **buses** drop off at the monument at the intersection of Tarbert Street and Centennial Avenue; while Catch-a-Bus offer a door-to-door service. Atomic and Southern Link **shuttles** both stop outside the **visitor centre**, 22 Centennial Ave (Mon–Fri 9am–5pm, Sat & Sun 10am–3pm; ⓣ03/448 9515, ⓦwww.alexandra.co.nz), which has leaflets (50c) on a number of walks in the local mountains, and the *Mountain Biking* pamphlet detailing five local trails that are open all year. You can also book here for guided 4WD tours of the surrounding rugged terrain (see "Activities", above). The **post office**, 66 Tarbert St (ⓣ03/448 7500), has poste restante facilities; and there's **internet** access at the library, corner of Skird and Tarbert streets, and *Smith City Cyber Café*, Limerick Street (both open standard business hours).

There's plenty of low-cost **accommodation** in Alexandra, including **motels**: try the soothing *Alexandra Garden Court*, Manuherikia Road (ⓣ & ⓕ03/448 8295; ❸), a fifteen-minute walk from the centre, with six fully self-contained units and a swimming pool set in extensive landscaped gardens; or the slightly more central, small and friendly *Kiwi Motel*, 115 Centennial Ave (ⓣ03/448 8258, ⓕ448 6201; ❹). The French provincial-style *Rocky Range Lodge*, 2km south of town, signposted off SH8 (ⓣ & ⓕ03/448 6150, ⓣ0800/153 293; ❾), is the luxury pick, perched high on a hill amid schist outcrops with stunning panoramic views; dinner can be arranged for an extra $65.

Campers need to head for the *Alexandra Holiday Park* on Manuherikia Road/SH85 (ⓣ03/448 8297, ⓕ448 8294; huts ❷, cabins ❸), a large well-kept and tree-sheltered site offering tent sites for $9.50, single-bed huts and cabins, as well as mountain bikes for rent; or the pleasant *Pine Lodge Holiday Camp*, 31 Ngapara St (ⓣ03/448 8861, ⓕ448 8276; tent sites $9.50, flats ❷, motel units ❸), beside a deer park; both are fifteen minutes' walk from the centre.

The best **places to eat** hereabouts are in Clyde, 8km to the north (see p.911); in town go for the licensed *Briar & Thyme*, 26 Centennial Ave (book for dinner ⓣ03/448 9189; Oct–April daily; May–Sept Tues–Sat), which specializes in classy lunches like camembert and vegetable turnovers or oven-baked blue cod (around $15 each), as well as elegant dinners ($15–25), in a comfortable historic house with a wine bar. For something more low-key try the *Red Brick*, in the Supervalue car park on the corner of Limerick Street and Ennis Street, a mellow café, licensed and open daily for a good range of lunch ($10–20) and dinner ($14–25) dishes, plus great desserts. Fans of quality burgers and seafood at low prices should eat at the nautically themed *Nuno's*, 73 Centennial Ave

(Ⓣ03/448 5444; closed Mon & Tues), which does the best greasies in town to eat-in or take out and also has a passable bar.

North of Alex: the Maniototo Plain

The most interesting route to the east coast from Alexandra is through the **Maniototo**, a generic name for the flat high country shared by three shallow valleys and the low craggy ranges that separate them, which have been made famous by the paintings of the artist **Grahame Sydney** (Ⓦwww.grahamesydney.com), whose work is considered a national treasure, prints of which are available throughout the entire region; well worth a look between Ranfurly and Alexandra is the Oturehua Store, its windows stuffed with produce in the old 1940s and 50s packaging where you can pick up a Sydney print, or have one sent home for you.

Despite easy road access, the Maniototo seems a world apart, largely ignored by foreign visitors, though it is a common summertime destination for Dunedinites who appreciate the dry climate and the quality of the light some 500 metres up.

Predictably, Europeans first came to the area in search of gold. They found it near **Naseby**, but returns quickly declined and farming on the plains became more rewarding. This was especially true when **railway** developers looking for the easiest route from Dunedin to Alexandra chose a way up the Taieri Gorge and across the Maniototo. The line arrived in **Ranfurly** in 1898 and that soon took over from Naseby as the area's main administrative centre, an honour held to this day. Passenger trains ran through the Maniototo until 1990, but by the end of 1991 all the track had been pulled up; the route has now been fashioned into the **Otago Central Rail Trail** (see p.916).

The main road through the Maniototo is SH85 from Alexandra to Palmerston, which is fast, largely straight and paved, and usually known as "**The Pigroot**"; it began life as the easiest route from the east coast to the Central Otago Goldfields. Scattered on the way are a handful of old gold-mining communities, among them **St Bathans**, **Naseby** and the aforementioned Ranfurly, each worth a brief visit for their laid-back atmosphere, calm seclusion and subtle reminders of how greed transforms the land. In between you'll see dozens of small cottages, many abandoned – a testament to the harsh life in these parts.

These days the highway also provides access to a rugged route further northeast to the Waitaki Valley (see p.720), via Dansey's Pass. The only public transport through these parts is the Catch-a-Bus service (Ⓣ03/471 4103; daily except Sat) between Dunedin and Wanaka which leaves Dunedin at 8am, arriving in Wanaka around noon and then setting back at 1pm.

Omakau, Ophir and St Bathans

Heading northeast from Alexandra you are immediately into the high country plain passing through inconsequential hamlets until you reach the twin settlements of **Omakau** and **Ophir** after 20km. These are mainly of interest for those on the Otago Central Rail Trail and in need of accommodation: try the *Omakau Domain Camping Ground*, Alton St, Omakau (Ⓣ03/447 3814; tents $8), or *Ophir Lodge Backpackers*, 1 Macdonald St, Ophir (Ⓣ & Ⓕ03/447 3339, Ⓔblgaler@xtra.co.nz; Sept–May; dorms ❶, rooms ❷), a small, comfortable and well-set-up hostel a couple of kilometres from the trail.

The first place with genuine appeal is the minute yet strangely attractive former gold town of **ST BATHANS**, 80km north of Alexandra and accessed 17km along a mostly sealed loop road from Becks. St Bathans began life as a

Otago Central Rail Trail

One of the finest ways to explore the Maniototo is on the **Otago Central Rail Trail** (Ⓦwww.hike.org/walks/Otago-Central-Rail.html), a relatively little-known 150km route – open to walkers, cyclists and horse-riders – from Clyde to Middlemarch and passing through almost all the towns of importance with the exception of St Bathan's and Naseby.

A **mountain bike** is definitely the way to go (some sections are rough), but there are currently no rental facilities nearby, so you'll need to obtain one from Alexandra (see p.913) or Dunedin (see p.727), or bring you own. Walkers are better advised to tackle shorter sections through gorges with plenty of tunnels and viaducts, avoiding the long flat bits: go for the stretch between Lauder and Auripo in the northern section, or the run from Daisybank to Hyde in the east. Both are around 10km, though unless you are prepared to hitch you'll have to hike back; remember to take a torch for the tunnels.

The route is fully outlined in one overall *Otago Central Rail Trail* leaflet ($0.50) and a series of six section leaflets ($0.50 each).

boom town called Dunstan Creek in 1863, following a gold strike at the foot of Mount St Bathans. Within six months two or three hundred miners were working the area, and the tent town comprised twenty stores, four pubs and a bank. The population peaked at 2000, but when the gold ran out in the 1930s, everything went with it. These days it's virtually a ghost town with just three permanent residents and a straggle of ancient buildings strung in a crooked line along a single road. Two of the residents manage the atmospheric 1882 *Vulcan Hotel* (Ⓣ03/447 3629; bunks ❶, rooms ❹), where local farmers and the occasional visitor prop up the old wooden bar, which serves *St Bathans Gold*, a single malt bottled on the premises. The pub offers good cheap snacks and dinners, and simple B&B accommodation, though be warned that the place is haunted; doubters should book Room 1.

The prettiest thing about the area is the striking **Blue Lake** right beside the town, where mineral-rich water has flooded a crater left by the merciless sluicing of Kildare Hill, which used to be 120m high until it was entirely washed away. A short track leads from the *Vulcan* to a vantage point over the intensely azure lake, now used for water-skiing, swimming and picnics.

Just up the street from the lake and the hotel, the former post office is once again performing that role as part of Despatches, a kind of mini-museum-cum-Victorian-gift shop that also books **horse riding** with St Bathans Horse Treks (Ⓣ & Ⓕ03/447 3512): rides range from $30 for a couple of hours to $180 for an overnight jaunt sleeping in a musterer's hut.

Apart from the hotel, the only other **accommodation** hereabouts is the *Constable Cottage and Gaol* (Ⓣ & Ⓕ03/447 3558, Ⓔlauderdale@xtra.co.nz; ❺–❻), a self-contained former police house and its gaol let separately or together: all meals can be provided by prior arrangement.

Naseby

The small settlement of **NASEBY**, 25km east of St Bathans and 14km off SH85, clings to the Maniototo Plain some 600m above sea level. Surrounding the town, the dark-green swathe of **Naseby Forest** stands out from the tussock-covered hills to the north and the farmland plains to the south. Managed for its exotic timber – mainly European larches, Douglas firs and pines – it is the highest forest of its kind on the South Island. A number of pleasant picnic spots and forest **walks** (750m–3km one way; 30min–90min; or a circuit walk of 10km, 6hr) are easily accessible from Naseby, signposted throughout the forest with times, distances and destinations, and also listed in the *Naseby Forest* leaflet and map available free from Earnslaw Ore in the middle of town on Derwent Street (Mon–Fri 9am–4pm, April–Sept 1pm–4pm; ⓣ03/444 9995). To witness the effects of former sluicing at their most dramatic, follow the **One Tree Hill Track** (1.6km; 1hr return), starting only five minutes' walk north of the Timberlands HQ, which snakes uphill along the eastern side of Hogburn Gully, past dramatic honey-coloured cliffs entirely carved by water; a free sheet on the walk is available from the visitor centre. If you feel particularly energetic and fancy a bit of **mountain biking**, then try Naseby Mountain Bike Hire ($25 half day, $40 full day) who operate from opposite the *Royal Hotel*, 1 Eam St (ⓣ03/444 9990); they also do half-day guided bike trips for $100 around the forest.

At its 4000-strong peak in 1865, Naseby was the largest gold-mining town on the Maniototo, but today numbers have dropped to around 150. It functions as a quiet holiday town in summer and the country's centre for the Scottish sport of curling (a sort of bowls on ice played on a local pond) in winter, but is little more than a collection of small houses (many of them originally built by miners from sun-dried mud brick), with a shop, a garage, a couple of hotels, a café, a great campsite and a good pub. There are also a swimming dam, an impressive ice rink for winter use, and a couple of tiny museums, both at the junction of Earne Street and Leven Street. The **Maniototo Early Settlers Museum** (Nov–May Sat–Sun 1.30–3.30pm, or by arrangement; ⓣ03/444 9558; $2) features a large number of black-and-white photos of past residents' lives alongside a small collection of items left by Chinese miners, while the **Jubilee Museum** (daily 10am–5pm; $1 token available from the general store across the street) houses the remains of an old watchmaker's shop together with displays on the local gold rush of the 1860s and 1870s plus the history of the town since then. On the northwestern outskirts of town, just outside the forest boundary and about ten minutes' walk from the centre, is the **swimming dam**, a popular cooling-off spot in summer, surrounded by mature Douglas fir and larch trees. The **Maniototo Ice Rink** (early June to mid-Aug; $10 including skate rental) at the southern end of town on Channel Road is New Zealand's largest outdoor rink, and is a popular venue for skating, ice hockey and particularly curling. If you happen to catch the season, pop along armed with the *Spectators Guide to Curling* leaflet, available free from the Ranfurly visitor centre; or join in. Curling equipment is available for rent ($5 for two hours plus $6 for a stone and broom).

If you want to break your journey here, there's basic **accommodation** at the *Ancient Briton* pub in Leven Street (ⓣ03/444 9992; rooms ❸–❹), which has a number of neat, good-quality motel units and power sites ($10), all in a quiet spot out the back. The pub serves breakfast for around $14 and hearty cheap dinners in enormous portions. There's also the pretty and very tranquil *Naseby Larchview Camping Park* (ⓣ & ⓕ03/444 9904; tent and powered sites $10, cabins & vans ❷–❸), in the forest about five minutes' walk from town; and the *Monkey Puzzle House*, corner of Derwent and Oughter streets (ⓣ & ⓕ03/444 9985; half board ❹), a comfortable if somewhat chintzy B&B with guest-share bathrooms, a lounge full ofVictoriana and free use of skates in winter.

The best place for **snacks** and **main meals** is the Royal Hotel, 1 Eam St. where you can pick up cheap pub grub in the form of sandwiches, fish and steak, usually with chips.

Dansey's Pass

The metalled Kyeburn Diggings Road, running east out of Naseby, continues as a narrow barren and beautiful route climbing northeast across the Kakanui Mountains via **Dansey's Pass** (about 40km from Naseby), to eventually emerge in the Waitaki Valley, where SH83 gives access to Mount Cook in the west and the coast in the east. Though reasonably well maintained, the route is sometimes closed in summer and always unsafe in winter, so check in Naseby before setting out. Old gold workings are visible from the roadside, where water jets from sluices have distorted the schist and tussock landscape, leaving rock dramatically exposed.

At Kyeburn Diggings, 16km from Naseby, you'll come across the charming **Dansey's Pass Coach Inn** (Ⓣ & Ⓕ03/444 9048, Ⓦwww.danseyspass.co.nz; ❻), a comfortable lodge at the foot of the pass but in the middle of nowhere, built from local schist stone in 1862 and the only remnant of a 2000-strong gold-rush community. The stonemason was reputedly paid a pint of beer for each stone laid. The inn offers good beer, affordable lunches and fairly pricey dinners, as well as nicely modernized en-suite accommodation, which is booked up most weekends throughout the year. They also rent out mountain bikes ($8 per hour, $24 a half day), and in winter will take folk cross-country skiing up at the pass. There's **budget accommodation** at the far end of the route, about 15km north of the pass itself, at the excellent small and quiet *Dansey's Pass Holiday Camp* (Ⓣ03/431 2564, Ⓕ431 2560; tent & powered sites $10, cabins ❷–❸), down by the riverside.

Ranfurly

Back on SH85 and 5km beyond the Naseby turn-off lies the compact town of **RANFURLY**, the largest settlement on the Maniototo Plain, famed so it claims for its Art Deco heritage – an arsonist torched most of the town's buildings and they were replaced in the Art Deco period, a few years before Napier – though with precious little to show for it except for a few places to stay and eat. The elegant **former train station** on Charlemont Street East has a free audio-visual show on the region and pictorial displays tracing the history of the town and the Otago Central Railway. In summer, anyone with a 4WD or high-clearance vehicle can set out from here to explore part of the magnificent **Old Dunstan Road** (unsafe May–Sept), the original route to the Central Otago goldfields before the Pigroot was opened. Traversing the Rock and Pillar and Lammerlaw ranges fills you with admiration for those gold prospectors who guided their horse-drawn drays and bullock wagons through some of the harshest land in the country, all for the sake of a dream. From Ranfurly head 20km south to Patearoa and from there a further 25km to Paerau (aka Styx), where a 50km section of the Old Dunstan Road begins its gruelling journey to Clarks Junction and the easier SH87 heads towards Dunedin.

The **visitor centre**, Charlemont St E (daily 10am–4.30pm; Ⓣ & Ⓕ03/444 9970, Ⓔmaniototo.vic@xtra.co.nz), stocks leaflets on the whole district and can offer further advice on **accommodation**. Opposite the railway station there's the large colonial *Ranfurly Lion Hotel* (Ⓣ03/444 9140, Ⓕ444 9142; dorms ❶, rooms ❸–❹), with a range of single and double rooms (some ensuite) plus a pleasant and very cheap backpackers across the road. There's a bar, a good but fairly cheap restaurant, and guests get free use of a spa pool. The clean and sheltered *Ranfurly Motor Camp*, Reade Street, off Pery Street, two minutes' walk from the town centre (Ⓣ03/444 9144; tent sites $10, dorms ❶, cabins ❷, tourist flats ❸), has a covered swimming pool. About ten minutes' walk west of the centre, in a park-like setting, is the small and quiet *Ranfurly*

Motel, Davis Avenue, off Caulfield Street (Ⓣ & Ⓕ03/444 9383; ❹). Twelve kilometres east from Ranfurly, on the road to the tiny settlement of Waipiata and close to the rail trail, is *Peter's Farm Hostel* (Ⓣ03/444 9083; Dec–April; tent sites $10, dorms ❶, rooms ❷), a comfortable and very relaxing farm with free use of bikes, kayaks, fishing rods and gold pans; plus several good walks nearby. Phone ahead to enquire about winter opening, to get directions and for a free pick-up from Ranfurly.

The best **eating** in town is at the BYO *Korner Shop* on Northland Street (SH85), which does meals throughout the day and good coffee, and at the *Highland Wine Bar*, 8 Charlamonte St, opposite the railway station, which dishes up some reasonably priced hearty staples and serves a much-needed drink.

Macraes Gold Mine, Middlemarch and SH85 to Dunedin

At Kyeburn, 15km east of Ranfurly, the slow **route to Dunedin** (SH87) branches south off SH85 and twists through the eastern Maniototo, a barren yet scenic landscape squeezed between the towering Rock and Pillar Range and the Taieri River. Fifty kilometres south of Kyeburn you'll reach the tiny and decaying community of **Middlemarch**, the Sunday-only terminus of the **Taieri Gorge Railway**, which makes a spectacular two-hour run between here and Dunedin (see p.227 for details). Anyone planning to tackle the Otago Central Rail Trail from east to west should definitely consider starting by riding the railway either to Middlemarch or to **Pukerangi** (the weekday turnaround point), 18km to the south. Either way you can spend the first night in Middlemarch. Opposite the station at 5 Snow Ave you'll find **accommodation** at *Shannon-Lea* (Ⓣ & Ⓕ03/464 3762, Ⓔalistermdl@xtraco.nz; bunks ❶, room ❸–❹), a house converted into a combined hostel and lodge; enquire at the shop on the main street. Alternatively, cross the tracks to *Blind Billy's Holiday Camp*, Miro Street (Ⓣ03/464 3355, Ⓦwww.middlemarch.co.nz/blind_billys.html; tent sites $8, dorms ❶, cabins & vans ❷, motel units ❹), a campsite with cooking facilities in a converted railway carriage and seats outdoors beside the piano. There are also simple dorms, a cabin, a couple of basic on-site vans and an old-fashioned but spacious two-bedroom motel unit.

The most renowned of Otago's operating gold mines, the huge opencast **Macraes Gold Mine**, lies on windswept hills between Ranfurly and Palmerston and can be visited on a two-hour tour which also takes in a historic reserve and a fully operational stamper battery. Bookings (Ⓣ03/465 2400; $15) are essential and there is a minimum charge of $70, making visits prohibitive except for groups.

Should you want to **eat or stay** in the area, the historic and cheap *Stanley's Hotel* (Ⓣ & Ⓕ03/465 2400; B&B ❹), another schist-stone construction, has a restaurant and bar, a few rooms with shared bathrooms, and a swimming pool.

Back on SH85 it's a further 14km from Dunback to Palmerston, where SH1 heads south to Dunedin and north towards Oamaru.

Southeast along SH8: Alexandra to Dunedin, via Roxburgh

The fastest route from Alexandra to the coast is SH8, partly because it's a shorter road than SH85, but also because there are fewer enticing stop-offs en route. The road follows the meandering course of the Clutha River, passing through rugged hill country between the Old Man and Lammerlaw ranges to the east, and the Knobby Blue Mountain range to the west. Along the way are a couple of mildly interesting gold towns, Roxburgh and Lawrence, both served by the major **bus** companies and **shuttles** (notably Atomic Shuttle and Catch-a-Bus) running between Queenstown or Alexandra and Dunedin.

Roxburgh and Lawrence

Thirteen kilometres south of Alexandra you pass through the ironically named **Fruitlands**, a tiny settlement where orchards were once planted in the hope that they'd flourish, only to fail and be replaced by grazing sheep. From the ridge to the west of the road you get a good view of the 27-metre-tall **Old Man Rock**, an extraordinary stone obelisk from which the Old Man Range takes its name. A characterful reminder of the gold-mining days, the roadside *Fruitlands Gallery* (daily 10am–5pm), occupies a restored stone pub of 1866 and functions as a fully licensed and BYO **café** exhibiting local arts and crafts.

Some 15km further on, a signposted turn-off leads to an **observation point** high above the immense **Roxburgh Dam** and power station, which, when completed in 1956, was New Zealand's most massive, and is still only pushed into second place by its cousin upriver at Clyde. From the lookout you get a great view over the shimmering turquoise of Lake Roxburgh, which backs up for over 30km. Also of interest in the area are walks in the Teviot Valley (a free leaflet is available from local visitor centres), which concentrates on a dirt road and tracks beside the river. Not far from Roxburgh is the most interesting part of the valley walks, two gravestones beside the road, one with the legend, "Somebodies Darling Lies Here", the other reading "Died 1865, stone erected 1903." Presumably the occupier of the second grave buried "somebodies" darling before himself expiring. The walk up and around this part of the pretty valley takes about an hour.

Eight kilometres south of the dam, and hemmed in by orchards, farmland and opencast coal mines, the bland former gold town of **ROXBURGH** occupies the flat western bank of the Clutha River at the foot of a precipitous hillside, in turn dominated by the parched Umbrella Mountains further west. Soon after the discovery of gold here in 1862, Roxburgh turned its attention to fruit growing. The vast orchards now yield bountiful crops of peaches, apricots, apples, raspberries and strawberries, all harvested by an annual influx of seasonal pickers; the season's surplus is sold from a phalanx of roadside stalls from early December through to May. Roxburgh is one of the only towns of significant size between Alexandra and Dunedin, and there are a couple of budget **places to stay**: the pool-equipped *Roxburgh Family Motor Camp*, 11 Teviot St (Ⓣ03/446 8093; tent sites $8, dorms ❶, cabins ❷), in a quiet spot near the town centre; and the central *Villa Rose*, 79 Scotland St (Ⓣ03/446 8402; dorms ❶, rooms ❷), a backpackers in a villa equipped with dorms and several doubles, and frequented by orchard workers. The best accommodation, however, is to be had at the *Roxburgh Lodge*, Lake Roxburgh Village (Ⓣ03/446 8220, Ⓔlakerox@xtra.co.nz; ❹–❺), which offers wonderful en-suite motel-style rooms and a very good licensed **restaurant** for breakfast, lunch and dinner (open to non-residents).

From Roxburgh SH8 runs 24km south to **Raes Junction** (where SH90 spurs off southwest to Tapanui and Gore), and continues 26km to **LAWRENCE**, Otago's original gold town. It's hard to believe that this sleepy farming town, with its population barely nudging 550, was once the scene of frenetic activity, as 12,000 gold-seekers scrambled to try their luck in the gold-rich Gabriels Gully, discovered by Gabriel Read on May 23, 1861 (see p.907). This short-lived boom (it was over in barely a year) is recalled in a scattering of Victorian buildings, hastily constructed in a variety of materials and styles.

The combined **visitor centre** and **Goldfields Museum** on Ross Place/SH8

(ⓣ03/485 9222; Mon–Fri 9am–4.30pm, Sat & Sun 10am–4pm) brings something of those heady days to life through imaginative displays, rents out gold pans ($5 per day), and dispenses information on the town. An occasionally steep road walk to **Gabriels Gully** (8.5km round trip; 2.5hr return) is signposted nearby and leads through old gold workings before returning along a ridge with broad views of the town and its surroundings. Along the way the **Pick and Shovel Monument** commemorates Read and the pioneer miners, and a noticeboard illustrates how the area would have looked in its gold-mining heyday. A climb up the steep rise of **Jacob's Ladder** gives a good view of the gully, long since filled with tailings that reach nearly 20m in depth. From here the road follows the ridge, dips into the gully once more and returns to town.

If you are just passing through you may be satisfied with something to **eat** from one of the tearooms along the single main street, or more exalted fare from the smart new *Jazzed on Java* café, 26 Ross Place, which serves imaginative lunches, great coffee and has **internet** access. For budget **accommodation** head for *Oban Guest House*, 1 Oban St (ⓣ & ⓕ03/485 9259, ⓔobanhouse@xtra.co.nz; dorms ❶, rooms ❷–❸), a pleasant backpackers in a big old house; or the creekside *Gold Park Motor Camp*, 1km south of the main road on Harrington Street (ⓣ03/485 9850; tents $12 per site, cabins ❷), is a fairly basic campsite with cabins in a picturesque setting. Bed and breakfast can be sought just south of town on SH8 at *Marama* (ⓣ & ⓕ03/485 9638, ⓔmarama.k@xtra.co.nz; ❸–❹) where there are two units which can be treated as self-contained or B&B. Guests have use of the tennis court, bikes fishing rods and even golf clubs.

From Lawrence it's another 33km southeast to the junction with SH1 on the east coast, which strikes north towards Dunedin or south to Balclutha (see p.756).

Travel details

Buses

The following lists the direct scheduled bus services in the area and doesn't include the scores of tour buses which ply the Queenstown to Milford Sound route daily – see the relevant accounts for details of these.

From Alexandra to: Lawrence (8–10 daily; 1hr 15min); Queenstown (8–10 daily; 1hr 30min); Dunedin (7–9 daily; 3hr).

From Arrowtown to: Queenstown (10 daily; 40min).

From Lawrence to: Alexandra (8–10 daily; 1hr 15min); Cromwell (8–10 daily; 1hr 45min); Dunedin (6–8 daily; 1hr 20min).

From Cromwell to: Alexandra (8–10 daily; 30min); Lawrence (8–10 daily; 1hr 45min); Queenstown (10 daily; 1hr); Wanaka (4 daily; 45–60min).

From Glenorchy to: Queenstown (3–7 daily; 1hr).

From Queenstown to: Alexandra (7–9 daily; 1hr 30min); Arrowtown (10 daily; 40min); Christchurch (6-7 daily; 7hr–9hr); Cromwell (7–9 daily; 1hr); Dunedin (6–8 daily; 4–5hr); Franz Joseph Glacier (1 daily; 8hr); Glenorchy (3–7 daily; 1hr); Invercargill (2–3 daily; 2hr 30min–5hr); Kingston (1–2 daily; 45min); Milford Sound (2 daily; 5hr 15min); Mount Cook (1 daily; 4hr); Te Anau (2 daily; 2hr 15min); Wanaka (1 daily; 1hr 45min).

From Wanaka to: Christchurch (3–4 daily; 6hr 20min–9hr 20min); Cromwell (4 daily; 45min–1hr); Dunedin (2 daily; 4hr 15min); Queenstown (1 daily; 1hr 45min); Ranfurly (1 daily; 2hr).

Flights

Apart from scheduled services to the South Island's main centres, most flights are geared towards the lucrative Milford Sound market (see p.937), with nearly a dozen fiercely competitive companies flying out of Wanaka and Queenstown daily.

From Queenstown to: Auckland (3–4 daily; 2hr 30min); Christchurch (4–6 daily; 50min); Milford Sound (5 daily; 35min); Mount Cook (1 daily; 40min); Te Anau (3 daily; 30min); Wanaka (3 daily; 20min).

From Wanaka to: Queenstown (3 daily; 20min).

14

Fiordland

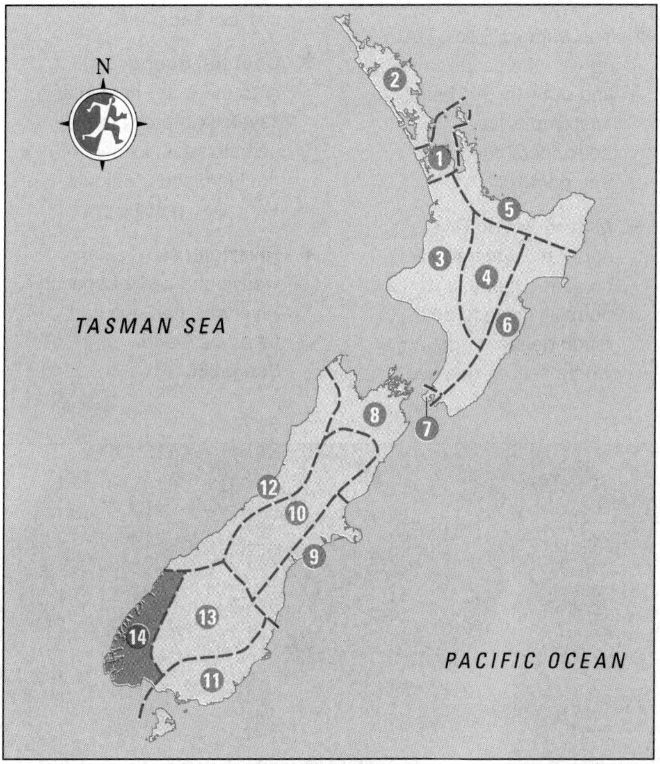
N
TASMAN SEA
PACIFIC OCEAN
1
2
3
4
5
6
7
8
9
10
11
12
13
14

CHAPTER 14

Highlights

* **Te Anau** Ride four-wheel bikes through the mud in the back hills of Te Anau to get to places in a day that you couldn't reach in several days' walking. See p.927
* **The Milford Track** Put up with the sandflies to find out why this beautiful tramp is New Zealanders' favourite. See p.943
* **Milford Sound** Dive under the water to see creatures that you would normally have to go much deeper to get anywhere near, take a scenic flight over it, or get an overnight boat trip into Milford Sound so that you'll be there when the last plane has departed and you can truly appreciate the silence. See p.946
* **Doubtful Sound** Get out onto the water here in a kayak to appreciate the unmatchable scenery of the Fiordlands National Park. See p.951
* **Riverton** Learn to flax weave and carve bone in Riverton, the Paua capital of the world. See p.960

14

Fiordland

For all New Zealand's scenic grandeur, no single region quite matches the concentration of stupendous landscapes found in its southwestern corner. Almost the entirety of **Fiordland** falls within the generous boundaries of the Fiordland National Park, a land of superlatives, boasting New Zealand's two deepest lakes, its highest rainfall and some of the world's rarest birds. This hasn't gone unnoticed at the United Nations, which has gathered pretty much the whole region — along with the Mount Aspiring National Park and parts of south Westland and the Mount Cook area –- into the **Te Wahipounamu World Heritage Area**.

The **Fiordland National Park**, New Zealand's largest, stretches from Martins Bay, once the site of New Zealand's remotest settlement, to the southern forests of Waitutu and Preservation Inlet where early gold prospectors set up a couple of short-lived towns. The 12,500 square kilometres of the park embraces breathtaking scenery, a raw and heroic landscape with deep, icy and mountain-fringed lakes in the east and a western coastline of fourteen hairline fiords gouged out over the last two million years by glaciers creaking off the tail of the Southern Alps.

Maori legend tells how the **fiords** were formed at the hands of the great god Tu-to-Rakiwhanoa (see box on p.928), while scientific explanations point to a complex underlying geology, which evolved over the last 500 million years. When thick layers of seabed sediment were compressed and heated deep within the earth's crust, hard crystalline granite, gneiss and schist were formed. As the land and sea levels rose and fell, layers of softer sandstone and limestone were overlayed; during glacial periods, great ice sheets deepened the valleys and flattened their bases to create the classic U-shape, invaded by the sea lapping at their mouths.

After a few days in the inhospitable conditions created by Fiordland's copious rainfall and pestilent **sandflies** (*namu*), you'll appreciate why there is little evidence of permanent Maori settlement in these parts, though they certainly spent summers hunting here and passed through in search of greenstone (*pounamu*). **Cook** was equally suspicious of Fiordland when, in 1770, he sailed up the coast on his first voyage to New Zealand. Anchorages were hard to come by: the glowering sky put him off entering Dusky Sound; slight, shifting winds hardly encouraged entry into what he dubbed Doubtful Harbour; and, uncharacteristically, he missed Milford Sound altogether.

Paradoxically, for a region that's now the preserve of hardy trampers and a few anglers, the southern fiords region was once the best-charted in the country. Cook returned in 1773, after four months battling the southern oceans, and spent five weeks in Dusky Sound. His midshipman, George Vancouver,

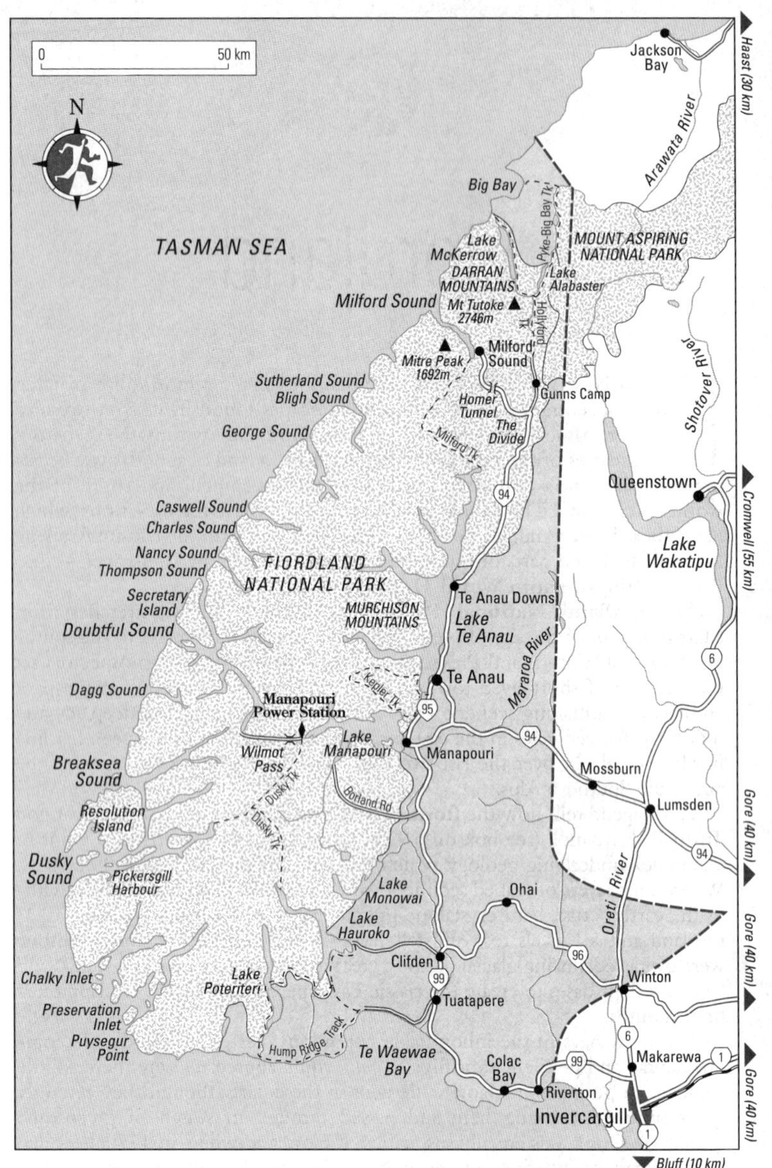

returned in 1791, with the first bloodthirsty sealers and whalers hot on his heels. Over the mountains, **Europeans** seized, or paid a pittance for, land on the eastern shores of lake Te Anau and Manapouri for the meagre grazing it offered, while **explorers** headed for the interior. More egotistical than their seafaring kin, they conferred their own names on the passes, waterfalls and valleys they came across – Donald Sutherland lent his name to New Zealand's highest waterfall and Quentin McKinnon scaled the Mackinnon Pass (but failed to persuade cartographers to spell his name correctly).

One feature of Fiordland you can't miss is the **rain**: the region is sodden for much of the year. Milford Sound is particularly favoured, being deluged with up to seven metres of rainfall a year – the second-highest in the world (after the mountains of Tahiti). Fortunately the area's settlements are in a relative rain shadow and receive less than half the precipitation of the coast. Despite its frequent soakings, **Milford Sound** sees a concentration of noisy traveller activity and is undoubtedly the most popular destination, with at times the distinct atmosphere of a Vietnam war film due to the large number of planes and choppers swooping in and out. However, the Sound is still quite beautiful particularly off-season or when its raining, with ribbons of water plunge from hanging valleys directly into the fiords – where colonies of red and black coral grow and dolphins, fur seals and Fiordland crested penguins gambol. Many visitors on a flying visit from Queenstown see little else of Fiordland, but a greater sense of remoteness is gained by driving along the dramatically scenic **Milford Road** between the sound and the lakeside town of **Te Anau**. Better still, trudge here along the **Milford Track**, widely promoted as the "finest walk in the world", though others in the region – the **Hollyford Track**, the **Kepler Track** and the **Dusky Track** – constantly threaten to steal this title. A second lakeside town, **Manapouri**, is the springboard for trips to the West Arm hydro-electric power station, **Doubtful Sound** and the isolated fiords to the south. From Manapouri, the Southern Scenic Route winds through the western quarter of Southland through minor towns along the southwestern coast of the South Island.

Almost all **buses** in Fiordland ply the corridor from Queenstown through Te Anau to Milford Sound: most are tour buses (in various guises), stopping at scenic spots and regaling passengers with a jocular commentary, but others are scheduled services that disgorge trampers at the **trailheads**. Elsewhere, services are skeletal. Drivers are well disposed to giving **lifts**, though the Milford Road from Te Anau to Milford Sound is notoriously fallow ground for hitchers and, bearing in mind the number of diversions along the way, teaming up with like-minded souls and renting a car for the day, or joining a tour bus, is a much better bet. The only **flights** you are likely to take are the scenic jaunts from Milford Sound to Te Anau or Queenstown, although others do exist.

Te Anau

The growing town of **TE ANAU** straggles along the shores of its eponymous lake, one of New Zealand's deepest and most beautiful. To the west, the lake's watery fingers claw deep into bush-cloaked mountains so remote that their most celebrated inhabitant, the takahe (see box on p.932), was thought extinct for half a century. Civilization of sorts can be found on the lake's eastern side, predominantly in Te Anau, which has set itself up in recent years as a viable alternative to Queenstown because it is a more convenient access point to Milford Sound, Doubtful Sound, the scenic walks, lakes and mountains. The town is the major way station on the route to Milford Sound and serves as a base and recuperation spot for the numerous tramps, including several of the most famous and worthwhile in the country. Top of most people's list is the

Tu-to-Rakiwhanoa and Te Namu

Fiordland came into being when the great god **Tu-to-Rakiwhanoa** worked with his axe to carve the rough gashes of the southern fiords around Preservation Inlet and Dusky Sound, leaving Resolution and Secretary islands where his feet stood. His technique improved further north, where he formed the more sharply defined lines of Nancy Sound, Caswell Sound and, the most famous of all, Milford Sound (Piopiotahi), the summit of Tu's skill.

After creating this spectacular landscape, Tu was visited by Te-Hine-nui-to-po, the goddess of death, who feared that the vision created by Tu was so wonderful that people may wish to live in Piopiotahi forever. To remind humans of their mortality, she liberated *namu*, or **sandflies**. The place of this liberation, Te Namu-a-Te-Hine-nui-te-po, at the end of the Milford Track, is now known as Sandfly Point. And the pesky critters have certainly had the desired effect. In 1773, when James Cook entered Dusky Sound, he was already familiar with the sandfly:

The most mischievous animal here is the small black sandfly which are exceedingly numerous and are so troublesome that they exceed everything of the kind I ever met with, wherever they light they cause swelling and such an intolerable itching that it is not possible to refrain from scratching and at last ends in ulcers like the small Pox. The almost continual rain may be reckoned another inconvenience attending this Bay.

Milford Track, which is reached across the lake from here, as is the newer **Kepler Track**, while the **Dusky Track**, accessible from Lake Hauroko, covers part of Lake Manapouri and ends at Supper Cove by Dusky Sound. To the north, the Milford Road passes The Key, the western end of the Routeburn, Greenstone and Caples tracks (see p.886), beyond that there's the Hollyford Valley and its tramp to the Tasman Sea, and at the southeastern end of the national park is the new, privately run Humpridge Track.

Arrival, information and transport

Buses either drop off around town or stop on the town's main shopping and restaurant street, known as Town Centre. The **visitor centre**, at the junction of Town Centre and Lake Front Drive (daily: Oct–March 8am–5pm; April–Sept 8.30am–5pm; ⓣ03/249 7416, ⓦwww.fiordlandtravel.co.nz), is part of the offices of **Fiordland Travel** (ⓣ03/249 7416 & 0800/656 501), who run the visitor centre on Sundays and Mondays, and operate a number of cruises on Lake Te Anau, Lake Manapouri and Milford Sound. The **Fiordland National Park visitor centre** is 500m south along Lake Front Drive (daily: late Dec–mid Jan 8am–8pm; Mid Jan–April 8.30am–5pm; April–Oct 8.30am–4.30pm; Oct– late Dec 8.30am–6pm; ⓣ03/249 7921, ⓦwww.doc.gov.nz, fiordlandvc@doc.govt.nz), and has a **Great Walks Booking Desk** (ⓣ03/249 8514, ⓕ249 8515; Oct–April 8.30am–5pm; April–Oct 8.30am–4.30pm), as well as plenty of general information. From here, the DOC run an excellent summer visitor programme (Jan 3–27) of hour-long evening talks ($3) plus half-day ($7–35), full-day ($40–85), evening ($30), unhurried conservation-themed trips in the forests, all of which need to be booked in advance. Also remember that the Routeburn and Milford Tracks have serviced huts (from 23 Oct–24 April) and need to be booked in advance. Bev's Tramping Gear Hire, 16 Homer St (May–Oct daily 9am–1pm & 5–7pm or by arrangement; ⓣ & ⓕ03/249 7389), is the place to **rent** any **gear** you need: individual items are charged by the day, or you can save a few dollars with special packages aimed at Great Walks trampers. For some useful further information and the town generally try Ⓦwww.fiordland.org.nz.

Getting around Te Anau is no problem: everywhere in town is easily walkable, and there's a plethora of transport to the various trailheads. If you yearn for pedals, though, **bikes** can often be rented from your accommodation or, failing that, from Fiordland Mini Golf & Bike Hire, 7 Mokonui St (Ⓣ03/249 7211; around $25 half day, $30 per day), whose tandems ($10 an hour) make exploring fun. For ranging slightly further afield (Manapouri springs to mind), local **taxis/shuttles** may fill the gap (Te Anau Taxi and Tours; Ⓣ03/249 7777). Alternatively you can hire a **car**, though financially speaking you're almost certainly better with an organized trip. Rent-a-Dent (Ⓣ03/249 8363; around $100 per day) does a good 24-hour deal aimed primarily at Milford Sound trippers, while the Mount Cook Te Anau Travel Office and Information Centre, Lake Front Drive, diagonally opposite the Fiordland Travel Visitor Centre (daily 8am–6pm; Ⓣ03/249 7516, Ⓕ249 7518), are a Hertz agent offering cars at similar rates; the latter doubles as the Manapouri Airport check-in desk and booking centre for onward travel and trips.

Accommodation

Good motels string the length of Lake Front Drive, while slightly more downmarket places line Quintin Drive a block back. There are also a number of reasonable budget options and a few good B&Bs. At more expensive places, **rates** tend to drop dramatically between June and August, and may be negotiable in the shoulder seasons (mid-April to May & Sept).

Hotels and motels

Alpenhorn Motel 35–37 Quintin Drive Ⓣ & Ⓕ03/249 7147. Well-priced concrete-block motel with full kitchen, in-house video and courtesy pick-up. ❹–❺

Arran Motel 64 Quintin Drive Ⓣ & Ⓕ03/249 8826. Motel cum B&B with attractive en-suite rooms, some cooking facilities and the added bonus of either a cooked or continental breakfast, plus courtesy car to and from the local transport options. ❺

Campbell Autolodge 42–44 Lake Front Drive Ⓣ03/249 7546, Ⓕ249 7814. Quite attractive place with lake views and flower-bedecked one-bedroom units, each with bath, shower and full kitchen, microwave, TV and phone. Bargain rates June–Aug, rest of the year ❹–❻

The Cat's Whiskers 2 Lake Front Drive Ⓣ & Ⓕ03/249 8112, Ⓔi.t.maher@paridise.net.nz. Excellent and very welcoming lakeside guesthouse with three pleasantly decorated en-suite rooms: one with a bath, and all with TV and full cooked breakfast. ❺–❻

Edgewater XL Motel 52 Lake Front Drive Ⓣ03/249 7258, Ⓕ249 8099. Fairly basic waterfront motel with one- and two-bedroom units, full kitchen, TV, barbecue and free use of canoes. ❺

Explorer Motor Lodge 6 Cleddau St Ⓣ03/249 7156, Ⓕ249 7149. These spacious studios and one-bedroom units come complete with microwaves. The decor is slightly faded and quirky, with walls at weird angles. Discounts during the off-season. ❺–❼

Lakefront Lodge 58 Lake Front Drive Ⓣ & Ⓕ03/249 7728, Ⓔanne@lakefront.co.nz. Brand-new, luxurious motel units, some with spa bath and all with every convenience, including room service. Prices drop considerably outside the Oct–April season. ❺–❻

Luxmore Hotel cnr of Mokonui St and Town Centre Ⓣ03/249 7526, Ⓕ249 7272. Big, posh central hotel that deals with lots of the more expensive coach tours and offers standard and (newer) superior doubles and twins with ensuites and all the usual paraphernalia, as well as a variety of eating options. ❻–❼

B&Bs and homestays

Barnyard Backpackers Mount Yorke Rd, 8km south at Rainbow Reach Ⓣ & Ⓕ03/249 8006. En-suite units with excellent views in a lovely lodge hand-built from natural timbers and with a licensed à la carte restaurant and bar on site. Horse trekking along the Waiau River is also available. Dorms ❶, rooms ❷

House of Wood 44 Moana Crescent ⓣ03/249 8404, ⓕ249 7676. Four tastefully decorated, modern rooms, one with bathroom, make up this fine homestay, which takes its design cues from an alpine chalet. Guests share the welcoming hosts' cosy lounge and it is only two minutes' walk from the town centre. ❺

Kepler Cottage William Steven Rd off the Te Anau, Manapouri Highway, just a couple of kilometres from town (ⓣ03/249 7185, ⓔkepler@teanau.co.nz. A very comfortable modern, rural homestay on the edge of the town limits, with plenty of space and friendly hosts. ❺

Rob & Nancy Marshall 13 Fergus Square ⓣ & ⓕ03/249 8241, ⓔrob.nancy@xtra.co.nz. Pleasant, peaceful homestay rooms and a self-contained apartment five minutes' walk from town. Cooked breakfast is accompanied by fresh home-made bread and dinners are available by prior arrangement. Homestay ❹–❺, apartment ❺

Hostels and campsites

Fiordland Holiday Park Milford Rd, 2km east ⓣ & ⓕ03/249 7059, ⓔfiordland.holiday.park@xtra.co.nz. Small attractive site with a range of well-priced cabins and tourist flats. A courtesy bus does daily Kepler Track drop-offs and there's free gear storage. Tent & powered sites $7.50, cabins & flats ❸

Mountain View Holiday Park 128 Te Anau Terrace ⓣ & ⓕ03/249 7462. Cramped, central park that's most in demand for its fine on-site accommodation. Tent & powered sites $12, cabins & units ❸–❺

Te Anau Backpackers Lodge 48 Lake Front Drive ⓣ03/249 7713, ⓔhostel@xtra.co.nz. Shabby former motel saved by a friendly atmosphere and small dorms, mostly with their own bathroom and kitchen. They're well set up for trampers, being five minutes' walk from the DOC office; what's more, pots and cutlery are available on free loan, gear is stored at no charge, and baggage can be sent on to Queenstown for about $5 per piece. As well as dorms, there are nice doubles and free use of shonky bikes. Dorms ❶, rooms ❷

Te Anau Holiday Park Manapuri Rd, 1km south ⓣ03/249 7457, ⓕ249 7536. Te Anau's largest site, with spacious camping areas, dorms, and a range of cabins and units. There are also basic bikes for rent ($5 per hour), a sauna ($5 for 30min) and the *Jintz* bar and grill (Oct–April) to keep you fed and amused. Tent sites $11, powered sites $12, dorms ❶, cabins ❷, motel units ❺

YHA Mokonui St ⓣ & ⓕ03/249 7847, ⓔyhatanau@yha.org.nz. Within one block of the lake and Town Centre, this modern comfortable hostel is now the best place to stay in town because it has been moved about 1km towards the centre and turned into a two-storey building with large dorms, double rooms (including ensuites), free gear storage, helpful and informative staff, a booking office and a lawn for camping. Tent sites $11, dorms ❶, rooms ❷–❸

Sights and activities

There is little in Te Anau itself to distract you from simply admiring the scenery across the lake and taking gentle strolls along its shore. Ten minutes' walk south, a statue of Milford Track explorer Quintin McKinnon heralds the Fiordland National Park visitor centre (see p.928), where a short video (20min; $3) introduces the **Fiordland National Park Visitor Centre and Museum** inside the centre (same hours; free), with its fascinating displays on the construction of the Homer Tunnel and the undersea life of the national park, including an eighteenth-century cannon salvaged from Dusky Sound.

Across the road you can drop $1 in a turnstile to view the dismal tank of fish which masquerades as the **Underground Trout Aquarium**, or stroll on to the **Lake Henry Walk** in the Ivor Wilson Park planted with native and exotic trees (about 20min circular walk). Once back at the visitor centre head a kilometre or so along the Te Anau lakeside path to the DOC's **Te Anau Wildlife Centre**, 178 Manapouri Rd (unrestricted entry; $1 donation box), where you can amble through the park-like setting and see parakeets, morepork and other bush birds, notably the takahe in specially constructed enclosures (see box on p.932 for more on the centre's ground-breaking work). If you're feeling particularly energetic then follow the path past the control gates at Dock Bay and head up along the shores of Lake Te Anau toward Brod Bay

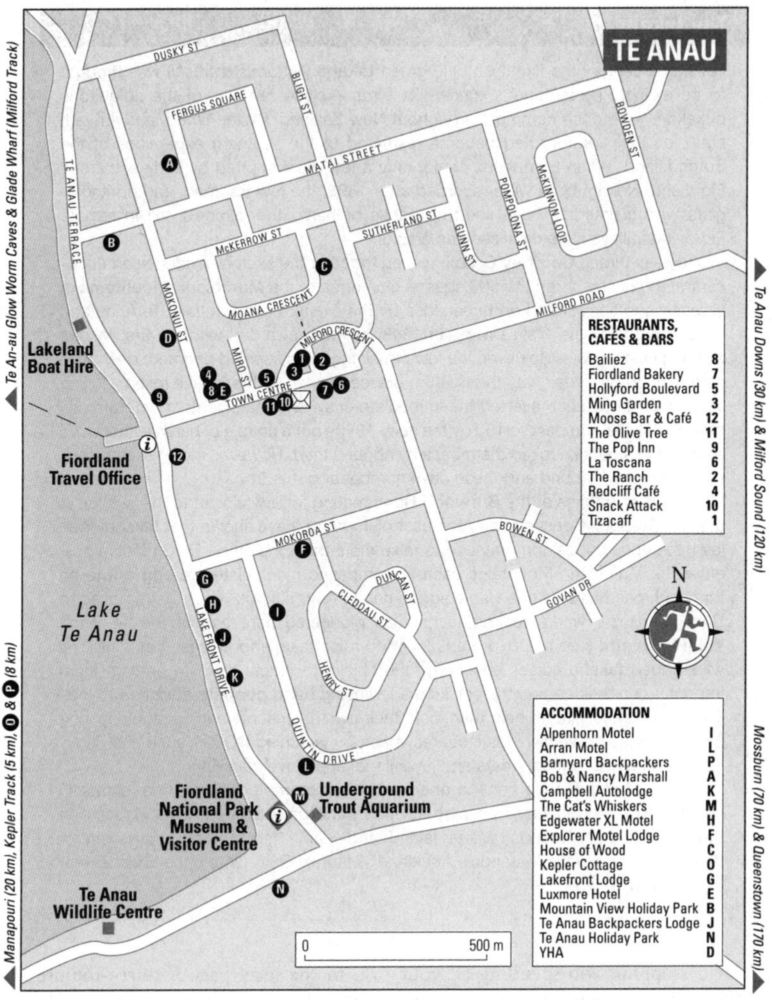

(1hr 30min one way, or water taxi to the bay and walk back ☎03/249 8364; $15); or better still in the opposite direction along the Waiau River, past the Balloon Loop, dropping in at the wetland viewing platform (for twitchers) and on to the *Shallow Bay Hut* (where you can use the toilets), overlooking Lake Manapouri (about 17km; 4hr one way), and return by taxi (see p.928).

Te Anau's main paying attraction is the **Te An-au Glow Worm Caves** (guided tours only: daily 2pm, Oct–April 8.15pm; May–Sept 6.45pm; around 2hr 30min; $44–51), which has recently been improved and refurbished. There are a couple of nice waterfalls,a sort boat ride and the glow-worm grotto is impressive, but its main appeal lies in its ability to occupy long evenings in Te

The takahe

For half a century the flightless blue-green **takahe** (*Notornis mantelli*) was thought to be extinct. These plump, turkey-like birds – close relatives of the ubiquitous pukeko – were once common throughout New Zealand. By the time Maori arrived, however, their territory had become restricted to the southern extremities of the South Island. When Europeans came, only a few were spotted by early settlers in Fiordland. No sightings were recorded after 1898; the few trampers and ornithologists who claimed to have seen its tracks or heard the takahe's call in remote Fiordland valleys were dismissed as cranks.

One keen birder, **Geoffrey Orbell**, pieced together the sketchy evidence and concentrated his search on the 500 square kilometres of the **Murchison Mountains**, a virtual island surrounded on three sides by the western arms of Lake Te Anau and on the fourth by the Main Divide. In 1948, he was rewarded with the first takahe sighting in fifty years. However, the few remaining birds seemed doomed: deer were merrily chomping their way through the grasses on which the takahe relied. Culling of the deer population averted the immediate crisis and management programmes brought takahe numbers to 160 by the early 1990s but a couple of harsh winters and a plague of stoats knocked them back by about a third. However, more recently they have recovered ground and these days number about 220.

Meanwhile, studies at the **Burwood Bush** rearing facility (closed to the public), in the Red Tussock Conservation Area east of Te Anau, have shown that takahe often lay three eggs but seldom manage to raise more than one chick. DOC officers now enter the Murchison Mountains each November to manipulate the **egg quota** so that each pair has only one viable egg to hatch. Any "surplus" eggs are removed to Burwood Bush, where rearing techniques pioneered here and at the **Te Anau Wildlife Centre** (see p.930) are employed to raise takahe for release back into the wild. Taped takahe noises encourage the chicks to hatch; then, to prevent them imprinting on their carers, the chicks are fed using **hand puppets** designed to look like adult takahe. And to help them hold their own against marauding stoats, young birds have their defensive instincts reawoken by watching DOC "Punch and Judy" shows, featuring stuffed stoats and juvenile takahe glove puppets.

Fear of having all their eggs in one basket has prompted the DOC to establish several takahe populations on predator-free **sanctuary islands** – Maud Island in the Marlborough Sounds, Mana Island and Kapiti Island (both northwest of Wellington), and Tiritiri Matangi in Auckland's Hauraki Gulf – where the birds appear to be breeding well.

Anau stopping you spending all your cash in the local bars. A thirty-minute boat trip takes you across to the western side of Lake Te Anau where you are herded into a visitor centre and taken through the caves in small groups on foot and by punt, spending thirty minutes in a 200-metre length of the Aurora cave system which tunnels under the Murchison Mountains.

A good alternative to activities from the town is the **Highride Four-Wheeler Adventure** (Ⓣ03/249 8599 & 0800/822 882 or book at the visitor centre), a three-hour guided tour, including the shuttle from Te Anau, that takes in the high backcountry and includes some stunning views of lakes Manapouri and Te Anau. No experience is necessary but make sure you feel confident on your bike before you agree to get under way on the trip proper ($98; 3 trips daily, 9.30am, 2pm & 6pm), which includes a welcome tea break.

In Te Anau the **Tawaki Dive Company**, 44 Caswell St (Ⓣ & Ⓕ03/249 9006, Ⓦwww.tawakidive.co.nz), offer one of the more exciting and rewarding **scuba** trips (for those who have PADI or SSI dive qualification) in Milford

Sound, as well as four to five day PADI courses. The beauty of diving in the Sounds is that the layer of tannin-stained fresh water on top of the sea water blocks out much of the light, making creatures and plants, used to certain conditions, suppose they are deeper than they actually are, thus enabling the divers to see them (visibility can be 10m easily) without having to plumb the extreme depths. Some of the rarities in Milford Sound's confined catchment area are black coral (white but with a black skeleton), brachiopods (living dinosaurs), purple and white nudribranchs, scarlet wrasse and telescope fish (trips from Te Anau around $225, full day; lunch $10; maximum 4; plus opportunities to explore the Milford–Te Anau Rd on the return journey).

Lake cruises and flights

Having exhausted the possibilities on shore, it pays to get **cruising** on the lake. If you're going tramping, this can best be accomplished en route to the start of the Kepler or Milford tracks (see below & p.940). The operators who provide trailhead transport also provide a number of other trips. Sinbad Cruises (Ⓣ03/249 7106) run the usual to Milford ($60) and Kepler ($15) drop-offs and scenic cruises of the lake ($45), evening cruises ($45), overnight specials ($55) and *Mount Luxmore Hut* day walks on the Kepler ($25), all on the idiosyncratic, home-made gaff ketch *Manuska*, under the captaincy of Murray – a chatty, knowledgeable lake-version of the typical Kiwi bushman. Fiordland Travel (Ⓣ0800/656 501) have acquired the old Bluff-Stewart Island ferry, a powerful catamaran, which does drop-offs and cruises, including a trip for day walkers on the Milford Track ($110) in association with Trips 'n'Tramps (Ⓣ03/249 7081, Ⓔtrips@teanau.co.nz). Fiordland Travel also include in their portfolio of other excursions runs out to Te Anau Downs ($38) and on to Glade Wharf ($50), which can be completed as a $70 round trip.

Fiordland Wilderness Experiences (Ⓣ03/249 7700 & 0800/200 434, Ⓔfiordland.sea.kayak@clear.net.nz) will get you paddling either on guided trips or independently (**kayak rental** costs about $50 a day) on lakes Te Anau or Manapouri as well as their more spectacular trips to Doubtful, Milford and Dusky sounds. Their one-day guided trip ($95) on Te Anau or Manapouri offers manageable paddling and stunning views at an easily attainable level. Lakeland Boat Hire, The Boat Hire Wharf, Te Anau Terrace between Dusky Street and Matai Street (Ⓣ03/249 8364), operate a water taxi to the Brod Bay on the Kepler Track for walkers (around $20 one way, $25–30 return) and rent out small **catamarans** ($25; 1hr), **pedaloes** or **canoes** for a gentle tootle along the banks in the summer (around $20; 1hr).

For an aerial view of southern Fiordland or a quick route to the track heads, try fixed-wing **flights** with Waterwings Airways, Lake Front Drive (Ⓣ03/249 7405, Ⓕ249 7939), who run float planes into Supper Cove and fly just about anywhere – from local runs (10min; $55) to Kepler Track overflights (20min; $110), Milford Sound overflights ($295), Doubtful Sound overflights (40min; $195), and a fly'n'boat option that involves jetboating down the Waiau River to Lake Manapouri and then flying back to Te Anau via the hidden lakes. Air Fiordland (Ⓣ03/249 7505, Ⓕ03/249 7080) use more conventional planes and concentrate more on Milford Sound, offering various combinations of flights, bus rides, kayak trips and cruises, as well as trips over Doubtful Sound, Mount Aspiring and Lake Wanaka ($230–370).

The waterside helipad of Southern Lakes Helicopters, Lake Front Drive (Ⓣ03/249 7167, Ⓔslheli@teanau.co.nz), launches several **helicopter flights** (from around $110), from around ten minutes to a couple of hours and include flights to Milford, Doubtful and Dusky sounds with landings in a narrow canyon known as Campbell's Kingdom or on snow high in the hills. They're also responsible for various flight/walk/cruise combinations and do drop-offs for the tracks. Fiordland Helicopters (Ⓣ03/249 7575, Ⓔfiord.heli@xtra.co.nz) offer a variety of scenic trips from Te Anau (ten minutes to over an hour) and track transport, with prices depending on numbers.

The Kepler Track

The **Kepler Track** (67km; 3–4 days), finished in 1988, was intended to take some of the load off the Milford and Routeburn tracks. Tracing a wide loop through the Kepler Mountains on the western side of Lake Te Anau, the track takes in one full day of exposed sub-alpine ridge walking and some lovely virgin beech forest, and has the added advantage of being easily accessible (on foot if you are keen) from Te Anau. Throughout its length it is well graded and maintained but the long haul up to *Mount Luxmore Hut* makes this a strenuous tramp, and sections can be closed after snowfalls. DOC's *Kepler Track* leaflet (free) is adequate, but for more detailed information, consult the 1:50,000 *Kepler Track Trackmap*.

Access and accommodation

The Kepler Track is one of the Great Walks and through the summer season (Nov to mid-April) its three main **huts** ($20 or £50 for 3 nights if pre-booked at the DOC centre, $30 per night if purchased on the track) – Mount Luxmore (50 bunks), Iris Burn (50 bunks) and Moturau (40 bunks) – all come with a

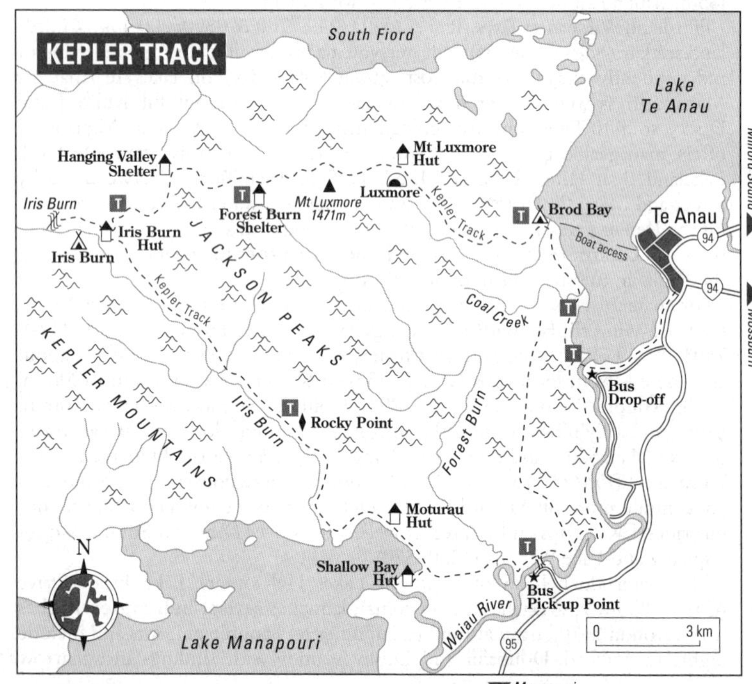

warden, gas rings and flush toilets. You don't need to book specific nights in particular huts, but a Great Walks hut **pass** for the required number of nights must be bought in advance from the Great Walks Booking Desks in Te Anau, Glenorchy or Queenstown. During the winter, these huts lose their warden and their gas rings and revert to backcountry huts ($10). In addition there is the simple *Shallow Bay Hut* ($5), just off the track beside Lake Manapouri.

Camping ($9) is permitted at only two places, Brod Bay and Iris Burn, making for one very short and two very long days – assuming you walk the track anti-clockwise – but getting the bulk of the climbing over with on the first long day.

Trailhead transport

It is possible to start the Kepler from Te Anau, but most people avoid the 5km walk around the southern end of Lake Te Anau by taking the Fiordland Tracknet **shuttle bus** (Ⓣ03/249 7777; mid-Oct to April; $5), which picks up at accommodation around town at 8.30am and 9.30am and drops off at the Control Gate, the source of the Waiau River. On the return leg, most trampers stop 11km short of the Control Gates at the swingbridge over the Waiau's Rainbow Reach. Fiordland Tracknet pick up at Rainbow Reach at 10am, 3pm and 5pm and charge $8 back to Te Anau.

You can skip another 5km of lakeside walking by cutting across Lake Te Anau to Brod Bay: Lakeland Boat Hire (Ⓣ03/249 8364) operate an early **boat** departing from the Te Anau wharf at 8.30am and 9.30am; and Sinbad Cruises (Ⓣ03/249 7106) sail the *Manuska* across at 9am. Both services charge $15.

The route

If you're setting out from Te Anau, head south along Lake Front Drive, then right, following the lakeshore and taking the first right to the Control Gates. From the **Control Gates to Brod Bay** (5.5km; 1hr–1hr 30min; flat) the track follows the lakeshore around Dock Bay and over Coal Creek, passing through predominantly beech and kamahi forests but with a fine stand of tree ferns. Brod Bay has good swimming off a sandy beach and makes a lovely place to camp. Non-campers must press on from **Brod Bay to Mount Luxmore Hut** (8.5km; 3–4hr; 880m ascent), following a signpost midway along the beach. The path climbs fairly steeply for a couple of hours to limestone bluffs, from where it is almost another hour to the bushline and fine views over Te Anau and Manapouri lakes and the surrounding mountains. The hut is almost an hour from the bushline.

With the hard ascent done, the section from **Mount Luxmore Hut to Iris Burn Hut** (19km; 5–6hr; 300m ascent, 900m descent) is testing but OK by comparison. Overall it makes a long day, and this is an exposed, high-level section where any hint of bad weather should be treated seriously. The track climbs to just below the summit of Mount Luxmore (from where you can scramble up to the 1471m peak), then descends to Forest Burn Shelter before following a ridge to Hanging Valley Shelter and turning sharply south to trace another open ridge towards Iris Burn. The Iris Burn is reached by zigzagging west into the forested Hanging Valley then following the stream to the hut and campsite in a large tussock clearing.

The track from **Iris Burn Hut to Moturau Hut** (17km; 4–6hr; 300m descent) starts behind the *Iris Burn Hut* and makes a steady descent through beech forest and riverside clearings beside Iris Burn. About halfway you pass toilets at Rocky Point, then enter a short gorge before hugging the river for several magical kilometres. Just before Iris Burn spills into Lake Manapouri, the track swings east and skirts Shallow Bay to the pleasant lakeside *Moturau Hut*. The hut is seldom full since some trampers prefer the simpler and older **Shallow Bay Hut** (free; 6 bunks) about forty minutes further on, while others continue from **Moturau Hut to Rainbow Reach** (6km; 1hr 30min; flat) through gentle beech forest to catch the last shuttle bus.

Walkers who persevere with the final stretch along the Waiau River from **Rainbow Reach to the Control Gates** (11km; 2–3hr; negligible ascent) are in for an easy forest walk with opportunities for fishing and swimming.

Eating and drinking

Diners have little culinary genius to look forward to in Te Anau, with a couple of café exceptions, but there are plenty of **no-frills places** selling decent food at reasonable prices, either in the many bars and restaurants within the tourist hotels or the more mundane, purpose-built eateries. The **drinking** picture is much the same, and entertainment is mostly BYO.

Fiordland Bakery Town Centre, adjacent to *La Toscana*. Produces some excellent Trampers Bread for the tracks (lasting 3–4 days), particularly the four-grain. The bakery café also offers a generous all-day breakfast (around $8). Mon–Sat 7am–4.30pm, daily from late Dec-Easter.

Luxmore Hotel cnr of Town Centre and Mokonui St ☎03/249 9034. The *Bailiez Café Bar* here is a pleasant bar offering brews and wholesome bar meals from 11am daily, while attached is an informal, busy, fine-dining arm with a broad menu and wine list. Upstairs, the *Highlights Buffet Restaurant*, so named because it has big windows and a high octagonal ceiling, serves buffet-style nosh to the mostly coach-party crowds. Due to the sheer size of the kitchen staff the standard of food in all the different styles of eatery is fair but worth particular attention are the sea- and fresh-water options, the venison and burgers.

Hollyford Boulevard Town Centre. Reasonably priced pseudo-American burger and grills joint which, under threat of litigation, was forced to change its name from the infinitely more catchy *Planet Hollyford*. Licensed. Avoid the attached *Boulevard Café*, dominated by coach parties.

Ming Garden Loop Road ☎03/249 7770. The best of the Chinese restaurants in town, serving, dinner-only, authentic eat-ins and takeaways including venison with black pepper, spring lamb with ginger, shredded duck with ginger and spring onions, and bean curd in oyster sauce hotpot. The combi-menu is excellent and the atmosphere a welcome relief from the rest of the town. Licensed.

Moose Bar & Café Lake Front Drive. Standard pub meals for lunch and dinner, enlivened by the bar atmosphere and busy at weekends.

The Olive Tree Café Jailhouse Mall, 52 Town Centre. Licensed and open all day, this stylish café is one of the top spots to stop at. They produce some rich and delicious Mediterranean mains, a lovely green chicken curry, some excellent pizza and pasta dishes and tasty brunches, as well as eye-opening coffee and sticky home-made cakes.

The Pop Inn 92 Tenau Terrace. A lakeside café that opens early with cheap bagels, home-made muffins and pies and an endless supply of chips, as well as cooked breakfasts. They also do snack boxes for trips and offer internet access. Closed Jul–Aug.

The Ranch Milford Rd. Rumbustious locals haunt with bog-standard, but plentiful and cheap, Kiwi grub and drinks deals, which has its own local, music-only radio station, and offers lively DJ-run entertainment from Wednesday to Saturday. Worth braving the silent walk across to the bar just for the breath of life that follows.

Redcliff Café 12 Mokonui St ☎03/249 7431. Very highly regarded, and rightly so, late-afternoon and evening favourite serving an excellent range of modern Kiwi variations on world cuisine, bistro and café food, veggie options and in quantities to satisfy trampers' appetites. Particular favourites are open sandwiches, minted braised lamb, wild venison and home-made ice cream. The cosy bar area acts as a local meeting spot, has occasional live bands and comedy nights and is a good place to drop by for some of the best coffee in town, plus there's a garden bar. Licensed; closed June-August.

Snack Attack 90 Town Centre. Open daily from 8am–8pm, with no frills, is this extremely cheap fish-and-chip and snack eat-in- or takeaway-café, favoured by the locals when they fancy a bit of fried something or other.

La Toscana 108 Town Centre. Reasonable Italian restaurant that tries hard to please with a wide range of good pizza and pasta dishes. Licensed &

BYO for wine only, plus takeaway.

Tizacaff 9 The Lane. Apart from the rotten name and slightly garish decor, this is a smashing little all-day café with some wholesome, big-portioned, home-made snacks, cakes, soups and sandwiches, BBQ dinner options (summer only), all-day breakfasts and good veggie alternatives. Everything is under $20, there's feisty coffee to wake you up, and wine and beer to send you off.

Milford Sound and around

Milford Sound is the most northerly and most celebrated of Fiordland's fifteen fiords, with vertical sides towering 1200m above the sea and waterfalls plunging from hanging valleys. While many of the other fiords approach Milford for their spectacular **beauty**, none come close for **accessibility** which has perhaps in recent years been its downfall. Before the road was pushed

Monorails and soggy roads

A visit to **Milford Sound** is undoubtedly one of the highlights of most visitors' South Island experience. For most, the journey to this remote spot is half the enjoyment, but tour operators catering to short-stay-must-see tourists are constantly on the lookout for new ways to get punters in and out quickly. Milford Sound's topography largely prevents much greater development of the airport, so developers have concentrated on two schemes: shortening the Queenstown to Milford journey by means of a monorail; and linking the Hollyford Valley with Jackson Bay and Haast to the north. Both schemes threatened the dynamics of the whole region.

The **monorail** plan was originally mooted by the Ngai Tahu *iwi*, which claims land rights over much of the Greenstone Valley, the shortest route from Queenstown to The Divide, just 40km east of Milford Sound. An alliance of greenies and outdoor enthusiasts – recognizable from their bumper stickers proclaiming "Hands off the Greenstone Valley" – raised enough public concern to force the shelving of the plans in 1994. But by 1996 a second and more feasible proposal, again backed by the Ngai Tahu, was on the table: a $120-million state-of-the-art monorail would link Mount Nicholas Station, at the southwestern crook of Lake Wakatipu, with the Milford Road 50km north of Te Anau, via the Von and Mararoa valleys. Detractors claim that the inconvenience of transferring between catamaran, monorail and bus would offset any time gains, while investors still need to obtain consent for a thirty-kilometre section of the route which passes through the DOC-managed Snowdon State Forest. For every supporter of the venture in Queenstown, there is an opponent in Te Anau – a town that relies as heavily on Milford-bound traffic for its livelihood as Queenstown does on its jetboating, bungy-jumping reputation. More importantly, the plans are actively opposed by almost every wilderness walker, tramper and environmentalist in New Zealand (and abroad) because of the disastrous effect it would have on the infra-structure, ambience, plant- and animal-life of this unique environment.

More recently, a revised proposal supported by the Ngai Tahu Holdings Corporation (representatives of the local Maori), Skyline Enterprises Ltd and various others have suggested a combined **road** and **electric-gondola** option (costing $80 million), along the lines of the 1996 proposal. The current Hollyford Valley Road was approved in 1936, but only 16km of it were built as a spur off the SH94 to Milford; between the Hollyford end of this spur and existing roads around Jackson Bay lie around 80km of valley floor, across which a new toll-road could be constructed. Fortunately, the plan was rejected by the Queenstown council for being incomplete, and the project is hopefully now on the backburner permanently.

△ Doubtful Sound

through in 1952 visitors had to arrive by boat or walk the much-lauded **Milford Track** to reach the head of the fiord, but the opening of the Homer Tunnel paved the way for the phalanx of tourist buses that disgorge patrons onto fiord cruises. The tiny little airport hardly seems to rest for a second as planes buzz angrily in and out, while all day in the summer and around the middle of the day during spring and winter, the crowds can certainly detract from the grandeur of the spot – but don't let that, or anything else for that matter, put you off. Even torrential rain adds to the atmosphere of this magical place, as an ethereal mist descends, periodically lifting to reveal the waterfalls at their thunderous best.

Like the other sounds, Milford is a drowned glacial rather than a river valley, making it technically a fiord. Maori know it as **Piopiotahi** ("the single thrush"), and attribute its creation to the god Tu-to-rakiwhanoa, who was called away before he could carve a route into the interior, leaving high rock walls. These precipitous routes are now known as the Homer and Mackinnon passes, but were probably first used by Maori who came here to collect *pounamu*. The first European to sail into Piopiotahi was probably sealer John Grono who, in 1823, named the fiord Milford Haven after his home port in south Wales. The main river flowing into the Welsh Milford was the Cleddau, so naturally the river at the head of the fiord took that name too.

The earliest settler was Scot **Donald Sutherland**, who arrived with his dog, John O'Groat, in 1877; he promptly set a series of thatched huts beside the freshwater basin of what he called the "City of Milford", funding his explorations by guiding the small number of visitors who had heard tell of the scenic wonder hereabouts. By 1890 Sutherland had married a Dunedin widow, Elizabeth Samuel, and together they built a twelve-room hotel to serve the growing number of steamer passengers – "ashfelters" (city dwellers) and "shadow catchers" (photographers) – who flocked to admire the beauty of his remote home and to walk the newly opened Milford Track.

The predations of today's influx of visitors and the operation of a small fishing fleet have necessitated strategies to preserve the fiord's **fragile ecosystem**. Like all fiords, Milford Sound has an Entrance Sill at its mouth, in this case only 70m below the surface as compared to the deepest point of almost 450m. This effectively cuts off much of the natural recirculation of water and hinders mixing of sea water and the vast quantities of fresh water that pour into the fiord. The less-dense tannin-stained fresh, surface layer (up to 10m deep) builds up, further diminishing the penetration of light, which is already reduced by the all-day shadow cast by the fiord walls. The result is a relatively barren inter-tidal zone that protects a narrow – but wonderfully rich and extremely fragile – band of light-shy red and black **corals**; these normally grow only at much greater depths, but thrive here in the dark conditions. Unfortunately, Milford's fishing fleet use crayfish pots, which tend to shear off anything that grows on the fiord's walls. A marine reserve has been set up along the northeastern shore, where all such activity is prohibited, but really this is far too small and conservation groups are campaigning for its extension.

The road to Milford Sound

The 120-kilometre road from Te Anau to Milford Sound has to be one of the world's finest, though this hasn't stopped folk from hatching outlandish plans to circumvent it (see box on p.937). This two-hour drive can easily take a day if you grab every photo opportunity. Anywhere else the initial drive beside Lake Te Anau would be considered obscenely scenic, but it is nothing com-

The Hollyford Track

The **Hollyford Track** (54 km; 4 days) is long, but mostly flat, and over the past couple of years much improved which means it's not as muddy as of old. DOC's *Hollyford Valley* **leaflet** ($1) is fine for following it, though the 1:75,000 *Hollyford Track Trackmap* is more detailed. The track follows Fiordland's longest valley from the end of the Hollyford Valley road to Martins Bay. The track suffers from being essentially a one-way tramp, requiring four days' backtracking – unless you're flash enough to fly out from the airstrip at Martins Bay or tough enough to continue around a long, difficult and remote loop known as the **Big Bay–Pyke route** (9–10 days total; consult the DOC's Big Bay–Pyke Route leaflet for details). The joy of the Hollyford is not in the sense of achievement that comes from scaling alpine passes, but in the appreciation of the dramatic mountain scenery and the kahikatea, rimu and matai **bush** with an understorey of wineberry, fuchsia and ferns. At Martins Bay, Long Reef has a resident **fur seal** colony, and from September to December you might spot rare Fiordland crested **penguins** (tawaki) nesting among the scrub and rocks.

Trampers who hate carrying a big pack, prefer more comfortable lodgings and having hearty meals cooked for them should consider a **guided walk** with Hollyford Valley Walk, PO Box 360, Queenstown (☎03/442 3760 & 0800/832 226): small groups are led by knowledgeable guides, and nights are spent at the relatively luxurious *Martins Bay Lodge* and the similar standard *Pyke Lodge* (3–4 days plus fly-out $1290–1570); those in a mad rush can even fly from Queenstown, see the seal colonies, jetboat upriver for a night at the *Martins Bay Lodge* and fly back to Queenstown for around $600.

Accommodation and access

The six DOC **huts** ($5) are each equipped with platform bunks, mattresses, water and toilets and do not need to be booked, though hut tickets or an annual hut pass should be bought in advance.

Buses on the Te Anau–Milford run will drop off at Marian Corner, where the Hollyford and Milford roads part company, or head down to the end of the Hollyford Road, by arrangement. Hollyford Track (☎03/249 9080 & 0800/832 226) run most mornings between November and May, to the Road End, as does Fiordland

pared to the Eglinton Valley, where the road penetrates into steeper, bush-clad mountains and winds through a sub-alpine wonderland to the bare rock walls of the seemingly impassable head of the Hollyford River. The Homer Tunnel then cuts through to the steep Cleddau Valley, the home straight down to Milford Sound.

Maori parties must have long used this route on their way to seek *pounamu* at Anita Bay on Milford Sound, but no road existed until two hundred unemployment-relief workers with shovels and wheelbarrows were put on the job in 1929. The greatest challenge was to puncture the headwall of the Hollyford Valley: work on the 1200-metre-long **Homer Tunnel** began in 1935, but was badly planned from the start. Working at a one-in-ten downhill gradient, the builders soon hit water and were forced to pump out continuously; a pilot tunnel allowing the water to drain westwards was finished in 1948 – when the whole project was relegated to the too-hard basket until 1952. After a concerted push, the road was finally completed in 1953, and officially inaugurated the following year, opening up Milford Sound to road traffic for the first time.

Despite recent improvements, such as passing bays for buses, the tunnel remains rough-hewn, forbiddingly dark and is often choked with diesel fumes (which make the headlights of oncoming vehicles appear to change from red

Tracknet (☎03/249 7777) from mid-October to April; both charge around $40, or $35 to the Hollyford Road turn-off, leaving an extra 16km to tramp. Hollyford Track also operate **flights** (which must be pre-booked) to and from Martins Bay or the Hollyford Airstrip (both around $300); or, since many people fly out from Martins Bay, you can fly standby from Milford Sound – and walk the track in reverse – for under $100. Both Air Fiordland (☎03/249 7505; $300 for two) and Milford Sound Helicopters (☎03/249 7845; about $550 for four) offer the same services to the bay and airstrip. Finally, you can avoid most of the long day's walk beside the attractive but samey Lake McKerrow with Hollyford Track's **jetboat service** (4–7 people; $70 each for four or more) to the head of Lake McKerrow; if you're really pushed for time, a similarly priced run up the Hollyford River can further reduce the walk by a day.

The route

The track from **Road End to Hidden Falls Hut** (9km; 2hr 30min–3hr; negligible ascent) follows a disused section of road which soon crumbles into a track with some riverbank walking to the *Hidden Falls Hut* (20 bunks). Keen walkers will probably want to push on from **Hidden Falls Hut to Alabaster Hut** (11km; 3–4hr; 100m ascent) through ribbonwood and beech to Little Homer Saddle and past Little Homer Falls. From **Alabaster Hut to Demon Trail Hut** (13km; 3–4hr; negligible ascent), you soon pass a side track to the nicely sited *McKerrow Island Hut* (20 bunks), before continuing beside Lake Alabaster to *Demon Trail Hut* (12 bunks). The section from **Demon Trail Hut to Hokuri Hut** (10km; 5–6hr; 100m ascent) is probably the toughest on the walk, following the shore of Lake McKerrow on rough ground with some tricky stream crossings, to *Hokuri Hut* (12 bunks). The path continues from **Hokuri Hut to Martins Bay Hut** (11km; 4–5hr; negligible ascent), by way of the scant remains of Jamestown, a cattle-ranching settlement that prospered briefly in the 1870s. Passing the small airstrip served by Hollyford Track's flights, you'll stumble across some of the dozen dwellings that comprise Martins Bay; no one lives here permanently, but they are used by opportunistic whitebaiters and hunters. Continuing parallel to Martins Bay, and occasionally glimpsing the Hollyford River through wind-shorn trees, you reach the new *Martins Bay Hut* (20 bunks).

to yellow to white). The sub-alpine section of the road is one of the world's most **avalanche**-prone. Since the last death on the road, in 1984, there has been a sophisticated avalanche-monitoring system in place and, if necessary, explosives are dropped from helicopters to loosen dangerous accumulations of snow while the road is closed. This mostly happens between May and November, when motorists are required to carry chains (available from service stations in Te Anau for around $30). Whatever the season, drivers should bear in mind that there is heavy bus traffic, which tends to be Milford-bound from around 11am to noon and Te Anau-bound between 3 and 5pm. Apart from the store in the Hollyford Valley, 8km off your route, there is nowhere to buy **food** until you reach Milford, so be prepared. Also, buying petrol at Milford is an exercise in throwing money away so fill up your car before you start your journey.

Along the road there are a dozen simple DOC **campsites** ($5), almost all with giardia-free stream water, long-drop toilets and fireplaces. Two are between Te Anau and Te Anau Downs, and the remaining ten pack into the next 50km, either on the grassy flats of the Eglinton Valley or in the bush nearby. Mackay Creek, Totara Creek and East Branch Eglinton, all around 55km north of Te Anau, are particularly good.

Heading north from Te Anau, there's little reason to stop in the first 30km to **Te Anau Downs Harbour**, where boats stop off en route to the start of the Milford Track. The road then cuts east away from the lake, before veering north into the **Eglinton Valley** through occasional stands of silver, red and mountain beech interspersed with open flats of red tussock grass. Surprisingly in a national park, these plains are grazed, an anomaly resulting from longstanding leases which had to be honoured. The mountains that hem in the valley are picturesquely reflected in the roadside **Mirror Lakes**, if its not too windy, 56km north of Te Anau, just before you hit the underwhelming **Avenue of the Disappearing Mountain** where the road slopes up, creating the illusion of the mountain ahead growing smaller as you approach.

As you get nearer to the head of the valley the road steepens to **The Divide**, at 532m the lowest east–west crossing of the Southern Alps. From the car park, with its toilets and walkers' shelter, you can walk to **Key Summit** (919m; 2–3hr return) for fine panoramic views over three valley systems. For those travelling by bus, a noticeboard details the times of passing services (Kiwi Discovery come through at roughly 11.20am Milford-bound & 4pm Te Anau-bound; ⓣ03/442 7340 & 0800/505 504), though it's best to book a **pick-up** beforehand. Pressing on towards Milford, you descend into the valley of the Hollyford River, which is best seen from a popular viewpoint just before the Hollyford Road shoots off north. The Milford Road continues west towards the Hollyford's source, a huge glacial cirque in which an Alpine Club hut marks the start of a walk to the Gertrude Saddle (4hr return), where you'll be rewarded by great views of the Darran Mountains and Mount Tutoko (2756m), Fiordland's highest point.

A kilometre further on, the **Homer Tunnel**, home of many curious kea, forges through the rock, emerging at the top of a long switchback down to the Cleddau River. Roughly 10km on from the tunnel all buses stop at **The Chasm**, while their passengers stroll (15min return) to the near-vertical rapids where the Cleddau has scoured out a deep, narrow channel. Tantalizing glimpses through the foliage reveal sculpted rocks hollowed out by churning stones or tortured into free-standing ribs that resemble flying buttresses.

The Hollyford Valley

The Milford Road drops down from The Divide into the Hollyford Valley, which runs 80km from its headwaters in the Darran Mountains north to the Tasman Sea at Martins Bay. A 16km spur road (originally planned to reach Haast – see box on p.836) provides access to the Hollyford Track (see box on pp.940–941) and a couple of other diversions. The first of these is a walk or more of a scramble to **Lake Marian** (5km return; 2–3hr; 400m ascent), which starts 1km along the Hollyford Valley spur road and climbs to a beautiful alpine lake, passing some wonderful cataracts (30–40min return) where boardwalks are cantilevered out from the rock wall.

The only settlement is 8km along the valley road at **Gunns Rest**, home to the idiosyncratic, knowledgeable and entertaining Murray Gunn, who operates a shop (daily 8.30am–8pm) packed with some of the things you'll need for tramping and a lot more besides: postcards, good books, maps, some rare greenstone (Bowenite Tangiwai) and souvenirs. Murray also runs the *Hollyford Camp* (no phone; bunks ❶, rooms ❷), a huddle of simple old 1930s cabins which served as married family's quarters for the long-suffering road-builders. Each cabin has a double room and a four-berth bunk room, linked by a kitchen/lounge area equipped with a coal-burning range and cold water supply. The **museum** (shop hours; $1, free to *Hollyford Camp* guests) is yet another Murray Gunn venture – a collection of photos, pioneer artefacts and some interesting paraphernalia relating to the building of the Milford road and the Homer Tunnel, the one-time community at Martins Bay, and the devastating floods that periodically afflict the region.

The road runs 8km beyond Gunns Camp to the Road End – the beginning of the Hollyford Track and a shorter walk to **Humboldt Falls** (20–30min return), a three-step cascade leaping some two hundred metres and apparently the highest falls near a road in Australasia.

The Milford Track

More than any other Great Walk, the **Milford Track** has become a Kiwi icon and it sometimes seems that walking it is the dream of every New Zealander. Unlike other major tramps where foreigners, and particularly Europeans, predominate, Kiwis are in the majority here.

Its exalted reputation is partly accidental and partly historical. It seems likely that southern **Maori** paced the Arthur and Clinton valleys in search of *pounamu*, but there is little direct evidence. The first **Europeans** to explore this section of Fiordland were Scotsmen Donald Sutherland and John Mackay who, in 1880, blazed a trail up the Arthur Valley from Milford Sound. The story goes that while working their way up the valley they came upon the magnificent Mackay Falls and tossed a coin to decide who would name it, on the understanding that the loser would name the next waterfall. Mackay won the toss but rued his good fortune when, days later, they stumbled across the much more famous and lofty Sutherland Falls. They may well have climbed the adjacent Mackinnon Pass, but the honour of naming it went to **Quintin McKinnon** who, with his companion Ernest Mitchell, reached it in 1888 after having been commissioned by the Otago Chief Surveyor, C. W. Adams, to cut a path up the Clinton Valley.

The route was finally pushed through in mid-October 1888 and the first **tourists** came through the next year, guided by McKinnon. The greatest fillip came in 1908 when a writer submitted her account of the Milford Track to the editor of London's *Spectator*. She had declared it "A Notable Walk" but, in a fit of editorial hyperbole, the editor retitled the piece "The Finest Walk in the World". From 1903 until 1966 the government, through its Tourist Hotel Corporation (THC), held a monopoly on the track, allowing only guided walkers; the huts were supplied by a team of packhorses, which weren't finally retired until 1969.

Wider **public access** was only achieved after the Otago Tramping Club challenged the government's policy by tramping the Milford in 1964. Huts were built in 1966 and the first independent parties came through later that year.

Practicalities

The Milford Track (54km; 4 days) has become a victim of its own hype. There is no doubt that it is a wonderful route through some of Fiordland's finest scenery, but many trampers disparage it as over-regimented, expensive, and not especially varied, while other complaints focus on the huts, which are badly spaced and lurk below the tree line among the sandflies. While these criticisms aren't unfounded – the tramp costs around $250 in hut and transport **fees** alone – the track is extremely well managed and maintained, the huts are clean and unobtrusive, and, because everyone's going in the same direction, you can go all day without seeing a soul. The Milford is also tougher than many people expect, packing the only hard climb and a dash for the boat at Milford Sound into the

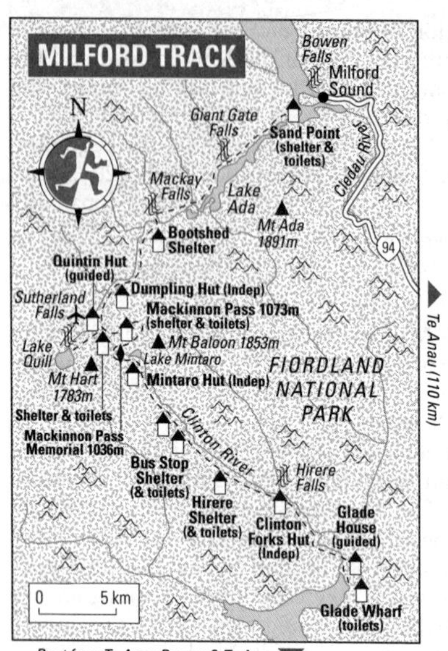

last two days. Nevertheless, almost anyone of any age can walk the track, though the DOC recommends that unfit aspirants build up to it over 6–8 weeks. As the Mackinnon Pass can only be crossed when avalanche conditions do not prevail check the likely weather at the DOC office before you start out.

The DOC's *Milford Track* **leaflet** (provided free when you book – see below) is adequate for route-finding, though the 1:75,000 *Milford Track Trackmap* provides much more information. The 1:250,000 *Fiordland National Park* **map** is too small a scale to be of much use.

Booking and accommodation

Independent walkers tackling the Milford Track during the late-October to late-April tramping season are subject to a rigid system of advance-booking **accommodation passes** – use the DOC's Great Walks Booking Desks in Queenstown, Glenorchy and Te Anau – for the three special category huts. Bookings are made for specific days and you can only walk the track from south to north, spending the first night at *Clinton Forks Hut*, the second at *Mintaro Hut* and the third at *Dumpling Hut*. No backtracking or second nights are allowed and there is strictly **no camping**. Numbers are limited to forty per day, so you'll need to book as far ahead as possible (a month or more if you are adaptable, six months if you need a specific departure date or are part of a large group), but this does have the huge advantage that you are guaranteed a bed. Huts all have wardens and are equipped with flush toilets, running (but not drinking) water, heaters and gas rings, but not pans and plates; the cost is $105 for the three nights, and family discounts of thirty percent apply throughout the season. Credit-card phone or mail bookings are taken for the following season from July 1 and can be made through the Great Walks Booking Desk, the DOC, PO Box 29, Te Anau (See Te Anau, Arrival, Information and Transport; ⓣ03/249 8514, ⓔgreatwalksbooking@doc.govt.nz); pick up your accommodation passes from Te Anau before 11.30am on the day of departure. If the track is closed due to bad weather or track conditions, full refunds are made but new bookings can only be taken if there is space.

Outside the season the huts revert to backcountry prices ($10). They are unstaffed with heating but no clothes-drying or cooking facilities; bookings are not required and annual hut passes are valid.

Trailhead transport

The initial stretch of the Milford Track is a doddle and you'll find a late start is a good way of avoiding just hanging about at the first hut full of unbearable anticipation at the prospect of the next day. Both ends of the Milford Track can only be realistically approached **by boat**. There are several possibilities, but all must be arranged and paid for before, or at the same time as, accommodation passes are issued. Independent walkers can catch the Milford Tracknet Bus at 9.45am to Te Anau Downs ($12) or the 10.30am Fiordland Travel Coach in Te Anau; both meet the Fiordland Travel Launch at Te Anau Downs, 30km north of Te Anau. The morning launch departs at 10.30am ($38) for the journey across Lake Te Anau (1hr 15min) to the start of the track at Glade Wharf, the afternoon launch departs at 2pm ($50), for the start of the track. At the Milford end of the track, the majority catch either the 2.30pm or the 3.15pm *Anita Bay* launch from Sandfly Point (Nov to mid-April; around $20) for the journey to Milford Sound (20min). **Buses** back to Te Anau can be picked up at 9.15am, 3pm and 5.15pm (3hr; $37).

Other operators offer different ways to approach and leave the track. They can all be booked individually, but most have combined to marginally undercut the total price you'd pay for independent arrangements. Probably the best way to start from Te Anau is on the *Manuska*, a wooden ketch run by Sinbad Cruises (10.30am; 5–6hr; $60; Ⓣ03/249 7106), which sails under canvas whenever possible to Glade Wharf. Sea Kayak Fiordland meet track walkers and give them some paddling on the sound before mini-busing them back to Te Anau (Ⓣ03/249 7700, Ⓔfiordland.sea.kayak@clear.net.nz; $49; 2.30–6.30pm daily).

If money is no object, you can **fly** in to Glade Wharf with Waterwings Floatplane (Ⓣ03/249 7405; around $250) or one of the several companies who fly out of Milford Sound, Te Anau or Queenstown.

Guided walks

For many years, the only way to walk the Milford Track was on a **guided walk**. Some would argue that this is still the case, with just your personal effects to carry and comfortable beds to sleep in. Accommodation is in clean, plain huts which aren't exactly luxurious, but do boast hot showers, duvets on the bunks, three-course dinners with wine and cooked breakfasts. Staff prepare the huts, cook the meals, make up the lunches and tidy up after you. All you have to do is walk, but there's a price to pay for all this pampering. The **Milford Track Guided Walk**, PO Box 185, Te Anau (Nov to mid-April; Ⓣ03/441 1138 & 0800/659 255, Ⓔmtinfo@milfordtrack.co.nz), is a six-night, five-day affair and costs $1690, or $1490 in the low season (Oct–Nov & Mar–April). For that you get an introductory talk with dinner and a night at the *Te Anau Travel Centre*, transport to the trailhead, accommodation and food on the track, a night at the *Milford Sound Hotel* (used only for this purpose), a cruise and a return bus ride to Te Anau.

Anyone wanting a taste of the track without having to walk more than a couple of kilometres can stay overnight at **Glade House**, the first of the guided walkers' huts on the track. Bus and boat transport are scheduled to leave time to explore the Clinton River and eat a three-course dinner – all for $190 (book through Milford Track Guided Walk).

The route

The track starts at the head of Lake Te Anau and follows the Clinton River into the heart of the mountains, climbing over the spectacular Mackinnon Pass before tracing the Arthur River to Milford Sound.

The first day is a doddle. **Glade Wharf to Clinton Forks Hut** (8km; 2hr; 50m ascent) starts along a 2km 4WD track which serves Glade House. The path then crosses a long swingbridge to the right bank of the gentle, meandering Clinton River; keen anglers can spend an hour or two fishing for trout in the deep pools. The track runs through dense beech forest, only occasionally giving glimpses of the mountains ahead beyond *Clinton Forks Hut*.

From **Clinton Forks Hut to Mintaro Hut** (13.5km; 4–5hr; 350m ascent), the track follows the right bank of the Clinton River to its source, Lake Mintaro, right by the *Mintaro Hut*. Again this is easy going, and, by the time you reach a short side track to Hidden Lake, the Mackinnon Pass should be visible ahead. The track steepens a little to Bus Stop Shelter, then flattens out to *Pompolona Hut*. From here it's a further hour to *Mintaro Hut* where, if it looks like it will be a good sunset, it pays to drop your pack and head up the Mackinnon Pass.

The walk so far does nothing to prepare you for the day from **Mintaro Hut to Dumpling Hut** (14km; 5–6hr; 550m ascent, 1030m descent). Though the surface of the broad path is firm and well graded, bushwalking neophytes will find the haul up to Mackinnon Pass (1hr 30min–2hr) very strenuous. Long breath-catching pauses provide an opportunity to admire the wonderful alpine scenery, notably the headwall of the Clinton Valley, a sheer glacial cirque of grey granite. As the bush drops away behind you, the slope eases to the saddle at Mackinnon Pass, a great place to eat lunch, though you'll have the company of kea and the incessant buzzing of pleasure flights from Milford. A memorial to McKinnon and Mitchell marks the low-point of the saddle, from where the path turns east and climbs to a shelter (with toilets and a gas ring) just below the dramatic form of Mount Balloon. From there it is all downhill, and steeply too, initially skirting the flank of Mount Balloon then following a recent re-routing of the path beside the picturesque Roaring Burn and down to the Arthur River. The confluence is marked by **Quintin Hut**, which was originally built by the Union Steamship Company as an overnight shelter for sightseers from Milford visiting the Sutherland Falls. Though it remains a private hut, toilets and shelter are provided for independent walkers – who mostly dump their packs for the walk to the base of the 560m **Sutherland Falls** (4km; 1hr–1hr 30min return; 50m ascent), the highest in New Zealand. *Quintin Hut* has an airstrip and anyone with $50 to spare can take a **scenic flight** (minimum 4 people; 20min) to view Lake Quill (which feeds the Sutherland Falls), the Mackinnon Pass and the Clinton Valley. *Dumpling Hut* is another hour's walk from *Quintin Hut*.

After a tiring third day, you're in for an early start and a steady walk from **Dumpling Hut to Sandfly Point** (18km; 5–6hr; 125m decent) to meet your launch or kayak at 2pm. After rain this can be a magnificent walk, as the valley walls stream with waterfalls and the Arthur River is in spate. The track follows the tumbling river for a couple of hours to the Boatshed (toilets), before crossing the Arthur River on a swingbridge and cutting inland to the magnificent MacKay Falls. More a steep cascade than a waterfall, they are much smaller than the Sutherland Falls but equally impressive, particularly after rain. Don't miss Bell Rock, a water-hollowed boulder that you can crawl inside. The track subsequently follows Lake Ada, created by a landslip 900 years ago, and named by Sutherland after his Scottish girlfriend. A small lunch shelter midway along its shore heralds Giant Gate Falls, which are best viewed from the swingbridge that crosses the river at the foot of the falls. From here it is roughly an hour and a half to the shelter at Sandfly Point.

Milford Sound

After all the superlatives feted on Milford Sound, initial impressions can be a little deflating. The smattering of buildings that comprise the small settlement are hardly in keeping with such magnificent surroundings and the best of the fiord can only really be seen from the water. Nevertheless, it is a fine spot on the edge of a basin where the Cleddau and Arthur rivers surge into the fiord, and the whole scene is dominated by the triangular glaciated pinnacle of **Mitre Peak** (1694m), named for its resemblance to a bishop's mitre when viewed from this angle. It's worth bearing in mind that at the height of the summer, in good weather this area is buzzing with coaches, boats and flights.

Arrival and getting around

The most worthwhile way to get here, and the one which conveys the greatest sense of place, is to **walk** the Milford Track (see p.943), though **drivers** and **cyclists** do get the freedom to stop, sightsee and camp at the numerous basic campsites along the dramatic road from Te Anau (see p.939). Failing either of those, you can fly, hop on a bus, or do a combination of both, often with a cruise on the fiord thrown in (see box on p.948 for a rundown of the options).

There isn't much to Milford Sound. The airport, fishing harbour, new cruise terminal, post office, pub and café, and an extremely expensive petrol station are scattered along the shore. Though they are not more than a few hundred metres apart, there is a sporadic free **shuttle bus** connecting them all.

Accommodation and eating

The only place on dry land where you can stay, as opposed to overnight cruises (see "Trips to Milford Sound", p.948) is *Milford Sound Lodge* (ⓣ & ⓕ 03/249 8071, ⓔ milford.sound.lodge@xtra.co.nz; tent sites $10, dorms ❶, rooms ❸), under ambitious management that has slowly turned this once unappealing dump into a really worthwhile stopping point on the approach to Milford Sound, almost 2km from the wharf and linked to it by a courtesy bus. Rooms have been refurbished and the bathrooms are practically a work of art. Unfortunately the *THC Milford Sound Hotel* is closed to the public, used only by people on expensive guided trips.

Eating well in Milford has never been great but it is getting better. The ever-improving *Milford Sound Lodge* café sells filling meals and groceries at inflated prices (due to transport costs). The *Mitre Peak Café* (daily: 8.30am–late) is also owned by the *Lodge* and eschews the usual Kiwi tearoom traditions in favour of good coffee, filling snacks and tasty mains, as well as knocking through to the pub (which they also own), in order to create a café/bar that is relaxing, makes the best of its surroundings, and allows you to watch the weather sweeping along the fiord. So far the food is passable, but if it improves at the same rate as the *Lodge* has done then it will become a must-stop destination.

Around Milford

You are pretty much surrounded by water here, and you should waste little time before getting out on it. If tales of his pioneering days have inspired you, pay homage at **Donald Sutherland's grave**, hidden among the staff accommodation behind the pub. Otherwise, there's a five-minute stroll up to a **lookout** behind the *THC Hotel*, or a boardwalk and track beside the cruise terminal leads to the 160-metre **Lady Bowen Falls** (15min return), named after the wife of George Bowen, New Zealand's governor in the 1860s. Though most impressive in spate, when the upturned lip sends a spume out across the fiord, the falls are worth the walk at any time to observe the village's source of water and hydroelectricity. Three old graves at the foot of the falls guard the remains of nineteenth-century sealers and whalers.

Trips to Milford Sound

As **Milford Sound** is on most visitors' itineraries, there's no shortage of operators willing to get you there from almost anywhere in the country. **From Queenstown**, a stream of luxury **buses** make the tiring four-to-five-hour drive via Te Anau to Milford, complete with frequent photo-opportunity stops and a relentless commentary, decanting their passengers for a cruise on the fiord then running them back again. Trips **from Te Anau** involve the middle (and most interesting) section of Queenstown-based trips and are appreciably shorter, generally taking a leisurely eight rather than a hurried twelve hours. Most tours also include a **cruise** on the sound once you get there – see p.950 for a run-down of the various vessels that ply its waters.

From Te Anau

The cheapest trips are those which don't include cruises – good value if you're going kayaking: try the track-transport specialists Fiordland Tracknet (Ⓣ03/249 7777; Nov–May), who will get you there and back for $37, but you'll have to put up with detours to the trailheads. The big boys such as Fiordland Travel (Ⓣ03/249 7416 & 0800/656 510, Ⓔreservations@fiordlandtravel.co.nz), InterCity (Ⓣ03/249 7559 & 0800/731 711), Milford Explorer (Ⓣ03/249 7516 & 0800/800 904) and Red Boat Cruises (Ⓣ03/441 1137 & 0800/657 444, Ⓔteanau.travel@xtra.co.nz) all run luxury **bus and cruise** packages for around $100, though there are small reductions for backpackers and substantial standby **discounts** outside the peak season. A trip to Milford and an overnight cruise, on the *Milford Mariner*, MV *Friendship* or *Milford Wanderer*, tends to be much more expensive around $320 a pop, while overnight cruises alone cost about $155-255.

The most interesting possibilities include trips with Fiordland Wilderness Experiences (Ⓣ03/249 7700; $95), involving four hours' kayaking on the fiord; Kiwi Discovery (Ⓣ03/442 9792 & 0800/100 792; around $99), with a bus and boat ride; Topline Tours (Ⓣ03/249 8059), who offer a luxury little bus and then cruise or walk followed by either a plane or bus trip back ($65–200); and Trips 'n' Tramps (Ⓣ03/249 7081 & 0800/305 805, Ⓔtrips@teanau.co.nz; around $105), concentrating on

The only other sight attached to terra firma is the **Milford Sound Underwater Observatory**, which can be visited as part of a cruise run either by Red Boat Cruises or Fiordland Travel ($62; see "Trips to Milford Sound", above), or by shuttle (Ⓣ03/249 7400; 9.15am–5pm; $35–40, subject to availability). It's a floating platform moored to a sheer rock wall in Harrison Cove, part of the marine reserve about a third of the way along the fiord. A series of explanatory panels on the surface prepare you for the main attraction, a spiral staircase which takes you nine metres down through the relatively lifeless freshwater surface layer to a circular gallery where windows look out into the briny heart of the fiord. Sharks and seals have been known to swim by, but most of the action happens immediately outside in window-box "gardens", which have been specially grown from locally gathered **coral** and plant species. Lights pick out colourful fish, tubeworms, sea fans, huge starfish and rare red and black coral. This might all sound a little naff – but unless you're an experienced diver or you've got $500 to spare, this is the only chance you'll get to see these corals, which elsewhere in the world grow only at depths greater than forty metres. Cruises only stop for around twenty minutes, which isn't really long enough, so if you're really interested, a water taxi's your best bet. A new attraction at the Observatory site is **Submarine Adventure** (Ⓣ0800 478 262, Ⓦwww.submarines.co.nz; $400 per person, 4 passengers max; 4–5 trips daily; 1 hr), a ride down to 100m below the surface in a cut-down sub originally designed for the

relaxed short bushwalks along the way before usually meeting up with the *Milford Wanderer*.

From Queenstown

Trips typically start at 7am and seldom get back before 8pm. Many shy away from such a long day and opt instead for a more expensive package involving the forty-minute **flight** to Milford's small airfield, a **cruise** and a **return flight**, but the best option available involves staying in and travelling from Te Anau. A good compromise, if you don't have your own transport, is to fly there and bus back only as far as Te Anau (from around $220 with Kiwi Discovery; ☎03/442 7340), since flights back are oversubscribed, sending prices up as high as $390. Travellers locked into the Kiwi Experience or Magic Bus circuit have to pay extra to do the Milford Sound leg; if you can get a group of four or five together, you can get here as cheaply, and with greater flexibility, by renting a car from Queenstown (see p.849).

Prices for the **bus/cruise/bus trips** kick off at $139–325 with Kiwi Discovery and Kiwi Experience (☎03/442 9708), both of whom run comparable trips on smaller buses; but, best value of all, the BBQ Bus (☎03/442 1045; around $160) run full-day trips, with stops for short bushwalks and a barbecue in the Hollyford Valley. More upmarket tours using air-conditioned vehicles, complete with prerecorded multilingual commentary, are offered by several companies, including Fiordland Travel (☎03/442 7500 & 0800/656 503; $170), whose unusual wedge-profiled coaches give the best all-round views.

Magnificent though it is, the Milford road scenery is upstaged by the aerial views of the top end of Lake Wakatipu and the Routeburn and Greenstone tracks from the **flights to Milford**. Mount Cook Airlines do a four-hour fly/cruise/fly package for around $295; other operators include Air Fiordland (☎03/442 3404), Air Wakatipu (☎03/442 4148) and Milford Sound Scenic Flights (☎03/442 3065 & 0800/101 767). Any flights overflying the Olivine Ice Plateau and the Red Hills are likely to be more spectacular.

North Sea, with see-through domes at each end. Powerful lights illuminate what otherwise only divers see, but the domes have the unfortunate effect of making everything look considerably smaller than it should appear.

Fiord cruises, kayaks and flights

Dramatic though it is, the view from the shore of Milford Sound pales beside the incomparable spectacle from the water, with waterfalls plunging hundreds of metres into the fiord. It is still difficult to grasp the heroic scale of the place, unless your visit coincides with that of one of the great cruise liners – even these formidable vessels are totally dwarfed by the cascades and cliff faces.

The majority of cruises explore the full 22km of Milford Sound, all calling at waterfalls, the seal colony and overhanging rock faces; at Fairy Falls, boats nose up to the base of the fall, while suitably attired passengers are encouraged to edge out onto the bowsprit and collect a cup of water. Longer trips sometimes anchor in Anita Bay (Te-Wahi-Takiwai, "the place of Takiwai"), a former greenstone-gathering place at the fiord's mouth, but still sheltered from the wrath of the Tasman Sea. In short, having come this far, it's essential to get out on the water by some means or other – even if it means putting up with corny cruise commentaries. There are three main options, all of which should be booked a few days in advance: a two- to four-hour cruise around the fiord, an overnight cruise, or kayaking. All boats leave from an incongruous, cavernous new building at the wharf.

Two large companies and one single-boat operator run **cruises** on the fiord. Red Boat Cruises (Ⓣ03/249 7926 & 0800/657 444) operate five well-appointed boats, some carrying several hundred passengers and all bombarding you with a running commentary. Most cruises go to the Tasman Sea (2–6 daily; 1hr 45min; $45), but the longer cruise to the observatory (daily 12.25pm; 2hr 30min; $62) is preferable, taking you out to the mouth of the fiord and returning to Harrison Cove for a quick look at the underwater observatory. Fiordland Travel (Ⓣ03/442 7500) run similar cruises to the Tasman Sea (2–4 daily; 1hr 45min; $45–55) and longer ones on the *Milford Wanderer* (Oct–April 2 daily; 2hr 30min; $55–60) and an observatory cruise ($62). The smaller company is Mitre Peak Cruises (Ⓣ03/249 8110 & 0800/744 633, Ⓔin@milfordsound.org), who operate a smaller more intimate boat and run either two hour trips ($52–57), or one hour forty minute trips ($47) with an extra $20 for a combination including the observatory.

Fiordland Travel run backpacker-orientated **overnight trips** on the *Milford Wanderer* (Oct–April daily 5pm–9am; $155), a motor-driven, seventy-berth replica of a sailing scow with cosmetic sails. It makes an impressive sight as it ploughs along the fiord to Anita Bay for some fishing, canoeing and bushwalking before spending the night in Harrison Cove. On-board accommodation is somewhat institutional, with cramped four-bunk rooms equipped with sheets, sleeping bags and towels, but a hearty three-course evening meal is served (drinks extra). A more luxurious time can be had on Fiordland Travel's *Milford Mariner*, which has private cabins with ensuites and will set you back $250 (dinner, bed, breakfast and kayaking), while their smaller overnighter, the MV *Friendship*, a more intimate experience (includes the same extras), is a mere $155 in a quad-bunked shared cabin.

Fine though the cruises are, the elemental nature of Milford Sound can best be appreciated without the throb of an engine. The best **kayaking** is with Fiordland Wilderness Experiences who run full-day, guided trips on Milford Sound, with an ecological slant (Ⓣ03/249 7700 & 0800/200 434, Ⓔfiordland.sea.kayak@clear.net.nz; $80 from Milford, $95 from Te Anau). Alternatively, Rosco's Milford Sound Sea Kayaks (Ⓣ03/249 8840) offer an extensive range of kayaking trips taking single and double sea kayaks to Harrison Cove and Sandfly Point (mid-Oct to mid-April; $80–250). Both companies organize transport from Te Anau and will pick up trampers coming off the Routeburn, Greenstone or Caples tracks at The Divide.

Scenic **flights** over Fiordland's magnificent alpine terrain are run by a vast phalanx of companies based in Queenstown, Wanaka and Te Anau, so book the one closest to where you are staying. Of the squadron of options, most operators do a good job because the scenery does the work for them, but the following are the most reliable: Air Fiordland (Ⓣ03/249 7505); Glenorchy Air (Ⓣ03/442 2207); Milford Sound Flightseeing (Ⓣ03/442 2686); Milford Sound Scenic Flights (Ⓣ03/442 3065); Queenstown Air, Glacier Southern Lakes Helicopters (Ⓣ03/442 3016); Aspiring Air (Ⓣ03/443 7943); Wanaka Flightseeing (Ⓣ03/443 8787); Wanaka Helicopters (Ⓣ03/443 1085); Waterwings Airways (Ⓣ03/249 7405); and Air Milford (Ⓣ03/442 2351). All run flights to the mouth of the sound over Sutherland Falls and a grand tour. The flights vary in price dependent upon length, starting point, destination, the number of passengers, the cost of fuel and the mode. On average, a ten-minute jaunt in a plane will cost $55–60, a helicopter $70-100, a twenty minute ride in a plane about $110–130, a helicopter $150, and so on.

Manapouri and the southern fiords

There is no shortage of contenders for the title of New Zealand's most beautiful lake, and sloshing 178m above sea level, **Lake Manapouri** is definitely among them, with its long and indented bush-clad shoreline contorted into three distinct arms. The lake has a vast catchment area, guzzling all the water that flows down the Upper Waiau River from Lake Te Anau and unwittingly creating a massive hydroelectric generating capacity – something which almost led to its downfall.

The one good thing to come from the hydroelectric project has been the opening up of **Doubtful Sound**, following the construction of the Wilmot Pass supply road. What was previously the preserve of the odd yacht and a few deerstalkers and trampers is now accessible to anyone prepared to take a boat across Lake Manapouri and a drive over the Wilmot Pass. Costs are unavoidably high and you need to be self-sufficient (no burger joints or corner shops here), but any inconvenience is easily outweighed by glorious isolation and pristine beauty. Wildlife is a major attraction, not least the resident pod of bottlenose dolphins, who frequently come to play around ships' bows and gleefully cavort near kayakers. Fur seals slather the outer islands, Fiordland crested penguins come to breed here in October and November, and the bush, which comes right down to the water's edge, is alive with kaka, kiwi and other rare bird species.

Cook spotted Doubtful Sound in 1770 but didn't enter as he was "doubtful" of his ability to sail out again in the face of winds buffeted by the steep-walled fiord. The breeze was more favourable for the joint leaders of a Spanish expedition, Malaspina and Bauza, who in February 1793 sailed in and named Febrero Point, Malaspina Reach and Bauza Island.

In fact, Cook seemed more interested in **Dusky Sound**, 40km south, where he spent five weeks on his second voyage in 1773, while his crew recovered from an arduous crossing of the Southern Ocean. At Pickersgill Harbour, Cook endeavoured to ward off scurvy by using manuka leaves to brew a kind of "spruce beer" which, helped along with a touch of brandy, apparently tasted like champagne; obviously, the captain hadn't supped champagne for some time. On Astronomer's Point nearby, it is still possible to see where Cook's astronomer had trees felled so he could get an accurate fix on the stars; not far from here is the site where 1790s castaways built the first European-style house and boat in New Zealand. Marooned by the fiord's waters, Pigeon Island shelters the ruins of a house built by Richard Henry, who battled from 1894 to 1908 to save endangered native birds from introduced stoats and rats.

Manapouri

The scattered community of **MANAPOURI**, 20km south of Te Anau, drapes itself prettily around the shores of the lake of the same name which, in the 1960s became a cause célèbre for conservationists opposed to the raising of the lake level as part of the massive West Arm hydroelectric power scheme (see box on p.952). With the power station complete, the lake left at its original level and the passage of three decades, there is little tangible evidence of the passions that once threatened the community's cohesion, but scratch below the surface and you'll find a lingering antipathy between economic rationalists and environmentalists.

Electricity, aluminium and brickbats

Lake Manapouri's **hydroelectric** potential had long been recognized, but nothing was done to realize it until the 1950s. Consolidated Zinc Pty of Australia wanted to smelt their Queensland bauxite into **aluminium** – a tremendously power-hungry process – as cheaply as possible, and their beady eyes alighted upon **Lake Manapouri**. They approached the New Zealand government, who agreed to build a power station on the lake, at taxpayers' expense, while Consolidated Zinc's subsidiary Comalco built a smelter at Tiwai Point, near Bluff, 170km to the southeast. The scheme entailed blocking the lake's natural outlet into the Lower Waiau River and chiselling out a vast powerhouse 200m underground beside Lake Manapouri's West Arm, where the flow would be diverted down a 10km tailrace tunnel to Deep Cove on Doubtful Sound. By the time the fledgling **environmental movement** had rallied its supporters, the scheme was well under way, but the government underestimated the anger that would be unleashed by its secondary plan to boost water storage and power production by raising the water level in the lake by 12m. The threat to the natural beauty of the lake sparked **national protests**, culminating in the presentation to parliament of a 265,000-signature petition, after which the plan was reluctantly dropped. The full saga is recounted in Neville Peat's book *Manapouri Saved* (see "Books" in Contexts, p.1004).

The **West Arm Power Station** took eight years to build. Completed in 1971, it remains one of the most ambitious projects ever carried out in New Zealand. Eighty percent of its output goes straight to the **smelter** – which consumes something like fifteen percent of all the electricity used in the country, and yet Comalco are charged only a third of what domestic users pay. It is widely perceived to be an unnecessary drain on the country's resources and every time a new power station is proposed, the cry goes up for the plug to be pulled on the smelter. Nevertheless, a second parallel tailrace tunnel is now being drilled to increase the station's capacity which has only ever been six-sevenths of what was originally intended. The most likely explanation is that the engineers got their sums wrong and then realized if they ever did run at full power the turbine chamber would flood. Meanwhile locals are keeping an eye on the project as its budget spirals out of control; they fear that to try and recuperate lost money the government will agree to another smelting plant or something even less environmentally friendly.

Arrival and information

To get to Manapouri without your own transport, hop on the Spitfire Shuttle (contact Fiordland Travel ⓣ03/249 7416), which leaves Te Anau at 8.30am and returns from Manapouri around 3pm as part of the Te Anau to Invercargill return run, or try the Fiordland Travel buses (around $6 each way) plying the West Arm and Doubtful Sound runs, who'll take you if their cruise passengers don't fill the bus.

The road from Te Anau reaches Manapouri as Cathedral Drive and then becomes Waiau Street, passing almost everything of interest on the way to the offices of Fiordland Travel, Pearl Harbour (daily: Nov–Feb 7.30am–8pm; March–Oct 8am–5.30pm; ⓣ03/249 6602 & 0800/656 502, ⓕ249 6603), the closest thing the village has to an **information centre**, and the jumping-off point for lake cruises. The sole shop and the post office both occupy the same building as the *Cathedral Café* on Cathedral Drive – find one and you've found the lot.

Accommodation and eating

Most people prefer to stay in Te Anau but there is a reasonable selection of **places to stay** in Manapouri, but not much choice for **eating**, so if you are staying at a place that provides food, take advantage of it. Failing that, the *Manapouri Motor Inn* now houses the *Beehive Café* which dishes out generous if uninspired café fare while the bar offers ordinary meals ($12–25). Your best bet is the *Cathedral Café*, Cathedral Drive (☎03/249 6619), which serves teas and snacks, but also stays open for 18–20 evening meals (in the summer only) until 8pm, later if you make a reservation.

Beechwood Lodge 40 Cathedral Drive ☎03/249 6993, www.beechwoodlodge.com. Pound-for-pound the best place to stay in the settlement, this purpose-built, wooden house in which the en-suite guest rooms (one double, one twin) have lake views. There is internet access, wonderful breakfasts including muffins and home-made bread, and the hosts are friendly and helpful. He's a fishing guide so there is alway the chance he'll let slip where you can pick up some lake-fresh supper. ❻–❼

The Cottage Waiau St ☎03/249 6838 & 0800/677 866. Attractive ensuites in a cutesy house with a cottage garden close to the wharf. Continental breakfast is included, cooked is $5 extra, and $30 dinners are available. ❹

Deep Cove Hostel Deep Cove, Doubtful Sound ☎03/216 1340. This two- and four-bed bunkroom accommodation overlooking Doubtful Sound is available only during school holidays. There are mattresses, all eating and cooking utensils and good hot showers, but the nearest place to buy food is Manapouri, so bring everything you'll need. The one-way fare with Fiordland Travel's Doubtful Sound service from Manapouri is around $55. ❺

Manapouri Glade Motel and Motor Park Murrell Ave ☎03/249 6623. Appealingly old-fashioned, peaceful and neatly tended motor park located right where the Waiau River meets the lake. Tent and powered sites go for $9. Cabins ❷, motel units ❸–❹

Manapouri Lake View Motels and Motor Park 50 Manapouri–Te Anau Highway, 1km from the wharf (☎03/249 6624). Fully equipped motor park with spa and swimming pool and excellent vistas. Tent and powered sites cost around $9 or there are cabins and units. Cabins ❷–❸, motel units ❹

Around town

The several dozen houses that constitute Manapouri cluster at the outlet of the Waiau River, which the hydroelectric shenanigans have turned into a narrow arm of the lake now known as Pearl Harbour.

Apart from cruises and kayak trips (see below), the only thing to do in Manapouri is to saunter along some of the **walking trails** detailed in the DOC's *Manapouri Tracks* leaflet ($1, from some accommodation and the Fiordland Travel office). On the Manapouri side there's the **Pearl Harbour to Fraser's Beach** trail (45min), which follows an easy track through lakeshore beech forest with fantails and silvereye flitting about the thin understorey. For all the other tracks, you'll need to rent yourself a row boat to get across the Waiau River: Adventure Charters (☎03/249 6626; daily 8am–6pm), at the Mobil station on Waiau Street, are happy to oblige. Boats cost $5 per person per day, or you can pay another $3 each and stay on the other side overnight, either camping or in one of the two DOC huts (both $5).

The most frequently walked is the **Circle Track** (3hr loop; 7km; 330m ascent) initially contouring west around the lake then turning southeast to climb the ridge up to a point with stupendous views over the lake then north back the to start.

The lake: cruises and kayaking

Most of the lake cruises are operated by Fiordland Travel (☎03/249 6602 & 0800/656 502), who run three to four-hour trips across Lake Manapouri to the impressive, if controversial, **West Arm Power Station** (Oct–April, 12.30pm daily; $52 from Manapouri, $65 from Te Anau); work on a second tailrace over the next few years is likely to disrupt tour schedules, so check the latest with Fiordland Travel. The ride across the lake terminates at a visitor centre, which highlights the European "discovery" of Fiordland, its flora and fauna and, more predictably, the construction of the power station. A bus then takes you down a narrow, 2km-long tunnel to a viewing platform in the Machine Hall. All you can see are the exposed sections of seven turbines, but there's an interesting model of the whole system and some panels assaulting you with yet more statistics; read quickly before you're whisked back to the bus for the return trip.

For greater independence, you'll need **kayak rental**: Adventure Charters (☎03/249 6626; daily 8am–6pm) rent reasonable-quality single and double sea kayaks for around $50 per day, $45 overnight; or Fiordland Wilderness Experiences, 66 Quintin Drive, Te Anau (☎03/249 7700), rent out better boats for about the same.

The southern fiords

To fully appreciate the beauty and sense the isolation of the **southern fiords**, you really need to spend a few days among them, travelling either by boat or kayak. If time is limited, plump for a full-day trip to Doubtful Sound; with more time to spare, a few days weaving between these mystical waterways is an unforgettable experience.

The Dusky Track

At its most extensive, the **Dusky Track** is one of the **longest** and **most remote** tracks in New Zealand. The high cost of transportation and the commitment involved make it one of the least-walked tracks, but anyone with sufficient experience and stamina shouldn't miss this opportunity to walk from one of New Zealand's largest lakes (Manapouri) to its longest fiord (Dusky Sound). DOC's *Dusky Track* **leaflet** ($1) is the best single resource for this walk, though tricky route-finding makes the 1:50,000 *Wilmot* (S148) and *Heath* (S157) **maps** invaluable adjuncts.

There are three basic elements, each following a major river valley and connecting to form an inverted Y. Any two of these can be combined to make a tramp of four to six days, or all three can be attempted in eight to ten days. On a tramp of this length it is especially important to have plenty of spare food and stove fuel in case of bad weather or flooding. In **summer**, be prepared for a lot of stream crossings and precarious walkwires to negotiate. In **winter** you can also expect snow and ice, which often render the track impassable, though you will be advised of conditions when you notify either the Tuatapere or Te Anau DOC office of your intentions; remember to check in on your return from the track.

Accommodation and access

There is no need to book **huts** on the Dusky, all eight huts are backcountry ($10) and operate on a first-come-first-served basis. All have twelve bunks (except the 6-bunk *West Arm Hut*), tank water and long-drop toilets; only *Halfway Hut* lacks mattresses.

There are four ways of tackling the track: walk in from Lake Hauroko, via Supper Cove and on to Lake Manapouri; doing it the other way round; flying in to Supper Cove and walking out to Manapouri (ignoring Lake Hauroko), or doing this in reverse. Most trampers enter the region by boat across Lake Hauroko with Lake Hauroko Tours (☎03/226 6681; Nov–April Mon & Thurs at 9am; around $60), who'll also drive you in from Tuatapere (see p.958). For walkers coming in the opposite direction, pick-ups from *Hauroko Burn Hut* are on the same days at noon, but must be confirmed in advance.

From Lake Hauroko, it's three days' walk to *Loch Maree Hut*, which is poised at the junction of the three "legs". Some trampers then turn west to **Supper Cove** (1 day) and leave (or arrive) with Waterwings Airways' scheduled **flights** (☎03/249

Fiordland Travel run a full-day trip to **Doubtful Sound** (ⓣ03/249 6602 & 0800/656 502; 1 daily; $185 from Manapouri, $198 from Te Anau; lunch $18 extra; and an overnight cruise $340 ex Manapouri, $353 ex Te Anau): after the inevitable power-station treatment on Lake Manapouri, you're transferred onto a bus for the 20km ride over Wilmot Pass – the costliest stretch of road in the country and completely unconnected to any other road – to Deep Cove, where the tailrace tunnel spews out vast quantities of lake water. Here you board a three-hour cruise to the mouth of the fiord, where fur seals loll on the rocks, and into Hall Arm, where bottlenose dolphins often congregate. The overnight cruise on the *Fiordland Navigator*, designed to look like a traditional sailing scow, is an unwelcome recent addition to the Sound where previously there were only a few boats and a number of silent, low-impact kayaks.

For a more in-depth encounter with the fiords, join one of the superb multi-day **trips** organized by Fiordland Ecology Holidays (ⓣ03/249 6600, ⓔeco@xtra.co.nz; 3–7 days; $195–295 per day; book as far in advance as you can). The skipper of the motor-sailer *Breaksea Girl* spent twelve years running DOC's research vessel in these waters and holds passionate views on the non-extractive use of the fiords. Fishing is out and, though snorkelling and scuba

7405; Nov–April daily 11am; $195), Fiordland Helicopters (ⓣ03/249 7575, ⓦwww.fiordlandhelicopters.co.nz; slightly more expensive), or South West Helicopters (ⓣ03/249 7402), while others head north to **West Arm** (3 days) to pick up Fiordland Travel's daily **launch** across Lake Manapouri (ⓣ03/249 6602 & 0800/656 502; $52), also worth confirming in advance.

The route

You won't want to hang around the *Hauroko Burn Hut*, and mid-morning boat drop-offs leave you plenty of time to walk from **Hauroko Burn Hut to Halfway Hut** (12km; 4–6hr), following Hauroko Burn as it runs through a short gorge and gradually steepens to *Halfway Hut*. The second day from **Halfway Hut to Lake Roe Hut** (7km; 3–5hr) goes easily for a couple of hours then climbs above the bushline and follows snow poles to the magnificently sited *Lake Roe Hut*. On the third day, from **Lake Roe Hut to Loch Maree Hut** (10km; 4–6hr), the track veers west along the tops of the Pleasant Range, with spectacular views to Dusky Sound, before descending very steeply to *Loch Maree Hut*.

Trampers wishing to walk from **Loch Maree Hut to Supper Cove Hut** (12km; 6hr) continue west from Loch Maree following the Seaforth River. At low tide, the last rough section of track can be avoided by cutting across the flats to *Supper Cove Hut* – where it is traditional to take out the dinghy and fish for your supper. Anyone not flying out has to retrace their steps to *Loch Maree Hut*.

From **Loch Maree Hut to Kintail Hut** (11km; 4–5hr), you follow the Seaforth River upstream on fairly difficult ground that can be boggy and becomes impassable when the river is high. The next day, the route from **Kintail Hut to Upper Spey Hut** (7km; 5–6hr) involves a steep ascent to the scenic sub-alpine Centre Pass, then an equally precipitous descent to *Upper Spey Hut*. The last day takes you fairly painlessly from **Upper Spey Hut to West Arm Hut** (11km; 4–5hr), down the Spey River to the Wilmot Pass road between West Arm and Doubtful Sound. Forty minutes' walk brings you to the wharf at West Arm – hopefully in time to catch the last launch (usually at around 4.30pm). Otherwise you'll have to spend the night at *West Arm Hut* 200m east of the power-station visitor centre.

diving are in, care is taken to minimize the impact on this fragile environment. Trips typically take in Doubtful, Dusky and Breaksea sounds, spending time with dolphins and seals and calling at places frequented by Cook and by turn-of-the-century bird conservationist Richard Henry. A worthy alternative to cruising is to take a research holiday (also run by Fiordland Ecology Holidays, and also booked way in advance), monitoring skinks and weevils, short- and long-tailed bats and native birds on Breaksea and the surrounding small islands (no experience required; around $1100 for 5 days).

A similar ethical vein flavours the energetic and excellent **kayaking trips** run by Fiordland Wilderness Experiences (Ⓣ03/249 7700, Ⓔfiordland.sea.kayak@clear.net.nz), who sometimes run joint trips with Fiordland Ecology Holidays which enable kayakers to reach unsullied waters by hitching a ride aboard the *Breaksea Girl* (around $200–220 per day). Otherwise, their regular guided trips involve the usual bus ride from Te Anau, boat ride from Manapouri, 4WD trek over the Wilmot Pass and then idyllic kayaking on the almost silent Doubtful Sound and camping out in one of its spectacular remote arms where they have set up comfortable, ecologically-minded, camping sites. On day two you'll be paddling and sailing back with a satisfied glow (Tues, Sat & most Thurs departures; 2 days for $260). For even remoter alternatives there are also two- to five-day guided trips at $95 a day, to Breaksea and Dusky Sounds, and freedom rentals for experienced paddlers. Adventure Charters offer a variation on the theme with cruise and kayak options on the Sound (Ⓣ03/249 6626, Ⓔinformation@fiordlandadventure.co.nz; 2 days for around $230; 1 day for $170), involving sitting in their boat *Adventurer I* and then kayaking along either behind or in front of it.

During the **winter months** (May–Sept), the *Milford Wanderer* (Ⓣ03/249 6602 & 0800/656 502) leaves its beat on Milford Sound and indulges in some leisurely cruises around the southern fiords: prices range from around $400 for a three-day jaunt to $1500 for a week-long saunter around Preservation Inlet, Dusky, Doubtful and Breaksea sounds and/or Stewart Island, depending on who wants to go where and how much dosh they've got.

The Southern Scenic Route

The vast majority of visitors to Te Anau and Manapouri retrace their steps to Queenstown and miss out on the fringe country, where the fertile sheep paddocks of Southland butt up against the remote country of the Fiordland National Park. The minor towns of the region are linked by the understated **Southern Scenic Route**, small roads where mobs of sheep are likely to be the biggest cause of traffic problems. From Te Anau it runs via Manapouri to SH99, following the valley of the Waiau River to the cave-pocked limestone country around **Clifden**. A minor road cuts west to Lake Hauroko, access point to both the Dusky Track and the new Humpridge Track, while the Southern Scenic Route continues south through the small service town of **Tuatapere** to estuary-side little **Riverton** and on to Invercargill.

Spitfire shuttle **buses** do the trip through Manapouri, Tuatapere and Riverton on Saturday (Ⓣ03/249 7505, Ⓔek@spitfire.co.nz; 8.30am from Te Anau, arriving at Invercargill around 11am; around $40); they also do track drop-offs and pick-ups for all the road-accessed tracks including the Dusky, making a few stops along the way.

The **eastern continuation** of the Southern Scenic Route through the Catlins to Dunedin is covered in Chapter Eleven, starting on p.727.

Borland Road and Lake Monowai

Some 35km south of Manapouri, **Borland/Lake Monowai Road** cuts west to Lake Manapouri's South Arm. Built in 1963, it provides hunting, fishing, mountain-biking and tramping access to a huge swathe of untouched country south of Lake Manapouri.

Passing the dam which controls the flow of water from Lake Manapouri down the Waiau River, the road runs 12km to the *Monowai River Lodge* (Ⓣ & Ⓕ03/225 5191, freephone 0800/877 222; dorms ❶, rooms ❸), a superb lagoonside retreat geared to both the rod-and-gun set and backpackers. The fully self-contained lodge – complete with piano – sleeps twelve, and when not booked by groups, individual rooms are rented out; failing that, there are beds in rustic but comfortable bunkhouses. The lodge also operates Fiordland Adventures (same phone & fax numbers), offering mountain bikes for rent ($30 per day), 4WD trips and advice on walks off Borland/Lake Monowai Road.

Immediately past the lodge, a spur runs 6km to **Lake Monowai**, the water level of which was artificially raised as part of an early, small-scale hydro scheme in 1925. The scars can still be seen on its shores, where there's a primitive **campsite** ($4) with long-drop toilets and barbecues. Monowai is a popular spot for fishing – mostly done from boats to avoid snagging lines in the submerged skeletons of drowned trees. Back on Borland Road it is another 4km west to *Borland Lodge* (Ⓣ03/225 5464; $17), a youth adventure centre where you can stay in twin chalets (bring your own bedding). They also rent out reasonably priced tents and stoves to those wanting to explore the excellent **walking** country and huts hereabouts, all detailed in DOC's *Lake Monowai/Borland Road* leaflet ($1).

Beyond *Borland Lodge*, the increasingly narrow, steep and landslip-prone road can be driven another 40km to **Lake Manapouri's South Arm**, where there are toilets and a shelter (Oct–May; key from the DOC in Tuatapere or Te Anau). Close to the end of the road, a spur (open to trampers only) leads 15km over the Percy Saddle to **West Arm** and eventually to Doubtful Sound.

Clifden and Lake Hauroko

Back at the junction with the main highway, it is 32km further south to **CLIFDEN**, barely a town at all but of some interest for the historic **Clifden Suspension Bridge**, one of the longest in the South Island, built over the Waiau River in 1899 and in use until the 1970s. The north abutment overshadows a free campsite and barbecue area. Clifden most likely gets its name from low cliffs made of the same limestone that is riddled with the **Clifden Caves** (unrestricted access, signposted off Clifden Gorge Road), where Maori once camped on summer foraging trips. Suitably equipped with torches and treading carefully, you can explore the stalactite and glow-worm grottoes at your leisure, using ladders installed in the steepest sections.

Languishing at the end of a dirt road, 30km west of Clifden, **Lake Hauroko** is New Zealand's deepest lake (462m). Low bush-clad hills surround the lake, leaving it open to the "sounding winds" immortalized in its name. There are no facilities at First Bay, the road end, just a primitive campsite midway between Clifden and Lake Hauroko and, at the north end of the lake, the *Hauroko Burn Hut* (accessible by boat, or on foot via the Dusky Track – see p.954).

To explore the lake and its environs, call the Wairaurahiri Jet (ⓣ03/236 1137) or Wairaurahiri Wilderness Jet (ⓣ03/225 8174 & 0800/270 556), both of which run day-trips across Lake Hauroko, followed by **jetboating** 27km of the Grade III Wairaurahiri River down to the coast, and exploring the bush around Percy Burn. Transport can be arranged from Tuatapere (see below) or Clifden, and trips are priced by the boat-load ($400 for up to 3 people, $500 for 4 or 5).

Tuatapere and around

Two sawmills and one feeble stand of beech and podocarp forest is the only evidence that **TUATAPERE**, on the banks of the Waiau River 14km south of Clifden, could once have justified its epithet of "The Hole in the Forest". As the largest town in southwestern Southland, the "sausage capital" of the area makes a good geographical though otherwise poor base for exploring the very southern limits of Fiordland. It is generally hoped that the **Tuatapere Humpridge Track** (see box, opposite) will draw travellers to the area and that in preparation for the track, or in a state of exhaustion after it, they will feel encouraged to stay in the town but this seems highly unlikely in its present state. The best advice is to hit the road after you've bought some sausages.

The Town

Maori legend records the great war canoe Takitimu being wrecked on the Waiau River bar at Te Waewae Bay some six hundred years ago. Maori set up summer foraging camps along the river and used these as way-stations on the route to the *pounamu* fields around Milford Sound, but it wasn't until European **pioneers** arrived around 1885 that Tuatapere came into being. By 1909 the **railway** had arrived from Invercargill, bringing with it increasingly sophisticated steam-powered haulers that made short work of clearing the surrounding bushland. More recently, foresters' attention shifted west to the fringes of the Fiordland National Park where, in the 1970s, the Maori owners proposed clear felling stands of rimu. Environmentalists prevailed upon the Conservation Minister who eventually, in 1996, agreed to pay compensation in return for a sustainable management policy. The bush's last stand – a riverside clump of beech, kahikatea and totara on the Domain – forms one station on the **Tuatapere Walkway**, a 5km stroll around town guided by a leaflet from the DOC. If you want to see a rose-coloured version of pioneer history then try out the local museum next to the visitor centre (daily 9am–5pm; free) where the displays are well presented if one-sided.

Practicalities

For such a small town, Tuatapere is thinly spread. The riverside town centre holds the Tuatapere **information centre**, 31 Orawia (daily 9am–5pm; ⓣ03/226 6399), which is there to help with accommodation, transport and the like, and there is a **visitor centre** of sorts at 18 Orawia Rd, though for how much longer is unknown. Bookings for the track should be done through the recommended phone and web lines though the Tuatapere Trust Booking Office, at 31 Orawia Rd (ⓣ03/226 6739, ⓦwww.humpridgetrack.co.nz), will open in the season.

The Tuatapere Humpridge Track

Once known as the **Waitutu Tracks**, the combined name for two historic paths that sliced through the largest area of lowland rain forest in New Zealand: the predominantly easy-going and well graded **South Coast Track** from Bluecliffs Beach on Te Waewae Bay southwest to Big River, and the tougher **Hump Track** which rises above the bushline en route from Bluecliffs Beach to Lake Hauroko, have, in part, been combined to make the **Tuatapere Humpridge Track** (which must be booked in advance, ⓣ03/226 6739, ⓦwww.humpridgetrack.co.nz or at the office in Tuatapere, see Practicalities). The new track doesn't actually combine both its predecessors but it does make them impossible to explore so it has become the only alternative. The **map** on the DOC's *Waitutu Tracks* leaflet ($1) is adequate for these walks.

For history buffs, the South Coast Track in particular was one of the country's most interesting. The route followed a portion of the 100km track cut in 1896 to link Orepuki, 18km southeast of Tuatapere, with Cromarty and Te Oneroa, gold-mining settlements in the southernmost fiord of Preservation Inlet. This paved the way for wood cutters, who arrived en masse in the 1920s. Logs were transported to the mills on tramways, which crossed the burns and gullies on **viaducts** built of Australian hardwood – four of the finest have been faithfully restored, three on the track, including the one over Percy Burn that spans 125m and is now the star attraction on the Humpridge Track.

Bluecliffs Beach **trailhead access** is by road from Tuatapere with Lake Hauroko Tours (ⓣ03/226 6681; $30) or by jetboat (Wairaurahiri Jet ⓣ03/225 8318; or Wairaurahiri Wilderness Jet ⓣ03/225 8174; $140 return). The entire track is now supposed to take **three days** but in all honesty it's a bit of a slog at both start and finish, so explore the possibility of spending an extra day in one of the two huts available. Following its rebirth as the Humpridge Track there are now two excellent **huts** (40 bunks, $40 per person per night), at Port Craig Village and Okaka. The huts have lights, gas cookers, tables, hot and cold running water, four-bunk rooms, and ablution blocks with flush toilets and wash basins.

The Tuatapere Humpridge Track

The track begins at Bluecliffs Beach Car Park and day one is an 18km up-hill slog (8–9hr, 600m ascent) through podocarp/beech forest to the **Okaka Hut** on the Hump Ridge. Views are spectacular and there's always the chance of Hectors dolphins at the start, but it's a long day and you'll be glad of your bed at the end of it. For those feeling particularly energetic there is an extra little loop climb above the hut which will provide some enhanced views of the coast and surrounds. Day two wanders along an up-and-down section to the recommended lunch spot, where they've carefully provided a toilet and some mountain and coastline views. You'll be walking through limestone tors and past mountain tarns which all adds to the magic. After lunch you continue to descend, in a roundabout way, through the Edwin Burn Viaduct and then the spectacular Percy Burn Viaduct, a good photo opportunity, and its less awesome cousin, before hugging the coastline round to **Port Craig Village** (around 7hrs, 18km). The third day is another 17km (6–7hr) of going pretty much down hill, with occasional rises, through towering coastal rimu and then down on to sandy beaches, until you finally reach the car park from whence you began. As walks go it's spectacular and easily accessible but it's also gruelling and not for beginners who aren't fit. Also there's some trouble with the Maori land crossed at the end of the walk, meaning you have to stick to the beach, avoiding the incoming tide (check with DOC).

There is as yet no worthwhile **accommodation** in the town, though a motel is being built. The best **eating** around, and that's not saying much, is to be found at the *Waiau Hotel*, 47 Main St, and the *99 Café* just up the road, but most sensible of all is to go to the butchers, 75 Main St (Mon–Fri 8am–12.30pm & 1.30–5pm) for some of their famous sausages (a mutton and beef mix) and cook them yourself.

Around Tuatapere

There is no reason to spend much time in Tuatapere itself, though you might use it as a base for jetboat trips on Lake Hauroko (see p.957) or as a springboard for **Te Waewae Bay**, a large bite out of the Southland coastline 10km to the south where Hector's dolphins frequently frolic and the occasional southern right whale drifts past. **Bluecliffs Beach**, at its western end, 28km from Tuatapere, is the start of the Tuatapere Humpridge Track (see box on p.959).

Colac Bay and Riverton

South of Tuatapere, SH99 follows the wind-ravaged cliffs behind the wide and moody Te Waewae Bay, where fierce southerlies have sculpted some much-photographed macrocarpa trees into compact forms not unlike giant broccoli. Beyond the small town of Orepuki, the road cuts inland, regaining the sea 45km southeast of Tuatapere, at the quiet community of **Colac Bay** – a name eighteenth-century whalers derived from the name of the local Maori chief, Korako. Swimming aside, there's little reason to stop here, and you might as well press on a further 12km to **RIVERTON** (Aparima), one of the country's oldest settlements. Used by whalers from New South Wales as early as the last decade of the eighteenth century, the town was formally established in 1836 by another whaler, John Howell – who is also credited with kick-starting New Zealand's now formidable sheep-farming industry. The town also boasts a proliferation of somewhat shambolic Art Deco buildings.

Strung along a spit between the sea and the Jacob's River Estuary (actually the mouth of the Aparima and Pourakino rivers), where fishing boats still harbour, Riverton has a relaxed almost comatose feel that might just lull you into staying for a day or so. The town is trying to pitch itself as some kind of paua capital, with a giant paua shell at the eastern entrance to town, buildings painted in shell-like colours, plans to inlay the streets with bits of shell and, should you be in need of any, shops selling the **shells** by the score, best of which is the Factory Shop, on the outskirts of town heading toward Invercargill (Mon–Fri 8am–5pm, Sat & Sun 10am–4pm). Alternatively, the Maori Craft Studio, 130 Palmerston St (Ⓣ03/234 9965, Ⓦwww.solo1nz.faithweb.com), although it looks like a shop, is actually a great place to learn to **weave flax** in the traditional Maori-style or **carve bone** (both $90, including overnight accommodation). You should reserve an hour for the interesting local history and hoard of knick-knacks in the **Early Settlers Museum**, 172 Palmerston St (Ⓣ03/234 8520; daily 2–4pm; gold coin donation requested). Otherwise, you'll have to seek diversion on the water: one-hour scenic and historic rides up the Pourakino River are offered by Pourakino Jet Boat Tours (Ⓣ03/224 6130; around $65–70); or let one of the many boat charters take you out trout or salt-water **fishing** (check at the visitor centre to see which ones are awake).

Practicalities

Local information, including a leaflet detailing leisurely beach and hilltop walks, is available in the **Riverton Visitor Information Centre** (Nov–April daily 10.30am–4.30pm; May–Oct 2–4pm; ⓣ03/234 8520), 172 Palmerston St, in the museum opposite the Super Saver market. They will make an effort to help anyone who calls and keep most local information within their grasp, or at least at the end of a phone call.

Easily the best **place to stay** is *The Riverton Rock*, at 136 Palmerston St (ⓣ03/234 8886 & 0800/248 886, ⓕ234 8816), where beautifully decorated but expensive standard (❹) and en-suite (❺) rooms occupy a recently renovated 1870s building, and there's also a bunkroom (❶ a bunk); campervans can park outside for $15, and everyone gets to use the well-equipped kitchen area and spacious, comfortable lounge overlooking the lagoon. If they're full, make for the *Riverton Caravan Park and Holiday Homes* on Roy Street (ⓣ03/234 8526; tent sites $9, bunkhouse ❶, cottages & chalets ❷–❸). Of the limited range of **places to eat**, the most appealing is the *Nostalgia Country Café*, 108 Palmerston St (closed winter weekday evenings), which is good for coffee, light meals, their speciality home-made pies and predominantly seafood specials. Alternatively there's the stylish *Beach House Café and Bar*, on Rocks Highway, 2km west of Riverton town centre, with lovely views out over the estuary, where you can pick up delicious lunches and dinners from a blackboard menu of predominantly tasty seafood, veggie and steak options or some gorgeous desserts.

Beyond Riverton, SH99 heads into the hinterland of Invercargill, 40km away.

Travel details

Buses

From Manapouri to: Clifden (1 weekly; 1hr 30min); Te Anau (2 daily; 20min); Riverton (1 weekly; 5hr); Tuatapere (1 weekly; 3hr).
From Milford Sound to: Te Anau (2–5 daily; 2hr 15min); The Divide (2–5 daily; 1hr 30min); Queenstown (2 daily; 5hr 15min).
From Te Anau to: Dunedin (1 daily; 5hr); Manapouri (2 daily; 20min); Milford Sound (2–5 daily; 2hr 15min); Invercargill (2 daily; 3hr); Manapouri (2 daily; 20min); Queenstown (3–5 daily; 2hr 15min); Te Anau Downs (2 daily Nov–April; 30min); The Divide (2–5 daily; 1hr 20min).
From The Divide to: Milford Sound (2–5 daily; 1hr 30min); Te Anau (2–5 daily; 1hr 20min).
From Tuatapere to: Invercargill (1 weekly; 2hr 30min); Riverton (1 weekly; 1hr 30min).

Flights

From Milford Sound to: Queenstown (5–20 daily; 35min).
From Te Anau to: Queenstown (3 daily; 30min).

Contexts

contexts

History

White New Zealanders have long thought of their country as a model of humanitarian colonization. Most Maori take a different view, however, informed by generations of their ancestors witnessing the theft of land and erosion of rights that were guaranteed by a treaty with the white man. Schoolroom histories have long been faithful to the European view, even to the point of influencing Maori mythology, but in the last couple of decades revisionist historians have largely discredited what many New Zealanders know as fact. Much that is presented as tradition, on deeper investigation turns out to be late nineteenth-century scholarship, often the product of historians who bent what they heard to fit their theories and, in the worst cases, even destroyed evidence. What follows is inextricably interwoven with Maori legend and can be understood more fully with reference to the section on Maoritanga (see p.982).

Pre-European history

Humans from southeast Asia first started exploring the South Pacific around five thousand years ago, gradually evolving a distinct culture as they filtered down through the islands of the Indonesian archipelago. A thousand years of progressive island hopping got them as far as Tonga and Samoa, where a distinctly Polynesian society continued to evolve, the people honing their seafaring and navigational skills to the point where lengthy sea journeys were possible. Around a thousand years ago, Polynesian culture reached its classical apotheosis in the Society Islands, a group west of Tahiti. This was almost certainly the hub for a series of migrations heading southwest across thousands of kilometres of open ocean, past the Cook Islands, eventually striking land in what is now known as **New Zealand** (**Aotearoa**).

It is thought that the first of these Polynesian people, the ancestors of modern **Maori**, arrived in double-hulled canoes between 1000 and 1100 AD, as a result of a migration that was planned to the extent that they took with them the *kuri* (dog) and food plants such as taro (a starchy tuber), yam and kumara (sweet potato). It seems likely that there were several migrations and there may have even been two-way traffic, although archeological evidence points to a cessation of contact well before 1500 AD. The widely believed story of a legendary "Great Fleet" of seven canoes arriving in 1350 AD seems most likely to be the product of a fanciful Victorian adaptation of Maori oral history, which has been readopted into contemporary Maori legend.

Arriving Polynesians found a land so much colder than their tropical home that many of the crops and plants they brought with them wouldn't grow. Fortunately there was an abundance of large quarry in the form of marine life and flightless birds, particularly in the South Island, where most settled. The people of this **Archaic Period** are often misleadingly known as "Moa Hunters" and while some undoubtedly lived off these birds, they didn't exist in other areas. By 1300, settlements had been established all around the coast, but it was only later that there is evidence of horticulture, possibly supporting the contention that there was a later migration bringing plants for cultivation. On the other hand, it may just signal the beginning of successful year-round food storage allowing a settled living pattern rather than the short-lived campsites used by earlier hunters. Whichever is the case, this marks the beginning of the **Classic Period** when *kainga* (villages) grew up close to the kumara grounds, often supported by *pa* (fortified villages) where the people could retreat when under attack. As tasks became more specialized and hunting and horticulture began to take up less time, the arts – particularly carving and weaving (see pp.986–989) – began to flourish and warfare became endemic, digs revealing an armoury of mere, patu and taiaha (fighting clubs) not found earlier. The decline of easily caught birdlife and the relative ease of growing kumara in the warmer North Island marked the beginning of a northward population shift, to the extent that when the Europeans arrived, ninety-five percent of the population was located in the North Island, mostly in the northern reaches, with coastal settlements reaching down to Hawke's Bay and Wanganui.

European contact and the Maori response

Ever since Europeans had ventured across the oceans and "discovered" other continents, many were convinced of the existence of a *terra australia incognita*, an unknown southern land thought necessary to counterbalance the northern continents. In 1642, the Dutch East India Company, keen to dominate any trade with this new continent, sent Dutchman **Abel Tasman** to the southern oceans where he became the first European to catch sight of the South Island of Aotearoa. He anchored in Golden Bay, where a small boat being rowed between Tasman's two ships was intercepted by a Maori war canoe and four sailors were killed. Without setting foot on land Tasman turned tail and fled up the west coast of the North Island and went on to add Tonga and Fiji to European maps. He named Aotearoa "Staten Landt", later renamed Nieuw Zeeland after the Dutch maritime province.

New Zealand was ignored for over a century until 1769 when Yorkshireman **James Cook** sailed his *Endeavour* into the Pacific to observe the passage of Venus across the sun. He continued west arriving at "the Eastern side of the Land discover'd by Tasman" where he observed the "Genius, Temper, Disposition and Number of the Natives" and meticulously charted the coastline – the only significant errors were to show Banks Peninsula as an island and Stewart Island as a peninsula – and encouraged his botanists, Banks and Solander, to collect numerous samples.

Cook and his crew found Maori a sophisticated people with a highly formalized social structure and an impressive ability to turn stone and wood into fabulously carved canoes, weapons and meeting houses – and yet they were tied to Stone Age technology, with no wheels, roads, metalwork, pottery or animal husbandry. Cook found them aggressive, surly and little inclined to trade, but after an initial unfortunate encounter near Gisborne (see p.444) and another off Cape Kidnappers, near Napier (see p.460), he managed to strike up friendly and constructive relations with the "Indians". These "Indians" now found that their tribal allegiance was not enough to differentiate them from the Europeans and subsequently began calling themselves *maori* (meaning "normal" or "not distinctive") while referring to the newcomers as *pakeha* ("foreign").

Offshore from the Coromandel Peninsula, Cook deviated from instructions and unfurled the British flag, claiming formal possession without the consent of Maori, but was still allowed to return twice in 1773 and 1777. The French were also interested in New Zealand, and on his 1969 voyage Cook had passed **Jean Francois Marie de Surville** in a storm without either knowing of the other's presence. Three years later, **Marion du Fresne** spent five amicable weeks around the Bay of Islands, before most of his crew were killed, probably after inadvertently transgressing some *tapu* (taboo).

The establishment of the Botany Bay penal colony in neighbouring Australia aroused the first commercial interest in New Zealand and from the 1790s to the 1830s New Zealand was very much part of the Australian frontier. By 1830 the coast was dotted with semi-permanent **sealing** communities which, within thirty years, had almost clubbed the seals into extinction. Meanwhile the British navy was rapidly felling giant kauri trees for its ships' masts, while others were busy supplying Sydney shipbuilders. By the 1820s **whalers** had moved in, basing themselves at Kororareka (now Russell, in the Bay of Islands), where they could recruit Maori crew and provision their ships. This combination of rough whalers, escaped convicts from Australia and all manner of miscreants and adventurers combined to turn Russell into "the Hellhole of the Pacific", a lawless place populated by what Darwin, on his visit in 1835, found to be "the very refuse of Society".

Before long, the Maori way of life had been entirely disrupted. Maori were quick to understand the importance of guns and **inter-tribal fighting** soon broke out on a scale never seen before. Hongi Hika from Ngapuhi *iwi* of the Bay of Islands was the first chief to acquire firearms in 1821, adding 300 muskets to his stock by trading the gifts showered on him by London society when he was presented to George IV as an "equal". Vowing to emulate the supreme power of the imperial king, he set about subduing much of the North Island, using the often badly maintained and inexpertly aimed guns to rattle the enemy, who were then slaughtered with the traditional mere. Warriors abandoned the old fighting season – the lulls between hunting and tending the crops – and set off to settle old scores, resulting in a massive loss of life. The quest for new territory fuelled the actions of Ngati Toa's **Te Rauparaha** (see p.965), who soon controlled the southern half of the North Island.

The huge demand for firearms drove Maori to sell the best of their food, relocating to unhealthy areas close to flax swamps, where flax production could be increased. Even highly valued tribal treasures – *pounamu* (greenstone) clubs and the preserved heads of chiefs taken in battle – were traded. Poor living conditions allowed European **diseases** to sweep through the Maori population time and again, while alcohol and tobacco abuse became widespread, Maori women were prostituted to Pakeha sailors, and the tribal structure began to crumble.

Into this scene stepped the **missionaries** in 1814, the brutal New South Wales magistrate, **Samuel Marsden**, arriving in the Bay of Islands a transformed man with a mission to bring Christianity and "civilization" to Maori, and to save the souls of the sealers and whalers. Subsequently Anglicans, Wesleyans and Catholics all set up missions throughout the North Island, playing a significant role in protecting Maori from the worst of the exploitation and campaigning in both London and Sydney for more policing of **Pakeha** actions. In return, they destroyed fine artworks considered too sexually explicit and demanded that Maori abandon cannibalism and slavery; in short Maori were expected to trade in their Maoritanga and become Brown Europeans. By the 1830s, self-confidence and the belief in Maori ways was in rapid decline:

the *tohunga* (priest) was powerless over new European diseases which could often be cured by the missionaries, and Maori had started to believe the Pakeha, who were convinced that the Maori race was dying out. They felt they needed help.

The push for colonization

Despite Cook's discoverery claim in 1769, imperial cartographers had never marked New Zealand as a British possession and it was with some reluctance – informed by the perception of an over-extended empire only marginally under control – that New South Wales law was nominally extended to New Zealand in 1817. The effect was minimal; the New South Wales governor had no official representation on this side of the Tasman and was powerless to act. Unimpressed, by 1831 a small group of northern Maori chiefs decided to petition the British monarch to become a "friend and the guardian of these islands", a letter that was later used to justify Britain's intervention.

Britain's response was to send the pompous and less-than-competent **James Busby** as British Resident in 1833, with a brief to encourage trade, stay on good terms with the missionaries and Maori, and apprehend escaped convicts for return to Sydney. Feeling that New Zealand was becoming a drain on the colony's economy, the New South Wales governor, Bourke, withheld guns and troops, and Busby was unable to enforce his will. Busby was also duped by the madness of Baron de Thierry, a Brit of French parents, who claimed he had bought most of the Hokianga district from Hongi Hika and styled himself the "sovereign chief of New Zealand", ostensibly to save Maori from the degradation he foresaw under British dominion. In a panic, Busby misguidedly persuaded 35 northern chiefs to proclaim themselves as the "**United Tribes of New Zealand**" in 1835. As far as the Foreign Office was concerned, this allowed Britain to disclaim responsibility for the actions of its subjects.

By the late 1830s there were around two thousand Pakeha in New Zealand, the largest concentration around Kororareka in the Bay of Islands, where there were often up to thirty ships at anchor. Most were British, but French Catholics were consolidating their tentative toehold, and in 1839 James Clendon was appointed American consul. Meanwhile, land speculators and colonists were taking an interest for the first time. The Australian emancipationist, William Charles Wentworth, had "bought" the South Island and Stewart Island for a few hundred pounds (the largest private land deal in history, subsequently quashed by government order) and British settlers were already setting sail. The British admiralty finally began to take notice when it became apparent that the Australian convict settlements, originally intended simply as an out-of-sight, out-of-mind solution to their bulging prisons, looked set to become a valuable possession.

It was a combination of these pressures and Busby's continual exaggeration of the Maori inability to control their own affairs that goaded the British government into action. The result was the 1840 **Treaty of Waitangi** (see box on p.191, and also p.969), a document that purported to guarantee continued Maori control of their lands, rights and possessions in return for their loss of sovereignty, a concept poorly understood by Maori. The annexed lands became a dependency of New South Wales until New Zealand was declared a separate colony a year later.

The Treaty of Waitangi: in English and Maori

The main points set out in the **English treaty** are as follows:

- The chiefs cede sovereignty of New Zealand to the Queen of England.
- The Queen guarantees the chiefs the "full exclusive and undisturbed possession of their Lands and Estates Forests Fisheries and other properties which they may collectively or individually possess".
- The Crown retains the right of pre-emption over Maori lands.
- The Queen extends the rights and privileges of British subjects to Maori.

However, the **Maori translation** presents numerous possibilities for misunderstanding, since Maori is a more idiomatic and metaphorical language, where words can take on several different meanings. The main points of contention are as follows:

The preamble of the English version cites the main **objectives** of the treaty being to protect Maori interests, to provide for British settlement and to set up a government to maintain peace and order. On the other hand, the main thrust of the Maori version is that the all-important rank and status of the chiefs and tribes will be maintained.

In the Maori version, the concept of **sovereignty** is translated as *kawanatanga* (governorship), a word Maori linked to their experience of the toothless reign of British Resident James Busby. It seems unlikely that the chiefs realized just what they were giving away.

In the Maori text, the Crown guaranteed the *tangata whenua* (people of the land) the possession of their properties for as long as they wished to keep them. In English this was expressed in terms of **individual rights** over property. This is perhaps the most wilful mistranslation and, in practice, there were long periods when Maori were coerced into selling their **land**, and when they refused, lands were simply taken.

Pre-emption was translated as *hokonga* – a term simply meaning "buying and selling", with no explanation of the Crown's exclusive right to buy Maori land, which was clearly spelled out in the English version. This has resulted in considerable friction over Maori being unable to sell any land that the government didn't want, even if they had a buyer.

The implications of **British citizenship** may not have been well understood: it is not clear whether Maori realized they would be bound by British law.

Settlement and the early pioneers

Even before the Treaty was signed, there were moves to found a settlement in Port Nicholson, the site of Wellington, on behalf of the **New Zealand Company**. This was the brainchild of **Edward Gibbon Wakefield**, who desperately wanted to stem American-style egalitarianism and hoped to use New Zealand as the proving ground for his theory of "scientific colonization". This involved preserving the English squire-and-yokel class structure by encouraging the settlement of a cross-section of English society, though without the "dregs" at the bottom. It was supposed to be a self-regulating system, whereby the company would buy large tracts of land cheaply from the government then charge a price low enough to encourage the relatively wealthy to invest, yet high enough to prevent labourers from becoming landowners. The revenue from land sales was then to fund the transportation of cheap labour to work the land, but the system ended up encouraging absentee landlordism as English "gentlemen", arriving to find somewhere altogether more rugged and less refined than they had been promised, hot-footed it to Australia or America.

Between 1839 and 1843 the New Zealand Company dispatched nearly 19,000 settlers and established them in "**planned settlements**" in Wellington, Wanganui, Nelson and New Plymouth. This was the core of Pakeha immigration, the only substantial non-Wakefield settlement being **Auckland**, a scruffy collection of waterside shacks which, to the horror of New Zealand Company officials, became the capital after the signing of the Treaty of Waitangi. Maori welfare and social justice had no place in all this, despite the precarious position of Pakeha settlements, which were nothing but tiny enclaves in a country still under Maori control. Transgressing the protocols of the local *iwi* was likely to have graver implications than offending the Pakeha government.

The company couldn't buy land direct from Maori, but the government bought up huge tracts and sold it on, often for ten or twenty times what they paid for it. Maori must have been well aware that they were being swindled and could have negotiated better prices themselves, but sold almost the whole of the South Island in a number of large blocks. Some was bought by two more organizations expounding the Wakefield principle: the dour Free Church of Scotland founded **Dunedin** in 1848, while the Canterbury Association established **Christchurch** in 1850, fashioning it English, Anglo-Catholic and conservative. In 1850 the New Zealand Company foundered, leaving well-established settlements which, subject to the hard realities of colonial life, had failed to conform to Wakefield's lofty theories and were filled with sturdy workers from labouring and lower middle-class backgrounds.

In 1852 New Zealand achieved self-government and set about dividing the country into six **provinces** – Auckland, New Plymouth, Wellington, Nelson, Canterbury and Otago – which took over land sales and encouraged migrants with free passage, land grants and guaranteed employment on road construction schemes. The same people drawn to the Wakefield settlements heeded the call, hoping for a better life away from the oppression and drudgery of working-class Britain. The new towns were alive with ambitious folk prepared to work hard to realize their high expectations, but many felt stymied by the low-quality land they were able to buy. At this point Maori still held the best land and were doing quite nicely growing potatoes and wheat for both local consumption and export to Australia, where the Victorian gold rush had created a huge demand. Pakeha were barely able to compete, and with the slump in export prices in the mid-1850s, many looked to pastoralism. The Crown helped out by halving the price of land, allowing poorer settlers to become landowners but simultaneously paving the way for the creation of huge pastoral runs and putting further pressure on Maori to sell land.

Maori discontent and the New Zealand Wars

The first five years after the signing of the Treaty were a disaster, first under governor Hobson then under the ineffectual FitzRoy. Relations between Maori and Pakeha began to deteriorate immediately, as the capital was moved from Kororareka to Auckland and duties were imposed in the Bay of Islands. The consequent loss of trade from passing ships precipitated the first tangible expression of dissent, a famous series of incidents involving the Ngapuhi leader **Hone Heke**, who repeatedly felled the most fundamental symbol of British authority, the flagstaff at Russell (see p.193). The situation was normalized to some degree by the appointment of **George Grey**, the most able of New Zealand's governors and a man who did more than anyone else to shape the country's early years. He was economical with the truth and despotic, but possessed the intelligence to use his deceit in a most effective (and often benign) way. As Maori began to adapt their culture to accommodate Pakeha in a way that few other native peoples have – selling their crops, operating flour mills and running coastal shipping – Grey encouraged the process by establishing mission schools, erecting hospitals where Maori could get free treatment, and providing employment on public works. In short, he did what he could to uphold the spirit of the Treaty, thereby gaining enormous respect among Maori. Sadly, he failed to set up any mechanism to perpetuate his policies after he left for the governorship of Cape Town in 1853. Under New Zealand's constitution, enacted in 1852, Maori were excluded from political decision-making and prevented from setting up their own form of government; although British subjects in name, they had few of the practical benefits and yet were increasingly expected to comply with British law.

By now it was clear that Maori had been duped by the Treaty of Waitangi: one chief explained that they thought they were transferring the "shadow of the land" while "the substance of the land remains with us", and yet he now conceded "the substance of the land goes to the Europeans, the shadow only will be our portion". Growing **resistance** to land sales came at a time when settler communities were expanding and demanding to buy huge tracts of pastoral land. With improved communications Pakeha became more self-reliant and dismissive of Maori, who progressively began to lose faith in the government and fell back on traditional methods of handling their affairs. Self-government had given landowners the vote, but since Maori didn't hold individual titles to their land they were denied suffrage. Maori and Pakeha aspirations seemed completely at odds and there was a growing sense of betrayal, which helped to replace tribal animosities with a tenuous unity. In 1854, a month before New Zealand's first parliament, Maori held inter-tribal meetings to discuss a response to the degradation of their culture and the rapid loss of their land. The eventual upshot was the 1858 election of the ageing **Te Wherowhero**, head chief of the Waikatos, as the Maori "King", the leader of the **King Movement** (see box in Chapter Three, p.238) behind which Maori could rally to hold back the flood of Pakeha settlement. Initially just the Waikato and central North Island *iwi* supported the King, but soon Taranaki and some Hawke's Bay *iwi* joined in a loose federation united in vowing not to sell any more land. This brave attempt to challenge the changes forced upon them gave Maori a sense of purpose and brought with it a resurgence of ancient customs such as tattooing. While some radical Maori wanted to completely rid the country of the white menace, most were moderates and made peaceful overtures that Pakeha chose to regard as rebellious.

By now, most settlers felt that the Treaty of Waitangi had no validity whatsoever and sided with the land sellers to drive the government to repress the Maori landholders. There had been minor skirmishes over land throughout the country, but matters came to a head in 1860, when the government used troops to enforce a bogus purchase of land at Waitara, near New Plymouth. The fighting was temporarily confined to Taranaki but soon spread to consume the whole of the North Island in the **New Zealand Wars**, once known by Pakeha as the Maori Wars and by Maori as *te riri Pakeha* (white man's anger). Maori were divided: most of the supporters of the King movement, particularly the Waikatos, traced their *whakapapa* (genealogy) back to the Tainui canoe and some others chose this opportunity to settle old grievances by siding with the government against their traditional enemies. Through the early 1860s the number of Pakeha troops was tripled to around 3000, providing an effective force against Maori who failed to adopt a co-ordinated strategy. The warrior ethic meant there was no place for more effective guerrilla tactics, except in the east of the North Island, where **Te Kooti** (see box, p.238) kept the government troops on the run. Elsewhere Maori frequently faced off against ranked artillery and, though there were notable successes, the final result was inevitable. Fighting had abated by the end of the 1860s but peace wasn't finally declared until 1881, when the Maori fastness of the "King Country" (an area south of Hamilton which still goes by that title) was finally opened up to Pakeha once again.

British soldiers had been lured into service with offers of land and free passage and, as a further affront to defeated Maori, many of them were settled in the solidly Maori Waikato. Much of the most fertile land was **confiscated** – in the Waikato, the Bay of Plenty and Taranaki – with little regard to the owners' allegiances during the conflict. By 1862 the Crown had relinquished its right of preemption and individuals could buy land directly from Maori, who were forced to limit the stated ownership first to ten individuals and later to just one owner. With their collective power smashed, there was little resistance to voracious land agents luring Maori into debt then offering to buy their land to save them.

Between 1860 and 1881 the **non-Maori population** rose from 60,000 to 470,000, swamping and marginalising Maori society. An Anglo-Saxon world view came to dominate all aspects of New Zealand life, and by 1871 the Maori language was no longer used for teaching in schools. A defeated people were widely thought to be close to extinction: Anthony Trollope in 1872 wrote "There is scope for poetry in their past history. There is room for philanthropy as to their present condition. But in regard to their future – there is hardly a place for hope."

Meanwhile, as the New Zealand Wars raged in the North Island, **gold fever** had struck the South. Flakes had been found near Queenstown in 1861 and the initial rushes soon spread to later finds along the West Coast. For the best part of a decade, gold was New Zealand's major export, but the gold provinces never had a major influence on the rest of the country, nor does the gold era retain the legendary status it does in California and Victoria. The major effect was on population distribution: by 1858 the shrinking Maori population had been outstripped by the rapidly swelling horde of Pakeha settlers, most settling in the South Island where relations with Maori played a much smaller part. The South Island prospered, with both Christchurch and Dunedin consolidating their roles, serving the surrounding farms and more distant sheep stations. Dunedin became the largest town in the country, the influx of the "New Iniquity" radically changing the city's staunch front of the "Old Identity".

Consolidation and social reform

The 1870s were dominated by the policies of **Julius Vogel**, an able Treasurer who started a programme of borrowing on a massive scale to fund public works. Within a decade what had previously been a land of scattered towns in separately governed provinces was transformed into a single country unified by improved roads, an expanding rail system, 7000 kilometres of telegraph wires and numerous public institutions. Almost all the remaining farmable land was bought up or leased from Maori and acclimatization societies sprang up with the express aim of anglicizing the New Zealand countryside and improving **farming**. New Zealand quickly began to realize the agricultural expectation created by fertile soils, a temperate climate and relatively high rainfall. Arable farming was mostly abandoned and pastoralism was taking hold, particularly among those rich enough to afford to buy and ship the stock. With no extensive market close enough to make perishable produce profitable, **wool** became the main export item, stimulated by the development of the Corriedale sheep, a Romney-Lincoln cross with a long fleece. Wool continued as the mainstay until 1882, when the first refrigerated meat shipment left for Britain, signalling a turning point in the New Zealand economy and the establishment of New Zealand as Britain's offshore larder, a role it maintained until the 1970s.

From 1879 until 1896 New Zealand went into the "long depression", mostly overseen by the conservative "Continuous Ministry" – the last government composed of colonial gentry. During this time **trade unionism** began to influence the political scene and bolstered the Liberal Pact (a Liberal and Labour alliance), which, in 1890, wrested power from those who had controlled the country for two decades and ushered in an era of unprecedented social change. Its first leader, **John Ballance**, firmly believed in state intervention and installed **William Pember Reeves**, probably New Zealand's most radically socialist MP, as his Minister of Labour. Reeves was instrumental in pushing through sweeping reforms to working hours and factory conditions that were so progressive that no further changes were made to labour laws until 1936. On his own initiative, with no apparent demand from workers, he introduced the world's first **compulsory arbitration system**, which went on to award numerous wage rises, so increasing the national prosperity. He had become too radical for most of his colleagues, however, and only remained in office until 1896. When Ballance died in 1892 he was replaced by **Richard "King Dick" Seddon**, a blunt Lancastrian who became, along with Grey, one of the country's greatest, if least democratic, leaders. Following Ballance's lead he introduced a graduated income tax and repealed property tax, hoping to break up some of the large estates (something eventually achieved much later, as technological changes made dairying and mixed farming more prosperous). New Zealand was already being tagged the "social laboratory of the world", but more was to come.

In 1893, New Zealand was the first nation in the world to enact full **female suffrage**, undoubtedly in line with the liberal thinking of the time, but apparently an accident nonetheless. The story goes that Seddon let an amendment to an electoral reform bill pass on the assumption that it would be rejected by the Legislative Council (an upper house which survived until 1950), thus diverting the ill will of suffragists. Others contend that female suffrage was approved not for any free-thinking liberal principle but in response to the powerful quasi-religious temperance movement, which hoped to "purify and improve the tone of our politics", effectively giving married couples double the vote of the single man who was often seen as a drunken layabout. In 1898 Seddon further astonished the world by weathering a ninety-hour continuous debate to squeeze through legislation guaranteeing an **old age pension**. Fabian Beatrice Webb, in New Zealand that same year, allowed that "it is delightful to see a country with no millionaires and hardly any slums".

By the early twentieth century, the radical impetus had faded along with the memory of the 1880s depression, and Pakeha could rest easy in the knowledge that their standard of living was one of the highest in the world. But things were not so rosy for Maori, whose numbers had dropped from an estimated 200,000 at Cook's first visit to a low of 42,000 in 1896. However, as resistance to European diseases grew, numbers started rising, accompanied by a new confidence buoyed by the rise of Maori parliamentary leadership. **Apirana Ngata**, **Maui Pomare** and **Te Rangi Hiroa** (**Peter Buck**) were all products of Te Aute College, an Anglican school for Maori, and all were committed to working within the administrative and legislative framework of government, convinced that the survival of Maoritanga depended on shedding those aspects of the traditional lifestyle that impeded their acceptance of the modern world.

Seddon died in 1906 and the flame went out of the Liberal torch, though the party was to stay in power another six years. This era saw the rise of the "**Red Feds**", international socialists of the Red Federation who began to organize Kiwi labour. They rejected the arbitration system that had kept wage rises below the level of inflation and prevented strikes for a decade, and encouraged **strikes**. The longest was at Blackball (see p.794) on the West Coast, where prime movers in the formation of the Federation of Miners, and subsequently the Federation of Labour, led a three-month stoppage.

The 1912 election was won by William Massey's Reform Party, with the support of the farmers or "cow cockies". Allegiances were now substantially polarized and 1912 and 1913 saw bitter fighting at a series of strikes at the gold mines of Waihi, the docks at Timaru and the wharves of Auckland. As workers opposed to the arbitration system withdrew their labour, the owners organized scab labour, while the hostile Farmers' Union recruited mounted "specials" to add to the government force of "special constables". All were protected by naval and military forces as they decisively smashed the Red Feds. The Prime Minister even handed out medals to strike-breaking dairy farmers. Further domestic conflict was only averted by the outbreak of war.

Coming of age: 1916-1945

Though New Zealand had started off as an unwanted sibling of Mother England, it had soon transformed itself into a devoted daughter who could be relied upon in times of crisis. New Zealand had supported Britain in South Africa at the end of the nineteenth century and was now called upon to do the same in **World War I**. Locally born Pakeha now outnumbered immigrants and, in 1907, New Zealand had traded its self-governing colony status for that of a Dominion, giving it control over its foreign policy; but the rising sense of nationalism didn't dilute a patriotism for the motherland far in excess of its filial duty. Altogether ten percent of the population were involved in the war effort, 100,000 fighting in the trenches of Gallipoli and elsewhere. Seventeen thousand failed to return, more than were lost in Belgium, a battleground with six times the population.

At home, the **Temperance Movement** was back in action, attempting to curb vice in the army brought on by the demon drink. Plebiscites in 1911, 1914 and 1919 narrowly averted national prohibition but the "wowsers" succeeded to the point that from 1917 pubs would close at 6pm for the duration of the war. Six o'clock closing entered the statute books in 1918: not until

1967 did its repeal end half a century of the "**Six o'clock swill**", an hour or so of frenetic after-work consumption in which the ability to tank down as much beer as possible was raised to an art form. This probably did more to hinder New Zealand's social development than anything else: pubs began to look more like lavatories, which could be hosed down after closing, and the predilection for quantity over quality encouraged breweries to churn out dreadful watery brews.

The wartime boom economy continued until around 1920 as Britain's demand for food remained high. Things looked rosy, especially for Pakeha returned servicemen, who were rehabilitated on newly acquired farmland; in contrast, Maori returned servicemen got nothing. These highly mortgaged and inexperienced farmers began to suffer with the rapid drop in produce prices in the early 1920s, fostering a sense of insecurity which pervaded the country. Political leadership was weak and yet New Zealand continued to grow with ongoing improvements in infrastructure – hydroelectric dams and roads – and enormous improvements in farming techniques, such as the application of superphosphate fertilizers, sophisticated milking machines and tractors. New Zealand remained a prosperous nation but was ill-prepared for the **Great Depression**, when the Wall Street Crash sent shock waves through the country. The already high national debt skyrocketed as export income dropped and the Reform government cut pensions, health care and public works' expenditure. The budget was balanced at the cost of producing huge numbers of unemployed. Prime Minister Forbes dictated "no pay without work" and sent thousands of men to primitive rural relief camps for unnecessary tasks such as planting trees and draining swamps in return for a pittance. With the knowledge of the prosperous years to come it is hard to conjure the image of lines of ragged men awaiting their relief money, malnourished children in schools and former soldiers panhandling in the streets.

Throughout the 1920s the Labour Party had gradually watered down some of its socialist policies in an attempt to woo the middle-ground voter. In 1935 they were swept to power and ushered in New Zealand's second era of massive social change, picking up where Seddon left off. Labour's leader **Michael Joseph Savage** felt that "Social Justice must be the guiding principle and economic organization must adapt itself to social needs", a sentiment translated by a contemporary commentator as aiming "to turn capitalism quite painlessly into a nicer sort of capitalism which will eventually become indistinguishable from socialism". State socialism was out, but "Red Feds" still held half the cabinet posts. Salaries reduced during the depression were restored; public works programmes were rekindled, with workers on full pay rather than "relief"; income was redistributed through graduated taxation; and in two rapid bursts of legislation Labour built the model **Welfare State**, the first in the world and the most comprehensive and integrated. State houses were built and let at low rental, pensions were increased, a national health service provided free medicines and health care, and family benefits supplemented the income of those with children.

Maori welfare was also on the agenda and there were moves to raise their living standards to the Pakeha level, partly achieved by increasing pensions and unemployment payments. Much of the best land had by now been sold off but legal changes paved the way for Maori land to be farmed using Pakeha agricultural methods, while maintaining communal ownership. In return, the newly formed **Ratana Party**, who held all four of the Maori Parliamentary seats, supported Labour, keeping them in office until 1949.

New Zealand's perception of its world position changed dramatically in 1941 when the Japanese bombed Pearl Harbor. The country was forced to recognize its position half a globe away from Britain and in the military sphere of America. As in World War I, large numbers of troops were called up, amounting to a third of the male labour force, but casualties were fewer and on the home front the economy continued to boom. Foreign wars aside, by the 1940s New Zealand was the world's most prosperous country, with a fabulous quality of life and the comfortable bed of the Welfare State to fall back on.

More years of prosperity

The Reform Party and the remnants of the Liberals eventually combined to form the **National Party** which, in 1949, wrested power from Labour. With McCarthyite rhetoric, National branded the more militant unionists as Communists and succeeded in breaking much of the power of the unions during the violent and emotional **1951 Waterfront Lock-out**. From the late 1940s until the mid-1980s, National became New Zealand's natural party of government, disturbed only by two three-year stints with Labour in power. The conservatism always bubbling under had now found its expression. Most were happy with the government's strong-arm tactics, which emasculated the militant unions and the country settled down to what novelist C.K. Stead viewed as the Kiwi ideal: "to live in a country with fresh air, an open landscape and plenty of sunshine; and to own a house, car, refrigerator, washing machine, bach, launch, fibre-glass rod, golf clubs, and so on." Such a life had huge appeal for Brits still suffering rationing after World War II, and between 1947 and 1975, 77,000 British men, women and children became "**ten pound poms**", making use of the New Zealand government's assisted passage to fill Kiwi job vacancies.

While the egalitarian myth still perpetuated by many Kiwis may never have existed, by most measures New Zealand's wealth was evenly spread, with few truly rich and relatively few poor. The exception at least in economic terms were Maori, many now migrating in huge numbers to the cities, especially Auckland, responding to the urban labour shortages and good wages after World War II. By the 1970s the deracination of urban Maori was creating social unrest which, left unchannelled, resulted in high Maori unemployment and a disproportionate representation in prisons. Increasing contact between Maori and Europeans exposed weaknesses in the Pakeha belief that the country's race relations were the best in the world. Pakeha took great pride in Maori bravery, skill, generosity, sporting prowess and good humour, but were unable to set aside the discrimination which kept Maoris out of professional jobs.

On the economic front the major changes took place under **Walter Nash**'s 1957–60 Labour government, when New Zealand embarked on a programme designed to relieve the country's dependence on exports. A steel rolling mill, oil refinery, gin distillery and glass factory were all set up and an aluminium industry was encouraged by the prospect of cheap power from hydroelectric project on Lake Manapouri (see box, p.953). When **Keith Holyoake** took over at the helm of the next National government, Britain was still by far New Zealand's biggest export market but was making overtures to the economically isolationist European Common Market. New Zealand was becoming aware that Britain was no longer the guardian she once was. This was equally true in the **military** sphere, where New Zealand began to court its Pacific allies, signing the anti-Communist SEATO (South-East Asia Treaty Organization) document, and the ANZUS pact, which provided for mutual defence of Australia, New Zealand and the US.

Dithering in the face of adversity 1972–1984

In a landslide victory, the third **Labour government** took control in 1972. Again it was to last only a single three-year term, largely due to the difficulties of having to deal with international events beyond its control. Most fundamental was the long-expected entry of Britain into the Common Market. Some other export markets had been found but New Zealand still felt betrayed. Later the same year oil prices quadrupled in a few months and the treasury found itself with mounting fuel bills and decreasing export receipts. The government borrowed heavily but couldn't avoid electoral defeat in 1975 by National's obstreperous and pugnacious **Robert "Piggy" Muldoon**, who denounced Labour's borrowing and then outdid them. In short order New Zealand had dreadful domestic and foreign debt, unemployment was the highest for decades, and the unthinkable was happening – the standard of living was falling. People began to leave in their thousands and the "brain drain" almost reached crisis point. Muldoon's solution was to "**Think Big**" a catch-all term for a number of capital-intensive petrochemical projects designed to utilize New Zealand's abundant natural gas to produce ammonia, urea fertilizer, methanol and synthetic petrol. Though undoubtedly self-aggrandizing it made little economic sense. Rather than use local technology and labour to convert New Zealand vehicles to run on compressed natural gas (a system already up and running), Muldoon chose to pay international corporations to design and build huge prefabricated processing plants which were then shipped to New Zealand for assembly, mostly around New Plymouth.

Factory outfalls often jeopardized traditional Maori shellfish beds, and where once *iwi* would have accepted this as inevitable, a new spirit of protest saw them win significant concessions. Throughout the mid-1970s Maori began to question the philosophy of Pakeha life and looked to the Treaty of Waitangi (see box, p.191) to correct the grievances that were aired at occupations of traditional land at Bastion Point in Auckland (see p.77), and Raglan, and through a petition delivered to parliament after a march across the North Island.

Maori also found expression in the formation of **gangs** – Black Power, the Mongrel Mob and the bike-oriented Highway 61 – along the lines graphically depicted in Lee Tamahori's film *Once Were Warriors*, which was originally written about South Auckland life in the 1970s. Fortified suburban homes still exist and such gangs continue to be influential among Maori youth, a position now being positively exploited to bring wayward Maori youth back into the fold.

Race relations were never Muldoon's strong suit and when large numbers of illegal **Polynesian immigrants** from south Pacific islands – particularly Tonga, Samoa and the Cook Islands – started arriving in Auckland he responded by instructing the police to conduct random street checks for "over-stayers", many of whom were deported. Muldoon opted for a completely hands-off approach when it came to sporting contacts with South Africa and in 1976 let the pig-headed rugby administrators send an All Black team over to play racially selected South African teams. African nations responded by boycotting the Montreal Olympics, putting New Zealand in the unusual position of being an international pariah. New Zealand signed the 1977 Gleneagles Agreement requiring it to "vigorously combat the evil of apartheid" and yet in 1981 the New Zealand Rugby Union courted a **Springbok Tour**, which sparked New Zealand's greatest civil disturbance since the labour riots of the 1920s.

Modern New Zealand

Muldoon's big-spending economic policies were widely perceived to be unsuccessful, and when he called a snap election in 1984, Labour were returned to power under **David Lange**. Just as National had eschewed traditional right-wing economics in favour of a "managed economy", Labour now changed tactics, addressing the massive economic problems by shunning the traditional left-of-centre approach. Instead, they grasped the baton of Thatcherite economics and sprinted off with it. Under Finance Minister Roger Douglas's **Rogernomics**, the dollar was devalued by twenty percent, exchange controls were abolished, tariffs slashed, the maximum income tax rate was halved, a Goods and Services Tax was introduced, Air New Zealand and the Bank of New Zealand were privatized, and state benefits were cut. Unemployment doubled to twelve percent, a quarter of manufacturing jobs were lost, and the moderately well-off benefited at the expense of the poor; nevertheless, market forces and enterprise culture had come to stay. As one of the world's most regulated economies became one of the most deregulated, the longstanding belief that the state should provide for those least able to help themselves was cast aside.

In other spheres Labour's views weren't so right-wing. One of Lange's first acts was to refuse US ships entry to New Zealand ports unless they declared that they were nuclear-free. The Americans would do nothing of the sort and withdrew support for New Zealand's defence safety net, the **ANZUS** pact. Most of the country backed Lange on this but were less sure about his overtures towards Maori who, for the first time since the middle of the nineteenth century, got legal recognition for the Treaty of Waitangi. Now, Maori grievances dating back to 1840 could be addressed.

The rise in apparent income under Rogernomics created consumer confidence and the economy boomed until the **stock market crash** of 1987, which hit New Zealand especially hard. The country went into freefall and all confidence in the reforms was lost. Labour's position, consolidated in the 1987 election, now became untenable, and in the 1990 election National's **Jim Bolger** took the helm. Throughout the deep recession National continued Labour's free-market reforms, cutting welfare programmes (a policy dubbed "Ruthanasia" after its perpetrator Ruth Richardson) and extracting teeth from the unions by passing the Employment Contracts Act, which established the pattern of individual workplaces coming to their own agreements on wages and conditions. By the middle of the 1990s the economy had improved dramatically and what for a time had been considered a foolhardy experiment was seen by monetarists as a model for open economies the world over. Meanwhile, the gap between the rich and the poor continues to widen and New Zealand's classless society is increasingly exposed for the myth it always was.

While many have relished the good life, those at the bottom of the pile have suffered. In her resignation speech, **Cath Tizard**, the most popular and charismatic Governor-General New Zealand has had for years, levelled a thinly veiled attack at the government for its record on health care, but succeeded only in raising anti-monarchist hackles at her vice-regal intervention. Nonetheless, the kind of **republican rabble-rousing** championed across the Tasman in recent years largely falls on deaf ears in Aotearoa, where, despite the maturing of the nation in the last decade or so, and a progressive realignment with the Pacific and Asia, most seem happy to maintain links with Britain.

Ever since New Zealand achieved self-government from Britain in 1852, it had maintained a first-past-the-post Westminster style of parliament, with the exception of the scrapping of the upper house in 1950 and the provision for four (now seven) **Maori seats**. Maori can chose to vote for their general or Maori candidate but not both. In the depths of the recession in 1993, New Zealand voted for **electoral reform**, specifically Mixed Member Proportional representation (MMP), which purports to give smaller parties an opportunity to have some say. In the two MMP elections since then, this has certainly proved to be the case. In 1996, National and Labour shared the majority of the vote, but the balance of power was held by New Zealand First, a new Maori-dominated party who eventually formed a coalition with National under **Jim Bolger**. A new Maori spirit entered parliament, with far more Maori MPs than ever before and maiden speeches received with a *waiata* (song) from their *whanau* (extended family group) in the public gallery. Unfortunately, most were political neophytes and NZ First self-destructed in short order after a spate of scandals. Bolger's poor handling of the situation saw his support wane, and he was replaced in a palace coup, in which **Jenny Shipley** became New Zealand's first female prime minister. Her brand of right-wing economics and more liberal social views succeeded in holding the coalition together but failed to bolster the polls on the lead up to the 1999 election. Suddenly, out of left-field came the **Green Party**, long-sidelined but newly resurgent under MMP. The vagaries of the MMP system meant that, on a nail-biting election night, the Greens were teetering between getting no seats at all and racking up six seats, a tally they eventually achieved with the counting of special votes. They formed a government with Labour and the Alliance under **Helen Clark**, and sent New Zealand's first Rastafarian MP to parliament, one **Nandor Tanczos**. Resplendent in waist-length dreads and a new hemp suit he has become both a bogeyman for the opposition and something of a hero to disenfranchised youth. As if the political landscape weren't topsy-turvy enough, the staunchly conservative Wairarapa district returned the world's first transgender MP, Carterton's former mayor, **Georgina Beyer**.

Nine years in opposition left Labour (the senior coalition partner) with a considerable agenda for change. Logging of beech forests on the West Coast had been stopped, the Employment Contracts Act had been replaced by more worker-friendly legislation, and they'd unilaterally abolished knighthoods. They had failed to deliver on education and health care, but Clark seemed to weather every brickbat and minor scandal, so the government's rating remained high as they went into the next election in November 2002.

Meanwhile, Maoritanga looks set to play an ever increasing role in the life of all New Zealanders as Maori consolidate the gains of the past few years. In the twenty-first century the number of New Zealanders who consider themselves Maori may well surpass the number of Pakeha, and it remains to be seen just how significant that will be.

Chronology of New Zealand

c.1000AD ▸ Arrival of first **Polynesians**.

c.1350 ▸ mythical arrival of the "Great Fleet" from Hawaiki.

1642 ▸ Dutchman **Abel Tasman** sails past the West Coast but doesn't land.

1769 ▸ Englishman **James Cook** circumnavigates both main islands and makes first constructive contact.

1772 ▸ French sailor **Marion du Fresne** and 26 of his men killed in the Bay of Islands.

1809 ▸ Whangaroa Maori attack the *Boyd*; most of the crew killed.

1814 ▸ Arrival of **Samuel Marsden**, the first Christian missionary.

1830s ▸ Sealing and whaling stations dotted around the coast.

1833 ▸ James Busby installed as British Resident at Waitangi.

1835 ▸ Independence of the United Tribes of NZ proclaimed.

1840 ▸ **Treaty of Waitangi** signed; capital moved from Kororareka to Auckland.

1840s ▸ Cities of Auckland, Christchurch, Dunedin, Nelson, New Plymouth, Wanganui and Wellington all established

1852 ▸ NZ becomes a self-governing colony divided into six provinces.

1858 ▸ Settlers outnumber Maori.

1860–65 ▸ **Land Wars** between Pakeha and Maori.

1860s ▸ Major gold rushes in the South Island.

1865 ▸ Capital moved from Auckland to Wellington.

1867 ▸ Maori men given the vote.

1870s ▸ **Wool** established as the mainstay of the NZ economy.

1876 ▸ Abolition of provincial governments. Power centralized in Wellington.

1882 ▸ First **refrigerated meat shipment** to Europe. Lamb becomes increasingly important.

1890 ▸ NZ become "social laboratory" with introduction of compulsory arbitration and graduated income tax.

1893 ▸ Full **women's suffrage**; a world first.

1898 ▸ Old age pension introduced.

1910s ▸ Rise of organized labour under the socialist Red Federation. Strikes at Blackball, Waihi and Auckland.

1914–18 ▸ NZ takes part in WWI with terrible loss of life.

1917 ▸ **Temperance Movement** gets pubs closed after 6pm. Only repealed in 1967.

1920s ▸ Initial prosperity evaporates as the Great Depression takes hold.

1935 ▸ M.J. Savage's Labour government ushers in the world's first **Welfare State** with free health service, family benefits, state housing and increased pensions.

1941 ▸ Bombing of Pearl Harbor

and WWII begins NZ's military realignment with the Pacific region.

1947 ▸ New Zealand becomes fully independent from Britain.

1950 ▸ Parliament's upper house abolished.

1951 ▸ NZ joins **ANZUS** military pact with the US and Australia.

1950s ▸ NZ comfortable as one of the world's most prosperous nations.

1957–60 ▸ Infrastructure improvements: steel mill, oil refinery, and numerous hydroelectric power stations built or planned.

1960s ▸ Start of **immigration from Pacific Islands**. Major **urbanization of Maori** population.

1972-75 ▸ Third Labour government. NZ economy struggles to cope with huge oil price hikes and Britain's entry in to the Common Market.

1975 ▸ **Waitangi Tribunal** established to consider Maori land claims.

1975–84 ▸ National's Robert "Piggy" Muldoon tries to borrow NZ out of trouble, investing heavily in ill-considered petrochemical projects.

1976 ▸ African nations boycott Montreal Olympics because of NZ's rugby contacts with South Africa.

1977 ▸ NZ signs Gleneagles Agreement banning sporting ties with South Africa.

1981 ▸ **Springbok Tour**. Massive protests as a racially selected South African rugby team tours NZ.

1983 ▸ NZ signs Closer Economic Relations (CER) Treaty with Australia.

1984 ▸ The "Hikoi" land march brings Maori grievances into political focus.

1984 ▸ Labour regains power under David Lange. Widespread privatization and deregulation of NZ's protectionist economy. Refusal to allow American nuclear warships into NZ ports severely strains US-NZ relations.

1985 ▸ French secret service agents bomb Greenpeace flagship the **Rainbow Warrior** in Auckland Harbour.

1987 ▸ New Zealand becomes a **Nuclear-Free Zone**

1987 ▸ Stock market crash devastates NZ economy.

1990–96 ▸ Jim Bolger leads National government, pressing on with Labour's free-market reforms and further dismantling the welfare state.

1996 ▸ First **MMP election** returns an alliance of National and NZ First.

1997 ▸ Jenny Shipley ousts Bolger to become NZ's **first woman Prime Minister**.

1999 ▸ **Labour** regain power under Helen Clark in coalition with the Alliance and the Green Party. The Greens' Nandor Tanczos installed as NZ's first Rastafarian MP and Labour's Georgina Beyer becomes the world's first transgender MP.

2000 ▸ New Zealand becomes first non-US country to successfully defend the **America's Cup**.

2001 ▸ New Zealand in the tourist spotlight as first *Lord of the Rings* movie released to general acclaim.

Maoritanga

When the Pakeha first came to this Island, the first thing he taught the Maori was Christianity. They made parsons and priests of several members of the Maori race, and they taught these persons to look up and pray; and while they were looking up the Pakehas took away our land.

Mahuta, the son of the Maori King Tawhiao, addressing the New Zealand Legislative Council in 1903.

The term **Maoritanga** embodies Maori lifestyle and culture – it is the Maori way of doing things, embracing social structure, ethics, customs, legends and art, as well as language (see p.1017). In the Anglo-European dominated society that New Zealand has always been, and to a large extent still is, it has been easy to see Maori culture as harping back to some fond-remembered idyll of the past, but Maoritanga has remained very much alive, and in the last couple of decades has seen a dramatic resurgence. By most measures, Maori make up over ten percent of New Zealand's population, but Maori–Pakeha marriage since the early nineteenth century has left a complex inter-racial pool; many third- or fourth-generation Pakeha can claim a Maori forebear or two, and some contend that there are no full-blooded Maori left. Maori ancestry remains the foundation of Maoridom, but a sense of Maori belonging has become a question of cultural identity as much as bloodlines.

Until very recently, white New Zealanders liked to promote the image of the two races living in harmony as one people, citing scenes of Maori and Pakeha elbow to elbow at the bar and Maori rugby players in the scrum alongside their Pakeha brothers. Pakeha prided themselves on successful integration that seemed a world away from the apartheid of South Africa or the virtual genocide exacted on North American and Australian aboriginal peoples; after all, Maori could claim all the benefits of Pakeha plus dedicated seats in parliament, extra university grants and various other concessions. Yet this denied the undercurrent of Maori dissatisfaction over their treatment since the arrival of the first Europeans; the policy of **assimilation** relied entirely on Maori conforming to the Pakeha way of doing things and made no concession to Maoritanga. Maori adapted incredibly quickly to Pakeha ways but were rewarded with the loss of their **land**. It is impossible to overestimate the importance of this: Maori spirituality invests every tree, every hill and every bay with a kind of supernatural life of its own, drawn from past events and the actions of the ancestors. It is by no means fanciful to equate the loss of land with the diminution of Maori life-force; little surprise, then, that much of the spirit went out of Maori people.

It is only really since the 1980s that the Pakeha paternal view has been challenged, with the country reacting by adopting **biculturalism**. As Maori rediscover their heritage and Pakeha open their eyes to what has been around them for generations, knowledge of Maoritanga and some understanding of the language is seen as desirable and even advantageous. The government has increasingly channelled resources towards the "flax roots" of Maoridom, fostering a rapid take-up in the learning of Maori language, a resurgence in interest in Maori arts and crafts and a growing pride in Maoridom. At the same time, Maori have won back customary rights to fisheries and resources, and parcels of land have been returned to Maori ownership. Nonetheless, there is a sense in some quarters that Maori are only getting as much as the Pakeha-dominated government feels it is prepared to give back.

For many Pakeha, however, there is considerable unease over what is perceived as the government's soft stance on Treaty of Waitangi land claims (see box on p.191). Some envisage a future where Maori will own the land (including private land not currently up for redistribution under Treaty claims), will reclaim the rights granted them by the Treaty, and will have more influence than Pakeha. Quite frankly, they're afraid. So far, reaction to the strengthening Maori hand in this climate of conciliation has only been voiced quietly, and just how this scenario will pan out remains to be seen. True power-sharing and biculturalism seems a long way off, and Maori aspirations for "sovereignty" – a separate Maori government and judiciary – look far-fetched at present, but the Maori juggernaut is moving fast.

Maori legend

Maori culture remains highly oral, with chants, storytelling and oratory central to ceremonial and daily life. This was doubly so when Europeans arrived and first recorded the traditions and legends normally passed down verbally. Different tribal groups often had different sets of stories, or at least variations on common themes, but European historians with pet theories to promote often distorted the stories they heard and even destroyed conflicting evidence, creating their own Maori folklore. This generalizing trend served the purpose of creating a common Maori identity, and many of the stories have been accepted back into the Maori tradition, leaving a patchwork of authentic and bowdlerized legends. Nonetheless, there are fixed themes common to most.

Creation

From the primal nothingness of **Te Kore** sprang **Ranginui** the sky father and **Papatuanuku** the earth mother. They had numerous offspring, principally the major gods: **Haumia Tiketike**, the god of the fern root and food from the forest; **Rongo**, the god of the kumara and cultivation; **Tu Matauenga**, the god of war; **Tangaroa**, the god of the oceans and sealife; **Tawhirimatea**, the god of the winds; and **Tane Mahuta**, the god of the forests. Through long centuries of darkness the brothers argued over whether to separate their parents and create light. Tawhirimatea opposed the idea and fled to the skies where his anger is manifested in thunder and lightning, while Tane Mahuta succeeded in parting the two, breaking their primal embrace and allowing life to flourish. Rangi's tears filled the oceans and even now it is their grief which brings the dew, mist and rain.

Having created the creatures of the sea, the air and the land, the gods turned their attentions to humans and, realizing that they were all male, had to create a female. They fashioned clay into a form resembling their mother and the responsibility again fell to **Tane**, who breathed life into the nostrils of the first woman, the Dawn Maiden, **Hinetitama**. It is from their union that the whole human race is descended.

Maui the trickster and Kupe the navigator

Maori mythology is littered with half-human demigods, and none is more celebrated than **Maui-Tikitiki-a-Taranga**, whose exploits are legend throughout Polynesia. With an armoury of spells, guile and boundless mischief, Maui gained a reputation as a trickster, using his abilities to turn any situation to his advantage. Equipped with the powerful magic jawbone of his grandmother, he set about taming his world, believing himself invincible. He even took on **the sun**, which had taken to passing so swiftly through the heavens that the people had no time to tend their fields before it disappeared back into its fiery pit. Maui vowed to solve the problem and, with the aid of his older brothers, plaited super-strong ropes which they tied across the sun's pit before dawn. As the sun rose into the net, Maui set upon the sun with his magic jawbone, beating him and imploring him not to go so fast. The sun was weakening rapidly and, in return for his release, agreed to do as Maui asked.

In the New Zealand context, Maui's master work was the creation of **Aotearoa**. With his reputation for mischief, Maui's brothers would often leave him behind when they went fishing, but one morning he stowed away under the seats. Far out at sea he revealed himself, promising to improve their recent poor catch. Maui egged them on until they were well beyond the normal fishing grounds before dropping anchor. In no time at all Maui's brothers filled their canoe with fish, but Maui still had some fishing to do. They scorned his hook (secretly armed with a chip of his grandmother's jawbone) and wouldn't lend him any bait, so Maui struck his own nose and smeared the hook with his own blood. Soon he had hooked a fabulous fish which, as it broke the surface, could be seen stretching into the distance all around them. Chanting an incantation, Maui got the fish to lie quietly on the surface where it became the North Island, known as Te ika a Maui, the fish of Maui. As Maui went off to make an offering to the gods, his brothers began to cut up the fish and eat it, hacking mountains and valleys into the surface. To fit in with the legend, the South Island is often called Te waka a Maui, the canoe of Maui, and Stewart Island is the anchor, Te punga o te waka a Maui.

With more historical veracity, Maori trace their ancestry back to **Hawaiki**, the semi-legendary source of the Polynesian diaspora, for which the Society Islands and the Cook Islands are the most likely candidates. According to legend, the first visitor to Aotearoa's shores was **Kupe**, the great Polynesian navigator. In one version of the tale he was determined to kill a great octopus that kept robbing his bait; drawn ever further out to sea in pursuit, he finally reached landfall on the uninhabited shores of Aotearoa, the "land of the long white cloud". He named numerous features of the land, then returned to Hawaiki with instructions on how to retrace his voyage.

Social structure and customs

Maori society remains **tribal** to a large extent, though the deracination resulting from the widespread move from the tribal homelands to the cities has eroded some of the closer ties. In urban situations the finer points of Maoritanga are having to be rediscovered, but the basic tenets remain strong and formal protocol still reigns for ceremonies as diverse as funeral wakes, meetings and Maori exhibition openings.

The most fundamental and tightest division in Maori society is the extended family or **whanau** (literally "birthing"), which extends from immediate relatives to cousins, uncles and nieces several times removed. A dozen or so *whanau* jointly form a localized sub-tribe or **hapu** (literally "gestation or pregnancy"), perhaps the most important tribal group, comprising dozens of extended families of common descent. *Hapu* were originally economically autonomous and today continue to conduct communal activities, typically through their *marae* (see p.986). Neighbouring *hapu* are likely to belong to the same tribe or **iwi** (literally "bones"), a looser association of several thousand Maori spread over a fairly large geographical area. The thirty-odd major *iwi* are even more tenuously linked by their common ancestry traced back to semi-legendary canoes, or *waka*. In troubled times, especially during the eighteenth-century New Zealand Wars, *iwi* from the same *waka* would band together for protection. Together these are the **tangata whenua** (literally "the people of the land"), a term that may refer to Maori people as a whole, or just to one *hapu* if local concerns are being aired.

The literal meanings of *whanau*, *hapu* and *iwi* can be viewed as a metaphor for the Maori view of their relationship with their ancestors or **tupuna**, who are considered to exist through their genetic inheritors; the past is very much a part of the present. Evidence of this is seen in the respect accorded the **whakapapa**, an individual's genealogy tracing descent from the gods via one of the migratory *waka* and through the *tupuna*. The *whakapapa* is often recited at length on formal occasions such as **hui** (meetings).

Maori traditional life is informed by the parallel notions of **tapu** (taboo) and **noa** (mundane, not *tapu*). These are not superstition but a belief system designed to impose a code of conduct: transgressing *tapu* brings ostracism and ill fortune and is thought to cause sickness. Objects, places, actions and even people can be *tapu*, demanding extra respect – for example, the body parts of a chief, especially the head, menstruating women, sacred items to do with ritual, earrings, pendants and hair combs, burial sites, and the knowledge contained in the *whakapapa* are all *tapu*. There is a practical aspect too, with the productivity of fishing grounds and forests traditionally maintained by imposing *tapu* at critical times. The direct opposite of *tapu* is *noa*, a term applied to ordinary items which, by implication, are considered safe; a new building is *tapu* until a special ceremony renders it *noa*.

People, animals and artefacts, whether *tapu* or *noa*, possess **mauri** (life force), **wairau** (spirit) and **mana**, a term loosely translated as prestige, but embodying wider concepts of power, influence and charisma. Birthright brings with it a degree of *mana* which can then be augmented through battle or brave deeds, and lost through inaction or defeat. Wartime cannibalism was partly ritual but by eating an enemy's heart a warrior absorbed his *mauri*; likewise personal effects gain *mana* from association with the *mana* of their owner, accruing more as they are passed down to descendants. Any slight on the *mana* of an individual was felt by the whole *hapu*, which must then exact **utu** (a need to balance any action with an equal reaction), a compunction which often led to bloody feuds, sometime escalating to war and further enhancing the *mana* of the victors. Pakeha found this a hard concept to grasp and deeds which they considered deceitful or treacherous could be correct in Maori terms.

The responsibility for determining *tapu* fell to the **tohunga** (priest or expert), the most exalted of many specialists in Maoritanga, who is conversant with tribal history, sacred lore and the *whakapapa*, and considered to be the earthly presence of the power of the gods.

Marae

The rituals of *hapu* life – *hui*, **tangi** (funeral wakes) and **powhiri** (formal welcomes) – are conducted on the **marae**, a kind of combined community, cultural and drop-in centre (and much more), where the cultural values, protocols, customs and vitality of Maoritanga find their fullest expression. Strictly, a *marae* is simply a courtyard, but the term is often applied to the whole complex, comprising the **whare runanga** (meeting house, or *whare nui*), *whare manuhiri* (house for visitors), *whare kai* (eating house) and possibly even an old-fashioned **pataka** (raised storehouse). Marae belonging to one or more *hapu* are found all over the country, though they're concentrated in rural areas where a larger number of Maori live. In recent years, pan-tribal urban *marae* have started up, partly to help wayward Maori youth find their roots but also to cope with the growing awareness of Maoritanga on the part of urban Maori, many of whom have lost their *whakapapa*.

Visitors, whether Maori or Pakeha, may not enter *marae* uninvited, so unless you have Maori friends, you're only likely to visit on a commercially run **tour**. Invited guests are expected to provide some form of **koha** (donation) towards the upkeep of the *marae*, but this is included in tour fees. Remember that the *marae* is sacred and due reverence must be accorded the **kawa** (protocols) governing behaviour. There's no need to feel intimidated, though, as you aren't expected to know *kawa* and will be instructed as to what is required of you.

Following long tradition, **manuhiri** (visitors) approaching the marae are ritually challenged to determine friendly intent. This **wero** might involve a fearsome warrior (often the teenager you see driving away after the show) bearing down on you with twirling **taiaha** (long club), flickering tongue and bulging eyes. The women then make the **karanga** (welcoming call), which is followed by their **powhiri** (sung welcome), which breaks the *tapu* and acts as a prelude to ceremonial touching of noses or **hongi**, binding the *manuhiri* and the *tangata whenua* both physically and spiritually. On commercial trips, the welcoming ceremony is followed by a concert comprising songs, dances and chants, and a **hangi** (a feast cooked in an earth oven).

Arts and crafts

Although the origins of **Maori art** lie in the traditions of eastern Polynesia, over half a millennium of isolated development has resulted in a unique richness and diversity. Eastern Polynesia has no suitable clay, so Maori forebears had already lost the skills of pottery and focused their talents on wood, stone and weaving, occasionally using naturalistic designs but most often the highly **stylized forms** that make Maori art unmistakable.

As with other *taonga* (treasures), many superb examples were taken out of the country by Victorian and later collectors, but there is a determined move on the part of *iwi* and the Department of Maori Affairs to restore as many *taonga* as possible to New Zealand, including over a hundred severed heads which are scattered through museums all over the world.

Wood carving

Maori handiwork finds its greatest expression in **wood carving**, a discipline applied with as much care to a water bailer or ornamental comb as it is to the pinnacles of Maori creativity, *waka* (canoes) and *whare whakairo* (carved houses).

The earliest examples of wood carving feature the sparse, rectilinear styles of ancient eastern Polynesia, but by the fifteenth century these had been replaced by the cursive style still employed by more traditional carvers today. In the Northland forests, kauri wood was used, but in the rest of the country the durable yet easily worked totara was the material of choice. Carvers worked with shells and sharp stones in the earliest times, but the artist's scope increased dramatically with the invention of tools fashioned from **pounamu** (greenstone, a form of jade; see box on p.821), and again with the transition to steel tools. Some would say that the quality of the work declined with the coming of the Europeans: not just through the demand for quickly executed "tourist art", but as a consequence of pressure to remove the phallic imagery that the missionaries considered obscene. As early as 1844, carving had been abandoned altogether in areas with a strong missionary presence, and it continued to decline into the early years of the twentieth century, when Maori pride was at its lowest ebb. By the end of the 1920s the situation had become so lamentable that Maori parliamentarian Apirana Ngata established Rotorua's pan-tribal **Maori Arts and Crafts Institute**, viewed as the foundation on which Maoritanga could be rebuilt, and still the guardian of what is now a much more secure art.

The role of a carver has always been a highly respected one, with seasoned and skilled exponents having the status of *tohunga* and travelling the country both to carve and to teach. The work is a *tapu* activity and *noa* objects must be kept away – cooked food is not allowed near, and carvers have to brush away shavings rather than blow them – though women, previously banned, have now become carvers.

Maori carving exhibits a distinctive **style**, not just in its visual elements but in the approach to the material. Typically, relief forms are determinedly hewn from a single piece of wood with no concession to the natural forms, shapes and blemishes of the material. There is no attempt to represent perspective and while landscapes are represented, they are not actually depicted – figures stand alone. Unadorned wood is rare, carvers creating a stylistic rather than symbolic bed of swirling spirals, curving organic forms based on fern roots or sea shells, and interlocking latticework. Superimposed on this are the key elements, often inlaid with paua shell. The most common is the ancestor figure, the **hei tiki**, a grotesquely distorted, writhing human form, either male, female or of indeterminate gender, often stylized to the point of unrecognizability except for the challenge of a protruding tongue and the threat of a hand-held *mere*. Almost as common are the mythical *manaia*, a beaked birdlike form, often with an almost human profile. Secondary motifs such as the *pakake* (whale) and *moko* (lizard) also occur.

While the same level of craftsmanship was applied to all manner of tools, weapons and ornaments, it reached its most exalted expression in *waka taua* (**war canoes**), sleek and formidable vessels that were the focus of community pride and endeavour. Gunwales, bailers and paddles would all be fabulously decorated, but the most detailed work was reserved for the prow and sternpost, usually a matrix of spirals interwoven with *manaia* figures. As guns and the European presence altered the balance of tribal warfare in the 1860s, the *waka taua* was superseded in importance by the *whare whakairo* (**carved meeting house**). Originally the chief's residence, the *whare* gradually adopted the symbolism of the *waka* – some even incorporated wood from *waka*. Each meeting house could be seen as the tangible manifestation of the *whakapapa*, usually representing a synthesis of the ancestors: the ridge-pole is the backbone; the rafters form the ribs, enclosing the belly of the interior; the gable figure is the head; and the barge boards represent arms, often decorated with finger-like decoration. Inside, all wooden surfaces are carved and the spaces are filled with intricate woven panels known as *tukutuku*.

Greenstone carving

When not using wood, Maori carvers work in **pounamu** (greenstone). In pre-European times complex trade routes developed to supply Maori throughout the land from the sources on the West Coast and in Fiordland; the South Island even became known as Te Wai Pounamu, the Water of Jade. The stone was fashioned into adzes, chisels and clubs for hand-to-hand combat; tools which soon took on a ritual significance and demanded decoration. Pounamu's hardness dictates a more restrained carving style and *mere* and *patu* in particular tend to be only partly worked, leaving large sweeping surfaces ending in a flourish of delicate swirls. Ornamental pieces range from simple drop pendants worn as earrings or neck decoration, to *hei tiki*, worn as a breast pendant and, for women, serving as a fertility charm and talisman for easy childbirth. Like other personal items, especially those worn close to the body, an heirloom *tiki* possesses the *mana* of the ancestors and absorbs the wearer's *mana*, becoming *tapu*.

Tattooing

A stylistic extension of the carver's craft is exhibited in *moko*, an ornamental and ceremonial form of **tattooing** that largely died out with European contact. Women would have *moko* just on the lips and chin, but high-ranking men often had their faces completely covered, along with their buttocks and thighs; the greater the extent and intricacy of the *moko*, the greater the status. A symmetrical pattern of the traditional elements – crescents, spirals, fern-root and other organic forms – were painfully gouged into the flesh with an *uhi* (chisel) and mallet, then soot rubbed into the open wound. In the last decade or so the tradition of full-face *moko* has been revived both as an identification with Maoritanga and as an art form in its own right; since 1999, *moko* artists have been eligible for government funding through the Creative New Zealand organization.

Weaving and clothing

While men were busy carving, the women dedicated themselves to weaving and the production of clothing. When Polynesians first arrived in these cool, damp islands their paper mulberry plants didn't thrive and they were forced to look for alternatives. In time, they found *harakeke* (New Zealand **flax**), which became the foundation of all Maori fibre-work. The strong, pliable fibres were used as fishing lines and cordage for lashing axe-heads onto hafts, and most importantly for protection from the elements and floor matting. With the arrival of the Pakeha, Maori quickly adopted European clothes, but they continued to wear cloaks on formal occasions and these now constitute the basis of contemporary design.

Flax will grow on marshy land all over the country and so the long, spindly leaves were almost always on hand. They were used in something close to their raw form for *raranga* (plaiting) into *kete*, handle-less baskets used for collecting shellfish and kumara, triangular canoe sails, sandals and *whariki*, patterned floor mats still used in meeting houses. For finer work, the flax must be treated by trimming, soaking and beating, a laborious process that produces a wonderfully strong and pliable fibre. Most fibre is used in its natural form, but Maori design requires some **colouring**: black is achieved by soaking in a dilute extract of the bark from a *hinau* tree then rubbing with a black swamp sediment known as *paru*; the red-brown range of colours requires boiling in a dye derived from the bark of the *tanekaha* tree then fixed by rolling in hot ashes; and the less popular yellow tint is produced from the bark of the Coprosma species. Economic necessity and consideration for the tree species concerned have seen the introduction of synthetic dyes, but traditional dyes are still used whenever possible.

Natural and coloured fibres are both used in *whatu kakahu* (**cloak-weaving**), the crowning achievement of Maori women's art, the finest cloaks ranking alongside the most prized *taonga*; the immense war canoe now in the Auckland Museum was once exchanged for a particularly fine cloak. The technique is sometimes referred to as finger-weaving as no loom is used, the women working downwards from a base warp strung between two sticks. Complex weaving techniques are employed to produce a huge array of different textures, often decorated with *taniko* (coloured borders), cord tags tacked onto the cloth at intervals and, most impressive of all, **feathers**. Feather cloaks (*kahu huruhu*) don't appear to have been common before European contact, though heroic tales often feature key players in iridescent garments undoubtedly made from bird feathers. The appeal of the bright yellow feathers of the *huia* probably saw to its demise, and most other brightly coloured birds are now too rare to use for cloaks, so new feather cloaks are very rarely made. Existing examples have become the most prestigious of garments, and you'll come across some fine examples in museums, the base cloth often completely covered by a dense layer of kiwi feathers bordered by zig-zag patterns of tui, native pigeon and even parakeet feathers. More robust *para* (rain capes) were made using the water-repellent leaves of the cabbage tree, and a form of coarse canvas which could reportedly resist spear thrusts was used for *pukupuku* (war cloaks). Some *pukupuku* were turned into *kahu kuri* (dog-skin cloaks) with the addition of strips of dog skin, arranged vertically so that the natural fur colours produced distinctive patterns.

As with other aspects of Maoritanga, weaving and plaiting have seen a resurgence. Cloaks are still an important element of formal occasions, whether on the *marae* for *hui* and *tangi*, or elsewhere for receiving academic or state honours. Old forms are reproduced directly, and also raided as inspiration for contemporary designs, which interpret traditional elements in the light of modern fashion, sometimes incorporating non-traditional colours and designs.

The haka and Maori dance

Opposing rugby teams quiver as the New Zealand All Blacks perform the ferocious, thigh-slapping, foot-stomping, tongue-poking, eye-bulging chant *Ka mate, Ka mate, Ka ora, Ka ora* ("It is death, it is death, It is life, it is life"), from the intimidating Te Rauparaha Haka. This is just the best known of many posture dances (often wrongly referred to as war dances) designed to demonstrate the fitness and prowess of warriors. It was composed by Te Rauparaha himself (see p.249) as he lay in a kumara pit trying to avoid detection by his enemies. Its use by what are often predominantly Pakeha sides might seem inappropriate, but it is so entrenched that there was considerable backlash when in 1996 the All Black coach suggested the *haka* may be changed to mollify southern Maori who were decimated by Te Rauparaha.

At commercial **Maori concerts** (predominantly in Rotorua but also in Christchurch, Queenstown and elsewhere) there will always be some form of *haka*, usually the Te Rauparaha version, which is almost always performed by men. Though women aren't excluded from the *haka*, they normally concentrate on **poi dances**, where balls of *raupo* (bulrush) attached to the end of strings are swung around in rhythmic movements originally designed to improve co-ordination and dexterity.

The drums of eastern Polynesia don't appear to have made it to New Zealand, and both chants and the *haka* go unaccompanied. To the traditional bone flute, Pakeha added the guitar, which now accompanies **waiata** (songs), relatively modern creations whose impact comes as much from the tone and rhythm as from the lyrics (which you probably won't understand anyway). The impassioned delivery can seem at odds with music that's often based on Victorian hymns: perhaps the most well known are *Pokarekare ana* and *Haere Ra*, both post-European contact creations. Outside the tourist concert party, Maori music has developed enormously in recent years to the point where there are tribal and Maori language music stations almost exclusively playing music written and performed by Maori, often rap and hip-hop with a Pacific twist.

Wildlife and the environment

New Zealand is still perceived as a green and pleasant land, as it has been by many thousands of immigrants, first from the Polynesian Islands, then Europe and now the Pacific rim of Asia. Although relatively small it boasts an enormous diversity: unspoiled sub-tropical forest, rich volcanic basins (and volcanoes), mudpools and geysers, intricate and rugged coastline with golden sand beaches and spectacular alpine regions. This diverse landscape supports an extraordinary variety of animals and plant life, with almost ninety percent of the flora not found anywhere else in the world. Thanks to the efforts of a vociferous minority, since the late 1800s, examples of the many habitats, plants and wildlife are still easily accessible, protected within national parks and scenic reserves. For more on green issues, see p.1000.

Beginnings

Land has existed in the vicinity of New Zealand for most of the last 500 million years: the earliest rocks found in the country are thought to have originated in the continental forelands of Australia and Antarctica, part of Gondwanaland, the massive continent to which New Zealand belonged. The oceanic islands were created by continental drift, the movement of the large plates that form the earth's crust, which created a distinct island arc and oceanic trench about 100 million years ago.

Roughly 26 million years ago, the land that makes up New Zealand rose further from the sea, and the landscape you see today was formed by **volcanic** activity and continuous movement along fault lines, particularly the Alpine Fault of the South Island. The essential geology of the two islands is different: the North Island is at the edge of two tectonic plates, where one has slid beneath the other, resulting in prolific volcanic activity; the South Island is the site of two tectonic plates crashing into each other, causing rapid **mountain** building. Today New Zealand experiences about four hundred **earthquakes** every year, roughly a quarter of them strong enough to be noticeable. The volcanoes on the North Island, some still impressively active (the last eruption was Ruapehu in 1996), extend from the Bay of Plenty to the dormant volcanic cone of Mount Taranaki on the West Coast.

Isolated from man and other mammals, New Zealand would have been the perfect place to study the **evolution** of species. It's hardly surprising that so many botanists considered the oceanic islands as laboratories where they could perfect their theories. The country was separated from all other land masses for so long that, uniquely, **birds** occupied the position in the food chain usually held by mammals. Darwinism would suggest that with no predators the birds became fearless, learning to walk amid the dense bush, gradually becoming flightless and growing in size. If allowed to develop unhindered, perhaps they would have evolved into a serious competitor to mammals, but their perfect adaptation to the environment brought their downfall with the arrival of man and other aggressive, fast-moving mammals.

No ground-based mammals colonized the islands until Maori gave rats and dogs passage in their canoes, possibly in about 1000 AD although some theories suggest earlier. Maori were also responsible for hunting the large, flightless **moa** into extinction, and clearing great swathes of **bush** with fire. At that time both islands were almost entirely covered in dense **forest** composed of over a hundred species of tree, the floor carpeted by moss and lichen with a thick tangled undergrowth of **tree fern**, some species over ten metres high. Amongst the trees and ferns were twining creepers, nikau palms and palm lilies, all intermingled and forming an impenetrable bush alive with native birds.

The changes to the land brought by Maori pale in comparison with the incursions of the Europeans. Right from Cook's first exploratory visits, when he brought with him the pig, the sheep and the potato, Europeans tampered with the delicate balance of New Zealand in an attempt to turn it into a "New England". In the early 1800s whalers and sealers bloodied the coastal waters, while logging campaigns cleared vast swathes of native trees, leaving land suitable only for grazing cattle; later, gold prospectors diverted streams and carved chunks out of hillsides. Perhaps the greatest environmental changes were made by immigrant farmers, who had introduced over fifty species of **mammal** to New Zealand by the start of World War I, including rabbits, weasels, mountain goats, cats, dogs, frogs, mice, possums and wallabies. These animals decimated native animal and plant life in the increasing competition for food. Imported plants, such as blackberry, pine and gorse, had just as much effect: allowed to grow wild, they choked and destroyed hundreds of unique plants vital to the ecology of the islands.

The coast, islands and sea

New Zealand's indented coastline, battered by the Tasman Sea and the Pacific Ocean, is a meeting place of warm and cold currents, which makes for an environment suited to an enormous variety of **fish**. Tropical fish species such as barracuda, marlin, sharks and tuna are attracted by the warm currents, locally populated by **hoki**, **kahawai**, **snapper**, **orange roughy** and **trevally**. The cold Antarctic currents bring blue and red **cod**, blue and red **moki**, and fish that can tolerate a considerable range of water temperatures, such as the **tarakihi**, **grouper** and **bass**, all avidly sought after by an army of weekend anglers.

Many people visit New Zealand with the express intention of seeing the sea mammals that grace the waters, and most leave satisfied. The rare **humpback whale** is an occasional visitor to the shores of Kaikoura and Cook Strait, while **sperm whales** are common year round in the deep sea trench near Kaikoura. **Orca** are seen regularly wherever there are dolphins, seals and other whales, namely Banks Peninsula, Kaikoura, Dunedin, Stewart Island, the Marlborough Sounds, Cook Strait, the Bay of Plenty and the Bay of Islands. One frequent visitor is the **pilot whale**: up to 200 pass by Farewell Spit each year and some strand themselves there. Despite the efforts of the locals to refloat them, a few die nearly every year. Pilot whales are also seen in Cook Strait and the Bay of Plenty.

Common dolphins congregate all year round in the Bay of Plenty, Bay of Islands and around the Coromandel Peninsula. Of the three other species seen in New Zealand, **bottlenose dolphins** hang around Kaikoura and Whakatane most of the year, while **dusky dolphins**, the most playful, can be spotted near the shore of the Marlborough Sounds and Kaikoura, from October to May. At any time of year you might get small schools of tiny **Hector's dolphins** accompanying your boat around Banks Peninsula, the Catlins and as far down as Invercargill.

Until recently there were few opportunities to see the Hooker's (now called New Zealand) **sea lion** except on remote Antarctic islands; now these rare animals with their round noses and deep, wet eyes are appearing once more around the Catlins and Otago Peninsula. If you do see them, though, be careful: they bite and can move fast over short distances, so don't go any closer than ten metres and avoid getting between them and the sea. The larger New Zealand **fur seal** is in much greater abundance around the coast, easily spotted basking on rocks or sand and gracefully turning in the waters, their broader, pointy heads popping above the surface. You're most likely to come across them in the Sugar Loaf Marine Reserve, the Northland Coast, the Bay of Plenty, near Kaikoura, the Otago Peninsula and in Abel Tasman National Park. Both seals and sea lions can become aggressive during the breeding season (Dec–Feb), so remember to keep your distance (at least 30m) at these times. If you are lucky enough to visit the Nuggets in the Catlins, you may be rewarded by a sighting of one of the few **elephant seals** still breeding on the New Zealand coast; more extensive colonies exist on the offshore islands.

Also drawn by the fish-rich waters of the coast are a number of visiting and native seabirds, the most famous being the graceful and solitary **royal albatross**, found on the Otago Peninsula, and, just offshore, the smaller **wandering albatross**. A far more common sight are **little blue penguins**, which you're almost guaranteed to see on any boat journey, all year round. The large **yellow-eyed penguin** is confined to parts of the east coast of the South Island, from Christchurch to the Catlins, while the **Fiordland crested penguin** with its thick yellow eyebrows is rarely seen outside Fiordland and Stewart Island. Other common sea birds include **gannets**, their yellow heads and white bodies unmistakable as they dive from great heights into shoals of fish; and **cormorants** and **shags** (mostly grey or black), usually congregating on cliffs and rocky shores. On and around islands you're also likely to see the **sooty shearwater**, **titi** (also known as "mutton birds"), while the **black oystercatchers** and the black and white **variable oystercatchers**, both with orange cigar beaks and stooping gait, can be spotted searching in pairs for food on the foreshore almost everywhere.

The highlands

Thanks to the impact of introduced species on the environment (see p.1000), to really appreciate the picture that greeted first the Maori and then the European immigrants, you need to visit one of New Zealand's many scenic reserves or national parks. In the Tongariro, Whanganui, Taranaki, Nelson Lakes, Arthur's Pass and Mount Cook national parks, all **highland forest** areas, **tawhairauriki** (mountain beech) grow close to the top of the tree line, straight trees up to 20m high, with sharp dark leaves and little red flowers. Also at high altitudes, often in mixed stands, are **tawhai** (silver beech), whose grey trunks grow up to 30m. Slightly lower altitudes are favoured by the other members of the beech family, the black and red varieties. Often mixed in with them is the thin, straggly **manuka** (tea tree), which grows in both Alpine regions and on seashores.

New Zealand has five hundred species of flowering alpine plant that grow nowhere else in the world. Most famous are the large white mountain daisies, **Mount Cook lilies** – the largest in the world, – and a white-flowered yellow-centred member of the buttercup family. Another interesting plant found on the high ground of the South Island is the **vegetable sheep**, a white hairy plant that grows low along the ground and, at a great distance, could just about be mistaken for grazing sheep.

One of the oldest of New Zealand's unique creatures inhabits caves and rock crevices above the snow line: the **weta** (also known as the "Mount Cook flea"), an insect that has changed little in 190 million years. There are several species, the most impressive being the giant weta, which is the heaviest insect in the world, weighing up to 71g and about the size of a small thrush. Weta aren't dangerous, despite their vicious-looking mandibles (they're said to have been the model for Ridley Scott's *Alien*). Though weta also inhabit the bush, they're hard to spot and you're most likely to see them in museums and zoos.

The red-beaked, green **takahe**, a close relative of the more common pukeko, is one of the most famous of the country's flightless birds. Thought to have been extinct until 1948, its survival is currently in the hands of the DOC, who have set up protection programmes in a few highland regions (see p.932). Another highland forest bird to watch out for is the **New Zealand falcon** or bush hawk, seen sometimes in the north of the North Island and more often in the high country of the Southern Alps, Fiordland and the forests of Westland. It has a heavily flecked breast, chestnut thighs and a pointed **head**.

New Zealand boasts the only flightless **parrot** in the world, the green and blue, nocturnal **kakapo**. Once widespread, it's now very rare and predominantly seen in the forests and highlands of Fiordland. You're much more likely to come across the **kea**, regarded as the only truly alpine parrot in the world (see p.691), though its range encompasses both lowland and highland forests. Known for killing sheep (an alleged recently acquired habit), making off with people's possessions and then ripping them apart or eating them, the kea is green with distinctive orange patches on the underside of its wings and a crimson abdomen. Finally, of the smaller birds in the sub-alpine areas, the yellow and green **rock wren** and the **rifleman**, a tiny green and blue bird with spiralling flight, are commonly seen in the high forests of the South Island.

The lowlands

These days the majority of New Zealand is covered by grazing land, grasslands and plains that are dominated by tall and low **tussock**. Fortunately, there remains a great variety of native trees in the **mid- to lowland forests** of Northland, the Coromandel Peninsula, along the west coasts of both islands, around Wellington and on Stewart Island. There are also sixty different endemic native flowering plants in lowland areas, whose blooms mostly range from white to yellow, their relative lack of colour due to the fact that there were no bees to cross-pollinate until the Europeans arrived. Much colour in gardens, parks and mixed forest comes from introduced species such as roses, azaleas and rhododendrons.

New Zealand's best-known tree, the **kauri**, is found in mixed lowland forest, particularly in Northland (see p.225). With a lifespan of two to four thousand years, this magnificent king of the forest rises to thirty metres, two-thirds of its height being straight, branchless trunk. Maori canoe-builders treat the kauri

The kiwi

The kiwi is a member of the ratite family, which includes the ostrich, emu, rhea, cassowary and the long-extinct moa, and if action is not taken soon the kiwi will join the moa on the list of **terminated** animals. A stout muscular bird, shy and nocturnal, it inhabits the forest floor. Sadly there are probably fewer than 15,000 wild birds left in the country and currently the numbers are going down, not up. It sleeps for up to twenty hours a day, which probably explains why it normally lives to the age of 20 or 25. The females are bigger than the males and lay huge eggs, equivalent to around a fifth of their body weight. After eighty days, the eggs hatch and the chicks live off the rich yolk; neither parent feeds them and they emerge from the nest totally independent.

The kiwi is one of the few birds in the world with a well-developed sense of **smell**. At night you might hear them snuffling around in the dark, using the nostrils at the end of their bill to detect earthworms, beetles, cicada larvae, spiders and also koura (freshwater crayfish), berries and the occasional frog. Armed also with sensitive bristles at the base of its bill and a highly developed sense of hearing, the kiwi can detect other birds and animals on its territory and will readily attack them with its claws.

The **Brown Kiwi** (*Apteryx australis*), the largest species, is famous for its big nose, bad temper and for being a tough fighter against intruders on their territory. They live in a wide range of vegetation, including exotic forests and rough farmland on the North Island. In 1993 the **Tokoeka** or **Okarito Brown**, which is almost identical, was identified as a separate species. Inhabiting the South Island and Stewart Island, the southern tokoeka are the most communal of the kiwi family and can be seen poking about along the tideline within a few metres of one another. A subspecies, the **Haast Tokoeka**, are found only in Fiordland.

The **Little Spotted Kiwi** or **Kiwi Pukupuku** (*Apteryx owenii*) is the smallest and rarest of the kiwi, found on only six offshore islands, including Kapiti Island. Predators and land clearance are largely responsible for the low numbers, although a programme to remove predators from the offshore islands has seen their fortunes revive. This species is mellow and docile by nature and pairs often share daytime shelter, going their separate ways to feed, grunting to one another as they pass. Little Spotted Kiwi rarely probe for food, instead finding prey on the ground or in the forest litter. In spring, during courtship, birds stand with bills crossed and pointing downwards while shuffling around each other, grunting, for up to twenty minutes. The best time to hear them is just after dark from high points around an island. Listen carefully for the male's shrill whistle and the female's gentle purr.

The **Great Spotted Kiwi** or **Roa** (*Apteryx haastii*) inhabit regions of snow-covered peaks, herb fields, with rocky outcrops, valleys of red tussock and mountains clothed in beech forest and alpine scrub. Their severe living conditions account for the many legends that surround them. Early European explorers told stories of remote kiwi the size of a turkey with powerful spurs on its legs, whose call was louder than any other of the species. Their harsh home has also helped preserve these big handsome birds, keeping them safe from the pigs, dogs and stoats that have killed so many other kiwi species.

Should you want to help save these symbols of New Zealand you can make a **donation** of $2 direct to the Department of Conservation, Royal Forests and Birds Protection Society and Bank of New Zealand programme.

with great reverence and have always enacted solemn ceremonies before hacking them down for transformation into giant canoes; European shipbuilders coveted the trees for making ocean-going traders and warships. The tree is also the source of the kauri gum, dug from ancient forests and exported in the late nineteenth and early twentieth century.

Open spaces along forest edges and river banks are often alive with tui (see p.997) sucking nectar from golden clusters of **kowhai**, the national flower, which hangs from an eponymous tree whose wood was once fashioned into Maori canoe paddles and adze handles. Another useful tree, the **maire,** stands up to 20m tall and is covered with whitish bark, thick narrow leaves and tiny pink flowers that look like open umbrellas. Its wood is heavy and close-grained, ideal for war clubs, and when burned it gives off very little smoke. Now quite rare, the 30m **matai** was also once used by Maori as a source of timber for canoe prows and by settlers for buildings; it can be identified by a thick, dark grey bark that flakes off.

North of Banks Peninsula and on the North Island grows New Zealand's only native **palm**, the **nikau**, whose slender branchless stem bears shiny leaves of up to 30cm, long pink spiky flowers and red fruit. Early European settlers used to use the berries as pellets in the absence of ammunition.

The **pohutukawa** is an irregularly branched 20m tree found as far south as Otago, seen in forests around the coast and at lake edges. Bearing bright crimson blossoms from November to January, it's often known as "New Zealand's Christmas tree". Another well-known red-blooming tree is the gnarled **rata**, found in quantity in South Island forests and in ones and twos around the North Island. It starts out life as a climber, its windblown seeds establishing it high in other trees, and then its aerial roots gradually take over the host, eventually draining it of life.

One native pine which was heavily milled for its timber and yet is still widespread throughout mixed forests is the majestic **rimu** (red pine), growing to 50–60m with small green flowers, red cones and tiny green or black fruit. Charcoal from rimu used to be mixed with oil and rubbed into tattoo incisions.

A common shade-loving tree found in stands in the forests is the **tawa**, with a long, thin blackish trunk and spear-shaped leaves. The tree produces black berries which, although initially unpleasant, develop a better flavour some time after picking. Also common throughout the country's mixed forests is the **totara**, which usually lives for a thousand years and was often used by Maori to make war canoes. The tree's thick brown bark was also used: it peels in long lengths, suitable for weaving baskets.

The **ti kouka** grows beneath the forest canopy, usually in moist areas and often along the edges of farmland. These 10- to 20m trees with long, thin grey trunks and spear-shaped leaves are also known as "cabbage trees", a reference to the shoots that were eaten by Captain Cook and his men. The tree also produces hundreds of white flowers in spectacular clusters. Below, on the forest floor grow an enormous variety of **ferns**, many of them hard to tell apart. The most famous, adopted as a national emblem, is the **ponga** (silver fern). Reaching about 10m in height, it has long fronds that are dull green on top and silvery white underneath.

Lowland wildlife

Next to the sea, the mid to lowland forests contain the broadest range of **wildlife**. One of the country's oldest inhabitants is the **tuatara**, a lizard-like reptile dating back at least 260 million years, making it, to all intents and purposes, a mini dinosaur. It's nocturnal so you're unlikely to see one in the wild, although they have been reintroduced to many pest-free offshore islands – your best chance of spotting one is in a zoo or kiwi house. Tuatara are about sixty centimetres in length and live for over a hundred years, feeding off insects, small mammals and birds' eggs.

New Zealand's national bird, the flightless **kiwi** (see box on p.995), is also mostly found in the mid to lowland forests. It has been on the endangered list for many years, and these days the only place you're likely to see one in the wild is on Stewart Island; however, they can be seen in specially designed kiwi houses all over the country, such as Otorohanga (see p.251) and Napier (see p.460). Of the other flightless birds in New Zealand the most common is the **weka**, which has four subspecies found in a variety of habitats throughout the country. The North Island bird flourishes in Poverty Bay and has been reintroduced around Auckland and in the forests. The South Island bird is found on the west coast of the South Island and Fiordland; and the bluff weka has thrived on the Chatham Islands and is being reintroduced in Canterbury. The last sub-species is ever present on Stewart Island. The bird is slimmer than the kiwi, and dark brown with marked golden flecks, especially on the heavily streaked breast. Like the kiwi, the weka grubs around at dusk but can be seen regularly during the day: many are bold enough to approach trampers and take titbits from their hands. The bird's whistle is a loud and distinctive "kooo-li".

The **kaka** is a member of the parrot family and closely related to the kea, though it does not venture from its favoured lowland forest environments in Northland, around Nelson, the Marlborough Sounds, the West Coast and Stewart Island. You can recognize the bird by its colour: bronze with a crimson belly and underside of the tail and wings.

When walking among the forests of New Zealand, it is not unusual to hear the cry of the **morepork**, an owl that's named after the distinctive sound of its call. A small brown bird, it sometimes appears in town and city gardens. Alongside the morepork is the distinct musical "mackmacko" of the **bellbird**, a shy green and blue, curve-billed bird. In contrast, the **fantail**, another common forest dweller, is more likely to be seen than heard, constantly opening and closing the tail that gives it its name. Often flying alongside walkers on trails, the bird is not keeping you company but feeding on the insects you disturb.

The **tui**, with its white throat and mostly green and purple velvet-like body, is renowned for mimicking the calls of other birds and the copious consumption of nectar and fruit. Its song has greater range than the bellbird and contains some rather unmusical squeaks, croaks and strangled utterances. Just as noisy is the **saddleback**, a rare but pretty bird, mostly black except for a tan-coloured saddle, whose chattering call welcomes you if you stumble into its patch of the forest. The thrush-sized saddleback belongs to the endemic family of wattle birds, of which the North Island kokako is also a member – see below.

Among the smaller birds regularly glimpsed as they flit around the forest the most distinctive are the **robin** family, which range from black with a cream or yellow breast to all black, depending how on far south you have travelled. They have a prolonged and distinctive song lasting for up to thirty minutes with only brief pauses for breath.

The New Zealand pigeon, the **kereru**, was a favourite Maori food but these days it is prohibited to kill and eat them. It is a very ancient New Zealand species, which seems to have no relatives elsewhere. A handsome large bird with metallic green, purple and bronze colouring and a pure white breast, you'll often see it flashing along in the low-lying forests. Another of New Zealand's oldest birds is the rare **kokako**, an abysmal flyer that lives around the Pureora Forest, Little Barrier Island (see p.259) and Rotorua (see p.311). If you're lucky you'll see it grouchily walking around the forest floor or climbing trees for another crack at flying, or catch a glimpse of its distinctive bright blue wattle.

Rivers, lakes and wetlands

New Zealand is riddled with **rivers**, most of them short and flowing rapidly down to the sea. There are some slower, meandering rivers on the east coast of the South Island, however, which make for a unique environment. The braided rivers in Canterbury and the Waitaki/Mackenzie Basin have distinctive wide shingle beds and multiple channels, providing a breeding ground for many birds, insects, fish and plants. Numerous **lakes** provide rich habitats for fish and birds; many of New Zealand's **wetlands**, on the other hand, have been drained for agriculture and property development, although some areas are preserved as national parks and scenic reserves. It's in low wetland areas that you're likely to come across the tallest of the native trees, the **kahikatea** (white pine), which reaches over 60m. There's a particularly fine stand in the central western North Island close to Te Awamutu.

One bird you're bound to see in the vicinity of a lake is the takahe's closest relative, the **pukeko**, a bird which is still in the process of losing the power of flight. The pukeko is mostly dark and mid-blue with large feet and an orange beak, and lets out a high-pitched screech if disturbed.

New Zealand is renowned for its great fresh-water fishing, with massive brown and rainbow **trout** and **salmon** swarming through the fast-flowing streams. All introduced species, these fish have adapted so well to their conditions that they grow much larger here than elsewhere in the world; as a result, many native species have been driven out. Another delicacy commonly found in New Zealand's waters are native **eels**, much loved by Maori who built complicated eel traps along many rivers.

Keeping the fishermen company along the river banks of the Mackenzie country and Canterbury are **black stilt** or **kaki**, one of the world's rarest wading birds. A thin black bird with round eyes and long red legs, the stilt is incredibly shy – if you do see one in the wild, keep well away. Usually found in swamps and beside riverbeds, the best place to see them is in the specially created reserve near Twizel (see p.714). A slightly more adaptable member of the family is the **common pied stilt**, a black and white bird that has been more successful in resisting the attentions of introduced mammals, particularly feral cats.

Another inhabitant of the Canterbury braided riverbank is the **wrybill**. This small white and grey bird uses its unique bent bill to turn over stones or pull out crustaceans from mud. In winter the species migrates to Auckland and the mudflats of Kaipara, Manukau and the Firth of Thames. The wrybill's close cousin, the **banded dotterel**, favours the sides of rivers, lakes, open land with sparse vegetation and coastal lagoons and beaches. It is a small brown and white bird with a dark or black band around its neck and breeds only in New Zealand, though it does briefly migrate to Australia.

The **blue duck** is one of four endemic species with no close relatives anywhere in the world. Its Maori name, **Whio**, is a near perfect representation of the male bird's call. You can spot it by its blue-grey plumage, with chestnut on both breast and flanks; it also has an unusual bill with a black flexible membrane along each side, and beady yellow eyes. Mountainous areas are where it makes its home, preferring the swift mountain streams and approaching the coast only where the mountains are close to the sea. Unfortunately this is now an endangered species, preyed upon by mammals and forced to compete for food with the salmon and trout in the rivers.

Green issues

The fact that New Zealand is, at least by European standards, apparently both clean and green is more by accident than design, a result of its isolation and relatively short human history. And although many New Zealanders are trying to preserve the country's environment, their efforts are often hampered by a vacillating government and the paramount interests of big business – wildlife has had to pay the price for some short-sighted and flagrant profiteering.

Traditionally meat, wool and dairy products have been New Zealand's main exports, but today a greater proportion is made up of forestry, machinery, aluminium and chemicals, all of which take their toll on the environment in terms of land usage, pollution and energy demands. Today none of the animals or crops and few of the trees harvested are endemic to New Zealand: the countryside is a confusion of native, European and Australian birds, exotic and indigenous trees, and a profusion of plants and animals from each hemisphere. Since human habitation began, forty-three indigenous birds have been consigned to the ranks of the extinct, and New Zealand now accounts for eleven percent of the world's endangered bird species.

Land usage

People came to New Zealand to build a new life in a green land and visitors today arrive with many romantic images in mind. With a population of only 3.6 million, you would expect human interference to be limited but the country is in fact one of the most bizarre ecological disasters in the history of man. **Forest cover** has been reduced from about 85 percent since human colonization, while nearly three-quarters of the land area is given over to the production of food and commercial forestry, the latter essential to the national economy. Most of the trees are quick-growing **radiata pine**, an American species introduced because it is more profitable than any native variety; these days just ten percent of native forest remains.

The increase in demand for forestry- and wet-land goes unabated, even though commercial timber milling turns areas into virtual lunar deserts dotted with tree stumps. A by-product is added air pollution from fume-spitting, eighteen-wheeler logging trucks. And despite a sustained programme to eradicate them, pests like **possums**, wild deer, goats and rabbits pose a serious threat to the country's economic welfare.

Pollution

Influenced by commerce, past governments have favoured some decidedly unfriendly **environmental policies**, although the current Labour coalition is now trying to redress the balance. Despite a record of admirable moral stands, such as banning ships and submarines carrying nuclear warheads from its shores (see p.976), governments have usually managed to disregard environ-

Possums

During 1837–40 the first **Australian brushtail opossums** (*Trichosurus vulpecula*, more commonly known as **possums**) were introduced and liberated in New Zealand by private individuals and Acclimatization Societies wanting to establish a fur industry. Up until 1930 the spread of these nocturnal marsupials was accelerated by further releases, both authorized and illegal, of New Zealand-bred stock.

As early as the 1890s people were advocating control because the potential for damage to orchards and gardens was becoming evident. However, in 1920 a Professor of Botany and Zoology at the then Victoria University College of Wellington released a report supporting the possum, and stating that the harm to native forests was negligible. There followed a series of ineffective regulations until 1947, when heavier penalties for harbouring and liberating opossums were brought into effect and all restrictions on the trapping or killing of possums were cancelled. Finally, in 1951, a control measure was introduced – a bounty was to be paid on all killed possums from which skins had not been taken – a scheme that continued until 1960.

Possums number in excess of 70 million, even pushing sheep into second place, and it is thought that they currently munch their way through 21,000 tonnes of vegetation every day. They are also carriers of bovine TB, an added menace to the dairy, beef and deer industries. They pose a threat to the survival of native bush and to the indigenous fauna that rely on the tree fruits and flowers for food, to say nothing of the eating of eggs and killing of chicks.

Most travellers will encounter possums either when walking the tracks or when driving. Road-kill possum is know colloquially as "road pizza": the relatively cute-looking, furry little creatures engender an almost pathological hatred in even the most mild mannered Kiwis who will swerve all over the road in order to run them over. Many believe a return to the old possum hunter days would provide the best solution to the problem with hunters getting a few dollars for each pelt and creating employment. The Department of Conservation continue with the controversial policy of poisoning which in the past has led to casualties amongst non-targeted bird species. But whatever the solution it is clear that if the possums are allowed to continue unchecked they will turn New Zealand into a barren wasteland.

mental initiatives related to air pollution and industrial emissions – in fact, New Zealand has the second-worst record for CO2 emissions in the OECD. Although it's perceived abroad as a country with enviably clean air, its quality in many cities, if measured, is shocking (check out Christchurch in the winter), and there have been massive increases in asthma and other respiratory problems amongst the young. It is interesting to note that in Auckland over 450,000 cars a day create amounts of **air pollution** that exceed the World Health Organization's recommended safety levels, and that for fifty days of each year Auckland's air pollution is worse than that of London. This is not helped by the fact that New Zealand was the last OECD country to improve its motor vehicles emissions policy and still imports automobiles that would not be allowed off the boat in many other countries. This has even led to a ban on swimming in some of Auckland suburban bays after a couple of days rain, because the high levels of heavy metals deposited in the atmosphere by car pollution reappear in the run-off water that sloshes into storm drains that empty directly into the bays.

And it's not just cars. Greenpeace rates the **industrial pollution** from the

Tasman pulp and paper mill in Kawerau as one of the country's worst problems. The mill is apparently responsible for the largest discharge of toxic organochlorine chemicals in the country and the nearby river has been contaminated by some of the most harmful chemicals known to man – it's known as the "black drain" by the locals. New Zealand also scores badly on **waste disposal** and the monitoring of chemical usage and contaminated sites – with 700 potentially contaminated sites, it is on a par with the USA. Every day more than a billion litres of sewage and industrial waste is discharged into rivers and the sea. Another **poisoning** issue of some import is the use of the chemical 1080 to kill possums, actually banned in every other country in the world. Despite claims to the contrary, it is becoming apparent that the poison is having a more widespread effect than was intended. More and more reports are being brought to the public's attention about the death of farmers' stock and native birds because of 1080, which it would appear is killing the very things it was introduced to preserve.

Further short-sightedness is sadly evident in the use of intensive **farming techniques** and the massive amounts of phosphates piled onto soil that has been heavily exploited this century. Some rivers and lakes, in regions such as the Waikato, are either polluted by high nitrate levels or have few natural features left. The amalgamation of the country's **dairy farmers** under one umbrella, Fontera, has also had a detrimental effect on the environment as increasing amounts of people are drawn to the huge profits dairy farming now seems to offer, resulting in a marked increase in nitrogen run-off into streams, rivers and lakes. This contamination of once crystal-clear water means that it is now not safe to swim or drink water that was once famed for its purity.

Thankfully, there is a strong groundswell of informed opinion leaning towards **organic smallholdings** in tandem with a rising consumer demand for natural, untreated food. The food industry has even introduced a carefully monitored "eco-label", where rigorous standards provide an independent endorsement of the quality of food production. However, more recently, under threat of trade sanctions from the US, the New Zealand government sanctioned trials of GM crops and produce a real missed opportunity to stand alone as a GM-free nation and, in all probability, command higher prices for its all-natural produce.

Energy

New Zealand is about 70 percent energy self-sufficient, but the known reserves of gas and oil are thought to be good for only another twenty to thirty years and coal will also run out sometime in the next century. Demand for energy is currently on the increase, thanks to energy-intensive processes like luminium smelting (near Invercargill) and the Taranaki petrochemical indus-
y, together with a general increase in energy demand of 57 percent, despite
y a 17 percent population rise over the last 25 years.

hough the nation is surrounded by sea water and buffeted by high winds,
forts to exploit **alternative power sources** have been token at best with
ent Palmerston North wind-farm being a notable exception (see p.293).
lectricity is, on the face of it, an environmentally friendly way of cop-
the demands for power from an ever increasing population, but the
f unique environments to create lakes and grand dams has destroyed

numerous natural habitats. Perhaps the most important environments at risk are the riverbanks, where threatened species of birds live, nest and feed.

Preserving the environment

Much of New Zealand is utilized for farming and forestry, and land constantly swallowed up by urban sprawl, so what remains of pre-colonized New Zealand is under increased pressure.

Although not enough was done, as early as the 1880s it was realized that humans were having a detrimental effect on the land and that measures needed to be taken to preserve the environment. Pressure was exerted by the eco warriors of the time to conserve the forest, wetlands and volcanic areas by gazetting them as **national parks**. In this way, native flora and fauna could be preserved, encouraging regeneration and restocking. In 1887 Te Heuheu Tukino IV (Horonuku) set the ball rolling by giving the nucleus of the Tongariro National Park to the nation, in order to preserve the integrity of a venerated tribal area. The newest national parks are Kahurangi, formed in 1996, and Rakiura, which became one in 2002 to ensure the preservation of an areas of great natural beauty at the northwestern tip of the South Island and at the southern most extreme of the South Island.

A further effort to take back land and alleviate pressure on the national parks has seen the creation of small **scenic reserves** or managed areas, zones given over to preserving or regenerating native bush. There are hundreds of them dotted around the country, each concerned with regenerating a particular aspect of the local environment so that it can sustain native fauna. The process requires great vigilance as the stands grow slowly and are constantly under threat from development and introduced animals. It takes at least a hundred years for the bush to grow to maturity.

In another positive step, the Department of Conservation has made efforts to clear pests from **offshore islands**, in order to translocate endangered native species and ensure their survival. The creation of these environmental sanctuaries/havens saves many animals and plants from extinction and provides an opportunity to build up numbers of species on the brink of oblivion. Once the native birds become familiar with their new environment they become less fearful and allow their curiosity full rein, inspecting visitors at close quarters – just as they would have done when Maori first arrived over a thousand years ago.

Books

Kiwis are avid readers, and almost equally keen writers, producing more glossy picture books and wildlife guides than you would think possible. In a climate of growing confidence and with a more honest approach to issues that concern and reflect on New Zealanders lives there have been an increasing number of excellent novels too, despite the tiny home readership and the great difficulty of breaking into the international market.

Almost all of the following titles can be easily found in bookstores. Where two publishers are given, these refer to UK and US publishers respectively; titles that are published only in New Zealand are denoted NZ. Note that Hodder Headline titles are published by Hodder Moa Becket in New Zealand.

Travel and impressions

Mark Lawson *The Battle for Room Service: Journeys to all the Safe Places* (Picador). On the basis that Timaru is rumoured to be the most activity-challenged city in New Zealand, itself the world's most differently interesting place, Lawson selects this modest South Island city as the first port of call, and first chapter, of his wonderfully entertaining world tour of such dull places.

Austin Mitchell *The Half-gallon, Quarter-acre, Pavlova Paradise* (OUP). A humorous and insightful vision of 1960s New Zealand as seen through the eyes of a British Labour MP and self-declared Kiwi commentator. Though wildly out of date, in many ways the lifestyles and values he describes still have the ring of truth, and the book stands as a measure of how much New Zealand has progressed, and at the same time how little.

Paul Theroux *The Happy Isles of Oceania* (Penguin). Another misanthropic diatribe from Mr Theroux, and one which really put Kiwi noses out of joint. This time he kicks off in New Zealand and subsequently rides a clutch of hobby-horses through the Pacific. Some worthwhile observations on trekking in the South Island and a little historical context on the Polynesian migrations go some way towards saving the book.

History, society and politics

James Belich *The New Zealand Wars* (Penguin). An extraordinary, well-researched, and in-depth demolition job on the received version of the course and outcome of the colonial wars, which re-examines the Victorian and Maori interpretation of the conflict. A book for committed historians and those fanatically interested in the subject, since it gives more detail than most people will ever need to know.

Roger Booth *Bruno* (Canterbury University Press, NZ). A no-nonsense biography of Bruno Lawrence, a

New Zealand film star, musician and icon who died of cancer in 1995. The book details his occasionally bizarre life and provides an interesting insight into the New Zealand film and entertainment industry.

Alistair Campbell *Maori Legends* (Viking Sevenseas, NZ). A brief retelling of selected stories in an accessible way with some evocative illustrations.

R.D. Crosby *The Musket Wars* (Reed). An account of the massive upsurge in inter-*iwi* conflict before the start of European colonization, that was exacerbated by the introduction of the musket and led to the death of 23 percent of the Maori population, a proportion far greater than that of Russian casualties in World War II.

Alan Duff *Out of the Mist and Steam* (Tandem Press). Duff, author of *Once Were Warriors* (see p.1007), has comprised a strangely vivid memoir of his life that falls short of autobiography but gives the reader a good idea where all the material for his novels came from.

A.K. Grant *Corridors of Pua* (Hazard Press, NZ). A light-hearted look at the turbulent and fraught political history of the country from 1984 to the introduction of MMP.

Tom Hewnham *By Batons and Barbed Wire* (o/p). A harrowing account of the 1981 Springbok Tour of New Zealand that stirred up more social hatred than any other event and proved conclusively that there is more to New Zealand society than just a bunch of good blokes and "Hail fellow well met".

Hineani Melbourne *Maori Sovereignty: The Maori Perspective* (Hodder Headline); and its companion volume *Maori Sovereignty: The Pakeha Perspective* by Carol Archie (Hodder Headline). Everyone from grass-roots activists to statesmen get a voice in these two volumes, one airing the widely divergent Maori visions of sovereignty, the other covering the equally disparate pakeha view on the subject. They assume a fairly good understanding of Maori structures and recent New Zealand history, but are highly instructive nonetheless.

Claudia Orange *The Story of the Treaty* (Bridget Williams Books, NZ). A concise, illustrated exploration of the history and myths behind what many believe to be the most important document in New Zealand history, the Treaty of Waitangi. Well written but probably more than the casual traveller needs to know. Much the same criticism applies to the author's *The Treaty of Waitangi* (Allen & Unwin, NZ), which covers the lead-up to the signing, and the treaty's first sixty years.

Margaret Orbell *A Concise Encyclopaedia of Maori Myth and Legend* (Canterbury University Press, NZ). A fairly comprehensive rundown on many tales and their backgrounds that rewards perseverance even though it's a little dry.

Jock Phillips *A Man's Country? The Image of the Pakeha Male* (Penguin). Classic treatise on mateship and the Kiwi bloke. This thorough exploration ranges through the formative pioneering years, rugby, wartime camaraderie, the development of the family-man ideal and now Nineties man. It comes to life with the partial dismantling of the stereotype in the light of developments of the last thirty years.

Keith Sinclair *The History of New Zealand* (Penguin). A highly readable general history of New Zealand with comprehensive coverage of the social factors that have shaped the country, as well as the prime movers. Maori oral history gets a brief and informative look-in, and there's plenty on uneasy Maori–pakeha relations, but it's not been updated to take into account recent political changes and the Maori renaissance.

D.C. Starzecka (ed) *Maori Art and Culture* (British Museum Press). A kind of Maori culture primer, with concise and interesting coverage of Maori history, culture, social structure, carving and weaving, spiced up by excellent colour photos of artefacts from the British Museum's collection.

David Wilkie *Year of the Dove* (Quion Press, NZ). The edited diaries of a Kiwi anaesthetist who, after his divorce, volunteered to become a health professional in Vietnam during the war. It is a fascinating view of what happened to the man, how he fell in love and what on earth possessed the NZ government to support this well-documented tragedy.

Ross Wiseman *The Spanish Discovery of New Zealand in 1576* (Discovery Press, NZ). Wiseman puts the case for pre-Abel Tasman European discovery based on wreckage from ships, Spanish-sounding Maori names and a clutch of other circumstantial but convincing evidence.

Fiction

Barbara Anderson *All the Nice Girls* (Vintage, NZ). A short, insightful comedy of manners-cum-romance about a naval officer's wife who goes off the rails in 1960s Auckland, by a writer known for her clarity and vibrancy.

Anonymous *The Spin* (Hodder Headline). Allegedly written by a government insider, hence the anonymity. Though Kiwis were shocked at the antics of barely disguised current politicians, it's all pretty tame by world standards, and only mildly revealing about the behaviour of elected representatives behind closed doors.

Graeme Aitken *Fifty Ways of Saying Fabulous* (Headline). An extremely funny book about burgeoning homosexuality in a young farm boy, who lives in a world where he is expected to clean up muck and play rugby. Brilliant and touching, but it loses its way in the final third and serves up an anticlimactic ending.

Eric Beardsley *Blackball 08* (Collins, NZ). Entertaining and fairly accurate historical novel set in the West Coast coal-mining town of Blackball during New Zealand's longest ever labour dispute.

Graham Billing *Forbrush and the Penguins* (Oxford University Press, NZ). Described as the first serious novel to come out of Antarctica, it is the compelling description of one man's lonely vigil over a colony of penguins and the relationship he develops with them. Well worth the effort.

Samuel Butler *Erewhon* (Penguin). Gulliver's Travels-style journey to a utopian land, initially set in the Canterbury high country (where Butler ran a sheep station) but increasingly devoted to a satirical critique of mid-Victorian Britain.

Catherine Chigey *In a Fishbone Church* (Victoria University Press, NZ). A high-minded, broad-ranging novel spanning physical borders and time, learning about the past and dealing with it, maybe, by focusing on one family.

Ian Cross *The God Boy* (Penguin). This first and only novel of note from Ian Cross is widely considered to be New Zealand's equivalent to *Catcher in The Rye*. It concerns a young boy trapped between two parents who hate each other and describes the violent consequences of this situation.

Barry Crump *A Good Keen Man*; *Hang on a Minute Mate*; *Bastards I Have Met*; *Forty Yarns and a Song* (Hodder Headline). Just a few of the many New Zealand bushman books by the Kiwi equivalent of Banjo Patterson, who writes with great humour, tenderness and style about the male-dominated world of hunting, shooting, fishing, drinking, and telling tall stories. Worth reading for a picture of a New Zealand and a lifestyle that have now largely disappeared.

Sigrid Crump *Bushwoman* (Reed Books, NZ). Light, fresh and highly evocative account of a young German woman's solo travels on foot in New Zealand's backcountry during the 1960s and 70s. Infusing each page with her deep love of the Kiwi bush and fiercely independent spirit, Barry Crump's sister-in-law leaves you full of admiration.

Alan Duff *Once Were Warriors* (Virago/Random House). A shocking and violent book in the social realism, kitchen-sink drama style, set in 1970s south Auckland and adapted in the 1990s for Lee Tamahori's film of the same name. At its heart are good intentions concerning the predicament of urban Maori, but at times this is a clumsy book with an oddly upbeat ending. Duff has also published a sequel, *What Becomes of the Broken Hearted* (Virago/Random House), which lacks the conviction, immediacy and passion of the first novel.

Denis Edwards *Connor is Free* (Penguin). A pretty run-of-the-mill thriller, but it will divert you during long bus, train or plane journeys.

Fiona Farrell *Six Clever Girls Who Became Famous Women* (Penguin). A second novel of some quality and style has the girls of the title reunited in mid-life to confront what they have achieved and come to terms with their present and the possibilities of the future.

Janet Frame *An Angel at My Table* (Random House). Though undoubtedly one of New Zealand's most accomplished novelists, Frame is perhaps best known for this three-volume autobiography, dramatized in Jane Campion's film which, with wit and a self-effacing honesty, gives a wonderful insight into both the author and her environment. Her superb novels and short stories use humour alongside highly disturbing combinations of events and characters to overthrow readers' preconceptions. For starters, try *Faces in the Water*, *Living in the Maniototo*, *Scented Gardens for the Blind*, *Daughter Buffalo* and *Owls Do Cry* (all The Women's Press).

Maurice Gee *Crime Story*; *Going West; Prowlers*, *The Plumb Trilogy* (Penguin). These from an underrated but highly talented writer. Despite the misleadingly light titles, Gee's focus is social realism, taking an unflinching, powerful look at motivation and unravelling relationships.

Patricia Grace *Potiki* (Penguin). Poignant and poetic tale of a Maori community redefining itself through a blend of traditional and modern values, while its land is threatened by coastal development. Exquisite writing by an outstanding author who ranks among the finest in New Zealand today. She has also written several other novels and short-story collections.

Patricia Grace *Baby No Eyes* (Penguin). A magical weaving of actual, controversial events with stories of family history told from four points of view, where a deceased baby becomes a living character acting as the eyes of a stranger to further increase the reader's understanding of Maori ways and traditions.

Patricia Grace *Dogside Story* (Talanoa, NZ). Short-listed for the 2001 Booker Prize, this is a wonderful story concerning the power of the land and the power of *whanau* at the turn of the Millennium.

Peter Hawes *Leapfrog with Unicorns* (Vintage Press, NZ) and *Tasman's Lay* (Hazard Press, NZ). Two from the unsung hero, cult figure and probably only member of the absurdist movement in New Zealand, who writes with great energy, wit and surprising discipline about almost anything that takes his fancy. It's not much of a secret that Peter is also W.P. Hearst who has written the not-to-be-missed *Inca Girls Aren't Easy* (Vintage), a series of joyous, sad and slippery tales.

Stuart Hoar *The Hard Light* (Penguin). A black novel that begins in Dunedin and travels to Europe in Word War II. The characters are uniformly self-destructive, the conclusions bleak and yet it is strangely compelling with just a wisp of hope in the last few sentences.

Keri Hulme *The Bone People* (Picador). Celebrated winner of the 1985 Booker Prize, and a wonderful first novel set along the wild beaches of the South Island's West Coast. Mysticism, myth and earthy reality are transformed into a haunting tale peopled with richly drawn characters.

Witi Ihimaera *Bulibasha – King of the Gypsies* (Penguin). The best introduction to one of the country's finest Maori authors. A rollicking good read, energetically exploring the life of a rebellious teenager in 1950s rural New Zealand, where two mighty sheep-shearing families are locked in battle. It's an intense look at adolescence, cultural choices, family ties and the abuse of power, culminating in a masterful twist. Look out also for the excellent *The Matriarch* (Penguin) and *The Uncle Story* (Talanoa, NZ) by the same author.

Phil Kawana *Dead Jazz Guys* (Huia Publishers, NZ). A relatively new kid on the block, writing short stories about the young urban Maori, family, drugs and sex. Poignant and intelligent writing in a collection of mixed quality.

Fiona Kidman *The Book of Secrets* (Picador). Historical novel tracing one family's heritage through the reclusive granddaughter of a Scot who left the highlands with commanding preacher Norman McLeod, eventually ending up in Northland's Waipu.

Elizabeth Knox *The Vintner's Luck* (Victoria University Press). A very curious book indeed that for no great reason became an international best seller, all about "a man, his vineyard, love, wine and angels."

Shonagh Koea *The Grandiflora Tree* (Penguin). A savagely witty yet deeply moving study of the conventions of widowhood, with a peculiar love story thrown in. First novel from a journalist and short-story writer renowned for her astringent humour.

Deborah Nourse Lattimore *Punga: The Goddess of Ugly* (School and Library Binding, NZ). A pacey, lively and beautifully illustrated story, telling of two sisters trying to learn the beautiful *haka*, which incorporates Maori legend from an outsider's point of view.

Katherine Mansfield *The Collected Stories of Katherine Mansfield* (Penguin). All 73 short stories sit alongside 15 unfinished fragments in this 780-page tome. Concise yet penetrating examinations of human behaviour in apparently trivial situations, often transmitting a painfully pessimistic view of the world, and startlingly modern for their time.

Ngaio Marsh *Opening Night*; *Artists in Crime*; *Vintage Murder* (Fontana). Just a selection from the doyenne of New Zealand crime fiction. Since 1934 she has been airing her anglophile sensibilities and killing off innumerable individuals in the name of entertainment, before solving the crimes with Inspector Allen. Perfect mindless reading matter for planes, trains and buses. A recently published collection of five of her novels within one cover is sufficient to exemplify her talents and keep you occupied on a half-way-round-the-world journey.

Ronald Hugh Morrieson *Came a Hot Friday* (OUP). Superb account of the idiosyncrasies of country folk and the two smart spielers who enter their lives, in a comedy thriller focusing on crime and sex in a small country town.

John Mulgan *Man Alone* (Penguin). Seminal and soberly written boy's-own novel about one man's restless and peripatetic times working the New Zealand back blocks between the wars, as the country lurched from its pioneering days into the modern world. First published in 1939, it is often regarded as one of the first truly Kiwi novels and had a huge influence on New Zealand writing, its evocation of the Kiwi male quickly becoming an archetype.

Vincent O'Sullivan *Let the River Stand* (Penguin). Deftly conjuring the minutiae of homestead and rural school life in a Waikato farming community of the 1930s, Sullivan weaves disparate tales around the life of his gawky anti-hero, Alex. Tragic, humorous and captivating. *Believers to the Bright Coast* (Penguin) is O'Sullivan's disappointing follow-up and little more than an impenetrable confusion repeating the themes and obsessions of the first.

Emily Perkins *Not Her Real Name* (Picador). Sub-Mansfield short-story writer who inexplicably picked up an award for this. Though lacking the subtlety and incisiveness of the master, this uneven collection shows some promise. Sadly, however, this promise subsequently failed to materialize in her first novel, *Leave Before You Go* (Picador).

Frank Sargeson *The Stories of Frank Sargeson* (Penguin). Though not well-known outside New Zealand, Sargeson is a giant of Kiwi literature. His writing, from the 1930s to the 1980s, is incisive and sharply observed, at its best in dialogue, which is always true to the metre of New Zealand speech. This work brings together some of his finest short stories. *Once is Enough, More than Enough* and *Never Enough!* (all Penguin) make up the complete autobiography of a man sometimes even more colourful than his characters; Michael King has written a fine biography, *Frank Sargeson: A Life* (Viking).

Maurice Shadbolt *Strangers and Journeys* (Hodder/Atheneum). On publication in 1972 this became a defining novel in New Zealand's literary ascendancy and its sense of nationhood, putting Shadbolt in the same league as Australia's Patrick White. A tale of two families of finely wrought characters, whose lives interweave through three generations. Very New Zealand, very human and not overly epic. Later works, which have consolidated Shadbolt's reputation, include *Mondays Warriors, Season of the Jew* and *The House of Strife* (Hodder/Atheneum).

C.K. Stead *The Singing Whakapapa* (Penguin). Highly regarded author of many books and critical essays who is sadly little known outside New Zealand and Australia. A combination of a powerful historical novel about an early missionary and a dissatisfied modern descendant who is searching for meaning in his own life by exploring the past. An excellent and engaging read. His 1998 collection of short stories, *The Blonde with Candles in her Hair*, was less critically acclaimed, but still entertaining and readable.

Paul Thomas *Old School Tie* (Hodder Headline). Smart thriller with some neat comedic touches but a bit clichéd, just like his last book, *Inside Dope* (Hodder Headline), and lacking any really sympathetic characters. Another relaxing read, ideal while waiting for a bus.

Damien Wilkins *The Miserables* (Faber). One of the best novels to come out of New Zealand, shorn of much of the colonial baggage of many writers. It is surprisingly mature for a first novel, sharply evoking middle-class New Zealand life from the 1960s to the 1980s through finely wrought characters.

Anthologies

Fergus Barrowman (ed) *The Picador Book of Contemporary New Zealand Fiction* (Picador). A good combination of extracts and short stories from most of the best living writers in the country.

Warwick Brown *100 New Zealand Paintings* (Godwit Publishing, NZ). As the title suggests, with some excellent reproductions and a good bit of information.

Warwick Brown *100 New Zealand Artists* (Godwit Publishing, NZ). The companion to the above but also allowing room for sculptors, printmakers, photographers and graphic artists.

James Burns (ed) *Novels and Novelists 1861–1979, a Bibliography* (Textbook Binding, NZ). A sweeping and comprehensive introduction to the history of the New Zealand novel and the characters who have made it such a powerful art form.

Bill Manhire (ed) *100 New Zealand Poems* (Godwit Publishing, NZ). A very manageable selection of Kiwi verse which provides an excellent introduction to the poetry of the nation.

C.K. Stead (ed) *Contemporary South Pacific Stories* (Faber and Faber). A great collection from authors as diverse as European Kiwi, Maori, Fijian-Indian, Samoan, Tongan and Cook Islanders, with a brilliant introduction.

Hone Tinwhare (trans Frank Stewart) *Deep River Talk: Collected Poems* (Talanoa, NZ). Tinwhare is a respected and established Maori poet with a bawdy sense of humour which is reflected in the collected old and new poems, showcased in this anthology.

Ian Wedde and Harvey McQueen (eds) *The Penguin Book of New Zealand Verse* (Penguin). A comprehensive collection of verse from the earliest European settlers to contemporary poets, and an excellent introduction to Kiwi poetry; highlights are works by James K. Baxter, Janet Frame, C.K. Stead, Sam Hunt, Keri Hulme, Hirini Melbourne and Apirana Taylor.

Reference and specialist guides

Rosemary George *The Wines of New Zealand* (Faber and Faber). Entertaining and informative look at New Zealand's most important wine regions, the history, the people and the product.

Les Hill & Graeme Marshall *Images of Silver* (The Halcyon Press, NZ). Inspirational fishing picture book with great shots of anglers in action all over the country.

John Kent *North Island Trout Fishing Guide* and *South Island Trout Fishing Guide* (Reed, NZ). Laden with information on access, seasons and fishing style, and illustrated with maps of the more important rivers.

Terry Sturm (ed) *The Oxford History of New Zealand Literature* (Oxford University Press). A massive and comprehensive guide to non-fiction, novels, plays and poems by a variety of academics, which is fascinating for anyone with an academic interest in the subject but otherwise as dry as an old stick.

Vic Williams *The Penguin New Zealand Wine Guide* 2001–2002 (Penguin). A comprehensive breakdown of over 1200 wines from the land of the long white cloud that will keep you interested and turn you into a big fan, if you are not already.

Flora, fauna and the environment

D.H. Brathwaite *Native Birds of New Zealand* (Caxton Press, NZ). Brilliant colour photographs and lots of information pinpointing thirty rare birds that, with a little effort and some patience, you can observe while travelling around.

Andrew Crowe *Which Native Tree?* (Viking Pacific, NZ). Great little book, ideal for identification of New Zealand's common native trees – though not tree ferns – with diagrams of tree shape, photos of leaves and fruit, and an idea of geographic extent.

John Dawson *New Zealand Coast and Mountain Plants* (Victoria University Press, NZ). A luxuriant book filled with colourful and unusual illustrations.

Susanne & John Hill *Richard Henry of Resolution Island* (John McIndoe, NZ). Comprehensive and very readable account of a man widely regarded as New Zealand's first conservationist. The book serves as a potted history of this underpopulated area of Fiordland, peopled by many of the key explorers.

Geoff Moon *The Reed Field Guide to New Zealand Birds* (Reed, NZ). Excellent colour reference book, with ample detail for species identification.

Geoff Moon *The Reed Field Guide to New Zealand Wildlife* (Reed, NZ). Separate chapters, stuffed with colour photos, cover forest, open country, the coast and offshore islands, but facts are too thin on the ground for it to succeed as a reference work.

Rod Morris & Hal Smith *Wild South: Saving New Zealand's Endangered Birds* (Century Huchinson/TVNZ). A fascinating companion volume to a 1980s TV series following a band of dedicated individuals trying to preserve a dozen of New Zealand's wonderfully exotic bird species, including the kiwi, kakapo, takahe and kea.

Murdoch Riley *New Zealand Trees and Ferns* (Viking Sevenseas, NZ). An excellent, pocket-size guide with colour illustrations identifying the most-often-seen trees and ferns.

Neville Peat *Manapouri Saved* (Longacre Press, NZ). Full and heartening coverage of one of New Zealand's earliest environmental battles when, in the 1960s, a petition signed by ten percent of the country succeeded in persuading the government to cancel its hydroelectric plans for Lake Manapouri.

Tramping

Moir's Guide (NZ Alpine Club, NZ). Probably the most comprehensive guide to tramping in the South Island. It is divided into two volumes: North, covering hikes between Lake Ohau and Lake Wakatipu; and South, which concentrates on walks around the southern lakes and fjords including the Kepler Tracks, plus the less popular Dusky and George Sound tracks.

Pearl Hewson *New Zealand's Great Walks* (Hodder Headline). Pearl is a no-nonsense DOC officer working out of the Wellington Office and what she doesn't know about the Great Walks isn't worth knowing. This is a practical, concise guide which concentrates her experiences into a useful aid to trampers.

Mark Pickering *Wild Walks* (Shoal Bay Press, NZ). Sixty short and easily accessible walks on the North Island, mixed in with historical anecdotes and precise descriptions of the local environment.

Philip Temple *BP Pocket Tramping Guides* (BP). A series of inexpensive, lightweight paperback guides giving handy and informative track notes, with information on the history, flora and fauna, for the major New Zealand tramps. Titles cover the Routeburn, Milford, Copland, Hollyford and Abel Tasman tracks.

Cycling and adventure sports

Mike Bhana *New Zealand Surfing Guide* (Reed, NZ). Pragmatic handbook to the numerous prime surf spots around the New Zealand coast, with details on access, transport, the best wind and tide conditions and expected swells.

Graham Charles *New Zealand Whitewater: 120 Great Kayaking Runs* (Craig Potton, NZ). An indispensable, comprehensive and entertaining guide to New Zealand's most important kayaking rivers. River maps and details on access are supplemented by quick reference panels with grades, timings, and handy tips like which rapids not to even think about running.

Bruce Ringer *New Zealand by Bike* (The Mountaineers, NZ). The definitive Kiwi cycle touring guide with 14 regional tours (with many side-trips) which can all be knitted together into a greater whole. Plenty of maps and altitude profile diagrams.

Marty Sharp *A Guide to the Ski Areas on New Zealand* (Random House). Exactly what you'd expect, with full descriptions of the fields complete with tow plans and information on access, local towns and ski rental.

Ken Sibly and Mark Wilson *4 Wheel-drive South Island* (Shoal Bay Press, NZ). A book for adventurous drivers who know how to use their off-road vehicles, covering seventy public, but treacherous, roads.

Paul Simon and Jonathan Kennett *Classic New Zealand Mountain Bike Rides* (Kennett Bros, NZ). All you need to know about off-road biking in New Zealand with details of over four hundred rides. Paul Simon runs the www.mountainbike.co.nz site.

Film

In the wake of *Lord of the Rings* films, all shot in New Zealand at the same time, the Kiwi film industry has enjoyed another of its intermittent revivals, previously most notable during the relatively short period of time in 1988–1994 when *The Navigator*, *An Angel at my Table*, *The Piano*, *Once Were Warriors* and *Heavenly Creatures* all gained international recognition and success. Yet while each of the directors involved went on to greater successes, usually in Hollywood, along with one or two of the actors, the renaissance in New Zealand itself effectively then faded away like a closing shot. In fact, New Zealand was primarily used as a relatively inexpensive back-drop for American TV series like *Hercules* and *Xena Warrior Princess* and for movies that needed the big outdoors. As a result the local film industry, with a few notable exceptions, was known only for technical back-up and providing a few extras.

In many ways this role hasn't changed all that significantly since Peter Jackson brought *Lord of the Rings* to New Zealand, despite the production company using 150 locations in 40 different areas, local technical expertise, a local special effects company and a number of Kiwi actors, though none in major roles. But it is to be hoped that the interest generated in New Zealand as a country will engender an enthusiasm for its home-grown cinema, just as *The Navigator* did back in 1988, leading to another flourishing of this small, highly individual film industry.

Recommended films

An Angel at my Table Jane Campion, 1990. Winner of the Special Jury prize at the Venice Film Festival. One of the most inspiring events in New Zealand film, based on the brilliant autobiographies of Janet Frame (see "Books", p.1007).

Bad Blood Mike Newell, 1981. A New Zealand/British collaboration set in New Zealand in World War II that relates the true story of Stan Graham, a Hokitika man who breaks the law by refusing to hand in his rifle and kills several policemen subsequently sent to arrest him. The tension builds subtly, although the message is morally ambivalent with the anti-hero (a Kiwi cowboy) hunted down by the police and the army, a fact discussed in a bar room scene giving voice to farmers' vision of the Kiwi spirit. It takes the whole German army to tie up hundreds of British troops in the war but it only takes one New Zealander.

Bad Taste Peter Jackson, 1988. Winner of the special jury prize at the Paris Film Festival. Aliens visit earth to pick up flesh for an intergalactic fast-food chain and have a wild old time. A witty and irreverent spoof that derides many of the alien-to-earth films that take themselves too seriously.

Broken English Gregor Nicholas 1996. A tough, uncompromising movie about Croatian immigrants and the relationship between a young Croatian girl and a Maori, with excellent performances and a powerful message about discrimination.

Came a Hot Friday Ian Mune, 1984. Rightly regarded as the best comedy ever to come out of New Zealand, concentrating on two incompetent confidence tricksters whose luck runs out in a sleepy country town.

Crush Alison Maclean, 1992. A competitor at Cannes. An offbeat, angst-ridden psychological drama set around Rotorua, where the boiling mud and gushing geysers underline the manipulative tensions and sexual chaos that arise when an American femme fatale enters the lives of a New Zealand family.

Desperate Remedies Peter Wells and Stewart Main, 1993. An acclaimed winner of the Certain Regard Award at Cannes that comments wryly on the intrigues and desires of a group of different people whose lives all somehow interconnect.

Flying Fox in a Freedom Tree Martyn Sandersson, 1989. Winner of the best screenplay award at Tokyo. A moving film about a young Samoan who rejects the old ways and his father who is obsessed with money and success.

The Frighteners Peter Jackson 1996. New Zealand-filmed and directed, but Hollywood-financed, this special-effects extravaganza stars Michael J Fox as a psychic investigator involved in a series of mysterious deaths in a small town. It seems to contain all the Jackson ingredients but somehow fails to satisfy.

Goodbye Pork Pie Geoff Murphy, 1980. A much loved and underrated comedy/road movie following the adventures of two young men in a yellow mini, the cops they infuriate, and the mixed bag of characters they encounter.

Heavenly Creatures Peter Jackson, 1994. Winner of the Silver Lion at Venice and an Oscar Academy-Award nominee for best original film script. An account of the horrific Parker/Hulme matricide in the 1950s that follows the increasingly self-obsessed passion, friendship and secrets of two adolescent girls. An evocative and explosive film that brings all Jackson's subversive humour to bear on the strait-laced real world and, best of all, the girls' fantastic imaginary one. Kate Winslet's film debut.

The Navigator Vincent Ward, 1988. A well-received competitor at Cannes, this atmospheric and stylistically inventive venture employs all Ward's favourite themes and characters, including the innocent visionary, in this case a boy who leads five men through time from a fourteenth-century Cumbrian village to New Zealand in the twentieth century in a quest to save their homes.

Once were Warriors Lee Tamahori, 1994. A surging fly-on-the-wall style comment on the economically challenged Maori situation in modern south Auckland, bringing to mind kitchen-sink dramas of the 1950s and 1960s. More a study of class than a full-blown racial statement, it revels in the ordinary drudgery that creates despair, with a warts-and-all story about human weakness and strength of spirit against a background of urban decay. A true reflection of part of New Zealand life, giving expression to many of the conflicts and fears that rest beneath the surface of wider society. Based on the novel by Alan Duff (see "Books", p.1007).

Patu Merata Mita, 1983. A powerful documentary recording the year of opposition to the 1981 Springbok rugby team tour of New Zealand, which goes some way to showing just what extraordinary passions were ignited by the event.

The Piano Jane Campion, 1993. With Holly Hunter (Oscar winner), Harvey Keitel, Sam Neill and Anna Paquin (another Oscar winner) as the young girl, this is the film that made Campion bankable in Hollywood consolidation, a moody evocative winner of the Palme d'Or, Cannes. With a mixture of grand scenes and personal trauma it knowingly synthesizes paper-back romance, erotica and Victorian melodrama – and includes Keitel's apparent attempt at the worst Scottish accent of all time.

Rain Christine Jeffs, 2002. An evocative, dark portrayal of lazy summer beach holidays that grows more complicated when a young girl decides to compete for a man with her unhappily married mother.

Scarfies Robert Sarkies, 2000. Surprise hit of the year in NZ and art houses worldwide, a darkly funny story about students taking over a deserted house in Dunedin only to discover a massive dope crop in the basement. Things get progressively more unpleasant when the dope grower returns.

Sleeping Dogs Roger Donaldson, 1977. Perhaps the birth of the real New Zealand film industry based on C.K. Stead's book *Smith's Dream*. Sam Neill plays a paranoid anti-hero hunted by the repressive forces of the state for being a nonconformist. Although a slick thriller, the film struggles to get beyond its fast-paced rush to its violent conclusion.

Smash Palace Roger Donaldson, 1981. Like *Sleeping Dogs*, this is another Kiwi man-alone, in this case a dissection of a marriage break-up and custody chase that follows a racing driver attempting to get his child back at any price. A serious film with touches of humour, it suffers from being slick and a little too like *Kramer Versus Kramer* on speed (or in *Speed*).

Stickmen Hamish Rothwell, 2001. A softer version of the Brit-flick *Lock, Stock and Two Smoking Barrels*, owing it much in terms of style but concentrating on the pool rooms of New Zealand for its action.

The Ugly Scott Reynold, 1996. Shown at the 1997 Cannes Film Festival, and winning rave reviews in the US, this movie revolves around a serial killer who has been locked away and wants to convince the world he is cured. An edgy comment on incarceration, reform and mistrust.

Utu Geoff Murphy, 1983. One of the official selections at Cannes, this portrays a Maori warrior in the late 1800s setting out to revenge himself on the conquerors of New Zealand, in the form of a Pakeha farmer. A tense, well-acted representation of many modern as well as historic issues.

Vigil Vincent Ward, 1984. A Cannes competitor, this dark, rain-soaked story portrays a young girl's coming of age and her negative reaction to a stranger who is trying to seduce her mother, adding to tension of her own sexual awakening.

Whakataratara Paneke Don C. Selwyn, 2001. The Maori *Merchant of Venice*, with English subtitles, an ambitious home-grown film that brings much local acting talent to the screen in an involved, if overly long, epic.

Language

language

Language

English and te reo Maori, the Maori language, share joint status as New Zealand's official languages, but on a day-to-day basis all you'll need is English, or its colourful Kiwi variant. All Maori speak English fluently, often slipping in numerous Maori terms that in time become part of everyday Kiwi parlance. You may find television, radio and newspaper articles – especially those relating to Maori affairs – initially confusing without a basic grounding, but with the aid of our glossary (see p.1022) you'll soon find yourself using Maori terms all the time.

A basic knowledge of Maori pronunciation will make you more comprehensible and some understanding of the roots of place names can be helpful. You'll need to become something of an expert, though, to appreciate much of the wonderful oral history, and stories told through waiata (songs), but learning a few key terms will enhance any Maori cultural events you may attend.

To many Brits and North Americans, **Kiwi English** is barely distinguishable from its trans-Tasman cousin, "Strine", sharing much of the same lexicon of slang terms, but with an accent marginally closer in tone to South African English. Australians have no trouble distinguishing the two accents, repeatedly highlighting the vowel shift which turns "bat" into "bet", makes "yes" sound like "yis" and causes "fish" come out as "fush". This vowel contortion is carried to new levels in remoter country areas, but there is really very little regional variation, only Otago and Southland – the southern quarter of the South Island – distinguishing themselves with a rolled "r", courtesy of their predominantly Scottish founders. Throughout the land, Kiwis add an upward inflection to statements, making them sound like questions; most are not, and to highlight those that are, some add the interrogative "eh?" to the end of the sentence, a trait most evident in the North Island, especially among Maori.

Maori

For the 50,000 native speakers and 100,000 who speak it as a second tongue, **Maori** is very much a living language, gaining strength all the time as both Maori and Pakeha increasingly appreciate the cultural value of te reo, a language central to Maoritanga and forming the basis of a huge body of magnificent songs, chants and legends, lent a poetic quality by its hypnotic and lilting rhythms.

Maori is a member of the Polynesian group of languages and shares both grammar and vocabulary with those spoken throughout most of the South Pacific. Similarities are so pronounced that Tupaia, a Tahitian crew member on Captain Cook's first Pacific voyage in 1769, was able to communicate freely with the Aotearoa Maori they encountered. The Treaty of Waitangi was written in both English and Maori, but te reo soon began to lose ground to the point where, by the late nineteenth century, its use was proscribed in schools. Maori parents keen for their offspring to do well in the Pakeha world frequently promoted the use of English, and Maori declined further, exacerbated by the mid-twentieth-century migration to the cities. Though never on the brink of extinction, the language reached its nadir in the 1970s when perhaps only ten percent of Maori could speak their language fluently. The tide began to turn towards the end of the decade with the inception of kohanga reo **pre-schools** (literally "language nests") where Maoritanga is taught and activities are conducted in Maori. Originally a Maori initiative, it has now crossed over and progressive Pakeha parents are increasingly introducing their kids to biculturalism at an early age. Fortunate kohanga reo graduates can progress to the small number of state-funded Maori-language primary schools known as kura kaupapa. For decades, Maori has been taught as an option in secondary schools, and there are now state-funded tertiary institutions operated by Maori, offering graduate programmes in Maori studies.

The success of these programmes has bred a young generation of Maori speakers frequently far more fluent than their parents who, shamed by the loss of their heritage, are beginning to attend Maori evening classes. Legal parity means that Maori is now finding its way into officialdom too, with government departments all adopting Maori names in recent years and many government and council documents being printed in both languages. The increasing knowledge and awareness has spawned Maori TV and radio broadcasts. With the backing of the Labour government, a new nationwide Maori TV channel started broadcasting in 2002.

In your day-to-day dealings you won't need **to speak Maori**, though both native speakers and Pakeha may well greet you with kia ora (hi, hello), or less commonly haere mai (welcome). On ceremonial occasions, such as *marae* visits, you'll hear the more formal greeting tena koe (said to one person) or tena koutou katoa (to a group).

Maori words used in place names are listed below, while those in common use are listed in the general glossary (see p.1022). If you are interested in learning a little more, the best handy reference is Patricia Tauroa's The Collins Maori Phrase Book (HarperCollins) which has helpful notes on pronunciation, handy phrases and a useful Maori–English and English–Maori vocabulary.

Maori place names

The following is a list of some of the most common words and elements you will see in **town and place names** throughout New Zealand. A.W. Reed's A Dictionary of Maori Place Names (Reed) gives more detailed coverage of the same field.

Cloud - **Ao**
Road or path - **Ara**
River or valley - **Awa**
Wind - **Hau**
Fish - **Ika**
Small - **Iti**
Food, or eat - **Kai**
Home, village - **Kainga**
Rippling - **Kare**
Bad - **Kino**
White, clear - **Ma**
Stream - **Manga**
Bird - **Manu**
Headland - **Mata**
Mountain - **Maunga**
Speeches - **Mihi**
Sea, lake - **Moana**
Island or anything isolated - **Motu**
End - **Muri**
Big - **Nui**
The place of - **O**
Sand, beach - **One**
Fortified settlement - **Pa**
Ridge - **Pae**
Flat, earth, floor - **Papa**
Chants - **Patere**
Hill - **Puke**
Spring - **Puna**

North - **Raki**
Sky - **Rangi**
Long, high - **Roa**
Lake - **Roto**
Hole, cave, pit, two - **Rua**
Top - **Runga**
Light - **Tahu**
Sea - **Tai**
Man - **Tane**
Sacred - **Tapu**
Peak - **Tara**
The - **Te**
Cave - **Tomo**
Water - **Wai**
Canoe - **Waka**
Bay, body of water - **Whanga**
Land or country - **Whenua**

Pronunciation

Laziness and arrogance have combined to give Pakeha – and consequently most visitors – a distorted impression of Maori pronunciation, which is usually mutated into an Anglicized form. Until the 1970s there was little attempt to get it right, but with the rise in Maori consciousness since the 1980s, coupled with a sense of political correctness, many Pakeha now make some attempt at Maori pronunciation. As a visitor you will probably get away with just about anything, but by sticking to a few simple rules and keeping your ears open, the apparently unfathomable place names will soon trip off your tongue. The key to **pronunciation** is in knowing where to split long compound words; scanning the place name elements above) should help a great deal, and it is worth remembering that all syllables end in a vowel. Each syllable is then stressed equally, so that, for example, Waikaremoana comes out as a flat Wai-ka-re-mo-ana. The other trick for the unwary is that Maori words don't take an "s" to form a plural, so you'll find many plural nouns in this book – kiwi, tui, kauri, Maori – in what appears to be a singular form; about the only exception is Kiwis (as people), a Maori word wholly adopted into English.

Maori was solely a spoken language before the arrival of British and French missionaries in the early nineteenth century, who transcribed it using only fifteen letters of the Roman alphabet. The five **vowels** come in long and short forms; the long form is sometimes signified in print by a macron – a flat bar above the letter – but usually it is simply a case of learning by experience which sound to use. When two vowels appear together they are both pronounced, though substantially run together. For example, "Maori" should be written with a macron on the "a" and be pronounced with the first two vowels separate, turning the commonly used but incorrect "Mow-ree" into something more like "Maao-ri".

The eight **consonants**, **h**, **k**, **m**, **n**, **p**, **r**, **t** and **w**, are pronounced much as they are in English. Finally, there are two digraphs: **ng**, pronounced much as in "sing", and **wh**, which sounds either like an aspirated "f" as in "off", or like the "wh" in "why", depending on who is saying what and in which part of the country.

Glossary

ACC - Accident Compensation Commission.
ANZAC - Australian and New Zealand Army Corps; every town in New Zealand has a memorial to ANZAC casualties from both world wars.
Aotearoa - Maori for New Zealand, the land of the long white cloud.
Ariki - Supreme chief of an *iwi*.
Bach - (pronounced "batch") Holiday home, originally a bachelor pad at work camps and now something of a Kiwi institution that can be anything from shack to palatial waterside residence.
Back-blocks - Remote areas.
Biddy-bid - A burr-bearing bush (from Maori piripiri).
Blat - Travel at great speed.
Bludger - Someone who doesn't pull their weight or pay their way, a sponger.
Boomer - Excellent.
Bro - Brother, term of endearment widely used by Maori.
Captain Cooker - Wild pig, probably descended from pigs released in the Marlborough Sounds on Cook's first voyage.
Chilly bin - Insulated cool box for carrying picnic supplies and beer to the beach or cricket match.
Chook - Chicken.
Choice - Fantastic.
Chuddy - Chewing gum, also "chutty".
Chunder - Vomit.
Coaster - (Ex-) resident of the West Coast of the South Island.
Cocky - Farmer, comes in "Cow" and "Sheep" variants.
Crib - South Island name for a bach.
Cuz or **Cuzzy** - Short for cousin, see "bro".
Dag - Wag or entertaining character.
Dairy - Corner shop selling just about everything, open seven days and sometimes 24 hours.
Dally - Semi-derogatory name for descendants of Dalmatian immigrants from the Balkans.
Dob in - Reporting one's friends and neighbours to the police; there is currently a dobber's charter encouraging drivers to report one another for dangerous driving.
Docket - Receipt.
Domain - Grassy reserve, open to the public.
Fizz boat - Small powerboat.
Flicks - Cinema, movie theatre.
Flog - Steal.
Footie - Rugby, usually union rather than league, never soccer.
Freezing works - Slaughter house.
Give it a burl - Try it.
Godzone - New Zealand, short for "God's own country".
Gorse in your pocket - To be slow to pay your share.
Good as (gold) - First rate, excellent.
Good on ya - Expression of approbation or encouragement, frequently appended with "mate".
Greasies - Takeaway food, especially fish and chips.
Greenstone - A type of nephrite jade known in Maori as pounamu.
Haka - Maori dance performed in threatening fashion before All Black rugby games.
Handle - Large glass of beer.
Hangi - Maori feast cooked in an earth oven (see p.982).
Hapu - Maori sub-tribal unit. Several make up an *iwi*.
Hard case - See "dag".
Hard yacker - Hard work.
Hollywood - A faked or exaggerated sporting injury used to gain advantage.
Hongi - Maori greeting, performed by pressing noses together.
Hoon - Lout, yob or delinquent.
Hori - Offensive word for a Maori.
Hui - Maori gathering or conference.
Iwi - Largest of Maori tribal groupings.
Jandals - Ubiquitous Kiwi footwear, thongs or flip-flops.
Jug - Litre of beer.
Kai - Maori word for food, used in general parlance.

Kaimoana - Seafood.
Karanga - Call for visitors to come forward on a *marae.*
Kaumatua - Maori elders, old people.
Kawa-Marae - Etiquette or protocol on a *marae.*
Kete - Traditional basket made of plaited flax that is seeing something of a resurgence in popularity.
Kiore - Polynesian rat.
Koha - Donation.
Kohanga - Reo pre-school Maori language immersion (literally "language nest").
Kumara - Sweet potato.
Kuri - Polynesian dog, now extinct.
Lay-by - Practice of putting a deposit on goods until they can be fully paid for.
Log of wood - Slang for the Ranfurly Shield, New Zealand rugby's greatest prize.
Mana - Maori term indicating status, esteem, prestige or authority, and in wide use among all Kiwis.
Manaia - Stylized bird or lizard forms used extensively in Maori carving.
Manchester - Linen section of a department store and its contents.
Manuhiri - Guest or visitor, particularly to a *marae.*
Maoritanga - Maori culture and custom, the Maori way of doing things.
Marae - Literally "courtyard" but much more. Place for conducting ceremonies in front of a meeting house. Also a general term for a settlement centred on the meeting house.
Mauri - Life force or life principle.
Mere - War club, usually of greenstone.
Metalled - Graded road surface of loose stones found all over rural New Zealand.
MMP - Mixed member proportional representation – New Zealand's new electoral system.
Moko - Old form of tattooing on body and face that has seen a resurgence among Maori gang members.
Ngati - Tribal prefix meaning "the descendants (or people) of". Also Ngai and Ati.
No fear - Expression indicating refusal or disagreement.
OE - Overseas experience, usually a year spent abroad by Kiwis in their early twenties.
Pa - Fortified village of yore, now usually an abandoned terraced hillside.
Paddock - Field.
Pakeha - A non-Maori, usually white and not usually expressed with derogatory intent. Literally "foreign" though it can also be translated as "flea" or "pest". It may also be a corruption of pakepakeha, which are mythical human-like beings with fair skins.
Pashing - Kissing or snogging.
Patu - Short fighting club
Paua - Abalone, a type of shellfish with a wonderful iridescent shell.
Pavlova - Meringue dessert with a fruit and cream topping.
Pike out - To chicken out or give up.
Piss - Beer.
Pissed - Drunk.
Piss head - Drunkard.
Plunkett rooms - Childcare centre.
Poms - Folk from Britain; not necessarily offensive.
Powhiri - Traditional welcome onto a *marae.*
Puckerooed - Broken. Derived from the Maori for broken, pakaru.
Puku - Maori for stomach, often used as a term of endearment for someone amply endowed.
Queen Street farmer - City businessman owning rural property.
Ranch slider - Sliding glass door giving onto the garden or decking.
Rangatira - General term for a Maori chief.
Rapt - Well-pleased.
Rattle your dags - Hurry up.
Root - Vulgar term for sex.
Rooted - To be very tired or beyond repair, as in "she's rooted, mate" – your car is irreparable.
Rough as guts - Uncouth, roughly made or operating badly, as in "she's running rough as guts, mate".
Scroggin - Trail mix, essentially nuts and raisins.
Sealed road - Bitumen-surfaced road.
Section - Block of land usually surrounding a house.
She'll be right - Everything will work out fine.
Shoot through - To leave suddenly.
Shout - To buy a round of drinks or generally to treat folk.
Skull - To knock back beer quickly.
Slutted - Greatly annoyed.

Smoko - Tea break.
Snarler, snag - Sausage.
Spinner - A jerk.
Squiz - A look, as in "Give us a squiz".
Station wagon - Estate car.
Stoked - Very pleased.
Taiaha - Long-handled club.
Tall poppy - Someone who excels. "Cutting down tall poppies" is to bring overachievers back to earth – every Kiwi's perceived duty.
Tane - Man.
Tangata whenua - The people of the land, local or original inhabitants.
Tangi - Mourning or funeral.
Taniwha - Fearsome water spirit of Maori legend.
Taonga - Treasures, prized possessions.
Tapu - Forbidden or taboo. Frequently refers to sacred land.
Te reo Maori- Maori language.
Tiki - Maori pendant depicting a distorted human figure.
Tiki tour - Guided tour.
Togs - Swimming costume.
Tohunga - Maori priests, experts in Maoritanga.
Tukutuku - Knotted latticework panels decorating the inside of a meeting house.
Tupuna - Ancestors; of great spiritual importance to Maori.
Ute - Car-sized pick-up truck, short for "utility".
Varsity - University.
Wahine - Woman.
Waiata - Maori action songs.
Wairau - Spirit.
Waratah - Stake, a term used to describe snow poles on tramps.
Waka - Maori canoe.
Wero - Challenge before entering a *marae*.
Whakapapa - Family tree or genealogical relationship.
Whanau - Extended family group.
Whare - Maori for a house.
Whare runanga - Meeting house.
Whare whakairo - Carved house.
Within cooee - Within reach.
Wop-wops - Remote areas.
Yahoo - To be or act like a lout.

Index

and small print

Index

Map entries are in colour

A

B

C

D

E

F

G

H

I

J

K

L

M

N

O

P

Q

R

Twenty Years of Rough Guides

In the summer of 1981, Mark Ellingham, Rough Guides' founder, knocked out the first guide on a typewriter, with a group of friends. Mark had been travelling in Greece after university, and couldn't find a guidebook that really answered his needs.There were heavyweight cultural guides on the one hand – good on museums and classical sites but not on beaches and tavernas – and on the other hand student manuals that were so caught up with how to save money that they lost sight of the country's significance beyond its role as a place for a cool vacation. None of the guides began to address Greece as a country, with its natural and human environment, its politics and its contemporary life.

Having no urgent reason to return home, Mark decided to write his own guide. It was a guide to Greece that tried to combine some erudition and insight with a thoroughly practical approach to travellers' needs. Scrupulously researched listings of places to stay, eat and drink were matched by careful attention to detail on everything from Homer to Greek music, from classical sites to national parks and from nude beaches to monasteries. Back in London, Mark and his friends got their Rough Guide accepted by a farsighted commissioning editor at the publisher Routledge and it came out in 1982.

The Rough Guide to Greece was a student scheme that became a publishing phenomenon. The immediate success of the book – shortlisted for the Thomas Cook award – spawned a series that rapidly covered dozens of countries. The Rough Guides found a ready market among backpackers and budget travellers, but soon acquired a much broader readership that included older and less impecunious visitors. Readers relished the guides' wit and inquisitiveness as much as the enthusiastic, critical approach that acknowledges everyone wants value for money – but not at any price.

Rough Guides soon began supplementing the "rougher" information – the hostel and low-budget listings – with the kind of detail that independent-minded travellers on any budget might expect. These days, the guides – distributed worldwide by the Penguin group – include recommendations spanning the range from shoestring to luxury, and cover more than 200 destinations around the globe. Our growing team of authors, many of whom come to Rough Guides initially as outstandingly good letter-writers telling us about their travels, are spread all over the world, particularly in Europe, the USA and Australia. As well as the travel guides, Rough Guides publishes a series of dictionary phrasebooks covering two dozen major languages, an acclaimed series of music guides running the gamut from Classical to World Music, a series of music CDs in association with World Music Network, and a range of reference books on topics as diverse as the Internet, Pregnancy and Unexplained Phenomena. Visit **www.roughguides.com** to see what's cooking.

Rough Guide Credits

Text editors: Geoff Howard, Ann-Marie Shaw, Oilivia Swift, Gavin Thomas, Clifton Wilkinson
Series editor: Mark Ellingham
Editorial: Martin Dunford, Jonathan Buckley, Kate Berens, Ann-Marie Shaw, Helena Smith, Judith Bamber, Olivia Swift, Ruth Blackmore, Geoff Howard, Claire Saunders, Gavin Thomas, Alexander Mark Rogers, Polly Thomas, Joe Staines, Richard Lim, Duncan Clark, Peter Buckley, Lucy Ratcliffe, Clifton Wilkinson, Alison Murchie, Matthew Teller, Andrew Dickson, Fran Sandham (UK); Andrew Rosenberg, Stephen Timblin, Yuki Takagaki, Richard Koss, Hunter Slaton, Julie Feiner (US)
Production: Susanne Hillen, Andy Hilliard, Link Hall, Helen Prior, Julia Bovis, Michelle Draycott, Katie Pringle, Zoë Nobes, Rachel Holmes, Andy Turner, Michelle Bhatia
Cartography: Melissa Baker, Maxine Repath, Ed Wright, Katie Lloyd-Jones
Cover art direction: Louise Boulton
Picture research: Sharon Martins, Mark Thomas
Online: Kelly Cross, Anja Mutic-Blessing, Jennifer Gold, Audra Epstein, Suzanne Welles, Cree Lawson (US)
Finance: John Fisher, Gary Singh, Edward Downey, Mark Hall, Tim Bill
Marketing & Publicity: Richard Trillo, Niki Smith, David Wearn, Chloë Roberts, Demelza Dallow, Claire Southern (UK); Simon Carloss, David Wechsler, Megan Kennedy (US)
Administration: Tania Hummel, Julie Sanderson

Publishing Information

This third edition published October 2002 by **Rough Guides Ltd**,
62–70 Shorts Gardens, London WC2H 9AH.
Penguin Putnam, Inc. 375 Hudson Street, NY 10014, USA.
Distributed by the Penguin Group
Penguin Books Ltd,
80 Strand, London WC2R ORL
Penguin Putnam, Inc.
375 Hudson Street, NY 10014, USA
Penguin Books Australia Ltd,
487 Maroondah Highway, PO Box 257, Ringwood, Victoria 3134, Australia
Penguin Books Canada Ltd,
10 Alcorn Avenue, Toronto, Ontario, Canada M4V 1E4
Penguin Books (NZ) Ltd,
182–190 Wairau Road, Auckland 10, New Zealand
Typeset in Bembo and Helvetica to an original design by Henry Iles.

Printed in Italy by LegoPrint S.p.A

1080pp includes index
A catalogue record for this book is available from the British Library.

ISBN 1-85828-896-7

SMALL PRINT

Help us update

We've gone to a lot of effort to ensure that the third edition of **The Rough Guide to New Zealand** is accurate and up-to-date. However, things change – places get "discovered", opening hours are notoriously fickle, restaurants and rooms raise prices or lower standards. If you feel we've got it wrong or left something out, we'd like to know, and if you can remember the address, the price, the time, the phone number, so much the better.

We'll credit all contributions, and send a copy of the next edition (or any other Rough Guide if you prefer) for the best letters. Everyone who writes to us and isn't already a subscriber will receive a copy of our full-colour thrice-yearly newsletter. Please mark letters: **"Rough Guide New Zealand Update"** and send to: Rough Guides, 62–70 Shorts Gardens, London WC2H 9AH, or Rough Guides, 4th Floor, 345 Hudson St, New York, NY 10014. Or send an email to **mail@roughguides.com**

Have your questions answered and tell others about your trip at **www.roughguides.atinfopop.com**

Acknowledgements

This book is dedicated to Guy Harper. **The authors** would like to thank our editor, Geoff Howard, for his tireless efforts and patience, and Ann-Marie Shaw, Olivia Swift, Gavin Thomas and Clifton Wilkinson for all stepping in when the need was greatest, and Kate Berens for overseeing the whole project. Thanks also to those readers who wrote or emailed their thoughts and experiences, especially Ursula Payern and Peter Zürcher for their long and helpful letter. Cheers also to those who accosted us in the field, sometimes with great suggestions, other times just to tell us they disagreed with our opinions; and all the staff of visitor centres around the country who gave up their time to help. Finally, thanks to Ed Wright for cartography, Sharon Martins and Louise Boulton for picture research, Michelle Bhatia, James Morris and Katie Pringle for typesetting, and Ken Bell for proofreading.

Paul would like to thank all those who shared experiences and huts on numerous tramps throughout the country, helped pass long bus journeys and shared meals across the land. In particular, thanks to Sharon Alexander for putting up with shitty weather and endless gravel roads while researching the Western North Island; Richard and Raewyn for friendship and advice in Wellington; James, Tania, Annie, Peter, Simon, Helen, Mel and the mythical Clifford for assistance sussing out the Auckland bars and clubs; and Tracey for nearly being there and restaurant advice. Cheers, too, to all the friends and acquaintances around New Zealand and elsewhere (both old and new) who have suggested favourite restaurants, waxed lyrical about everything from hostels to luxurious retreats and generally helped make this third edition what it is. And most of all thanks to Irene for continued support and forbearance over long evenings spent at the computer and even longer research trips down country.

Tony and Laura would like to thank Peter Hawes and Elizabeth Barker for their invaluable input; Singapore Airlines; Topcat; Southern Air; Suzanne Miller, Ann Shepherd, Catherine Connew and Richard Maloney of the DOC; David Hindley; Stephen O'Neil; Peter Kitchen (Kitch); Evan Bloomfield, Barbara Hughs (ENABLE); and Jennifer Beaston and Bronwyn Grant. Mention must also be made of the wonderful Tony at ACE Rentals (Auckland); Renny Rentals (Christchurch) who were fantastically helpful; Rae White of the Saltmarsh Partnership; Hamish (you know who you are) for giggles and a guiding hand; all the people who helped us, took us in, looked after our home while we were away and to anyone who walked, talked or supped with us and generally made their feelings known on how to improve the book.
Tony would like to offer special thanks to Violet and Don for their support and good wishes.

Readers' letters

Lastly, thanks to anyone who wrote or emailed or provided help and information, especially those listed below (apologies for any misspellings):

Beatriz Alonso, Ruth Amos, Mary Beth Armstrong, Hilary and Alan Bill, Linda Bain, Chris Boyle, Mark Brabyn, Joyce Bregman, John Bridge, Sophie Brookes, Merran Buchanan, Karen Bull, Janet Bullen, Anne Busby, Kate Campbell, Dan Carter, Christine Chinetti, Chiyang Chua, Jenny Cook, Nigel Coventry, R.M. Cross, Silvia Crotti, Dave Delia, Pravasi Dhyan, Stephen Emanuel, Andrew Fogg, Joyce van Gelder, Norbert Gintner, Margaret Gorrie, Lise Goyette, Hugh Gray, Katinka Gregoire, Janet and Tim Gripper, Kelly Gross, Siobhan Hanley, Heather Hapeta, Richard Hardy, Rachel and Michael Hemingway, Sue Herbert, Alan and Bill Hilary, John and Jacqueline Hindly, V.A. Huggins, Robyn Jebson, Graeme Jenkinson, Mark Jones, Duers Jonnson, Warren and Marita Jowett, Glena Llewellyn, Tony Loosmore, Dave Loten, Lenore Malone, Roger Meadows, Jamie Mc Cormick, Wallace McMillan, Miki, Trixie and Murray Montagu, Mary Morwood, Peter Moss, Gillian Nahum, Sinead Nally, Stephen and Jackie Newbould, Ina and Stefan Noll, Lynne O'Neill, Carol Orbell, Linda Ott, Sally Parker, Ursula Payern, Perry and Tracey, Karen Pigott, Ceri Powell, Natalie Prensa, Edward and Barbara Priestley, Paul Prowting, Helen Quaggin, Fioan Hesse and Steven Ramm, Charlotte Renner, Frank and Cathrin Sallie, Jonathan Schofield, P.A.E. Sedding, Nathan Smith, Andy Spence, Tom Stainer,

Annette and Thomas Steinbach, Catherine Stephenson, Alan & Viv Swithenbank, Catherine Taylor, Thelma Taylor, Katherine Trippe, Emer Twomey, Rick Volden, Robert Volger, Jane Ward, Maja Hostettler Wildisen, Anne Wilmot, Alan Yeo, Peter Zürcher.

Photo Credits

Cover Credits

Front main image Milford Sound © Stone
Front (small top image) Maori Anglican church, Mission Bay © Robert Harding
Front (small bottom image) Jet Boat © Robert Harding
Back (top) Moeraki Boulders, East Otago © Trip
Back (lower) Giant Gate Falls, Fiordland © Imagestate

Colour introduction

Rainbow and rugby shirts © NZ Tourism
Maori Carving, Rotorua, © Paul Whitfield
Wai-O-Tapu Thermal Reserve, Artist's Palate © Jerry Dennis
Theatre Wall Motif, Stewart Island © Norma Joseph/Robert Harding
Te Papa © Focus New Zealand
Elephant Rocks © Tony Mudd
Lord of the Rings © Courtesy of Image Net
Bungy-jumping off the Kawarau Bridge, Queenstown © Jeremy Bright/Robert Harding
Paua Shell House © Focus New Zealand

Things not to miss

Karori Wildlife Sanctuary, Wellington © Tourism New Zealand
The Routeburn Track © Nick Wood/Robert Harding
Kiwi © Focus New Zealand
Rugby © Tourism New Zealand
Farewell Spit © Focus New Zealand
Tree Fern © Paul Whitfield
Wine, Marlborough/Blenheim © Focus New Zealand
Hot Water Beach © Robert Francis/Robert Harding
Petrified forest, the Catlins coast © Maurice Joseph/Robert Harding
Surfing © Surfing NZ Magazine/Craig Levers
Milford Sound © Gavin Hellier/Robert Harding
Wanganui River © Jerry Dennis
Abel Tasman Kayaking © Focus New Zealand
Dune Rider, Te Paki sand dunes. Northland © Paul Whitfield
Waiotapu Thermal Area, Rotorua © Jerry Dennis
The Kauri Museum, Matakohe © Kauri Museum
"Lost World" abseil, Waitomo Caves © Waitomo Adventures Ltd
Canoeing, Tawhai Falls, Tongariro National Park © Tourism New Zealand
Yellow-eyed Penguins, Taiaroa Heads, Otago Peninsula © Jerry Dennis
Moeraki Boulders, Oamaru © Paul Whitfield
Jetboat on the Shotover River © Jerry Dennis
Bungy jumping on the Kawarau River © Robert Harding
America's Cup 2000 finals © Tourism New Zealand
Te Papa © Te Papa
Little Arch, Oparara Basin, near Karamea © Paul Whitfield
Dunedin Gallery © Dunedin Gallery
Tongariro Crossing © Paul Whitfield
White Island © Paul Whitfield
Christchurch Arts Centre © Focus New Zealand
Hangi © Paul Almasy/CORBIS
Ice Hole, Foxes Glacier, Westland © Maurice Joseph/Robert Harding
Maori Carver, Christchurch © Robert Harding
Taieri Gorge Railway © Focus New Zealand
Daily Telegraph Buidling, Napier, Hawke's Bay © Jerry Dennis
Whale diving off Kaikoura © Jerry Dennis

Black and white photos

Auckland yachts and Sky City © Tourism New Zealand
Poor Knights Island © Focus New Zealand
Caving, Waitomo © Focus New Zealand
Wai-O-Tapu © Paul Whitfield
Swimming with dolphins © Jerry Dennis
Gannet colony, Cape Kidnappers © New Zealand Tourism Board
Beehive and Parliament House, Wellington © Chris Whitehead
Abel Tasman National Park, Nelson © Tourism New Zealand
Oamaru © Focus New Zealand
Church of the Good Shepherd, Lake Tekapo © Jeremy Bright/Robert Harding
Dunedin © Focus New Zealand
Routeburn Track © Jerry Dennis
Lady Bowen Falls © Paul Whitfield
Tiritiri Matangi © Focus New Zealand

Hundertwasser toilets © Focus New Zealand
Egmont National Park © Focus New Zealand
Maori cultural performance, Tamaki Village © Paul Whitfield
Driving Creek Railway © Focus New Zealand
Lake Waikaremoana © Focus New Zealand
Te Papa © Te Papa
Commercial Hotel, Murchison © Paul Whitfield
Yellow-eyed penguin, Dunedin © Tourism New Zealand
Arthur's Pass © Tony Mudd
Otago Peninsula © Focus New Zealand
Franz Josef Glacier, Westland © Tourism New Zealand
Post Office, Arrowtown © Jerry Dennis
Doubtful Sound © Focus New Zealand

TRAVEL • MUSIC • REFERENCE • PHRASEBOOKS

Rough Guides travel

Europe

Algarve
Amsterdam
Andalucia
Austria
Barcelona
Belgium & Luxembourg
Berlin
Britain
Brittany & Normandy
Bruges & Ghent
Brussels
Budapest
Bulgaria
Copenhagen
Corsica
Costa Brava
Crete
Croatia
Cyprus
Czech & Slovak Republics
Devon & Cornwall
Dodecanese & East Aegean
Dordogne & the Lot
Dublin
Edinburgh
England
Europe
First-Time Europe
Florence
France
French Hotels & Restaurants
Germany
Greece
Greek Islands
Holland
Hungary
Ibiza & Formentera
Iceland
Ionian Islands
Ireland
Italy
Lake District
Languedoc & Roussillon
Lisbon
London
London Mini Guide
London Restaurants
Madeira
Madrid
Mallorca
Malta & Gozo
Menorca
Moscow
Norway
Paris
Paris Mini Guide
Poland
Portugal
Prague
Provence & the Côte d'Azur
Pyrenees
Romania
Rome
Sardinia
Scandinavia
Scotland
Scottish Highlands & Islands
Sicily
Spain
St Petersburg
Sweden
Switzerland
Tenerife & La Gomera
Turkey
Tuscany & Umbria
Venice & The Veneto
Vienna
Wales

Asia

Bali & Lombok
Bangkok
Beijing
Cambodia
China
First-Time Asia
Goa
Hong Kong & Macau
India
Indonesia
Japan
Laos
Malaysia, Singapore & Brunei
Nepal
Singapore
South India
Southeast Asia
Thailand
Thailand Beaches & Islands
Tokyo
Vietnam

Australasia

Australia
Gay & Lesbian Australia
Melbourne
New Zealand
Sydney

North America

Alaska
Big Island of Hawaii
Boston
California
Canada
Florida
Hawaii
Honolulu
Las Vegas
Los Angeles
Maui
Miami & the Florida Keys
Montréal
New England
New Orleans
New York City
New York City Mini Guide
New York Restaurants
Pacific Northwest
Rocky Mountains
San Francisco
San Francisco Restaurants
Seattle
Southwest USA
Toronto
USA
Vancouver
Washington DC
Yosemite

Caribbean & Latin America

Antigua & Barbuda
Argentina
Bahamas
Barbados
Belize
Bolivia
Brazil
Caribbean
Central America
Chile
Costa Rica
Cuba
Dominican Republic
Ecuador
Guatemala
Jamaica
Maya World
Mexico
Peru
St Lucia
Trinidad & Tobago

Africa & Middle East

Cape Town
Egypt
Israel & Palestinian Territories
Jerusalem
Jordan
Kenya
Morocco
South Africa, Lesotho & Swaziland
Syria
Tanzania
Tunisia
West Africa
Zanzibar
Zimbabwe

Dictionary Phrasebooks

Czech
Dutch
European Languages
French
German
Greek
Hungarian
Italian
Polish
Portuguese
Russian
Spanish
Turkish
Hindi & Urdu
Indonesian
Japanese
Mandarin Chinese
Thai
Vietnamese
Mexican Spanish
Egyptian Arabic
Swahili

Maps

Amsterdam
Dublin
London
Paris
San Francisco
Venice

Rough Guides publishes new books every month!

Music

Acoustic Guitar
Blues: 100 Essential CDs
Cello
Clarinet
Classical Music
Classical Music: 100 Essential CDs
Country Music
Country: 100 Essential CDs
Cuban Music
Drum'n'bass
Drums
Electric Guitar & Bass Guitar
Flute
Hip-Hop
House
Irish Music
Jazz
Jazz: 100 Essential CDs
Keyboards & Digital Piano
Latin: 100 Essential CDs
Music USA: a Coast-To-Coast Tour
Opera
Opera: 100 Essential CDs
Piano
Reading Music
Reggae
Reggae: 100 Essential CDs
Rock
Rock: 100 Essential CDs
Saxophone
Soul: 100 Essential CDs
Techno
Trumpet & Trombone
Violin & Viola
World Music: 100 Essential CDs
World Music Vol1
World Music Vol2

Reference

Children's Books, 0–5
Children's Books, 5–11
China Chronicle
Cult Movies
Cult TV
Elvis
England Chronicle
France Chronicle
India Chronicle
The Internet
Internet Radio
James Bond
Liverpool FC
Man Utd
Money Online
Personal Computers
Pregnancy & Birth
Shopping Online
Travel Health
Travel Online
Unexplained Phenomena
Videogaming
Weather
Website Directory
Women Travel
World Cup

Music CDs

Africa
Afrocuba
Afro-Peru
Ali Hussan Kuban
The Alps
Americana
The Andes
The Appalachians
Arabesque
Asian Underground
Australian Aboriginal Music
Bellydance
Bhangra
Bluegrass
Bollywood
Boogaloo
Brazil
Cajun
Cajun and Zydeco
Calypso and Soca
Cape Verde
Central America
Classic Jazz
Congolese Soukous
Cuba
Cuban Music Story
Cuban Son
Cumbia
Delta Blues
Eastern Europe
English Roots Music
Flamenco
Franco
Gospel
Global Dance
Greece
The Gypsies
Haiti
Hawaii
The Himalayas
Hip Hop
Hungary
India
India and Pakistan
Indian Ocean
Indonesia
Irish Folk
Irish Music
Italy
Jamaica
Japan
Kenya and Tanzania
Klezmer
Louisiana
Lucky Dube
Mali and Guinea
Marrabenta Mozambique
Merengue & Bachata
Mexico
Native American Music
Nigeria and Ghana
North Africa
Nusrat Fateh Ali Khan
Okinawa
Paris Café Music
Portugal
Rai
Reggae
Salsa
Salsa Dance
Samba
Scandinavia
Scottish Folk
Scottish Music
Senegal & The Gambia
Ska
Soul Brothers
South Africa
South African Gospel
South African Jazz
Spain
Sufi Music
Tango
Thailand
Tex-Mex
Wales
West African Music
World Music Vol 1: Africa, Europe and the Middle East
World Music Vol 2: Latin & North America, Caribbean, India, Asia and Pacific
World Roots
Youssou N'Dour & Etoile de Dakar
Zimbabwe

Rough Guides music guides & CDs

The ideas expressed in this code were developed by and for independent travellers.

Learn About The Country You're Visiting

Start enjoying your travels before you leave by tapping into as many sources of information as you can.

The Cost Of Your Holiday

Think about where your money goes - be fair and realistic about how cheaply you travel. Try and put money into local peoples' hands; drink local beer or fruit juice rather than imported brands and stay in locally owned accommodation. Haggle with humour and not aggressively. Pay what something is worth to you and remember how wealthy you are compared to local people.

Embrace The Local Culture

Open your mind to new cultures and traditions - it will transform your experience. Think carefully about what's appropriate in terms of your clothes and the way you behave. You'll earn respect and be more readily welcomed by local people. Respect local laws and attitudes towards drugs and alcohol that vary in different countries and communities. Think about the impact you could have on them.

Exploring The World – The Travellers' Code

Being sensitive to these ideas means getting more out of your travels - and giving more back to the people you meet and the places you visit.

Minimise Your Environmental Impact

Think about what happens to your rubbish - take biodegradable products and a water filter bottle. Be sensitive to limited resources like water, fuel and electricity. Help preserve local wildlife and habitats by respecting local rules and regulations, such as sticking to footpaths and not standing on coral.

Don't Rely On Guidebooks

Use your guidebook as a starting point, not the only source of information. Talk to local people, then discover your own adventure!

Be Discreet With Photography

Don't treat people as part of the landscape, they may not want their picture taken. Ask first and respect their wishes.

We work with people the world over to promote tourism that benefits their communities, but we can only carry on our work with the support of people like you. For membership details or to find out how to make your travels work for local people and the environment, visit our website.

www.tourismconcern.org.uk

TourismConcern
Campaigning for Ethical and Fairly Traded Tourism

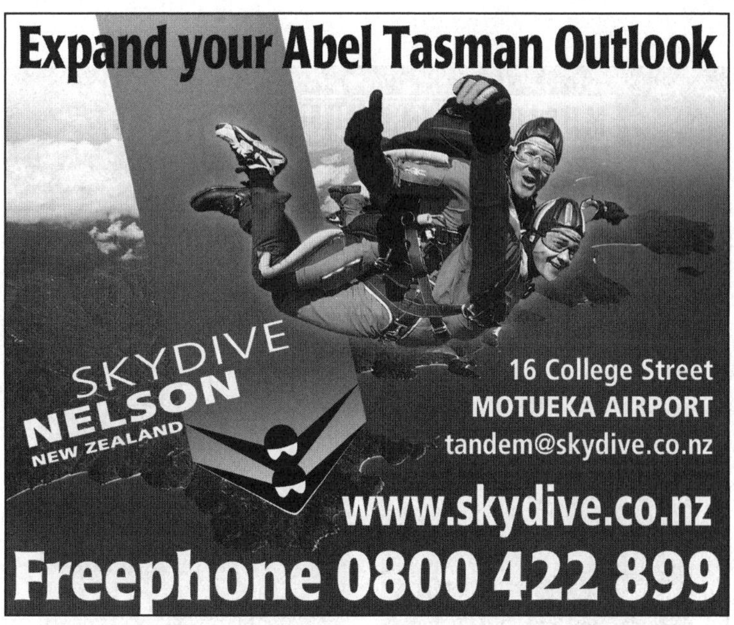

Expand your Abel Tasman Outlook
SKYDIVE
NELSON
NEW ZEALAND
16 College Street
MOTUEKA AIRPORT
tandem@skydive.co.nz
www.skydive.co.nz
Freephone 0800 422 899

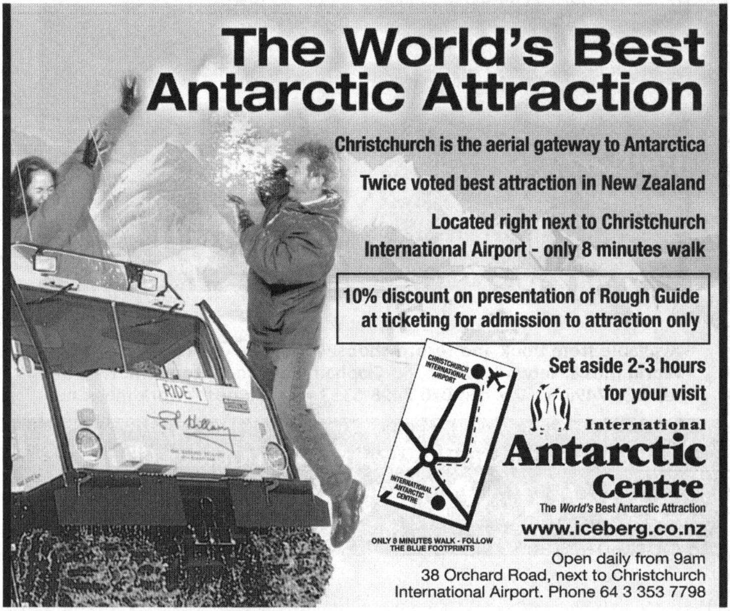
The World's Best
Antarctic Attraction
Christchurch is the aerial gateway to Antarctica
Twice voted best attraction in New Zealand
Located right next to Christchurch
International Airport - only 8 minutes walk
10% discount on presentation of Rough Guide
at ticketing for admission to attraction only
Set aside 2-3 hours
for your visit
RIDE 1
CHRISTCHURCH INTERNATIONAL AIRPORT
INTERNATIONAL ANTARCTIC CENTRE
ONLY 8 MINUTES WALK - FOLLOW THE BLUE FOOTPRINTS
International
Antarctic
Centre
The World's Best Antarctic Attraction
www.iceberg.co.nz
Open daily from 9am
38 Orchard Road, next to Christchurch
International Airport. Phone 64 3 353 7798